Lecture Notes in Computer Science 11339

More information about this series at http://www.springer.com/series/7407

Gabriele Mencagli · Dora B. Heras et al. (Eds.)

Euro-Par 2018: Parallel Processing Workshops

Euro-Par 2018 International Workshops
Turin, Italy, August 27–28, 2018
Revised Selected Papers

Editors
Gabriele Mencagli
University of Pisa
Pisa, Italy

Dora B. Heras
CiTIUS
Santiago de Compostela, Spain

Workshop Editors *see next page*

ISSN 0302-9743 ISSN 1611-3349 (electronic)
Lecture Notes in Computer Science
ISBN 978-3-030-10548-8 ISBN 978-3-030-10549-5 (eBook)
https://doi.org/10.1007/978-3-030-10549-5

Library of Congress Control Number: 2018965409

LNCS Sublibrary: SL1 – Theoretical Computer Science and General Issues

This Springer imprint is published by the registered company Springer Nature Switzerland AG
The registered company address is: Gewerbestrasse 11, 6330 Cham, Switzerland

Workshop Editors

Auto-DaSP
Valeria Cardellini
University of Rome Tor Vergata
Italy
cardellini@ing.uniroma2.it

CBDP
Emiliano Casalicchio
University of Rome La Sapienza
Italy
emiliano.casalicchio@uniroma1.it

COLOC
Emmanuel Jeannot
Inria Bordeaux Sud-Ouest
France
emmanuel.jeannot@inria.fr

Euro-EDUPAR
Felix Wolf
TU Darmstad
Germany
wolf@cs.tu-darmstadt.de

F2C-DP
Antonio Salis
Engineering Sardegna
Italy
antonio.salis@eng.it

FPDAPP
Claudio Schifanella
University of Turin
Italy
schi@di.unito.it

HeteroPar
Ravi Reddy Manumachu
University College Dublin
Ireland
ravi.manumachu@ucd.ie

LSDVE
Laura Ricci
University of Pisa
Italy
ricci@di.unipi.it

Med-HPC
Marco Beccuti
University of Turin
Italy
beccuti@di.unito.it

PDCLifeS
Laura Antonelli
ICAR-CNR
Italy
laura.antonelli@icar.cnr.it

RePara
Josè Daniel Garcia Sanchez
Universidad Carlos III de Madrid
Spain
josedaniel.garcia@uc3m.es

Resilience
Stephen L. Scott
Tennessee Technological University
USA
sscott@tntech.edu

Preface

Euro-Par is an annual, international conference in Europe, covering all aspects of parallel and distributed processing. These range from theory to practice, from small to the largest parallel and distributed systems and infrastructures, from fundamental computational problems to full-fledged applications, from architecture, compiler, language and interface design and implementation to tools, support infrastructures, and application performance aspects. The Euro-Par conference itself is complemented by a workshop program, where workshops dedicated to more specialized themes, to cross-cutting issues, and to upcoming trends and paradigms can be easily and conveniently organized with little administrative overhead.

This year, 12 workshop proposals were submitted, and after a careful revision process, which was led by the workshop co-chairs, all of them were accepted.

The workshops took place on the two days before the Euro-Par conference and the program included the following 12 workshops:

1. Workshop on Autonomic Solutions for Parallel and Distributed Data Stream Processing (Auto-DaSP)
2. Workshop on Container-Based Systems for Big Data, Distributed, and Parallel Computing (CBDP)
3. Workshop on Data Locality (COLOC)
4. Workshop on Parallel and Distributed Computing Education for Undergraduate Students (Euro-EDUPAR)
5. Workshop on Fog-to-Cloud Distributed Processing (F2C-DP)
6. Workshop on Future Perspective of Decentralized Applications (FPDAPP)
7. Workshop on Algorithms, Models, and Tools for Parallel Computing on Heterogeneous Platforms (HeteroPar)
8. Workshop on Large-Scale Distributed Virtual Environments (LSDVE)
9. Workshop on Advances in High-Performance Bioinformatics, Systems Biology (Med-HPC)
10. Workshop on Parallel and Distributed Computing for Life Sciences: Algorithms, Methodologies, and Tools (PDCLifeS)
11. Workshop on Reengineering for Parallelism in Heterogeneous Parallel Platforms (RePara)
12. Workshop on Resiliency in High Performance Computing with Clouds, Grids, and Clusters (Resilience)

All workshops together received a total of 109 submissions from 40 different countries. Each workshop had an independent Program Committee, which was in charge of selecting the papers. The workshop papers received more than three reviews per paper on average (361 reviews in total). Out of the 109 submissions, 65 papers were selected to be presented at the workshops. One of the accepted papers was not included in the final proceedings because the authors decided to withdraw it. Thus, the acceptance rate was 58%.

The success of the Euro-Par workshops depends on the work of many individuals and organizations. We therefore thank all workshop organizers and reviewers for the time and effort that they invested. We would also like to express our gratitude to the members of the Organizing Committee and the local staff, especially the volunteer PhD students, who helped us. Sincere thanks are due to Springer for their help in publishing the proceedings.

Lastly, we thank all participants, panelists, and keynote speakers of the Euro-Par workshops for their contribution to a productive meeting. It was a pleasure to organize and host the Euro-Par workshops 2018 in Turin.

September 2018

Gabriele Mencagli
Dora B. Heras

Organization

Euro-Par Steering Committee

Chair

Luc Bougé	ENS Rennes, France

Co-chair

Fernando Silva	University of Porto, Portugal

Full Members

Marco Aldinucci	University of Turin, Italy
Dora Blanco Heras	CiTIUS, Santiago de Compostela, Spain
Emmanuel Jeannot	LaBRI-Inria, Bordeaux, France
Christos Kaklamanis	Computer Technology Institute, Greece
Paul Kelly	Imperial College, UK
Thomas Ludwig	University of Hamburg, Germany
Tomàs Margalef	Autonomous University of Barcelona, Spain
Wolfgang Nagel	Dresden University of Technology, Germany
Francisco F. Rivera	CiTIUS, Santiago de Compostela, Spain
Rizos Sakellariou	University of Manchester, UK
Henk Sips	Delft University of Technology, The Netherlands
Domenico Talia	University of Calabria, Italy
Jesper Larsson Träff	Vienna University of Technology, Austria
Denis Trystram	Grenoble Institute of Technology, France
Felix Wolf	Technische Universität Darmstadt, Germany

Honorary Members

Christian Lengauer	University of Passau, Germany
Ron Perrott	Oxford e-Research Centre, UK
Karl Dieter Reinartz	University of Erlangen-Nuremberg, Germany

Observers

Ramin Yahyapour	GWDG/University of Göttingen, Germany
Krzysztof Rzadca	University of Warsaw, Poland

Euro-Par 2018 Organization

Co-chairs

Marco Aldinucci	University of Turin, Italy
Luca Padovani	University of Turin, Italy
Massimo Torquati	University of Pisa, Italy

Workshops

Gabriele Mencagli	University of Pisa, Italy
Dora B. Heras	CiTIUS, Santiago de Compostela, Spain

Logistics

Katia Lupo	University of Turin, Italy
Claudio Mattutino	University of Turin, Italy
Sergio Rabellino	University of Turin, Italy

Additional Reviewers

Alonso, Pedro
Antonelli, Laura
Assari, Pouria
Badia, Jose
Besozzi, Daniela
Bianco, Simona
Castelló, Adrián
Cazzaniga, Paolo
Ciric, Vladimir
De Salve, Andrea
Denoyelle, Nicolas
Di Napoli, Claudia
di Somma, Vittorio
Ferrero, Giulio
Fey, Florian
Follia, Laura
Galizia, Antonella
Hagedorn, Bastian
Jung, Jason
Klomp, Rick
Lastovetsky, Alexey
Maiorano, Francesco
Marques, Diogo
Matos, David
Mercanti, Ivan
Oliva, Gennaro
Oppermann, Julian
Pennisi, Marzio
Perez Abreu, David
Piccialli, Francesco
Sahal, Radhya
Sangiovanni, Mara
Santini, Francesco
Saurabh, Nishant
Schiano di Cola, Vincenzo
Schmidt, Jan
Sommer, Lukas
Spagnuolo, Carmine
Su, Li
Talia, Domenico
Tao, Dingwen
Tessier, Francois
Tonellotto, Nicola
Totis, Niccolò
Veltri, Pierangelo
Wang, Haomiao

Contents

F2C-DP - Workshop on Fog-to-Cloud Distributed Processing

FPDAPP - Workshop on Future Perspective of Decentralised Applications

Auto-DaSP - Workshop on Autonomic Solutions for Parallel and Distributed Data Stream Processing

Workshop on Autonomic Solutions for Parallel and Distributed Data Stream Processing (Auto-DaSP)

Workshop Description

Auto-DaSP is a forum for researchers and practitioners working on parallel and autonomic solutions for Data Stream Processing applications, frameworks, and programming support tools. The data streaming domain belongs to the Big Data ecosystem, where the so-called *data velocity*, i.e., the rate at which data arrive at the system for processing, represents one of the most challenging aspects to be addressed in the design of applications and frameworks. High-volume data streams can be efficiently handled through the adoption of novel high-performance solutions targeting today's commodity parallel hardware. However, despite the large computing power offered by the affordable hardware available nowadays, high-performance data streaming solutions need to be equipped with smart logics in order to adapt the framework/application configuration to rapidly changing execution conditions and workloads. This turns out in mechanisms and strategies to adapt the queries and operators placement policies, intra-operator parallelism degree, scheduling strategies, load shedding rate and so forth, and fosters novel interdisciplinary approaches that exploit Control Theory and Artificial Intelligence methods. The workshop calls the attention of the data stream processing and the distributed and parallel computing research communities in order to stimulate integrated approaches between these two disciplines.

The second edition of the International Workshop on Autonomic Solutions for Parallel and Distributed Data Stream Processing (Auto-DaSP 2018) was held in Turin, Italy. For the second time, this workshop was organized in conjunction with the Euro-Par annual series of international conferences. The format of the workshop included a keynote followed by technical presentations. The workshop was attended by around 20 people on average.

This year we received 8 submissions for reviews, from authors belonging to 7 distinct countries. After an accurate and thorough peer-review process, we selected 5 papers for presentation at the workshop. The review process focused on the quality of the papers, their scientific novelty and applicability to existing Data Stream Processing problems and frameworks. The acceptance of the papers was the result of the reviewers' discussion and agreement. All the high quality papers were accepted, and the acceptance rate was 62%. The accepted articles represent an interesting mix of techniques to solve recurrent as well as new problems in Data Stream Processing, such as efficient handling of data streams, distributing DSP tasks that involve machine learning steps, management of fault tolerance and its impact on performance, architectures and strategies to support runtime elasticity and address latency constraints.

The workshop program was completed by the invited talk titled "The Long Road Towards Elastic Distributed Stream Processing" given by Leonardo Querzoni from Sapienza University of Rome, Italy.

Last but not least, we would like to thank the Auto-DaSP 2018 Program Committee, whose members made the workshop possible with their rigorous and timely review process. We would also like to thank Euro-Par for hosting the workshop and our emerging community, and the Euro-Par workshop chairs for the valuable help and support.

Organization

Auto-DaSP Chairs

Valeria Cardellini	University of Rome Tor Vergata, Italy
Gabriele Mencagli	University of Pisa, Italy
Massimo Torquati	University of Pisa, Italy

Program Committee

Muhammad Intizar Ali	National University of Ireland, Ireland
Marcos Assunção	Inria, France
Pablo Basanta-Val	Universidad Carlos III de Madrid, Spain
Daniele Bonetta	Oracle Labs, Switzerland
Daniele Buono	IBM T. J. Watson Research Center, USA
Marco Danelutto	University of Pisa, Italy
Tiziano De Matteis	ETH Zurich, Switzerland
Daniele De Sensi	University of Pisa, Italy
J. Daniel Garcia	University Carlos III of Madrid, Spain
Dalvan Griebler	Pontifícia Universidade Católica do Rio Grande do Sul, Brazil
Bingsheng He	National University of Singapore, Singapore
Christoph Hochreiner	TU Wien, Austria
Peter Kilpatrick	Queen's University Belfast, Northern Ireland
Dave Lillethun	Seattle University, USA
Francesco Lo Presti	University of Rome Tor Vergata, Italy
Matteo Nardelli	University of Rome Tor Vergata, Italy
Yongluan Zhou	University of Southern Denmark, Denmark

Additional Reviewer

Li Su	University of Copenhagen, Denmark

TPICDS: A Two-Phase Parallel Approach for Incremental Clustering of Data Streams

Ammar Al Abd Alazeez(✉), Sabah Jassim, and Hongbo Du

Department of Applied Computing, The University of Buckingham, Buckingham MK18 1EG, UK
{1405097, sabah.jassim, hongbo.du}@buckingham.ac.uk

Abstract. Parallel and distributed solutions are essential for clustering data streams due to the large volumes of data. This paper first examines a direct adaptation of a recently developed prototype-based algorithm into three existing parallel frameworks. Based on the evaluation of performance, the paper then presents a customised pipeline framework that combines incremental and two-phase learning into a balanced approach that dynamically allocates the available processing resources. This new framework is evaluated on a collection of synthetic datasets. The experimental results reveal that the framework not only produces correct final clusters on the one hand, but also significantly improves the clustering efficiency.

Keywords: Big data · Data stream clustering algorithms
Distributed and parallel frameworks

1 Introduction

Recent advances in information and networking technologies and their applications in almost every sector of life have led to a rapid growth of the massive amount of data known as *Big Data* [1]. One of the most important characteristics of big data is its *velocity*, which means that data may arrive and require processing at different speeds. While for some applications, the arrival and processing of data can be performed in an offline batch processing style, others require continuous and real-time analysis of collections of incoming data (known as data chunks) ([2–4]). Data stream clustering is defined as a grouping of data in light of frequently arriving new data chunks for understanding the underlying group patterns that may change over time [5].

It is the sheer volume of data arriving at high and variable speeds of accumulation that deems normal clustering algorithms inefficient and incapable of dealing with the demand [6]. Therefore, distributed and parallel algorithms are the ultimate solution for analysing big data streams in reality, which is evident in the more recent research work ([4, 7, 8]). Distributed and parallel solutions offer several benefits such as reduction of the overall response time, improved scalability of solutions and suitability for applications of distributed nature such as sensor networks, social media, Internet of Things (IoT), etc. [9].

Multi-core processor commodity computers are widely used nowadays. At a higher but affordable price, a computer can have up to 72 core processors. As the computer

G. Mencagli et al. (Eds.): Euro-Par 2018 Workshops, LNCS 11339, pp. 5–16, 2019.
https://doi.org/10.1007/978-3-030-10549-5_1

hardware technology advances, cheaper and more core processors will become available. The question then is how to utilise the available processing resources on board of a local machine. In this paper, we argue that algorithms for data stream clustering should be first implemented on a multi-core parallel processing framework by making the best use of the available processors in a local machine before running the algorithms in a distributed network of computers.

This paper is therefore concerned with how to parallelise most recent techniques for clustering data streams. In general, the paper promotes a two-phase parallel approach for incrementally clustering data streams (TPICDS) where processors will incrementally maintain local clustering models in parallel at the online phase, and local cluster models can be merged into a global cluster model at the offline phase. In particular, the paper investigates the parallelisation of a recent algorithm EINCKM [10] in the TPICDS framework because of the algorithm's modular structure and performance over other existing algorithms. The work consists of two parts. In the first part, the paper investigates how the EINCKM algorithm adapts three typical parallelisms in existence. Based on a performance evaluation of the adapted parallelisms inside the algorithm, the paper further proposes a parallel pipeline with optimised and dynamic allocations of processing resources. Experimental results show that the proposed solution not only produces correct final clusters, but also significantly improves the efficiency.

The rest of this paper is organised as follows. Section 2 explains the related work on distributed and parallel data stream clustering algorithms in the literature, and propose the TPICDS approach at the end. Section 3 explains the EINCKM algorithm adaptation of the existing parallelisms. Section 4 presents the proposed optimised and dynamic parallel pipelines. Section 5 concludes the work and outlines possible future directions of this research.

2 Related Work

2.1 Computational Approaches

Two approaches for mining data streams are in existence: incremental and two-phase learning. With the incremental methods (e.g. STREAM [11]), a global model of clusters is iteratively developed to reflect current modifications made by incoming data chunks. The two-phase approach (e.g. CluStream [12]) divides the clustering process into two phases, i.e. an online phase where the data records are summarised into small intermediate *micro-clusters*, and an offline phase where the micro-clusters are processed into final clusters at a query point [13]. While the incremental algorithms always provide an accumulated view of global clusters at the arrival point of an incoming data chunk at the expense of continuous clustering, the two-phase algorithms provide such a view of clusters at the point of the query without constantly finding final clusters. Therefore, it can be argued that incremental algorithms are more suited for real-time response systems [4].

2.2 Data Stream Clustering Algorithm EINCKM

EINCKM is a prototype-based algorithm for clustering data streams and identifying outlier objects [10]. Taking the incremental learning approach, the algorithm divides the clustering process into three sequential steps: *Build Clusters*, *Merge*, and *Prune*. *Build Clusters* uses the K-Means method to find the clusters in the input data chunk. *Merge* integrates the newly formed clusters with existing ones. *Prune* detects outliers and checks the concept drift using a fading function. The algorithm applies a heuristic-based method to estimate the number of clusters, a radius-based technique to merge overlapped clusters, and a variance-based mechanism to prune outliers. The algorithm is modular and adaptable to further improvements. However, the algorithm is a sequential algorithm where the three key operations must be performed in order. It is, therefore, useful to explore how to parallelise the algorithm.

2.3 Distributed and Parallel Frameworks

Depending on how the input data is organised, two categories of distributed and parallel data stream clustering algorithms exist: object-based where the data record is a complete data object and attribute-based where each data item is an attribute value. Each category may take either incremental or two-phase learning approach.

For the incremental learning of object-based clusters, the central site receives the input data streams, divides it into chunks and sends them to the remote sites. Upon receiving the local clustering models from the remote sites, the central site produces the final output clusters. Bandyopadhyay *et al.* have used this approach for clustering data streams in a peer-to-peer environment [14]. Gao *et al.* showed an enhanced Apache Storm framework for clustering social media data, by adding another process between the central site and the participant remote sites for synchronising changes to the local models to avoid a bottleneck in communications [15]. Incremental learning of clusters from attribute streams is similar. The only differences are that each remote site receives an input attribute stream directly without the central site to distribute the data and that upon receiving the local cluster models, the central site integrates the local attribute models into a global object-based cluster model. Rodrigues *et al.* used this approach in the ODAC algorithm to cluster attribute streams [16]. The incremental learning is simple, easy to implement and efficient. However, extensive communication with the central site can result in bottlenecks. Besides, integrating all attribute clusters with a central site becomes infeasible when the dimensionality of data streams are high.

In the two-phase learning of object-based clusters, the local models are saved in a local buffer memory on each remote site, and are sent to the central site when there is a query from the user or there are significant changes in the local models [17, 18]. However, heavy computation is needed with the central site to obtain the final output clusters due to the large number of micro-clusters. Guerrieri and Montresor presented an improvement by making the remote sites communicate to reduce the number of micro-clusters [19]. Karunaratne *et al.* also made an improvement using Apache Storm where the remote sites save their local clustering models in a globally shared memory so that the designated second central site processes the local clusters into the final clusters [19]. The two-phase learning of clusters from attribute streams is similar to

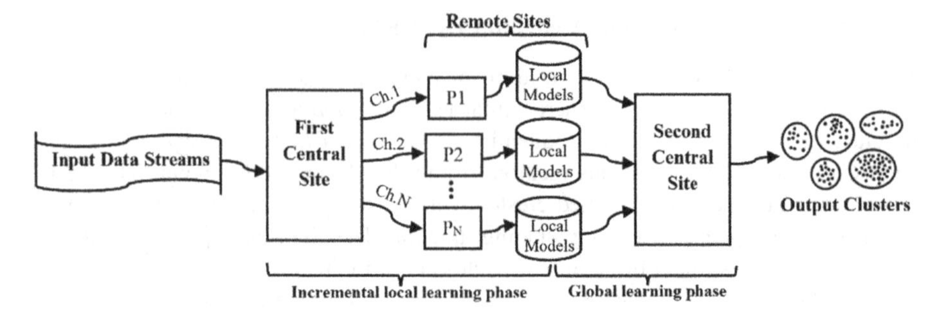

Fig. 1. Proposed TPICDS framework

incremental learning by using buffers for local models. Gama *et al.* adopted this approach in the DGClust algorithm to cluster data streams in sensor networks [20]. The algorithm reduces data dimensions and hence communications needed.

2.4 The Proposed TPICDS Framework

The proposed framework TPICDS combines the two computational approaches in the two-phase hybrid system. At the online phase, the first central site receives the data streams, divides it into chunks, and sends then to the remote sites. Each remote site receives its own data chunk, creates and maintains its own local cluster models in the incremental fashion. At the offline phase, the second central site receives the local models from the remote sites and presents the final global clusters (see Fig. 1). Our research aims to embed the EINCKM algorithm within the proposed framework where the second central site uses the same merge strategy to form the global clustering model.

3 Adapting EINCKM to the Existing Parallelisms

In this section, we first briefly summarise three typical parallel frameworks that already exist. We then describe how the EINCKM algorithm can intuitively adapt to each framework. We then evaluate the performance of each adaptation empirically using synthesised datasets.

3.1 Existing Parallel Frameworks

Three typical parallel frameworks exist. The replication, hereby known as embarrassingly parallel or basic parallelism (BP), simply makes multiple copies of the entire algorithm and then runs each copy on each processor [21]. Each processor must complete all operations of the algorithm before receiving next new data inputs. The framework has the pros of being simple, and directly employs the principle of divide and conquer by sharing the processing of input data by the available processors. We use this framework as a basic benchmark for performance evaluations later.

The parallel pipeline (PP) is an improvement of the basic parallelism to streamline several processors in a pipeline [22], which works as follows. A present processor receives the output of a previous processor as its input, processes the data, generates the output, and passes it on to the next processor. Each processor has a certain degree of independence so that when the next processor processes its output, the present processor takes and processes its next data input. This framework not only divides the workload among different processors but also further improve the degree of parallelism within a sequential pipeline.

MapReduce parallel pipeline (MRPP) is a further modification of PP [23]. First, data stored in memory are divided into partitions, and each partition is sent to a different processor (Mapping). Each processor processes the data within the partition and the processed outputs are then hashed to fewer processors on another layer to further process them (Reducing). The hashing can be determined by the relevance of the outputs.

3.2 Algorithm Adaptation

All adaptations of the algorithm to the existing frameworks mentioned above require dividing the available processing resources into central and remote sites (in this context, a site is a single core processor on the same computer). The adaptation of the algorithm to the basic parallelism is straightforward: each remote site finds the clusters from the incoming chunk, merges them with its own existing clusters, prunes them, and saves the resulting clusters into its own local buffer memory.

The adaptation of the algorithm to the PP framework is done as follows. We first divide all the available remote sites into groups of *three* sites, and then arrange the three sites into a pipeline. We then designate the first of the three sites for the *Build Clusters* function, the second for the *Merge* function, and the third for the *Prune* function. When the *Build Cluster* site finishes the current chunk, it sends the clusters to the *Merge* site. When the *Merge* site merges the clusters from the chunk with the existing ones, the *Build Cluster* site starts discovering clusters from the next chunk. When the *Merge* site finishes its task of merging clusters, it sends the results to the *Prune* site, and then starts working on the new clusters from the *Build Cluster* site. The *Prune* site works in a similar fashion.

For the adaptation of the MRPP framework, the first central site in TPICDS performs the mapping operation. The remote sites for the *Build Cluster* function is modified to include a further function for the hashing, i.e. assigning similar local clusters to a specific *Merge* site. More precisely, a *Build Cluster* site checks the closest cluster's centroids and send them to the same merger site, and a *Merge* site receives clusters from different *Build Cluster* sites to build a *regional model* of clustering. After that, the *Prune* site conducts the pruning of regional models and sends them to the second central site in TPICDS. The difference between the PP adaptation and the MRPP adaptation is that the *Merge* site in the PP framework receives clusters only from the *Build Cluster* site within the same pipeline, whereas the *Merge* site in the MRPP merges clusters from more than one *Build Cluster* site in different pipelines.

3.3 Empirical Evaluation

In order to evaluate empirically the performance of each adaptation, we created two collections of synthetic datasets, DS1 and DS2. Each collection include six datasets of different sizes, i.e. 100,000, 200,000, 500,000, 1,000,000, 1,500,000 and 2,000,000 data points of two dimensions. To simulate various sizes, shapes and numbers of clusters, we used Gaussian distributions to randomly generate spherical shape clusters with different means, variances and number of members. DS1 and DS2 respectively have four and thirty clusters. We acknowledge the limitations of synthesised datasets in expressing the characteristics of data in reality, but synthesised datasets do allow us to check the correctness of clustering by comparing the resulting clusters to known clusters.

A computer with 12 2.8 GHz core processors and 16 GB memory under Microsoft Windows7 was used to conduct the experiment. MATLAB 2017a was used to implement the adapted algorithms and program the experiment scripts. For each experiment, we randomly selected data points from the dataset to form data chunks of 1000 data points. The random selection simulates the situation where there is no control on the order of the arriving data points. To minimise the random effect of the selected data points to the performance of the algorithms for a specific experiment, we repeated each experiment 100 times, and then take the average of the speeds of execution in seconds. The processors on the machine are configured as follows. For the BP framework, we allocate three processors each of which has the entire EINCKM algorithm. For the PP and MRPP frameworks, we allocate three processors (one for *Build Cluster*, one for *Merge*, and one for *Prune*) to form one parallel stream. We allocate two processors serving as the two central sites in TPICDS. Figure 2 shows the performance of the adapted EINCKM algorithms in terms of execution time.

Among the adapted algorithms, the BP adaptation is slower than the PP and MRPP. The two pipeline adaptations show consistent faster speeds due to the additional parallelism gained from the pipeline frameworks. However, the MRPP adaptation consumes more time than the PP adaptation in mapping and hashing similar local clusters to a merger. The PP adaptation, however, may still have potential delays because the processor configuration on each pipeline was fixed, and some processors within the pipeline may have to wait for the outputs from other processors. Therefore, optimised and dynamic allocations of processors to the needed steps should be the right way to further exploit the parallelism.

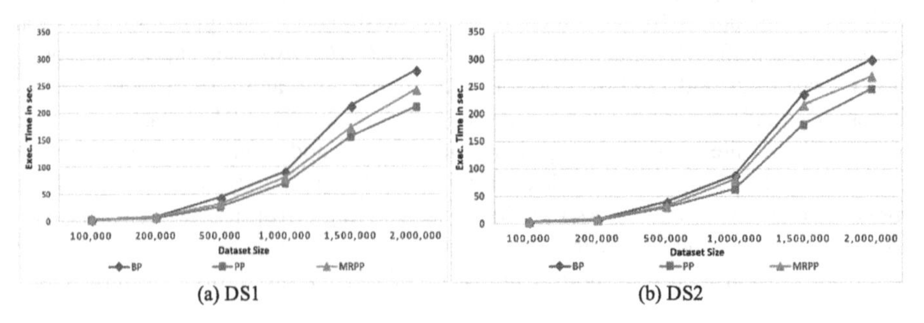

Fig. 2. Adapted algorithms performance in execution time

4 Optimised and Dynamic Parallel Pipeline Frameworks

4.1 An Optimised Parallel Pipeline Framework

The idea behind optimised parallel pipeline (OPP) framework is to decide how many processors should be statically allocated for each step of the EINCKM algorithm by analysing the time complexity of the algorithm. The time complexity of the entire algorithm is estimated by the sum of the time complexity for each of the three key functions [10]. Let R represent the number of chunks, N the total number of data points in a chunk plus the outliers, K the number of clusters, I the number of iterations until the clusters converge, T the number of clusters of the previous iteration, n the maximum number of data points in a new/existing cluster, k the number of clusters from a new chunk, and S the number of output clusters of merge function. The time complexity is $O(NKI)$ for the *Build Cluster* function, $O\left((Tn + kn)^2\right)$ for the *Merge* function, and $O(Sn)$ for the *Prune* function. The expressions indicate that the *Merge* function takes the longest amount of time in the worst case. This is followed by the *Prune* function. The *Build Cluster* function needs relatively the minimum amount of time because the values for N, K and I are normally small. In order to confirm the results of the theoretical analysis, we tested each function separately on synthesised data chunks of different sizes. Figure 3 illustrates the execution time for each function at different chunk sizes for DS1 and DS2 datasets. The test results confirm the theoretical analysis results.

According to this understanding, we configure the 12-core machine in the following way: two processors for the *Build Cluster* function, four processors for the *Merge* function, and three processors for the *Prune* function (see Sect. 4.3 for performance test results), plus two processors serving as the two central sites.

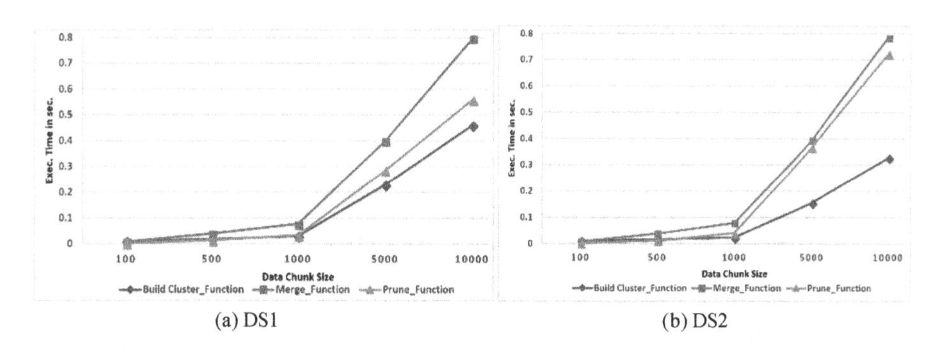

Fig. 3. Comparison of execution time among the key functions of EINCKM

4.2 Dynamic Parallel Pipeline Framework

The worst-case measure of time complexity does not always reflect the reality. Dynamic scheduling of resources based on actual execution of each individual step makes more sense in deciding how many processors should be allocated to resolve the bottleneck at the time. Therefore, a dynamic parallel pipeline (DPP) framework is proposed. In this framework, a minimum number of processors are initially allocated as the *baseline* processors for performing the clustering task. One central processor is then designated to the role of *scheduler* by monitoring occupancy rates of the buffers being used by the existing processors. A number of spare processors are held in reserve. A spare processor can be assigned to join the baseline processors for a specific function by the scheduler according to the need for additional assistance as indicated by the level of free buffer memory.

We encountered two immediate problems: (a) how to select the right number of baseline processors, and (b) how to decide if there is a need for allocating additional resources. To solve the first problem, we allocate by default one processor for each of the three key functions of the algorithm. To solve the second problem, we monitor the size of the buffers, decide where the possible bottleneck may occur and then take a decision to add/move a processor one at a time. For each iteration, the scheduler checks the use of two buffers (Bf1 and Bf2). If the buffer use, i.e. use of the storage space of the buffer, is below a minimum threshold (*Min_Thr*), the buffer is about to become empty and hence more processors are needed by the function that outputs *into* the buffer. If the buffer usage is above a maximum threshold (*Max_Thr*), it means that the buffer is about to become full and more processors are needed for the function that inputs *from* the buffer. Figure 4 shows four decision rules for the two possible situations: (a) there are processors in the reserve (assigning a processor), and (b) there are no processors in the reserve (moving a processor).

Dynamic Parallel Pipeline Algorithm:

Algorithm Steps:

$if\ size(Reserve) > 0\ then$ // **(a) First situation when have reserved processors**

$if\ size(Bf1) < Min\_Thr\ \&\ size(Bf2) < Min\_Thr\ then\ add\ processor\ to\ Build\ Cluster_s$

$elseif\ size(Bf1) < Min\_Thr\ \&\ size(Bf2) > Max\_Thr\ then\ add\ processor\ to\ Prune_s$

$elseif\ size(Bf1) > Max\_Thr\ \&\ size(Bf2) < Min\_Thr\ then\ add\ processor\ to\ Merge_s$

$elseif\ size(Bf1) > Max\_Thr\ \&\ size(Bf2) > Max\_Thr\ then\ add\ processor\ to\ Prune_s/Merge_s$

$else$ // **(b) Second situation when do not have reserved processors**

$if\ size(Bf1) < Min\_Thr\ \&\ size(Bf2) < Min\_Thr$
$then\ take\ one\ processor\ from\ Prune_s\ /\ Merge_s\ and\ add\ it\ to\ Build\ Cluster_s$

$if\ size(Bf1) < Min\_Thr\ \&\ size(Bf2) > Max\_Thr$
$then\ take\ one\ processor\ from\ Merge_s\ and\ add\ it\ to\ Prune_s$

$if\ size(Bf1) > Max\_Thr\ \&\ size(Bf2) < Min\_Thr$
$then\ take\ one\ processor\ from\ Prune_s\ and\ add\ it\ to\ Merge_s$

$if\ size(Bf1) > Max\_Thr\ \&\ size(Bf2) > Max\_Thr$
$then\ take\ one\ processor\ from\ Build\ Cluster_s\ and\ add\ it\ to\ Prune_s\ /\ Merge_s$

Fig. 4. Dynamic parallel pipeline framework

4.3 Experimental Results and Discussion

We used the two collections of datasets to test the performance of the OPP and the DPP frameworks. The results in Fig. 5 show that both OPP and DPP are consistently faster than the PP framework, confirming that optimised and dynamic allocations of processing resources are better than the even distribution of the resources among the processing steps. At the same time, the DPP framework performs better than the OPP one because the statically allocated processors in OPP does not reflect the dynamic reality.

One issue that affects the performance of the DPP framework is the setting of the two thresholds for the buffer use. For the tests presented in Fig. 5, we set *Min_Thr* = 20% and *Max_Thr* = 80%. Setting the range between the two thresholds too low means too many scheduling activities for additional resources. Setting the range too big means increasing the risk of the buffers being empty or full causing time delay in the process. Other factors such as the speed of data arrival and buffer sizes also play a role. A proper sensitivity study regarding the thresholds and the search for optimal thresholds certainly require further research.

We also compare the DPP version of the EINCKM algorithm against the BP versions of three typical existing algorithms of the same category, i.e. STREAM, Adapt.KM [24], and Inc.KM [25]. The results show faster execution time by the EINCKM algorithm than that by the Adapt.KM and the Inc.KM algorithms due to the dynamic allocations of processing resources to the right place in the EINCKM algorithm. The EINCKM algorithm speed is close to that, but slower than that of the STREAM algorithm (see Fig. 6). This is mainly because the STREAM algorithm does not consider the concept drift issue and nor identify outliers as the EINCKM does.

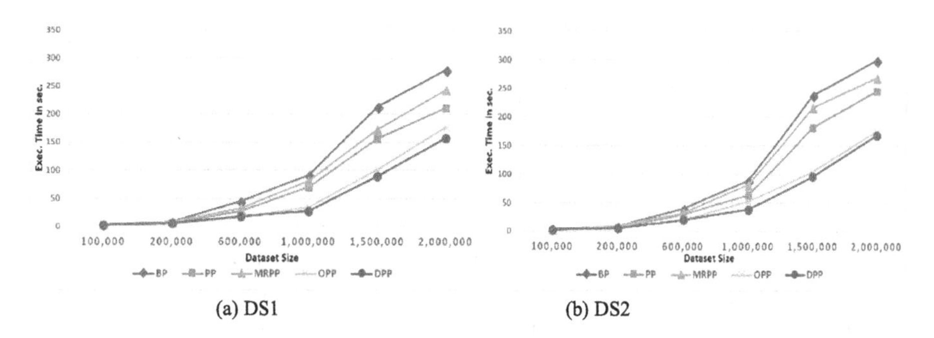

(a) DS1 (b) DS2

Fig. 5. The ratio between ideal time and the measured parallel frameworks

Regarding the correctness of the output clusters, we confirm that all the five versions of parallel EINCKM algorithm produce correct global clusters after the whole datasets are processed. We have evidence to demonstrate the correctness of the final global cluster models by comparing the output clusters by the algorithms against the ground truth clusters in terms of the correctness metrics such as purity, entropy, and the sum of square errors measurements. However, because of the constraints of the limited space, we are unable to present the evidence here.

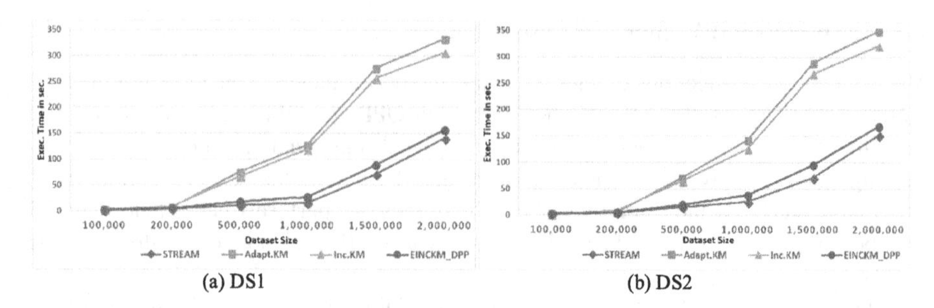

(a) DS1

(b) DS2

Fig. 6. Comparison between algorithms

Next generation of online real-time systems required big data platforms to process a huge amount of continuously arriving data under computational constraints [26]. This kind of systems raises new issues regarding the current big data infrastructures. One of the main issues is that most current platforms are not intentionally built to consider real-time performance issues. Another main issue is the lack of clear computational models for processing big data that could be supported by the current frameworks [8]. Recent attempts to address these issues include a study of analysing patterns in data stream processing and associating the patterns with performance requirements [4], and an effort in improving the computational model for distributed stream processing and formalising the model through extensions to the Storm framework for real-time application [27]. Our proposed parallel frameworks can be considered as another attempt to address the infrastructure issue for real-time applications at least on the local individual machine level. The strengths and limitations of the proposed framework have not been, but can only be realistically evaluated within the context of a large-scale distributed processing environment.

5 Conclusion and Future Work

This paper made two main contributions: (a) adapting a newly developed data stream clustering algorithm EINCKM to existing parallel frameworks, and (b) developing static and dynamic allocation schemes for utilising available processors, both within a two-phase learning approach (TPICDS). The adaptation is made easier because the algorithm has a modular structure, making it easy to adapt pipeline frameworks. The evidence shows that the static and dynamic allocations of processing resources is more efficient than simple adaptations.

The understandings we take from our work are of two folds. Firstly, there is a room to utilising as much as possible the available resources within a single computer before we bring in a group of computers to share the workload distributedly. Secondly, the two learning approaches for data stream clustering are artificially separated. The paper shows that a hybrid way of merging them in a parallel pipeline is possible.

Future work includes an immediate sensitivity analysis for the buffer thresholds and more extensive testing of the proposed dynamic parallel pipeline version of the EINCKM algorithm, and further improvements to dynamic allocation of resources by using more sophisticated techniques including machine learning techniques. Reclaim of processors into the reserve should also be considered when the speed of incoming data arrival slows down and there is no need to use a large number of processors to share out a small amount of workload. Another important work is the integration and testing of the dynamic parallel pipeline on a single computer with a distributed network environment.

Acknowledgements. The first author wishes to thank the University of Mosul and Government of Iraq/Ministry of Higher Education and Research (MOHESR) for funding him to conduct this research at the University of Buckingham.

References

1. Liu, C., Ranjan, R., Zhang, X., Yang, C., Georgakopoulos, D., Chen, J.: Public auditing for big data storage in cloud computing – a survey. In: 2013 IEEE 16th International Conference on Computational Science and Engineering, pp. 1128–1135, December 2013
2. Olshannikova, E., Ometov, A., Koucheryavy, Y.: Towards big data visualization for augmented reality. In: 2014 IEEE 16th Conference on Business Informatics, pp. 33–37, July 2014
3. Kaur, N., Sood, S.K.: Efficient resource management system based on 4Vs of big data streams. J. Big Data Res. **9**, 98–106 (2017)
4. Basanta-Val, P., Fernandez-Garcia, N., Sanchez-Fernandez, L., Arias-Fisteus, J.: Patterns for real-time stream processing. IEEE Trans. Parallel Distrib. Syst. **28**(11), 1–91 (2017)
5. Yogita, Y., Toshniwal, D.: Clustering techniques for streaming data – a survey. In: 3rd IEEE International Advance Computing Conference (IACC), pp. 951–956 (2012)
6. Sliwinski, T.S., Kang, S.-L.: Applying parallel computing techniques to analyze terabyte atmospheric boundary layer model outputs. J. Big Data Res. **7**, 31–41 (2017)
7. Yusuf, I.I., Thomas, I.E., Spichkova, M., Schmidt, H.W.: Chiminey: connecting scientists to HPC, cloud and big data. J. Big Data Res. **8**, 39–49 (2017)
8. Lv, Z., Song, H., Basanta-val, P., Steed, A., Jo, M.: Next-generation big data analytics: state of the art, challenges, and future research topics. IEEE Trans. Industr. Inf. **13**(4), 1891–1899 (2017)
9. Aggarwal, C.C.: Data Streams: Models and Algorithms, Book. Yorktown Hieghts, NY 10598. Kluwer Academic Publishers, Boston/Dordrecht/London (2007)
10. Al Abd Alazeez, A., Jassim, S., Du, H.: EINCKM: an enhanced prototype-based method for clustering evolving data streams in big data. In: Proceedings of the 6th International Conference on Pattern Recognition Applications and Methods, ICPRAM, pp. 173–183 (2017)
11. Guha, S., Mishra, N., Motwani, R., O'Callaghan, L.: Clustering data streams. In: IEEE FOCS Conference, pp. 359–366 (2000)
12. Aggarwal, C., Han, J., Wang, J., Yu, P.: A framework for clustering evolving data streams. In: Proceedings of the 29th VLDB Conference, Germany, pp. 1–12 (2003)
13. Silva, J., Faria, E., Barros, R., Hruschka, E., Carvalho, A.: Data stream clustering: a survey. ACM Comput. Surv. (CSUR), 1–37 (2013)
14. Bandyopadhyay, S., Giannella, C., Maulik, U., Kargupta, H., Liu, K., Datta, S.: Clustering distributed data streams in peer-to-peer environments. J. Inf. Sci. **176**(14), 1952–1985 (2006)
15. Gao, X., Ferrara, E., Qiu, J.: Parallel clustering of high-dimensional social media data streams. arXiv, pp. 323–332 (2015)

16. Rodrigues, P.P., Gama, J., Pedroso, J.P.: Hierarchical clustering of time-series data streams. IEEE Trans. Knowl. Data Eng. **20**(5), 615–627 (2008)
17. Zhou, A., Cao, F., Yan, Y., Sha, C., He, X.: Distributed data stream clustering : a fast EM-based approach. 1-4244-0803-2/07/$20.00 ©2007, pp. 736–745. IEEE (2007)
18. Yeh, M.Y., Dai, B.R., Chen, M.S.: Clustering over multiple evolving streams by events and correlations. IEEE Trans. Knowl. Data Eng. **19**(10), 1349–1362 (2007)
19. Guerrieri, A., Montresor, A.: DS-means: distributed data stream clustering. In: Kaklamanis, C., Papatheodorou, T., Spirakis, Paul G. (eds.) Euro-Par 2012. LNCS, vol. 7484, pp. 260–271. Springer, Heidelberg (2012). https://doi.org/10.1007/978-3-642-32820-6_27
20. Gama, J., Rodrigues, P.P., Lopes, M.L.: Clustering distributed sensor data streams using local processing and reduced communication. Intell. Data Anal. **15**(1), 3–28 (2011)
21. Talistu, M., Moh, T.S., Moh, M.: Gossip-based spectral clustering of distributed data streams. In: 2015 International Conference on High Performance Computing Simulation (HPCS), pp. 325–333 (2015)
22. Fu, T.Z.J., Ding, J., Ma, R.T.B., Winslett, M., Yang, Y., Zhang, Z.: DRS: dynamic resource scheduling for real-time analytics over fast streams. In: Proceedings of International Conference on Distributed Computing Systems, pp. 411–420, July 2015
23. Jin, C., Patwary, M.A., Agrawal, A., Hendrix, W., Liao, W., Choudhary, A.: DiSC: a distributed single-linkage hierarchical clustering algorithm using MapReduce. In: Proceedings of the International SC Workshop on Data Intensive Computing in the Clouds (DataCloud), pp. 1–10 (2013)
24. Bhatia, S.K., Louis, S.: Adaptive K-Means clustering. Am. Assoc. Artif. Intell. 1–5 (2004)
25. Chakraborty, S., Nagwani, N.K.: Analysis and study of incremental K-means clustering algorithm. In: Mantri, A., Nandi, S., Kumar, G., Kumar, S. (eds.) HPAGC 2011. CCIS, vol. 169, pp. 338–341. Springer, Heidelberg (2011). https://doi.org/10.1007/978-3-642-22577-2_46
26. Stoica, I.: Trends and challenges in big data processing. Proc. VLDB Endowment **9**(13), 1619–1622 (2016)
27. Basanta-Val, P., Fernández-García, N., Wellings, A.J., Audsley, N.C.: Improving the predictability of distributed stream processors. Future Gener. Comput. Syst. **52**, 22–36 (2015)

Cost of Fault-Tolerance on Data Stream Processing

Valerio Vianello[1(✉)], Marta Patiño-Martínez[1], Ainhoa Azqueta-Alzúaz[1], and Ricardo Jimenez-Péris[2]

[1] Universidad Politécnica de Madrid, Madrid, Spain
{vvianello,mpatino,aazqueta}@fi.upm.es
[2] LeanXcale, Madrid, Spain
rjimenez@leanxcale.com

Abstract. Data streaming engines process data on the fly in contrast to databases that first, store the data and then, they process it. In order to process the increasing amount of data produced every day, data streaming engines run on top of a distributed system. In this setting failures will likely happen. Current distributed data streaming engines like Apache Flink provide fault tolerance. In this paper we evaluate the impact on performance of fault tolerance mechanisms of Flink during regular operation (when there are no failures) on a distributed system and the impact on performance when there are failures. We use the Intel HiBench for conducting the evaluation.

Keywords: Data streaming · Fault tolerance · Evaluation · HiBench

1 Introduction

Data streaming has become a popular data processing model in the last decade with the increase of the amount of data that is produced every second that must be processed on the fly. Typical examples of streaming applications include quick detection of price changes in the stock market, credit card fraud detection, detection of attacks by inspecting network traffic among others. Data streaming engines run on top of distributed systems in order to process the high volumes of data produced every second (from thousands to millions of events per second). Distributed streaming engines like StreamCloud [8], Borealis [4] and Flink [1] have incorporated fault-tolerance mechanisms in order to ensure the availability of the system when a failure happens. Fault-tolerance mechanisms resort to checkpointing the state of the data streaming application and the data streams in order to be replayed when the system recovers after the failure, ensuring that all the data is processed. In this paper, we evaluate the performance overhead that the fault-tolerance mechanisms introduce during regular operation running the Intel HiBench benchmark [10] with Flink on top of a distributed system. We also evaluate the time the system needs to resume regular processing and the impact on performance till the system returns to regular operation (the

G. Mencagli et al. (Eds.): Euro-Par 2018 Workshops, LNCS 11339, pp. 17–27, 2019.
https://doi.org/10.1007/978-3-030-10549-5_2

system processes all the queued records during the failure). These performance evaluation is important for practitioners in order to dimension the system when fault-tolerance mechanisms are present and understand the behavior of the system when it recovers.

The rest of the paper is organized as follows. First we present an introduction to Flink (Sect. 2) then, the fault-tolerance mechanisms of Flink are described (Sect. 3). Section 4 presents the performance evaluation. Finally conclusions are presented in Sect. 5.

2 Flink Architecture

Apache Flink is an open-source distributed and fault-tolerant stream processing framework. A Flink program transforms the incoming data streams and returning results through sinks that can write them to different destinations. The transformations are also known as operators and the set of operators linked by the incoming and outgoing data streams form a topology that logically is a DAG (directed acyclic graph).

Flink provides several built-in operators which can be classified as stateless or stateful. Stateless operators do not keep any state. They simply transform the incoming data. Examples of stateless operators are *map, filter and union.* Stateful operators keep events in memory (windows) apply a function and produce an output (time windows) or a number of records are received (record based windows). Examples of stateful operators are *fold, aggregates, join.*

At the core of the Flink architecture there are two components that are JobManager and TaskManager. The JobManager is the master of a Flink cluster. More than one JobManager can be started in a Flink cluster to provide high availability. The JobManager is not directly involved in data processing, it is in charge of coordinating the distributed execution. The TaskManager runs topologies (or part of them) and manages the data exchange using streams.

Figure 1 shows how a client application (Flink Program) runs on a Flink cluster made by one JobManager and two TaskManagers. Each TaskManager (process) has its own Memory and Network Manager and can be configured with several task slots. On one hand, task slots are used to split and isolate TaskManager dedicated memory for different topologies. On the other hand, they fix the maximum number of concurrent sub-task (part of a topology) that can be running on a given TaskManager. In Fig. 1, TaskManagers are configured with three task slots, it means that three sub-tasks from three different topologies can be executed by the TaskManager. It is worth noting that Flink allows the deployment of different sub-tasks of a given topology to share the same task slot. The JobManager keeps track of the registered topologies and their corresponding dataflow graph. It also schedules the tasks and decides on which TaskManager they are executed. On the client side, a Flink program is used to build an optimized dataflow graph from the topology and deploy it on the Flink cluster sending it to the JobManager.

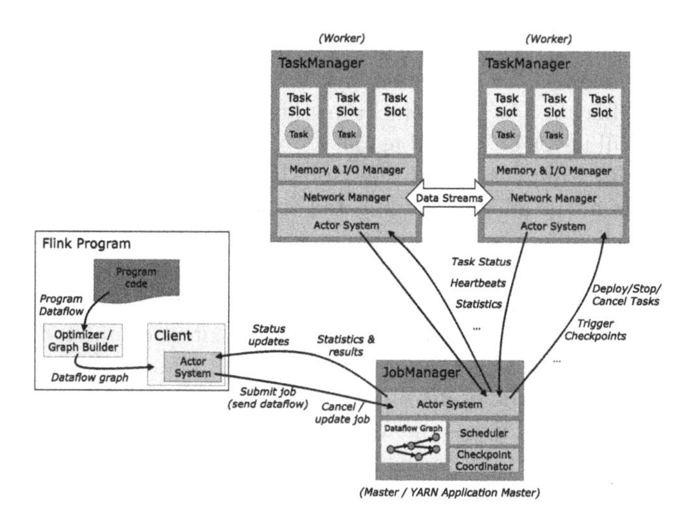

Fig. 1. Apache Flink runtime [7].

3 Fault Tolerance

Fault tolerance in Flink [6] is based on durable data sources and state checkpointing. A durable data source is able to replay records from a specified point in time in the past. Typically, a durable data source reads records from a persistent messaging system, such as Apache Kafka [3] or RabbitMQ [12], so in case a failure happens Flink can go back in time and re-read the input streams. Flink uses state checkpointing to save the state of topologies into a persistent storage. This state is recovered in case of failures. The persistent state must be accessible by all JobManagers and TaskManagers running in the Flink cluster in order to recover the state after a failure, hence a distributed filesystem, such as Hadoop Distributed File System [2], can be used for this purpose. This approach is similar to the one in [11]. Flink allows users to set different parameters to tune the checkpointing duration like the time between two consecutive checkpoints, the maximum time to wait for a checkpoint to be completed, the number of stored checkpoints.

A snapshot of an operator is taken when a special tuple, called barrier, is received from all its input streams. Then, the operator sends the barrier in all its outgoing streams. The JobManager injects the barriers in the streams at the data sources in order to take a distributed consistent snapshot. When a sink receives barrier n from all its incoming streams, it informs the snapshot coordinator. When the snapshot coordinator (the JobManager) receives this message from all the sinks in the topology, the n-th snapshot is completed. The snapshot can be taken synchronously or asynchronously. The former has an impact on the performance. If the snapshot is taken asynchronously, the state is copied as a background process and the operator immediately sends the barrier in its output streams. Once the state is copied, the operator informs the snapshot coordinator.

A snapshot is considered complete when the coordinator is informed by all sinks that they have received the corresponding barriers and stateful operators have completed their backup. At this point, the state at the sources corresponding to that snapshot will never be needed again.

When a failure happens, and the JobManager detects that one of the TaskManagers is not available, the affected topology is undeployed and a new deployment is scheduled on the available task slots. The JobManager cannot re-deploy the topology if there are not enough task slots left, in this case the topology is suspended until new TaskManagers join the Flink cluster making available their task slots. After a redeployment, the latest completed snapshot is selected (n). The state for checkpoint n is read from persistent storage and the streams are resent from the n offset.

Flink ensures at least once semantics. That is some tuples may be processed more than once. That is, records sent after the latest completed snapshot might be processed more than once.

Flink has recently introduced end-to-end exactly once semantics, where each incoming event affects the final result exactly once. For this purpose Flink uses a two-phase commit protocol that together with new special sink components, durable data source and checkpoint is able to ensure that there are no duplicate results in case of failures happen [5].

4 Evaluation

The goal of the performance evaluation is to evaluate the overhead that the fault-tolerance introduces in a regular processing and the cost of recovery. For this purpose the *HiBench* big data benchmark is used [9] and deployed in a cluster.

4.1 Benchmark

The *Hibench* provides a set of topologies already implemented for Apache Flink among them we picked the one that has window operators (*Fixwindow*) in order to test the performance of window operations in streaming frameworks. The benchmark creates records representing the visits of users to a web server. Each record has a total of 200 bytes and among the other fields it includes a timestamp taken at record creation time and the IP address of the client. Figure 2 depicts the graph representing the *Fixwindow* topology. The *Kafka source* source operator fetches records from the remote Kafka server. The *Map* operator projects *Timestamp* and *IP* fields of records from the input stream to the output stream ones. *KeyBy* partitions the stream using the *IP* field. *Window* stores events from each partition for a given amount of time. *Reduce* counts the elements in the window and emits one record with the *IP*, oldest *Timestamp* among the records in the window, and the number of elements in the window. The second *Map* operator adds a *Timestamp* to the record and writes it into Kafka.

The benchmark evaluates the latency of the operation calculating for each output record the difference in time between the *Timestamp* added in Flink by the latest Map in the topology and the *Timestamp* added by the benchmark at record creation time.

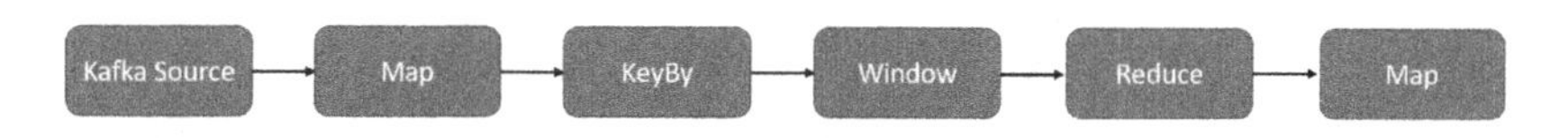

Fig. 2. HiBench fixwindow topology.

4.2 Setup

The evaluation was performed in a cluster with six homogeneous nodes. Each node is equipped with 2 CPU sockets with Intel XEON E5-2620 v3 with 6 cores (12 virtual cores), a total of 24 virtual cores, 128 GB RAM divided into 8 slots. Each slot contains a 16 GB RAM card. Each node is equipped with a directly attached SSD Intel SD3510 480 GB. All of them connected by a 1Gbit Ethernet. The software running on the nodes is: Intel HiBench 7.0, Flink 1.4.2, Kafka 2.10-0.8.2.2, Hadoop 2.6.5 and Zookeeper 3.4.8. Figure 3 shows where this software is running. *Node1* runs the HiBench benchmark. We used from 2 to 5 instances of the benchmark to increase the load. *Node2* runs HDFS to store Flink checkpoints and the HiBench data seed and Zookeeper for coordinating the Kafka cluster and the JobManager of Flink. *Node3* and *Node4* run 6 Kafka Brokers each. *Node5* and *Node6* run 12 JobManagers each. JobManagers are configured with 2 task slots (for a total availability of 48 task slots) and 8 GB of memory.

The experiments are run with different configurations and loads summarized in the Table 1. Varying the number of HiBench instances generates loads from 200,000 records per second up to 500,000 records per second. We ran experiments with and without Flink checkpointing mechanism in order to measure the overhead of the checkpointing mechanism during regular operation. Checkpoints are taken every second and stored in HDFS. Later, failures are injected in both configurations and the time for recovery is measured.

Table 1. Experiments configurations.

Input load (r/sec)	Window size	Checkpointing	Fault injection
200k–500k	50 Records	No	No
200k–500k	30 to 50 Records	HDFS	No
200k–500k	30 to 50 Records	HDFS	Yes
200k–500k	50 Records	HDFS + RocksDB	No
200k–500k	50 Records	HDFS + RocksDB	Yes

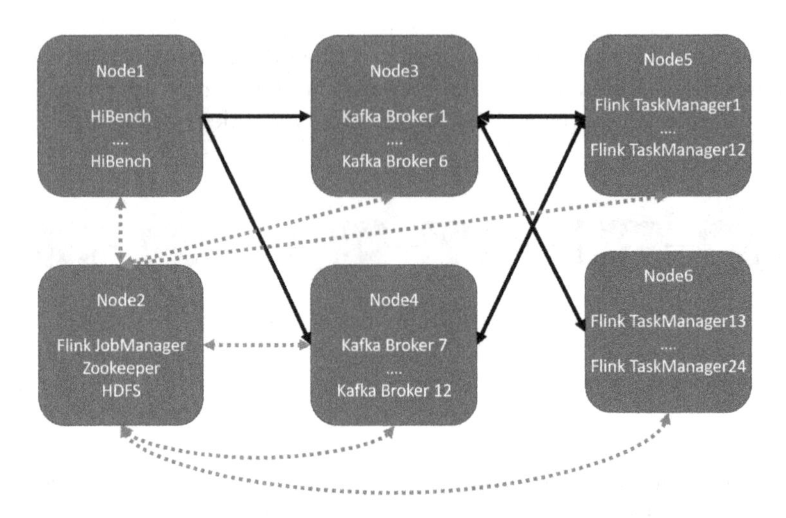

Fig. 3. Evaluation setup.

4.3 Performance Evaluation Results

For all experiments we show measure both latency (on the left axis) and throughput (on the right axis). The latency represents the difference in time between the timestamp of the newest record that falls in a window and the timestamp taken when the result record of the window is generated; it is measured in milliseconds and we report the mean value per second. The throughput shows the number of result records created per second, that is the number of windows that are triggered per second. The x-axis shows the time evolution during an experiment. Second 0 in the x-axis corresponds to the first output received from Flink. First, we run experiments without the checkpointing mechanism. Figure 4 reports the results of these experiments with four different loads.

In all cases, Flink is able to process the load with a very low latency that is always smaller than 200 ms. The maximum throughput is around 40K, 70K, 80K and 100K records per second for the increasing load. This maximum is reached twice with a load of 200K records per second (Fig. 4a), three times with 300K (Fig. 4b) and four times with 400K and 500K per second (Figs. 4c and d). These peaks happen because the load is increased by adding more HiBench instances but, the key space remains the same causing the same windows (there is a window per key) to be triggered more times. As the load increases, windows are filled at a faster pace.

Figure 5 shows the experiments with the checkpointing mechanism enabled in Flink and the same workloads. Comparing Figs. 4a and 5a we observe that the latency of the window processing with the checkpointing mechanism enabled is almost equal to the baseline case. This happens because Flink stores the snapshot of the state asynchronously and if the load is not too high it is able to perform both operations without a noticeable penalty on the latency. However, as the load increases, the latency increases up to 1 second with a load of 300K (Fig. 5b) and

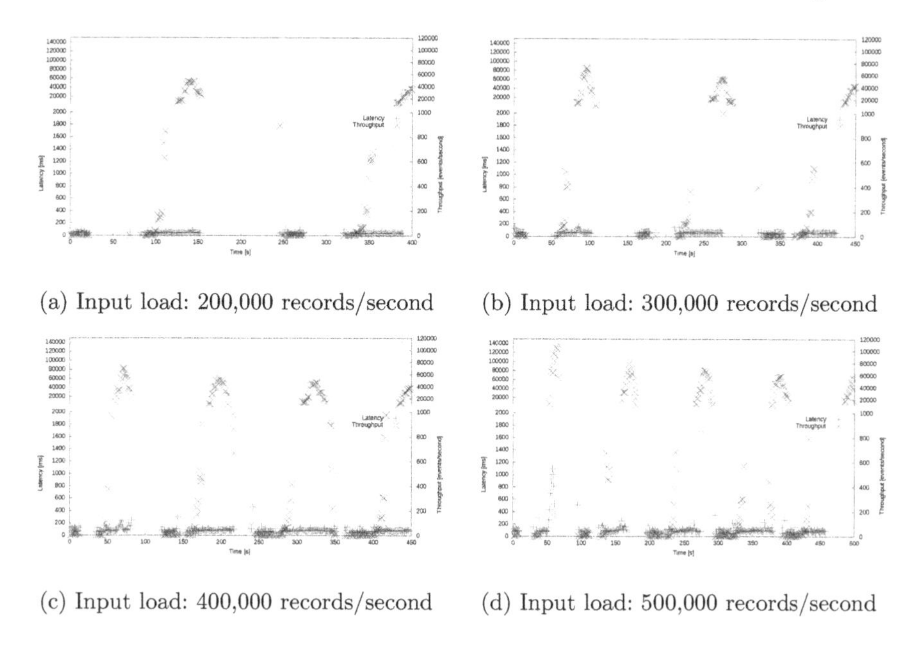

(a) Input load: 200,000 records/second

(b) Input load: 300,000 records/second

(c) Input load: 400,000 records/second

(d) Input load: 500,000 records/second

Fig. 4. Experiments results with checkpointing disabled.

up to 2 s when the load increases to 400k and 500k records per second (Fig. 5c and d). This happens because there are more concurrent windows to checkpoint and taking and storing the snapshot consumes CPU cycles that cannot be used to process the input load and therefore, the processing time of records increases.

Figure 6 shows the CPU utilization per core in one of the two nodes used for running Flink in the experiments with 200k and 500k record per second checkpointing the state to HDFS. It can be observed that with 200K the CPU usage is on average 40% while with a load of 500K the system is almost saturated with 70% CPU usage on average.

Figure 7 presents the results of the experiments with failures in order to measure impact of failures when the system recovers. The fault is injected by killing one of the TaskManagers running the topology 90 s after the first outputs are produced. Flink takes around 90 s to detect the failure and resume processing that is, detect the failure of the TaskManager, undeploy the topology, redeploy the topology on the available task-slots, load the state and restart the normal processing. During that period there is no throughput (Figs. 7a, b and c). Then, the latency is very high in all setups: up to 1 min with a load of 200 records per second and reaching up to 2 min with the other configurations. This happens because the data needs to be resent from the source and there are a lot of data that are waiting to be processed while the system recovers. These data are processed in 60 s with a load of 200K records (after second 210 latency is below 200 ms), 150 s with a load of 300K records, 170 s for a load of 400K. The system

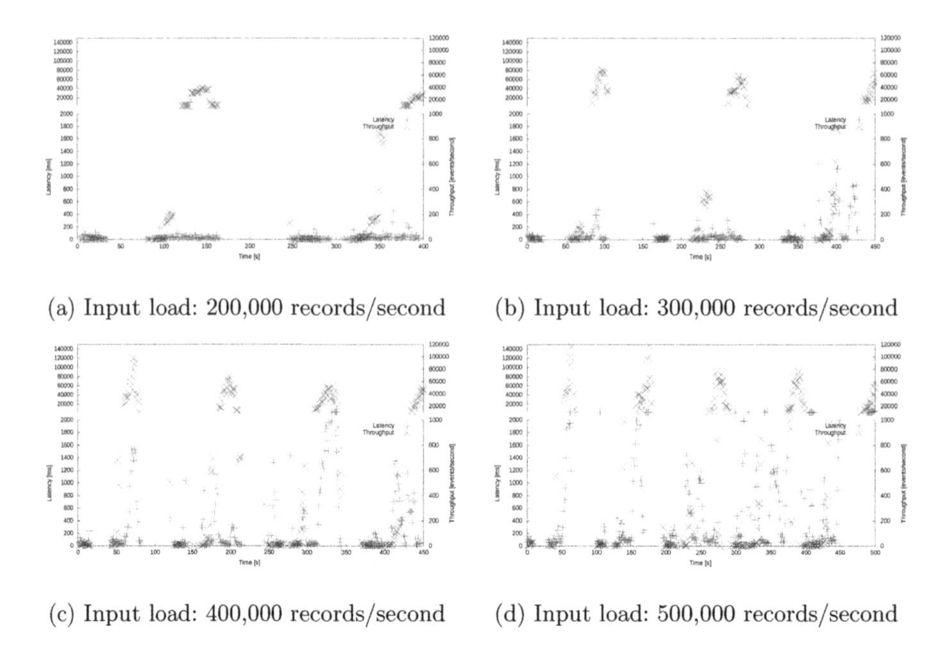

(a) Input load: 200,000 records/second (b) Input load: 300,000 records/second

(c) Input load: 400,000 records/second (d) Input load: 500,000 records/second

Fig. 5. Performance with checkpointing on HDFS

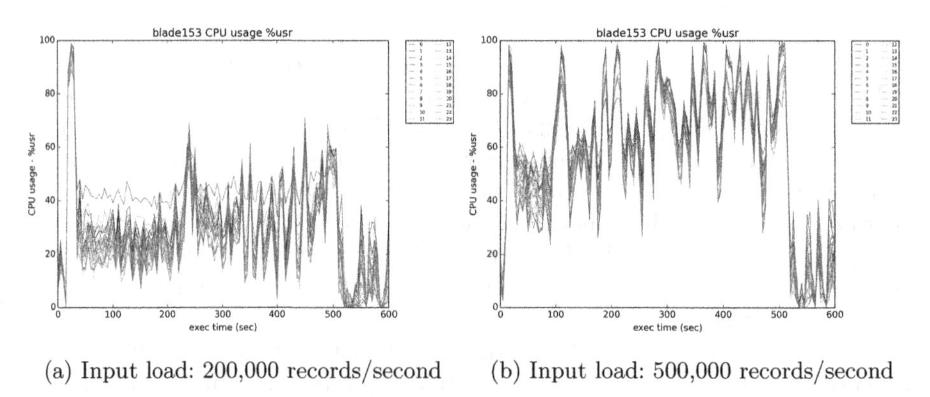

(a) Input load: 200,000 records/second (b) Input load: 500,000 records/second

Fig. 6. CPU utilization on one of the Flink nodes

is not able to return to regular latencies after 260 s with a load of 500K records, showing latencies higher than 20 s during that period.

Figure 8 reports the CPU usage per core in the two nodes running Flink when the input load rate is 500,000 record per second. Both nodes have a CPU consumption similar to the one of Fig. 6b (checkpoint enabled without faults) at the beginning of the experiment before the failure. When the failure happens, CPU usage goes to 0 and after the recovery both nodes are completely saturated processing the pending load.

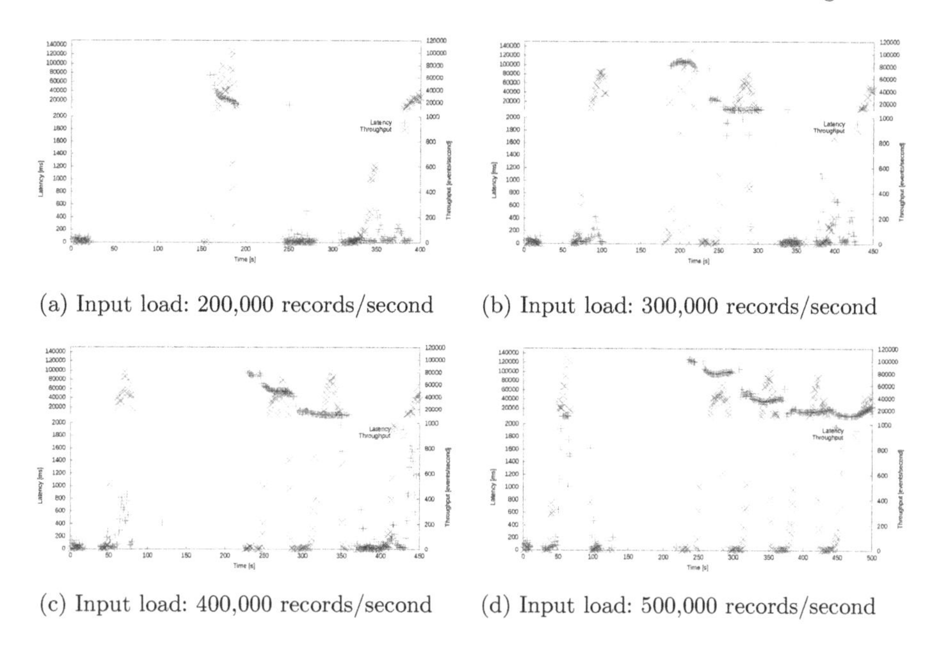

(a) Input load: 200,000 records/second (b) Input load: 300,000 records/second

(c) Input load: 400,000 records/second (d) Input load: 500,000 records/second

Fig. 7. Performance with checkpointing on HDFS and fault injection

To study the impact of the state size to be checkpointed on the latency, we run a set of experiments, with the checkpointing, with different window size 30, 40 and 50 records. The window size represents the state to be checkpointed. Figure 9 shows the latency graphs with the four loads.

The latency for different window sizes is similar for low loads (200K records per second). As the load increases, the latency increases first for the larger windows (with 300K records) and then for all the window sizes with a high load (500K records per second). As expected the window size has an impact on the time to retrieve and store the checkpoint and therefore in the regular latency.

Table 2 reports the latency percentiles (75% and 95%) for each of the experiments with different window size. For the window size of 50 records we also report the latency percentiles when there is no checkpointing. The 75% percentile is smaller than 200 ms in any configuration when the input load is either 200,000 or 300,000 records per second. When the load is 400,000 records per second, the latency (75% percentile) when the state is 40 or 50 records reaches up to 768 ms in the case of 50-records window. With the highest workload, the 75% percentile latency is between 3 and 10 times higher than the case with no checkpointing depending on the state size. The 95% percentile shows latency values much greater than the 75% percentile due to the peaks in the latency that happen when there are many windows triggered at the same time. The impact of the window size on latency is clearly shown with the largest window comparing the latencies with and without checkpointing. The latency is at least double when chekpointing is enabled.

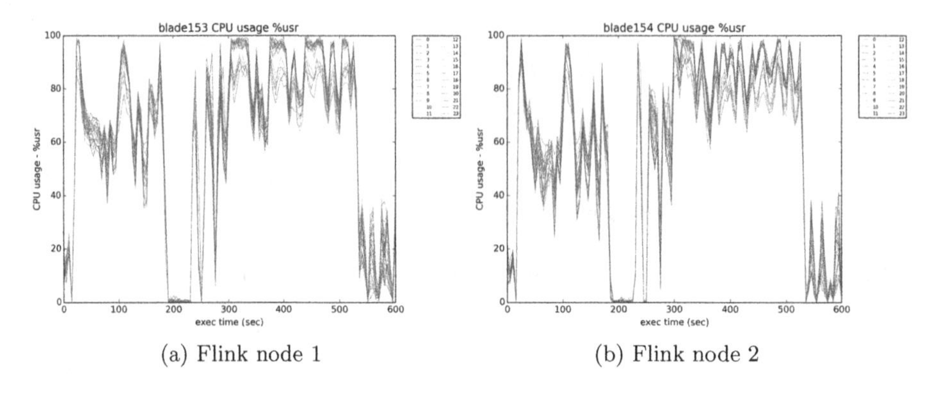

(a) Flink node 1 (b) Flink node 2

Fig. 8. CPU usage on Flink nodes with failures

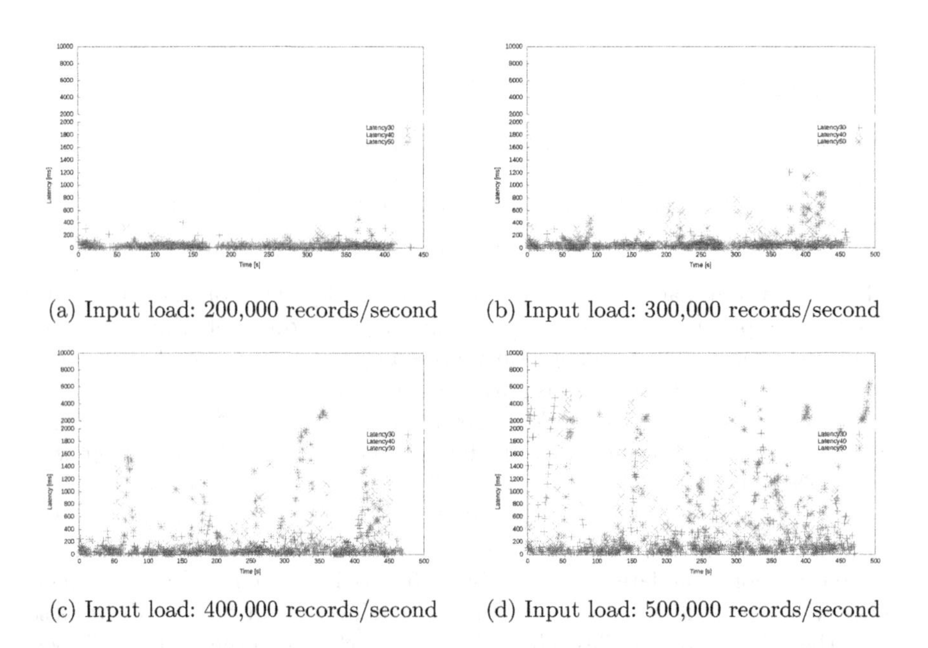

(a) Input load: 200,000 records/second (b) Input load: 300,000 records/second

(c) Input load: 400,000 records/second (d) Input load: 500,000 records/second

Fig. 9. Latency varying the window size

Table 2. Latency. Percentiles 75% and 95%

Input Load (r/sec)	Window size 30	Window size 40	Window size 50	Window size 50 no chekpointing
200k	25–113 ms	32–281 ms	34–286 ms	73–158 ms
300k	60–279 ms	125–855 ms	172–947 ms	89–215 ms
400k	127–622 ms	391–2062 ms	768–4186 ms	108–282 ms
500k	681–2499 ms	885–3194 ms	1922–4982 ms	212–1060 ms

5 Conclusions

This paper describes and evaluate the fault tolerance mechanisms available in Apache Flink, the current de facto standard for streaming processing engines. The paper focuses on the overhead of these mechanisms on the latency and throughput through a comprehensive set of experiments. The analysis of the results shows that when the fault tolerance mechanisms are enabled, the latency can grow up the 10 times the baseline values. In presence of failures the system is able to recover quite quickly if it has enough available resources to process the peak on the input load after that the failure happens. As future work, we are interested in evaluating the performance of the system in presence of multiple topologies deployed at same time and the overhead of the exactly once end-to-end protocols.

Acknowledgments. This research has been partially funded by the European Commission under projects CloudDBAppliance, CrowdHealth and BigDataStack (grants H2020-732051, H2020-727560 and H2020-779747), the Madrid Regional Council, FSE and FEDER, project Cloud4BigData (grant S2013TIC2894), the Ministry of Economy and Competitiveness (MINECO) under project CloudDB (grant TIN2016-80350).

References

1. Apache flink. https://flink.apache.org/. Accessed 11 May 2018
2. Apache hadoop. http://hadoop.apache.org/. Accessed 11 May 2018
3. Apache kafka. https://kafka.apache.org/. Accessed 11 May 2018
4. Balazinska, M., Balakrishnan, H., Madden, S., Stonebraker, M.: Fault-tolerance in the borealis distributed stream processing system. ACM Trans. Database Syst. **33**(1), 3:1–3:44 (2008)
5. Flink an overview of end-to-end exactly-once processing in apache flink. https://flink.apache.org/features/2018/03/01/end-to-end-exactly-once-apache-flink.html. Accessed 11 May 2018
6. Flink checkpointing. https://ci.apache.org/projects/flink/flink-docs-release-1.4/dev/stream/state/checkpointing.html. Accessed 11 May 2018
7. Flink runtime. https://ci.apache.org/projects/flink/flink-docs-release-1.4/concepts/runtime.html. Accessed 11 May 2018
8. Gulisano, V., Jiménez-Peris, R., Patiño-Martínez, M., Soriente, C., Valduriez, P.: Streamcloud: an elastic and scalable data streaming system. IEEE Trans. Parallel Distrib. Syst. **23**(12), 2351–2365 (2012)
9. Hibench, a big data benchmark suite. https://github.com/intel-hadoop/HiBench. Accessed 11 May 2018
10. Huang, S., Huang, J., Dai, J., Xie, T., Huang, B.: The HiBench benchmark suite: characterization of the MapReduce-based data analysis. In: 22nd International Conference on Data Engineering Workshops, pp. 41–51 (2010). https://doi.org/10.1109/icdew.2010.5452747
11. Kwon, Y., Balazinska, M., Greenberg, A.: Fault-tolerant stream processing using a distributed, replicated file system. Proc. VLDB Endow. **1**(1), 574–585 (2008). https://doi.org/10.14778/1453856.1453920
12. Rabbitmq. https://www.rabbitmq.com/. Accessed 11 May 2018

Autonomic and Latency-Aware Degree of Parallelism Management in SPar

Adriano Vogel[1(✉)], Dalvan Griebler[1,3], Daniele De Sensi[2], Marco Danelutto[2], and Luiz Gustavo Fernandes[1]

[1] School of Technology, Pontifical Catholic University of Rio Grande do Sul, Porto Alegre, Brazil
adriano.vogel@acad.pucrs.br
[2] Department of Computer Science, University of Pisa, Pisa, Italy
[3] Laboratory of Advanced Research on Cloud Computing, Três de Maio Faculty, Três de Maio, Brazil

Abstract. Stream processing applications became a representative workload in current computing systems. A significant part of these applications demands parallelism to increase performance. However, programmers are often facing a trade-off between coding productivity and performance when introducing parallelism. SPar was created for balancing this trade-off to the application programmers by using the C++11 attributes' annotation mechanism. In SPar and other programming frameworks for stream processing applications, the manual definition of the number of replicas to be used for the stream operators is a challenge. In addition to that, low latency is required by several stream processing applications. We noted that explicit latency requirements are poorly considered on the state-of-the-art parallel programming frameworks. Since there is a direct relationship between the number of replicas and the latency of the application, in this work we propose an autonomic and adaptive strategy to choose the proper number of replicas in SPar to address latency constraints. We experimentally evaluated our implemented strategy and demonstrated its effectiveness on a real-world application, demonstrating that our adaptive strategy can provide higher abstraction levels while automatically managing the latency.

Keywords: Autonomic computing · Stream processing
Parallel programming · Adaptive degree of parallelism

1 Introduction

Stream processing applications gained even more attention in the recent computing age due to the increasing use of techniques to collect data from different sources (*e.g.*, sensors, cameras, radars). These applications are characterized by a continuous flow of data and high variance of input data rates [2,3]. In addition to that, due to the growing of data generation, parallel programming can

G. Mencagli et al. (Eds.): Euro-Par 2018 Workshops, LNCS 11339, pp. 28–39, 2019.
https://doi.org/10.1007/978-3-030-10549-5_3

be used in stream processing applications as an option for increasing performance. A set of programming frameworks and libraries were developed to allow the stream parallelism exploitation on multi-core systems. Examples are Intel Thread Building Blocks (TBB) [14], FastFlow [1,7], and StreamIt [17]. Despite the coding abstraction introduced by these programming frameworks, they are still not abstract enough for application programmers, which are the ones focused on developing the stream processing application [10] and which may not be parallel programming experts.

To raise the abstraction level on stream parallel applications, the SPar [9] DSL (domain-specific language) was designed for parallelizing stream processing application in a simpler and more productive way than the state-of-the-art alternatives [10]. SPar maintains the sequential structure of C++ codes and programmers identify regions that can run in parallel. The programmer can annotate these regions by using C++11 attributes, and the SPar compiler will parse such annotations and generate the associated parallel code. Some regions can be executed concurrently by a number of entities called *replicas*. In SPar, as well as in other state-of-the-art frameworks, the number of concurrent entities (i.e., the degree of parallelism) is static and must be manually set by the programmer. Choosing a proper number of replicas is a complex task, since the best choice depends both on the arrival rate of the data but also on the performance requirements for the specific application. For example, while having more replicas can improve the throughput, it could also increase the latency required to process the stream items. Unfortunately at moment being, SPar and other state-of-the-art frameworks (TBB, FastFlow, and StreamIt) do not provide any automatic and latency-aware strategy for selecting the most appropriate number of replicas.

In this work, we propose a strategy to automatically set, without any user intervention, the number of replicas to be used in parallel applications with SPar. The optimal number of replicas will be selected according to the latency requirements of the application. The main contributions of this work are:

- An extension of the SPar DSL [9,10] with a new parallelism abstraction. This abstraction is achieved by a strategy to automatically adapt the number of replicas in SPar that is fully abstracted from the application programmer. The adaptation mechanism is designed based on a feedback loop, through which a specific latency Quality of Service (QoS) is provided. The application is monitored at run-time and the adaptation strategy periodically takes actions to optimize the number of replicas, considering the latency of stream items. Consequently, the adaptation strategy concerns stream processing applications sensitive to latency.
- An experimental evaluation of the effectiveness of the strategy running on a stream processing application.

The remainder of this paper is organized as follows: the next section presents the scenario of this study. The need for low latency in stream processing applications is emphasized in Sect. 3. Section 4 presents the strategy that manages the latency by adapting the number of replicas. In Sect. 5 we present our experimental evaluation. Then, the related work is discussed in Sect. 6. Eventually, in Sect. 7 we draw the conclusion and discuss some possible future directions for this work.

2 An Overview of SPar

SPar[1] is a DSL for stream parallelism that offers high-level C++11 attributes to enable automatic parallelization by means of source code annotations. The parallel code is generated by SPar compiler through source-to-source transformations [9]. SPar relies on the FastFlow runtime, a high-level and pattern-based parallel programming library [1,7]. SPar's compiler generates parallel code using FastFlow library through source-to-source transformations. SPar also allows code parallelism by simply adding annotations in the original sequential code. By doing so, SPar relieves the programmers from the effort in dealing with advanced concepts such as scheduling, load balancing and parallelism strategies. Since SPar is based on the C++ standard interface, application programmers do not need to learn a new language for parallelizing their code, and can just focus on the functional parts of their applications.

SPar provides five attributes, which we describe in the following to exploit key aspects of stream parallelism (Listing 1.1 presents a use case example). The `ToStream` attribute represents the beginning of a stream region with the production of the stream elements. Inside the *ToStream* section, it is possible to add a number of `Stages`, which represents different and subsequent phases of the computation over the stream elements. The data needed by each stage can be indicated by using the `Input` attribute. Similarly, by using the `Output` attribute, the programmer can specify the variables representing the data produced by the stage.

```
1 [[spar::ToStream]] while(1){
2  i = read_item();
3  [[spar::Stage,spar::Input(i),spar::Output(i),spar::Replicate(n)]]
4  {
5    i = filtering(i);
6  }
7  [[spar::Stage,spar::Input(i)]]{
8   write_item(i);
9  }
10 }
```

Listing 1.1. SPar example.

Each stage can be executed by multiple threads. To define how many threads (replicas) should be used for a stage, the `Replicate` attribute can be used. As SPar currently supports stateless stream operators, each replica is independent from the others and they can operate in parallel without any need of synchronization among them. During the source-to-source compilation process, some flags can be specified to customize the behaviour of the generated code. For

[1] SPar home page: https://gmap.pucrs.br/spar.

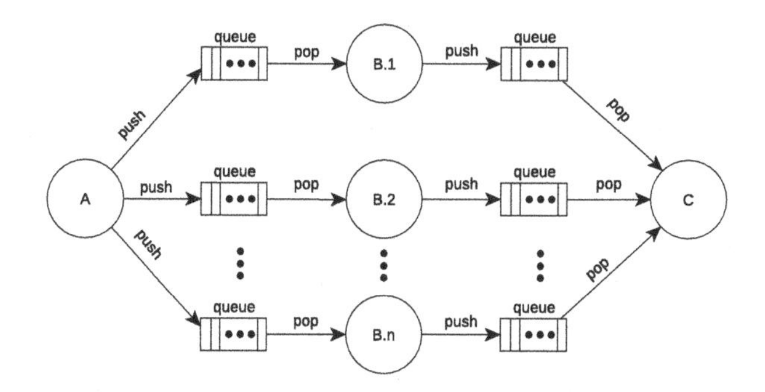

Fig. 1. Farm - communication queues inside SPar runtime.

example, to change the way in which the elements are scheduled to the replicas or to preserve the order of the stream elements among different stages [9].

In Listing 1.1, we show a trivial example of a sequential code enhanced by means of SPar annotations. This application generates the stream, applies a function over each stream element, and then outputs the results. In Fig. 1, we can visualize the association between the different parts of the code and the execution unit, which will be executed in parallel.

In this specific example, n replicas are activated (which corresponds to B.1 to B.n in Fig. 1), each of which receive data from the previous stage and sends produced results to the subsequent stage. Communications between stages occur through shared queues. By default, SPar schedules the stream items to the workers with a round-robin policy. However, other scheduling strategies can be used and this behaviour can be customized during the source-to-source compilation process. For example, to improve load balancing, it is possible to schedule stream items in an *on-demand* fashion so that an element is scheduled to a specific worker when it is not already processing another element.

3 The Impact of Parallelism on Latency

In this section we describe the relationship between the number of replicas and the performance in a stream processing application. We consider the *Lane Detection* application [11], a video processing application used to identify road lanes in videos recorded, for example, by self-driving vehicles. This application has a similar structure to that shown in Fig. 1 (3 stages) where one stage is replicated by a number of times. In the experiments, we used as input a video file (5.25 MB - 640 × 360 pixels) to simulate a typical execution of a video streaming application. We execute this application on a multi-core machine composed by 12 cores with 2-way Simultaneous MultiThreading (SMT) for a total of 24 hardware threads.

Firstly, we show in Fig. 2(a) the throughput of the application (i.e. how many stream elements per second are processed) for different number of replicas. The number of replicas is statically chosen and never modified during the execution.

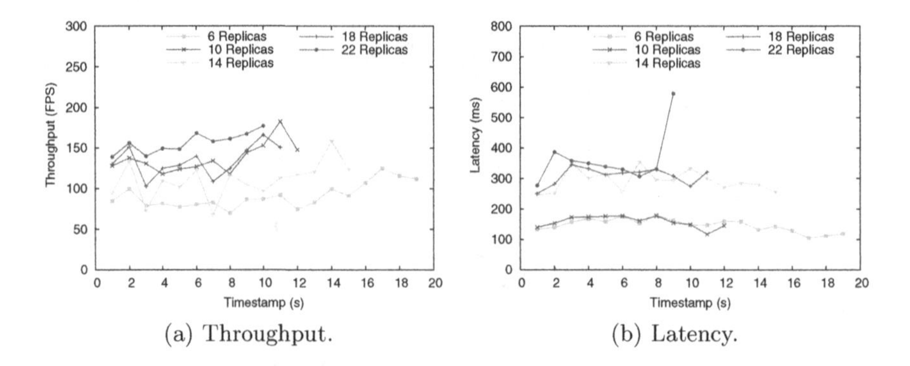

(a) Throughput. (b) Latency.

Fig. 2. Lane detection characterization.

These results prove that the use of SMT is beneficial for the throughput of this kind of application since the best throughput is obtained by using 22 replicas.

As shown in Fig. 2(b), increasing the number of replicas may have detrimental effects on the latency of the application. It is worth noting that a significant increase in the latency (as well as a decrease in the throughput) can be observed when more than 10 replicas are used. Moreover, it is possible to note a significant increase in the oscillation of the latency when using more replicas. These effects are caused by the contention between stages running on two SMT cores corresponding to a same physical core.

There can be seen a correlation between throughput and latency. Achieving a high throughput using many replicas tends to increase the latency. On the other hand, using too few replicas decreases the throughput and latency. Consequently, a balance between the two performance goals is required. The challenge is that a high throughput is commonly pursued, and at the same time low latency may also be necessary. In this work, the goal is to manage latency in replicated stages.

4 Autonomous Degree of Parallelism

In the previous section we have seen how the number of replicas affects the latency of stream items. Responding in real-time according to latency constraints and the actual rates cannot be done manually by the programmer. As a consequence, we are abstracting from programmers the aspects related to the number of replicas and latency for latency sensitive applications.

We implemented a strategy in the SPar's runtime that monitors and manages the latency of stream items by adjusting the number of replicas. Figure 3 shows the architecture we use to adapt the number of replicas considering the monitored latency of stream items. This adaptive mechanism is based on a feedback loop [13] that at each *control step*, monitors the application and takes decision so to optimize the execution of the application at the next step. By doing so, it is possible to be reactive to select the best number of replicas even in presence of workload fluctuations, which is common in data streaming applications. The

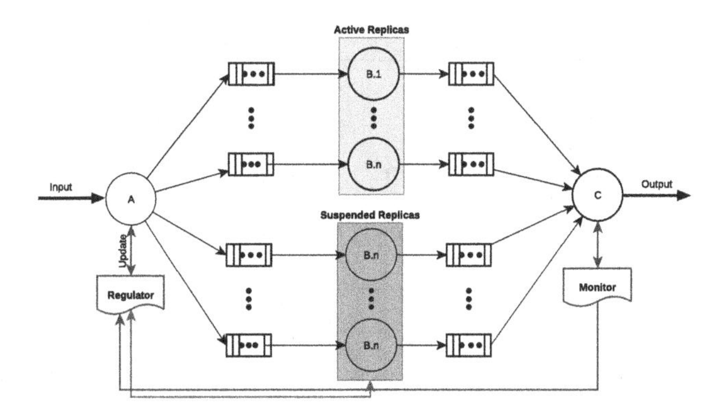

Fig. 3. Latency - Regulator and Monitor.

implemented strategy works on a single replicated stage. However, this strategy can also work in more complex compositions formed by several replicated stages, and each stage can use the adaptive mechanisms under a global strategy. Also, SPar replicates stateless stages, in case of an internal state, it would need to be handled by other means.

A *monitor* routine is attached to the last stage of the application. It monitors the latency of each stream element and calculates the average latency of the elements processed in each iteration of the feedback loop. The latency calculated by the monitor is read by a *regulator* connected to the first stage of the application. The regulator, by using the information collected by the monitor, decides which actions to take at the next step of the feedback loop in order to enforce the latency required by the user.

In Algorithm 1 we show the regulator used in this work. It calls the monitor for the current latency and when it is higher than the target one, the number of replicas is reduced. On the other hand, the regulator increases the number of replicas if the latency is significantly lower than the constraint. The part that dynamically regulates the parallelism was implemented using low-level calls to the FastFlow runtime library for changing the status of the replicas (active, suspended). The regulator changes the number of replicas at run-time without restarting the application. In order to avoid oscillation in the number of replicas, a threshold value is used so that the number of replicas is not increased when the latency is lower but close to the constraint. This strategy of the regulator tries to maximize throughput while the latency constraint is met, pursuing a balance between throughput and latency requirements.

By considering the example in Fig. 3, if executed on a machine with N cores, we would activate at most $N-2$ replicas. Indeed, as we shown in Fig. 2(b), when the replicas share the computing resources with other stages of the application, this could lead to detrimental effects for both latency and throughput of the application. The regulator we shown in Algorithm 1 assumes that at most one stage is replicated. If more stages are replicated, the strategy should find the best number of replicas for each of them. We will consider this scenario in our future

Algorithm 1. Parallelism Regulator

```
1: procedure REGULATOR( )
2:     while true do
3:         Sleep(timeInterval)                          ▷ Wait until the next iteration
4:         if Latency > Constraint then                 ▷ Latency is too high
5:             SuspendReplica()
6:         else if Latency < Constraint − Threshold then
7:             WakeUpReplica()
```

work. Moreover, the implemented strategy works on stateless computations. In case of a stateful scenario, the internal state would need to be handled manually.

An important part of the configuration is the scaling factor (SF), which is how many threads/replicas are added or remove when adjusting the degree of parallelism. In the literature, the most common SF value is 1 threads/replicas. Our implementation is tested with SF of 1 and 2, thus in lines 5 and 7 of Algorithm 1, 1 or 2 replicas can be suspended or awaken on each iteration.

Another relevant aspect is how often the algorithm should consider the possibility of adding/removing replicas. The most common approach is time-driven that, at fixed time intervals, it decides if changing the number of active replicas. The choice of the time interval is critical and depends from the application. In general, a shorter time interval allows to react quickly to changes in the application. In [4,8,15], the authors used time intervals ranges from 0.1 to 5 s. For our scenario, we consider 1 s as the default time interval. We experimentally saw that this configuration avoids too many changes in the number of replicas, but also maintain a correct level of sensitivity to application fluctuations. The impact on latency caused by the different choices of the time interval is left to be evaluated in the future.

5 Results

Stream processing applications may run only pursuing the maximum throughput without considering the latency. However, it is not suitable for those latency sensitive applications that need to rapidly return their results. At the same time, using a minimal number of replicas for reducing the latency tends to result in a low throughput as well as inefficient usage of computational resources. Therefore, our regulator tries to improve the throughput by increasing the number of replicas when the latency is below the constraint. We tested our strategy for latency with the same application and input used in Sect. 3. In this experiments, the scaling factor (SF) of the parallelism regulator was 1 or 2, meaning that on each reconfiguration one or two replicas can be activated or suspended. Also, we used a control step of 1 s, which is a time interval sensitive enough to react without compromising the overall execution. Another aspect tested is related to the thresholds of the latency constraint presented in Sect. 4. In our scenario, the best thresholds were 10% and 20%.

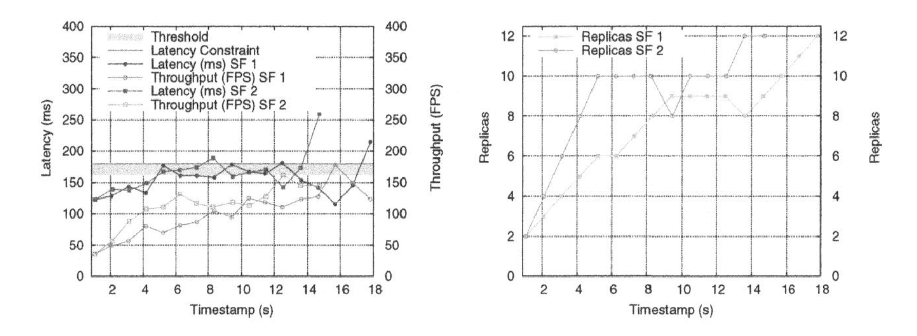

Fig. 4. Threshold 10% - Latency constraint of 180 ms (Left) and replicas used (Right).

In Fig. 4, we show on the left side the throughput and latency of the application, while on the right side we plot the number of replicas used during the execution. In this experiment, we set a latency constraint of 180 ms with a 10% threshold. As we can see from the Fig. 4, the number of replicas is reduced when the latency increases, and the number of replicas is changed several times due to oscillations in the input video. Comparing the configurations, we observed that SF of 2 reacts faster to changes and increases the throughput at the price of more latency violations.

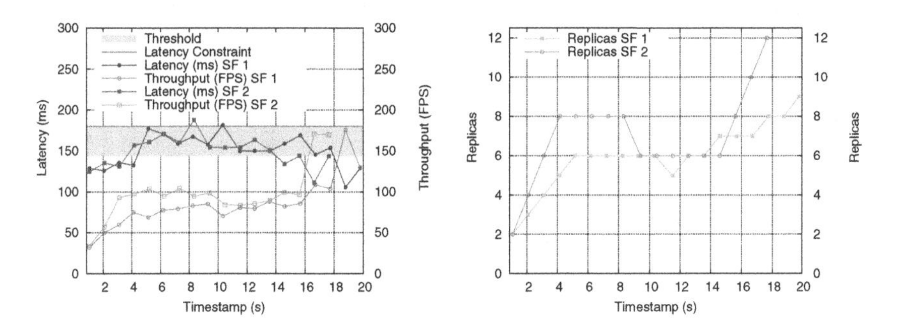

Fig. 5. Threshold 20% - Latency constraint of 180 ms (Left) and replicas used (Right).

In Fig. 5 is presented an experiment with the same latency constraint but using a threshold of 20%. In this experiment, fewer latency violations occurred because the threshold of 20% is more conservative, which avoids adding more replicas when the latency is close to the constraint. Comparing thresholds 10% and 20%, we noted that the effectiveness of threshold 20% in managing the latency did not decrease the application throughput significantly. Moreover, SF of 1 is more stable by avoiding to overreact in the face of latency oscillations caused by the application workload fluctuations.

An experiment tolerating higher latency (200 ms) is shown in Figs. 6 and 7. Despite the different constraint, the performance trend from the configurations is

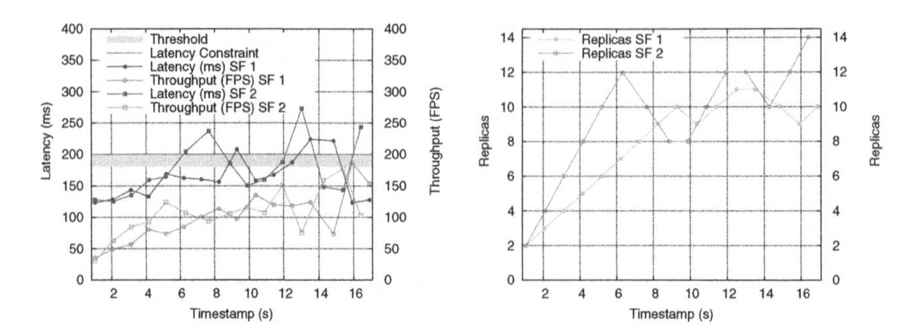

Fig. 6. Threshold 10% - Latency constraint of 200 ms (Left) and replicas used (Right).

similar. The threshold of 10% resulted in too many re-configurations that caused latency violation by using too many replicas. Thanks to fewer latency violations, SF of 1 was most suited than SF of 2. Considering the SF of 1, that yielded the best trade-off between latency and throughput, the results revealed a similar throughput regarding the thresholds 10% and 20%. Using the threshold of 20%, it only violated the latency constraint in the last seconds of the execution. This event is not caused by the adaptive mechanism but by the application, and it also occurred with a static number of replicas as seen in Fig. 2(b). Consequently, the adaptive mechanism was unable to respond because the latency violations occurred right before the application termination.

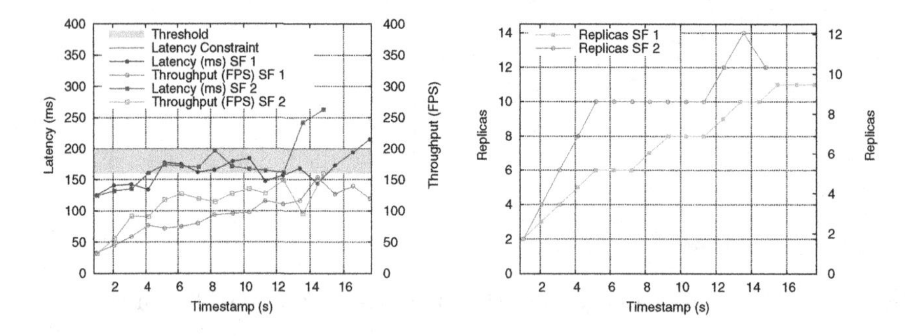

Fig. 7. Threshold 20% - Latency constraint of 200 ms (Left) and Replicas used (Right).

Considering these results, we can highlight that latency-sensitive stream processing applications with fluctuations perform better using SF of 1 and higher thresholds. In fact, an acceptable performance depends on the constraints and on the user requirements. Often in stream processing applications, a high throughput does not mean that users will actually have a better experience [6]. Consequently, it is important to support custom configurations (*e.g.*, throughput, latency) and to adapt the application at run-time while maintaining high-level parallelism abstractions.

6 Related Work

In this section, we present and contextualize the related studies that present efforts for autonomous properties in the stream processing scenario. De Sensi et al. [5,6] propose `Nornir`, a simple programming interface and runtime support for dynamically and automatically control the resources allocated to the application according to the user needs. `Nornir` enables the application to change number of cores, clock frequency and placement of threads during run-time. It also aims to satisfy bounds regarding power consumption and throughput, even in presence of changes in the input rate, in the application phases, or external interference. `Nornir` is validated using simulations and real-world benchmarks from the PARSEC suite. In SPar, we do not focus on power-aware computing. With respect to `Nornir`, we provide the possibility to express latency constraints by adapting the number of replicas.

De Matteis et al. [4] present elastic properties for data stream processing regarding performance (latency) and energy efficiency (number of cores and frequency). Elasticity support is stated as a solution for an efficient usage according to QoS requirements and so reducing the operating cost. The proposed model was implemented in the FastFlow runtime, which is a framework for stream processing targeting shared-memory multi-core architectures and also used by our target SPar runtime. In this work, the authors use a controller thread to monitor the application and to change the number of replicas and the clock frequency of the CPUs when needed.

In Gedik et al. [8], the authors show aspects related to parallelism in pipeline stages and they presented the motivation and challenges for elastic degree of parallelism during run-time. They proposed an elastic auto-parallelization solution, which adjusts the number of replicas aiming to achieve high throughput without wasting computational resources. Elasticity is implemented by requiring the programmer to define a threshold and a congestion index in order to decide whether to add or not more replicas.

Heinze et al. [12] emphasizes the complexity involved in determining the right point to increase or decrease the degree of parallelism. The authors investigated issues and requirements related to elasticity in the data stream for auto-scaling (scaling in or out) and they manage latency in a distributed system by keeping the system utilization in a range (min, max).

Selva et al. [16] show an approach related to the adaptation in run-time for streaming languages. The StreamIt language is extended to allow the programmer to specify the desired throughput and the runtime controls the execution. Moreover, it was implemented an application and system monitor that checks the throughput and system bottleneck, respectively. Using the implemented strategy, the system can adapt the execution based on previous observations.

Our research differs from existing works because we provide autonomous degree of parallelism and latency-aware management for the SPar DSL, shown in Sect. 2. De Sensi et al. [6] and De Matteis et al. [4] used the FastFlow framework to implement autonomic management of energy consumption on parallel applications. Besides providing a new strategy for implementing the latency-aware degree of parallelism, we integrated our strategy in the SPar's runtime system, adding therefore a new parallelism abstraction for its users.

We have a different scenario and target architecture compared to Gedik et al. [8] and Heinze et al. [12] because they focused on distributed systems while SPar targets multi-core environments. While Selva et al. [16] optimize the placement and throughput in StreamIt, we abstract parallelism complexities and focus on latency constraints for the SPar DSL. Moreover, the available solutions do not focus on parallelism abstractions and can be complicated to be used even for experts in parallel programming.

There is a demand to relieve end-users from the need to set a degree of parallelism and to enable their applications to run transparently without the manual intervention. We aim to free programmers from defining the degree of parallelism by implementing a strategy that supports an adaptive degree of parallelism in any application sensitive to latency parallelized by using SPar.

7 Conclusion

In this study, we extended SPar with a new parallelism abstraction. This was accomplished by implementing a strategy that adapts, without any programmer intervention, the number of replicas in order to have a latency lower than that specified by the application programmer. This is particularly useful for stream processing applications, which are characterized by fluctuations in the input rates. Our strategy monitors the execution and adapts the degree of parallelism. The manual, complex, and time-consuming definition of the degree of parallelism is no longer required in SPar. Experimental results demonstrated the effectiveness of our solutions when adjusting the number of replicas at run-time. Although the result trends are expected to occur in different scenarios, the presented results are limited to the tested application and environment.

In this study we proposed a strategy to control applications where only one stage is replicated. In the future, we plan to extend this work to consider applications with a more complex structure. Moreover, we aim to evaluate our latency-aware approach in other latency sensitive applications, specially those running for long time periods. Eventually, we will improve the adaptive strategy, for example, by using proactive rather than reactive approaches, to minimize the number of times the number of replicas is changed at run-time.

Acknowledgements. This study was financed in part by the Coordenação de Aperfeiçoamento de Pessoal de Nivel Superior - Brasil (CAPES) - Finance Code 001, by the EU H2020-ICT-2014-1 project RePhrase (No. 644235), and by the FAPERGS 01/2017-ARD project ParaElastic (No. 17/2551-0000871-5).

References

1. Aldinucci, M., Meneghin, M., Torquati, M.: Efficient Smith-Waterman on multi-core with FastFlow. In: Euromicro Conference on Parallel, Distributed and Network-Based Processing, pp. 195–199 (2010)
2. Andrade, H., Gedik, B., Turaga, D.: Fundamentals of Stream Processing: Application Design, Systems, and Analytics. Cambridge University Press, Cambridge (2014)
3. Chakravarthy, S., Qingchun, J.: Stream Data Processing: A Quality of Service Perspective: Modeling, Scheduling, Load Shedding, and Complex Event Processing. Advances in Database Systems, vol. 36. Springer, Boston (2009). https://doi.org/10.1007/978-0-387-71003-7
4. De Matteis, T., Mencagli, G.: Keep calm and react with foresight: strategies for low-latency and energy-efficient elastic data stream processing. SIGPLAN Not. **51**(8), 13:1–13:12 (2016)
5. De Sensi, D., De Matteis, T., Danelutto, M.: Simplifying self-adaptive and power-aware computing with Nornir. Future Gener. Comput. Syst. **87**, 136–151 (2018)
6. De Sensi, D., Torquati, M., Danelutto, M.: A reconfiguration algorithm for power-aware parallel applications. ACM Trans. Architect. Code Optim. **13**(4), 43 (2016)
7. FastFlow : FastFlow (FF) Website (2017). http://mc-fastflow.sourceforge.net/. Accessed Dec 2017
8. Gedik, B., Schneider, S., Hirzel, M., Wu, K.L.: Elastic scaling for data stream processing. IEEE Trans. Parallel Distrib. Syst. **25**(6), 1447–1463 (2014)
9. Griebler, D., Danelutto, M., Torquati, M., Fernandes, L.G.: SPar: a DSL for high-level and productive stream parallelism. Parallel Process. Lett. **27**(1), 20 (2017)
10. Griebler, D., Hoffmann, R.B., Danelutto, M., Fernandes, L.G.: High-level and productive stream parallelism for Dedup, Ferret, and Bzip2. Int. J. Parallel Program., 1–19 (2018)
11. Griebler, D., Hoffmann, R.B., Danelutto, M., Fernandes, L.G.: Higher-level parallelism abstractions for video applications with SPar. In: Parallel Computing is Everywhere, Proceedings of the International Conference on Parallel Computing, ParCo 2017, pp. 698–707. IOS Press, Bologna (2017)
12. Heinze, T., Pappalardo, V., Jerzak, Z., Fetzer, C.: Auto-scaling techniques for elastic data stream processing. In: IEEE International Conference on Data Engineering Workshops, pp. 296–302 (2014)
13. Hellerstein, J.L., Diao, Y., Parekh, S., Tilbury, D.M.: Feedback Control of Computing Systems. John Wiley & Sons, Chichester (2004)
14. Reinders, J.: Intel Threading Building Blocks: Outfitting C++ for Multi-core Processor Parallelism. O'Reilly Media, Sebastopol (2007)
15. Schneider, S., Hirzel, M., Gedik, B., Wu, K.L.: Auto-parallelizing stateful distributed streaming applications. In: Proceedings of the International Conference on Parallel Architectures and Compilation Techniques, pp. 53–64 (2012)
16. Selva, M., Morel, L., Marquet, K., Frenot, S.: A monitoring system for runtime adaptations of streaming applications. In: Euromicro International Conference on Parallel, Distributed and Network-Based Processing, pp. 27–34 (2015)
17. Thies, W., Karczmarek, M., Amarasinghe, S.: StreamIt: a language for streaming applications. In: Horspool, R.N. (ed.) CC 2002. LNCS, vol. 2304, pp. 179–196. Springer, Heidelberg (2002). https://doi.org/10.1007/3-540-45937-5_14

Consistency of the Fittest: Towards Dynamic Staleness Control for Edge Data Analytics

Atakan Aral(✉) and Ivona Brandic

Institute of Information Systems Engineering,
Vienna University of Technology, Vienna, Austria
{atakan.aral,ivona.brandic}@tuwien.ac.at
http://rucon.ec.tuwien.ac.at/

Abstract. A critical challenge for data stream processing at the edge of the network is the consistency of the machine learning models in distributed worker nodes. Especially in the case of non-stationary streams, which exhibit high degree of data set shift, mismanagement of models poses the risks of suboptimal accuracy due to staleness and ignored data. In this work, we analyze model consistency challenges of distributed online machine learning scenario and present preliminary solutions for synchronizing model updates. Additionally, we propose metrics for measuring the level and speed of data set shift.

Keywords: Edge computing · Data analytics · Consistency · Staleness

1 Introduction

Traditional way of data production and consumption is being revolutionized by new generation Internet based services such as smart cities, buildings, grids, factories and many other applications of Internet of Things. In this ongoing paradigm shift, not only volume of data explodes, but also it is generated in distributed fashion and consumed in real-time. Accordingly, the way such data is processed and analyzed is also subject to change [17,28]. Many applications require near real-time reaction based on streaming data. Such applications, including *intelligent traffic management*, *spam or fraud detection*, *transactive energy control* and *computational advertising*, require fast response to the events detected in distributed streams. Hence, traditional batch processing, where data is aggregated in a central processing facility (e.g. massive cloud data center), is no longer feasible for such applications due to the high cost of data transmission [26]. This cost includes both network delay and bandwidth usage.

Edge computing paradigm, which aims to bring processing power of cloud to the closer proximity to where data is being generated or used, intrinsically matches above-described requirements. One realization of this approach is so-called Cloudlets [27] that are located in business promises such as restaurants

G. Mencagli et al. (Eds.): Euro-Par 2018 Workshops, LNCS 11339, pp. 40–52, 2019.
https://doi.org/10.1007/978-3-030-10549-5_4

or public offices, much like wireless access points today, and serve as a local cloud to nearby clients. Another possibility is to utilize micro data centers that contain multiple servers and provide computational capabilities at the edge of the network [10]. Regardless of the implementation choices, edge computing will benefit near real-time data stream processing (DSP) tasks in two distinct ways: (i) it replaces sensor-to-cloud round trips and consequent network latency; (ii) it saves significant bandwidth capacity by confining majority of data transmission to the local area network. Distributing DSP tasks that involve machine learning (ML) steps, however, is not straightforward. One particular issue is to maintain a consistent ML model that can be updated as data streams evolve. Our aim in this work is to better understand the model consistency challenges with distributed online machine learning (DOML) scenario and provide initial ideas for potential solutions. To that end, we provide background information on the DOML paradigm and non-stationarity along with a motivational scenario in Sect. 2. We introduce a novel inference accuracy optimizing mechanism for synchronizing model updates, which we call *consistency of the fittest*, in Sect. 3. Furthermore, in Sect. 4, we propose three metrics for measuring the level of non-stationarity and in the subsequent Sect. 5, present preliminary numerical results. Finally, we discuss related work in Sect. 6 and conclude the paper in Sect. 7. To the best of our knowledge, this study is the first to address ML model consistency challenges within edge computing context and also the first attempt to quantitatively measure the extent of non-stationarity in ML models.

2 Background

2.1 Distributed Online Machine Learning

When real time decision making and high velocity data streams are involved, DOML is a viable alternative to centralized data processing/ML techniques. In this scenario, data originating from geographically distributed sources (e.g. IoT sensors, client computers, streaming media publishers, etc.) are processed at a nearby edge computing node. Here, both inference and online training steps are executed in each node. The former is about deriving conclusions (e.g. classification, prediction) from a ML model, whereas the latter is the continuous process of improving and adapting that model. Figure 1 demonstrates such distributed architecture where `DS` are data streams and `EN` are edge nodes. Based on input data (i) to the current ML model at each `EN`, actions (ii) are determined and sent back to the distributed actuators (e.g. traffic control signals, in-home smart devices). One issue in this scenario is that each `EN` has access to only a local fragment (`DS`) of all generated data, hence local model (iii) trained with that fragment is suboptimal. A centralized parameter server is typically implemented in order to easily combine and synchronize new information learned by distributed `EN`s as a global ML model [13]. This model can be hosted at a cloud data center (`DC`) and updated in iterative fashion based on contributions from `EN`s. Stale models at `EN`s should be replaced with the current global model

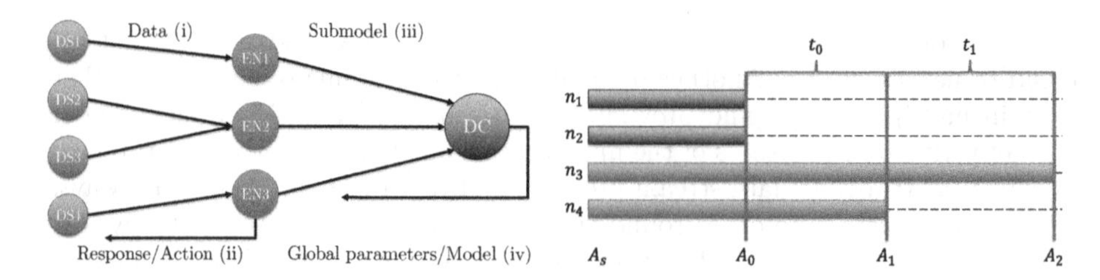

Fig. 1. DOML architecture.

Fig. 2. Example scenario where two of the four edge nodes (in blue) are straggling. (Color figure online)

(iv) so that they are more accurate in their inference and they build upon a global checkpoint avoiding multiple branches of models.

2.2 Non-stationarity

Data set shift (or concept drift) is defined as the discrepancy between training and test data of a ML model [25]. It can be observed in the joint distribution of inputs or outputs due to non-stationarity of the environment. In many real world applications, assumptions made in learning phase may become invalid over time. For instance, frauds or spammers may change their methods, which invalidates detection algorithms or in a financial forecasting model, external events such as mergers and acquisitions may change the learned dependencies between stock prices. However, each application has its own characteristics and rate of evolution. *Data horizon* is defined as the urgency of including new evidence and updating the model, whereas, *data obsolescence* is the velocity that old data becomes irrelevant to the model [23]. We address these concepts more formally in Sect. 4. Two well-known solutions for learning data coming from non-stationary processes are to periodically retrain the model and to incrementally update it. We consider the latter in DOML due to high computation overhead of the former. Use of a static model in an application area with short data horizon and rapid data obsolescence is impractical since inference accuracy will decrease over time. Moreover, in the case of DOML, it is also not efficient to update global model with each new data due to high communication cost. Hence, we consider a scenario similar to previous work [3,17], where local models at each edge node are updated online, whereas, global model is periodically synchronized via a central node. We propose dynamic periodicity of ML model synchronization for DOML, where quorum size and staleness bound are controlled to maximize expected model accuracy. We also define metrics to measure data horizon and obsolescence to analyze in which application areas proposed technique is the most beneficial. Accuracy is used to represent ML model performance in this paper, however, any other metric such as precision, recall or f-measure is viable.

2.3 Motivational Scenario: Transactive Energy Control

Digital transformation of the electricity grid results in so-called smart grids [8, 9], which provide many capabilities such as distributed generation, pervasive control, load management, self-healing, emission control, etc. Also enabled by smart grids, transactive energy control is defined as *a system of economic and control mechanisms that allows the dynamic balance of supply and demand across the entire electrical infrastructure using value as a key operational parameter* [20]. A NIST report [19] estimates that digitization and modernization of the power grid until 2030, will bring cost benefits that are the three to five times the required investment. In this endeavor, ML has many areas of application such as clustering users and producers into power profiles, detecting theft of electricity, understanding user behaviour, predicting supply and demand, etc. High volume and frequency of data generated by smart meters and sensors, their country-wide dispersion, and cruciality of fast decisions make smart grids challenging for traditional data processing, but an ideal application area for DOML. In conjunction with edge computing, DOML can address scalability issues by alleviating network load meanwhile reducing response time through data processing in high-bandwidth and low-latency proximity. In that sense, DOML is very promising for enabling massive scale smart grids.

Let us consider energy supply and demand forecasting as an example task in this scenario. Accurate and real-time predictions are crucial for optimizing the generation and distribution of electricity, which is considered as a perishable good since it cannot be stored on a wide scale. Some example optimization scenarios include, coping with short-term spikes in demand, dynamically controlling voltage based on geographical demand to reduce losses, or increasing the utilization of generators. ML algorithms such as logistic regression, neural networks (e.g. LSTM), and support vector machines (SVM) can be adapted to forecast time-series data and all have successful applications in the literature [15,30,31]. Data originating from generators or consumers in close proximity can be collected in edge nodes as denoted with (i) in Fig. 1, and forecasts can be made locally to give quick responses (ii). Non-stationarity is a particular challenge in this area, which may stem from structural changes such as joining/leaving producers, forming/dissolving links in grid network, and technological advances or quantitative changes such as evolving consumption habits, unexpected events, and seasonality. Trained ML model that is used in forecasting local supply and demand at each edge node, has to be updated frequently with global knowledge from the centralized parameter server in order to avoid staleness and consequent accuracy drop. However, it is not trivial to collect all updates from edge nodes (iii) and decide when local forecast models have to be updated (iv). Both too late and too early updates may cause inaccurate prediction of supply or demand, and consequently inadequate or excessive electricity generation.

3 Consistency of the Fittest

3.1 Problem Definition

We focus on the decision problem of when to synchronize local models at edge nodes in DOML, so that they are informed about global knowledge which is learned collectively by others. Iterations at edge nodes may finish at different times due to heterogeneity of edge resources and volatility of streaming data, leaving us with decision *which (or how many) responses to wait for at each iteration, before updating global model and sending it to edge nodes.* Too long synchronization period (e.g. waiting until all nodes respond) may cause suboptimal inference performance because edge nodes are obliged to the stale model for a longer time. Too short period, on the other hand, has the disadvantage of losing updates from straggler nodes as well as additional communication cost. Moreover, optimal period differs both over time and between applications due to changes in environment such as streaming rate, selection and capacity of edge nodes, unexpected events and failures, etc. Existing quorum- and bound-based approaches (described in Sect. 6) overlook such environmental dynamicity.

3.2 Dynamic Periodicity of Synchronization

The main idea behind the proposed technique is to push global model to the edge nodes when either all responses are received or waiting for the future responses is expected to result in lower average inference performance statistically based on previous outcomes. Consider a small-scale example with four nodes in Fig. 2. Here, at the beginning of the time period t_0, edge nodes n_1 and n_2 have already completed their iteration and sent their model updates to the parameter server, however, n_3 and n_4 are late. Stale model already distributed to nodes (M_S) have current accuracy A_s whereas incorporating currently received information results in a model (M_0) with accuracy A_0. First possibility is to push M_0 immediately to distributed nodes so that they will avoid staleness of M_S (assuming $A_s < A_0$). However, this would mean updates from remaining nodes will be ignored for this iteration and they will restart online training from M_0. The second option is to wait until n_4 responds (as it is predicted to be earlier than n_3), update the model with its contribution to M_1 with accuracy A_1, and then push that model. In that case, resulting model can be more accurate ($A_0 < A_1$), but M_S has to be tolerated until the end of time period t_0. Moreover, A_s and A_1 may also decrease over time due to staleness of models. Here, the decision should be made by considering expected magnitude of contribution by n_4 as well as expected length of t_0. A similar trade-off applies for n_3, as well. More formally, we are looking for the future response i among k stragglers such that average accuracy given in objective function in (1) is maximized. Here, τ_i is the waiting time for response i, and ϵ is the time period in consideration for accuracy (e.g. time until next iteration ends). The optimization problem, considering its small size in terms of parameters, can be efficiently solved via linear program solvers.

$$\begin{aligned} &\underset{i}{\text{maximize}} && \frac{A_s \tau_i + A_i (\epsilon - \tau_i)}{\epsilon} \\ &\text{where} && \tau_i = \sum_{j=0}^{i-1} t_j \\ &\text{subject to} && i \in \mathbb{Z},\ 0 \leq i \leq k. \end{aligned} \tag{1}$$

$$\begin{aligned} &\underset{i}{\text{maximize}} && \int_0^{\tau_i} A_s(x)\, dx + \int_{\tau_i}^{\epsilon} A_i(x)\, dx \\ &\text{where} && \tau_i = \sum_{j=0}^{i-1} t_j \\ &\text{subject to} && i \in \mathbb{Z},\ 0 \leq i \leq k. \end{aligned} \tag{2}$$

For simplicity, A_s and A_i are assumed to be constant in (1), however they are functions of time. A more realistic objective function with this consideration is given in (2). Here, ϵ in denominator is also replaced since it does not affect the objective being a constant. Multiple accuracy functions and response times need to be calculated or predicted so that aforementioned objective function can be evaluated. We propose efficient mechanisms for these in the rest of this section.

Characteristic Function. We first learn a characteristic function, $C(x)$, for the accuracy drop of a static model over time. We then utilize the same function for all predicted accuracy values to emulate the impact of staleness on them. In order to obtain $C(x)$, we test the same model at different time steps, log average accuracy value of all edge nodes at each step, and fit a curve to these values. Based on our evaluation with multiple ML tasks on real world streaming data sets, we assume that $C(x)$ follows a sigmoidal function. However, any other curve can be fitted if it better describes data. We propose a four parameter logistic regression that is given by (3). Here, y is the performance value (e.g. accuracy, precision, recall, f-measure, percentage error etc.) of the ML model and x is the time of measurement. Four parameters, a, b, c, and d correspond to lower limit of y, upper limit of y, time of inflection, and the slope of the curve at time c, respectively. We normalize the range of the characteristic function to $[0, 1]$ so it can be used with different models by simply multiplying with initial accuracy as in (4). Characteristic function is specific to the application area as well as ML algorithm used, thus curve fitting should be repeated when one of these changes.

$$y = a + \frac{b - a}{1 + \left(\frac{x}{c}\right)^d} \tag{3}$$

$$A(x) = C(x)A \tag{4}$$

$$R_i = \frac{A_i - A_{i-1}}{A_{i-1}} \tag{5}$$

Initial Accuracy. Second part of the problem is to predict initial accuracy of the model (A_i) that includes updates from prospective response i along with all preceding. A_i corresponds to the performance of M_i with test data that is collected immediately after its training data. Since M_s and M_0 are already available, their accuracy (A_s and A_0) can be directly computed with the test data collected from all edge nodes. For predicting $A_{i \geq 1}$, however, we resort to time series prediction. Time series data is collected at each response, i, by logging accuracy of current model, A_{i-1}; and accuracy of current model updated with the response, (A_i). We then calculate the magnitude of contribution as improvement rate, R_i as given in (5). Through historical trends of R for each node, time series forecasting algorithms such as autoregressive integrated moving average (ARIMA) [4] can estimate the next value, R_{i+1}. Given estimated R_{i+1} and A_i, it is possible to calculate prospective accuracy value A_{i+1} before response $i+1$ is received by solving (5) for A_i and replacing i with $i+1$.

Response Time. We model response characteristics of each edge node as a time series where observed response times are the data points. A time series forecasting algorithm can be used to estimate next response time from which elapsed time is subtracted to obtain time-to-response. We employ support vector machine regression algorithm, which demonstrates good accuracy in the similar task of forecasting time-to-failure of edge computing servers [1].

4 Metrics for Non-stationarity

Consistency of the fittest technique is fairly generic with regard to applicable ML algorithms. It is compatible with any algorithm as long as (i) training is online; (ii) ML model is updatable with submodels; and (iii) its performance is measurable through accuracy or error rate. Majority of online regression, clustering, and classification algorithms meet these criteria and we employ some of the most prevalent ones such as SVM, Bayesian networks, and naive Bayes, in our evaluation (Sect. 5). However, impact of the proposed technique would be proportional to the non-stationarity of the data stream. Furthermore, edge computing brings new communication challenges to model consistency that greatly increases the significance of measuring the extent of non-stationarity, with respect to centralized or high-bandwidth environments. To the best of our knowledge, there is no other work as of today that handles data set shift in high granularity and proposes metrics for data horizon or obsolescence. Hence in this section, we introduce four metrics for that purpose.

Slope of the Characteristic Function (SCF) is the decrease rate of the ML model performance represented with the slope of the characteristic function at the point of inflection. This corresponds to the absolute value of d in (3) and can be used to evaluate both data horizon and obsolescence.

Time of Inflection (TOI) is the time it takes to observe significant drop in the performance of a static model. More formally, it is the point in the characteristic function such that the second derivative is equal to zero, i.e. x such that $C''(x) = 0$. This corresponds to c in (3) and can also be used to evaluate both concepts.

Contribution of Updates (COU) is the magnitude of contribution observed in the performance when the model is updated with the most recent data. We measure it as the average percentage increase in accuracy (or decrease in error) of the ML model divided by elapsed time since previous update. This metric can be used to measure data horizon.

Depreciation by Stale Data (DSD) is the sensitivity of the ML model to the freshness of data. To measure DSD, we gradually add older data to the training set and observe its accuracy. It is calculated as the average rate of deterioration (or slope) per addition. This metric can be used to measure data obsolescence.

5 Numerical Results

In line with the motivational scenario described in Sect. 2.3, we train a SVM regression model for the demand forecasting in electricity market of New South Wales, Australia. We utilize `Elec2` data set described in [12]. Our training set consists of 100 half-hourly data points and we forecast five subsequent data points. After initial training, we run the model to predict demands that are increasingly toward the future and calculate accuracy at each step. Accuracy function used in this experiment is %100−Symmetric Mean Absolute Percentage Error (SMAPE), which is defined in (6). SMAPE is chosen for having an upper and lower bound on the values it can get, in contrast to other widely used error metrics such as mean absolute percentage error (MAPE) and mean squared error (MSE). Here, p_t and a_t are the predicted and actual values at time step t.

$$\text{Accuracy} = \%100 - \frac{\%100}{n} \sum_{t=1}^{n} \frac{|p_t - a_t|}{|p_t| + |a_t|} \tag{6}$$

Figure 3 demonstrates that the accuracy of a static model drops following a sigmoidal characteristic function, $C(x)$, due to staleness. However, updating the model via retraining at time step 10, delays the accuracy drop. Hence, it is possible to maintain an accurate model through repeated updates. This experiment also shows that $C(x)$ is still valid after the model is updated. Note that, we present unnormalized $C(x)$ to facilitate comparison to accuracy values. Only for this experiment, we use model retraining as SVM is not an updatable model.

As an additional scenario, we consider availability prediction of massively distributed client computers for service reliability. We utilize failure traces [14] from the `SETI@home` volunteer computing project to train a Dynamic Bayesian

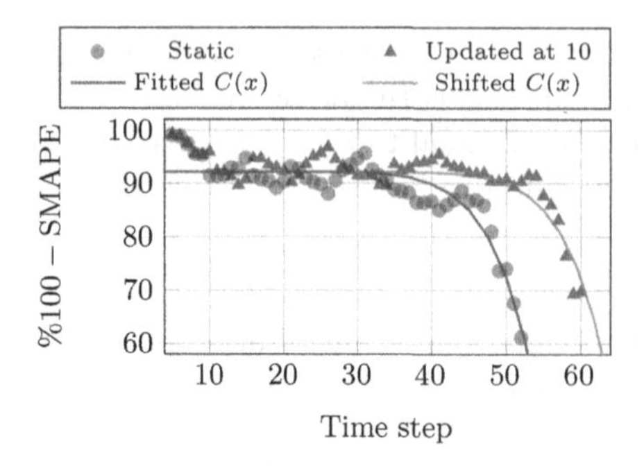

Fig. 3. Regression accuracy in `Elec2` data set as the SVM model stales.

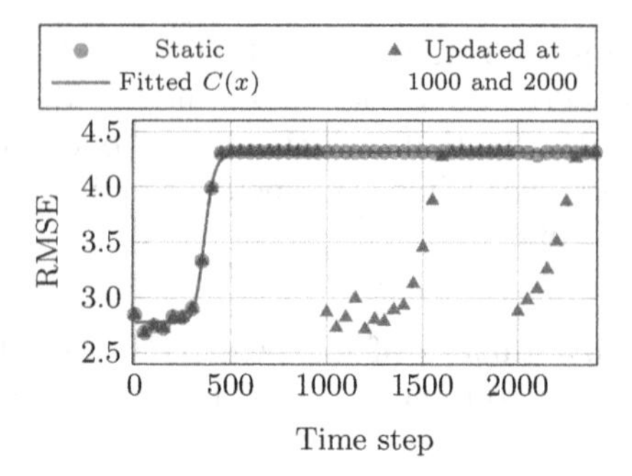

Fig. 4. Prediction error in `SETI@home` data set as the DBN model stales.

Network (DBN) model for failure dependencies between nodes and predict availability rates through this model. To demonstrate the use of approach with different performance metrics, we use Root Mean Squared Error (RMSE) as in (7), which is one of the most widely used quality measures for estimators. As shown in Fig. 4, a sigmoidal characteristic function also fits to the increasing error rate. Figure demonstrates the impact of two model updates at time steps 1000 and 2000 against a static model. Initial model maintains the same performance for significantly longer time (around 250 time steps or two days) in comparison to the electricity price forecasting scenario (around 30 time steps or 15 min). This suggests less stationarity, more general ML model, or both.

We report calculated metrics for the first two scenarios in Table 1a. It also includes five variation of the first scenario with 10 to 50 forecast data points. Results from the second scenario at the bottom row are not directly comparable with others due to the use of a different ML model and they are intended for informative purposes only. COU and DSD are in percentage and TOI unit is the number of time steps. SCF has no unit by definition of slope. As expected, extending the forecast horizon results in steeper (SCF) and earlier (TOI) accuracy drop. Moreover, models become slightly more sensitive to stale data (DSD),

Table 1. Non-stationarity metric values (a) and their intercorrelation (b). TOI unit is number of time steps, whereas COU and DSD are in percentage. SCF is unitless.

DS	ML (#P)	SCF	TOI	COU	DSD
[12]	SVM (10)	6.702	91.682	8.244	22.49
[12]	SVM (15)	7.408	84.037	3.302	23.71
[12]	SVM (20)	8.264	78.034	10.32	24.81
[12]	SVM (40)	8.394	67.497	5.636	23.54
[12]	SVM (50)	10.97	37.941	3.738	25.38
[14]	DBN	14.27	363.83	32.00	2.430

(a)

	SCF	TOI	COU	DSD
TOI	**-0.9879**			
COU	-0.3849	0.4654		
DSD	**0.8571**	-0.7731	-0.1505	
#P	**0.8212**	**-0.9489**	-0.4506	0.6325

(b)

whereas no trend in COU is detected. In Table 1b, on the other hand, the correlation between the pairs of metrics are given. There exists strong (positive and negative) correlation between SCF, TOI, and DSD. SCF and TOI are also strongly correlated with the number of forecast data points (indicated by #P).

$$\text{RMSE} = \sqrt{\frac{1}{n}\sum_{t=1}^{n}(p_t - a_t)^2} \tag{7}$$

$$F_1 = \frac{2 \cdot TP}{2 \cdot TP + FN + FP} \tag{8}$$

Finally in Figs. 5 and 6, we present average results of 10 repetitions from our DOML simulation. To that end, we randomly split `Elec2` to five sets to represent distributed data streams. We train and update five naive Bayes classifiers, which instead represent ML models at edge nodes. The classification is for the prediction whether the electricity price will go up or down based on demand, supply, time of the day, etc. In Fig. 5, we report F_1 scores given by (8), in the case that there is no synchronization and each edge node maintains its own ML model. In Fig. 6, on the other hand, scores of global models are presented. It is clear that use of a parameter server and a global model not only increases classification accuracy (by 13% on average) but also smooths the fluctuations arising from local non-stationary. However, a static global model stales over time and loses its accuracy. We also provide results from two dynamic models that combine local models from three (random) and five (all) edge nodes, respectively. Updating the model significantly increases accuracy (by 3.3% with 5 nodes) even when some nodes are not considered (by 2.1% with 3 nodes).

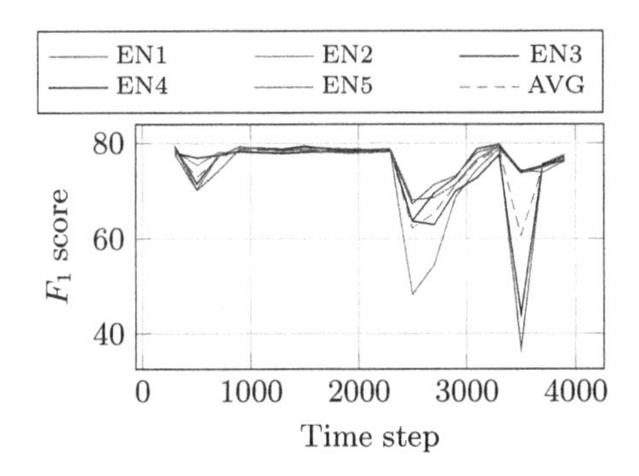

Fig. 5. Classification scores in the case that each edge node is trained separately.

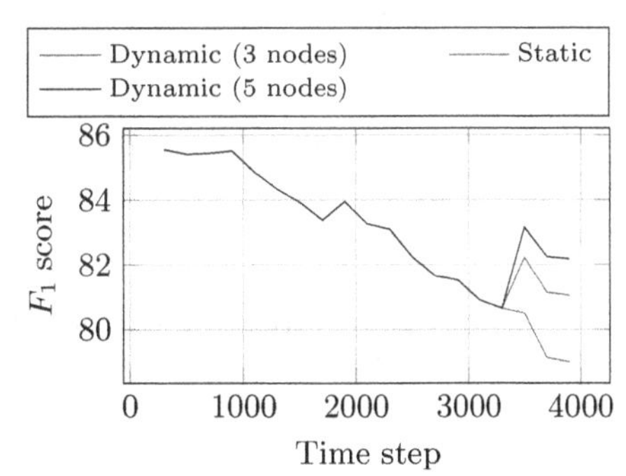

Fig. 6. Classification scores in the case that a global model is maintained.

6 Related Work

To cope with memory and bandwidth boundedness of traditional stream processing algorithms, several distributed stream processing engines including Apache Storm, Samza, Flink, and Spark Streaming, are proposed. They provide distributed, scalable, and fault-tolerant ways to handle streaming data flow. However, none of these explicitly deal with the problem of data set shift. When processing is distributed and occurs at the source (i.e. horizontal parallelism), a centralized parameter server [13,17] is typically implemented in order to easily combine and synchronize new information learned by distributed nodes as a global model, and to avoid multiple stale models. The unique issue in the geo-distributed case is that arrival times of updates from local nodes may exhibit high variation. State-of-the-Art staleness management techniques can be categorized as quorum and bound based ones. The works in the former category [11,29], allow to continue synchronization as long as certain number of updates is reached, whereas the latter approaches [7,13,16,28] allow asynchronous execution unless the level of staleness is over the predefined bound. Apache SAMOA (Scalable Advanced Massive Online Analysis) framework is proposed [21] to act as an abstraction for the aforementioned distributed stream processors and it provides rudimentary snapshot-based model consistency. However, none of these techniques are capable of providing the dynamicity in model update times and adaptability to data set shift that are necessitated by high volatility of DOML.

An overview of ML techniques and adaptability mechanisms under data set shift is studied in [32]. The focus is on traditional, centralized ML models, hence consistency issues stemming from distributed learning are not considered. Another work [22] investigates data set drift issues in classification algorithms. They propose the terminology, which we incorporate in this paper, and survey the types and common causes of data set shift as well as methods to detect its occurrence. In the context of edge computing, there exists architectures for DSP that support autonomous stateful migration [5,6,24]. However, management of model consistency across multiple nodes is not yet studied to the best of our knowledge. In [18], a data storage management mechanism to cope with limited capacity of edge nodes is proposed. It evaluates the sensitivity of time series forecasting algorithms (but not ML techniques as in this work) to the amount of input data and address the trade-off between storage space and forecast accuracy. Other works on DSP within the edge computing context can be found in a recent comprehensive survey [2].

7 Conclusion

We present a novel technique for efficiently scheduling machine learning model updates from a global parameter server to many distributed edge nodes. Proposed algorithms can be integrated into consistency management modules of DOML tools to outsource implementation challenges. This also applies to data collection from the pervasive edge nodes, which is required by the proposed non-stationarity metrics. Our preliminary evaluation results for both schedulers and metrics are highly promising. In the future, we plan to implement the algorithms as an extension to the prospective Apache SAMOA framework. Another side of the consistency problem left as future work, is how to distribute load to nearby edge nodes so that iterations complete in intended times without too much deviation between nodes. Factors to consider in this regard are resource capacity and transient unavailability of edge nodes as well as streaming rate of data. Depending on the environment, it may be necessary to redistribute load after each iteration based on previous outcomes.

Acknowledgements. The work described in this paper has been funded through the Haley project (Holistic Energy Efficient Hybrid Clouds) as part of the TU Vienna Distinguished Young Scientist Award 2011 and Rucon project (Runtime Control in Multi Clouds), FWF Y 904 START-Programm 2015.

References

1. Aral, A., Brandic, I.: Dependency mining for service resilience at the edge. In: ACM/IEEE Symposium on Edge Computing, pp. 228–242. IEEE (2018)
2. de Assuncao, M.D., da Silva Veith, A., Buyya, R.: Distributed data stream processing and edge computing: a survey on resource elasticity and future directions. J. Netw. Comput. Appl. **103**, 1–17 (2018)
3. Ben-Haim, Y., Tom-Tov, E.: A streaming parallel decision tree algorithm. J. Mach. Learn. Res. **11**, 849–872 (2010)
4. Box, G.E., Jenkins, G.M., Reinsel, G.C., Ljung, G.M.: Time Series Analysis: Forecasting and Control. Wiley, Hoboken (2015)
5. Brogi, A., Mencagli, G., Neri, D., Soldani, J., Torquati, M.: Container-based support for autonomic DSP through the Fog. In: Auto-DaSP, pp. 17–28 (2017)
6. Cardellini, V., Presti, F.L., Nardelli, M., Russo, G.R.: Decentralized self-adaptation for elastic data stream processing. Future Gener. Comput. Syst. **87**, 171–185 (2018)
7. Cipar, J., Ho, Q., Kim, J.K., Lee, S., Ganger, G.R., Gibson, G., et al.: Solving the straggler problem with bounded staleness. In: HotOS, vol. 13, p. 22 (2013)
8. Erol-Kantarci, M., Mouftah, H.T.: Energy-efficient information and communication infrastructures in the smart grid: a survey on interactions and open issues. IEEE Commun. Surv. Tutor. **17**(1), 179–197 (2015)
9. Farhangi, H.: The path of the smart grid. Power Energy Mag. **8**(1), 18–28 (2010)
10. Greenberg, A., Hamilton, J., Maltz, D.A., Patel, P.: The cost of a cloud: research problems in DC networks. Comput. Commun. Rev. **39**(1), 68–73 (2008)
11. Hara, T., Madria, S.K.: Consistency management among replicas in peer-to-peer mobile ad hoc networks. In: 24th IEEE Symposium on Reliable Distributed Systems, pp. 3–12. IEEE (2005)
12. Harries, M.: SPLICE-2 Comparative Evaluation: Electricity Pricing. Technical report, The University of New South Wales, Sydney 2052, Australia (1999)
13. Ho, Q., Cipar, J., Cui, H., Lee, S., Kim, J.K., Gibbons, P.B., et al.: More effective distributed ML via a stale synchronous parallel parameter server. In: Advances in Neural Information Processing Systems, pp. 1223–1231 (2013)

14. Javadi, B., Kondo, D., Vincent, J., Anderson, D.: Mining for statistical availability models in large-scale distributed systems: an empirical study of SETI@home. In: IEEE/ACM MASCOTS (2009)
15. Kim, K.: Financial time series forecasting using support vector machines. Neurocomputing **55**(1–2), 307–319 (2003)
16. Lee, J.H., Sim, J., Kim, H.: BSSync: processing near memory for machine learning workloads with bounded staleness consistency models. In: International Conference on Parallel Architecture and Compilation, pp. 241–252. IEEE (2015)
17. Li, M., Andersen, D.G., Park, J.W., Smola, A.J., Ahmed, A., Josifovski, V., et al.: Scaling distributed machine learning with the parameter server. In: USENIX Conference on Operating Systems Design and Implementation, pp. 583–598 (2014)
18. Lujic, I., De Maio, V., Brandic, I.: Efficient edge storage management based on near real-time forecasts. In: ICFEC, pp. 21–30. IEEE (2017)
19. McDonald, J., McGranaghan, M., Denton, D., Ellis, A., Imhoff, C., et al.: Strategic R&D opportunities for the smart grid. Technical report, NIST Steering Committee for Innovation in Smart Grid Measurement Science and Standards (2013)
20. Melton, R., Knight, M., et al.: GridWise Transactive Energy Framework (version 1). Technical report, The GridWise Architecture Council, WA, USA, PNNL-22946 (2015)
21. Morales, G.D.F., Bifet, A.: Samoa: scalable advanced massive online analysis. J. Mach. Learn. Res. **16**(1), 149–153 (2015)
22. Moreno-Torres, J.G., Raeder, T., Alaiz-Rodríguez, R., et al.: A unifying view on dataset shift in classification. Pattern Recognit. **45**(1), 521–530 (2012)
23. Parker, C.: Machine learning from streaming data: two problems, two solutions, two concerns, and two lessons (2013). https://blog.bigml.com/2013/03/12/
24. Patel, P., Ali, M.I., Sheth, A.: On using the intelligent edge for IoT analytics. IEEE Intell. Syst. **32**(5), 64–69 (2017)
25. Quionero-Candela, J., Sugiyama, M., Schwaighofer, A., Lawrence, N.D.: Dataset Shift in Machine Learning. The MIT Press, Cambridge (2009)
26. Ranjan, R.: Streaming big data processing in datacenter clouds. IEEE Cloud Comput. **1**(1), 78–83 (2014)
27. Satyanarayanan, M., Bahl, P., Caceres, R., Davies, N.: The case for VM-based cloudlets in mobile computing. IEEE Pervasive Comput. **8**(4), 14–23 (2009)
28. Xing, E.P., Ho, Q., Dai, W., et al.: Petuum: a new platform for distributed machine learning on big data. IEEE Trans. Big Data **1**(2), 49–67 (2015)
29. Yu, H., Vahdat, A.: Design and evaluation of a conit-based continuous consistency model for replicated services. ACM TOCS **20**(3), 239–282 (2002)
30. Zeger, S.L., Qaqish, B.: Markov regression models for time series: a quasi-likelihood approach. Biometrics **44**(4), 1019–1031 (1988)
31. Zhang, G.P.: Time series forecasting using a hybrid ARIMA and neural network model. Neurocomputing **50**, 159–175 (2003)
32. Žliobaitė, I.: Learning under concept drift: an overview. Technical report, Vilnius University (2010). eprint arXiv:1010.4784

A Multi-level Elasticity Framework for Distributed Data Stream Processing

Matteo Nardelli(✉), Gabriele Russo Russo, Valeria Cardellini, and Francesco Lo Presti

Department of Civil Engineering and Computer Science Engineering, University of Rome Tor Vergata, Rome, Italy
{nardelli,russo.russo,cardellini}@ing.uniroma2.it, lopresti@info.uniroma2.it

Abstract. Data Stream Processing (DSP) applications should be capable to efficiently process high-velocity continuous data streams by elastically scaling the parallelism degree of their operators so to deal with high variability in the workload. Moreover, to efficiently use computing resources, modern DSP frameworks should seamlessly support infrastructure elasticity, which allows to exploit resources available on-demand in geo-distributed Cloud and Fog systems. In this paper we propose E2DF, a framework to autonomously control the multi-level elasticity of DSP applications and the underlying computing infrastructure. E2DF revolves around a hierarchical approach, with two control layers that work at different granularity and time scale. At the lower level, fully decentralized Operator and Region managers control the reconfiguration of distributed DSP operators and resources. At the higher level, centralized managers oversee the overall application and infrastructure adaptation. We have integrated the proposed solution into Apache Storm, relying on a previous extension we developed, and conducted an experimental evaluation. It shows that, even with simple control policies, E2DF can improve resource utilization without application performance degradation.

Keywords: Data Stream Processing · Elasticity · Hierarchical control

1 Introduction

Exploiting on-the-fly computation, Data Stream Processing (DSP) applications can elaborate unbounded data flows so to extract high-value information as soon as new data are available. A DSP application is represented as a directed (acyclic) graph, with data sources, operators, and final consumers as vertices, and streams as edges. Importantly, these applications are usually long running and often subject to strict latency requirements that should be met in face of variable and high data volumes to process. To deal with operator overloading, a commonly adopted stream processing optimization is data parallelism, which consists in scaling-out or scaling-in the number of parallel instances for the operators, so that each instance can process a subset of the incoming data flow in parallel [7].

G. Mencagli et al. (Eds.): Euro-Par 2018 Workshops, LNCS 11339, pp. 53–64, 2019.
https://doi.org/10.1007/978-3-030-10549-5_5

To execute the application, its operators are deployed on computing resources, which host the operator instances. We consider the emerging environment, where distributed Cloud and Fog computing resources can be acquired and released on demand. Specifically, Fog computing enriches powerful but distant Cloud data centers with micro-data centers located at the network periphery, closer to the users/devices that produce and consume data. Therefore, the abundant presence of geo-distributed computing nodes can be exploited so to decentralize the application execution as well, thus reducing the application latency and the movement of high data volume. In this environment, DSP frameworks should be able to scale their applications, by changing the operators parallelism (*application elasticity*), as well as to accordingly provision computing resources (*infrastructure elasticity*) [1]. While the application elasticity allows to better distribute computing capacity among DSP operators, the infrastructure elasticity allows to avoid resource wastage while guaranteeing that enough computing capacity is available when needed.

In this paper, we present *Multi-level Elastic and Distributed DSP Framework* (E2DF), which extends our hierarchical architecture for application-level elasticity [2] so to introduce infrastructure management capabilities. In E2DF, the application control system and the infrastructure control system are organized according to the Monitor, Analyze, Plan and Execute (MAPE) architectural pattern for self-adaptive systems. Differently from existing works [10,12] that consider multi-level elasticity in a clustered environment, our solution is designed for a geo-distributed operating environment. To manage a high number of geo-distributed nodes in a scalable manner, our infrastructure and application control systems are realized through a two-level hierarchical pattern.

Our main contributions are as follows:

- we present the infrastructure control system of E2DF. It relies on a high-level MAPE-based *Infrastructure Manager* that coordinates the run-time adaptation of subordinated MAPE-based *Region Managers*, which locally control the elasticity of computing resources within a single micro-data center;
- we present simple control strategies for each component of E2DF, namely a *local* policy for the Region Managers, and a *global* policy for the Infrastructure Manager;
- we implement and evaluate E2DF on top of our extension [2,4] of Apache Storm. Our results are promising and show the effectiveness of the proposed E2DF framework, which allows to reduce the amount of used computing resources, while keeping an acceptable level of application performance.

This paper is organized as follows. We review related work in Sect. 2. In Sect. 3, we present the hierarchical distributed architecture of E2DF for the autonomous control of application and infrastructure elasticity. In Sect. 4, we present simple control policies for each component of E2DF. In Sect. 5, we evaluate the ability of E2DF to dynamically manage applications and computing resources. We conclude in Sect. 6.

2 Related Work

Run-time adaptation of DSP applications has attracted attention in recent years [1], mainly focusing on the application elasticity and the adaptation policies and mechanisms that support it. Some works, e.g., [6,8], exploit best-effort threshold-based policies based on the utilization of either the system nodes or the operator instances. Other works, e.g., [3,9,11,16], use more complex centralized policies to plan the scaling decisions. Heinze et al. [9] estimate latency spikes caused by operator reallocations through a model and use it to define a heuristic placement algorithm. Lohrmann et al. [11] propose a scaling strategy that enforces latency constraints by relying on a predictive queueing theory model. Stela [16] relies on throughput-based metric to identify the operators that need scaling. In [3] we formulate a centralized optimization problem for the run-time elasticity management of DSP applications that takes into account reconfiguration costs.

Current open-source DSP frameworks (e.g., Flink, Heron, Samza, Storm, Spark Streaming) manage the DSP application distribution, execution, and adaptation. However, as regards the application elasticity, most of them (except Heron and Spark Streaming) only support the manual scaling of operators, which can lead to sub-optimal application performance and operating costs. Dhalion, a framework on top of Heron, provides application elasticity by scaling out/in operators so to satisfy their throughput; Spark Streaming supports elastic scaling of the number of executors. As regards the infrastructure elasticity, the above frameworks can take advantage of the elasticity support of Cloud infrastructures [5]. However, in most cases the reconfiguration is enacted by restarting the DSP application, thus causing downtime and possible state loss. Moreover, elasticity decisions at the two different levels are, when available, independent and uncoordinated, which could led to sub-optimal adaptation.

Only few solutions explicitly consider the reconfiguration of DSP applications in Fog and Cloud geo-distributed environments. SpanEdge [14] uses Cloud and Fog data centers and follows a master-worker architecture implemented in Storm, but it does not support operator migrations. Firework [17] provides only elasticity of computing resources. Decentralized solutions for the elasticity of DSP applications do not suffer as their centralized counterpart from network latencies in geo-distributed environments. Among them, Mencagli [13] presents a game-theoretic strategy where the control logic is distributed on each operator. In [2] we propose a hierarchical distributed architecture for the autonomous control of elastic DSP applications and present distributed self-adaptation policies also based on reinforcement learning; in this paper, we extend that architecture to support elasticity also at the infrastructure level.

The works most closely related to our own have been presented in [10,12], which consider multi-level elasticity both at the application and infrastructure level. Liu et al. [10] propose a stepwise profiling framework that evaluates the efficiency of possible configurations of parallelism. Similarly to us, their goal is to avoid resource wastage; however, they do not propose auto-scaling policies. Lombardi et al. [12] consider at the same time the elasticity at the operator and resource levels, where scaling actions can be executed either in a reactive or proactive fashion, and implement their proposal in Storm. Differently from us, all these works are designed for a traditional clustered system and therefore could suffer from scalability issues in a geo-distributed environment. The E2DF framework we propose is a first step towards coordinated multi-level elasticity in geo-distributed Cloud and Fog systems.

3 System Architecture

The MAPE loop represents a well-know architectural pattern to organize the autonomous control of a software system, where four components (Monitor, Analyze, Plan, and Execute) are responsible for the primary functions of self-adaptation. When the controlled system is geo-distributed, as in Fog computing, a centralized MAPE loop, where analysis and planning are carried on by a single component, may suffer from scalability issues. As described in [15], different patterns to decentralize the MAPE components have been used in practice. Among them, the hierarchical control pattern is of particular interest. It revolves around the idea of a layered architecture, where each layer works at a different level of abstraction. In this pattern, multiple MAPE control loops work with time scales and concerns separation. Lower levels operate on a shorter time scale and deal with local adaptation. Exploiting a broader view on the system, higher levels steer the overall adaptation by providing guidelines to the lower levels.

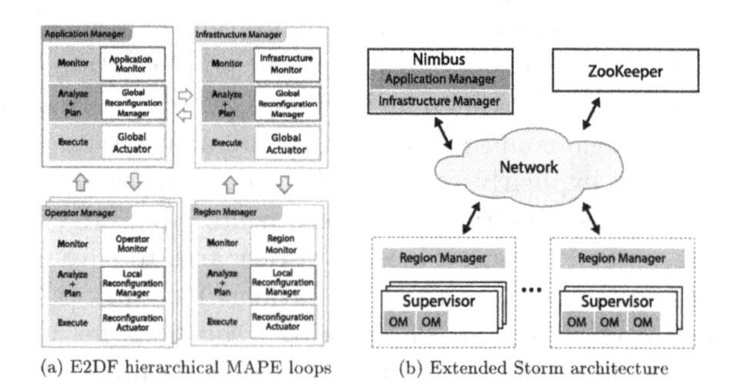

(a) E2DF hierarchical MAPE loops (b) Extended Storm architecture

Fig. 1. System architecture

Multi-level Elastic and Distributed DSP Framework (E2DF) includes two management systems that are organized according to a two-level hierarchical pattern: the Application Control System, which adapts the DSP operators deployment, and the Infrastructure Control System, which realizes resource elasticity. Figure 1a illustrates the conceptual architecture of E2DF, highlighting the hierarchy of the multiple MAPE loops and the system components in charge of the MAPE loop phases. The Infrastructure Control System includes a centralized *Infrastructure Manager* (IM), which cooperates with multiple decentralized

Region Managers (RM). Similarly, the Application Control System comprises a centralized *Application Manager* (AM) and decentralized *Operator Managers* (OM). Besides controlling the applications and computing resources in E2DF, the IM and AM can interact to adapt their behavior at run-time. Specifically, the IM can expose different views of the computing resources upon which the AM can run the application. In such a way, the IM can dynamically partition resources among applications. Differently from the approaches where the infrastructure is adapted without considering the application needs, the IM-AM interaction enables to realize cross-level optimizations. For example, when the IM detects that computing resources are underutilized, it can propose the AM to consolidate the managed applications on a reduced number of resources. Similarly, the AM can prevent the IM from terminating underutilized nodes when the latter execute critical DSP operators.

Infrastructure Control System. The *Region Manager* (RM) realizes the lower level MAPE loop of the Infrastructure Control System. It is a distributed entity that oversees resource elasticity within a single region (i.e., data center, micro-data center). To this end, it monitors the computing nodes used by E2DF within the region through the *Resource Monitor*. Then, through the *Local Reconfiguration Manager*, it analyzes the monitored data and determines if new resources should be acquired or leased ones should be released. When the RM determines that some adaptation should occur, it issues an adaptation request to the higher layer.

At the higher level, the *Infrastructure Manager* (IM) coordinates the resource adaptation among the different computing regions through a global MAPE loop. By means of the *Infrastructure Monitor* it collects aggregated monitoring data from the different available regions. Then, through the *Global Reconfiguration Manager*, it analyzes the monitored data and the reconfiguration requests received by the multiple RMs, and decides which reconfigurations should be granted. For example, the Global Reconfiguration Manager can decide that it is more convenient to acquire resources from a specific region, so it will inhibit scaling operations proposed for other regions. According to its internal policy, the Global Reconfiguration Manager can interact with the AM and adapt its behavior accordingly. For example, it may suggest the AM to consolidate the managed DSP operators on fewer computing nodes (the AM can accordingly accept or deny the request). Using the *Global Actuator*, the IM communicates its reconfiguration decisions to each RM, which can, finally, scale the computing infrastructure by means of the their local *Reconfiguration Actuators*.

Application Control System. The Application Control System manages the run-time adaptation of a DSP application. Similarly to the Infrastructure Control System, it implements a hierarchical MAPE loop where an Application Manager oversees subordinate Operator Managers. At the lower level, the *Operator Manager* (OM) controls the reconfiguration of a single DSP operator and proposes reconfiguration requests to the higher level. At the higher level, the *Application Manager* (AM) is the centralized entity that coordinates the adaptation request aiming to obtain good overall DSP application performance. We refer the reader to [2] for further details.

Integration of E2DF in Storm. We have implemented the proposed E2DF architecture in EDF [2], our extension of Apache Storm. EDF, by relying on Distributed Storm [4], enhances the official Storm release by introducing an infrastructure-level and application-level monitoring system and by supporting run-time stateful operator scaling and migration (i.e., it enables the application elasticity while preserving its integrity). Due to space limitations, we omit a detailed description of EDF and Distributed Storm and refer the reader to [2,4]. As represented in Fig. 1b, we introduce the E2DF components into the Storm architecture. More precisely, the AM, IM, and OM are implemented within existing Storm components, whereas the RM constitutes a new component to be deployed in every region along with Storm Supervisors.

The IM runs within Nimbus, i.e., Storm's master node. As soon as it is created, it runs its MAPE control loop and waits for requests by the RMs and AMs. The RMs are statically defined, one per region; each RM executes its local policy and operates autonomously with one another. To acquire and release resources, the Reconfiguration Actuator of the RM can be implemented to manage virtual machines or software containers. In our current implementation, it uses software containers, managed through Docker. In such a way, each Storm worker node runs within a container that can be quickly spawn and terminated at run-time. The RM first retrieves monitoring information about CPU utilization of the computing resources used by Distributed Storm within the region. Then, it uses the local policy to determine whether a resource scaling operation should be performed, and possibly forwards the request to the IM. Should the reconfiguration be performed, the Reconfiguration Actuator of the RM scales the computing resources using the Docker APIs.

When a new application is submitted to Storm, Nimbus creates one AM and multiple OMs (one per operator). While the AM runs in Nimbus, the OMs are assigned to the available worker nodes by the Storm scheduler. As soon as the AM is created, it determines the initial application placement on the set of worker nodes. At run-time, Nimbus executes periodically the AM, which analyzes the monitored application response time, acquired from Distributed Storm, and collects the reconfiguration requests coming from the decentralized OMs. Then, the global policy is executed so to coordinate and grant the reconfiguration actions. To enact the deployment changes, the Global Actuator of the AM relies on the `rebalance` command of Storm and on the stateful migration mechanisms of Distributed Storm, which allow to preserve the operators internal state while reconfiguring. Each OM collects information about the managed operator (e.g., resource usage) and relies on its local policy to identify beneficial reconfigurations and to propose them to the AM. Should a reconfiguration be performed, the OM Reconfiguration Actuator adapts the operator deployment (e.g., by changing its replication degree), while preserving the operator internal state.

4 Multi-level Elasticity Policy

The proposed two-layered architecture identifies different macro-components (i.e., AM-OM, IM-RM) that cooperate to adapt the deployment of DSP applications and infrastructures at run-time. The E2DF architecture is general enough to not limit the specific internal policies and goals for these components. By properly selecting the internal policy for each component, the proposed solution can address the needs of different execution contexts, thus encompassing applications with different requirements, infrastructures with different kind of computing resources, and different user preferences. For example, the planning components can be either activated periodically or on event-basis, can rely on optimization problem formulation or heuristics that minimize the application response time, maximize its availability, or a combination thereof.

Since the control components (i.e., AM, OM, IM, RM) work at different abstraction layers, we need two-layered control policies as well. Specifically, we will consider *local policies*, associated with RM and OM, which are concerned with low-level adaptation actions and exploit a fine grained view on a subset of the controlled entities (i.e., the replicas of a single operator and the computing resources in a given region, respectively). The local policy does not directly enact planned adaptation actions, which instead are communicated to the higher level components, i.e., AM and IM. These components are each equipped with a *global policy* that works at the granularity of the whole application/infrastructure. On the basis of the overall monitored performance and the application performance requirements (e.g., coming from a SLA), the global policies identify the most effective reconfigurations proposed by the decentralized agents, providing an implicit coordination mechanism among the independent local policies.

As a proof-of-concept of the proposed architecture, we present simple heuristic elasticity policies whose overall adaptation goal is to preserve the application performance in face of varying workloads, avoiding computing resources wastage.

4.1 Infrastructure Control Policy

The Infrastructure Control System manages the computing resources (e.g., containers, VM) allocated for the execution of DSP applications. As a proof-of-concept policy, we consider a simple threshold-based approach, which is the most commonly used one in Cloud auto-scaling systems [5]. The *local policy* executed by the RM in each region r considers: (i) C_n, the *capacity* of each node n, defined as the maximum number of application operators' instances it can host (e.g., proportional to the number of CPU cores); (ii) A_n, the number of operators instances currently assigned to each node; and (iii) U_n, the CPU utilization of each node.[1] For each region r, we consider a target capacity C_r, which should always be available for deploying new operator replicas. Hence, we require that $\sum_{n \in Nodes(r)} (C_n - A_n) \geq C_r$. Whenever this constraint is violated,

[1] The policy can be easily extended to consider other load metrics (e.g., related to memory or network bandwidth utilization).

the RM proposes to add one or more computing resources to satisfy the capacity requirement. For simplicity, we assume that, if the RM can pick different kinds of resources, it will choose the one with minimum capacity C_n, in order to have a fine-grained control over the resource allocation. On the other hand, when the available capacity in the region exceeds the minimum required amount, the RM searches for computing resources to turn off. Specifically, the RM searches for nodes that do not host application operators' instances, and, if any, issues a request to the IM for terminating them.

Moreover, the local policy searches for nodes that host one or more application operators' instances, but seem to be under-loaded. Specifically, the RM looks for nodes whose CPU utilization does not exceed a predefined threshold $\bar{U}_{low,r}$ (i.e., $U_n \leq \bar{U}_{low,r}$). The replicas running on those nodes might be easily migrated elsewhere, in order to consolidate the active computing nodes. The RM issues a request to the IM for freeing and terminating these nodes.

Finally, the local policy communicates to the IM its proposed actions. The IM *global policy* can accept/reject adaptation requests based on functional and non-functional requirements. For the sake of simplicity, to evaluate the proposed framework, we rely on a simple global policy, which accepts all the actions proposed by the RM, except for those requiring the termination of a computing resource currently occupied by one or more DSP applications, which require special attention. When the RM proposes to turn off such a node, the IM will in turn issue a request to the involved AMs for migrating their operators to different nodes. The IM also removes the node from the list of available resources, to avoid that other operators are assigned to it by any AM. After a configurable time interval, if the AM has not moved away the operators from the under-loaded node, the scale-in procedure is canceled and the node considered available again.

4.2 Application Control Policy

Relying on a local policy executed by the OMs, and on a global policy executed by the AM, the Application Control System manages the DSP applications elasticity and placement. The OM *local policy* implements the Analyze and Plan phases of the decentralized MAPE loop, which controls the execution of a single DSP operator. Running on a decentralized component, this policy has only a local view of the system, which consists of the status (i.e., resource utilization) of each operator replica and of a restricted suitable set of computing nodes (i.e., located in the same region). By analyzing this information, the policy can plan a reconfiguration of the operator deployment, by changing the number of its replicas. We adopt a simple threshold-based policy for planning scaling actions [2]. Let us denote by S_α the resource utilization of replica α, which measures the fraction of CPU time used by α. When the utilization of α exceeds a usage threshold $S_{\text{s-out}} \in [0, 1]$ (i.e., $S_\alpha > S_{\text{s-out}}$), the OM proposes to add a new replica. The new replica is allocated on the least utilized computing resource within the same region of the other operator replicas. Conversely, the OM proposes a scale-in operation, which removes one of the running n replicas, when the sum of their utilization divided by $n-1$ is significantly below the usage threshold, i.e., when

$\sum_{\alpha=1}^{n} S_\alpha/(n-1) < cS_{\text{s-out}}$, being $c < 1$. The replica to be removed is randomly chosen between the two replicas with the highest utilization. Similarly to the RM local policy, the OM proposes reconfiguration actions to the high-level AM, which can accept or reject them, based on its global policy.

The AM determines the initial application deployment. To this end, it uses a placement policy that assigns the operators on an initial number of R_{init} computing nodes, aiming to balance the number of operator per node. To perform run-time adaptation, the AM adopts a *global policy* that implements the Analyze and Plan steps of the centralized MAPE loop. Its main goal is to coordinate the actions of the decentralized OMs, so to satisfy the DSP application performance requirements, while minimizing the allocated resources (or their cost). In particular, it monitors the application response time and analyzes its behavior, possibly by comparing it against a user-defined target performance. It can leverage this information to decide whether, e.g., a higher parallelism could be beneficial for the application, or the resource usage costs should be reduced. To this end, the policy determines which reconfiguration plans, proposed by the decentralized OMs, should be accepted. For the sake of simplicity, in this work we consider a very simple global policy, which only rejects reconfigurations when they try to acquire an already used resource (e.g., just assigned to another operator). More sophisticated approaches (e.g., based on a token bucket to limit the number of performed reconfigurations) can be proposed as well [2].

5 Evaluation

We evaluate the ability of E2DF to realize the multi-level elasticity. To more easily investigate the proposed architecture, we equip E2DF with the proposed proof-of-concept policies, and consider a single deployment region, where Storm worker nodes are allocated as Docker containers. Each container allows the worker node to run on a single CPU core, for no more than 50% of the time. Each worker node has capacity $C_n = 1$, thus can host a single operator instance. The Docker containers are executed on a single host machine, equipped with an Intel i7-4710HQ CPU and 16 GB of RAM.

As a reference application, we consider a simple *Word Count* topology, defined as a sequence of a source and 3 operators. The *datasource* emits random sentences at a variable rate; the *split* emits a tuple for each word in the received sentences; the *counter* traces how many times each word has appeared; the final *consumer* publishes statistics to a RabbitMQ queue. Specifically, as shown in Fig. 2a, the source emits data at a rate that grows from 5 to 550 tuples/s and then decreases back to the initial value.

To show the potentialities of E2DF, we evaluate three different execution scenarios. In the baseline one, neither the infrastructure nor the application parallelism is adapted at run-time. We provisioned both the infrastructure and the application so to handle the peak load; we run 16 worker nodes and 15 total operator replicas for the reference application (namely, 2 replicas for *split*, 6 for *counter* and 6 for *consumer*). As a second scenario, we consider the case where the worker nodes are statically provisioned, but the operators parallelism can be adapted at run-time (i.e., only application-level elasticity). Finally, in the third scenario, we evaluate E2DF with all the self-adaptation features enabled, exploiting infrastructure-level elasticity as well. For the experiments, we let the IM and RM run once per minute, and the AM and OM twice per minute. For the RM policy, we set $C_r = R_{init} = 5$, and $\bar{U}_{low,r} = 0.1$. As regards the OM policy, we set $S_{\text{s-out}} = 0.7$, and $c = 0.75$.

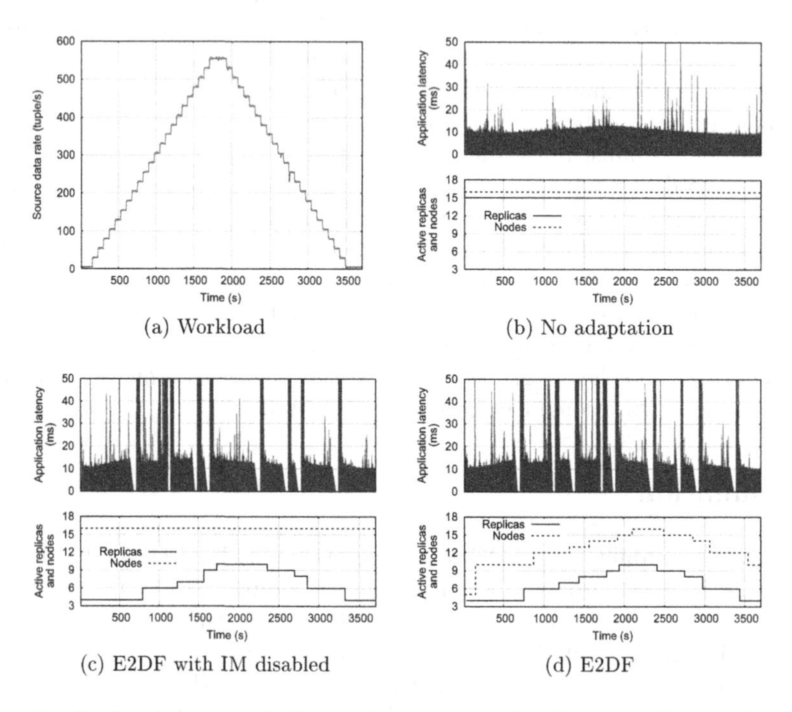

Fig. 2. Application latency and allocated resources with different self-adaptation capabilities (b–d), when the application is subject to a linearly growing and decreasing input rate (a).

Results. Figure 2 reports the application latency, the application parallelism, and the number of active worker nodes throughout our experiments. Figure 2b illustrates the baseline scenario, when both the worker nodes and the operator replicas are statically provisioned. In this case, the average application latency throughout the experiment is 11.4 ms. Such a configuration is likely to waste resources by using the same computational power in face of different levels of incoming load. Our second experiment confirms this observation: indeed, the Application Control System, starting with a single replica per operator, adapts the number of operator replicas used by the DSP application at run-time (see Fig. 2c). Application elasticity allows to use, on average, 55% less replicas during the experiment, with only limited performance degradation: the average application latency in this setting is 19.3 ms.[2] Nonetheless, in this experiment we are likely to still over-provision the infrastructure resources, keeping 16 active worker nodes all the time.

The third scenario allows to evaluate the benefits of exploiting the full self-adapting capabilities of E2DF, i.e., when it can adapt the application and the infrastructure. The application performance is almost identical to that observed in the previous experiment, while the number of active worker nodes (and so the resource usage cost, in a real scenario) is reduced on average by 24%. As shown in Fig. 2d, the number of running worker nodes is readily adjusted as the application acquires or releases worker slots. These results demonstrate that our simple policies are effective in limiting the resource wastage, at the same time avoiding significant performance degradation.

6 Conclusions

In this paper, we presented Multi-level Elastic and Distributed DSP Framework (E2DF), a hierarchical approach for controlling DSP application elasticity and infrastructure elasticity. Designed according to the decentralized MAPE control pattern, our solution relies on a two layered approach with separation of concerns and time scale between layers. At the lower level, distributed components control the adaptation of DSP operators and computing resources within a deployment region. At the higher level, a per-application manager oversees and coordinates the DSP application adaptation, while a global IM supervises the management of computing resources across different regions. We prototyped the proposed solution within Distributed Storm and proposed proof-of-concept policies to evaluate the benefits of the proposed hierarchical and distributed architecture. The results show that our simple yet effective policies allow to significantly reduce resource wastage with respect to statically provisioned applications and infrastructures.

As future work, we will further investigate the presented hierarchical approach. We plan to design more complex decentralized policies, considering different (stringent and possibly conflicting) optimization objectives, and a larger set of constraints (e.g., related to network bandwidth). We will also investigate the interaction between the application-level and infrastructure-level elasticity. In particular, we will study the multi-agent optimization problem that arises from the interaction of the ACS and ICS, recurring to techniques specifically targeted to this class of systems (e.g., Multi-Agent Reinforcement Learning).

[2] We can observe evident spikes in the measured application latency after each reconfiguration; they are due to the *pause-and-resume* stateful reconfiguration protocol adopted by Distributed Storm. Therefore, we compute our statistics excluding the first 2 min after each reconfiguration.

References

1. de Assunção, M.D., da Silva Veith, A., Buyya, R.: Distributed data stream processing and edge computing: a survey on resource elasticity and future directions. J. Netw. Comput. Appl. **103**, 1–17 (2018)
2. Cardellini, V., Lo Presti, F., Nardelli, M., Russo Russo, G.: Decentralized self-adaptation for elastic data stream processing. Future Gener. Comput. Syst. **87**, 171–185 (2018)
3. Cardellini, V., Lo Presti, F., Nardelli, M., Russo Russo, G.: Optimal operator deployment and replication for elastic distributed data stream processing. Concurr. Comput. Pract. Exp. **30**(9), e4334 (2018)
4. Cardellini, V., Grassi, V., Lo Presti, F., Nardelli, M.: Distributed QoS-aware scheduling in storm. In: Proceedings of ACM DEBS 2015, pp. 344–347 (2015)
5. Chen, T., Bahsoon, R., Yao, X.: A survey and taxonomy of self-aware and self-adaptive cloud autoscaling systems. ACM Comput. Surv. **51**, 61 (2018)
6. Fernandez, R.C., Migliavacca, M., Kalyvianaki, E., Pietzuch, P.: Integrating scale out and fault tolerance in stream processing using operator state management. In: Proceedings of ACM SIGMOD 2013, pp. 725–736 (2013)
7. Gedik, B., Schneider, S., Hirzel, M., Wu, K.L.: Elastic scaling for data stream processing. IEEE Trans. Parallel Distrib. Syst. **25**(6), 1447–1463 (2014)
8. Gulisano, V., Jiménez-Peris, R., Patiño Martínez, M., Soriente, C., Valduriez, P.: StreamCloud: an elastic and scalable data streaming system. IEEE Trans. Parallel Distrib. Syst. **23**(12), 2351–2365 (2012)
9. Heinze, T., Roediger, L., Meister, A., Ji, Y., et al.: Online parameter optimization for elastic data stream processing. In: Proceedings of ACM SoCC 2015, pp. 276–287 (2015)
10. Liu, X., Dastjerdi, A.V., Calheiros, R.N., Qu, C., Buyya, R.: A stepwise auto-profiling method for performance optimization of streaming applications. ACM Trans. Auton. Adapt. Syst. **12**(4), 24 (2018)
11. Lohrmann, B., Janacik, P., Kao, O.: Elastic stream processing with latency guarantees. In: Proceedings of IEEE ICDCS 2015, pp. 399–410 (2015)
12. Lombardi, F., Aniello, L., Bonomi, S., Querzoni, L.: Elastic symbiotic scaling of operators and resources in stream processing systems. IEEE Trans. Parallel Distrib. Syst. **29**(3), 572–585 (2018)
13. Mencagli, G.: A game-theoretic approach for elastic distributed data stream processing. ACM Trans. Auton. Adapt. Syst. **11**(2), 13 (2016)
14. Sajjad, H.P., Danniswara, K., Al-Shishtawy, A., Vlassov, V.: SpanEdge: towards unifying stream processing over central and near-the-edge data centers. In: Proceedings of 2016 IEEE/ACM Symposium on Edge Computing, pp. 168–178 (2016)
15. Weyns, D., et al.: On patterns for decentralized control in self-adaptive systems. In: de Lemos, R., Giese, H., Müller, H.A., Shaw, M. (eds.) Software Engineering for Self-Adaptive Systems II. LNCS, vol. 7475, pp. 76–107. Springer, Heidelberg (2013). https://doi.org/10.1007/978-3-642-35813-5_4
16. Xu, L., Peng, B., Gupta, I.: Stela: enabling stream processing systems to scale-in and scale-out on-demand. In: Proceedings of IEEE IC2E 2016, pp. 22–31 (2016)
17. Zhang, Q., Zhang, Q., Shi, W., Zhong, H.: Firework: data processing and sharing for hybrid cloud-edge analytics. IEEE Trans. Parallel Distrib. Syst. **29**(9), 2004–2017 (2018)

CBDP - Workshop on Container-Based Systems for Big Data, Distributed and Parallel Computing

Workshop on Container-Based Systems for Big Data, Distributed and Parallel Computing (CBDP)

Workshop Description

CBDP is a forum for researcher working on systemic aspects of Big data, Distributed and Parallel computing and that, today. are adopting container technologies. Nowadays, in Big data, distributed and parallel computing, there is a shift from a Virtual Machine centric to a Container centric model. Containers enable micro-service software architectures, containers are used to deploy and run enterprise, scientific and big data applications, to architect IoT and edge/fog computing systems, and are used by cloud providers to internally manage their infrastructure and services. The scientific objective of the workshop is to collect high quality contributions that: advance the state of the art of container technologies; propose new solutions for architecting high performance distributed and/or parallel container based systems; put forward resource management techniques like scaling and migration; enhance the state of the art in container security; show successful use of container technologies in fields like Big Data processing, Cloud Computing, Parallel computing, Distributed Computing and Internet of Things.

The 2018 edition of the CBDP workshop was held in Tourin, Italy in conjunction with the Euro-Par annual series of international conferences. The format of the workshop includes a keynote, followed by technical presentations.

This year, the keynote was about "Self-adaptation for Streaming Analytics at the Edge". Data Stream Processing (DSP) systems are commonly used to process big data streams from sensors and devices and there is a need to push streaming analytics capabilities to the edges of the network in order to cut down the latency. This scenario requires to devise effective solutions to manage and self-adapt at run-time the execution of DSP applications in the presence of unforeseeable variations of demand in time and space. The talk addressed the related challenges and presented a two-layered hierarchical solution for the autonomous control of elastic DSP applications deployed in geo-distributed Cloud and Fog/edge environments.

The papers presented in this edition covered different aspect of big data and distributed computing, like: vertical scalability for big data applications, QoS-aware resource allocation, network function containerization, containerized databases and storage systems.

Last, but certainly not least, I would like to thanks Stefano Iannucci for co-chairing the workshop with me, the CBDP Steering Committee and the CBDP 2018 Program Committee, who made the workshop possible. I would also like to thank Euro-Par for hosting our community, and Euro-Par workshop chairs Dora Blanco Heras and Gabriele Mencagli for their help and support. The organization of the workshop has been partially supported by the BigData@BTH project (grant number 20140032 Knowledge Fundation, Sweden).

Organization

Steering Committee

Sherif Abdelwahed	Virginia Commonwealth University, USA
Robert Bohn	NIST, USA
Alan Sill	Texas Tech University, USA
Vlado Stankovski	University of Ljubljana, Slovenia
Kurt Tutschku	Blekinge Institute of Technology, Sweden

Program Chairs

Emiliano Casalicchio	Blekinge Institute of Technology, Sweden and Sapienza University of Rome, Italy
Stefano Iannucci	Mississippi State University, USA

Program Committee

Danilo Ardagna	Politecnico di Milano, Italy
Valeria Cardellini	University of Rome Tor Vergata, Italy
Edlira Dushku	Sapienza University of Rome, Italy
Salvatore Filippone	Cranfield University, UK
Eva Garcia-Martin	Blekinge Institute of Technology, Sweden
Fabio de Gasperi	Sapienza University of Rome, Italy
Roberto Gioiosa	Oak Ridge National Laboratory, USA
Abdelouahed Gherb	Ecole de Technologie Superieure, Canada
Håkan Grahn	Blekinge Institute of Technology, Sweden
Gabriele Gualandi	Sapienza University of Rome, Italy
Dharmesh Kakadia	International Institute of Information Technology, Hyderabad and Microsoft Research, India
Parisa Heidari	Ecole Polytechnique de Montreal, Canada
Elisa Heymann	Universitat Autonoma de Barcelona, Spain
Briland Hitaj	Sapienza University of Rome, Italy
Wubin Li	Ericsson Research, Canada
Lars Lundberg	Blekinge Institute of Technology, Sweden
Vida Ahmadi Mehri	Blekinge Institute of Technology, Sweden

A Resource Allocation Framework with Qualitative and Quantitative SLA Classes

Tarek Menouer[1(✉)], Christophe Cérin[1], Walid Saad[1,2], and Xuanhua Shi[3]

[1] Université Paris 13, Sorbonne Paris Cité, Paris, France
{tarek.menouer,christophe.cerin,walid.saad}@lipn.univ-paris13.fr
[2] ENSIT, LATICE Laboratory, University of Tunis, Tunis, Tunisia
[3] Huazhong University of Science and Technology, Wuhan, China
xhshi@hust.edu.cn

Abstract. This paper presents a new resource allocation framework based on SLA (Service Level Agreements) classes for cloud computing environments. Our framework is proposed in the context of containers with two qualitative and two quantitative SLAs classes to meet the needs of users. The two qualitative classes represent the satisfaction time criterion, and the reputation criterion. Moreover, the two quantitative classes represent the criterion over the number of resources that must be allocated to execute a container and the redundancy (number of replicas) criterion. The novelty of our work is based on the possibility to adapt, dynamically, the scheduling and the resources allocation of containers according to the different qualitative and quantitative SLA classes and the activities peaks of the nodes in the cloud. This dynamic adaptation allows our framework a flexibility for efficient global scheduling of all submitted containers and for efficient management, on the fly, of the resources allocation. The key idea is to make the specification on resources demand less rigid and to ask the system to decide on the precise number of resources to allocate to a container. Our framework is implemented in C++ and it is evaluated using Docker containers inside the Grid'5000 testbed. Experimental results show that our framework gives expected results for our scenario and provides with good performance regarding the balance between objectives.

Keywords: Scheduling and resource management
Optimization · Performance measurement and modelling
New economic model · Cloud computing
Containers to support high performance computing
and industrial workloads

1 Introduction

Nowadays, different forms of cloud computational resources exist such as virtual machines (VMs), containers, or bare-metal resources, having each their own characteristics. Container technology is relatively new in production systems

G. Mencagli et al. (Eds.): Euro-Par 2018 Workshops, LNCS 11339, pp. 69–81, 2019.
https://doi.org/10.1007/978-3-030-10549-5_6

but it is not a new concept. Container is a light-weight OS-level virtualization technique that allows to run an application and its dependencies in a resource-isolated process.

This paper presents a new opportunistic scheduling and resource allocation system based on an economic model related to different classes for SLAs (Service Level Agreements). The objective is to address the problems of companies that manage a private infrastructure of machines i.e. a cloud platform, and would like to optimize the scheduling of several containers submitted online by users. Each container is executed using a set of computing resources.

To specify the user desired SLAs classes, we propose to modelled each class by 3 services. This choice is motivated by our experience with the Fonds Unique Interministériel (FUI) Wolphin project [6]. It is based on the observation that hosting solutions do not allow manufacturers or cloud providers to offer to their users a fair or accurate invoice, i.e. a precise invoice with respect to the waiting time, the nodes reputation, consumption of resources and the number of replicas. The AlterWay company, coordinator of the Wolphin project, noticed that the project must respond to the following usages with regard to the deployed services: (i) Premium service is designed to users who want to get a 'high quality' service; (ii) Advanced service is designed to users who want to get an 'average quality' service; and (iii) Best effort service is designed to users who want to get a 'low/less quality' service.

In this work, we decompose the scheduling and allocation problems into 4 steps, namely selection of a container in a queue, selection of candidate nodes, computation of resources and allocation on a node. One can view the scheduler has a program that repeats forever these 4 steps. The third step is new, compared to the existing state-of-art research because, to the best of our knowledge, none of the existing cloud scheduler computes, dynamically, the number of resources allocated to a container. This is the first contribution of the paper. The user do not request for a fixed number of resources. The second contribution is related to the new economic model sustained by the 4 SLA classes regrouped in 2 qualitative and 2 quantitative SLA classes. The third contribution of the paper is the experiments that we conduct with Docker containers. We have implemented a new scheduler, based on the Docker API, for the creation of containers and we execute traces representative from the High Performance Computing (HPC) world and traces representative of Web hosting companies.

The organization of the paper is as follows. Section 2 presents some related works. Section 3 describes our framework architecture. Section 4 presents our qualitative and quantitative SLA classes. Section 5 describes how the SLA classes are used by our framework. Section 6 introduces exhaustive emulation that allows the validation of our proposed framework. A last, a conclusion and some future works are given in Sect. 7.

2 Related Work

In the literature, all problems of resources allocation or resources management refer to the same class of scheduling problems. They consist generally in associating a user's request to one or several computing cores. Most of these problems are NP-hard [13].

In the context of containers scheduling on cloud computing, there exists several studies, as those presented in [10,14,16]. However, to the best of our knowledge, all frameworks schedule containers according to a fixed configuration in term of computing resources. From an industrial point of view, we may cite, as examples, the schedulers inside Google Kubernetes [16], Docker Swarm [10] and Apache Mesos [14].

Google Kubernetes [16] is a scheduler framework which represents an orchestration system for containers based on pods concept. Pods are a group of one or more containers. They are always co-located and co-scheduled and run in a shared context. Moreover, they will be run on the same physical or virtual machine. The principle of Kubernetes scheduling can be summarized in two steps. First, filter all machines to remove machines that do not meet certain requirements of the pod. Second, classify the remaining machines using priorities to find the best fit to execute a pod.

Docker Swarm [10] is an important container scheduler framework developed by Docker. Docker is the technology used by the FUI Wolphin project [6] which is the support of our work. The Swarm manager is responsible for scheduling the containers on the agents or nodes. Swarm also has two steps to finally selecting the node that will execute the container. First, it uses filters to select suitable nodes to execute the container. Then, it uses, according to a ranking strategy, the most suitable one. Actually, Swarm has three ranking strategies: (i) Spread strategy which executes a container on the node having the least number of containers, (ii) Bin packing strategy, in contrast with spread, chooses the node with the most packed containers on it, and (iii) Random strategy which chooses a node randomly.

The field of Virtual Machines (VMs) scheduling may also serve as a reference for containers scheduling. Various approximation approaches are applied in the work of Tang et al. [12]. Authors propose an algorithm that can produce high-quality solutions for hard placement problems with thousands of machines and thousands of VMs within 30 seconds. This approximation algorithm strives to maximize the total satisfied application demand, to minimize the number of application starts and stops, and to balance the load across machines.

Targeting the energy efficiency and SLA compliance, Borgetto et al. [2] present an integrated management framework for governing Cloud Computing infrastructures based on three management actions, namely, VM migration and reconfiguration, and power management on physical machines. By incorporating an autonomic management loop, optimized using a wide variety of heuristics ranging from rules over random methods, the authors demonstrated that the proposed approach can save energy up to 61.6% while keeping SLA violations acceptably low.

In contrast to these related and above-mentioned studies, our proposed framework combines scheduling and allocation strategies with qualitative and quantitative SLA classes. The SLA classes are proposed to answer the needs of different users. The benefit of our framework consists to use the different SLA classes to: (i) select the first container that must be executed; (ii) decide the cloud node that must execute the selected container; (iii) compute dynamically the number of resources allocated to the considered container and (iv) decide the number of replicas for a container and choose nodes which execute the considered container and it's redundancy replicas.

A preliminary work has been published in [9]. In this paper, we consider the following improvements: (i) we consider 4 SLA classes instead of 2 SLA classes to have an economic model with several classes; (ii) the general scheduling schema is composed of 4 steps instead of 3 to satisfied all the SLA classes; and (iii) experiments are emulation on Grid'5000 testbed, with Docker containers, instead of simulations. In other words, this work introduces a more general and realistic framework compared to [9].

3 Architecture

The goal of our framework is to give answers to the problem stated as follows: *in cloud computing environment, how to use a set of qualitative and quantitative SLA classes to optimize the global scheduling of containers submitted online by users?*

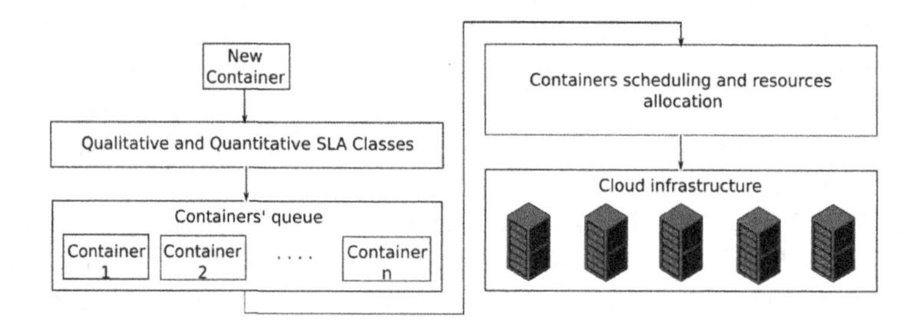

Fig. 1. Framework's architecture

Figure 1 depicts the architecture of our framework. Each time a new container is submitted online, the user must firstly select its services in the qualitative and quantitative SLA classes. Then, the new submitted container is inserted in the containers' queue. After that, our framework, schedules and allocates resources to each container according to its configuration in term of SLA classes. Finally, the submitted container is executed in the most appropriate cloud node.

4 Qualitative and Quantitative SLA Classes

As said before, our framework is based on SLA classes to configure each new submitted container. Our SLA classes are regrouped in two qualitative and two quantitative classes. Each class is proposed with 3 services: Premium, Advanced and Best effort.

The two qualitative classes address: (i) the satisfaction time criterion, that means, the user waiting time before the execution of the user container; and (ii) the reputation criterion, that means the node choice of the user to execute his container. Moreover, the two quantitative classes address: (i) the number of resources criterion, that means the number of resources must be allocated to execute a container; and (ii) the redundancy criterion which set the number of time that a container is executed to ensure fault tolerance.

In our context, to satisfy the user needs according to its SLAs classes, we propose to represent each service by one priority value as following: (i) Premium service: priority value = 3; (ii) Advanced service: priority value = 2; and (iii) Best effort service: priority value = 1. As we have 4 SLA classes (2 qualitative and 2 quantitative), each container is represented by 4 priorities values, each value represent the assignment of the service in one SLA class. For the first qualitative SLA class (satisfaction time), the modeling of our 3 services is motivated by the fact that users are regrouped in 3 categories:

- Premium service: It is designed for users who wish to find a solution as soon as possible without considering the price of the operation,
- Advanced service: It is designed for users that have a limited financial budget but still wish to have a solution in the smallest reasonable execution time,
- Best effort service: It is designed to users who have no time constraints, but want to pay for the minimum possible price.

For the second qualitative SLA class (reputation), our modeling based on 3 services is motivated by the fact that nodes are different according to the cloud infrastructure. Generally the differences between nodes is based on reputation criterion as: (i) security of sites; (ii) reliability of hardware; and (iii) reliability of network. In this context, users are also regrouped in 3 categories:

- Premium service: It is designed for users which execute their containers in nodes with high reputation;
- Advanced service: It is designed for users which execute their containers in nodes with an average reputation;
- Best effort service: It is designed to users who have no constraints about the reputation of the cloud nodes. The goal is to has a low cost price.

For the first quantitative SLA class (number of resources), the modeling of our 3 services is motivated by the fact that the need of resources for each user is different. Generally users are regrouped in 3 categories:

- Premium service: It is designed to users with long service that needs many computing cores.
- Advanced service: It is designed to users with short service that need some computing cores.
- Best effort service: It is designed to users with micro service that do not need many computing cores. Its service life is less than the frequency of metrics' collection.

For the second quantitative SLA class (redundancy replicas), the modeling of our 3 services is motivated by the fact that users are regrouped also in 3 categories according of the number of redundancy replicas of containers:

- Premium service: It is designed for users who execute their containers with a big number of redundancy replicas in different nodes to be sure that at the end of the execution, they get a solution;
- Advanced service: It is designed for users who execute their containers with average number of redundancy replicas in different nodes;
- Best effort service: It is designed to users who execute their containers without constraint about the number of replicas.

5 Scheduling and Resources Allocation Based on SLA Classes

As many other scheduling system proposed in the literature, we sketch to use a containers' queue to store all submitted containers. To schedule and allocate resources to containers, our framework goes through four phases according to the qualitative and quantitative SLA classes:

1. Container scheduling: It is based on a combination between qualitative and quantitative classes. To select the first container which must be executed we propose to use the PROMETHEE II (*Preference Ranking Organization METHod for Enrichment Evaluations*) algorithm;
2. Container reputation: It is based on the qualitative reputation class, to select a set of nodes that can execute the container and its redundancy replicas;
3. Container allocation: It is based on the quantitative number of resources class, to set dynamically the number of resources must be allocated to the selected container;
4. Container 'redundancy replicas': It is based on the quantitative 'redundancy replicas' class, to set the number of replicas for a container. This phase is also used to assign a container and its replicas to cloud nodes using the bin packing heuristic.

5.1 Container Scheduling

To select the first container which must be executed we propose to use, in this paper and for convenience, the PROMETHEE II algorithm [11] because it is a multi-criteria decision algorithm. It is also possible to use for example a CPLEX solver [4] in order to solve the decision problem, or any other techniques. In our context, if the selected container (c_x) can not be executed because of a lack of resources for example, the container c_x wait in the container's queue and a new container is selected by the PROMETHEE II algorithm. Remind that PROMETHEE II is an algorithm which permits the building of an outranking between different alternatives [11]. It is used in this step because it is known to provide with a 'good' compromise between qualitative and quantitative criteria and it is mathematically well founded. Indeed, the PROMETHEE II has been used with success to solve many problems [1]. It is based on a comparison, pair by pair, of possible decisions (containers) along the qualitative criteria (satisfaction time and reputation) and the quantitative criteria (number of resources and redundancy replicas). More details about the use of PROMETHEE II algorithm in our context is presented in [9]. PROMETHEE II algorithm has a complexity of $\mathcal{O}(q.n \log(n))$ [3] (where q represents the number of criteria and n the number of possible decisions (alternatives)).

5.2 Container Reputation

This step is used by our framework to select nodes that must execute a container and its copies according to the container service. Indeed, our framework classifies statically all nodes which form the cloud infrastructure in 3 categories: (i) High reputation nodes; (ii) Average reputation nodes; and (iii) Low reputation nodes.

Then, each service in the qualitative reputation class uses nodes category, as following: (i) Premium service uses the high reputation nodes category; (ii) Advanced service uses the average reputation nodes category; and (iii) Best effort service uses the low reputation nodes category.

5.3 Container Allocation

Our framework uses the quantitative number of resources class to set, for each container, the number of resources. In this step, we propose to use the same idea as the introductory work presented previously in [9], which is applied for any kind of nodes in the cloud (heterogeneous and not heterogeneous nodes). The principle is to set, for each container, a range on resources demand instead of specifying a fixed quantity of resources. It means that each service in the quantitative number of resources class has a number of resources bounded between the min and max parameters. The bound of cores for each service is proposed to be sure that each container, with low service in the number of resources class, cannot be executed with more cores than a container with a high service in the number of resources class.

To compute the bound of cores, we propose first to set N as the number of resources of the smallest machine of the infrastructure. N is set in this way to be sure that in any situation, the container is executed on one cloud node. After setting N, each service in the SLA quantitative number of resources class calculates the min and max number of resources. As we have 3 services, we propose to manage 3 intervals with the same distance as follows:

- *Best effort* class : Min number of resources $= 1$; and Max number of resources $= \frac{1}{3} \times N$,
- *Advanced* class : Min number of resources = Max number of resources of the Best effort service + 1; and Max number of resources $= \frac{2}{3} \times N$,
- *Premium* class : Min number of resources = Max number of resources of the Advanced service + 1; and Max number of resources $= N$.

After bounding the number of resources for each service in the quantitative number of resources class, we use a function that set, dynamically, the number of resources for a container (c_x) at time t using: (i) bounds cores (min and max cores) in each service; (ii) number of containers saved in the containers' queue at time t with the same reputation service as the container c_x; and (iii) number of free cores available in all the candidates nodes that can execute the container c_x at time t.

Let r_i be the number of resources that must be allocated to container c_i with quantitative number of resources priority p_i. We suppose that the containers' queue has n containers $(c_1, c_2, \cdots, c_n)$ with the same reputation service as c_i. Lest set $(p_1, p_2, \cdots, p_n)$ the quantitative number of resources priorities associated to the previous n containers saved in the queue and wc the number of waiting cores in all candidates nodes that can execute c_i (with the same reputation service as c_i). Then r_i is computed as presented in the formula 1.

$$r_i = \frac{p_i * wc}{\sum_{j=0}^{n} p_j} \tag{1}$$

The formula 1 computes, at each time t, a fair partitioning of all waiting cores between containers according to their quantitative number of resources services. Next, the system checks if $r_i >$ Max cores (Max_{cores}) of its quantitative number of resources service, then $r_i = Max_{cores}$, else if $r_i < (Min_{cores})$ of its quantitative number of resources service, $r_i = Min_{cores}$.

For example, let us consider an infrastructure composed of 3 nodes with the Premium service in the reputation class, and 9 waiting cores in $node_1$, 6 waiting cores in $node_2$ and 6 waiting cores in $node_3$. The total number of waiting cores is 21. Let us also use the following three containers which have Premium service in the reputation class and have the following configuration:

- Container c_1: *Premium* service on the quantitative number of resources class (priority = 3), Min cores = 7 and Max cores = 9;
- Container c_2: *Advanced* service on the quantitative number of resources class (priority = 2), Min cores = 4 and Max cores = 6;
- Container c_3: *Best effort* service on the quantitative number of resources class (priority = 1), Min cores = 1 and Max cores = 3.

The number of resources is set as following:

- Container $c_1 : r_1 = \frac{3*21}{3+2+1} = 10$. As $10 > 9$ (max cores for *Premium* service), we set $r_1 = 9$. Then, the number of waiting cores will be equal to (9-9)+6+6 = 12. Now, in the queue, only 2 containers are saved: c_2 and c_3.
- Container $c_2 : r_2 = \frac{2*12}{2+1} = 8$. As $8 > 6$ (max cores for *Advanced* service), we set $r_2 = 6$. Then, the number of waiting cores will be equal to 0+(6-6)+6=6. Now, in the queue there is only the container c_3.
- Container $c_3 : r_3 = \frac{1*6}{1} = 6$.

5.4 Container Replicas

In our framework each container and its replicas are executed in different nodes of the same reputation category nodes. That means, we cannot execute a container and it's redundancy replicas in the same cloud node. To compute the number of redundancy replicas for each container, our framework sets an empirical value for each service in the quantitative redundancy replicas class. The unique constraint is that the highest service has the biggest value for the number of replicas. For example, we may have the following setting:

- Premium service, our framework sets 3 redundancy replicas for each container;
- Advanced service, our framework sets 2 redundancy replicas for each container;
- Best effort service, our framework sets 1 redundancy replica for each container.

We propose to add in our framework the redundancy replicas class to manage some fault tolerance issues. For example, if one cloud node ($node_x$) is stopped for different reasons, all containers who are executing on $node_x$ are also stopped. In this case, if the user chooses a high service in the redundancy replicas class, he will be granted that another copy of his container is running in another node. In reality, the usual practical assumption is that there is very low likelihood that all nodes will stop at the same time.

In our system, we guarantee that each container or its redundancy replicas are executed in fifferent nodes. To assign a container to a cloud node, our framework applies the well known bin packing principle which is a combinatorial *NP-hard* problem [5]. The principle of the bin packing heuristic consists, for each new container c_i, to assign it to the node n_j which has the less available free resources. This means that we select the node (not yet visited) that has the smallest number of idle cores and that can execute the container c_i.

The goal of using this heuristic is to minimize the number of active nodes to reduce the cost of exploiting the infrastructure.

5.5 Complexity Analysis

Based on above mentioned arguments, the overall time complexity of our approach is the complexity of the 4 steps: $\mathcal{O}(q.n\log(n))$, NP-hard problem, $\mathcal{O}(n)$ and $\mathcal{O}(n)$ respectively and for n being the node number of the architecture.

6 Experimental Evaluation

In this section, we introduce emulation result of our framework to check if it meets our expectations. For the emulation, we have used the Docker container technology inside the Grid5000 platform [7], an experimental large-scale testbed for distributed computing in France. For our experimental evaluation, we reserved an infrastructure composed of 480 computing cores distributed in 15 nodes (Intel Xeon CPU). The 15 nodes are split as following: (i) 5 nodes form high reputation category; (ii) 5 nodes form average reputation category; and (iii) 5 nodes form low reputation category.

In this experimental evaluation, each container is submitted by one of the following three users, each user has a particular services in the SLA classes:

- Premium user: Premium service for all qualitative and quantitative SLA classes;
- Advanced user: Advanced service for all qualitative and quantitative SLA classes;
- Best effort user: Best effort service for all qualitative and quantitative SLA classes.

Each container runs a unique simple parallel application which load computing cores. The number of cores occupied by each container is set automatically by our framework as presented in Subsect. 5.3. However, each container has also a Sequential Life Time (SLT) set when the container is submitted and it is equal to 5 min. Then, according to the number of cores allocated for each container (N), the Parallel Life Time (PLT) which represent the real executing time of the container is computed as being $PLT = \frac{SLT}{N}$.

Moreover, in this series of emulation, we introduce the performance of our framework according to the submitting containers type. In this context, we propose two types of experiments: (i) containers submitted at the same time; and (ii) containers submitted online. The first one stresses the behavior of our framework. The second one represents a "normal" operating mode.

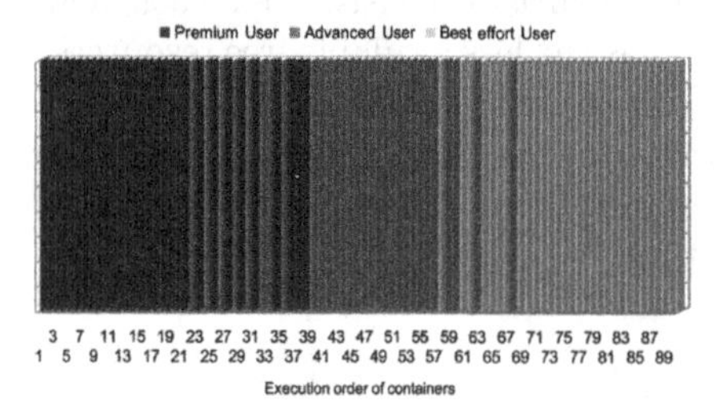

Fig. 2. Submission of 90 Docker containers at the same time

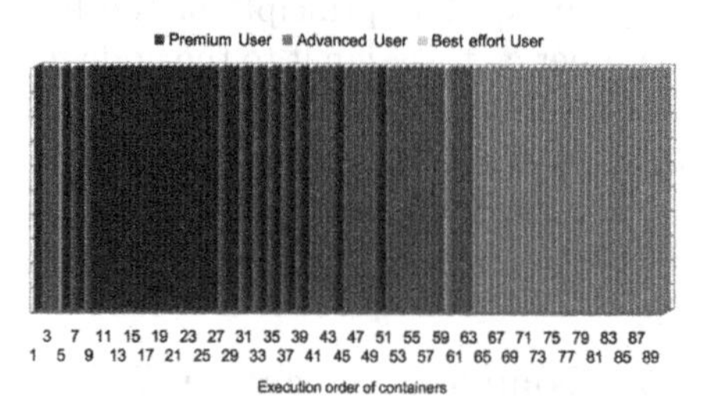

Fig. 3. Submission of 90 Docker container online with a fixed frequency

6.1 Containers Submitted at the Same Time

Figure 2 shows the order of execution of 90 containers submitted at the same time by 3 users, each user submits 30 containers. As a result, it is clear that our framework starts by the execution, firstly, of containers submitted by the Premium user, then containers submitted by the Advanced user. Finally, our framework executes containers submitted by the Best effort user. This result confirms that our framework respects the priorities of containers. We note also that when our framework cannot execute a container which has a high service priority, as the container submitted by the Premium user, for lack of resources, our framework executes another container, for a user who has a lower service request in order to optimize the global scheduling of all containers. The goal is not to stop the scheduling process when a container is not executed and to wait.

6.2 Containers Submitted Online

Figure 3 shows the order of execution of 90 containers submitted online with a fixed frequency. Each 3 s 3 containers are submitted by 3 different users. That means, each 3 s, each user submits one container. Figure 4 shows the order of execution of 90 containers submitted according to the Google Cluster Data traces [15] patterns. The Google traces information (May 2011), are related to the submission frequency time of requests on cluster of about 12.5k machines. In our case, the 90 containers are submitted using the same submission frequency time as the first 90 requests submitted in Google traces. The 90 containers are distributed as follows: (i) 2 containers submitted by Premium user and (ii) 88 containers submitted by Advanced user. In a complementary way, Fig. 5 shows the order of execution of 90 containers submitted according to the real-world trace files of an international company called Prezi [17]. These traces represent the submission frequency time of the web oriented applications. In our case, the 90 containers are submitted using the same submission frequency time as the first 90 web oriented applications submitted in Prezi traces. The 90 containers are distributed as follows: (i) 10 containers submitted by Premium user, (ii) 13 containers submitted by Advanced user and (iii) 67 containers submitted by Best effort user. According to Figs. 3, 4 and 5, we note that there is an overlap between the execution of containers. This expected overlap is due to the fact that containers are submitted online by different users.

6.3 Comparison Between the Average Number of Cores Allocated for Each User

To the best of our knowledge, there is no framework which configures dynamically the number of cores that must be allocated to each container. This explains that it is impossible to compare the performance obtained using our framework with another state-of-art framework. However, in Table 1 we shows a comparison between the average number of cores assigned to each user. As a result, we note that our framework assigns, for each submission type, more cores to the user with highest services. We note also that the user with the low service gets always the smallest number of cores.

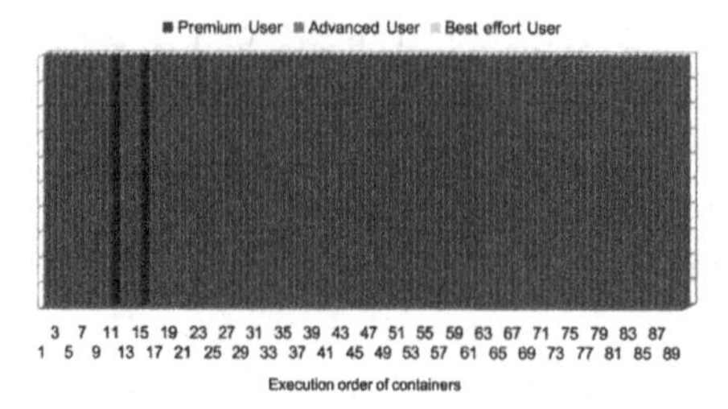

Fig. 4. Submission of 90 Docker containers according to Google traces frequency

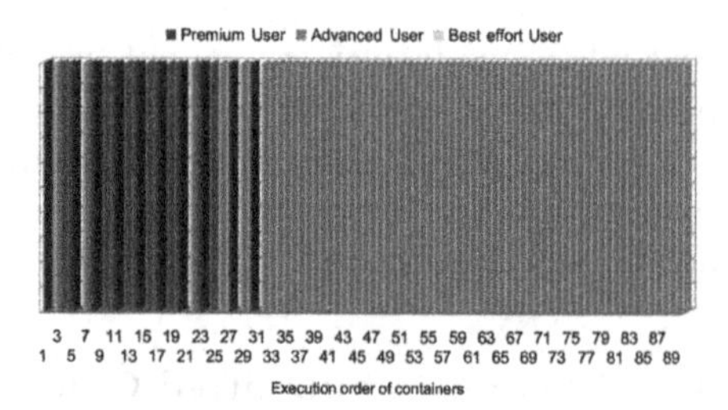

Fig. 5. Submission of 90 Docker container according to Prezi traces frequency

Table 1. Comparison between the average number of cores allocated for each user

Submitting type	Average number of cores allocated for each user		
	Premium user	Advanced user	Best effort user
Submission at the same time	27.1	15.26	6.16
Submission online with a fixed frequency	27.63	15.26	5.33
Submission online according to Google traces	32	13.7	-
Submission online according to Prezi traces	30.4	17.15	3.98

7 Conclusion

We have presented, in this paper, a new framework adapted for cloud computing environments in the context of containers technologies. The novelty of our framework relies on SLA classes to optimize the global scheduling and the allocation of resources for containers. Our solution proposes to users two qualitative and two quantitative SLAs classes with three services for each class (Premium, Advanced and Best effort). In our framework, the number of resources are computed, dynamically, according to the quantitative number of resources class.

As a first perspective, we propose to compute the number of resources by taking into consideration the submitted container history. It is challenging to efficiently decide when and how to reconfigure the cloud in order to dynamically adapt to the changes. Such a challenge has been identified as a MAPE-K (Monitoring, Analysis, Planning, Execution, and Knowledge) control loop by IBM, deeply investigated in [8], resulting in the concept of autonomic computing that could be used in our case.

We may also wonder if the approach is flexible enough in the context of multiple cloud providers. This question poses the problem of the adoption of our economic model. We also propose, as a perspective, to add to our framework a consolidation heuristic which allows to set dynamically the number of active cloud nodes in the infrastructure. This means that, according to the global load of nodes, the framework decides the number of active nodes to reduce the energy consumption.

Acknowledgements. This work is funded by the French *Fonds Unique Ministériel (FUI)* Wolphin Project. We thank Grid5000 team for their help to use the testbed.

References

1. Behzadian, M., Kazemzadeh, R., Albadvi, A., Aghdasi, M.: Promethee: a comprehensive literature review on methodologies and applications. Eur. J. Oper. Res. **200**(1), 198–215 (2010)
2. Borgetto, D., Maurer, M., Costa, G.D., Pierson, J., Brandic, I.: Energy-efficient and SLA-aware management of IaaS clouds. In: International Conference on Energy-Efficient Computing and Networking, e-Energy 2012, Madrid, Spain, p. 25 (2012)
3. Calders, T., Assche, D.V.: Promethee is not quadratic: an o(qnlog(n)) algorithm. Omega **76**, 63–69 (2018)
4. IBM CPLEX solver: https://www.ibm.com/products/ilog-cplex-optimization-studio
5. Garey, M.R., Johnson, D.S.: Computers and Intractability: A Guide to the Theory of NP-Completeness. W. H. Freeman & Co., New York (1979)
6. Fui-22 wolphin project: https://lipn.univ-paris13.fr/~menouer/wolphin.html
7. Grid5000: https://www.grid5000.fr/
8. Huebscher, M.C., McCann, J.A.: A survey of autonomic computing–degrees, models, and applications. ACM Comput. Surv. **40**(3), 7:1–7:28 (2008)
9. Menouer, T., Cerin, C.: Scheduling and resource management allocation system combined with an economic model. In: IEEE International Symposium on Parallel and Distributed Processing with Applications (IEEE ISPA) Guangzhou, China (2017)
10. Peinl, R., Holzschuher, F., Pfitzer, F.: Docker cluster management for the cloud-survey results and own solution. J. Grid Comput. **14**(2), 265–282 (2016)
11. Deshmukh, S.C.: Preference ranking organization method of enrichment evaluation (promethee). Int. J. Eng. Sci. Invent. **2**, 28–34 (2013)
12. Tang, C., Steinder, M., Spreitzer, M., Pacifici, G.: A scalable application placement controller for enterprise data centers. In: Proceedings of the 16th International Conference on World Wide Web, Banff, Alberta, Canada, pp. 331–340, May 2007
13. Ullman, J.: NP-complete scheduling problems. J. Comput. Syst. Sci. **10**(3), 384–393 (1975)
14. The apache software foundation. mesos, apache. http://mesos.apache.org/
15. Google cluster data traces. https://github.com/google/cluster-data/
16. Kubernetes scheduler. https://kubernetes.io/
17. Prezi real-world traces. http://prezi.com/scale/

Automated Multi-Swarm Networking with Open Baton NFV MANO Framework

Jun-Sik Shin[1(✉)], Mathias Santos de Brito[2,3], Thomas Magedanz[2], and JongWon Kim[1(✉)]

[1] EECS, Gwangju Institute of Science and Technology (GIST), Gwangju, South Korea
{jsshin, jongwon}@nm.gist.ac.kr

[2] NGNI, Fraunhofer FOKUS, Berlin, Germany
{mathias.santos.de.brito, thomas.magedanz}@fokus.fraunhofer.de

[3] DCET, Universidade Estadual de Santa Cruz, Ilhéus, Brazil

Abstract. Container-based Network Functions Virtualization (NFV) and multi-site/multi-cluster service orchestration are a critical topic in the field of ICT infrastructure. Academia, Industry and Open Source projects are actively working on the technology. With the trends, Open Baton, an implementation of the ETSI NFV MANO Reference Architecture, started efforts to orchestrate network services over multiple Docker Swarm clusters. To achieve that, Open Baton would require an additional feature to configure an overlay networking over multiple swarm clusters, since Docker Swarm does not support multi-cluster service. In this paper, we discuss our design and implementation of the Multi-Swarm Networking Helper in Open Baton, which configures an L2 overlay networking over multiple Docker Swarm clusters by leveraging on a third-party Docker networking driver.

Keywords: Multi-cluster networking · Container networking
Service orchestration with NFV MANO

1 Introduction

Container-based NFV (Network Functions Virtualization) is a topic of interest in the field of ICT infrastructure. NFV researches previously focused on bare-metal-based PNF (Physical Network Functions) to address performance issues in VM (Virtual Machine)-based VNF (Virtual Network Functions). However, PNF occupies much hardware resources, and it is difficult to isolate multiple of them in a single box. Therefore, an NFV research line started to focus on Containerized Network Function (CNF), because of advantages of this technology, such as scalability, agility and resource efficiency, delivering a performance equivalent or near to the performance observed when using bare-metal.

Network service orchestration is another popular topic in NFV domain. According to the definition of the European Telecommunications Standard Institute (ETSI), network service orchestration is lifecycle management (deployment, update and remove)

G. Mencagli et al. (Eds.): Euro-Par 2018 Workshops, LNCS 11339, pp. 82–92, 2019.
https://doi.org/10.1007/978-3-030-10549-5_7

of a network service, a composition of network functions such as firewall and load balancer, over resource cluster(s) [1]. Single-cluster service orchestration based on Virtual Machines matured with the efforts of researchers and open source communities, a natural step forward is to extend it to multi-site/multi-cluster service orchestration based on containers, which is currently an active research topic.

In this paper, we demonstrate an Open Baton NFV MANO (MANagement and Orchestration) framework [2] to orchestrate CNF-based multi-cluster service over Docker Swarm. We extended the Open Baton Docker Swarm VIM/VNFM, under development at Fraunhofer FOKUS, to allow it to orchestrate multi-cluster services over Docker Swarm clusters. In our scenario, the CNFs of a given service should work on an L2 overlay network regardless of the type of the service (single-cluster or multi-cluster). However, the default networking of Docker Swarm has not enough features to support multi-cluster services. Therefore, it is required an additional networking feature for Open Baton to allow the configuration of multi-Swarm Networking, as an overlay network created over multiple Docker Swarm clusters.

In this paper, we present the Multi-Swarm Networking Helper, an additional feature compliant to Open Baton MANO Framework. The feature configures multi-Swarm networking by leveraging on the Weave Net driver, a third-party Docker networking plugin, during the deployment phase of a network service in Open Baton. We then evaluate the functional aspects of the implementation in a real multi-site testbed.

2 Backgrounds and State-of-the-Art

Since the introduction of the concept of container-based NFV, A research line claims that container is more appropriate than a virtual machine for deploying network functions. [3, 4] showed CNF has higher performances concerning resource utilization, agility, and scalability compared to VNF. With the advantage of CNF, the authors of [4] suggested Glasgow Network Function that is a container-based NFV platform targeted for orchestrating Linux Container (LXC)-based CNFs over resource-constrained edge boxes. Even though Glasgow Network Function made great progress on CNF orchestration, the design was hard to be aligned with OpenBaton. At the same time, researchers are also focusing on multi-site VNF orchestration. [5–7] insisted that previous NFV studies not show proper solutions to support multi-domain/multi-site VNFs orchestration. The authors suggested their own multi-domain VNFs orchestration framework. However, the works are not appropriate to be applied for CNF orchestration, because the designs do not consider addressing different characteristics of CNF orchestration. The multi-site/multi-cluster orchestration of CNFs combining two domains has still challenged regarding implementation.

OpenStack project, a popular open source cloud operating system, has developed its subprojects, Tacker and Tricircle, for supporting multi-site VNF orchestration. OpenStack Tacker acting as NFVO as well as VNFM orchestrates VNFs over multiple OpenStack clusters. In the other hands, OpenStack Tricircle can configure service (tenant)-level L2/L3 overlay networks over multi-site OpenStack clusters. Combining two projects could orchestrate VNF-based multi-site services, but it has not supported container-based service orchestration yet. A proposal about Kubernetes VIM plugin is actively being discussed for OpenStack Tacker to be able to orchestrate multi-site services consisting of CNFs as well as VNFs. Meanwhile, Docker Swarm and Kubernetes approach a different way to coordination of multi-site clusters. They federate multiple clusters at the level of Identity and API, but container networking over multiple clusters is not focused.

With trends on containerized NFV, the Open Baton community developed Docker VIM (Virtual Infrastructure Manager), and VNFM (Virtual Network Function Manager) to support Docker container-based infrastructures. Open Baton is an open source NFV MANO framework developed and supported by Fraunhofer FOKUS. It is a reference implementation of ETSI MANO specification [8]. However, Docker VIM/VNFM should manage each of Docker-enabled boxes independently. It increases the management complexity of the resources and makes Open Baton user need to be aware of too much detail of the underlay resources for deploying a service. To resolve this issue, Open Baton could leverage on a container orchestration tool taking care of multiple boxes. For that purpose, we selected Docker Swarm among many tools including Kubernetes and Fleet, because Docker Swarm is very easy to install and use, also, we could alleviate our efforts on applying research developed with Docker into Docker Swarm. For that purpose, a version of a VIM and VNFM were developed to support Docker Swarm Clusters and expose them as a Point-of-Presence (PoP) in Open Baton. However, Open Baton's current version of the Docker Swarm VIM/VNFM does not support communication between two containers, part of the same deployment, in different clusters due to the lack of multi-cluster support in the default network driver of Docker Swarm. Especially, overlay networks configured by the default driver are isolated from the outside of a cluster.

One typical approach to enable containers in different sites to communicate with each other is to include multi-site boxes into a container cluster. Then the container orchestration tool could natively configure overlay networks across multi-sites. However, this approach has limitations for supporting use cases that require managing multiple clusters separately, for example, individual operation of each site or applying different policies to sites. Besides, adding multi-site worker boxes into a Docker Swarm cluster could degrade performance, resulting from manager-worker communication across multi-sites. Adding cluster managers, in contrast, results in performance reduction due to the consensus algorithm for synchronizing states among managers. Thus, this approach has limitations of scalability and performance in large-scale and widely distributed multi-site infrastructure. Therefore, OpenBaton's current version of Docker Swarm VIM/VNFM needs to be extended to support interconnection between containers running in multiple Swarm Clusters.

3 Requirements and Design

To explain our proposal, described in Sect. 1, we assume an example scenario that depends on multi-cluster service orchestration. This scenario consists of multiple Docker Swarm clusters registered to Open Baton as PoPs. Open Baton user selects one network service descriptor, which specifies the configuration and behavior of the virtual network functions of a service, through the Open Baton NFVO Dashboard. Then, the user can select the clusters for each VNFs in the belonging to the network service. If the user selects the same cluster for all VNFs, then the service is a single-cluster service. If not, the service is a multi-cluster service. NFVO starts the deployment process according to the descriptor and the user's selection. In case of single-cluster, Open Baton creates an overlay network with the default networking driver of Docker Swarm. However, for multi-cluster service, Open Baton utilizes the Multi-Swarm Networking Helper to configure a Multi-Swarm Networking. After creating the network, Open Baton deploys the VNFs.

To realize the use case with the Multi-Swarm Networking Helper, Open Baton must consider the following:

- For a multi-cluster service, Open Baton utilizes Multi-Swarm Networking Helper to configure Multi-Swarm Networking.
- For a single-cluster service, Open Baton configures default Docker Swarm networking.
- Regardless of service types, all VNFs in a network service should work on an L2 overlay network.
- Do not modify common NFVO procedures for network service orchestration.
- Multi-Swarm Networking does not introduce any additional parameters in the Network Service Descriptor and VNF Descriptor.

Before considering Open Baton, we had to find a way for Docker Swarm to enable an overlay network over multiple clusters. We considered three approaches: (1) to configure a relay container in each cluster. In this approach, all containers need to send packets destined to other clusters to the relay container working in the same cluster. The relay container can pass the packets to another relay container in the destination cluster; (2) to configure a Linux networking stack including Linux Bridge and internal firewall to inter-connect boxes in different clusters, whenever a container and a network is changed (creation, deletion, update). This approach requires the configuration of a forwarding table, neighbors table and a VXLAN tunnel on the Linux Bridge inside the network namespaces of the overlay networks; (3) to use the Weave Net driver that is one of the third-party network plugins for Docker Swarm. Weave Net driver manages an internal router in each box, and the router maintains networking information in the box such as the network list and attached containers. Those routers in the same cluster make peer relationships with each other and exchange the information. Then the driver configures an L2 overlay networking over the cluster according to the exchanged information. In this approach, we extend the scope of Weave Net router from a single cluster to multi-clusters by making peer relationships among Swarm manager boxes located in different clusters.

Among the candidates, we select to leverage on the Weave Net third-party driver. The third party driver could reduce the number of interaction between NFVO and Docker Swarm Boxes compared to other approaches. The driver required the addition of new steps to allow setting up the peers within Open Baton VIM/VNFM. After that, the driver automatically configures an overlay network over multi-clusters. In contrast, other approaches demand the NFVO to keep monitoring networking-related events in Swarm clusters, and directly configures Linux networking stack in all boxes whenever events occur. If the NFVO handles detailed configuration of all boxes, then advantages by leveraging Docker Swarm as cluster resource orchestrator are decreased. For this reason, we decided to use the Weave Net driver approach, which is more suitable for our solution.

Implementing the approach into Open Baton has different issues. One of the main issues is duplicated IP addresses of containers in different clusters owing to default IPAM (IP Address Management) of Docker Swarm. Each Swarm cluster has a default IPAM. However, the IPAM does not know the IP addresses used in other clusters. Therefore, containers in different clusters may have the same IP address. To avoid this problem, Open Baton should divide L2 subnet into smaller IP allocation ranges and assign different range to each participating cluster to accommodate a multi-cluster service and reduce unassigned IP ranges, while creating an overlay network. Also, another design issue is to select the MANO component where we implement the feature for identifying multi-cluster services and calculating IP allocation ranges. The feature requires to find the number of clusters participating in the given service. We used the Docker Swarm VNFM rather than the NFVO and the Docker Swarm VIM. The NFVO seems the most proper element since it can randomly generate an IP subnet for a network while knowing the number of clusters. Therefore, the NFVO can easily calculate IP allocation ranges and pass these ranges to the VIM/VNFM when creating a network. However, it violates the requirement not to modify common NFVO procedures for the network service orchestration. By the way, the VIM does not receive any clues about the service being orchestrated by the NFVO, other than about the resources necessary to deploy a VNF. Thus, it cannot ask the number of clusters used by a network service to the NFVO. In contrast, VNFM can find a service identifier from the given VNF, so it can query the NFVO to get information about the network service. In this context, we introduce Multi-Swarm Networking Helper doing all additional steps including service classification, network service descriptor query to NFVOm calculation of IP allocation ranges, and creating multi-Swarm networks with the third-party driver. VNFM can create both single-cluster and multi-cluster services with the help of Multi-Swarm Networking Helper.

The designed procedure using Open Baton for deploying a network service is shown in Fig. 1. Open Baton user selects a network service and the clusters for each VNFs, and then the NFVO starts the procedure for creating the network service. The NFVO requests the VIM to create an overlay network, the VIM, then skips this step, the reason is that the VIM does not know if the network belongs to a single-cluster network service or a multi-cluster one. For each VNF in the service, the NFVO sends a request with the VNF descriptor to the VNFM to deploy it. The VNFM then contacts the Multi-Swarm Networking Helper. The Helper extracts the service identifier from the given VNF descriptor and takes the network service record (NSR) that contains information of the service by sending a request to NFVO. The Helper classifies whether the service is deployed in single-cluster or multi-clusters, based on the cluster lists included in the received NSR. If the service is a single-cluster service, then the VNFM creates a network using the default networking driver and the containerized VNF in the target cluster. If not, the Helper divides a subnet into multiple IP allocation ranges based on the number of clusters and returns one of the ranges to the VNFM. VNFM creates a network with the subnet using the assigned range with the Weave Net third-party driver. The Helper configures an internal router for making peers with the other

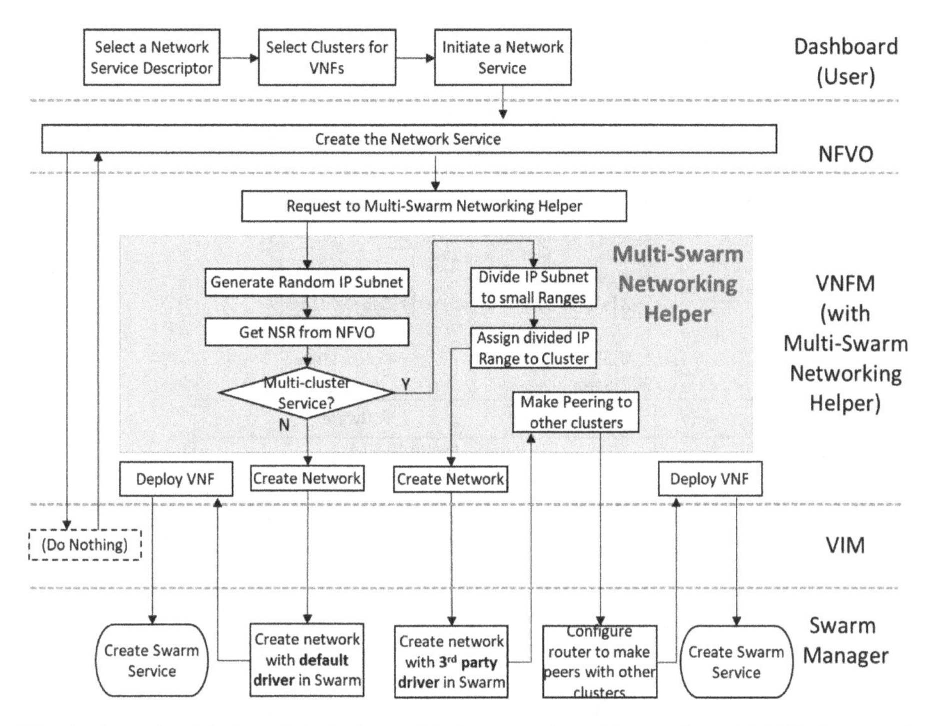

Fig. 1. Procedural design of deploying multi-cluster service with open baton MANO framework

clusters listed in the NSR. After those configurations, multi-Swarm networking becomes available, so VNFM creates the containerized VNF on the network. With this design, Open Baton satisfies the requirements previously established.

However, our design currently has limitations. We only consider the deployment procedure of service orchestration. We assume that multiple services do not share one overlay network, and all boxes in Docker Swarm clusters has pre-installed Weave Net third-party driver. Also, clusters configured with other software such as OpenStack cannot utilize it, because the design depends on Docker Swarm and Weave Net third-party driver.

4 Implementation and Verification

In this section, we describe the implementation of the Multi-Swarm Networking Helper in Open Baton based on the design proposed, and also verify its functionality on our testbed. For implementation and functional validation, we prepared a small-sized multi-site testbed consisted of two sites within the K-ONE (Korea OpenNetworking Everywhere) Playground. K-ONE Playground is a miniaturized multi-site Edge-Cloud testbed in South Korea. It consists of five sites, each of them comprising a K-Cluster that is a cluster consisted of multiple resource boxes. Those K-Clusters are inter-connected through L3 WAN supporting 1 Gbps networking provided by KREONET research network [9].

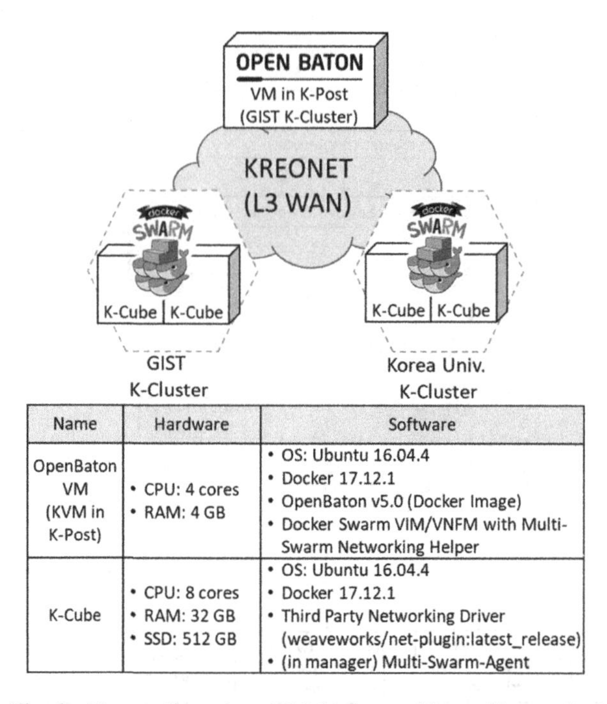

Name	Hardware	Software
OpenBaton VM (KVM in K-Post)	• CPU: 4 cores • RAM: 4 GB	• OS: Ubuntu 16.04.4 • Docker 17.12.1 • OpenBaton v5.0 (Docker Image) • Docker Swarm VIM/VNFM with Multi-Swarm Networking Helper
K-Cube	• CPU: 8 cores • RAM: 32 GB • SSD: 512 GB	• OS: Ubuntu 16.04.4 • Docker 17.12.1 • Third Party Networking Driver (weaveworks/net-plugin:latest_release) • (in manager) Multi-Swarm-Agent

Fig. 2. The configuration of Multi-Swarm Networking testbed

Figure 2 shows the configuration of our testbed. Open Baton is deployed on an OpenStack VM (KVM) in K-Post box of GIST K-Cluster. We use a Docker image of Open Baton version 5.0 for deploying the NFVO. Docker VIM and VNFM work in the K-Post box, and they register to the NFVO via RabbitMQ. We used two K-Cube boxes from GIST (Gwangju, South Korea) K-Cluster and another two boxes from Korea University (Seoul, South Korea) K-Cluster. We configured the Docker Swarm clusters in two different sites and registered the clusters in Open Baton. Next, we installed Weave Net third-party driver to all boxes along with the Multi-Swarm-Agents in the Swarm Manager boxes. The Multi-Swarm-Agent acts as an intermediator between MANO and the third-party driver in the Swarm Manager box. The agent provides a REST APIs to Open Baton and configures the internal routers according to received requests. As a result, we ended up with Docker Swarm clusters in two different sites, being network services orchestrated upon them by Open Baton with Multi-Swarm Networking Helper.

In this testbed, we verify the functionality of Multi-Swarm Networking Helper by showing a simple scenario. We deploy a network service consisted of two containerized VNFs configured to be deployed in different clusters via Open Baton NFVO dashboard. For each CNFs, we used a customized Docker image of Ubuntu OS with networking test tools. Then, Open Baton NFV MANO with Multi-Swarm Networking Helper automatically configures an L2 overlay networking over two sites, so two CNFs can do L2-based networking each other.

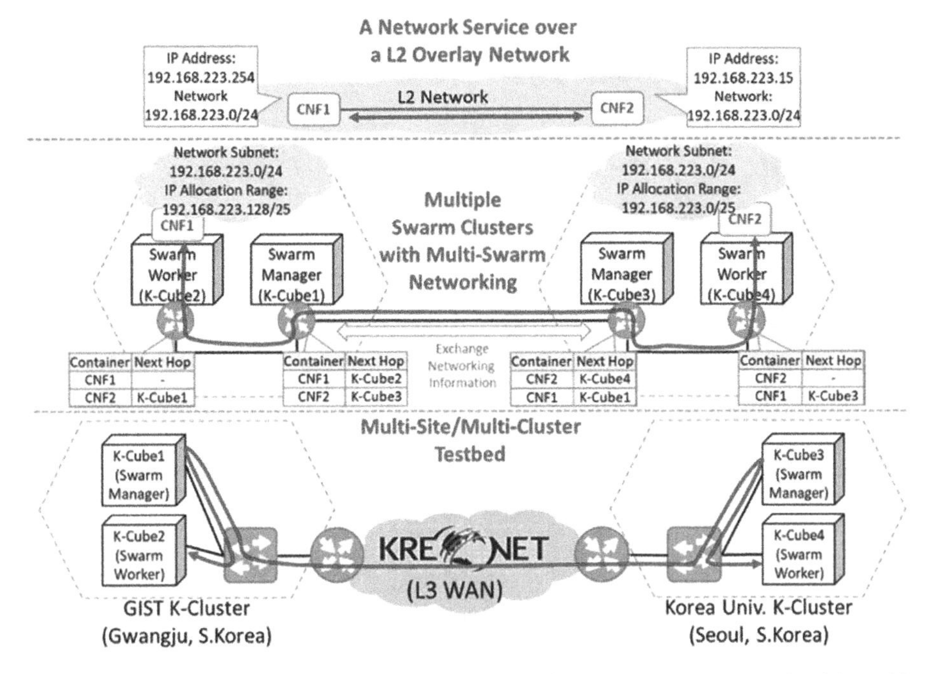

Fig. 3. Verification of multi-cluster service orchestrated by Open Baton MANO with Multi-Swarm Networking Helper

Figure 3 shows the result of the functional validation. From a service perspective, two CNFs in different clusters have IP addresses of the same subnet and can directly communicate with each other through the L2 network. In what concerns Docker Swarm, two clusters had the networks created with Weave Net third-party driver. The networks, despite being on the same subnet, they are using different IP allocation ranges. For intra-cluster networking, internal routers in a cluster exchange networking information just after the network creation, and the third-party driver configures VXLAN-based overlay network over the boxes of the cluster accordingly. For multi-Swarm networking, the Multi-Swarm Networking Helper makes peer relationships between routers in the Swarm manager boxes of the different clusters. The peered routers exchange information and spread it to Swarm worker boxes. All routers know the next hop router for packets destined to containers in different clusters. After the exchange, the driver creates VXLAN tunnels among routers in the Swarm manager boxes. As a result, an L2 overlay network extends to multiple Swarm clusters. Consequently, Open Baton NFV MANO can orchestrate multi-cluster services with Multi-Swarm Networking Helper and Weave Net third-party driver. Furthermore, CNFs of network services always work in the same way regardless of their location in underlay clusters.

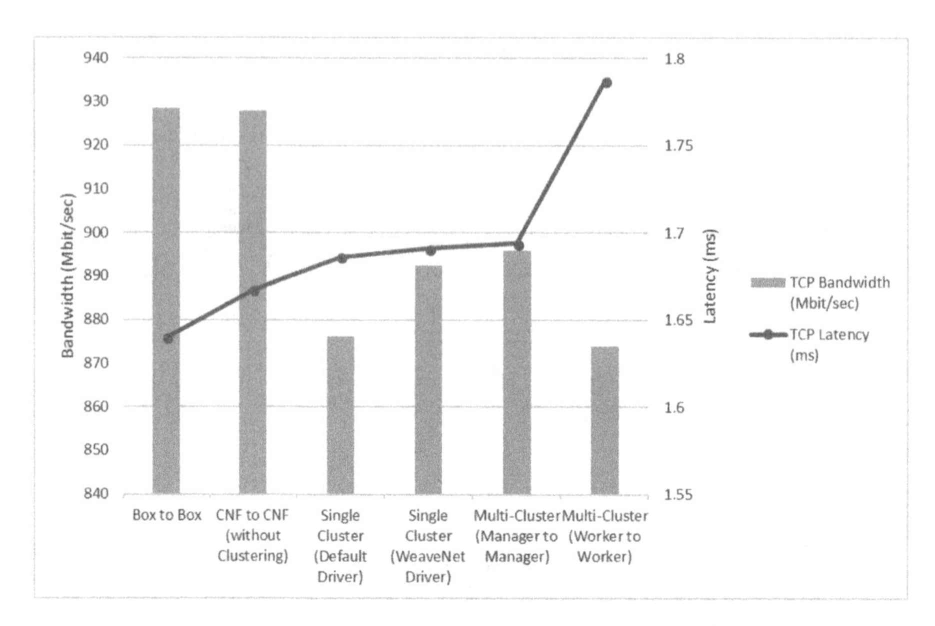

Fig. 4. TCP networking performance in different cases of multi-site container networking

We perform an additional experiment for measuring TCP bandwidth and latency in different cases of multi-site networking to verify the performance. To measure TCP performance, we use Qperf (version 0.4.11)[1] that is a benchmark tool designed for TCP/UDP as well as RDMA and other protocols. We consider six test cases of measuring TCP performance: (1) typical TCP/IP networking between bare metal boxes in different sites, as a reference point for other cases. (2) TCP/IP networking between two containers without clustering. (3) overlay networking with the default driver and single cluster over two sites. (4) overlay networking with Weave Net driver and single cluster over two sites. (5) multi-Swarm networking configured by multi-Swarm networking helper, and containers in manager boxes of two clusters in two sites. (6) multi-Swarm networking, and containers in worker boxes of two clusters in two sites.

Figure 4 shows the result of the performance measurement. Comparing the case 2 and 3 shows that overlay networking in Docker Swarm cluster decrease networking performance, due to network namespaces, virtual switches, internal firewall rules and virtual extensible LAN (VxLAN) tunnels additionally configured in each clustered box. Meanwhile, default driver and the third-party driver working under the same configuration have the equivalent performance as shown in the case 3 and 4. Multi-cluster service, in the case 5 and 6, shows TCP networking performance can be slightly changed according to locations of containers. As we explained in the feature verification, all packets destined to other clusters are sent to the manager box, and its internal router routes them to another manager box in the destination cluster. So, the additional hops are added to a networking path crossing the clusters. The results show that the

[1] https://github.com/linux-rdma/qperf.

additional two hops decrease approximately 20 Mbit/sec of TCP bandwidth and increase 0.1 ms of TCP latency. However, the amount of the decrease tends to be stationary, because the number of additional hops is at most two and the hops are between boxes in a cluster. Thus, we anticipate the overhead of multi-Swarm networking accounts for a relatively small portion of the performance degradation in large-scale infrastructures, where sites are widely distributed, and inter-site traffic is massive. Consequently, we insist on our solution, multi-Swarm networking orchestrated by OpenBaton MANO framework, has reasonable networking performance to support multi-cluster services.

5 Conclusion and Outlook

In this paper, we described a new approach to enable an overlay networking over multiple Swarm clusters with Weave Net third-party Docker networking driver to allow communication between containers. We also discussed the design and implementation of Multi-Swarm Networking Helper in Open Baton, automating the configuration of Multi-Swarm networking. We verified that Open Baton was able to deploy multi-cluster services with the support of our solution, and multi-Swarm networking has reasonable networking performance for multi-cluster services.

However, we only covered multi-cluster service deployment that is one part of the orchestration process. Therefore, we will improve Multi-Swarm Networking Helper to support all aspect of orchestration for Multi-Cluster services. Besides, we plan to implement a VIM and VNFM for Kubernetes that is the de-facto container orchestration engine in the market. After that, we will work on deploying CNFs over heterogeneous container-based clusters.

Acknowledgements. This work was supported by Institute for Information & Communications Technology Promotion (IITP) grants funded by the Korea government (MSIT) (No. 2015-0-00575, Global SDN/NFV Open-Source Software Core Module/Function Development and No. 2017-0-00421, Cyber Security Defense Cycle Mechanism for New Security Threats), by Fraunhofer FOKUS and Universidade Estadual de Santa Cruz. Shin acknowledges Erasmus Mundus TEAM Programme for financial and administrative supports during mobility in Fraunhofer FOKUS.

References

1. ETSI: Network Function Virtualisation (NFV); Terminology for Main Concepts in NFV. ETSI GS NFV 003 v1.2.1, ETSI Group Specification, December 2014
2. Carella, G.A., Magedanz, T.: Open Baton: a framework for virtual network function management and orchestration for emerging software-based 5G networks. IEEE Newsletter, July 2016
3. Felter, W., Ferreira, A., Rajamony, R., Rubio, J.: An update performance comparison of virtual machines and Linux containers. In: Proceedings of 2015 IEEE International Symposium on Performance Analysis of Systems and Software, pp. 171–172. IEEE (2015)

4. Cziva, R., Pezaros, D.P.: Container network functions: bringing NFV to the network edge. IEEE Commun. Mag. **55**(6), 24–31 (2017)
5. Francescon, A., Baggio, G., Fedrizzi, R.: X-MANO: cross-domain management and orchestration of network services. In: Proceedings of 2017 IEEE Conference on Network Softwarization. IEEE (2017)
6. Vilata, R., et al.: Fully automated peer service orchestration of cloud and network resources using ACTN and CSO. In: Proceedings of Optical Fiber Communications Conference and Exhibition. IEEE (2017)
7. Bonafiglia, R., Castellano, G., Cerrato, I., Risso, F.: End-to-end service orchestration across SDN and cloud computing domains. In: Proceedings of 2017 IEEE Conference on Network Softwarization. IEEE (2017)
8. ETSI: Network Function Virtualisation (NVF); Management and Orchestration, ETSI GS NFV 001 v1.1.1. ETSI Group Specification, December 2014
9. Shin, J., Kim, J.: K-Cluster-based Playground for SDN/NFV/Cloud Integration. In: Proceedings of the 27th Joint Conference on Communications and Information, KICS (2017)

The Impact of the Storage Tier: A Baseline Performance Analysis of Containerized DBMS

Daniel Seybold(✉), Christopher B. Hauser, Georg Eisenhart, Simon Volpert, and Jörg Domaschka

Institute of Information Resource Management, Ulm University, Ulm, Germany
{daniel.seybold,christopher.hauser,georg.eisenhart, simon.volpert,joerg.domaschka}@uni-ulm.de

Abstract. Containers emerged as cloud resource offerings. While the advantages of containers, such as easing the application deployment, orchestration and adaptation, work well for stateless applications, the feasibility of containerization of stateful applications, such as database management system (DBMS), still remains unclear due to potential performance overhead. The myriad of container operation models and storage backends even raises the complexity of operating a containerized DBMS. Here, we present an extensible evaluation methodology to identify performance overhead of a containerized DBMS by combining three operational models and two storage backends. For each combination a memory-bound and disk-bound workload is applied. The results show a clear performance overhead for containerized DBMS on top of virtual machines (VMs) compared to physical resources. Further, a containerized DBMS on top of VMs with different storage backends results in a tolerable performance overhead. Building upon these baseline results, we derive a set of open evaluation challenges for containerized DBMSs.

Keywords: Container · YCSB · Benchmarking · DBMS · MongoDB

1 Introduction

The raise of containers, containerization, and container orchestration [3] has a great influence on the structure of distributed applications, and greatly eased the operation of such systems by finally leveraging the realisation of continuous deployment. Support for containers is offered beside traditional virtual machine offerings by Amazon Elastic Container Service[1] and OpenStack Magnum[2].

Much of the success of containers is a consequence of the fact that they enable a quick installation of pre-packaged software components, which is a prerequisite for handing overload (scale out), bug fixing (software upgrade), and

[1] https://aws.amazon.com/ecs/.
[2] https://wiki.openstack.org/wiki/Magnum.

G. Mencagli et al. (Eds.): Euro-Par 2018 Workshops, LNCS 11339, pp. 93–105, 2019.
https://doi.org/10.1007/978-3-030-10549-5_8

replacing failed components (fault tolerance). All of these concepts work fine for mostly stateless components such as load balancers, web and application servers, message queues, and also caches. Yet, despite recent attention in the field [2,14], it is currently unclear to what extent containerization is suited for and beneficial to the operation of stateful applications. Database management systems (DBMS) are an important representative of this type of applications and a crucial part of Big Data and IoT applications.

While the containerization of DBMS particularly eases the usage of features of modern DBMS such as horizontal scalability or high availability, at least two challenges remain: *(a)* The general runtime overhead of containerized DBMS is unknown. *(b)* The container eco-system offers a myriad of different storage backends and their impacts on performance are also unclear.

Only with an answer to these baseline questions, it is beneficial to think about more sophisticated questions such as placement of state and data migration. This paper is an initial step to identify further research and engineering challenges with respect to containerized DBMS. Our contributions are as follows: *(i)* We introduce three different operational models for DBMS ranging from bare metal to containers in virtual machines. *(ii)* We analyse the landscape of storage backends for containers and their pros and cons. *(iii)* For three operational models and two storage backends we evaluate the performance for the well known MongoDB[3] DBMS under various workloads. In contrast to related work, our main focus is not on a performance comparison between containerized and virtualised execution. *(iv)* Based on the outcome of the evaluation, we propose open challenges for modelling and evaluating DBMS performance.

The remainder of this document is structured as follows: Sect. 2 discusses the containerization of stateful applications. Section 3 defines the evaluation methodology, while Section 4 presents the evaluation environment. Section 5 discusses the results and derives open evaluation challenges for containerized DBMS. Section 6 presents related work, and Sect. 7 concludes.

2 Challenges for Containerization of Stateful Applications

Containerization in the context of cloud computing is besides *hardware virtualization* for virtual machines (VMs) so called *operating-system (OS) virtualization* for containers. In hardware virtualization a hypervisor manages the resource allocation and operating state of virtual machines. OS-Virtualization uses operating system features to create lightweight isolated environments, known as containers. Container engines allocate resources and access to *e.g.* networking and storage, the popular Docker[4] engine. Orchestrators manage VMs or containers across hypervisors or container engines [1,3,15]. These virtualization approaches provide the different operational models depicted in Fig. 1(a) where each operation model combines the benefits and drawbacks of the respective virtualization approaches: Hardware virtualization securely isolates with fixed

[3] https://www.mongodb.com/de.
[4] https://www.docker.com.

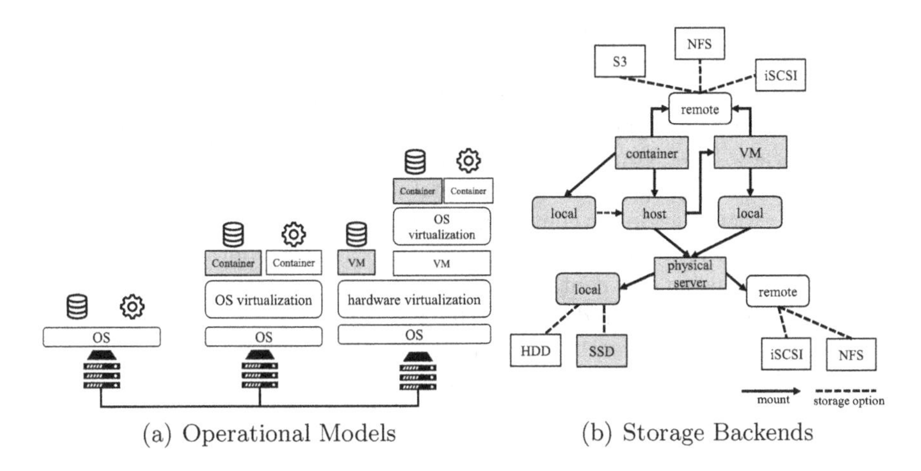

(a) Operational Models (b) Storage Backends

Fig. 1. Containerization of stateful applications

hardware-oriented offers; OS virtualization provides less strong isolation with soft hardware limits [12].

In multi-tier applications, stateful components require to store data temporarily or even durably, *i.e.* by instantiating (distributed) DBMS or stateful caches. Figure 1(b) lists potential storage backends for VMs and containers, which leads to challenging decisions when deploying stateful containers, especially in large-scale set-ups. Challenges in this field include *(i)* performance aspects such as throughput and latency, *(ii)* support for scalability, *i.e.* considering parallel read/write access, and *(iii)* failure strategies and recovery mechanisms. Since VMs and containers isolate customers to share infrastructure, performance interferences may occur whenever resources (*e.g.* storage) are utilised, which are not directly under control of the container engine and the underlying kernel.

The focus of our work evaluates the performance aspect of containerized DBMS with respect to different storage backends for containerized DBMS on physical hardware over DBMS in VMs to containerized DBMS on top of VMs. The performance and runtime overhead of these approaches are evaluated in the following.

3 Evaluation Methodology

In this section, we define an extensible evaluation methodology for the identification of potential performance overhead of common operation models for containerized DBMS. In the following, the methodology is defined on a conceptual level, while Sect. 4 describes the technical implementation.

3.1 System Architecture

In order to provide a concise analysis of the potential performance overhead of containerized DBMS in the cloud, we define an extensible system architecture, which comprises three common operational models for DBMS, highlighted in the grey boxes in Fig. 1(a). Each operational model is defined by its virtualisation, *i.e.* OS virtualisation for container, hypervisor for VMs or container on top of VMs. Further, we apply two storage backends for the containerized DBMS, namely *local* for using the container filesystem and *host* for using the hosting resource filesystem as depicted in Fig. 1(b). For the VM-based DBMS, we apply the local filesystem provided by the hypervisor. The resulting resource configurations are depicted in Table 1. While *remote* storage is also a common storage configurations for containerized DBMS, it is omitted in this work to reduce the interference factor of the network and will be targeted in future evaluations. In addition, we do not use any container-specific network virtualisation as the focus relies on compute, memory and storage.

Table 1. Operational models and storage backends

ID	Operational model [*physical (P), container (C), VM*]	Storage backend [*local (L), host (H), remote (R)*]
P-C-L	Physical + container	Local
P-C-H	Physical + container	Host
VM-L	VM	local
VM-C-L	VM + container	Local
VM-C-H	VM + container	Host

3.2 Workload and DBMS

In favour of emulating container-centric workloads, we define a *write-heavy (w-h)* workload, emulating the storage of sensor data and a *read-heavy (r-h)* workload, emulating a social media application with mostly reads and barely update operations. Both workloads are defined in a *memory-bound* version, *i.e.* the whole data set fits into memory and a *disk-bound* version, *i.e.* the data is larger than the available memory. As workload generator, we select the Yahoo Cloud Serving Benchmark (YCSB) [4], which is widely used in performance studies on NoSQL DBMSs. YCSB offers web-based workloads based on create, read, update and delete (CRUD) operations, enabling the emulation of container-centric workloads [10].

As exemplary containerized DBMS, we select document-oriented MongoDB for our evaluation as it is a NoSQL DBMS[5]. MongoDB emphasizes its operation on virtualised resources[6]. Records are stored as *documents* within *collections.*

[5] https://db-engines.com/de/ranking.

[6] https://www.mongodb.com/containers-and-orchestration-explained.

While MongoDB supports a distributed architecture, we select a single node setup for our evaluation to reduce potential interference factors such as network jitter or MongoDB specific data distribution algorithms. Yet, our methodology can easily be extended for a distributed setup and also MongoDB can be exchanged with any desired DBMS.

3.3 Metrics

For each evaluation scenario the following metrics are collected to analyse the results: *throughput* in operations per seconds and *latency* per operation type in μs. Each evaluation scenario is repeated ten times to ensure significant results and for the all metrics the minimum, maximum, average and standard deviation are provided. In addition, system metrics (CPU, RAM, I/O, network) are monitored during each evaluation scenario for MongoDB and the YCSB to provide reliable results by ensuring that none of the system resources creates a bottleneck.

3.4 Evaluation Execution

Our methodology comprises the memory-bound (mb) and disk-bound (db) evaluation scenarios. Each scenario starts with the w-h workload, followed by the r-h workload. Each workload is executed against the resource combinations of operational models and storage backends presented in Table 1. Hence, the execution (E) of the memory-bound and disk-bound scenarios can be expressed as *scenario:E(mb(wh,r-h)), e.g. P-C-L:E(mb(wh,r-h))* and *P-C-L:E(db(w-h,r-h))*.

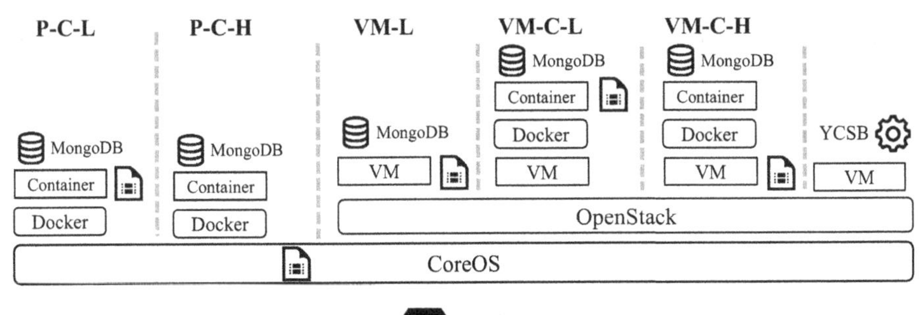

Fig. 2. Evaluation environment

4 Evaluation Environment

Based on the introduced evaluation methodology in Sect. 3, the following presents its implementation for a private, OpenStack-based cloud[7] (version Pike) with full and isolated access to all physical and virtual resources. In order to reduce potential resource interference and to guarantee reproducible results, we use the availability zones feature of OpenStack to dedicate one physical host for spawning the required VMs and containers. The resulting evaluation environment for the specified evaluation scenarios is depicted in Fig. 2. In the following, the implementation details for the resources, MongoDB and YCSB are presented.

Table 2. Evaluation scenario resources

Resource	Virtualisation	OS	Cores	RAM	FS	Storage
Physical host	-	CoreOS 1632	16[a]	64 GB	Ext4	512 GB[b]
MongoDB container	Docker 18.04	Ubuntu 16.04	4	4 GB	overlay2	40 GB
MongoDB VM	KVM, QEMU 1.5.3	Ubuntu 16.04	4	4 GB	Ext4	40 GB
YCSB VM	KVM, QEMU 1.5.3	Ubuntu 16.04	4	2 GB	Ext4	10 GB

[a] 2x Intel Xeon E5-2630 v3 8-Core Haswell 2.4 Ghz
[b] 2x 256 GB SSD of type SAMSUNG MZ7WD240HAFV-00003

4.1 Resources

As depicted in Fig. 2, all containers and VMs are located on the same physical host, which has enough resources for running the YCSB VM and the DBMSs without resource interference (*i.e.* no overbooking). Further, this set-up only uses the host-internal network interfaces and avoids the overhead of the OpenStack network service. Accordingly, all containers are configured to use the host network interface via `--network host`. The available resources of the respective physical host, container and VMs are described in Table 2. In order to ensure comparable results, the container resources on the physical host (*i.e.* P-C-L and P-C-H) are limited to 4 cores and 4 GB RAM. The containers on CoreOS use the kernel version 4.14.19-coreos while the VM and container inside the VMs use the kernel version 4.4.0-127-generic.

4.2 MongoDB and YCSB

The evaluation scenarios are based on a vanilla deployment of MongoDB and the YCSB to ensure a baseline performance evaluation of MongoDB containerization. The relevant configurations for MongoDB and the YCSB are listed in Table 3. Further, the YCSB operation distribution for the *w-h* workload are 100% write operations and for the *r-h* workload 95% read operations and 5% update operations. Table 3 also highlights overall collection size of each workload

[7] https://www.openstack.org/.

Table 3. YCSB VM details

MongoDB configuration	Value	YCSB configuration	Value
Version	3.6.3 (CE)	Version	0.12[a]
Services	1 × mongod	Record size	1 KB
Storage engine	WiredTiger	# of records (memory-bound)	2.000.000
Replication	off	# of records (disk-bound)	10.000.000
		# of operations	10.000.000
		# of threads	20
		Distribution	Zipfian

[a] https://github.com/brianfrankcooper/YCSB/releases/tag/0.12.0

version as the number of records for the *memory-bound* version results in a 2 GB MongoDB collection, while the *disk-bound* version results in a 10 GB MongoDB collection. The MongDB binding of YCSB is configured with the write concern option[8] `w = 1` and `j = false`, *i.e.* write operations are acknowledged by MongoDB after they are put into memory.

4.3 Portability and Reproducibility

The execution of each scenario is fully automated by utilizing ready to deploy artifacts, which are together with the results publicly available[9]; their release as open research data is currently under way. For the Docker images we make use of the Docker native capabilities of building images based on Dockerfiles. The VM images are generated by Packer[10]. Packer processes a Packerfile, which is similar to a Dockerfile, but uses a multitude of different virtualization providers to generate and store the image. In our case we are using OpenStack Glance[11]. This approach enables fellow researchers to reproduce, validate and extend our scenarios by changing the cloud provider or benchmark a different DBMS.

5 Results and Discussion

In the following, we present and discuss the results of the memory- and disk-bound evaluation scenarios (*cf.* 1) based on defined metrics in Sect. 3.3.

5.1 Evaluation Results

The throughput results are depicted in Fig. 3 and latency results in the Fig. 4. Each plot represents the results of the respective scenario, *i.e.* memory-bound

[8] https://docs.mongodb.com/manual/reference/write-concern/.
[9] https://github.com/omi-uulm/Containerized-DBMS-Evaluation.
[10] https://packer.io.
[11] https://docs.openstack.org/glance/pike/.

or disk-bound and the respective workload, *i.e.* w-h or r-h. For the latency plots of the r-h workloads, the first bar of each operational model always represents the read latency while the second bar represents the update latency. As remark, the results reflect the best case operational models as the DBMS and the YCSB are operated on the same, isolated physical host (*cf.* Sect. 4.1).

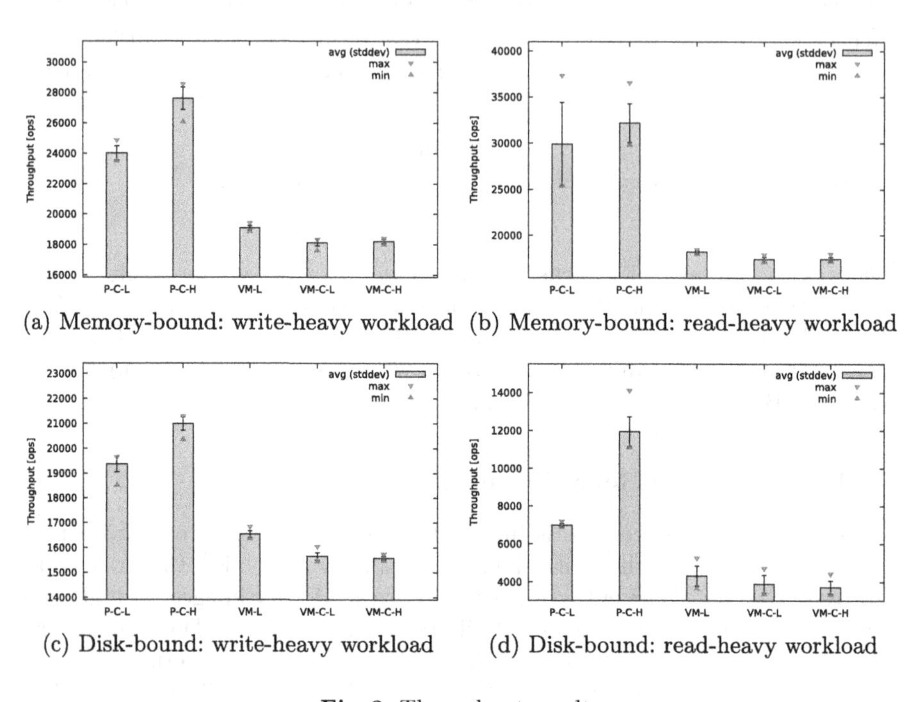

(a) Memory-bound: write-heavy workload (b) Memory-bound: read-heavy workload

(c) Disk-bound: write-heavy workload (d) Disk-bound: read-heavy workload

Fig. 3. Throughput results

The results shows a significant throughput and latency overhead for operating a DBMS on top of VMs instead of using physical hardware. These results confirm previous performance studies of memory-bound workloads for former Docker versions [5]. A novel insight is shown by the results for the DBMS operated in a container on VM the (VM-C-L,VM-C-H) as the performance only decreases slightly compared to DBMS directly operated on VMs (VM-L), *e.g.* VM-C-H achieves 6% less throughput than VM-L for the w-h workload and 13% for r-h of the disk-bound scenario. Hence, if VMs are the only available resource, operating the DBMS in container on top of the VMs can be beneficial to exploit container orchestrators or the soft resource limits to operate additional containerized applications next to the DBMS on the same VM [12].

The second insight of the results is the performance overhead of the internal Overlay2 filesystem of Docker. The container on physical hardware with the Overlay2 filesystem (P-C-L) shows significantly less throughput and higher latencies compared to the container using the host filesystem (P-C-H). This finding most clearly applies for the r-h workload of the disk-bound scenario (*cf.* Figs. 3(d) and 4(d)). The Overlay2 overhead is also present on container running on VMs (VM-C-H) but to a lower extent.

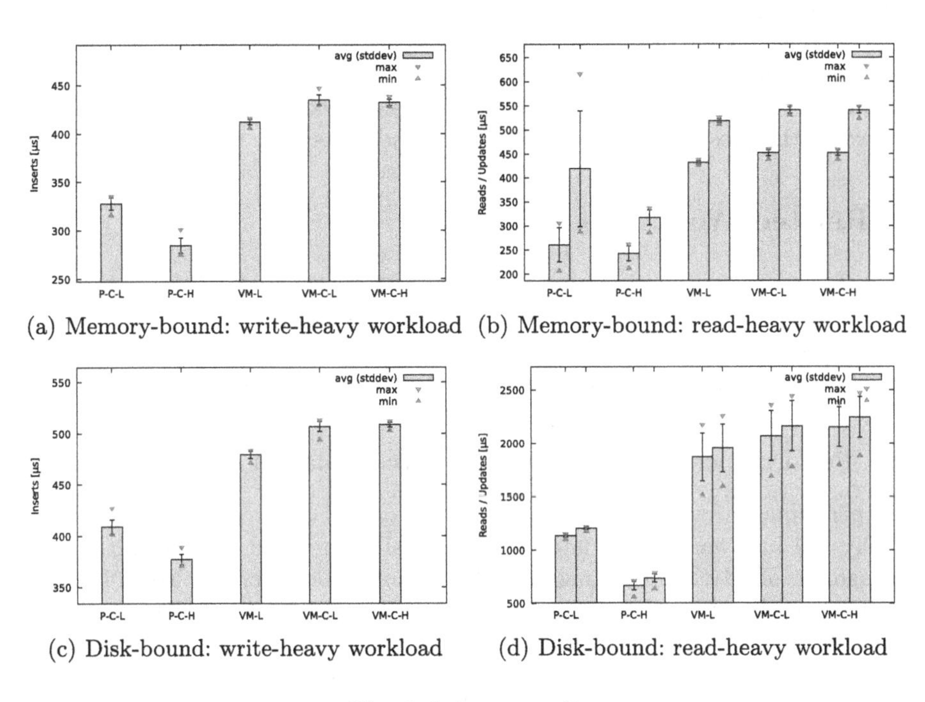

(a) Memory-bound: write-heavy workload (b) Memory-bound: read-heavy workload

(c) Disk-bound: write-heavy workload (d) Disk-bound: read-heavy workload

Fig. 4. Latency results

5.2 Open Evaluation Challenges

The results of our baseline evaluation, show that containers are suitable to operate DBMS, even on top of VMs. Yet, the operational models reveal significant performance deviations, also dependent on the memory- or disk-bound scenarios. Hence, the selection of the operational model in conjunction with the storage backend is a crucial decision for the DBMS operator, which has to be driven by the available operational models, the targeted performance and the demand of optional orchestration features.

Based on our methodology and the presented baseline results, we derive a set of open evaluation challenges, which have to be addressed to drive the selection process of the operational model for containerized DBMS: *(i)* The performance of the presented operational models needs to be evaluated based on public cloud offerings by considering additional hypervisors and containers with respect to memory- and disk-bound DBMS workloads. *(ii)* The presented storage backends require a dedicated evaluation with respect to different local and remote container storage drivers. This also comprises local and remote block storage of the host resource. *(iii)* As the DBMS performance deviation of the operational models VM-L, VM-C-L, and VM-C-H are in a tolerable margin, the advantages of VM-C-L and VM-C-H have to be analysed with respect to orchestration and the co-location with suitable applications. *(iv)* The presented methodology needs to be extended for additional DBMS to evaluate their containerization feasibility and container orchestration features with respect to the scalability and elasticity of distributed DBMS [11]. Further, container orchestration features for high availability and migration of containerized DBMS need to be evaluated in the context of the presented operational models and storage backends.

6 Related Work

With the increasing usage of containers besides VMs in cloud offerings, different comparative analysis of their performance overhead and resource isolation capabilities have been conducted. Moreover, the containerization of DBMS moved into the focus, especially in combination with container orchestrators.

6.1 Performance Overhead and Resource Isolation

The performance overhead of VMs in contrast to Docker containers running on physical hardware is evaluated by [5]. SysBench[12] is used to compare the throughput of MySQL running on VMs against containerized MySQL. The results show that VMs cause a higher performance overhead as Docker containers for disk-intensive workloads. Further, the usage of the Docker AUFS storage driver causes a higher performance overhead as the usage of Docker volumes.

A related performance comparison of KVM VMs, Docker and LXC containers and a lightweight VM approach based on OSv[13] is provided by [7]. The evaluation is based on different resource-specific micro-benchmarks and the results accord to [5] for the lower performance of VMs for disk-intensive workloads.

An analysis and evaluation of the Docker storage drivers with respect to filesystem performance is presented by [13]. The results demonstrate that the choice of the storage driver can influence the filesystem performance significantly where the Btrfs storage driver achieves the best performance but less stability as the other storage drivers.

The comparative analysis of the resource isolation capabilities of VMs and containers is provided by [8,12,16]. While [12] apply resource-specific micro-benchmarks, [8,16] use DBMS and respective DBMS workloads to evaluate the resource capabilities. All of these evaluation indicate a stronger resource isolation of VMs, especially for disk-bound workloads.

While existing performance evaluations focus either on micro-benchmarks or apply DBMS only for the evaluation of the resource isolation, our evaluation provides an evaluation across multiple operational model and storage backends. In addition, the operation of container on top of VMs is emphasized by [12] but so far no performance evaluation has considered this operational model.

[12] https://github.com/akopytov/sysbench.
[13] http://osv.io/.

6.2 Containerization of DBMS

The containerization of DBMS in combination with container orchestrators provides multiple adaptation actions to automate the operation of NoSQL DBMSs [2]. Hereby, the orchestration features of Kubernetes are enhanced with distributed DBMS-specific adaptation rules for proactive and low-cost adaptations to avoid the transfer of data between nodes. While container orchestrators typically manage the disk storage internally, modifying the persistent storage within container orchestrators is difficult and hinders their adoption for DBMS [6]. Therefore, [6] present a persistent storage abstraction layer for container orchestrators, which eases the usage of containerized DBMS across different container orchestrators. Yet, the usage of container orchestrators and their internal handling of persistent storage can introduce additional performance overhead for DBMS. Hence, [14] analyse the performance overhead of using remote storage for containerized DBMS within Kubernetes.

While the usage of containerized DBMS with container orchestrators eases the automation of DBMS operation, there is potential performance overhead added by the different handling of the persistent storage of the container orchestrator. While, [14] provide a fist step into analysing this overhead for remote storage, we provide a baseline evaluation for container local and host storage backends. In addition, we apply a memory- and disk-bound workload to identify the suitability of container for the respective DBMS workloads.

7 Conclusion and Future Work

The evolvement of container leads to a variety of new operational models for distributed applications in the cloud. While containers work fine for stateless applications, stateful applications such as database management systems (DBMS) are receiving increasing attention recently. As DBMS add the persistence aspect to the operational model, storage backends for containers are evolving. Yet, the performance impact of these new operational and storage backends remains unclear for containerized DBMS. Hence, we analyse current operational and storage backends in the context of containerized DBMS. and derive a baseline evaluation methodology for a comparative evaluation of operational models and storage backends. Hereby, we define a memory- and a disk-bound scenario, which is applied on three operational models (container on physical hardware, virtual machines (VMs) and container on VMs) in combination with two storage backends (container filesystem and host filesystem), resulting in 20 evaluation configurations. The evaluation is executed in a private OpenStack with a containerized MongoDB. The results show a significant performance overhead of container running on VMs in contrast to container running on physical hardware. Yet, running container on VMs with different storage backends only causes a tolerable performance impact in contrast to running the DBMS directly on the VM. Further, the usage of the container internal filesystem causes a significant performance overhead compared to using the host filesystem.

Based on these baseline results, we conduct that container are suitable to operate DBMS but additional evaluations are required to get a clear understanding of potential performance bottlenecks. Therefore, we derive a set of open evaluation challenges, which will be addressed in future work: *(i)* evaluating additional operational models implementations; *(ii)* evaluating additional storage backends; *(iii)* consolidation of containerized DBMS and processing applications on top of VMs and *(iv)* the feasibility of DBMS containerization and orchestration for different DBMS. These challenges will be addressed within [9].

Acknowledgements. The research leading to these results has received funding from the EC's Framework Programme HORIZON 2020 under grant agreement number 731664 (MELODIC) and 732667 (RECAP).

References

1. Baur, D., Seybold, D., Griesinger, F., Tsitsipas, A., Hauser, C.B., Domaschka, J.: Cloud orchestration features: are tools fit for purpose? In: UCC, pp. 95–101. IEEE (2015)
2. Bekas, E., Magoutis, K.: Cross-layer management of a containerized NoSQL data store. In: 2017 IFIP/IEEE Symposium on Integrated Network and Service Management (IM), pp. 1213–1221. IEEE (2017)
3. Burns, B., Grant, B., Oppenheimer, D., Brewer, E., Wilkes, J.: Borg, omega, and kubernetes. Queue **14**(1), 10 (2016)
4. Cooper, B.F., Silberstein, A., Tam, E., Ramakrishnan, R., Sears, R.: Benchmarking cloud serving systems with YCSB. In: ACM Symposium on Cloud computing, pp. 143–154. ACM (2010)
5. Felter, W., Ferreira, A., Rajamony, R., Rubio, J.: An updated performance comparison of virtual machines and linux containers. In: ISPASS, pp. 171–172. IEEE (2015)
6. Mohamed, M., Warke, A., Hildebrand, D., Engel, R., Ludwig, H., Mandagere, N.: Ubiquity: extensible persistence as a service for heterogeneous container-based frameworks. In: Panetto, H., et al. (eds.) OTM 2017. Lecture Notes in Computer Science, pp. 716–731. Springer, Cham (2017). https://doi.org/10.1007/978-3-319-69462-7_45
7. Morabito, R., Kjällman, J., Komu, M.: Hypervisors vs. lightweight virtualization: a performance comparison. In: IC2E, pp. 386–393. IEEE (2015)
8. Rehman, K.T., Folkerts, E.: Performance of containerized database management systems. In: DBTEST, p. 6. ACM (2018)
9. Seybold, D.: Towards a framework for orchestrated distributed database evaluation in the cloud. In: Proceedings of the 18th Doctoral Symposium of the 18th International Middleware Conference, pp. 13–14. ACM (2017)
10. Seybold, D., Domaschka, J.: Is distributed database evaluation cloud-ready? In: Kirikova, M., et al. (eds.) ADBIS 2017. CCIS, vol. 767, pp. 100–108. Springer, Cham (2017). https://doi.org/10.1007/978-3-319-67162-8_12
11. Seybold, D., Wagner, N., Erb, B., Domaschka, J.: Is elasticity of scalable databases a myth? In: IEEE Big Data, pp. 2827–2836. IEEE (2016)
12. Sharma, P., Chaufournier, L., Shenoy, P., Tay, Y.: Containers and virtual machines at scale: a comparative study. In: Proceedings of the 17th International Middleware Conference, p. 1. ACM (2016)

13. Tarasov, V., et al.: In search of the ideal storage configuration for docker containers. In: FAS* W, pp. 199–206. IEEE (2017)
14. Truyen, E., Reniers, V., Van, D., Landuyt, B.L., Joosen, W., Bruzek, M.: Evaluation of container orchestration systems with respect to auto-recovery of databases (2017)
15. Verma, A., Pedrosa, L., Korupolu, M., Oppenheimer, D., Tune, E., Wilkes, J.: Large-scale cluster management at google with borg. In: Proceedings of the Tenth European Conference on Computer Systems, p. 18. ACM (2015)
16. Xavier, M.G., De Oliveira, I.C., Rossi, F.D., Dos Passos, R.D., Matteussi, K.J., De Rose, C.A.: A performance isolation analysis of disk-intensive workloads on container-based clouds. In: PDP, pp. 253–260. IEEE (2015)

Towards Vertically Scalable Spark Applications

Luciano Baresi and Giovanni Quattrocchi(✉)

Politecnico di Milano, Dipartimento di Elettronica, Informazione e Bioingegneria, Piazza Leonardo Da Vinci 32, Milan, Italy
{luciano.baresi,giovanni.quattrocchi}@polimi.it

Abstract. The dynamic provisioning of virtual machines (VMs) supported by many cloud computing infrastructures eases the scalability of software applications. Unfortunately, VMs are relatively slow to boot and public cloud providers do not allow users to vary their resources (vertical scalability) dynamically. To tackle both problems, a few years ago we presented a solution that combines the management of VMs with the use of containers specifically targeted to the efficient runtime management of the resources provisioned to Web applications. This paper borrows from this solution and addresses the problem of provisioning resources to big data, Spark applications at runtime. Spark does not allow for the runtime scalability of the resources associated with its executors, but resources must be provisioned statically. To tackle this problem, the paper describes a container-based version of Spark that supports the dynamic resizing of the memory and CPU cores associated with the different executors. The evaluation demonstrates the feasibility of the approach and identifies the trade-offs involved.

Keywords: Containers · Big data · Spark · Resource allocation

1 Introduction

The virtualization and softwarization of computing resources fostered by cloud computing has made the on-demand allocation/deallocation of computing means extremely easy. One can smoothly provision virtual machines (VMs) dynamically to cope with different workloads and meet stated qualities of service and/or cost constraints [7]. Many approaches [10,15] use different techniques to foresee and modify the number of allocated VMs properly and smartly, but unfortunately, Mao et al. [11] demonstrate that a VM on a public cloud infrastructure takes on average six minutes to boot. This is a too long delay when one thinks of the dynamic provisioning of resources to modern applications: for example, if the

---

This work has been partially supported by the GAUSS national research project (MIUR, PRIN 2015, Contract 2015KWREMX) and by project EEB (Italian Technology Cluster For Smart Communities, CTN01_00034_594053).

G. Mencagli et al. (Eds.): Euro-Par 2018 Workshops, LNCS 11339, pp. 106–118, 2019.
https://doi.org/10.1007/978-3-030-10549-5_9

workload increases, users do not want to wait for six minutes before being able to interact with the system properly. Instead of booting new VMs, one could alternatively think of adding resources to running VMs, but this is not possible since VMs usually come in fixed configurations and the resources associated with them (vertical scalability) cannot be changed. To overcome these two problems, that is, the latency of newly provisioned resources and the resizing of running ones, we proposed a solution [4] that pairs VMs and containers [16] for the fast and fine-grained allocation of resources to web applications. The idea is to deploy containerized web applications in a cluster of VMs, where each container is equipped with a lightweight control-theoretical planner to quickly (i.e., in a few seconds) provision and scale (vertically) the resources associated with it.

Starting from these ideas, this paper addresses a different, but similar problem: the dynamic provisioning of resources for big data applications. These applications are batch applications executed on top of special-purpose frameworks, which slice input data and carry out the computation on each slice by means of parallel processes executed on a distributed cluster of (virtual) machines. Specifically, we address Spark [19] applications, since Spark is the most widely used framework for big data applications: it is more flexible than Hadoop [2] and can support more complex computations. It uses a master-slave architecture, and multiple distributed *executors*—Java processes dedicated to data processing—are deployed onto the cluster. The response time of these applications is defined as the time they take to process the entire set of inputs; resources are usually estimated to meet *deadlines*, that is, thresholds on response times [18].

Spark does not allow one to specify deadlines and allocates resources (i.e., CPU cores and memory) to executors statically at the beginning of the execution; by default it always uses all available resources. This means that the resources that are allocated to applications must be planned carefully since runtime deviations are not allowed. The only dynamism managed by Spark refers to switching off preallocated executors if they remain idle for a user-defined amount of time, and on again if some tasks have to wait for too long (and idle executors are available), respectively. In addition, the resources provisioned to executors (e.g. CPU cores) cannot be changed. The scalability is only horizontal and based on simple time-outs, and on the availability of preallocated executors.

In contrast, this paper discusses and evaluates the feasibility of adding vertical scalability to Spark executors. It presents xSpark[1], a container-based extended version of Spark that allows for the fine-grained allocation of resources (CPU cores and memory) to applications, and that also supports the vertical scalability of executors (containers).

The rest of the paper is organized as follows. Section 2 surveys what industry tools offer in terms of dynamic resource allocation and introduces some related work. Section 3 motivates the need for vertical scalability and the use of containers as enabling technology. Section 4 describes the architecture of xSpark and how it supports the dynamic allocation (vertical scalability) of both CPU

[1] This paper extends [5] with an in-depth description of the technical details of xSpark that enable the vertical scalability of resources.

cores and memory. Section 5 presents the assessments we carried out and Sect. 6 concludes the paper.

2 Related Work

Spark only provides limited functionality to adjust the resources allocated to applications. By default, and at each execution, Spark always uses all the resources in the cluster. This means that when applications are running, and a new application is submitted for execution, it must wait since all resources are already taken. Alternatively, at submission time, Spark offers three parameters for allocating a smaller amount of resources to a specific application, leaving resources available to other subsequent application. Parameter `total-executor-cores` sets an upper bound to the total amount of CPU cores that an application can use, while parameter `num-executors` sets the number of executors. Therefore, the ratio between these two parameters gives the average number of cores allocated to each executor. Finally, parameter `executor-memory` sets the memory allocated to each executor.

The memory and cores allocated to executors cannot be changed at runtime since the vertical scalability of executors is not supported by Spark. However, Spark offers a *dynamic resource allocation* mode—governed by parameter `spark.dynamicAllocation.enabled`—to scale the number of executors at runtime. At submission time, parameter `spark.dynamicAllocation.initialExecutors` is used to set the initial amount of executors (instead of parameter `num-executors`) and parameters `spark.dynamicAllocation.min|maxExecutors` set the allowed range. To scale the number of executors Spark uses a simple heuristic based on utilization: if an executor remains idle for a predefined amount of time, it is decommissioned. If idle executors exist and a task remains pending for too long, a new executor is commissioned using a backlog algorithm: the first time Spark allocates an executor, if another request is triggered shortly (yet another parameter) the number of allocated executors is doubled, and so on. These time-outs are set statically and cannot vary at runtime.

As for additional resource management solutions, Spark can be paired with external resource managers—such as Mesos [8] and YARN [17]. Mesos sends resource offers (*push-based* scheduler) to its clients and manages both CPU cores and memory, while YARN waits for resource requests (*pull-based* scheduling) and only considers memory (each executor is bound to a single core). They both support containers to launch executors, but they do not offer any form of vertical scalability. Mesos also provides an optional fine-grained mode, where each task is containerized, but the runtime overhead is heavy, and this is why the use of this feature is deprecated in Spark 2.0.

xSpark offers two major improvements with respect to both Spark alone and Spark equipped with Mesos or YARN. First, it supports dynamic resource provisioning with respect to deadlines. This is not possible with existing industrial tools that only scale resources according to the utilization of the system. Second, it supports the vertical scalability of executors with respect to both CPU cores, by means of containers, and memory, through the use of off-heap memory. This allows one to be precise and fast when scaling resources and also to minimize the overhead needed for creating/destroying executors. As for Mesos and YARN, xSpark is complementary to them: it is built on top Spark alone and we plan to extend our control capabilities to Mesos and YARN in the future.

Even if they do not target Spark specifically, it is also worth mentioning few works that exploit containers to provide the vertical scalability of resources [3,14]. Lakew et al. [9] rely on Linux containers to build fast and fine-grained controllers for the management of multiple resources. They exploit vertical scalability to meet performance indicators while optimizing resources for both interactive and non-interactive applications. Barna et al. [6] propose a methodology to build autonomic systems for containerized multi-tier applications. They exploit layered queuing networks to create self-tuning controllers for applications composed of heterogeneous components such as web services, databases, and big data elements. These solutions could be used to manage the resources allocated to a complete Spark instantiation, but they cannot manage the resources allocated to the different applications since they have no visibility of them. xSpark can do that since besides working on dynamic resource management, we have also changed the architecture and processing model behind Spark to work at a lower granularity level.

3 Vertical Scalability with Containers

The advent of cloud computing infrastructures has significantly simplified the runtime management of computing resources, and solutions from both industry [1] and academia [13,15] have proliferated. These solutions use virtual machines (VMs) to change the amount of CPU cores and memory allocated to applications and fulfill set quality requirements. Public cloud providers however only provision virtual machines with a fixed amount of memory and CPU cores. VMs can simply be created or deleted, and thus only the *horizontal scalability* of resources is supported. *Vertical scalability*, that is, the capability of modifying the amount of resources associated with a VM while it is in operation, is limited by the fact that users have no access to the hypervisor.

Another limitation of VM-based resource management is that it is too slow. According to Mao et al. [11], cloud providers require some 6 min to launch a new VM. Since new resources cannot be allocated faster than that, this *delay* imposes stringent limitations on how frequently allocated resources can change, and thus on how quickly these systems can meet user expectations.

These problems can be solved by adopting containers [12] as means to manage resources since they can be launched faster than VMs and can support both horizontal and vertical scalability. Containers can be booted in few seconds (depending on the application type) and scaled vertically in hundreds of milliseconds [16]. Resource managers can then be as fast as their actuators and adopt control periods that are less than a second: this is the case of the control-theoretical solution presented in Sect. 4.

In addition, VMs are usually dedicated to only one process at a time since the simultaneous execution of independent application components cannot be easily managed, and unexpected resource contention may arise. With containers instead, a single machine can be used more efficiently to deploy multiple parts of the same application—or of different applications—since each container is provisioned individually and is isolated from the others.

Containers alone are not sufficient to making Spark executors scale vertically. xSpark exploits Docker containers to achieve vertical scalability and embeds then into Spark to scale the number of CPU cores allocated to executors at runtime. However, memory allocation is limited by the Java Virtual Machine (JVM), which sets a static upper bound to allocated memory at startup time, and this value cannot be changed without restarting the virtual machine itself. For this reason we extended Spark to allow for the dynamic resizing of *off-heap* memory, as discussed in Sect. 4.3. xSpark exploits vertical scalability to control the execution time of Spark applications in order to allocate resources efficiently and fulfill user deadlines. A similar result could be achieved through horizontal scalability, but with less efficiency since vertical scalability is faster and works at a finer level.

4 xSpark

xSpark[2] extends Spark and uses containers (i.e., Docker) to support a more flexible and advanced management of resources. xSpark enriches command `submit` with an additional parameter `deadline` to specify the required execution time. Since the goal of xSpark is to minimize the use of resources without violating deadlines, xSpark interprets this input as a constraint on execution: finishing before the deadline would mean that fewer resources could have been used, while violating it means that too few resources are provisioned (or are available).

This section describes xSpark atop virtual machines, but our tool can also be deployed on bare-metal to favor performance over flexibility.

4.1 Hierarchical Architecture

Figure 1 shows the master/slave architecture of xSpark: white boxes represent the existing components we modified, gray boxes are container-related components, and dark-gray boxes correspond to new, control-related components.

The *Master Node* hosts a *Stage Scheduler*, a *Task Scheduler*, and a heuristic-based *Application Level Controller* for each running application (Fig. 1 assumes the existence of two applications). Spark logically splits applications into *stages*[3], a key entity for xSpark. In fact, xSpark has modified component *Stage Scheduler* to intercept the beginning and end of each stage and uses the heuristic embedded in *Application Level Controller* to compute an execution *deadline* for each stage.

[2] The source code of xSpark is available at https://github.com/deib-polimi/xSpark.

[3] A Spark stage is a set of pipelined operations that do not require shuffling data among nodes.

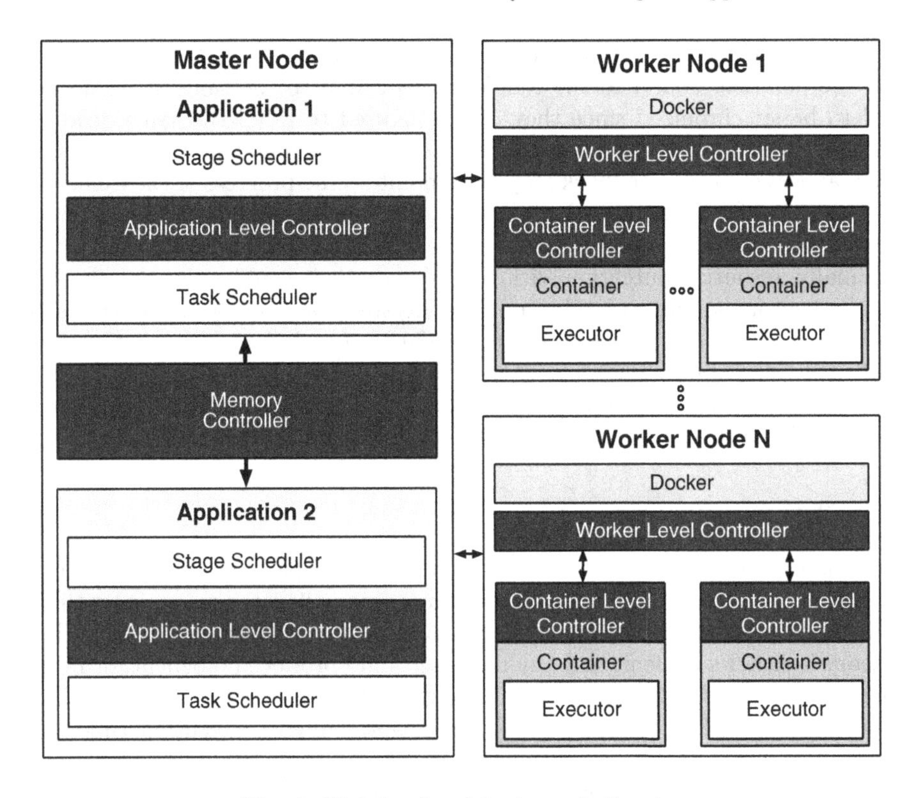

Fig. 1. High-level architecture of xSpark.

The heuristic considers the remaining amount of time, with respect to the global deadline set at application level, and some performance data collected through a profiling phase. Since xSpark needs to know the internals of each stage, this preliminary activity is used to create the actual execution flow (direct acyclic graph) of each stage and some performance metrics (e.g., the duration of each stage, number of input/output records).

After estimating execution deadlines, the actual execution of an application's stages start in the different worker nodes. Since stages can be composed of diverse operations, we advocate that resource allocation should be controlled at stage level (and not at application level). Therefore, xSpark executors are dedicated to single stages, while Spark executors can execute the tasks of any stage. This way, the resources (dynamically) provisioned to a given executor can only impact the performance of the stage associated with it, and xSpark can even obtain a finer-grained control of the execution of the different stages, and thus of the whole application. This allows xSpark to control stages individually and to equally distribute computation and data over the whole set of nodes.

As described in Sect. 4.2, executors are wrapped in containers and individually controlled by a control-theoretical planner (*Container Level Controller*). The planner uses CPU quotas to provide computing resources to make the execution times of stages last as close to estimated deadlines as possible. Note that the planners bound to the executors dedicated to the same stage do not need to be synchronized since they are configured to fulfill the same deadline and the workload (i.e., the tasks to be processed) is equally split among them. The planners exploit a feedback loop that monitors the progress of the executors (i.e., number of completed tasks over the total) and allocates processing power (i.e., CPU quotas) accordingly.

Finally, resource contention within a *Worker Node* could occur because different executors bound to specific applications/stages are deployed onto the same machine. For this reason, xSpark uses a *Worker Level Controller* that gathers all the core allocation requests from the control-theoretical planners and, if their sum is greater than available cores, scales them down according to different configurable strategies, such as Earliest Deadline First or proportionally.

4.2 CPU Cores

Vertical scalability is the key feature provided by xSpark: it enables continuous control over executing applications by managing allocated resources without restarting/deallocating containers, thus reducing the associated overhead. While memory is either sufficient, and any increase would produce no benefit, or insufficient, provisioned computing resources, given the high degree of parallelism embodied in Spark applications, can significantly impact execution time: the more CPU cores one allocates, the faster the application should execute.

Spark deploys executors onto *Worker Nodes* (virtual/physical machines) and uses Java Virtual Machines to execute them. The allocation of CPU cores is static and managed by a simple, internal, pool of threads. xSpark instead deploys each executor in a container by using *Docker* to allow xSpark to dynamically change the computing resources provisioned to an executor without interfering with the other executors running on the same node.

Docker provides three ways to allocate CPU cores dynamically: reservations, shares, and quotas. All these methods are extremely fast (few hundreds of milliseconds [16]), but they heavily differ in terms of granularity and reliability. Reservations allocate specific cores to containers. For example, given a machine with 8 cores, *container1* can be pinned to the first 5 cores, while *container2* to the remaining 3 cores and cannot use any of the cores allocated to *container1* if not used. CPU reservation is deterministic since each container can only use the cores allotted to it while granularity is limited to full cores.

With shares, each container uses at least a number of cores that is proportional to its *shares* but if there is no contention, and additional cores are available, a single container can even exploit all available cores. For example, if *container1* has 70 shares and *container2* 30 shares, in case of resource contention *container2* uses some 70% of the cores of the machine while *container1* just 30%. However, if *container2* only needed 20% of available cores, *container1* could use the remaining 80%. Thus, shares are not always deterministic, since the actual number of used cores depends on both set shares and the number of cores used by each container. The solution is extremely fine-grained since it can allocate fractions of cores.

Quotas provide the most powerful way of provisioning cores to containers and guarantees both determinism and appropriate granularity. Each container is associated with a *period* and a *quota*, where the latter represents the percentage of CPU time allocated to the container within the period. Setting a quota larger than the period means that the container should use more than one core at a time, but the sum of all quotas must always be less than set period times the number of available cores. For example, given a single-core CPU and a period of 100 ms, if *container1* is given a quota of 30 ms and *container2* a quota of $70ms$, then 70% of the CPU time is reserved for *container2* and 30% for *container1*. This mechanism is thus deterministic and very fine-grained.

xSpark associates each executor (container) with a control-theoretical planner that computes the amount of CPU cores needed at each control period. Since the faster, finer-grained, and more deterministic actuation capabilities are, the more precise these planners can be, xSpark uses quotas as allocation mechanism and associates all containers with the same period.

4.3 Memory

One of the main problems when executing a Spark job is how to determine the amount of memory to allocate to each executor. Spark allows one to specify this value statically by using parameter `spark.executor.memory`, which changes the size of the heap memory of all executors. When the heap memory of an executor gets saturated, the process crashes and the JVM is restarted.

When executing multiple applications, if their number is known, one can simply equally partition available memory to the applications, that is, $h = \frac{M}{|A|}$, where A is the set of running applications, h is the amount of heap memory allocated to an application $a \in A$, and M is the total memory available. Unfortunately, the number of applications to execute and when to execute them are often not known a priori, and thus the amount of memory associated with each executor inevitably impacts the maximum number of applications that can be run in parallel. This were not a problem if the heap memory could be scalable vertically, but unfortunately JVM's do not allow one to resize it at runtime: a given configuration can only be changed by restarting the JVM. Note that Spark postpones the launch of an application if requested memory cannot be provided.

To solve this problem, xSpark uses *off-heap memory* to add flexibility and be able to change memory boundaries dynamically. Although on-heap memory offers better performance, Spark can use off-heap memory to both support execution and store data. Objects stored in off-heap memory are managed directly by the operating system, are not part of the process heap, and are not garbage collected. As said, accessing off-heap data is slightly slower than on-heap data, but it is faster than reading and writing from/to disk (see Sect. 5).

Since Spark *does not* provide any means to resize the memory used by off-heap objects at runtime, xSpark offers a *Memory Controller*, which is deployed on the *Master Node*. Each executor is associated with a fixed quantity of on-heap memory plus a quota of off-heap memory that can then be adjusted at runtime. This quota is decremented when a new application is submitted for execution and is incremented when an application terminates.

5 Evaluation

This section describes the experiments we conducted to evaluate the solutions we conceived for the dynamic allocation of both CPU cores and off-heap memory. The assessment is based on the following three questions: (Q1) is the vertical scalability of cores appropriate for controlling the response time of Spark applications? (Q2) what can we achieve by vertically scaling resources? (Q3) how does the use of off-heap memory impact the performance of xSpark when compared against the use of on-heap memory?

5.1 Vertical Scalability of CPUs

To answer Q1 we used two applications taken from the SparkPerf[4] benchmark suite: *sort-by-key* and *aggr-by-key*. These applications perform simple aggregation and sorting operations over a randomly generated dataset. We executed them on a single AWS EC2 *m4.4xlarge* VMs with 8 CPUs[5] and 64 GB of memory. We executed each application with 8 different configurations, and repeated each experiment three times, for a total of 24 executions. We started by allocating 1 core to each application. Then, we randomly changed the number of allocated cores every second by using a uniform distribution in the range between 1 and 3 to get an expected average value of 2 cores. As for the other experiments, we kept changing the number of allocated cores every second, and we kept increasing the expected value from 2 to 8 cores.

Figure 2 shows the results of our experiments; the blue dotted line renders the duration of the execution and refers to the left-hand y-axis, while the red crossed line corresponds to the speedup (over one core) and refers to the right-hand y-axis. The charts witness that vertically scaling the number of CPU cores assigned to an executor strongly impacts the response time of Spark applications with a close to linear speed-up.

To answer Q2 we studied how xSpark exploits vertical scalability to control the execution time of applications. To do that we tried to control the two aforementioned applications and a more complex one called *PageRank*, a graph-based algorithm that was taken from another benchmark suite called SparkBench[6]. We executed the three applications with different deadlines and datasets and we obtained an error as low as 1%, where the error was computed as $(deadline - actualDuration)/deadline$. An error equals to 0 means that xSpark was able to allocate the minimum amount of CPU cores and fulfill the deadline.

[4] Available at https://github.com/databricks/spark-perf.
[5] 8 cores without hyperthreading or 16 virtual cores if enabled.
[6] Available at https://github.com/CODAIT/spark-bench.

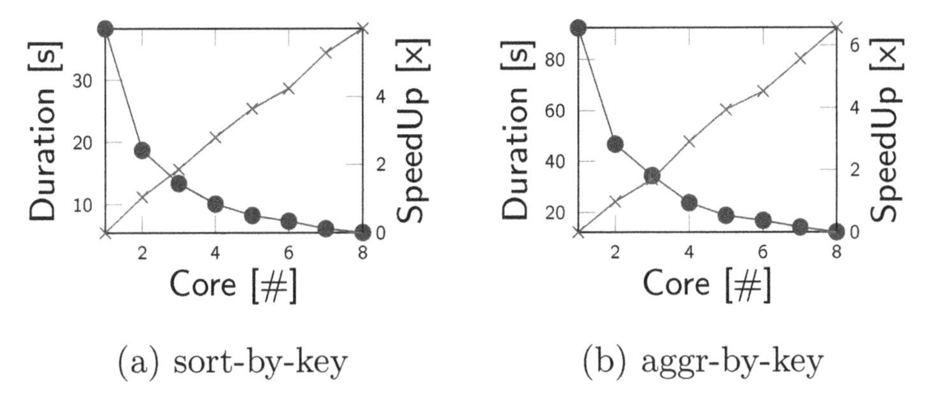

Fig. 2. CPU allocation over application duration (dots represent execution times while crosses refer to speedups).

To better visualize how xSpark works Fig. 3 shows the details of a controlled executor while processing PageRank. Note that during its life-cycle an executor can execute different stages in a row (in this case 9 stages). In this chart, the black and gray lines, which refer to the left-hand y-axis, show the actual stage completion percentage (i.e., number of tasks completed over the total) and the imposed one, that is the set-point of the control theoretical planners. The blue line, which refers to the right-hand y-axis, shows the core allocated to the executor. The E-labeled green vertical lines represent stage ends (actual stage durations), while the red dashed vertical lines represent stage deadlines (the last one correspond to the application deadline). The fast and fine-grained vertical scalability provided by containers allows xSpark to make all the executors (closely) follow the prescribed progress rates for each stage and thus terminate the execution very close to the foreseen deadline (Table 1).

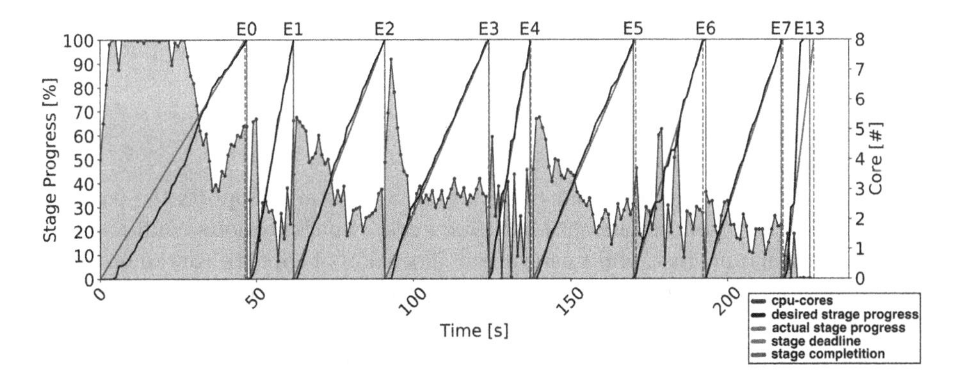

Fig. 3. Controlling PageRank.

Table 1. Off-heap impact.

App	On-heap	Off-heap	CPUTime	Delay
aggr-by-key	100%	0%	5166	-
	50%	50%	5502	6%
	10%	90%	6289	21%
PageRank	100%	0%	2013	-
	50%	50%	2051	2%
	10%	90%	2150	7%

5.2 Vertical Scalability of Off-Heap Memory

To answer Q3 we compared the performance of *aggr-by-key* and *PageRank* when only using on-heap memory or on-heap and off-heap memory. To carry out these experiments we used *Standard_D14_v2* VMs provided by Microsoft Azure, each of them had 16 CPUs, 112 GB of memory. The applications were executed with three distributions of on-heap and off-heap memory with fixed core allocation: *all on-heap* (100/0), *balanced on-heap and off-heap* (50/50) and *almost all off-heap* (10/90). To evaluate the differences among the different memory configurations, we rely on metric *CpuTime*, that is, the execution time times the number of used cores: needless to say, the higher this value is, the worse it is. Moreover, *aggr-by-key* was configured to use off-heap memory only for processing, while PageRank was instructed to use off-heap memory for both processing and storing data.

In the case of *aggr-by-key*, when decreasing the on-heap memory allocated to executors, up to 90%, *CpuTime* increased by 21% (from 5166 to 6289). This significant difference is caused by disk swapping since cached datasets were persisted onto disk. In contrast, when running *PageRank*, which used off-heap memory also for storing data, the impact of disk swapping was dramatically reduced (*CpuTime* only increases by 7%). This is in many cases a negligible performance reduction given that the use of off-heap memory allows xSpark to vertically scale the memory allocated to executors and foster the parallelism among applications.

6 Conclusions

This paper introduces xSpark, our extension to Spark that supports the vertical scalability of the resources allocated to executors. xSpark exploits containers to provide the dynamic, fast, and fine-grained allocation of cores to containers, and off-heap memory to allow for resizing the memory associated with executors. Our preliminary assessment shows that xSpark can control the execution time of Spark applications precisely and that the use of off-heap memory has limited impact on the execution time of applications.

References

1. Amazon EC2 Autoscaling. https://aws.amazon.com/autoscaling/
2. Apache Hadoop (2017). http://hadoop.apache.org
3. Al-Dhuraibi, Y., Paraiso, F., Djarallah, N., Merle, P.: Autonomic vertical elasticity of Docker containers with ELASTICDOCKER. In: IEEE 10th International Conference on Cloud Computing (CLOUD), pp. 472–479 (2017)
4. Baresi, L., Guinea, S., Leva, A., Quattrocchi, G.: A discrete-time feedback controller for containerized cloud applications. In: Proceedings of the 24th ACM International Symposium on Foundations of Software Engineering, pp. 217–228. ACM (2016)
5. Baresi, L., Guinea, S., Leva, A., Quattrocchi, G.: Fine-grained Dynamic Resource Allocation for Big-Data Applications. Technical report (2018). http://hdl.handle.net/11311/1057275
6. Barna, C., Khazaei, H., Fokaefs, M., Litoiu, M.: Delivering elastic containerized cloud applications to enable DevOps. In: Proceedings of the 12th International Symposium on Software Engineering for Adaptive and Self-Managing Systems, SEAMS 2017, pp. 65–75. IEEE Press (2017)
7. Dustdar, S., Guo, Y., Satzger, B., Truong, H.L.: Principles of elastic processes. IEEE Internet Comput. **15**, 66–71 (2011)
8. Hindman, B., et al.: A platform for fine-grained resource sharing in the data center. In: Proceedings of the 8th USENIX Conference on Networked Systems Design and Implementation, NSDI 2011, pp. 295–308. USENIX (2011)
9. Lakew, E.B., Papadopoulos, A.V., Maggio, M., Klein, C., Elmroth, E.: KPI-agnostic control for fine-grained vertical elasticity. In: 17th IEEE/ACM International Symposium on Cluster, Cloud and Grid Computing, pp. 589–598. IEEE (2017)
10. Liu, J., Shen, H., Narman, H.S.: CCRP: customized cooperative resource provisioning for high resource utilization in clouds. In: Proceedings of the 3rd IEEE International Conference on Big Data (Big Data), pp. 243–252 (2016)
11. Mao, M., Humphrey, M.: A Performance study on the VM startup time in the cloud. In: Proceedings of the IEEE 5th International Conference on Cloud Computing, pp. 423–430. IEEE (2012)
12. Merkel, D.: Docker: lightweight linux containers for consistent development and deployment. Linux J. (2014)
13. Nikravesh, A.Y., Ajila, S.A., Lung, C.H.: Towards an autonomic auto-scaling prediction system for cloud resource provisioning. In: Proceedings of the International Symposium on Software Engineering for Adaptive and Self-Managing Systems, pp. 35–45. IEEE Press (2015)
14. Rao, J., Bu, X., Xu, C.Z., Wang, K.: A distributed self-learning approach for elastic provisioning of virtualized cloud resources. In: IEEE 19th International Symposium on Modeling, Analysis & Simulation of Computer and Telecommunication Systems (MASCOTS), pp. 45–54. IEEE (2011)
15. Seracini, F., Menarini, M., Krueger, I., Baresi, L., Guinea, S., Quattrocchi, G.: A comprehensive resource management solution for web-based systems. In: Proceedings of the 11th International Conference on Autonomic Computing (2014)
16. Soltesz, S., Pötzl, H., Fiuczynski, M.E., Bavier, A., Peterson, L.: Container-based operating system virtualization: a scalable, high-performance alternative to hypervisors. In: Proceedings of the 2nd ACM SIGOPS/EuroSys European Conference on Computer Systems, vol. 41, pp. 275–287. ACM (2007)

17. Vavilapalli, V.K., et al.: Apache Hadoop yarn: yet another resource negotiator. In: Proceedings of the 4th annual Symposium on Cloud Computing. ACM (2013)
18. Verma, A., Cherkasova, L., Kumar, V.S., Campbell, R.H.: Deadline-based workload management for MapReduce environments: pieces of the performance puzzle. In: NOMS, pp. 900–905. IEEE (2012)
19. Zaharia, M., Chowdhury, M., Franklin, M.J., Shenker, S., Stoica, I.: Spark: cluster computing with working sets. In: Proceedings of the 2nd Conference on Hot Topics in Cloud Computing, HotCloud 2010. USENIX (2010)

COLOC - Workshop on Data Locality

Workshop on Data Locality (COLOC)

Workshop Description

A well-known handicap for HPC applications running on modern highly parallelized and heterogeneous HPC platforms is that an increasing amount of time is spent in communication and data transfers; thus, it is necessary to design, implement and validate new approaches to optimize process placement and data locality management. COLOC is a forum for exposing contribution from HPC application developers interested in exploring new ways to optimize their code; HPC centers and clusters managers to enhance cluster usage and application efficiency; Academics and researchers in scientific computing.

The different areas or research interest include, but are not limited to:

- Modeling node topology
- Modeling network and communication
- Performance analysis of applications to understand affinity
- Affinity metrics
- Runtime support for extracting affinity from application
- Code analysis in order to understand communication pattern
- Algorithm to improve locality
- Language, abstraction and compiler support for data locality
- Data structure and library support to better manage memory access
- Runtime-system and dynamic locality management
- System-scale locality optimization
- Validating locality optimization at thread or process level
- Memory management
- Locality management in large-scale application

We have received 6 submissions and we have accepted 5. All of them are published in this proceedings. The workshop also included the invited talk *Why don't we have data close to the computation? Let's understand and optimize data locality problem* from Fabio Baruffa, Intel.

The workshop also featured the SPPEXA http://www.sppexa.de Poster Session on Data Locality. Karl Fürlinger (LMU, München) was the poster chair. 8 posters where accepted and presented by young researchers:

- Ari Rasch, WWU Münster: Utilizing Data Locality on Multi- and Many-Core Devices via Multi-Dimensional Homomorphisms
- Roger Kowalewski, LMU München: Scalable Hybrid Sorting on Distributed Many-Core Architectures using PGAS
- Huihui Sun, WWU Münster: Improving Vectorization in the Presence of Aggregated Conditions
- Richard Schulze, WWU Münster: Exploiting Data Locality for High-Performance BLAS Routines on Multi- and Many-Cores

- Yusuke Tanimura, AIST Japan: Towards Faster and Secure Data Staging From/To Object Storage for AI and Big Data Analytics
- Jannis Klinkenberg, RWTH Aachen: Assessing Task-to-Data Affinity in the LLVM OpenMP Runtime
- Pascal Jungblut, LMU München: Increasing locality by interleaving host and on-device patterns
- Florian Schmaus, FAU Erlangen: Efficient Micro-Parallelism Using Work-Stealing with Affinity Hints

Organization

Program Chair

Emmanuel Jeannot	Inria, France

Program Committee

George Bosilca	UTK, USA
Florina Ciorba	University of Basel, Switzerland
Matthias Diener	UIUC, USA
Anshu Dubey	Argonne Natl Lab, USA
Karl Fürlinger	LMU, München, Germany
Brice Goglin	Inria, France
Aleksandar Ilic	INESC-ID/IST, Univ. de Lisboa, Portugal
Vitus Leung	Sandia National Laboratories, USA
Hatem Ltaief	KAUST, Saudi Arabia
Farouk Mansouri	DDN, France
Naoya Maruyama	LLNL, USA
Hartmut Mix	Technische Universität Dresden, Germany
Marc Perache	CEA, France
Eric Petit	Intel, France
Didem Unat	Koç University, Turkey

Progress Thread Placement for Overlapping MPI Non-blocking Collectives Using Simultaneous Multi-threading

Alexandre Denis[1], Julien Jaeger[2], and Hugo Taboada[1,2](✉)

[1] Inria, LaBRI, Univ. Bordeaux, CNRS, Bordeaux-INP, Talence, France
{alexandre.denis,hugo.taboada}@inria.fr
[2] CEA, DAM, DIF, 91297 Arpajon, France
{julien.jaeger,hugo.taboada}@cea.fr

Abstract. Non-blocking collectives have been proposed so as to allow communications to be overlapped with computation in order to amortize the cost of MPI collective operations. To obtain a good overlap ratio, communications and computation have to run in parallel. To achieve this, different hardware and software techniques exists. Dedicated some cores to run progress threads is one of them. However, some CPUs provide Simultaneous Multi-Threading, which is the ability for a core to have multiple hardware threads running simultaneously, sharing the same arithmetic units. Our idea is to use them to run progress threads to avoid dedicated cores allocation. We have run benchmarks on Haswell processors, using its Hyper-Threading capability, and get good results for both performance and overlap only when inter-node communications are used by MPI processes. However, we also show that enabling Simultaneous Multi-Threading for intra-communications leads to bad performances due to cache effects.

1 Introduction

MPI is the standard interface for communications in HPC applications. It is used by applications for inter-node (i.e. network) and intra-node (processes on the same node) communications. The cost of communications is one of the main obstacles to get a good speedup for parallel applications. To amortize the cost of MPI communications, application programmers try to overlap communications with computation by using non-blocking communication primitives, and let them progress in background while keeping the CPU busy with computation.

Initially the non-blocking communications were only available for point-to-point communications. The extension of the non-blocking communications to collective operations (i.e. primitives that involve more than two nodes, such as broadcast, reduce, scatter, gather, ...) is an addition of the latest major MPI version [11]. It opens the door to computation/communication overlap for collective operations too. However, collective communications are more CPU-hungry than

G. Mencagli et al. (Eds.): Euro-Par 2018 Workshops, LNCS 11339, pp. 123–133, 2019.
https://doi.org/10.1007/978-3-030-10549-5_10

point-to-point communications, as they have to handle the collective algorithms, and even some computations for reduction collectives. Therefore, it is harder to make them progress in background.

Most processors nowadays include *Simultaneous Multi-Threading* [4] (SMT, commercially known as *Hyper-Threading* on *Intel* processors), which is the ability for a core to have multiple *hardware threads* running simultaneously, sharing the same arithmetic units. A lot of scientific applications don't use all hardware threads, leaving them idle. Thus it seems like a natural idea to use these idle *hardware threads* to make communication progress. Since communication typically doesn't use arithmetic units, it is expected that placing progress threads on *hardware threads* will bring background progression for free. We distinguish the case of *network* (inter-node) communication, where the progression thread merely execute the algorithm for the collective operation, the rendez-vous protocol, programs DMA on the NIC, but overall doesn't burn a lot of CPU cycles; and the case of *shared-memory* (intra-node) communication, where the transfer is essentially a `memcpy`, which may be heavier on the CPU.

This paper focuses on what happens when placing MPI non-blocking collective progress threads on *hardware threads*. We show that using *SMT* for network communications leads to good results for both performance and progression. We also show that using *SMT* for intra-node (shared memory) communications leads to bad performances due to cache effects.

The rest of the paper is organized as follows. Section 2 presents related work about computation/communication overlap in general, and for collective communication in particular. Section 3 describes how communication progression works inside the MPC framework. Section 4 presents progress threads placement for inter-node and intra-node communications and results on Haswell processors, using Hyper-Threading. Then, Sect. 5 explains how intra-node communications can interfere on the computation when Hyper-Threading are used to make communication progression, before concluding in Sect. 6.

2 Related Works

The topic of communication progression has already been studied for some aspects in the literature. Several strategies do exist for background progression of point-to-point communications, such as offloading the communication to hardware [13,15] and let the hardware do the progression; use of a thread [5] or process [8] dedicated to communication progression; opportunistic scheduling of communication tasks [3,14].

MPI non-blocking collective communications are more difficult to make progress in the background, since not only the data transfer but the collective algorithm too needs to progress, which makes it harder to rely on hardware. There is specific work [2] for hardware-assisted progression on Blue Gene, or offloading shared memory collectives to a kernel module [9] (although authors only address performance of blocking collectives, not progression of non-blocking collectives). The reference NBC implementation [7] relies on a progress thread, with some tricks [6] to improve overlap on InfiniBand, but without any study about the impact of progress thread placement.

Hyper-Threading usage for non-blocking operations progression has already been studied in [10], with the use of `MONITOR/MWAIT` instructions on progress threads in order to avoid resource contention with the computational thread on the same physical core using another Hyper-Thread on process based MPI (network communication on intra node). However, `MONITOR/MWAIT` being privileged instructions usable only from kernel, this approach may not be used broadly on production clusters. Moreover, these instructions are inherently slow, which reserve them for coarse grain cases. Our approach is different because we rely only on bare Hyper-Threading accessible from user-space, and study different placements for both process based MPI (intra-node communications on network) and thread based MPI (intra-node communication with `memcpy`).

3 Non-blocking Collective Progression Inside the MPC Framework

The MPC [12] framework provides implementations for several parallel programming languages, such as MPI, OpenMP or POSIX threads. MPC provides two flavors for MPI: a process-based implementation and a thread-based implementation. Moreover, MPC also provides its own user thread scheduler. This scheduler handles the threads of all programming languages implemented in MPC, or build on top of the POSIX threads implementation provided by MPC, and allows to bypass the system scheduler.

MPC uses a tuned version of libNBC [7] to implement MPI 3 Non-Blocking Collectives. One progress thread is created for each MPI process. Thus, with the thread-based version of MPI, the MPC scheduler has the knowledge of all MPI processes and all progress threads present on a node. This knowledge allows to easily implement different placement algorithms for all these threads. The default behavior is for MPI "thread" to be bound with a scatter policy, and their corresponding progress threads to be bound to the closest idle cores (or to the same core if no idle cores are available).

In this implementation, a MPI non-blocking collective is decomposed in MPI point-to-point non-blocking calls fulfilling the collective algorithm. When a MPI non-blocking collective is called, each MPI process creates a *schedule* containing requests for the point-to point non-blocking calls corresponding to its part of the collective algorithm, and attach it to its associated progress thread. Thus, the progress threads handle the communication described by the schedules while MPI processes continue to execute computation. However, MPC has a non-preemptive scheduler, thus it is not able to make communication progress on the same core as the application with a seamless interleaved scheduling. A solution is to dedicate some cores to communication progression. In this paper we investigate the use of hardware threads instead of full cores for communication progression.

4 Progress Threads Placement for MPI Communications on Hyper-Threads

In this Section, we benchmark various placement schemes for placement of progress threads, using SMT or not, for network communications and shared-memory communications.

We will use Haswell processors featuring *Hyper-Threading*, the incarnation of *Simultaneous Multi-Threading* in Intel processors. It consists in allowing execution of two different threads (or more depending on the architecture) at the same time on a single core. Generally, applications do not use Hyper-Threading to perform more computation because it leads to Floating-Point Unit (FPU) contention. However, progress threads do not need the FPU to make communication progression, or scarcely for floating-point reduction operations. Thus, progress thread placement using Hyper-Threading seems to be a good idea.

After describing our experimental setup, we present results and observations on the use of Hyper-Threading to perform communications for the two distinct cases: pure network communications, and pure intra-node communications.

4.1 Benchmark

We implemented our own micro-benchmarking tool to evaluate the performance of different progress threads placement. This tool performs a non-blocking collective communication overlapped with a matrix-matrix multiply. It works similarly to the Intel MPI Benchmarks [1] except that the problem size is fixed, allowing us to have the same computation workload for the different progress threads placement. We arbitrary set the buffer size to 2 MB and sized the computation workload to reach perfect overlap when we have progress threads dedicated cores.

We ran our benchmark on a many-core architectures: an Intel Xeon E5-2698 v3 @2.30 GHz with 32 cores per node, and 128 GB of RAM (Haswell).

While our placement policy for MPI processes stays the same (scatter policy), we test three different progress threads placement configurations:

- "dedicated-core": each progress thread is bound on another dedicated core. We use twice more cores than both the other cases.
- "no-smt-bind": the progress threads are bound on the MPI process core and Hyper-Threading is disabled.
- "smt": each progress thread is bound on its MPI process core but on another Hyper-Thread.

For each configuration, we measure the time of the computation (t_{cpu}), the communication time (t_{comm}) and the total execution time (t_{ovrl}), all times measured when overlapping communication with computation. We get t_{ovrl} close to the maximum of t_{cpu} and t_{comm} in case of good overlap; it is closer to the sum in case operations get serialized. Please note that t_{comm} and t_{cpu} may vary depending on threads placement if computation slows down communication or

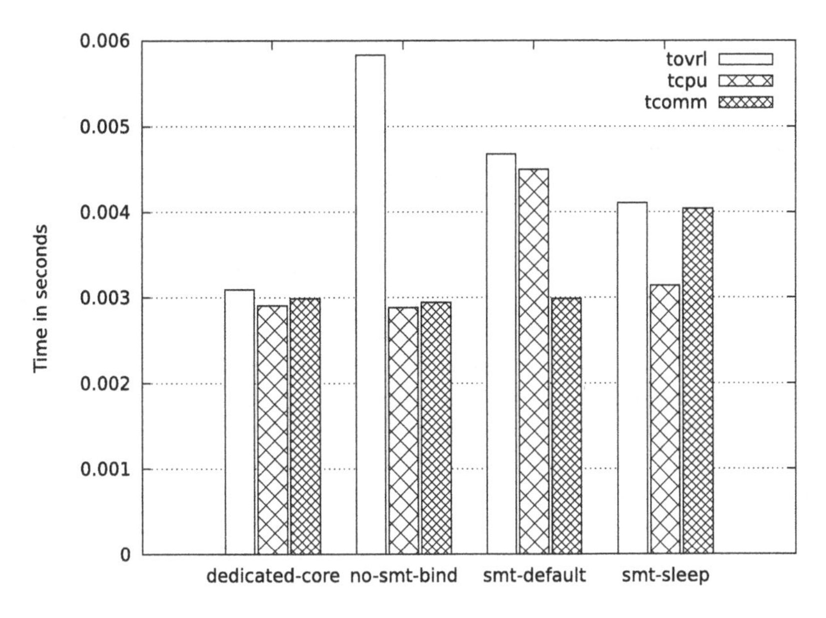

Fig. 1. Result of dedicated-core, no-smt-bind, smt-default and smt-sleep for `Ialltoall` operation with constant-size buffer of 2 MB on 8 nodes with 8 MPI processes.

if computation slows down communication when both are run at the same time. We use the same overlap definition as the Intel MPI Benchmarks [1]:

$$overlap\_ratio = 100 * \frac{max(0, min(1, (t_{comm} + t_{cpu} - t_{ovrl})}{min(t_{comm}, t_{cpu}))}$$

4.2 Inter-node Communications on Hyper-Threads

To study the impact of using hyper-threads only for inter-node communications, we ran our benchmark on 8 Haswell nodes, with only one MPI process per node. This is a usual configuration when MPI is combined with a threaded programming model (e.g. OpenMP) handling intra-node communications.

The results for inter-node communications are depicted in Fig. 1. The best results are obtained for the "dedicated core" placement, with an overlap ratio of 96% for an execution time of 3.0 ms. This is the expected behavior since a dedicated core for each progress thread makes the communication progress run smoothly in background, leading to an almost perfect overlap. However, this configuration uses twice as many cores as the other cases.

For the "no-smt-bind" placement, no overlap happens and the execution time doubles (5.8 ms). This is the expected behavior since MPC being non-preemptive, computation and communication end up serialized if computation thread and progress thread are placed on the same core. We observe that communications need some CPU resources to progress, not necessarily for the network itself, but at least to execute the algorithm of the collective and for the rendez-vous protocol for large messages.

The "smt" placement with default settings leads to an overlap ratio of 94% for an execution time of 4.6 ms. While the overlap ratio is good, we also observe that the t_{cpu} increases significantly. This is due to our MPI implementation. When Hyper-Threading is enabled, MPC creates an OS thread per logical core (Hyper-Thread). By default, this thread is populated with an idle user thread, spending its time busy waiting for work. As nothing is planned for this thread, it will permanently hinder the CPU with its busy waiting, thus slowing down the computation done on the other *hardware thread* sharing the same core.

To assess this behavior, we inserted a `usleep` call ($2\,\mu s$) to diminish the impact of this busy waiting in the idle thread.

With this version, called smt-sleep in Fig. 1, we observe an improvement of t_{ovrl} by a factor of 1.42 over the default MPC configuration (no-smt-bind) and an overlap ratio of 98%. In this version, t_{cpu} is only marginally impacted, which shows this tuning successfully mitigates contention between communication and communication. Since the idle thread is sleeping most of the time, the computation thread is indeed not hindered and the computation time is back to normal. However, when progression happens, the sleep calls reduce progression performance and the communication time is higher. Hence, it is possible to find a trade off to get best of both worlds.

As a summary, placing progress thread on hyper-threads improves both execution time performance and overlap ratio for network inter-node communications. It alleviates the need for dedicated cores for communication progression.

4.3 Intra-node Communications on Hyper-Threads

The common way to achieve intra-node communications is to copy a buffer from the source to the destination. For process based MPI implementation, such as Open MPI, MPICH, MVAPICH, Intel MPI or NewMadeleine, this can be performed using a shared memory segment across all the processes in the node. This technique allows MPI ranks to copy the buffer directly in the shared memory segment.

In the MPC framework, with the thread-based flavor, all MPI ranks are threads. This implies that the whole memory is shared in the same address space. Copies of buffers can be performed directly with a single *memcpy* call.

We ran our benchmark on one single Haswell node, with one MPI rank per core. We test two different thread placement configurations: the "no-smt-bind and the"smt" placement described in the Sect. 4.1. For each configurations, we measure the computation time (t_{cpu}), the communication time (t_{comm}) and the total execution time (t_{ovrl}) when overlapping communications with computation.

The results are depicted in Fig. 2. For both "no-smt-bind" and "smt" placement, we observe that $t_{ovrl} = t_{cpu} + t_{comm}$, which means no overlap happens. We also observe a 44% increase of the total time t_{ovrl} when placing progress threads on hyper-threads, due to the huge increase of computation time. This is a completely different behavior than with inter-node communication.

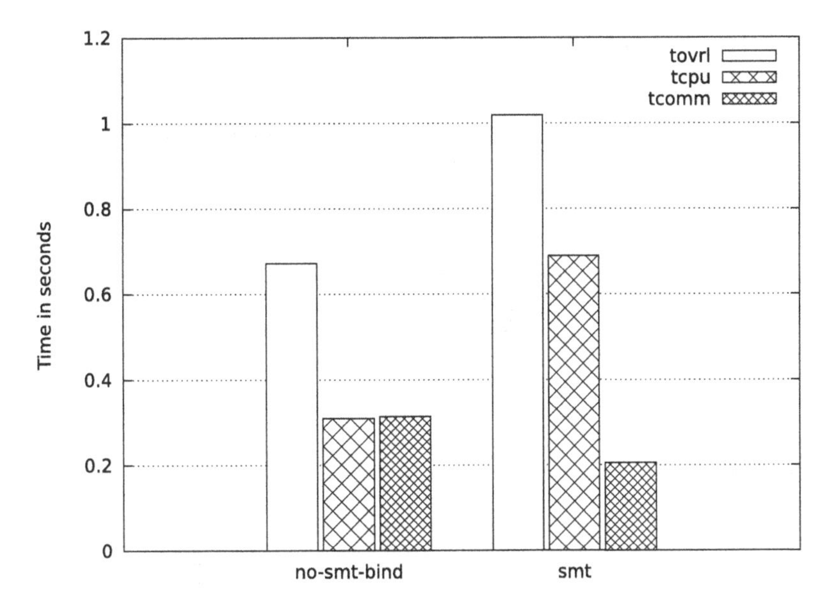

Fig. 2. Result of no-smt-bind and smt for `Ialltoall` operation with constant-size buffer of 2 MB on 1 nodes with 32 MPI processes.

From this observation, it is clear that placing progress threads on hyper-threads has a huge impact on computation performance when communications take place in shared memory. We investigate this issue in the Sect. 5.

5 Cache Effects with Hyper-threading

In this Section, we investigate how a communication thread on a hyper-thread negatively impacts the computation performance on the same core. We focus on cache effects caused by multiple hardware threads on the same core competing for cache lines, an effect known as *cache thrashing*.

We implemented a micro-benchmark to confirm our assumptions that cache effects occur when Hyper-Threading is used to perform the progression of intra-node communications. The benchmark runs a 1024×1024 matrix multiplication in a thread bound to a single core; we call it the *computation thread*. Another thread is created to simulate the progression of intra-node communications by performing a `memcpy` call in a loop; we call it the *memcpy thread*. We focus on the impact of this thread on the *computation thread*.

We test three different threads placement configurations:

- "cache-not-shared": the *computation thread* is bound on a single core and the *memcpy thread* is bound on another socket. Threads do not share any cache.
- "no-smt-bind": the *computation thread* is bound on a single core and the *memcpy thread* is bound on the same core. Hyper-Threading is disabled.

– "smt" the *computation thread* is bound on a single core and the *memcpy thread* is bound on the same core but on the other Hyper-Thread.

For each configuration, we run our tests with three buffer sizes for the *memcpy thread*, 4 KB, 128 KB and 2 MB on a dual socket Haswell processor, with 16 cores per socket and 2 Hyper-Thread per core.

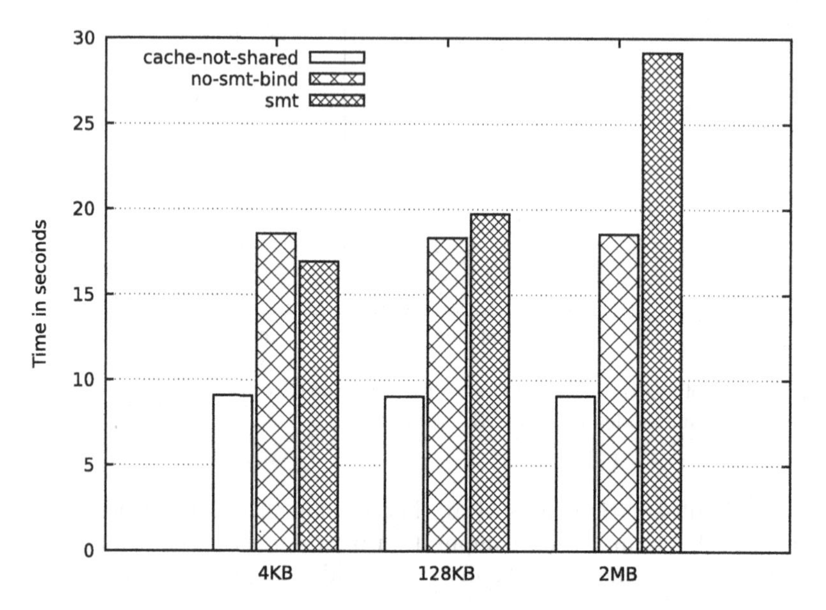

Fig. 3. Result of Time dgemm for no-smt-bind and smt configurations for 4 KB, 128 KB and 2 MB on a 32 core Haswell processor.

We measure the time of the computation for these three different threads placements with different buffer sizes. We observe in Fig. 3 that for all buffer sizes, we obtain a 9 s execution time with the "cache-not-shared" placement. This time doubles when we use the "no-smt-bind". The reason is that the first two placements do not compete for the caches. In the first case, the two threads are not located on the same socket. In the second case, the two threads are located on the same core, but without Hyper-Threading, execution is interleaved. Hence, when the *computation thread* runs, the *memcpy thread* is paused, and, after context switching between these threads, the *memcpy thread* runs while the *computation thread* is paused. If data may be removed from the caches after context switching, no competition for the cache occurs while a thread is running between context switches. However, for the "no-smt-bind" placement, the two threads share the same core without Hyper-Threading. Thus, all the workload from both threads are running on the same resources. Since we fixed the *memcpy thread* to run as long as the *computation thread*, it doubles the workload per core, hence also doubling the execution time.

For the "smt" placement, the *memcpy thread* is bound to the same core as the *computation thread* but on another Hyper-Thread. We observe a different behavior. Execution time is slower when the buffer size increases whereas the execution time remains constant between buffer sizes for the other placements. The computation is slower when the *memcpy thread* manipulates a larger amount of data: it is a typical symptom of *cache thrashing*.

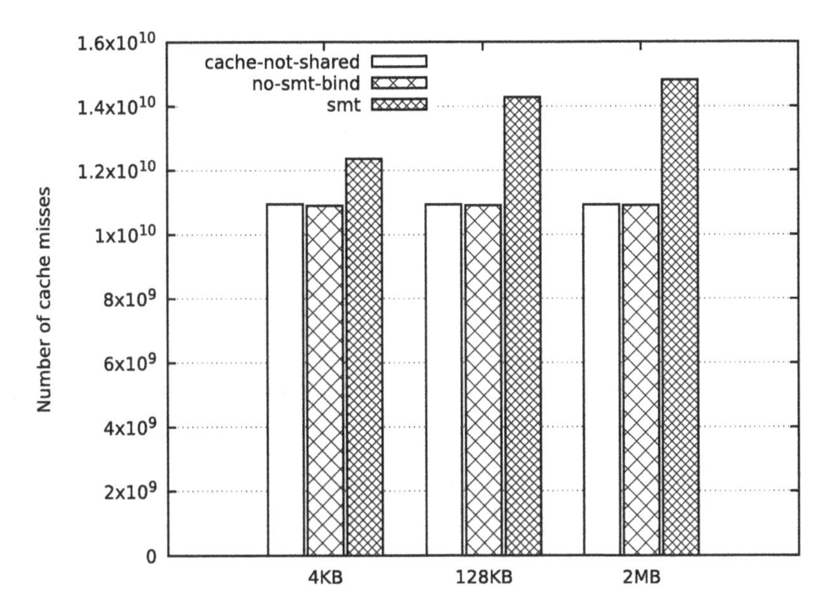

Fig. 4. Result of cache L1 miss for cache-not-shared, no-smt-bind and smt configurations for 4 KB, 128 KB and 2 MB on a 32 core Haswell processor.

To assess this hypothesis, we use the Performance Application Programming Interface (PAPI) [16] to collect the L1 cache misses. We see in the Fig. 4 that the number of cache misses is constant between both "no-smt-bind" and "cache-not-shared" placements. This is expected because the *computation thread* and the *memcpy thread* do not share the caches for the "cache-not-shared" placement. For the "no-smt-bind" placement, these threads are scheduled one after the other and no additional cache misses occurs.

For the "smt" placement, we observe additional cache misses compare to the two previous placements. This is due to Hyper-Threading being enabled. Both threads are executed on the same core simultaneously sharing the caches. Both of them needs to fetch their cache lines to execute their jobs. Contention happens and leads to additional cache misses because the *memcpy thread* evicts cache lines of the *computation thread*.

It is now common to use non-temporal memory operations for shared memory operations in MPI libraries. The non-temporal memory copy, introduced with SSE2 instruction set, do not store in cache data sent to memory (i.e. it forces a *write around* cache policy). However, only the *write* operation bypasses the cache, not the *read*. Benchmarks with non-temporal memory copy exhibits the same results as with regular memory copy.

These results demonstrate that using Hyper-Threading for communication progression in shared-memory causes a flood of cache misses, which severely degrades the performance of computation on the same core.

6 Conclusion and Future Work

Overlapping communications with computation is the key to amortize the cost of communications, especially for collective communications which are heavier than point-to-point communications. Approaches for progression relying on a progress thread per MPI rank may suffer from competition between communication and computation.

In this paper, we have studied the placement of progress threads for MPI non-blocking collective on hyper-threads and compared it against dedicated cores. We have brought a comprehensive benchmark and full performance analysis of using hyper-threads for communication progression on Haswell processor.

We have tested several progress thread placements and obtained an overlap ratio of 98% of *network* communications when placing progress threads on hyper-threads. We have shown that this scheme leads to performance degradation for *shared memory* communication, and highlighted its cause in cache thrashing.

As a consequence of this work, the optimal placement for a network communication and a shared-memory communication is not the same, which is not achievable through the use of a single progress thread making progress for all communications. As future works, we plan to have communication progression rely on *tasks* rather than on a thread, which will allow for a greater flexibility in placement.

References

1. IMB-NBC benchmarks. https://software.intel.com/fr-fr/node/561946. Accessed 10 May 2018
2. Almási, G., et al.: Optimization of MPI collective communication on BlueGene/L systems. In: Proceedings of the 19th Annual International Conference on Supercomputing, ICS 2005, pp. 253–262. ACM, New York (2005). https://doi.org/10.1145/1088149.1088183
3. Denis, A.: pioman: a pthread-based Multithreaded Communication Engine. In: Euromicro International Conference on Parallel, Distributed and Network-based Processing. Turku, Finland, March 2015. https://hal.inria.fr/hal-01087775
4. Eggers, S.J., Emer, J.S., Levy, H.M., Lo, J.L., Stamm, R.L., Tullsen, D.M.: Simultaneous multithreading: a platform for next-generation processors. IEEE Micro **17**(5), 12–19 (1997)
5. Hoefler, T., Lumsdaine, A.: Message progression in parallel computing - to thread or not to thread? In: Proceedings of the 2008 IEEE International Conference on Cluster Computing. IEEE Computer Society, October 2008

6. Hoefler, T., Lumsdaine, A.: Optimizing non-blocking Collective Operations for InfiniBand. In: Proceedings of the 22nd IEEE International Parallel & Distributed Processing Symposium, CAC'08 Workshop, April 2008
7. Hoefler, T., Lumsdaine, A., Rehm, W.: Implementation and performance analysis of non-blocking collective operations for MPI. In: Proceedings of the 2007 International Conference on High Performance Computing, Networking, Storage and Analysis, SC07. IEEE Computer Society/ACM, November 2007
8. Lai, P., Balaji, P., Thakur, R., Panda, D.: ProOnE: a general purpose protocol onload engine for multi- and many-core architectures, June 2009
9. Ma, T., Bosilca, G., Bouteiller, A., Goglin, B., Squyres, J.M., Dongarra, J.J.: Kernel assisted collective intra-node MPI communication among multi-core and many-core CPUs. In: IEEE (ed.) 40th International Conference on Parallel Processing (ICPP-2011), Taipei, Taiwan, September 2011. https://hal.inria.fr/inria-00602877
10. Miwa, M., Nakashima, K.: Progression of MPI Non-blocking Collective Operations Using Hyper-Threading, pp. 163–171 (03 2015)
11. MPI Forum: MPI: A Message-Passing Interface Standard Version 3.0, September 2012
12. Pérache, M., Jourdren, H., Namyst, R.: MPC: a unified parallel runtime for clusters of NUMA machines. In: Luque, E., Margalef, T., Benítez, D. (eds.) Euro-Par 2008. LNCS, vol. 5168, pp. 78–88. Springer, Heidelberg (2008). https://doi.org/10.1007/978-3-540-85451-7_9
13. Rashti, M.J., Afsahi, A.: Improving communication progress and overlap in MPI Rendezvous protocol over RDMA-enabled interconnects. In: 22nd International Symposium on High Performance Computing Systems and Applications, HPCS 2008, pp. 95–101. IEEE (2008)
14. Si, M., Peña, A., Balaji, P., Takagi, M., Ishikawa, Y.: MT-MPI: multithreaded MPI for many-core environments. In: Proceedings of the International Conference on Supercomputing, June 2014
15. Sur, S., Jin, H., Chai, L., Panda, D.: RDMA read based rendezvous protocol for MPI over InfiniBand: design alternatives and benefits. In: Proceedings of the Eleventh ACM SIGPLAN Symposium on Principles and Practice of Parallel Programming, pp. 32–39. ACM New York (2006)
16. Terpstra, D., Jagode, H., You, H., Dongarra, J.: Collecting performance data with PAPI-C. In: Müller, M.S., Resch, M.M., Schulz, A., Nagel, W.E. (eds.) Tools for High Performance Computing 2009, pp. 157–173. Springer, Heidelberg (2010). https://doi.org/10.1007/978-3-642-11261-4_11

A Methodology for Handling Data Movements by Anticipation: Position Paper

Raphaël Bleuse[1,2(✉)], Giorgio Lucarelli[1(✉)], and Denis Trystram[1]

[1] Univ. Grenoble Alpes, CNRS, Inria, Grenoble INP, LIG, 38000 Grenoble, France
{giorgio.lucarelli,denis.trystram}@imag.fr
[2] FSTC/CSC, University of Luxembourg, Luxembourg City, Luxembourg
raphael.bleuse@uni.lu

Abstract. The enhanced capabilities of large scale parallel and distributed platforms produce a continuously increasing amount of data which have to be stored, exchanged and used by various tasks allocated on different nodes of the system. The management of such a huge communication demand is crucial for reaching the best possible performance of the system. Meanwhile, we have to deal with more interferences as the trend is to use a single all-purpose interconnection network whatever the interconnect (tree-based hierarchies or topology-based heterarchies). There are two different types of communications, namely, the flows induced by data exchanges during the computations, and the flows related to Input/Output operations. We propose in this paper a general model for interference-aware scheduling, where explicit communications are replaced by external topological constraints. Specifically, the interferences of both communication types are reduced by adding geometric constraints on the allocation of tasks into machines. The proposed constraints reduce implicitly the data movements by restricting the set of possible allocations for each task. This methodology has been proved to be efficient in a recent study for a restricted interconnection network (a line/ring of processors which is an intermediate between a tree and higher dimensions grids/torus). The obtained results illustrated well the difficulty of the problem even on simple topologies, but also provided a pragmatic greedy solution, which was assessed to be efficient by simulations. We are currently extending this solution for more complex topologies. This work is a position paper which describes the methodology, it does not focus on the solving part.

Keywords: Scheduling · Affinity · Data movements · Heterogeneity Topology · HPC

This work has been partially supported by a DGA-MRIS scholarship, and is partially funded by the joint research programme UL/SnT-ILNAS on Digital Trust for Smart ICT.

G. Mencagli et al. (Eds.): Euro-Par 2018 Workshops, LNCS 11339, pp. 134–145, 2019.
https://doi.org/10.1007/978-3-030-10549-5_11

1 Introduction

In High Performance Computing (HPC), the demand for computation power is steadily increasing [27]. To meet up the challenge of always more performances, while being constrained by ever growing energy costs, the architecture of supercomputers also grows in complexity at the whole machine scale. This complexity arises from various factors: firstly, the size of the machines (supercomputers now integrates millions of cores); secondly, the heterogeneity of the resources (various architectures of computing nodes, mixed workloads of computing and analytics, nodes dedicated to I/O, etc.); and lastly, the interconnection topology. The architectural evolutions of the interconnection networks at the whole machine scale pose two main challenges that are described as follows. First, the community proposed several types of topologies including hierarchies and heterarchies (which are based on structural well-suited topologies), the trend today is to create mixed solutions of tree-like machines with local structured toplogies [22]; and second, the interconnection network is usually unique within the machine (which means that the network is shared for various mixed data flows). Sharing such a single multi-purpose interconnection network begets complex interactions (e.g., network contention) between running applications. These interactions have a strong impact on the performances of the applications [4,15], and hamper the understanding of the system by the users [11]. As the volume of processed data increases, so does the impact of the network.

We propose in this work a *generic framework for interference-aware scheduling*. More precisely, we identify two main types of interleaved flows: the flows induced by data exchanges for computations, and the flows related to I/O. Rather than explicitly taking into account these network flows, we address the issue of harmful or inefficient interactions by constraining the shape of the allocations. Such an approach aims at taking into account the complexity of the new HPC platforms in a qualitative way that is more likely to scale properly. The scheduling problem is then defined as an optimization problem with the platform (nodes and topology) and the jobs' description as input. The objective is to minimize the maximum completion time, maximize the throughput or optimize any other relevant objective while enforcing constraints on the allocations.

The purpose of this paper is to describe the methodology for interference-aware scheduling. The design of an algorithm and the corresponding simulations/experiments are another side of this subject. We are currently studying efficient solutions for assessing this methodology, but this paper does not focus on this point.

2 General Problem Setting

Modelization. A platform is of a set $\mathcal{V}$ of m nodes divided in two sets: m^{C} nodes dedicated to computations $\mathcal{V}^{\mathrm{C}}$, and $m^{I/O}$ nodes that are entry points to a high performance file system $\mathcal{V}^{I/O}$. The nodes are indexed by $i \in 0, \ldots, m-1$.

This numbering provides an *arbitrary ordering* of the nodes. We distinguish two interesting distributions of the nodes:

1. *coupled I/O*, where some compute nodes are also entry points for the I/O operations (i.e., $\mathcal{V}^{I/O} \subseteq \mathcal{V}^{\mathrm{C}} = \mathcal{V}$);
2. *separate I/O*, when there is no overlap between compute and I/O nodes (i.e., $\mathcal{V}^{I/O} \cap \mathcal{V}^{\mathrm{C}} = \emptyset$).

We also distinguish two ways of interacting with the I/O nodes, namely, *shared I/O* when any number of jobs can access an I/O node at any time, and *exclusive I/O* when an I/O node is exclusively allocated to a job for the job's lifespan. We further annotate node symbols with $\star^{I/O}$ ($\star^{\mathrm{C}}$, resp.) if there is a need to distinguish I/O nodes (compute nodes, resp.).

The nodes communicate thanks to an interconnection network with a given *topology* (i.e., the connected graph of the interconnection) or by a hierarchical topology (tree-like interconnection). The localization of every node within the topology is known. We define the distance that intrinsically derives from a topology as follows:

Definition 1 (Distance). *The distance* $\operatorname{dist}(i, i')$ *between two nodes* i *and* i' *(either compute or I/O) is defined as the minimum number of hops to go from* i *to* i'. *For hierarchical topologies, the distance is defined as the number of traversed levels (switches) to go from* i *to* i'.

Batch schedulers are a critical part of the software stack managing supercomputers: their goal is to efficiently allocate resources (nodes from $\mathcal{V}$ in our case) to the jobs submitted by the users of the platform. The jobs are queued in a set $\mathcal{J}$ of n jobs. Each job j requires a number of compute nodes q_j^{C} and some I/O nodes $q_j^{I/O}$. The I/O nodes requirements can either be a number of nodes (*unpinned I/O*), or a dedicated subset of $\mathcal{V}^{I/O}$ (*pinned I/O*). The number of allocated nodes is fixed (i.e., the job is *rigid* [17]). We denote by $\mathcal{V}(j)$ the nodes allocated to the job j. Each job j requires a certain time p_j to be processed, and it is *independent* of every other jobs. Once a job starts executing, it runs until completion (i.e., it *cannot be preempted*). Finally, any compute node is able to process at most one job at any time.

Before presenting the constraints we consider in this work, we need to precisely define the network flows we target. We distinguish two types of flows, directly deriving from the fact that we are dealing with two kinds of nodes.

Definition 2 (Communication types). *We distinguish two types of communications (see Fig. 1):*

compute communications *are the communications induced by data exchanges for computations. Such communications occur between two compute nodes allocated to the same application.*

I/O communications *are the communications induced by data exchanges between compute nodes and I/O nodes. Such communications occur when compute nodes read input data, checkpoint the state of the application, or save output results.*

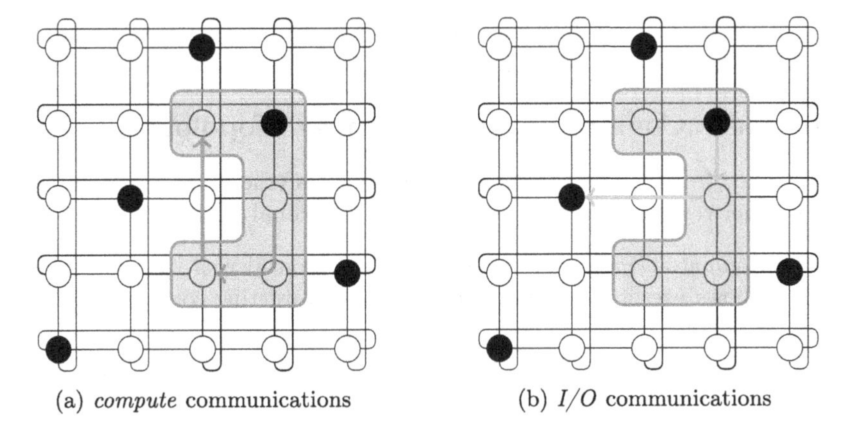

(a) *compute* communications (b) *I/O* communications

Fig. 1. Figuration of the two distinguished types of communications. Note that some communications stay within the allocation, while others do not. White nodes represent compute nodes, and black nodes represent I/O nodes.

As stated in the introduction, we do not aim at finely modeling the context of execution. We propose here to model the platform in such a way that network interactions are *implicitly* taken into account. We enrich the scheduling problem with alien geometric constraints on the allocations deriving from the platform topology or the application structure.

Most scheduler implementations are naive, in the sense that they allocate resources greedily. This is known to impact performances [15], and is the core difference between parallel machine scheduling and packing problems. Constraining the allocations to enhance performance is however no new idea. For example, Lucarelli et al. studied the impact of enforcing contiguity or locality constraints in backfilling scheduling [23]. They showed that enforcing these constraints can be done at a small computational cost, and has minimum negative impact on usual metrics such as makespan (i.e., maximum completion time), flow-time (i.e., absolute time spent in the system), or stretch (i.e., time spent in the system relative to each job size). One may refer to [9,14] for a detailed definition of classic optimization objectives in scheduling.

We go further with this model as we target heterogeneous machines, and distinguish network flows. We seek the following properties for the constraints:

- It *captures part of the execution context*: enforcing the constraint should help minimize nocuous effects arising from the execution context.
- It *derives from minimal reliable data*: constraints on the allocations are enforced ahead of the scheduling decisions. As a result, the proposed constraints only use the topology of the interconnection network and the size of the allocation as input data.
- It is *cheap to compute*: enumerating the list of allocations respecting some constraints cannot be a performance bottleneck for the scheduler.

We study in more detail in the two following sections how to consider these constraints for structured topologies and for hierarchical topologies.

3 Intrinsic Constraints for Structured Topologies

For the sake of clarity, we consider here a 2D-torus (the same constraints also hold for other regular topologies like higher-dimensional torus or hypercubes).

Avoiding Compute-Communication Interactions. Considering this classification of network flows, we first expose three constraints targeting compute communications.

Definition 3 (Connectivity). *An allocation π is said to be* connected *iff there exists a subset $\mathcal{V}_\pi$ of $\mathcal{V}^{I/O}$ such that $\left(\pi \cap \mathcal{V}^C\right) \cup \mathcal{V}_\pi$ is connected in the graph-theory sense. $\mathcal{V}_\pi$ may be empty.*

The *connectivity* constraint ensures, for a given allocation, that there exists a path without interference between any pair of compute nodes of the allocation. This however, with regard to the interconnection topology, can either require support for dynamic routing or demand to the application to implement its own routing policy. Moreover, it may lead to islets of isolated compute nodes. Hence, although satisfactory from the graph theoretical point of view, the connectivity constraint is not sufficient to ensure that compute communication do not interfere. We propose the *convexity* constraint with the goal of overcoming these limits.

Definition 4 (Convexity). *An allocation is said to be* convex *iff it is impossible for compute communications from any other potential allocation to share an interconnect link with respect to the underlying routing algorithm.*

By taking into account the effective routing policy, and by forbidding any potential sharing, the *convexity* constraint does forbid interactions.

Note that the convexity constraint dominates the connectivity constraint, as stated in the following Proposition.

Proposition 1. *Given any topology, any convex allocation is connected (Fig. 2).*

Definition 5 (Contiguity [6,23]**).** *An allocation is said to be* contiguous *if and only if the nodes of the allocation form a contiguous range with respect to the nodes' ordering.*

One has to note that the contiguity constraint is intrinsically unidimensional as it relies on the nodes' ordering. For topologies such as trees, lines or rings the ordering is natural. On higher dimension topologies, no natural ordering exists, and an arbitrary mapping is needed. An usual strategy to order nodes is to use space-filling curves (e.g., Z-order curve [24], Hilbert curve [20], etc.) as they enforce a strong spatial locality. Albing proposes various orderings that may be more suited for HPC use cases, and a method to evaluate them [3]. Contiguity is an interesting relaxation of convexity as it offers good spatial locality properties for a reasonable computing cost. It is however unable to ensure that no jobs could interact.

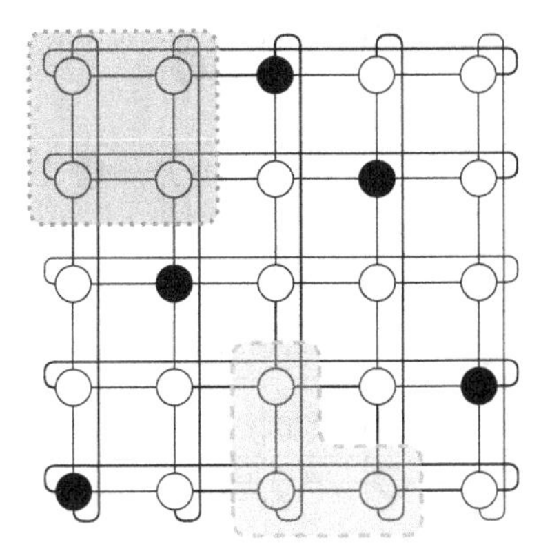

Fig. 2. Example of a convex allocation (dotted orange contour), and a non-convex, but connected allocation (dashed blue contour). The underlying topology is a 2D-torus, with dimension-order routing. White nodes represent compute nodes, and black nodes represent I/O nodes. (Color figure online)

Avoiding I/O-Communication Interactions. The constraints exposed so far are well suited to take into account the compute communications, but not the I/O communications. Indeed, the compute communications may occur between any pair of compute nodes within an allocation: we usually describe this pattern as all-to-all communications. I/O communications, on the other hand, generate traffic towards few identified nodes in an all-to-one or one-to-all pattern. Hence, we propose the *locality* constraint, whose goal is to limit the impact of the I/O flows to the periphery of the job allocations (see Fig. 3). We must emphasize that the locality constraint proposed here is not related to the locality constraint previously described by Lucarelli et al. [23].

Definition 6 (Locality). *A given allocation for a job j is said to be* local *iff it is connected, and every I/O nodes from $\mathcal{V}^{I/O}(j)$ are adjacent to compute nodes from $\mathcal{V}^{C}(j)$, with respect to the underlying topology. In other words, $\mathcal{V}^{I/O}(j)$ is a subset of the closed neighborhood of $\mathcal{V}^{C}(j)$.*

Interestingly, the locality constraint enforces a bound on the number of concurrent jobs that can target a given I/O node.

Proposition 2. *Given any topology, any I/O node i, at any time, the number of local jobs targeting i cannot exceed the number of adjacent compute nodes of i.*

As a consequence, if the I/O nodes can be shared, the number of concurrent jobs targeting a given I/O node is bounded by the degree of this I/O node. This identity obviously also holds for exclusive I/O, but has limited interest in this case.

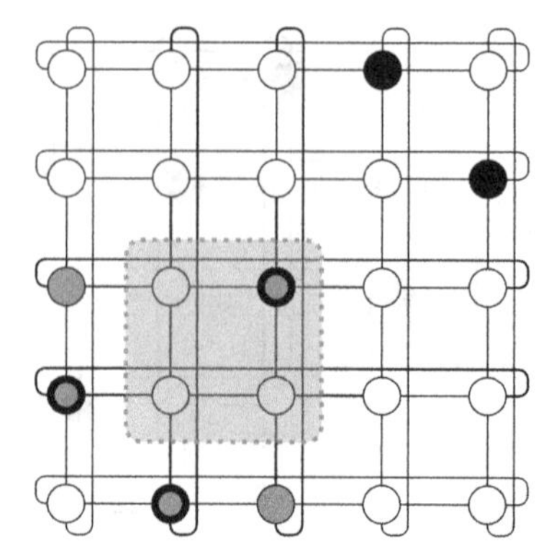

Fig. 3. Given an allocation (dotted orange contour) for a job j, the allocation is local iff j uses a subset of the I/O nodes marked with the orange dot. Foreign compute nodes potentially impacted by I/O communications of j are depicted in gray: these nodes can only be in the neighborhood of the allocation thanks to the locality constraint. The underlying topology is a 2D-torus, with dimension-order routing. White nodes represent compute nodes, and black nodes represent I/O nodes.

4 Intrinsic Constraints for Hierarchical Topologies

Hierarchical platforms are composed of computing nodes and communication switches. The interconnect is a tree where the leaves are the computing nodes, and the internal nodes correspond to the switches. A group of leaves connected by the same switch is a *cluster*. The communications inside a cluster are negligible while external communications require to cross all the switches along the unique path from a node to another. Figure 4 depicts a model of hierarchical platform.

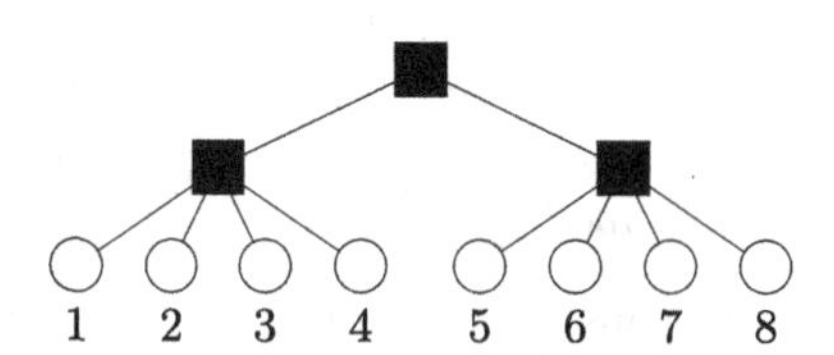

Fig. 4. Example of a hierarchical topology. White nodes represent compute nodes, and black nodes represent internal nodes (switches).

Avoiding Compute-Communication Interactions. In tree-like topologies the three constraints introduced for torus topologies should be revisited. Specifically, the convexity constraint is not relevant for hierarchical topologies since it implies that the internal nodes (switches) should be exclusively used by a single application, which significantly affects the platform utilization. On the other hand, the contiguity constraint can be naturally applied, by considering an arbitrary order of the children of any internal node and then numbering the leaves from left to right. Finally, the definition of connectivity constraint does not directly apply to hierarchical topologies.

The main characteristic of the hierarchical topologies is that there is no reason to distinguish among nodes that are connected under a common switch. However, the distance among two nodes of the same allocation is very important. In what follows, we define two new constraints that are better suited to tree-like topologies.

Definition 7 (Proximity). *A given allocation* π *for a job* j *satisfies the* proximity *constraint iff the quantity* $\max_{i,i' \in \pi} dist(i, i')$ *is minimized.*

In other words, the maximum distance among any two computing nodes assigned to the job j should be minimum. Hence, the allocation affects the minimum number of levels of the tree (see Figs. 5b and c).

Definition 8 (Compacity). *A given allocation* π *for a job* j *is called* compact *iff the quantity* $\sum_{i,i' \in \pi} dist(i, i')$ *is minimized.*

Intuitively, the compacity constraint intents not only to use the minimum number of levels in the tree, but also to consider two qualitative properties of the allocation (see Fig. 5c). First, compacity implies that an allocation spans as few clusters as possible. Second, if a cluster is used, the compacity constraint aims at maximizing the number of nodes allocated within this cluster.

Avoiding I/O-Communication Interactions. In the previous presentation of hierarchical topologies, the I/O nodes have been implicitly placed at the switch levels, as it is common in many existing architectures [1]. Let notice that our analysis also holds where the I/O nodes are located at the leaves level as it is the case in some architectures like in the interconnect of the private cloud [25].

5 Related Work

Tackling the nocuous interactions arising from the context of execution—or, more specifically, network contention—can be seen as a scheduling problem with uncertainties. Within this framework, there exist two main approaches to abate the uncertainty: by either preventing some uncertainties from happening (proactive approach), or by mitigating the uncertainties impact (reactive approach) [5]. We start reviewing some related works in the prevention/mitigation of interactions before discussing monitoring techniques.

Interactions Prevention. Some steps have been taken towards integrating more knowledge about the communication patterns of applications into the batch scheduler. For example, Georgiou et al. studied the integration of TreeMatch into SLURM [19]. Given the communication matrix of an application, the scheduler minimizes the load of the network links by smartly mapping the application's processes on the resources. This approach however is limited to tree-like topologies, and does not consider the temporality of communications. Targeting the

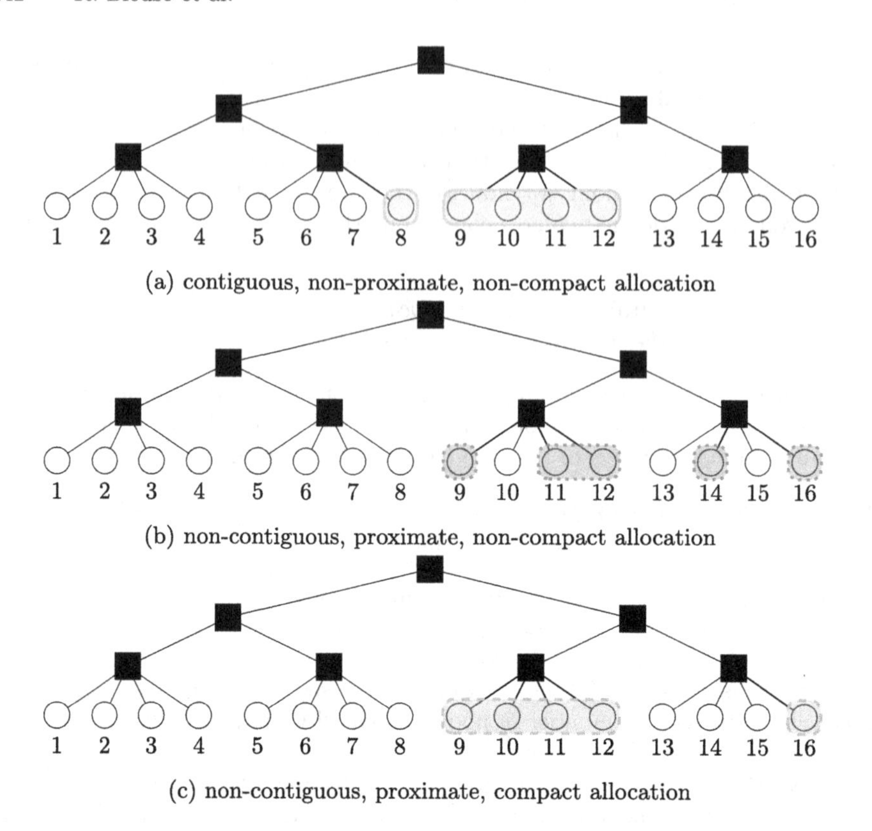

Fig. 5. Figuration of the constraints on a hierarchical topology. The depicted allocations contain five compute nodes (i.e., $q_j = 5$). White nodes represent compute nodes, and black nodes represent internal nodes (switches).

mesh/torus topologies, the works of Tuncer et al. [29] and Pascual et al. [26] are noteworthy. Another way to prevent interactions is to force the scheduler to use only certain allocation shapes with good properties: this strategy has been implemented in the Blue Waters scheduler [15]. The administrators of Blue Waters let the scheduler pick a shape among 460 precomputed cuboids.

Yet, the works proposed above only target compute communications. HPC applications usually rely on highly tuned libraries such as MPI-IO, parallel netCDF or HDF5 to perform their I/O. Tessier et al. propose to integrate topology awareness into these libraries [28]. They show that performing data aggregation while considering the topology allow to diminish the bandwidth required to perform I/O. The CLARISSE approach proposes to coordinate the data staging steps while considering the full I/O stack [21].

Interactions Mitigation. Given a set of applications, Gainaru et al. propose to schedule I/O flows of concurrent applications [18]. Their work aim at mitigating I/O congestion within the interconnection once applications have been allocated computation resources. To achieve such a goal, their algorithm relies on past I/O patterns of the applications to either maximize the global system utilization, or minimize the maximum slowdown induced by sharing bandwidth. Deeper in the I/O stack, at the I/O node level, the I/O flows can be reorganized to better match the characteristics of the storage devices [8].

Application/Platform Instrumentation. The approaches discussed above require the knowledge of the application communication patterns (either compute or I/O communications). A lot of effort has been put into developing tools to better understand the behavior of HPC applications. Characterizing I/O patterns is key as it allows the developers to identify performance bottlenecks, and allows the system administrator to better configure the platforms. Some tools, such as Darshan [10], instrument the most used I/O libraries, and record every I/O-related function call. The gathered logs provide valuable data for postmortem analysis. Taking a complementary path, Omnisc'IO aims at predicting I/O performances during execution [13]. The predictions rely on a formal grammar to model the I/O behavior of the instrumented application.

These instrumentation efforts allow for a better use of the scarce communication resources. However, as they are application-centric, they fail to capture inter-application interactions. Monitoring of the platform is a way of getting insight on the inter-application interactions [2,16]. For example, the OVIS/LDMS system deployed on Blue Waters collect 194 metrics on every 27648 nodes every minute [2]. Among the metrics of interest are the network counters: the number of stalls is a good indicator of congestion [12].

6 Conclusion and Future Work

The goal of this paper was to propose a methodology for handling data communications in modern parallel platforms for both structured topology and hierarchical interconnects. Our proposal was to identify relevant constraints that can easily be integrated into an optimization problem. We have successfully applied this methodology for a specific topology (line/ring of processors) [7].

Defining constraints that work well for any kind of topologies has been troublesome. This raises the question to know if a topology-agnostic heuristic can be designed at a reasonable cost with decent performances. If not, it would be interesting to classify the topologies, and propose class-specific constraints and heuristics. We are currently working on the design of a generic heuristic that can address several topologies.

The proposed constraints are strongly expected to have a positive impact on the performances as they implicitly emphasize data locality. We however did not verify through experiments that these constraints indeed have a positive impact on the network usage. The benefits from these experiments will be twofold: first, validate the proposed constraints; second, provide a feedback to design better suited constraints.

References

1. TGCC Curie Supercomputer. http://www-hpc.cea.fr/en/complexe/tgcc-curie.htm
2. Agelastos, A., et al.: The lightweight distributed metric service: a scalable infrastructure for continuous monitoring of large scale computing systems and applications. In: SC, pp. 154–165. IEEE, November 2014
3. Albing, C.: Characterizing node orderings for improved performance. In: PMBS@SC, pp. 6:1–6:11. ACM (2015)
4. Bhatele, A., Mohror, K., Langer, S.H., Isaacs, K.E.: There goes the neighborhood: performance degradation due to nearby jobs. In: SC, pp. 41:1–41:12. ACM, November 2013
5. Billaut, J.C., Moukrim, A., Sanlaville, É.: Flexibility and Robustness in Scheduling. Control Systems, Robotics and Manufacturing, Wiley (2008)
6. Błądek, I., Drozdowski, M., Guinand, F., Schepler, X.: On contiguous and non-contiguous parallel task scheduling. J. Sched. **18**(5), 487–495 (2015)
7. Bleuse, R., Dogeas, K., Lucarelli, G., Mounié, G., Trystram, D.: Interference-aware scheduling using geometric constraints. In: Aldinucci, M., Padovani, L., Torquati, M. (eds.) Euro-Par 2018. LNCS, vol. 11014, pp. 205–217. Springer, Cham (2018). https://doi.org/10.1007/978-3-319-96983-1_15
8. Boito, F.Z., Kassick, R.V., Navaux, P.O.A., Denneulin, Y.: Automatic I/O scheduling algorithm selection for parallel file systems. Concurr. Comput. Pract. Exp. **28**(8), 2457–2472 (2016)
9. Brucker, P.: Scheduling Algorithms, 5th edn. Springer, New York (2007)
10. Carns, P.H., Harms, K., Allcock, W.E., Bacon, C., Lang, S., Latham, R., Ross, R.B.: Understanding and improving computational science storage access through continuous characterization. ACM Trans. Storage **7**(3), 8:1–8:26 (2011)
11. Chen, N., Poon, S.S., Ramakrishnan, L., Aragon, C.R.: Considering time in designing large-scale systems for scientific computing. In: CSCW, pp. 1533–1545. ACM, February 2016
12. Deveci, M., et al.: Exploiting geometric partitioning in task mapping for parallel computers. In: IPDPS, pp. 27–36. IEEE, May 2014
13. Dorier, M., Ibrahim, S., Antoniu, G., Ross, R.B.: Using formal grammars to predict I/O behaviors in HPC: the Omnisc'IO approach. IEEE Trans. Parallel Distrib. Syst. **27**(8), 2435–2449 (2016)
14. Drozdowski, M.: Scheduling for Parallel Processing. Computer Communications and Networks. Springer, London (2009). https://doi.org/10.1007/978-1-84882-310-5
15. Enos, J., et al.: Topology-aware job scheduling strategies for torus networks. In: Cray User Group, May 2014. https://cug.org/proceedings/cug2014_proceedings/includes/files/pap182.pdf
16. Evans, R.T., Browne, J.C., Barth, W.L.: Understanding application and system performance through system-wide monitoring. In: IPDPS Workshops, pp. 1702–1710. IEEE, May 2016
17. Feitelson, D.G., Rudolph, L., Schwiegelshohn, U., Sevcik, K.C., Wong, P.: Theory and practice in parallel job scheduling. In: Feitelson, D.G., Rudolph, L. (eds.) JSSPP 1997. LNCS, vol. 1291, pp. 1–34. Springer, Heidelberg (1997). https://doi.org/10.1007/3-540-63574-2_14
18. Gainaru, A., Aupy, G., Benoit, A., Cappello, F., Robert, Y., Snir, M.: Scheduling the I/O of HPC applications under congestion. In: IPDPS, pp. 1013–1022. IEEE, May 2015

19. Georgiou, Y., Jeannot, E., Mercier, G., Villiermet, A.: Topology-aware resource management for HPC applications. In: ICDCN, pp. 17:1–17:10. ACM (2017)
20. Hilbert, D.: Ueber die stetige Abbildung einer Line auf ein Flächenstück. Math. Ann. **38**(3), 459–460 (1891)
21. Isaila, F., Carretero, J., Ross, R.B.: CLARISSE: a middleware for data-staging coordination and control on large-scale HPC platforms. In: CCGrid, pp. 346–355. IEEE, May 2016
22. Kathareios, G., Minkenberg, C., Prisacari, B., Rodríguez, G., Hoefler, T.: Cost-effective diameter-two topologies: analysis and evaluation. In: SC, pp. 36:1–36:11. ACM, November 2015
23. Lucarelli, G., Machado Mendonça, F., Trystram, D., Wagner, F.: Contiguity and locality in backfilling scheduling. In: CCGRID, pp. 586–595. IEEE Computer Society, May 2015
24. Morton, G.M.: A computer Oriented Geodetic Data Base; and a New Technique in File Sequencing. Technical report, IBM Ltd., March 1966. https://domino.research.ibm.com/library/cyberdig.nsf/0/0dabf9473b9c86d48525779800566a39
25. Ngoko, Y.: Heating as a cloud-service, a position paper (industrial presentation). In: Dutot, P.-F., Trystram, D. (eds.) Euro-Par 2016. LNCS, vol. 9833, pp. 389–401. Springer, Cham (2016). https://doi.org/10.1007/978-3-319-43659-3_29
26. Pascual, J.A., Miguel-Alonso, J., Antonio, L.J.: Application-aware metrics for partition selection in cube-shaped topologies. Parallel Comput. **40**(5), 129–139 (2014)
27. Strohmaier, E., Dongarra, J., Simon, H., Meuer, M.: TOP500 list. https://www.top500.org/lists/
28. Tessier, F., Malakar, P., Vishwanath, V., Jeannot, E., Isaila, F.: Topology-aware data aggregation for intensive I/O on large-scale supercomputers. In: COMHPC@SC, pp. 73–81. IEEE (Nov 2016)
29. Tuncer, O., Leung, V.J., Coskun, A.K.: PaCMap: topology mapping of unstructured communication patterns onto non-contiguous allocations. In: ICS, pp. 37–46. ACM, June 2015

Scalable Work-Stealing Load-Balancer for HPC Distributed Memory Systems

Clement Fontenaille[1,2(✉)], Eric Petit[3], Pablo de Oliveira Castro[1], Seijilo Uemura[1], Devan Sohier[1], Piotr Lesnicki[2], Ghislain Lartigue[4], and Vincent Moureau[4]

[1] Li-PaRAD, University of Versailles, Versailles, France
clement.fontenaille@uvsq.fr
[2] Atos-Bull, Paris, France
[3] Intel Corporation, Santa Clara, USA
[4] CORIA-CNRS, University of Normandie, Saint-Étienne-du-Rouvray, France

Abstract. Work-stealing schedulers are common in shared memory environments. However, large scale distributed memory usage has been limited to specific *ad-hoc* implementations preventing a broader adoption. In this paper we introduce a new scalable work-stealing algorithm for distributed memory systems as well as our implementation as the TITUS_DLB library. It is based on Kleinberg's small-world graph. It allows to control the communication patterns and associated runtime overheads while providing efficient heuristics for victim selection and results routing. To validate our approach, we present the DLB_Bench benchmark which emulates arbitrary workload distribution and imbalance characteristics. Finally, we compare TITUS_DLB to the *ad-hoc* solution developed for the YALES2 computational fluid dynamics and combustion solver. We achieve up to 54% performance gain over thousands of cores.

1 Introduction

In high-end HPC machines, the current architecture trend is to dramatically increase the number of cores. Managing large scale concurrency is a challenge for many HPC applications and runtimes, which eventually hit a *scalability wall.*

Load balancing systems optimize workload distribution and resource usage to improve the scalability of unbalanced applications.

Work-stealing, as presented in [7,8], is an asynchronous distributed decentralized dynamic load balancing algorithm.

In order to implement scalable work-stealing for large scale distributed memory systems, we take into account an overlooked limitation of the classical victim selection strategy: random victim selection may trigger the connexion of all possible pairs of processes, and the expected memory and time overhead limits scalability.

G. Mencagli et al. (Eds.): Euro-Par 2018 Workshops, LNCS 11339, pp. 146–158, 2019.
https://doi.org/10.1007/978-3-030-10549-5_12

In this paper, we introduce the TITUS_DLB library: a new scalable approach to the work-stealing algorithm for dynamic load-balancing targeting large scale computations on distributed memory systems.

We control runtime overheads by constraining the communication pattern of the work-stealing algorithm to a scalable, low diameter, family of overlay networks: the Kleinberg's small-world sparse neighboring graph class. This overlay network provides short paths, allowing for efficient scheduling. Moreover, to return the data resulting from the execution of relocated computation, we propose a scalable results routing strategy.

Using a synthetic benchmark which emulates arbitrary workload characteristics and distribution, we study the efficiency of our scheduler in various configurations up to 3584 cores. We also evaluate the performance of our implementation compared to a hierarchical work-sharing approach in use in the ill-balanced computation of detailed chemistry from the YALES2 computational fluid dynamic and combustion application and achieve up to 54% speedup at 3584 cores.

2 Context and Objectives

We address load balancing using a relocatable tasks representation of a given computation.

Tasks are indivisible self-contained units of sequential work. They consume exclusive input data and produce results data. Relocating a task requires relocating its input data. Each task is spawned by its owner process initially holding the required input data. We do not address tasks dependencies. A task is completed when the produced results have been stored in its owner's memory. The execution time of each task is presumed to be irregular and unpredictable.

Parallel work resolution is completed as soon as the global set of tasks has been executed and the termination detection algorithm has converged.

We are interested in minimizing the parallel resolution time. We measure the time spent between the beginning of parallel work and the termination detection on each process. The maximum of these measured times is the parallel resolution time. Assuming homogeneous processor capabilities, we deduce the parallel efficiency against an hypothetical resolution time with perfect scheduling and zero overhead, i.e. the average work per process.

Blumofe *et al.* [5] introduce the *work first principle*: they observe that the available parallelism in parallel programs is vastly superior to the parallelism exploited for its execution, *i.e.* scheduling efficiency is driven by the work scheduling overhead, rather than that of the critical path scheduling overhead. As a first step towards an efficient and scalable distributed task scheduling algorithm for such applications, we address the problem of scheduling a set of tasks available for computation. All tasks are spawned before parallel resolution begins, and the critical path of the scheduled computation is the resolution time of the longest task to solve, which is assumed to be a small fraction of the average work per process.

The presented implementation of our algorithm does not yet support the benchmarks generally adopted for dynamic task scheduling (see Sect. 6.1), and focuses on the elaboration of a scalable communication pattern for this specific problem.

2.1 Context

Work-stealing approaches define two process states: processes who own work are workers, while the others are thieves. Thieves attempt to acquire work from workers using a work stealing protocol.

Following the *work first principle* [8], we attempt to minimize the amount of time spent by workers on non-working activities, and move the scheduling overhead to thieves. Work stealing protocols have been proposed which rely on RDMA to access task data and operate load balancing without affecting the execution of tasks on the worker's end [7,15].

In [22], Woodall *et al.* outline an important limitation of RDMA capable hardware: the first communication between two processes (the connection) incurs a much longer response time than the subsequent communications as well as some memory overhead. Amortizing this pair connexion overhead is a necessity for the elaboration of a scalable distributed algorithm.

We use an overlay network to constrain the communication pattern of our scheduler in order to control and amortize the overhead of RDMA connexion. As in [14,17,20], work-stealing is local to a thief's neighborhood as work spreads among thieves through the edges of the overlay network.

2.2 Work-Stealing Algorithm Description

A worker is a process that locally holds work. A worker manages two sets of local tasks: tasks are executed from the private set and thieves acquire tasks from the shared set. When one of these sets is empty, the worker re-balances them. Processes do not hold any information about tasks spawned by other processes nor about the global set of tasks.

A thief is a process that holds no work. Termination detection is performed before each theft attempt. The thief then selects a victim, as discussed in Sect. 4 and performs the work stealing protocol. When an attempt succeeds, the theft policy selects a number of tasks from the remote set of tasks to relocate.

In the studied context, the termination detection protocol is a non-blocking barrier: when a process detects that all its owned tasks have completed, local completion is reached and the barrier is entered. If local completion has been reached, the process checks the advancement of the termination detection barrier before each theft.

3 Related Work

Static load balancing approaches compute a balancing strategy before computation. These approaches do not apply to unpredictable workloads, and are subject to system noise at scale.

Dynamic load balancing redistribute workload during computation [8,20]. It is a well studied topic and an important part of task-based runtime systems, which can use both workload-specific and platform-specific information to provide portable scheduling performance.

Maintaining a centralized knowledge of the load has a limited scalability and entails an uneven usage of network leading to contention [2]. Hierarchical approaches [2,14] alleviate this issue by distributing the load balancing responsibility across a hierarchy of master processes. By contrast, work-stealing is a decentralized scheduling algorithm which principles are theoretically sound and have been well studied for shared memory execution models [8,21]. Cilk [8], X-Kaapi [9], and Intel TBB [13] are a few examples which all feature work-stealing.

Many approaches for distributed memory systems using work-stealing have been proposed [7,15,17,20]. They perform very well at spreading work across a large distributed memory system, but do not address pair initialization overheads. They rely on hybrid programming using threads, alleviating the issue, or have been tested with limited scalability or on very specific use cases such as the GRAPH500 BFS [3] or UTS [18] in which tasks do not produce individual results.

Charm++ [1] supports a variety of dynamic scheduling policies, and allows for the composition of tuned *ad-hoc* solutions, making each solution designed with specific heuristic for a given application.

ADLB [14] or YALES2 introduce a hierarchy of basic working actors (threads and/or processes) and scheduling decision makers. Such hierarchical work-sharing is the most efficient approach in use in large scale HPC applications today. However, these approaches approaches may yield uneven resource usage, over-synchronization (jitter on the higher level of the hierarchy impacts overall performance), and require careful tuning and adaptation at large scale [14].

In this paper, we present a general-purpose non-hierarchical scalable approach to load-balancing that spreads the scheduling overhead and related network usage among the distributed system. Our algorithm uses a scalable overlay network to constrain the victim selection with interesting properties discussed in Sect. 4.

4 Work-Stealing on Smallworld Graph

In this section we discuss how Kleinberg's small-world graphs [11] are a good candidate for our constrained work-stealing algorithm.

They are built on top of a regular spanning lattice, *e.g.* a two-dimensional grid, that defines $D(u, v)$ as the lattice distance between any two nodes (u, v) in the system. Random edges are added to the spanning lattice and called shortcuts, resulting in interestingly low diameter graphs. Figure 1a shows an example of such graph.

Graph generation time and memory overhead is $O(d * |V|)$ as long as $d << |V|$. The graph representation can be scattered across processes, resulting in memory overhead of $O(d)$ per process.

Using such a graph $G = \{V, E\}$ to constrain victim selection in a work stealing protocol allows to connect a large number of nodes using a low and constant number of connections for each process: the degree d of the graph.

J. Kleinberg shows that G has a small diameter, $\delta = O(\log_d(|V|))$, with high probability. In other terms, it exists with high probability a path of length at most $\log_d(|V|)$ between any pair of nodes. Intuitively, this property allows work to spread efficiently in the graph.

4.1 Work Spreading

Work Reachability Criterion. Consider a worker u and a thief v at a distance Δ. The minimum number of thefts required for the worker's tasks to reach the thief is Δ. Assuming that a proportion p of the remote tasks are stolen at each successful theft, the minimum number of available tasks on u for at least one task to reach v is $O(p^{\Delta})$.

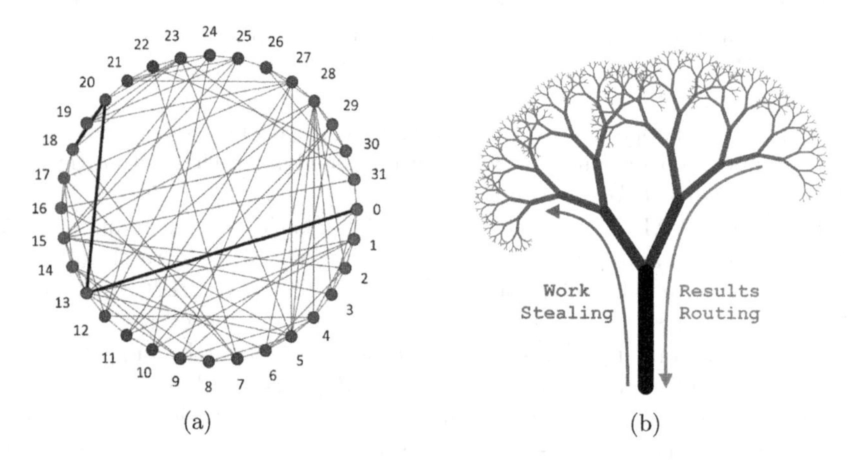

Fig. 1. (a) Example of small world graph and the generated route from node 0 to node 18 (b) Illustration of work fragmentation and results coarsening

In particular, if one worker owns all the tasks W, ensuring that all processes may participate in the computation requires that the amount of parallel tasks is at least $Wp^{\Delta} > 1 \Leftrightarrow \Delta < \log_{p^{-1}} W$.

To cope with workloads polynomial in the size of the system, $W = O(|V|^{\alpha})$ with $\alpha > 1$, a suitable overlay network must have low diameter $\Delta = O(\log |V|)$ which is satisfied.

Resilience to Jitter. The work-stealing algorithm allows spreading work through disjoint path in parallel without synchronization. J. Kleinberg shows that multiple short paths exist in such a small-world graph [12]. As such, while an homogeneous random source of jitter impacts the efficiency of a number of thefts, it is unlikely to globally slow down the work spreading process.

Data Locality. Kleinberg's graphs are randomly generated graphs built on top of a notion of distance which can be mapped to the actual hardware network topology. They are more heavily clustered than simple random graphs because of a bias toward short-length connections in the system, providing optimal route length for a simple routing strategy presented in section.

Perarnau and Sato [19] observe that given latency estimates, using a similar bias when selecting a victim for a theft promotes low-latency thefts and obtain significant performance gains.

In the experiments presented in Sect. 5, the small-world graph is built on top of the 1-dimension lattice formed by the MPI rank numbering. Assuming that the rank numbering, often based on *hwloc* [6], takes into account the physical distance in the network, a higher distance in terms of this lattice distance is likely to correspond to an equivalent or higher communication latency.

4.2 Results Routing and Coarsening

At each routing step the message is forwarded to the closest neighbor - in terms of lattice distance - to its destination [11]. J. Kleinberg shows that routes are found shortest when the probability for two nodes u, v to be connected by a shortcut is proportional to $D(u, v)^{-p}$, with p the dimension of the lattice. Figure 1a shows an example of routing. We measured that our implementation of this strategy finds routes through a 10000 nodes 64-regular random small-world graph with an average of 2.87 jumps, with maximum length of 6, over a million of random source-destination tuples.

After each theft, work is fragmented in two chunks. After computing, each chunk's resulting data has to be routed back to their owner. This effect is represented graphically in Fig. 1b. In order to mitigate congestion due to the sheer amount of routed chunks, we leverage the following routing properties:

- Whenever any two sets of resulting data belonging to the same owner are routed to the same node, they will be routed through the same nodes for the remainder of their routes.
- As sets of results from the same owner get closer to their destination, the probability to be routed to the same nodes increase.

Our results routing protocol aggregates buffered results chunks by next hop in route. As a consequence, the number of communications is asymptotically smaller than the number of chunks to route (i.e. the number of successful theft performed to balance load).

4.3 Memory and Communication Management

We use GASPI [10], an explicit Partitioned Global Address Space - PGAS - approach: accesses to remote memory locations are issued through traditional communication function calls. GASPI communication phases can occur in a traditional MPI program. It offers fine grained one-sided communication and a notification mechanism, allowing a truly asynchronous implementation.

Each process allocates dedicated memory segments which can be remotely accessed through read, write, atomic, and collective operations. A worker's set of shared tasks is stored in the *TASK* segment. A *TMP* segment receives task resulting data as they are computed. The *RESULTS* segment receives results chunks as they are routed and implements a simple lock-based remote memory reservation protocol. Metadata are stored on each segment in order to implement the related functionalities.

The set of private tasks is stored in a private memory buffer. Tasks are executed last-to-first, and balancing the sets of private and shared tasks is a local memory copy. Accessing the *TASK* segment of a given process requires obtaining a lock through a remote atomic compare and swap operation. If such a lock attempt succeeds, the thief performs two remote read operations. The first read operation acquires metadata information. Then, using this information the remote set of shared tasks is copied to the local *TASK* segment. The lock ownership on the remote *TASK* segment is then transfered to the victim. Workers check the state of the *TASK* segment between the execution of tasks, if a theft occurred and the lock ownership has been transfered, the set of shared tasks is empty and all data have been copied. half the set of local private tasks is then moved to the *TASK* segment, metadata are updated, and the lock is released. In Sect. 6.1, we provide hints for refining this strategy.

5 Use Cases and Experiments

We ran experiments on the Myria cluster at CRIANN, a Tier-2 computing center. Each compute node has 28 Intel Broadwell Xeon cores. Nodes are connected with Intel Omni-Path. We run on a maximum of 3584 cores on 128 compute nodes.

Pair Initialization Connection. In the presented experiments, we generate small world graphs with an average degree of $4log_2(|V|)$. It is an arbitrary choice - among those which satisfy $d << |V|$ - which implications at scale should be investigated further. We establish all connections allowed by the small-world overlay network and measure a 18 s of pair connection time at 3584 cores. This does not represent a significant overhead for typical HPC applications. This pair connection time is excluded from the presented performance.

5.1 DLB_Bench: A Synthetic Proto-Benchmark

We introduce DLB_bench, a dynamic load balancing benchmark that allows us to assess the performance of our scheduler against arbitrarily challenging initial work distribution. In this paper, we spread 70% of the tasks among 10% of processes (Fig. 2) following a gaussian distribution.

Due to our small-world overlay network, some processes are not connected to any work owner and most resulting data have to be routed to a small and clustered set of ranks.

Table 1 presents the various workload profiles considered in this study.

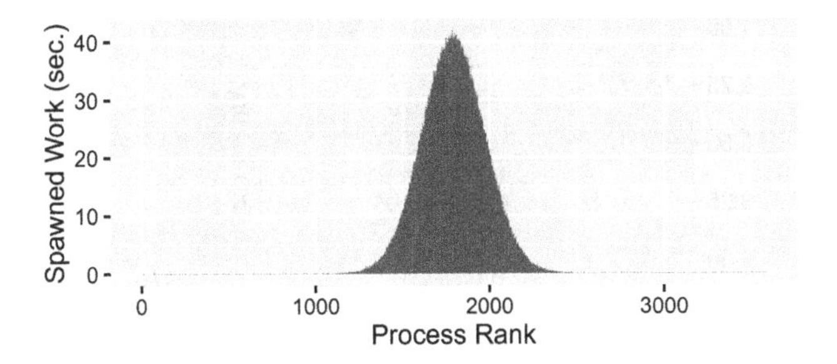

Fig. 2. DLB_Bench: workload distribution

Table 1. DLB_Bench: workload profiles

Average work per process	Average problem size per process	Tasks per process	Shared task segment size	Cycle/byte
10 s	4, 16, 32 MB	2 k, 8 k, 16 k	2, 8, 16 MB	750, 3 k, 6 k
5 s	2, 8, 16, 32 MB	1 k, 4 k, 8 k 16 k	1, 4, 8, 16 MB	375, 1.5 k, 3 k, 6 k
1 s	1, 4, 8, 16 MB	500, 2 k, 4 k, 8 k	0.5, 2, 4, 8 MB	150, 600, 1.2 k, 2.4 k

Workloads and Efficiency. Table 1 presents the workloads simulated using DLB_Bench. It is a weak-scaling experiment: overall problem size and overall work duration scales with the number of cores. Per process values are given and are referred to using average work (W/n) and problem size per process (S/n). We measure the efficiency of our load-balancer for each of the 11 selected workload profiles up to 3584 cores, and present the performance of the median execution - in terms of parallel efficiency - out of 5 repetitions. We did not observe significant performance variability for workload profiles where work per process is 5 and 10 s.

Figure 3 presents the parallel efficiency for the simulated workload characteristics of Table 1.

Down to 5 s of average work per core, our load balancing strategy generally shows high efficiency. As expected, a performance loss appears with low arithmetic intensity problems due to data transfer time overhead. When scheduling 1 s of average parallel work, the scheduling overhead becomes significant. To achieve more than 75% parallel efficiency on the studied workloads up to 3584 processes, we observe that the presented implementation requires both more than 1 s of execution time and a minimum of about 400 cycles per byte arithmetic intensity. Further investigation, which we do not present in details due to lack of space, suggest that these figures can be improves by suggestions presented in Sect. 6.1.

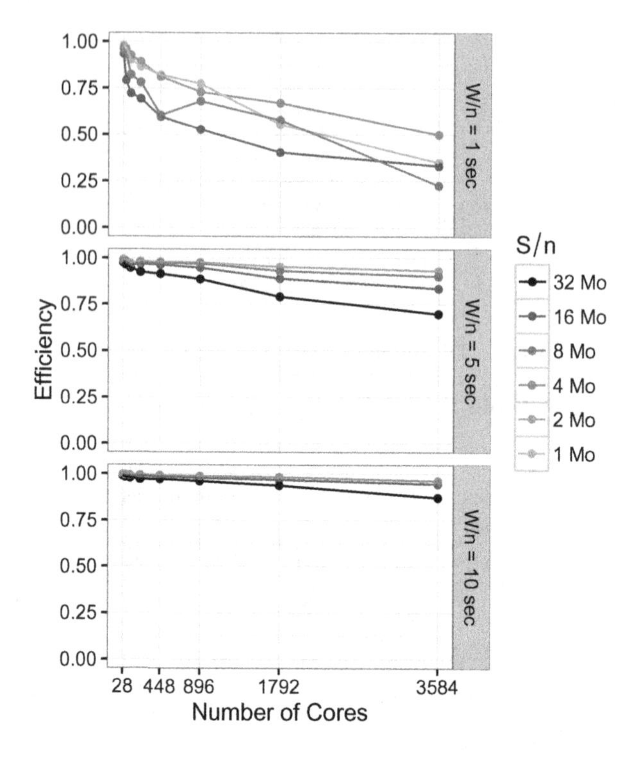

Fig. 3. DLB_Bench weak scaling efficiency

5.2 YALES2 Multi-physics Solver

YALES2 is a scalable multi-physics solver for HPC developed at CORIA. The code features many different solvers, collaborations with several academic laboratories and industrial partners, and it is used to solve large scale HPC problems in industrial companies such as SAFRAN, SOLVAY or ADWEN. It aims at modeling reactive flows in complex burners from primary atomization of the liquid fuel up to pollutant production. Detailed chemistry, in which tens of species are transported and react with each other, has gained a lot of interest due to the enabling available computational power. However, combustion is a localized and dynamic phenomenon that occurs in thin reaction zones at the sub-millimeter scale. Integrating the stiff chemical reactions requires few data and incurs high arithmetic intensity in the reaction zones, entailing an unbalanced workload.

YALES2 features a scalable *ad-hoc* task-based hierarchical work-sharing scheduler. Processes are attributed to a group using workload estimation based on previous iterations in order to provide approximated inter-group load balancing. However, the quality of this approximation drops at high number of cores and for very dynamic use-cases where reaction zones prediction is hard. At group level, processes operate a round-robin master/slave scheduling policy: masters distribute their work to their group and pass on the master token.

Table 2. Preccinsta: Workload profiles at 3584 cores

Mesh size	Average work per core range over 10 iterations	Problem size per core	Tasks per core	Shared tasks segment size	Average cycle/byte
14 M	0.15–0.23 s	0.28 MB	655	448 KB	1484
110 M	0.47–0.65 s	2.2 MB	5171	448 KB	550

Despite its high scalability, it does not satisfy the *work-first principle* [8]: workers pro-actively distribute their work among processes in their group and communication volume scales proportionally to the amount of work for any workload profile and imbalance.

We interfaced our approach in place of this built-in load-balancer, allowing us to test and evaluate our strategy in a real-life application at large scale, and demonstrate its efficiency empirically.

Workload. Figure 4 presents a typical workload distribution of an iteration of the studied experiment. Compared to the DLB_Bench workload presented in Fig. 2, work is less imbalanced, and initial task owners are distributed more evenly across the system. While the number of tasks spawned on each process is roughly the same and all the tasks carry the same amount of input data, the source of the imbalance is the unpredictability of each task's execution time.

Table 2 shows the main characteristics of scheduled workload. There is little variation in the amount of work and relative imbalance from one iteration to another.

Experimental Results. Figure 5 presents the performance of TITUS_DLB compared to the original load balancing strategy implemented in Yales2. Starting with a 14 million elements mesh, we refine the mesh in order to obtain a 110 millions elements test case. The total amount of work scales with the number of elements. Using these two use cases, we perform a strong scaling experiment up to 3584 cores. We run the first 10 time step iterations of the simulation, and measure the time spent in the chemistry simulation phase. In order to exclude

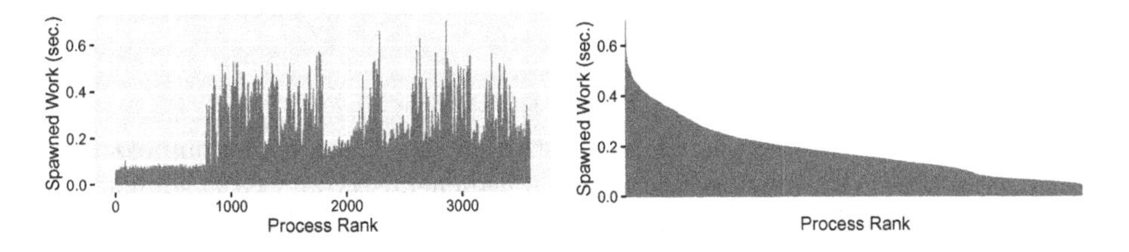

Fig. 4. Preccinsta: work distribution (Sorted)

pair initialization time for the original scheduler, we exclude the first iteration from these results. We compute parallel efficiency and speedup over the original scheduler from the sum of these times for the other 9 iterations.

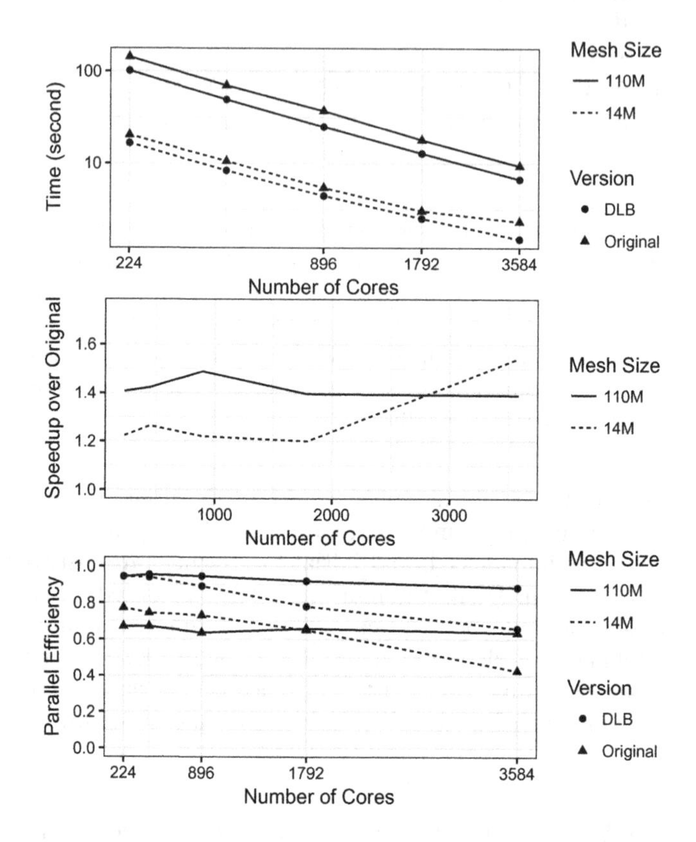

Fig. 5. Compared strong scaling performances of TITUS_DLB against Yales2's built-in dynamic scheduler for two mesh sizes

In all tested configurations, TITUS_DLB outperforms the original dynamic scheduler significantly, and up to 54% at 3584 core. The best efficiency achieved by the built-in dynamic scheduler on 3584 cores is 65% on the 110 M element case. TITUS_DLB achieves 88% efficiency, speeding up execution by 39%.

6 Conclusion

We propose a dynamic load-balancing strategy for large scale computations which we successfully demonstrate on a coupled chemistry and CFD simulation.

The small-world based communication pattern we introduce allows an efficient implementation of the work-stealing algorithm for large scale distributed computations.

The TITUS_DLB Library and DLB_Bench are released under open-source LGPL3.0 license at https://github.com/EXAPARS/TITUS.

6.1 Future Work

We are interested in developing an analytical model to provide a theoretical analysis of the presented approach.

We intend to extend the scope of the presented approach by allowing tasks to be spawned dynamically, providing support for a wider variety of problems, such as dynamic tasks decomposition and fork-join parallelism, allowing us to compare the performance of the proposed approach to existing dynamic task scheduling strategies through usually adopted benchmarks such as UTC and BFS.

The development of DLB_Bench gives us the opportunity to study and compare the performance of existing approaches in various configurations, which may be included in future publications.

Moreover, we plan to optimize our implementation to use shared-memory communication for intra-node communications and explore various algorithmic improvement. Some shared work-queue and associated work stealing protocol may provide lock-free algorithms as well as not require the victim to take action in between thefts. Small-world generation and victim selection strategies may take more finely data locality into account in the form of expected or average latency. Lock-free memory allocators can be found in the literature [16], which may be adapted to our results returning strategy, further alleviating contention at scale. Finally, in [4], Berenbrink *et al.* show that a number of theft policies are viable in the classical work-stealing scheme, which may be explored in this context.

Acknowledgment. This work has been funded by the European FP7 Exa2ct project, ATOS, and the ECR lab, a collaboration between CEA, UVSQ, and Intel. The authors thank the GASPI and GPI-2 development team for their very good support and advice. The authors also thank CRIANN, IT4I and BSC for the compute resources and assistance.

References

1. Acun, B., et al.: Parallel programming with migratable objects: Charm++ in practice. In: Proceedings of the International Conference for High Performance Computing, Networking, Storage and Analysis, pp. 647–658. IEEE Press (2014)
2. Augonnet, C., Thibault, S., Namyst, R., Wacrenier, P.A.: StarPU: a unified platform for task scheduling on heterogeneous multicore architectures. Concurr. Comput. Pract. Exp. **23**(2), 187–198 (2011)
3. Bader, D.: Designing scalable synthetic compact applications for benchmarking high productivity computing systems. Cyberinfrastructure Technol. Watch. **2**, 1–10 (2006)
4. Berenbrink, P., Friedetzky, T., Goldberg, L.A.: The natural work-stealing algorithm is stable. SIAM J. Comput. **32**(5), 1260–1279 (2003)

5. Blumofe, R.D., Leiserson, C.E.: Scheduling multithreaded computations by work stealing. J. ACM (JACM) **46**(5), 720–748 (1999)
6. Broquedis, F., et al.: hwloc: a generic framework for managing hardware affinities in HPC applications. In: 2010 18th Euromicro International Conference on Parallel, Distributed and Network-Based Processing (PDP), pp. 180–186. IEEE (2010)
7. Dinan, J., Larkins, D.B., Sadayappan, P., Krishnamoorthy, S., Nieplocha, J.: Scalable work stealing. In: Proceedings of the Conference on High Performance Computing Networking, Storage and Analysis, p. 53. ACM (2009)
8. Frigo, M., Leiserson, C.E., Randall, K.H.: The implementation of the Cilk-5 multithreaded language. In: ACM Sigplan Notices, vol. 33, pp. 212–223. ACM (1998)
9. Gautier, T., Lima, J.V., Maillard, N., Raffin, B.: Xkaapi: a runtime system for data-flow task programming on heterogeneous architectures. In: 2013 IEEE 27th International Symposium on Parallel & Distributed Processing (IPDPS), pp. 1299–1308. IEEE (2013)
10. Grünewald, D., Simmendinger, C.: The GASPI API specification and its implementation GPI 2.0. In: 7th International Conference on PGAS Programming Models, vol. 243 (2013)
11. Kleinberg, J.: The small-world phenomenon: an algorithmic perspective. In: Proceedings of the Thirty-Second Annual ACM Symposium on Theory of Computing, pp. 163–170 (2000)
12. Kleinberg, J., Rubinfeld, R.: Short paths in expander graphs. In: Proceedings of the 37th Annual Symposium on Foundations of Computer Science, pp. 86–95. IEEE (1996)
13. Kukanov, A., Voss, M.J.: The foundations for scalable multi-core software in Intel Threading Building Blocks. Intel Technol. J. **11**(4), 309–322 (2007)
14. Lusk, E.L., Pieper, S.C., Butler, R.M., et al.: More scalability, less pain: a simple programming model and its implementation for extreme computing. SciDAC Rev. **17**(1), 30–37 (2010)
15. Machado, R., Lojewski, C., Abreu, S., Pfreundt, F.J.: Unbalanced tree search on a manycore system using the GPI programming model. Comput. Sci. Res. Dev. **26**, 229–236 (2011)
16. Michael, M.M.: Scalable lock-free dynamic memory allocation. ACM Sigplan Not. **39**(6), 35–46 (2004)
17. Min, S.J., Iancu, C., Yelick, K.: Hierarchical work stealing on manycore clusters. In: 5th Conference on Partitioned Global Address Space programming Models (2011)
18. Olivier, S., et al.: UTS: an unbalanced tree search benchmark. In: Almási, G., Caşcaval, C., Wu, P. (eds.) LCPC 2006. LNCS, vol. 4382, pp. 235–250. Springer, Heidelberg (2007). https://doi.org/10.1007/978-3-540-72521-3_18
19. Perarnau, S., Sato, M.: Victim selection and distributed work stealing performance: a case study. In: Parallel and Distributed Processing Symposium, vol. 28. IEEE (2014)
20. Quintin, J.-N., Wagner, F.: Hierarchical work-stealing. In: D'Ambra, P., Guarracino, M., Talia, D. (eds.) Euro-Par 2010. LNCS, vol. 6271, pp. 217–229. Springer, Heidelberg (2010). https://doi.org/10.1007/978-3-642-15277-1_21
21. Tchiboukdjian, M., Gast, N., Trystram, D., Roch, J.L., Bernard, J.: A Tighter Analysis of Work Stealing. Angorithms and Computation, pp. 291–302 (2010)
22. Woodall, T.S., Shipman, G.M., Bosilca, G., Graham, R.L., Maccabe, A.B.: High performance RDMA protocols in HPC. In: Mohr, B., Träff, J.L., Worringen, J., Dongarra, J. (eds.) EuroPVM/MPI 2006. LNCS, vol. 4192, pp. 76–85. Springer, Heidelberg (2006). https://doi.org/10.1007/11846802_18

NUMAPROF, A NUMA Memory Profiler

Sébastien Valat[1(✉)] and Othman Bouizi[2(✉)]

[1] CERN, Meyrin, Switzerland
sebastien.valat@cern.ch
[2] INTEL, Meudon, France
othman.bouizi@intel.com

Abstract. The number of cores in HPC systems and servers increased a lot for the last few years. In order to also increase the available memory bandwidth and capacity, most systems became NUMA (Non-Uniform Memory Access) meaning each processor has its own memory and can share it. Although the access to the remote memory is transparent for the developer, it comes with a lower bandwidth and a higher latency. It might heavily impact the performance of the application if it happens too often. Handling this memory locality in multi-threaded applications is a challenging task. In order to help the developer, we developed NUMAPROF, a memory profiling tool pinpointing the local and remote memory accesses onto the source code with the same approach as MALT, a memory allocation profiling tool. The paper offers a full review of the capacity of NUMAPROF on mainstream HPC workloads. In addition to the dedicated interface, the tool also provides hints about unpinned memory accesses (unpinned thread or unpinned page) which can help the developer find portion of codes not safely handling the NUMA binding. The tool also provides dedicated metrics to track access to MCDRAM of the Intel Xeon Phi codenamed Knight's Landing. To operate, the tool instruments the application by using Pin, a parallel binary instrumentation framework from Intel. NUMAPROF also has the particularity of using the OS memory mapping without relying on hardware counters or OS simulation. It permits understanding what really happened on the system without requiring dedicated hardware support.

Keywords: NUMA · Memory · Profiler · Instrumentation · Pin Access · Remote · MCDRAM · KNL

1 Introduction

In the late 2000s, the number of cores in servers and HPC systems increased a lot, with commonly at least two CPUs per server. There is now up to 72 cores in one CPU if we consider the up-to-date Intel® Xeon Phi™ codenamed Knight's Landing (KNL). In order to avoid hitting the memory wall [17], most of the current architectures became NUMA (Non-Uniform Memory Access) meaning

G. Mencagli et al. (Eds.): Euro-Par 2018 Workshops, LNCS 11339, pp. 159–170, 2019.
https://doi.org/10.1007/978-3-030-10549-5_13

that each processor has its own memory. This way we can easily increase the memory bandwidth of the system to feed the cores. This architecture now applies inside the socket itself like for the Intel KNL which can be configured to run as up to 4 NUMA domains or looking at some AMD® processors (*e.g.* Ryzen™ 1950X).

Nowadays, all the commonly available NUMA architectures are ccNUMA (Cache Coherent NUMA) meaning that the synchronization between the NUMA domains is automatically handled by the architecture without requiring any intervention from the developer. This is certainly one of the reasons for the wide adoption of this kind of architecture as all existing programs can run out of the box on them. Even if it is simple to make an application running on NUMA machines, it is hard to extract the full performance of the machine because of the data remote access costs.

There are now some studies about using OpenMP on multiple NUMA domains [15], some are also explicitly tuning the OpenMP runtime for this usage [5]. Using multi-threaded applications over NUMA domains fully rely on the developer to well place the data in memory to efficiently exploit the architecture and ideally limit the remote memory accesses. Strictly avoiding them is not always a good thing; it is sometimes better to spread the data over multiple NUMA domains to get more memory bandwidth. This is where the knowledge of the developer is needed and the automation becomes limited.

As we will show in the next section, on most of the operating systems, the semantic to set up the memory placement is by default implicit. It relies on the first touch policy which can lead to many mistakes. Without any profiling tools, the developer must rely on his confidence and on global timings measurement to believe that he made the placement right. This is where we present the NUMAPROF tool. It provides a profiling backend associated with a graphical interface annotating the source code with various metrics. Such a tool can also be useful for developers working on NUMA-aware runtimes like MPC [10].

Section 2 will first look on the related work by listing the available NUMA profiling tools. Section 3 will contrast our contribution. As our tool mainly targets the Linux operating system we will describe the available API in Sect. 4. Section 5 will provide the technical details about NUMAPROF. We will lastly provide an analysis example by using NUMAPROF on an application and show some findings.

2 Related Work

Some NUMA profiling tools already exist and we can find several papers on this topic. We first found NUMATOP [19] which is the "simplest" one. It is an application similar to `top` which counts the number of local and remote accesses of all running applications and displays the result into the terminal. The tool relies on hardware counters to determine the local and remote accesses. It is interesting for looking for the processes placement when running multiple applications on the same node and check their binding. As a limitation, it does not provide any details on the source of the remote accesses inside the application.

SNPERF [11] provides charts with memory accesses on each NUMA domain over time within a given process. It relies on hardware counters of the Origin 2000™ architecture. This is useful to check if the memory bandwidth is balanced over the nodes. This tool is not available on the web and is hardware dependent on an uncommon architecture.

Memphis [9] is a tool making deep instrumentation using AMD Opteron™ hardware counters. It uses event sampling to report the domain access count onto source code lines. For this property, it looks like what we want. But it is now unavailable and its code is dependent on a specific old hardware. From the paper it also looks not providing a graphical interface to exploit the profiles it generates.

For another approach, there is MemProf [7] which, this time, focuses on access patterns. The tool tracks each thread memory access flow by using a kernel module and tracking threads binding to detect specific bad patterns in the application. Again, it relies on specific hardware feature from AMD®: Instruction Based Sampling (IBS) [6].

One can think about a tool based on Valgrind [13] and we can find such a tool: NUMAgrind [18]. This time, the tool is based on an architecture simulation, so, not relying on specific hardware counters. It simulates all the cache details and also the page affinity. This approach is interesting because it allows simulating any kind of architecture with the drawback of neglecting the effective operating system memory mappings. Last, it relies on Valgrind which does not allow to run threads in parallel, making the overhead really big for a large number of cores. This is an issue to simulate something on the KNL, for example. The tool is not available any more on the Internet.

Still looking for hardware simulation we can also find SIMT [14] which fully simulates the architecture details. This tool simulates the interconnect protocol and can be used for architecture design but can also give some hints about applications on those architectures.

Lastly, we found HPCToolkit [8] which is really close to what we want to provide with NUMAPROF and is also open source. It uses hardware counters and events sampling to track the application. It then provides a nice reporting by annotating the source code and the call stacks in a graphical interface. Interestingly, it provides all the usage information of a variable in one go: allocation site, first touch site and all access site. It also provides a summary of the access pattern over threads so the developer can look at how the memory accesses are distributed and might find some reordering or packing to improve data locality. This is something we do not have in NUMAPROF. Due to its usage of hardware counters it has a low overhead but becomes dependent on specific hardware. It has the advantage of providing a kind of cost estimation due to the sampling approach which is something we do not yet have in NUMAPROF. The NUMA part of the tool described in the paper is not available in the public release.

Really close to our approach for the backend implementation we also found Tabarnac [4] which also instrument the memory accesses. It then generate a static web page as output with limited charts.

We finally took inspiration and codes from MALT [16], a malloc tracker, for its web-based interface providing global metrics and source annotation. Web GUI are interesting as it can be easily forwarded via the ssh-port forward, avoiding the latency of rendering when forwarding a full X application. It also helps to quickly implement the interface and open possibility to work with multiple people connected onto the same interface.

3 Contribution

Looking on the available tool we notice a few things. Many of them rely on dedicated hardware counters which make them quickly outdated and not being able to be used on up-to-date architectures. This way, they also, most of the time, rely on sampling which might miss some details of the code.

On the other side we have tools working on hardware emulation which is nice as allowing simulation of any kind of hardware on our workstation. But it has the disadvantage to miss the real memory mapping built by the operating system we run on. Also a lot of them are not yet/anymore available.

Last, all the listed tools, except HPCToolkit and Tabarnac (non interactive), provide raw text output which might be hard to interpret. To be useful, the tool needs to come up with an attractive graphical interface annotating the source code with the extracted metrics.

In order to overcome these issues, we want to build NUMAPROF following those rules:

- We do not rely on hardware counters.
- We keep track of the real mapping of the operating system.
- We must run in parallel.
- We provide a graphical interface to look on the profile annotating the code lines.
- We want to make it Open-Source to be available to the community, available at [3].

With NUMAPROF we allow checking what the operating system does for the mapping. This can be useful to validate codes but also runtimes which are supposed to help handling multithreading. Being independent on hardware counters ensure a better support over time by not being dependent on a specific architecture. On this aspect we also provide dedicated efforts on handling the huge pages semantic when considering the first touch measurements which is explicitly handled by none of the listed tools.

Although we could have used Valgrind to make the binary instrumentation, it would lead to large overhead when running on nodes like the Intel KNL handling up to 288 threads. Hence, we proceed by using Pin [12]. This tool does an on-the-fly binary instrumentation providing services very similar to Valgrind but with multi-threading support and being a little bit faster. It is also easy to use, just as Valgrind, wrapping the command line we want to run and making an on the fly instrumentation. NUMAPROF instruments all the memory accesses and check the NUMA distance of each access to build the profile.

In addition to the local and remote metric, the tool also adds a new metric: unpinned. This permit to track cases where the running thread is not bound to a specific domain and making "random" accesses generating "random" placement of the memory. Compared to other tools we also searched to provide information on the source lines making the first touch. Hence, we pinpoint the source of the remote accesses. Lastly, we also provide access counter on memory allocation site to detect which allocated chunks lead to incorrect accesses.

The tool also provide dedicated metrics to handle the case of the MCDRAM from Intel Knight-Landing helping profiling on this architecture.

Our tool currently does not provide caches simulation so we report raw accesses not considering cache effects. This might be done in a second step to get more meaningful metrics when considering spin locks which in practice stay in the cache not generating effective remote accesses (eg. in the OpenMP runtime).

4 NUMA Linux API

This section will describe the Linux NUMA API to understand what we want to observe and which operations we need to intercept to track the NUMA state of the application.

We first remember that most operating systems allocate a virtual segment when an application makes a big allocation. It then fills it, on the fly, with physical pages when the application starts to really access it. This is called the first touch policy. Operating systems like Linux decide during this first access which NUMA page to map, by default by looking at the current thread location. This way the operating system tries to automatically fit the data accesses by considering the memory usage will later be done in the same way. This approach is nice but leads in some ways to problems because it is implicit and many non-expert developers might not know what they are really doing. We will show that our tool is specifically tuned to track those problems.

Hopefully, the user can change the first touch policy of a segment by using the `membind` system call. It setups a strict binding (`MPOL_BIND`) of a segment to a specific NUMA domain or forces page interleaving (`MPOL_INTERLEAVE`). It can lastly set a preferred domain (`MPOL_PREFERRED`) which will be chosen and neglected if there is no free pages any more on this domain. This `membind` call is specific to Linux. In last resort, the user can also provide a detailed mapping by using the `move_pages` system call providing the mapping for each page of the targeted segment.

By default, the threads are spawned randomly on a core and can move depending on decisions from the operating system scheduler. But, as the memory is linked to the process, the OS has no knowledge of the link between data and threads. When a thread moves to another NUMA domain, there is no information permitting to also move the related data. The only available real solution is to bind the threads on a specific core, to place the data accordingly and keep this state for the whole execution.

This thread mapping can be handled via the `sched_setaffinity` system call which is also not POSIX. This call takes a mask as parameters to allow the thread to run on the given cores (or CPU threads if using hyper-threading). This mapping is automatically done when the user sets the `OMP_PROC_BIND` environment variable for OpenMP.

The user can also handle the thread and memory binding by selecting its behaviour through the command wrapper `numactl`.

Again, we see with this interface that nothing links the threads to the data so the placement policy is implicit meaning that nothing prevents the user from mistakes and nothing can notify the user if he does the thing wrong. This is where tools like NUMAPROF can be useful. Also, all the aforementioned interfaces are Linux dependent so our tool will target only this operating system.

5 Implementation Details

This section will give details about the NUMAPROF implementation going from the backend up to the graphical interface.

5.1 Metrics

As many other tools, NUMAPROF provides the local/remote access metric. But it also track the unpinned accesses, meaning the thread is not bound to a specific NUMA domain and can move on other nodes. It also tracks if a page has been first-touched by such a thread, meaning the page is "randomly" placed on the machine generating later random accesses.

NUMAPROF also finds the code location where the page placement was made, which happened at the first touch. Lastly, it counts the access metrics on the allocation site, meaning we can quickly know which allocated segments are concerned by remote memory accesses.

To summarize, we provide the listed metric for each access call site and allocation site:

first-touch. Counts the number of first touch on the given location.
unpinned first-touch. Counts the number of unpinned first touch on the given location.
local. Counts the local memory accesses when the thread is on the same NUMA domain as the page.
remote. Counts the remote memory accesses when the thread is on a different NUMA domain than the page.
unpinned-page. Counts the cases of a thread bound to a NUMA domain but the page is not.
unpinned-thread. Counts the cases of a thread not bound accessing a bound page.
unpinned-both. Counts the cases of a non-bound thread accessing a non bound page.

MCDRAM. Counts accesses to local MCDRAM memory. MCDRAM is considered when the accessed NUMA domain has no cores.

MCDRAM has two sub-counters which are local and remote to consider the case of the KNL which can be configured with 4 NUMA domains each having its local MCDRAM.

5.2 Thread Tracking

In order to build our metrics we first need to track the thread placement. For this, we need to check the thread location at spawning time. Thanks to Pin we can intercept the spawning of a thread and place our handler on it. From there we extract the thread binding by using the `sched_getaffinity` system call. From the cores/threads affinity, we extract the NUMA affinity of the thread and keep track of this state. A thread which can move onto more than one NUMA domain will be considered as unpinned. If the thread is not bound, we pursue without needing to check on every access where he is running to determine the local or remote memory access. We just track its memory accesses as unpinned.

We lastly need to track the thread movement if there are changes during the run. In the Linux OS this can happen on the call of `sched_setaffinity` which we intercept thanks to Pin. We do not manage a possible change from outside the process. But, in this case there is nothing to do except to provide a function to be called by the user.

Threads can also set up a memory policy (`set_mempolicy`) possibly assigning a remote memory domain to the process. We intercept this policy and consider the thread bound if it is restricted to one domain.

All the thread movement (which are rare) will be logged in the profile so the user can check if it matches his expectation. This is also a new feature from NUMAPROF compared to existing tools.

5.3 Memory Access Tracking

As said, thanks to Pin, we probe all the memory accesses and check if they are remote or local. We already know where the thread is, thanks to the tracking described in the previous section. We now need to know where the page is. On Linux this can be done by using the `move_pages` system call which is normally used to move the pages. If we do not provide a mapping in parameters, the call returns the current location of the pages. Notice we can request a list of pages in one call.

To limit the overhead we cannot make a system call for every memory access so we need to cache the information. As a workaround, we build a shadow page table rebuilding the same structure used in the kernel. Then we can easily detect the first access (first touch) and use the cached value on next accesses. We do not remove entries in this table so we can use it in a lock-free manner having to take locks only when we add new entries in the tree. This permit to maintain scalability.

The page table entries are allocated when intercepting calls to mmap. To track the state of the pages we also need to track calls to munmap (resp. mremap) to flag the related pages as released (resp. to move them). While flagging the page as free, we do not remove the tree structures if empty to keep the algorithm read lock-free.

We also implemented a dedicated support for huge pages. At first touch we request the binding with move_pages for all the pages of the given huge page. If all the pages are available on the same NUMA domain, we consider it is a huge page, so, accounting the first touch only once for the huge page.

One last thing, to improve the performance of the tool we do not probe the local stack memory accesses, as we know they are local. This provides in practice a speedup of a factor 2, greatly reducing the high overhead of the tool.

5.4 Instruction and Allocation Counters

We report the metrics globally, per thread, per call site (instruction) and per allocation site. For the call site, we maintain an std::map indexed by the instruction memory address. This structure is not lock-free so we need to take locks on every access. In order to make the profiler scalable we cache the entries of this tree into each thread. In this way, each thread can quickly update the counters in the cache and then sometimes (when there are too many entries in the cache) flush it into the global tree by taking locks.

For the allocations we again need a way to quickly find in a lock-free manner the pointer to the counters. For this, we extend the shadow page table by making an entry for every eight addressed bytes. This pointer is used to point the corresponding allocation site. We used the same approach as the instruction with a cache in the thread to store local copies of the counters and then flush the cache when it becomes too big. This limits the number of atomic operations. Notice we can up to double the memory consumption by using this approach. To limit this effect we use two storage methods. For allocation fully using a page, we use only one pointer and allocate the list of eight bytes entries only if the page contains small allocations.

To maintain this page table pointers we need to track the call to malloc, free, calloc, realloc...

5.5 Scalability

One can check the scalability of the tool on the Hydro [2] application running on an Intel KNL. The Fig. 1 shows that the tool scales up to 64 threads with an overhead of a factor 27x. There is then a slight increase with an overhead of 60x on 256 threads. In any case this is far better than what we observe with the Valgrind's memcheck tool due to the serialization of the threads.

5.6 Graphical Interface

NUMAPROF takes back the idea from MALT by providing a dynamic web-based interface. It provides global metrics summarizing the application like the

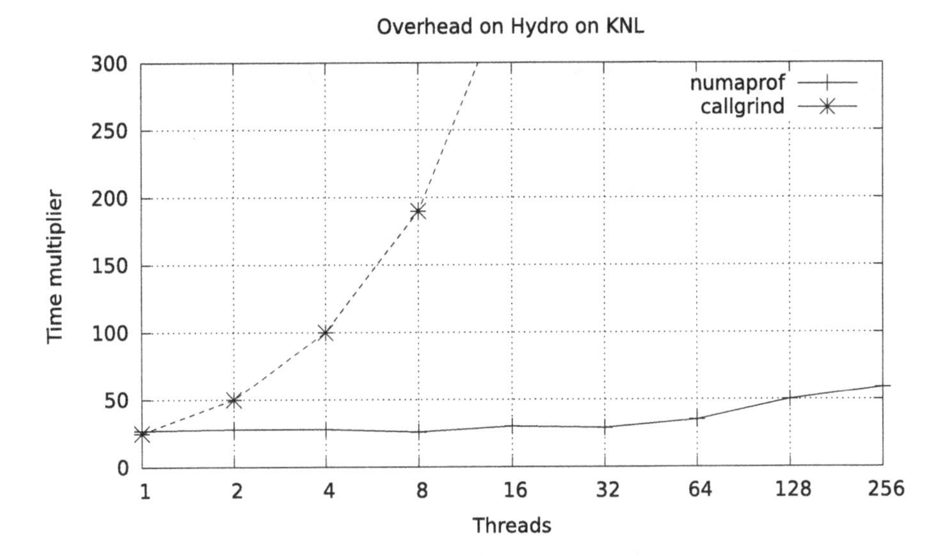

Fig. 1. NUMAPROF and Valgrind overhead on HydroC code on KNL.

global local/remote/unpinned metrics and an access matrix. The access matrix is provided to quickly check if the memory accesses are on the diagonal or form a line pointing intensive accesses to one NUMA domain. Second, the interface provides the per thread metrics to quickly see how the first touch and accesses are balanced. It also provides the pinning log and access matrix for each thread. Finally, and most important feature, the GUI provides annotation of the source code to project the counters onto the source lines as shown in Fig. 2. This is the core part of the tool.

6 Use Case Example: Hydro

We tested the tool onto some applications: AMG2013, HACC, Cloverleaf and it mostly shows that those applications were well optimized making only local memory accesses. On huge pages they showed some remote accesses when the array splitting not to match with 2 MB limits of huge pages but we observed by testing that this does not impact too much the application performance.

We then tested the Hydro [2] application (commit d1303337624) which is less tuned. On this application NUMAPROF observed interesting things. Firstly, in August 2017 we observed that when running the application on an Intel KNL was not allocating memory on the MCDRAM (in FLAT mode) when it should. Searching deeper on the issues pointed a bug form the kernel which ignored the `MPOL_PREFERRED` semantic when the huge pages are enabled. This bug was known by Red Hat [1] and has been fixed end of 2017. Moving to the right policy makes the application going down from 42.8 s to 28.0 s.

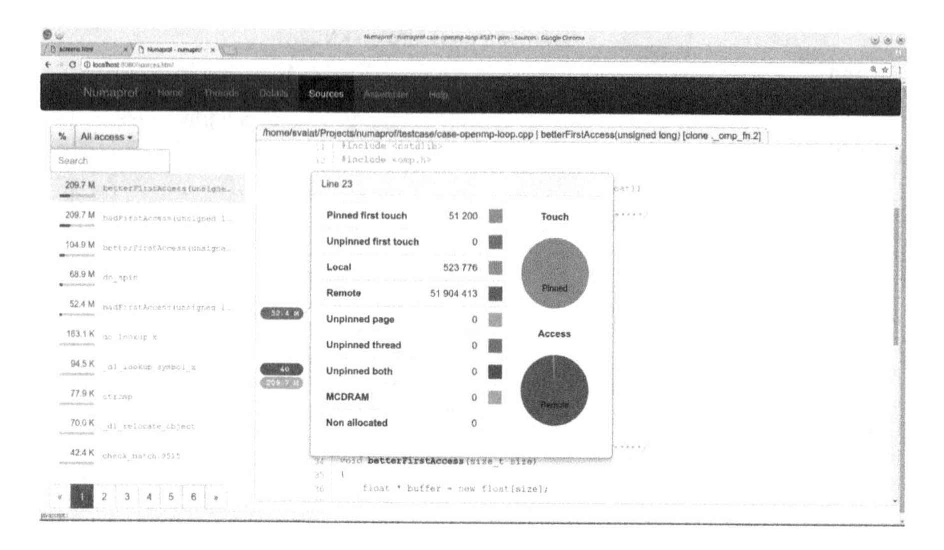

Fig. 2. NUMAPROF graphical interface, source code annotation.

Starting the real analysis, we first looked at the access matrix from Fig. 3 showing a wrong placement of some segments. The test is done on an Intel KNL with MCDRAM activated which explains the two vertical lanes, the second one being MCDRAM accesses. We see that there are issues with the blocs allocated into the main memory but also a mis-distribution of the blocks into the MCDRAM shown by the vertical lines meaning all the threads accessed data on the same NUMA domain.

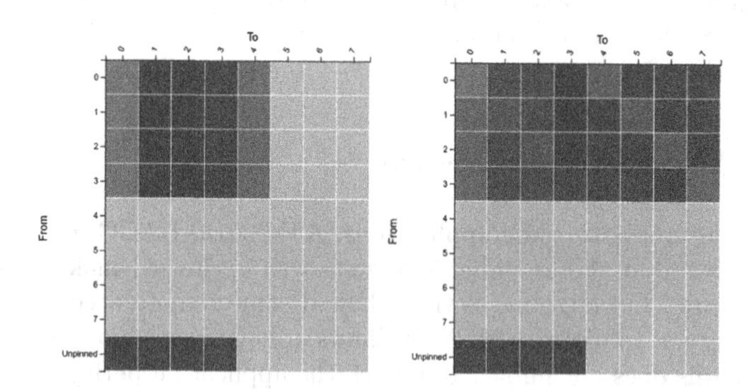

Fig. 3. HydroC access matrix before and after optimisation.

Looking at the annotated sources, we can search for remote memory accesses and more precisely on the related allocation call sites. We first found the allocation of the ThreadBuffers in the `Domain::setTiles` function which is not done in parallel. It maps all the allocated memory onto the first NUMA domain. This can be fixed by adding a `pragma omp parallel` section in place of the loop.

Second, we noticed remote memory accesses onto the Tile objects. Here there is a missing feature of NUMAPROF, we would like to have the call stack. Anyway, reading back the code leads to the call of `Tile::godunov()` which is called from `Domain::computeTimeStep()` in a loop indexed by i. If we look a little bit at the beginning of the loop, we now see that the index i is modified via the `m_mortonIdx` array. This is not done at the allocation time meaning the allocation and access orders mismatched. We can fix this by using the same index indirection in the allocation loop where we make the `new Tile`.

This slightly improves the access matrix making it more diagonal as shown by Fig. 3. This also translates onto performance by lowering the runtime to 22.9 s. This is a time reduction of 18% achieved without knowing the code in advance and by working for half an hour.

The tool still reports remote memory accesses. Most of them come from a spin lock into the OpenMP runtime. The rest mostly comes from access to global floating point constants which are stored in the data section of the binary. In other words, it is a false negative as those constant and spin locks will be in practice stored into the cache if accessed in a loop.

7 Conclusion

We showed the need to NUMA profiling tools and didn't find our wish in the existing ones. Hence, NUMAPROF was built in a simple way on top of the Pin instrumenter which quickly provided a useful tool coming with a nice web-based graphical interface. The source annotation and global metrics like access matrix had been useful to optimize the Hydro application gaining 18% of performance in half an hour without knowing the code before. Notice that the overhead of the tool was 60x on 256 threads.

Of course there is still a lot of work to be done. We mainly consider adding a cache simulator not to report too many memory access which are stored in the cache and do not slow down the application. Also we still have margins to improve the performance of the tool to reduce the overhead by mostly improving the internal caching mechanism and maybe packing the access and flushing them in groups. The tool is flexible enough that adding support of more memory levels like the 3D Xpoint should be easy.

This methodology is not limited to x86 architecture. It can be applied to other architectures by adding support of DynamoRIO [20], which is similar to Pin. As a complement one can also consider using Valgrind.

The tool is available under open source license at http://memtt.github.io/.

References

1. Huge pages and preferred policy kernel bug. https://access.redhat.com/solutions/3155591
2. Hydro. https://github.com/HydroBench/Hydro
3. Numaprof. https://www.github.com/memtt/numaprof

4. Beniamine, D., Diener, M., Huard, G., Navaux, P.O.A.: TABARNAC: Tools for Analyzing Behavior of Applications Running on NUMA Architecture. Research Report 8774, Inria Grenoble Rhône-Alpes, Université de Grenoble, October 2015. https://hal.inria.fr/hal-01202105
5. Clet-Ortega, J., Carribault, P., Pérache, M.: Evaluation of OpenMP task scheduling algorithms for large NUMA architectures. In: Silva, F., Dutra, I., Santos Costa, V. (eds.) Euro-Par 2014. LNCS, vol. 8632, pp. 596–607. Springer, Cham (2014). https://doi.org/10.1007/978-3-319-09873-9_50
6. Drongowski, P.J.: Instruction-based sampling: A new performance analysis technique for amd family 10h processors (2007). http://developer.amd.com/Assets/AMD_IBS_paper_EN.pdf
7. Lachaize, R., Lepers, B., Quema, V.: MemProf: A memory profiler for NUMA multicore systems. In: Presented as Part of the 2012 USENIX Annual Technical Conference (USENIX ATC 12), pp. 53–64. USENIX, Boston, MA (2012)
8. Liu, X., Mellor-Crummey, J.: A tool to analyze the performance of multithreaded programs on NUMA architectures. SIGPLAN Not. **49**(8), 259–272 (2014)
9. McCurdy, C., Vetter, J.: Memphis: Finding and fixing NUMA-related performance problems on multi-core platforms. In: IEEE International Symposium on Performance Analysis of Systems Software (ISPASS), pp. 87–96 (2010)
10. Pérache, M., Jourdren, H., Namyst, R.: MPC: a unified parallel runtime for clusters of NUMA machines. In: Luque, E., Margalef, T., Benítez, D. (eds.) Euro-Par 2008. LNCS, vol. 5168, pp. 78–88. Springer, Heidelberg (2008). https://doi.org/10.1007/978-3-540-85451-7_9
11. Prestor, U.: Evaluating the memory performance of a ccNUMA system. http://www.cs.utah.edu/~uros/snperf/thesis.pdf
12. Roy, A., Hand, S., Harris, T.: Hybrid binary rewriting for memory access instrumentation. SIGPLAN Not. **46**(7), 227–238 (2011)
13. Seward, J., Nethercote, N.: Using valgrind to detect undefined value errors with bit-precision. In: Proceedings of the Annual Conference on USENIX Annual Technical Conference, ATEC 2005, pp. 2–2, USENIX Association, Berkeley, CA, USA (2005)
14. Tao, J., Schulz, M., Karl, W.: A simulation tool for evaluating shared memory systems. In: 36th Annual Simulation Symposium, 2003, pp. 335–342, March 2003
15. Terboven, C., an Mey, D., Schmidl, D., Jin, H., Reichstein, T.: Data and thread affinity in openmp programs. In: Proceedings of the 2008 Workshop on Memory Access on Future Processors: A Solved Problem? MAW 2008, pp. 377–384, ACM, New York, NY, USA (2008)
16. Valat, S., Charif-Rubial, A.S., Jalby, W.: Malt: A malloc tracker. In: Proceedings of the 4th ACM SIGPLAN International Workshop on Software Engineering for Parallel Systems, SEPS 2017, pp. 1–10. ACM, New York, NY, USA (2017)
17. Wulf, W.A., McKee, S.A.: Hitting the memory wall: implications of the obvious. SIGARCH Comput. Archit. News **23**(1), 20–24 (1995)
18. Yang, R., Antony, J., Rendell, A., Robson, D., Strazdins, P.: Profiling directed NUMA optimization on Linux systems: a case study of the GAUSSIAN computational chemistry code. In: IEEE International Parallel Distributed Processing Symposium, pp. 1046–1057, May 2011
19. Yao, J.: Numatop: A tool for memory access locality characterization and analysis. https://01.org/sites/default/files/documentation/numatop_introduction_0.pdf
20. Zhao, Q., Rabbah, R., Amarasinghe, S., Rudolph, L., Wong, W.F.: Ubiquitous memory introspection. In: Proceedings of the International Symposium on Code Generation and Optimization, CGO 2007, pp. 299–311. IEEE Computer Society, Washington, DC, USA (2007)

ASPEN: An Efficient Algorithm for Data Redistribution Between Producer and Consumer Grids

Clément Foyer[1,2(✉)], Adrian Tate[1], and Simon McIntosh-Smith[2]

[1] Cray EMEA Research Lab, Bristol, UK
cfoyer@cray.com
[2] High Performance Computing Research group, Department of Computer Science, University of Bristol, Bristol, UK

Abstract. HPC applications and libraries have frequently moved parallel data from one distribution scheme to another, for reasons of performance. In modern times, a resurgence of interest in this *data redistribution* problem has emerged due to the need to relocate data distributed across one Producer grid onto a different distribution scheme across a Consumer grid. In this paper, we study the efficient algorithms to perform redistribution, and show how the best methods from the literature are still dependent on the number of processors in both grids. We describe a new algorithm ASPEN that exploits more cyclic patterns and relations in the distribution, is not dependent on the total number of processors and is thus well suited for use in a workflow management systems. We describe a preliminary implementation of the algorithm within such a workflow system and show performance results that indicate a significant performance benefit in data redistribution generation.

Keywords: Data distribution · Redistribution · Data placement
Data locality · Memory layout · Communication pattern
Parallel programming · Distributed memory

1 Introduction

Explicit data movement libraries and tools are used in HPC applications, coupled models, ensembles and workflows, to communicate data between distinct applications through various means. In many HPC workflows, a simulation running on M nodes (the *Producer Grid* or *Producer*) writes a large amount of data to another job running on a (possibly) distinct set of resources (the *Consumer Grid* or *Consumer*). Although this data movement pattern is far from new, it has become a common concern in modern times due to the prevalence of data-intensive workflows, coupled climate/environment applications and combined workflows of HPC with Data Analytics or AI. Many approaches exist to provide data movement between programs including in-situ frameworks, job couplers, in-memory databases and file-system approaches. In this paper we describe a

G. Mencagli et al. (Eds.): Euro-Par 2018 Workshops, LNCS 11339, pp. 171–182, 2019.
https://doi.org/10.1007/978-3-030-10549-5_14

library for communication of data between jobs over the interconnect fabric. Moving data over the interconnect, direct from DRAM has the benefit that many fewer data copies are incurred, but has the significant hurdle of needing to explicitly manage the parallel data movement in order to move the data. This problem of explicit data redistribution management is the focus of this paper.

A good deal of work (reviewed in Sect. 3) has explored the cost and benefits of explicit data redistribution, typically to a different distribution scheme within *the same processor grid.* While sharing many qualities with the classical data redistribution problem, so called *Producer-Consumer redistribution* or *M:N node redistribution* exhibits significant additional complications arising from the fact that the two grids reside in different jobs and lack awareness of the other's characteristics including distribution scheme. Cray has developed a library called the *Universal Data Junction* (UDJ)[1] that provides the missing information and allows distinct jobs in distinct grids to package, send and receive parallel (distributed) data over the high-performance interconnect as well as other resources that may be preferred.

In this work, we focus on the algorithmic machinery that is required in order to allow a Producer and a Consumer Grid to communicate the correct data, at minimal expense in a scalable fashion. The reason to place so much emphasis on the cost of redistribution is that the operations cannot easily be offloaded or performed asynchronously and thus incur direct overhead on the simulation code, which is often intolerable. In Sect. 3 we show that classical algorithms and those in the literature display running times that are proportional to the number of *remote* processors from the perspective of either the Producer (i.e. *remote* means Consumer) or the Consumer (i.e. *remote* means Producer) grid. In the Exascale era, it is expected that simulation jobs may run on millions of compute cores. Hence, this dependence on remote grid size is intolerable. In Sect. 4 we describe a new approach that exploits three types of periodicity in cyclic data distributions, resulting in a lower complexity redistribution algorithm and one that does not depend on remote grid sizes. In Sect. 5 we show the results of our new approach versus the classical algorithm and some of the most used and well-regarded algorithms published in the literature.

2 Background

We define the regular redistribution problem in the same way as [1] using updated producer-consumer terminology: given a d-dimensional array A on a set of Producer resources (processors and memory) $\mathscr{R}_{producer}$ that uses some distribution scheme $\mathscr{D}_{producer}$ we wish to move all the data to another set of resources $\mathscr{R}_{consumer}$ using some other distribution scheme $\mathscr{D}_{consumer}$. $\mathscr{D}_{producer}$ and $\mathscr{D}_{consumer}$ represent arbitrary array element mappings across each dimension of the array.

The global array indices of A are given by $G_1, \ldots, G_d$. The set of distribution schemes of primary interest are BLOCK, CYCLIC, 1-d BLOCK CYCLIC and

[1] https://gitlab.com/cerl/universal-data-junction.

k-d BLOCK-CYCLIC. Since BLOCK, CYCLIC and 1-d CYCLIC are special cases of k-d BLOCK-CYCLIC, we study only the latter in this paper. Like [1,7] we use a *Local Data Descriptor* approach, but we choose to ignore this representation since it is an implementation feature not relevant to the algorithmic descriptions. Local data sizes of A on rank p are given by $L_1^p, L_2^p, \ldots, L_d^p$. Processors compose a d-dimensional processor grid $p_1 \times \cdots \times p_d$ where $p_i (1 \leq i \leq d)$ gives the number of processors in the grid dimension i. We will discuss two such processor grids $\mathscr{G}^{producer}$ and $\mathscr{G}^{consumer}$ where the resources are assumed to be distinct though this is not necessary. We define the mapping $G2L(p, d)$ as the function that maps global indices to the local indices for processor p in dimension d, and the inverse relation $L2G(p, d)$ mapping local indices to global indices.

The non-triviality of redistribution of cyclic data can be illustrated by the graphic example of Fig. 1. A 2-d array is divided into 2-d partitions using some block sizes b_1^1, b_2^1. The blocks of this partitioning are distributed using a 2d block-cyclic distribution scheme across a producer grid of size 4×4. We denote the block ownership by labelling the blocks by processor owner, round-robin style along each dimension (Fig. 1a). We wish to redistribute the same 2-d data across a different consumer grid of size 3×3 using different block sizes b_1^2, b_2^2 labelled similarly (Fig. 1b). For any process pair (p, c) where p is in the producer grid and c is the consumer grid, we can overlay the global data owned by each processor to begin to ascertain shared indices, e.g., producer process $(0, 0)$ (Fig. 1b) and consumer process $(0, 0)$ (Fig. 1c) superimposed in Fig. 1d. The intersection of the superimposed data in Fig. 1e represents the global indices that these two processors must directly exchange over the network (i.e., producer $(0, 0)$ must send these indices and consumer $(0, 0)$ must receive these indices). The d-dimensional situation is a direct extension of the illustrated 2-dimensional case.

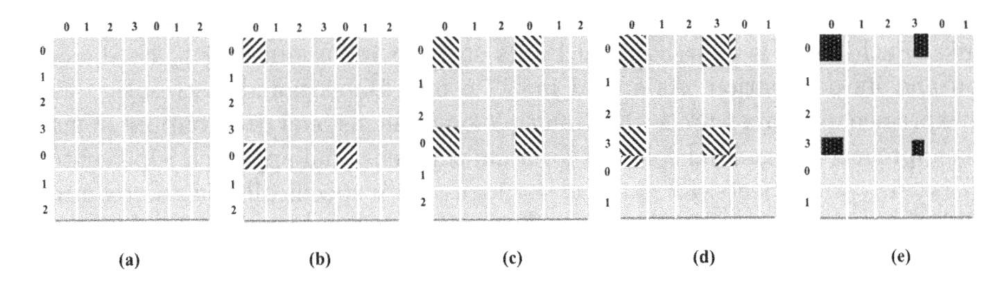

Fig. 1. Example of non-triviality of data index calculations for trivial distribution across 4×4 producer and 3×3 consumer grids

3 Related Work

The question of parallel data redistribution has been addressed many times, both statically and dynamically as this question was central when dealing with the imposed data distributions of early distributed memory programming models such as High Performance Fortran (HPF) [4].

Extensive analysis has been performed on both the nature of block-cyclic distribution, and its relevance to distributed memory relations as it stands as a generalisation of both block distribution and cyclic distribution. Multiple improvements have been proposed taking advantage of certain characteristics of this kind of data distribution [1,2,6,7]. These solutions also focused on the message scheduling part of array redistribution, which is out of scope for this paper. Petitet and Dongarra [5] described techniques for redistribution taking into account the severe alignment restrictions induced by the architecture, as well as further treatment of the scheduling.

Thakur et al. compared different solutions and presented solutions both specific and general varying the size of the blocks but restricted to fixed size process grids [8,9]. The presented techniques rely either on computing the source and destination for each element of the array outside of where it was possible to use improvements due to any common factors between the two block-cyclic sizes. Hsu et al. [3] also described some optimisations for specific cases where the two block-cyclic distributions have a common factor, but with irregular number of processors. In their more generic approach [2] the authors provide a thorough proof of the algorithm. Our version, although very close in the principle, is based on LDD usage and does not enforce the sizes to be relatively prime numbers, allowing simpler generation of the final scalar product.

4 Data Redistribution Algorithms

From the literature, the redistribution problem has been expressed as: given two possibly different regular distributions of data over two grids P and C with distributions D_P and D_C, for each pair of processes $(p \in P, c \in C)$ find the intersecting elements in $D_p \cap D_c$. The general idea when addressing the redistribution problem is to compute the intersecting `blocks` of data between the ranks. Each block is characterized by its starting index, its length, its dimension and its destination. As stated in [7], a multidimensional distribution can be expressed as a cross-product of multiple one-dimensional distributions. Using this approach, the general solution for a multidimensional approach is presented in Sect. 4.1, while Sects. 4.2, 4.3 and 4.4 focus more specifically on the required block comparisons.

4.1 General Problem

Algorithm 1 presents the outer loop over the dimensions needed to generate the block sets describing how to scatter the local data. In this algorithm, `ComputeIntersection` refers to any of the algorithms presented in Sects. 4.2, 4.3 and 4.4. The version described here considers the computation of the complete redistribution. It is however possible to pass to Algorithms 2 or 3 the remote process coordinates in order to compute the unique intersection with the local process. As the full description of the intersecting blocks is created with a crossproduct, any empty returned $\texttt{block}^{\texttt{d}}$ would allow the algorithm to finish early in this case.

Algorithm 1. Base algorithm for redistribution

```
/* Each rank performs the following for each dimension d                */
input : Producer Grid P, Consumer Grid C, Producer Distribution D_P,
        Consumer Distribution D_C
output: Set of blocks^d
1 for d ← 1 to ndims(Data) do
2 |  blocks^d ← ComputeIntersection(P^d, C^d, D^d_P, D^d_C);
3 end
```

Algorithm 2. Classical Redistribution Algorithm

```
/* Each rank performs the following for each dimension d                */
input : Producer Grid P^d, Consumer Grid C^d, Producer Distribution D^d_P,
        Consumer Distribution D^d_C
output: Int_rank consists of tuples (remoteRank, start, end)
1  N_local ← Number of local blocks owned by this rank;
2  for remote ← 1 to |C^d| do
3  |  N_remote ← Number of local blocks on remote rank;
4  |  for localBlockId ← 1 to N_local do
5  |  |  localBlock ← getBlock(D^d_P, localBlockId);
6  |  |  for remoteBlockId ← 1 to N_remote do
7  |  |  |  remoteBlock ← getBlock(D^d_C, remoteBlockId);
8  |  |  |  Left ← max(localBlock.start, remoteBlock.start) ;
9  |  |  |  Right ← min(localBlock.end, remoteBlock.end) ;
10 |  |  |  if Left < Right then
11 |  |  |  |  Int_rank ← Int_rank ∪ (remote, Left, Right) ;
12 |  |  |  end
13 |  |  end
14 |  end
15 end
```

4.2 Classical Algorithm

This algorithm presents the naïve way of computing the intersection, by taking each block of the given local distribution and looking for an overlap by comparing its boundaries with those of each block of the remote distribution. This comparison is performed for each process of the remote grid.

The total number of operations is given by

$$\mathtt{Ops}_{Classical} = D \cdot L \cdot R \cdot N^{local} \cdot N^{remote} \tag{1}$$

where N^{local} represents the number of local blocks and L represents the number of processes in the local grid dimension, respectively remote blocks and remote grid dimensions are N^{remote} and R.

Algorithm 3. FALLS Redistribution Algorithm

```
/* Each rank performs the following for each dimension d                    */
input  : Producer Grid P^d, Consumer Grid C^d, Producer Distribution D^d_P,
         Consumer Distribution D^d_C
output: Int_rank consists of tuples (remoteRank,start,end)
1  S_local ← local stride between blocks;
2  S_remote ← remote stride between blocks;
3  S ← lcm(S_local, S_remote);
4  N_local ← Number of local blocks owned by this rank;
5  for remote ← 1 to |C^d| do
6     N_remote ← Number of local blocks on remote rank;
7     for localBlockId ← 1 to max(N_local, S/S_local) do
8        localBlock ← getBlock(D^d_P, localBlockId);
9        firstIndex ← max(0, ⌈(localBlock.start − remoteOffset − remoteBlocksize)/S_remote⌉);
10       lastIndex ←
         min(1 + (localBlock.start + localBlocksize − remoteOffset)/S_remote, N_remote, S/S_remote);
11       for remoteBlockId ← firstIndex to lastIndex do
12          remoteBlock ← getBlock(D^d_C, remoteBlockId);
13          Left ← max(localBlock.start, remoteBlock.start);
14          Right ← min(localBlock.end, remoteBlock.end);
15          if Left < Right then
16             for disp ← 0 to |Data^d|/S do
17                start ← Left + disp × S;
18                end ← Right + disp × S;
19                Int_rank ← Int_rank ∪ (remote, start, end);
20             end
21          end
22       end
23    end
24 end
```

4.3 FALLS Algorithm

This algorithm is the best version found in the literature for *M:N node redistribution.* The same idea is expressed in [1,7], and summarized in Algorithm 3. Although comparing boundaries block-by-block, these articles present a huge improvement over the classical algorithm in terms the number of block comparisons required.

The bounds are reduced by using the fact that the intersection of two block cyclic distributions can be expressed as the union of some set of block cyclic distributions, each origin being the beginning of the intersection, each block length being the length of the intersecting block and the distance between blocks[2] is equal to the lower common multiple of the two original strides. The result is that it is only necessary to compare blocks within one stride S. In other words,

[2] Later referred to simply as *stride.*

for each element x in the found intersection then $x + n(S)$ is also inside the intersection, where n is all integers for which $x + n(S)$ remains smaller than the extent of the full array. Additionally, it is only necessary to compare the blocks in the onwards direction and those already checked can be ignored.

Compared to the classical algorithm, the reduction of the bounds reduces drastically the number of blocks to be considered when evaluating the intersection for big grids of data. The total number of operations is given by

$$\texttt{Ops}_{\text{FALLS}} = D \cdot L \cdot R \cdot \hat{N}^{local} \cdot \hat{N}^{remote} \tag{2}$$

where the $\hat{N}^{local}$ and $\hat{N}^{remote}$ represent the reduced number of local blocks due to searching only with one S. In theory then, Eq. 2 resembles Eq. 1 but in practice, $\hat{N}$ and N typically differ greatly with $\hat{N} \ll N$.

4.4 ASPEN Algorithm Description

To improve redistribution performance, we develop a scheme that can exploit further qualities of the periodic nature of the distributed data, and the known relationships between adjacent blocks. We call the approach *Adjacent Shifting of PEriodic Node data* or ASPEN. To illustrate the approach we first describe the two remaining weaknesses of the existing algorithms.

Periodicity of Remote Block Data. In the Algorithms 2 and 3 each local block's position in the global scheme is compared against multiple remote blocks (all remote blocks in the case of Algorithm 2 and many fewer than all remote blocks in the case of 3). In fact, the need to perform more than one comparison ignores periodic qualities of the data distribution since the constant stride should enable a direct periodic comparison. Consider the code in Algorithm 3 lines 11–14. This code searches over the loop of remote blocks (Algorithm 3 line 11) to generate all remote *RemoteBlockIDs*, then inside that loop *remoteBlock* is extracted using $getBlock(D_C^d, remoteBlockId)$ (Algorithm 3 line 12). $Left$ and $Right$ are then both generated using various extents of *localBlock* and *remoteBlock* (Algorithm 3 lines 13 and line 14). We can avoid this logic if we generate a *periodic offset* as follows

$$offset \leftarrow localBlock.start \mod remoteBlocksize$$

Offset can be seen visually in Fig. 2 and appears in Algorithm 4 line 8.

The $offset$ can be used to indirectly obtain the same information, without doing explicit comparisons to individual remote blocks, by checking the inequality

$$localBlock.start - offset + remoteBlocksize \leq localBlock.end \tag{3}$$

If condition Eq. 3 is true, then this particular local and remote block comparison overlaps on the left-hand side of the local block. This can be understood by seeing that the blue box of Fig. 2 would be non-empty when Eq. 3 holds.

Algorithm 4. ASPEN Redistribution Algorithm

```
   /* Each rank performs the following for each dimension d                */
   input  : Producer Grid P^d, Consumer Grid C^d, Producer Distribution D^d_P,
            Consumer Distribution D^d_C
   output: Int_rank consists of tuples (remoteRank,start,end)
 1 S_local ← local stride between blocks;
 2 S_remote ← remote stride between blocks;
 3 S ← lcm(S_local, S_remote);
 4 N_local ← Number of local blocks owned by this rank;
 5 for localBlockId ← 1 to max(N_local, S/S_local) do
       /* GTL is a global to local index conversion function.              */
 6     localBlock ← getBlock(D^d_P, localBlockId);
 7     remote ← (localBlock.start / remoteBlocksize) mod |C^d|;
 8     offset ← localBlock.start mod remoteBlocksize;
 9     Left ← localBlock.start;
10     if localBlock.start − offset + remoteBlocksize ≤ localBlock.end then
11         Right ← min(localBlock.start − offset + remoteBlocksize, |Data^d|);
12         diff ← Right − Left;
13         for ps ← Left to |Data^d| by S do
14             start ← G2L(ps);
15             end ← G2L(min(ps + diff, |Data^d|));
16             Int_rank ← Int_rank ∪ (remote, start, end);
17         end
18         Left ← Right;
19         remote ← (remote + 1) mod |C^d|;
20     end
21     for Left to min(localBlock.end, |Data^d|) by remoteBlocksize do
22         Right ← min(Left + remoteBlocksize, localBlock.end, |Data^d|);
23         diff ← Right − Left;
24         for ps ← Left to |Data^d| by S do
25             start ← G2L(ps);
26             end ← G2L(min(ps + diff, |Data^d|));
27             Int_rank ← Int_rank ∪ (remote, start, end);
28         end
29         remote ← (remote + 1) mod |C^d|;
30     end
31     Right ← min(localBlock.end, |Data^d|);
32     if Left ≤ Right then
33         diff ← Right − Left;
34         for ps ← Left to |Data^d| by S do
35             start ← G2L(ps);
36             end ← G2L(min(ps + diff, |Data^d|));
37             Int_rank ← Int_rank ∪ (remote, start, end);
38         end
39     end
40 end
```

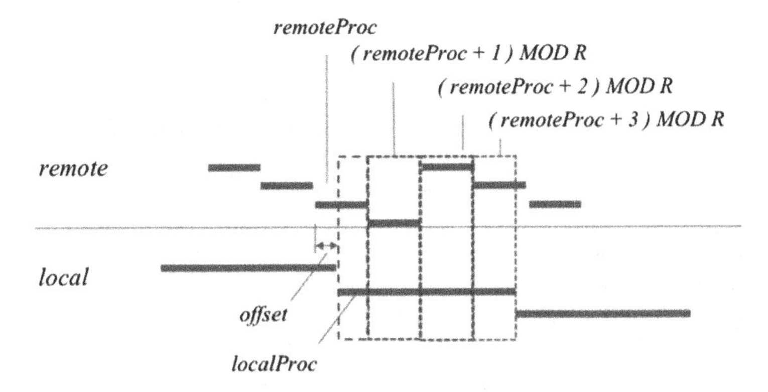

Fig. 2. Illustration of Adjacent shifting and periodic relations. *offset* is a periodic difference that will mean a local-remote comparison is valid for this local block when *offset* is greater than a threshold. The leftmost part of local data maps to processor *RemoteProc*. Adjacent data on the local processor can be known to then map to *RemoteProc+1* (and repeated for any further adjacent blocks); R represents the Remote grid dimension. (Color figure online)

When it holds, $remoteBlocksize - offset$ elements will be shared with processor *remote*. This is how ASPEN exploits the periodic nature of remote data to avoid looking at all remote blocks.

Properties of adjacent Sub-blocks. In the case that condition Eq. 3 holds, some number of elements are shared with processor *remote*. Instead of resetting knowledge with respect to the rest of the local block, ASPEN exploits the fact that if a set of global indices $g_l, \ldots, g_r$ of length less than *localBlockSize* map to processor *remote*, and if some set of global indices $\{g_{r+1}, \ldots, g_{r+p}\}$ with $p + (r - l) \leq localxBlockSize$ then `localProc` will also share indices with processor $(remoteProc{+}1) \mod |C^d|$. Similarly, if several blocks of size `remoteBlockSize` fit into the `localBlock`, then each full block will map to the next processor in the remote grid. This approach is how ASPEN assigns contiguous local sub-blocks to adjacent processors in the remote grid (adjacency shifting). Hence the loop over remote processors in Algorithm 2 line 6 and Algorithm 3 line 11, does not appear in 4. The number of operations in Algorithm 4 is given by

$$\texttt{Ops}_{\text{ASPEN}} = D \cdot L \cdot \hat{N}^{local} \tag{4}$$

Comparing this to Eq. 2, we see a factor of $R{\cdot}\hat{N}^{remote}$ reduction in operations. The missing R term in particular will affect scalability since each grid will not require distinct calculations for each process element in the size of the remote grid. Theoretically then, we expect ASPEN to scale significantly better with larger Producer or Consumer grids involved in redistribution.

5 Results

The followings tests were run on Cray XC30 systems, each node featuring two INTEL XEON HASWELL E5–2698 with 16 cores each (2.30 GHz). The benchmark was made of MPI applications computing independently the complete redistribution from one 2D grid of processes to another 2D grid, varying dimensions, shape and size of each grid. The data was a fixed size 2D square grid of ten thousand by ten thousand elements. Because this benchmark aimed at evaluating the redistribution performance, the computation were only executed on the indices and no actual communication of data occurred.

Each case of block-cyclic to block-cyclic distribution was run many times for all 4 methods: the naïve, the implementation of the algorithm presented in [1], the FALLS algorithm, the ScaLAPACK redistribution computation algorithm, and the ASPEN version[3]. The correctness of computed intersection was checked by comparing with the naïve approach results, and on later work in the *Universal Data Junction* library unit tests.

The main loop as show in Algorithm 1 was timed. In order to limit the impact of system related issues, all memory needed for the creation of intersection description sectors were pre-allocated before any measure of timing was taken. Nevertheless, outliers may appear because of cache misses.

The process grids were made of 2 to 32 processes per grid, and the block-cyclic sizes were one of 1024 by 1024, 256 by 256, 30 by 50 or 654 by 321. The objective was to highlight performance behaviour in regular-to-irregular redistributions, and the impact of partial blocks on the performance.

ASPEN showed to be very robust over disturbance induced by irregularity in structures. The main factor of influence over the execution time are the number of remote processes per rank. As shown in Fig. 3, while the number of blocks is scaled by a factor ≈ 8.5 and ≈ 5 in each dimension, timings scaled linearly for

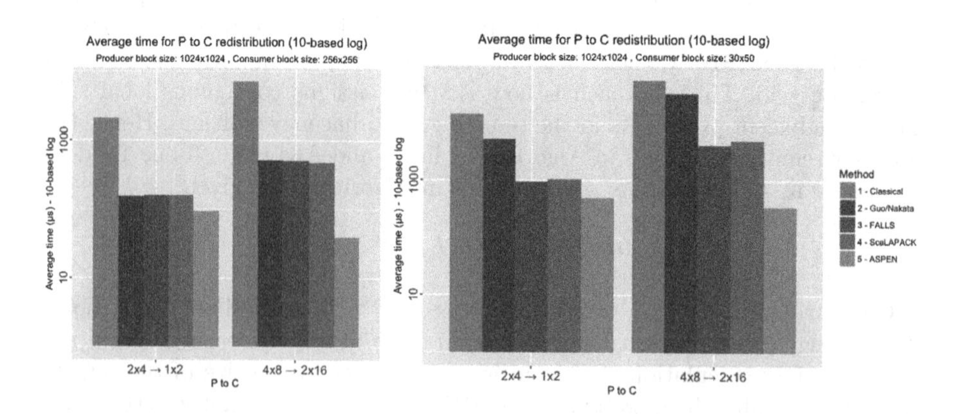

Fig. 3. Data redistributions for different blocksize and different grid sizes

[3] For all methods except classical, changing total data size does not affect the performance.

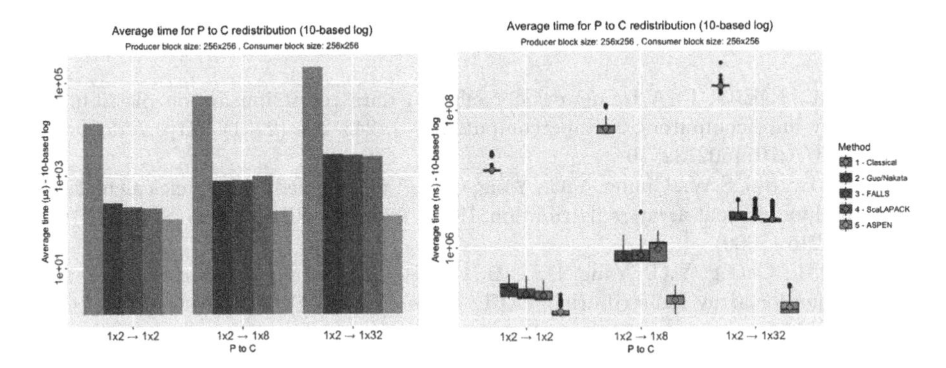

Fig. 4. Data redistributions for different blocksize and different grid sizes

ASPEN, which is not dependent on the remote number of blocks nor on remote grid dimension while for all other algorithms scale with the square (or worse) of grid length.

The results shown in Fig. 4 suggest a strong influence on performance by the number of remote processes. Since the R term can become significant even with small grids, we see the time begin to rise even for modest grid exchanges. With ASPEN, the R term is absent and this effect is limited. With large grid sizes, we expect to see this effect becoming critically significant.

6 Conclusion and Further Work

We have demonstrated that the ASPEN algorithm can generate redistributions more efficiently (both theoretically and in practice) when moving cyclic data across distinct processor grids. As there is a growing requirement to perform such redistributions across larger grids, the ASPEN algorithm is likely to be impactful. The total cost of moving data across jobs will depend on many factors, such as cost of generating the redistribution, cost of buffering data and message latencies. Subsequent work will study all of these factors by describing the ASPEN algorithmic framework integrated into the Universal Data Junction library, which will be used to send complex distributed data across production HPC jobs. We will investigate and implement ASPEN for redistribution of data using Gaussian grids and in complex workflow situations such as many-Producer, many-Consumer.

Acknowledgement. This work was partly funded by the EXPERTISE project (http://www.msca-expertise.eu/), which has received funding from the European Union's Horizon 2020 research and innovation programme under the Marie Skłodowska-Curie grant agreement No 721865.

References

1. Guo, M., Nakata, I.: A framework for efficient data redistribution on distributed memory multicomputers. J. Supercomput. **20**(3), 243–265 (2001). https://doi.org/10.1023/A:1011602732570
2. Hsu, C.H., Bai, S.W., Chung, Y.C., Yang, C.S.: A generalized basic-cycle calculation method for efficient array redistribution. IEEE Trans. Parallel Distrib. Syst. **11**(12), 1201–1216 (2000)
3. Hsu, C.H., Chung, Y.C., Yang, D.L., Dow, C.R.: A generalized processor mapping technique for array redistribution. IEEE Trans. Parallel Distrib. Syst. **12**(7), 743–757 (2001)
4. Loveman, D.B.: High performance fortran. IEEE Parallel Distrib. Technol. Syst. Appl. **1**(1), 25–42 (1993)
5. Petitet, A.P., Dongarra, J.J.: Algorithmic redistribution methods for block-cyclic decompositions. IEEE Trans. Parallel Distrib. Syst. **10**(12), 1201–1216 (1999)
6. Prylli, L., Tourancheau, B.: Fast runtime block cyclic data redistribution on multiprocessors. J. Parallel Distrib. Comput. **45**(1), 63–72 (1997)
7. Ramaswamy, S., Simons, B., Banerjee, P.: Optimizations for efficient array redistribution on distributed memory multicomputers. J. Parallel Distrib. Comput. **38**(2), 217–228 (1996)
8. Thakur, R., Choudhary, A., Fox, G.: Runtime array redistribution in HPF programs. In: Proceedings of the Scalable High-Performance Computing Conference, pp. 309–316. IEEE (1994)
9. Thakur, R., Choudhary, A., Ramanujam, J.: Efficient algorithms for array redistribution. IEEE Trans. Parallel Distrib. Syst. **7**(6), 587–594 (1996)

Euro-EDUPAR - Workshop on Parallel and Distributed Computing Education for Undergraduate Students

Workshop on Parallel and Distributed Computing Education for Undergraduate Students (Euro-EDUPAR)

Workshop Description

Parallel and Distributed Computing (PDC) is omnipresent. It is in all the computational environments, from mobile devices and laptops to clusters, data centers and supercomputers. It becomes now vital to train new generations of scientists and engineers in the use of these environments: PDC-related topics must be incorporated in Computer Science (CS) and Computer Engineering (CE) programs. In 2010 the IEEE Computer Society Technical Committee on Parallel Processing launched the Curriculum Initiative on Parallel and Distributed Computing, with Core Topics for Undergraduates, and in 2011 started the workshop EduPar. Motivated by differences in education in different parts of the world, Euro-EDUPAR aims to analyze PDC Education in a European context. The 4th European Workshop on Parallel and Distributed Computing Education for Undergraduate Students (Euro-EDUPAR) invited unpublished manuscripts on topics pertaining to the teaching of PDC-related topics in the CS and CE curricula as well as in Computational Science with PDC or HPC concepts, with emphasis on European undergraduate teaching.

Eight papers were submitted and, following a review of each paper by at least four members of the Program Committee, four papers were accepted for presentation. The final program also featured a keynote presentation by William Gropp from University of Illinois at Urbana-Champaign on thinking about parallelism and programming. Moreover, Arnold Rosenberg from University of Massachusetts gave an update on the curriculum guidelines of the NSF-supported Center for Parallel and Distributed Computing Curriculum Development and Educational Resources (CDER). Martina Barnas from Indiana University Bloomington chaired a panel on the question of gender balance in our field, leading to a lively discussion among the audience and three further panelists, including Valeria Cardellini from University of Rome Tor Vergata, Arnold Rosenberg from University of Massachusetts, and Denis Trystram from Grenoble Institute of Technology. Overall, the workshop generated good interest and was held in a pleasant environment thanks to the great support of the Euro-Par 2018 organizers.

Organization

Steering Committee

Henri E. Bal	Vrije Universiteit, The Netherlands
Alexey Lastovetsky	University College Dublin, Ireland
Christian Lengauer	University of Passau, Germany

Pierre Manneback	University of Mons, Belgium
Sushil K. Prasad	Georgia State University, USA
Yves Robert	École Normale Supérieure de Lyon, France
Arnold L. Rosenberg	University of Massachusetts, USA
Rizos Sakellariou	University of Manchester, UK
Cristina Silvano	Politecnico di Milano, Italy
Paul G. Spirakis	University of Liverpool, UK
Denis Trystram (Chair)	Grenoble Institute of Technology, France
Mateo Valero	Barcelona Supercomputing Center, Spain
Vladimir Voevodin	Moscow State University, Russia

General Co-chairs

Denis Trystram	Grenoble Institute of Technology, France
Arnold L. Rosenberg	University of Massachusetts, USA

Program Co-chairs

Felix Wolf	Technische Universität Darmstadt, Germany
Rizos Sakellariou	University of Manchester, UK

Program Committee

Jorge G. Barbosa	University of Porto, Portugal
Marian Bubak	AGH Krakow PL and University of Amsterdam, The Netherlands
Aurélien Cavelan	University of Basel, Switzerland
Sunita Chandrasekaran	University of Delaware, USA
Gennaro Cordasco	Universita' della Campania "L. Vanvitelli", Italy
Efstratios Gallopoulos	University of Patras, Greece
Chryssis Georgiou	University of Cyprus, Cyprus
Domingo Giménez	University of Murcia, Spain
Thilo Kielmann	Vrije Universiteit Amsterdam, The Netherlands
Alexey Lastovetsky	University College Dublin, Ireland
Vania Marangozova-Martin	Grenoble University, France
Tomas Margalef	Universitat Autonoma de Barcelona, Spain
Svetozar Margenov	Bulgarian Academy of Sciences, Bulgaria
Lena Oden	Forschungszentrum Jülich, Germany
Marcin Paprzycki	Polish Academy of Sciences, Poland
Dana Petcu	West University of Timisoara, Romania
Geppino Pucci	DEI - Universita' di Padova, Italy
Erven Rohou	Inria, France

Emil Slusanschi	University Politehnica of Bucharest, Romania
Juan Touriño	University of A Coruna, Spain
Jesper Larsson Träff	Vienna University of Technology, Austria
Vladimir Voevodin	Moscow State University, Russia

Getting Started with CAPI SNAP: Hardware Development for Software Engineers

Lukas Wenzel, Robert Schmid, Balthasar Martin, Max Plauth(✉), Felix Eberhardt, and Andreas Polze

Operating Systems and Middleware Group, Hasso Plattner Institute for Digital Engineering, University of Potsdam, Potsdam, Germany
{lukas.wenzel,robert.schmid,max.plauth,felix.eberhardt, andreas.polze}@hpi.uni-potsdam.de, balthasar.martin@student.hpi.uni-potsdam.de

Abstract. To alleviate development of FPGA-based accelerator function units for software engineers, the OpenPOWER Accelerator Work Group has recently introduced the CAPI Storage, Network, and Analytics Programming (SNAP) framework. However, we found that software engineers are still overwhelmed with many aspects of the novel hardware development framework. This paper provides background and instructions for mastering the first steps of hardware development using the CAPI SNAP framework. The insights reported in this paper are based on the experiences of software engineering students with little to no prior knowledge about hardware development.

Keywords: FPGA · Programming environment · Tutorial

1 Introduction

Embracing heterogeneous computing, hardware vendors are seeking new approaches for augmenting general purpose *Central Processing Units* (CPUs) with accelerator hardware to satisfy the ever-growing demand for compute capacity. *Field-Programmable Gate Arrays* (FPGAs) can be used in many application scenarios while being orders of magnitude more power-efficient compared to *Graphics Processing Units* (GPUs) [1]. With the Zynq SoCs, Xilinx has successfully demonstrated the consolidation of FPGA-based programmable logic with ARM-based CPU cores [17]. Following this trend of tightly coupling programmable logic accelerators with CPUs, IBM has introduced the *Coherent Accelerator Processor Interface* (CAPI) [12], making hardware accelerators such as FPGAs first-class citizens by integrating them into the processors coherent memory hierarchy.

Unfortunately, the benefits of FPGAs come at the cost of high development efforts, as it is very time consuming and difficult for software engineers to implement FPGA-based *Accelerator Functional Units* (AFUs). To optimize hardware

G. Mencagli et al. (Eds.): Euro-Par 2018 Workshops, LNCS 11339, pp. 187–198, 2019.
https://doi.org/10.1007/978-3-030-10549-5_15

designs, detailed knowledge about the targeted FPGA is required. Furthermore, additional effort is necessary to establish communication channels with the host application, as well as for interfacing with peripheral hardware available on the FPGA extension card. To alleviate these issues, the *OpenPOWER Accelerator Work Group* has recently introduced the *CAPI Storage, Network, and Analytics Programming* (SNAP) framework. On the side of the host application, it enables simple integration of AFUs by providing a ready-to-use job infrastructure. Complementing the hardware side, the framework provides libraries for accessing hardware components such as DRAM, NVMe flash storage and network interfaces. Covering both the software and hardware side of FPGA development, as well as the ensuing build process, the CAPI SNAP framework enables developers to focus their efforts on implementing their AFUs using Vivado HLS C/C++.

However, even with all these support mechanisms in place, we found that even graduate students in software engineering are still overwhelmed by many aspects of the novel framework, including the initial setup of the development environment, simulation of AFUs, as well as deployment on actual hardware. To help breaking down the remaining barriers for software engineers, this paper provides guidance for mastering the first steps of hardware development using the CAPI SNAP framework. The instructions reported in this paper are based on the insights of graduate students in software engineering, collected over the course of multiple student projects, with the participants having little to no prior knowledge about hardware development. The instructions apply to on-premise setups as well as to the *SuperVessel Cloud for OpenPower* [2] service.

Hereinafter, this paper is structured as follows: Enabling tight integration of accelerators, Sect. 2 introduces the basic concepts of CAPI. Section 3 provides an overview of the major traits of the CAPI SNAP framework. Afterwards, Sect. 4 reports best practices for getting started with the framework. Finally, Sect. 5 discusses related work, before an outlook is provided in Sect. 6.

2 Understanding CAPI

The *Coherent Accelerator Processor Interface* (CAPI) is an interface standard introduced with the IBM POWER8 architecture [12]. It enables accelerators to partake in the processors coherent view on the memory hierarchy. Prior to CAPI, accelerator resources had to be mapped to specific IO memory areas, where data had to be copied to and from explicitly. CAPI-enabled accelerators can access the same virtual address space as its controlling process, drastically curtailing the overhead for interacting with accelerators [13]. In its initial version, CAPI is layered on top of PCIe 3.0. In the upcoming POWER9 architecture, CAPI will be extended to support custom I/O facilities in addition to PCIe 4.0.

2.1 Architecture

CAPI involves several components on the host CPU as well as on the accelerator side. The FPGA side is comprised of *Accelerator Function Units* (AFUs), implementing the application logic, as well as the *Power Service Layer* (PSL), which is a fixed design provided by IBM for supported FPGA cards [5].

The PSL communicates with the host part of the CAPI hardware, the *Coherent Accelerator Processor Proxy* (CAPP) via PCIe. The CAPP is part of the POWER CPU and from the point of view of the memory subsystem, it has the same status as a processor core. The software side of CAPI consists of a driver in the linux kernel, exposing installed CAPI accelerator cards as *cxl* devices. To encapsulate the interaction with raw *cxl* devices, the *libcxl* provides a user-land C API with the same functionality. Given sufficient privileges, any user application can interact with the AFUs on a cxl device by linking against *libcxl*.

2.2 Development

AFUs have to be expressed in low-level hardware description languages such as VHDL or Verilog, differing significantly from imperative languages like C in that most statements have concurrent semantics. The interface between PSL and AFU facilitates efficient communication, however its complexity imposes high efforts on AFU developers. Demonstrating the degree of complexity, Fig. 1 illustrates the state machine of a simple AFU for adding of two numbers stored in host memory. The AFU-PSL interface consists of five semi-independent sets of signals:

- The *Job-Interface* is controlled by the PSL and indicates job control and reset commands issued by the host.
- The *MMIO-Interface* exposes a register view of the AFU to the host, which can map this view into its virtual memory to control and monitor the AFU.
- The *Command-Interface* is controlled by the AFU, which can issue a variety of read or write commands with different side effects on the cache hierarchy.
- The *Response-Interface* and *Buffer-Interface* are controlled by the PSL and are used to complete pending commands (e.g. read and write).

For further details on implementing AFUs directly on top of CAPI, please refer to the tutorial "Tinkering with CAPI" by Keneth Wilke [14].

3 The CAPI SNAP Framework in a Nutshell

While CAPI provides the technical foundations for tightly coupling accelerators with CPUs (see Sect. 2), the technology is hard to adopt for software engineers. With the goal of making it as easy as possible for software engineers to leverage CAPI-enabled FPGA hardware acceleration, the *CAPI Storage, Network, and Analytics Programming* (SNAP) framework [10,11] has been introduced recently. The framework assists developers in various aspects explicated hereinafter. Also the acceleration paradigms supported by the framework are discussed.

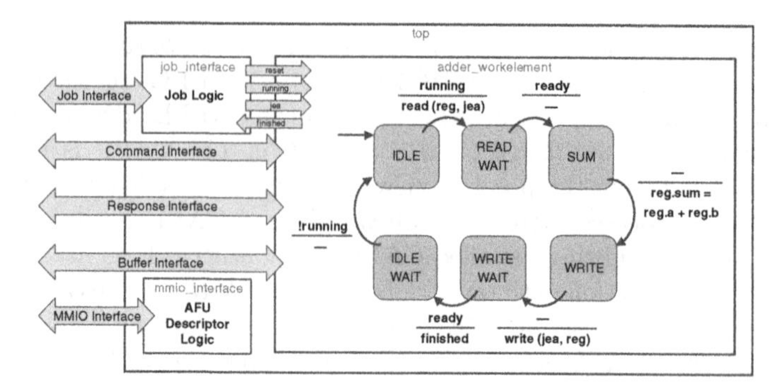

Fig. 1. The state diagram of a simple adder AFU demonstrates the complexity of developing AFUs directly on top of CAPI.

3.1 Core Features

High-Level Language Support. Having to implement application logic using low-level hardware description languages such as VHDL or Verilog, and switching from procedural to state-based thinking is very challenging for most software engineers. CAPI SNAP lowers the hurdles significantly by providing high-level language support based on HLS C/C++.

Job Interface. Calling an action using CAPI requires a lot of complexity in the calling application in order maintain all required communication channels. The framework provides a simple API for interacting with AFUs, allowing actions to be issued by creating a job based on a filled parameter struct, e.g. via the blocking call `snap_action_sync_execute_job(action, &job, timeout)`.

Hardware Abstraction. All FPGA extension cards supported by CAPI SNAP offer peripheral hardware components such as DRAM, NVMe storage or network interfaces. Without the framework, developers would have to implement interface logic and data movers for leveraging the peripheral components, also requiring data movers for interacting with host memory. As illustrated in Fig. 2, the CAPI SNAP framework hides a lot of this complexity by providing simple interfaces, abstracting away the specific details of both peripheral components and the specifics of the FPGA chip itself.

Automated Build Process. Using the Xilinx Vivado Design Suite [16] as a foundation, the development workflow for CAPI SNAP based AFUs is comprised of many stages, including software development, hardware development, hardware simulation as well as hardware deployment. As visualized in Fig. 3, each stage requires its own complex set of tools — originating from various sources (Vivado, CAPI SNAP and CAPI) — in order to create functional builds. Orchestrating all of these tools properly is a very complex task, which is being taken

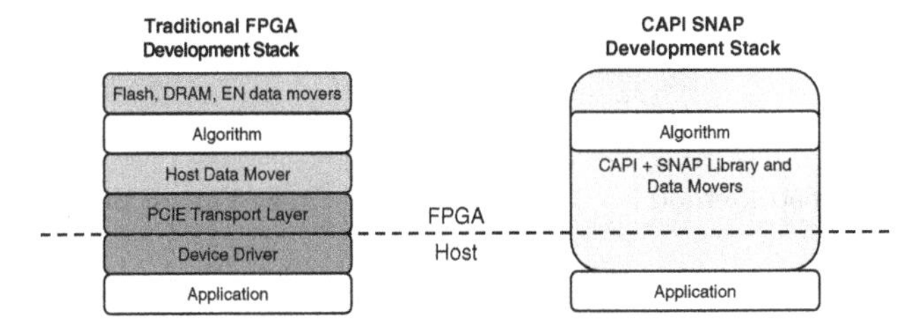

Fig. 2. CAPI SNAP hides complexity on the layers between AFUs and the host application, as well as for accessing peripheral components on the FPGA card. Illustration adapted from [6].

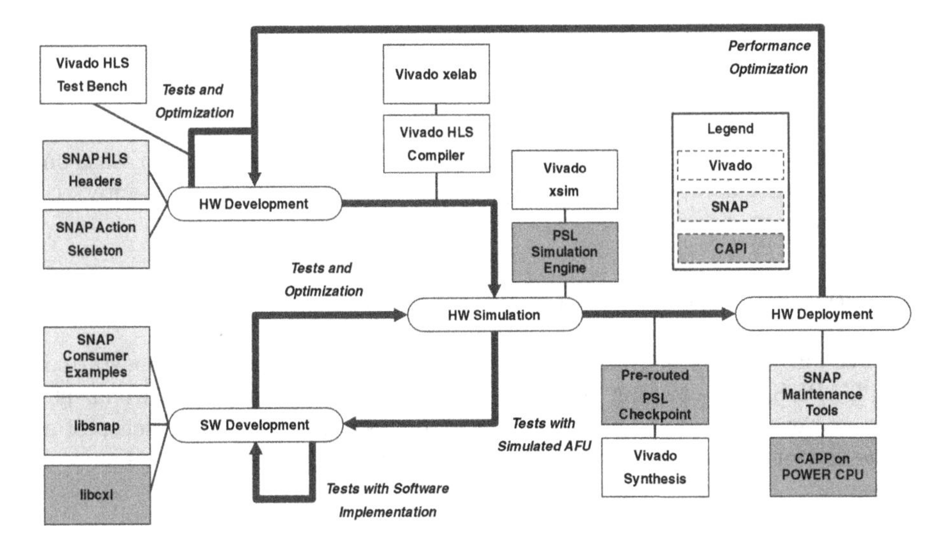

Fig. 3. CAPI SNAP automates the complex build process by orchestrating a wide range of tools originating from various sources.

care of by the CAPI SNAP framework, freeing up many resources on the developers end.

3.2 Acceleration Paradigms

In addition to the well-established *Offload* paradigm commonly used in the field of GPU computing (see Fig. 4a), the availability of peripheral components on the FPGA card enables the CAPI SNAP framework to support a variety of acceleration methods. The *Egress* and *Ingress* methods (see Fig. 4b and c, respectively) can be applied in scenarios where data streams leaving or entering the system (e.g. via network or persistent storage) need to be processed on-the-fly. Use cases for these methods include transparent encryption or compression, as well as media-processing tasks. The *Funnel* method (see Fig. 4d) is eligible in scenarios where the input bandwidth of all external sources exceeds the ingestion

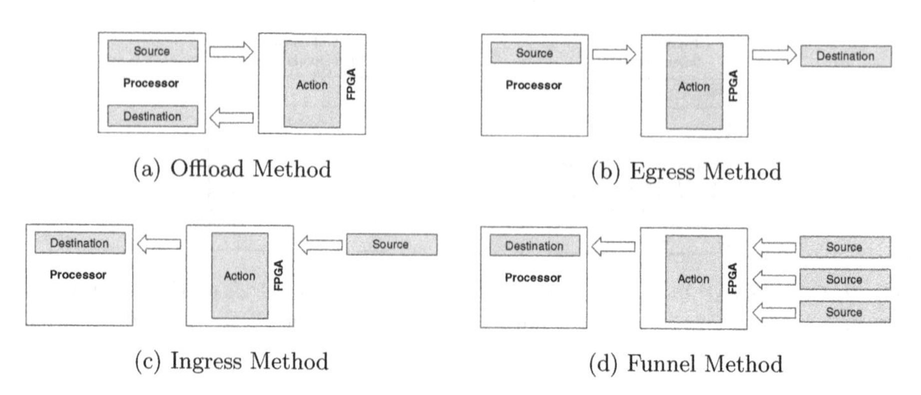

(a) Offload Method

(b) Egress Method

(c) Ingress Method

(d) Funnel Method

Fig. 4. Due to the availability of peripheral components on the FPGA card, CAPI SNAP supports various acceleration paradigms next to traditional offloading.

capabilities of the host. Potential use cases include filter or aggregation tasks on incoming sensor data, as well as database-like operations such as joins, intersections, and merges on large datasets residing on external storage.

4 Getting Started with CAPI SNAP

This section provides an overview of the most important steps for getting started with CAPI SNAP, covering the *basic setup* of the development environment, setup and execution of a *simulation model* for testing purposes, the setup of a *test bench* for validation, as well as deployment and invocation of AFUs on real *hardware*.

4.1 Basic Setup

Setting up a development environment for CAPI SNAP involves several components, including the *Vivado Design Suite*, the *Power Service Layer Checkpoint*, the *Power Service Layer Simulation Engine*, and last but not least the *CAPI SNAP Framework* itself. In the following, the setup process of all these components is documented.

Vivado Design Suite. The Xilinx Vivado Design Suite [16] provides the foundation for the CAPI SNAP framework. Being the centerpiece, the Vivado IDE is used to synthesize and layout actions, for providing *High Level Synthesis* (HLS) C/C++ support, as well as for simulating designs without the actual hardware using *xsim* (Vivado Simulator).

Power Service Layer Checkpoint. On the FPGA, the Power Service Layer (PSL) manages the communication with the host (see Subsect. 2.1). This includes translating memory addresses, handling interrupts and virtualizing AFUs if necessary. Since the PSL component needs to be part of the FPGA bitstream, IBM provides the PSL for download as a pre-routed checkpoint (`.dcp`) file [5]. Care should be taken to pick the correct checkpoint file for the FPGA card at hands, since each card requires a different checkpoint file.

Power Service Layer Simulation Engine. In order to augment the Vivado Simulator *xsim* with CAPI-like behavior, the *Power Service Layer Simulation Engine* (PSLSE) is required additionally, which is is freely available for download [4]. The PSLSE implements the PSL in software and connects the (locally hosted) simulation server with the desired action. The host application then communicates with the (locally hosted) PSLSE server instead of actual hardware. Since hardware synthesis is a very time-consuming process, simulation is usually preferred over hardware deployment for quick testing purposes during development.

CAPI SNAP Framework. After having downloaded the CAPI SNAP framework from [11], the Vivado environment must be established by sourcing the `settings64.sh` script and exporting the location of a valid license file. To ensure that every terminal session has a Vivado environment, the lines in Listing 1.1 might be added to the local shell initialization script (e.g. `~/.bashrc`).

```
1 source /opt/Xilinx/Vivado/2016.4/settings64.sh
2 export XILINXD_LICENSE_FILE=<path to Xilinx license>
```

Listing 1.1. Setup of the Vivado environment in a new terminal session.

The SNAP build process requires the locations of several dependencies. These should be specified in the `snap_env.sh` script in the SNAP root directory. The setup is finally completed by executing `make snap_config` in the CAPI SNAP root directory. This opens an interactive menu to specify the build configuration. After saving the choices and leaving the menu, SNAP shows a summary of the chosen configuration similar to Listing 1.2.

```
1  =======================================================
2  == SNAP SETUP                                                ==
3  =======================================================
4  =====Checking Xilinx Vivado:===========================
5  Path to vivado         is set to: /opt/Xilinx/Vivado/2016.4/bin/vivado
6  Vivado version         is set to: Vivado v2016.4 (64-bit)
7  =====CARD variables====================================
8  FPGACARD               is set to: "FGT"
9  FPGACHIP               is set to: "xcku060-ffva1156-2-e"
10 PSL_DCP                is set to: "/tmp/cards/FGT/b_route_design.dcp"
11 =====SNAP PATH variables===============================
12 SNAP_ROOT              is set to: "/tmp/snap"
13 ACTION_ROOT            is set to: "/tmp/snap/actions/hdl_example"
14 =====SNAP simulation variables=========================
15 SIMULATOR              is set to: "xsim"
16 =====SNAP function variables===========================
17 NUM_OF_ACTIONS         is set to: "1"
18 SDRAM_USED             is set to: "FALSE"
19 NVME_USED              is set to: "FALSE"
20 ILA_DEBUG              is set to: "FALSE"
21 FACTORY_IMAGE          is set to: "FALSE"
```

Listing 1.2. Output yielded from the execution of `make snap_config`.

Depending on which card is used, the variable FPGACARD has to be set correspondingly. At the time of writing, valid options for FPGACARD are N250S, ADKU3, and S121B for the Nallatech 250S, the Alpha Data KU3, and the Semptian NSA-121 FPGA-cards, respectively. The variables SNAP_ROOT and SIMULATOR are set automatically, making xsim the default simulator. However, ACTION_ROOT and the CAPI SNAP function variables (SDRAM_USED, NVME_USED) have to be set based on the action that should be build. Per default, the example hdl_example is build, requiring neither access to DRAM nor NVMe storage.

4.2 Simulating an Action

Simulation is a powerful tool during the development phase, as it enables developers to test the correct communication between AFUs and the host application by tracing the flow of binary signals. Simulation speed itself is much slower than the execution on real hardware. Therefore the simulation model does not include the PSL nor any part of the host side hardware. Nevertheless these components are essential for a host application to access the AFU under test. This issue can be sidestepped by using the PSLSE server. The PSLSE implements a higher level and thus faster model of the internal CAPI components. It provides a modified version of the *libcxl*, which uses the PSLSE server to access the virtual device instead of real CAPI hardware. The simulated PSL merely acts as a proxy, whose behavior on the signal level is controlled by the PSLSE server.

After CAPI SNAP has been configured, a simulation model of the user design can be built by running `make model` from the SNAP_ROOT directory. In this step, all framework components and the user design are compiled into a simulation model as well as a simulator configuration. The setup of the PSLSE server and its connection to the simulator is automated by the sim make target.

Executing `make sim` creates an interactive terminal session with the environment correctly set up to run applications on the simulated hardware. Before the action can be tested, it needs to be initialized as part of the discovery process implemented by the snap_maint tool. Afterwards the actual host application can interact with the simulated hardware action.

Leaving this session also stops the underlying simulation environment. During the simulation, traces of all signals are recorded in a wave database. Afterwards, the detailed operation of the hardware action can be explored by viewing the recorded traces with the `xsim --gui hardware/sim/xsim/latest/top.wdb` command.

4.3 Debugging in the Test Bench

Simulation is only rarely feasible for debugging AFUs implemented in HLS C/C++: The HLS code will be converted into VHDL/Verilog blocks that are quite hard to match to the HLS code. To facilitate debugging and validation of HLS code, setting up a test bench in Vivado enables developers to validate the correct behavior of their code by executing HLS code like a regular C/C++ program in a software debugger.

In order to enable software-based execution in the test bench, a main function needs to be added to the HLS code as explicated in Listing 1.3. To avoid the synthesis of the main function in later development steps, the function should be enclosed by the preprocessor conditional `#ifdef NO_SYNTH ... #endif`.

```
1 #ifdef NO_SYNTH
2 int main()
3 {
4     bf_halfBlock_t left = 0xda7a, right = 0xb10c;
5     printf("encrypt(0x%08x, 0x%08x) -> ", left, right);
6     bf_encrypt(left, right);
7     printf("0x%08x, 0x%08x\n", left, right);
8 }
9 #endif
```

Listing 1.3. In order to use CPU-based execution in the work bench, the HLS code needs to be augmented with a main function.

Before the test bench can be executed, the tested HLS source file needs to be added as a simulation source by right clicking *Test Bench* in the project explorer and selecting *Add Files*. Furthermore, the SNAP specific `CFLAGS` documented in Listing 1.4 must be set up by opening the *Project/Project Settings* dialog and editing the `CFLAGS` of the HLS source file in the *Simulation* tab. Afterwards, the execution can be started by pressing the *Run C Simulation* icon in the toolbar. After the execution has started, the *Debug* view will be entered, where the usual functionality of a C/C++ debugger is available.

```
1 -DNO_SYNTH -I./include -I../../software/include -I./<action_directory>/include
```

Listing 1.4. `CFLAGS` necessary for the work bench setup.

4.4 Running on Hardware

Once the AFU has been successfully tested in the test bench and the simulator, it can be deployed to the FPGA hardware. For that purpose, the command `make image` needs to be executed from the `SNAP_ROOT` directory in order to synthesize bitstream images. Synthesizing the bitstream image is a compute-intensive process and can take any time from several minutes up to a couple of hours, depending on the complexity of the action at hands. Once the build process has successfully finished, the resulting bitstream files can be found in the `hardware/build/Image` folder. The file ending in `*.bit` can be flashed to the FPGA using a JTAG programmer; the `*.bin` file is intended to be flashed using the `capi-flash-script`.

Programming via JTAG Programmer. For a new FPGA card straight from the factory, the operating system will not detect it as a CAPI-enabled device, since the pre-installed image on the factory partition of the FPGA doesn't support CAPI. Hence, a suitable image needs to be flashed onto the user partition using an external JTAG programmer. While this process is slightly cumbersome, it usually has to be performed only once in the lifetime of the FPGA card. Afterwards, new bitstreams can be flashed from the host system.

On the machine connected to the JTAG programmer, a light-weight version of Vivado including the hardware server tool `hw_server` is sufficient. Once the Vivado *Hardware Manager* has successfully connected to the FPGA, the activity LEDs on the programmer should turn on.

If the FPGA card has not been detected as a CAPI device yet, the user partition of the FPGA will be cleared upon each power cycle of the POWER machine. Hence, for initialization purposes, a bitstream image needs to be flashed after the system has been powered on, but before the operating system performs the PCIe walk. The timespan in between the power cycle and booting the operating system kernel should be sufficient to finish the programming process before the host operating system has completed the boot process. Once this procedure has been completed, the FPGA should be appear under `/dev/cxl`.

Programming from the Host Machine. Once the FPGA is detected as a CAPI-device appearing under `/dev/cxl`, the `capi-flash-script` utility can be used to flash new bitstreams directly from the host. The tool is part of the `capi-utils`, which are available on GitHub [3].

5 Related Work

There are several technologies for leveraging FPGA compute resources in applications using high-level programming languages. The approaches can be loosely or tightly coupled. Intel offers a tightly coupled integration with *The Open Programmable Acceleration Engine* (OPAE) [9]. In many aspects, the approach is similar to IBM CAPI SNAP. It consists of libraries and kernel drivers offering resource management and abstraction of the underlying FPGA technology to the application developer. The OPAE C-Library [7] (`libopae-c`) is used by the applications to communicate with the FPGA. The building blocks on the FPGA device are comprised of a static part, the FPGA Management Engine (FME) and as many slots with accelerated function units (AFUs) as the device supports [9]. The AFUs an be partially reconfigured during runtime. One slot and one AFU form a function which can either be physical or virtual. The kernel driver supports SR-IOV so that virtual functions can be assigned to virtual machines [18]. The OPAE and CAPI SNAP are similar but also differ in several aspects, f.e. in OPAE there is no Job Management, the interface to the AFUs is given via a freely defined 256 KB Registers which have to be mapped into the address space of the host process to communicate.

There are also other approaches for leveraging FPGA accelerators using high-level programming languages. With *SDAccel* [15] Xilinx offers a development environment to execute C, C++ and OpenCL Kernels on FPGA Hardware. The *Intel FPGA SDK for OpenCL* [8] offers a similar development environment. Due to the lack of coherent host memory access, both technologies offer a more loosely coupled integration of the FPGA resources.

6 Outlook

To alleviate the complexity of developing FPGA-based accelerator functions for software engineers, the *OpenPOWER Accelerator Work Group* has recently introduced the *CAPI Storage, Network, and Analytics Programming* (SNAP) framework. Over the course of multiple graduate student projects, we have observed that the high level of abstraction provided by CAPI SNAP in conjunction with HLS, the framework enabled students to implement common algorithms in hardware and evaluate these accelerator-based resources within one semester. However, even though CAPI SNAP is well documented and comes with many examples, we have noticed that graduate students in software engineering found themselves challenged with certain details of the novel hardware development framework. At the same time, we also found that the framework helped students to improve their understanding of hardware development, as CAPI SNAP allowed them to concentrate on implementing application logic using a hardware description language without having to consider the complexity of any interface and management logic. In this paper, we consolidated these insights into a getting started guide, providing the background knowledge and the first instructions necessary for breaking down the remaining barriers for software engineers.

With the CAPI SNAP framework being a relatively young technology compared to well-established frameworks for heterogeneous computing, we think that it offers great potential for bridging the gap between hardware development and software engineering, allowing software engineers to tap into the extended solution space offered by the more flexible resources that FPGAs can offer. For users without access to IBM POWER systems and CAPI-supported FPGA cards, we recommend using the *SuperVessel Cloud for OpenPower* [2] service, which offers cloud-based access to CAPI-enabled resources for academic researchers. Also, we would like to stress that the active community behind CAPI SNAP has been very open-minded and forthcoming regarding feedback we provided. In general, the community-character is a welcome change to the closed, vendor-specific nature of other ecosystems met in the field of GPU-computing.

Since the limited space of a paper does not offer the ideal venue for a detailed hands-on guide, this paper is augmented with an extended online tutorial, which is available at https://www.dcl.hpi.uni-potsdam.de/capi-snap. The extended online tutorial covers several aspects of the CAPI SNAP framework, including setup, configuration and debugging in greater detail. Furthermore, it provides an additional section that documents the process of developing a new HLS-based AFU step-by-step, using the blowfish encryption algorithm as an exemplary workload.

Acknowledgements. We would like to thank everyone at IBM who held close contact and helped us during the project, including but not limited to: Frank Haverkamp, Jörg-Stephan Vogt, Sven Boekholt, Thomas Fuchs, Bruno Mesnet, Nicolas Mäding, and Bruce Wile.

References

1. Fowers, J., Brown, G., Cooke, P., Stitt, G.: A performance and energy comparison of FPGAs, GPUs, and multicores for sliding-window applications. In: Proceedings of the ACM/SIGDA International Symposium on Field Programmable Gate Arrays, FPGA 2012, pp. 47–56. ACM, New York (2012)
2. IBM China Research Lab: SuperVessel Cloud for POWER/OpenPower. https://ptopenlab.com/
3. IBM Corporation: capi-utils package. GitHub. https://github.com/ibm-capi/capi-utils
4. IBM Corporation: Power Service Layer Simulation Engine (PSLSE). GitHub. https://github.com/ibm-capi/pslse
5. IBM Corporation: PSL Checkpoint Files for the CAPI SNAP Design Kit. https://www-355.ibm.com/systems/power/openpower/tgcmDocumentRepository.xhtml?aliasId=CAPI
6. IBM Corporation: CAPI SNAP Education Series: Module #1 - CAPI SNAP Overview (2017) (Presentation)
7. Intel Corporation: Github Organisation for the Open Programmable Acceleration Engine. https://github.com/OPAE
8. Intel Corporation: Intel FPGA SDK for OpenCL, December 2017. https://www.altera.com/en_US/pdfs/literature/hb/opencl-sdk/aocl_programming_guide.pdf
9. Luebbers, E., Liu, S., Chu, M.: Simplify Software Integration for FPGA Accelerators with OPAE (White Paper). https://01.org/sites/default/files/downloads/opae/open-programmable-acceleration-engine-paper.pdf
10. OpenPOWER Accelerator Work Group: CAPI Storage, Network, and Analytics Programming (SNAP) Framework. IBM developerWorks. https://developer.ibm.com/linuxonpower/capi/snap/
11. OpenPOWER Accelerator Work Group: CAPI Storage, Network, and Analytics Programming (SNAP) Framework Repository. GitHub. https://github.com/open-power/snap
12. Stuecheli, J., Blaner, B., Johns, C.R., Siegel, M.S.: CAPI: a coherent accelerator processor interface. IBM J. Res. Dev. **59**(1), 7:1–7:7 (2015)
13. Wile, B.: Coherent Accelerator Processor Proxy (CAPI) on POWER8, October 2014. presented at Enterprise 2014
14. Wilke, K.: Tinkering with CAPI. Such Programming, January 2016. https://www.suchprogramming.com/tinkering-with-capi/
15. Xilinx Corporation: The Xilinx SDAccel Development Environment. https://www.xilinx.com/publications/prod_mktg/sdx/sdaccel-backgrounder.pdf
16. Xilinx Corporation: Vivado Design Suite. Product Website. https://www.xilinx.com/products/design-tools/vivado.html
17. Xilinx Inc.: Xilinx Introduces Zynq-7000 Family, Industry's First Extensible Processing Platform, March 2011. Press Release
18. Zhang, Z.: Getting Started With Open Programmable Acceleration Engine, August 2017. Webinar. https://www.brighttalk.com/webcast/10773/275799?utm_source=Intel+-+Data+Center+Group&utm_medium=brighttalk&utm_campaign=275799

Studying the Structure of Parallel Algorithms as a Key Element of High-Performance Computing Education

Vladimir Voevodin, Alexander Antonov(✉), and Nina Popova

Lomonosov Moscow State University, Moscow, Russia
{voevodin,asa}@parallel.ru, popova@cs.msu.su

Abstract. Since the computing world has become fully parallel, every software developer today should be familiar with the notion of "parallel algorithm structure." If in recent years, students have studied a basic introduction to algorithms; today, parallel algorithm structure must become a vital part of computer science education. In this work we present two years of experience teaching a "Supercomputer Modeling and Technologies" course, and running practical assignments at the Computational Mathematics and Cybernetics faculty of Lomonosov Moscow State University, aimed at teaching students a methodology for analyzing parallel algorithm properties.

Keywords: Structure of parallel algorithms · High-performance computing education · Parallel programming · Educational curricula · Computer science curricula · Undergraduate students

1 Introduction

Today, computing technologies are used in all areas of science, industry and economics, which imposes strict requirements on higher education systems training computer science specialists in all countries. One recent example is India's "National Supercomputing Mission" [1], during which the government set a 7-year target for training 20,000 specialists in the area of parallel and distributed computer technologies. The demand for actively developing education in the areas of computational sciences, high-performance computing, and mathematical modeling using supercomputers is evidenced throughout the entire global educational community [2–5].

The results described in Sects. 4, 5 were obtained in Lomonosov Moscow State University with the financial support of the Russian Science Foundation (Agreement № 14-11-00190). The research is carried out using the equipment of the shared research facilities of HPC computing resources at Lomonosov Moscow State University supported by the project RFMEFI62117X0011.

G. Mencagli et al. (Eds.): Euro-Par 2018 Workshops, LNCS 11339, pp. 199–210, 2019.
https://doi.org/10.1007/978-3-030-10549-5_16

A number of major national and international projects can be noted that offer recommendations for developing training materials in these areas [6–10]. Interesting results have been discussed at international seminars dedicated to the issue: EduHPC, EduPAR, Euro-EduPAR [11]. Books have been published that are entirely dedicated to the best materials and pedagogical practices in the area of PDC [12]. These activities are fueling growth in the number of educational courses and programs, with the mathematical modeling industry engaging specialists from various applied areas. This is further promoted by the emergence of new areas where high-performance computing is in high demand. The most recent examples where industries received a development boost thanks to HPC technologies are deep learning, artificial intelligence, and big data analytics.

This work consists of 5 sections. In Sects. 2 and 3 we give a brief overview of supercomputer education at the Computational Mathematics and Cybernetics faculty of Lomonosov Moscow State University, and describe how the "Supercomputer Modeling and Technologies" course is organized. Sections 4 and 5 describe two versions of practical assignments that are part of the course, which allow for two different perspectives on studying the structure of algorithms. From our point of view, focusing on the study of parallel algorithm structure in the form presented is a new approach, representing the key content of this work. Section 6 contains recommendations and conclusions based on two years of experience from teaching this course and conducting practical assignments in the form presented.

This approach to studying the structure of parallel algorithms is in line with existing proposals on the content of educational curricula, e.g., Computer Science Curricula [13], NSF/IEEE-TCPP Curriculum Initiative on Parallel and Distributed Computing [14], and can be used at many universities.

2 Supercomputer Education at MSU

Lomonosov Moscow State University provides a good basis for supercomputer education. MSU's supercomputer center is currently the most powerful in Russia. It is centered around the Lomonosov-2 (4.9 Petaflops) and Lomonosov (1.7 Petaflops) supercomputers and IBM Blue Gene/P (28 Teraflops). The basics of parallel computations are taught at several faculties within MSU: Computational Mathematics and Cybernetics, Mechanics and Mathematics, Physics, Chemistry, Bioengineering and Bioinformatics, and a few others.

CMC faculty is a leading educational center in Russia offering specialist training that combines applied mathematics, computational technologies and information science. It has about 2000 full-time students, with about 200 PhD candidates. Training at the faculty is provided as part of an integrated Master's degree program: for their first four years, students study within a Bachelor's degree program, followed by two years in one of twenty-two available Master's degree programs. This dual-level system offers basic fundamental training for students during years 1–4, with deeper specialization as a part of the Master's degree programs. Studying supercomputer-related disciplines is mandatory for all students at the faculty.

3 The Supercomputer Modeling and Technologies Discipline

The "Supercomputer Modeling and Technologies" course is the only general lecture course for all 22 Master's degree programs at CMC faculty. It is taught to second-year Master's degree students with a total of about 240 students taking the course. All students are expected to have basic knowledge of mathematical modeling, parallel computing systems and supercomputer architecture, and the basics of parallel computing.

The discipline totals 7 credits. The course consists of a lecture module, seminars and several practical assignments. Lectures are conducted for two academic hours a week from September to November. Two hours of seminars are also conducted each week. The seminars are used to discuss problem definitions and implementation details, to offer consultations on assignments, and for students to present reports on the assignments they have completed.

The course lasts for one semester, and two full cycles have been completed to date in the fall semesters of 2016 and 2017. Teachers from the various departments at the CMC faculty are invited to take part in delivering lectures, along with representatives from leading IT companies.

Students are offered three practical assignments as part of the course, of which two are mandatory. The first assignment requires studying and describing the structure and properties of parallel algorithms. The second assignment involves implementing a parallel algorithm to solve a three-dimensional hyperbolic equation using MPI and OpenMP. The third assignment is given by the lecturers in specific subject areas, and students can choose which lecturer's assignment they would like to perform. While the second and third assignments are classical assignments that directed to parallel implementations; the first one requires additional clarifications and is central to this work: Sects. 4, 5 and 6 of this article describe two options for the first assignment that are aimed at studying the properties of parallel algorithms.

The first assignment is indeed unusual and non-trivial, so students were allowed to work in pairs. Any parallel computers could be chosen as the target computing platform. By default, all students were provided access to MSU's supercomputers: Lomonosov [15] and IBM Blue Gene/P. Some students were granted access to the Lomonosov-2 supercomputer [16], clusters with Intel Xeon Phi (KNL) and/or NVIDIA P100 processors, clusters with the new "Angara" interconnect and several others. This enabled comparison of results across different processors (multicore/manycore Intel, NVIDIA GPU, IBM PowerPC), and various communication networks (InfiniBand, proprietary) with different network topologies (fat tree, 3-dimensional torus, flattened butterfly).

The results verification form is an important part of the assignment. The goal was not just to grade the work, but to make sure that students completed their assignments at a good level of quality. In fact, the idea was to teach students to find a proper approach to this kind of assignment. Instead of immediately grading the work, the tutors formulated their comments; the students would incorporate the feedback and send the assignment results back for further review.

This interaction was repeated as necessary, usually limited only by the deadline for grading course results at the end of the term. This is very different from the traditional assignment grading process. The purpose is not so much about making sure the course materials are absorbed correctly. Rather what is most important is to teach students an effective approach to analyzing algorithm properties in a proper and high-quality manner. This requires tutors to have a much higher level of qualification and to dedicate more time to the assessment, but the final results are comparable in quality with the best teaching practices.

4 Version of the Practical Assignment: Description of Parallel Algorithm Properties

Assignment: *Describe the structure and properties of the chosen algorithm.*

While this wording sounds extremely simple, it masks a number of small but important nuances. It is also important to note that in order to successfully complete this assignment, students need to use knowledge previously obtained over various disciplines at the faculty.

4.1 Methodological Comments on the Assignment

What does it mean to describe an algorithm's structure and properties? This is not a simple question, as there is no universally recognized standard specifying which properties of an algorithm are important and exactly how they must be described. The students were offered the algorithm description structure used by the AlgoWiki Open Encyclopedia of Algorithm Properties [17,18]. This description structure was developed as a universal one that can be applied to any algorithm, giving particular emphasis to the properties related to parallelism.

Some sections of the AlgoWiki description were left out of this assignment due to their complexity (for example, sections describing the data locality or dynamic characteristics of an algorithm's implementation). Ultimately, the following structure was recommended for students to use in their descriptions of the algorithm's properties:

1. General description of the algorithm.
2. Mathematical description of the algorithm.
3. Computational kernel of the algorithm.
4. Macro structure of the algorithm.
5. Implementation scheme of the serial algorithm.
6. Serial complexity of the algorithm.
7. Information graph.
8. Parallelism resource of the algorithm.
9. Input and output data of the algorithm.
10. Properties of the algorithm.
11. Scalability of the algorithm and its implementation.
12. Existing implementations of the algorithm.
13. References.

Notably, a number of examples are available in AlgoWiki for each item, which helped students to complete the assignment. The first ten items in the description require studying the algorithm's theoretical properties, while items 11 and 12 are oriented towards studying the properties of its specific implementations. The main focus of the assignment was not on the actual algorithm description (this part could simply be taken from textbooks), but on studying its properties — primarily the algorithm's information structure and parallelism resource. These properties are rarely described in the literature, so this part of the assignment required conducting independent research.

The central task in describing the algorithm properties would be to build and analyze an information graph (Item 7 of the above structure) [19,20]. Figure 1 shows the example information graph of the Cooley-Tukey algorithm with input and output data.

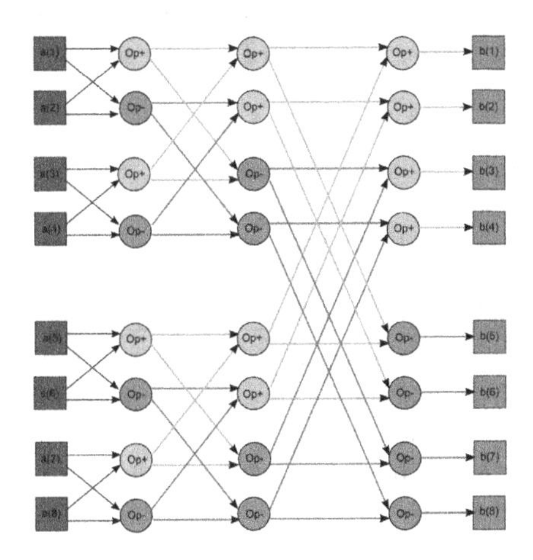

Fig. 1. The information graph of the Cooley-Tukey algorithm for n = 8. Op+ denotes the addition of two complex numbers, while Op- denotes the subtraction of two complex numbers followed by multiplying the result by another complex number (a twiddle factor). The edges correspond to the transmission of data between the vertices.

An information graph is vital for studying algorithm properties, as it contains all the necessary information about its parallel structure. The skills for working with an information graph are also very important in practice, as they help to evaluate an algorithm's parallel complexity and an application's parallelism resource, to understand the algorithm's bottlenecks and to find different options for parallel implementation. This is why special attention was paid to information graph analysis — both when formulating the student assignments and when checking the completed work.

To prepare a specific description, the students were asked to choose one of 30 preselected algorithms, specifically: Jacobi's method for the singular value decomposition, Gram-Schmidt orthogonalization process, fast discrete Fourier transform, and others. These algorithms are all certainly different in complexity. However, the essence of the assignment was not about developing algorithms, nor even about implementing them, so the complexity of the algorithm itself didn't affect the complexity of the assignment so much.

4.2 Organization and Results of the First Practical Assignment

This version of the assignment was completed by 246 Master's degree students in 2016, during their second year of education. As a result, each of the 30 proposed algorithms was described by 4–5 groups of 1–2 students each. The students could use any literature or online sources in their algorithm descriptions, as long as they were appropriately cited. Moreover, when the assignment was distributed, each algorithm was accompanied by references to well-known sources that explain the algorithm. This addressed two issues at once: the students would get a reliable source of information, and both the student and the tutor would be guaranteed to have an unequivocal understanding of which specific algorithm was to be described.

Due to the volume of the work produced, the resulting descriptions were verified in two independent stages. The first stage involved a purely formal verification of the descriptions for compliance with the requirements. This included checking for the presence of all relevant description sections, the clarity of the formulas, the information content of any drawings used, the inclusion of all parameters and conditions under which the algorithm properties were studied, references to sources, etc. The content of the algorithm descriptions was not checked at this stage, to reduce the requirements for inspector qualifications and the time needed to perform the verification. The second stage of the verification required a review of content. The algorithm description was checked for accuracy, the proper definition and description of its properties, proper formulas and the accuracy of the results. These checks required much more time and substantially higher tutor qualifications.

The technical evaluation was successfully supported by useful features of AlgoWiki, based on MediaWiki technology. The students prepared algorithm descriptions in their personal spaces and interacted with tutors using a built-in collaboration mechanism. This facilitated communication student — tutor, in addition to tracking every stage of the assignment, including any changes made in the descriptions, tutor comments, date of response to tutor feedback, etc.

The final grades of the 146 groups comprising the 246 students were distributed as follows: 59 works received a 5 (Excellent) grade; 36 were graded at 4 (Good), 48 received a 3 (Satisfactory) grade, and three works were evaluated as 2 (Unsatisfactory). Thus, the average grade for the assignment was 4.03, which indicates a generally high level of description quality given the complexity and novelty of the assignment.

Remarkably, some of the student works were completed with such a high quality level that they were included in the AlgoWiki Encyclopedia. In some cases, the students went beyond the assignment formulation, conducting additional studies of other issues related to parallelism. Moreover, some of the students became so engaged in studying the selected algorithms that they continued enhancing their results even after the semester ended.

5 Version of the Practical Assignment: Studying Algorithm Scalability

Assignment: *Studying the scalability of algorithms and their implementations on various computing platforms when changing the size of the problem and the number of processors available.*

5.1 Methodological Comments on the Assignment

When performing the second version of the assignment as part of the "Supercomputer Modeling and Technologies" course, students needed to perform a series of computational experiments, collect the relevant data, interpret it correctly, then draw a conclusion on the algorithm's level of scalability. Additionally, they needed to determine from the data obtained, which combination of problem size and the quantity of processors maximized performance.

Graph algorithms were chosen as the subject of study in 2017. Five key problems were considered: Single Source Shortest Path, Breadth-First Search, Page Rank, Minimum Spanning Tree, and Strongly Connected Components.

The students could choose one of several available algorithms for each problem. For example, the options for the "Single Source Shortest Path" problem were the Bellman-Ford, Dijkstra's and Delta-Stepping algorithms. Since the objective of this assignment was not to study parallel programming technologies, up to 5 different ready-made implementations were offered for each algorithm, which were to be used in computational experiments on the chosen computer platform. As a result, each student chose a unique combination within which scalability [21] was to be examined:

Problem → Algorithm → Implementation → Computing platform.

Computer performance for these algorithms is frequently measured in TEPS (Traversed Edges Per Second), indicating the number of graph edges the computer can pass (process) in one second using a given implementation of a given algorithm. This parameter was used in our assignment to assess performance.

Special attention was paid to processing large graphs, which are common in practical applications: social networks, road maps, chemical compounds and many other real-life objects are described using graphs with millions and billions of vertices and edges. At the same time, as the graph size increases, its implementation performance can drop substantially, as data no longer fit in cache memory at different levels; hence the interest in carefully measuring the dependence between the size of the problem, number of processors and performance.

Another important issue is that dynamic characteristics of graph algorithms can change significantly with changes in the structure and properties of the graphs being processed. For this reason, each student needed to study scalability for two types of graphs: RMAT and SSCA2. These are synthetic graphs reflecting different properties of real-life graphs: RMAT graphs are suitable for modeling the structure of social networks [22], while SSCA2 graphs are good for describing a set of interconnected communities [23]. To obtain input RMAT/SSCA2 graphs of an arbitrary size, students were provided ready-made parallel generators.

As a result, the assignment for each student was formulated as follows: for each of the two graph types: RMAT and SSCA2, within the chosen combination "Problem → Algorithm → Implementation → Computing platform," it was required to:

- build a chart showing the dependence (MTEPS) on the number of processors (or threads) used and the graph size;
- find the combination of processor number and graph size that maximizes performance.

Since the assignment was focused on analyzing large graphs, the maximum performance point was to be calculated only for those problem sizes where the graph did not fit entirely within cache memory. Figure 2(a) shows the dependence experimentally determined by one of the students for the Breadth First Search algorithm without considering this requirement, where maximum performance is achieved on a small graph of 2^{12} vertices.

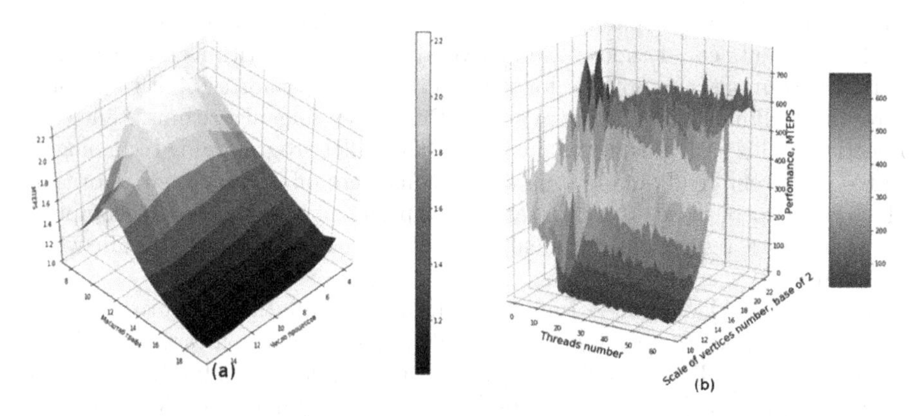

Fig. 2. Particular aspects of the assignment: (a) impact of cache memory on maximum performance value, (b) value fluctuations in the absence of multiple runs

One has to note the substantial computing resources needed to perform the assignment properly. The assignment required the programs to be run multiple times: the performance values were to be assessed for different graph sizes and different processor numbers, for each of the two graph types (RMAT and SSCA2). Moreover, performance values on nearly every computer would change from one run to another, so ideally several experiments needed to be conducted and the maximum value chosen, otherwise the resulting chart would contain obvious artifacts, like the example shown in Fig. 2(b).

To motivate students to conduct a more thorough analysis of the scalability figures obtained, it is useful to show the results obtained by other students using other algorithms, other implementations and other computers (an example is shown in Table 1). When comparing their maximum performance figures to other results, students begin to ask the question: "Why am I doing worse?" Finding the answer would require analyzing the entire chain "Problem → Algorithm → Implementation → Computing platform," which helps students realize the need for a comprehensive approach for studying scalability.

Table 1. Comparison of maximum performance for different algorithms solving the "Single Source Shortest Path" problem using different implementations on different platforms.

Algorithm	Implementation	Computing Platform	MTEPS	GraphType	GraphSize
Bellman-Ford	RCC for GPU	Lomonosov	1309.0	SSCA2	2^{20}
Bellman-Ford	Ligra	Lomonosov-2	1035.0	RMAT	2^{21}
Delta Stepping	PBGL MPI	Cluster/"Angara"	809.5	SSCA2	2^{21}
Delta Stepping	GAP	Lomonosov-2	616.0	RMAT	2^{21}
Bellman-Ford	RCC for CPU	Lomonosov	435.0	SSCA2	2^{21}
Bellman-Ford	RCC for CPU	Lomonosov-2	426.0	RMAT	2^{21}
Bellman-Ford	Graph500 MPI	Lomonosov	350.0	RMAT	2^{20}
Dijkstra's	PBGL MPI	IBM BlueGene/P	8.9	SSCA2	2^{20}
Dijkstra's	PBGL MPI	Lomonosov	5.3	SSCA2	2^{21}

5.2 Organization and Results of the First Practical Assignment

This version of the first practical assignment was performed in 2017 by 143 groups of Master's degree students and the grades were distributed as follows: 121 works received a 5 (Excellent) grade; 15 were graded at 4 (Good), 5 received a 3 (Satisfactory) grade, and two works were evaluated as 2 (Unsatisfactory). The average grade for scalability description was 4.78. This is much higher than the average for the 2016 assignment (4.03), which is not surprising: the scalability study assignment was simpler and more familiar than the task of studying and describing algorithm properties. In addition, when students described algorithm properties in 2016, they had to present, among other things, their considerations for algorithm's scalability, as this was required in the description structure (Item 11). At the same time, the assignment form chosen in 2017, turned out successfully in a different way. By combining a simple assignment statement with the need to interpret the obtained data, we achieve our goal: students begin to think not just about the scalability analysis methodology and the notions of weak and strong scalability, but also to learn the techniques for studying parallel program scalability in practice. Moreover, when analyzing scalability data, students recognize the need for the joint (and specifically joint) study of the various algorithm properties, implementations and computing platforms.

6 Lessons Learnt from the 2-Year Experience

Let's look at some important issues that one must keep in mind when using similar assignments in the future. Some of them we chose to point out to students at the very beginning, when distributing the assignments; others were faced during the course of work, causing difficulties for students or tutors.

When describing algorithm properties, it is important to realize that not just floating point arithmetic matters, but also read-write memory operations which determine the execution time for many algorithms. In particular, it is necessary to describe the computational core and sequential complexity of algorithms.

When defining the information structure of an algorithm, it is important to define a level of details for operations. Otherwise, the students could produce a linear graph of 3–4 vertices reflecting the sequential stages of the algorithm: while this isn't necessarily wrong, it clearly isn't very informative either.

Some algorithms are based on other, simpler algorithms. In these cases, it was advisable to use "macro-operations" that corresponded to simpler algorithms, as they could be more traditional, expressive and clear for describing and understanding the structure of the original algorithms.

The information structure of the algorithms could be expressed in different ways, with no set standards. However, the students were best off using a system of axes related to the loop nesting structure: in that case, the information graph reflects the computation structure used in the program and is more intuitive.

Describing an algorithm's potential parallelism is challenging for the students. This is not a habitual notion, and students don't always immediately learn to look at the algorithm structure in general. Methodological materials need to be developed that contain sample descriptions of potential parallelism, clearly showing what kind of results is expected from the students.

When studying scalability, it is important to draw the students' attention to explain all of the feature points on the performance charts: peaks, inflection points, asymptote starting points, etc. Detailed analysis is not simple, but if peculiarities consistently repeat between runs, then there must be an explanation.

For self-written programs independently, the students needed to clarify the testing technology for the program implementing the given algorithm. This is important, as the results presented will otherwise not be trustworthy.

7 Conclusion

Overall, we consider the two-year track record in teaching the "Supercomputer Modeling and Technologies" course along with the practical assignments to be a highly positive experience. A spacious inter-disciplinary approach to problems under study, supported by specific practical assignments on actual supercomputers, creates a solid foundation for using the knowledge gained in further professional activities. Indeed, obtaining good results required serious efforts from both students and professors. But it was worth it! Students must use knowledge and skills from previous courses, which is a good way to bring them closer to completing their Master's degree studies.

Practical assignments can easily be adapted to the specific environment of another faculty by using a different set of algorithms, placing particular emphasis on studying different algorithm properties, analyzing their own implementations, studying existing source codes, focusing on the scalability of a specific computing platform, and many other aspects.

The courses implemented in 2016 and 2017 are considered to be a pilot program. Given the positive results achieved, we are planning to modify the topics covered during the lecture part of the course, including areas such as supercomputer climate modeling, high-performance image processing methods, deep learning, and big data analytics.

Acknowledgments. We are sincerely grateful to our colleagues form the Faculty of Computational Mathematics and Cybernetics and the Research Computing Center who helped us to deliver the lectures and organize the practical assignments—completing the educational program in this form without their help would simply have been impossible.

References

1. National Supercomputing Mission. https://www.nsmindia.in/. Accessed 4 May 2018
2. Secretary of Energy Advisory Board. Report of the Task Force on Next Generation High Performance Computing, U.S. Department of Energy. August 18, 2014. https://www.energy.gov/sites/prod/files/2014/10/f18/SEAB%20HPC%20Task%20Force%20Final%20Report.pdf. Accessed 4 May 2018
3. Ezell, S.J., Atkinson, R.D.: The Vital Importance of High-Performance Computing to U.S. Competitiveness. http://www2.itif.org/2016-high-performance-computing.pdf. Accessed 4 May 2018
4. SIAM Working Group on CSE Education. SIAM: Graduate Education for Computational Science and Engineering (2014). http://www.siam.org/students/resources/report.php. Accessed 4 May 2018
5. Chapman, B., et al.: DOE: assessment of workforce development needs in office of science research disciplines. http://science.energy.gov/~/media/ascr/ascac/pdf/charges/ASCAC_Workforce_Letter_Report.pdf. Accessed 4 May 2018
6. Dongarra, J., et al.: Applied Mathematics Research for Exascale Computing, US - DOE Report, March 2014. https://science.energy.gov/~/media/ascr/pdf/research/am/docs/EMWGreport.pdf. Accessed 4 May 2018
7. Future Directions in CSE Education and Research. Report from a Workshop Sponsored by the Society for Industrial and Applied Mathematics (SIAM) and the European Exascale Software Initiative (EESI-2). http://wiki.siam.org/siag-cse/images/siag-cse/f/ff/CSE-report-draft-Mar2015.pdf. Accessed 4 May 2018
8. Voevodin, V., Gergel, V., Popova, N.: Challenges of a systematic approach to parallel computing and supercomputing education. In: Hunold, S., et al. (eds.) Euro-Par 2015. LNCS, vol. 9523, pp. 90–101. Springer, Cham (2015). https://doi.org/10.1007/978-3-319-27308-2_8
9. Supercomputing Education in Russia. Final report on the national project "Supercomputing Education", Supercomputing Consortium of the Russian Universities (2012). http://hpc.msu.ru/files/HPC-Education-in-Russia.pdf. Accessed 4 May 2018

10. Voevodin, Vl.V., Gergel, V.P.: Supercomputing education: the third pillar of HPC. In: Computational Methods and Software Development: New Computational Technologies, vol. 11, no. 2, pp. 117–122. Moscow State University Press, Moscow (2010)
11. 3rd European Workshop on Parallel and Distributed Computing Education for Undergraduate Students (Euro-EDUPAR). http://www.cs.man.ac.uk/~rizos/euroedupar/. Accessed 4 May 2018
12. Prasad, S.K., Gupta, A., Rosenberg, A.L., Sussman, A., Weems Jr., C.C. (eds.): Topics in Parallel and Distributed Computing: Introducing Concurrency in Undergraduate Courses. Morgan Kaufmann, San Francisco (2015)
13. Computer Science Curricula 2013. https://www.acm.org/binaries/content/assets/education/cs2013_web_final.pdf. Accessed 4 May 2018
14. NSF/IEEE-TCPP Curriculum Initiative on Parallel and Distributed Computing. http://www.cs.gsu.edu/~tcpp/curriculum. Accessed 4 May 2018
15. Sadovnichy, V., Tikhonravov, A., Voevodin, Vl., and Opanasenko, V.: "Lomonosov": supercomputing at Moscow State University. In: Contemporary High Performance Computing: From Petascale Toward Exascale, pp. 283–307. Chapman & Hall/CRC Computational Science), CRC Press, Boca Raton (2013)
16. MSU Supercomputers: "Lomonosov-2". http://hpc.msu.ru/?q=node/159. Accessed 4 May 2018
17. Open Encyclopedia of Parallel Algorithmic Features. http://algowiki-project.org/en. Accessed 4 May 2018
18. Antonov, A., Voevodin, V., Dongarra, J.: Algowiki: an open encyclopedia of parallel algorithmic features. J. Supercomput. Front. Innov. **2**(1), 4–18 (2015)
19. Voevodin, V.: Mathematical Foundations of Parallel Computing. Series in Computer Science, vol. 33. World Scientific Publishing Co. (1992)
20. Voevodin, V., Voevodin, Vl.: Parallel Computing. BHV-Petersburg, St. Petersburg (2002)
21. Antonov, A., Teplov, A.: Generalized approach to scalability analysis of parallel applications. In: Carretero, J., et al. (eds.) ICA3PP 2016. LNCS, vol. 10049, pp. 291–304. Springer, Cham (2016). https://doi.org/10.1007/978-3-319-49956-7_23
22. Chakrabarti, D., Zhan, Y., Faloutsos, C.: R-MAT: a recursive model for graph mining. In: Proceedings of 4th International Conference on Data Mining, Brighton, UK, pp. 442–446 (2004). https://doi.org/10.1137/1.9781611972740.43
23. Bader, D.A., Madduri, K.: Design and implementation of the HPCS graph analysis benchmark on symmetric multiprocessors. In: Bader, D.A., Parashar, M., Sridhar, V., Prasanna, V.K. (eds.) HiPC 2005. LNCS, vol. 3769, pp. 465–476. Springer, Heidelberg (2005). https://doi.org/10.1007/11602569_48

From Mathematical Model to Parallel Execution to Performance Improvement: Introducing Students to a Workflow for Scientific Computing

Franziska Kasielke[1(✉)] and Ronny Tschüter[2]

[1] Faculty of Computer Science, Technische Universität Dresden, 01062 Dresden, Germany
{franziska.kasielke,ronny.tschueter}@tu-dresden.de
[2] Center for Information Services and High Performance Computing, Technische Universität Dresden, 01062 Dresden, Germany

Abstract. Current courses in parallel and distributed computing (PDC) often focus on programming models and techniques. However, PDC is embedded in a scientific workflow that incorporates more than programming skills. The workflow spans from mathematical modeling to programming, data interpretation, and performance analysis. Especially the last task is covered insufficiently in educational courses. Often scientists from different fields of knowledge, each with individual expertise, collaborate to perform these tasks. In this work, the general design and the implementation of an exercise within the course "Supercomputers and their programming" at Technische Universität Dresden, Faculty of Computer Science is presented. In the exercise, the students pass through a complete workflow for scientific computing. The students gain or improve their knowledge about: (i) mathematical modeling of systems, (ii) transferring the mathematical model to a (parallel) program, (iii) visualization and interpretation of the experiment results, and (iv) performance analysis and improvements. The exercise exactly aims at bridging the gap between the individual tasks of a scientific workflow and equip students with wide knowledge.

Keywords: Workflow for scientific computing · Teaching
Parallel programming · Performance analysis · Heat transfer

1 Introduction

Besides theory and experiment, simulation is the third pillar of science [8]. The increasing numerical complexity of simulation models results in a high computational effort. Furthermore, the memory demands of scientific simulations often exceed the amount of memory accessible by a single process. These factors render sequential execution infeasible. *Parallel and distributed computing* (PDC)

G. Mencagli et al. (Eds.): Euro-Par 2018 Workshops, LNCS 11339, pp. 211–221, 2019.
https://doi.org/10.1007/978-3-030-10549-5_17

enables fine-granular and large-scale simulations on highly parallel computer systems. As a consequence, PDC acts as a central service for computational science and has to be an integral part of educating future scientists. However, the task of training students in PDC is more than just teaching programming skills. Developers of parallel scientific applications need a profound knowledge about:

- Mathematical modeling to express the problem by, e.g., algebraic operators, differential operators, and/or functions,
- Computer science (CS) and computer engineering (CE) to transfer the mathematical model into statements of a programming language, and
- Visualization and interpretation of experiment results to gain knowledge out of raw data.

Additionally, performance analysis and improvements of scientific applications are important aspects. Despite these aspects being an integral part of the daily work of scientists, they are often missed in education. Scientific applications need to be tuned in order to leverage the full potential of computer systems, as well as to scale parallel applications to a larger amount of processes.

In summary, in order to successfully implement scientific applications a *workflow for scientific computing* has to cover all aspects: mathematical modeling, programming, working with HPC systems, data visualization and interpretation, as well as performance analysis and improvement [4].

In this work, a lecture and, especially, an associated exercise at Technische Universität Dresden is presented. Both lecture and exercise introduce students to the workflow for scientific computing. In addition, current feedback revealed that students experience a lack of practical programming exercises in their courses. Therefore, the exercise also aims to improve their programming skills. The specific contributions of this work comprise:

- The general design and goals of the course "Supercomputers and their programming" and, especially, one of the associated exercises at Technische Universität Dresden,
- The implementation of the exercise in order to address current limitations/ drawbacks in the education of students,
- Bridging the gap between domain scientists and computer experts by
  - Introducing students to a complete workflow of implementing scientific applications,
  - Emphasize on both mathematical modeling as well as programming skills, and
- Reporting on experiences gained during the course and exercises.

The remainder of this work is organized as follows: In Sect. 2, design aspects of the course and one of the associated exercises are described in detail. The implementation of these aspects within the exercise is presented in Sect. 3. The feedback from current students and tutors is summarized in Sect. 4. Additionally, an outlook on future enhancements is given.

2 Design of the Exercise: Workflow for Scientific Computing

The course "Supercomputers and their programming" at Technische Universität Dresden, Faculty of Computer Science, is characterized by a heterogeneous audience. This course addresses undergraduate and graduate students of computer science, information systems engineering, mathematics, computational science and engineering, as well as natural and engineering sciences. The focus is on strategies and methods for parallel processing including common programming models, architecture and networking concepts, and required algorithmic components of parallel and distributed computing. Furthermore, the course is influenced by experiences of the interdisciplinary application area at the Center for Information Services and High Performance Computing (ZIH). At Technische Universität Dresden, the academic year consists of a summer and a winter semesters. Each semester includes a teaching period of 15 weeks. Both, the lecture and the associated exercise, take place once a week with a duration of 90 min each.

Since the students attending the course come from different fields of science, their existing knowledge varies widely. Either the students have comprehensive expertise in (parallel) programming and only basic to none expertise in numerical modeling of scientific applications, or vice versa. An exercise comprising two sessions was created to bridge this gap. The idea of this exercise is to convey expertise in both areas: numerical modeling of scientific applications as well as parallel programming including performance analysis and improvement. Based on the example of a heat transfer simulation, the students practically pass through a complete, albeit simplified, workflow for scientific computing. Considering the entire workflow for scientific computing represents the unique characteristic of this exercise.

In the following subsections, the design of the exercise is described in more detail: the mathematical model, the parallel implementation and execution, as well as visualization and performance analysis aspects. The implementation of these aspects within the exercise is explained in Sect. 3.

2.1 Mathematical Model

For convenience and without loss of generality, in the exercise the heat transfer simulation in a two-dimensional space is considered. The propagation of thermal energy in a given two-dimensional space is described by the following parabolic partial differential equation:

$$\frac{\partial}{\partial t}u(x,y,t) = a \cdot \left(\frac{\partial^2}{\partial x^2}u(x,y,t) + \frac{\partial^2}{\partial y^2}u(x,y,t)\right), \qquad (1)$$

where a denotes the thermal diffusivity. A visualization of the heat distribution in a two-dimensional space with a source of heat at the center of the region is shown in Fig. 1.

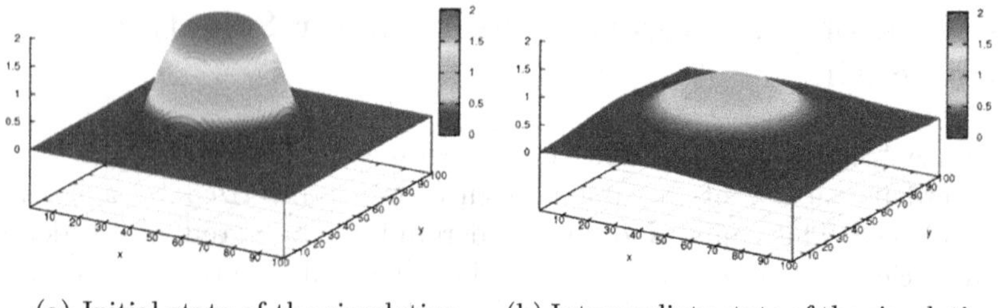

(a) Initial state of the simulation (b) Intermediate state of the simulation

Fig. 1. Heat distribution in a two-dimensional space, heat source at the center

The finite difference method is used to obtain the numerical solution of Eq. 1. The continuous partial differential equation is approximated with a discrete equation. The heat distribution u is determined on a grid $\Omega = \{(x_i, y_j, t_k)\}$, with $x_i := i \cdot \Delta x$ $(i = 1, \ldots, n_x)$, $y_j := j \cdot \Delta y$ $(j = 1, \ldots, n_y)$, and $t_k := k \cdot \Delta t$ $(k = 1, \ldots, n_t)$, where Δx, Δy, and Δt denote the increments in x-, y-, and t-direction. The heat distribution in a given cell (x_i, y_j) of the grid at a given time step t_k is denoted as $u(x_i, y_j, t_k) := u|_{i,j}^k$. Approximating the time derivative by the forward differencing scheme and the space derivatives by the 2nd order central differencing scheme yields:

$$\frac{u|_{i,j}^{t+1} - u|_{i,j}^t}{\Delta t} = a \cdot \left(\frac{u|_{i+1,j}^t - 2u|_{i,j}^t + u|_{i-1,j}^t}{\Delta x^2} + \frac{u|_{i,j+1}^t - 2u|_{i,j}^t + u|_{i,j-1}^t}{\Delta y^2} \right). \quad (2)$$

The solution of Eq. 2 requires the specification of boundary conditions. Well-known representatives are Dirichlet and Neumann boundary conditions. The Dirichlet boundary condition specifies the value by a function, whereas the Neumann boundary condition specifies the value by the normal derivative of the function. Periodic boundary conditions represent a special case. For the sake of simplicity, periodic boundary conditions are assumed, given by:

$$\begin{aligned} u|_{0,j}^t &= u|_{n_x,j}^t, \quad & u|_{n_x+1,j}^t &= u|_{1,j}^t \quad (\forall j = 1, \ldots, n_y), \\ u|_{i,0}^t &= u|_{i,n_y}^t, \quad & u|_{i,n_y+1}^t &= u|_{i,1}^t \quad (\forall i = 1, \ldots, n_x). \end{aligned} \quad (3)$$

2.2 Parallel Implementation and Execution on HPC Resources

The implementation of the heat distribution (Eq. 2) with periodic boundary conditions uses two two-dimensional grids of the size $n_x \times n_y$. One is the present grid, the other one is the temporary grid. For calculation of the heat distribution at the boundaries according to Eq. 3, these grids are expanded at the boundaries resulting in a grid size of $(n_x + 2) \times (n_y + 2)$.

The heat distribution is computed for all inner cells in the present grid for one time step, the results are saved in the temporary grid. After completing the calculations of one time step, the boundary cells are updated with the new values (according to Eq. 3). The present and the temporary grid are swapped in order to prepare computations of the next time step. A visualization of this computing scheme is shown in Fig. 2.

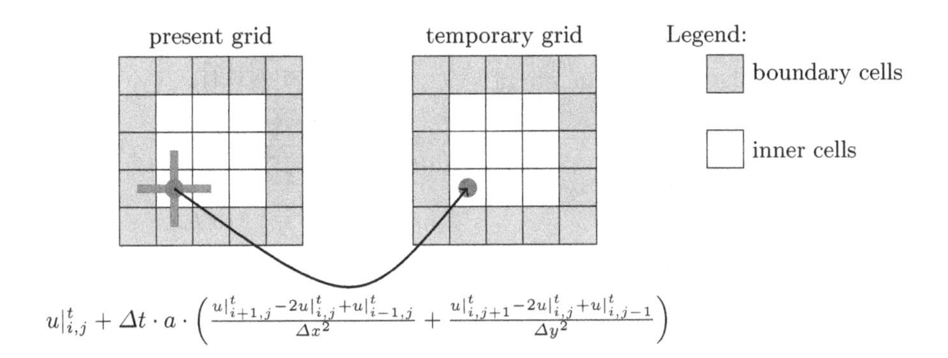

Fig. 2. Computing the heat distribution at one time step using the present (left-hand side) and the temporary (right-hand side) grid

The heat distribution is parallelized using the Message Passing Interface (MPI) [6]. MPI is widely used and proved its performance on a wide range of hardware platforms. It is assumed that the available processes $P_1, \ldots, P_k$ can be arranged in a two-dimensional cartesian grid. The computational grid is evenly partitioned over the process grid. The partitioning of the computational grid over four processes is shown in Fig. 3.

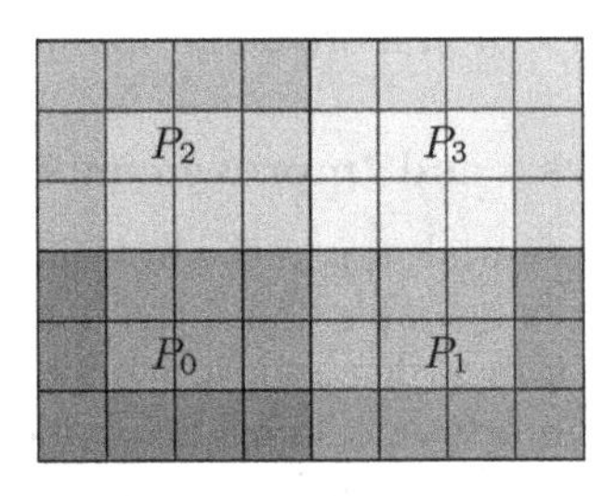

Fig. 3. Partitioning of the computational grid over four processes

Each process works on its own parts of the present and temporary grid. Communication is necessary for computing the heat distribution at the boundaries of the partial present grid. Therefore, the grids of the processes are extended by halo cells at the boundaries. The required data transfers of a process P_i $(i \in 1, \ldots, k)$ including the neighborhood relations are shown in Fig. 4.

After finishing the simulation, the overall energy of the system is computed by gathering and adding the final values of all inner grid cells. A loss of energy

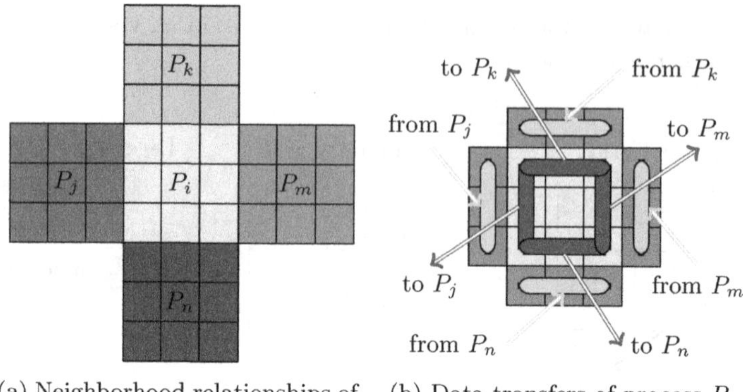

(a) Neighborhood relationships of process P_i

(b) Data transfers of process P_i

Fig. 4. Neighborhood relations and corresponding data transfers of process P_i

in the system between the start and the end of the simulation detects failures in the implementation.

The parallel implementation of the heat distribution is executed on *Taurus*. This Bull HPC system at Technische Universität Dresden, Germany, consists of 2,085 nodes with a total theoretical peak performance of 2,087 TFLOP/s.

2.3 Visualization and Interpretation of the Simulation Results

The numerical solution of the heat distribution is written to a file periodically. A simple visualization tool is offered in the exercise. The correct distribution of the heat energy in the computational domain over time can be determined intuitively. The tool is described in more detail in Subsect. 3.3.

2.4 Performance Analysis and Improvements

Performance analysis is an essential step in the workflow for scientific computing. Due to the increasing numerical complexity of the underlying simulation models scientific applications show a high demand on compute resources. Performance analysis and corresponding improvements of the applications can help to reduce execution times or increase applications' scalability. This enables time critical use case scenarios like weather forecasts. Additionally, if the simulation requires less time it often directly translates into reduced cost in terms of energy. In the exercise, students use established tools (e.g., Score-P [5], Cube [2], Vampir [3]) for the performance analysis of the parallel heat distribution application.

3 Implementation of the Exercise: Workflow for Scientific Computing

In this section, the implementation of an exercise within the course is highlighted. Within this exercise students learn the basic concepts of PDC, e.g., domain decomposition, communication, and synchronization between processing elements. Another important aspect of this exercise is teaching students to build upon existing libraries and tools instead of starting from scratch. Additionally, students are introduced to the concepts of working with HPC systems.

3.1 Mathematical Model

The exercise starts with a brief introduction to the numerical solution of the heat distribution. In a slide set, the mathematical model (as shown in Sect. 2.1) is presented to the students. Typically, students with a science background are more familiar with these aspects than CS/CE students.

3.2 Parallel Implementation and Execution on HPC Resources

In the exercise, the students implement a heat distribution simulation in the C programming language and use MPI in order to parallelize the application. Due to time constraints, the students would not be able to implement the application from scratch. Therefore, they receive a source code skeleton from the tutors. This skeleton already contains the basic program structure (see Listing 1.1). However, essential parts of the source code (e.g., domain decomposition, data transfer between processes) are left blank and marked to be implemented by the students. The programming exercises start with fairly simple tasks, such as, initializing the MPI environment (`MPI_Init`), determining the number of all MPI processes (`MPI_Comm_size`) or the global MPI rank (`MPI_Comm_rank`). More challenging tasks include parallel I/O (`MPI_File_open`, `MPI_File_set_view`, `MPI_File_read`, `MPI_File_write`, `MPI_File_close`) to read/write data from/to files. In order to distribute data over participating processes, the students create cartesian topologies and associated MPI communicators (`MPI_Dims_create`, `MPI_Cart_create`). The implementation of the halo update after each iteration requires the determination of the neighbor ranks in the cartesian communicator (`MPI_Cart_shift`) and subsequent data exchanges with the appropriate neighbor ranks (`MPI_Isend`, `MPI_Recv`, `MPI_Wait`). In addition, the update of the vertical halo cells makes use of derived datatypes (`MPI_Type_vector`, `MPI_Type_commit`, `MPI_Type_free`). Finally, a collective operation (`MPI_Reduce`) computes the overall energy of the system.

For some students, this exercise is the first opportunity to work on HPC systems. Using HPC systems differs fundamentally from the experience students gained by working on their local machines.

First, HPC systems typically provide a wide range of software components (e.g., libraries, compilers, tools). Often multiple versions of software components are available. Therefore, the students are introduced to the idea and usage of environment modules. In the exercise, students use the *LMOD* module system to select the compiler and MPI runtime.

Second, in contrast to a local system, multiple users share the compute resources of a HPC machine. Therefore, a job scheduling system allocates

Listing 1.1. Pseudo code illustrating the algorithm of the heat distribution simulation

```
/* initialize grid from file */
loadGridFromFile();

/* initialize temporary grid */
initializeTempGrid();

/* heat distribution calculation phase */
for ( count = 0; count < max_steps; count++ ) {
    /* save intermediate result to file */
    if ( count % 20 ) {
        saveGridToFile();
    }
    heatCalculation();
}

/* save result to file */
saveGridToFile();
```

resources for each application run (job) initiated by the user. Taurus is operated with the *Slurm* job scheduling system. The students write their own job script to request appropriate compute resources (e.g., select compute nodes from partitions equipped with Haswell CPUs). Afterwards, the students learn how to submit, cancel, and monitor their jobs.

3.3 Visualization and Interpretation of the Simulation Results

As shown in Listing 1.1, every 20 iterations the heat simulation writes its intermediate results to a file. At the end of the application run, also the final heat distribution is written to this file. Consequently, the result file contains a series of snapshots. Each snapshot represents an individual state of the heat distribution at a specific simulation time step. In this exercise, the students use a prepared bash script to generate a movie showing the heat flow over time. The bash script opens the result file. Within the main loop of the bash script an individual snapshot is read and converted to a PNG image using *Gnuplot*. Two of these PNG images are illustrated in Fig. 5. Finally, the bash script calls *ffmpeg* to create an MP4 video based on the series of PNG images.

3.4 Performance Analysis and Improvements

Tasks with respect to performance analysis and improvements complement the overview of the workflow for scientific computing. The goal is to monitor the application and observe its runtime behavior. Therefore, the students recompile the application with the Score-P [5] measurement infrastructure. For the presented example, Score-P automatically enables compiler instrumentation for user

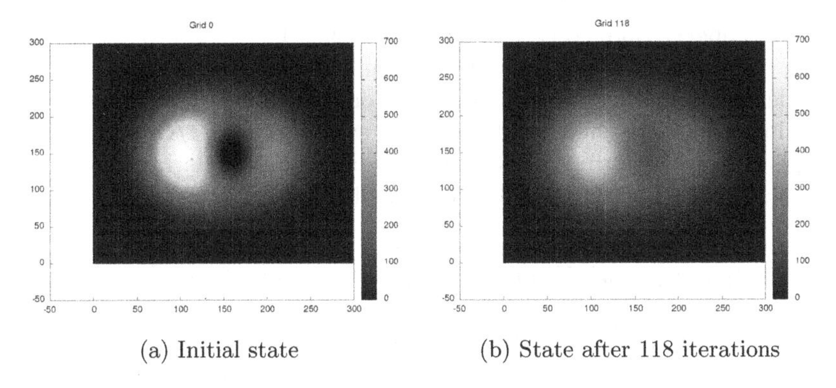

Fig. 5. Visualization of the result data generated by the heat distribution simulation code

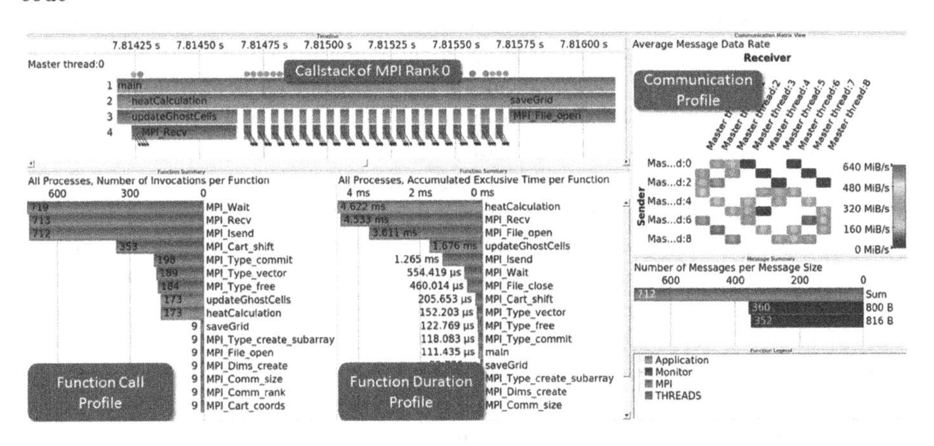

Fig. 6. Trace visualization of the time interval of 20 iterations in the heat simulation, at the end of this interval the application starts writing intermediate results to a file

functions within the source code and intercepts calls to the MPI library. As a consequence, calls to MPI and user functions trigger the measurement system at application runtime. Whenever triggered, the measurement system collects performance data (e.g., timestamp, function name, hardware performance counter) and stores the information as a *profile* (aggregated data) or *trace* (log of individual events). Guided by the tutors, the students use established tools, e.g., Cube [2] and Vampir [3], to visualize and analyze this performance data. The visualization of a trace in the Vampir analysis tool is shown in Fig. 6. The students learn how to interpret profiles and traces, correlate performance patterns with source code, and gain knowledge about the application behavior. Based on this knowledge, students and tutors discuss about ideas to improve the performance of the application. For example, the performance analysis of the initial application reveals that most of the runtime is spent in MPI. On the one hand, this performance issue stems from inefficient usage of MPI routines (e.g., the result file is opened and closed for each snapshot). On the other hand, the ratio between communication and computation can be improved. After the discussion, the students can modify the source code in order to resolve performance problems or investigate the effects of different file systems on the I/O performance of the application. Comparing the performance data collected during the run of the initial and modified application directly reveals the effectiveness of the changes.

4 Conclusion and Future Work

In this work, the idea behind an exercise in the course "Supercomputers and their programming" is presented. In this exercise, the students from computer science, information systems engineering, mathematics, computational science and engineering, as well as natural and engineering sciences are practically introduced to a complete workflow for scientific computing. While working on a simplified example, the students familiarize with the general idea of the workflow for scientific computing. This workflow can be applied to other problems of computational science as well. The students learn to work with mathematical models, transfer these models into statements of programming languages, use HPC systems, visualize and interpret result data generated by simulation runs, as well as analyze and improve the performance of scientific applications.

In the course "Supercomputers and their programming" the students are introduced to theoretical background in the field of parallel and distributed computing. The exercise described in this work supplements the gained knowledge from the course with practical experiences. With completion of the exercise the students are well prepared for their future scientific work. The exercise presents a holistic training for students and is often the first practical experience with a complete workflow for scientific computing. This workflow represents a general methodology and can be applied to other scientific problems as well. The feedback from the students is very positive. In contrast to common curriculums, the course covers not only theoretical knowledge. Moreover, in this exercise the students have to implement, execute, and analyze a parallel program on a HPC system. The students highly appreciate the chance to gain skills or improve their expertise in parallel programming. Furthermore, the tutors noticed that the exercise encourages the cooperation between students from different courses of study. The students benefit from each others expertise and complement their knowledge. Furthermore, the tutors also benefit from the close cooperation with the students. First contacts are established for acquiring student workers or thesis topics.

While the feedback of the exercise is very positive, there are options to enhance the practical session. For example, the parallel implementation can be extended to shared-memory parallelism by an hybrid MPI+OpenMP version. Multi-core architectures with shared memory are omnipresent. Although, OpenMP [7] is theoretically introduced in the lecture, it is currently not part of the exercises. A practical implementation of the shared memory paradigm would complement the course. The visualization approach presented in the exercise can be improved as well. Students would benefit from replacing the self-implemented visualization approach by established frameworks (e.g., VisIt [1]) and their file formats.

References

1. Childs, H., et al.: VisIt: An end-user tool for visualizing and analyzing very large data. In: High Performance Visualization-Enabling Extreme-Scale Scientific Insight, pp. 357–372 (2012)
2. Geimer, M., Saviankou, P., Strube, A., Szebenyi, Z., Wolf, F., Wylie, B.J.N.: Further improving the scalability of the scalasca toolset. In: Jónasson, K. (ed.) PARA 2010. LNCS, vol. 7134, pp. 463–473. Springer, Heidelberg (2012). https://doi.org/10.1007/978-3-642-28145-7_45
3. Knüpfer, A., et al.: The Vampir performance analysis tool-set. In: Resch, M., Keller, R., Himmler, V., Krammer, B., Schulz, A. (eds.) Tools for High Performance Computing, pp. 139–155. Springer, Heidelberg (2008). https://doi.org/10.1007/978-3-540-68564-7_9
4. Koumoutsakos, P., Chatzi, E., Krzhizhanovskaya, V.V., Lees, M., Dongarra, J., Sloot, P.M.A.: The art of computational science, bridging gaps - forming alloys. Preface for ICCS 2017. Procedia Comput. Sci. **108**, 1–6 (2017)
5. Mey, D., et al.: Score-P: a unified performance measurement system for petascale applications. In: Bischof, C., Hegering, H.G., Nagel, W.E., Wittum, G. (eds.) Competence in High Performance Computing. Springer, Heidelberg (2012). https://doi.org/10.1007/978-3-642-24025-6_8
6. MPI Forum: Message Passing Interface (MPI), May 2018. http://mpi-forum.org/
7. OpenMP: The OpenMP API specification for parallel programming, May 2018. http://openmp.org/
8. Riedel, M., Streit, A., Wolf, F., Lippert, T., Kranzlmüller, D.: Classification of different approaches for e-science applications in next generation computing infrastructures. In: 2008 IEEE Fourth International Conference on eScience, pp. 198–205 (2008). https://doi.org/10.1109/eScience.2008.56

Integrating Parallel Computing in the Curriculum of the University Politehnica of Bucharest

Mihai Carabaş, Adriana Drăghici, Grigore Lupescu, Cosmin-Gabriel Samoilă, and Emil-Ioan Sluşanschi(✉)

University Politehnica of Bucharest, 313 Splaiul Independenţei, Bucharest, Romania
{mihai.carabas,adriana.draghici,cosmin.samoila,emil.slusanschi}@cs.pub.ro,
grigore.lupescu@gmail.com

Abstract. The continuous shift of hardware computing architectures, from single to many-core processors, as well as the blurring of the hardware - software interface, has made the introduction of parallel and distributed computing topics in the undergraduate curriculum an essential requirement for any quality computer science program. The University Politehnica of Bucharest offers a unique approach, employing a heterogeneous hardware and software teaching and computing infrastructure, to its over 450 students enrolled in undergraduate studies of Computer Science and Electrical Engineering. In this study we present two of the most important lectures covering PDC topics at the UPB.

Keywords: Parallel programming · Python
Performance optimization · GPU computing · PDC
Undergraduate education

1 Introduction

Given the current evolution of the IT industry, Parallel and Distributed Computing is seen as an essential topic for any IT professional. University "Politehnica" of Bucharest is one of the oldest and most prestigious engineering school in Romania. Over the last 20 years, the Computer Science and Engineering Department has conferred a special importance to the PDC curricula. The importance of parallel and distributed systems as well as a distinction between parallel versus distributed systems is discussed in [20,23], and the approach offered by the UPB is consistent with the view presented therein, since our curriculum already contains different courses for distributed and parallel systems. Most courses containing PDC issues are taught in the first three years of CS and touch a wide audience of around 400–500 students per year. Similar lectures are being offered around the world by various CS groups in Tennessee [19], Cadiz [24], or Cluj-Napoca [22].

This paper is structured as follows. In Sect. 2 we outline the PDC curriculum in the UPB undergraduate CS and EE programs. In turn, Sect. 3 presents the

G. Mencagli et al. (Eds.): Euro-Par 2018 Workshops, LNCS 11339, pp. 222–234, 2019.
https://doi.org/10.1007/978-3-030-10549-5_18

practical activities in two of the lectures concerned with PDC. Section 4 presents the student progress evaluation process, whereas Sect. 5 outlines the interest and involvement of the IT industry in Romania and abroad towards the PDC issues being taught to our undergraduate students. In Sect. 6 we enumerate the lessons learned through the years while offering the PDC curriculum, and we conclude in 7 with some conclusions and an outline of possible improvements to our present approach.

2 Parallel and Distributed Computing Curriculum

In the bachelor program of the UPB, we can find three main lectures where Parallel and Distributed Computing issues are presented to the students, namely the Parallel and Distributed Algorithms (PDA), Computer Systems Architecture (CSA), and Parallel Processing Architectures (PPA). In this paper we will focus on the Computer Systems Architecture and Parallel Processing Architectures lectures as introduced in Sects. 2.1 and 2.2 respectively. Section 2.3 briefly goes through other PDC graduate courses, not covered thoroughly in this paper. The number of students taking the PDA and CSA lectures ranges from 350 to 450 each year – these two lectures being compulsory for all students enrolled at the Computer Science and Engineering Department. The PPA lecture gathers from 130 to 150 students, in the Advanced Computer Architectures specialization of our bachelor Computer Science Program.

2.1 Computer Systems Architecture

The Computer Systems Architecture lecture is presented in the sixth semester of bachelor study. This lecture presents the fundamentals of design and structure of numerical computing systems. The main topics covered include:

- Processor Memory Switches descriptions of computing systems.
- Various taxonomies of computing systems.
- Fundamentals of SIMD and MIMD design, architectures, and applications.
- Hierarchical and non-hierarchical switches.
- Switches for inter-processor and processor-memory communication.
- Inter-cluster and intra-cluster communication protocols.
- The roof-line model.
- Advanced CPU and GP-GPU computing architectures.
- Debugging and performance evaluation and analysis of computer programs.
- Profiling and tracing computer codes on modern processing platforms.
- Parallel correctness challenges.
- Benchmarking computing systems.
- Analysis of top 500 systems architectures over the years.

The practical activities over the course of the entire semester deal with three different topics, namely concurrent programming in Python, serial code optimization, profiling and OpenCL programming in C. The lecture as well as the practical activities are being update continuously. More details are given in Sect. 3.

2.2 Parallel Processing Architectures

The PPA lecture is given in the ninth semester of bachelor study. The main objective of this lecture is the assimilation of fundamental concepts concerning parallel processing architectures design, programming and configuration. During this lecture students learn to analyze parallel processing models, as well as synchronization issues in complex parallel and distributed systems. During the lecture, the following topics are discussed:

- The evolution of parallel processing systems.
- The concepts of concurrency and parallelism.
- Indicators for evaluating parallel structures.
- Parallel systems classifications.
- General characteristics of parallel processing systems.
- Mathematical models of parallel computation.
- Relationships between parallel architectures and parallel algorithms.
- Parallel computation limits and levels of parallelism.
- Synchronization in parallel and distributed systems.
- Parallel system architectures with practical examples.

In this lecture, the practical activities are split between two phases: the first six weeks of the semester in which students learn and practice advanced issues on OpenMP, MPI, and PThreads programming, while the remaining eight weeks of the semester are spent working in teams of two or three on software projects in which they are attempting to parallelize given serial computer programs.

2.3 Graduate Lectures on PDC

The graduate lectures gather from 25 to 40 students, in the Advanced Computer Architectures [1] and Parallel and Distributed Processing Systems specializations [10] of our bachelor Computer Science Program.

Parallel Programming is a lecture outlining a series of programming paradigms in the context of modern parallel computer architectures. It offers an overview of parallel programming models considering issues such as productivity, performance, and portability and presenting a number of models for communication, synchronization, memory consistency and runtime systems. Various parallel programming paradigms with shared- and distributed-memory, parallel global address shared space, and other atypical paradigms are presented.

High Performance Scientific Computing presents state-of-the-art parallel computing architectures in the context of modern parallel programming paradigms. Topics include mathematical modeling, numerical methods and data structures employed in HPC, from systems of differential equations, automatic differentiation, optimization problems, solving systems of nonlinear equations, to basic linear algebra and chaotic systems. The lecture also tackles scientific applications requiring HPC systems with examples from research and industry.

3 Practical Activities

3.1 Computer Systems Architecture

The CSA practical activities follow the structure of most of the courses in our faculty's curriculum for the first six semesters, consisting of weekly two-hour labs and three or four homework assignments every two or three weeks. Through the years such a structure received positive feedback from students and proved very efficient in the development of their technical skills and on their understanding and application of the subjects presented during lectures. In terms of organization, our activities bring something new to the students: they are split into three, formerly four, distinct topics and technologies, the homeworks require not just coding but also analysis and performance evaluation and they offer the students a chance to enrich their presentation skills.

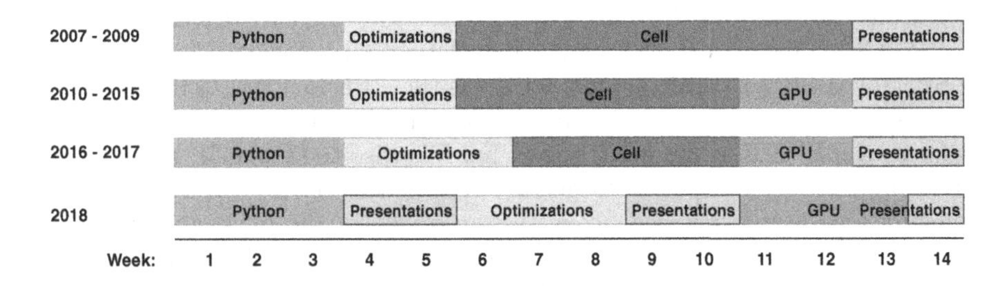

Fig. 1. CSA Practical activities through the years.

The topics taught during CSA's lab activities cover concurrency and multi-threaded programming (in Python), optimizations and profiling (in C), parallelization of computationally intensive programs, using Cell, OpenCL [21], or CUDA [16]. We adapted this structure based on technological evolution, as shown in Fig. 1. For conciseness, throughout this article we will refer to these parts of the CSA's activities using the technology/language used for them.

The last two weeks of the semester were dedicated to presentation sessions, in which students chose a topic related to the course or the lab and presented it in 10 min. The presentations were extremely varied and up to date to the newest trends in high performance computing, parallelism and concurrency and even embedded systems (e.g. a cluster build out of Raspberry Pi boards). This year, we replaced these presentations with ones in which they present their homeworks, a decision we discuss in Sect. 6.

The main reason we chose Python was the desire to present *concurrency* concepts in multi-thread programming in a widely used language. Due to its quick learning curve, a simple threading API and the fact that we are focusing on correctness of concurrent programs and not on parallelization performance, Python is the right choice for our needs. The concepts learned during the lab exercises and from the homework assignment can be easily applied to other languages too.

During the weeks dedicated to concurrent programming students learn Python's basic syntax and data structures, how to create and manage threads and how to protect the access to shared resources using locks and semaphores, events, conditions and synchronized queues.

The first of the three labs dedicated to *program optimization* offers an introduction into Intel and AMD general purpose CPU architectures, with exercises meant to detect the actual size of the line of cache and of the LLC – Last Level Cache – of the processors in the lab. The second lab is treating a number of serial optimizations of the well-known matrix multiply kernel, on CPUs, from improving access to vectors, to loop order optimization and block-matrix optimizations. This section concludes with a lab on performance optimization using dedicated software tools such as Valgrind, perf and Intel Parallel Studio. Therefore, students learn about the specifics of CPU architectures, serial optimization techniques, and how to identify performance bottlenecks using specialized tools.

We have chosen the OpenCL programming paradigm as it is a natural transition from the previous *IBM Cell architectures* we used to teach. Similar to the IBM CELL framework there is a clear distinction between *device* GPU (as the SPE for IBM Cell) and the *host* CPU (as the PPE for IBM Cell). From the execution point of view the *host* is responsible for managing the *device* hardware similar to the PPE that managed the SPEs. Likewise the OpenCL kernels need to be compiled for the specific target *device* and sent out by the HOST which highlights how a true heterogeneous system works in the back-end. Although OpenCL programming is a difficult topic, it is worth learning since it offers students a deeper understanding of the advantages and limitations of most co-processing architectures, like GPUs, FPGAs, ASICs, etc.

While CUDA is the de-facto standard when it comes to the HPC industry, *OpenCL* provides a better understanding of the underlying interactions in components of a heterogeneous system. Since we also touch upon the systems programming side, we consider OpenCL is better suited in Academia than CUDA. OpenCL was designed to support any number of devices (e.g. CPU, GPU, FGPA, ASIC) from any vendor, while CUDA is a closed ecosystem targeting only NVIDIA GPU hardware. Thus, our students learn how to query for platforms and devices of different vendors, how to allocate and manage buffers as well as how to perform cross compilation of kernels. They also understand that the software stack induces latency and can significantly impact performance. The transition from OpenCL to CUDA is easy, since for beginners CUDA represents a simplification of the OpenCL API. We offer three OpenCL labs: the first focuses on the host side interactions with the device (queries, buffer allocation, kernel enqueue), and the next two focus more on the underlying architecture of a GPU and how to design an efficient kernel program.

3.2 Parallel Processing Architectures

The PPA labs consist of two different parts, namely a hands-on section of labs and a team project. The hands-on section tackles advanced issues concerning PThreads, OpenMP [15], MPI programming [18], and concludes with a profiling and parallel debugging lab. The team project is focused on deploying, under our team's supervision, shared as well as distributed memory programming techniques on serial applications chosen by the students. The projects conclude with presentations in front of the class outlining the benefits and drawbacks of each particular programming approach, as well as the influence of the underlying machine and system architecture on the performance of the chosen application.

4 Student Assessment and Evaluation

4.1 Lab Activity and Homeworks

During the two-hour lab activities of the **Computer Systems Architecture** lab students get the chance to practice their coding and apply the concepts learned during the lectures or from the lab's wiki page [3]. The exercises also challenge them to look for performance issues, optimizations and also understand the architectures their code runs on. During each lab, the teaching assistants present and explain the main concepts in the first 15–30 min and then help the students with their tasks (individual explanations, debugging, discussions about their results).

We use the wiki as support for labs and homeworks. On each lab's page we offer an overview of the topic, examples, links to additional resources and tasks. Most of the labs also provide a code skeleton the students can build upon. Only the lab about the profiling tools has less coding and its flow is tutorial-like, with students having precise instructions on what to create, click, and run.

The first concurrency lab focuses on exercising Python syntax and its challenge is teaching the fundamentals of a new language in just two hours. Therefore, we varied the difficulty and the amount of tasks through the years. We first offered many short tasks that covered a lot of concepts but the students' feedback showed us that it is more important to provide the tasks a story and not require the use of that many language features, so the current exercises simulate a coffee machine. The second concurrency lab starts with a simple exercise that requires the creation of threads that concurrently modify a list, and then requires the implementation of well-known concurrency problems, like producer-consumer or dining philosophers. In the third lab students work with events, conditions and barrier objects to implement a gossiping algorithm and a master-slave scenario.

The Cell labs provided code skeleton that the students adapted and the tasks covered all the topics presented on the wiki: creation and management of SPE threads, vectorization, data transfers using DMA, double buffering, mailboxes and caches. The exercises were compiled and run on our cluster. Students understood the concepts but their performance during the labs was hindered by C programming aspects such as data alignment. Therefore, we have included in the optimization labs some tasks for allocations and pointer casts.

The purpose of the OpenCL GPU/CPU labs is to understand the main differences between programming on a CPU and on a GPU. For a typical lab, students have a skeleton code on which they will have to fill in the gaps for the proper execution to take place. The labs gradually go from a high level view of

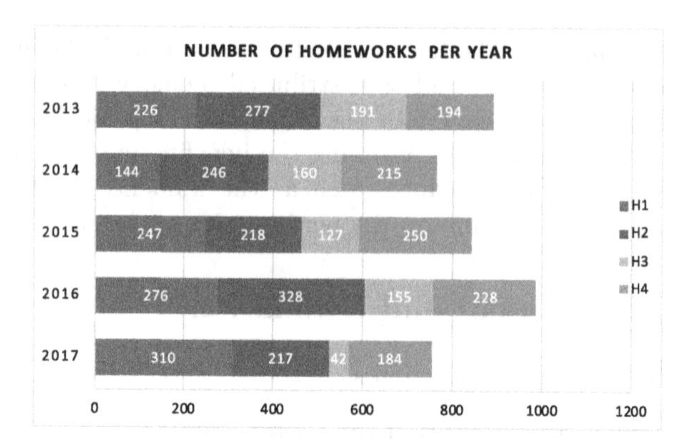

Fig. 2. Number of submitted CSA homeworks (H1, H2, H3 and H4) in the last five years. In 2016 and 2017 the students had to choose between H3 (Cell) and H4 (GPU), they were not required to do both.

the OpenCL stack to the low level details of kernel programming on a certain architecture.

The common themes of the **Computer Systems Architecture** homework assignments are the following: threads that concurrently access each other's data in order to apply an algorithm for the Concurrency track, implementing a BLAS [2] operation in several ways (basic, optimized, basic compiled with flags) and comparing the performance against the library's implementation for the Optimization track, parallelization of a serial algorithm in OpenCL. The Cell homeworks revolved around image and video processing and required the use of DMA transfers. The students also had to perform optimizations using vector operations and double buffering. With the exception of the concurrency homework, the students have to provide relevant graphs and explanations about their solution's performance. For the Python track, we encourage students not only to write correct concurrent code, but also respect a coding style and document it. To ease the evaluation and to help them, their homeworks are also tested with Pylint [11], a Python code analysis tool. As an incentive, we offer bonus points to homeworks exhibiting high Pylint scores.

We are addressing a large number of students each semester, which makes it overwhelming to evaluate more than 500 homeworks per semester only for one course, as presented in Fig. 2. Moreover, the fact that the CSA homeworks require running the solutions on various architectures and also measuring their performance, makes it more difficult to integrate with VMChecker, an automatic grading system. We use VMChecker only for OpenCL GPU assignments, while for the rest we provide public tests and scripts that automate the runs, so that students can test their solutions before submitting them on the course's platform. Over-subscription of cluster queues by students is one disadvantage to using VMChecker for the GPU assignments, since it requires constant monitoring so that the system remained responsive (i.e. queues not full). The end result is faster grading but the trade-off comes from deploying and managing the system.

For the **Parallel Processing Architectures** projects, students are divided in groups of two or three and decide on the project's topic, usually the parallelization of CPU-intensive applications written mostly in C or C++. Then each week we decide together with the students on the tasks they have to do until the subsequent week. The parallelization paradigms they use include PThreads, OpenMP and MPI, and usually, each member of the team is in charge of one parallelization strategy. At the end of the semester, each team presents before the entire class the results, outlining the lessons learned, the benefits as well as the drawbacks of each programming paradigm in the context of their particular software application. The projects are done in teams, however grading is individual, to ensure fairness and accountability of our student's effort.

4.2 Computing Infrastructure

Computing infrastructure is one of the key elements in applying theoretical aspects shown in lectures, especially in computer architecture and parallel programming. For our courses we need a variety of platforms (e.g. x86 CPUs, embedded ARM CPUs, specialized PowerPC CPUs, or GPUs) for students to be able to compare them and a high number of units (CPUs/GPUs) in order to assess the performance of parallel implementations. Therefore, we rely on the Computing Cluster of our department, where all the HPC resources are aggregated, as summarized in Table 1.

Table 1. The CS computing cluster.

Nodes	Node type	CPU	GPU	RAM
32	IBM HS21	Intel Xeon E5405	–	16 GB
28	IBM HS22	Intel Xeon E5630	–	32 GB
16	IBM LS22	AMD Opteron 2435	–	16 GB
4	IBM QS22	Cell BE Broadband	–	8 GB
8	IBM PS703	IBM Power7	-	32 GB
4	IBM iDataPlex dx360M3	Intel Xeon X5650	8 NVidia Tesla M2070	32 GB
3	HPE ProLiant BL460c	Intel Xeon E5-2670	7 NVidia Tesla K40m	128 GB

The storage infrastructure of the CS Cluster is currently composed of multiple systems with different capacities, such as: an IBM Storage Fibre Channel DS3950 with 30 TB, a Dell PowerVault with 120 TB, and a HPE MSA P2000 with 6 TB of storage space. On these storage servers we installed, over time, multiple file system solutions for distributed and parallel computing systems. Among others, we explored NFS, Lustre FS, and GlusterFS. Lustre FS did not scale because of the significant configuration and restart times. GlusterFS was a good solution, however once we reached 30 million files, the system slowed down significantly.

The current NFS solution employs 10 Gbps links, with fast disks which offer good scaling for about 20 TB of data and multiple millions of user files.

Network connectivity within the cluster is ensured by 56 Gbps Infiniband links connecting computational nodes to the centralized storage; normal Gigabit Ethernet links for network and storage connectivity; and 10 Gigabit Ethernet links for network, storage and Internet connectivity. Currently the uplink uses 2x10 Gbps Ethernet links.

The hardware infrastructure described previously is complemented by the use of the Moodle [7] open-source learning system. Our Moodle implementation integrates students database information with automatic accounts creation, course creation based on the CS curricular structure, and course enrollment for students based on their contracts. Moodle fulfills most of our needs with: storage for resources (documents, slides), interactivity with students via forums and feedbacks and assignments upload and grading. For the collaborative design and deployment of lab materials we use a Dokuwiki [4] instance on the same server. During the Dokuwiki integration with our Moodle system and our student database, our team also contributed back to upstream with different features that would help others implement a similar system. In the near future we plan to integrate automatic programming assignment verification using the VMchecker [14] tool.

Cluster management is currently achieved using Open Grid Scheduler [9], and will shortly be migrated to Torque [13]. We offer our students and users interactive, as well as non-interactive (i.e. batch-mode) use of our systems. Having a significant number of compute nodes as well as a big number of end-users places a high demand on our software stack (e.g. compilers, libraries, applications, tools). Thus, the management of different software versions is done by employing the `module` feature. It basically sets/unsets environment variables depending on the desired version of software being selected. Best performance for all our packages is obtained by compiling most of the stack directly from sources and creating our own RPMs for each cluster node architecture.

4.3 Final Examination and Feedback

The final examinations for both CSA and PPA typically consist of two different parts: a theoretical section of 50 min, where students are required to answer to 10 questions from the entire lecture; and a practical section of 45 min in which students have to solve a practical assignment linked to the lab activity. The total scores of the lab activity, homeworks, theoretical and practical examination are then added together to give the final grade for each lecture participant. During the last two weeks of the semester, students offer their feedback to our team - of course the information is available for us only after the end of the examination period. Student feedback is a constant source of improvement of our activity, and a good indication of the interest towards PDC subjects in our Department. Over the last years, we have thus constantly striven to offer our students access to the most advanced processor and parallel systems architectures.

5 Industry Involvement

Between the eighth and ninth semesters of their bachelor program, students are required to spend at least twelve weeks in internships or summer-schools on topics related to their chosen field of study. Over the years, a number of summer-schools have been organized in our Department, on topics ranging from High Performance Computing, Embedded Systems, Security, Mobile Development, Artificial Intelligence, GPU programming, Machine learning to Computer Vision and 3D-Graphics technologies. The industry has also diversified its internship offer to students, with topics on Business software development, Cloud programming, Artificial Intelligence, Embedded Systems, IoT, Mobile, Gaming, Networking, Telecommunications. To this end, the "Stagii pe Bune" [12] and "Junio.ro" [6] platforms were jointly developed by people from our Department and from the IT industry. More recently, students apply to internships abroad. Participation in Google, Facebook, and Microsoft internship programs is constantly growing. Some examples of companies, typical programming requirements, and representative technologies covered by their internships are given in Table 2.

Table 2. Internship listings.

Company	Requirements	Technologies
NXP	C/C++, Python, OpenCL, knowledge of microprocessors architecture	Automotive, IoT
Intel	C/C++, Python, Bash, Profiling skills	Microarchitecture Design and Optimizations
BitDefender	Algorithms, C/C++	Big Data Analysis, System Programming
Adobe	Algorithms, C/C++	Big Data Tehnologies, Application Design

Each year our team is considering the requirements and feedback received from the industry when redesigning or adapting our curricula for the next year. This process is smoothed by our integration of a significant number of teaching assistants (TAs) directly from industry professionals. Thus our students can learn where different types of problems presented at our laboratories occur in the daily life of an IT engineer. Another advantage of having input directly from an industry that is evolving so fast is having an objective view of how our teaching materials helps our students fulfill their job requirements.

6 Lessons Learned

Through the years our team has adapted to the feedback received from students in previous generations. For example, we introduced specific sections in the practical exercises of the labs based on common mistakes or challenging parts of the student assignments. To illustrate this point: we observed misunderstandings on how the threads run, a tendency for busy waiting and a wrong usage of events. We therefore provided more explanations and examples in the lab's wiki and offered exercises based on code skeletons, that showed incorrect approaches and asked students to improve them.

To encourage students to submit more homeworks, we developed a system of soft deadlines for two or three weeks after they are published, and only then impose a final hard deadline. Nonetheless, we observed that most students start working on homeworks in the last few days before the soft deadline, which had a significant impact on our hardware resources. Therefore, a few years ago we introduced a further incentive for submitting homeworks early – in the form of bonus points – an approach which proved quite successful.

To better assess the students' understanding of their homework and also tackle the plagiarism problem, we introduced this year the requirement for homework presentations in front of the class. To improve the uniformity of the TA's evaluation, we created homework evaluation guidelines, as well as typical errors and questions which should be posed to students during their evaluation. Over the years we have used automatic grading systems along with MOSS [8] and Etector [5] code plagiarism detection systems.

At the end of each semester, our entire team takes part in a debrief where we discuss all the problems we encountered during the lecture, practical activities and homework assignments. Possible improvements, owners and solutions are offered, and each point is then taken under consideration at the setup meeting of our group in the next academic year.

7 Conclusions and Outlook

7.1 Conclusions

The team at the Computer Science and Engineering Department of the UPB is striving to improve the presentation of PDC concepts in its undergraduate curricula. In the lectures, students are taught general architecture and design aspects of PDC, while in the practical activities they explore various software approaches best suited to illustrate those general concepts. Assignments and homeworks are then meant to check that the relevant desired skills have been learned by our students. In this article, we outline the content of the lectures, the student evaluation process, as well as the lessons learned over time, and the improvements we introduced in our content and approach. The IT industry is exhibiting a particular interest in our graduates, and their PDC skills are highly appreciated. This is also due to the fact that we have continued to evolve our Materials and Methods constantly, as new technologies emerge. At the same time however, we aim for our students to have a fundamental understanding of how parallel and distributed processing architectures work, from both the hardware and software perspective. As new architectures emerge continuously, driven now by emerging domains such as AI or IoT, the essential building blocks remain the same – and PDC is one of those blocks.

7.2 Outlook

We are constantly adapting our curriculum as the industry evolves. One interesting direction are cross-API intermediate languages such as SPIR which provide the underlying runtime for several APIs, such as OpenCL, Vulkan, SyCL, OpenMP, or OpenACC. Moreover, we are considering the addition of a section exemplifying the interaction of OpenCL with popular data analytics and machine learning frameworks such as Anaconda, by using the PyOpenCL [17] wrapper, thus linking together the CSA labs on Python and OpenCL.

Acknowledgements. The authors would like to thank Professor Nicolae Tăpuş, Alexandru Herişanu, Răzvan Dobre, Vlad Spoială, Dan Dragomir, Alexandru Olteanu, and Voichiţa Iancu for their valuable contributions to the CSA and PPA curriculum. This work is partially supported by project Sovarex, ID: 10PS/2017.

References

1. ACA master program. https://cs.pub.ro/index.php/education/courses/68-mas/aca?layout=. Accessed 14 May 2018
2. BLAS Basic Linear Algebra Subprograms. http://www.netlib.org/blas/. Accessed 14 May 2018
3. CSA wiki. http://cs.curs.pub.ro/wiki/asc/. Accessed 8 May 2018
4. Dokuwiki homepage. https://www.dokuwiki.org/dokuwiki. Accessed 14 May 2018
5. ETector homepage. http://www.etector.org/show.cgi. Accessed 14 May 2018
6. Junio homepage. https://junio.ro. Accessed 27 Apr 2018
7. Moodle homepage. https://moodle.org. Accessed 14 May 2018
8. Moss - for a Measure Of Software Similarity. https://theory.stanford.edu/~aiken/moss/. Accessed 14 May 2018
9. Open Grid Scheduler. http://gridscheduler.sourceforge.net/. Accessed 14 May 2018
10. PDPS master program. https://cs.pub.ro/index.php/education/courses/70-mas/pdps?layout=. Accessed 14 May 2018
11. Pylint homepage. https://www.pylint.org/. Accessed 25 Apr 2018
12. Stagii pe bune homepage. https://stagiipebune.ro. Accessed 27 Apr 2018
13. Torque Resource Manager. http://www.adaptivecomputing.com/products/open-source/torque/. Accessed 14 May 2018
14. VMChecker. https://github.com/rosedu/vmchecker. Accessed 25 Apr 2018
15. Chandra, R., Dagum, L., Kohr, D., Maydan, D., McDonald, J., Menon, R.: Parallel Programming in OpenMP. MK Inc., San Francisco (2001)
16. Cook, S.: CUDA Programming: A Developer's Guide to Parallel Computing with GPUs, 1st edn. MK Inc., San Francisco (2013)
17. Pierro, M.D.: Portable parallel programs with Python and OpenCL. Comput. Sci. Eng. **16**, 34–40 (2014)
18. Message Passing Interface Forum. MPI: A message-passing interface standard. Technical report, Knoxville, TN, USA (1994)

19. Ghafoor, S., Brown, D.W., Rogers, M.: Integrating parallel computing in introductory programming classes: an experience and lessons learned. In: Heras, D.B., Bougé, L. (eds.) Euro-Par 2017. LNCS, vol. 10659, pp. 216–226. Springer, Cham (2018). https://doi.org/10.1007/978-3-319-75178-8_18
20. Paprzycki, M., Wasniowski, R., Zalewski, J.: Parallel and distributed computing education: a software engineering approach. In: Ibrahim, R.L. (ed.) CSEE 1995. LNCS, vol. 895, pp. 187–204. Springer, Heidelberg (1995). https://doi.org/10.1007/3-540-58951-1_104
21. Munshi, A., Gaster, B., Mattson, T.G., Fung, J., Ginsburg, D.: OpenCL Programming Guide, 1st edn. Addison-Wesley Professional, Upper Saddle River (2011)
22. Niculescu, V., Bufnea, D.: Experience with teaching PDC topics into Babeş-Bolyai University's CS courses. In: Heras, D.B., Bougé, L. (eds.) Euro-Par 2017. LNCS, vol. 10659, pp. 240–251. Springer, Cham (2018). https://doi.org/10.1007/978-3-319-75178-8_20
23. Raynal, M.: Parallel computing vs. distributed computing: a great confusion? (position paper). In: Hunold, S., et al. (eds.) Euro-Par 2015. LNCS, vol. 9523, pp. 41–53. Springer, Cham (2015). https://doi.org/10.1007/978-3-319-27308-2_4
24. Tomeu-Hardasmal, A.J., Salguero, A.G., Capel, M.I.: Integration of ICT in concurrent and parallel programming lectures. In: Hunold, S., et al. (eds.) Euro-Par 2015. LNCS, vol. 9523, pp. 114–124. Springer, Cham (2015). https://doi.org/10.1007/978-3-319-27308-2_10

F2C-DP - Workshop on Fog-to-Cloud Distributed Processing

Workshop on Fog-to-Cloud Distributed Processing (F2C-DP)

Workshop Description

Future service execution in different domains (e.g. smart cities, e-health, smart transportation, etc.), will rely on a large and highly heterogeneous set of distributed devices, located from the edge to the cloud, empowering the development of innovative services. In such envisioned scenario, the main objective for the workshop was to set the ground for researchers, scientists and members of the industrial community to interact each other, fueling new discussions in the emerging area coming out when shifting distributed services execution towards the edge. Analyzing the way existing programming models and distributed processing strategies may support such a scenario and to what extent these solutions should be extended or just replaced, is also fundamental to support the expected evolution in edge computing.

The workshop aimed at bringing together the community of researchers interested in new applications, architectures, programming models, applications and systems based on these computing environments, with emphasis on research topics like Machine and Deep Learning, BlockChain, Function-as-a-Service, Security and Privacy. The workshop was organized with the support of the mF2C, a H2020 funded project, and was the second edition, that has been held in Turin, Italy, in conjuction with the Euro-Par annual series of international conferences. The workshop format included a keynote speaker, technical presentations and a panel. The workshop was attended by around 25 people. The workshop received eight submissions, from authors belonging to more than 15 distinct countries. Each of them was reviewed at least three times. The program committee took into account the relevance of the papers to the workshop, the technical merit, the potential impact, and the originality and novelty. From these submissions, and taking into account the reviews, seven papers were selected for presentation in the workshop (87% acceptance ratio). The papers focused on different aspects of the fog to cloud computing platforms: application requirements and specifications, architecture, programming models, and deployment with containers. The workshop included also a keynote presentation and a panel that discussed technology and business challenges posed by the fog to cloud paradigm.

We would like to thank the Euro-Par organizers for their support in the organization, specially to the Euro-Par workshop chairs, Dora Blanco and Gabriele Mencagli. We would like to thank also Giovanni Frattini (Engineering R&D) for his keynote presentation, Massimo Coppola (ISTI/CNR) and Filippo Gaudenzi (UniMi) for their participation in the panel, as well as to all the program committee members.

Organization

Organizing Committee

Rosa M. Badia	Barcelona Supercomputing Center, Spain
Xavier Masip	Universitat Politecnica de Catalunya, Spain
Ana Juan Ferrer	ATOS Research, Spain

Program Chair

Antonio Salis	Engineering Sardegna, Italy

Program Committee

Eva Marin	Universitat Politecnica de Catalunya, Spain
Toni Cortes	Barcelona Supercomputing Center, Spain
Jens Jensen	Sciences and Technology Facilities Council, UK
John Kennedy	Intel, Ireland
Matija Cankar	XLAB, Slovenia
Admela Jukan	TU Braunschweig, Germany
Cristovao Cordeiro	SIXSQ, Switzerland
Yaser Jararweh	Carnegie Mellon University, USA
Roberto Cascella	ECSO, Belgium
Massimo Coppola	Institute of Information Science and Technologies (ISTI/CNR), Italy
Filippo Gaudenzi	University of Milan, Italy
Gianluigi Zanetti	CRS4, Italy
Marcello Coppola	ST Microelectronics, France
Eduardo Monteiro	University of Coimbra, Portugal
Eduardo Quinones	Barcelona Supercomputing Center, Spain

Benefits of a Fog-to-Cloud Approach in Proximity Marketing

Antonio Salis[1(✉)], Glauco Mancini[1], Roberto Bulla[1], Paolo Cocco[1], Daniele Lezzi[2], and Francesc Lordan[2]

[1] Engineering Sardegna Srl, Cagliari, Italy
{antonio.salis,glauco.mancini,roberto.bulla,paolo.cocco}@eng.it
[2] Barcelona Supercomputing Center (BSC), Barcelona, Spain
{daniele.lezzi,francesc.lordan}@bsc.es

Abstract. The EC H2020 mF2C Project is working to the development of a software framework that enables the orchestration of resources and communication at fog level, as an extension of cloud computing and interacting with the IoT. In order to show the project functionalities and added-values three real world use cases have been chosen. This paper introduces one of the mF2C use cases: Smart Fog Hub Service (SFHS) use case, in the context of an airport, with the objective of proving that the adoption of the fog-to-cloud approach brings relevant benefits in terms of performance and optimization of resource usage, thus giving an objective evidence of the impact of the mF2C framework.

Keywords: Cloud computing · Fog computing · Fog-to-cloud
Distributed systems · IoT · Proximity marketing · 3G
4G/LTE · Wi-Fi

1 Introduction

By 2020 the installed base of the Internet of Things (IoT) devices is forecasted to grow to almost 31 Billion worldwide, with an annual economic impact of $3.9T to $11.1T by 2025 [4]. The forecast scenario includes diverse settings and use cases including factories, cities, retail environments, and healthcare. At the same time, 50% of IoT spending will be driven by discrete manufacturing, transportation, logistics, and utilities where predictions say that IoT will have the most transformative effect on industries that are not technology-based today. The most critical success factor of all these use cases depend on secure, scalable and reliable end-to-end integration solutions that encompass on-premise, platforms [1], legacy and cloud systems. While consumer applications will attract the most attention and create significant value, Business-to-Business (B2B) applications will generate nearly 70% of potential value enabled by IoT [3]. Also, in the airport industry an increase in the number of passengers is foreseen, where more than 4 billion passengers will concentrate in the airports with an average of two connected devices for each passenger [2]. Current technology infrastructures and

G. Mencagli et al. (Eds.): Euro-Par 2018 Workshops, LNCS 11339, pp. 239–250, 2019.
https://doi.org/10.1007/978-3-030-10549-5_19

architectures have not been designed to process in real time the great amount of information data that is being made available from such a number of devices with a so high concentration. As one of the first technical response to such technological challenges fog computing is emerging as an architectural model that places itself between the cloud and the IoT, in the Cloud-to-Things Continuum. In this paper we present a service implemented following the fog-to-cloud approach of the mF2C project, that acts as a smart hub to provide real time information in public environments. A prototype is being implemented in the context of an airport testbed that collects data from the passengers and provides information to enable proximity marketing (shops, restaurants, etc.) as well as analytics computed in the cloud. This setting could be reused in other public domains like train stations, shopping centers, etc. This paper describes the design possible scenarios, the networking particular elements of this use case, and some tests on different design scenarios that have been run. The results of these tests demonstrate that the capabilities and performance obtained by the mF2C adoption overcome the other possible choices, fulfilling the real-time requirement, enabling the distribution of processing of data, reducing traffic load and latency between cloud and hub. This paper is structured as follows. Section 2, introduces the mF2C Smart Fog Hub in an airport use case. Section 3 describes the comparison of the potential technical solutions, and Sect. 4 describes the experimental results and related benefits coming from the fog-to-cloud approach. Finally, Sect. 5 concludes the paper.

2 Fog Hub in Airport Use Case

The EC Horizon 2020 program in 2016 has funded a new research initiative (mF2C)[1] bringing together relevant industry and academic players in the cloud arena, aimed at designing an open, secure, decentralized, multi-stakeholder management framework for F2C (Fog-to-Cloud) computing, including novel programming models, privacy and security, data storage techniques, service creation, brokerage solutions, SLA policies, and resource orchestration methods [7,8]. There is an increasing demand on evaluating and identifying new market sectors and opportunities, and interest at the IoT evolution as a potential arena where current commercial cloud services offering could be enriched and differentiated. In this perspective a relevant focus in setting up hubs in public environments (e.g. airports, train stations, hospitals, malls and related parking areas) is suggested, capable of tracking the presence of people and other objects in the field, and developing added value services for proximity marketing, prediction of path/behavior of consumers, and taking real time decisions. This kind of environments can be implemented with a recommendation system, in order to produce a new and personalized pleasant experience for end-users.

The foreseen hub can be easily considered as a fog environment that embeds cloud connectivity to either process large amount of data or request extra-data, perhaps data coming from other fogs located in near sites (e.g. airport,

[1] http://www.mf2c-project.eu.

train/main bus/ harbor station), and that could interact sharing data and customer behavior gathered to improve the effectiveness of marketing proposals, given that the identity of objects/customers is protected.

This scenario has been named as the Smart Fog-Hub Service (SFHS). The use case is experimental and extends the concept of a "cloud hub" to a new concept of "fog hub", driven by real market needs [9].

The system is under development in the Engineering Labs, and will be moved to the Cagliari Elmas Airport in 2019. In the final configuration the fog elements will be positioned in the field in order to create a grid for Wi-Fi coverage.

The field (Fig. 1) includes check-in area, security control area, lounges and departure gates. Check-in and departure gates host several shops and other frequented places like bars and restaurants[2].

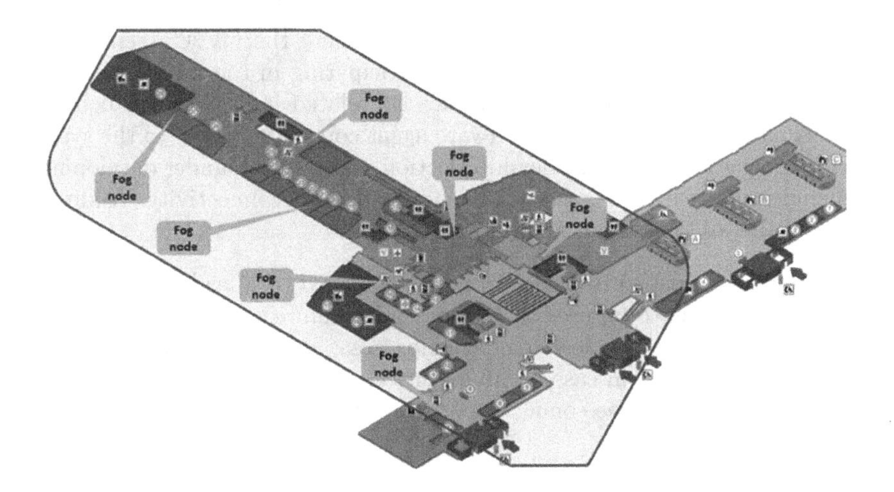

Fig. 1. Use case scenario in the airport.

According to the current architecture specifications, the system has the following elements, as depicted in Fig. 3:

- A cloud layer, based on a OpenStack[3] instance, wired connected with the fog layers, that provides scalable computing power for machine learning algorithms used for the recommendation system.
- A first fog layer, which acts as aggregator, based on a NuvlaBox mini[4], equipped with 8 GB RAM, that provides real-time computing and storage resources to the edge elements.

[2] http://www.cagliariairport.it.
[3] https://www.openstack.org.
[4] http://www.sixsq.com/products/nuvlabox/.

- A second fog layer, which acts as access node, based on six RaspberryPi3[5] with 1 GB RAM, that provide session management and fast response to the edge devices.
- Android smartphones at the edge, connected to the access node with Wi-Fi, and using an Android app to interact with the system; in this phase they are used as data generator.

A core element of the system architecture is constituted by the mF2C framework, able to manage and coordinate the orchestration of all existing and potentially available resources, from the edge up to the cloud, when executing a service, according to the service requirements and user needs. This is structured in a hierarchical architecture (Fig. 2), where resources are grouped into layers, and an mF2C agent entity deploys the management functionalities in every component within the system. In practical scenarios there are different layers, from layer 0 at cloud, to layer N as closest to the edge, where the mF2C agent runs in all devices capable of supporting it, and participating in the mF2C system. In case of devices not able to run the agent, the related information is collected, processed and distributed by the software agent connecting them to the system. The clustering strategy and leadership election policy is still under development, but includes elements like spatial distance and data connectivity. Additional features of the mF2C system architecture are:

- A fog area (or cluster) is the set of nodes managed by a leader, with election of a backup node, to be used in case of leader failure,
- Only one node acts as a leader in each fog area, and only one backup, which substitute the leader in case of failure or loose of connection,
- Only IoT devices can be connected to any of the agents in the mF2C system

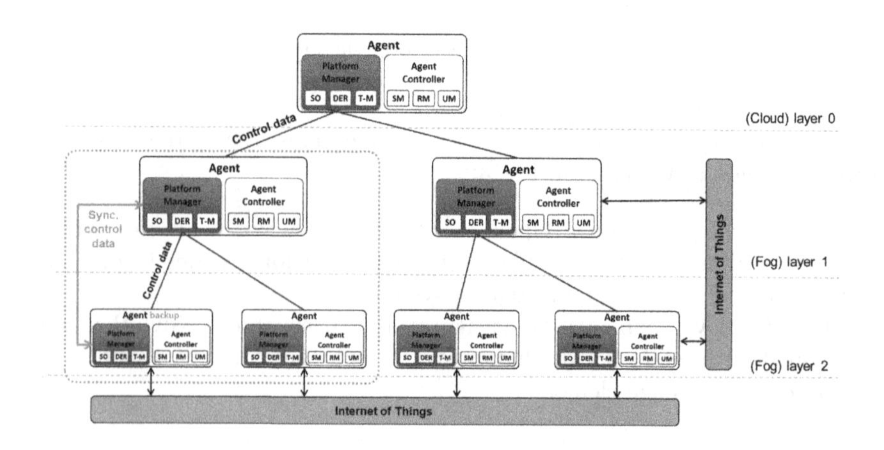

Fig. 2. mF2C architecture for IT-1.

[5] https://www.raspberrypi.org/products/raspberry-pi-3-model-b/.

The whole set of management and control functionalities of the agent is split into two main blocks, the Platform Manager (PM), and the Agent Controller (AC). The PM provides high-level functionalities, and manages the inter-agent communications, with the capacity to take decisions with a more global view. Agent Controller (AC) has a local scope, dealing with local resources and services. At run time, when a service is requested to any of the mF2C agents, the PM is responsible for deciding if this task can be executed in that agent, or forwarded down to any of the agents in the area if the agent is a leader or up to the higher hierarchical layer. If the task is forwarded, the communication is also done through the PMs of the agents. The request is passed to the AC only when an agent can execute the forwarded task, using the agent's local resources.

In the use case, an mF2C agent software runs in all cloud and fog elements and provides management and control functionalities. An Android app is installed in the smartphone and implements security and privacy features to preserve managed data both at rest and in transit, with a security level comparable to the ones adopted by the mF2C agent. In particular, the Distributed Execution Runtime (DER) in the mF2C agent is responsible for optimizing services/tasks execution on the available resources. This component is based on the COMPSs [5] framework and orchestrates the execution of the requests coming from the mobile app, to optimally exploit the available computing resources. The tasks generated by the execution of the applications are distributed, in parallel, on the resources selected by other components of the mF2C platform. DataClay in the mF2C agent performs the system data management.

At application level the following business processes have been identified and under development:

- App installation and device registration.
- Position calculation, check for Points of Interest (PoI) & notification.
- Position data sync in fog & cloud.
- Airport events notification (flight call, but also invitation to move closer to the gate).
- Recommendations generation based on user similarities (and recalculations with data caching).
- Reporting (real-time and history) with the dashboard.
- Configuration of Points of Interest (PoI) and promotions (in case of shops).
- Filtering and calculating data in position data streams.

The overall idea is to track and engage all people and objects in the field and use a Collaborative Filtering[6] based recommender system to get the best possible customer experience, with suggestion on the best way to use available services, e.g. suggest the moment for shorter waiting times in Security Control to departing people, to move close to the gate or notify the final call, or recommend relevant proposals and offerings in shops close to the user. All these suggestions can be refined according to behavior and choices done by passengers.

[6] http://recommender-systems.org/collaborative-filtering/.

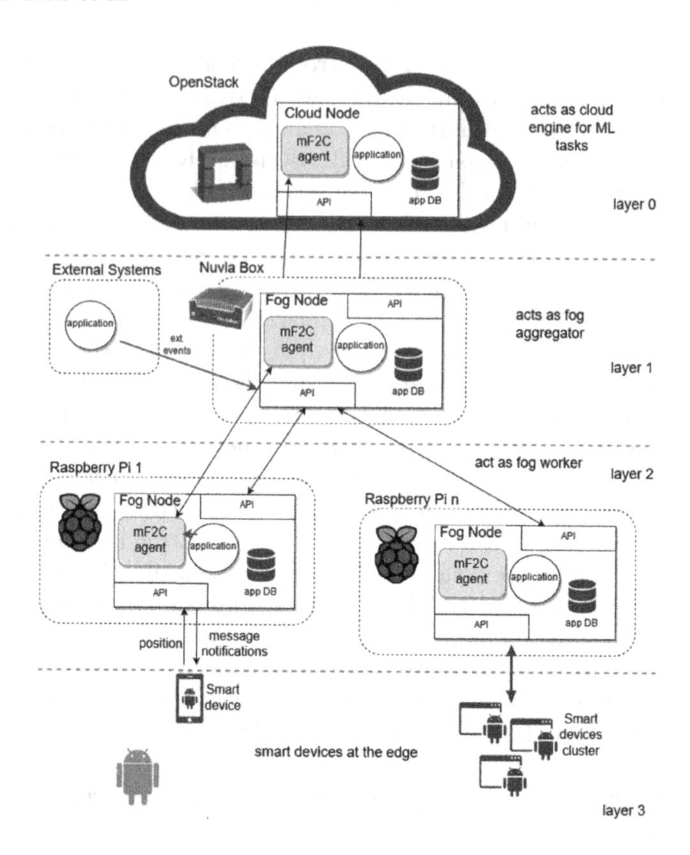

Fig. 3. Use case 3 system architecture.

The recommender system will play a major role for the personalization of the traveler's experience, machine learning based features like users similarity will be used to suggest items that other users liked but the current user has not interacted with yet. A particular care has been provided for the privacy and security of personal data: the recommender system uses algorithms that works perfectly without any personal information.

3 Architecture Evaluation

Given the nature of the chosen use case and the business processes listed above, some characteristics emerge in terms of processing demand:

- Real-time requirements for position calculation and check for PoIs nearby.
- Massive calculation in the case of machine learning algorithms for Collaborative Filtering.

While the processing demand from the machine learning can be offloaded using the Fog-to-Cloud approach to ask for more computing power when needed and keep the latest data, the real-time requirements for position tracking and engaging (with notifications) need to be managed immediately, starting from the smartphone owned by the users.

The typical loop is the following:

- Calculate PoIs in proximity, given object position (x, y)
- Notify the user in case of PoIs nearby

This is a small processing that every object runs every few seconds with immediate response, but that requires much higher processing capacity as the number of devices in the field grows.

Since the smartphone is the selected device, the possible scenarios of implementation are:

1. Wi-Fi connectivity and mF2C support.
2. 3G connectivity and direct connection to a public cloud.

The first case corresponds to the architecture shown in the previous section, with Wi-Fi connection between the smartphone and RaspberryPi3 devices, with wired connections between the other layers. In this scenario the only network link that requires attention is the Wi-Fi, that will be used in open space; further copper or fiber connections can be ignored. In the other case the smartphone uses 3G networking to connect directly to the public cloud that hosts the relevant services. Here 3G connectivity is the most critical link, while intra cloud communications could be ignored.

Both communication means try to satisfy the growing expectation of ubiquitous connectivity for a broad range of services. At the same time, wireless transmission means are highly variable in terms of bandwidth, latency, battery usage.

The following are the main features of Wi-Fi communications with respect to the proximity processing:

- IEEE 802.11g /n /ac standards are quite adequate to support the real-time requirement and sustain the fast growing number of devices to be managed in the field;
- The newest standards based on 5 Ghz frequency and MIMO (multiple input multiple output) features enable wider bandwidth and faster response times
- Slow start events like first hop do not affect the overall speed of the communication channel;
- The Wi-Fi protocol is the preferred communication protocol for indoor communication and adequate for the proximity processing request;
- Wi-Fi connections are more battery efficient than 3G/4G.

Table 1 summarizes the main features of Wi-Fi current technology.

The following are the main features of 3G/4G radio communications [7] with respect to the proximity processing:

[7] Ilya Grigorik, High Performance Browser Networking, O'Reilly, 2013.

Table 1. Wi-Fi release history and main features

802.11 protocol	Freq (Ghz)	Bandwidth (Mhz)	Data rate (Mbit/s)	Max MIMO streams	Median Latency - (msec)
b	2.4	20	1, 2, 5,5, 11	1	6,22
g	2.4	20	6, 9, 12, 18, 24, 36, 48, 54	1	6,22
n	2.4	20	7,2, 14,4, 21,7, 28,9, 43,3, 57, 8, 65, 72, 2	4	6,22
n	5.0	40	15, 30, 45, 60, 90, 120, 135, 150	4	0,90
ac	5.0	20, 40, 80, 160	Up to 866,7	8	0,90

- Intermittent network access, like polling, is a performance waste on mobile networks, as it uses the packet based communication mean in the worst way;
- Real time analytics like proximity processing demand high battery usage against all battery optimizations implemented in 3G/4G;
- Intermittent network access carries a large latency cost due to the Radio Resource Control (RRC) state transitions
- In case of an HTTP request like in our scenario, also the DNS, TCP, TLS and HTTP protocols can increase the overall latency in the communication;
- TCP implementation on top of 3G shows poor performances due to the 3-way handshaking nature of TCP and related slow start, in practice it triples response times, compared with native TCP implementation;
- 3G and 4G/LTE, in order to make the best use of bandwidth, have a kernel that waits for data (buffer more requests) to have bigger packets instead of sending smaller packets immediately

Table 2 summarizes the latency of a single HTTP request on 3G/4G network:

Table 2. Latency overhead of a HTTP request

	3G	4G/LTE
RRC Control plane	200–2500 ms	50–100 ms
DNS lookup	200 ms	100 ms
TCP handshake	200 ms	100 ms
TLS handshake	200–400 ms	100–200 ms
HTTP request	200 ms	100 ms
Total latency overhead	200–3500 ms	100–600 ms

From the data presented above Wi-Fi seems to be much better than 3G, only the latest 4G promise to compete with Wi-Fi over peak throughput and latency, use battery in a more efficient way and be more adequate in indoor environments.

4 Experimental Results and Benefits from mF2C

All information reported seems to determine that the Wi-Fi network connection, together with the fog-to-cloud approach, brings the best performance, thus being the preferred solution for the Smart Fog Hub in the Airport for the proximity calculations.

In order to validate this assumption an experimental benchmarking has been defined with a client-server sample with the following characteristics:

- The client simply calls a request with a position (x, y) asking for the list of available Points of Interest within 5 m,
- The server receives the request, calculates the available PoIs and return a JSON array with them.

This client-server sample has been run in the following environments:

- (Client) XIAOMI REDMI NOTE2 smartphone with Android 5.0.2, and app Rest Api Client for HTTP requests
- (Server - 1. option) RaspberryPi3 with ARM Cortex A53 64-bit cpu and 1 GB Ram
- (Server - 2. option) VM running in a Public cloud on OVH-Paris, with 4 cpu and 4 GB Ram, with minimum load. The average ping from the RaspberryPi3 to the VM is about 35 ms.

A VM running a service that provides the PoIs search has been prepared and deployed on both server targets. The available Wi-Fi connectivity is based on 802.11g at 2.4 Ghz.

The following scenarios have been prepared for tests:

(A) Smartphone connects with Wi-Fi to RaspberryPi3, the "Rest Api" app calls the service locally.
(B) Smartphone connects with Wi-Fi to RaspberryPi3, the "Rest Api" app calls the service in the public cloud.
(C) Smartphone connects with 3G to the public cloud and the "'Rest Api" app calls the service.
(D) Smartphone connects with 4G/LTE to the public cloud and the "Rest Api" app calls the service.

In every test run a sequence of calls has been performed with a delay of 5 s between consecutive calls.

Test results have confirmed the statements of the previous chapter: the mF2C (A) with Wi-Fi connectivity approach over-performed 3G and 4G/LTE network communications. Figures 4 and 5 present the test environment and summary of response times collected.

The (A) scenario, currently used for the mF2C project, performed the best, with a pretty stable and fast response. Times are in line with the real-time requirement, but they could be improved with the use of 5.0 Ghz frequencies and latest version that offer both a much wider frequency range and is still largely

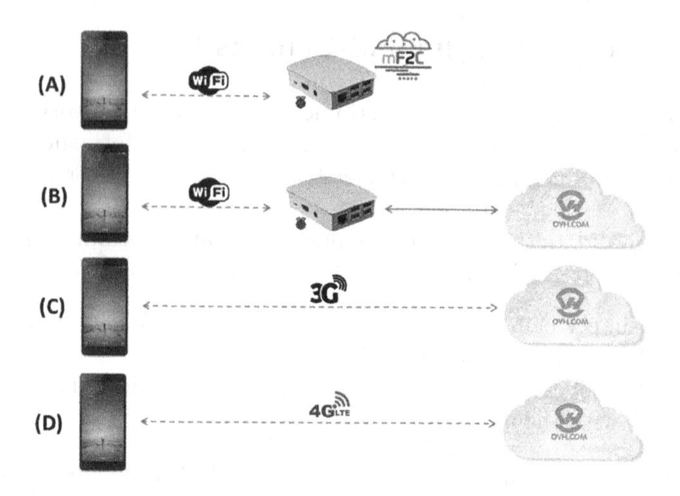

Fig. 4. Test environment in the different approaches.

interference free in most environments. The (B) scenario returned good values, since it benefited from the four-cpu configuration and the minimum cpu load, but with a high latency between the RaspberryPi3 and the Public cloud. Times are 2X compared with the (A) scenario, but still within the real-time requirement. The (C) scenario scored the worst, with a median response time near 3 s, which does not fulfil the real-time proximity requirement. The (D) scenario scored the third, just within the limits of the real-time requirement. The sampling showed a very stable response time, coming both from the low cpu load of the cloud and low traffic on the 4G/LTE channel. Times are 3.5X compared with the (A) scenario.

As final evaluation both theoretical aspects and experimental results confirm that Wi-Fi must be preferred to radio communications like 3G or 4G/LTE, as it fulfills completely the real-time requirement. As second aspect the fog-to-cloud approach of the (A) scenario presents the best performance, thus it would clearly highlight the benefits of the adoption of the fog support. The ability to move close to the edge the computation makes the difference: even if with a smaller computing element like a RaspberryPi3 the overall performance is fully respondent to the requirement and leaves room for additional load that could come from the adoption of augmented reality features.

It is remarkable to notice the benefits coming from the distributed processing supported by the COMPSs and DER runtime support embedded into the mF2C agent, that enables the optimization of computing, moving and balancing the load at different levels of the fog hierarchy. Another benefit coming from the mF2C support is related to the distributed data management: DataClay [6] mechanisms such as replication guarantee that nodes requesting some data will have a way to access it, even if the originating node is not available at a given time. At the same time these replicas can follow different synchronization policies

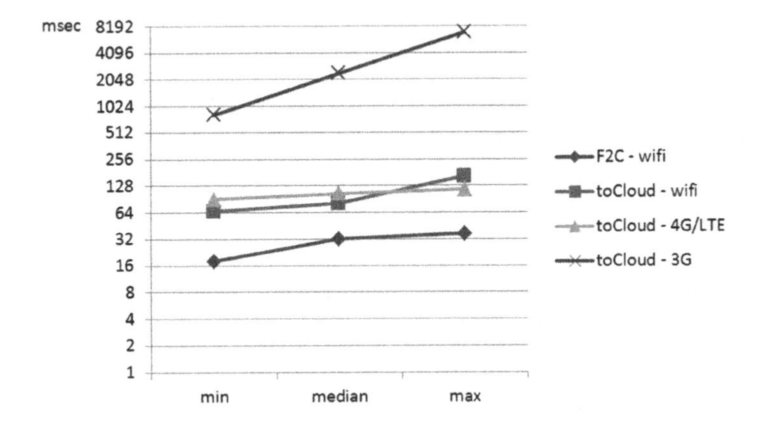

Fig. 5. Comparison of response times with different approaches.

depending on the particular data, while avoiding single points of failure. All the mentioned benefits of orchestration, distribution and optimization in the resource usage would not be possible with the direct link of the edge devices to a centralized cloud-based architecture.

5 Conclusions

The relevant increase in the number of IoT devices is going to generate a huge amount of data. While consumer market will attract most attention, B2B applications will generate more revenues. But the successful development of business depends on critical factors like security, reliability and fast response of proposed solutions. So the arise of the fog computing concept as an architectural model that makes the glue between the cloud and the IoT, extends cloud computing and services to IoT objects to the ends of the network.

The experimental use case on Smart Fog Hub Service (SFHS) has been described, detailing the main business needs and the objectives of using proximity marketing and a personalized customer centric approach based on the use of Collaborative Filtering and a recommendation system. Both the system and application architecture defined for iteration-1 have been presented, with a detailed vision of the mF2C framework, its hierarchical architecture, resource clustering in layers and agent splitting into PM and AC blocks. Then some critical requirements of the use case have been analyzed in depth, particularly the real-time calculation of object positions and check for Points of Interests nearby. For this reason two different approaches have been defined, one with the fog-to-cloud support, the other with direct cloud connection. At the same time different wireless communications means have been evaluated with their characteristics.

Finally, a benchmark has been defined for the experimental evaluation of different scenarios, where results have confirmed that the mF2C approach together with Wi-Fi network connection brings the best performance, compared with other approaches based on direct cloud connection and 3G/4G usage.

Acknowledgments. This work is supported by the H2020 mF2C project (730929).

References

1. Boston Consulting: Internet of things market to reach $267b by 2020. https://iotsources.com/applications/iot-market-to-reach-267b-by-2020-use-cases-drive-demand/
2. IATA: 2036 forecast reveals air passengers will nearly double to 7.8 billion (2017). http://www.iata.org/pressroom/pr/Pages/2017-10-24-01.aspx
3. McKinsey Global Institute: The internet of things: mapping the value. https://tinyurl.com/y7dmutgz
4. McKinsey Global Institute: What's new with the internet of things? https://tinyurl.com/y8fk4sft
5. Lordan, F., Lezzi, D., Ejarque, J., Badia, R.M.: An architecture for programming distributed applications on fog to cloud systems. In: Heras, D.B., Bougé, L. (eds.) Euro-Par 2017. LNCS, vol. 10659, pp. 325–337. Springer, Cham (2018). https://doi.org/10.1007/978-3-319-75178-8_27
6. Marti, J., Queralt, A., Gasull, D., Barcelo, A., Costa, J.J., Cortes, T.: Dataclay: a distributed data store for effective inter-player data sharing. J. Syst. Softw. **131**, 129–145 (2017)
7. Masip-Bruin, X., et al.: mF2C: towards a coordinated management of the IoT-fog-cloud continuum. In: Proceedings of the ACM Smartobjects 2018 (MobiHoc) Conference (2018). https://doi.org/10.1145/3213299.3213307
8. Ramirez, W., et al.: Evaluating the benefits of combined and continuous fog-to-cloud architectures. Comput. Commun. **113**, 43–52 (2017)
9. Salis, A., Mancini, G.: Making use of a smart fog hub to develop new services in airports. In: Heras, D.B., Bougé, L. (eds.) Euro-Par 2017. LNCS, vol. 10659, pp. 338–347. Springer, Cham (2018). https://doi.org/10.1007/978-3-319-75178-8_28

Multi-tenant Pub/Sub Processing for Real-Time Data Streams

Álvaro Villalba[1,2(✉)] and David Carrera[1,2(✉)]

[1] Technical University of Catalonia (UPC), Barcelona, Spain
[2] Barcelona Supercomputing Center (BSC), Barcelona, Spain
{alvaro.villalba,david.carrera}@bsc.es

Abstract. Devices and sensors generate streams of data across a diversity of locations and protocols. That data usually reaches a central platform that is used to store and process the streams. Processing can be done in real time, with transformations and enrichment happening on-the-fly, but it can also happen after data is stored and organized in repositories. In the former case, stream processing technologies are required to operate on the data; in the latter batch analytics and queries are of common use.

This paper introduces a runtime to dynamically construct data stream processing topologies based on user-supplied code. These dynamic topologies are built on-the-fly using a data subscription model defined by the applications that consume data. Each user-defined processing unit is called a Service Object. Every Service Object consumes input data streams and may produce output streams that others can consume. The subscription-based programing model enables multiple users to deploy their own data-processing services. The runtime does the dynamic forwarding of data and execution of Service Objects from different users. Data streams can originate in real-world devices or they can be the outputs of Service Objects.

The runtime leverages Apache STORM for parallel data processing, that combined with dynamic user-code injection provides multi-tenant stream processing topologies. In this work we describe the runtime, its features and implementation details, as well as we include a performance evaluation of some of its core components.

Keywords: Big Data · Analytics · Stream processing
Real-time data processing · Programming models
Internet of Things · IoT

1 Introduction

In the last years, Big Data and Internet of Things (IoT) platforms are clearly converging in terms of technologies, problems and approaches. IoT ecosystems generate a vast amount of data that needs to be stored and processed, becoming a Big Data problem. Devices and sensors generate streams of data across a

G. Mencagli et al. (Eds.): Euro-Par 2018 Workshops, LNCS 11339, pp. 251–262, 2019.
https://doi.org/10.1007/978-3-030-10549-5_20

diversity of locations and protocols that in the end reach a central platform that is used to store and process it. Processing can be done in real time, with transformations and enrichment happening on-the-fly, but it can also happen after data is stored and organized in repositories.

This situation implies an increasing demand for advanced data streams management and processing platforms. Such platforms require multiple protocols support for extended connectivity with the objects. But also need to exhibit uniform internal data organization and advanced data processing capabilities to fulfill the demands of the application and services that consume these streams of data.

To provide answer to this growing demand, ServIoTicy[1] is a state-of-the-art platform for hosting real-time data stream workloads in the Cloud. It provides multi-tenant data stream processing capabilities, a REST API, data analytics, advanced queries and multi-protocol support in a combination of advanced data-centric services. The main focus of ServIoTicy is to provide a rich set of features to store and process data through its REST API, allowing objects, services and humans to access the information produced by the devices connected to the platform. ServIoTicy allows for a real time processing of device-generated data, and enables for simple creation of data transformation pipelines using user generated logic. Unlike traditional service composition approaches, usually focused on addressing the problems of functional composition of existing services, one of the goals of the ServIoTicy is to focus on data processing scalability. Other components that can be connected to ServIoTicy provide added capabilities to automatically create compositions of high-level services using existing tools [13].

The core of the ServIoTicy runtime relies on a novel programming model that allows users to dynamically construct data stream processing topologies based on user-supplied code. These topologies are built on-the-fly according to a data subscription model defined by the applications that consume data. Once a stream subscriber finishes its work, it is freed from the platform until it is needed again. Each user-defined processing unit is called a Service Object (SO). Every Service Object consumes input data streams and may produce output streams that others can consume. Data streams can originate in real-world devices or they can be outputs of Service Objects deployed in the platform.

Advanced streaming and analytics platforms such as ServIoTicy are complex pieces of software that integrate a large set of components under the hood. They hide their complexity behind simple REST APIs and multi-protocol channels. ServIoTicy leverages Apache STORM runtime for parallel data processing, auto-scaling and operation placement, that combined with dynamic user-code injection provides multi-tenant stream processing topologies.

This paper provides insights on the performance properties of ServIoTicy as an starting point for the construction of advanced cloud provisioning strategies and algorithms. The work presented here focuses on the processing topologies built in ServIoTicy, although some details about other platform components are also provided.

[1] servioticy.com.

The source code of ServIoTicy is freely available as an open source project[2] in GitHub. The platform is also available for single node testing as a vagrant box, downloadable from a github repository[3].

The main contributions of this paper are:

- A technique for user-code injection on a data stream processing runtime that allows for multi-tenant stream processing on-the-fly. This runtime is the core of the ServIoTicy platform.
- An insight on the performance of the code-injection technique, including response time end-to-end in a processing pipeline and across stages.

The next sections of the paper are organized as follows: Sect. 2 introduces a set of abstractions defined in ServIoTicy for managing data associated to objects; Sect. 3 describes in detail the stream processing runtime of ServIoTicy; Sect. 4 presents the evaluation methodology and the experiment included in the paper; Finally, Sect. 5 goes through the related work and Sect. 6 provides some conclusions and future lines of work.

2 Abstractions Used in ServIoTicy

Several abstractions are used in ServIoTicy to embrace the different entities involved in the existence of IoT ecosystems.

- Web Object: Web Objects are physical objects sitting on the edge of ServIoTicy and capable of keeping for example HTTP-based bi-directional communications, such that the object will be able to both send data to the platform and receive activation requests and notifications.
- Service Object: Service Objects are standard internal ServIoTicy representations of Web Objects. This entity serves mainly for data management purposes and has a well-defined and closed API. That API is needed in order to streamline and standardize internal access to Service Objects, which can in turn represent a variety of very different Web Objects providing very different capabilities.
- Sensor Update: Sensor Updates are the unit of data sent by a Web Object to its Service Object. It contains the different synchronously sensed values and a timestamp that is maintained all over the pipelines. A subscription or a query to a Service Object will get the data in this format.

3 Data Processing Pipelines

Service Objects store their associated data in abstractions called *streams*. The unit of data that can be observed for one stream is called a *Sensor Update* (SU). Applications can subscribe to or query data associated to any stream. Streams can be of two different types:

---

[2] https://github.com/serviotic y.
[3] https://github.com/serviotic y/serviotic y-vagrant.

- Simple data streams store data generated in the physical world by a sensing device, assuming that a device with N sensors will generate N streams of data that will be grouped in a Service Object abstraction that represents the device.
- Composite data streams represent transformations (aggregate, merge, filter or join, among other possibilities) performed on other data sources (either by devices located in the physical world or by Service Objects existing in the ServIoTicy platform). They can be thought about as a virtual (non-physical) sensor of the SO.

From an API perspective there is no difference between a simple stream and a composite stream, as they both support queries and subscriptions. Therefore, the inputs of composite stream can be streams or other composite streams. These chained transformations of SUs are called *Data Processing Pipelines.*

3.1 Data Structures

The structure of a Sensor Update that corresponds to a given stream is basically composed of a series of *Channels* associated to the dimensions of the data represented by the stream (e.g. a geo-location stream may contain two channels representing the latitude and the longitude correspondingly), and a timestamp reported by the data source as the time at which the Sensor Update was generated.

The composite stream structure is similar to the structure of a SU. It contains channels, and each channel contains a so-called 'current-value' field that represents the output value that the composite stream will emit after ingesting a new SU, assuming that the output is not filtered. In a SO document, the content of a 'current-value' field is a string with a JavaScript variable assignment using any mix of basic operator and functions from the Math object, String object, Array object, as well as shorthand conditional expressions (a = b ? true: false). The result of the assignment to 'current-value' will always be numeric, a Boolean, a string or an array of the previous types. It will be stored and emitted to its subscribers.

3.2 Stages of the Processing Pipeline

Once a SU reaches a composite stream as one of its inputs, it goes through a number of stages in order to transform it into a new output SU. This process of ingesting a SU and processing it until a new SU is produced can be summarized as the following set of stages:

1. Subscriber dispatching: A sensor update gets into the processing pipeline, along with its origin information. This stage looks for the subscribers of its origin and if they are composite streams, they are requested and sent to the next stage with the SU.
2. Data Fetching: The composite stream may need access to the data stored by other streams that are inputs involved in the data transformation. In each stage, the sources needed by the stream are queried and their data made available for the rest of the stages, altogether with the original SU. References to fields on the Sensor Updates are made using JSONPaths.

3. Transformation & filtering: Data transformation is performed by taking all the SUs extracted from all the data sources, and operating on their associated data using JavaScript algebraic operations and its Math object functions, String object operations, Array object operations, and boolean operations, to finally obtain a single value for the new SU to emit. Also, before and after the transformation SUs are discarded if a defined filter assertion is false, and no further stages would follow.
4. Store, trigger actions and emit: Finally, the generated SU gets stored and emitted to the stream subscribers. Additionally, in this final stage, actions to be sent back to SOs are triggered. Such actions will end up being sensor actuations that will be driven through the WOs that embed the actual physical objects.

In ServIoTicy, basic physical object actuation is driven through SOs. When a SO gets an action invoked through the SO actions API, the action is initiated on the corresponding WO, that will act as a proxy for the physical actuator. If a user needs to be able to manually request the execution of a composite action (involving multiple SOs), it is necessary to create a SO that includes the desired action and references to the individual SOs representing each of the physical objects to be actuated, so that the composite action can be properly triggered.

3.3 Design Principles

The data processing pipelines introduced in this work are intended to be scalable in accordance with other works found in the literature [15]. In particular, the key design principles considered for the data processing pipelines were:

- Event-driven: A new SU calculation is triggered in a stream when it receives a SU.
- Lock-free: A stream that needs of several different SUs to generate a new one will not lock until all of them are received. It makes use of the received SU, and queries the last SUs from the other needed streams.
- Real-time data processing oriented: Each new SU is processed individually without waiting for a batch.

The approach followed by ServIoTicy is an asynchronous model for which only one of the sources needs to issue a sensor update to trigger the processing of the composite stream. It enforces a high rate of updates and avoids locking the generation of new updates because one sensor is idle. This situation would lock an entire pipeline.

3.4 Time, Data Consistency and Efficiency

A composite stream can take as inputs the most recent SU from any stream declared in the platform, either from its own Service Object or from any other Service Object. In the context of a particular data stream, that receives SUs as inputs and stores data associated to its outputs in the platform, some restrictions need to be in place to keep chronological consistency of the data being produced by a given composite stream.

More formally, let S be a composite stream that takes as inputs the SUs generated by N streams. Let $su_i^{t_i}$ be the most recent SU associated to the ith stream that is a data source for S, where $0 \leq i < N$, and let be t_i the associated timestamp to $su_i^{t_i}$. Also, let $su_s^{t_s}$ be the most recent SU associated to the stream S. Notice that it is possible that $\exists_i$ such that $i = s$ if S consumes its own previously generated data to produce new outputs.

Then we can define $SU_{s,in}^t = \{su_0^{t_0}, su_1^{t_1}, \ldots, su_{n-1}^{t_{n-1}}\}$ as the set of N inputs that S will use to produce one new output $SU_{s,out}^t$ with timestamp t. This output will be defined as a function $SU_{s,out}^t = f(SU_{s,in}^t)$ that is user-defined.

Given these definitions, ServIoTicy needs to guarantee that the function f is calculated (and an output $SU_{s,out}^t$ emitted) only once for the same set of input values, and that at least one of the SUs in $SU_{s,in}^t$ needs to be updated (with a more recent timestamp) to trigger the computation again. Furthermore, it is necessary that the set $SU_{s,in}^t$ satisfies that $\exists su_i^{t_i} \in SU_{s,in}^t$ such that $t_i > t$ to initiate the computation of f to emit $SU_{s,out}^t$.

This restriction can be enforced by checking all the elements of $SU_{s,in}^t$ everytime that an element of the set is updated. But this approach can result in performing large amounts of costful operations just to decide that the conditions were not satisfied and that no new output needs to be emitted.

To mitigate this problem, ServIoTicy relaxes the previously stated restriction to the form $t_j > t$ where $0 \leq j < N$ and $su_j^{t_j}$ is the actual element in $SU_{s,in}^t$ that triggered the computation. This relaxation is possible because if an element exist in the set other than the one triggering the computation that has a more recent timestamp than t, then this it is very unlikely that this element has been computed before in time, because then t would have to be as recent as its timestamp. Otherwise, if the element with more recent timestamp has not yet triggered the computation, then it means that the SU has been stored for the source stream and it must be awaiting in a queue its time to be processed, and therefore it will trigger the computation soon.

3.5 Execution Trees of the Data Processing Pipelines

The structure of a pipeline created using the ServIoTicy subscription model is by definition a directed graph. In practice, though, it behaves more like a set of trees. The reasoning behind this statement is discussed in this section.

When an update reaches a stream, if it is newer than the last generated update, the computation will be triggered. But if the received update is as new as the last generated update, the computation will be discarded. Consider a stream that has several inputs and they originally come from the exact same entry stream to the pipeline (source). When one of the inputs receives an update, at some point all the other inputs will receive an update with the same timestamp and the subsequent computations will always be discarded. Only the first update to reach the stream will trigger the computation.

From this reasoning it can be deduced that the set of paths of the triggered computations from a single source will always end up looking like a tree. For example Fig. 1(a) represents the graph of a valid pipeline. The computations that would be generated from the subscriptions $d \rightarrow c$ and $h \rightarrow e$ are discarded for the explained reasons. Therefore the execution graphs look like in Fig. 1(b), and updates from d to c and from h to e will only be queried.

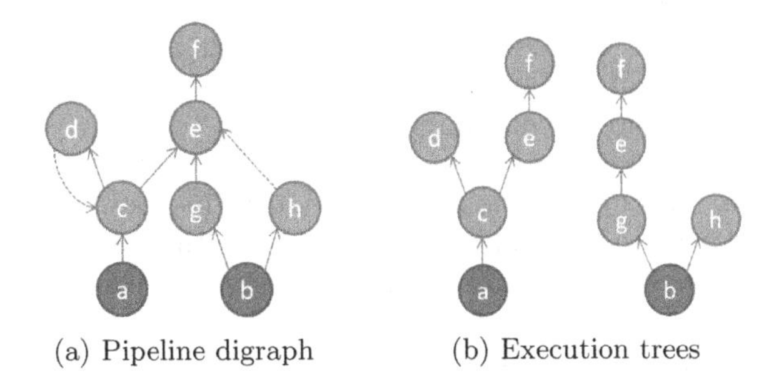

(a) Pipeline digraph (b) Execution trees

Fig. 1. Relation between a pipeline and its execution trees

Another interesting property of a pipeline is the novelty of its generated data, and it is useful for evaluating the quality of a stream. A stream generates novel data when it has an input with a source that no other input of the same stream has. The further a stream is in a path from the last new source addition, the less novel its generated SUs are. For example in Fig. 1(a), c, g, h and e are 1 level more novel than f and d. See that e gets data sourced on b from two inputs, but theres also another input sourced on a. On the other hand f and d are one vertex away from the most novel source. At the levels of data novelty of this example, getting data from f or d is not a problem. The problem comes when the distance from the most novel stream is too far away will always take too much time to process an SU that will not add much value to what it is already evaluated, and will generate several discarded computations which will end up being time consumed without a result. Novel data means faster dispatch, less noise in the pipeline and more added value on the data.

3.6 Runtime Implementation and User-Code Injection

The software that dispatches the incoming SUs and executes the pipelines runs on STORM. STORM topologies are static, but the pipelines can easily change over time, add connections between them, and have arbitrary sizes. For this reason the STORM topology in ServIoTicy runs the stages described in Sect. 3.2, common to all the pipelines to be processed. On the subscribers dispatch stage, the target streams are requested, with the code to be executed in them (previously deployed by the owner of the Service Object using the REST API). In the different execution stages (filters and transformation), the JavasScript code related to it is executed on a JavaScript engine. The JavaScript engine used is Rhino.

4 Evaluation

This section presents a performance evaluation of the implementation of the ServIoTicy Data Pipelines.

4.1 Evaluation Methodology and Infrastructure

In the experiment we explored the performance of several randomly-generated topologies. We present here the average results for all of them and the specific results of one illustrative case. A number of SUs were submitted to the topologies, and we measured the time it took for each SU to be propagated to all the streams that were subscribed directly or indirectly to the SU.

To drive the evaluation we developed a tool to automate the generation and deployment of randomly generated Data Processing Pipelines. The tool provides several control knobs to customize the properties of the topologies being generated. The most relevant controls are the number of streams, the number of composite streams, the number of operands per stream and how the operands are distributed between the streams.

The tests were run on two sets of nodes: one set for running the client emulators and one set for running the servers of the system under test. The 'server' set was composed of 16 two-way 4-core Xeon L5630 @2.13 GHz Linux boxes, for a total of 8 cores per node and 16 hardware threads because hyperthreading was enabled. Each 'server' machine was enabled with 24 GB of RAM. The 'client' set was composed of 2 two-way 6-core Xeon E5-2620 0 @2.00 GHz Linux boxes, for a total of 12 cores per node and 24 hardware threads because hyperthreading was enabled. Each 'server' machine was enabled with 64 GB of RAM. All nodes were connected using GbE links to a non blocking 48port Cisco 3750-X switch. The ServIoTicy data processing runtime was deployed on 2 server machines, and 1 client machine was used to generate the SUs. The REST API used the other nodes to host its components. For the data processing pipelines we used Apache STORM v0.9.2-incubating, Kafka v0.8.2.2 and ZooKeeper v3.4.5.

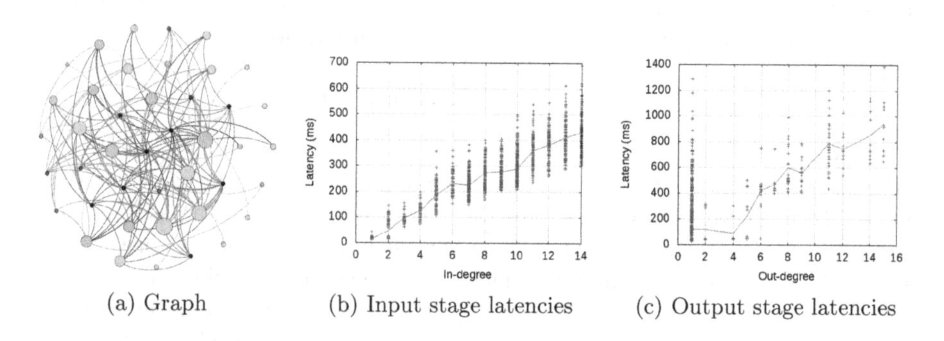

(a) Graph (b) Input stage latencies (c) Output stage latencies

Fig. 2. Topology number 3 and its related experiments results

4.2 Experiment

For this experiment, we generated six different testing topologies for ingesting data produced by a Service Object. The characteristics of these topologies are summarized in Table 1. They can be grouped based on their size (small, medium or large), and we randomly produced 2 samples of each complexity level. Based

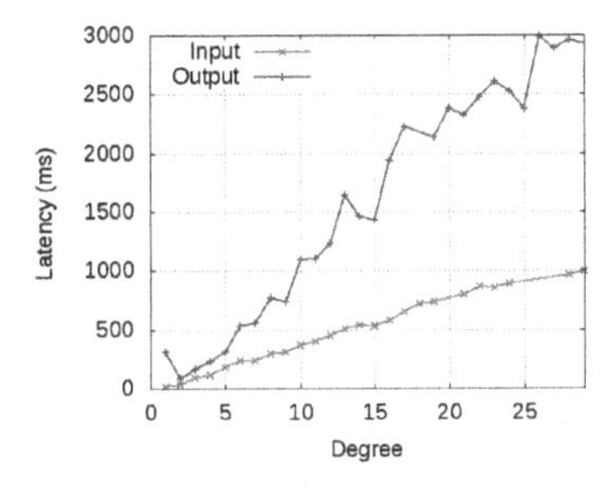

Fig. 3. Stage latency by degree

on our experience, topologies 1 and 2 emulate two realistically sized situations. Topologies 3 and 4 are large cases. Finally, topologies 5 and 6 are extreme cases. A graphical representation of topology number 3 is shown in Fig. 2(a). In this figure, dark nodes indicate a high out-degree and big nodes represent high in-degree. The in and out degree related properties are also very relevant for this experiment, as they have a big impact on the metrics taken.

Table 1. Pseudo-random topologies

Type	Small		Medium		Big	
Id	1	2	3	4	5	6
Max in-degree	9	8	14	16	29	24
Mean in-degree	1.42	1.94	3.54	3.51	5.28	6.18
In-degree std. dev	2.22	2.63	4.36	5.05	7.43	7.38
Max out-degree	4	7	15	15	25	28
Mean out-degree	1.42	1.94	3.54	3.51	5.28	6.18
Out-degree std. dev	1.07	2.14	4.59	4.44	7.71	9.48
Edges	30	37	149	151	423	458
Nodes	21	19	42	43	80	74
Sources	11	9	17	18	30	24
Sinks	4	7	15	15	25	28
Density	0.14	0.21	0.17	0.16	0.13	0.16
Connectivity	1	1	1	1	1	1
Edge-connectivity	1	1	1	1	1	1

For each data source, 10 Sensor Updates were sent to the platform in sequence: a new update was generated only after the previous pipeline computation was finished. During the topology execution, two metrics were measured for each stream. The first metric is the execution time to perform all the data queries required to complete the processing, named the *input stage*. This metric measures the effect of using several inputs to generate a new update. The second metric is the time difference between the instant at which a new update is emitted and the time at which all subscribers have received it: this metric measures how the topology processing time is affected by the number of subscribers at each stage of the processing pipeline. This is named in this section as the *output stage*.

Other stages were also measured, such as the injected code processing time or the time an update remained unaccessed in Kafka. The function to generate a new update was always a summation of the inputs, and so had complexity $O(n)$, being n the in-degree. However, these measures resulted on negligible times and have not been included in the discussion.

Figures 2(b) and (c) show all the latencies measured for topology number 3. Each dot in the plot represents one execution of a topology node with a given in- or out-degree that corresponds to the value in the X-axis. The average latency for each degree is also drawn in both charts as a solid line. As it can be observed, latency grows linearly with the degree level as some sequential operations are required for each operation. Although the communication is made asynchronous, the stages need to be closed before jumping to the next step for the topology, and therefore it is necessary to wait for all on-the-fly operations to complete at some point, what results in a waiting time that is proportional to the number of initiated operations and therefore the degree of the stage.

Finally, Fig. 3 shows the average latency on the input and output stages for every related degree, across all six topologies. As it can be observed, the latency of both the input and output stages grow linearly, but in a higher pace in the output stage. While the in-degree latencies look almost the same to Figs. 2(b), the out degree grows faster. The reason for this worse performance is that this Figure reports average values that are affected by the higher latencies of the bigger topologies. Therefore, the time of the output stage not only depends on the out-degree, but also on the total size of the topology. And in particular, the topology length is the most important factor that affects the performance of the topologies. The larger the topology is, the more operations are run in parallel in the topology and therefore the largest the response times of the components, resulting in a slightly higher latency to complete the processing of an update.

5 Related Work

In the last years several stream processing platforms have emerged, being Apache Storm [2] the most popular and it is used in this contribution as a platform runtime. Storm is a distributed, reliable, and fault-tolerant stream processing system, which was open sourced by Twitter after acquiring BackType and now distributed by the Apache Software foundation. ZeroMQ or Netty are the messaging interfaces between the computation units. In the last versions multi-tenancy was added in terms of several tenants deploying isolated topologies. This topologies are always in memory whether are being used or not, and there is not data subscription between tenants. Also open-source and distributed by the Apache Software Foundation are Apache Samza [10] and Apache Flink [1] and Apache

S4 [12]. Apache Samza uses Kafka for the whole messaging between the computation units and YARN for resource management. Apache Flink is a streaming dataflow engine that provides data distribution, communication, and fault tolerance for distributed computations over data streams. It has two APIs, one for data streams and another for data sets or batch processing. Flink also bundles libraries for domain-specific use cases like complex event processing and machine learning. Apache S4 is an already deprecated project started by Yahoo with a very similar topology based philosophy to Storm and an architecture resembling the Actors model. Microsoft Research developed a proprietary solution for complex event processing called StreamInsight [7]. It also leverages a programing model for temporal data streams, operator algebra and continuous queries. Other relevant foundations on stream processing in real-time from Microsoft come the CEDR [9] project. It is centered in the problem of keeping time consistency on event streaming. Other well known research related projects on data streams are Aurora [6] and its forks Medusa [8] and Borealis [5]. None of this projects are maintained anymore. From the perspective of data stream sharing, StreamGlobe [11] offers a Grid Computing solution using a P2P approach. It consist then in stream sharing between machines but not multi-tenancy.

Data Centric view of the IoT is not something new for ServIoTicy as it was widely covered in the survey presented in [14]. What ServIoTicy uniquely provides is an open source solution that challenges the features of commercial solutions such as Xively [4] and Evrythng [3], while extending their capabilities with the ability to inject user-defined code into its stream processing runtime.

6 Conclusions

In this paper we have introduced a multi-tenant data stream processing mechanism on top of Apache STORM that enables the tenants to share data streams between them. STORM provides auto-scaling capabilities that make it particularly suitable for cloud deployments. The ServIoTicy runtime allows for users to deploy custom service codes inside Service Objects in the form of composite streams, and subscribe those streams to multiple sources of data (either outside the platform on real-world devices or in other streams defined in the ServIoTicy platform by other users). The user-code will be automatically injected in the STORM topology and executed when a unit of data is generated from a source to which the composite stream is subscribed. The runtime is designed to be highly scalable, following a lock-free model that combines operations triggered by new data being generated inside or outside the platform, with queries performed over historic data logged for existing Service Objects. The design imposes some restrictions mainly related to the timestamps of the updates being processed, and some optimizations are applied to improve the scalability of the platform. A basic evaluation of the runtime is included in this work, showing how acceptable response times of less that 100 ms can be delivered by basic composite streams, and that for most realistic pipelines can be processed in the range of less than a second. The work presented in this paper is, to our knowledge, the first multi-tenant IoT data processing platform for the Cloud.

Acknowledgments. This work is partially supported by the European Research Council (ERC) under the EU Horizon 2020 programme (GA 639595), the Spanish Ministry of Economy, Industry and Competitivity (TIN2015-65316-P) and the Generalitat de Catalunya (2014-SGR-1051).

References

1. Apache Flink official website. http://flink.apache.org
2. Apache Storm official website. http://storm.apache.org
3. evrythng official website. evrythng.com
4. Xively official website. xively.com
5. Abadi, D.J., et al.: The design of the borealis stream processing engine. In: CIDR, vol. 5, pp. 277–289 (2005)
6. Abadi, D.J., et al.: Aurora: a new model and architecture for data stream management. VLDB J. Int. J. Very Large Data Bases **12**(2), 120–139 (2003)
7. Ali, M., Chandramouli, B., Goldstein, J., Schindlauer, R.: The extensibility framework in Microsoft StreamInsight. In: 2011 IEEE 27th International Conference on Data Engineering (ICDE), pp. 1242–1253. IEEE (2011)
8. Balazinska, M., Balakrishnan, H., Stonebraker, M.: Load management and high availability in the medusa distributed stream processing system. In: Proceedings of the 2004 ACM SIGMOD International Conference on Management of Data, pp. 929–930. ACM (2004)
9. Barga, R.S., Goldstein, J., Ali, M., Hong, M.: Consistent streaming through time: a vision for event stream processing. arXiv preprint cs/0612115 (2006)
10. Kleppmann, M., Kreps, J.: Kafka, Samza and the unix philosophy of distributed data
11. Kuntschke, R., Stegmaier, B., Kemper, A., Reiser, A.: StreamGlobe: processing and sharing data streams in grid-based P2P infrastructures. In: Proceedings of the 31st International Conference on Very Large Data Bases, pp. 1259–1262. VLDB Endowment (2005)
12. Neumeyer, L., Robbins, B., Nair, A., Kesari, A.: S4: distributed stream computing platform. In: 2010 IEEE International Conference on Data Mining Workshops (ICDMW), pp. 170–177. IEEE (2010)
13. Pedrinaci, C., Liu, D., Maleshkova, M., Lambert, D., Kopecky, J., Domingue, J.: iServe: a linked services publishing platform. In: The 7th Extended Semantic Web Ontology Repositories and Editors for the Semantic Web Workshop, vol. 596, June 2010. http://oro.open.ac.uk/23093/
14. Qin, Y., Sheng, Q.Z., Falkner, N.J.G., Dustdar, S., Wang, H., Vasilakos, A.V.: When things matter: a data-centric view of the internet of things. CoRR abs/1407.2704 (2014). http://arxiv.org/abs/1407.2704
15. Stonebraker, M., Çetintemel, U., Zdonik, S.: The 8 requirements of real-time stream processing. ACM SIGMOD Rec. **34**(4), 42–47 (2005)

A Review of Mobility Prediction Models Applied in Cloud/Fog Environments

David H. S. Lima[1,3](✉), Andre L. L. Aquino[2], and Marilia Curado[1]

[1] Centre for Informatics and Systems (CISUC),
DEI/FCTUC - University of Coimbra, Coimbra, Portugal
{dhlima,marilia}@dei.uc.pt

[2] LaCCAN/CPMAT – Computer Institute,
Federal University of Alagoas (UFAL), Maceió, Brazil
alla@laccan.ufal.br

[3] Federal Institute of Alagoas (IFAL), Rio Largo, Brazil

Abstract. Cloud and Fog Computing are two emerging technologies that have being used in various fields of application. On one hand, Cloud Computing has the problem of big latency, being especially problematic when the application requires a rapid response in the edge network. On the other hand, Fog Computing distributes the computational data processing tasks to the edge network to reduce the latency, but it still faces challenges especially when dealing with support for mobile users. This work aims to present a review of the works in Cloud/Fog Computing that use mobility prediction techniques in their favor in order to deal with users mobility problem. Additionally we present the potential of applying the techniques in Cloud/Fog environments.

Keywords: Cloud Computing · Fog computing · Mobility prediction

1 Introduction

In recent years, humans have become more connected. In the next few years it is expected that billions of new devices, each one with the capacity to collect information, communicate and interact with the environment, to be inserted into the world. Cloud [4] and Fog [9] computing are both new technologies that aim to deal with those kind of devices.

Cloud Computing has the objective of deploying computational systems in highly distributed environments and deal with configuration of resources. Therefore, Cloud Computing is not a good choice to deal with applications that need frequent communication or real time response. For this purpose, Fog Computing was proposed. Fog Computing is implemented in the edge of the network and it provides low latency, location awareness and improves Quality of Service (QoS) for streaming and real time applications.

A major challenge is that most of those new devices will be mobile, so it will be an important issue to know how to deal with this characteristic. Integrating

G. Mencagli et al. (Eds.): Euro-Par 2018 Workshops, LNCS 11339, pp. 263–274, 2019.
https://doi.org/10.1007/978-3-030-10549-5_21

mobility prediction with Cloud/Fog Computing studies can be a solution to face this problem. In this work we present an overview of three research fields (Handover, Computation Offloading and Resource Management) in Cloud/Fog computing presenting state-of-the-art works and additionally we discuss how the usage of mobility prediction techniques makes sense in their context.

The remainder of this paper is organized as follows. Section 2 presents an overview of human mobility prediction and some of its applications. Section 3 discusses how mobility prediction can be applied in Cloud/Fog Environments to improve their capabilities. Finally, Sect. 4 discusses challenges and open issues in applying Human Mobility studies to the Cloud/Fog computing field and presents conclusions and future works.

2 Human Mobility Prediction

To improve urban mobility, accessibility and quality of life, it is important to understand how people travel and conduct their activities. This issue has been one of the major focus of city planners, geographers and transportation planners. Human mobility is important to characterize mobility patterns such as walking home, driving to working places or utilizing public transportation system and it could be applied in several fields as epidemic control, urban planning, traffic and forecasting systems. Urban human mobility prediction refers to the estimation of the person's next location.

Current human mobility models can be classified into two groups: trace-based and synthetic models [18]. The trace-based models generally use GPS (Global Positioning System) traces, Bluetooth connectivity observations or Call Detail Records (CDR). A problem that we found in the use of trace-based models is that the data are collected in a specific place, as a consequence, their applicability can be limited. Synthetic models are defined on mathematical basis what makes them widely used in simulations. A drawback in this approach is that it often has limited similarity with a mobility behavior in the real world. Figure 1 presents a taxonomy of the presented models.

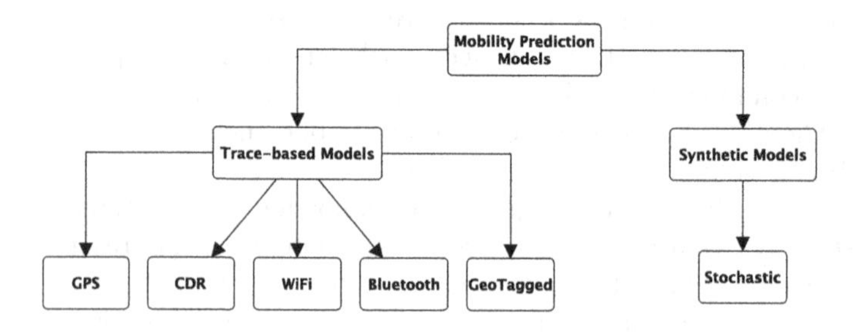

Fig. 1. Taxonomy of presented models

To define which data collection technique will be used, it is important to take in consideration what kind of application will be conducted and what is the minimum acceptable accuracy that the user expects. Many other studies started to use GPS data to track people. With the popularization of the usage of smartphones, it becomes very easy to obtain GPS data from users. An advantage of using GPS data is its accuracy in outdoor locations and also it is a low cost way to obtain data. A drawback is that if the user is using GPS embedded in a smartphone he/she tends to keep the GPS signal turned off to save battery. In the literature it is possible to find articles that use GPS signal embedded in smartphones [35], taxis [37], public transportation [26] and private vehicles [15].

It is also possible to use WiFi Scanning to predict human mobility [25]. While people are walking, their devices could automatically connect to WiFi Access Points (APs). As soon as they connect, this information becomes available in real time and the model can detect where the user is. When the user connects to another AP the system will know his/her trajectory. Nowadays, it has become very popular the usage of Call Data Records (CDR) in human mobility studies [36]. CDRs are recorded every time that a voice-call or SMS or any Internet activities occurs. Each CDR record is composed by the user id, the cell id of the handling tower and the date and time of the phone activity.

Other kinds of data used are from social networks. Existing works take advantage of check-ins or geotags posted on social networks like Twitter [11], Flickr [7] and Foursquare [1], to try to infer the user's movement. They use the last and before last information to try to create the possible user's route. Additionally they use information of possible Points of Interests and probabilities of most visited places to deduce the user's route.

The most common used mobility models are Lévy Walks [29] and Radiation Model [34]. A Lévy Walk is a random walk in which the step-lengths have a probability distribution that is heavy-tailed. Intuitively, the Lévy walks consist of many short flights and occasionally long flights where a flight is defined to be a longest straight line trip of a human from one location to another without a directional change or pause.

The Radiation Model is a stochastic process that captures local mobility decisions to help to analytically derive commuting and mobility fluxes that require as input only information on the population distribution. It predicts mobility patterns according to mobility and transport patterns observed in a wide range of phenomena. Given its parameter-free nature, the model can be applied in areas where there is a lack of previous mobility measurements, significantly improving the predictive accuracy of most of the phenomena affected by mobility and transport processes. Other works in literature propose their own human mobility prediction models.

The study of human mobility creates several possibilities to apply the acquired knowledge. Several areas could take advantage of this field. It is clearly that the direct application of this kind of study is in the characterization of human trajectory. With the proposed models it is possible to determinate with high accuracy what trajectory a person or a group will take in a certain moment in a certain day.

In network research field it can help in different aspects of network operation such as handover, resource management, routing and in a better independent deployment of connectivity models [19]. It is possible to apply human mobility in a network to achieve large scale dissemination in a dynamic Device to Device based communication network [2,14]. Human mobility prediction can also be applied in the field of Mobile Cloud Computing [16,24]. For example, it is possible to apply the user's next location to determine which cloud is the best one to migrate an application that the user is executing [3,33]. Delay Tolerant Networks (DTNs) and Opportunistic Networks (OppNets) can also benefit from the usage of human mobility detection [20,31]. This kind of networks need an inter-contact time to have an opportunity to forward message from one device to another. If the user's next location is known the node can determine which is the best receiver based on its location.

3 Application of Mobility Prediction in Cloud/Fog Computing

This section presents and discusses some research areas of Cloud and Fog Computing and how human mobility prediction can be used in order to improve their capabilities. We list the usage of human mobility prediction technique in Handover, Computation Offloading and Resource Management in Cloud/Fog Computing. In the presented works, mobility prediction was used as an Input source for decision algorithms. With this information the algorithms could determinate how to better deal with the user's mobility and what actions it should take to avoid resource (time, computing resources, money) wasting. Table 1 presents a summary of the presented papers and contributions.

Table 1. Summary of presented papers

Research fields	How mobility prediction was used?	Mobility predictioncontributions
Handover	– Takes RSS strength in consideration to define the next fog node – Determines to which fog node the packets will be transmitted	– Decrease the handover rate – Determine the best fog node to accept node's handover request – Send data directly to the destination fog node
Computation offloading	– Infer the next user's location to proactive migrate services – As input source to offloading decision-making systems	– Select the best cloud/fog to offload the tasks – Partial offloading approach – Determine if it has enough time to offload the task – Recreate routes
Resource management	– As input source to resource allocation decision-making systems	– Determine the best location for cloud/fog nodes – Allocate resources according to user's next location to have resources close to them

3.1 Handover in Cloud/Fog Environments

One of the main challenges in mobile environments is how to deal with handover procedures. Handover, or handoff, is the process where a node maintains its connection active while moving from one point of attachment to another. The idea is that the equipment should select the best base station to connect. One simple rule to determine the best base station is the received signal strength (RSS) level, in other words, the equipment will select the base station with the strongest signal [5]. In case another base station provides a higher RSS than the current base station, the user equipment will change its association. This can occur if the user equipment moves away from the current base station, for example. Other metrics besides RSS can be used. Many studies have been conducted in order to evaluate the best time to perform a handover procedure [12].

Bao et al. [6] proposed a framework known as Follow Me Fog (FMF) to support a seamless handover timing scheme among different computation access points. The proposed framework has a mechanism to pre-migrate a job when a handover procedure is expected to happen. The FMF framework constantly monitors RSSs from different fog nodes to determine when a job needs to be migrated. When the RSS from the current fog node is decreasing while, at the same time, the RSS from a neighbor fog node is increasing, the computation jobs are migrated before the connection redirection. As a result, the service can be resumed when the mobile device is redirected to the new fog node. The authors developed a prototype and their evaluation demonstrated that FMF can achieve a latency reduction of 36.5% when a mobile device is handed over from one fog node to another.

Chen and Tsai [10] presented a new mobility management mechanism using an integrated strategy of Follow Me Cloud (FMC) and Follow Me Edge (FME) called Follow Me Cloud-Cloudlet (FMCL) for smart cities. The FMCL approach aims to reduce the total transmission time if some data packets are pre-scheduled and pre-stored into the cache of a cloudlet when an user is switching from the previous Fog-RAN (Radio Access Network) to the serving Fog-RAN. FMCL is evaluated through simulation in terms of the total transmission time, the throughput, the probability of packet loss, and the number of control messages. The proposed FMCL approach outperforms existing FMC results in terms of the total transmission time, the average throughput, and the probability of packet loss, but with higher overhead due to the amount of control messages.

Zhang et al. [38] presented an architecture for Fog RAN (FRAN) and then proposed a handover management mechanism using edge caching in FRAN. Authors argued that conventional handover schemes are mainly based on RSS, where handover decisions are made comparing it to a predefined threshold. Their proposed mechanism considers APs as a resource for mobile devices making the handover process problem a resource allocation problem. Using simulation the authors concluded that the proposed FRAN architecture in conjunction with the mobility management scheme can significantly decrease the signaling overhead of handover compared to conventional RANs.

Handover management brings several challenges in Cloud/Fog scenarios. For instance, the higher the mobility of an user, the higher his/her handover rate will be. Other problem must occur is if a node stays attached for a short period of time, as there might not be sufficient time for the system to complete the handover procedure. Human mobility prediction could be used to improve the performance of handover procedures. If the user's next location is known, the handover procedure can be performed in an optimal way. In a scenario where there is a dense network with several fog nodes, as expected in 5G networks, when the node starts to move and his/her next location is known by the network, the closest fog node can be responsible to accept his/her handover process and this way optimize this procedure. Other possible usage of mobility prediction is when the node that is moving has packets to receive. Instead of waiting to send those packets to the node, the sender can send them directly to the destination fog node to be cached until the node complete his/her handover procedure.

3.2 Computation Offloading in Cloud/Fog Environments

Computation offloading is a process where tasks that demand a large amount of resources can be executed over a Cloud/Fog infrastructure in order to overcome the resource limitation problem of mobile devices and to try to reduce the total execution time. Due their limited and non-scalable processing power, mobile devices take longer time to execute intensive computations when compared to the same computations executed over the cloud. Transmission time for offloading computations and retrieving the results is an important factor which determines whether the offloading process will be beneficial [8]. Besides the advantage of the increase in the computational power when users offload their task, they also benefit from the decreasing in their energy consumption.

Farris et al. [13] formulated the proactive migration problem at the network edge. They applied prediction schemes of user mobility patterns to improve their results. The authors defined two integer linear optimization problems aiming at the one hand to minimize Quality of Experience (QoE) degradation due to service migration and on the other hand, minimize the cost of proactive replication. The proposed algorithms were evaluated in terms of probability of user reactive migration and average number of replicas per user.

Lee and Shin [22] developed an offloading decision-making technique based on a mobility model of each individual user known as Mob-Aware. This mobility model takes advantage of the regularity of user's mobility pattern and it is characterized by a sequence of networks to which users are connected. The Mob-Aware decision maker gathers previous user movements and network changes corresponding to the movements, builds a mobility model with gathered data, and then makes offloading decisions. The authors evaluated their technique using a trace-based simulation with real log data traces from 14 Android users. The results showed that their technique, when users are highly mobile, can increase the performance of mobile devices in terms of response time and energy consumption.

Li et al. [23] presented a mobility prediction based offloading heuristic to mobile device clouds. As nodes are usually connected via wireless technology and can change their locations from time to time, the connections between devices are usually unstable and the applications offloaded may fail. The authors proposal has the objective of guaranteeing that users are able to continue the applications offloaded seamlessly regardless of the mobility of the nodes. Based on the simulation results, it was shown that in a Mobile Cloud Computing environment, due to the mobility of nodes, it is very difficult to build a robust and effective environment for client nodes to offload computation-intensive applications. With the help of mobility prediction, the proposed heuristic can complete the applications offloaded as soon as possible and with the least risk of failure.

Shi et al. [32] proposed a cloudlet service model and formulated the service scheduling problem in cloudlets aiming to find the optimal service running sequence which minimizes the average service response time during the whole running process of the service for a user. The authors presented an algorithm known as Mobility Prediction-based Markov Decision Process (MPMDP) that takes user's mobility prediction into account and uses Markov Decision Process to make a decision on which cloudlet the services should run. Their proposal was evaluated by simulation using real world traces. The results showed that MPMDP achieves a lower average response time compared with previous schemes.

Having information about user mobility is essential to optimize computation offloading. If a node is moving and it needs to offload some task, it will be better if it offloads its task to a Cloud/Fog closer to its final destination. In this way, the node will be able to receive its results only when it finishes moving, avoiding unnecessary communication in the network. Other possible approach is, instead of full offloading a task to a cloud/fog close to its final destination, the node could partially offload the task, in other words, it could divide the task in some parts and then offload those parts during its trajectory. Those parts could be send to clouds/fogs that are in the node's way. Another issue in computation offloading is that users must know for how long they will stay at a determinate place. With this information they can decide if it worth to offload their task at that moment. If they realize that they will not stay long enough to finish the offload process, the user can decide to wait until he/she arrived in an area that he/she will stay long enough to finish the process. Mobility prediction can also be used to recreate routes in a effective way, since a user can be in a different place than the one that he/she initially the offloading process.

3.3 Resource Management in Cloud/Fog Environments

Resource management is one of the main research fields in Cloud/Fog Computing. Providing resources at the edge of networks (closer to end-devices) brings several benefits such as low latency. Resource management brings two different perspectives: where is the best place to allocate the resources, and when and how much resource it is necessary to allocate. The main ideas behind resource management is that it has to meet the agreed QoS constraints and minimize the resource waste. To achieve this, placement and scheduler strategies can play a major role by keeping log of the status of available resources.

Gao et al. [17] studied the resource allocation problem for cloud-based cache-enabled small cell networks. In the proposed model, the contents that users request are stored both at the cloud pool and at the cache storage of each small base station. Additionally the cloud pool can predict the users' mobility patterns and determine the resource allocation scheme in a period of time. The authors formulated the problem using Game Theory. To solve this problem, they proposed a machine learning based resource allocation method. Simulation results show that the proposed algorithm achieves up to 58.2% and 26.1% gains, respectively, in terms of network throughput compared to random and the nearest algorithms.

Karimzadeh et al. [21] proposed an architecture called MOBaaS (Mobility and Bandwidth Availability Prediction as a Service). MOBaaS is composed by two algorithms that have the objective of predict user(s) mobility and network link bandwidth availability. The information provided by MOBaaS can be used in order to generate triggers for on-demand deploying, provisioning, disposing of virtualized network components and also for self-adaptation procedures and optimal network function configuration during run-time operation. Authors implemented MOBaaS on the OpenStack platform and their results confirmed the feasibility and the effectiveness of the prediction algorithms and the proposed architecture.

Mustafa et al. [27] introduced a solution to reduce the effect of resources mobility on the performance of vehicular cloud, using an efficient resource management scheme based on vehicles mobility prediction. Their mobility prediction model is based on an Artificial Neural Network that enables the vehicular cloud to take pre-planned procedures. The main objective is to reduce the negative impact of sudden changes in vehicles locations on vehicular cloud performance. Simulation results show that the proposed approach has leveraged the performance of vehicular cloud effectively without overusing available vehicular cloud resources when compared to other resources management approaches introduced in the literature.

Ojima and Fujii [28] proposed a resource management for Mobile Edge Computing using user mobility prediction. User mobility prediction is executed using linear Kalman filter for estimation of the connectivity. With mobility prediction, users can select the more stable Edge Server during task request and task collection decreasing the failing rate that implies users to proceed the tasks again. Simulation results have shown that this process has improved the success rate.

Plachy et al. [30] presented an algorithm to enable flexible selection of communication path together with a dynamic Virtual Machine placement. The authors use mobility prediction for dynamic VM (Virtual Machine) placement and to find the most suitable communication path according to expected users' movement. The authors compared their approach to state of the art ones. The proposed algorithm leads to reduction of the task offloading delay between 10% and 66% while energy consumed by user's equipment is kept at similar level.

Adding knowledge about user mobility can optimize the resource allocation and placement in a Cloud/Fog infrastructure. As the location of data centers is crucial to optimize resource utilization and to improve performance of services, QoE can be enhanced in terms of content access latency, by placing user content at locations where they will be present in the future. This approach can be used, for example, when some kind of event is occurring and it will be necessary for the infrastructure to reserve resources to serve every node. In this kind of applications fogs or clouds could be able to reserve an amount of their resources for a specific node or for a group of nodes that are going to a place near the cloud/fog. Thinking in a cloudlet infrastructure, for example, if users are far away from cloudlets due to their mobility, it can lead to a poor network connectivity, consequently, their user experience will be poor. The main idea is that services and applications allocate the resources according to user's future locations, this way the resources will usually be close from the users.

4 Final Considerations

This work presented an overview of Handover, Computation Offloading and Resource Management research fields in Cloud/Fog Computing presenting some state-of-the-art works. Additionally we discussed how mobility prediction techniques could be used to improve Cloud/Fog Computing capabilities.

Cloud and Fog Computing already have interesting results in the literature and, as presented in the previous sections, researchers are already dealing with mobility issues in their works. As still exists open issues, mobility prediction problem will continue to be a hot research topic. Having mobile devices and mobile resources creates lots of challenges such as how to handle the unreliable connectivity with those resources, how to provide seamless handovers, which model better fits to predict node's next place. Having mobile resources introduce another level of complexity in resource management algorithms.

The combination of mobility prediction with Cloud/Fog Computing brings many advantages as showed before, but it still has some open issues. It is necessary to create strategies to deal with mobility prediction failure, in other words, how the system will behave if the user's next location is wrong. Another point is understanding users' behavior and mobility patterns to better planning application scheduling, in other words, it is important to know the perfect timing to instantiate or migrate resources to decrease the waiting time.

Besides the usage of user mobility prediction, it should be of great value the usage of virtualization technologies as Network Function Virtualization (NFV) and Software Defined Network (SDN) to deal with problems in cloud and fog environments. Both technologies can help in the virtualization process and can also improve the performance of the system. As future works we aim to characterize this interaction and further analyze how mobility prediction could be more helpful in this new scenario.

Acknowledgements. The work presented in this paper was partially carried out in the scope of the MobiWise project: From mobile sensing to mobility advising (P2020 SAICTPAC/0011/2015), cofinanced by COMPETE 2020, Portugal 2020 - Operational Program for Competitiveness and Internationalization (POCI), European Union's ERDF (European Regional Development Fund) and the Portuguese Foundation for Science and Technology (FCT).

References

1. Abbasi, O.R., Alesheikh, A.A., Sharif, M.: Ranking the city: the role of location-based social media check-ins in collective human mobility prediction. ISPRS Int. J. Geo-Inf. **6**(5), 136 (2017)
2. Agarwal, R., Gauthier, V., Becker, M., Toukabrigunes, T., Afifi, H.: Large scale model for information dissemination with device to device communication using call details records. Comput. Commun. **59**, 1–11 (2015)
3. Ahmed, E., Akhunzada, A., Whaiduzzaman, M., Gani, A., Ab Hamid, S.H., Buyya, R.: Network-centric performance analysis of runtime application migration in mobile cloud computing. Simul. Model. Pract. Theory **50**, 42–56 (2015)
4. Armbrust, M., Fox, A., Griffith, R., Joseph, A.D., Katz, R., Konwinski, A., Lee, G., Patterson, D., Rabkin, A., Stoica, I., Zaharia, M.: A view of cloud computing. Commun. ACM **53**(4), 50–58 (2010)
5. Arshad, R., Elsawy, H., Sorour, S., Al-Naffouri, T.Y., Alouini, M.S.: Handover management in 5G and beyond: a topology aware skipping approach. IEEE Access **4**, 9073–9081 (2016)
6. Bao, W., Yuan, D., Yang, Z., Wang, S., Li, W., Zhou, B.B., Zomaya, A.Y.: Follow me fog: toward seamless handover timing schemes in a fog computing environment. IEEE Commun. Mag. **55**(11), 72–78 (2017)
7. Beiro, M.G., Panisson, A., Tizzoni, M., Cattuto, C.: Predicting human mobility through the assimilation of social media traces into mobility models. EPJ Data Sci. **5**, 30 (2016)
8. Bhattacharya, A., De, P.: A survey of adaptation techniques in computation offloading. J. Netw. Comput. Appl. **78**, 97–115 (2017)
9. Bonomi, F., Milito, R., Zhu, J., Addepalli, S.: Fog computing and its role in the internet of things. In: Proceedings of the First Edition of the MCC Workshop on Mobile Cloud Computing, MCC 2012, pp. 13–16. ACM, New York (2012)
10. Chen, Y.S., Tsai, Y.T.: A mobility management using follow-me cloud-cloudlet in fog-computing-based RANs for smart cities. Sensors **18**(2), 489 (2018)
11. Comito, C., Falcone, D., Talia, D.: Mining human mobility patterns from social geo-tagged data. Pervasive Mob. Comput. **33**, 91–107 (2016)
12. Drissi, M., Oumsis, M.: Performance Evaluation of Multi-criteria Vertical Handover for Heterogeneous Wireless Networks. In: Intelligent Systems and Computer Vision, pp. 1–5 (2015)
13. Farris, I., Taleb, T., Bagaa, M., Flick, H.: Optimizing service replication for mobile delay-sensitive applications in 5G edge network. In: IEEE International Conference on Communications, pp. 1–6 (2017)
14. Flores, H., et al.: Social-aware device-to-device communication: a contribution for edge and fog computing? In: ACM International Joint Conference on Pervasive and Ubiquitous Computing: Adjunct, pp. 1466–1471. ACM (2016)
15. Gallotti, R., Bazzani, A., Rambaldi, S., Barthelemy, M.: A Stochastic Model of Randomly Accelerated Walkers for Human Mobility. Nat. Commun. **7**, 1–7 (2016)
16. Gani, A., Nayeem, G.M., Shiraz, M., Sookhak, M., Whaiduzzaman, M., Khan, S.: A review on interworking and mobility techniques for seamless connectivity in mobile cloud computing. J. Netw. Comput. Appl. **43**, 84–102 (2014)
17. Gao, T., Chen, M., Gu, H., Yin, C.: Reinforcement learning based resource allocation in cache-enabled small cell networks with mobile users. In: IEEE/CIC International Conference on Communications in China, pp. 1–6 (2017)

18. Hess, A., Hummel, K.A., Gansterer, W.N., Haring, G.: Data-driven human mobility modeling: a survey and engineering guidance for mobile networking. ACM Comput. Surv. **48**(3), 38:1–38:39 (2015)
19. Jahromi, K.K., Zignani, M., Gaito, S., Rossi, G.P.: Simulating human mobility patterns in urban areas. Simul. Model. Pract. Theory **62**, 137–156 (2016)
20. Karamshuk, D., Boldrini, C., Conti, M., Passarella, A.: Human mobility models for opportunistic networks. IEEE Commun. Mag. **49**(12), 157–165 (2011)
21. Karimzadeh, M., et al.: Mobility and bandwidth prediction as a service in virtualized LTE systems. In: IEEE International Conference on Cloud Networking, pp. 132–138 (2015)
22. Lee, K., Shin, I.: User mobility model based computation offloading decision for mobile cloud. J. Comput. Sci. Eng. **9**(3), 155–162 (2015)
23. Li, B., Liu, Z., Pei, Y., Wu, H.: mobility prediction based opportunistic computational offloading for mobile device cloud. In: IEEE International Conference on Computational Science and Engineering, pp. 786–792 (2014)
24. Li, W., Zhao, Y., Lu, S., Chen, D.: Mechanisms and challenges on mobility-augmented service provisioning for mobile cloud computing. IEEE Commun. Mag. **53**(3), 89–97 (2015)
25. Lind, P.G., Moreira, A.: Human mobility patterns at the smallest scales. Commun. Comput. Phys. **18**(2), 417–428 (2015)
26. Mazimpaka, J.D., Timpf, S.: How they move reveals what is happening: understanding the dynamics of big events from human mobility pattern. ISPRS Int. J. Geo-Inf. **6**(1), 15 (2017)
27. Mustafa, A.M., Abubakr, O.M., Ahmadien, O., Ahmedin, A., Mokhtar, B.: Mobility prediction for efficient resources management in vehicular cloud computing. In: IEEE International Conference on Mobile Cloud Computing, Services, and Engineering, pp. 53–59 (2017)
28. Ojima, T., Fujii, T.: Resource management for mobile edge computing using user mobility prediction. In: International Conference on Information Networking, pp. 718–720 (2018)
29. Pirozmand, P., Wu, G., Jedari, B., Xia, F.: Human mobility in opportunistic networks: characteristics, models and prediction methods. J. Netw. Comput. Appl. **42**(SI), 45–58 (2014)
30. Plachy, J., Becvar, Z., Strinati, E.C.: Dynamic resource allocation exploiting mobility prediction in mobile edge computing. In: IEEE International Symposium on Personal, Indoor, and Mobile Radio Communications, pp. 1–6 (2016)
31. Rao, W., Zhao, K., Zhang, Y., Hui, P., Tarkoma, S.: Towards maximizing timely content delivery in delay tolerant networks. IEEE Trans. Mob. Comput. **14**(4), 755–769 (2015)
32. Shi, L., Fu, X., Li, J.: Mobility prediction-based service scheduling optimization algorithm in cloudlets. In: Sun, X., Chao, H.-C., You, X., Bertino, E. (eds.) ICCCS 2017. LNCS, vol. 10603, pp. 619–630. Springer, Cham (2017). https://doi.org/10.1007/978-3-319-68542-7_53
33. Shiraz, M., Sookhak, M., Gani, A., Shah, S.A.A.: A study on the critical analysis of computational offloading frameworks for mobile cloud computing. J. Netw. Comput. Appl. **47**, 47–60 (2015)
34. Simini, F., González, M.C., Maritan, A., Barabási, A.L.: A universal model for mobility and migration patterns. Nature **484**(7392), 96–100 (2012)
35. Terroso-Saenz, F., Valdes-Vela, M., Gonzalez-Vidal, A., Skarmeta, A.F.: Human mobility modelling based on dense transit areas detection with opportunistic sensing. Mob. Inf. Syst. **2016**, 1–15 (2016)

36. Yang, X., Zhao, Z., Lu, S.: Exploring spatial-temporal patterns of urban human mobility hotspots. Sustainability **8**(7), 1–18 (2016)
37. Zhang, F., Zhu, X., Guo, W., Ye, X., Hu, T., Huang, L.: Analyzing urban human mobility patterns through a thematic model at a finer scale. ISPRS Int. J. Geo-Inf. **5**(6), 78–95 (2016)
38. Zhang, H., Qiu, Y., Chu, X., Long, K., Leung, V.C.M.: Fog radio access networks: mobility management, interference mitigation, and resource optimization. IEEE Wirel. Commun. **24**(6), 120–127 (2017)

An Architecture for Resource Management in a Fog-to-Cloud Framework

Souvik Sengupta(✉), Jordi Garcia(✉), and Xavi Masip-Bruin(✉)

Advanced Network Architectures Lab (CRAAX), UPC BarcelonaTech, Vilanova i la Geltrú, Spain
{souvik,jordig,xmasip}@ac.upc.edu
https://www.craax.upc.edu

Abstract. Fog-to-cloud (F2C) platforms provide an excellent framework for the efficient resource management in the context of smart cities. In such a scenario, a vast number of heterogeneous resources, including computing devices and IoT sensors, are considered in coordination to provide the best facilities. One of the most critical and challenging tasks in this framework is appropriately managing the set of resources available in the smart city. Many devices with different features should be efficiently classified, organized, and selected, to fulfill the requirements during services execution. In this paper, we present the design of an architecture for resource management as part of a core module in an F2C system. In this architecture, we classify both, the system resources and services and, based on the users' preferences and sharing policies; we discuss the process of resource selection according to a predefined cost model. The cost model could consider any cost dimension, such as performance, energy consumption, or any eventual business model associated with the F2C system.

Keywords: Fog-to-Cloud (F2C) · Internet of Things (IoT)
Resource management

1 Introduction

In the current era of the smart world, we are and will be surrounded by a broad set of smart objects, thus gradually, day by day, entering into and forming part of an ever smart environment. In these days, significant research and industrial activities are focusing on making everything much smarter. Many of these activities are using cutting-edge technologies. In this endeavor, the Internet of Things (IoT) [9] is the most promising and enabling technology. In these days, almost all of the computing and small electronic devices have the facilities to connect to the Internet. Indeed, in [15], authors already provided various statistics to represent the increment rate and future trends of using the IoT devices. So following these trends and statistics, it is clear that, as we are gradually entering into the

G. Mencagli et al. (Eds.): Euro-Par 2018 Workshops, LNCS 11339, pp. 275–286, 2019.
https://doi.org/10.1007/978-3-030-10549-5_22

smart environment, the number of IoT devices is also drastically increasing. By looking at the smart environment system, it is noticeable that all these massive numbers of IoT devices and other computing devices are highly distributed and scattered over the network. For that reason, correct management of this massive amount of devices intended to provide latency-sensitive services to the end users efficiently - is one of the most challenging tasks. To that end, the Fog-to-Cloud (F2C) concept recently came up aimed at optimizing resource utilization while efficiently executing services.

In order to better understand what the F2C paradigm is, we represent in Fig. 1 our view of smart city. In this figure, a smart city may consist of multiple numbers of Fog Areas, each consisting of several heterogeneous IoT devices and other computing devices. Most interestingly, all these devices are diverse in nature. So, the management of this vast number of devices intended to provide real-time services delivery efficiently is the most crucial issue. By considering these challenges and problems, our primary intention is to find out a suitable and proper resource management strategy particularly suiting the F2C paradigm. By identifying the resource and service classification and also by focusing on the functionalities of the different management module (i.e., categorization, resource sharing, resource collector etc.), in this paper, we are proposing the outlined structure for managing the resources in the system. This adequate resource management strategy architecture is envisioned as the initial step for defining the proper resource management strategy in the F2C.

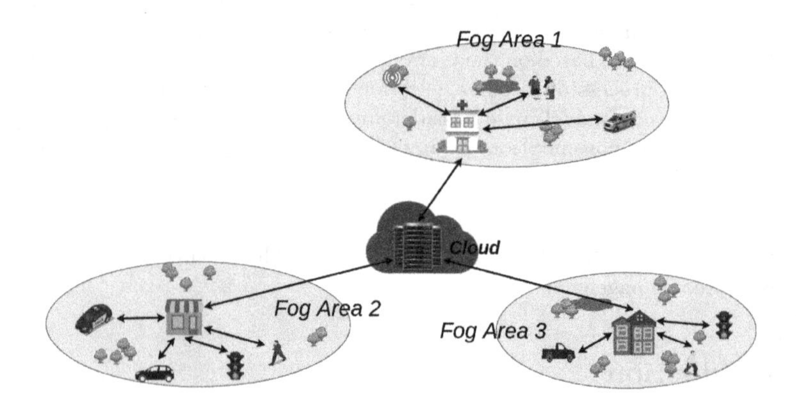

Fig. 1. The Fog-to-Cloud (F2C) computing paradigm in a smart city.

The rest of the paper is organized as follows. We discuss the background of our research work in Sect. 2. The core concepts of the F2C computing are presented in Sect. 3. In Sect. 4, we present the resource management architecture for the coordinated F2C paradigm. Following the previous sections, in Sect. 5 we briefly discuss the future directions of our work by focusing on the various aspects of designing the cost model in the F2C paradigm. Finally, some concluding remarks of our research work are given in Sect. 6.

2 State of the Art

With the recent advancement in modern technology and considering the smart city scenario, many applications need real-time service provisioning support and a massive amount of processing and storage capacity. So to fulfill these requirements, the new coordinated F2C system has emerged. In this system, IoT, fog, and cloud technologies are potentially equal and play the crucial role to bring more efficiency in the smart city scenario. Most importantly, in a smart city scenario, the diversity and heterogeneity in the system resources and services generate key challenges in building an efficient resource management strategy in the F2C paradigm.

In [14], to improve the efficiency of fog resource utilization and satisfy the users' QoS requirements, the authors proposed a dynamic resource allocation strategy for fog computing based on 'priced timed Petri nets'. Whereas in [10], considering the IoT devices and the fog computing platform the authors proposed a simulator. The simulator toolkit measures the impact of a resource management strategy in fog computing by considering the latency, network congestion, energy consumption, and cost. Defining the cost model is one of the critical tasks of any computing platform. In [1], authors proposed a cost model for the fog computing platform, where they proposed the process for determining the cost of accessing the resources to execute some tasks. Considering the virtualization techniques, in [2], the authors proposed an architecture and a strategy for resources provisioning in fog computing environment. Authors in [8] proposed the linear programming based heuristic algorithm to build a cost-efficient resource management strategy for the framework, which they have considered. In that algorithm, they addressed the computation complexity in a fog computing supported medical cyber-physical system.

Similarly, in the cloud computing paradigm, some research has been done to tackle the cloud resource allocation and scheduling problem, both in academia [22] and industry [21]. In [4,20], authors designed some work-flows for allocating the cloud resources and achieve some specific goals. Furthermore, in [23], a resource management strategy has been described by considering the application performance and cost. Whereas in [18], the authors proposed a scheduling algorithm for cloud resources to enhance the cloud resource utilization and guaranteeing some execution deadlines. In [11], the authors presented a distributed cloud resource allocation algorithm by optimizing the service response time. Also, in [16], authors proposed a combinatorial double auction-based model for allocating cloud resources.

Finally, like as the fog and cloud paradigms, in some other related computing paradigms, some research has been done to find out the most efficient resource management strategy. For instance, in [6], the authors proposed an auction-based market-oriented resource scheduling algorithm for managing the resources in a grid computing platform. Some research work has also been done on the combined, fog to cloud, or cloud-edge platforms, to manage the system resources. For example, by minimizing the service-latency, authors in [19] proposed the QoS-aware service allocation problem in the combined fog-to-cloud architecture.

Also, in [17], for a performance-sensitive application, the authors presented a framework for managing the cloud-edge resources and guaranteeing the QoS factor of their considering system. Though several numbers of research works have been already conducted on tackling the resources in different individual computing paradigms, we have not still found any comprehensive, cost-effective strategy to managing the resources in such coordinated F2C computing platform.

3 Architectural View: The F2C Framework

In smart cities, the combined F2C computing paradigm has emerged as a reference architecture for optimizing resource utilization and improving services execution. The main rationale for F2C is to combine the whole set of resources brought in by putting together cloud computing and fog computing [5], seeking for higher QoS delivery and a much better resource utilization. By following Fig. 1, it can be easily identified that in a modern smart city several Fog Areas may be defined to build the coordinated F2C platform. Each Fog Area builds upon a vast amount of different IoT devices and considers a particular node is acting as a fog service provider and thus responsible for providing the fog services to the users of the corresponding Fog Area. This particular node is known as Leader Fog Node. Similarly, many different cloud providers may control the provisioning of cloud facilities to the citizens of a smart city.

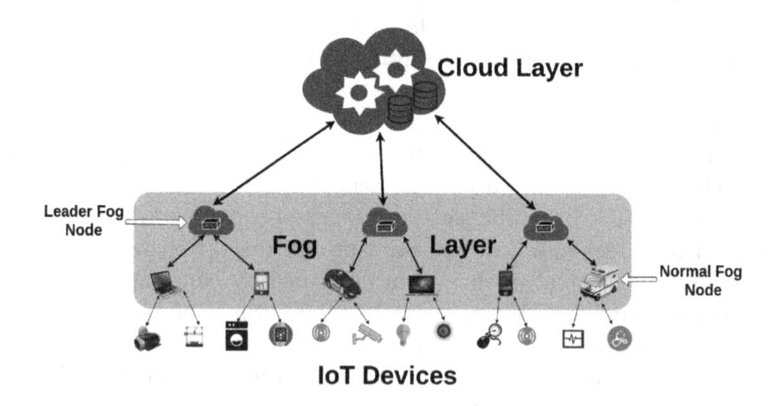

Fig. 2. Fog-to-Cloud (F2C) computing architecture: Hierarchical representation.

In [12], the authors represent the F2C platform as a combined, hierarchical and layered architecture, where cloud resources reside at the top layer and fog resources at the bottom, right above the IoT devices. Indeed, according to the envisioned architecture, the IoT layer resides at the bottom of the layered architecture and includes the whole set of IoT devices. The architecture considers several intermediate fog layers, which are built by grouping various edge devices. Hence, in this section, by considering all the key potential issues in the smart city scenario, we represent the hierarchical structure of the F2C architecture as shown in Fig. 2. Following the hierarchical structure and considering the depicted smart city scenario we argue that for each Fog Area, the Leader Fog Node is acting as a gateway for coordinating with the upper layer resources.

Also in the same paper [12], authors highlighted the need to have a comprehensive devices control and management strategy to build an efficient F2C system in their research work. As mentioned previously, we identify heterogeneity as the main challenge of managing the vast amount of devices. So, in this paper, by knowing the system resources and services, we present the model for managing the system resources and efficiently providing services delivery in the F2C paradigm. Consequently, in the next section, we describe the proposed model for the resource management strategy in the F2C paradigm. Moreover, we briefly discuss the various modules involved in the resource management strategy of the F2C paradigm.

4 Proposed Model: Resource Management Strategy for the F2C Paradigm

Before we intensely focus on the resource allocation strategy in the F2C platform, it is relevant to briefly discuss on the various modules and aspects, which are mandatory to build a proper plan for managing the resources in the F2C paradigm. Consequently, in this section, we represent the strategical model for managing resources in the F2C platform.

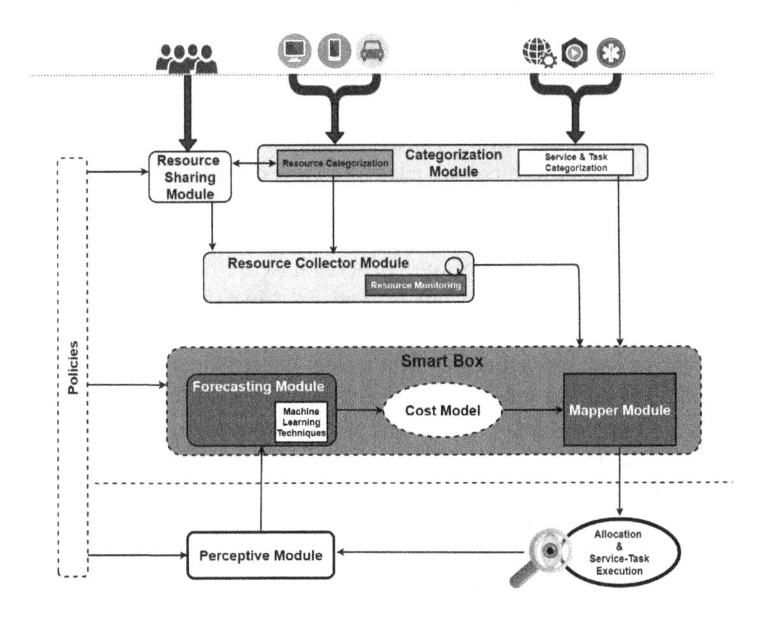

Fig. 3. Resource management strategy in the F2C paradigm.

In Fig. 3, we represent the framework for managing the resources in the Fog-to-Cloud (F2C) computing platform. According to the diagram, there are several components or modules are working together to achieve the proper resource management strategy in the F2C paradigm. Considering the various potential issues in a smart city scenario, in the next, we briefly discuss the functionalities of each component or module.

4.1 Categorization Module

As earlier mentioned, the most significant challenge, for managing resources in a smart city scenario is the diversity and variety of the whole set of resources from the edge up to the cloud. Simultaneously, many different services may be considered in a smart city scenario. Undoubtedly, by successfully and efficiently providing all these services to its citizens, the city becomes much more smarter. Unfortunately, services have different characteristics (i.e., free or chargeable services), contexts (i.e., governmental, health, educational, etc.) and even different requirements (i.e., resource requirements for executing the services). That kind of diversity creates notable difficulties to build up the proper resource management strategy in the F2C paradigm for an appropriate matching with the smart services. So, before forming the appropriate resource management strategy, it is pretty relevant to identify the classification and categorization of the system resources and services involved in the F2C paradigm. Hence, in this subsection, we first put the focus on the resource categorization, and later on, we briefly represent the service categorization.

Resource Categorization. The enormous diversity and heterogeneity of the system resources create some serious challenges for managing them into the F2C paradigm. For that reason, it is essential to know the system resources properly by understanding their characteristics and build a proper catalogue of them. Following the hierarchical structure of the coordinated F2C platform in a real smart city scenario, it can be easily identified that the devices working at the lower layer (i.e., IoT or fog layer) are mostly resource-constrained devices. Thus, their computation, storage and processing capabilities are different from those at upper layers (i.e., cloud layer) devices. Most interestingly, in the F2C visualized scenario this evaluation is even more elaborated, leveraging the various layers foreseen for fog. Indeed, according to the hierarchical structure of the F2C platform, different layers include devices with different characteristics. Thus, considering all these potential issues and the hierarchical layered structure of the F2C paradigm, we propose to define a novel taxonomy for characterizing the different F2C resources.

In Fig. 4 we represent the categorization model of the F2C system resources. Initially, in the F2C system, several attributes and characteristics are considered to classify the system resources, including **Device attributes** (i.e., hardware, software, network specification, etc.), **IoT components & Attached components** (i.e., sensors, actuators, RFID tags, or additional attached device components), **Security & Privacy aspects** (i.e., device hardware security, network security and data security), **Cost Information** (i.e., chargeable device, non-chargeable device), and **History & Behavioral information** (i.e., participation role, mobility, life span, reliability, information of the device location, etc.).

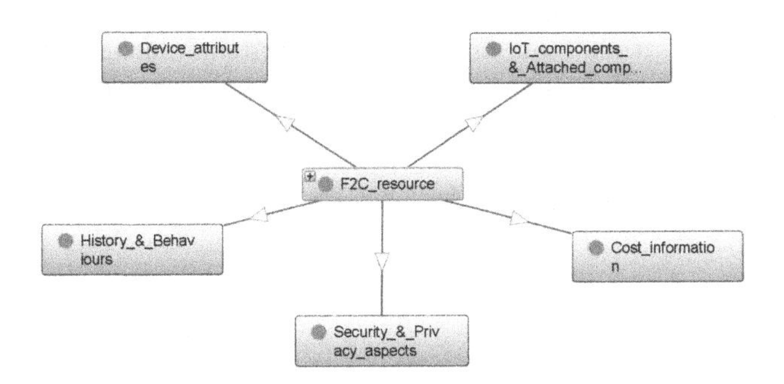

Fig. 4. Generalized resource categorization model in the F2C paradigm.

Service and Task Categorization. In any computing platform, before knowing the characteristics of services, it is relevant to identify the definition of 'Service' and 'Task' because in the context of a system both of them are quite closely related to each other. In [3], according to the authors, the 'Task' means performing some certain job(s) or function(s). Whereas, in [7], the authors define the 'Service' is a composite made up of small blocks of functionalities. According to them, the system is providing the service to the users, by executing some task. Therefore, following the F2C computing platform in the smart city environment, we found that service characterization is the composite form of two steps: one is the service classification, and the other is task classification. Combining these two steps, we get the proper taxonomic model for service-task in the F2C platform.

In addition, as said before, diversity also refers to the services concept. Formally speaking, in order to provide service(s), it is necessary to execute some task(s) or perform some job(s). And, to that end, it is necessary to meet some specific requirements (i.e., resource components requirements, time requirements etc.). Interestingly, each of the tasks having various kind of requirements. In Fig. 5, we represent the combined form of service-task categorization model in the F2C paradigm. By considering all the potential issues in a smart city and also following the various characteristics and attributes of the services, initially, we classify the services according to five different aspects: **Context of services** (i.e., governmental, educational, transport, etc. related services), **Service location** (from where the services are offered, i.e., cloud or fog etc.), **Secure & Reliableness** (i.e., based on the security preferences, services can be classified),

Data Characteristics (i.e., based on the amount of data processing requirement, services can also be classified), and **Cost information** (i.e., based on the service offering cost, services can be further classified into chargeable or non-chargeable services). As earlier mentioned, in any system services are offered by executing some task(s). Therefore, not only services in the F2C system should be classified according to their characteristics and attributes, but similarly, tasks can also be classified according to their **Execution requirements** (i.e., network bandwidth capacity, time requirements, processor requirements, etc.) and their **Priority** (i.e., high, medium, or low). So combining the service and task classifications in the considering system, we represent the Service-Task Categorization model in the F2C paradigm.

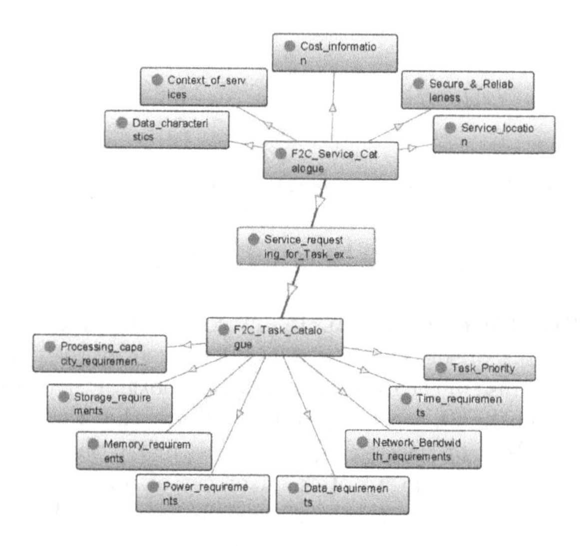

Fig. 5. Generalized service and task categorization model in the F2C paradigm.

In the F2C paradigm, both of the categorization models help to identify the characteristics and attributes of the resources and services. Explicitly, that helps to define the proper resource-service mapping mechanism and build the proper resource management strategy in the coordinated F2C platform.

4.2 Resource Sharing Module

Following the smart city scenario, it can be easily identified that many citizens in the smart city, are only using the F2C system for only accessing some smart services. Whereas, many of them are joining the F2C system by contributing their devices to execute some task, in order to provide the service. Also, some of them may enter into the F2C system for accessing the facilities as well as contributing their devices to execute the task. So, mainly in the F2C system, devices may participate as either 'Consumer', 'Contributor', or 'Both'. For each device, before contributing their resource components to the F2C system, it is necessary to define the resource sharing model. Based on the owner preference, system policies, and availability of their resource-components, a resource sharing model can be determined. For a specific device, the sharing model can be defined as the abstract or 'shareable-amount' view of the whole set of available resource components of the corresponding device. In the F2C paradigm, the virtualization technology enables the provision to make such an abstraction for a particular device. In the F2C platform, the responsibility of the Resource Sharing Module is to provide the information about the amount of participating resource-components to the system. Explicitly that information also helps to manage the system resources efficiently, and adequately provide the services.

4.3 Resource Collector Module

Before deciding and allocating the proper and suitable resources for executing the task and providing the service, it is essential to have an overview of the available amount of resource-components. Initially, the Resource Collector Module obtains the information about the resource characteristics from the Resource Categorization Module. However, the Resource Sharing Module is enriching the Resource Collector Module by providing the information about the actual amount of participating resource-components. In the F2C platform, this module is in-charge of continuous monitoring the status of currently available participating resources, and also it is continuously generating a landscape of the system and providing the information about the characteristics.

4.4 Smart Box and Perceptive Module

In the proposed F2C resource management framework, the Smart Box is one of the most important and intelligent composite components. The sole function of this component is to allocate the best available resource to execute the requested task(s) and provide the service(s). In the F2C architecture, togetherly the Mapper Module, Cost Model, and Forecasting Module define the Smart Box.

Initially, for the first time (i.e., the first time a resource is executing a new task or first time a new resource is performing a task), the resource in the F2C system is allocated based on the predefined Cost Model. Considering the hierarchical distributed F2C architecture in a smart city scenario, we identified that it is a pretty challenging job to define a proper Cost Model in such a distributed paradigm. Following [8,13] and considering all the potential critical issues in a smart city scenario, we identify that the Cost Model in the F2C paradigm could be defined by considering various aspects, i.e., the system deployment cost, resource usage cost, SLA, etc. In addition, we can find that there is a trade-off between cost and QoS parameters; for example, the higher security requirement cost for a system means that the QoS metrics should be degraded. Following these various aspects we identified that the cost of the F2C system could be mainly classified as following: **Deployment cost** - cost for deploying the system; **Task execution cost** - can be measured by following the resource usage for executing the task, i.e., bandwidth usage cost, power cost, computation cost, etc.; **SLA related cost** - the cost which is calculated by negotiation agreement for services, between the service providers and users. Also, we can classify the cost, according to the dependency on the QoS parameter. So considering all these potential issues the Cost Model can be designed in the F2C system and which helps to denote the resources by providing some weight on them. Finally, based on this weights, the appropriate and best resource should be allocated to execute the task(s) and provide the service(s).

For building an efficient and enhanced resource allocation mechanism, it is necessary to understand the historical information of past execution. For this reason, in the running F2C system it is essential to keep tracking the information of resource usage for executing the task(s). So, following Fig. 3, it can be easily identified that the Perceptive Module is always monitoring the task-service execution procedure in the F2C paradigm and collecting the actual information of resource usage during task(s) execution. After collecting this information, the Perceptive Module is continuously updating this information to the Smart Box. Based on the past execution information, available resource information, and information about the service-task requirements, the Forecasting Module predicts the updated resource usage for executing the newly requested task(s). Using some machine learning techniques the Forecasting Module will be able to predict the resource usage for executing the newly requested task(s) and then passes this information to update the Cost Model. Now after getting this information, the Cost Model calculates the new cost of the resource(s) and denoted with the new weight. After that, the Mapper Module will be able to propose new and more accurate allocation options for task(s) execution.

5 Future Directions and Opportunities

In the previous section, we have proposed the strategical architecture for resource management in the F2C platform, as part of a smart city management scenario. We have presented the different modules of the architecture which are potentially involved in building the model. We have seen that there are several technical issues to be addressed, such as virtualization techniques, defining and managing user and system policies and preferences, and analyzing the effectiveness of different cost models, just to name a few. In fact, by focusing on various service-oriented system architectures, we found that cost is one of the most important aspects to be considered. As we have already seen, an enormous number of devices are participating in the F2C platform and contributing their resource-components to provide some services, so it is pretty relevant that these resources might get some revenue for providing the services in the F2C system. So, we believe that it is necessary to define the generalized cost model for the F2C system that might help to find and to allocate the most appropriate resource(s), in order to execute some task. In the F2C platform, also by considering the cost model and policies, it is possible to create the various strategy for managing the resources. By comparing the different resource management strategies, it is possible to build the generalized, approximate and optimal solutions for managing the resources in the F2C paradigm.

6 Conclusion

In this paper, we have proposed the strategical architecture for managing the resources in a coordinated Fog-to-Cloud computing platform. The proposed model is illustrated in a smart city scenario for the sake of better understanding. We also briefly described the different modules and their functionalities envisioned in the proposed model. By addressing the various challenges in the smart city scenario, we have defined the resource and service-task categorization module for the F2C system. This work is presented as the initial step to determine and design a comprehensive resource management strategy in the F2C paradigm, but still, lots of work and many challenges remain to be addressed.

Acknowledgement. This work was supported by the Spanish Ministry of Economy and Competitiveness and the European Regional Development Fund, under contract TEC2015-66220-R(MINECO/FEDER) and by the H2020 EU mF2C project reference 730929.

References

1. Aazam, M., Huh, E.N.: Fog computing micro datacenter based dynamic resource estimation and pricing model for IoT. In: IEEE 29th International Conference on Advanced Information Networking and Applications. IEEE (2015)
2. Agarwal, S., Yadav, S., Yadav, A.K.: An efficient architecture and algorithm for resource provisioning in fog computing. Int. J. Inf. Eng. Electron. Bus. **8**(1), 48–61 (2016)
3. Barker, J., Marxer, R., Vincent, E., Watanabe, S.: The third 'chime'speech separation and recognition challenge: dataset, task and baselines. In: IEEE Workshop on Automatic Speech Recognition and Understanding. IEEE (2015)
4. Bessai, K., Youcef, S., Oulamara, A., Godart, C., Nurcan, S.: Bi-criteria workflow tasks allocation and scheduling in cloud computing environments. In: IEEE 5th International Conference on Cloud Computing. IEEE (2012)
5. Bonomi, F., Milito, R., Natarajan, P., Zhu, J.: Fog computing: A platform for internet of things and analytics. In: Bessis, N., Dobre, C. (eds.) Big Data and Internet of Things: A Roadmap for Smart Environments. SCI, vol. 546, pp. 169–186. Springer, Cham (2014). https://doi.org/10.1007/978-3-319-05029-4_7
6. Ding, L., Chang, L., Wang, L.: Online auction-based resource scheduling in grid computing networks. Int. J. Distrib. Sens. Netw. **12**(10), 1550147716673930 (2016)
7. Graves, T.: The Service-oriented Enterprise. Tetradian Books, Colchester (2009)
8. Gu, L., Zeng, D., Guo, S., Barnawi, A., Xiang, Y.: Cost efficient resource management in fog computing supported medical cyber-physical system. IEEE Trans. Emerg. Top. Comput. **5**(1), 108–119 (2017)
9. Gubbi, J., Buyya, R., Marusic, S., Palaniswami, M.: Internet of things (IoT): a vision, architectural elements, and future directions. Futur. Gener. Comput. Syst. **29**(7), 1645–1660 (2013)

10. Gupta, H., Vahid Dastjerdi, A., Ghosh, S.K., Buyya, R.: iFogSim: A toolkit for modeling and simulation of resource management techniques in the internet of things, edge and fog computing environments. Softw. Pract. Exp. **47**(9), 1275–1296 (2017)
11. Keller, M., Karl, H.: Response time-optimized distributed cloud resource allocation. In: Proceedings of the 2014 ACM SIGCOMM Workshop on Distributed Cloud Computing. ACM (2014)
12. Masip-Bruin, X., Marín-Tordera, E., Tashakor, G., Jukan, A., Ren, G.J.: Foggy clouds and cloudy fogs: a real need for coordinated management of fog-to-cloud computing systems. IEEE Wirel. Commun. **23**(5), 120–128 (2016)
13. Mazrekaj, A., Shabani, I., Sejdiu, B.: Pricing schemes in cloud computing: an overview. Int. J. Adv. Comput. Sci. Appl. **7**(2), 80–86 (2016)
14. Ni, L., Zhang, J., Jiang, C., Yan, C., Yu, K.: Resource allocation strategy in fog computing based on priced timed petri nets. IEEE Internet Things J. **4**(5), 1216–1228 (2017)
15. Riggins, F.J., Wamba, S.F.: Research directions on the adoption, usage, and impact of the internet of things through the use of big data analytics. In: 48th Hawaii International Conference on System Sciences. IEEE (2015)
16. Samimi, P., Teimouri, Y., Mukhtar, M.: A combinatorial double auction resource allocation model in cloud computing. Inf. Sci. **357**, 201–216 (2016)
17. Shekhar, S., Gokhale, A.: Dynamic resource management across cloud-edge resources for performance-sensitive applications. In: Proceedings of the 17th IEEE/ACM International Symposium on Cluster, Cloud and Grid Computing. IEEE Press (2017)
18. Shin, S., Kim, Y., Lee, S.: Deadline-guaranteed scheduling algorithm with improved resource utilization for cloud computing. In: 12th Annual IEEE Consumer Communications and Networking Conference. IEEE (2015)
19. de Souza, V.B.C., Ramírez, W., Masip-Bruin, X., Marín-Tordera, E., Ren, G., Tashakor, G.: Handling service allocation in combined fog-cloud scenarios. In: IEEE International Conference on Communications. IEEE (2016)
20. Wu, Z., Liu, X., Ni, Z., Yuan, D., Yang, Y.: A market-oriented hierarchical scheduling strategy in cloud workflow systems. J. Supercomput. **63**(1), 256–293 (2013)
21. Yi, S., Kondo, D., Andrzejak, A.: Reducing costs of spot instances via checkpointing in the amazon elastic compute cloud. In: IEEE 3rd International Conference on Cloud Computing. IEEE (2010)
22. Yu, L., Cai, Z.: Dynamic scaling of virtual clusters with bandwidth guarantee in cloud datacenters. In: The 35th Annual IEEE International Conference on Computer Communications. IEEE (2016)
23. Yu, L., Shen, H., Sapra, K., Ye, L., Cai, Z.: CoRE: cooperative end-to-end traffic redundancy elimination for reducing cloud bandwidth cost. IEEE Trans. Parallel Distrib. Syst. **28**(2), 446–461 (2017)

Enhancing Service Management Systems with Machine Learning in Fog-to-Cloud Networks

Jasenka Dizdarević(✉), Francisco Carpio, Mounir Bensalem, and Admela Jukan

Technische Universität Braunschweig, Braunschweig, Germany
{j.dizdarevic,f.carpio,m.bensalem,a.jukan}@tu-bs.de

Abstract. With the fog-to-cloud hybrid computing systems emerging as a promising networking architecture, particularly interesting for IoT scenarios, there is an increasing interest in exploring and developing new technologies and solutions to achieve high performances of these systems. One of these solutions includes machine learning algorithms implementation. Even without defined and standardized way of using machine learning in fog-to-cloud systems, it is obvious that machine learning capabilities of autonomous decision making would enrich both fog computing and cloud computing network nodes. In this paper, we propose a service management system specially designed to work in fog-to-cloud architectures, followed with a proposal on how to implement it with different machine learning solutions. We first show the global overview of service management system functionality with the current specific design for each of its integral components and, finally, we show the first results obtained with machine learning algorithm for its component in charge of traffic prediction.

Keywords: Machine learning · Fog-to-Cloud · Service management

1 Introduction

In the recent years, integration of the fog and cloud computing into fog-to-cloud hybrid computing systems has became an important research subject, especially regarding their presence in Internet of Things (IoT) scenarios. Both cloud and fog computing satisfy different system requirements, complementing each other. In these integrated solutions, cloud servers are used for analyzing and processing large amounts of data that require high computing power and where service execution is not time sensitive. Fog nodes include less powerful devices, but also with computing power and data storage capabilities, which allows them to process data from multiple sensors while minimizing latency and reducing the amount of data which needs to be transported to the cloud. Some of the efforts devoted to the development of an integrated fog to cloud (F2C) system include the OpenFog Consortium [1] and the mF2C H2020 EU project [2].

G. Mencagli et al. (Eds.): Euro-Par 2018 Workshops, LNCS 11339, pp. 287–298, 2019.
https://doi.org/10.1007/978-3-030-10549-5_23

In order to ensure high performance of F2C solutions it is necessary to explore new emerging technological solutions, such as Machine Learning (ML). At the moment there is no determined definition of how machine learning should be used in a F2C system, but it is evident that both fog and cloud enriched with ML capabilities would improve the system performances with the ability to make decisions and take actions individually based on algorithmic sensing of patterns in locally captured sensor data in the case of fog nodes, and centrally captured data in the case of the cloud nodes. In this paper, we propose ML implementation as a mean of improving a specific area of F2C - service management. Since the architecture of a F2C system is still a relatively new research field, without strictly defined standards and guidelines, in order to observe ML behavior for this purpose, we also propose an architectural component of F2C that would be in charge of service related functionalities.

With most of the research efforts in fog computing and fog-to-cloud based systems being more focused on the integrated architecture and communication aspects of these new systems, and not just on the particular problem of managing services, we relied on previous work done in this area in order to propose a design of our service management component. A comprehensive survey on service management and handling Web services and distributed services was conducted in [3], offering an overview of well known *service-oriented architectures* concepts. Some of the available service management solutions are cloud oriented such as [4,5] or they present completely novel approaches as the one proposed in [6], where authors developed a concept of managing services that simplifies service operations by sharing different tasks and functionalities of a global service among multiple distributed agents. Also, some papers focus on the service management in IoT solutions, so for example in [7] authors propose *Management Server Service* as a part of their IoT system architectural design for handling service related tasks.

In this paper, we propose possible ways of using ML in a specific part of fog-to-cloud computing system - components that are in charge of managing service related functionalities. For this purpose, we propose a Service Management System (SMS) integral unit, composed of multiple components, each of them representing a different functionality. In the following sections we analyze possible ML application areas in these components.

The rest of this paper is organized in the following way. Section 2 introduces the Service Management System for fog-to-cloud based systems. Section 3 covers possible Service Management System components where different machine learning algorithms can be used and show the preliminary results with Sect. 4 concluding the paper.

2 Service Management System

As the main F2C architecture component in charge of service related functionalities, we propose a Service Management System (SMS), shown in Fig. 1, as an integral component that can be deployed on all nodes/devices with computing

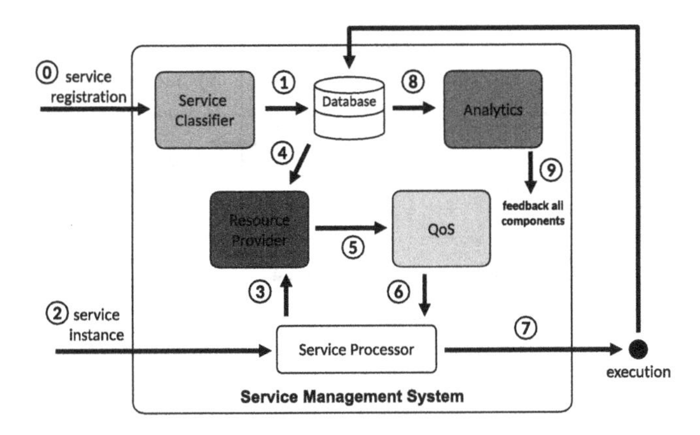

Fig. 1. Service Management System architecture

capacities, both in the cloud and the fog. Different SMS tasks include classifying different types of services, executing different phases of the service lifecycle, deciding in which F2C system node will the execution take place, gathering and measuring network data from different nodes, and ensuring quality of the service.

Figure 1 shows the components that comprise the Service Management System: Service Classifier, Service Processor, Resource Provider, QoS, Analytics and a Database. When a new service registers to the system, regardless of the node, it will first be passed on to the Service Classifier component where different services will be classified based on different requirements they have, and this information will be saved in a database. Once the service is registered, the system will be ready for receiving new instances of the service for executions. When one of these service instances arrive, the Service Processor component of SMS, which controls the service lifecycle, have to be previously registered. The Service Processor will then communicate with the Resource Provider, the component that decides where a service instance will be executed. For this decision, it first has to read the information from the database on the availability of the nodes, where he can obtain the information, whether it is possible to use multiple nodes, as well as the information from the Analytics on traffic prediction. Nodes represent different devices with different levels of computing and processing capabilities, allocated in different abstract layers of F2C system. To decide whether it is possible to use these nodes, it will contact the QoS component. Based on the recommended nodes from the Resource Provider and the possibility of using them, the Service Processor will get the information where the service instance should be executed and deploy it accordingly. The results of the execution are saved in the database, so the Analytics component can use them to update the Resource Provider and the QoS.

In the following section we will propose how some of these component's functionalities can be improved with machine learning solutions, which should result with the improvement of the entire F2C system performances.

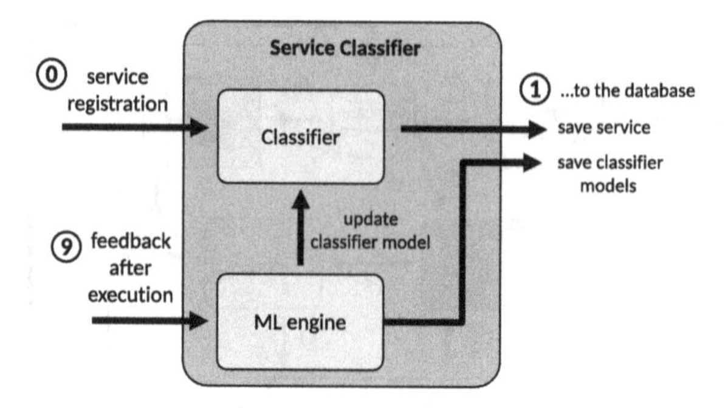

Fig. 2. Service Classifier component

3 Components Implementing Machine Learning Algorithms in Service Management System

In the Service Management System, we propose different methods of implementing machine learning in the components where traditional heuristic algorithms are not enough for taking complex decisions. These components include Service Classifier, Resource Provider, QoS and Analytics. The numerical results are shown for the Analytics and its implementation of ML for traffic prediction, while for the other components we propose the current design, with numerical results being the next step to prove the validity of the design.

3.1 Service Classifier

In [9] a service classification was proposed based on user defined requirements. The goal was service differentiation based on their requirements to be able to allocate resources. The service classification method proposed here was grouping the services into classes according to information defined by the user. However, what was not taken into consideration, and in most service classification modules, is that service requirements can be different from one execution to another which makes the classification process dynamic and non trivial. As a result, we need to learn from a previous execution of the service in the network to achieve an accurate classification. The Service Classifier, shown in Fig. 2, is responsible for the categorization of new services registered into the F2C system based on the information specified by the user about the service requirements. Some requirements necessary for the service to be successfully executed are unknown to the user, such as the network load, network topology, resource load, etc. Thus, in the beginning the Classifier needs to execute the service in the network and then extract some information to enhance the classification process. Afterwards, service categories are stored in the database.

After the test executions, the Analytics component, which collects information about services and node performance, will contact Service Classifier in order to feedback the results from the execution which will update the ML engine for

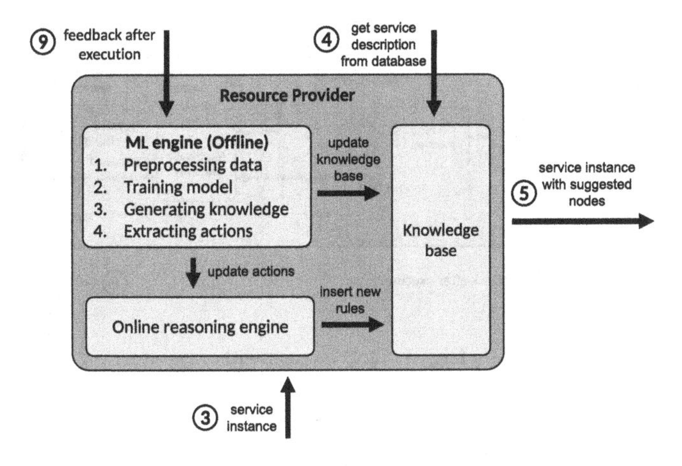

Fig. 3. Resource Provider component

the future classifications. The ML engine, in response, preprocesses the data and extracts the features that will then train and tune a model offline. The model obtained is used to update the Classifier which works online with new incoming services. Moreover, it is also used to update the categories that are already stored in the database. For the next step the presented component design should be implemented with the choice of an adequate ML algorithm in order to test the effectiveness and performances.

3.2 Resource Provider

The service instances that have already been registered, as described previously, upon arriving for execution to the Service Processor component of SMS, initialize the communication between the Service Processor and the Resource Provider, the component that decides where the execution will take place.

Figure 3, shows the global picture of the Resource Provider component, which includes three main parts: a knowledge base (KB), an online reasoning engine and a ML engine working offline. So, when the Service Processor receives a service instance, it requests for a node recommendation from the Resource Provider. The Resource Provider will obtain this information about the particular service from the database, generate node suggestions and send them to the QoS component to decide where to execute this service instance. When a new service instance is requested, the online reasoning engine generates recommendations based on predefined rules and then stores the recommendations for each service instance in the KB. If the information on the instance already exists in the KB, the Resource Provider will directly send the suggestions to the QoS. After the execution, the system collects statistics about the network: feedback about the suggested nodes, traffic prediction, holding time, etc.

The gathered data is used to feed the ML engine working offline which is responsible for recognizing data patterns to improve the reasoning engine and

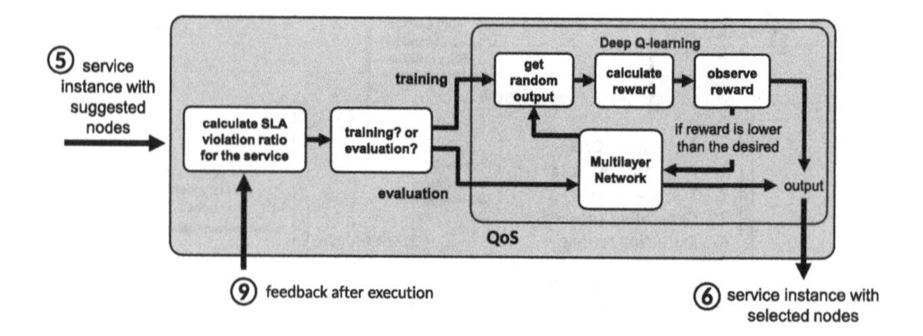

Fig. 4. QoS component

to improve the previous recommendations. This process is also shown in Fig. 3. First, we preprocess data by adding labels and normalizing values. Then, we train an ML model which will be used to generate recommendations based on the history of the network. After that, we update the KB by the new recommendations and finally we use those new recommendations to extract new actions that can be used by the online reasoning engine to recommend nodes for newly registered services. As with the previous component, the future steps include testing of the proposed design.

3.3 Quality of Service

As mentioned above, in order for the Resource Provider to make a decision on service instance execution, it will have to communicate with the QoS component.

This communication happens in the following step, after the Resource Provider suggests the list of nodes to be used for the service instance execution, the service instance is sent to the QoS component. The design of this block in shown in Fig. 4. The QoS component checks which of those nodes can actually be used for the service execution or if they have to be discarded in case they are not satisfying requirements to be considered as the potential solutions. In order to make this decision, the QoS component also gets informed about the existing Service Level Agreement (SLA) violations which are assumed to be stored in the Analytics component each time a service execution finishes. SLA management is out of the scope of our work with the assumption that SLA violations are detected and stored after the execution of the service. After making the decision on which nodes should be acceptable for the service instance execution, a modified service instance is returned to the Service Processor with the updated list of suitable nodes. The SLA violations are not considered by the Resource Provider component itself because the Resource Provider only takes into account the individual information from the nodes and the QoS analyses if the service as a global entity could be used for these devices.

The decision whether a certain resource can or cannot be used for a certain service, is based on the number of SLA violations that had occurred in previous executions of that specific service. With this information, the QoS Component uses reinforcement learning to allow or block the use of a specific node. The process that takes place in QoS component in order to decide whether the suggested nodes by the Resource Provider should be used, includes utilization of the number of service executions and the number of SLA violations. This information is used to calculate a ratio which is then passed on as the input for the Deep Q-learning (DQL) algorithm. Then, it has to be decided whether that input is taken for training or for evaluation (the decision process being described below). In the case of training, the DQL algorithm will initially get a random output, which determines which nodes are accepted. Based on the output, a reward is calculated following the next function:

$$r_t = \sum_{n=0}^{N} y_n(-2x_s + 1) + (1 - y_n)(x_s - 1), \tag{1}$$

where the N is the total number of nodes specified in the service instance, y_n is 1 when the node n is chosen, 0 otherwise, and x_s is the input ratio. The calculated reward is observed by the network and in case it is lower than a specific threshold, a new random output is generated and the process is repeated. When the reward is greater or equal than desired, the output is being used to modify the list of accepted nodes for the service instance. On the other hand, in the case of evaluation, the QoS component will directly ask the network about an optimal output for a specific input. How to decide if an input is taken for the training or for the evaluation is based on the quantity of already acquired knowledge in the network. For now, this decision is only based on a certain number of service executions.

While the QoS component could use the reward function without the need of using deep learning, the output would be only determined by that function, missing other non-trivial factors like the relation between the failure of the execution of a service and the nodes that were involved. For that reason, the proposed algorithm can be used to learn in every situation by taking random decisions and helping the optimization of the decision making process in the evaluation period. To be noted, at the moment the presented algorithm is a relatively simple version that could be used for testing of the proposed system. In the future, the reward function, the input, the output or how the decision to opt for a training or evaluation case is taken could change in order to improve the effectiveness of the algorithm.

3.4 Analytics

One of the most important SMS components which is used to update all the others is the Analytics component. It is responsible for gathering data generated from devices which allows it to offer an overview of network statistics. This component includes traffic prediction module which is used to enhance effectiveness of other modules by predicting traffic flows based on old statistics stored in the database. The need of automating the process of obtaining the analytics and the existence of datasets collected in this component opens the door for ML and AI to be implemented. Automation can dynamically extract insights from network statistics and implement the right algorithms with achieving a high performance results, instead of this task being handled by a developer, especially in the cases when patterns are not visible for a human being. The Analytics might include several features to provide a better view of the network such as device locations, device connections and signal coverage, but, we focused on gathering the data about the traffic and then generating insights to produce a real time visibility as one of the more interesting features. In this context, we studied only this feature of the Analytics, which analyzes the network traffic and leave the other features for the future research. In our system this feature is called Traffic prediction.

Traffic Prediction. In this paper, we focus on a service traffic prediction which we located in a F2C architecture as a part of the Analytics component. As a first requirement for this component to implement ML we need a dataset that represents the history of traffic demand at each instant of sampling, obtained from the SMS database. In our case, the goal is to study the temporal evolution of the traffic demand in a network, and to see how it can later be used to improve Analytics component of F2C system. It is necessary to use historical data which can be a real data or data that is modelled theoretically. We referenced several models that were used to analyze the traffic in different networks such as mobile cellular networks in order to generate out own dataset. [10] introduced a model to simulate the traffic variation for a base station in real cellular networks. The model used sinusoid superposition modelling method to describe the temporal traffic variation. [11] studied the network traffic in 10 data centers of different organization types (university, enterprise and cloud data centers). The study shows that the lognormal distribution can fit the time series of data center traffic. Thus, we use Eq. (2) to generate the mean values, then we use the lognormal distribution to generate traffic demands for each mean value.

$$Mean(t) = a_0 + \sum_{k=1}^{n} a_k \sin(w_k t + \phi_k) \tag{2}$$

In our case, $Mean(t)$ presents the total traffic demands in the data center, a_0 is the mean value of all traffic demands during 24 h, w_k is the frequency components of traffic, a_k and ϕ_k represent the amplitudes and phases, n is the number of frequency components. Table 1a summarizes the different values used to generate the mean values. As a result, we obtain the following equation:

$$Mean(t) = 100 + 70 \sin\left(\frac{\pi}{12} t + 3.11\right) + 30 \sin\left(\frac{\pi}{6} t + 2.36\right) \tag{3}$$

Time series prediction has been studied for a long time using traditional statistical techniques to solve forecasting problems. In the last two decades, recurrent neural networks proved to have good performance results in time series predictions due to their ability to capture short and long term dependencies. Our goal was to predict multiple future values based on a sequence of previous

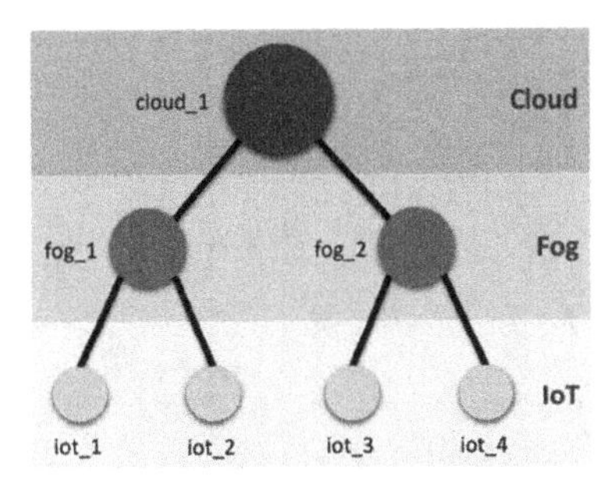

Fig. 5. Tested F2C architecture

demands. As we used recurrent neural network, we were able to create a multi-step forecasting model. This allowed prediction of all of the values in the time window using only one model. We generated data gathered in a two-month period to train and to test a Long Short Term Memory (LSTM) network. The data was then divided into 67% for training and 33% for testing.

Table 1. Experiment parameters and results

(a) Parameters

param.	*iot_1*	*iot_2*	*iot_3*	*iot_4*
n	2	3	3	3
w_1,w_2,w_3	$\frac{\pi}{12}$, $\frac{\pi}{6}$, 0	$\frac{\pi}{12}$, $\frac{\pi}{6}$, $\frac{\pi}{3}$	$\frac{\pi}{12}$, $\frac{\pi}{6}$, $\frac{\pi}{2}$	$\frac{\pi}{12}$, $\frac{\pi}{6}$, $\frac{\pi}{2}$
a_0	100	100	100	100
a_1,a_2,a_3	70,30,0	70,20,20	60,20,15	60,25,15
ϕ_1,ϕ_2,ϕ_3	3.11,2.36,0	5,1,1	7,5,2	1,1,1

(b) Test Score (RMSE)

	smooth	**noisy**
iot_1	0.046	0.238
iot_2	0.074	0.242
iot_3	0.095	0.261
iot_4	0.087	0.257
fog_1	0.077	0.340
fog_2	0.186	0.376
cloud_1	0.125	0.529

After this step, we used a Keras API running on the top of Tensorflow to obtain the forecast results. Generally, recurrent neural networks need a periodic data to be able to offer good forecasting results. As a result, the data was mapped into sequences of length 24 to be able to capture the data relationship during a whole day. The LSTM network has three layers: input, hidden and output layer. The model consists of an input layer, one hidden layer with 48 units and an output layer with hyperbolic tangent function as an activation function. We used mean square error as a loss function and the Root Mean Square Error (RMSE) to measure the accuracy. The RMSE is defined as follow:

$$RMSE = \sqrt{\frac{\sum_{k=1}^{n}(\hat{y}_k - y_k)^2}{n}} \tag{4}$$

RMSE has the same unit as the data and it estimates the difference between true values and predictions.

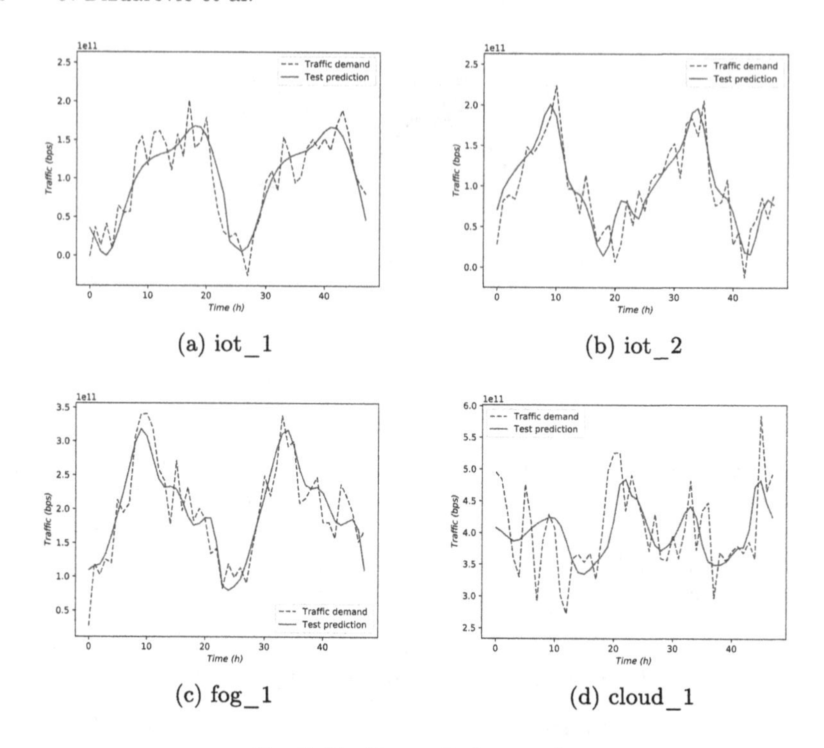

Fig. 6. Traffic prediction results

Performance Evaluation. In this section, we evaluate the performance of the traffic predictor algorithm previously proposed running independently in each node of the F2C architecture shown in Fig. 5. We assume that traffic is generated by devices connected to the IoT nodes or by the IoT nodes themselves, and this traffic is sent to the cloud through the fog nodes. The IoT layer, we assumed that consists of nodes that present processing capable devices, which would allow ML to be implemented in this layer. As a result the distribution of traffic in higher network layers can be modeled as the sum of traffic flows coming from nodes in the lower layers. We assume there are no additional constraints (link capacity, node capacity, etc.), so we are able to send all the generated traffic to the cloud. In this paper, we evaluate the performance of LSTM with 4 different traffic flows generated by the four IoT devices using Eq. 2. Then, for instance, the node fog_1 receives together the traffic generated by the iot_1 and iot_2, and the cloud receives the traffic from fog_1 and fog_2. We evaluate the performance of the prediction algorithm for these three layers in two cases: with smooth artificially generated traffic without random noise and with the same shape but adding random noise.

The numerical results, shown in Table 1b, show that the RMSE is low when the traffic is predicted in the IoT layer without noise, but it is doubled when the noise is added. However, when the prediction is tested in the fog or in the cloud layer, RMSE increases in all cases being with noise the worst case and the cloud the layer with worse performance. Figure 6a and b show the traffic generated by the *iot_1* and *iot_2* devices for the case when there is random noise. Here, it can be seen how the prediction relatively well matches with the real traffic. When we add both traffics to the *fog_1* node, see in Fig. 6c, the LSTM network still can perform well but with worse performance compared with the previous case. Finally, when the traffic in the fog layer is added to the *cloud_1* node, the algorithm can not catch some of the periodical raises. This can be explained by the effect of noise which is accumulated from different traffic flows to make it difficult to the algorithm to differentiate between periods and noise. Since the traffic in the upper layers is the sum of traffics coming from different nodes and having a different periodicity, it results with a more complicated function. Also, each traffic has its own noise the sum of noises makes the traffic more random, so that the prediction become less efficient. That is why in the results we can see better prediction in the nodes close to the traffic generation.

4 Conclusion

With the interest in fog computing and architectural solutions that integrate fog and cloud, the focus is on developing and exploring new approaches and technologies, that would lead to significant improvements of these integrated F2C systems. With that in mind, in this paper, we proposed an architectural design of a service management component for a F2C system, and explored a ways how different machine learning algorithms could be used in different composite components of service management. In order to improve Analytics component we implemented LSTM network to evaluate the performance of the traffic prediction algorithm running independently in each node of the F2C architecture. The traffic generated by nodes representing IoT devices was observed for two cases, with and without noise added to the traffic. The results have shown that closer the prediction is to the source of generated data, the prediction results will be better in both cases. So the best prediction was achieved when it was performed in IoT layer without added noise, with the assumption that IoT layer consists of nodes with processing capabilities. Fog layer whose nodes were used as the aggregating points for multiple IoT generated traffic flows also performed well in terms of being able to predict close to real traffic. The worst traffic prediction was achieved in the cloud layer, which received aggregated flows from the fog layer. As a further step, QoS component improvement was implemented with a Deep Q-Learning algorithm, enabling it to make decisions whether a use of a certain node will be allowed or blocked, based on number of SLA violations that had occurred in previous executions of a specific service. The numerical results and improvement of decision making process for this algorithm are planned for the future. Additionally, in this paper, we propose the utilization of ML in components tasked with service classification and resource provisioning, with the implementation part as a goal for future work.

Acknowledgment. This work has been partially performed in the framework of mF2C project funded by the European Union's H2020 research and innovation programme under grant agreement 730929.

References

1. OpenFog Consortium. http://www.openfogconsortium.org/. Accessed Apr 2018
2. mF2C Project. http://www.mf2c-project.eu/. Accessed 20 Apr 2018
3. Papazoglou, M.P., van den Heuvel, W.J.: Web services management: a survey. IEEE Internet Comput. **9**(6), 58–64 (2005). https://doi.org/10.1109/MIC.2005.137
4. Amanatullah, Y., Lim, Y., Ipung, H.P., Juliandri, A.: Toward cloud computing reference architecture: cloud service management perspective. In: International Conference on ICT for Smart Society, Jakarta, pp. 1–4 (2013). https://doi.org/10.1109/ICTSS.2013.6588059
5. Guo, J., Chen, I.R., Tsai, J.J.P., Al-Hamadi, H.: A hierarchical cloud architecture for integrated mobility, service, and trust management of service-oriented IoT systems. In: 2016 Sixth International Conference on Innovative Computing Technology (INTECH), Dublin, pp. 72–77 (2016). https://doi.org/10.1109/INTECH.2016.7845021
6. Castro, A., Villagra, V.A., Fuentes, B., Costales, B.: A flexible architecture for service management in the cloud. IEEE Trans. Netw. Serv. Manag. **11**(1), 116–125 (2014). https://doi.org/10.1109/TNSM.2014.022614.1300421
7. Agyemang, B., Xu, Y., Sulemana, N., Liu, N.: Resource-oriented architecture toward efficient device management and service enablement. In: 2017 IEEE International Conference on Systems, Man, and Cybernetics (SMC), Banff, AB, pp. 2561–2566 (2017). https://doi.org/10.1109/SMC.2017.8123010
8. Yin, Y., Wang, L., Gelenbe, E.: Multi-layer neural networks for quality of service oriented server-state classification in cloud servers. In: 2017 International Joint Conference on Neural Networks (IJCNN), 14–19 May 2017. https://doi.org/10.1109/IJCNN.2017.7966045
9. Hwang, J., Liu, G., Zeng, S., Wu, F.Y., Wood, T.: Topology discovery and service classification for distributed-aware clouds. In: 2014 IEEE International Conference on Cloud Engineering (IC2E), March 2014. https://doi.org/10.1109/IC2E.2014.86
10. Zhang, X., Wang, S., et al.: An approach for spatial-temporal traffic modeling in mobile cellular networks. In: Teletraffic Congress (ITC 27). IEEE (2015)
11. Maltz, D.A., Benson, T., Akella, A.: Network traffic characteristics of data centers in the wild. In: IMC '10 Proceedings of the 10th ACM SIGCOMM Conference on Internet Measurement. ACM, New York (2015)

A Knowledge-Based IoT Security Checker

Marco Anisetti[1], Rasool Asal[2], Claudio Agostino Ardagna[1], Lorenzo Comi[1], Ernesto Damiani[1,3], and Filippo Gaudenzi[1(✉)]

[1] DI – Università degli Studi di Milano, Milan, Italy
{marco.anisetti,claudio.ardagna,lorenzo.comi,ernesto.damiani, filippo.gaudenzi}@unimi.it

[2] British Telecommunications, London, UK
rasool.asal@bt.com

[3] Centre on Cyber-Physical Systems, Khalifa University, Abu Dhabi, UAE
ernesto.damiani@kustar.ac.ae

Abstract. The widespread diffusion of ubiquitous and smart devices is radically changing the environment surrounding the users and brought to the definition of a new ecosystem called Internet of Things (IoT). Users are connected anywhere anytime, and can continuously monitor and interact with the external environment. While devices are becoming more and more powerful and efficient (e.g., using protocols like zigbee, LTE, 5G), their security is still in its infancy. Such devices, as well as the edge network providing connectivity, become the target of security attacks without their owners being aware of the risks they are exposed to. In this paper we present *IoT Security Checker*, a solution for IoT security assessment coping with the most relevant IoT security issues. We also provide some preliminary analysis showing how the IoT Security Checker can be used for verifying the security of an IoT system.

1 Introduction

Internet of Things (IoT) is changing the world where we live and the way in which we interact. Current environment composed of billions of interconnected devices points to scenarios where everything can be a data source or an actuator. According to Gartner, there will be more than 20 Billions devices by 2020 and every sector, from private life to public services, will be influenced and significantly improved by IoT technologies.[1] Baby-monitor, fitness bands, dog-tracker, smart-locker are already common goods with large adoption. Their exponential rate of adoption makes IoT devices and infrastructure the target of new security attacks [4], introducing many concerns about the risks an IoT systems need to face. The heterogeneity, variety, and complexity of IoT systems require the support of high security standards, which conflicts with the intrinsic insecurity of devices that are often under the control of non-expert users. Several studies and articles [4,6,10,13] reported on security threats and flaws affecting an enormous amount of devices, resulting in large-scale attacks and data breach [5].

[1] https://www.gartner.com/newsroom/id/3598917.

G. Mencagli et al. (Eds.): Euro-Par 2018 Workshops, LNCS 11339, pp. 299–311, 2019.
https://doi.org/10.1007/978-3-030-10549-5_24

IoT security does not only concern the application layer, where IoT devices play the role of sensors or actuators, but it also affects lower layers of the stack such as network, hardware, and the center of the architecture (e.g., cloud) [2,3].

In this paper, we present the IoT Security Checker (Sect. 5), a scanner supporting pentesters in carrying out a complete and structured analysis aimed to identify IoT device vulnerabilities. IoT Security Checker identifies IoT devices and collects information driving such analysis. It relies on public information sources such as Shodan [8], Censys (https://censys.io/), and National Vulnerability Database (https://nvd.nist.gov/).

The remaining of the paper is organized as follow. Section 2 describes the main security issues affecting IoT solutions. Section 3 describes an IoT classification used as a reference by the IoT-Security Checker. Section 5 describes the architecture and processes implemented by the IoT Security Checker, while an experimental scenario is reported in Sect. 6. Section 7 presents the related work on IoT security. Finally Sect. 8 draws our conclusions.

2 Security Attack Surfaces

IoT security introduces new requirements and challenges due to: *(i)* lack of control on the production environment, *(ii)* limited resources of the devices, *(iii)* limitations on the connectivity, reachability, power consumption, *(iv)* difficulties in imposing security best practices that consider the entire IoT environment. The goal of providing a secure IoT environment is a complex task that requires to consider both the plurality of devices and the heterogeneity of the IoT infrastructure and edge network. Device hardening requires a security-by-design approach involving the whole development-cycle, from hardware design to software/firmware implementation. This scenario is further complicated by the fact that security features need not to hinder the IoT functioning, especially preserving resource consumptions.

In this context, Open Web Application Security Project (OWASP) has identified the top ten IoT vulnerabilities (https://www.owasp.org/index.php/Top_IoT_Vulnerabilities), as well as several possible attack surfaces (https://www.owasp.org/index.php/OWASP_Internet_of_Things_Project#tab=IoT_Attack_Surface_Areas) that are summarized in the following.

- *Ecosystem Access Control* refers to access control mechanisms, enrollment and decommissioning procedures.
- *Device Memory* refers to the possibility of having clear-text credentials stored in memory and the management of cipher keys.
- *Device Physical Interfaces* refers to the firmware extraction and updates, and to removal storages and reset operations.
- *Device Web Interface* refers to all features and services offered by the device over the web.
- *Device Firmware* refers to the presence of credentials, sensitive information, keys stored inside the firmware.

- *Device Network Services* refers to all security issues related to connectivity and includes communication channels, UDP services and CLI (command line interface) to interact with the device.
- *Administrative Interface* refers to all possible attacks and threats related to the admin console, which may involve web attacks and restrict access and accounting techniques to improve security.
- *Local Data Storage* refers to the need to encrypt data at rest and to guarantee integrity.
- *Cloud Web Interface* refers to all services that are not offered by the devices, but rather connected to them and, in turn, with the user through an interface.
- *Third-party Backend APIs* refers to all issues related to the possibility of data breach using third parties. It points to the need of encrypted channels and anonymized data.
- *Update Mechanism* refers to techniques that should prevent all attacks during update operations, which may modify or replace device firmware and software.
- *Mobile Application* refers to all applications connected to the devices.
- *Ecosystem Communication* refers to all techniques that permit to monitor the status of an IoT device, including deprovisioning and update notifications.
- *Network Traffic* refers to all security issues that are related to the network and communication choices made during the design (e.g., radio or cabled communications).
- *Hardware (Sensors)* refers to all possible physical tampering and damages that may be applied to sensors and devices.
- *Privacy* refers to those devices leading to personal information, such as location or medical data, leak.
- *Authentication* refers to all authentication mechanisms offered by the IoT: administrative access, user access through the web, cloud applications, mobile applications, peer to peer IoT exchange information, to name but a few.
- *Vendor Backend APIs* refers to all possible attacks and vulnerabilities that may affect the APIs provided by the vendors.

Clearly, IoT attack surfaces are not limited to IoT devices. They also include processes involving devices, cloud or mobile applications enabling interaction with devices, as well as considered environments. Furthermore, the whole IoT stack from physical layer to service layer may be the target of an attack. IoT attack surfaces can be organized in four main categories that we identified in this paper as follow:

- *Third-Party Services.* This category involves all attack surfaces that depend on services and apps that may be used to collect or manage IoT devices (e.g. smarphone apps, data logger, cloud apps).
- *Physical Environment.* This category involves all attack surfaces that are correlated to environmental or physical damages a device may cause or suffer.
- *Device Logic.* This category includes all attack surfaces related to software, interfaces, and services embedded in or provided by IoT devices.
- *Communication Channel.* This category includes all attack surfaces related to the communication channel such as ZigBee and BLE.

3 Devices Classification

Although IoT is today a shared concept, there are different definitions. In this paper, we consider the ETSI definition that is built on the concept of Machine to Machine (M2M). It separates the communication (*M2M communication*) and the devices (*M2M device*), where *M2M devices* are defined as devices running M2M application(s) using M2M communication capabilities. This section analyzes some of the M2M device characteristics and tries to provide a classification over them that will be used in Sect. 5.

In 2017, NSfocus (https://blog.nsfocusglobal.com/categories/exposed-iot-assets-in-china-analysis/) carried out an analysis on public device endpoints in China based on information collected by most famous scan engines (Shodan, NTI, Zoom Eye). The output of this analysis was a list of 12 IoT categories, which we reassembled into six macro-categories used by the IoT Security Checker to classify the discovered IoT devices.

- **IP-Camera** refers to all devices recording or playing video content such as web cams, DVR and streaming devices such as baby monitors.
- **Router** refers to switches, modems, routers and any other network appliances.
- **Defense** refers to all devices that aim to protect a system (e.g., firewalls, IDSs, IPSs).
- **Printer** refers to all printing and fax devices that may be exposed to the Internet to provide a higher interoperability.
- **ICS** refers to all Industrial Control System (ICS) that plays a fundamental role in smart grids and industry 4.0.
- **Generic** refers to all devices that cannot be ranked in any of the above categories, but expose well-known protocols such as XMPP, CoAP, MQTT.

4 Device Mining

Given the classification in Sect. 3, a preliminary knowledge extraction is needed to support further analysis on the IoT devices. The scope of this knowledge extraction is to identify a set of properties that describe every IoT category in terms of *(i)* keywords, *(ii)* manufacturer, *(iii)* ports, and *(iv)* vulnerabilities, thus enhancing the vulnerability assessment carried out with our IoT Security Checker.

The knowledge extraction is based on text mining done on information retrieved by Shodan [8] and composed of 3 main steps as follow:

1. Create a keyword and manufacturer list for each category.
2. Create a port list for each category.
3. Create a vulnerability list for each category.

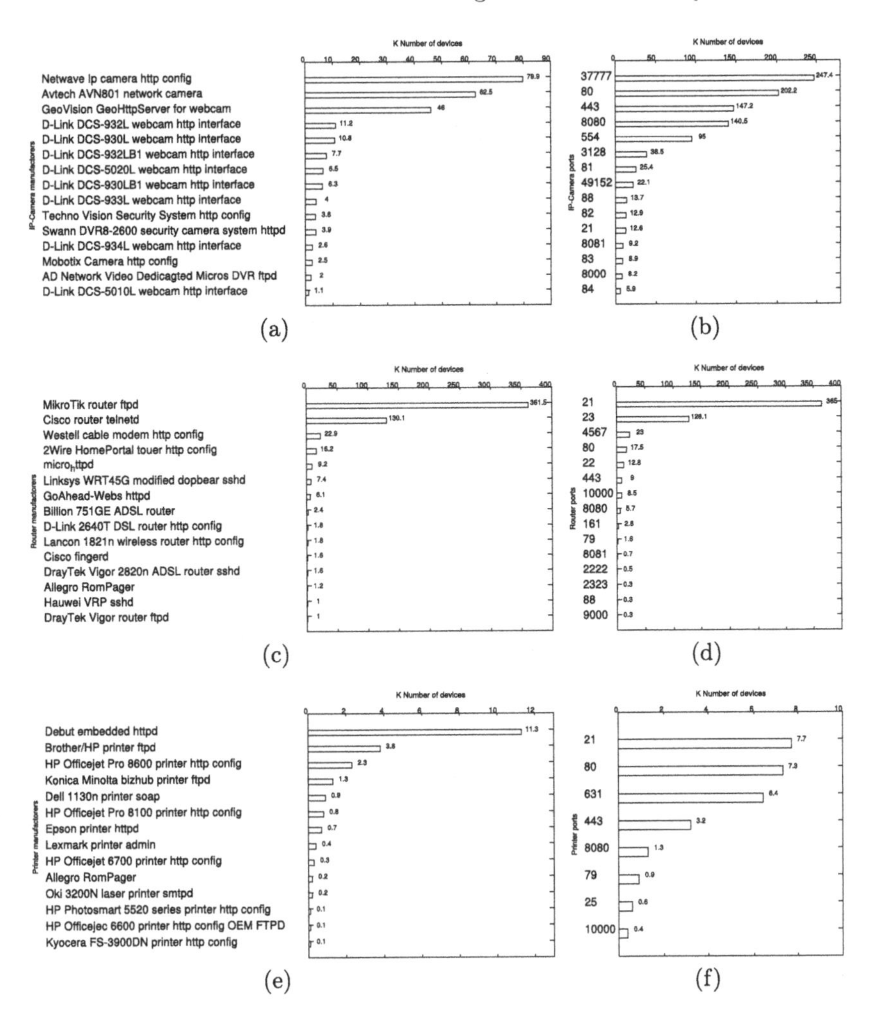

Fig. 1. Distribution of manufacturers and ports over three categories: IP-Cameras (a, b), Routers (c, d), Printers (e, f).

Based on Shodan public information, an analysis on the main services and ports used by IoT devices has been carried out. Figure 1(a) reports the top 15 IP-Cameras manufacturer found by Shodan using the filter "device:webcam", while Fig. 1(b) shows the distribution of ports used by IP-Cameras. Manufacturer and ports for routers has been identified using the filter "device:switch", device:broadband+router" and "device:load+balancer"; filters "device:print+server" and "device:printer" have been used for category printer. Results from categories router and printer are shown in Fig. 1(c), (d), (e), (f), while the complete results of ports analysis are summarized in Table 1.

Table 1. Matching between categories and ports from Shodan analysis

Category	Ports
IP-Camera	81, 82, 83, 84, 88, 443, 554, 37777, 49152, 143
Router	1900, 21, 80, 8080, 1080, 9000, 8888, 8000, 49152, 81, 8081, 8443, 9090, 8088, 88, 82, 11, 9999, 22, 23, 7547
Printer	80, 631, 21, 443, 23, 8080, 137, 445, 25, 1000
Firewall	8080, 80, 443, 81, 4433, 8888, 4443, 8443
ICS	47808, 20000, 44818, 1911, 4911, 2404, 789, 502, 102
Generic	5222, 5683, 1883, 8883

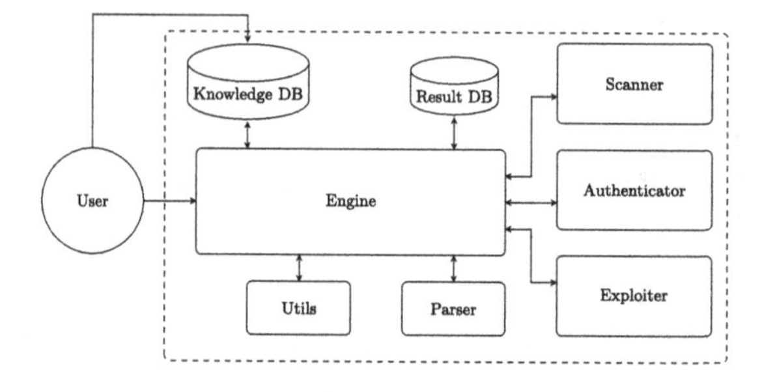

Fig. 2. IoT Security Checker architecture.

5 IoT Security Checker

The IoT Security Checker helps pentesters in identifying vulnerable devices in a given network, using discovery mechanism and known exploits. In the following, we describe the IoT Security Checker architecture, execution flow, and target exploit.

5.1 Architecture

Figure 2 shows the internal modules of IoT Security Checker.

Knowledge DB contains all information and data acquired during the mining phase in a NO-SQL DB. It can be updated in real time as new information is collected.

Scanner manages and starts the host discovery process. The scanning operations are run using masscan (https://github.com/robertdavidgraham/masscan).

Authenticator executes a dictionary attack on the following services: FTP, Telnet, SSH, HTTP basic. The dictionary is built based on the knowledge extraction in Sect. 4.

Exploiter executes a set of exploits of well-know IoT vulnerabilities. As for dictionary, the exploit list derives from the knowledge extraction in Sect. 4.

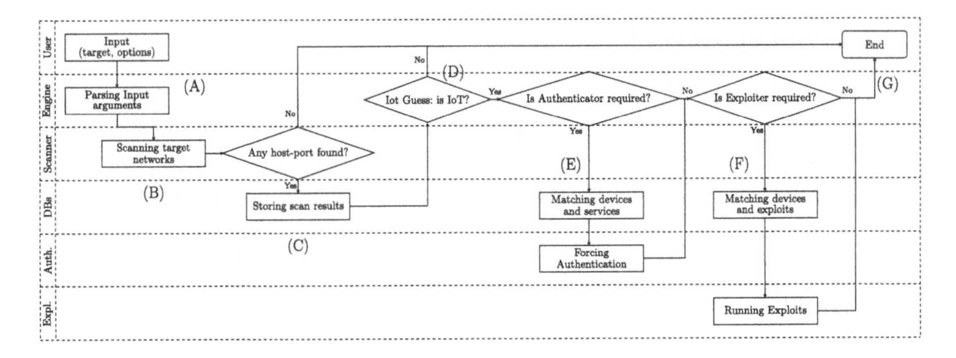

Fig. 3. IoT Security Checker execution flow

Engine manages all operations and exchanges of information through all modules. The user can set up the scan and then the Engine is in charge of starting the scanning, redirect data to the parser and DBs, setting up the execution of the Exploiter and Authenticator based on the results.

Utils provides a set of functionalities for input/output validation.

Parser includes all parsers that translate and filter outputs from one module and give them as input to another module. It also includes a human-readable translation parser for the final output.

Result DB stores all the information about the found services, hosts, and devices. It is used as the target list by Authenticator and Exploiter, or to store the final evaluation of the target devices. The host table storing the scanner results has the following structure:

- *Timestamp.* It is the timestamp when the scanner returned the result.
- *IP.* It is the IP of the found services; we note that there might be several rows with the same IP since the primary key is composed of the pair (IP, Port) representing the service.
- *Port.* It is the port where the service is listening.
- *Service.* It is the type of found service (e.g., SSH, HTTP)
- *Banner.* It is the discovered banner for the related service.
- *Info.* It contains extra information found during the scanning of the given service.
- *Error.* It contains any possible errors during the scanning operations.

5.2 System Flow

Figure 3 annotates the architecture in Fig. 2 with the flow of a single execution of the IoT Security Checker. Before starting the flow execution, the IoT Security Checker must be initialized by loading the knowledge. The IoT Security Checker can then be configured by the user by simply specifying the target.

Once the input parameters[2] are set (A), based on the parameters and the knowledge, the Engine launches the appropriate scanning (B). If no services/hosts are found, the execution ends; otherwise, they are stored in the result DB (C). The Engine analyzes all results based on the knowledge to identify whether they are IoT devices or not (D); this process is called the *IoT guess*. In case IoT devices are found, the Authenticator runs the appropriate vocabulary attacks based on the available services (E). The Authenticator stores the attack results in the Result DB and then the Exploiter runs the available exploits only on those appropriate services (F-G). The results are stored in the Result DB and finally shown to the user (H-I).

5.3 Target Exploit

The IoT Security Checker implements a set of exploits as follows.[3]

- *Cisco-PVC-2300*: the web camera Cisco PVC-2300 is affected by several vulnerabilities that may allow an unauthenticated user to login and access to multiple functionalities. The developed exploit tries to login and download the device configuration to read username and password.
- *Dlink*: a set of Dlink webcams are affected by different vulnerabilities that mainly permits OS command injection. The developed exploit tests each of these vulnerabilities.
- *h264-dvr-RCE*: a set of devices identified by the caption "Cross Web Server", which have been used by several companies, may suffer Remote Command Injection. This vulnerability allows an attacker to execute any commands on the vulnerable device. The exploit verifies the vulnerabilities attempting to create a file on the target device.
- *Humax-HG100R*: the Humax Wifi Router is vulnerable to Authentication Bypass attack by sending specific crafted request to the management console. If the console is publicly exposed, an attacker can exploit it and may get access to confidential information.
- *Rom-0*: a set of network appliances from companies such as ZTE, TP-Link, ZynOS, and Huawei are vulnerable to Authentication Bypass attacks. An attacker can access confidential data sending a crafted HTTP request to the /rom=o resource.
- *TV-IP410wn*: Trendnet TV-IP410WN webcams are vulnerable to Remote Command Execution attacks. The developed exploit verifies these vulnerabilities by executing the *ls* command on the target device.

[2] All input parameters are described in details at https://github.com/c0mix/IoT-SecurityChecker.

[3] We took inspiration from the following articles: https://media.blackhat.com/us-13/US-13-Heffner-Exploiting-Network-Surveillance-Cameras-Like-A-Hollywood-Hacker-WP.pdf, http://www.kerneronsec.com/2016/02/remote-code-execution-in-cctv-dvrs-of.html, https://www.exploit-db.com/exploits/42732/, https://rootatnasro.wordpress.com/2014/01/11/how-i-saved-your-a-from-the-zynos-rom-0-attack-full-disclosure/, https://medium.com/@lorenzo.comi93/break-into-2k-ip-camera-cb65bbac9e8c.

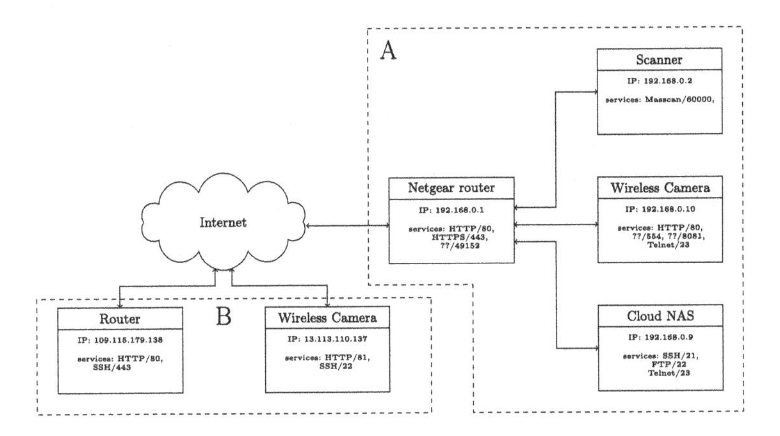

Fig. 4. IoT Security Checker experimental scenario

A zero-day vulnerability affecting some webcams and baby monitors (*IPcamera* vulnerability in the following) has been discovered during the development of the IoT Security Checker and now classified as CVE-2017-17101. It is based on Credential Injection through the camera web app. An attacker can obtain full admin access by using a crafted HTTP request, for instance, accessing video streams and changing credentials.

6 Experimental Scenario

We run the IoT Security Checker in a simulated environment that have been built specifically to test the tool functionalities. Figure 4 shows the networks with all nodes. The experimental environment is composed of a private network (A) containing the *scanner* node, an IPcamera wireless cam and a Cloud NAS. All nodes access internet through a Netgear router. A Wireless cam and a router (B) are added to the scenario and reachable from the private network through Internet.

The IoT Security Checker was executed from the scanner node with the following command,

```
sudo python3 IoT-SecurityChecker.py target.txt -m 300
-w 15 -E ALL -B ALL -T 2 -o result.csv
```

where:
target.txt contains three different targets: *(i)* the private network (192.168.0.0/24) and the two public IPs (109.115.179.138, 13.113.110.137).
-m 300 -w 15 instructs masscan how to run the scan. These parameters require to use no more than 300 packages per second and wait 15 s once the scan is done to get the results.

Table 2. Pairs (host, port) found after network scan (1); hosts, ports and information after process IoT guess (2)

host	port
192.168.0.1	80
192.168.0.1	443
192.168.0.10	8081
13.113.110.137	81
192.168.0.10	23
109.115.179.138	443
192.168.0.9	21
192.168.0.9	23
192.168.0.10	554
192.168.0.9	22
13.113.110.137	22
109.115.179.138	80
192.168.0.10	80
192.168.0.1	49152

(a)

host	port	keywork	classification
109.115.179.138	443	SSH	
13.113.110.137	22		Routers
13.113.110.137	81		IP-camera
13.113.110.137	22	SSH	
192.168.0.1	49152		IP-camera
192.168.0.1	49152		Routers
192.168.0.10	23		Routers
192.168.0.10	554		IP-camera
192.168.0.10	8081		Routers
192.168.0.9	21		Routers
192.168.0.9	22		Routers
192.168.0.9	23		Routers
192.168.0.9	22	SSH	

(b)

Table 3. Final results from IoT Security Checker.

192.168.0.10	23	Telnet	TelnetAuthenticator	Telnet Access found username: adm password:
192.168.0.9	23	Telnet	TelnetAuthenticator	Telnet Access found username: adm password:
192.168.0.9	22	SSH	SSHAuthenticator	SSH Access found username: test password: admin
192.168.0.9	21	FTP	FTPAuthenticator	FTP Access found username: anonymous password:
192.168.0.9	21	FTP	FTPAuthenticator	FTP Access found username: user password: test
13.113.110.137	81	HTTP	HttpAuthenticator	Http Access found username: test password: test
109.115.179.138	80	HTTP	Rom-0	http://109.115.179.138:80/rom-0
192.168.0.10	80	HTTP	IPcamera	http://192.168.0.10:80 new credentials are admin:hacked

-B ALL -E ALL -T 2 instructs Authenticator (-B) and Exploiter (-E) to run all possible authentications and exploits, but using a maximum of two threads. **-o results.csv** requires to store the final results in file result.csv.

The first phase of the analysis scans the network based on what specified in *target.txt*. The scan returns a set of (host, port) as described in Table 2(a). Each pair is then analyzed to identify possible IoT devices (process *IoT guess*). Table 2(b) reports the results with service and IoT device classification for each part after the IoT guess.

Following the IoT Security Checker flow described in Fig. 3, using the result from IoT guess, the *authenticator* module attempts to authenticate to all available services. Authentication attacks were successful over telnet protocol on hosts 192.168.0.9 and 192.168.0.10: they have been accessed with username "adm" and empty password. Attacks on SSH were tried on hosts 192.168.0.9, 13.113.110.137,

109.115.179.138; access was granted only on 192.168.0.9. Attacks on HTTP basic authentication were tried on hosts 192.168.0.1, 109.115.179.138, 13.113.110.137, 192.168.0.10; a single attack was successful on 13.113.110.137 (access was granted on port 81 with credentials "test:test").

After vocabulary attacks, the IoT Security Checker attempted to attack the devices using the exploits described in Sect. 5.3 based on HTTP.

No host was vulnerable to *h264-dvr-RCE*, *Cisco-PVC-2300*, *TV-IP410wn*, *Humax-HG100R* and Dlink. Host 109.115.179.138 was vulnerable to *Rom-0*, while host 192.168.0.10 to *IPcamera*. Table 3 reports the final results returned by the IoT Security Checker; each row of the table shows a security issue.[4]

7 Related Work

IoT security and vulnerability scanning are hot research topics. Kumar et al. [6] and Zhao et al. [13] presented an overview of the main IoT security issues focusing of the importance of a holistic view over the three-layer system structure. A real use case is described by Seralathan et al. [10], where the authors analyze the security of a general webcam taking into consideration the camera itself, as well as its mobile and cloud applications and communication channels. Shodan [8], a public information source on IoT devices, is widely used in IoT security research [1,7,9,12]. Markowsky et al. [7] analyzed the router status in the Indian Autonomous System Number (ASN) space, identifying misconfiguration or Rom-0 vulnerability. Williams et al. [12] defined a pattern to analyze webcams, smart-tv, and printers. First these devices are identified using Shodan and then a vulnerability scan is used to assess possible vulnerabilities. A similar approach is used by Samtani et al. [9], where Shodan is adopted to identify SCADA system and then Nessus is run to find potential vulnerabilities. The authors however introduced a text-mining approach that filters the results from Shodan to enhance the SCADA recognition process. Al-Alami et al. [1] presented an overall view of IoT devices in Jordan with a specific focus on security using Shodan. Solutions based on Shodan support a fast and wide analysis, but limited to public-accessible devices. Visoottiviseth et al. [11] presented an assessment tool based on Kali Linux called PENTOS. Pentos permits to scan a private network and subsequently assess the found services and hosts. PENTOS is completely manual; indeed the pentesters set the scanning at the beginning and then choose the assessment to run. The IoT Security Checker, being based on a knowledge, automatically identifies IoT devices and sets the appropriate assessment based on their characteristics.

[4] The logs of this experiment are available at https://github.com/c0mix/IoT-SecurityChecker.

8 Conclusions

This paper presented IoT Security Checker, a vulnerability scanner for IoT devices. The tool, using a knowledge built on public information, can help pentesters in providing an IoT security assessment. The modularity of the tool permits to easily extend the knowledge, and the available vocabulary and exploits. Future work will consider the development of an intelligent knowledge that can be automatically built and updated, driving a more effective assessment. Furthermore, IoT Security Checker will be extended towards assurance verification and monitoring of IoT devices and infrastructures.

Acknowledgements. This project was partly supported by the program "piano sostegno alla ricerca 2015-17" funded by Università degli Studi di Milano.

References

1. Al-Alami, H., Hadi, A., Al-Bahadili, H.: Vulnerability scanning of IoT devices in Jordan using Shodan. In: Proceedings of IT-DREPS 2017, pp. 1–6 (2017). https://doi.org/10.1109/IT-DREPS.2017.8277814
2. Anisetti, M., Ardagna, C.A., Damiani, E., Gaudenzi, F., Veca, R.: Toward security and performance certification of open stack. In: Proceedings of IEEE CLOUD 2015, June 2015. https://doi.org/10.1109/CLOUD.2015.81
3. Anisetti, M., Ardagna, C., Damiani, E., Gaudenzi, F.: A semi-automatic and trustworthy scheme for continuous cloud service certification. IEEE TSC (2017)
4. Ardagna, C.A., Damiani, E., Schütte, J., Stephanow, P.: A case for IoT security assurance. In: Di Martino, B., Li, K.-C., Yang, L.T., Esposito, A. (eds.) Internet of Everything. IT, pp. 175–192. Springer, Singapore (2018). https://doi.org/10.1007/978-981-10-5861-5_8
5. Kolias, C., Kambourakis, G., Stavrou, A., Voas, J.: DDoS in the IoT: Mirai and other botnets. Computer **50**(7), 80–84 (2017). https://doi.org/10.1109/MC.2017.201
6. Kumar, N., Madhuri, J., ChanneGowda, M.: Review on security and privacy concerns in Internet of Things. In: Proceedings of ICIOT 2017, pp. 1–5 (2017). https://doi.org/10.1109/ICIOTA.2017.8073640
7. Markowsky, L., Markowsky, G.: Scanning for vulnerable devices in the Internet of Things. In: Proceedings of IEEE IDAAC 2015, vol. 1, pp. 463–467, September 2015. https://doi.org/10.1109/IDAACS.2015.7340779
8. Matherly, J.: The Complete Guide to Shodan: Collect. Analyze. Visualize. Kindle Publisher (2016)
9. Samtani, S., Yu, S., Zhu, H., Patton, M., Matherly, J., Chen, H.: Identifying supervisory control and data acquisition (SCADA) devices and their vulnerabilities on the Internet of Things (IoT): a text mining approach. IEEE Intell. Syst., 1 (2018). https://doi.org/10.1109/MIS.2018.111145022
10. Seralathan, Y., et al.: IoT security vulnerability: a case study of a web camera. In: Proceedings of ICACT 2018, pp. 172–177, February 2018. https://doi.org/10.23919/ICACT.2018.8323686

11. Visoottiviseth, V., Akarasiriwong, P., Chaiyasart, S., Chotivatunyu, S.: PENTOS: penetration testing tool for Internet of Thing devices. In: Proceedings of IEEE TENCON 2017, pp. 2279–2284 (2017). https://doi.org/10.1109/TENCON.2017.8228241
12. Williams, R., McMahon, E., Samtani, S., Patton, M., Chen, H.: Identifying vulnerabilities of consumer Internet of Things (IoT) devices: a scalable approach. In: Proceedings of IEEE ISI 2017, pp. 179–181 (2017). https://doi.org/10.1109/ISI.2017.8004904
13. Zhao, K., Ge, L.: A survey on the Internet of Things security. In: Proceedings of CIS 2013, pp. 663–667 (2013). https://doi.org/10.1109/CIS.2013.145

MAD-C: Multi-stage Approximate Distributed Cluster-Combining for Obstacle Detection and Localization

Amir Keramatian, Vincenzo Gulisano, Marina Papatriantafilou(✉), Philippas Tsigas, and Yiannis Nikolakopoulos

Chalmers University of Technology, Gothenburg, Sweden
{amirke,vinmas,ptrianta,tsigas,ioaniko}@chalmers.se

Abstract. Efficient distributed multi-sensor monitoring is a key feature of upcoming digitalized infrastructures. We address the problem of obstacle detection, having as input multiple point clouds, from a set of laser-based distance sensors; the latter generate high-rate data and can rapidly exhaust baseline analysis methods, that gather and cluster all the data. We propose MAD-C, a distributed approximate method: it can build on any appropriate clustering, to process disjoint subsets of the data distributedly; MAD-C then distills each resulting cluster into a data-summary. The summaries, computable in a continuous way, in constant time and space, are combined, in an order-insensitive, concurrent fashion, to produce approximate volumetric representations of the objects. MAD-C leads to (i) communication savings proportional to the number of points, (ii) multiplicative decrease in the dominating component of the processing complexity and, at the same time, (iii) high accuracy (with RandIndex > 0.95), in comparison to its baseline counterpart. We also propose MAD-C-ext, building on the MAD-C's output, by further combining the original data-points, to improve the outcome granularity, with the same asymptotic processing savings as MAD-C.

Keywords: Point cloud processing · Approximations · Fog computing

1 Introduction

LIDAR (LIght Detection And Ranging), used in e.g. autonomous vehicles and production environments, is a 3D scanning method to measure ranges with rotating pulsed lasers. A LIDAR sensor produces hundreds of thousands of points (*point clouds*) per rotation, at rates of several MBps. In the presence of occlusions, multiple such sensors could join local views from various angles into a consistent global view, an overlooked benefit, to the best of our knowledge, that can enhance resiliency and availability.

Challenges. Single-source point cloud object detection can be achieved with clustering methods [13]. With multiple LIDAR sensors, a *baseline* approach of

G. Mencagli et al. (Eds.): Euro-Par 2018 Workshops, LNCS 11339, pp. 312–324, 2019.
https://doi.org/10.1007/978-3-030-10549-5_25

clustering the union of the sources' point clouds is impractical due to its cumulative data volumes and rates resulting in prohibitive (i) processing costs and latency (at least linear in the number of point-clouds' sizes) even for parallel clustering approaches [9,11], and (ii) communication bandwidth requirements. *Edge/fog* continuous data processing (i.e., distributed clustering local to each LIDAR) could overcome these limitations. However, two *opposing goals* make such an approach challenging: sharing fine-grained data (to maximize the accuracy) versus coarse-grained data (to minimize communication overheads).

Contributions. We propose MAD-C, a multi-stage approximate distributed cluster-combining method for obstacle detection and localization. First, it clusters each point cloud at the edge, i.e. at each LIDAR sensor. Then, it computes a local constant size geometric summary of each object and combines it with those of other LIDARs (in time depending only on the number of objects and sensors, not on the point-clouds' sizes). We show that MAD-C's summaries are computable in a continuous way and can be combined in an order-insensitive concurrent fashion, exploiting data parallelism. Our extensive experimental study covers a wide spectrum of scenarios, including very demanding cases, showing that the common view produced by MAD-C is very close to that of the aforementioned baseline. We also observe significant improvements in processing and communication efficiency, which is all the more important for edge/fog architectures and use of the algorithm in time-sensitive applications.

In the following, Sect. 2 describes the system model, problem and preliminary concepts; Sect. 3 and Sect. 4 introduce MAD-C, its properties and its algorithmic implementation. Experimental evaluation is presented in Sect. 5, related work discussion in Sect. 6 and conclusions in Sect. 7.

2 Preliminaries

System Model. We consider K ($\geq$ 1) asynchronous, interconnected nodes, each being at a known location and associated with a LIDAR and a processing unit (i.e. nodes are *edge/fog* devices). We assume the existence of a *spanning tree* for nodes to communicate and aggregate data. Each node knows its children and its parent. Let $\mathbb{S}$ denote the *sink* of the network (i.e., the tree-root), in charge of generating a global view from data from the other nodes. We first present our methods under the spanning tree and no-message-loss assumptions, for ease of the presentation. Later, we generalize using known results in distributed systems.

Each LIDAR, in each rotation, collects a *point cloud* centered at its location. The node can process the point-cloud locally, as well as communicate raw or processed data to others. Let $ptCloud_i$ be the point cloud from a full rotation of LIDAR L_i, consisting of n_i data points, as *node i's view.* A *(local) view* refers to an individual $ptCloud_i$ while a *merged point cloud* is the union of point clouds.

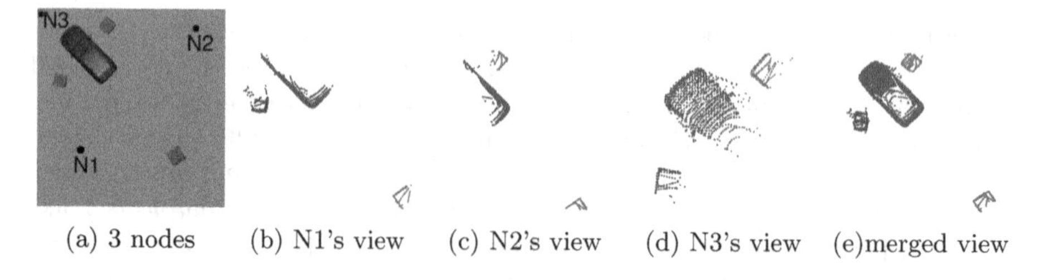

(a) 3 nodes (b) N1's view (c) N2's view (d) N3's view (e)merged view

Fig. 1. A scene with three LIDAR nodes

For simplicity and w.l.o.g we assume point clouds be obtained at the same time and views are expressed in the same coordinate system[1].

Problem Description. Using point clouds from K LIDARs, We want to detect objects, with low communication cost, while ensuring high quality of detection, data parallelism, as well as continuous, stream-compliant processing. The goal is to find a *map* that: (i) enumerates the objects and (ii) for each object, provides a representation (e.g. volumetric, or expressed as clusters of points). Besides detection and localization, this map can be used in scenarios with e.g. geo-fences.

Evaluation Criteria: (i) complexity in time, communication overhead and *(ii) accuracy* of the outcome. For the former we estimate the number of processing steps and the amount of information that needs to be communicated among the nodes. For the latter we use *Rand Index*, which is a similarity measure between two clusterings [15].

Example. *Figure 1(a) is to introduce running example to illustrate the problem and the functionality of our proposed methods. Parts 1(b–d) respectively visualize the local views of the 3 LIDARs. Figure 1(e) shows the merged point cloud. Notice that (i) there is at least one object missing in each local view and (ii) the views are complementary regarding the objects that are not occluded; e.g. they display almost non-overlapping segments of the car. Therefore, engaging more nodes to collect point clouds can result in higher accuracy.*

Background. Given a point cloud, there are several algorithms that segment the data points in it into *scene objects* [4,13], that our proposed methods can build on. Taking, e.g. Euclidean clustering, a point cloud would be partitioned into a set of clusters that correspond to objects and noise-points. To describe our methods we use the latter and for self-containment we paraphrase the definition from [13] (Ch. 4): Given n points in 3D space, a *Euclidean clustering* is a partitioning of them into some (unknown) number of disjoint sets (i.e. clusters),

[1] Else, pre-processing can transform them into a canonical system: depending on each LIDAR's disposition, a rotation matrix and a translation can be applied on its point-cloud, in constant time, in conjunction with the data-reading, along with filtering away ground points, a common pre-processing phase [8].

each containing at least a predefined number of points ($minPts$), so that pairs of points p_i and p_j are clustered together if $||p_i - p_j||_2 < \epsilon$, a predefined threshold. Points that don't belong to any cluster are characterized as *noise*.

3 The MAD-C Algorithm

We now describe MAD-C and how it meets the challenges described in Sect. 1. Due to space limitations, the proof arguments are briefly sketched. We consider a *baseline* that gathers all point-clouds and performs Euclidean clustering of these n points, with complexity $O(n \log n)$ expected processing steps [4,13].

In a nutshell, each node L_i in MAD-C locally detects objects in $ptCloud_i$ and forwards compact summaries of the local objects. The summaries get merged with the ones of other nodes along a spanning tree, up to $\mathbb{S}$, which then can deliver the set of global objects. Compared to the *baseline*, MAD-C drastically reduces data communication, while it pipelines and distributes the analysis.

In the following we address how to efficiently (i) generate local maps, i.e. summaries of the local clusters in the local views; and (ii) gradually merge the maps in a deterministic fashion, despite network asynchrony.

Efficient Maps and Summarization of Local Clusterings. Consider two local clusters c_1 and c_2 from two views. How can we determine whether to *merge* them without having to calculate pairwise distances of points in c_1 and c_2? Simply considering distances between their centroids doesn't work, as the size and shape of clusters matter. Hash-based similarity checks don't apply either, since point clouds have different elements. To address these issues efficiently, MAD-C works on summaries of local clusters.

A summary of a cluster c should ideally (i) use small space (independent of $|c|$), (ii) be built incrementally as new points are added, (iii) be shared with peers as soon as all c's points are found and (iv) express the *volume* that c occupies, to allow comparisons and merging with close/overlapping clusters.

We noticed that *bounding ellipsoids* satisfy these requirements. With this in mind, and inspired by contour surfaces of a three-variable Gaussian distribution, which form 3D ellipsoids, we propose to fit Gaussian distributions to local clusters and represent them as *bounding ellipsoids*.

A Gaussian distribution is characterized by a mean vector $\mu \in \mathbb{R}^3$ (center of the distribution) and a covariance matrix $\Sigma \in \mathbb{R}^{3\times3}$ (spread of the distribution). The family of ellipsoids corresponding to the surface plots of a three-variable Gaussian distribution are characterized through $(x-\mu)^T \Sigma^{-1}(x-\mu) = \alpha^2$, where α is a constant (i.e. a parameter of MAD-C) which we call the *confidence step*. The unit eigen-vectors of Σ define the directions of the principal axes of the ellipsoid centered at μ [7]. The Gaussian fit through maximum likelihood estimation [7], allows to calculate a bounding ellipsoid incrementally by calculating N (c's number of points), $S = \sum_1^N p_i$ (cumulative vector sum of c's points) and $\tilde{\Sigma} = \sum_1^N p_i p_i^T$ (cumulative sum of outer products of c's points). As soon as c is complete, μ and Σ of the bounding ellipsoid $\mathbb{E}$ can be calculated through S/N and $\tilde{\Sigma}/N - \mu\mu^T$ respectively (Algorithm 1, l. 10).

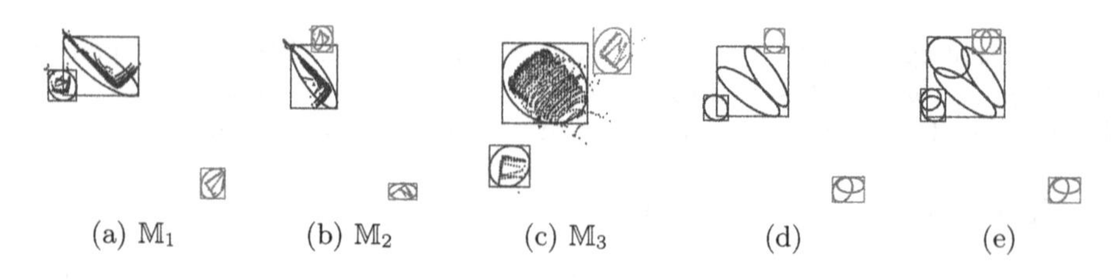

Fig. 2. (a,b,c) are local maps. (d) $\mathbb{M}_w = \mathrm{C}(\mathbb{M}_1, \mathbb{M}_2)$, (e) $\mathbb{M}_w = \mathrm{C}(\mathbb{M}_w, \mathbb{M}_3)$

Example. *Figure 2a, b, and c respectively show the local maps corresponding to Fig. 1b, c, and d. Ellipses symbolically illustrate the bounding ellipsoids. The delimiting boxes are explained later in this section.* We need some definitions to introduce next steps and properties of MAD-C.

Definition 1. *A map $\mathbb{M}$ is a set of objects. An object $\mathbb{O}$ is a set of ellipsoids. $||\mathbb{M}||$ denotes the number of ellipsoids in $\mathbb{M}$.*

In MAD-C, a node L_i produces a *local map* $\mathbb{M}_i$, i.e. a set of singletons, each containing a bounding ellipsoid approximating a local cluster in L_i's view (excluding noise points). The calculation of each ellipsoid's parameters can be embedded in the calculation of the clustering, at constant overhead per point.

Observation 1. *The representation of a bounding ellipsoid of cluster c is of size independent of $|c|$. The cost of calculating its parameters μ and Σ is constant per point in c. The representation of a map $\mathbb{M}_i$ is of size linear in $|\mathbb{M}_i|$.*

Algorithm 1. GenLocalMap(i)

1: $\mathbb{A}$: Euclidean clustering algorithm
2: α: confidence step in MAD-C
3: **while** $\exists$ p just clustered by $\mathbb{A}$ **do**
4:     c : local cluster where p belongs
5:     **if** c is new **then**
6:         $c.N = 0; c.S = 0_{[3\times 1]}; c.\tilde{\Sigma} = 0_{[3\times 3]}$
7:     $c.N = c.N + 1;\ c.S \leftarrow c.S + p;$
8:     $c.\tilde{\Sigma} = c.\tilde{\Sigma} + p * p^T$
9: **for** $c \in$ detected clusters at L_i **do**
10:     $\mu = c.S/c.N;\ \Sigma = c.\tilde{\Sigma}/c.N - \mu\mu^T;$
11:     $\mathbb{E}$: an ellipsoid with a unique id
12:     $\mathbb{E}.\mu \leftarrow \mu; \mathbb{E}.\Sigma \leftarrow \alpha^2\Sigma;$
13:     Initialize $\mathbb{O}$ to contain $\mathbb{E}$
14:     **for** $d \in \{x, y, z\}$ **do**
15:         $\mathbb{O}.b_d = [\min proj_d\mathbb{E}, \max proj_d\mathbb{E}]$
16:     $\mathbb{M}.addSingleton(\mathbb{O})$

Algorithm 2. UnifyChildren(i)

1: M_w = GenLocalMap(i)
2: **for all** Child $\mathbb{C}$ **do**
3:     get($\mathbb{M}_\mathbb{C}$); M_w = Merge($M_w, \mathbb{M}_\mathbb{C}$)
4: send M_w to parent (if any)
5: **Function** Merge($M_w, \mathbb{M}_\mathbb{C}$)
6: $\mathbb{M}_r \leftarrow M_w \cup \mathbb{M}_\mathbb{C}$
7: **for all** $\mathbb{O}_i \in M_w, \mathbb{O}_j \in \mathbb{M}_\mathbb{C}$ **do**
8:     **if** overlap($\mathbb{O}_i.b, \mathbb{O}_j.b$) **then**
9:         **if** $\exists\mathbb{E} \in \mathbb{O}_i \wedge \exists\mathbb{E}' \in \mathbb{O}_j | \mathbb{E} \cap \mathbb{E}'$ **then**
10:             $\mathbb{M}_r$.Merge($\mathbb{O}_i, \mathbb{O}_j$) *with:*
11:             $\mathrm{b}_d = \mathbb{O}_i.\mathrm{b}_d \cup \mathbb{O}_j.\mathrm{b}_d, d \in \{x, y, z\}$
12: **RETURN** $\mathbb{M}_r$

Combining Ellipsoids and Maps from Multiple Nodes. While passing maps along the tree, each node merges its *working map* M_w (initially its local map), with maps from its children, then it forwards the result to its parent (cf. Algorithm 2; shadowed lines are explained later in this section).

If merging is performed on the local point clouds rather than summaries, two local clusters become one if at least a pair of points (one from each) are within ϵ distance. Similarly, objects in the M_w and each child map $\mathbb{M}_{\mathbb{C}}$ are compared to detect if they contain ellipsoids satisfying such *matches*. If so, those objects are *merged*; i.e. the union of their ellipsoids is recognized as one object in M_w. In Sect. 4 we explain how (i) to integrate ϵ in an ellipsoid's representation, (ii) to check if two ellipsoids intersect and (iii) merge two objects, all in constant time.

If the baseline is performed on the merged point cloud excluding noise, then it generates clusters consisting of one or more local clusters because local clusters do not break into smaller pieces in the merged point cloud. Hence:

Lemma 1. *Applying the baseline on $\cup_{i=1}^{K} ptCloud_i$ results in clusters, each containing local clusters from local views. Likewise, the objects returned by $\mathbb{S}$ are sets of ellipsoids, each of the latter corresponding directly to a local cluster.*

Example. *Figure 2d shows the result of* MERGE $(\mathbb{M}_1, \mathbb{M}_2)$. *Figure 2e shows the* MERGE *result of the latter and* $\mathbb{M}_3$.

Lemma 2. *Operation* MERGE *on maps containing ellipsoids with unique identities, satisfies the reflexive, symmetric and associative properties.*

This follows through line 7 of Algorithm 2: if $\mathbb{O}_i$ and $\mathbb{O}_j$ have intersecting ellipsoids, they will be merged regardless of the order of execution, implying that MERGE satisfies properties of *conflict-free replicated data types* [12].

Corollary 1. *The network topology and timing asynchrony does not affect the final map at $\mathbb{S}$. Moreover, the* MERGE *operations can be executed using non-atomic multicasting, similar to gossiping or selective flooding, guaranteeing* eventually consistent *final outcome and inherent fault-tolerance properties.*

Corollary 1 implies the *spanning tree assumption can be lifted* and besides the sink node, any other node can construct the global map, if nodes broadcast their views in the network. We now study the processing and communication overhead of MAD-C, with a single sink.

Observation 2. $||\mathbb{M}||$ *equals* $||\mathbb{M}_1||+||\mathbb{M}_2||$ *if* $\mathbb{M}$ *is the result of* MERGE$(\mathbb{M}_1, \mathbb{M}_2)$.

Lemma 3. *Comparing objects $\mathbb{O}_1$ and $\mathbb{O}_2$ needs at most $\theta(|\mathbb{O}_1| \times |\mathbb{O}_2|)$ comparisons. $O(||\mathbb{M}_1|| ||\mathbb{M}_2||)$ processing steps is an upper bound on the computational cost of merging maps $\mathbb{M}_1$ and $\mathbb{M}_2$.*

This is because the number of comparisons for merging two maps is at most: $\left(\Sigma_{i=1}^{|\mathbb{M}_1|} \Sigma_{j=1}^{|\mathbb{M}_2|} |\mathbb{M}_1(i)||\mathbb{M}_2(j)|\right) \leq (\Sigma_{i=1}^{|\mathbb{M}_1|} |\mathbb{M}_1(i)|)(\Sigma_{j=1}^{|\mathbb{M}_2|} |\mathbb{M}_2(j)|) = ||\mathbb{M}_1|| ||\mathbb{M}_2||$, while the cost of comparison and merging is constant (see Sect. 4). This bound is an overestimation of a worst-case because it counts unnecessary comparisons as well. The exact bound is data-dependent and hence harder to estimate in a data-agnostic way, yet we experimentally study the number of comparisons in Sect. 5. In the following we study the role of topology in the above (still worst-case estimations), while later in this section we explain how to avoid unnecessary comparisons.

Let γ be the number of actual objects and K be the number of LIDARs. In each local view, while some objects might be entirely occluded, others might split into smaller ones, though not changing the order of magnitude of objects $O(\gamma)$ detected in the view, for the same ϵ and $minPts$ (cf. Sect. 2) as the baseline.

Lemma 4. *MERGE's worst-case complexity is $O(\gamma^2 K^2)$ with a star or non-balanced tree topology and $O(\gamma^2 K \lg K)$ with a balanced binary tree.*

Recall that the expected cost of Euclidean clustering of n points is $O(n \log n)$ processing steps [4,13]. Let n_i be the size of *ptCloud*$_i$.

Corollary 2. *The overall computation cost of MAD-C is the sum of (i) the local clustering steps, $\sum_{i=1}^{K} O(n_i \log(n_i))$, (ii) MERGE operations steps, (Lemma 4, Lemma 3) and (iii) bounding ellipsoids calculation steps, $\sum_{i=1}^{K} O(n_i)$ (Observation 1).*

Lemma 5. *The total volume of data (e.g. in bytes) to be transferred between pairs of nodes in MAD-C is $O(\gamma K)$, $O(\gamma K^2)$, and $O(\gamma K lg K)$ under star, non-balanced tree, and balanced binary tree topologies, respectively.*

The above are determined through the ellipsoids to be transferred, using Observation 2 to find the number of ellipsoids that any node transfers to its parent.

Considering that (i) MAD-C relies on local clustering and assuming the latter is performed in parallel, and (ii) in the worst case, no MERGE operation takes place until the latest local clustering is completed, we have:

Corollary 3. *Completion time of MAD-C is determined by $\max_{i=1}^{K} O(n_i \log n_i)$, plus the time to complete MERGE operations and the time to transmit the maps.*

Avoiding unnecessary comparisons To avoid unnecessary one-to-one comparisons (e.g. when two objects occupy completely different parts of the scene), we propose *delimiting boxes* as a way of distinguishing objects, so that those that don't need to be compared, get grouped separately. An object's delimiting box is an axis-aligned rectangular shape that encapsulates all the ellipsoids corresponding to that object (Algorithm 2, l. 11). An ellipsoid's *delimiting box* is the smallest axis-aligned circumscribed rectangle encapsulating that ellipsoid, i.e. one closed interval for each axis (Algorithm 1, l.14).

Lemma 6. *If the delimiting boxes of $\mathbb{O}_i$ and $\mathbb{O}_j$ do not overlap, the two objects do not have overlapping ellipsoids.*

This follows from the definition of delimiting boxes and it helps to reduce the comparison costs, while the other properties shown in the analysis still hold.

MAD-C-ext: Delivering Data Point Labels Rather than Ellipsoids. The baseline determines a labeling/clustering tag for each data point in the merged point cloud. MAD-C too can be modified so that, as well as maintaining a M_w, each parent node combines point clouds from its children and its own, and it determines a labeling for the latter and forwards both to its parent.

4 Algorithmic Implementation of MAD-C

Ellipsoidal Overlap. Given a pair of ellipsoids $\mathbb{E}_a, \mathbb{E}_b$, the method described in [1] determines in constant time if they intersect. It characterizes $\mathbb{E}_a, \mathbb{E}_b$ respectively as $X^T AX = 0$ and $X^T BX = 0$, where A and B are 4×4 matrices derived from their centroids and covariance matrices by extending with a default row and column. $\mathbb{E}_a, \mathbb{E}_b$ overlap if there is at least an admissible eigenvector (one without a zero in the fourth dimension) of $A^{-1}B$ that satisfies both equations.

Aura: Integrating ϵ in Ellipsoids. If the minimum distance of pairs of points from two objects is less than ϵ, then they are grouped together by the Euclidean clustering algorithm. We target the same behaviour with the ellipsoidal models, adding an *aura* $\delta = \epsilon/2$ around them, simply by increasing lengths of the main axes by δ. This is achieved by manipulating the covariance matrix of the ellipsoid to be expanded. Suppose $V\Lambda V^T$ is the singular value decomposition of the covariance matrix. Since the lengths of the main axes of the ellipsoid are the entries in the diagonal matrix Λ, it suffices to update Λ to $\left(\Lambda^{0.5} + \delta.I\right)^2$.

Data Structure for Maps. Implementation of MAD-C requires a data structure supporting *maps*. As described in Sect. 3, a map is a set of objects, each being a set of ellipsoids. We employed a variant of disjoint-set data structure with path compression technique. In our implementation, ellipsoids are initially elements of a disjoint-set forest and objects are merged by merging their corresponding trees through a simple pointer operation, hence the merging cost is constant.

5 Experimental Evaluation

We study (i) how well the ellipsoids represent local objects, (ii) the quality of MAD-C's approximate clustering and (iii) the quality of the clustering from all the LIDAR nodes for both the baseline and MAD-C-ext. To complement MAD-C's MERGE and communication worst case costs (Lemmas 3, 4 and 5) we also empirically measure (i) the computational costs of the former (including that of maintaining maps on local nodes) and (ii) the communication costs of the latter.

Evaluation Data. Public LIDAR datasets are usually gathered by a single source. Therefore, we only use them to study how well the ellipsoids represent local objects. To that end, we use 30 randomly chosen point clouds from the KITTI dataset [5], collected by a Velodyne laser scanner in urban driving (Fig. 3).

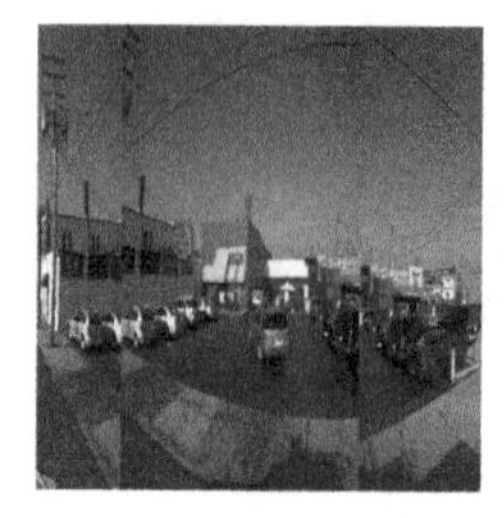

Fig. 3. KITTI-dataset scene.

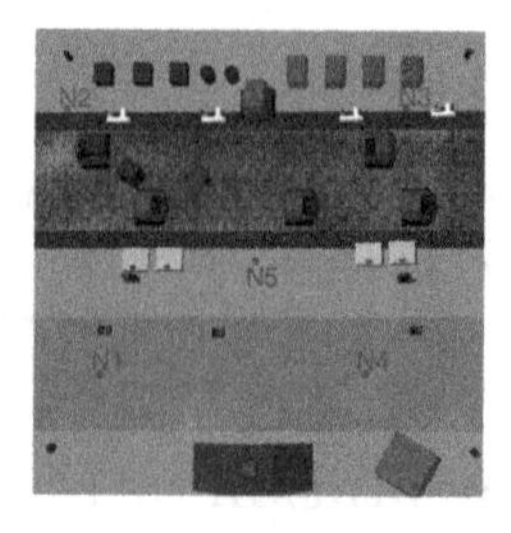

Fig. 4. Factory scene.

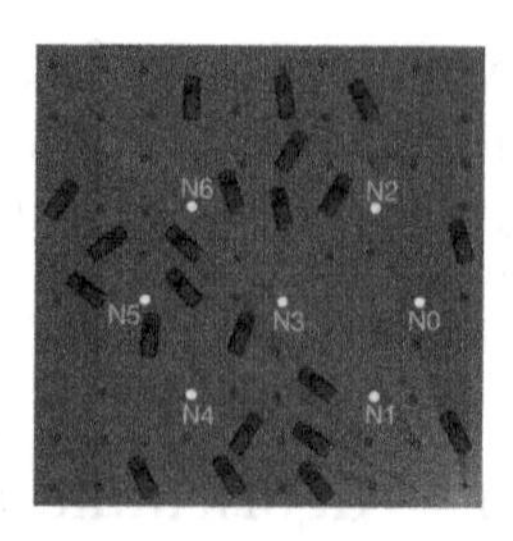

Fig. 5. Random scene.

We also use datasets generated by the Webots simulator (https://www.cyberbotics.com/overview), which simulates real-world LIDARs (VelodyneHDL-32e, in our case) and 3D scenes. One such scene resembles a factory environment (with Automated Guided Vehicles, lifting arm cranes and related objects) with four LIDARs placed at the corners of the scene and one in the middle (Fig. 4). Other scenes define random objects, as small as cubic boxes (with lengths of 80 cm) to objects as big as cars, over an area of $50 \times 50m^2$ with LIDARs placed at up to seven spots. Each object is randomly rotated around its vertical axes to vary the angle with which it is exposed to LIDARs (e.g. Fig. 5). To study MAD-C's operational costs, which depend on the number of scene's object and LIDARs (Lemmas 4 and 5), random scenes have a variable number of objects. We define 10 scenes for 10, 50 and 100 objects, for a total of 30 scenes. We use the notation Λ_i for any scene to specify it contains i LIDAR nodes. We exclude the point cloud portions falling outside the scenes' area.

Evaluation Setup. We implemented MAD-C in C++ and used GNU scientific library and Eigen for matrix algebra. For the baseline and local clusterings, we employed Euclidean clustering (cf. Sect. 2) algorithm in Point Cloud Library [14], with ϵ and $minPts$ respectively set to 0.35 and 10. With these values, the baseline reasonably detects all objects in the scenes and provides a reliable ground-truth. All experiments were run on an Ubuntu 14.04 virtual machine with one 3.1 GHz core and 4 GB of memory. We assume a *star topology*, i.e. $K-1$ nodes communicating with a *sink*. Execution of fog/edge devices was emulated by individually running them on the virtual machine and profiling the intermediate results (i.e. local maps) and the performance measurements. The Merge was performed afterwards. Corollary 3 suggests why this approximations hold.

We estimate *running times* by dividing the *rdtsc* [10] count, the number of *CPU cycles*, by the CPU frequency clock rate. To approximate the *communication times*, we divide the communication volume (sum of local point clouds' volumes for the baseline and sum of the maps' volumes in MAD-C) by the available bandwidth. Despite the latter being a coarse-grained approximation that favours the baseline (since the latter transfers about two orders of magnitude more data, which causes even higher communication overheads and possibly

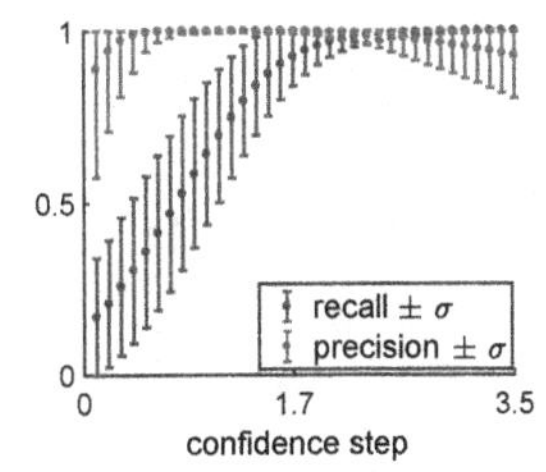

Fig. 6. Performance of the bounding ellipsoid (KITTI-dataset scenes)

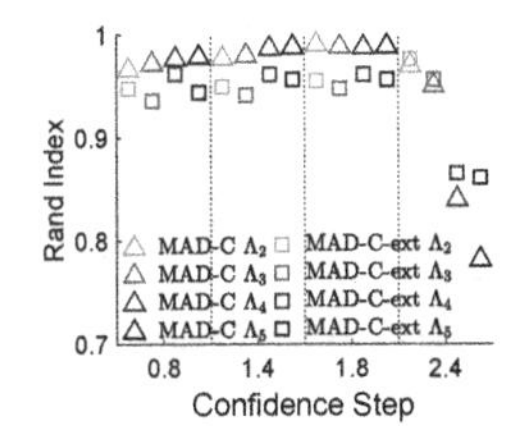

Fig. 7. Accuracy of MAD-C and MAD-C-ext (factory scene)

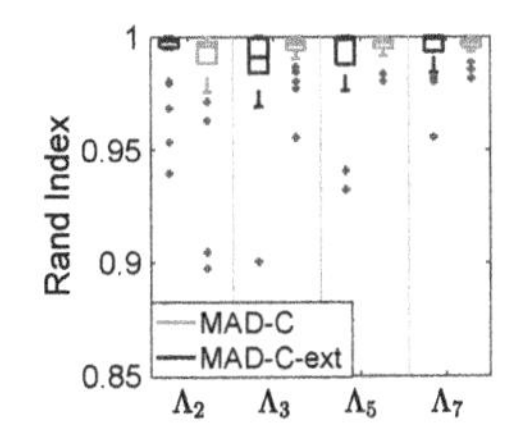

Fig. 8. Accuracy of MAD-C and MAD-C-ext (random scenes)

retransmissions, especially in multi-hop networks), we show that MAD-C still has better performance. We also count the *ellipsoid comparisons* in Algorithm 2 to see how effective the delimiting-box method is.

Estimating the Confidence Step α: Large α (i.e., large bounding ellipsoids) leads to high coverage of local objects. Yet, excessively large α, can lead to ellipsoids erroneously covering other objects' points. To study the trade-off, we employ *precision* and *recall*. For a local object and its bounding ellipsoid, they measure the ratio of the correctly covered points to all covered points and the ratio of the correctly covered points to the size of the point-set of the object, as detected by the baseline, respectively. As shown in Fig. 6 for the KITTI dataset (similar is the behaviour for the Webots simulations), when α is too small, local objects are partly covered (i.e. low average recall) or not covered at all (i.e. low average precision). This is not the case for higher values of α, until the precision decreases again when the bounding ellipsoids erroneously start overlapping other objects. We take $[0.8, 2.4]$ as the desirable range for α.

Accuracy of MAD-C and MAD-C-ext. As noted in Lemma 1, objects identified by the baseline contain one or more local objects from different views. Objects returned by the sink node in MAD-C, likewise, are composed of ellipsoids which in turn relate to local objects. Therefore, we take local objects as the basic elements on which MAD-C and the Euclidean clustering algorithm are executed and compare them using the *RandIndex* measure (cf. Sect. 2). Figure 7 presents the accuracy of MAD-C and MAD-C-ext, respectively, for two, three, four, and five nodes with α values 0.8, 1.4, 1.8, and 2.4 for the factory scene. Figure 8 shows their accuracy for $\alpha = 1.5$ for the random scenes; we use box plots to present accuracy for all the 30 scenes. As shown, both MAD-C's and MAD-C-ext's clustering outcomes are close to the baseline ones. In the remainder, the experimental study of processing and communication costs assumes $\alpha = 1.5$.

Execution cost of MAD-C. Figure 9 (left) shows MAD-C's and baseline's execution costs (Corollary 3) for the random scenes while Fig. 9 (middle) distinguishes MAD-C's costs for local clustering - $\mathbf{C}_1$ - and for the MERGE operation (including the calculations of the bounding ellipsoids) - $\mathbf{C}_2$. Notice

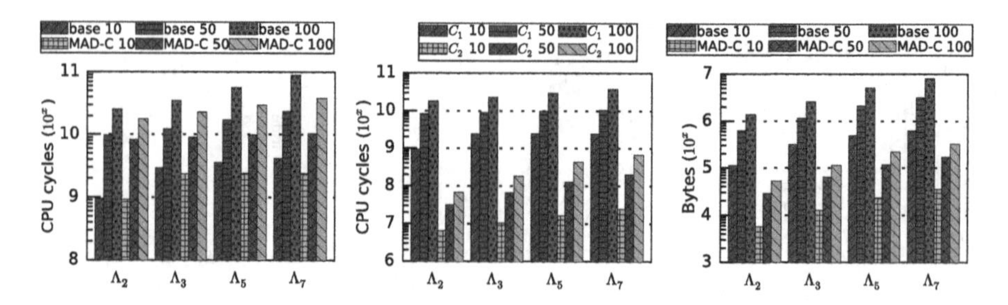

Fig. 9. MAD-C and baseline - avg. execution cost, MAD-C's execution costs decomposition and MAD-C vs baseline - avg. communication cost (random scenes).

Table 1. Average number of ellipsoid comparisons with/without the delimiting-box method.

	Λ_2		Λ_3		Λ_5		Λ_7	
10 obj.	16	168	46	599	92	1827	164	2951
50 obj.	72	3610	218	12738	487	38858	804	56477
100 obj.	105	12618	390	42481	1094	140380	2049	203423

Table 2. Execution times in seconds (100 objects).

	Λ_2	Λ_3	Λ_5	Λ_7
baseline	14	19	32	50
MAD-C	9	11	15	19

the logarithmic-scale y-axis, showing order(s) of magnitude difference between MAD-C and the baseline. Table 1 quantifies the effectiveness of the delimiting-box heuristic (Lemma 6), showing the average number of comparisons with (highlighting) and without the heuristic.

Communication Cost of MAD-C. Figure 9 (right) contrasts the required average volume of communication for both MAD-C (see Lemma 5) and the baseline for the random scenes. MAD-C improves by two orders of magnitude the average communication cost compared to that of the baseline.

Summary. In Table 2 we estimate the total execution time for 100 objects of MAD-C versus the baseline, assuming CPU frequency of 2 Ghz and communication bandwidth of 10 Mbps (similar to specification of devices in edge and fog computing). As observed, MAD-C offers a considerable improvement over the state-of-the-art, with a gap increasing accordingly to the number of LIDARs.

6 Related Work

Relevant clustering-based object detection algorithms for point clouds found in the literature are [4,13]. To cope with point clouds' large data volumes, parallel analysis techniques are given in [9,11]. All these can be leveraged by MAD-C since, as discussed, it integrates on top of *any* clustering algorithm. Variants of Octrees [3], voxel grids [13], and bounding boxes [6] are efficient tools for processing point clouds. MAD-C offers new opportunities due to the compact representation of bounding ellipsoids and their properties. ICP [2] performs geometric alignment of point clouds when the relative location and pose of sources is unknown, yet, in our work, we know this information.

7 Conclusions and Future Work

MAD-C is a multi-stage method to distributedly approximate detection and localization of objects with multiple LIDARs. Its core phase clusters disjoint subsets of data in a distributed and parallel fashion. Through summarization, it drastically reduces the volume of transmitted data while approximating efficiently the outcomes obtained by clustering all the raw data as a whole. The summaries, computable in a continuous way and with constant time and space overhead, can be combined in an order-insensitive concurrent fashion, allowing for more general-purpose uses of MAD-C. Future work will focus on the deployment of a MAD-C prototype on an IoT test-bed.

Acknowledgements. Work supported by SSF grant "FiC: Future Factories in the Cloud" (GMT14-0032) and VR grants "HARE: Self-deploying and Adaptive Data Streaming Analytics in Fog Architectures" (2016-03800) and "Models and Techniques for Energy-Efficient Concurrent Data Access Designs" (2016-05360).

References

1. Alfano, S., Greer, M.L.: Determining if two solid ellipsoids intersect. J. Guid. Control Dyn. **26**(1), 106–110 (2003)
2. Besl, P.J., McKay, N.D.: Method for registration of 3-D shapes. In: Sensor Fusion IV: Control Paradigms and Data Structures, vol. 1611, pp. 586–607. International Society for Optics and Photonics (1992)
3. Elseberg, J., Borrmann, D., Nüchter, A.: One billion points in the cloud-an octree for efficient processing of 3D laser scans. ISPRS J. Photogramm. Remote. Sens. **76**, 76–88 (2013)
4. Ester, M., Kriegel, H.P., Sander, J., Xu, X., et al.: A density-based algorithm for discovering clusters in large spatial databases with noise. In: KDD, vol. 96, pp. 226–231 (1996)
5. Geiger, A., Lenz, P., Stiller, C., Urtasun, R.: Vision meets robotics: the KITTI dataset. Int. J. Robot. Res. (IJRR) **32**(11), 1231–1237 (2013)
6. Geiger, A., Lenz, P., Urtasun, R.: Are we ready for autonomous driving? The KITTI vision benchmark suite. In: CVPR, pp. 3354–3361. IEEE (2012)
7. Hansen, N.: The CMA evolution strategy: a comparing review. In: Lozano, J.A., Larrañaga, P., Inza, I., Bengoetxea, E. (eds.) Towards a New Evolutionary Computation. STUDFUZZ, vol. 192, pp. 75–102. Springer, Heidelberg (2006). https://doi.org/10.1007/3-540-32494-1_4
8. Himmelsbach, M., Hundelshausen, F.V., Wuensche, H.J.: Fast segmentation of 3D point clouds for ground vehicles. In: Intelligent Vehicles Symposium, pp. 560–565. IEEE (2010)
9. Kumari, S., Goyal, P., Sood, A., Kumar, D., Balasubramaniam, S., Goyal, N.: Exact, fast and scalable parallel DBSCAN for commodity platforms. In: 18th International Conference on Distributed Computing and Networking, p. 14. ACM (2017)

10. Paoloni, G.: How to benchmark code execution times on Intel IA-32 and IA-64 instruction set architectures. Intel Corporation, p. 123 (2010)
11. Patwary, M.A., Palsetia, D., Agrawal, A., Liao, W.k., Manne, F., Choudhary, A.: A new scalable parallel DBSCAN algorithm using the disjoint-set data structure. In: Proceedings of the International Conference on High Performance Computing, Networking, Storage and Analysis, p. 62. IEEE Computer Society Press (2012)
12. Preguica, N., Marques, J.M., Shapiro, M., Letia, M.: A commutative replicated data type for cooperative editing. In: 29th IEEE International Conference on Distributed Computing Systems, ICDCS 2009, pp. 395–403. IEEE (2009)
13. Rusu, R.B.: Semantic 3D object maps for everyday manipulation in human living environments. KI-Künstliche Intelligenz **24**(4), 345–348 (2010)
14. Rusu, R.B., Cousins, S.: 3D is here: point cloud library (PCL). In: IEEE International Conference on Robotics and automation (ICRA), pp. 1–4. IEEE (2011)
15. Wagner, S., Wagner, D.: Comparing clusterings: an overview. Universität Karlsruhe, Fakultät für Informatik Karlsruhe (2007)

FPDAPP - Workshop on Future Perspective of Decentralised Applications

Workshop on Future Perspectives of Decentralized Applications (FPDAPP)

Workshop Description

Blockchain technologies (BCTs) make agreement amongst untrusted parties possible, without the need for certification authorities. Proposed frameworks have been put forward in sector as diverse as finance, health-care, notary, intellectual property management, identity, provenance, international cooperation, social good, and security to cite but a few. Smart contracts, i.e. self-enforcing agreements in terms of executable software running on blockchains, have been developed in several contexts. Such an under-definition computational model introduces innovative aspects, such as the economics and trust of the decentralised computation relying on the shared contribution of peers and their decentralised consensus.

The first edition of the FPDAPP workshop was held in Turin, Italy, in conjunction with the Euro-Par conference. FPDAPP aimed to foster the cross-fertilisation between the blockchain and the distributed/parallel computing communities, which can strongly contribute to each other development.

FPDAPP workshop rigorously explored and evaluated the potentiality of such novel decentralised frameworks and applications. Of particular interest was the evaluation and comparison of killer applications that are showing evidence of how Distributed Ledger Technologies can revolutionize their domains or developing new application areas. Evaluation and comparisons are broadly understood, form technical aspects regarding the novel decentralised computer to the possible impact on society, business and the public sector.

This year, we have received 10 articles for review. After a thorough peer-reviewing process focused on quality, innovative contribution, applicability to real world scenarios, we have selected 6 articles for presentation at the workshop. Each paper has been revised by at least 3 independent reviewers, members of the program committee. The final decision on the acceptance of the papers was the result of the reviewers' discussion and agreement, leading to a high quality of the selected articles, despite the acceptance ratio.

In addition to paper presentations, Massimo Morini (Banca IMI) and Nadia Fabrizio (Cefriel) gave two very interesting invited talks, while during the networking session all attendees (more than 35 during all the day) had the opportunity to share their ideas and activities and look for future collaborations. In the last session of the workshop we organized a panel on consensus mechanisms and decentralized governance. Panelist included the Turing Award Silvio Micali (MIT), Nadia Fabrizio (Cefriel), Massimo Morini (Banca IMI). The panel has been introduced by Paola Pisano, Deputy Mayor for Innovation and Smart City, City of Torino.

Finally, we would like to thank all members of the FPDAPP Program Committee, the speakers, and the participants, as well as Euro-Par for hosting our new community and the workshop general chairs for the provided support.

Organization

Program Chairs

Andrea Bracciali	Stirling University, UK
Claudio Schifanella	University of Turin, Italy

Program Committee

Marcella Atzori	University College of London/Ifin Sistemi
Stefano Bistarelli	University of Perugia, Italy
Guido Boella	University of Turin, Italy
Maple Carsten	University of Warkwick, UK
Boris Düdder	University of Copenhagen, Denmark
Fritz Henglein	University of Copenhagen, Denmark
Stefano Leone	Deloitte, Italy
Patrick McCorry	University College of London, UK
Carlos Molina	University of Cambridge, UK
Immaculate Motsi	University of Warkwick, UK
Jack Jackson	Everledger, UK
Petr Novotny	IBM, USA
Federico Pintore	University of Trento, Italy
Henrique Rocha	Inria, France
Massimiliano Sala	University of Trento, Italy
Thomas Sibut Pinote	Inria, France
Andrea Vitaletti	Sapienza University of Rome, Italy
Aleš Zamuda	University of Maribor, Slovenia
Santiago Zanella-Beguelin	Microsoft Research

A Suite of Tools for the Forensic Analysis of Bitcoin Transactions: Preliminary Report

Stefano Bistarelli, Ivan Mercanti(✉), and Francesco Santini

Dipartimento di Matematica e Informatica, University of Perugia, Perugia, Italy
{stefano.bistarelli,ivan.mercanti,francesco.santini}@unipg.it

Abstract. Crypto-currencies are nowadays widely known and used by more and more users, principally as a means of investment and payment, outside the restrict circle of technologists and computer scientists. However, as fiat money, they can also be used as a means for illegal activities, exploiting their pseudo-anonymity and easiness/speed in moving capitals. The aim of the suite of tools we propose in this paper is to better analyse and understand money flows in the Bitcoin block-chain, e.g., by clustering addresses, scraping them in the Web, identifying mixing services, and visualising all such information to forensic scientists.

1 Introduction

Following the popularity of Bitcoin [2,9], also other crypto-currencies have experienced a huge increase in acceptance/use (e.g., Ethereum, Litecoin, Ripple, Monero). Hundreds of new crypto-currencies (coins and tokens) have been offered to the market, currently reaching slightly less than two thousands proposals. Crypto-currencies are no longer relegated (only) to *darknet markets*[1] or technology enthusiasts, but are nowadays a matter of discussion and investment products known by a large part of the population who has access to ICT.

However, due to the pseudo-anonymity offered to users, Bitcoin[2] payments have also become an attractive and frequently used means for collecting money from illegal activities perpetrated by criminals. For instance, Bitcoin payments are requested by most of the last *ransomware*, as *WannaCry* [5] and *Petya*[3]. Other activities are represented by demanding payments for illegal services/goods, as software *exploits* or *Ransomware-as-a-Service* (*RaaS*) targeting a desired victim. A new frontier could be the use of crypto-currencies as tax heavens.

After introducing Bitcoin in Sect. 2, in the remainder of the paper we describe a work-in-progress suite of different software tools, whose aim is to facilitate

[1] Commercial Web-sites that are only reachable through overlay networks implemented by communication anonymisation projects as *Tor* or *I2P*.
[2] In this paper we focus on this crypto-currency.
[3] https://www.symantec.com/blogs/threat-intelligence/petya-ransomware-wiper.

G. Mencagli et al. (Eds.): Euro-Par 2018 Workshops, LNCS 11339, pp. 329–341, 2019.
https://doi.org/10.1007/978-3-030-10549-5_26

the analysis of bitcoin flows, and let the forensic scientist extract and visualise useful insights on target (pools of) addresses. Results on specific case studies have been already presented in [4–6]. We name the whole suite *BlockChain Vis*, inheriting from the visualisation module [6]. Section 5 wraps up the paper with final conclusions.

2 Bitcoin

The white-paper on Bitcoin[4] appeared in late 2008 [9], under the pseudonym "Satoshi Nakamoto". It consists of an open-source, peer-to-peer, digital currency. Money transactions do not require a third-party intermediary. The payer and payee directly interact without using their real identities, and no personal information is transferred from one to the other. However, differently from a fully anonymous transaction, a complete transaction record of every bitcoin transfer and every Bitcoin user's encrypted identity is maintained on a public ledger, called the block-chain. For this reason, Bitcoin transactions are pseudonymous, and not completely anonymous: Bitcoin addresses are pseudonyms of real individuals, and a user may have several pseudonyms.

The only way to create new bitcoins is through the mining process: miners are the nodes that verify the transactions and add them to the block-chain, grouped into "blocks" of information. The amount of bitcoins[5] created each time a miner discovers a new block represents a reward for its job. Besides it, also the fees of all the transactions in the mined block go to the miner.

Transactions. Transactions are the basic brick of the Bitcoin network: they represent the mechanism that allows a user to cede money to another user, e.g., from a buyer to a seller. This mechanism is possible thank to Bitcoin addresses. A Bitcoin address is an identifier of 26–35 alphanumeric characters, and it strictly derives from the hash of a generated public key (*pubkey* in the following) [2]. A private key is a random 256bit number, and the corresponding pubkey is generated through an *Elliptic Curve Digital Signature Algorithm* (*ECDSA* [7]).

A transaction input needs to store the proof it belongs to the address who wants to re-transfer the money received in a previous transaction. The output of a transaction contains the next destination of bitcoins instead. Thus, the ownership of the coins is expressed and verified through links to previous transactions. For example, Alice, in order to send 3 bitcoins (BTC) to Bob, must refer to other transactions she has previously received, which amount to at least 3 BTC.

Block-chain. Miners keep the block-chain consistent, complete, and unalterable: they repeatedly verify and collect newly broadcast transactions into a new block of transactions. Each block header contains information that chains it to the previous block in the block-chain, that is the hash of the previous block. Thank to

[4] We use "Bitcoin" for the protocol and network, and "bitcoin" for the coin.

[5] Halved every 210,000 blocks. Now it is 12.5 bitcoins.

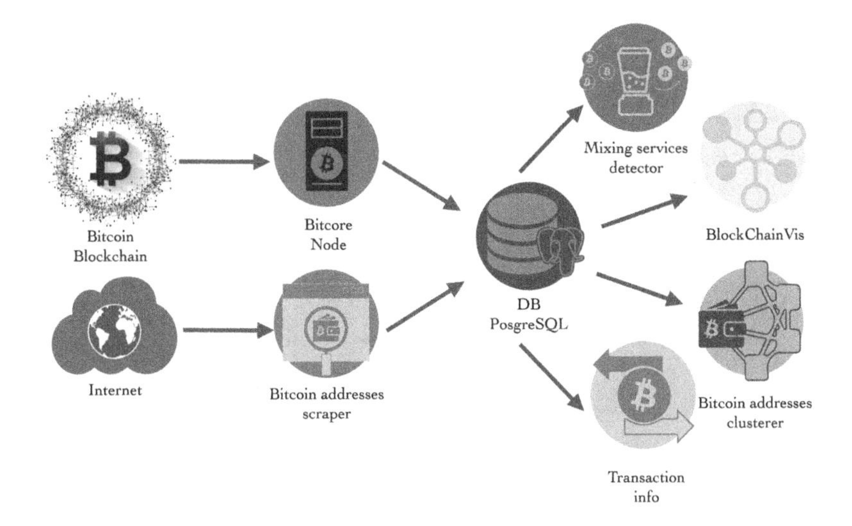

Fig. 1. A graphical summary of the BlockChainVis suite of tools.

this field, a block (and consequently the block-chain) is computationally impractical to be modified, since every block after it would also have to be regenerated. The remaining field of the header, i.e., the *nonce*, is obtained from the computation of the *proof-of-work* by miners. Once the header is filled with the nonce, its hash has to be less than a *target* number.[6] This proof is easy to verify (one hash operation), but extremely time-consuming to generate.

3 System Design and Implementation

The BlockChainVis architecture is designed to accommodate a modular and expandable framework with the purpose to build complex applications for the forensic analysis of the Bitcoin block-chain. Figure 1 summarises the tools.

The entire database of transactions is stored within PostgreSQL[7], even if it is possible to use OrientDB[8] as well. Moreover, we are currently moving the database to Accumulo[9]. The back-end of this suite is implemented on a machine with 512 Gbyte of RAM, 2 processors Intel(R) Xeon(R) CPU E5- 2620 v4 2.10 GHz 8 core (for a total of 32 threads); in particular, the implementation consists of three different virtual machines running, *(i)* Bitcore, *(ii)* PostgreSQL, and *(iii)* software dedicated to visualisation of Web-applications. In the remainder of this section we describe some of the modules in Fig. 1.

[6] Such a difficulty threshold is adjusted every 2016 blocks, in order to let a block mined every 10 min on the average.

[7] https://www.postgresql.org/.

[8] https://orientdb.com/.

[9] https://accumulo.apache.org/.

```
{
  "hex" : "data",        (string) The serialized, hex-encoded data for 'txid'
  "txid" : "id",         (string) The transaction id (same as provided)
  "hash" : "id",         (string) The transaction hash (differs from txid for witness transactions)
  "size" : n,              (numeric) The serialized transaction size
  "vsize" : n,             (numeric) The virtual transaction size (differs from size for witness transaction
  "version" : n,           (numeric) The version
  "locktime" : ttt,        (numeric) The lock time
  "vin" : [                (array of json objects)
     {
       "txid": "id",     (string) The transaction id
       "vout": n,          (numeric)
       "scriptSig": {      (json object) The script
         "asm": "asm",   (string) asm
         "hex": "hex"    (string) hex
       },
       "sequence": n       (numeric) The script sequence number
       "txinwitness": ["hex", ...] (array of string) hex-encoded witness data (if any)
     }
     ,...
  ],
  "vout" : [               (array of json objects)
     {
       "value" : x.xxx,             (numeric) The value in BTC
       "n" : n,                     (numeric) index
       "scriptPubKey" : {           (json object)
         "asm" : "asm",           (string) the asm
         "hex" : "hex",           (string) the hex
         "reqSigs" : n,             (numeric) The required sigs
         "type" : "pubkeyhash",   (string) The type, eg 'pubkeyhash'
         "addresses" : [            (json array of string)
           "address"        (string) bitcoin address
           ,...
         ]
       }
     }
     ,...
  ],
  "blockhash" : "hash",    (string) the block hash
  "confirmations" : n,       (numeric) The confirmations
  "time" : ttt,              (numeric) The transaction time in seconds since epoch (Jan 1 1970 GMT)
  "blocktime" : ttt          (numeric) The block time in seconds since epoch (Jan 1 1970 GMT)
}
```

Fig. 2. Getrawtransaction query.

3.1 Bitcore Node

Bitcore is a "full node"[10] Bitcoin client. The raw block-chain can be queried by using Insight API, and the result is presented to the user as a JavaScript Object Notation (JSON[11]) file, which is a simple text-document where the basic structure is a set of name-value pairs and an ordered list of values.

In Fig. 2 we can see the output of *getrawtransaction* query, which, by having a hash as parameter, allows for receiving all the information about a transaction; for instance, its block number, all the inputs and the outputs, the number blocks following in the block-chain (i.e., *confirmations*).

3.2 Bitcoin Addresses Scraper

The *Bitcoin addresses scraper* crawls the Web for Bitcoin addressees to be associated with real users, or to Web URL. The aim is to fully de-anonymise addresses where possible.

[10] Full nodes download every block in the block-chain, currently 170 Gb of raw data.
[11] http://www.json.org.

We use a set of scrapers [15] that crawl specific data form Web sites connected to the Bitcoin world:

- user-names on Bitcoin Talk[12] forum and Bitcoin-OTC[13] marketplace;
- physical coins created by Casascius (https://www.casascius.com) along with their Bitcoin value and status (opened, untouched);
- known scammers, by automatically identifying users that have significant negative feedback on the Bitcoin-OTC and Bitcoin Talk trust system.
- name tags on block-chain.info[14], e.g., *"Wannacry ransomware 1"*.

The tool helps users build lists of gambling addresses, online wallet addresses, mining pool addresses, and addresses which were subject to seizure by law enforcement authorities. All these addresses are entered in the database and they are used to de-anonymise further addresses by using the heuristics in Sect. 3.6.

3.3 Database of Transactions

Originally we had all block-chain in a OrientDB database. OrientDB is a widely used and open source NoSQL multi-model database. Unlike relational databases, a graph database does not utilise foreign keys or "join" operations. Instead, all relationships are natively stored as vertices of a graph. This results in deep traversal capabilities, increased flexibility and enhanced agility. However, from preliminary tests, this database is quite demanding in terms of RAM usage, which was not sufficient to calculate all the islands of transactions present in the block-chain, i.e., the strongly connected components.

For this reason, we are also testing a PostgreSQL database. Postgres, is an Object-Relational Database Management System (ORDBMS) with an emphasis on extensibility and standards compliance. As a database server, its primary functions are to store data securely and return that data in response to requests from other software applications.

3.4 Mixing Services Detector

Bitcoin is a good way to stay anonymous while making payments. Nevertheless, Bitcoin transactions are never truly anonymous. Bitcoin activities are recorded and available publicly via the block-chain. When a Bitcoin user pay for some service or good, she will of course need to provide her name and address to the seller for billing or delivery purposes. It means that a third party can trace her transactions and associate her address with her name. To avoid this, *mixing services* (also called *tumblers*) [13] provide the ability to interrupt a direct money-flow from one user to another by using addresses that do not belong to the original owner. Mixing services are used to mix one's funds with other people's

[12] https://bitcointalk.org/.
[13] https://bitcoin-otc.com/.
[14] https://blockchain.info/tags.

Table 1. Characteristics of some mixing services.

Service name	Fees	Return time	Minimum import	Maximum import
Helix light	2.5%	max 24 h	0.01 BTC	43 BTC
Bitcoin blender	1–3%	max 99 h	0.01 BTC	None
Coin cloud	1.25%	max 1 h	0.01 BTC	None
CoinMixer	1–3% + 0.0006 BTC	max 5 h	0.01 BTC	None
BitClock	2% + 0.0008 BTC	max 5 h	0.02 BTC	10 BTC

Table 2. Dataset characteristics.

Mixing services transactions	All transactions
Made with mixing services	Obtained from the Block-chain
Time range: 25 September 2017, 22 October 2017	Time range: 25 September 2017, 22 October 2017
Label with the name of the service	No label
973	7 852 074

money, intending to confuse the trail back to the original source. In traditional financial systems, the equivalent would be moving funds through banks located in countries with strict bank-secrecy laws, such as the Cayman Islands.[15]

The goal of this module (see Fig. 1) is to find mixing services in the Bitcoin network. In particular, to extract related behavioural-patterns in terms of payments, and consequently to understand how a mixing service works. In practice, this allows for tracking a desired bitcoin-flow also through a mixing service.

To experimentally find such patterns, we prepared some real bitcoin-payments using different mixing services: the final goals is to have identify those addresses that belong to tumblers. In Table 1 we can see the characteristics of the used mixing services. We extracted two databases to proceed with the investigation: one with all the transactions sending and receiving money from tumblers addresses, while the other one with all other transactions performed in the same time interval. The features of the two datasets are shown in Table 2.

Finally, we studied the behaviour of these addresses with Machine Learning, and in particular by using hierarchical clustering techniques considering the following nine features: input addresses, output addresses, balance, average balance, transaction ID, time of creation, number of inputs, number of outputs.

Unfortunately, in this way we were not able to spot a different behaviour between the two datasets. Hence, in a second experiment we focused on a Data-mining analysis instead; in the tumblers dataset we noticed that 4.9% of CoinMixer transactions generates 89.7% of the edges, and 14 transactions generated more than 1000 output addresses. These transactions have the following features:

[15] https://en.bitcoin.it/wiki/Mixing_service.

Table 3. Similarity of address sets (first six).

Transaction	TX 1	TX 2	TX 3	TX 4	TX 5	TX 6
TX 1	100%	98.16%	97.31%	96.05%	94.54%	93.28%

Table 4. Similarity of address sets (second eight).

Transaction	TX 7	TX 8	TX 9	TX 10	TX 11	TX 12	TX 13	TX 14
TX 1	92.58%	91.78%	90.91%	90.2%	89.55%	88.99%	88.28%	87.55%

(i) number of input addresses equal to 2, *(ii)* number of output addresses in the range [2530, 2534], *(iii)* they were collected one a day, for 14 consecutive days.

We decided to compare the sets of output addresses and we noticed that the similarity between the two datasets decreased day by day (see Tables 3 and 4). This feature allowed us to conclude that the output addresses are gradually renewed over time with new addresses that work in the same way as those deleted. These results clearly identify a behavioural pattern of the CoinMixer service, generated by a specific internal algorithm. Hence, through an analysis of transactions, and in particular of their output addresses, it is possible to also recover all similar past and future transactions.

3.5 BlockChainVis (Visualisation)

BlockChainVis [6] is a module dedicated to the visual analysis of flows of Bitcoin transactions. The aim of this module is to help analysing desired transaction flows in deep. The block-chain can be considered as Big Data. For this reason we turned our attention to Visual Analytics [16] (VA), that is the science of analytical reasoning facilitated by interactive visual-interfaces. The main objective of VA is to help the visualisation of problems like size and complexity. The goal is to rapidly visualise only the data of interest. Being VA task-oriented [16], we have identified nine main tasks: (i) find miners; (ii) find transaction sources and understand how they are connected; (iii) find the main addressees of transactions; (iv) find the "richest" and "poorest" addresses; (v) find the addresses with a break-even budget; (vi) find bitcoin flows from an arbitrary address; (vii) find bitcoin flows from a set of different addresses; (viii) filter the block-chain on intervals of time or block identifiers; (ix) filter the block-chain on specific transaction amounts of bitcoins, or on their number of involved addresses. To reach such tasks, in the initial window it is possible to select among three different kinds of visualisation: Single Transaction, Address Transactions, and Archipelago. The first view allows for manually inserting the hash of one desired transaction, and then the tool shows the input addresses (in the following mentioned simply as "inputs") and the output addresses (in the following, "outputs") as a graph. The second option is the dual of the former: it is possible to type in an address and the tool shows all the transactions that have such address as output, and all the

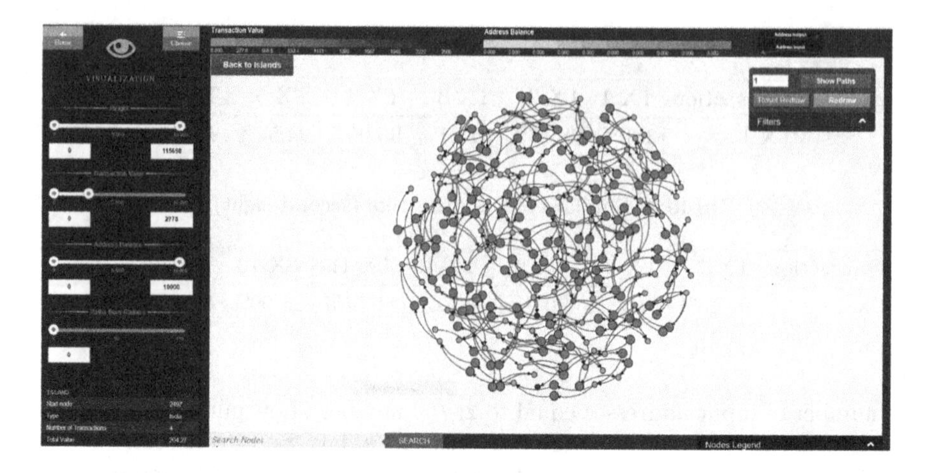

Fig. 3. Island visualisation.

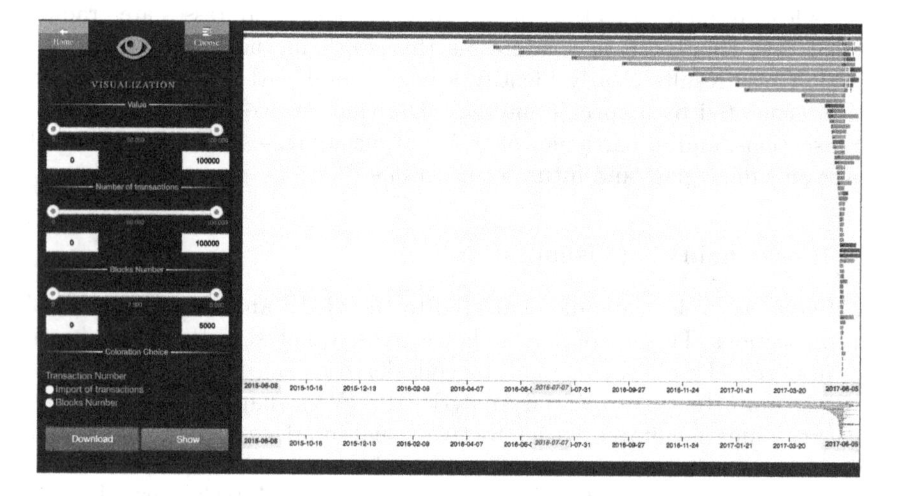

Fig. 4. Time visualisation.

inputs of these transactions. Hence, the first two options offer a more targeted view: the user already has some initial information. The Archipelago view is the third and most difficult one: it displays all the islands of the archipelago of Bitcoin transactions. An island is a connected component of a graph, where each couple of nodes is connected through a path, and each of the nodes is not connected to any other vertex of the super-graph of block-chain. Currently, we can visualise the Archipelago along time, as shown in Fig. 4. By clicking on any island of the archipelago, a summary of its statistics pops-up. Then, it is possible to enter into an island and visualise all its transactions, as shown in Fig. 3.

3.6 Bitcoin Addresses Clusteriser

The goal of the Bitcoin addresses clusteriser module is to find groups of addresses that belong to the same user. It incrementally reads the block-chain transactions from the DB and generates/updates clusters of addresses by using the following heuristics:

- The *Multi-Input Heuristic* [12] considers only transactions with more than one input. All the inputs of this transaction are considered belonging to the same owner. Formally: given a transaction $t(S_i \rightarrow R_i) \in T$ and $S_i = a_1, a_2, \ldots, a_n$ the set of input addresses. Given also the cardinality of the ensemble $|A_i| = n, n > 1$, then all input addresses belong to the same owner.
- The *Shadow Heuristic* [1] exploits the way in which clients manage the change, i.e., every time a transactions has a change, a new address (called *shadow*) is automatically created and used to collect back the change. This address belongs to same owner of the input address.
- The *Consumer Heuristic* [10] uses the concept of "consumer wallet", i.e., a client that by default allows for sending bitcoins to a single address, so it assembles transactions that have exactly 2 outputs. Given a transaction with 2 outputs, if there is an address appearing only in transactions that have 1 or 2 outputs, then this address and the input addresses are associated to the same owner.
- The *Optimal Change Heuristic* [10] is based on the assumption that clients try to use the outputs whose sum is closer to the value to be sent, then the change must be less than values of all other input addresses. Considering a transaction that has more than 2 outputs, if there is only one output whose value is lower than all input values, then this address and the input addresses are associated to the same owner.
- The *One-to-one Heuristic* considers only transactions having one input and one output. Given one of these transactions, and given a pool of addresses belonging to an *exchange service*[16], if the two addresses do not belong to the pool, they are considered belonging to the same owner.
- The *Multisig-one Heuristic* is based on multi-signature transactions[17]. Considering a transaction having a multisig output containing a pool of address where to unlock it, it is necessary to control 1 or all private keys referred by this pool of addresses, then the entire pool belongs to the same owner.
- The *Multisig-two Heuristic* considers multi-signature transactions that are already spent. Given a transaction which have a spent multi-signature output containing a set of addresses, where to unlock it is necessary to control more than one private keys, then the subset of addresses, that has actually used to

[16] Exchange services convert an amount of money in a given crypto-currency to a different crypto-currency (or fiat money).

[17] Multi-signature refers to requiring more than one key to authorise a Bitcoin transaction. https://en.bitcoin.it/wiki/Multisignature.

Table 5. Percentage of Bitcoin addresses that can be clustered.

Heuristic	Clustered addresses	% of clustered addresses
MI	83,867,895	72.61
OC	5,004,254	4.33
MS1	520,396	0.45
MS2	2,263	0.001
MI+OC	87,613,567	75.86
MI+MS1	84,372,511	73.05
MI+MS2	83,868,035	72.61
OC+MS1	5,523,007	4.78
OC+MS2	5,006,484	4.33
MS1+MS2	521,263	0.45
MI+OC+MS1	88,116,265	76.29
MI+OC+MS2	87,613,699	75.86
MI+OC+MS1	84,373,211	72.61
OC+MS1+MS2	5,523,859	4.78
MI+OC+MS1+MS2	88,116,388	**76.29**

unlock the output, belong to the same owner. This heuristics is not applied to 2-of-3 multi-signature because they could correspond to an escrow[18].

Table 5 shows how many addresses can be clustered using individual heuristics and their compositions. With only four heuristics, 76.29% of the total addresses in the block-chain can be clustered (last row in Table 5).

3.7 Transaction Information

The last module, i.e., *Transaction information*, is focused on providing additional information about transactions. First, it classifies transactions into standard and non-standard types, according to the Bitcore function *isStandard()*[19]. Then, it shows the distributions of standard and non-standard transactions in the block-chain. Our first results on classification are provided in [4].

This module also allows for interacting with a Bitcoin scripting compiler. The Bitcoin transaction language *Script* is a Forth-like [11] stack-based execution language. Script requires minimal processing and it is intentionally not Turing-complete (no loops) to lighten and secure the verification process of transactions. An interpreter executes a script by processing each item from left to right in the script. Data is pushed onto the stack, as well as operations, which can push or

[18] Buyer commits money into a 2-of-3 address with the seller and a third-party arbitrator.

[19] https://github.com/bitcoin/bitcoin.

pop one or more parameters on/from the execution stack, operate on them and possibly push their result onto the stack.

4 Related Works

Analysing and understanding the Bitcoin block-chain is as complicated as interesting and critical: several analysis tools have been developed. BitIodine [15] is a modular framework, which parses the block-chain, clusters and labels addresses and visualizes portions of transactions graph. Bitconeview [3] is a tool for the visual analysis of how and when a flow of Bitcoins mixes with other flows in the transaction graph. Blocksci [8] is an applications of block-chain analysis, that allow to get information from transactions graph. In [14] the authors present visualisation mechanisms for taint propagation in Bitcoin that display how cyber criminals launder money. Chainalysis[20] is a commercial Bitcoin forensic suites, that allows to detect and investigate cryptocurrency laundering and frauds.

5 Conclusion and Future Work

In this paper, we have provided a preliminary report on the BlockchainVis suite of tools, which is a modular framework to investigate the Bitcoin block-chain, cluster addresses, identify mixing services, visualise information about transactions, and allow for using scripting languages. In simple terms, we are currently developing several integrated tools that simplify the life of the forensic scientist, by automating some of the tasks performed to keep track of money flows and their sources/destinations.

Bitcore Node: We plan to build a graphical interface to display the most interesting information of Bitcore in real time, as the current broadcast transactions (called the *memory pool*). Some examples of what we want to do are in already-existing tools as bitcoind-status[21], MyPHP Bitcoin Node Status[22], Satoshi.info[23].

Database of Transactions: Since the bitcoin block-chain currently contains 320 million transactions, we have planned to test a third database system to increase the response time of queries: Accumulo (see footnote 9). Apache Accumulo is a highly scalable sorted, distributed key-value store based on Google's Bigtable[24]. Our idea is to have two different databases: a Postgres DB storing all the needed information, and an Accumulo DB with Graphulo[25] to store the

[20] https://www.chainalysis.com/.
[21] https://github.com/craigwatson/bitcoind-status.
[22] https://www.reddit.com/r/Bitcoin/comments/2zexq0/my_php_bitcoin_node_status_page/.
[23] https://statoshi.info/.
[24] https://cloud.google.com/bigtable/.
[25] https://graphulo.mit.edu/.

graph structure of transactions. In this way, the queries concerning the topology of the graph do not need to also load useless data in memory.

Mixing Services Detector: At the moment, this module is not fully automatised: in the future we plan to guide the user in reconnecting a broken flow of bitcoins and visualise it by using the tool in Sect. 3.5.

Bitcoin Addresses Clusteriser: We are currently implementing all the aforementioned heuristics and updating the database accordingly: we will highlight all the addresses of the same user in the visualisation.

Transaction Information: We are developing a compiler to study a particular transaction, called *pay-to-script-hash* (P2SH): transactions are sent to a script hash (address starting with 3) instead of a public-key hash (address starting with 1). The aim is to investigate such scripts.

Miner Analysis: We plan to build a new module that shows information about miners, e.g., the relationship between miners and hashrate.

In addition to what described in this Section, we will also extend the power of BlockchainVis by making it able to analyse not only Bitcoin, but also other crypto-currencies, as *Ethereum* for example.

Acknowledgment. This work is supported by project "REMIX" (funded by Banca d'Italia and Fondazione Cassa di Risparmio di Perugia) and project "ComPAArg" (funded by "Ricerca di Base 2015–2016", University of Perugia).

References

1. Androulaki, E., Karame, G.O., Roeschlin, M., Scherer, T., Capkun, S.: Evaluating user privacy in bitcoin. In: Sadeghi, A.-R. (ed.) FC 2013. LNCS, vol. 7859, pp. 34–51. Springer, Heidelberg (2013). https://doi.org/10.1007/978-3-642-39884-1_4
2. Antonopoulos, A.M.: Mastering Bitcoin: Unlocking Digital Crypto-Currencies. O'Reilly Media Inc., Sebastopol (2014)
3. Battista, G.D., Donato, V.D., Patrignani, M., Pizzonia, M., Roselli, V., Tamassia, R.: Bitconeview: visualization of flows in the bitcoin transaction graph. In: 2015 IEEE Symposium on Visualization for Cyber Security (VizSec), pp. 1–8, October 2015
4. Bistarelli, S., Mercanti, I., Santini, F.: An analysis of non-standard bitcoin transactions. In: Crypto Valley Conference on Blockchain Technology. IEEE Computer Society (2018, to appear)
5. Bistarelli, S., Parroccini, M., Santini, F.: Visualizing bitcoin flows of ransomware: WannaCry one week later. In: Proceedings of the Second Italian Conference on Cyber Security. CEUR Workshop Proceedings, vol. 2058. CEUR-WS.org (2018)
6. Bistarelli, S., Santini, F.: Go with the -bitcoin- flow, with visual analytics. In: Proceedings of the 12th International Conference on Availability, Reliability and Security, pp. 38:1–38:6. ACM (2017)
7. Johnson, D., Menezes, A., Vanstone, S.: The elliptic curve digital signature algorithm (ECDSA). Int. J. Inf. Secur. **1**(1), 36–63 (2001)

8. Kalodner, H.A., Goldfeder, S., Chator, A., Möser, M., Narayanan, A.: BlockSci: design and applications of a blockchain analysis platform. CoRR (2017). http://arxiv.org/abs/1709.02489
9. Nakamoto, S.: Bitcoin: a peer-to-peer electronic cash system (2008). http://www.hashcash.org/papers/hashcash.pdf. Accessed 28 Jan 2018
10. Nick, J.D.: Data-driven de-anonymization in bitcoin. Ph.D. thesis, ETH Zurich (2015). Master thesis. https://jonasnick.github.io/papers/thesis.pdf
11. Rather, E.D., Colburn, D.R., Moore, C.H.: The evolution of forth. In: ACM Sigplan Notices, vol. 28, pp. 177–199. ACM (1993)
12. Reid, F., Harrigan, M.: An analysis of anonymity in the bitcoin system. In: IEEE Third International Conference on Privacy, Security, Risk and Trust and IEEE Third International Conference on Social Computing, pp. 1318–1326 (2011)
13. Sampigethaya, K., Poovendran, R.: A survey on mix networks and their secure applications. Proc. IEEE **94**(12), 2142–2181 (2006)
14. Shumailov, I., Ahmed, M., Anderson, R.: Tendrils of crime: visualizing the diffusion of stolen bitcoins. In: The Fifth International Workshop on Graphical Models for Security (GramSec). LNCS. Springer (2018)
15. Spagnuolo, M., Maggi, F., Zanero, S.: BitIodine: extracting intelligence from the bitcoin network. In: Christin, N., Safavi-Naini, R. (eds.) FC 2014. LNCS, vol. 8437, pp. 457–468. Springer, Heidelberg (2014). https://doi.org/10.1007/978-3-662-45472-5_29
16. Wong, P.C., Thomas, J.: Visual analytics. IEEE Comput. Graph. Appl. **24**(5), 20–21 (2004)

On and Off-Blockchain Enforcement of Smart Contracts

Carlos Molina-Jimenez[1], Ellis Solaiman[2(✉)], Ioannis Sfyrakis[2], Irene Ng[3], and Jon Crowcroft[1]

[1] Computer Laboratory, University of Cambridge, Cambridge, UK
{carlos.molina,jon.crowcroft}@cl.cam.ac.uk
[2] School of Computing, Newcastle University, Newcastle upon Tyne, UK
{ellis.solaiman,ioannis.sfyrakis}@newcastle.ac.uk
[3] Hat Community Foundation, Cambridge, UK
irene.ng@hatcommunity.org

Abstract. Emerging blockchain technology is a promising platform for implementing smart contracts. But there is a large class of applications, where blockchain is inadequate due to performance, scalability, and consistency requirements, and also due to language expressiveness and cost issues that are hard to solve. In this paper we explain that in some situations a centralised approach that does not rely on blockchain is a better alternative due to its simplicity, scalability, and performance. We suggest that in applications where decentralisation and transparency are essential, developers can advantageously combine the two approaches into hybrid solutions where some operations are enforced by enforcers deployed on–blockchains and the rest by enforcers deployed on trusted third parties.

Keywords: Smart contracts · Blockchain · Monitoring
Enforcement · On chain · Off chain · IoT · Privacy · Trust

1 Introduction

This paper focuses on scenarios where two or more parties interact with each other to conduct business over the Internet. Typical scenarios involve consumers and providers where the latter sell tangible items or computing services to the former. A specific example is the selling of personal data collected from IoT sensors or social media applications to data consumers. We assume the business parties involved are reluctant to trust each other unguardedly, that is; without software mechanisms that assure (1) parties act according to some agreed upon rules, and (2) performed actions are indelibly recorded on means that make them undeniable and examinable, for example, to determine the sequence of actions that led to an unexpected outcome and subsequent dispute.

In conventional business, the mechanisms normally used in these situations are business contracts supported by *ledgers*. The contract stipulates what actions

G. Mencagli et al. (Eds.): Euro-Par 2018 Workshops, LNCS 11339, pp. 342–354, 2019.
https://doi.org/10.1007/978-3-030-10549-5_27

the parties are expected to execute, while the ledger is used to record the history of the actions that have been executed. It is widely accepted that equivalent mechanisms are also needed in electronic business. An emerging solution that is currently being explored to address this question is **smart contracts** built on the basis of blockchain technologies [4,25]. Examples of such technologies are Bitcoin [2], Ethereum [10] and Hyperledger [34]. However, blockchain-based smart contracts are only at their initial research stage, and plagued with questions about their scalability, performance, transaction costs and other questions that emerge from their decentralised nature.

This article makes the following contributions to help clarify some of these issues. (i) We explain that there are different approaches to implement smart contracts ranging from centralised to decentralised. (ii) We explain the advantages and disadvantages of these approaches and argue that their suitability in solving the problem depends on the particularities of the application, the assumptions made about the application, and the facilities offered by the blockchain technology available. (iii) We argue that there is a large class of applications that can benefit from a hybrid solution.

The remainder of this article is organised as follows: Sect. 2 presents a contract example to motivate the use of smart contracts. In Sect. 3, we introduce smart contracts and describe the difference between the centralised and decentralised variations. Section 4 discusses implementation alternatives of smart contracts. Section 5 places our work within past and current contexts. In Sect. 6, we present some concluding remarks and raise questions that in our view, need research attention.

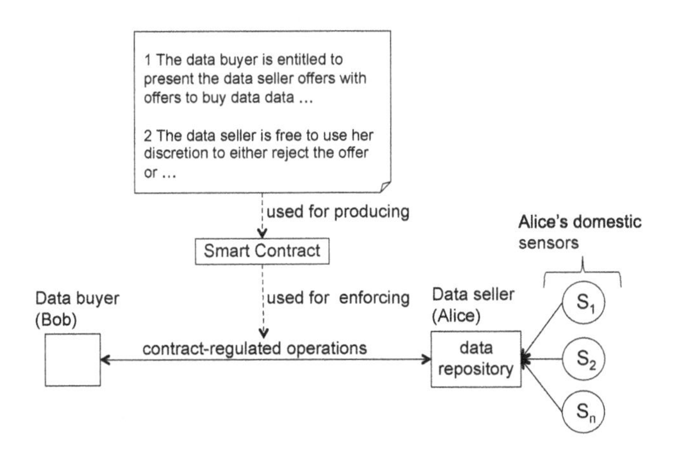

Fig. 1. Data trading regulated by a smart contract.

2 Motivating Scenario

An illustrative example of a contractually regulated IoT application of our research interest is shown in Fig. 1. Alice is a person in possession of personal data that she would like to sell and as such she plays the role of a *Data seller*. The *Data Buyer* (represented by Bob) is a company interested in buying data from Alice. Alice gathers her data from different sources, such as her social network activities, body sensors and domestic sensors, as envisioned in [35]. For simplicity and to frame the discussion, we assume that Alice is trading only her data collected from her domestic sensors. We assume that Alice stores her data in a personal repository, perhaps located in the cloud. Like in the "Hat" project [1], we assume Alice is the absolute owner of the data and that she is entitled to negotiate with potential buyers how to trade her data, i.e., to whom to sell it to, when, and under which conditions. The negotiation process can be as sophisticated as needed. Since this issue falls outside of the scope of this paper, we consider only a simple *accept or reject the offer as it is* negotiation process. An example of contractual clauses that Alice and Bob can use to regulate their data trading follows:

1. *The buyer (<u>Bob</u>) is entitled to present the data seller (<u>Alice</u>) with* ***offers to buy data*** *collected from Alice's domestic sensors.*
2. *The data seller is free to use her discretion to either* ***reject the offer*** *or* ***accept the offer*** *as it is.*
   (a) *The data seller is expected to* ***send a notification of offer acceptance*** *within 36 h of receiving the offer, when she decides to accept it.*
   (b) *Failure to send a notification will be considered as offer rejection.*
3. *The data buyer is obliged to* ***send the payment*** *to the data seller within 24 h of receiving the notification of acceptance.*
   (a) *Failure to meet his obligation will result in an abnormal termination of the agreement to be sorted out off line.*
4. *The data seller is obliged to* ***send a notification of payment acceptance*** *to the data buyer within 24 h of collecting the payment.*
   (a) *Failure to meet his obligation will result in an abnormal termination of the agreement to be sorted out off line.*
5. *The data seller is obliged to* ***make the data available*** *to the data buyer within 24 h of collecting the payment and* ***maintain the data repository accessible*** *during the following seven days.*
6. *The Data buyer is entitled to* ***place data requests*** *against the data seller repository without exceeding 24 data requests per day.*
7. *The data buyer is entitled to* ***close the repository*** *upon expiration of the seven day period.*
8. *This agreement will be considered successfully complete when the seven day period expires.*

The clauses include several contractual operations that we have highlighted in bold such as *offer to buy data, reject the offer, accept the offer, send a notification of offer acceptance, send payment*, etc. Though the clauses are relatively simple, they are realistic enough to illustrate our arguments.

3 Smart Contracts: Background

A smart contract is an event–condition–action stateful computer program, executed between two or more parties that are reluctant to trust each other unguardedly. It can be regarded as Finite State Machine (FSM) that keeps a state that models the development (from initiation to completion) of a shared activity. For instance, in [22,32], the state is used for modeling changes in rights, obligations and prohibitions as they are fulfilled or violated by the parties.

Research on executable contracts can be traced back to the mid 80s and early 90s [16,18]. In 1997, Szabo used the term smart contract [33] to refer to contracts that can be converted into computer code and executed. However, commercial interest in smart contracts emerged only in 2008 motivated by the publication of Satoshi's Bitcoin paper [24] that inspired the development of cryptocurrencies, smart contracts and other distributed applications. Satoshi departed from the centralised approach taken in previous research and demonstrated how smart contracts can be decentralised.

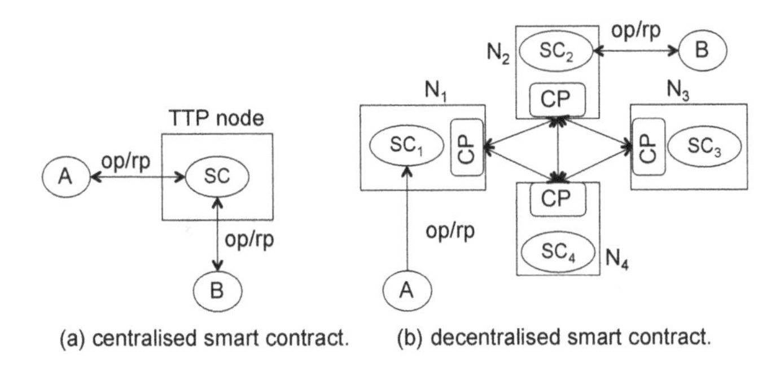

Fig. 2. Centralised and decentralised implementation of a smart contract.

3.1 Centralised and Decentralised Smart Contracts

Depending on the number of instances (copies) of the smart contract deployed to monitor and enforce the contract we distinguish between centralised and decentralised (distributed) approaches (Fig. 2). In the figure, A and B are business partners, for example, Alice and Bob of our contract example of Sect. 2. SC is the corresponding smart contract. *op* stands for operation executed against SC, *rp* is the corresponding response. *TTP node* is a node under the control of a Trusted Third Party. $N_1, \ldots, N_4$ are untrusted nodes. *CP* stands for Consensus Protocol. As shown in Fig. 2–(a), a contract can be implemented as a centralised application that uses a single instance of the smart contract (SC) running in the TTP node. Besides the disadvantages that a TTP introduces (single point of failure, trust placed on the TTP, etc.) this approach is comparatively simpler that the decentralised approach. The decentralised approach relies on a set of untrusted nodes instead of a single TTP that are used for running several identical instances (shown as $SC_1, \ldots, SC_4$) of the smart contract. In this approach, A and B are free to place their operation against any of the instances. The price that the decentralised approach pays for getting rid of the TTP is that the untrusted nodes must run a consensus protocol to verify that a given operation has been executed correctly, and to keep the states of $SC_1, \ldots, SC_4$ identical. Depending on the protocol used, its computational, communication and performance degradation cost might be unbearable [36] or its consistency guarantees inadequate [3] to the extent of rendering the decentralised approach unsuitable.

4 Implementation Alternatives

We will take the example of Sect. 2 and highlight the advantages and disadvantages of three implementation alternatives.

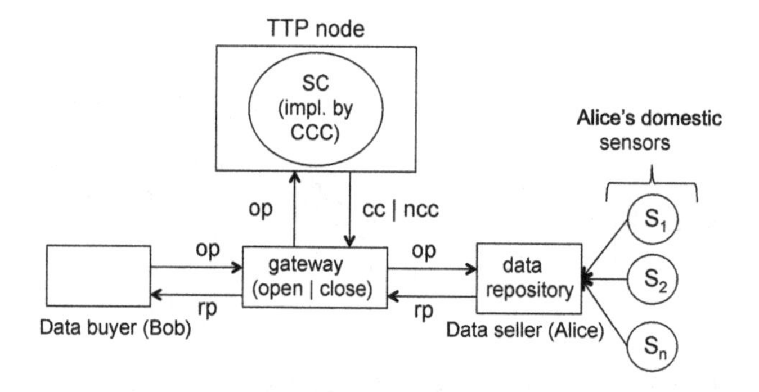

Fig. 3. Centralised smart contract.

4.1 Centralised Implementation

A centralised implementation is shown in Fig. 3. The role of the SC is played by the CCC (Contract Compliance Checker) developed at the University of Newcastle. We use CCC and SC synonymously in this section. The CCC is a FSM written in Java that accepts contractual clauses encoded as business rules written in the Drools language [22]. The state of the FSM is altered by the execution of contractual operations (op) initiated by the business partners, such as *offer to buy data*, and *send the payment*. The FSM running within the CCC keeps track of the state of the business process executed between Bob and Alice, and on this basis it determines if a given operation is contract compliant (cc) or non contract compliant (ncc). The CCC is used to control the *gateway* that grants access to Alice's data. For example, when Bob wishes to access Alice's data, he (i) issues the corresponding operation against the gateway, (ii) the gateway forwards the operation to the CCC, (iii) the CCC evaluates the operation in accordance with its business rules that encode the contractual clauses and responds with either cc

or *ncc* to open or close the gateway, respectively, (iv) the opening of the gateway allows Bob's operation to reach the data repository and retrieve the response (*rp*) that travels to Bob. Note that, to keep the figure simple, the arrows show only the direction followed by operations initiated by Bob.

It is worth elaborating the following points. Observe that in the architecture, all the operations are presented to the *SC* for evaluation. The operation rate is not a problem because the architecture involves only a single instance of the *SC*, i.e., there is no need to run consensus protocols. Likewise, the contract clauses, which are encoded in the Drools languages, are executed by a FSM implemented in Java. This means that we have a Turing complete programming environment that allows us to encode and implement clauses of arbitrary complexity. Unfortunately, the centralised approach introduces several drawbacks. For example, the contracting parties need to trust the TTP to collect undeniable and indelible records of the actions executed by the contracting parties and make them available upon request to parties that are entitled to see them, say to sort out disputes. At the technical level, the TTP is a single point of failure. Another issue is that the execution of the payment operation is centralised. We assume a conventional card payment mediated by a bank as opposed to cryptocurrency payment.

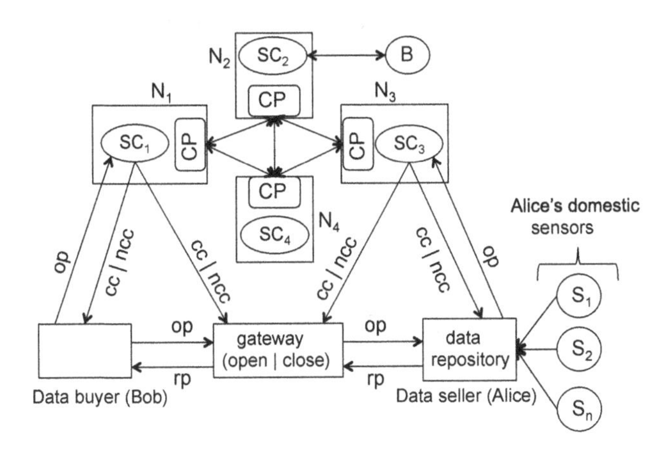

Fig. 4. Decentralised smart contract.

4.2 Decentralised Implementation

A decentralised architecture is shown in Fig. 4. Four instances of the smart contract ($SC_1, \ldots, SC_4$) are deployed in four nodes $N_1, \ldots, N_4$ (one each) of a blockchain platform. Each operation initiated by a business partner is executed against the contract; the contract determines if the operation is contract compliant (*cc*) or non contract compliant (*ncc*) and responds to both business partners accordingly. The response is also sent to the *gateway* to open or close it, accordingly.

To keep the figure simple, we show only the communication lines between the *Data buyer*, SC_1 and the *gateway*; and between the *Data seller*, SC_3 and the *gateway*. Yet we assume that a given operation can be presented to any of the four instances of the smart contract and that any of them can respond to the business partners and the *gateway*.

The salient feature of the decentralised implementation is the replication of the smart contract, consequently, there is no dependency on a single party. The cost to pay for this benefit is the execution of the consensus protocol among the instances which can significantly impact the performance of the smart contract in terms of number of operations (called transactions in blockchain terminology) per second that it can analyse, and the response time to complete a transaction. For example, Bitcoin, a public blockchain that uses a Proof of Work (PoW) consensus algorithm, can only process about 7 transactions per second. Another problem with Bitcoin is its consistency latency: its PoW algorithm offers only eventual consistency that might take Bitcoin about an hour (or longer) to approve and indelibly include a transaction in its blockchain [8]. Ethereum operating under PoW consensus suffer from similar drawbacks. Permissioned blockchains like Hyperledger rely on lighter consensus algorithms such as Proof of State (PoS). However, applications where eventual consistency is unsafe, demand strong consistency [3]. Strong consistency can only be delivered by communication intensive consensus protocols such as Byzantine Fault Tolerant protocols. Unfortunately, these protocols suffer from scalability issues [36]. Some smart contract applications (for example, applications that require instantaneous payment

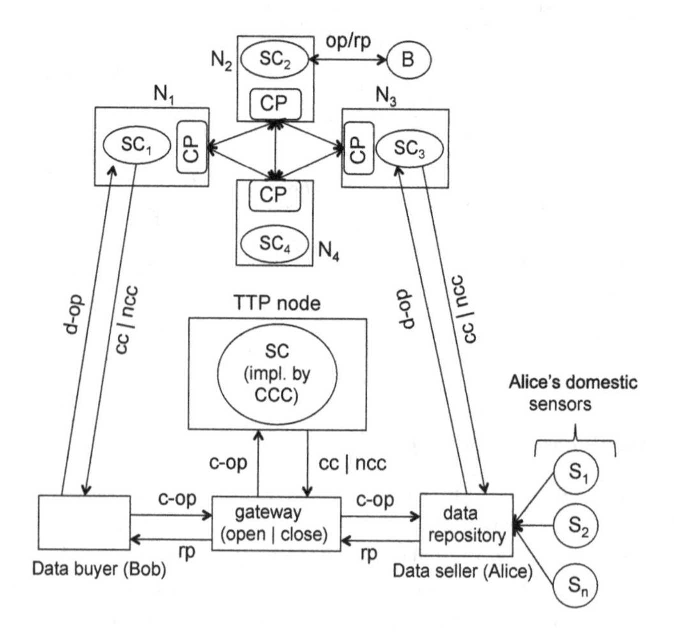

Fig. 5. Hybrid smart contract.

or the delivery of real time data) fall within this category. Another issue that impacts decentralised approaches that rely on public blockchains is the transaction fee incurred by each operation analysed by the smart contract. In this order, it would be insensible to take a decentralised implementation approach for the contract example of Sect. 2 if the data buyer was to place a large number of operations to retrieve small pieces of data under stringent time constraints.

4.3 Hybrid Implementation

Figure 5 shows the architecture of a hybrid implementation. It combines features from the centralised and decentralised approaches discussed, respectively, in Sects. 4.1 and 4.2. We separate the contractual operations into two classes: decentralised operations (*d–op*) that need blockchain support and operations that can be executed in a centralised fashion (*c–op*). *d–op* operations are encoded using the decentralised approach and enforced by the instances ($SC_1, \ldots, SC_4$) whereas operation of the *c–op* category are encoded using the centralised approach and enforced by the CCC.

The designer separates the contractual operation into *d–op* and *c–op* on the basis of several criteria. As examples, we can mention some key parameters related to the blockchain technology. The list is meant to be illustrative rather then exhaustive. Complementary advise is discussed in [9,38] where they take into account privacy concerns along with computation and data storage costs.

One decision criterion is the expressiveness of the language used for writing the contract. For instance, if the blockchain does not offer a Turing–complete language, the implementers needs to keep the *d–op* category simple. Bitcoin for example, offers only a stack–based opcode scripting language that does not support loops or flow control structures. In contrast, in a blockchain platform like Ethereum that offers a Turing–complete language the designer can afford to pass as much complexity to the decentralised part of the figure as she wishes to. Another decision criterion is the transaction fee which is an issue in private blockchains like Bitcoin and Ethereum but not in Hyperledger [37] when it is operated as a permissioned blockchain. For example, Bitcoin and Ethereum have already experienced average transaction fees of 54.90 and 4.15 USD, respectively [5]. Another central parameter to take into account is the performance of the blockchain, for example, the number of transactions per second and consistency requirements as explained in Sect. 4.2. Operations that demand strong consistency would be good candidates to be implemented as *c–op*. The performance of the blockchain is especially relevant to IoT applications where transactions must be automatically monitored to ensure that they perform under strict Quality of Service requirements. For example one could easily imagine an additional clause being added to the contract in Sect. 2 requiring the repository to process each request for data at a particular rate that would be too fast to be monitored using a smart contract deployed on a blockchain. In such a scenario, a centralised smart contract would be more logical, whereas the blockchain would be used to record important milestone events such as the sending and receipt of payments for received data. We envision that the centralised and decentralised integration can be operated in several ways, including the following:

Indelible Blockchain–Based Log. We can operate the blockchain–based part of Fig. 5 as a passive log that records events that the parties consider worth duplicating in the blockchain as well as in the TTP node. By passive we mean that $SC_1, \ldots, SC_4$ are not involved in enforcing activities—this is entirely the responsibility of the CCC. This arrangement is useful when one or more of the contracting parties is reluctant to trust the TTP blindly, say because it is deployed within the buyer's premises.

In this arrangement, the *d–op* set will include operations aimed at creating additional records while *c–op* will include all the contractual operations like in 4.1. The CCC and $SC_1, \ldots, SC_4$ operate independently from each other.

Cryptocurrency–Based Payment Channel. The data buyer of the example of Sect. 2 can take advantage of payment services offered by a public blockchain (for example, Bitcoin) and use the top part of Fig. 5 to pay in satoshis. This approach is recommended only when the payment operation is significantly larger than the transaction fees and is not repetitive. In this arrangement, the *d–op* set will include only the *send the payment* operation stipulated in clause 3. In this arrangement, the CCC requires the assistance of the smart contract running in the blockchain ($SC_1, \ldots, SC_4$) only to verify that the data buyer has fulfilled his obligation to pay. For instance, the data buyer application can submit his payment through Bitcoin, wait for the confirmation of his transaction, collect the evidence and submit it to the CCC.

Off-Blockchain Execution of Operations. In this arrangement the CCC running in the TTP node is used as an off the blockchain channel. The designer places in the *d–op* set only the contractual operations that need decentralised treatment and leaves the remaining in the *c–op*. Naturally, operations that cannot be executed in the decentralised blockchain because of the issues discussed in Sect. 4.2 need to be included in *c–op* set. A good candidate operation to place in the *d–op* set is *send the payment* (see Sect. 4.3). Another candidate is *close the repository* when the data seller wishes to generate indelible records about the closing time of her repository and completion of the contract. The remaining operations can be cheaply and efficiently enforced by the CCC, the inclusion of *place data requests* (clause 6), in the *c–op* set is highly desirable because its recurrence would incur high accumulative transaction fees.

It is worth clarifying that there are some similarities between the deployment shown in Fig. 5 and the lightning channels for executing off–blockchain payments in Bitcoin [27]. However, observe that in lighting networks the aim is to create channels for conducting micro–payment operations off the blockchain to save on transaction fees. In contrast, in Fig. 5 we use the CCC (a complete contractual enforcing tool) to execute most of the contractual operations off–blockchain.

Operations from both sets are independently converted to smart contracts and enforced at run time.

5 Related Work

An extended version of this paper can be found here [23]. Research on smart contracts was pioneered by Minsky in the mid 80s [18] and followed by Marshall [16]. Though some of the contract tools exhibit some decentralised features [17], those systems took mainly centralised approaches. Within this category falls [13,26]. To the same category belongs the model for enforcing contractual agreements suggested by IBM [15] and the Heimdhal engine [12] aimed at monitoring state obligations (see clause 5 of the contract example, *maintain the data repository accessible*). Directly related to our work is the Contract Compliant Checker reported in [22,32] which also took a centralised approach to gain in simplicity at the expense of suffering from all the drawbacks that TTPs inevitably introduce. Smart contracts were known as executable contracts or electronic contracts in [20,21,30], where the important issues of smart contract representation and verification were discussed. A pioneering implementation of a decentralised contract enforcer is discussed in [29]. The central idea is the use of a distributed middleware that is responsible for keeping indelible records of the operations executed by each party. The middleware (called Business to Business Objects [7]) is in essence an indelible ledger similar in functionality to the hyperledger used by current blockchains.

The publication of the Bitcoin paper [24] motivated the development of several platforms for supporting the implementation of decentralised smart contracts. Platforms in [2,10,34] are some of the most representative. A good summary of the features offered by these and other platforms can be found in [4]. Though they differ on language expression power, fees and other features discussed in Sect. 4.2 they are convenient for implementing decentralised smart contracts. The hybrid approach that we suggest addresses problems that neither the centralised or decentralised approach can address separately and was inspired by the off–blockchain payment channel discussed in [2,27]. Similar to our work also is Ekiden, a system for combining blockchains with Trusted Execution Environments (TEEs) [6]. The authors report significant performance improvements however they do not discuss the challenges of testing and verification hybrid smart contracts. The concept of logic–based smart contracts discussed in [14] has some similarities with our hybrid approach. They suggest the use of logic–based languages in the implementation of smart contracts capable of performing on–chain and off–chain inference. The difficulty with this approach is lack of support of logic–based languages in current blockchain technologies. In our work, we rely on the native languages offered by the blockchain platforms, for example, Ethereum's Solidity.

6 Conclusions and Future Research Directions

The central aim of this paper is to argue that conventional business contracts can be automated (at least partially) and that depending on several factors, the centralised approach suits some applications but others demand decentralised implementations or even hybrid implementations. We are only starting to explore hybrid implementation of smart contracts, yet on the basis of the study of the APIs (JSON–RPC) that Bitcoin, Ethereum and Hyperledger offer, the idea seems implementable [19]. Also, it is of practical interest as it would offer a pragmatic answer to the scalability problems that afflict current blockchain platforms. This approach opens several research questions.

An important issue is the interaction between the centralised (CCC) and decentralised components. In Fig. 5 they cannot communicate directly. We are currently working on a version of the CCC that can be deployed as a micro–service capable of interacting with the JSON-RPC Client API that blockchain technologies offer. Precisely, we are investigating how the hybrid architecture can be realised using the Ethereum blockchain and a CCC implemented as a decentralised application (DApp) [11]. The relationship (directly or indirectly) between the CCC and the blockchain raises several questions that need further investigation. They can interact directly, indirectly, tightly or loosely. Figure 5 suggests the latter where, for example, the CCC can fail and recover while the *send the payment* operation is taking place through the block–chain based smart contract (recall in Bitcoin it might take longer that 24 h to complete a transaction). However, in some applications a tight relationship might be desirable to hold or divert the progress of one of the contracts when its counterpart experiences an exception or fails. Therefore it is important to develop an understanding on how to separate the contractual operations into *c–op* and *d–op* in a manner that the two contracts collaborate instead of conflicting with each other. For contracts with scores of clauses, this issue might require the assistance of model–checking tools to ensure that the whole contractual clauses are consistent and that the two sets do not conflict with each other [28,31].

Another issue is the language for writing the contract. It is arguably accepted that declarative languages (rule based languages in particular) are more convenient than imperative languages to encode contractual clauses. This feature is enjoyed by the CCC. However, current blockchain platforms support only imperative languages (for example Ethereum's Solidity). This means that in our hybrid approach the contract will be written in two different languages which will make their interaction less intuitive. Therefore ideally blockchain platforms should support declarative languages, or alternatively developers should be offered a declarative language that can be automatically translated to languages like Solidity or Drools as needed.

Acknowledgements. Carlos Molina-Jimenez is collaborating with the HAT Community Foundation under support of Grant RG90413 NRAG/536. Ioannis Sfykaris was partly supported by the EU Horizon 2020 project PrismaCloud (https://prismacloud.eu) under GA No. 644962.

References

1. Hat: Hub-of-all-things. http://hubofallthings.com/home/. Accessed 10 Feb 2016
2. Antonopoulos, A.: Mastering Bitcoin. O'Reilly, second edn. (2017)
3. Bailis, P., Ghodsi, A.: Eventual consistency today: limitations, extensions, and beyond. ACM Queue **11**(3), 20 (2013)
4. Bartoletti, M., Pompianu, L.: An empirical analysis of smart contracts: platforms, applications, and design patterns (2017). https://arxiv.org/pdf/1703.06322.pdf
5. bitinfocharts: Cryptocurrency statistics (2018). https://bitinfocharts.com
6. Cheng, R., et al.: Ekiden: a platform for confidentiality-preserving, trustworthy, and performant smart contract execution. arXiv:1804.05141 [cs.CR] (2018)
7. Cook, N., Robinson, P., Shrivastava, S.: Component middleware to support non-repudiable service interactions. In: Proceedings of the IEEE International Conference on Dependable Systems and Networks (DSN 2004) (2004)
8. Decker, C., Seidel, J., Wattenhofer, R.: Bitcoin meets strong consistency. In: Proceedings of the 17th International Conference on Distributed Computing and Networking (ICDCN 2016) (2016)
9. Eberhardt, J., Tai, S.: On or off the blockchain? insights on off-chaining computation and data. In: (ESOCC 2017) (2017)
10. Ethereum: A next-generation smart contract and decentralized application platform (2017). https://github.com/ethereum/wiki/wiki/White-Paper. Acceepted 23 Oct 2017
11. Ethereum: Decentralized apps (dapps) (2018). https://github.com/ethereum/wiki/wiki/Decentralized-apps-(dapps)
12. Gama, P., Ribeiro, C., Ferreira, P.: Heimdhal: a history-based policy engine for grids. In: Proceedings of the 6th IEEE International Symposium on Cluster Computing and the Grid (CCGRID 2006), pp. 481–488. IEEE CS (2006)
13. Governatori, G., Milosevic, Z., Sadiq, S.: Compliance checking between business processes and business contracts. In: Proceedings of the 10th IEEE International Enterprise Distributed Object Computing Conference (EDOC 2006), pp. 221–232. IEEE Computer Society (2006)
14. Idelberger, F., Governatori, G., Riveret, R., Sartor, G.: Evaluation of logic-based smart contracts for blockchain systems. In: Alferes, J.J.J., Bertossi, L., Governatori, G., Fodor, P., Roman, D. (eds.) RuleML 2016. LNCS, vol. 9718, pp. 167–183. Springer, Cham (2016). https://doi.org/10.1007/978-3-319-42019-6_11
15. Ludwig, H., Stolze, M.: Simple obligation and right model (SORM) – for the runtime management of electronic service contracts. In: Bussler, C.J., Fensel, D., Orlowska, M.E., Yang, J. (eds.) WES 2003. LNCS, vol. 3095, pp. 62–76. Springer, Heidelberg (2004). https://doi.org/10.1007/978-3-540-25982-4_7
16. Marshall, L.F.: Representing management policy using contract objects. In: Proceedings of the IEEE First International Workshop on Systems Management, pp. 27–30 (1993)
17. Minsky, N.: A model for the governance of federated healthcare information systems. In: IEEE International Symposium on Policies for Distributed Systems and Networks (Policy 2010) (2010)
18. Minsky, N.H., Lockman, A.D.: Ensuring integrity by adding obligations to privileges. In: Proceedings of the 8th International Conference on Software Engineering, pp. 92–102 (1985)
19. Molina-Jimenez, C., Sfyrakis, I., Solaiman, E., Ng, I., Wong, M.W., Chun, A., Crowcroft, J.: Implementation of smart contracts using hybrid architectures with on-and off-blockchain components. arXiv:1808.00093 [cs.SE] (2018)

20. Molina-Jimenez, C., Shrivastava, S., Solaiman, E., Warne, J.: Contract representation for run-time monitoring and enforcement. In: IEEE International Conference on E-Commerce (CEC 2003) (2003)
21. Molina-Jimenez, C., Shrivastava, S., Solaiman, E., Warne, J.: Run-time monitoring and enforcement of electronic contracts. Electron. Commer. Res. Appl. **3**(2), 108–125 (2004)
22. Molina-Jimenez, C., Shrivastava, S., Strano, M.: A model for checking contractual compliance of business interactions. IEEE Trans. Serv. Comput. **PP**(99) (2011)
23. Molina-Jimenez, C., Solaiman, E., Sfyrakis, I., Ng, I., Crowcroft, J.: On and off-blockchain enforcement of smart contracts. arXiv preprint arXiv:1805.00626, May 2018
24. Nakamoto, S.: Bitcoin: a peer-to-peer electronic cash system (2008). http://nakamotoinstitute.org/bitcoin/. Accessed 13 Nov 2017
25. O'Hara, K.: Smart contracts-dumb idea. IEEE Internet Comput. **21**(2), 101 (2017)
26. Perrin, O., Godart, C.: An approach to implement contracts as trusted intermediaries. In: Proceedings of the 1st IEEE International Workshop on Electronic Contracting (WEC 2004), pp. 71–78 (2004)
27. Poon, J., Dryja, T.: The bitcoin lightning network: scalable off-chain instant payments, January 2016. https://lightning.network/lightning-network-paper.pdf
28. Sergey, I., Kumar, A., Hobor, A.: Scilla: a smart contract intermediate-level language: automata for smart contract implementation and verification, January 2018. https://arxiv.org/abs/1801.00687
29. Shrivastava, S.: An overview of the tapas architecture. http://tapas.sourceforge.net/deliverables/D5Extra.pdf, January 2005. supplement Delivery of the TAPAS (Trusted and QoS-Aware Provision of Application Services) IST Project No: IST-2001-34069
30. Solaiman, E., Molina-Jimenez, C., Shrivastav, S.: Model checking correctness properties of electronic contracts. In: Orlowska, M.E., Weerawarana, S., Papazoglou, M.P., Yang, J. (eds.) ICSOC 2003. LNCS, vol. 2910, pp. 303–318. Springer, Heidelberg (2003). https://doi.org/10.1007/978-3-540-24593-3_21
31. Solaiman, E., Sfyrakis, I., Molina-Jimenez, C.: High level model checker based testing of electronic contracts. In: Helfert, M., Méndez Muñoz, V., Ferguson, D. (eds.) CLOSER 2015. CCIS, vol. 581, pp. 193–215. Springer, Cham (2016). https://doi.org/10.1007/978-3-319-29582-4_11
32. Solaiman, E., Sfyrakis, I., Molina-Jimenez, C.: A state aware model and architecture for the monitoring and enforcement of electronic contracts. In: Proceedings of the IEEE 18th Conference on Business Informatics (CBI 2016) (2016)
33. Szabo, N.: Smart contracts: formalizing and securing relationships on public networks. First Monday **2**(9), September 1997
34. The Linux Foundation: Hyperledger (2017). www.hyperledger.org. Accessed Nov 2017
35. HATDex: Rumpel Platform (2018). http://www.hatdex.org/rumpel-platform/
36. Vukolić, M.: The quest for scalable blockchain fabric: proof-of-work vs. BFT replication. In: Camenisch, J., Kesdoğan, D. (eds.) iNetSec 2015. LNCS, vol. 9591, pp. 112–125. Springer, Cham (2016). https://doi.org/10.1007/978-3-319-39028-4_9
37. Wörner, D., von Bomhard, T.: When your sensor earns money: exchanging data for cash with bitcoin. In: Proceedings of the ACM International Joint Conference on Pervasive and Ubiquitous Computing (UbiComp 2014) (2014)
38. Zyskind, G., Nathan, O., Pentland, A.S.: Enigma: decentralized computation platform with guaranteed privacy. Tech. Report arXiv:1506.03471v1 [cs.CR], arXiv.org, January 2015

MaRSChain: Framework for a Fair Manuscript Review System Based on Permissioned Blockchain

Nitesh Emmadi(✉), Lakshmi Padmaja Maddali, and Sumanta Sarkar

TCS Innovation Labs, Hyderabad, India
{nitesh.emmadi1,lakshmipadmaja.maddali,sumanta.sarkar1}@tcs.com

Abstract. Current Manuscript Review Systems (Conference/Journal) rely on a centralized services (like EasyChair, iChair, HotCRP or EDAS), which manage the whole process that starts with manuscript submissions to notification of the results. As these review systems are centralized, the trust is based on a single entity. The fairness of the system hinges on the honesty of the central controlling authority. This dependency can be avoided by decentralizing the source of the trust. Bitcoin has shown the power of decentralization and shared database through blockchain technology, and currently is being studied for its immense impact on FinTech. We leverage blockchain to address the above concern and present a decentralized manuscript review system that provides trust and fairness. We call this system MaRSChain. As a proof of concept, we develop a prototype of MaRSChain system on top of Hyperledger Fabric platform. To the best of our knowledge, this is the first ever decentralized manuscript review system based on Blockchain.

Keywords: Manuscript review system · Blockchain
Consensus · Fairness · Trust · Smart contract

1 Introduction

Ever since the cryptocurrency Bitcoin [16] has shown the application of blockchain technology that rules out the need of central authority, it has drawn attention from both the industry and academia. Blockchain enables mutually distrusting parties form a peer to peer distributed network and maintain a common transaction ledger. A typical blockchain as in Bitcoin does not need verified identity of a peer, i.e., it is an open enrollment system. In other words it is a permission-less blockchain. Research has been carried out to embrace Blockchain's decentralization feature in several applications ranging from finance [10], supply chain [9], IoT [18], and to many other business use cases. A report by world economic forum predicted that 10% of global GDP would be stored on blockchain technology by 2025 [1]. The idea of permission-less blockchain may not be suitable for many enterprise applications, like banks, which require

G. Mencagli et al. (Eds.): Euro-Par 2018 Workshops, LNCS 11339, pp. 355–366, 2019.
https://doi.org/10.1007/978-3-030-10549-5_28

their users to be verified. To cater to this kind of applications, we need a permissioned model of blockchain, for example, Hyperledger Fabric [5]. With this permissioned blockchain many centralized services can be decentralized, which is now being explored. In this paper we focus on the applicability of permissioned blockchain to build a decentralized conference management system.

A conference management system (for example, EasyChair [2], EDAS [3], HotCRP [4] or iChair [7])[1] handles the life-cycle of a conference from manuscript submissions to acceptance/rejection notification. A conference program committee, first invites manuscripts for reviews and assigns the manuscripts to reviewers for evaluation. Based on the evaluations submitted by the reviewers, the conference program chairs decide on the manuscript acceptance. The accepted papers are invited for publication in the conference proceedings. Current systems are flexible, easy to use and have many features that make them powerful event managers for conducting international conferences. However, they are centralized services, thereby giving the hosting entity full control of the system. A malicious party in control of the system can manipulate decisions and results impacting fairness of the system. For instance, the controlling entity can assign papers to reviewers of his choice and hamper the fairness of reviews, or can change the results in the system. To address the above challenges, we propose a decentralized framework for fair manuscript review system based on permissioned blockchain. A conference review system is an application operating in controlled environment that employs parties with verified identities i.e., authors, reviewers, program chairs. Hence, a permissioned model of blockchain is suitable in case of applications where the distrusting parties involved have verified identities [15].

1.1 Related Work

Apart from the widely used conference management systems (such as EasyChair, EDAS, HotCRP or iChair), other notable systems are ConfiChair [13], P3ERS [12] and CryptSubmit [14]. ConfiChair proposes an architecture to build conference management systems in a privacy preserving manner in order to protect the privacy of entities (authors/reviewers/Program Chairs(PCs)) against untrusted cloud service providers. It preserves privacy and confidentiality using encryption mechanisms with key translations and mixes. P3ERS (Privacy Preserving Peer Review System) is a distributed peer review system with several group managers. P3ERS preserves privacy of all the users in the system with an improved group signature scheme. P3ERS considers an untrusted cloud service provider and actors within the system as potential adversaries and proposes a distributed architecture to host different services on different servers. It ensures privacy of authors and reviewers from PCs by creating separate services for them. These systems are still centralized and address privacy concerns within the conference system.

[1] EasyChair, EDAS and HotCRP are third party services whereas iChair is an open-source software that can be hosted by any of the program chairs of a forum.

*MaRSChain is listed in Hyperledger's inventory of usecases [6].

CryptSubmit proposes a manuscript review system with timestamped submissions and reviews. In this system, the hash of the submissions and reviews are timestamped on the public Bitcoin blockchain that lies outside the actual review system, still keeping the actual review system centralized. The manuscripts are timestamped outside the system and the review system does not guarantee proof of manuscript or review submissions into the system.

Centralized systems do not guarantee security against single point of failure and hence there is a need for decentralized manuscript review system. In this regard, we propose MaRSChain, a decentralized solution where the actual review process is done on the blockchain. Decentralization ensures that a malicious entity can not corrupt the system to modify/remove submissions and reviews from the system. Our solution aims to improve trust in the system by leveraging blockchain to decentralize the system. This is the first ever manuscript review system based on blockchain.

1.2 Our Contribution

In this paper, we propose MaRSChain, a framework to build a manuscript review system based on a permissioned blockchain. We leverage Hyperledger Fabric [5], a permissioned blockchain platform, to build our system. MaRSChain can be built on top of any permissioned blockchain platform which provides features described in this paper. We employ several smart contracts to handle submissions and reviews, validation of submissions and consolidation of reviews. In the usual centralized conference management systems, the PCs have immense power and control over the system. A malicious PC can manipulate reviewer assignments or can modify/remove reviews and etc.

MaRSChain promises:

- **Security against manipulation of manuscript reviewers assignment:** In a centralized system, a malicious PC can assign a manuscript to reviewers of his choice, in order to hamper the fairness of reviews. A decentralized solution ensures that a malicious PC can not manipulate the reviewers assignment.
- **Security against manipulation of manuscript reviews:** In a centralized system, a malicious PC can manipulate the reviews to influence the acceptance/rejection of a manuscript. Decentralization guarantees that a malicious party in the system can not manipulate reviews.
- **Confidentiality and privacy of manuscript submissions and reviews:** A permissioned blockchain employs encryption and pseudonymous identities along with access controls to better preserve confidentiality and privacy of the authors/reviewers.

2 System Overview

A conference/journal forum forms a peer-to-peer network of blockchain nodes. We refer to this blockchain network as Conference Blockchain (CBC). The entities in a CBC are listed below:

- Authors
- Reviewers
- Program Chairs

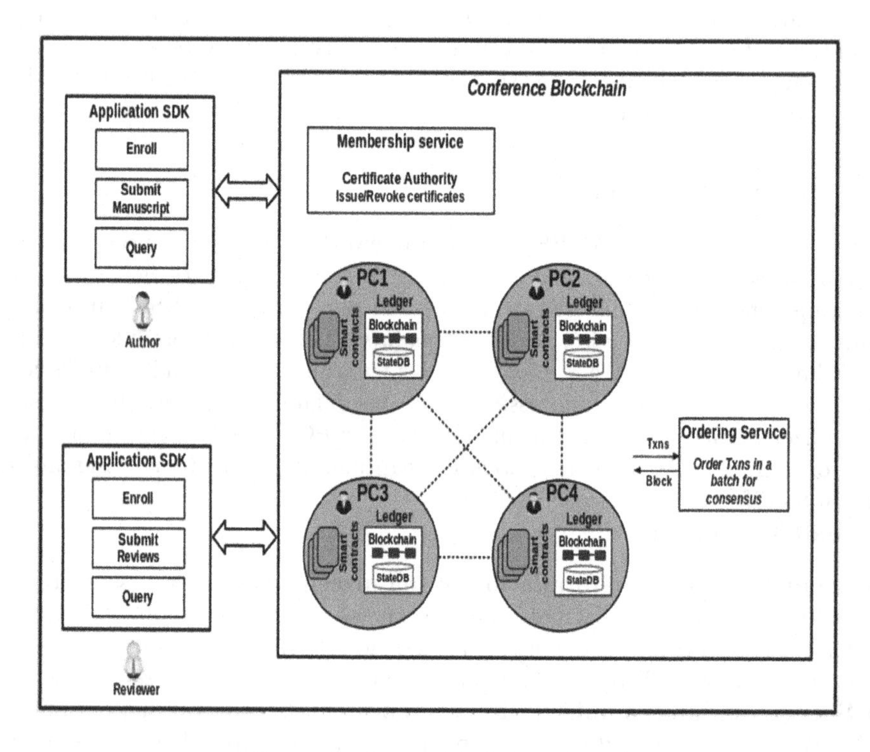

Fig. 1. Conference blockchain (CBC)

All the entities in CBC Blockchain are registered into the network by Membership Service. The Membership Service hosts a Certificate Authority that is responsible for issuing/revoking certificates to the entities. These certificates are identities of the entities and are used to transact on the blockchain ledger. Authors and Reviewers are end-users in the blockchain network. Users submitting manuscripts to the conference are authors. Reviewers review manuscripts submitted by the authors. PCs are the validating entities that are responsible for manuscript validation, reviewers assignment and reviews consolidation.

Operational Flow: A conference blockchain can be visualized as in Fig. 1. Below, we describe the operational flow of our system.

1. Manuscript Submission. All the inputs to the blockchain systems are signed transactions which are recorded in the blockchain. Authors submit their manuscripts to a conference as signed transactions. On receiving the manuscript transactions, the PC nodes in a CBC validate the transactions against submission policy (semantics, duplicates, signatures). If the transactions are valid, then the manuscripts are accepted by the conference for review and are recorded onto the blockchain ledger.

2. Reviewers Assignment. Once the manuscript acceptance window is closed, the PCs reach consensus on assigning the submitted manuscripts to reviewers for evaluation. For ease of implementation, we assume that this consensus is an offline process and all the PCs have agreed to the decision on reviewers assignment. A PC initiates the reviewer assignment transaction based on their decision for each of the manuscripts. All these transactions are validated by the PCs and their consensus reflects their agreement on reviewers assignments.

3. Review Submission. Reviewers evaluate the assigned manuscripts and submit their evaluations to the system in the form of transactions. Reviewers' evaluation transactions are validated by the PC nodes and the evaluations are updated in the system. An evaluation is a score awarded to the manuscript by the reviewer along with justifications (comments).

4. Results Declaration. Once the review window is closed and the reviews are received, the PCs consolidate the evaluation scores of each of the submissions and updates the results of the submissions. These scores reflect the decision of the conference. These scores and results are then notified to the authors.

3 Security of Our System

In this section, we describe security guarantees of our system.

3.1 Security Against Manipulation of Reviewers Assignment

In a centralized system, a malicious PC can affect the fairness of the reviews by assigning the manuscripts to reviewers of his choice in order to get his desired evaluation result. Consider a malicious PC submits a reviewers assignment transaction with the manipulated reviewers assignment to the system. The transaction submitted by malicious PC goes through consensus where each of the other PCs validate the transaction. A malicious assignment can easily be detected by the other PCs and the transaction is rejected during the consensus. This ensures protection against unfair reviewers assignment. The consensus algorithm ensures that a malicious PC can not influence reviewers assignment at his will without corrupting some other PCs.

3.2 Security Against Forgery or System Corruption

We assume that a malicious PC member is trying to manipulate review evaluations to impact the decision on a manuscript. This can be done either by forging review transactions of the reviewers or by corrupting all the PC nodes to exclude certain review transactions.

Consider a malicious PC member as an adversary trying to manipulate the review of a manuscript. To do so, the adversary has to do one of the following: forge signatures of reviewers or exclude reviews from ledger. The reviewers submit a review transaction digitally signed by reviewer's private key which is securely stored at his end. Security of a digital signature scheme ensures that a signature is very hard to be forged. Hence, protection against forgery is ensured. Excluding the review of a manuscript from the ledger either by denying the reviewers' transaction or by re-writing the ledger is one of the ways for the adversary to manipulate the review. Decentralized system coupled with consensus ensures that a single malicious party can not influence the system. The consensus algorithm ensures that a malicious PC can not force reviews exclusion without corrupting other PCs.

The digital signature schemes and secure consensus mechanisms ensure protection against malicious PCs. Hence, security against manipulation of reviews is guaranteed.

3.3 Privacy and Confidentiality of Authors and Reviewers

All the users in the blockchain network submit transactions to the system which are validated and recorded into a common ledger. In MaRSChain, an author can monitor transactions from other authors or reviewers and their review assignments. However, for fair reviews, the forums encourage anonymous submissions and blind reviews. Lack of information about the authors limits unwarranted behavior of reviewers in evaluation of manuscripts. Hence, privacy and confidential of data on blockchain is necessary.

Privacy of the users in blockchain can be viewed in two forms: Anonymity and Unlinkability. Anonymity of transaction refers to hiding of the a user's identity in an anonymity set of all the users i.e., an identity on the ledger should not directly be associated to particular user. Unlinkability refers to the association of multiple transactions of a single user i.e., two different transactions from a same user should not be related to each other. For anonymity and unlinkability, MaRSChain provides one-time pseudonymous identities to the users. All the transactions submitted to the blockchain are under pseudonymous identities. Thus, a transaction on the blockchain ledger can neither be linked to the user directly nor to other transaction by the same user. Only authorized parties (PCs) with the knowledge of a secret have the ability to link pseudonymous identity on the blockchain to the actual identity of the user.

To enable confidentiality of the transactions, a MaRSChain encrypts transaction payloads with one-time symmetric keys. The symmetric keys are only available to the users themselves and other authorized parties in the network

(PC nodes). Hence, an unauthorized adversary can not decrypt the transactions without the knowledge of secret key. Furthermore, access-control mechanisms that restrict access to transaction payloads provide another layer of security for the transactions.

Therefore, MaRSChain guarantees privacy and confidentiality of transactions.

4 Implementation

We develop a prototype of our MaRSChain system on top of Hyperledger Fabric platform (version 1.1.0-preview). We simulate various steps of a conference management system to illustrate the system operational flow Fig. 2. We remark that a MaRSChain system can be built on top of any permissioned blockchain platform. Note that our implementation assumes the program chairs decide offline on reviewers assignment. However, the final decision is recorded on the blockchain based on consensus. If the reviewer assignment transaction differs from the actually decided offline agreement, then the program chairs can easily detect and reject the transaction. This is to enable ease of implementation. This process can be made online, yet note that, this is off-chain process and only the final decision is recorded on the blockchain. Our blockchain system is instantiated with four PC nodes and the consensus requires majority of the nodes i.e., 3 out of 4 nodes, to endorse a transaction (refer Appendix B for more details).

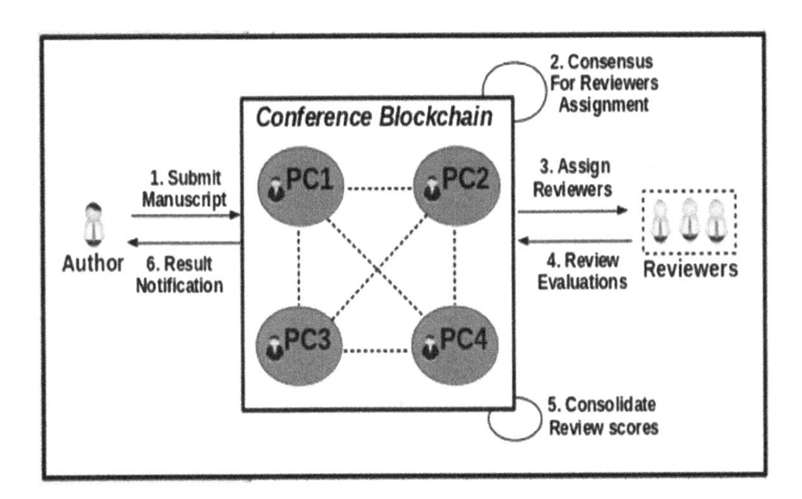

Fig. 2. CBC implementation flow

4.1 CBC Chaincode

In Hyperledger Fabric, the smart contracts are realized in chaincode that is deployed on the blockchain by peers. In this section, we describe various functionalities in our chaincode:

- ***submit_paper:*** Authors submit manuscripts by using client application to invoke *submit_paper.*

1: Manuscript submission to forum

Transaction: CBC_Submit_Txn=(*manuscript*, *author pseudonyms*)
Validation: Check if manuscript is already submitted to this forum
if *manuscript is present in the ledger* **then**
| *duplicate submission*; *rejected*
else
| *considered for submission*; *submitted*
end

- ***assign_reviewers:*** Once the manuscript submission window is closed, PCs decide on the reviewers assignment, one of the PCs invoke the *assign_reviewers* for each of the manuscripts to assign reviewers.

2: Reviewers Assignment

Transaction: CBC_Update_ReviewersList_Txn=(*manuscript_id*, *reviewers_list*)
Validation: Check if reviewers list is acceptable(as decided by program committee)
if *manuscript reviewers list is acceptable* **then**
| *update reviewers list for manuscript in CBC*
else
| *reject transaction*
end

- ***submit_review:*** Reviewers evaluate the assigned manuscripts and submit reviews by invoking *submit_review* through client application.

3: Review submission to forum

Transaction: CBC_Reviewer_Txn=(*manuscript_id*, *review_pseudonym_id*, *review*, *score*)
Validation: Check if review is submitted by assigned reviewer
if *reviewer in reviewers list* **then**
| *update review and score for manuscript*
else
| *reject transaction*
end

- ***make_decision:*** Once the review window is closed and the reviews are received, the PCs consolidate the reviews for each of the manuscripts by invoking *make_decision.*

4: Consolidate reviews of manuscripts

Transaction: CBC_Reviews_Consolidate_Txn=(*manuscripts*)
Validation: Check if manuscript status is "under-review"
for *all reviewedmanuscripts in CBC* **do**
    paper_final_score = (reviewer1_score + reviewer2_score + reviewer3_score)/3
    update manuscript final score in CBC;
    if *paper_final_score>3* **then**
        status updated to "accepted" in CBC
    else
        status updated to "rejected" in CBC
    end
end

- ***querySubmittedPaperInfo:*** Details of a submitted manuscript can be queried using *querySubmittedPaperInfo*.
- ***queryAllPaperIDs:*** List of all the manuscripts can be viewed using *queryAllPaperIDs*.
- ***queryPaperStatus:*** Status of a manuscript can be queried with *queryPaperStatus*.

The transactions corresponding to all the above functionalities can be seen in Appendix.

Our current implementation does not handle manuscript/review updations that are common in currently available review systems. Also, it is a common practice to re-consider acceptance/rejection of manuscripts with borderline threshold reviews. These features can be handled by introducing update transactions that can be linked to already submitted manuscript/review/decision.

Our system will be available in Hyperledger Fabric's Inventory of Usecases [6]. A detailed document describing the whole setup and other instructions will be available along with the implementation.

5 Conclusions and Discussions

We have proposed a framework to build a fair decentralized manuscript review system based on blockchain (MaRSChain). Our decentralized system ensures that a malicious party can not corrupt the system to hamper fairness of review process. As part of our future work, we plan to integrate a reputation system to strengthen MaRSChain further.

Another important problem in current conference management systems is to detect *double submissions* (plagiarism) and *concurrent submissions* (submission of a manuscript to multiple forums concurrently, during the review period) [17]. The current systems rely on some trusted third party services, for example iThenticate [8], to detect double submissions. iThenticate has access to publication content from several different publishers. It performs a "Similarity Check" [11] to check for plagiarism of the submissions i.e., double submission detection. To do this, a submission is compared against public domain data and a database of current and archived publications from publishing houses. As these services are centralized, the root of trust hinges solely on them. Therefore, double submissions can only be detected effectively as long as this third party is honest. Moreover, as the content of a submitted manuscript in a conference is not public, it is not possible to check concurrent submissions.

The nature of these problems is similar to "double spending" problem in cryptocurrencies. Cryptocurrencies handle double spending by enforcing a common ledger for all the miners to check against. This idea can be invoked in the conference systems too to detect double and concurrent submissions, i.e., we can enforce a common database of all publications from all the publishing houses. This database also includes the publications currently under review at all the conferences associated with the member publishing houses. Hence, whenever a manuscript is submitted to a conference, it can be compared with the list of manuscripts in this database to detect double and concurrent submissions. This effectively eliminates dependence on third party services for detecting double submission and also detects concurrent submission. However, the burden of maintaining huge database of publications makes this solution difficult to realize.

Acknowledgements. We would like to thank Vigneswaran R for his inputs towards the development of our system.

Appendix A CBC Transactions

Hyperledger Fabric supports chaincode execution through "*query*" and "*invoke*". A *query* is a chaincode execution which reads from the ledger but does not write into the ledger. Whereas, an *invoke* is capable of both, reading and writing. *invoke* transactions will be captured as transactions on blockchain. Here is the list of invoke and query transactions from our MaRSChain implementation:

- ***C*BC_Submit_Txn:**
  peer chaincode invoke -o 127.0.0.1:7050 -C CBC_Channel -n CBC_CC -c '{"Args":["submit_paper", "author1","author2", "author3","attach_01"]}'
- ***C*BC_Reviewer_Assignment_Txn:**
  peer chaincode invoke -o 127.0.0.1:7050 -C CBC_Channel -n CBC_CC -c '{"Args":["assign_reviewers", "paper_id","reviewer1", "reviewer2","reviewer3"]}'
- ***C*BC_Review_Txn:**
  peer chaincode invoke -o 127.0.0.1:7050 -C CBC_Channel -n CBC_CC -c '{"Args":["submit_review", "reviewer1","paper_id","rating"]}'
- ***C*BC_Reviewes_Consolidate_Txn:**
  peer chaincode invoke -o 127.0.0.1:7050 -C CBC_Channel -n CBC_CC -c '{"Args":["make_decision"]}'
- ***C*BC_Query_Manuscript_Txn:**
  peer chaincode query -o 127.0.0.1:7050 -C CBC_Channel -n CBC_CC -c '{"Args": ["querySubmittedPaperInfo", "paper_id"]}'
- ***C*BC_Query_Manuscripts_List_Txn:**
  peer chaincode query -o 127.0.0.1:7050 -C CBC_Channel -n CBC_CC -c '{"Args": ["queryAllPaperIDs"]}'
- ***C*BC_Query_Manuscript_Status_Txn:**
  peer chaincode query -o 127.0.0.1:7050 -C CBC_Channel -n CBC_CC -c '{"Args": ["queryPaperStatus", "paper_id"]}'

Appendix B Endorsement Policy

The classical blockchain systems relied on *order-execute architecture*, where the ordered transactions are executed by the peers sequentially. This has a drawback of decreased throughput. The current Hyperledger Fabric (v1.0.0+) employs *execute-order-validate architecture* to parallelize the validation of transactions by the peers. A transaction is executed by the peers in parallel and the result of the execution is provided as an endorsement to the user. The user collects and sends all the endorsements to the committers through an orderer. The committers validate the endorsements based on an endorsement policy(m out of n signatures) before committing the transactions into the ledger. Our implementation assumes a total of 4 PCs(3t+1), tolerating 1 malicious PC. Hence, our endorsement policy mandates 3 out of 4 endorsements for any transaction. The endorsement policy from our implementation can be seen below:

5: CBC Endorsement Policy

```
var epolicy = {
identities: [
{ role: { name: "member", mspId: "PC1MSP" }},
{ role: { name: "member", mspId: "PC2MSP" }},
{ role: { name: "member", mspId: "PC3MSP" }},
{ role: { name: "member", mspId: "PC4MSP" }}
],
policy: {
"3-of": [{ "signed-by": 0 }, { "signed-by": 1 }, { "signed-by": 2 }, { "signed-by": 3 }]
}
};
```

References

1. Deep Shift- Technology Tipping Points and Societal Impact. http://www3.weforum.org/docs/WEF_GAC15_Technological_Tipping_Points_report_2015.pdf
2. EasyChair. http://easychair.org/
3. EDAS. https://edas.info/
4. HotCRP. https://hotcrp.com/
5. Hyperledger Fabric. https://www.hyperledger.org/projects/fabric
6. Hyperledger Use Case Inventory. https://wiki.hyperledger.org/groups/requirements/use-case-inventory
7. iChair. https://www.baigneres.net/ichair/
8. iThenticate. http://www.ithenticate.com/
9. Provenance. https://www.provenance.org/whitepaper
10. Ripple. https://ripple.com/
11. Similarity Check. https://www.crossref.org/services/similarity-check/
12. Aïmeur, E., Brassard, G., Gambs, S., Schönfeld, D.: P3ers: privacy-preserving peer review system. Trans. Data Privacy, pp. 553–578 (2012). http://dl.acm.org/citation.cfm?id=2423656.2423659

13. Arapinis, M., Bursuc, S., Ryan, M.: Privacy supporting cloud computing: confichair, a case study. In: Proceedings of the First International Conference on Principles of Security and Trust. pp. 89–108 (2012). https://doi.org/10.1007/978-3-642-28641-4_6
14. Gipp, B., Breitinger, C., Meuschke, N., Beel, J.: Cryptsubmit: introducing securely timestamped manuscript submission and peer review feedback using the blockchain. In: Proceedings of the 17th ACM/IEEE Joint Conference on Digital Libraries. pp. 273–276 (2017). http://dl.acm.org/citation.cfm?id=3200334.3200370
15. Karl, W., Arthur, G.: Do you need a blockchain. https://eprint.iacr.org/2017/375.pdf
16. Nakmoto, S.: Bitcoin: a peer-to-peer electronic cash system (2008)
17. Schulzrinne, H.: Double submissions: publishing misconduct or just effective dissemination? SIGCOMM Comput. Commun. Rev. pp. 40–42 (2009). https://doi.org/10.1145/1568613.1568622
18. Shafagh, H., Burkhalter, L., Hithnawi, A., Duquennoy, S.: Towards blockchain-based auditable storage and sharing of iot data. In: Proceedings of the 2017 on Cloud Computing Security Workshop, pp. 45–50 (2017). https://doi.org/10.1145/3140649.3140656

Tamper-Proof Volume Tracking in Supply Chains with Smart Contracts

Ulrich Gallersdörfer(✉) and Florian Matthes

Technical University Munich, Arcisstraße 21, 80333 Munich, Germany
ulrich.gallersdoerfer@tum.de

Abstract. Complex supply chains involve many different stakeholders such as producers, traders, manufacturers, and consumers. These entities comprise companies and other stakeholders spanning different countries or continents. Depending on the involved goods, the origin and the responsible harvesting of these elements are essential. Due to their high complexity, these systems enable the introduction of resources with forged identity, tricking the participants of the supply chain into believing that they acquire goods with specific properties, e.g., environmentally friendly wood or resources which are not the result of child labor. We derive requirements from the global world trade of timber and timer-based products, in which the origin of a large portion of certified wood cannot be verified. A set of smart contracts deployed within the Ethereum platform allows for a transparent supply chain with validated sources. The platform enables the tracking of variations of the original good, tracing not only the raw material but also the resulting products. The proposed solution introduces a novel exchange contract and ensures a correct overall volume of assets managed in the supply chain.

Keywords: Blockchain · Volume tracking · Ethereum
Smart contracts · Supply chain · Logistics

1 Introduction

The manufacturing of products of daily use such as furniture or work material is the result of complex supply chains, involving multiple steps of different entities in the respective systems. Usually, mining facilities produce the raw materials for these products. These entities sell the resource, either with or without intermediaries to other manufacturers which purify the raw materials or create base components for further value creation. The process is repeated for each manufacturing step until a final product is being sold to end-customers. These procedures are time-consuming and tedious as a large number of stakeholders is involved [19].

Customers have high demands on products of their desire [4]. Not only should the product satisfy their needs in terms of functionality, design or appearance, but also the production should only involve environmentally friendly components and must avoid exploitation of child labor or unreasonably low wages [11].

G. Mencagli et al. (Eds.): Euro-Par 2018 Workshops, LNCS 11339, pp. 367–378, 2019.
https://doi.org/10.1007/978-3-030-10549-5_29

If their desires are satisfied, the willingness to pay for these products increases [17]. However, these requirements pose difficulties for some manufacturers. Due to their extensive network of suppliers, they often cannot verify the information they receive about incoming resources, leaving them unaware of any manipulations, fraud, or mislabeling [7]. As their customers are willing to pay more for environmentally sound products, they have an intrinsic interest in the production of such assets and therefore in a method to trace the origin of their base materials.

Other entities involved in the process also have an interest in removing fraudulent entities in the supply chain. Honest producers of base resources suffer from the introduction of intentionally mis-labeled goods on the market. Independent of the demand, a decrease of the overall supply could lead to higher market prices, increasing the profits of the original producers. Also, the society emphasizes the importance of environmentally sound and employee-friendly manufacturing and production of goods [3].

Blockchain technology promises to solve problems in the supply-chain industry [9]. A Blockchain network consists out of many interconnected computers which share a common state of a ledger [16]. The entities in the system define the rules for changing the state and appending new information to the ledger. As of the absence of a central entity, there is no way to forge or delete information afterward. As of these properties, the system can be used for creating decentralized currencies like Bitcoin [12] or individual Smart Contracts with platforms like Ethereum [20]. These contracts are software programs which are deployed and executed on the Blockchain. After the deployment, these contracts cannot be changed, assuring their integrity.

Many companies consider individual Smart Contracts as an opportunity to digitize supply chains and the involved goods. Companies such as Maersk [5] have already created concepts of Smart Contracts to trace the contents and ownership of containers transported by ships. These proposals focus on the digitalization of business processes, like the digitalization of the receipt of ownership, which does not fit with the above-stated problem. Other approaches like Everledger [10] do not cover the possibility of a good to be manipulated. We derive our requirements and goals of a use case we describe in following.

The supply chain we consider includes the group of enterprises and companies which harvest, trade and process resources made of wood from forests from different countries. The aim of the supply chain is the production of goods such as furniture or charcoal, generally speaking everything that can be made out of wood. Wood itself is often certified by authorities (such as the UN [14]) or NGOs (such as NEPCon [13]) which ensure that the wood originates from sustainable forests. In theory, these certifications ensure that only sustainable wood enters the supply chain. However, the chain itself is highly complex: Many different stakeholders are involved, the trading routes are opaque and it is very difficult to keep track of the flow of goods. The origin of the base resource wood is often non-transparent or fabricated, leaving manufacturers in the dark about the materials they use. Malicious entities in the system use these factors to introduce wood into the system without the required certification. This leads to a higher overall output of certified wood in contrast to the lower maximum volume that is allowed to be produced. Studies show that the volume of uncertified wood from certain regions increased over 50% [6]. This increased volume is the main problem in the supply chain. We derive our requirements from this specific case for our system.

One other paper gives a sound overview about the problem in timber tracking and discusses these issues [2]. The authors propose a Blockchain-based solution, writing each transportation operation in the Blockchain. They also outline possible limiting factors regarding the technology.

In this paper we propose a smart contract system enabling the participants of a supply chain to agree on

- the entities that are allowed to take part in the system
- the specification of the resources, products or goods handled on the supply chain
- the exchange rate between two types of resources
- how entities are selected for issuing new resources

while ensuring that

- no party can create a token/good if it has not the right to
- no resource, product or good can be spent twice
- the overall created volume remains the same when handed through the supply chain.

The system is implemented with Solidity for the platform Ethereum. We are confident that implementations in any other Blockchain platform supporting smart contracts are feasible, as the theoretical considerations remain constant.

After describing the various problems of the selected supply chain in detail in Sect. 2, we introduce the design of the system including the users and smart contracts involved in Sect. 3. We further discuss the processes and propose a bootstrapping mechanism. In Sect. 4 we discuss the limitations and the applicability of our proposed solution and end with an conclusion in Sect. 5.

2 Problem Statement

First, we introduce why a centralized approach under the supervision of NGOs or regulators is not feasible. Afterwards, common problems of traditional Blockchain-based solutions for supply chains are outlined. We describe the technical layout of the implementation, as it is important to understand the objective of the proposed solution.

2.1 Centralized Platform Issues

As there are already NGOs and governments in place that validate forest owners for a sustainable and environmentally-friendly approach, one might ask why these regulations do not prevent the introduction of mis-labeled materials? The problem is that only the producers itself are validated and the information provided by them can be validated very easily. Forests can be measured and an estimation gives a good indicator if the entity under validation is cheating. For intermediaries, this process is much harder, as the information itself can easily be tampered with without a convenient way to verify it. This imbalance leads to the possibility to introduce uncertified goods into the supply chain. Therefore, a digitalized system has to be put in place to track these streams and prevent the introduction of illegal resources.

A platform for a tamper-proof tracking and issuing of goods and resources is suited. However, it is the question if this platform should be run by a single entity or shared among all participants. There are different reasons against a centralized approach: The central authority is a worthwhile goal for attacks, as its shutdown paralyzes the system or renders the attacker able to manipulate account balances. These risks can be minimized, but one other issue remains: The missing trust in the central authority (CA) [8]. As there are many different entities which would qualify for this position, it would be impossible to agree on one entity because of the different interests of stakeholders. The CA could easily track every asset, could block single users or unilaterally introduce changes to the system. As of this, entities in the system are not interested in a centralized approach. As of that, we propose a decentralized system in which decisions are transparent.

2.2 Technical Issues

The overall goal is to propose a platform that enables to track assets and prove a valid origin. The platform is designed to be decentralized and governed only by its entities, however in many decentralized applications a proportion of centralism remains. A supply chain handles individual goods. Each and every asset transported in the supply chain could be identified by specific characteristics: Entities trace goods via serial number or specific material structures such as a DNA. However, these assumptions sometimes cannot be applied, as producers face different problems:

Combination of Different Goods. The combination or separation of goods leads, on a data level, to a creation of new good(s) and the destruction of old good(s). It is important to define the boundaries and rules for these processes, because if they are undefined, these procedure could lead to the creation of valid resources out of thin air on data level. Other questions arise: Which entity defines the new serial number of the defined product? Is it possible to sufficiently store all data associated with one single product, possibly comprising out of arbitrary amount of sub-products, goods and resources?

Loss of Information. In real world, the products or goods can lose the information that identifies them. This rarely happens to finished products at the end of manufacturing process, however it is possible that the association between two single goods (a base product and a manufactured product) gets lost as it is too costly to validate which base product was processed to a manufactured product. The information can also be lost as of the manufacturing process itself. Regular wood loses its DNA sequence when burned to produce coal. On a technical level, it is impossible to ensure the integrity of the information if the real-world processes are not sufficient to identify single entities.

Volume-Usage for Base Products. Manufacturers have reasons to not consider the single entity of a material (e.g. a tree), but measure the volume of these materials. They estimate their output for the given input volume, without tracking which entity winds up in which output. The complexity increases as base materials from different suppliers are combined, as it becomes impossible to refer the outputs to the resources of different suppliers. Additionally, the tracking is too costly to implement.

Entities of the system face another problem: All participants of the supply chain are required to use the platform for their transactions. If one user does not support the platform, the chain is interrupted. This leads to the fact that recipients of resources do not receive the equal amount on the platform.

3 System Design

In this section, we describe the design of the Blockchain-based supply chain network.

3.1 Entities

We identify all entities in the system by a regular Ethereum address. These addresses are either hashes of public keys or, in the case of smart contracts, random generated numbers. The owner of the identity also possesses the private key to express her will, in case of smart contracts code supplants the user. Therefore, we can store the identity about all involved entities or smart contracts with the data type `address`. In case the entity is a smart contract, the code decides upon the will of the address. Although both types of entities act in a similar way and have the same abilities, we separate between them for logical reasons. For clarity, we will refer to human entities as users and code entities as Smart Contracts (short: SC). An advantage of the equal treatment of entities in Ethereum is that the architects are able to replace users with Smart Contracts. A user has too many rights in SC A or one wants to impose a specific restriction for this specific user? One can create a SC B which replaces the user in SC A. The user is given the right to control SC B under the limits imposed in the code in SC B.

Users. First, we describe all human users in the system. As a general notice, we further refer to the goods represented on the Blockchain as tokens.

Regulators. The regulators are users in charge of validating all processes in the network. They can either be selected unilaterally by the entities deployed the system or can be selected via democratic processes within the system. We do not define any notion of how these regulators are selected or elected (as this varies between different supply chains), we define their tasks and responsibilities. Regulators select forest owners and validate their correct operation[1]. After a correct validation, they assign the right to create new tokens for a certain resource, either directly within the token contract or via a separate contract that regulates the amount of newly created tokens. Regulators also have the right to revoke access to the creation of new tokens if rules are violated. The regulators do not take part in the trade or exchange of tokens.

Trader. Traders are regular market participants in the supply chain. They are able to receive and send tokens they previously received. Their access to the system can be invitation only if necessary. We do not oppose any further restrictions to the traders in the system, as they do not have any rights to exchange tokens for other tokens or create new ones. The system designers can decide whether they want to include the traders in the democratic processes.

Creator of Goods. The producer is the creator of goods in the supply chain. She is responsible for creating new tokens and sending them alongside her real-world goods. Usually, a producer has the right to create only one type of good and therefore one type of token. Her rights to create tokens and the maximum specified amount per period depend on the decisions of the regulators. As her intrinsic motivation for a functional system, it is possible to involve the creator of the goods in the democratic processes of the system.

Manufacturer. The manufacturer has the same rights as the trader. However, she has the additional right to exchange one token for another at the exchange SC. The manufacturers are elected by a democratic process or are selected by other entities like the regulators. It is also possible to give traders and manufacturers the same rights, as we do not expect the trader to gain an advantage out of exchanging tokens for other tokens to which she has no real world product.

Smart Contracts. Further, we discuss the Smart Contracts specified in the system.

Central Authority Contract. In contrary to decentralized systems, our proposed solution contains a central authority SC controlling the system. As the governance of supply chains differ from industry to industry, we do not want to restrict the system to one specific design such as a majority vote. The owner of the contract, as mentioned before, can be replaced by any desired structure, i.e.

---

[1] Again, this process lies outside of the Blockchain and depends on the specific supply chain.

a democratic pattern or a 2 out-of 3 pattern. This decision has to be made by the architects of the specific implementation of the system. The central authority smart contract is the first contact in the system. It defines the available token and exchange contracts, is responsible for the selection of the regulators, and has the right to introduce new exchange rules or token contracts. It is also possible to deploy the contract in a way such that there is no governance afterwards possible; all rules and entities have to be agreed on before deployment on the Blockchain. Due to the transparency, the owner of the central authority contract can be reviewed by all participants of the system.

Tokens Contract. To enable compatibility with existing software components, the token contracts are modified ERC-20 token contracts [18]. ERC-20 SCs are widely accepted as they are mostly used in ICOs and other tokens on Ethereum. Our token SCs implement two additional functions: `createToken(uint amount)` and `modifyTokenAmount(address account, uint amount)`. The first function can only be executed by a producer or a regulated creation SC. It allows the creator of goods to create new tokens, because in ERC20 contracts the overall supply of the token is usually defined at the initialization of the contract. The second method is required for the exchange contract. The contract is responsible for the exchange of tokens, therefore reducing one amount on one contract and increasing the amount on another contract at the same time. The method allows the exchange SC to modify the balance of a single account. Besides the additional functionality, the token contract supports traditional methods as sending, checking account balances and sending amounts on behalf of another party.

Exchange Contract. The Exchange SC is the main contract for manufacturers which exchange their tokens for other tokens as they further processed the resources or created new products out of existing materials. The exchange SC is registered in the central authority contract and in all token contracts, otherwise it cannot manipulate the account balances in the existing token contracts. The contract also stores the exchange rates for pairs of tokens.

Regulated Creation Contract. The regulated creation SC is one example of a contract that regulates the usage of another contract, in this case a token contract and the right to arbitrary create new tokens of a producer. The user allowed to create new tokens is registered in the regulated creation contract, whereas the regulated creation contract is registered as an issuer in the token contract. In the regulated creation contract the regulators specify the maximum amount the user is allowed to issue, for example depending on their producing facility or other existing resources.

3.2 Processes

In this section, we describe recommended standard processes which occur while using the system.

Transfer of Goods. The transfer of goods is the basic process in the system. The system's main purpose is the transfer of goods on the Blockchain and is designed to be easy and comprehensible for every participant. The transfer of goods is facilitated in a regular way. The payment takes place with traditional arrangements such as bank transfer or cash. The shipment or transportation also happens in traditional ways. We do not create "digital twins" [1] on the Blockchain, as we do not want to track the individual component but rather the handled volume. A digital twin approach would be unnecessary, therefore the transfer of the digital good has to be executed manually. The sender just specifies the address of the receiver and the digital representatives are transfered. A easy rule applies: "If a good is bought and it is not accompanied with the same amount of the digital good, the good does not originate from a certified source." The transfer of goods is depicted in Fig. 1, in which malicious entities (red) are not able to introduce mis-labeled wood into the valid (green) supply chain. A red x marks where an operation fails on the Blockchain or in real world.

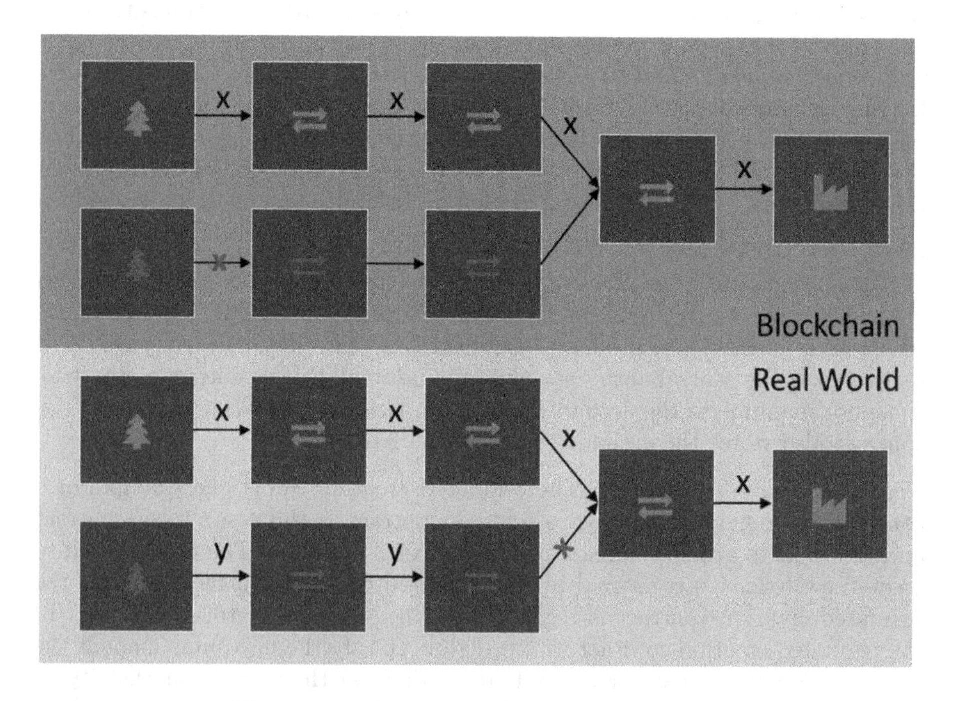

Fig. 1. Transfer of goods (Color figure online)

Exchange of Goods. The exchange of goods is a process required as the system supports many different digital goods. If a manufacturer wants to transform a good, she proceeds as always. The necessary physical steps stay identical. Additionally, she has to transform the digital good. To do so, she executes the method `exchange(uint Token1, uint token2)` to exchange one token for another. As of the atomic nature of the transaction, the exchange is either successful or aborts. It is not possible that the manufacturer keeps old tokens while creating new tokens or losing old tokens and not receiving new tokens. The tokens can only be manipulated for the account that sends the transaction, therefore manipulation is further restricted. The exchange of a single good by user #5 is shown in Fig. 2.

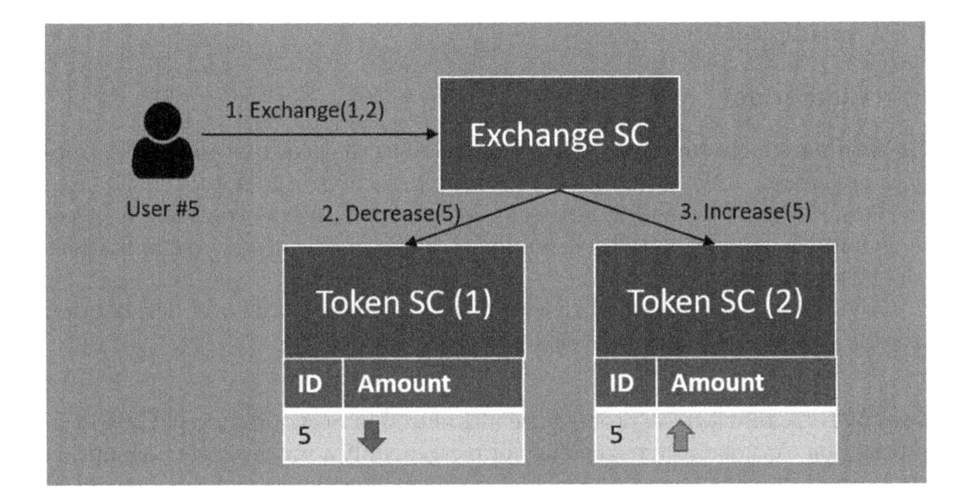

Fig. 2. Exchange of goods

3.3 Bootstrapping of the System

All participants of the supply chain have to use the proposed system or otherwise the system fails to provide all users the proposed functionality. If a supplier does not use the smart contract platform, the receiver of the goods cannot prove whether the good itself is from a valid source. The achieve a certain functionality, we have to ensure that a considerable amount of participants are using the system.

The idea for bootstrapping is as follows. From a game theoretical perspective, we have to encourage the users to participate in the Blockchain-based supply chain. Users which are just intermediaries do not gain an advantage of using the system, and they lose the ability to behave maliciously. It is questionable if the manufacturers of the base material do solely profit from introducing such a system if no other entities use the system. The only participants which heavily profit from the usage are large corporations which sell furniture or other goods made from sustainable wood. They have to prove to their customers the usage of economically friendly wood, otherwise their revenues would decrease. If the commercial customers are using the system, they can require that every merchant who provides them with wood has to use the system, which creates an incentive for all intermediaries to also use the system, as otherwise they would not be able to supply these companies. This also applies for other intermediaries which would start buying only from other suppliers which are able to actually provide certified wood in the system. If this happens, the easiest part is to convince the actual producers of the base material to introduce the system. They invest money in certifications and can increase their own revenue if they support a system that excludes their malicious competition from the market.

4 Discussion

4.1 Limitations

The introduced system exposes limitations due to the design of the Smart Contract architecture. We do not discuss limitations due to the nature of the used Blockchain technology and Smart Contract language such as transaction speed, anonymity, or susceptibility to errors. As technology advances, these limitations are likely to vanish.

Other limitations remain. The following list enables a brief overview of other possible strategic alignments of digital supply chains.

Loss of Information. A problem we introduced in Sect. 2 remains: The loss of information. As goods are recombined or merged, only a probabilistic assumption can be given about the origin of a single product. Furthermore, from a technical point of view we are not able to expand the platform in such way that it supports a provenance lookup. The introduction of meta-data is possible, but it remains unclear how the merging of meta-data from different sub-products would look like. As of our problem statement, this limitation is not relevant to our use case, as we are only interested in the consistent volume of goods managed by the system.

Exchange of Certified with Uncertified Products. Our system does not introduce digital twins, meaning that a digital good cannot be linked to a real-world good without doubt. As we only consider volumes, it would be possible for malicious entities to swap high quality (certified) wood with lower quality (uncertified) wood and sell it as certified. He would only benefit from that fact when a market exists for high quality wood outside of the supply chain where the entity is not required to send the tokens digitally. Again, our use case mainly focuses on prevention of volume manipulation. The damage incurred by swapping is low in comparison to volume manipulations.

Introduction of New Types of Products. An organizational problem could be the introduction of new products which require different amounts of other goods. First, the participants of the network have to agree to valid "exchange" rates: How much resources are required to create another product? Depending on the manufacturing process and the efficiency of the different manufacturers, these numbers can differ. This can lead to two problems: A manufacturer has to use more tokens than necessary on the Blockchain, basically "burning" tokens or it has to use less tokens than required, allowing the entity to introduce uncertified products into the supply chain. A way to mitigate the problem is that the manufacturer defines its conversion rates itself. In that case, other participants would have to validate whether these conversion rates are realistic or not. Generally, the participants have to be clear about their processes and the best way to mitigate risks is to develop sound exchange rates before implementing the system.

4.2 Applicability

We propose our solution for the use case of a timber-tracking supply chain. With limitations, one can apply the distributed application for other areas of supply chains.

Components for Electronic Devices. Electronic devices such as smart phones, notebooks or televisions consists of many base components which then again consist out of rare earths or other resources. Workers can get exploited in mining these goods, also the operators can exploit nature for their profit. With a system similar to our application, these drawbacks can be eliminated. The limitation would apply at that point in the supply chain as products are tracked on an individual level.

Ingredients of Food or Other Eatable Items. An additional supply chain system based on measurement of volumes is the food industry. By involving many stakeholders and intermediaries, the origin of base products such as wheat, corn as well as fish or meat can be used for malicious purposes. Some ingredients are intentionally mis-labeled, leading to a economical damage with potential health damages for consumers. For example, in 2013 horse meat was sold as beef which was unfit for human consumption [15]. With a proof, that meat originates from certified farms, one can complicate the manipulation.

5 Conclusion

In this paper, we present a solution for volume manipulation in large supply chains. The proposed exchange smart contract embedded in the system enables a transformation of base goods into other products according to predefined values, ensuring an overall sound maximum volume of base resources. Further advancements describe possible bootstrapping processes to introduce this digital solution in the industry. Future work can evaluate approaches to enable tracking of goods in supply chains on an individual level. Additional work has to be done to ensure a fully functional platform in case of non-participating entities.

References

1. Datta, S.P.A.: Emergence of digital twins. arXiv preprint arXiv:1610.06467 (2016)
2. Düdder, B., Ross, O.: Timber tracking: reducing complexity of due diligence by using blockchain technology (position paper). In: 2nd Workshop on Managed Complexity. CEUR-WS. org (2017)
3. Griggs, D., et al.: Policy: sustainable development goals for people and planet. Nature **495**(7441), 305 (2013)
4. Grunert, K.G.: Food quality and safety: consumer perception and demand. Eur. Rev. Agric. Econ. **32**(3), 369–391 (2005)
5. Hackius, N., Petersen, M.: Blockchain in logistics and supply chain: trick or treat? In: Proceedings of the Hamburg International Conference of Logistics (HICL), pp. 3–18. epubli (2017)
6. Hoare, A.: Tackling illegal logging and the related trade. Chatham House **2**, 21–47 (2015)
7. Hugos, M.H.: Essentials of Supply Chain Management. Wiley, Hoboken (2018)
8. Ireland, R.D., Webb, J.W.: A multi-theoretic perspective on trust and power in strategic supply chains. J. Oper. Manage. **25**(2), 482–497 (2007)
9. Korpela, K., Hallikas, J., Dahlberg, T.: Digital supply chain transformation toward blockchain integration. In: Proceedings of the 50th Hawaii International Conference on System Sciences (2017)
10. Lomas, N.: Everledger is using blockchain to combat fraud, starting with diamonds, https://techcrunch.com/2015/06/29/everledger (2015)
11. Miles, M.P., Covin, J.G.: Environmental marketing: a source of reputational, competitive, and financial advantage. J. Bus. Ethics **23**(3), 299–311 (2000)
12. Nakamoto, S.: Bitcoin: A peer-to-peer electronic cash system (2008)
13. NEPCon: FSC certification. https://www.nepcon.org/certification/fsc
14. News, U.: Un agricultural agency and european union step up efforts to combat illegal timber trade. URL: https://news.un.org/en/story/2016/05/529172-un-agricultural-agency-and-european-union-step-efforts-combat-illegal-timber
15. Premanandh, J.: Horse meat scandal-a wake-up call for regulatory authorities. Food Control **34**(2), 568–569 (2013)
16. Swan, M.: Blockchain: Blueprint for a New Economy. O'Reilly Media Inc., Newton (2015)
17. Vlosky, R.P., Ozanne, L.K., Fontenot, R.J.: A conceptual model of us consumer willingness-to-pay for environmentally certified wood products. J. Consum. Mark. **16**(2), 122–140 (1999)
18. Vogelsteller, F., Buterin, V.: ERC-20 token standard, September 2017, https://github.com/ethereum/EIPs/blob/master/EIPS/eip-20-tokenstandard.md
19. Wilding, R.: The supply chain complexity triangle: uncertainty generation in the supply chain. Int. J. Phys. Distrib. Logist. Manag. **28**(8), 599–616 (1998)
20. Wood, G.: Ethereum: a secure decentralised generalised transaction ledger. Ethereum Project Yellow Paper **151**, 1–32 (2014)

A Blockchain Based System to Ensure Transparency and Reliability in Food Supply Chain

Gavina Baralla[1], Simona Ibba[1], Michele Marchesi[2], Roberto Tonelli[2](✉), and Sebastiano Missineo[3]

[1] Department of Electrical and Electronic Engineering (DIEE), University of Cagliari, Cagliari, Italy
{gavina.baralla,simona.ibba}@diee.unica.it
[2] Department of Mathematics and Computer Science, University of Cagliari, Cagliari, Italy
marchesi@unica.it,roberto.tonelli@dsf.unica.it
[3] Strateghia srl, Rome, Italy
missineo@strateghia.it

Abstract. We propose a blockchain oriented platform to secure storage origin provenance for food data. By exploiting the blockchain distributed and immutable nature the proposed system ensures the supply chain transparency with a view to encourage local region by promoting the smart food tourism and by increasing local economy. Thanks to the decentralized application platforms that makes us able to develop smart contracts, we define and implement a system that works inside the blockchain and guarantees transparency, reliability to all actors of the food supply chain. Food, in fact, is the most direct way to get in touch with a place. The touristic activities related to wine and food consumption and sale in fact influence the choice of a destination and may encourage the purchase of typical food also once tourists are back home to the country of origin. Touristic destinations must therefore be equipped with innovative tools that, in a context of Smart Tourism, guarantee the originality of the products and their traceability.

Keywords: Blockchain · Smart tourism · Supply chain management
Product traceability

1 Introduction

Agrifood industry and land development are closely related. The food supply chain is a complex system in which citizens, institutions, businesses and tourists converge in a meeting based on two strategic axes: innovation and protection of product quality. In the field of food safety the guarantee of products quality is a key element. Traceability is considered a must and it is necessary not only from a regulatory standpoint: it allows monitoring the effectiveness of production, of

G. Mencagli et al. (Eds.): Euro-Par 2018 Workshops, LNCS 11339, pp. 379–391, 2019.
https://doi.org/10.1007/978-3-030-10549-5_30

processing, of logistics and sales systems in food chains and increases customer confidence and trust. The integrity of the food chain does not only include security problems, but it is also involved in the field of counterfeiting in order to limit the possibility of forgery and fraud. To address these requirements, a traceability system is needed to provide information on the origin, on processing, on retailing and on the final destination of food products. It is therefore necessary to have a product identity card which guarantees its originality, provenance and properties in a unmodifiable way and that certifies in a transparent and reliable way every single step in the production, supply and retail chain. In order to comlpy with all these needs we use an approach based on the blockchain technology as a means of safeguarding the local foodstuffs with special characteristics. In fact transparency, reliability and invariability of data are intrinsic properties of any blockchain technology, which is a digital ledger enabling a secure strategy for implementing and recording transactions, contracts and agreements is an excellent solution for those who wish to tell the history of their product in order to ensure reliability. We applied the blockchain technology to trace the food supply chain in Sardinia Region and we developed a system for protecting Made in Sardinia products food in a touristic context. It must be noted that the geographical characteristics of insularity of Sardinia characterize typical gastronomic products which are very original and connected to the agro-pastoral world. In Italy traditional agri-food products are defined as typical items whose methods of processing, preservation and maturing are performed homogeneously into a particular territory and according to traditional rules which are extended over time, for a period of at least 25 years. The platform we propose in this paper aims not only at ensuring the authenticity of typical Sardinian products, but also at improving their saling using on-line and on-site ordering in many of the major touristic points in Sardinia (beaches, ports, airports, archaeological sites, cultural heritage, etc.). The platform forecast a set of pop-up stores integrated through the development of a dynamic and innovative modular software system based on the blockchain technology within the framework of smart tourism.

The paper is structured as follows. Sections 2 and 3 present research background and related works. Section 4 explains the proposed platform based on blockchain technology and Sect. 5 describes the system architecture. In Sect. 6 proposed smart contracts are detailed through a pseudo-code. Section 7 discusses the use of the system to check the product traceability. Finally, Sect. 8 contains the conclusions.

2 Research Background and Setting

The concept of smart tourism is very recent. It is a logical consequence of the innovations and of the technological progress applied to traditional tourism, but not only that. Smart tourism is connected to the idea of smart destinations and more generally of smart cities. All those specific characteristics of urban or even rural areas typical of a smart city, and therefore useful to residents, can also be used by tourists in the context of mobility, sustainability and quality of visits [12,13]. According to [1] the smart tourism destinations could contribute to the improvement of tourists experiences proposing products and services tailored for each visitor with the understanding of its needs, wishes and desires. Our platform and project, that we called "Bertulas", aims at increasing the potential of smart tourism in the Sardinia Region through the creation of an innovative pop-up store system (POS), an interactive showcase of products for an effective contextual shopping that can improve the possibilities for tourists to discover the Sardinian food products. Pop-up stores are little local stores, runned by an exhibitor, that will be positioned in places of particular touristic interest in order to get the attention of potential customers inviting tourists to live an effective shopping experience, innovative and functional to specific needs. The exhibitor will be equipped with a tablet/laptop device connected to the network and channeled on a dedicated e-commerce site. Turists will able to pay in a secure way, using cryptocurrencies or by credit cards, and can choose a specific method of delivery: at their temporary residence in Sardinia or at their own home in any part of the world. Each movement of products, from local producer to customer, is mapped in a blockchain that has a double role: the role of public, transparent and unmodifiable ledger, and the role of control system which safeguards the originality of products. The latter role is implemented thanks to the computing resources available on the blockchain and will be explained later.

3 Related Works

The blockchain technology is mainly known as directly related to Bitcoin or other cryptocurrency and to financial transactions. In fact the blockchain technology can provide an appropriate solution in all those cases in which a system of relationships entirely based on a concept of trust and transparency is needed, even if the technology still suffers of various drowbacks, mainly related to the missing or the poor application of good practices of software engineering for blockchain-oriented software development [9]. Examples of blockchain technology application to smart cities or smart environments can be found in [10,11]. The first work attempts to respond to a topical issue in the scientific context: how can blockchain help smart cities? The second study models a blockchain-based solution in order to guarantee in a smart context the rights of temporary employees and the transparency in the management of job contracts.

The use of the blockchain technology in an agrifood context is proposed in [2]. The work is based on RFID and blockchain technology for sharing and transferring information about the production, the processing, the storage, the distribution and the selling of foodstuffs. A similar work is [3] in which authors analyze the limits of RFID technology proving it unreliable in the post supply chain because tags can be rather easily cloned in the public space. An experimental ethereum blockchain based on the proof-of-concept block validation is developed in the work, with an analysis of its cost performances: the cost of managing the ownership of a product with six transfers results in about one USD. In [4] Bateman focuses on the value of traceability. The paper presents an encrypted item (bar-codes, tags or serial number representing physical goods) of transaction and sends it out to all other nodes in the blockchain network. The nodes verify if this item of transactions is legitimate and add it to a ledger that then serves for future transactions. In the research of [5] the authors study the blockchain technology applied to a supply chain for a four-party logistic (4PL) firm to increase traceability and transparency. BigchainDB [6] provides the access to a huge distributed database, with many blockchain features, such as decentralized control, immutability and transfer of digital assets. In [7] the authors develop a food supply chain traceability system for real-time food tracing based on a blockchain, on the Internet of things and HACCP (Hazard Analysis and Critical Control Points) and provide a platform transparent, reliable, secure and useful to all the actors of the supply chain. The work of Kim and collaborators [8] is focused on ontologies as tools that can contribute to blockchain design applied to food provenance knowledge and traceability. Authors use the Ethereum blockchain platform for developing smart contracts supporting goods traceability and analyze the provenance of luxury goods produced and transported in international, big and complex supply chains. Blockverify [16] is a startup which applies the blockchain technology to improve anti-counterfeit measures in different industries, such as pharmaceuticals and luxury item's context.

4 The Blockchain Based Platform

In this section we provide an overview of how the system can be implemented by developing the following components:

- User-friendly and high-performance e-commerce platform containing all the eno-gastronomic products that can be purchased. The e-commerce system will be used both on the web and through a dedicated app.
- Dedicated on site exhibitors, named POS (pop-up stores), to be installed in the areas with the highest touristic presences in Sardinia and equipped with a laptop connected to the dedicated e-commerce website. These are real interactive showcases designed for a standalone use and dedicated to the sale and presentation of local, zero-mile, food and wine products.
- E-commerce system usable both through POS and through a dedicated app. The customers will obtain information about local companies and producers in order to buy further products as well as food and wine, for increasing the attractiveness of the territory and to favor the economic development in the context of a smart touristic region.

4.1 Blockchain Features for Chain-Food Applications

A record within the blockchain cannot be modified retroactively because of its structure. Not only transactions but also other information can be recorded within the blockchain, such as documents, identity management or food traceability. These characteristics render the blockchain technology ideal for managing the entire agri-food supply chain by avoiding the counterfeiting and ensuring the transparency, the quality, the origin and the integrity.

In our model it is possible both to assign a unique digital identity card for each product that must be traced, containing significant data related to the production and the supply chain, and to verify the originality.

The innovative commercial distribution process will allow the reduction of the typical steps of the commercial chain: in our scheme the transitions will be restricted and therefore the cost of storage on the blockchain will be limited.

Customers and all actors of the food chain can verify whether the data are correct, true and accurate. Each actor in the chain has his own interest in avoiding cheating from other actors and can easily check it. The system, based on Keyless Signature Infrastructure (KSI), improves the scalability and settlement time and uses the hash function to safeguard the integrity of data, and presents three main attributes: *the authenticity* it secures that the data has not been tampered with or modified, *the identity* it allows to uniquely identify the place where the item was recorded, *the proof of time* it allows to uniquely identify date and time at which the item was registered on the Blockchain.

By using KSI digital signatures our platform ensures the integrity of digital assets related to local products and their authenticity through the detection of unauthorized changes in software and configurations. At the same time allows to detect a violation to access of information through the analysis of the blockchain. In this context the blockchain is an enabling technology which allows for obtaining the satisfaction of security and availability of data. Information stored in blocks characterizes the state of the blockchain. The use of blockchain applied to food supply chain in the context of smart tourism is powerful and can lead important results and transformations in terms of procedure and process management opening the way for handling complex distributed applications.

4.2 Ethereum Blockchain and Smart Contracts

There are different possible choiches of blockchain for implementing our platform. We choose the Ethereum blockchain for our system since it offers the possibility to implement smart contracts in a simple way. Furthermore Solidity is up to now the most used coding language for writing smart contracts, it is continuously supported by the evolution of the Ethereum Virtual Machine with new versions of the compiler and is continuously documented. Examples of smart contracts source codes are freely available and validated on different online platforms, like Etherscan, and bugs and fixing are continuously managed and documented. Another solution could be a permissioned blockchain. We prefer to tackle the problem with a permissionless blockchain since this approcah solves completely the problem of customer's trust. In fact a permissioned blockchain may still give the sensation to the customer that a control which is indeed not needed (the various permissions) is applied to the food chain and may introduce the doubt that the central authority or some actor of the production chain can deny the free and complete access to all the desired information. On the contrary a permissionless and pervasively diffuse blockchain, such as Ethereum, give the sensation that nothing is hidded and all the information on the products are freele accessible increasing customer's trust. A contract in Ethereum, or smart contract, is a special typology of account. It is recorded in a block of the blockchain, and can receive and transmit messages from and to other account, by means of transactions. Messages can request the execution of a specific contract function. In the case of our agri-chain traceability, for instance, a message can contain the address of the receiver, the name of the function, and a list of parameters that ensure the reliability of the system and protect the originality of local products. For instance smart contracts can be used in the blockchain to record measurements of product coming from the producers. All actors of the food supply chain in our system are considered as senders and recipients of transactions. They are blockchain accounts and are defined by an alphanumeric code called address. The Ethereum blockchain provides a computational environment, programmable by the development of decentralized applications. Etherum smart contracts facilitate the exchange of money, goods, contents, properties, actions or anything else of value. Once activated on the blockchain, the smart contract operates independently and performs tasks automatically when specific conditions occur. Each smart contract is executed on the blockchain and then there are no risk of downtime, censorship, fraud or interference. Different blockchains have the ability to execute programs, but often they are very limited. Ethereum instead allows developers to implement any type of computation since the EVM language is turing complete.

5 The System Architecture

The proposed system aims to certify the production and the supply chain concerning food local products by using blockchain technology and smart contract. The stakeholders involved are:

- *authority* as the system administrator
- *local producers*
- *suppliers* identified as central or peripheral warehouses
- *retailers* identified as pop-up stores and the e-commerce application

In our application, we assume the Sardinian Region as the authority, namely the system administrator which inserts and monitors information about all the other stakeholders. Each actor who want to work into the system, must be therefore authorized and certified. The administrator also records information about every food product involved that will be certified by the system. The local producer must communicate with the authority a list or a single food product which may produce as well. For each stored record a payment of a fee is required. All this information will be stored in the blockchain as will be described later. According to [14,15] a total of 193 agri-food products are recognized as traditional. Given the shelf life, only part of these products will be sold through the system.

Figure 1 reports a state diagram describing the supply chain of the local agri-food products. A local producer places on the market the product (S0) that will be purchased at the end by the consumer (S4). A local producer can send the product both to a POS (S1) or to a Central Warehouse (S2). It is possible to have one or more peripheral warehouse (S3). We assume that a consumer can buy a product in site by a POS or online through the e-commerce website.

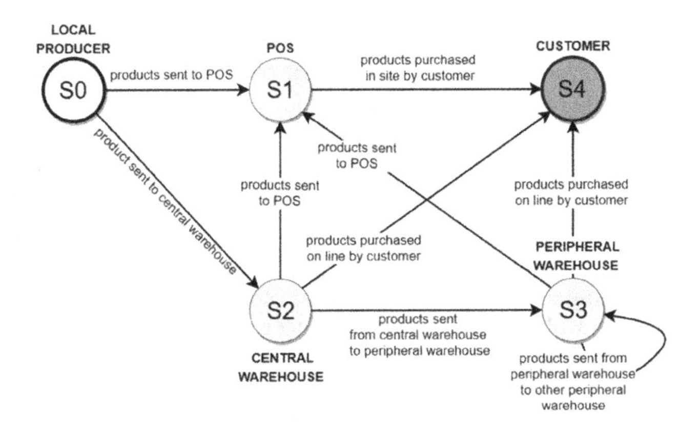

Fig. 1. The state diagram describing products agri-food chain.

6 Proposed Smart Contracts

We devised two smart contracts to automate the storage of information related to the agri-food supply chain where we have different involved stakeholders. As explained before, we have a detailed description for each local product contained into a file and we store all the information in the blockchain using hash codes. In fact a hash code can be used to verify the integrity of the data and for example can be used to check the integrity of the file containing the list of local products. By using hashing properties, it is possible to verify the integrity of the data by comparing the hash codes. We choose as algorithm of encryption the SHA256.

We propose two different smart contracts: *ProductChain* and *SupplyChain* that we describe through a pseudocode in Contract I and Contract II respectively. In the *ProductChain* contract all information about stakeholders is inserted by the authority, as well as information on products, with their origin and manufacturing, and then it is stored in the blockchain. Local producers can insert information about production batch when a good is ready to sell. We assume that the *ProductChain* contract manages the entire production chain. The *SupplyChain* contract instead manages the supply chain until the final consumer is reached. A customer can buy the product through a pop-up store or through the e-commerce, and at any time he/she can check the history of the product (form the production chain to the supply chain) because all transactions are recorded and available in the blockchain.

We list and show below the main steps planned which involve a blockchain transaction:

1. *the authority records information about agri-food local products.* The authority assigns to each product an identity code similar to a barcode. When the authority records information about products within the Ethereum Blockchain, it stores the hash of the file which describe the product. As explained before, only the authority, according to the function check of the designed smart contract, can insert information about stakeholders involved

and agri-food local products. To insert a product, the authority uses the *insert_record* function described through a pseudocode in the ProductChain contract. There is a different transaction for each new record and each transaction requires a fee.

2. *the authority validates local producers.* The authority, that in our case is the Sardinian Region, has the list of accredited producer in its local database with specific information. If a local producer wants to sell its product or a list of products by using the proposed system it has to ask for accreditation. The authority makes the following steps:
   (a) creation of a wallet for the local producer, in this way he can be identified by a specific address (*create_wallet* pseudocode);
   (b) addition of the address to an authorized author list and pairing of it to the identity code of the agri-food product or products (*enable_stakeholder* function);
   (c) creation of a transaction to store the hash code of the information about the local producer; likewise the agri-food local product, also the data related to a producer will be available in a public file, so that the hash code of this public file and the hash code stored in the blockchain can be compared to verify the integrity (*insert_record* function);
3. *the authority records information about other stakeholders involved such as their addresses (supplier, retailer).* The authority makes the following steps:
   (a) creation of a wallet for each stakeholder involved, such as a supplier or a retailer, so that it can be identified by a specific address *(create_wallet pseudocode)*;
   (b) addition of the address to an authorized authors list classifying it as enabled addresses *(enable_stakehoder function)*;
   (c) creation of a transaction to store the hash code of the information about each stakeholder; like the agri-food local product also the data related to the actor will be available in a public file, so that the hash code of this public file and the hash code stored in the blockchain can be compared to verify the integrity *(insert_record function)*;
4. *the local producer records information about the production batch.* The local producer, by using its address, can store information about the production batch:
   (a) calling of smart contract *ProductChain* and the function *insert_production_batch* providing as input its address and the products identification code; the function checks (through a *check_map_product function*) if the producer is enabled to record information about the production batch;
   (b) insertion of information giving a new transaction in the blockchain, about production batch including an identifying code for that production.
5. *the local producer records information about selling and address.* The local producer records within the blockchain, by using the smart contract SupplyChain, information about the sale:
   (a) call *send_product* function giving as input its address, the reference to the transaction within the blockchain about the production batch to send, the address of the recipient and the quantity of sending goods;

   (b) record of a transaction about selling if a function *check_property* is verified; that function checks if the stakeholder has the property and the quantity before selling.
6. *the recipient records information about receipt of goods.* The recipient records within the blockchain by using the smart contract *SupplyChain* information about the receipt:
   (a) calling of *receive_product* function giving as input its address, and the reference about the transaction shipment recorded within the blockchain by the sender;
   (b) record of a transaction about the receipt if a *check_receiving* function is satisfied, that function checks if the receiving is correct.
7. *the stakeholder records information about selling and recipient.* Steps fifth and sixth are repeated every time the product owner changes. Every step is registered with a transaction in the blockchain.

7 Product Traceability

In Fig. 2 we report a detail of the transactions that our application stores within the blockchain. We have indicated these transactions in pseudocode (see Contract I and Contract II in Appendix).

A consumer can buy a product through a pop-up store or through the specialized e-commerce. He/she can obtain information about the production chain and the supply chain in order to check authenticity, goodness and provenance of the product. The entire system is designed to certify the local agri-food product in order to prevent fraud and to promote the geographical area. All information about a product is stored in the blockchain and for each product the system recovers the information and shows it to the consumer that can verify the information by using a simple QR-code reader, or a specialized mobile app linked to the system. The customer can also manually verify the product information integrity comparing the hashcode stored in the blockchain with the hash code of the information displayed.

Our solution appears better than traditional solutions because all the infrastructure is already there and is the blockchain itself. There is no need to pay for cloud solutions or for service providers. Furthermore maintenance is avoided and customer's trust is maximized because all the infrastructure has not an ownership. There are no actors able to manipulate data as it could be for owned or rented infrastructures. In the specific case of the Sardinia Region, but this is valid also for others authorities, our solution minimizes the role of the central authority increasing customer's trust. The authority needs to be entrusted only for actors and products accreditations and authorizations, using already existing and used systems and infrastructures, which is a minimal requirement enforced by law. After that no intermediary is involved into the certification chain which is completely controlled through smart contracts in a completely trasparent and freely accessible way and unmodifiable.

It performs also better with respect to other solutions provided in a blockchain framework because only hashed information is inserted into the blockchain reducing gas costs and payload.

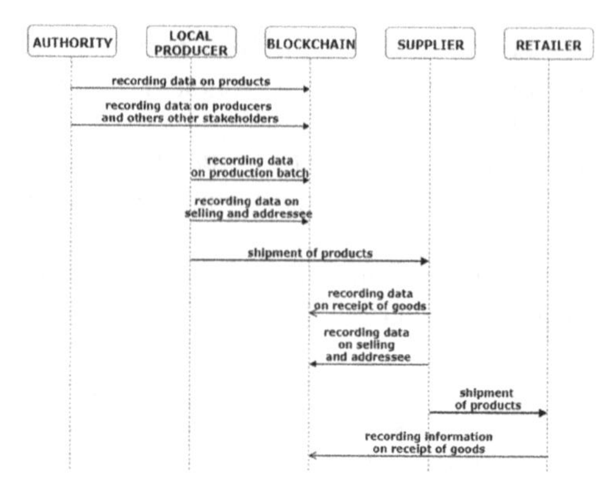

Fig. 2. Transactions recorded on blockchain.

8 Conclusions

The proposed platform aims at increasing the potential of the Sardinia Region as a smart tourism region and starts with the awareness that the typical local products are highly significant in order to offer to tourists a full sensory experience and able to tell, even with the taste, the uniqueness of Sardinian culture. The system is based on the blockchain technology and uses the Ethereum platform to implement a product agri-food chain by using smart contracts. The system in fact aims at ensuring the authenticity of typical Sardinian products and to sell them with online and on-site methods in many touristic places of the region through a system of pop-up stores. We know in fact, that to reach the end consumer each product deals with a complex production and distribution network and in the most recent period the need of transparency for end users is increasing even more rapidly. Sometimes some information about provenance exist, but we do not know if they are trustworthy because they are hard to verify. However, in most of the cases we ignore the supply chain process and its impacts on environment, health or safety fields. Currently there is a strong need to rely on someone who can guarantee the entire origin of goods and products. Moreover, given the complexity of the supply chain it would be desirable to have specialized entities for each different supply chain aspect causing the increase of product price. We proposed to solve the problem of traceability through the decentralized and reliable blockchain technology as a means of safeguarding the local foodstuffs with special characteristics and in order to create their digital identity card. We analyzed the use of blockchain technology for the food supply chain in Sardinia Region and we developed a system for protecting Made in Sardinia products food. The cost of managing products with blockchain technology will be minimal given the reduced number of transactions with the use of zero-mile products. The platform then ensures to the consumer to check the authenticity of the product before the purchase giving details on both production chain and supply chain. This application is now under implementation for being applied only to typical products, but it can be extended to different product types. The described system is supervised by a central authority, but it can be redesigned as decentralized system according to the blockchain vision.

Appendix

CONTRACT I - ProductChain

```
INPUT: authority_address, input_address;
function check (input_address)
START
if (input_address == authority_address) then
   return true
else
   exit
end if
END
function insert_record (new_record)
START
if true ← function check (input_address) then
   return id_transaction ← (record_a_transaction(sha256(new_record)))
else
   exit
end if
END
function create_wallet (stakeholder_information)
START
if true ← function check (input_address) then
   return stakeholder_address ← wallet(stakeholder_information)
else
   exit
end if
END
function enable_stakeholder (stakeholder_address, product_code,
stakeholder_type)
START
if true ← function check(inputaddress) then
   if (stakeholder_type == local_producer) then
      map_product[k, v] ← put(stakeholder_address, product_code);
      producer_list ← add(stakeholder_address);
      return true;
   end if
else
   exit
end if
END
function insert_production_batch (stakeholder_address, product_code, production_
information)
START
if true ← function check_map_product (stakeholder_address, product_code) then
   return id_transaction_batch ← record_a_transaction(sha256(
   production_information))
else
   exit
end if
END
```

CONTRACT II - SupplyChain

```
INPUT: input adressee_list, producer_list;
function send_product (stakeholder_address, id_transaction_batch,
addresee_address, product_quantity)
START
if true ← function check_property (id_transaction_batch, stakeholder_address,
product_quantity)) then
   return id_transaction_ship ← record_a_transaction(
   addresee_address, shipping_information)
```

```
else
    exit
end if
END
function receive_product (stakeholder_address, id_transaction_ship)
START
if true ← function check_receiving (
stakeholder_address, id_transaction_ship) then
    return id_transaction_batch ← record_a_transaction(
    stakeholder_address, id_transaction_ship)
else
    exit
end if
END
```

References

1. Buhalis, D., Amaranggana, A.: Smart tourism destinations enhancing tourism experience through personalisation of services. In: Tussyadiah, I., Inversini, A. (eds.) Information and Communication Technologies in Tourism, pp. 377–389. Springer, Cham (2015). https://doi.org/10.1007/978-3-319-14343-9_28
2. Tian, F.: An agri-food supply chain traceability system for China based on RFID & blockchain technology. In: 2016 13th International Conference on Service Systems and Service Management (ICSSSM), pp. 1–6. IEEE, June 2016
3. Toyoda, K., Mathiopoulos, P.T., Sasase, I., Ohtsuki, T.: A novel blockchain-based product ownership management system (POMS) for anti-counterfeits in the post supply chain. IEEE Access (2017)
4. Bateman, A.: Tracking the value of traceability. Supply Chain. Manag. Rev. **9**, 8–10 (2015)
5. Jeppsson, A., Olsson, O.: Blockchains as a solution for traceability and transparency (2017)
6. McConaghy, T., et al.: BigchainDB: a scalable blockchain database. white paper, BigChainDB (2016)
7. Tian, F.: A supply chain traceability system for food safety based on HACCP, blockchain & Internet of things. In: 2017 International Conference on Service Systems and Service Management (ICSSSM), pp. 1–6. IEEE, June 2017
8. Kim, H.M.: IoT and blockchain aware ontologies for supply chain provenance (2016)
9. Porru, S., Pinna, A., Marchesi, M., Tonelli, R.: Blockchain-oriented software engineering: challenges and new directions. In: Proceedings of the 39th International Conference on Software Engineering Companion, pp. 169–171. IEEE, May 2017
10. Ibba, S., Pinna, A., Seu, M., Pani, F.E.: CitySense: blockchain-oriented smart cities. In: Proceedings of the XP2017 Scientific Workshops, p. 12. ACM, May 2017
11. Pinna, A., Ibba, S.: A blockchain-based decentralized system for proper handling of temporary employment contracts. arXiv preprint arXiv:1711.09758 (2017)
12. Lopez de Avila, A.: Smart destinations: XXI century tourism. Presented at the ENTER2015 Conference on Information and Communication Technologies in Tourism, Lugano, Switzerland, 4–6 February 2015 (2015)
13. Gretzel, U., Sigala, M., Xiang, Z., Koo, C.: Smart tourism: foundations and developments. Electron. Mark. **25**(3), 179–188 (2015)

14. http://www.regione.sardegna.it/documenti/1_38_20160920145158.pdf . Accessed 10 Nov 2017
15. http://www.regione.sardegna.it/documenti/1_38_20170912114152.pdf . Accessed 10 Nov 2017
16. http://blockverify.io/ . Accessed 10 Nov 2017

Selecting Effective Blockchain Solutions

Carsten Maple[1] and Jack Jackson[2(✉)]

[1] University of Warwick, Coventry CV4 7AL, UK
[2] Everledger, London WC2H 9JQ, UK
jack.jackson@linace.ox.ac.uk

Abstract. Distributed ledger technologies (DLT) are becoming increasingly popular and seen as a panacea for a wide range of applications. However, it is clear that many organisations, and even engineers, are selecting DLT solutions without fully understanding their power or limitations. Those that make the assessment that blockchain is the best solution are provided little guidance on the vast array of types of blockchain; whether permissioned, permissionless or federated; which consensus algorithm to use; and a range of other considerations. This paper aims to addresses this gap.

Keywords: Distributed ledger technology · Blockchain anatomy
Blockchain selection · Consensus determination protocol

1 Introduction

A distributed ledger is a form of database which is stored across a number of computing devices within a network. Each node independently maintains an identical copy of the shared ledger. The distribution is typically unique, as records are independently constructed and held by each participant; as opposed to information sourcing from a central authority. Each participant in the network places a vote reflecting their calculated output, allowing the group to come to a consensus regarding the *true* data output. Once consensus has been reached, the distributed ledger can then be updated by all parties. Distributed ledger technology (DLT), affords a level of dexterity which is currently not facilitated by centralized systems. A popular form of distributed ledger technology is known as blockchain. Blockchain technologies are distinguishable from DLT by the nature in which they store information. Data on a blockchain is grouped together and organised into a series of cryptographically interconnected *blocks*. A blockchain is an append-only structure, meaning that it only permits further data contribution to the ledger. Once a block of data is committed to the blockchain, it is impossible to alter or delete the information contained within. The immutable nature of blockchain means that the technology is well suited for: records management, transaction processing and auditing. Because of this, we are seeing the widespread adoption of this technology across a number of high risk supply

G. Mencagli et al. (Eds.): Euro-Par 2018 Workshops, LNCS 11339, pp. 392–403, 2019.
https://doi.org/10.1007/978-3-030-10549-5_31

chains, where fraudsters have long taken advantage of opaqueness in the product life-cycle; typically with expensive ramifications. The nature of communications in such systems can help to eliminate intermediaries, allowing individuals and organisations to interact freely with one another. Considering that many industry infrastructures consist of such middlemen (such as distributors in supply chain networks), this could vastly decrease the operational costs associated with running a business; consequently, providing a more open, transparent and competitive marketplace. The implementation of blockchain technology is also valuable within industries that are continuously subjected to rigorous regulation, as the meeting of such requirements can be both time consuming and expensive for an organisation.

The first notable implementation of DLT came in the form of the Bitcoin whitepaper [1], written by Satoshi Nakamoto. Since then DLT such as blockchain have become a panacea for a wide range of applications. They are often perceived as the cornerstone of technological innovation across industries. As such, many organisations show interest in implementing the technology within their industry. Companies wishing to adopt such mechanisms are faced with the challenge of selecting an appropriate configuration for their functional requirements. As the solutions landscape continues to grow, it becomes increasingly important that engineers and decision-makers within an organisation fully understand the power and limitations of the various technologies on offer [7,8,13,14].

In this paper we present an anatomy of blockchain solutions, analysing their key technological features. This paper begins by considering existing work within the field, before proposing and analysing a generic anatomy. This is followed by a brief discussion of a number of developed platforms, before concluding and proposing areas for future work.

2 Existing Work

Since the rise in popularity of DLT, a number of papers have been published analysing various areas within the field, such as: consensus, scalability, mining difficulty and architecture. Pass et al. [2] conducted an analysis on the original blockchain consensus mechanism [1], proving strength of consistency within an asynchronous network environment. Their paper provided proof that Nakamoto's protocol satisfied their definitions for chain quality, growth, consistency (and the upper-bound on chain growth). More generally, Glaser [6] provided a framework for blockchain-enabled systems which was heavily grounded in hard use cases. Zheng et al. [5] extend upon this, educating readers on the key features of a blockchain product, with respects to both architecture and consensus. Their focus was directed towards the benefits of using blockchain technology, referencing a number of widely adopted consensus mechanisms. This paper builds upon such work, educating readers on the selection process, in respects to which anatomical structures are most appropriate given their functional (business) requirements. Similarly, Vukolić [3] draws contrast between traditional proof-of-work (PoW) blockchains and those grounded in byzantine-fault-tolerance (BFT) schemes. Notable emphasis is place upon the computational expense associated with each of the discussed mechanisms. The scalability constraints placed upon each approach are critically analysed, addressing a long-term problem within the DLT community.

In a more critical sense, Kraft [4] focuses on analysing the computation inefficiencies within existing blockchain technologies. In his paper, Kraft identified inefficiencies within the mining processes of both Bitcoin and Namecoin. He proposes a mechanism which is designed to work "*perfectly*" across both constant and exponentially growing hash rates. Comparisons between his mechanism and more traditional methods are drawn from three core metrics: mining difficulty, average block-time and name expiration. The majority of academic work within the field of DLT has been focused on analysing one core metric of the technology. Very little work has been directed at educating readers in the identification process for the appropriate solution for their requirements. This paper builds upon a number of previous works, allowing us to address this knowledge gap.

3 An Anatomy of Blockchain Solutions

We now consider some of the key features of a blockchain network. The feature list contained within this section does not fully encompass the topology of all blockchain solutions. Instead, they are a select subset of features used by us to create a generalized anatomy of a blockchain solution. Each block within a blockchain network contains a series of transactions, accompanied by the signature of the sending network participant. Participation within a network is controlled by the permission-determination protocol adopted by the network. Network participants are often offered incentives to maintain the ledger. Within public networks this can be achieved through mining. Consensus mechanisms are used within blockchain networks to ensure that the ledger is maintained in a valid and correct state, reflecting the *true* series of transactions taking place.

3.1 Blocks

Each block within a blockchain network contains both a header and a body. The block header typically consists of information equivalent to metadata. The header is usually used to support the identification and verification of blocks and their body contents. The block body usually contains information surrounding the transactions within the block. However, the format of data and information contained within both the header and body, varies between implementation.

For example, within the Bitcoin [1] network, the header contains information pertaining to the block version, which is an indication as to which set of validation rules it follows. The header also contains: a hash of all transactions within the block, a universal timestamp, a target threshold of a valid block hash, a 4-byte field and a 256-bit hash from its parent block. Each block has only one parent. The block body contains a series of transactions accompanied by a transaction counter. The maximum number of transactions contained within a block is dependent upon the size of both the block and the transaction contained within.

In contrast, the Ethereum [14,15] network block contains vastly different content. The block head within an Ethereum block (based on the yellow paper [15]) contains the: parent hash, ommers hash, beneficiary, state root, transactions root, receipts root, logs bloom, difficulty, number, gas limit, gas used, timestamp, extra data, mix hash and nonce. Whilst the body contains a list of transactions and an ommers list.

3.2 Smart Contracts

In essence, smart contracts [18] are a protocol which allow for the contribution, verification and implementation of actions within a contract. Smart contracts can be implemented to ensure the effectuation of embedded regulation, contractual terms, business rules and other codifiable instructions. This allows for the enforcement of obligations along with the auditable tracking of that enforcement on the blockchain, in addition to transparency and third party integration. This creates a unique value proposition for users, as well a proven platform on which to further integrate partners' systems and processes.

In the event that manual checks are required, smart contracts are capable of triggering an event which notifies relevant parties that action is necessary. This also extends to situations in which a combination of document submission and manual checking is required. When critically analysing these processes, it would be a waste of time to have a human perform an analysis if other supporting documents are either not present or invalid. A smart contract is capable of managing such scenarios, by first ensuring all supporting documents are present and valid, before prompting the human interaction with the process. Essentially, enabling effective time-management across an organisation.

While many blockchain platforms use smart contracts, such as: Ethereum [14,15], Corda [13] and Hyperledger Fabric [12], not all do; with Monero [7] being a prime example of this.

Monero is a platform which claims to offer superior security and privacy to its competitors, through the implementation of mechanisms such as ring signatures. Implementing smart contracts into a platform increases the attack surface of the network. All of which is counter-intuitive for a privacy-focused platform such as Monero.

3.3 Transaction Signing

Transaction signing is used within networks to provide assurance surrounding the validity of transactions. Networks build their transaction signing mechanisms upon a wide range of cryptographic mechanisms. One such example, is elliptic curve (EC) cryptography. Elliptic curves can be applied within asymmetric cryptography, to allow network participants to maintain ownership of their own public and private keys. Parties use their private keys to sign transactions using the elliptic curve digital signature algorithm (ECDSA). Signed transactions are then broadcast across the network for peer verification. Digital signature algorithms (DSA) such as ECDSA are used to ensure the authenticity of both the source and integrity of data. A great example of elliptic curves being implemented for transaction signing can be seen in the secp256k1 elliptic curve, which is implemented within: Bitcoin [1], Ethereum [14,15] and Zcash [8]. Numerous different types of elliptic curves are used by blockchain networks in the signing process, including the Ed25519 curve used within Monero [7].

3.4 Permissions

Permissions control access parameters around participation within a network, and can either encourage open contribution from the general population, or restrict admittance to pre-trusted entities. This is extremely useful from an engineering perspective as it provides flexibility, adaptive to the specification requirements of the proposed solution. Blockchain has three core permission-determination protocols: permissionless, permissioned and federated.

Permissionless blockchain networks [20] allow for external parties to participate within an open network, without the need for traditional registration mechanisms (permissionless access). This creates openness without imposing strong self-identification restraints on actors within the network. Since anyone can participate in the network freely, there is a requirement to offer a financial incentive for peer validation and system maintenance tasks. Incentives help to promote peer participation in the network, which in turn has a positive impact on the overall security provided by the system. For example, within the PoW consensus mechanism, a 51% network majority is required to enforce change.

Permissioned blockchains [20] are not controlled or manipulated by a single entity, but by a consortia of entities, which provide selected parties with authorization to participate within the network. This affords the consortia the power to *vet* participants to a degree. Since permissioned networks operate under the supervision of a trusted consortium of validators, the cost of verifying transactions is significantly reduced. The infrastructure also supports the updating of protocols with relative ease. As all nodes are well known and regulated, there is negligible risk of network performance degradation or outage.

Federated blockchains also restrict access to the network. However, there is a subtle difference in functionality from permissoned networks. For example, imagine that a network consisted of 15 nodes. Within a permissioned network each node would be required to sign transactions. However, within a federated network, only a subsection of the overall consensus contributing nodes are required to sign blocks. Flexibility is also afforded when assigning read permissions to the ledger. Conducting consensus in this nature reduces the computational cost associated with transaction signing and data redundancies even further.

3.5 Consensus

Consensus is the mechanism by which individuals within a network come to an agreement regarding a particular decision or view. Ideally, consensus mechanisms are capable of mitigating the actions of dishonest individuals or groups; whilst offering a level of redundancy in the event that a subset of parties are unable to respond. Within blockchain technology, consensus is used to provide a degree of consistency across transactions within a ledger. Each consensus mechanism has varying degrees of tolerance around the level of redundancy, resilience, speed and security involved in the performance of their functionality. Common consensus determination algorithms used within blockchain platforms include: PoW [1,3,19], proof-of-stake (PoS) [19], delegated proof-of-stake (DPoS), proof-of-authority (PoA), proof-of-elapsed-time (PoET) [16], byzantine fault tolerance (BFT) [3,9,11].

Proof-of-Work [1,3] is a piece of data that is both time consuming and costly to produce, but easily verifiable by peers. Producing a PoW is essentially a random process with a low probability of success; thus, it is down to trial and error. Perhaps the most notable implementation of PoW can be seen within the Bitcoin network [1]. Within Bitcoin, block references are obtained through the double hashing of the blocks header content, using the SHA-256 hash function. Hashing, mining difficulty and threshold functions for PoW schemes are outlined within [19]. Due to the nature of PoW, an adversarial party would require 51% of the networks hash-rate (or computing power) to compromise the system.

Although PoW is a decentralized protocol, within networks such as Bitcoin, PoW is executed by an ever increasing centralized system of miners. Practically speaking, most people do not have the computational resources to participate in the mining process. As a result, to guarantee stable returns for participation, most miners pool their resources. This has effectively created a centralized mechanism, revolving around so called *pool managers*. Currently, the Bitcoin network, the five biggest mining pools control over $\frac{3}{4}$ of all hashing power.

Proof-of-Stake [19] derives its consensus from the holdings of the cryptocurrency itself. For instance, if Bitcoin were to adopt PoS, users who hold the largest amount of Bitcoin would have the authority to make change across the network. Majority owners would also be able to mine an equivalent portion of their funds regardless of computing power. For an explanation of how the PoS algorithm works; including how it adjusts difficulty and provides proof of address ownership, read [19]. There is a known flaw within the PoW scheme in which newcomers to a network, without prior knowledge of the chain, can be tricked into validating an invalid chain, based on its larger length. PoS combats this by implementing a rule-set which disallows forking from a branching point more than N blocks in the past. Therefore, new participants in the network are provided with all information of prior block content. However, it must be noted that this requires a trade-off in the form of a centralization, trusted source. For a PoS mechanism to work effectively, there needs to be a way to select forgers (a transaction validator) from a user group. Simply selecting forgers based on their account balance would result in a system which is heavily skewed in favour of richer participants, who decide to stake more of their currency. To counter this problem a number of selection mechanisms have been created, such as randomized block and coin age based selection.

It is worth noting that a semi-centralized PoS algorithm known as delegated proof-of-stake also exists. Within DPoS, blocks are created by a select set of users within the system known as delegates. Stake within DPoS is used slightly differently than within PoS. For example, delegates may be *elected* based on their stake in proportion to the network. Additionally, delegates may receive votes from network participants. The voting power of participants is also reliant on their stake relative to the entire network. Delegates are rewarded for performing their role and punished for misbehaviour. There are two core functions performed by delegates: block building and signing. Each delegate is capable of individually generating blocks; however typically speaking, multiple delegates are required to sign a block. Signing is performed by a select subset of delegates. One notable exception to this rule is Tendermint [10], in which any user in the system canprovide a signature.

In essence, PoS systems are more computationally efficient than their PoW counterpart. A greater number of people are encouraged to run nodes and participate in the network as the cost of participation is affordable. As a result, they system becomes increasingly decentralized. Additional protection comes from the expense associated with executing an attack and the reduced incentive for attackers. An attacker would require a near majority of all network currency to manipulate the network. This is typically referred to as the *monopoly problem.*

Byzantine Fault Tolerance is commonly thought of in regard to the byzantine generals problem [9]. With respect to the byzantine generals problem, byzantine fault tolerance is achieved when loyal generals come to a majority agreement on their strategy. Typically byzantine faults are the most challenging to deal with, as no restrictions or assumptions are made around the behaviour a node can exhibit. The most successful approach to date is known as *practical byzantine fault tolerance* (PBFT) [11].

PBFT is the core for many algorithms used for tasks, such as: terminating reliable broadcast, group membership, view synchronous b-cast and state machine replication. PBFT processes can be categorised into three core types: clients, primary n replicas and backup n replicas. Any client within the system can be faulty. In accordance with the $1/3^{rd}$ corruption tolerance of BFT, the number of replicas present is calculated as follows; $n = 3f + 1$, where f is upper bound of faulty parties.

Practical Byzantine Fault Tolerant Consensus [11] is achieved through a three-phase protocol, ensuring the validity and integrity of the agreement. The first phase is known as pre-preparation. Within this phase an order of requests within the same view is agreed upon. The preparation phase that follows again agrees upon a request order within the same view, whilst also ensuring that request execution is performed in the pre-prepared order across different views. Garbage collection is also performed as part of the preparation phase. Finally a commit phase is executed, which again ensures the order of request execution in accordance with the preparation phase, whilst handling further garbage collection duties.

PBFT consumes less energy that both PoW and PoS mechanisms and also offers a higher level of performance in respects to latency and network throughput. Since it is a permissioned network protocol, its adversarial tolerance should not be compared to that of PoW, or permissionless PoS schemes. However, due to the nature of PBFT consensus, scalability becomes a significant issue. Therefore, we recommend using PBFT within small to medium size networks. PBFT is particularly effective within industries consisting of a strictly defined infrastructure.

Proof-of-Elapsed-Time (PoET) [16] is designed to achieve a distributed consensus in a *lottery-type* function. It was originally designed with the aim of creating a fair mechanism for distributing mining rights within permissioned networks.

PoET abide by a four-stage process flow. Firstly, each validator requests a randomly distributed wait-time period from a trusted enclave. Secondly, the validator with the shortest wait time wins the election and is awarded leadership for the transactional block in question. A function is used to create a timer for the transaction block that is guaranteed to have been created by the enclave. Another function is then used to verify the timer origin.

The enclave comes in the form of a secure CPU instruction-set, ensuring fairness in the randomness of selection across all participants. This is achieved through implementing in the low level, using Intel's Software Guard Extensions (SGX) [17]. This facilitates the PoET algorithm in providing random distribution of leadership across an entire population of participants, in a fair manner. An attestation of execution provides verification of a participants claim to leadership, providing a low cost for participation. This offers a strong incentive for participation in the network, as the algorithm is perceived to be fair, just and accessible (due to the low cost infrastructure). Perhaps the most notable implementation of PoET can be seen within the Hyperledger Sawtooth [16] network.

The following diagram provides a comparison between the aforementioned consensus mechanisms Fig. 1.

	Proof-of-Work	Proof-of-Stake	Distributed PoS	Practical BFT	Proof-of-Elapsed-Time	Proof-of-Weight
Node Identity Management	Open	Both	Both	Permissioned	Both	Implementation Dependent
Required Tools	Mining Equipement	None	None	None	Use of SGX in a Trusted Execution Environment	Implementation Dependent
Energy Consumption	High	Average	Average	Low	Low	Implementation Dependent
Performance	Limited / High-Latency	Average	Average	High	High	Implementation Dependent
Adversarial Tolerance	≤ 25% Computing Power	≤ 51% Stake	≤ 51% Validators	≤ 33.3% Faulty Replicas	Unknown	≤ 33.3% of Weighted Users
Scalability	High	High	High	Low	High	High
Implementation	Bitcoin	Peercoin	Bitshares	Hyperledger Fabric	Hyperledger Sawtooth	Filecoin

Fig. 1. Consensus protocol comparison

4 Developed Platforms

Once an engineer has determined that a blockchain solution is required it is then necessary for them to undertake the platform selection process. We discuss some of the key platforms here.

Corda [13] is an open-source DLT, which is targeted towards the financial industry. Corda is a permissioned private platform, offering a plugable consensus mechanism on a transactional level. This affords great flexibility to an engineer when developing an application built on Corda. The nature of consensus within the system means that no global broadcasting of data occurs. This is an attractive quality within heavily regulated industries, where information secrecy is pivotal. Corda has recently been endorsed by the famous insurance consrtium b3i. Smart contracts within Corda are grounded in legal prose; allowing for the self-execution and automation of event-driven, legally binding agreements between parties. This makes Corda ideal for financial records management and the automation of financial agreements.

Ethereum [14,15] is a decentralized platform which affords developers the ability to execute smart contracts within custom built blockchain networks. Ethereum allows for the creation of cryptocurrencies and storing of crypto-assets within the Ethereum Wallet. The wallet also allows for the writing, deployment and use of smart contracts. Perhaps the most interesting use case for Ethereum, can be seen within digital identity management systems. One great example of this is uPort, which aims to give users a more secure way to provide proof of their identity, by only offering critical information required to perform the desired function. For example, only providing an airport with the relevent information when boarding an aircraft. Ethereum is ideal for such a use-case as it has an easy-to-use smart contract mechanism.

Hyperledger Fabric [12] is an open source, modular platform, currently spearheaded by IBM (previously governed by the Linux Foundation). Fabric is a private permissioned platform, which supports the use of one or more networks. Each network manages the requirements of a different set of member nodes. Fabric offers users the ability to perform queries and updates to the ledger, through the use of a series of industry standard data store mechanisms, such as: key-based lookups, composite key queries and range-based searches. Fabric utilizes PBFT [11] and conducts consensus on a transactional level. Peers within Fabric networks are required to endorse transactions in accordance with a number of predefined policies. For a transaction within the network to be validated it must pass all policy checks and receive the signature of all endorsing peers submitting to the Fabric *ordering service*.

Fabric consists of channels, which contain the configuration block which defines policies, access controls and other information important to the blockchains function. Fabric channels allow for the derivation of cryptographic materials from multiple sources. An example of a real world implementation of Fabric can be seen within the Everledger organisation, in which Fabric is used to track and trace diamonds across the supply chain network.

Hyperledger Sawtooth [16] is also part of the Hyperledger family. However, it differs vastly from its sister Fabric network. Where Fabric was built for vast business networks, Sawtooth was developed as solution aimed at reducing the computational resource consumption within large distributed validator populations. It achieves this through implemented the proof-of-elapsed-time (PoET) consensus protocol. Since consensus is performed within the CPU, which are contained within most consumer electronics, realistically speaking, almost any device can participate within consensus. Considering that PoET consensus is also exceptionally lightweight, this makes Sawtooth ideal for use cases in which IoT devices (which typically contain limited computing power) are implemented. Sawtooth is a great choice for supply-chain networks with IoT device tracking during transit.

MultiChain [21] offers a platform for building both permissioned and permissionless blockchain networks. Multichain differentiates itself from most other blockchain networks through its use of *streams*, which come in three core formats: A NoSQL key-value database or document store, an ordered time series database, or an identity-driven database with author-based entry classification. If the purpose of the blockchain product is to store information as opposed to function execution, MultiChain provides a fast and lightweight solution. For this reason, MultiChain is particularly useful for document storage systems, in which simple CRUD functionality is required. Development on the MultiChain platform is also exceptionally easy. Streams can be created and added to the network without the need to write code.

Quorum [22], similarly to Corda, is a financial service facing blockchain network. However, unlike Corda, Quorum is actually a fork of an existing blockchain platform, Ethereum. The core changes Quorum makes within its fork, is the addition of a different consensus protocol, encrypted storage and the change to a permissioned access structure. Quorum still provides access to the standard Ethereum features, such as a distributed ledger and smart contracts. Quorum solves two major existing problems preventing permissioned network implementation upon the Ethereum platform. Firstly, within Ethereum anyone can connect to the network due to its permissionless nature. Secondly, all data inside of the smart contracts within Ethereum are visible to all participant nodes. Quorum addresses these issues by taking an off-chain approach to data storage. Quorum is particularly useful within use-cases in which privacy and security of transactions are a core concern (Fig. 2).

	Corda	Ethereum	Hyperledger Fabric	Hyperledger Sawtooth	Multichain	Quorum
Governance	R3	Ethereum Community	IBM	IBM	Coin Sciences	J.P. Morgan
Permissions	Permissioned (Private)	Permissionless	Permissioned (Private)	Both	Both	Permissioned
Consensus	Pluggable (Transaction Level)	Proof-of-work (Migrating to Proof-of-Stake)	Practical Byzantine Fault Tolerance	Proof-of-Elapsed-Time	Practical Byzantine Fault Tolerance (Alternative)	Istanbul Byzantine Fault Tolerance
Smart Contracts	Kotilin, Java, etc	Solidarity	GoLang, JavaScript, Python , Java, etc	GoLang, JavaScript, Python, Java, etc	N/A	Solidarity

Fig. 2. Platform comparison

5 Conclusion

In this paper we propose a format for outlining a generic blockchain anatomy. This anatomy ranges from permissions to consensus and can be referenced when assessing blockchain solutions architecture; assist in the design and implementation of business logic within the technology. We draw comparisons between existing technologies and protocols, providing solutions architects with a baseline upon which to build their products. However, this paper is meant to be used as a guideline, and is by no means a *bible* for building blockchain solutions. From a practical perspective, within industry, it is necessary to consider a multitude of factors outside that of the technological functionality; for example, cost.

In future work, we aim to address a number of other key topics for consideration when building ontop of blockchain technologies, such as: off-chain storage requirements, privacy preservation, integration with existing systems (particularly legacy) and ease of use. This should provide engineers with further information, upon which to effectively build their solutions. Platforms such as Monero [7] which focus heavily on security would make for an interesting starting point for such work.

References

1. Nakamoto, S.: Bitcoin: a peer-to-peer electronic cash system (2008). https://bitcoin.org/bitcoin.pdf
2. Pass, R., Seeman, L., Shelat, A.: Analysis of the blockchain protocol in asynchronous networks (2016). https://pdfs.semanticscholar.org/161c/24b98ce3af2c0f8a5e96d5055a367b81801e.pdf
3. Vukolić, M.: The quest for scalable blockchain fabric: proof-of-work vs. BFT replication (2015). https://allquantor.at/blockchainbib/pdf/vukolic2015quest.pdf
4. Kraft, D.: Difficulty control for blockchain-based consensus systems (2015). https://allquantor.at/blockchainbib/pdf/kraft2016difficulty.pdf
5. Zheng, Z., Xie, S., Dai, H., Chen, X., Wang, H.: An overview of blockchain technology: architecture, consensus, and future trends (2017). https://www.researchgate.net/profile/Hong-Ning_Dai/publication/318131748_An_Overview_of_Blockchain_Technology_Architecture_Consensus_and_Future_Trends/links/59d71faa458515db19c915a1/An-Overview-of-Blockchain-Technology-Architecture-Consensus-and-Future-Trends.pdf
6. Glaser, F.: Pervasive decentralisation of digital infrastructures: a framework for blockchain enabled system and use case analysis (2017). https://scholarspace.manoa.hawaii.edu/bitstream/10125/41339/1/paper0190.pdf
7. van Saberhagen, N.: CryptoNote v 2.0 (2013). https://cryptonote.org/whitepaper.pdf
8. Ben-Sasson, E., et al.: Zerocash: decentralized anonymous payments from bitcoin (extended version) (2014). http://zerocash-project.org/media/pdf/zerocash-extended-20140518.pdf
9. Lamport, L., Shostak, R., Pease, M.: The Byzantine generals problem (1982). https://people.eecs.berkeley.edu/~luca/cs174/byzantine.pdf
10. Kwon, J.: Tendermint: consensus without mining (2014). https://tendermint.com/static/docs/tendermint.pdf

11. Castro, M., Liskov, B.: Practical Byzantine fault tolerance (1999). http://pmg.csail.mit.edu/papers/osdi99.pdf
12. Cachin, C.: Architecture of the hyperledger blockchain fabric (2016). https://pdfs.semanticscholar.org/f852/c5f3fe649f8a17ded391df0796677a59927f.pdf
13. Hearn, M.: Corda: a distributed ledger (2016). https://docs.corda.net/_static/corda-technical-whitepaper.pdf
14. Ethereum Contributors. "White Paper" (2018). https://github.com/ethereum/wiki/wiki/White-Paper/3592dda1feca69cce8a9d9a624ea33b0999e1dcc
15. Ethereum Community. "Ethereum Yellow Paper" (2018). https://github.com/ethereum/yellowpaper/blob/e653258d1f94c6a29ff1c2c5b43e191f535fba49/README.md
16. Intel Corporation 2015–2017. https://sawtooth.hyperledger.org/docs/core/releases/1.0/architecture.html
17. Costan, V., Devadas, S.: Intel SGX Explained (2016). https://eprint.iacr.org/2016/086.pdf
18. Clack, C.D., Bakshi, V.A., Braine, L.: Smart contract templates: foundations, design landscape and research directions (2016). http://arxiv.org/abs/1608.00771
19. BitFury Group. Proof of Stake versus Proof of Work (2015). https://bitfury.com/content/downloads/pos-vs-pow-1.0.2.pdf
20. Yaga, D., Mell, P., Roby, N., Scarfone, K.: Blockchain technology overview (2018). http://img1.wsimg.com/blobby/go/60231649-12ce-4835-96f0-945ea7f2116c/downloads/1cb8a20ea_182905.pdf
21. Greenspan, G., Founder and CEO, Coin Sciences Ltd.: MultiChain private blockchain - White Paper (2015). https://www.multichain.com/download/MultiChain-White-Paper.pdf
22. Morgan Chase, J.P.: Quorum overview (2017). https://github.com/jpmorganchase/quorum/wiki/Quorum-Overview/0600693ce1453c7513c59154a2512c1efc2044eb

HeteroPar - Workshop on Algorithms, Models and Tools for Parallel Computing on Heterogeneous Platforms

Workshop on Algorithms, Models and Tools for Parallel Computing on Heterogeneous Platforms (HeteroPar)

Workshop Description

Heterogeneity is emerging as one of the most profound and challenging characteristics of today's parallel environments. From the macro level, where networks of distributed computers composed of diverse node architectures are interconnected with potentially heterogeneous networks, to the micro level, where deeper memory hierarchies and various accelerator architectures are increasingly common, the impact of heterogeneity on all computing tasks is increasing rapidly. Traditional parallel algorithms, programming environments and tools, designed for legacy homogeneous multiprocessors, will at best achieve a small fraction of the efficiency and the potential performance that we should expect from parallel computing in tomorrow's highly diversified and mixed environments. New ideas, innovative algorithms, and specialized programming environments and tools are needed to efficiently use these new and multifarious parallel architectures.

HeteroPar is a forum tailored for study of diverse aspects of heterogeneity and caters for researchers working on algorithms, programming languages, tools, and theoretical models aimed at efficiently solving problems on heterogeneous platforms. It includes broad range of topics pertaining to high performance heterogeneous computing from heterogeneous parallel programming paradigms, and algorithms, models and tools for energy optimization on heterogeneous platforms to fault tolerance of parallel computations on heterogeneous platforms.

The sixteenth edition of the workshop (HeteroPar'2018) was held on 27th August in Turin, Italy. For the tenth time, this workshop was organized in conjunction with the Euro-Par annual series of international conferences. The format of the workshop included a keynote followed by four sessions of technical presentations. The program committee (PC) comprised of 25 members with expertise in various aspects of high performance heterogeneous computing. The workshop was well-attended featuring an healthy average of 35 attendees.

We have received 26 articles for review this year from 16 countries. Each paper secured three reviews from members of the PC. After a thorough peer-reviewing process, we have selected 10 articles (an acceptance ratio of 38%) for presentation at the workshop. The review process focused on the quality of the papers, their innovative ideas and their applicability to the field of high performance heterogeneous computing.

The accepted articles covered a diverse range of topics, techniques, and applications exhibiting lucidly the depth, breadth, and growth of the heterogeneous computing field. The topics included realistic simulations of file replication strategies, anomaly detection using FPGA, GPU-accelerated optical coherence tomography, application-centric parallel memories, perturbations in heterogeneous systems, FPGA-accelerated change-point detection, merging publish-subscribe pattern and shared memory, a modular precision format, fast heuristic-based GPU compilation and benchmarking latest GPU and tensor cores.

Finally, I would like to thank the HeteroPar Steering Committee and the HeteroPar 2018 Program Committee, for their diligent efforts in ensuring the high quality and continued success of this workshop. I would also like to thank Euro-Par for hosting our community, and the Euro-Par workshop chairs Dora Blanco Heras and Gabriele Mencagli for their help and support.

Organization

Steering Committee

Domingo Giménez	University of Murcia, Spain
Alexey Kalinov	Cadence Design Systems, Russia
Alexey Lastovetsky	University College Dublin, Ireland
Yves Robert	Ecole Normale Supérieure de Lyon, France
Leonel Sousa	Universidade de Lisboa, Portugal
Denis Trystram	University Grenoble-Alpes, France

Program Chair

Ravi Reddy Manumachu	University College Dublin, Dublin, Ireland

Program Committee

Ana Lucia Varbanescu	University of Amsterdam, the Netherlands
Antonio Vidal	Universidad Politecnica de Valencia, Spain
Cristina Boeres	Universidade Federal Fluminense, Brasil
Dana Petcu	West University of Timisoara, Romania
Edgar Gabriel	University of Houston, USA
Emmanuel Jeannot	Inria, France
Erik Saule	University of North Carolina at Charlotte, USA
George Bosilca	ICL, University of Tennessee, USA
Hatem Ltaief	KAUST, Saudi Arabia
Helen Karatza	Aristotle University of Thessaloniki, Greece
Henk Sips	Delft University of Technology, the Netherlands
Ivan Milentijević	University of Nis, Serbia
Jorge Barbosa	Faculdade de Engenharia do Porto, Portugal
Louis-Claude Canon	Université de Franche-Comté, France
Olivier Beaumont	Inria Bordeaux Sud-Ouest, France
Oliver Sinnen	University of Auckland, New Zealand

Pierre Manneback	University of Mons, Belgium
Rafael Mayo	Universidad Jaume I, Spain
Ramin Yahyapour	University of Dortmund, Germany
Rizos Sakellariou	University of Manchester, UK
Shuichi Ichikawa	Toyohashi University of Technology, Japan
Thomas Rauber	University Bayreuth, Germany
Tom Scogland	Lawrence Livermore National Laboratory, USA
Toshio Endo	Tokyo Institute of Technology, Japan
Vladimir Rychkov	University College Dublin, Ireland

Evaluation Through Realistic Simulations of File Replication Strategies for Large Heterogeneous Distributed Systems

Anchen Chai[1,2(✉)], Sorina Camarasu-Pop[1], Tristan Glatard[4], Hugues Benoit-Cattin[1], and Frédéric Suter[2,3]

[1] Université de Lyon, CREATIS CNRS UMR5220, Inserm U1044, INSA-Lyon, Université Lyon 1, Lyon, France
chai@creatis.insa-lyon.fr
[2] IN2P3 Computing Center, CNRS, Lyon-Villeurbanne, France
[3] Inria, Lyon, France
[4] Department of Computer Science and Software Engineering, Concordia University, Montreal, Canada

Abstract. File replication is widely used to reduce file transfer times and improve data availability in large distributed systems. Replication techniques are often evaluated through simulations, however, most simulation platform models are oversimplified, which questions the applicability of the findings to real systems. In this paper, we investigate how platform models influence the performance of file replication strategies on large heterogeneous distributed systems, based on common existing techniques such as prestaging and dynamic replication. The novelty of our study resides in our evaluation using a realistic simulator. We consider two platform models: a simple hierarchical model and a detailed model built from execution traces. Our results show that conclusions depend on the modeling of the platform and its capacity to capture the characteristics of the targeted production infrastructure. We also derive recommendations for the implementation of an optimized data management strategy in a scientific gateway for medical image analysis.

Keywords: File replication · Platform model · Realistic simulation Evaluation

1 Introduction

File replication to multiple storage resources is a common technique to optimize data management in distributed systems. It reduces file transfer bottlenecks and increases file availability, with great impact on the application execution time [13]. Numerous file replication strategies were proposed and evaluated using simulations [1,9,14,16,20,21], focusing mostly on the optimization of file transfer durations (average or total duration by job). However, platform models are often oversimplified, leading to questionable accuracy of simulated transfer duration.

G. Mencagli et al. (Eds.): Euro-Par 2018 Workshops, LNCS 11339, pp. 409–420, 2019.
https://doi.org/10.1007/978-3-030-10549-5_32

Two platform models are commonly used in the literature. The *homogeneous* model [2,12] uses a nominal bandwidth (e.g., 1 Gb/s) for all the network links between storage and compute resources. The *hierarchical* model [8,17] uses different theoretical bandwidths for different link categories: for instance, 1 Gb/s for local links between computing resources and their local storage resource; 100 Mb/s for national links (compute and storage resources in the same country); 10 Mb/s for inter-country links. While these models might be good approximations for large distributed systems at a coarse level, the limited number of bandwidth values can hardly capture the heterogeneity and the complexity intrinsic to real production systems. In a previous work focusing on simulation accuracy [4], we have shown that the quality of simulated file transfer duration strongly depends on the accuracy of the platform topology and on the parametrization of the simulator. In particular, the homogeneous model can hardly capture the characteristics of a large grid infrastructure and, consequently, the accuracy of the simulation is rather poor when using such a model.

In this paper, we use two different platform models to evaluate file replication strategies: (i) a three-tier hierarchical model, representing the state-of-the-art platform and (ii) a model built from real execution traces. We focus on file management in the EGI e-Infrastructure (http://egi.eu), a large distributed system with hundreds of sites spread world-wide, and in particular on applications executed by the Virtual Imaging Platform (VIP) [11], a Web portal for medical image analysis and simulation. We aim at answering the following questions:

- What is the impact of replication strategies on file transfer durations?
- Does the answer to the above question depend on the platform model?
- What would be reliable recommendations for data placement in VIP?

The remainder of this paper is organized as follows. Section 2 provides some technical background on data replication strategies in general and, more particularly, in EGI and VIP. Section 3 describes our simulation studies with focuses on platform models, studied data placement strategies, and simulation scenarios. Section 4 presents the evaluation and the analysis of the simulation results. Recommendations for the targeted production system are given in Sect. 5. Finally, Sect. 6 summarizes our findings and details of our future work.

2 Technical Background on File Replication

Replication management encompasses both replica creation and replica selection. The former decides where and how many times to replicate a file, while the latter defines how to choose the best replica for a given file transfer. Both components can be implemented in various ways, depending on the features to optimize, e.g., file availability, transfer time, or network usage.

Replica creation strategies can be classified in two categories: *static* and *dynamic*. In static replication, decisions are made before launching the application and not changed during the execution. In [6,15], authors demonstrated that asynchronously replicating data to several remote sites before the application execution can significantly reduce its execution time. This process is named *file prestaging*. Static replication strategies are usually simple to implement, however, they are often inefficient in a dynamic environment such as a large grid infrastructure. In dynamic replication, decisions can adapt to changes of the infrastructure characteristics, e.g., storage capacity or network bandwidth. More replicas can be created on new nodes during the execution of the application and can be deleted when they are no longer required. Dynamic replication strategies often rely on information obtained at runtime, hence adding an extra overhead to the application execution time.

The Unified Middleware Distribution [7] is an integrated set of software components packaged for deployment as production services on EGI. Among them, the data management services allow users to upload files onto a Storage Element (SE), then replicate and register them in a File Catalog. However, the decisions about where to replicate files and how many replicas to create are left to the applications (users). The replica selection algorithm of the middleware selects replicas according to their distance to the computing site, that is, first in the SE local to the computing site, then in the same country as the job execution, and in last resort, randomly among all available replicas.

The replica creation strategy implemented in VIP relies on the experience and *a priori* knowledge of its administrators. VIP files are automatically replicated to a static predefined list of 3 SEs chosen among the ones considered as stable, with a general good network connectivity, and sufficiently large amounts of available storage space (generally at least 500 GB). This list is updated when one of the SEs needs to be replaced, is in downtime, is full, or faces any other issue preventing its usage. The number of replicas may also vary depending on the type and size of the files. Files larger more than 500 MB are usually replicated on the most available SEs.

3 Simulation Studies

The long-term objective of this study is to optimize data placement for scientific gateways such as VIP using large scale distributed heterogeneous infrastructures such as EGI. To this end, we propose to evaluate different simulation scenarios fed with realistic information coming from execution traces. We developed a simulator [18] based on the SimGrid toolkit [3] that is as close as possible to the actual behavior of several VIP services. Hereafter we detail the different components of these simulation scenarios.

3.1 Platform Models

We consider two platform models. First, we extend the realistic trace-based model proposed in [4]. This model determines an average bandwidth value for each network link between a SE and a computing site from file transfer logs of several application executions. This has been shown to give the best accuracy when simulating file transfers. However, some links were not used, and thus not in the logs, while they are needed to conduct the current study.

A naive solution to this issue would be to use the median of all the measured bandwidths for the missing links. However, this would neither reflect the hierarchical topology of the platform nor the overall connectivity of a site concerned by missing link(s). To address this limitation, we first define three categories of network links (local, national, and inter-country) to reflect the topology. For each category c we estimate the connectivity of a site S_i as the ratio between the median bandwidth of the known links to/from S_i and the median bandwidth of all the links: $\widetilde{B_i^c}/\widetilde{B^c}$. We weight this ratio by $|L_i^c|/|L_i|$, since the larger the number of known links, $|L|$, the more reliable the estimation. The overall connectivity of S_i with regard to the rest of the platform is then estimated by the following weighted sum:

$$C_i = \sum_c \left(\frac{|L_i^c|}{|L_i|} . \frac{\widetilde{B_i^c}}{\widetilde{B^c}} \right). \tag{1}$$

Finally, the bandwidth of a missing link of category c to/from S_i is computed as the median bandwidth in this category times the overall connectivity: $\widetilde{B^c} \times C_i$.

While this traced-based model is accurate, it is also complex to build. Therefore, we also consider a simpler model inspired from the state-of-the-art hierarchical model. If simulation results are consistent between the two models, then the building simplicity of this three-level hierarchical platform makes it a good candidate for further studies. To better reflect the connectivity of the production system, we enhance it by using average bandwidth values derived from logs instead of the theoretical values proposed in the literature. We use 1.3 Gb/s for local links, 255 Mb/s for national links, and 100 Mb/s for inter-country links.

3.2 Replication Strategies

We study data placement strategies based on (i) file prestaging and (ii) a dynamic replication strategy. In the file prestaging strategy, files are copied on three preselected SEs before the execution of the application. This corresponds to the current replication strategy used by VIP. We evaluate the impact of different prestaging lists on the performance of file transfers, with or without *a priori* information on the sites where jobs are executed.

Given the large scale of distributed systems such as EGI, allowing thousands of independent jobs to be executed in parallel, we believe that dynamic replication could further improve data placement during the execution of an application. Our idea is inspired by the "cache hit" mechanism. The first job executed in a computing site downloads the file, then copies and registers it onto the local SE associated to this site. Then, the subsequent jobs in the same site can directly benefit of a local file transfer hence optimizing the overall file transfer duration. This strategy derives of two observations made on EGI. First, when the application consists of a large number of jobs, a given site will execute more than one job in general. Second, the queuing time from a job submission to the job execution is highly variable. It means that if subsequent jobs have a much longer queuing time compared to the first job, they can directly benefit of the local transfer without any extra delay. More details are given in [5].

3.3 Simulation Scenarios

We simulate the execution of 15 workflows, each consisting of 100 jobs, to study the performance of file transfers. Realistic information are extracted from execution traces and injected as parameters in our simulator (e.g., the queuing time of jobs, execution site, source and destination of file transfers, ...).

To determine the impact of SE selection for each platform model, we study three categories of prestaging lists: (i) the current production setting, which corresponds to three SEs located in France, (ii) 50 randomly selected lists and (iii) four prestaging lists selected based on statistical information on the sites where the jobs of the 15 workflows were executed. These four lists contain the local SEs of the three sites hosting the largest number of jobs located in one or different countries or three sites hosting no jobs at all located in one or different countries, respectively. We always fix the number of SEs used to prestage files to three to match the number of replicas currently used in production. The impact of the number of SEs is let out of the scope of this paper.

In total, we simulate 220 scenarios (2 strategies $\times$ 2 platform models $\times$ 55 prestaging lists) for each of the 15 workflows.

4 Performance Evaluation

4.1 Impact of Dynamic Replication

We begin our evaluation by studying the cumulative distribution of the simulated durations of file transfers with and without dynamic replication. Each line in Fig. 1 corresponds to one list of 3 SEs used for file prestaging, using either the 3-level (top) or the trace-based (bottom) platform model. The same 50 random prestaging lists are used in all four scenarios.

For the 3-level model, we see that dynamic replication significantly decreases file transfer durations, as more jobs can download files from a local SE. Moreover, the performance does not depend on the SEs used for prestaging with a median duration of 5.1 s and a maximum value of 32.3 s. Without dynamic replication, the choice of the prestaging list has a stronger impact, leading to longer and more variable transfer durations. The median varies from 13 s to 21 s when utilizing different lists while the maximum varies from 123 s to 290 s.

For the trace-based model, we also see a reduction of file transfer durations when using dynamic replication, but the gap is less clear. Contrary to the 3-level model, the performance with dynamic replication varies more significantly depending on the prestaging list. For both models, the choice of the prestaging list always has a strong impact on performance when there is no dynamic replication. Median duration varies from 20 s to 44 s while the maximum and the longest duration is about 975 s when utilizing different lists.

4.2 Impact of Different Prestaging Lists on Static Replication

We saw that, globally, the choice of SEs used for prestaging mainly matters when there is no dynamic replication. To measure the impact of SE choice for file prestaging, we compare the 50 random prestaging lists, the 4 predefined lists and the current prestaging list used in production. The comparisons for the 3-level hierarchical (top) and trace based-model (bottom) are depicted in Fig. 2. We identify the best and the worst prestaging among these 55 lists based on the median simulated file transfers duration. The performance corresponding to the current production prestaging list is also identified (named "prod prestaging"). It utilizes 3 SEs in France, chosen according to the criteria described in Sect. 2. Note that we only evaluate the impact of the prestaging list w.r.t. the file transfer duration. Other aspects taken into account by VIP administrators (e.g., reliability, availability and storage space of each SE) are left as future work.

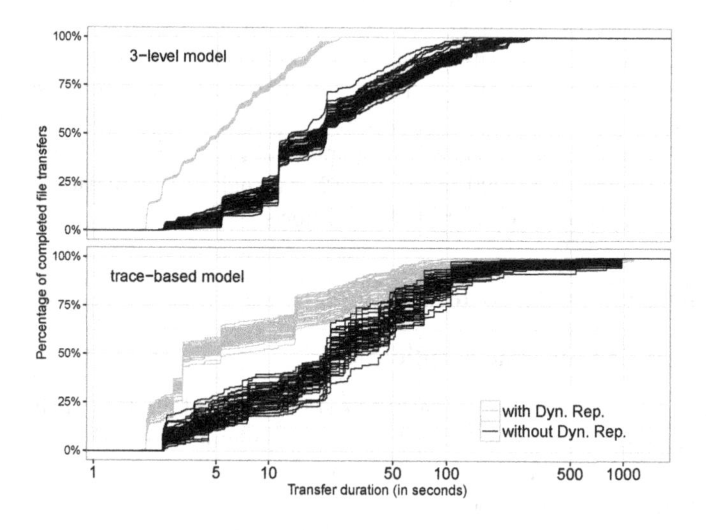

Fig. 1. Cumulative distribution of simulated file transfer durations with and without dynamic replication. Each line corresponds to a list of 3 SEs used for file pre-staging. The same 50 random prestaging lists are used in all four scenarios.

For the 3-level model, the "best prestaging" corresponds to one of the predefined lists: three SEs associated to the sites hosting the largest number of jobs located in three different countries, i.e., UK, Netherlands, and France. By selecting the most used sites, most of the jobs can directly download files from their local SEs. Moreover, scattering file replicas in different countries can efficiently reduce the number of downloads from a foreign country. Conversely, the "worst prestaging" for the 3-level model is given by three SEs associated to sites that do not execute any job and are located in different countries. Thus, most of the jobs download files from a foreign country, which leads to the worst performance.

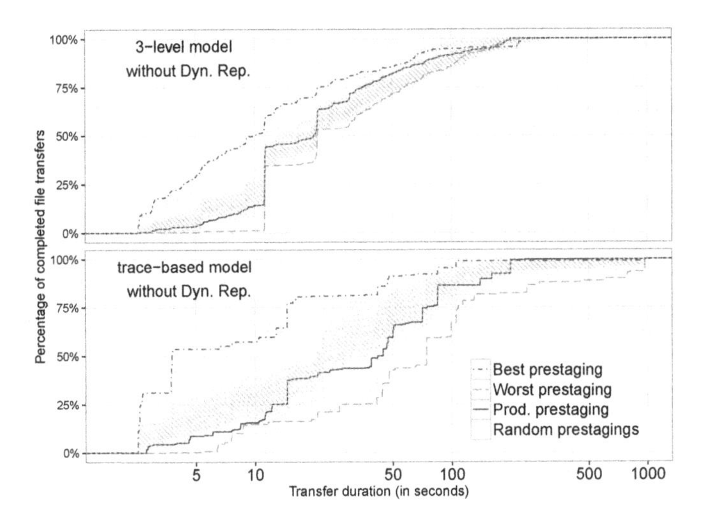

Fig. 2. Comparison of random, predefined, and the current production prestaging list without dynamic replication for two platform models

For the trace-based model, we find the exact same "best prestaging" and "worst prestaging" as for the 3-level model. It further validates the findings from the 3-level model. By collecting more historical information from the DIRAC [19] server that schedules the jobs, we find that UK, Netherlands, and France are the countries hosting the largest number of executed jobs in the Virtual Organization used by VIP. We can thus conclude that the best performance without dynamic replication is likely to be obtained by selecting the SE of the most used sites in different countries hosting the largest cumulative number of executed jobs for both models.

4.3 Impact of Platform Model on Replication Decisions

Figure 3 compares the duration of file transfers when using dynamic replication for the two models. We observe that dynamic replication leads to much more stable results in the 3-level model than in the trace-based model. In other words, in the 3-level model, a random selection of SEs to prestage files is enough: no improved SE selection strategy is required. However, for the trace-based model, we observe a greater variability which can be explained by the important heterogeneity in terms of network connectivity that is better captured by this model. While a local SE may have a poor connectivity in the trace-based model, the 3-level model will always assumes a very good connectivity, which is one of its known limitations.

Figure 4 compares the best performance achieved by predefined or randomly selected lists without dynamic replication for each model. As in simulation we have the complete *a priori* information about the sites on which jobs are going to be executed, the best predefined prestaging list is always better than the best random list that we obtained. Interestingly, we see that the gain is much larger in trace-based model. The more heterogeneous the platform is, the more important *a priori* information (e.g., the distribution of executed jobs on computing sites or in countries) is to optimize file transfers.

It is also interesting to note in Fig. 2 that the performance of the prestaging currently used in production is quite different between the 3-level and trace-based models. In the former, SEs are equivalent in the sense that a single bandwidth value is used for all the links in each category (i.e., local, inter-country, and intra-country). Performance will then be better for lists with SEs close to the sites executing most of the jobs. In the latter, each link is unique and the use of close SEs alone cannot ensure the best performance. The "prod prestaging" list illustrates this. It corresponds to three SEs in France, close to sites that execute more than 16% (which is more than the average sites) of the total number of jobs. However, the general connectivity for these three SEs is worse than the average. This explains why the performance of the "prod prestaging" list is better than most of the randomly selected prestaging lists in the 3-level model and worse in the trace-based model. It also shows that different platform models can lead to different qualitative assessments for similar scenarios.

5 Recommendations for File Replication in VIP on EGI

As we have seen, simulation results are not always consistent between the two models. A larger variability exists in the trace-based model even with dynamic replication. The relative performance of the current production configuration also differs from a model to another. Consequently, recommendations for VIP need to be based on the results obtained with the trace-based model.

Figure 5 compares the best and worst performance (with or without dynamic replication) to the current production setting. The performance with and without dynamic replication is depicted in black and gray, respectively.

Without dynamic replication, a careful selection of the SEs used for file prestaging reduces file transfer times. However, this requires *a priori* information on where jobs are going to be executed. For jobs submitted independently in large distributed systems, we cannot know in advance where they will be executed. However, we could attempt to predict it by leveraging historical data on where the jobs have been running over a given period of time.

Table 1. 95%-confidence interval for the statistics of the simulated release transfers durations of 55 prestagings with and without dynamic replication

	1st Qu.	Median	Mean	3rd Qu.	Max
With Dyn. Rep.	[2.6;2.7]	[3.5;4.3]	[25.6;30.7]	[19.8;24.7]	[1192.1;1301.4]
Without Dyn. Rep.	[8.3;11.2]	[22.9;28.23]	[60.5;71.2]	[57.8;66.9]	[974.4;974.8]

Dynamic replication always outperforms the current production configuration. To better quantify its gain, we computed in Table 1 the 95%-confidence

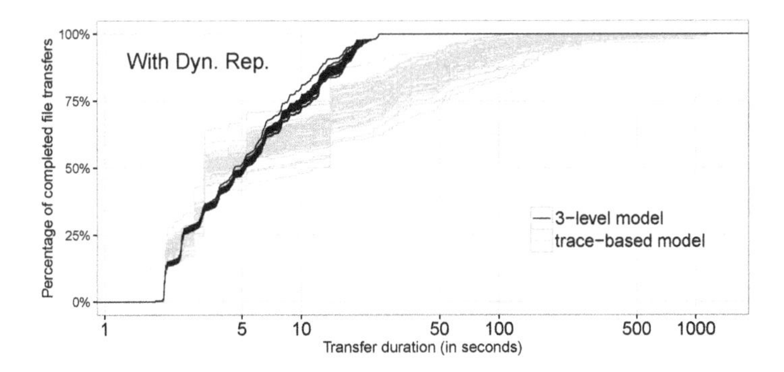

Fig. 3. Cumulative distribution of simulated file transfer durations with dynamic replication for two platform models

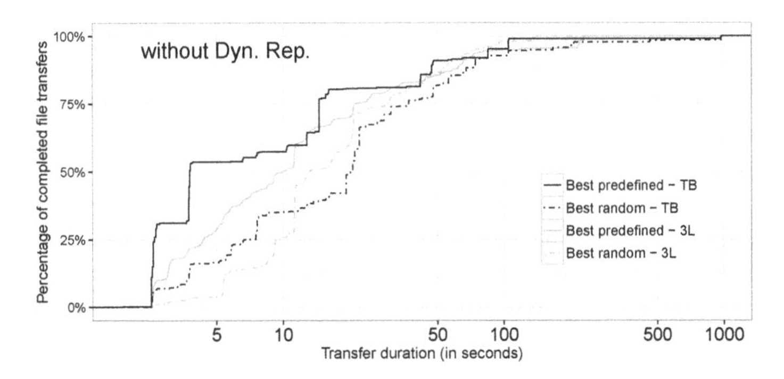

Fig. 4. Cumulative distribution of simulated file transfer durations without dynamic replication for two platform models. Best performance achieved by predefined or randomly selected lists is highlighted.

interval for the statistics on the simulated transfer durations over the 55 studied prestaging lists. We conclude that with dynamic replication, there is a 95% chance that 75% of file transfers will be 2.5 times shorter than without, regardless of the selected prestaging list.

However, the longest transfer duration seems to be worse with dynamic replication. In the proposed dynamic replication algorithm (details are given in [5]), the first job in a site tries to download the file using a timeout to reduce the impact of extremely long transfers [10]. If this timeout expires, this transfer is canceled and a new attempt is made with another SE. Then, the transfer time corresponds to the cumulative time of all transfer attempts (failed and successful). In the studied scenarios, the longest simulated transfer corresponds to a job executed on a site with poor connectivity to/from most SEs in the trace-based model. When using dynamic replication, the timeout expires 3 times, hence adding an overhead of three times the timeout value. This timeout is currently set to 110 s and corresponds to the third quartile of all measured transfer durations. This effect could be mitigated with a timeout value that makes a trade-off

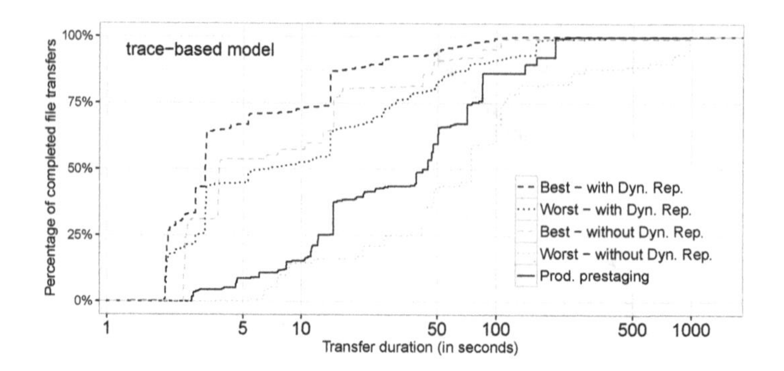

Fig. 5. Comparison of the best and the worst prestaging with the current production prestaging for trace-based model with or without dynamic replication

between the longest acceptable transfer duration and this extra overhead caused by retries. It is important to note that such an extreme case cannot be evaluated with the 3-level model that does not reflect the heterogeneity of the actual infrastructure.

To summarize, we can conclude from our observations that dynamic replication can globally reduce the duration of file transfers except for extreme cases where multiple transfer timeouts are hit successively. Such cases are only captured by the trace-based platform model. As the benefits of dynamic replication comes from the number of jobs that transfer files from a local SE thanks to the copy made by the first job, it may not be interesting for small applications. Finally, implementing such a dynamic replication strategy in the production environment would require non-negligible development effort for the correct handling of concurrent file access synchronization, as well as finding the optimal parameters (e.g., the timeout value and the maximum number of retries).

6 Conclusion

File replication is a widely used technique to optimize data management in distributed systems. Many replication strategies have been proposed in the literature to solve various optimization problems in which efficiency has mostly been evaluated through simulation. However, the often simplified configuration of simulators may critically question the findings derived from simulation results.

In this paper, we presented our efforts to improve the evaluation of file replication strategies by studying two platform models: a 3-level hierarchical model and a model built out of execution traces. We evaluated the impact of different strategies on file transfer durations and compared the results obtained with each model to cross-validate our findings. Last but not least, we proposed recommendations to optimize the replication management for VIP.

Simulation results show that the estimated impact of a strategy can be quite different when the platform model changes. In other words, the conclusion drawn from one model cannot be automatically transferred to another. We show that the instantiation of the two models leads to different qualitative decisions, even though they reflect a similar hierarchical topology. It emphasizes the fact that the realism of the platform model is key to the evaluation process.

By comparing the results obtained with each model, we found that selecting the sites hosting a large number of executed jobs to prestage files is a safe recommendation to optimize data management in the production system. In addition, adopting dynamic replication can further reduce the duration of file transfers except for extreme cases (very poorly connected sites) that our realistic simulations were able to capture.

All the simulation results presented in this article are available online along with all the code and data used to produce them [5]. This material allows readers and reviewers to reproduce and further investigate our results.

As future work, we plan to further improve the accuracy of our trace-based model by collecting more execution traces and evaluate different methods to fill the missing links. It would also be interesting to investigate the influence of the number of replicas and other important parameters (e.g., timeout value) for our strategy and take into account other parameters (e.g., transfer failure rate, storage space, etc.) in the simulation scenarios. We also plan to build probability distributions out of the real execution traces. Integrating them into the simulator would allow us to study different "what if" scenarios.

Acknowledgements. This work is partially supported by the LABEX PRIMES (ANR-11-LABX-0063) of Université de Lyon, within the program "Investissements d'Avenir" (ANR-11-IDEX-0007) operated by the French National Research Agency (ANR). The authors also thank EGI and France Grilles for their support and the provided resources.

References

1. Bsoul, M., Abdallah, A., Almakadmeh, K., Tahat, N.: A round-based data replication strategy. IEEE TPDS **27**(1), 31–39 (2016)
2. Camarasu-Pop, S., Glatard, T., Benoit-Cattin, H.: Simulating application workflows and services deployed on the european grid infrastructure. In: Proceedings of the 13th IEEE/ACM International Symposium on Cluster, Cloud, and Grid Computing, pp. 18–25 (2013)
3. Casanova, H., Giersch, A., Legrand, A., Quinson, M., Suter, F.: Versatile, scalable, and accurate simulation of distributed applications and platforms. J. Parallel Distrib. Comput. **74**(10), 2899–2917 (2014)
4. Chai, A., Bazm, M.M., Camarasu-Pop, S., Glatard, T., Benoit-Cattin, H., Suter, F.: Modeling distributed platforms from application traces for realistic file transfer simulation. In: Proceedings of the 17th IEEE/ACM International Symposium on Cluster, Cloud and Grid Computing, pp. 54–63 (2017)
5. Chai, A., Camarasu-Pop, S., Glatard, T., Benoit-Cattin, H., Suter, F.: Companion of article Evaluation through Realistic Simulations of File Replication Strategies for Large Heterogeneous Distributed Systems (2018). http://doi.org/10.5281/zenodo.1239677

6. Chervenak, A., et al.: Data placement for scientific applications in distributed environments. In: Proceedings of the 8th IEEE/ACM International Conference on Grid Computing, pp. 267–274 (2007)
7. David, M., et al.: Validation of grid middleware for the European grid infrastructure. J. Grid Comput. **12**(3), 543–558 (2014)
8. Dayyani, S., Khayyambashi, M.: RDT: a new data replication algorithm for hierarchical data grid. Int. J. Comput. Sci. Eng. **3**(7), 186–197 (2015)
9. Elghirani, A., Subrata, R., Zomaya, A.: A proactive non-cooperative game-theoretic framework for data replication in data grids. In: Proceedings of the 8th IEEE International Symposium on Cluster Computing and the Grid, pp. 433–440 (2008)
10. Glatard, T., Montagnat, J., Pennec, X.: Optimizing jobs timeouts on clusters and production grids. In: Proceedings of the 7th IEEE International Symposium on Cluster Computing and the Grid, pp. 100–107 (2007)
11. Glatard, T., et al.: A virtual imaging platform for multi-modality medical image simulation. IEEE Trans. Med. Imag. **32**(1), 110–118 (2013)
12. Gupta, H., et al.: iFogSim: a toolkit for modeling and simulation of resource management techniques in the internet of things, edge and fog computing environments. Softw. Pract. Exp. **47**(9), 1275–1296 (2017)
13. Lamehamedi, H., et al.: Data replication strategies in grid environments. In: Proceedings of the 5th International Conference on Algorithms and Architectures for Parallel Processing, pp. 378–383 (2002)
14. Lei, M., Vrbsky, S., Hong, X.: An on-line replication strategy to increase availability in data grids. Future Gener. Comput. Syst. **24**(2), 85–98 (2008)
15. Ranganathan, K., Foster, I.: Simulation studies of computation and data scheduling algorithms for data grids. J. Grid Comput. **1**(1), 53–62 (2003)
16. Sato, H., Matsuoka, S., Endo, T., Maruyama, N.: Access-pattern and bandwidth aware file replication algorithm in a grid environment. In: Proceedings of the 9th IEEE/ACM International Conference on Grid Computing, pp. 250–257 (2008)
17. Shorfuzzaman, M., Graham, P., Eskicioglu, R.: Adaptive popularity-driven replica placement in hierarchical data grids. J. Supercomput. **51**(3), 374–392 (2010)
18. Suter, F., Chai, A., Camarasu-Pop, S.: VIPSimulator: A Simulator of Gate Workflow Execution (2016). http://github.com/frs69wq/VIPSimulator
19. Tsaregorodtsev, A., et al.: DIRAC3 - the new generation of the LHCb grid software. J. Phys. Conf. Ser. **219**(6), 062029 (2010)
20. Vrbsky, S., Lei, M., Smith, K., Byrd, J.: Data replication and power consumption in data grids. In: Proceedings of the 2nd IEEE International Conference on Cloud Computing Technology and Science, pp. 288–295 (2010)
21. Yang, C.T., Fu, C.P., Hsu, C.H.: File replication, maintenance, and consistency management services in data grids. J. Supercomput. **53**(3), 411–439 (2010)

Modeling and Optimizing Data Transfer in GPU-Accelerated Optical Coherence Tomography

Tobias Schrödter[1,2(✉)], David Pallasch[2], Sandra Wienke[3], Robert Schmitt[4], and Matthias S. Müller[3]

[1] RWTH Aachen University, Aachen, Germany
tobias.schroedter@rwth-aachen.de
[2] Fraunhofer-Institute for Production Technology IPT, Aachen, Germany
[3] IT Center, RWTH Aachen University, Aachen, Germany
{wienke,mueller}@itc.rwth-aachen.de
[4] Laboratory for Machine Tools and Production Engineering (WZL), RWTH Aachen University, Aachen, Germany

Abstract. Signal processing of optical coherence tomography (OCT) has become a bottleneck for using OCT in medical and industrial applications. Recently, GPUs gained more importance as compute device to achieve video frame rate of 25 frames/s. Therefore, we develop a CUDA implementation of an OCT signal processing chain: We focus on reformulating the signal processing algorithms in terms of high-performance libraries like CUBLAS and CUFFT. Additionally, we use NVIDIA's stream concept to overlap computations and data transfers. Performance results are presented for two Pascal GPUs and validated with a derived performance model. The model gives an estimate for the overall execution time for the OCT signal processing chain, including compute and transfer times.

Keywords: GPU · OCT · Performance model · CUDA

1 Introduction

Tomographic imaging methods are of great importance in medical and industrial contexts. In medicine, one focus lies on imaging quality and processing speed, whereas in industry the possibilities for automation and cost efficiency are crucial. These various requirements have led to the development of a variety of different tomographic imaging techniques. Originating from ophthalmology, one of the techniques which gained importance in the last 25 years, is optical coherence tomography (OCT). Due to its resolution in the lower micrometer range, it is used in production metrology, i.e., for measuring coating thickness in terms of quality assurance. At the Fraunhofer IPT OCT systems for medical and industrial applications are developed, including the OCT itself as well as the corresponding signal processing.

G. Mencagli et al. (Eds.): Euro-Par 2018 Workshops, LNCS 11339, pp. 421–433, 2019.
https://doi.org/10.1007/978-3-030-10549-5_33

For monitoring processes in a production or biomedical environment, not only a high spatial resolution but also a high temporal resolution is needed. Currently, this is limited by the signal processing time for OCT systems. The goal is to achieve a frame rate of 25 frames/s, which corresponds to 40 ms of processing time. Increasing the frame rate beyond this value may not benefit the human eye while observing the process, but creates headroom for further image processing and evaluation, as well as accelerating processing volumetric data. GPUs with the possibility of executing massively parallel computations promise processing of high-resolution OCT images with video frame rate. Hence, we developed a GPU-parallel CUDA version of the signal processing based on an existing CPU implementation. Since the investigated OCT system has been designed to be cost-effective, we focused solely on consumer GPUs with Pascal architecture. For testing and validating the GPU implementation a middle class and a high-end GPU have been used. To validate the performance of our implementation, we derive a performance model for the OCT signal processing chain that covers runtime prediction of kernels and data transfers. This model can also be used to get an estimate which resolutions could be achieved with a given GPU.

Thus, our main contributions are:

- A CUDA-based GPU implementation of the OCT signal processing chain with focus on leveraging highly-optimized (BLAS) libraries
- A performance model which describes the computation and the data transfer of the GPU signal processing
- Investigation of two different NVIDIA GPUs in comparison to two CPU-parallel versions

The paper is structured as follows: Sect. 2 presents related work. The basics of OCT and the used signal processing functions are described in Sect. 3. The parallelization concepts using CUDA follow in Sect. 4. In Sect. 5, we derive a performance model for the given OCT signal processing chain. The performance results of our parallelization is presented in Sect. 6. Finally, we conclude and give a short outlook in Sect. 7.

2 Related Work

Due to the needed processing time, using GPUs has become an important factor during the development of OCT systems. So far, the main focus has lied on resampling the data [11,18], or using multiple GPUs one for computation and one for visualization [15,17]. These works do not elaborate on their strategies for implementing a GPU version of the OCT signal processing chain, especially leveraging BLAS libraries have not been reported yet. In addition, different libraries are available which are designed for tomographic signal processing such as the ASTRA Toolbox [1]. However, they do not include algorithms that are specifically needed for the signal processing of the Fraunhofer IPT OCT system.

While different techniques exist for performance models for GPUs [12], we focus on analytical-based models that illustrate a comprehensive approach. That means the model must cover the computational part, as well as the GPU-CPU data transfers, and should not be tied to a specific application. Various models have been established to describe the transfer times on distributed-memory systems [2–4]. The model of Boyer et al. [3] gives an estimate for the transfer time based on the GPU's bandwidth. A theoretical performance model, based on the Roofline Model [16], for GPU applications has been introduced as the so-called Boat Hull Model [13]. It gives an estimate of the floor of the attainable runtime for the computational part depending on the device specifications and some algorithm specific characteristics. To model concurrent copy and compute operations, Gómez-Luna et al. [8] have focused on (today) older NVIDIA architectures, where Werkhoven et al. [14] update this approach to (more) recent NVIDIA architectures with multiple copy engines. In this work, we combine the approaches of [3,13], and [14] to derive a complete model for the OCT signal processing chain as real-world application.

3 Optical Coherence Tomography

Optical coherence tomography is a cross-sectional tomographic imaging method and is mostly applied in ophthalmology, due to the possibility of creating contact free cross-sectional images of the eye [9]. In contrast to traditional imaging techniques, OCT offers a higher penetration depth than confocal microscopy and a better resolution than ultrasound imaging. Due to its destruction-free nature and the possibility of a complete fiber-optic setup, OCT has recently been introduced into new fields in biomedical imaging like cancer detection and tissue engineering, as well as in production technology for quality assurance.

OCT is an interferometric measurement technique, in which low-coherent light excites the material under investigation. Light, which is backscattered at different depths inside the sample, is overlapped with light from a reference path and interferes at the detector. The interference creates a modulated signal whose frequency depends on the depth of the reflection. In a Frequency-Domain-OCT (FD-OCT), a spectrometer is used to measure the interference and therefore obtain spectral resolved modulated data. The depths of the reflection can be computed by using a Fourier transformation on the modulated data, resulting in the depth profile of the sample. As this is only a brief overview of OCT we recommend [7] for further reading.

The OCT signal processing chain, as implemented in the OCT software at Fraunhofer IPT, is shown in Fig. 1. For controlling the line scan camera and the data acquisition boards only C++ interfaces are available, hence the driver is implemented in C++. The obtained signal is stored in vectors as `unsigned short` values and is processed serially on the CPU. From the line scan camera of the spectrometer the recorded spectrum of a 2D-scan (B-scan) is continuously written into the acquisition buffer. In the next step the data is processed and the results are written to the display buffer.

Due to physical effects, the modulated data recorded by the line scan camera is not equidistantly spaced [10]. Since Fourier transformations can only be

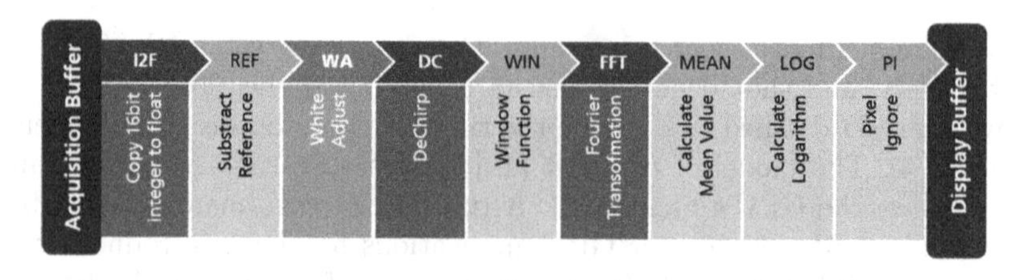

Fig. 1. Signal processing chain. Dark gray items display necessary operations of OCT signal processing, orange the bottleneck of the CPU implementation (WA).

applied if the data is sampled in an equidistant manner, the data must be rescaled (DC). To obtain the depth profile of the sample, the Fourier transformation (FFT) is applied. For this, we use the FFTW algorithm [6], in particular the real to complex transformation, where only the magnitude of the result is of interest. To reduce noise in the detected spectrum, the average of 1D-scans (A-scan) contained in the B-scan is computed and subtracted from the complete scan, here referred by white adjust (WA). Its implementation will be explained in Sect. 4.

As test data sets, we use different real-life OCT images that contain B-scans of a pill (1120 × 256 px, 1120 × 500 px) and cancerous tissue (2048 × 512 px). Since we are also interested in the performance for large data sets, one data set was artificially enlarged, by doubling the input data (up to 2048 × 8192 px). With these data sets also the correctness of the GPU implementation is assured.

In Fig. 2 the absolute runtimes of the serial reference OCT implementation are shown. The white adjust needs up to 40% of the execution time. FFT, DC and MEAN are further bottlenecks in the application. The red-dotted line indicates the time limit for processing data with a video frame rate. A B-scan of size 2018 × 1536 px is already too large to be processed in less than 40 ms. As the Fraunhofer IPT targets at larger data sets, a faster processing is needed.

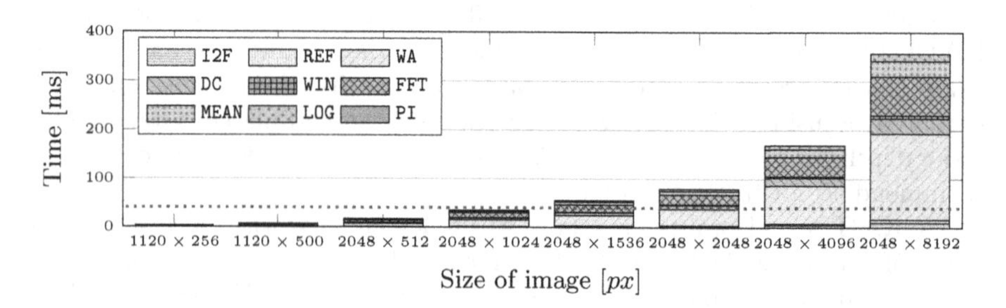

Fig. 2. Runtime of the reference implementation, split into the different processing steps. The red line indicates the target frame rate of 25 frames per second.

4 Parallelization with CUDA

Based on the existing serial CPU signal processing chain, we developed a massively-parallel GPU implementation with CUDA that focuses on matrix models. These models could also be applied to the original CPU implementation to parallelize it and speedup its runtime.

4.1 Signal Processing Chain

For our CUDA implementation of the signal processing chain, we focused on empowering the OCT application to leverage optimizations provided by the CUBLAS library. We remodeled the data alignment of the original CPU implementation (see Sect. 3) in matrix notation as shown in Eq. 1. Using the fact, that each A-scan is written continuously into the memory, we used a column-major ordered matrix.

$$\begin{bmatrix} A_1^1 & A_1^2 & \dots & A_1^{d_B} \\ A_2^1 & A_2^2 & \dots & A_2^{d_B} \\ \vdots & \vdots & \ddots & \vdots \\ A_{d_A}^1 & A_{d_A}^2 & \dots & A_{d_A}^{d_B} \end{bmatrix} \qquad (1)$$

We exemplify the data interpretation as matrix model by looking in-depth at the white adjust function (`WA` in Fig. 2) which is the hotspot of the CPU implementation. Originally, three consecutive for-loops are used to improve the image quality. The first loop computes the sum, the second one divides by the number of A-scans, and the third loop subtracts the result from the original data. The computation of the average can also be written as a matrix vector product, which can be computed by calling `gemv` provided by the BLAS library. It computes $y \leftarrow \alpha Ax + \beta y$ where A is the obtained B-scan, x is a vector of ones, $\alpha = \frac{1}{\text{\# A-scans}}$, and $\beta = 0$. The results stored in y are subtracted from each A-scan in A using the `ger` function: $A \leftarrow \alpha y x^T + A$. We assign x as vector of ones, reuse y and A from the previous step and set $\alpha = -1$. Thus, we rewrote three for-loops using two BLAS calls. Using BLAS calls also holds for rewriting `MEAN` and `REF` (see Sect. 3). To map code parts to CUBLAS-specific functions, we also applied matrix models to the functions `PI` and `WIN`, which could be reformulated using `cublasDdgmm` with a weighting vector as diagonal matrix.

For the function `FFT`, we exchanged the FFTW library that is used in the CPU version by NVIDIA's CUFFT library. It performs multiple Fourier Transforms in parallel since the A-scans are independent from each other. For functions which could not be remodeled in matrix notation, we used THRUST whenever possible. It provides a GPU-optimized version of `std::lib` algorithms. With THRUST, self-written transformations can be applied to each value of a data vector. In case of `LOG` and amplitude computations, which is part of `FFT` we used this to perform the needed operations. Finally, we provide self-written kernels for the remaining functions, namely `I2F` and `DC`. An overview of the used principles per function is given in Table 1.

Table 1. Overview of optimization principles for the signal processing functions.

Function	I2F	REF	WA	DC	WIN	FFT	MEAN	LOG	PI
Principle	kernel	CUBLAS	CUBLAS	kernel	CUBLAS	CUFFT+THRUST	CUBLAS	THRUST	CUBLAS

4.2 Data Transfer

To optimize the data transfer to and from the GPU, we keep unmodified data on the GPU and, thus, reduce the amount of data transferred. Data that is modified in each step (B-scans) is copied as a whole to the GPU, resulting in a high bandwidth. Furthermore, we use pinned memory with no ECC for all data transfers as we aimed for asynchronous data transfers. `OCT_sync` is the first code version that the parallelization of all kernels in the signal processing chain while relying on synchronous data transfers.

For the second (further optimized) code version `OCT_async`, we overlap data transfer and compute operations by using CUDA's streaming concept and asynchronous operations. Since the OCT B-scans are independent from each other, each CUDA stream processes one B-scan. Thus, the processing can be executed in one stream and another one moves data at the same time.

5 Performance Model

For validating the performance of the presented CUDA implementation, a performance model which takes the compute and data transfer times with synchronous and asynchronous transfers into account is derived. The results of the performance models also depend on the hardware, as GPU we used a Geforce GTX Titan X and a Geforce 1050 Ti, both of Pascal architecture. An overview of the specifications is given in Table 2.

5.1 Signal Processing

As part of an overall performance model, we take the Boat Hull Model [13] to abstract the OCT signal processing functions on the GPU. The model contains the compute and memory bound of the Roofline Model. As our analysis reveals that all functions are of low computational complexity, we only consider the memory bound. The estimated runtime m_0 for memory bound kernels is given by Eq. 2 with $d = c+u$, where d is the total amount of data accessed, and c and u are the coalesced and uncoalesced memory accesses respectively. The corresponding

Table 2. Specifications of the used GPUs.

	Architecture	Memory	MP	CUDA cores	GPU Clock rate	Mem. Clock rate	Mem. Bus Width
GTX Titan X	Pascal	12 GB	24	3072	1.08 GHz	3505 MHz	384 bit
GTX 1050 Ti	Pascal	4 GB	6	768	1.46 GHz	3504 MHz	128 bit

Table 3. Performance properties of the different used GPUs.

	$P_{coalesced}$	$P_{uncoalesced}$	b_{H2D}	α_{H2D}	b_{D2H}	α_{D2H}
GTX Titan X	230 GB/s	10 GB/s	6.1610 GB/s	0.030 ms	6.7084 GB/s	0.030 ms
GTX 1050 Ti	101 GB/s	12 GB/s	6.1614 GB/s	0.035 ms	6.7066 GB/s	0.050 ms

bandwidths are given by $P_{coalesced}$ and $P_{uncoalesced}$. If only scattered memory accesses occur, m_1 gives the estimated execution time.

$$m_0 = \frac{c}{P_{coalesced}} + \frac{u}{P_{uncoalesced}}, \quad m_1 = \frac{d}{P_{uncoalesced}} \tag{2}$$

To determine the on-device bandwidth we used the SHOC `deviceMemory` benchmark [5]. We used the maximum of the measurements of `readGlobalMemoryCoalesced` as bandwidth for the coalesced memory access $P_{coalesced}$, whereas the lowest value of `readGlobalMemoryUnit` and `writeGlobalMemoryUnit` represents $P_{uncoalesced}$. The latter measures the read or write bandwidth of uncoalesced, per thread contiguous, global memory accesses [5]. Since we optimized the algorithms by using high-performance libraries the particular memory access pattern cannot be reconstructed. Therefore, we needed to base values for c and u in the model on the assumption that the used libraries mainly use contiguous data access. From results of the NVIDIA profiler, we conclude that c is between 60% and 95% of the total data amount d depending on the signal processing function. The GPU-specific model parameters are listed in Table 3.

5.2 Data Transfer

Besides modeling the performance of the single GPU kernels, it is crucial to also incorporate the CPU-GPU data transfer into the performance evaluation for a better representation of the reality. First, we describe a general model for CPU-GPU data transfers where the hardware-dependent parameters are obtained by benchmarks. Later, we modified this model to take the OCT-specific data transfers into account.

For modeling the time of the data transfer, we generally used $T(d) = \alpha + \frac{d}{\beta}$ with data size d in Byte, latency α in seconds, and β the transfer bandwidth [3]. For modeling the data transfer to the GPU, it holds $d = 2B \times d_A \times d_B$, $\alpha = \alpha_{H2D}$, and $\beta = b_{H2D}$. The transfer of the data back to CPU is divided into two parts. First the processed data with $d_A \times d_B$ elements. Secondly, the computed spectrum with $(\frac{d_A}{2} + 1) \times d_B$ elements is copied to the CPU. Each element of the data sets is of type `float`, hence has a size of 4 B. Additionally, the latency α_{D2H} is needed twice, once for each copy operation, as displayed in Eq. 3.

$$T_{D2H}(d_A, d_B) = 2 \cdot \alpha_{D2H} + \frac{4B}{b_{D2H}} \times d_A \times d_B + \frac{4B}{b_{D2H}} \times (\frac{d_A}{2} + 1) \times d_B \quad (3)$$

We used the SHOC benchmarks `BusSpeedDownload` and `BusSpeedReadback` for b_{H2D} and b_{D2H}, and self-written latency benchmarks for α_{H2D} and α_{D2H}. The results are reported in Table 3. Of particular interest are the bandwidths for data sets of 0.5 MB to 64 MB, as our test data sets. Both GPUs reach the maximum of the transfer bandwidth at approx. 30 MB. As we are primarily interested in the performance of high-resolution OCT data sets, the highest attainable bandwidth is used as model parameter. Comparing the model and the results from the benchmark yield a deviation lower than 10%. This deviation occurs mainly at small data sizes since we used the highest attainable bandwidth as model parameter, hence, the transfer times for small data sets are underestimated.

5.3 Synchronous Data Transfer (`OCT_sync`)

The standard copy in CUDA is executed synchronously, meaning that the copy operation first has to be completed before the next processing step can start. For modeling the performance of systems with no overlapping computations or data transfers, the runtime T is the sum of the data transfer time from host to device and vise-versa (T_{H2D} and T_{D2H}) and the runtime of all kernels $T_{proc} = \sum m_0$. Thus, the total processing can be estimated by Eq. 4.

$$T = T_{H2D} + T_{proc} + T_{D2H} \quad (4)$$

5.4 Asynchronous Data Transfer (`OCT_async`)

Modeling data transfer of GPUs with two copy engines (as in the used Pascal GPUs) and no implicit synchronization is objective of [14]. The predicted runtime is the maximum of all possible combinations of overlap as described in Eq. 5. From Sect. 5.1 we concluded that the GPU is not utilized completely since all processing functions are memory bound. Hence, multiple compute operations of different streams can be executed concurrently on the GPU. Thus, the second term in Eq. 5 can be neglected since it describes the case that all computations are executed serially. The first term of Eq. 5 can also be eliminated since the time needed for the copy from device to host is always larger than the transfer from host to device, since more data needs to be transferred. Including the results from the previous steps yields the performance model for a GPU with two copy engines (as in our Pascal GPUs) for the OCT signal processing chain.

$$T = max(\cancel{T_{H2D} + \frac{T_{proc}}{\#streams} + \frac{T_{D2H}}{\#streams}}, \cancel{\frac{T_{H2D}}{\#streams} + T_{proc} + \frac{T_{D2H}}{\#streams}}, \frac{T_{H2D}}{\#streams} + \frac{T_{proc}}{\#streams} + T_{D2H}) \quad (5)$$

6 Results

For evaluating the performance of the OCT signal processing chain, we reduced the software system of Fraunhofer IPT to a test setup focusing on the signal processing functions included as shared libraries in the test suite. These implementations were compiled using either Microsoft's Visual Compiler 14.0 (MS VS), Intel's Compiler 17.0 (ICC) or CUDA 8.0, respectively. Additionally to the provided serial reference implementation (`MSVS`), BLAS libraries are utilized for CPU-parallel versions: `BLAS` (OpenBLAS + MS VS) and `ICC` (MKL + ICC). We used two different test set-ups: First a work station at Fraunhofer IPT, second a compute node of the RWTH Aachen cluster. The work station contains an Intel i7 3820 Sandy Bridge CPU with 3.6 GHz on 4 cores (8 threads) and 16 GB main memory. The compute nodes of the cluster are 2-socket Intel Broadwell EP E5-2650v4@2.2 GHz systems with an overall of 24 cores. Due to unbalanced data affinity, using only one socket with 6 threads and `close` thread binding yields the best-effort performance (`ICC_BW`). Future work will cover improved data affinity.

Runtime measurements on the CPU were tracked using the `boost::timer`, whereas CUDA calls were measured with CUDA events. The measured time also includes some overhead from the program flow of the processing chain. For `OCT_async`, we conducted an overall measurement of 100 runs and then derived the average runtime of a single execution. Furthermore, each of the measurements is the mean of 100 separate runs. We ensured that the standard deviation of measurements is within 10% of the reported mean and the measurements are roughly normally distributed. The number of used streams was set (up) to the number of multiprocessors as this lead to the best results in our tests (see Table 2). Times needed for initial copy operations of constant values to the GPU is not taken into account since it can be neglected when using OCT in real applications.

6.1 Model vs. Measurement

To validate the performance of `OCT_async`, we compare the measured runtimes with our predicted times from the model (see Eq. 5). For the Geforce GTX Titan X, the results are displayed in Fig. 3, tested to a maximum of 16 streams. Comparing `OCT_sync` with the predicted runtimes, shows an error of 5% to 8%. In case of `OCT_async`, the largest error (20%) occurs when using 4 streams, where our implementation has a better performance than predicted by the model. Using more than 4 streams lead to no further performance improvement, contrary more streams tend to lead to a slower processing time for smaller data sets. In case of the Geforce GTX 1050 Ti, the measured and predicted runtimes are shown in Fig. 4. The difference for `OCT_sync` is less than 5% for all tested data sets. Although the Geforce GTX 1050 has 6 multiprocessors, we tested it up to 4 streams, as our tests showed the best performance. The difference between model and reality is up 15%.

For both GPUs, `OCT_sync` is slower as predicted by the model. But when using multiple streams the measured execution time is faster than the model.

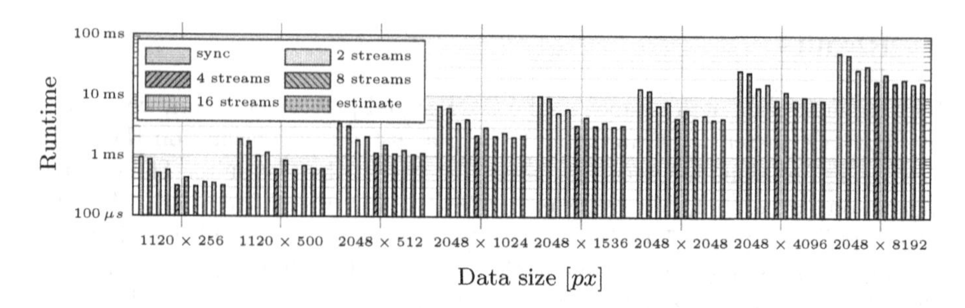

Fig. 3. Comparison of measured and predicted compute times on Geforce GTX Titan X with asynchronous data transfer.

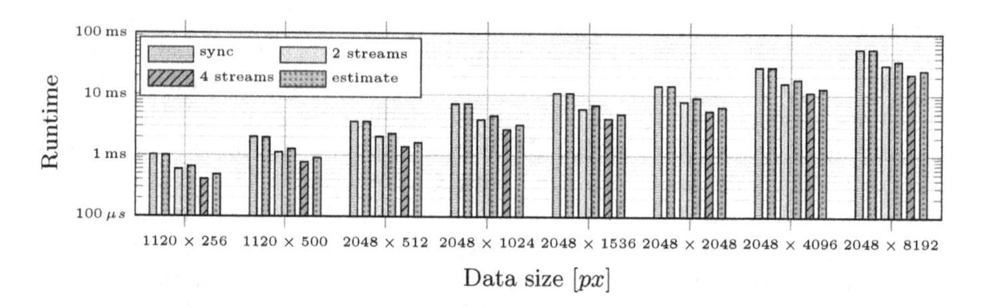

Fig. 4. Comparison of measured and predicted compute times on Geforce GTX 1050 Ti with asynchronous data transfer.

The error is mainly introduced in the prediction of T_{proc}, in particular in the functions where mostly scattered memory accesses occur, i.e. `DC`. The benchmarked $P_{uncoalesced}$ is based on more coalesced memory accesses than the compute kernels, leading to an overestimation of the runtime. However, the performance of our GPU implementations lies close to the predicted runtimes.

6.2 Performance Comparison

With the given (serial) reference implementation (`MSVS`), scans up to a size of 2048×1024 px could be processed with the desired frame rate. In Fig. 5, the processing times of the different implementations and data sizes are shown. Additionally, the speed-up compared to `MSVS` is displayed. The developed CPU parallel versions allow to process our data set with 2048×2048 px in less than 40 ms. They lead to a speed-up between 1.5 and 3, which means up to 3 times higher frame rate compared to the serial implementation. Due to higher clock frequency, we get nearly the same execution time for the Sandy Bridge as for the Broadwell node (`ICC` vs. `ICC_BW`). By using our new implemented GPU version with synchronous data transfer `OCT_sync`, all of the given test data sets could be processed faster than 40 ms with both GPUs. Overall the synchronous GPU

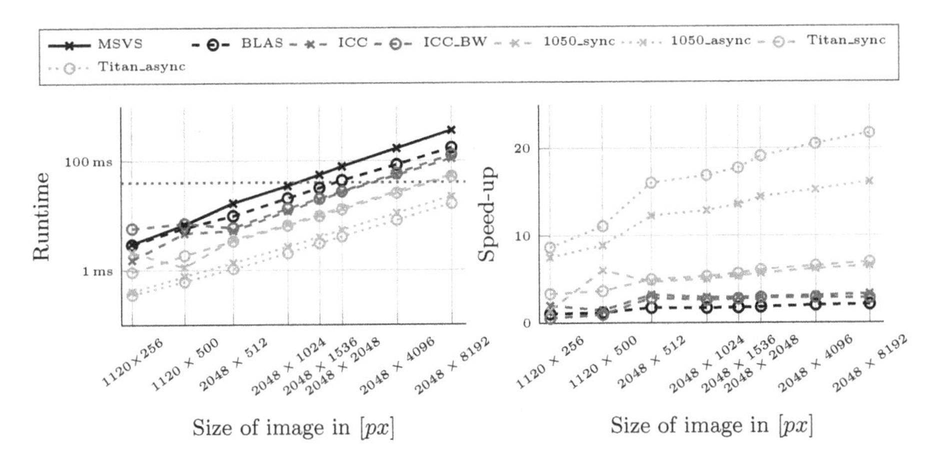

Fig. 5. Runtime comparison (log scale) of the different implementations and Speed-up compared to the serial reference implementation for the OCT signal processing chain.

implementation is 5 to 7 times faster than the provided reference implementation. Compared to the CPU-parallel version a speed-up of 2.5 to 3 is achieved. Now using `OCT_async` reduces the processing time by a factor of 2.5 for the Geforce GTX 1050 Ti compared to `OCT_sync`. Resulting in a speed-up of 8 to 16 compared to `MSVS`, and 4 to 5 compared to the CPU-parallel implementations. For the Geforce GTX Titan X, an additional speed-up of 3 could be noted compared to `OCT_sync`, hence, it can process the OCT signal 8 to 21 times faster than `MSVS`. Compared to the CPU-parallel versions `OCT_async` is 5 to 7 times faster.

7 Conclusion and Outlook

For creating tomographic images with OCT, the signal processing is the limiting factor to achieve a frame rate of 25 frames/s for smoothly displaying the result. In this work, we developed a GPU-parallel version of Fraunhofer IPT's OCT software using CUDA. We further created a corresponding performance model that includes runtime prediction of the OCT kernels and the PCIe data transfers.

For the porting of the signal processing kernels, we focused on re-formulating the algorithms in matrix notation to leverage highly-tuned libraries like CUBLAS. Furthermore, our optimizations included overlapping of data transfers and computations. With our CUDA implementation `OCT_sync`, we achieve a speed-up of factor 5 to 7 on consumer Pascal GPUs over the serial CPU version. Hence, the frame rate is increased from 3 frames/s to 20 frames/s for the largest data set. With `OCT_async`, 45 frames/s are reached for this data set, i.e., a speed-up of 5 compared to the CPU-parallel versions. Our performance model captures all important properties of these OCT GPU implementations. Deviations of measured and modeled performance results are below 15%. Using the model, we estimate that B-scans up to 2048×24576 px can be processed with video rate.

In future, to achieve further acceleration and enable video frame rates for volumetric 3D-scans, we will constantly optimize the code for both, CPU and GPU. Part of this is using the GPU to directly displaying the obtained signal, hence, saving two copy operations.

References

1. van Aarle, W., et al.: Fast and flexible x-ray tomography using the astra toolbox. Opt. Express **24**(22), 25129–25147 (2016)
2. Alexandrov, A., Ionescu, M.F., Schauser, K.E., Scheiman, C.: LogGP: incorporating long messages into the logp model for parallel computation. J. Parallel Distrib. Comput. **44**(1), 71–79 (1997)
3. Boyer, M., Meng, J., Kumaran, K.: Improving GPU performance prediction with data transfer modeling. In: 2013 IEEE International Symposium on Parallel Distributed Processing, Workshops and PhD Forum, pp. 1097–1106, May 2013
4. Culler, D.E., et al.: LogP: a practical model of parallel computation. Commun. ACM **39**(11), 78–85 (1996)
5. Danalis, A., et al.: The scalable heterogeneous computing (SHOC) benchmark suite. In: Proceedings of the 3rd Workshop on General-Purpose Computation on Graphics Processing Units, GPGPU-3, pp. 63–74. ACM, New York (2010)
6. Frigo, M., Johnson, S.G.: The design and implementation of FFTW3. Proc. IEEE **93**(2), 216–231 (2005). special issue on "Program Generation, Optimization, and Platform Adaptation"
7. Drexler, W., Fujimoto, J.G.: Optical Coherence Tomography: Technology and Applications. Springer, Heidelberg (2008). https://doi.org/10.1007/978-3-540-77550-8
8. Gómez-Luna, J., González-Linares, J.M., Benavides, J.I., Guil, N.: Performance models for asynchronous data transfers on consumer graphics processing units. J. Parallel Distrib. Comput. **72**(9), 1117–1126 (2012). accelerators for High-Performance Computing
9. Huang, D., et al.: Optical coherence tomography. Science **254**(5035), 1178–1181 (1991)
10. Izatt, J.A., Choma, M.A.: Theory of optical coherence tomography. In: Drexler, W., Fujimoto, J.G. (eds.) Optical Coherence Tomography. Biological and Medical Physics, Biomedical Engineering, pp. 47–72. Springer, Heidelberg (2008). https://doi.org/10.1007/978-3-540-77550-8_2
11. Van der Jeught, S., Bradu, A., Podoleanu, A.G.: Real-time resampling in fourier domain optical coherence tomography using a graphics processing unit. J. Biomed. Opt. **15**(3), 030511–030511-3 (2010)
12. Madougou, S., Varbanescu, A., de Laat, C., van Nieuwpoort, R.: The landscape of GPGPU performance modeling tools. Parallel Comput. **56**, 18–33 (2016)
13. Nugteren, C., Corporaal, H.: The boat hull model: enabling performance prediction for parallel computing prior to code development. In: Proceedings of the 9th Conference on Computing Frontiers, CF 2012. ACM Press (2012)
14. Van Werkhoven, B., Maassen, J., Seinstra, F.J., Bal, H.E.: Performance models for CPU-GPU data transfers. In: 2014 14th IEEE/ACM International Symposium on Cluster, Cloud and Grid Computing, pp. 11–20, May 2014

15. Wieser, W., Draxinger, W., Klein, T., Karpf, S., Pfeiffer, T., Huber, R.: High definition live 3D-OCT in vivo: design and evaluation of a 4D OCT engine with 1 GVoxel/s. Biomed. Opt. Express **5**(9), 2963–2977 (2014)
16. Williams, S., Waterman, A., Patterson, D.: Roofline: an insightful visual performance model for multicore architectures. Commun. ACM **52**(4), 65–76 (2009)
17. Zhang, K., Kang, J.U.: Graphics processing unit-based ultrahigh speed real-time fourier domain optical coherence tomography. IEEE J. Sel. Top. Quantum Electron. **18**(4), 1270–1279 (2012)
18. Zhang, K., Kang, J.U.: Real-time 4D signal processing and visualization using graphics processing unit on a regular nonlinear-k fourier-domain oct system. Opt. Express **18**(11), 11772–11784 (2010)

A Modular Precision Format for Decoupling Arithmetic Format and Storage Format

Thomas Grützmacher[1] and Hartwig Anzt[1,2(✉)]

[1] Karlsruhe Institute of Technology, Karlsruhe, Germany
thogru.kit@gmx.de
[2] University of Tennessee, Knoxville, USA
hartwig.anzt@kit.edu

Abstract. In this work, we propose to decouple the arithmetic format from the storage format in numerical algorithms. We complement this idea with a modular precision storage layout that allows runtime precision adaptation such that a value can be accessed faster if lower accuracy is acceptable. Combined with precision-aware numerical algorithms that use full precision in all arithmetic computations, this strategy can result in runtime savings without impacting the memory footprint or the accuracy of the final result. In an experimental analysis using the adaptive precision Jacobi method we assess the benefits of the modular precision format on a recent high-end GPU architecture.

Keywords: Mixed precision numerics · Modular precision ecosystem Customized precision · GPUs · Adaptive precision Jacobi

1 Introduction

Over the last decades, the scientific computing community witnessed a widening gap between the computational performance in terms of the number of floating-point operations per second (FLOPS) on the one side, and the memory throughput in terms of how fast data can be brought into the computational elements (bandwidth) on the other side. As a result, more and more algorithms are hitting the "memory wall," which means the performance being limited by the memory bandwidth, and the algorithms executing only at a fraction of the theoretical peak performance. Already today, sparse linear algebra powering a large fraction of the scientific simulations are memory bound on virtually all existing hardware architectures. To continue the success story of simulation-based research, it is therefore essential to develop novel strategies that allow to transfer the growing computational power into algorithm performance.

In this work, we introduce a disruptive paradigm change with respect to how data is stored and processed in numerical linear algebra. To reflect the imbalance between computational power and memory bandwidth, we propose to radically

G. Mencagli et al. (Eds.): Euro-Par 2018 Workshops, LNCS 11339, pp. 434–443, 2019.
https://doi.org/10.1007/978-3-030-10549-5_34

decouple the storage format from the arithmetic format. We complement this idea with the introduction of a "modular precision ecosystem" with demand-fitted memory access routines. The idea behind is to decompose the IEEE standard precision formats into segments, and to store those in a fashion that enables efficient access to the values at variable accuracy. This allows to maintain standard working precision in all arithmetic floating-point operations, but radically reduces the cost of accessing the data if lower accuracy is acceptable.

We structure the rest of the paper as follows. In Sect. 2 we review some existing work on mixed precision numerics before we introduce the idea of the modular precision format in Sect. 3. We start the experimental section with a review of the adaptive precision Jacobi that we employ to assess the efficiency of the modular precision format and the developed memory access routines. The experimental results we report in Sect. 4 are obtained from addressing a set of artificial test problems on a high-end NVIDIA GPU. We conclude in Sect. 5 with an outlook on future work.

2 Related Work on Mixed Precision Numerics

To illustrate the approach we take and its uniqueness, we address the iterative solution of linear systems, which is a common task in scientific computing. The quality of an iteratively generated solution depends on the condition number of the linear system and the floating-point format that is employed to represent the numbers. Generally, numerical errors due to rounding result in a less accurate solution if a lower precision format is used. For scientific simulation codes, IEEE double precision has become the de-facto standard. The numerical values are stored in a binary format where a certain number of bits is used for storing mantissa, exponent, and sign of the floating-point number representation [10].

While running an iterative solver in lower than double precision typically results in a solution approximation of inferior quality, this solution approximation can usually be generated much faster: The approximation accuracy stagnates after fewer iterations, and every iteration only reads and writes data in reduced precision, which, for memory bound algorithms, directly corresponds to runtime savings. Leveraging this property in a smart fashion can enable savings also when generating double precision solutions. The idea here is to combine different precision formats inside a single algorithm, and use double precision only if needed.

Among the most popular mixed precision strategies is the mixed precision iterative refinement technique [5,8,12]. There, the idea is to refine a solution approximation by solving a residual equation in lower than working precision. In many situations, double precision accuracy can be achieved [9]. Other recent work suggests the use of an incomplete factorization preconditioner computed in lower precision inside an iterative F-GMRES framework [6], and even extends this approach by cascading multiple formats of decreasing precision [7]. What all these approaches share is the tight coupling between working precision format and storage format. While this seems to be a natural choice, it ignores the hardware trend of the computational power growing at a much faster pace than the memory bandwidth.

In [2], a preconditioner stored in low precision is employed inside a high precision iterative solver. The numerical properties of the preconditioner are analyzed and, if the characteristics allow for it, stored in lower than working precision. This can be seen as a step towards decoupling storage format from arithmetic format, but as only IEEE standard formats are considered, the values have to be converted between the formats with careful protection against under- and overflow.

A different mixed precision strategy was presented in [3], where the distinct components in the solution vector are handled in different precision formats, each adapted to the component's convergence progress. The underlying idea is to truncate the double precision format by chopping off mantissa bits. The iteration process is started with few mantissa bits, and the mantissa length is then successively increased individually for each component as needed for convergence to a solution of double precision accuracy. This way, and in contrast to the previously-mentioned mixed precision strategies, the work in [3] does not refer to the IEEE standard precision formats, but, as part of a more experimental research, employs artificial precisions that arise by arbitrarily truncating the mantissa of the IEEE double precision format. The elegance of this approach is that the number of exponent bits remains unchanged, which virtually eliminates the danger of over- and underflow. Once read into the processing units, the values are converted to double precision by filling the truncated mantissa bits with zeros. The floating-point operations themselves all use double precision accuracy.

What [3] fails to address is a concept that handles the artificial precision format in memory. While this seems to be an implementation detail, the question of how data is accessed is performance-crucial, in particular on streaming architectures such as GPUs. There, each memory read accesses 128 bytes of contiguous memory, and utilizing only part of the data inevitably results in low performance [11]. Usually, mixed precision numerics duplicate the data (in different precision formats) in memory. However, this not only increases the memory footprint of the algorithm, but also makes it difficult to efficiently access different subsets of the values in different formats.

3 Modular Precision Format

The two key ideas of the modular precision format are (1) to completely decouple the storage format from the operating format, and (2) to abandon the IEEE-supported standard precision formats to store the data, but split the arithmetic format into segments, and store the segments of the values in the dataset in interleaved fashion such that the same segments of all values are consecutive in memory.

These two ideas can be addressed independently, however, they work efficiently in particular when used in combination. Decoupling the operational format from the storage format is motivated by the performance of many linear algebra routines being bound by memory bandwidth: If the algorithm can accept reading values with less accuracy, the data can be accessed much faster in a lower precision format. The arithmetic operations can still use high precision without impacting the performance as long as the algorithm remains memory bound. Decoupling the storage format from the operational format in an environment supporting IEEE standard precision requires to duplicate the data in memory if it is used in different precision formats over the algorithm execution. Also, as the IEEE standard formats differ in the exponent length (and therewith in the range or representable values), the conversion between the formats has to meticulously protect against under- and overflow.

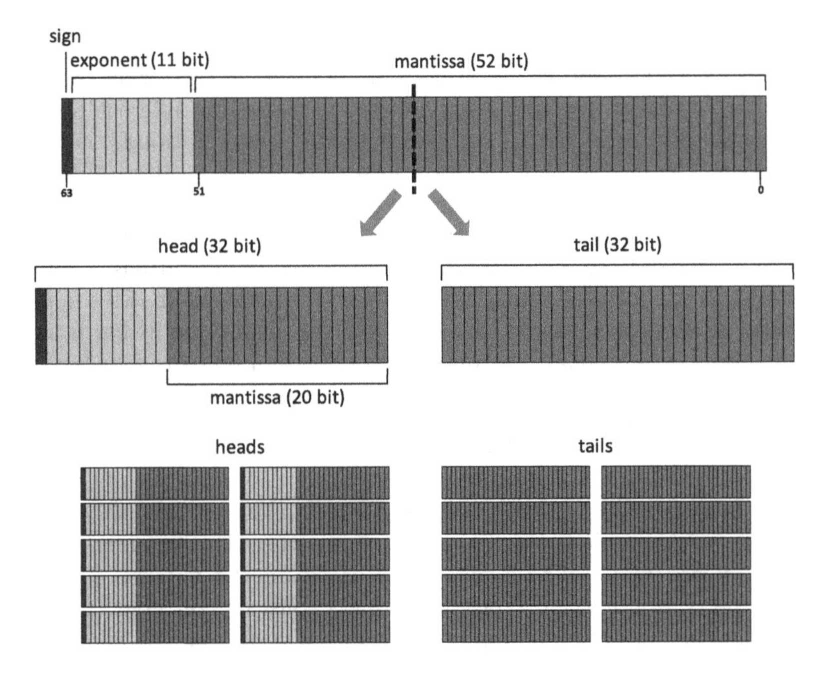

Fig. 1. Splitting an IEEE double precision number into "head" and "tail" (top) and storing head and tail of the data in the customized precision format in separate blocks (bottom).

The customized precision format based on mantissa segmentation ("CPMS") does not convert between IEEE standard formats, but instead splits the high precision number into segments. In Fig. 1 (top) we visualize this strategy for a 2-segment splitting of the IEEE double precision format. For this specific decomposition we refer to the two 32-bit segments as "head" and "tail" of the customized precision format. Other splittings are possible. As the CPMS strategy preserves the length of the exponent, the first 32 bits include less mantissa bits than the 32 bits of IEEE single precision [10]. Hence, the head of the 2-segment

CPMS carries less accuracy than the IEEE single precision format. The advantages of this strategy are that (1) for specialized data access routines, no format conversion is necessary; (2) preserving the length of the exponent avoids overflow/underflow; and (3) the data does not have to be duplicated in memory, but reading additional segments of the value will increase the value's accuracy.

We point out that by preserving the exponent bits of the IEEE standard precision format, the segmentation can not turn a valid number into "NaN" or infinity, as both are defined by all exponent bits being filled with "1 bits" [10].

To enable efficient access to the values in low precision, e.g. only the first segment of each value, it is important to separate the head from the tail in memory, and store the head of all values consecutively in memory, see bottom of Fig. 1. As long as considering all values under the accuracy of the head is acceptable, no access to the second part of the memory is necessary. We emphasize that the memory footprint for storing the values only is identical to storing the data in IEEE standard double precision, if the data is accessed in different precisions, an additional array is needed for storing the segment information for each value.

Obviously, the customized precision format could be realized independent of the format decoupling, but not only are the arithmetic operations in this non-standard format not natively supported by hardware, but also would this introduce additional rounding errors in the numerical operations. Combining CPMS with the idea of decoupling the arithmetic format eliminates the need of customized routines for a format that is not natively supported by hardware, and incurs no performance penalty as long as the algorithm remains memory-bound.

4 Experimental Evaluation

Problem Description and Algorithm Details. The problem we consider is the iterative solution of a sparse linear system via the adaptive precision Jacobi method proposed in [3]. The algorithm is based on the numeric property of the Jacobi relaxation method typically having a constant convergence rate, and the possibility to detect stagnation in the iteration vector on a component level. Concretely, this property establishes that, for any component of the approximate solution vectors at relaxation step k and $k-1$, there exists a $\theta_i < 1$:

$$\left|x_i^{\{k\}} - x_i^{\{k-1\}}\right| \le \theta_i \left|x_i^{\{k-1\}} - x_i^{\{k-2\}}\right| \le \theta_i^2 \left|x_i^{\{k-2\}} - x_i^{\{k-3\}}\right| \ldots. \quad (1)$$

Furthermore, due to the linear convergence rate of the Jacobi iteration, the ratios

$$c_i^{\{k\}} := \frac{z_i^{\{k-1\}}}{z_i^{\{k\}}} = \frac{\left|x_i^{\{k-1\}} - x_i^{\{k-2\}}\right|}{\left|x_i^{\{k\}} - x_i^{\{k-1\}}\right|}, \quad k \ge 2, \quad (2)$$

are, in general, different for the distinct components, but they remain constant up to convergence; i.e., $c_i^{\{2\}} = c_i^{\{3\}} = c_i^{\{4\}} = \ldots = c_i$, where we note that $c_i > 1$ is necessary for convergence [3]. The adaptive precision Jacobi presented in [3] utilizes this property by monitoring $z_i^{\{k\}}$ at component level and some periodicity ϕ, and use a stagnation test with some threshold $\tilde{\delta}$

$$\left| \frac{z_i^{\{k-\phi\}}}{z_i^{\{k\}}} - c_i^{\phi} \right| > \tilde{\delta} \tag{3}$$

that detects the necessity of mantissa extension [3].

While the test periodicity ϕ and the stagnation test threshold $\tilde{\delta}$ can be optimized for each problem individually, we use the default setting of $\tilde{\delta} = 0.9 \cdot \left(c_i^{\phi} - 1\right)$ and $\phi = 10$.

Experiment Environment and Test Matrices. The experimental analysis was conducted on a single node of the Piz Daint supercomputer[1] featuring an NVIDIA P100 GPU. The complete algorithm was implemented in the CUDA language [11] and compiled and executed with CUDA in version 8.0.

The test matrices we consider are all of size 1,000,000 × 1,000,000. They differ in the number of nonzeros they carry in each row, the bandwidth, and the condition number. The matrices are generated as band matrices with the aggregated number of nonzeros in a row on the main diagonal, and the values adjacent to the main diagonal set to −1.

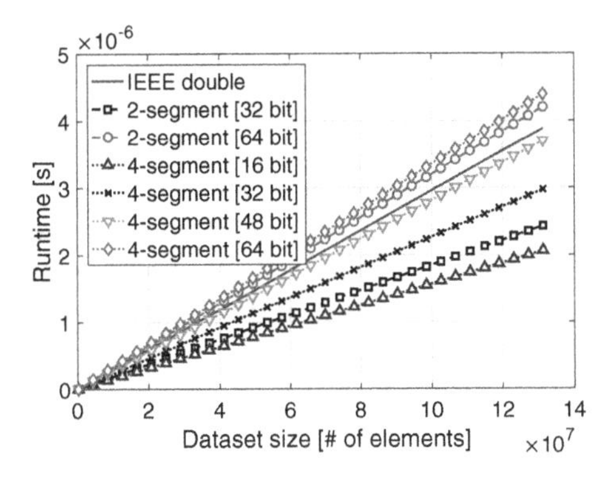

Fig. 2. Runtime for reading and writing data in double precision or customized precision with the accuracy of the data accesses indicated in the brackets.

Experimental Results. In a first experiment we assess the cost of reading and writing data not stored in IEEE-supported formats but in the 2-segment and the 4-segment `CPMS`, respectively. The access routines for `CPMS` are not natively supported by hardware, and the hardware-specific implementations we developed include the access to the segment information array, the element-individual decision of the segment access, some instruction logic to access the distinct segments

[1] https://www.cscs.ch/computers/piz-daint/.

in memory, the type cast to the double precision operating format, and the reassembling of the double precision format from head and mantissa segments.

The results in Fig. 2 reveal that reading 64-bit accuracy is 8% slower when using 2-segment CPMS and 13% slower when using 4-segment CPMS. The advantage of the customized precision format lies in the fact that the data access is much faster if reading the values with a shorter mantissa is acceptable. Reading 32-bit heads only is 1.6× faster than reading the data in double precision; Reading 16-bit heads is about 1.9× times faster.

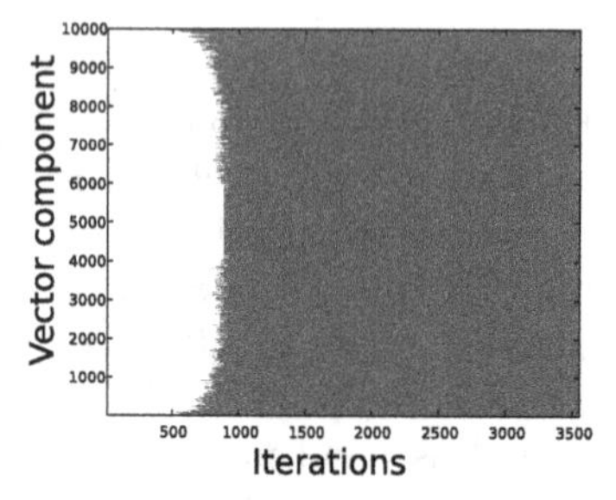

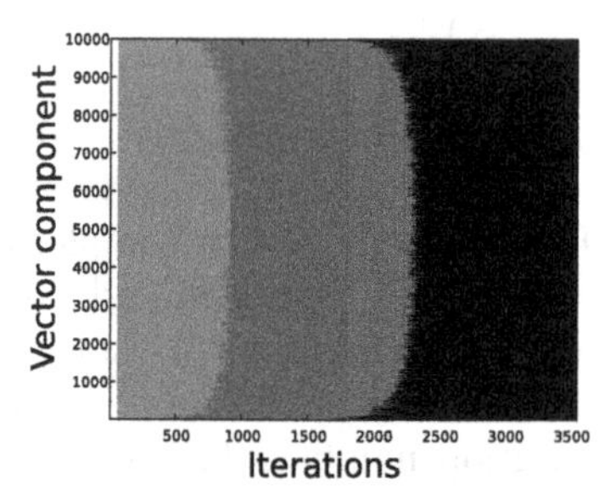

Fig. 3. Accuracy needs in adaptive Jacobi in a 2-segment (left) and a 4-segment (right) CPMS realization. The white-colored area indicates only the head is accessed, the blue areas indicate additional mantissa segment reads. (Color figure online)

Next, we realize the adaptive precision Jacobi in the modular precision format. In Fig. 3 we visualize for a small example problem with 129 nonzeros per row how the adaptive precision Jacobi method accesses the modular precision formats over the algorithm execution. Initially, the iteration process only reads the heads. As the execution progresses, mantissa segments are accessed on a component-individual basis once the stagnation test indicates the need for higher accuracy. The 16 bit head in the 4-segment modular precision format quickly becomes insufficient. We notice that the wavefront indicating the need for higher accuracy than 32 bits (which is reflected in the switch to 64 bits in the 2-segment modular precision and the switch to 48 bits in the 3-segment modular precision) is in both cases detected at the same iteration.

The experimental results presented in [3] reveal that the adaptive Jacobi can exhibit some convergence delay compared to a plain Jacobi as the mantissa extension detector may, depending on the test periodicity ϕ, not immediately identify stagnating components, and the threshold $\tilde{\delta}$ has to accept some rounding effects [3]. The question is whether this convergence delay, the overhead of the modular precision access routines, and the overhead of the stagnation detector is compensated by the faster access to reduced precision values in some relaxation steps. For this we compare the time-to-solution of the adaptive precision Jacobi with a reference implementation of plain Jacobi in IEEE double precision, both returning a solution approximation of the same accuracy. We consider different relative residual stopping thresholds as Jacobi relaxations are often employed as

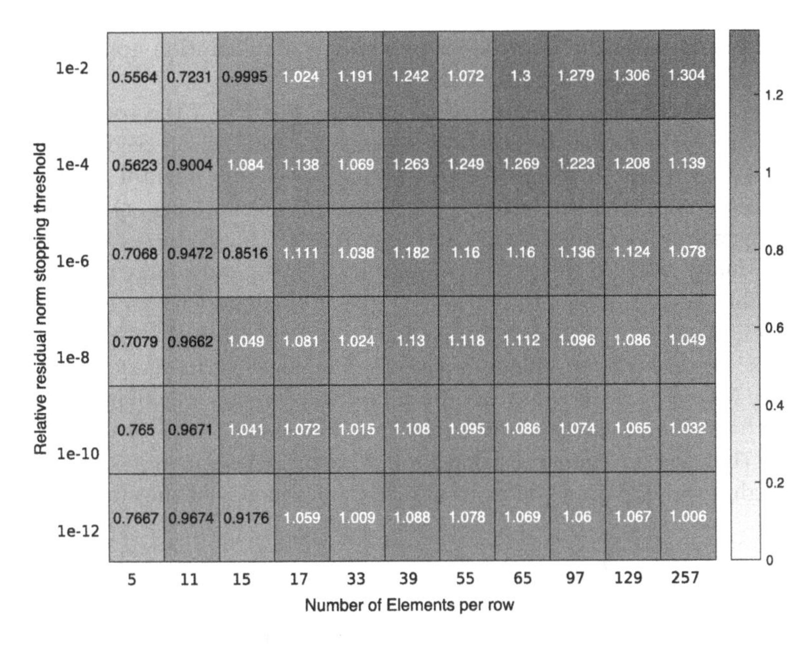

Fig. 4. Speedup factors of the adaptive precision Jacobi in a 2-segment modular precision realization.

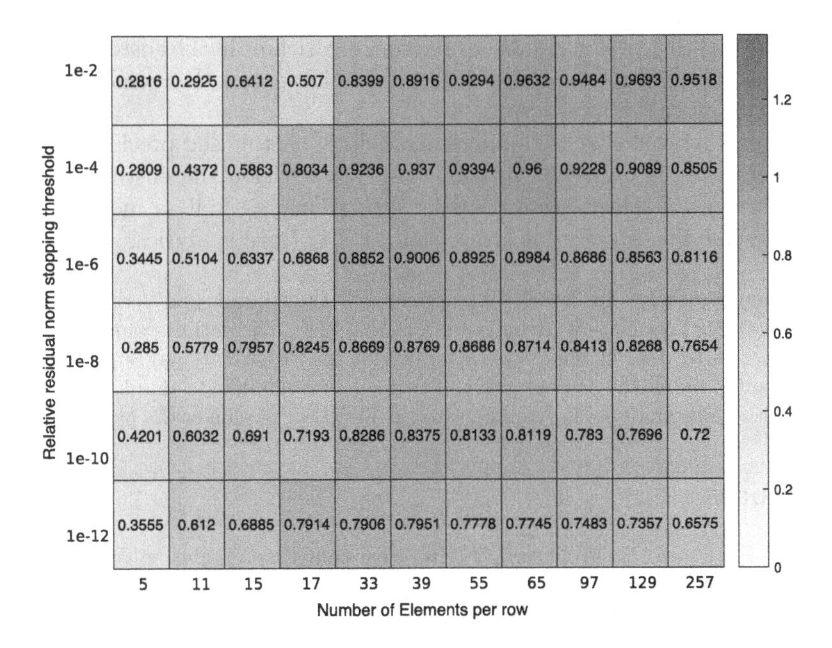

Fig. 5. Speedup factors of the adaptive precision Jacobi in a 4-segment modular precision realization.

smoother in multigrid methods or for providing rough solution approximations, e.g. in approximate sparse triangular solves [1,4].

Taking the plain Jacobi as reference, we report in Fig. 4 the speedup factors of the adaptive precision Jacobi in a 2-segment modular precision realization for the distinct matrix/threshold combinations. The experimental results reveal that the adaptive precision Jacobi is attractive (about 30% faster) in particular for settings where a significant amount of matrix data has to be accessed in every iteration (many nonzero elements in every matrix row), and a large residual norm is acceptable (few component iterations requiring the data with 64 bit accuracy). The faster access to the matrix values fails to compensate the overhead of the stagnation detection for problems with only few nonzeros in every row.

In Fig. 5 we report the same data for adaptive precision Jacobi in a 4-segment modular precision realization. Here, the reference Jacobi is always faster. This indicates that the modular precision format with finer segmentation is suitable only if high iteration counts allow to reduce the frequency of the stagnation test.

5 Concluding Remarks

We have presented the idea of radically decoupling the arithmetic format used in the floating-point operations from the format to store the data. We have proposed a customized precision format that allows to access values much faster in memory if reduced accuracy is acceptable. Experimental results on high-end GPUs revealed that realizing mixed precision algorithms in the customized precision format can render resource savings without impacting the memory footprint or the accuracy of the final result.

We are convinced that the application field of customized precisions is much wider than what is presented in this work. We envision the customized precision realization of selection and sorting algorithms, as well as memory-bound algorithms like PageRank that are central for Big Data analytics.

Acknowledgements. This work was supported by the "Impuls und Vernetzungsfond" of the Helmholtz Association under grant VH-NG-1241. The authors want to acknowledge the access to the PizDaint supercomputer at the Swiss National Supercomputing Centre granted under the project #d65. The authors would like to thank Goran Flegar and Enrique Quintana-Ortí for commenting on an earlier version of the paper.

References

1. Anzt, H., Chow, E., Dongarra, J.: Iterative sparse triangular solves for preconditioning. In: Träff, J.L., Hunold, S., Versaci, F. (eds.) Euro-Par 2015. LNCS, vol. 9233, pp. 650–661. Springer, Heidelberg (2015). https://doi.org/10.1007/978-3-662-48096-0_50
2. Anzt, H., Dongarra, J., Flegar, G., Higham, N.J., QuintanaOrtí, E.S.: Adaptive precision in block-Jacobi preconditioning for iterative sparse linear system solvers. Concurr. Comput. Pract. Experience **0**(0), e4460. https://doi.org/10.1002/cpe.4460. https://onlinelibrary.wiley.com/doi/abs/10.1002/cpe.4460, e4460 cpe.4460

3. Anzt, H., Dongarra, J., Quintana-Ortí, E.S.: Adaptive precision solvers for sparse linear systems. In: Proceedings of the 3rd International Workshop on Energy Efficient Supercomputing, pp. 2:1–2:10. ACM, New York (2015). https://doi.org/10.1145/2834800.2834802. http://doi.acm.org/10.1145/2834800.2834802
4. Anzt, H., Huckle, T.K., Bräckle, J., Dongarra, J.: Incomplete sparse approximate inverses for parallel preconditioning. Parallel Comput. **71**(Supplement C), 1–22 (2018). https://doi.org/10.1016/j.parco.2017.10.003. http://www.sciencedirect.com/science/article/pii/S016781911730176X
5. Buttari, A., Dongarra, J.J., Langou, J., Langou, J., Luszczek, P., Kurzak, J.: Mixed precision iterative refinement techniques for the solution of dense linear systems. Int. J. High Perf. Comput. Appl. **21**(4), 457–486 (2007)
6. Carson, E., Higham, N.J.: A new analysis of iterative refinement and its application to accurate solution of ill-conditioned sparse linear systems. SIAM J. Sci. Comput. **39**(6), A2834–A2856 (2017). https://doi.org/10.1137/17M1122918
7. Carson, E., Higham, N.J.: Accelerating the solution of linear systems by iterative refinement in three precisions. SIAM J. Sci. Comput. **40**(2), A817–A847 (2018). https://doi.org/10.1137/17M1140819
8. Göddeke, D., Strzodka, R., Turek, S.: Performance and accuracy of hardware-oriented native-, emulated- and mixed-precision solvers in FEM simulations. Int. J. Parallel Emergent Distrib. Syst. **22**(4), 221–256 (2007)
9. Higham, N.J.: Accuracy and Stability of Numerical Algorithms, 2nd edn. SIAM, Philadelphia (2002)
10. IEEE Computer Society: 754–2008 - IEEE Standard for Floating-Point Arithmetic
11. NVIDIA Corp.: CUDA C Programming Guide, 9.0 edn. http://docs.nvidia.com/cuda/cuda-c-programming-guide/index.html
12. Prikopa, K.E., Gansterer, W.N.: On mixed precision iterative refinement for eigenvalue problems. Proc. Comput. Sci. **18**, 2647–2650 (2013). https://doi.org/10.1016/j.procs.2013.06.002. http://www.sciencedirect.com/science/article/pii/S1877050913006108. 2013 International Conference on Computational Science

Benchmarking the NVIDIA V100 GPU and Tensor Cores

Matt Martineau(✉), Patrick Atkinson, and Simon McIntosh-Smith

HPC Group, University of Bristol, Bristol, UK
{m.martineau,p.atkinson,cssnmis}@bristol.ac.uk

Abstract. The V100 GPU is the newest server-grade GPU produced by NVIDIA and introduces a number of new hardware and API features. This paper details the results of benchmarking the V100 GPU and demonstrates that it is a significant generational improvement, increasing memory bandwidth, cache bandwidth, and reducing latency. A major new addition is the Tensor core units, which have been marketed as deep learning acceleration features that enable the computation of a $4 \times 4 \times 4$ half precision matrix-multiply-accumulate operation in a single clock cycle. This paper confirms that the Tensor cores offer considerable performance gains for half precision general matrix multiplication; however, programming them requires fine control of the memory hierarchy that is typically unnecessary for other applications.

1 Introduction

To fit within the anticipated power budgets for future supercomputing architectures, it is possible that clusters targeting exascale and beyond will be comprised of diverse heterogeneous architectures, including both CPUs and accelerator devices such as GPUs. Server-grade processors are constantly evolving in terms of core counts, vector widths, and memory architectures, in response to the needs of modern applications. Given the increasing complexity of heterogeneous devices, it is becoming more difficult to develop and optimise scientific applications that can exploit available supercomputing resources. The core aim of this paper is to uncover key architectural changes of the NVIDIA V100 GPU compared to its predecessors, and discuss the implications on performance.

Renewed investment in the machine learning space means that many areas of architecture design are focusing on the technological improvements that can also benefit low precision, approximate computation. A recent example of technological innovation targeting machine learning is the inclusion of Tensor cores in the new NVIDIA Volta V100 GPUs, a principal focus of this research. Two of the largest supercomputers in the world, Sierra and Summit [1], use dual-socketed POWER9 CPUs and NVIDIA Volta GPUs, supporting a peak performance of 72 and 122 PetaFLOP/s respectively. Through the use of micro-benchmarks and applications this paper will demonstrate that the V100 GPUs are a significant improvement over previous generations, offering impressive performance for current scientific workloads.

G. Mencagli et al. (Eds.): Euro-Par 2018 Workshops, LNCS 11339, pp. 444–455, 2019.
https://doi.org/10.1007/978-3-030-10549-5_35

2 Contributions

The following contributions are presented in the research:

- Benchmarking and analysis of many characteristics of the V100 GPUs compared to the previous generation of server-grade GPUs (Table 1).
- Analysis and evaluation of the Tensor cores, through the optimisation of a general matrix multiplication benchmark.
- A discussion regarding the applicability of Tensor cores to HPC.

3 Background

NVIDIA GPUs are throughput computing devices that support execution of thousands of parallel threads on lightweight processing elements called Streaming Multiprocessors (SMs). The GPU schedules multiple 32-wide units of execution, named warps, on the SMs.

Table 1. Hardware details of NVIDIA Tesla P100 and V100 devices

Device	Tesla P100	Tesla V100
SMs	56	80
FP32 cores/SM	64	64
FP64 cores/SM	32	32
Tensor cores/SM	-	8
GPU clock	1.189 GHz	1.245 GHz
Shared memory/SM	64 KB	96 KB
L2 cache size	4096 KB	6144 KB

The NVIDIA P100 GPU, presented in Fig. 1a, is the most powerful GPU in widespread use at the time of writing. The GPU introduces hardware double precision atomic instructions, and high bandwidth memory quoted to offer a theoretical 732 GB/s at peak. The NVIDIA V100 GPU (Fig. 1b) is the newest hardware from NVIDIA and introduces a number of features including:

- **Tensor cores** - Deep-learning focused cores that perform fast matrix-multiply-accumulate (MMA) operations.
- **Individual program counters per thread** - Numerous changes to synchronisation have been enabled as a consequence, including intra and inter GPU synchronisation that was not previously possible.
- **Increased memory bandwidth** - The high bandwidth memory (HBM2) has been optimised for a higher theoretical peak memory bandwidth.

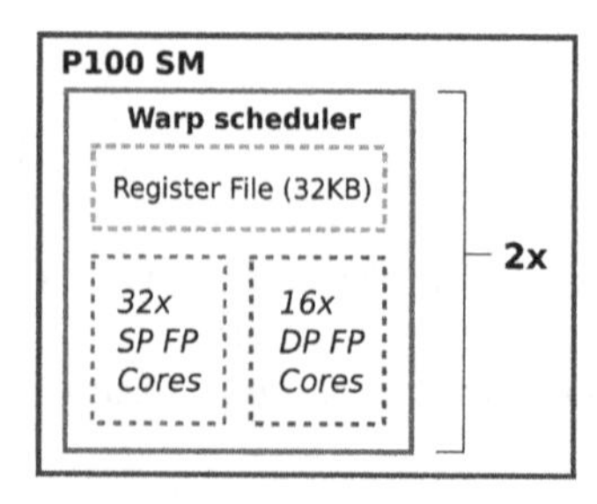

(a) P100 Warp Schedulers

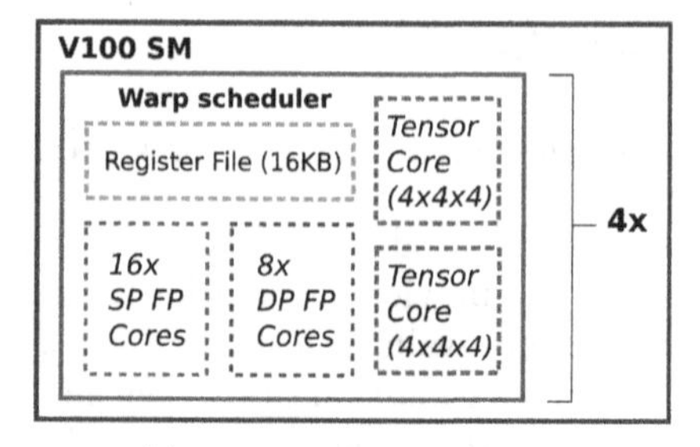

(b) V100 Warp Schedulers

Fig. 1. Balance of warp schedulers within each SM of P100 and V100 GPUs.

3.1 NVIDIA Volta GPU Tensor Cores

The available literature is not clear on the exact mechanisms that are used to fulfil a $16 \times 16 \times 16$ matrix multiplication using Tensor cores. In an NVIDIA V100 GPU, the SMs contain 8 Tensor cores, with each supporting a $4 \times 4 \times 4$ matrix-multiply-accumulate $(A * B + C = D, or\ A * B + C = C)$ operation per clock cycle.

The matrix multiplication step is performed in half precision, while the accumulation can be performed in either half or single precision. Although each of the SMs possesses 8 of the $4 \times 4 \times 4$ Tensor core units, the PTX ISA currently only supports warp-level operations of size $16 \times 16 \times 16$, $32 \times 8 \times 16$, and $8 \times 32 \times 16$ [10], exposed through the Warp Matrix-Multiply-Accumulate (WMMA) interface. This reduces the number of use cases for Tensor cores, as access to the individual $4 \times 4 \times 4$ units could allow for thread-level optimisation of routines, with the small blocking factor being far more useful to the general case.

4 Benchmarking

In this section we will benchmark the P100 and V100 GPUs to compare for generational improvements. All benchmarks are compiled with CUDA 9.0.

4.1 FLOP/s

Considering the NVIDIA V100 GPU with core clock speeds of 1.245 GHz, we can calculate the maximum FLOP/s achievable through single precision Fused-Multiply-Adds (FMAs): $2\ FLOPs \times 64\ threads \times 80\ SMs \times 1.245\,GHz = 12.7\ TFLOP/s$. Further to this, each of the 8 Tensor cores processes a $4 \times 4 \times 4$ MMA operation in a single cycle, performing 64 FMAs: $8\ Tensor\ Cores \times 128\ FLOPs \times 80\ SMs \times 1.245\,GHz = 102\ TFLOP/s$ for a mixed half and single precision operation. We observed a maximum of 25 TFLOP/s in half precision with FMAs, and 99 TFLOP/s using the MMA instructions.

4.2 Memory Bandwidth

The peak global memory bandwidth has been increased between the P100 and V100 by 1.23x; further, the achievable proportion of peak increases from roughly 80% on the P100 to around 93% on the V100. This is an important optimisation for many scientific workloads [7]. The number of warps in a thread-block required to saturate memory bandwidth has increased on the V100 to 4 warps from 3 warps on the P100 in single precision, or 8 warps from 5 warps in half precision (Fig. 2).

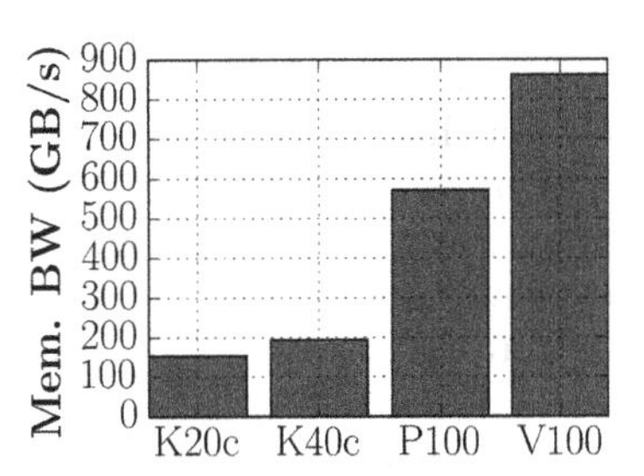

Fig. 2. NVIDIA GPU memory bandwidth.

4.3 Cache Bandwidth

The P100 GPU showed significant improvements to cache bandwidth over its predecessors [12] and through benchmarking we observed that the V100 continues this trend of increased memory bandwidth at the L1 cache level. To measure and compare the cache memory bandwidths between the P100 and the V100 we used the method outlined in [3], that is, we ran the STREAM Triad benchmark [9] multiple times over the same data-set to ensure cache-residency. The benchmark increasingly allocates more memory per CPU core or CUDA thread-block, which shows the bandwidth of each level of cache as the array saturates the available capacity, eventually spilling accesses into main memory.

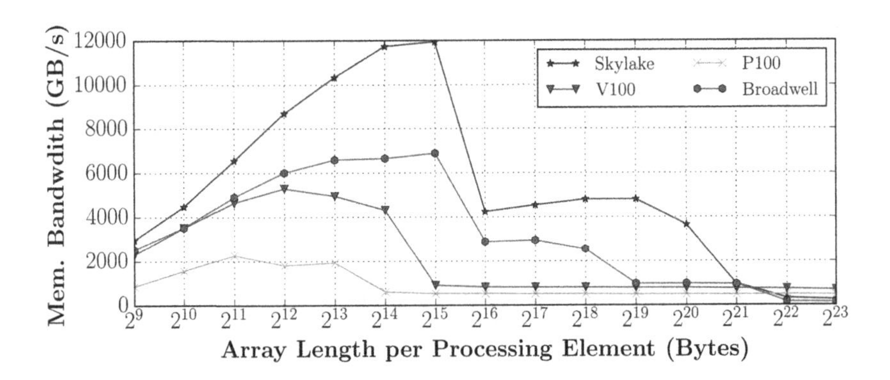

Fig. 3. Aggregate memory bandwidth as data per processing element doubles.

Figure 3 shows the aggregate bandwidth for several modern HPC processors. The L1 cache performance of the V100 GPU is 2.57x higher than the L1 cache performance of the P100, partly due to the increased number of SMs in the V100 increasing the aggregate result. However, when observing the memory bandwidth per SM, rather than the aggregate, the performance increase is 1.86x, suggesting there has been significant improvements made to the L1 cache. This performance increase has come from a change in hardware design as the Volta architecture features a unified shared memory/L1/texture cache, whereas the Pascal architecture has separate L1/texture and shared memory caches.

Figure 3 also compares the cache bandwidth to CPU architectures, 56 core Skylake, and 44 core Broadwell. The Xeon Skylake architecture outperforms the previous generation of CPUs (Broadwell) by roughly 1.7x, mainly due to the increase in vector width from 256-bit to 512-bit. The GPUs lag behind the CPU architectures in terms of unmanaged L1 cache performance; however, the shared-memory performance of the V100 and P100 architectures were observed to be 11.0 TB/s and 6.3 TB/s respectively, hence are comparable to the cache bandwidth of current CPU architectures.

4.4 Latency

Figure 4 shows the memory access latency of both the P100 and V100 GPUs alongside the performance of the Skylake CPU.

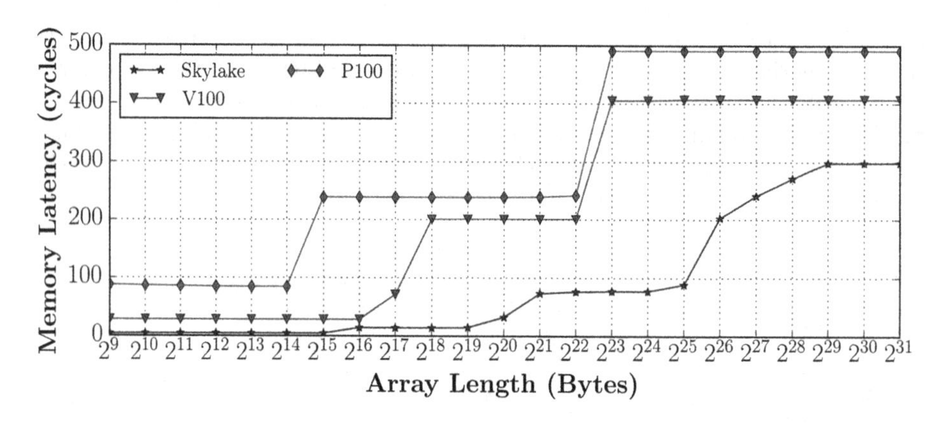

Fig. 4. Latency of memory accesses as array size is doubled.

For all levels of the memory hierarchy lower per-cycle latency is observed for the CPUs, compared to the GPUs. Further, the clock speed of the NVIDIA GPUs is around 3x lower than the CPU when executing on a single core without AVX, meaning that the CPUs move data significantly faster through the memory hierarchy. The GPU manages many more active threads and in-flight memory access requests than the CPU, in order to amortise the high latency for individual accesses. In spite of this, there has been a significant generational improvement in the L1 cache latency, as a consequence of the L1 and shared memories being combined in the new architecture.

4.5 Tensor Core Analysis

Throughout the paper we will refer to *tiles*, which represents a complete $16 \times 16 \times 16$ matrix-multiply-accumulation. Each of the 80 SMs in the V100 GPU contain 8 Tensor cores, where pairs of cores are situated on each of the 4 warp schedulers in an SM (Fig. 1b). Each of the cores is capable of performing a single sub-tile $4 \times 4 \times 4$ MMA instruction per cycle; so to perform an entire MMA for a $16 \times 16 \times 16$ tile, a total of 64 individual sub-tile MMAs are required. As a consequence, when a warp requests a $16 \times 16 \times 16$ MMA, there will be at least a 32 cycle latency for the two cores on a warp scheduler to fulfil the entire request.

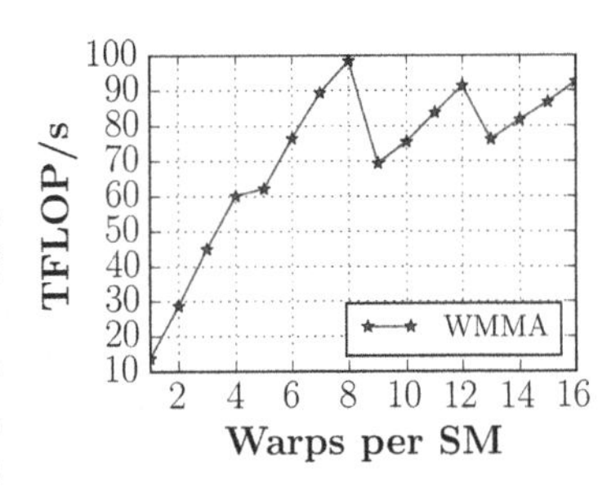

Fig. 5. Performance of MMA kernel as number of warps per thread block is increased.

In Fig. 5, we show the performance of increasing the number of warps resident on the GPU, for a benchmark kernel that performs a matrix multiplication without moving any data from global or shared memory. The performance scales linearly as the number of warps resident on each SM is increased from 1 to 4, and at 5 warps the performance plateaus. The results show that optimal MMA throughput is achieved when 8 warps are active on an SM.

4.6 Application Performance

The results of executing three optimised test applications written in CUDA can be seen in Fig. 6; `flow` is a 2D explicit hydrodynamics application, `hot` is a 2D implicit heat diffusion solver that uses the Conjugate Gradient method, and `neutral` is a 2D Monte Carlo neutral particle transport solver [7,8].

The applications are intended to represent the performance profiles of important HPC applications, and the results show a significant uplift in performance between the generations of hardware. The performance differences observed for both `flow` and `hot` track the memory bandwidth improvements of the architecture, as expected. The `neutral` application suffers from issues with memory latency due to poor reuse, and the performance observed on the V100 GPU is indicative of improved memory latency hiding in the new architecture, as well as improvements to compute throughput and memory bandwidth.

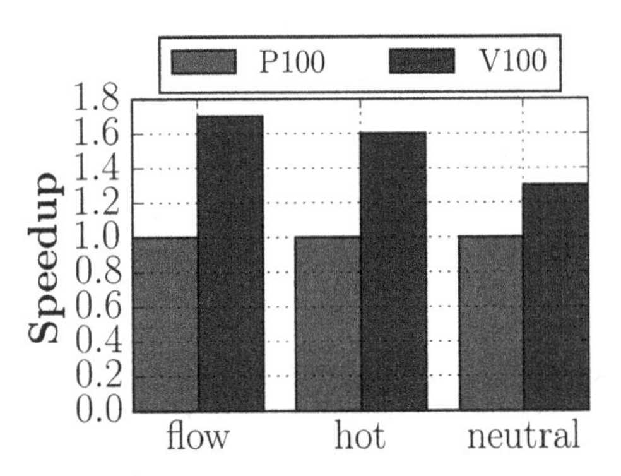

Fig. 6. Speedup observed for applications taken from the `arch` project.

4.7 cuBLAS Performance

Figure 7 presents the achieved FLOP/s for the varying precision cuBLAS routines, as the matrix size is increased. The half and single precision routines improve in performance, and asymptote upon reaching 8192^2. In contrast, for the Tensor core implementation we observe a sudden drop in performance once the matrix size exceeds 8192^2.

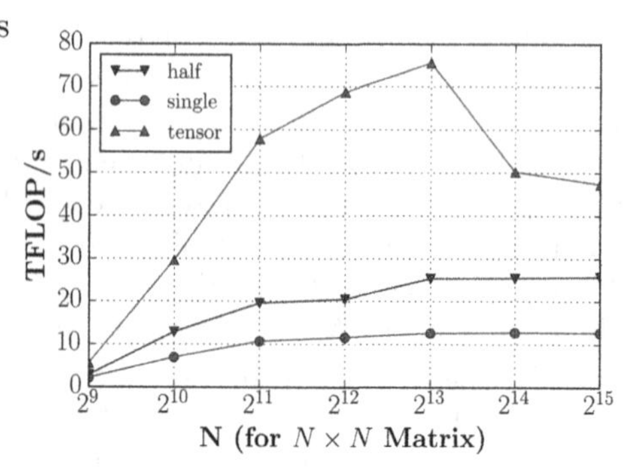

Fig. 7. cuBLAS Performance for increasing matrix sizes.

We compared the performance of calculating a single 16384^2 Tensor core MMA versus an equivalent calculation using 4 MMAs where the sub-matrices were 16384 wide on the k-th dimension and 8192 on the adjoining dimension. We observed a 1.35x improvement in performance, demonstrating that, in the short term, blocking cuBLAS for matrix sizes above 2^{13} is necessary even when the whole matrix is resident in high bandwidth memory.

5 Tensor Core Accelerated MMA

In a real application, the Tensor cores will more than likely be leveraged through the cuBLAS and cuDNN interfaces; however, an aim of this research is to uncover the current state of direct programming of the cores, and so we present the efforts taken to develop an optimised matrix multiplication as a canonical example.

5.1 Parallelisation and Decomposition for Tensor Cores

Our parallelisation strategy was influenced by the NVIDIA CUDA matrix multiplication sample, using 128×128 sub-matrices, containing 64 $16 \times 16 \times 16$ MMA tiles, enabling coalescence and saturation of shared memory. We chose a block size of 256 threads, where 8 warps co-operate in performing the instructions to complete the blocked 128×128 MMA.

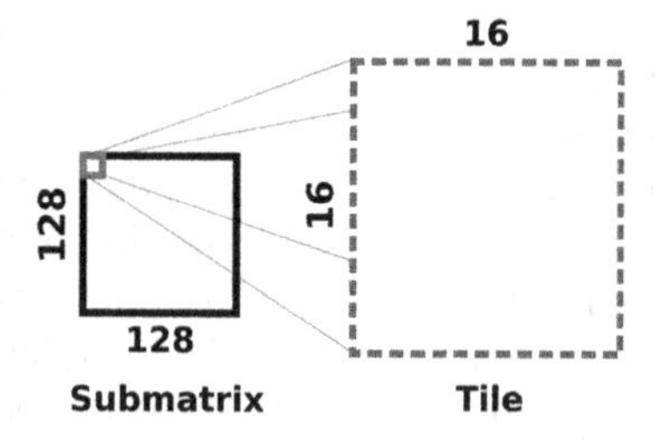

Fig. 8. Decompose 128×128 submatrices into 16×16 tiles.

The WMMA API is a significant departure from the conventional CUDA APIs, as the developer is expected to program operations at the warp level, rather than the thread level. As such, each CUDA block is responsible for performing 64 $16 \times 16 \times 16$ MMAs per sub-matrix along the k-th dimension, with each warp performing a single MMA at a time. Prior to performing the MMA operation, tiles are loaded from shared memory into WMMA fragments, which are groups of 16×16 registers, declared as in Listing 1.1.

Listing 1.1. WMMA fragments (`nvcuda::wmma` excluded for brevity).

```
fragment<matrix_a, 16, 16, 16, half, row_major> a;
fragment<accumulator, 16, 16, 16, float> c;
```

Our initial implementation allocated each of the warps within a CUDA block all 8 of the tiles in a row of the sub-matrix C. Each warp can fetch a single 16×16 fragment of A and multiply that by a whole row of B, achieving perfect reuse of A but no reuse of B. The result is that every warp is required to load the entirety of B from shared memory for every processed sub-matrix, with warps storing the results in an array of fragments for each tile in each row of the sub-matrix C.

Listing 1.2. WMMA load A and perform MMA sync.

```
load_matrix_sync(a, &Ashared[Aidx], shared_tile_lda);
mma_sync(c[cidx], a, b[bidx], c[cidx]);
```

In the main computational loop of the matrix multiplication, the A and B fragments were loaded and the MMA operation performed using the API calls in Listing 1.2.

5.2 Tiling and Register Optimisation

The scheme described in the previous section is inefficient in its management of fragments, introducing more shared memory requests than were actually required. It was possible to adjust the partitioning to increase the reuse of B and reduce shared memory accesses in favour of increasing register utilisation.

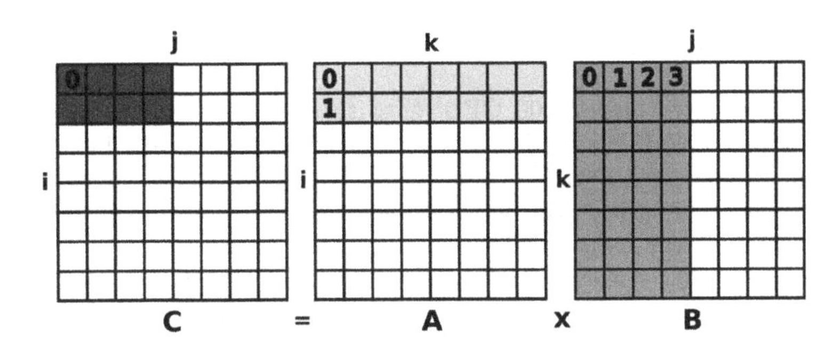

Fig. 9. The calculation of the first element of C, by multiplying the first element of A with the first chunk row of B, and then repeating the calculation for the first element of the second row of A.

Figure 9 depicts an optimisation where each warp is given a chunk of C, shaded orange, meaning the warp is only responsible for loading half of sub-matrix B per sub-matrix C. The result of this optimisation was a roughly 1.17x speedup for $N = 16384^2$.

5.3 Vector Loads

The matrix multiplication CUDA sample for the WMMA API adapted all reads from global memory to 128-bit wide loads; as such, each of the threads was responsible for reading 8 of the 16-bit floating-point numbers at once from global memory, and populating shared memory with them. As such, each warp reads 2 rows of a 128×128 sub-matrix.

Figure 10 shows that the memory bandwidth utilisation of a single warp resident on an SM greatly increases as the global load width is increased. This trend is true even if we have a single warp per warp scheduler on an SM, for 4 per SM on Volta, where the achieved memory bandwidth is 3.8x higher for 128-bit loads than scalar 16-bit loads.

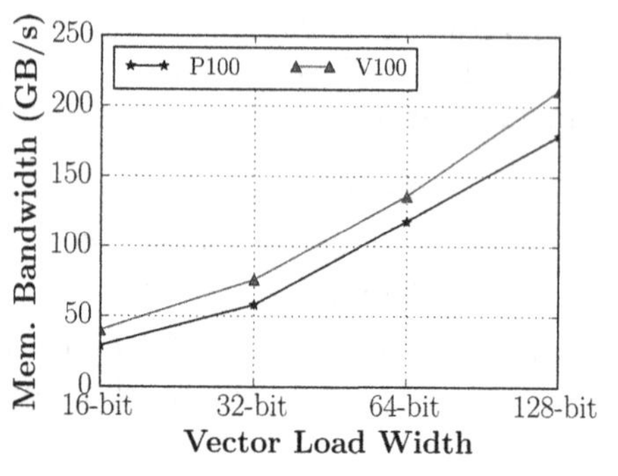

Fig. 10. Memory bandwidth of vector loads from global memory (16 to 128-bits) for one warp resident on each SM.

Through benchmarking we determined that, when the number of blocks issued for a particular kernel significantly over-subscribed the number of available SMs and warp schedulers, a single warp per block could saturate memory bandwidth using 128-bit vector loads, with half precision computation. For 64-bit vector loads, two warps were required to saturate memory bandwidth.

5.4 Shared Memory Optimisation

The shared memory on a V100 GPU, as with previous compute capabilities, is organised into 32 32-bit banks, which allow a warp to read 64 half precision values in a single cycle, two from each bank. If two threads access elements in the same bank, the latency of the resulting memory operation will increase to two cycles, a two-way bank conflict.

In Fig. 8, we show a section of a sub-matrix, where each individual tile stored in shared memory is read using a single WMMA API call. We can see in Fig. 11 that the individual banks, the orange bars, can contain 64 half precision elements, and so are distributed across an entire row of the half sub-matrix, or twice per row of the full sub-matrix. The banks line up perfectly so that the beginning of each row of the tile coincides with the beginning of the shared memory banks. As such, the 16 16-bit elements of each row of a tile reside within the same 8 32-bit banks of shared memory, meaning that, if a tile is allocated contiguously, warp-level accesses to that tile inherently lead to banks conflicts.

The exact manner in which the WMMA API moves data into fragments is not known; however, it is expected that the API uses all threads in a half-warp to access a number of rows in the tile. In theory, each thread could access 2

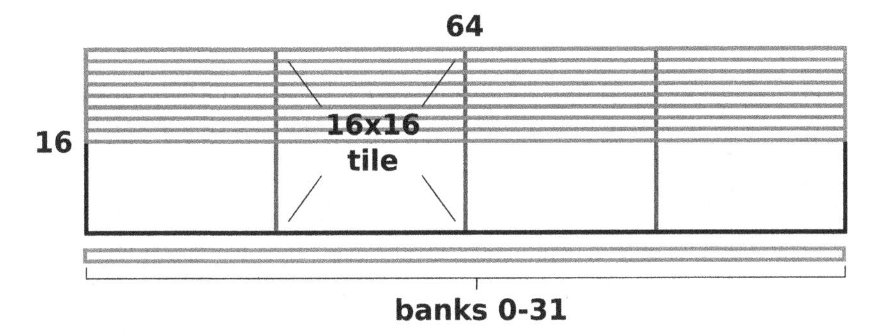

Fig. 11. A representation of the distribution of elements of the sub-matrix stored in the banks shared memory.

elements of each row of the tile, so the 16 threads would access 2 rows of the tile at once, resulting in a two-way bank conflict.

Padding, known as a skew factor, can be added to the leading dimension of the sub-matrix to avoid the data lining up. It is clear that a skew of 16 elements (16-bit elements of the sub-matrix) results in banks 0–7 containing row 0 of the tile, and banks 8–15 containing row 1, and so on. This ensures that rows 0–3 can be read in a single cycle by a single warp.

Given that the V100 allows the user to allocate up to 96 KB of shared memory per SM, and both A and B are 32 KB, there is enough space to pad both of the arrays in shared memory. In support of the analytic choice of 16, we demonstrate empirically that it is the best skew in Fig. 12.

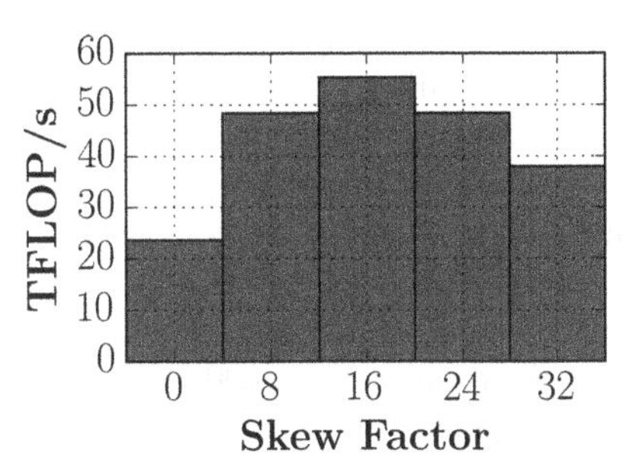

Fig. 12. Tuning skew factor for shared memory accesses where the sub-matrix size is 128×128, and the tile size is $16 \times 16 \times 16$.

While the preceding analysis appears specific to the optimisation of general matrix multiplications, or our particular choice of block size, it is important to recognise the generality of this particular issue. We anticipate that, in the majority of use cases, the utilisation of Tensor cores will require memory to be read in from global memory and reused within the available shared memory; as such, the fact that the tiles of the sub-matrices are 16×16 is expected to result in bank conflicts in general usage.

It is important that programmers are aware that bank conflicts are not fixed by the WMMA API. The 2.5x difference in performance observed between the 0 skew and 16 skew cases in Fig. 12 demonstrates that avoiding bank conflicts is an important part of programming with Tensor cores. Furthermore, due to the dramatic jump in computational throughput introduced by the Tensor cores, it is likely that tuning the use of shared memory, and potentially optimising for all levels of cache, will be essential for maximum performance.

6 Future Work

We expect that the majority of future research articles will focus on machine learning use cases for the Tensor cores, but we are hopeful that researchers will continue to investigate the potential for using them within HPC. As some of the largest pre-exascale supercomputers include V100 GPUs, it is important to discover use-cases or adaptations to existing algorithms that could leverage the Tensor cores. It will be important future work to understand the implication of attempting to include the WMMA API calls into code that is otherwise thread-level, as the shift in paradigm may make expressing some algorithms more challenging.

7 Related Work

An NVIDIA PARALLEL FORALL blog by Appleyard et al. [2] presents details about the Tensor hardware and API, and evaluates the performance of Tensor core accelerated routines in cuBLAS and cuDNN. The article by Harris [4] discussed mixed precision programming introduced in CUDA 8.0, providing technical details and demonstrating performance improvements for a number of use cases and libraries.

Through micro-benchmarking, Jia et al. [5] uncovered many of the architectural details of the Volta architecture such as the memory bandwidth/latency, warp scheduling policy, and instruction latencies. Markidis et al. [6] evaluated the Tensor core units in terms of programmability, performance, and precision, finding similar performance to the results presented here and exploring in detail the consequences of the loss in precision.

Reguly et al. [11] benchmarked the POWER8 GPUs in comparison to other hardware for a number of applications and benchmarks. Trott [12] performed an evaluation of the P100 GPU soon after release, and demonstrated that there were significant improvements in cache bandwidths and atomic performance.

8 Conclusion

The NVIDIA V100 GPU has been proven to be a significant improvement over its recent predecessor, the P100 GPU, introducing many new programmability improvements and offering exceptionally high memory bandwidth. Through benchmarking we observed that these memory bandwidth improvements have come at all levels of the memory hierarchy, but most notably the L1 cache, which offers considerably higher performance than the P100. We also observed gains in performance provided by the Tensor cores but that performance is now strongly coupled to the performance of the GPU memory hierarchy.

The Tensor cores can shift the balance of computational power within the devices to such an extent that it will be essential to carefully consider all levels of cache to successfully exploit the devices for computationally-bound algorithms.

This has important consequences for the future of HPC on those devices, as a significant amount of research is being conducted into the adaptation of algorithms into compute bound variations to support future scaling.

The organisation of the WMMA API to issue instructions at the warp rather than the thread level means that the individual $4 \times 4 \times 4$ Tensor cores cannot be directly programmed, and the developer will only have access to $16 \times 16 \times 16$ MMA instructions. In spite of this, the Tensor cores allow for a huge increase in compute performance when executing specific deep learning workloads, whilst other architectural changes bring benefits to HPC workloads.

References

1. Ang, J., Cook, J., Domino, S.P., Glass, M.W., Voskuilen, G.R.: Exascale co-design progress and accomplishments. New Front. High Perform. Comput. Big Data **30**, 3 (2017)
2. Appleyard, J., Yokim, S.: Programming Tensor Cores in CUDA 9 (2017)
3. Deakin, T., Price, J., McIntosh-Smith, S.: Portable methods for measuring cache hierarchy performance. In: IEEE/ACM Super Computing (2017)
4. Harris, M.: Mixed-Precision Programming with CUDA 8 (2017)
5. Jia, Z., Maggioni, M., Staiger, B., Scarpazza, D.P.: Dissecting the NVIDIA Volta GPU architecture via microbenchmarking, April 2018
6. Markidis, S., Chien, S.W.D., Laure, E., Peng, I.B., Vetter, J.S.: NVIDIA Tensor Core Programmability, Performance & Precision. CoRR abs/1803.04014 (2018). http://arxiv.org/abs/1803.04014
7. Martineau, M., McIntosh-Smith, S.: The arch project: physics mini-apps for algorithmic exploration and evaluating programming environments on HPC architectures. In: 2017 IEEE International Conference on Cluster Computing (CLUSTER), pp. 850–857, September 2017
8. Martineau, M., McIntosh-Smith, S.: Exploring on-node parallelism with neutral, a Monte Carlo neutral particle transport mini-app. In: 2017 IEEE International Conference on Cluster Computing (CLUSTER). IEEE (2017)
9. McCalpin, J.: Memory bandwidth and machine balance in current high performance computers. IEEE Computer Society Technical Committee on Computer Architecture (TCCA), pp. 19–25 (1995)
10. NVIDIA Corporation: Parallel Thread Execution ISA Version 6.1 (2017)
11. Reguly, I.Z., Keita, A.K., Giles, M.B.: Benchmarking the IBM Power8 processor. In: Proceedings of the 25th Annual International Conference on Computer Science and Software Engineering, pp. 61–69. IBM Corp. (2015)
12. Trott, C.R.: Early Experience with P100 on POWER8. Technical report, Sandia National Lab. (SNL-NM), Albuquerque, NM (United States) (2016)

SiL: An Approach for Adjusting Applications to Heterogeneous Systems Under Perturbations

Ali Mohammed(✉) and Florina M. Ciorba

Department of Mathematics and Computer Science,
University of Basel, Basel, Switzerland
{ali.mohammed,florina.ciorba}@unibas.ch

Abstract. Scientific applications consist of large and computationally-intensive loops. Dynamic loop scheduling (DLS) techniques are used to load balance the execution of such applications. Load imbalance can be caused by variations in loop iteration execution times due to problem, algorithmic, or systemic characteristics (also perturbations). The following question motivates this work: *"Given an application, a high-performance computing (HPC) system, and their characteristics and interplay, which DLS technique will achieve improved performance under unpredictable perturbations?"* Existing work only considers perturbations caused by variations in the HPC system delivered computational speeds. However, perturbations in available network bandwidth or latency are inevitable on production HPC systems. *Simulator in the loop* (SiL) is introduced, herein, as a new control-theoretic inspired approach to dynamically select DLS techniques that improve the performance of applications on heterogeneous HPC systems under perturbations. The present work examines the performance of six applications on a heterogeneous system under *all above system perturbations*. The SiL *proof of concept* is evaluated using simulation. The performance results confirm the initial hypothesis that *no single DLS technique can deliver best performance in all scenarios*, whereas the SiL-based DLS selection achieved improved application performance in most experiments.

Keywords: Performance · Load balancing · Loop scheduling
Heterogeneous computing systems · Perturbations · Simulation
Computationally-intensive applications · Simulator-in-the-loop

1 Introduction

Scientific applications are often characterized by large and computationally-intensive parallel loops. The performance of these applications on high-performance computing (HPC) systems may degrade due to load imbalance caused by problem, algorithmic, or systemic characteristics. Application (problem or algorithmic) characteristics include the irregularity of the number of

G. Mencagli et al. (Eds.): Euro-Par 2018 Workshops, LNCS 11339, pp. 456–468, 2019.
https://doi.org/10.1007/978-3-030-10549-5_36

computations per loop iterations due to conditional statements, where systemic characteristics include variations in delivered computational speed of processing elements (PEs), available network bandwidth or latency. Such variations are referred to as perturbations, and can also be caused by other applications or processes that share the same resources, or a temporary system fault or malfunction. Dynamic loop scheduling (DLS) is a widely-used approach for improving the execution of parallel applications using self-scheduling, that is *dynamic* assignment of the loop iterations to free and requesting processing elements. A wide range of DLS techniques exists, and can be divided into *nonadaptive* and *adaptive* techniques. The nonadaptive DLS techniques account for the variability in loop iterations execution times due to application characteristics. The nonadaptive DLS techniques include *self-scheduling* (SS), *fixed size chunking* (FSC) [14], *guided self-scheduling* (GSS) [18], *factoring* (FAC) [12], and *weighted factoring* (WF) [11]. The adaptive DLS techniques account for irregular system characteristics by adapting the amount of assigned work per PE request (chunk size) according to the application performance measured during execution. Adaptive DLS techniques include *adaptive weighted factoring* (AWF) [3], its variants *batch* (AWF-B), *chunk* (AWF-C), *batch-like* (AWF-D), *chunk-like* (AWF-E) [7], and *adaptive factoring* (AF) [2].

An *a priori* selection of the most appropriate DLS technique for a given application and system is challenging, given the various sources of load imbalance and the different load balancing properties of the DLS techniques. This observation raises the following question and motivates the present work: *"Given an application, an HPC system, and their characteristics and interplay, which DLS technique will achieve improved performance under unpredictable perturbations?"* Earlier work studied the flexibility of DLS (robustness to reduced delivered computational speed) and the selection of robust DLS using machine learning [20] with the SimGrid (SG) [8] simulation toolkit. The selection of DLS techniques for synthetic time-stepping scientific applications using reinforcement learning [4] was also studied using SG. The aforementioned existing work focuses on one source of perturbations (variation in delivered computing speed) in time-stepping applications to learn from previous steps. That approach may not be applicable to applications without time-steps, nor would it be feasible in a highly variable execution environment. Scheduling solutions using static optimizations, e.g., using evolutionary and genetic algorithms, can not dynamically adapt to the perturbations encountered during execution. Modern HPC systems are often heterogeneous production systems typically shared by many users. Therefore, perturbations in the available network bandwidth and latency in such systems are unavoidable.

In the present work, in an effort to select the most appropriate DLS for a given application and system, the performance of a scientific application (PSIA [10]) and five synthetic applications using nonadaptive and adaptive DLS techniques is studied on a heterogeneous HPC system, in the presence of perturbations. The present work makes the following contributions: (1) Proposes a novel *simulator in the loop* (SiL) approach for dynamically selecting a DLS technique during execution, based on the application characteristics and the present (monitored or predicted) state of the computing system; (2) Provides insights into the resilience of the DLS techniques to perturbations; and (3) Confirms the initial hypothesis that no single DLS ensures the best performance in all execution scenarios considered; The SiL performance is evaluated for the selected applications in simulation using SG.

This work is structured as follows. Section 2 contains a brief review of the selected DLS techniques, the SG simulation toolkit, as well as related work. The proposed SiL approach is discussed in Sect. 3. The experimental design and setup, and the performance results are described and discussed in Sect. 4. The work concludes and outlines potential future work in Sect. 5.

2 Background and Related Work

Loop Scheduling. The aim of loop scheduling is to achieve a balanced load execution among parallel PEs with minimum scheduling overhead. Loop scheduling can be divided into *static* and *dynamic*. In static loop scheduling, the loop iterations are divided and assigned to PEs before execution; both division and assignment remain fixed during execution. This work considers static (block) scheduling, denoted STATIC, each PE being assigned a chunk size equal to the number of iterations N divided by the number of PEs P. STATIC incurs *minimum* scheduling overhead, compared to dynamic loop scheduling, and may lead to load imbalance for non-uniformly distributed tasks and/or on perturbed systems.

In *dynamic loop scheduling* (DLS), free and requesting PEs are assigned, via self-scheduling, loop iterations during execution. The DLS techniques can be categorized into *nonadaptive* and *adaptive* techniques. The nonadaptive DLS techniques considered in this work are: SS [21], FSC [14], GSS [18], FAC [12], and WF [11]. While STATIC represents one scheduling extreme, SS represents the other scheduling extreme. In SS, the size of each chunk is one loop iteration. This yields a high load balance with potentially very large scheduling overhead. FSC assigns loop iterations in chunks of fixed sizes, where the chunk size depends on the standard deviation of loop iteration execution times σ as an indication of its variation and the incurred scheduling overhead h. GSS assigns loop iterations in chunks of decreasing sizes, where the size of a chunk is equal to the number of remaining unscheduled loop iterations R divided by the number of PEs N. FAC employs a probabilistic modeling of loop characteristics (standard deviation of iterations execution time σ and their mean μ) to calculate batch sizes that maximize the probability of achieving a load balanced execution. A PE's chunk size is equal to the batch size divided by N. When this information (σ and μ) is unavailable, FAC is practically implemented to assign half of the remaining loop iterations R in a batch. WF divides a batch into unequally-sized chunks, proportional to the relative PE speeds (weights). The PEs weights must be determined prior to the execution and do not change afterward. This work considers the *practical implementations* of FAC and WF. All nonadaptive DLS techniques account for variations in iteration execution times due to application characteristics.

The adaptive DLS techniques measure the performance of the application during execution and adapt the chunk calculation accordingly. Adaptive DLS techniques include AWF [3], its variants [7]: AWF-B, AWF-C, AWF-D, AWF-E, and AF [2]. AWF is designed for time-stepping applications. It improves WF by changing the relative weights of PEs during execution by measuring their performance in each time step and updating their weights accordingly. AWF-B relieves the time stepping requirement in AWF, and measures the performance after each batch to update the PE weights. AWF-C is similar to AWF-B, where weight updates are performed upon the completion of each chunk, instead of a batch. AWF-D is similar to AWF-B, and considers the total chunk time (equal to the chunk iteration execution times plus the associated overhead of a PE to acquire the chunk) and all the bookkeeping operations to calculate and update the PE weights. AWF-B and AWF-C only consider the chunk iterations execution times. AWF-E is similar to AWF-C by updating the PE weights on every chunk. Yet AWF-E is also similar to AWF-D by also considering the total chunk time also. Unlike FAC, AF dynamically estimates the values of σ and μ during execution and updates them based on the measured performance of the PEs.

Loop scheduling in simulation. SimGrid [8] (SG) is a versatile event-based simulation toolkit designed for the study of the behavior of large-scale distributed systems. It provides ready to use application programming interfaces (API) to represent applications and computing systems through different interfaces: MSG (SG-MSG), SimDag (SG-SD), and SMPI (SG-SMPI). SG uses a simple, fast CPU computation model and verified network models [22] which render it well suited for the study of computationally-intensive distributed scientific applications.

Various studies have used SG to study the performance of applications with DLS techniques in different scenarios [4,20]. To attain high trustworthiness in the performance results obtained with SG, the implementation of the nonadaptive DLS techniques in SG-SD has been verified [17] by reproducing the results presented in the work that introduced factoring [12]. In addition, the accuracy of the performance results obtained by simulative experiments against native experiments has recently been quantified [16]. This work employs the SG-SD interface to study the performance of scientific applications on a heterogeneous platform under perturbations.

Related Work. Robustness denotes the maintenance of certain desired system characteristics despite fluctuations in the behavior of its components or its environment [1], whereas, flexibility [20] denotes the robustness of DLS to variations in the delivered computational speeds. The performance of scientific applications under perturbations in the delivered computational speed is studied with nonadaptive DLS techniques [13,23]. The robust scheduling of tasks with uncertain communication time was also considered using a multi-objective evolutionary algorithm [6]. The selection of the best performing DLS during execution was studied for OpenMP multi-threaded applications [24], and for time-stepping applications using reinforced learning [4]. Further, machine learning was used to create a portfolio of DLS robustness to variations in the delivered computational speed on a homogeneous system [20].

Scheduling solutions based on optimization techniques, e.g., genetic and evolutionary algorithms, can not adapt to perturbations during execution. None of the aforementioned efforts considered perturbations in network bandwidth and latency. This work complements the previous efforts by studying the performance of scientific applications using nonadaptive and adaptive DLS techniques under different perturbations (variations in delivered computational speed, network bandwidth, network latency) on a heterogeneous computing system. A new approach, namely *simulator in the loop* (SiL) is introduced, to dynamically select DLS techniques that improve the performance of applications on heterogeneous system under multiple sources of perturbations.

3 Simulator in the Loop (SiL)

The SiL is inspired by control theory, where a controller (scheduler) is used to achieve and maintain a desired state (load balance) of the system (parallel loop execution), as illustrated in Fig. 1. The SiL concept is motivated by the well-known control strategy model predictive control (MPC) [19]. The MPC controller predicts the performance of the system with different control signals to optimize system performance. As shown in Fig. 1b, a call to the SiL simulator is inserted inside a typical scheduling loop. SiL leverages state-of-the-art simulation toolkits to estimate the performance of an application in a given execution scenario. The system monitor and estimator components read the system state during the execution and update the computing system representation accordingly. The above steps may be repeated several times during the execution of the loop, and its frequency can be aligned with the perturbations frequency or intensity.

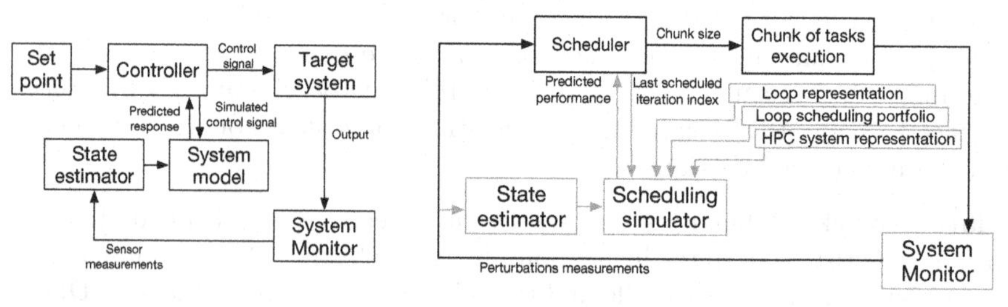

(a) A generic control system. **(b)** Proposed SiL approach for loop scheduling.

Fig. 1. The proposed *simulator in the loop* (SiL) approach for loop scheduling (b) is analogous to a typical control system (a). The components highlighted in mint color in (b) represent the SiL additions to a typical loop scheduling system. (Color figure online)

The SiL leverages the use of already developed state-of-the-art simulators to predict the performance dynamically during execution. Given that the main concern of this work is load imbalanced computationally-intensive applications, where the application data is replicated, the influence of complex memory hierarchy on their performance is minimal. Therefore, application performance can be predicted accurately via simulation. For instance, the percent error between native and simulative executions for a given application (PSIA [10]) using the SG-SD interface was found to be between 0.95% and 2.99% [16]. It is expected that the accuracy and speed of the simulators employed by SiL will improve as they are continuously being developed and refined. The cost of frequent calls to SiL can be amortized by launching parallel SiL instances to concurrently derive predictions for various DLS. Alternatively, this cost can be entirely mitigated by asynchronously calling SiL, concurrently to the application execution. Upon completion, SiL returns the recommended *best suited DLS technique* to the calling application that uses the recommended DLS to improve its performance.

The system monitor and estimator components can be implemented with a number of system monitoring tools [9], such as `collectl`. Such tools can periodically be instantiated to measure PE and network loads and to update the system representation in the simulator. The measured chunk execution times can also be used to estimate the current PE computational speeds. The PE loads can be estimated and predicted using autoregressive integrated moving average [15].

4 Evaluation and Analysis

Experimental Design and Setup. The design of factorial experiments is presented in Table 1. The applications performance is discussed below.

Applications. This work considers a real-world application and five synthetic applications. The parallel spin-image algorithm [10] (PSIA), is an application from computer vision. The PSIA is algorithmically load imbalanced and the computational effort of a loop iteration depends on the input data. The performance of PSIA has been studied in prior work [10] and enhanced for a heterogeneous cluster by using nonadaptive DLS techniques. The total number of PSIA loop iterations is 400,000. To represent the PSIA in simulation, the number of floating point operations (FLOP) of each loop iteration is counted using PAPI [5] counters. In SG-SD, each loop iteration is represented as a task [16]. Each of the five synthetic applications contains 400,000 parallel loop iterations, similar to the PSIA. The FLOP count in each loop iteration is assumed to follow five different probability distributions, namely: constant, uniform, normal, exponential, and gamma probability distributions. The probability distribution parameters used to generate these FLOP counts are given in Table 1.

Loop scheduling. Eleven loop scheduling techniques are used to assess the performance of the above six applications under test. These techniques represent a wide range of loop scheduling approaches, namely, *static* and *dynamic*. The dynamic loop scheduling (DLS) approach can further be distinguished into adaptive and nonadaptive. The DLS techniques can be implemented using centralized

Table 1. Design of factorial experiments

Factors	Values	Properties
Applications	Problem size	$N = 400{,}000$ iterations
	PSIA	$[5.9 \cdot 10^7, 6.6 \cdot 10^7]$ FLOP per iteration
	Constant	$2.3 \cdot 10^8$ FLOP per iteration
	Uniform	$[10^3, 7 \cdot 10^8]$ FLOP per iteration
	Normal	$\mu = 9.5 \cdot 10^8$ FLOP, $\sigma = 7 \cdot 10^7$ FLOP, $[6 \cdot 10^8, 1.3 \cdot 10^9]$ FLOP per iteration
	Exponential	$\lambda = 1/3 \cdot 10^8$ FLOP, $[948, 4.5 \cdot 10^9]$ FLOP per iteration
	Gamma	$k = 2$, $\theta = 10^8$ FLOP, $[4.1 \cdot 10^6, 2.7 \cdot 10^9]$ FLOP per iteration
Loop scheduling	STATIC	Static
	SS, FSC, GSS, FAC, WF	Nonadaptive dynamic
	AWF-B, -C, -D, -E, AF	Adaptive dynamic
Computing system	miniHPC (heterogeneous HPC cluster)	22 Intel Broadwell nodes ($22 \cdot 20$ cores), relative core weight = 1.398
		4 Intel Xeon Phi KNL nodes ($4 \cdot 64$ cores), relative core weight = 0.316
		$P = 224$ heterogeneous (112 Broadwell + 112 KNL) cores
		$P = 696$ heterogeneous (440 Broadwell + 256 KNL) cores
Perturbations	Nominal conditions	np (no perturbations)
	PE availability	pea-cm (constant mild): $\mu = 75\%$, $\sigma = 0\%$
		pea-cs (constant severe): $\mu = 25\%$, $\sigma = 0\%$
		pea-em (exponential mild): $\mu = 78\%$, $\sigma = 24 \cdot 10^{-3}\%$
		pea-es (exponential severe): $\mu = 31\%$, $\sigma = 89 \cdot 10^{-3}\%$
	Bandwidth	bw-cm (constant mild): $\mu = 1 \cdot 10^{-5}\%$, $\sigma = 0\%$
		bw-cs (constant severe): $\mu = 1 \cdot 10^{-7}\%$, $\sigma = 0\%$
		bw-em (exponential mild): $\mu = 1.1 \cdot 10^{-1}\%$, $\sigma = 9 \cdot 10^{-2}\%$
		bw-es (exponential severe): $\mu = 23 \cdot 10^{-2}\%$, $\sigma = 19 \cdot 10^{-2}\%$
	Latency	lat-cm (constant mild): $\mu = 1 \cdot 10^{-5}\%$, $\sigma = 0\%$
		lat-cs (constant severe): $\mu = 1 \cdot 10^{-7}\%$, $\sigma = 0\%$
		lat-em (exponential mild): $\mu = 1.2 \cdot 10^{-5}\%$, $\sigma = 1.5 \cdot 10^{-5}\%$
		lat-es (exponential severe): $\mu = 2.9 \cdot 10^{-7}\%$, $\sigma = 1.8 \cdot 10^{-7}\%$
	Combined	all-cm (constant mild): pea-cm, bw-cm, and lat-cm
		all-cs (constant severe): pea-cs, bw-cs, and lat-cs
		all-em (exponential mild): pea-em, bw-em, and lat-em
		all-es (exponential severe): pea-es, bw-es, and lat-es
Experimentation	Native[a]	PSIA on 224 cores under no perturbations (research report[b])
	Simulative	All applications on 224 cores under all perturbations (research report[b])
		All applications on 696 cores under all perturbations

[a] Direct experiments on real HPC systems.
[b] Mohammed A, Ciorba FM. SiL: An Approach for Adjusting Applications to Heterogeneous Systems Under Perturbations. arXiv preprint arXiv:1807.03577. p. 18 (2018)

or decentralized execution and control approach. The decentralized control approach was found to scale better by eliminating a centralized master, and hence, the master-level contention [17]. The DLS implemented using the decentralized control approach is considered in this work.

Computing system. miniHPC[1] consists of 26 compute nodes: 22 nodes each with one dual socket Intel Xeon E5-2640 v4 (20 cores) configuration and 4 nodes each with one Intel Xeon Phi Knights Landing 7210 processor (64 cores). All nodes are interconnected with Intel Omni-Path fabrics in a nonblocking two-level fat-tree topology.

Simulation. A computing system is represented in SG via an XML file denoted as `platform file`. SG registers each processor core for their representation as a `host` in the `platform file`. The computational speed of a processor core is estimated by measuring a loop execution time and dividing it by the total number of floating point operations included in the loop [16]. A Xeon core was found to be four times faster than a Xeon Phi core as indicated by the relative core weights (cf. Table 1). The network bandwidth and latency represented in the `platform file` are calibrated with the SG calibration procedure[2].

Perturbations. Three different categories of perturbations are considered in this work, namely *delivered computational speed*, *available network bandwidth*, and *available network latency*. Two intensities are considered, `mild` and `severe`, for each category. Two scenarios are considered for each intensity, where the value of the delivered computational speed is either `constant` or `exponentially` distributed. All perturbations (cf. Table 1) are considered to occur periodically, with a period of 100 s where the perturbations affect the system only during 50% of the perturbation period. The network (bandwidth and latency) perturbations commence with the application execution, whereas the delivered computational speed perturbations begin 50 s after the start of the application. Another perturbation category is created by combining all perturbations from the other individual categories. All perturbations are enacted in SG during simulation via the `availability`, `bandwidth`, `latency`, and `platform` files.

Performance of Scientific Applications Under Perturbations. The performance of the six applications of interest is shown in Fig. 2. One can see that STATIC, FSC, GSS, and FAC perform poorly on heterogeneous systems. WF is well suited for scheduling on heterogeneous systems. However, it can not adapt to accommodate the variability in the system due to perturbations, especially perturbations in the delivered computational speed. SS is resilient to perturbations in the delivered computational speed of the PEs. However, it is significantly influenced by the network latency variations, as can be seen in Fig. 2a `lat-cs` and `lat-es`. Perturbations in the network bandwidth show a very small influence on performance, as the PEs only communicate loop iterations indices to calculate the start index of the next chunk. Therefore, the communicated messages are small.

The adaptive techniques perform comparably, with a slight advantage for AWF-C as can be seen in Fig. 2e `all-cs` and in Fig. 2a `pea-cs` and `all-es`. However, in certain cases, other techniques outperform AWF-C. Specifically,

[1] miniHPC is a fully controlled non-production HPC cluster at the Department of Mathematics and Computer Science at the University of Basel, Switzerland.
[2] http://simgrid.gforge.inria.fr/contrib/smpi-calibration-doc/.

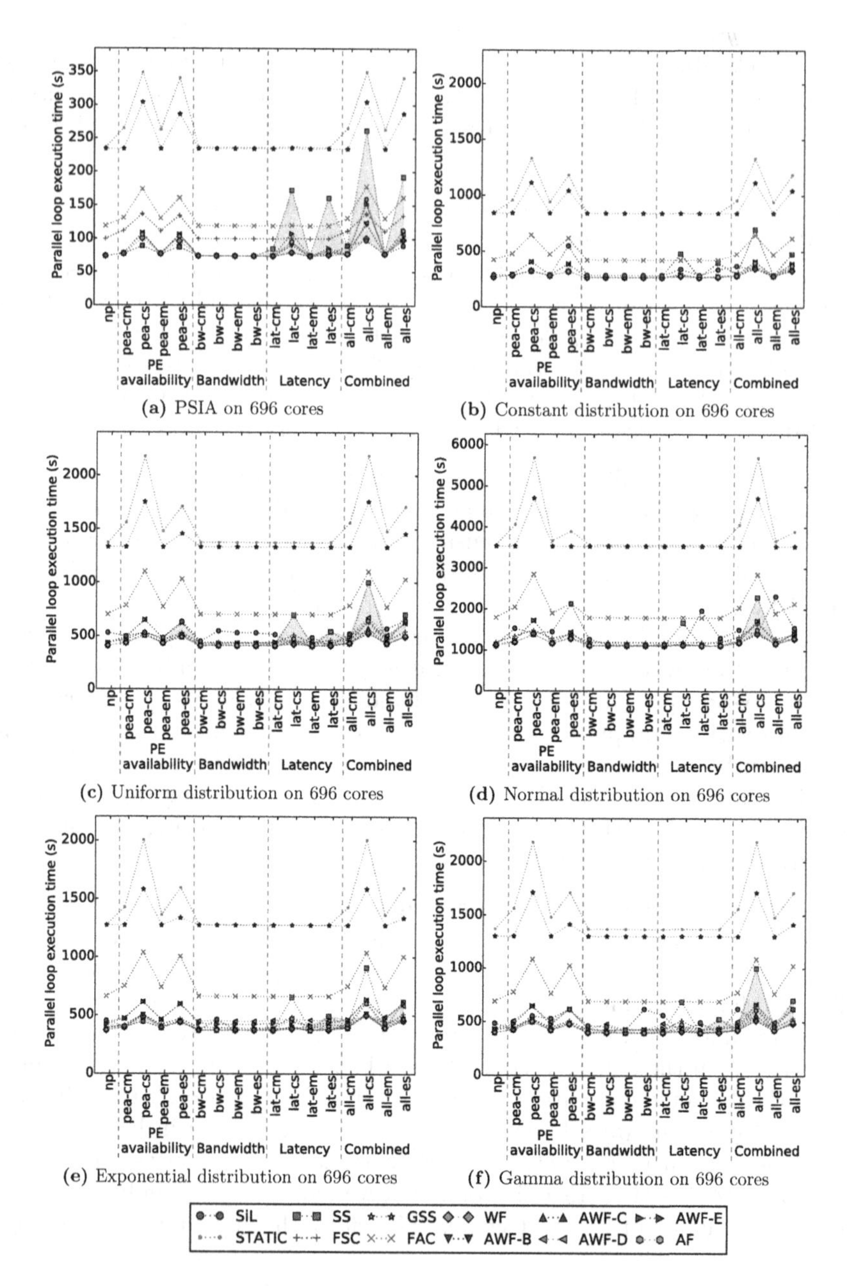

(a) PSIA on 696 cores

(b) Constant distribution on 696 cores

(c) Uniform distribution on 696 cores

(d) Normal distribution on 696 cores

(e) Exponential distribution on 696 cores

(f) Gamma distribution on 696 cores

Fig. 2. Performance results of the six applications of interest without (denoted with np) and with (the rest) perturbations using SiL and eleven loop scheduling techniques on 696 heterogeneous cores. The mint color shaded regions denote the upper and lower bounds of the performance with SiL if only one DLS technique were selected during execution in the particular execution scenario. (Color figure online)

WF outperforms AWF-C in Fig. 2a `lat-cs` and `all-cs`. *These results suggest that no single DLS outperforms all other techniques in all execution scenarios.* Therefore, the best strategy is to dynamically select a DLS based on the current application and system states.

The SiL is called every 50 s when there is a work request to select the best performing DLS. A closer analysis of the SiL-based results reveals that it resulted in the smallest execution time in most execution scenarios, especially for PSIA, as shown in Fig. 2a. The PSIA execution with SiL in the `all-es` scenario outperformed all other techniques, as the best DLS technique was changed during the execution according to the execution scenario. In other cases, the application performance with SiL was slightly slower than the minimum execution time achieved by other DLS. This is due to the fact that loop scheduling is, by definition, non-preemptive and the execution of already scheduled loop iterations can not be preempted to be resumed with the newly selected DLS.

Discussion. The advantage of the SiL approach is to dynamically select the DLS that is predicted to achieve the best performance. A combination of two or more DLS techniques throughout the application execution may result in a shorter execution time than that achievable by any single DLS technique alone as can be seen in Fig. 2a `all-es`. The SiL selected WF for the first 50 s in `all-es`, as can be seen in Fig. 3. After 50 s, the network was no longer perturbed, and SiL selects the SS technique to balance the load and achieve a better performance than any single DLS technique.

The performance results of simulative experiments of the PSIA on 224 heterogeneous cores (112 Broadwell cores and 112 KNL cores) have been verified by native experimentation under the *no perturbation* execution scenario. The raw results and details of the DLS selection for all the applications can be found online[3]. The native experimentation of application performance in other execution scenarios is planned as immediate future work. In certain cases, such as `all-em` in the application with normally distributed tasks, the SiL-based execution did not yield the best performance, due to the fact that DLS is non-preemptive. A simple heuristic that changes the selected DLS based on an application performance measurement may not cover all possible execution scenarios nor fully capture the application and computing system states. The DLS techniques selected

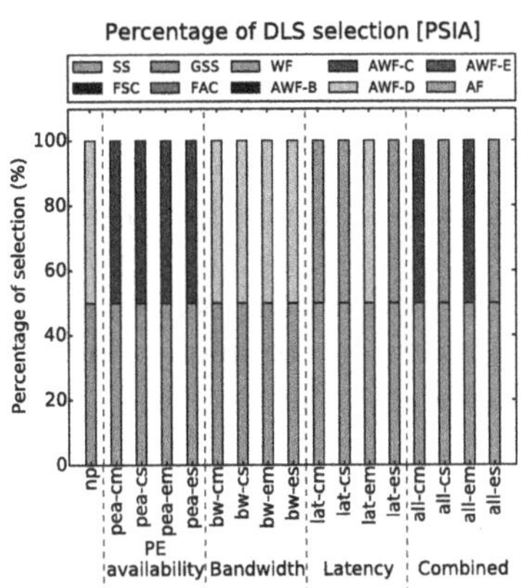

Fig. 3. DLS selection results for the PSIA application. Techniques such as FSC, GSS, and FAC, are not selected due to their poor predicted performance with SiL.

[3] Mohammed A, Ciorba FM. SiL: An Approach for Adjusting Applications to Heterogeneous Systems Under Perturbations. arXiv preprint arXiv:1807.03577. p. 18 (2018).

via SiL can be used as guidelines for a given application, computing system, and perturbation scenario. The SiL approach can proactively select the best suited DLS before any perturbations act on the system, when perturbations can be predicted in advance. The study and prediction of perturbations on HPC systems need further examination, as perturbations in HPC shared resources are inevitable. The cost of the SiL simulation depends on the problem size and the system size. Specifically, simulating the execution of 20,000 iterations on 9 PEs with SG-SD v. 3.16 built with Intel C compiler v. 17 executing on an Intel Broadwell E5 processor, with CentOS 7.2 operating system, required 0.34 s on average, whereas, it required 3.48 s for simulating the execution of 200,000 iterations on the same number of PEs. These costs can be amortized by calling the simulator asynchronously to the parallel loop execution.

5 Conclusion and Future Work

A new control-theoretic-inspired approach, namely simulator in the loop (SiL), was introduced to select a DLS dynamically that achieves the best performance, in an effort to answer the question of which DLS technique will achieve improved performance under unpredictable perturbations. The performance of six applications is studied under perturbations, and insights into the resilience of the DLS techniques to perturbations are provided. The performance results confirm the hypothesis that no single DLS technique can achieve the best performance in all the considered execution scenarios. Using the SiL approach improved the performance of applications in most considered experiments. SiL leverages state-of-the-art simulators to select the DLS predicted to result in the best performance of an application under perturbations. The results show that in the case of a system perturbed via multiple sources, a combination of two or more DLS techniques may result in improved performance than that achievable by any single DLS alone, such as the performance of the PSIA in the `all-es` execution scenario. However, due to applications being non-preemptively scheduled, changing the DLS during the execution may not result in the best performance. Further work is planned to realize and evaluate the performance of the SiL approach using native experimentation. Furthermore, experiments to investigate and enhance the performance of SiL, in terms of improving the DLS selection strategy and the period between SiL calls, are also planned as future work.

Acknowledgments. This work has been supported by the Swiss Platform for Advanced Scientific Computing (PASC) project SPH-EXA: Optimizing Smooth Particle Hydrodynamics for Exascale Computing and by the Swiss National Science Foundation in the context of the Multi-level Scheduling in Large Scale High Performance Computers (MLS) grant number 169123. The authors gratefully acknowledge Ahmed Eleliemy for sharing an initial implementation of the PSIA application.

References

1. Ali, S., Maciejewski, A.A., Siegel, H.J., Kim, J.K.: Measuring the robustness of a resource allocation. IEEE Trans. Parallel Distrib. Syst. **15**(7), 630–641 (2004)
2. Banicescu, I., Liu, Z.: Adaptive factoring: a dynamic scheduling method tuned to the rate of weight changes. In: Proceedings of the High Performance Computing Symposium, pp. 122–129 (2000)
3. Banicescu, I., Velusamy, V., Devaprasad, J.: On the scalability of dynamic scheduling scientific applications with adaptive weighted factoring. Cluster Comput. **6**(3), 215–226 (2003)
4. Boulmier, A., Banicescu, I., Ciorba, F.M., Abdennadher, N.: An autonomic approach for the selection of robust dynamic loop scheduling techniques. In: Proceedings of 16th International Symposium on Parallel and Distributed Computing, pp. 9–17 (2017)
5. Browne, S., Dongarra, J., Garner, N., Ho, G., Mucci, P.: A portable programming interface for performance evaluation on modern processors. Int. J. High Perform. Comput. Appl. **14**(3), 189–204 (2000)
6. Canon, L.C., Jeannot, E.: Evaluation and optimization of the robustness of DAG schedules in heterogeneous environments. IEEE Trans. Parallel Distrib. Syst. **21**(4), 532–546 (2010)
7. Cariño, R.L., Banicescu, I.: Dynamic load balancing with adaptive factoring methods in scientific applications. J. Supercomput. **44**(1), 41–63 (2008)
8. Casanova, H., Giersch, A., Legrand, A., Quinson, M., Suter, F.: Versatile, scalable, and accurate simulation of distributed applications and platforms. J. Parallel Distrib. Comput. **74**(10), 2899–2917 (2014)
9. Ciorba, F.M.: The importance and need for system monitoring and analysis in HPC operations and research. In: Proceedings of the 3rd bwHPC-Symposium: Heidelberg 2016, pp. 7–16. heiBOOKS (2017)
10. Eleliemy, A., Mohammed, A., Ciorba, F.M.: Efficient generation of parallel spin-images using dynamic loop scheduling. In: Proceedings of the 19th IEEE International Conference for High Performance Computing and Communications Workshops, pp. 34–41 (2017)
11. Flynn Hummel, S., Schmidt, J., Uma, R.N., Wein, J.: Load-sharing in heterogeneous systems via weighted factoring. In: Proceedings of the Annual ACM Symposium on Parallel Algorithms and Architectures, pp. 318–328. ACM (1996)
12. Flynn Hummel, S., Schonberg, E., Flynn, L.E.: Factoring: a method for scheduling parallel loops. Commun. ACM **35**(8), 90–101 (1992)
13. García-González, L.A., García-Jacas, C.R., Acevedo-Martínez, L., Trujillo-Rasúa, R.A., Roose, D.: Self-scheduling for a heterogeneous distributed platform. In: Proceedings of the International Conference on Parallel Computing, ParCo2017, pp. 232–241. IOS press (2018)
14. Kruskal, C.P., Weiss, A.: Allocating independent subtasks on parallel processors. IEEE Trans. Softw. Eng. **SE-11**(10), 1001–1016 (1985)
15. Mehrotra, R., Banicescu, I., Srivastava, S., Abdelwahed, S.: A power-aware autonomic approach for performance management of scientific applications in a data center environment. In: Khan, S., Zomaya, A. (eds.) Handbook on Data Centers, pp. 163–189. Springer, New York (2015). https://doi.org/10.1007/978-1-4939-2092-1_5

16. Mohammed, A., Eleliemy, A., Ciorba, F.M., Kasielke, F., Banicescu, I.: Experimental verification and analysis of dynamic loop scheduling in scientific applications. In: Proceedings of the 17th International Symposium on Parallel and Distributed Computing, p. 8 (2018)
17. Mohammed, A., Eleliemy, A., Ciorba, F.M.: Performance reproduction and prediction of selected dynamic loop scheduling experiments. In: Proceedings of the 2018 International Conference on High Performance Computing and Simulation, p. 8 (2018)
18. Polychronopoulos, C.D., Kuck, D.J.: Guided self-scheduling: a practical scheduling scheme for parallel supercomputers. IEEE Trans. Comput. **36**(12), 1425–1439 (1987)
19. Rawlings, J.B.: Tutorial: overview of model predictive control. IEEE Control Syst. **20**(3), 38–52 (2000)
20. Sukhija, N., Malone, B., Srivastava, S., Banicescu, I., Ciorba, F.M.: Portfolio-based selection of robust dynamic loop scheduling algorithms using machine learning. In: Proceedings of 2014 IEEE International Parallel and Distributed Processing Symposium Workshops, pp. 1638–1647 (2014)
21. Tang, P., Yew, P.C.: Processor self-scheduling for multiple-nested parallel loops. In: Proceedings of the International Conference on Parallel Processing, pp. 528–535 (1986)
22. Velho, P., Legrand, A.: Accuracy study and improvement of network simulation in the SimGrid framework. In: Proceedings of the 2nd International Conference on Simulation Tools and Techniques, p. 10 (2009)
23. Yang, Y., Casanova, H.: RUMR: robust scheduling for divisible workloads. In: Proceedings of the 12th IEEE International Symposium on High Performance Distributed Computing, pp. 114–123 (2003)
24. Zhang, Y., Voss, M., Rogers, E.S.: Runtime empirical selection of loop schedulers on hyperthreaded SMPs. In: Proceedings of the 19th International Parallel and Distributed Processing Symposium, p. 10 (2005)

Merging the Publish-Subscribe Pattern with the Shared Memory Paradigm

Loïc Cudennec(✉)

CEA, LIST, PC 172, 91191 Gif-sur-Yvette, France
loic.cudennec@cea.fr

Abstract. Heterogeneous distributed architectures require high-level abstractions to ease the programmability and efficiently manage resources. Both the publish-subscribe and the shared memory models offer such abstraction. However they are intended to be used in different application contexts. In this paper we propose to merge these two models into a new one. It benefits from the rigorous cache coherence management of the shared memory and the ability to cope with dynamic large-scale environment of the publish-subscribe model. The publish-subscribe mechanisms have been implemented within a distributed shared memory system and tested using an heterogeneous micro-server.

Keywords: S-DSM · Publish-Subscribe · Heterogeneous computing

1 Introduction

Distributed heterogeneous architectures are considered as a solution for different computing contexts that provides computational performance while saving the energy consumption. A mix of high-performance and low-power computing nodes are used in HPC and data centers, and a mix of low-power processors, specific accelerators (e.g. for deep learning), GPUs and FPGAs will be used in future embedded devices for autonomous vehicles or future industry. As for current distributed heterogeneous architectures, a part of the main challenges is the efficient programmability.

In such architectures, memories are physically distributed among the nodes, which makes the management of data between tasks more complex. For example it does not allow regular parallel applications with direct access to shared data: inter-node access requires explicit message passing from the user, which is usually addressed using hybrid programming. Distributed shared memory systems (DSM) offer an abstraction layer by federating memories into a global logical space. Data management is hidden by the runtime. The shared memory paradigm is convenient for programming HPC applications with quite a static topology and regular access patterns. However it is not well adapted to event-based applications in which volatile tasks get notified whenever an object state changes.

G. Mencagli et al. (Eds.): Euro-Par 2018 Workshops, LNCS 11339, pp. 469–480, 2019.
https://doi.org/10.1007/978-3-030-10549-5_37

Event-based applications are popular in web services, wireless networks and peer-to-peer (P2P) systems. It can be used to monitor a sensor, the output of a computation or a decision system. This makes the programming paradigm well adapted to new fields of computation such as the industry and the automotive world. The publish-subscribe mechanism relies on a set of mutable objects that can publish notifications to a set of subscribers. This paradigm fits to dynamic applications with unexpected and volatile access to shared data. However, what makes the strength of the paradigm is also a limitation it terms of data coherence management. First, data sharing is usually immutable, meaning that data is modified by the publisher while the subscribers are read-only. Second, the protocol is loosely coupled and the data coherence model is very permissive. It is quite difficult to ensure that the published version read by the subscribers is the current version in the distributed system, according to the causal model.

Upcoming distributed heterogeneous platforms will also run heterogeneous applications in terms of programming models. For example we can mix HPC simulation code with event-based monitoring GUI. In this paper, we propose to merge the publish-subscribe model with the shared memory model. We start from an in-house DSM, we extend the API and implement some distributed mechanisms on the atomic piece of shared data to raise publishing events. We implement a video processing application with the regular shared memory paradigm and the proposed mixed paradigm. Both implementations are then evaluated on a Heterogeneous Christmann RECS|Box Antares Microserver.

2 Shared Memory, Synchronization Objects and Events

Shared memory is a convenient programming paradigm in which a set of tasks can transparently access a set of data. The implementation of such system is quite straightforward on a physically shared memory but reveals to be complex on a distributed architecture. Software-Distributed Shared Memory (S-DSM) is used to federate distributed physical memory and provide a high level of abstraction to the application. In a S-DSM, the system is in charge of the location, the transfer and the management of multiple copies of data. It also provides objects and primitives to synchronize task execution and concurrent accesses. DSM in general have been studied since the late eighties to federate computer memories [7,8,12,14], clusters [1,3,16–18] and grids [4].

In a previous work [9], a S-DSM is proposed for heterogeneous distributed architectures such as micro-servers. This system allows tasks to allocate and access memory in a shared logical space. This is a super-peer distributed topology in which the user code is executed by S-DSM clients, connected to S-DSM servers. Allocated data can be split into *chunks* of any size, the atomic piece of data managed by the S-DSM. While the data is always locally allocated in a contiguous memory space on the clients to allow pointer arithmetic, the corresponding chunks are not necessarily contiguous in the shared logical space and can also be managed independently by the S-DSM servers afterwards. Accessing shared data follows the entry consistency scope paradigm [7]. In this paradigm, access must be protected in the user code using (1) the *READ* or *WRITE* primitive to enter the scope and (2) the *RELEASE* primitive to exit the scope. Outside this scope, data consistency is not guaranteed. The S-DSM can deploy different data coherence protocols on different chunks. In this paper we use the home-based 4-state MESI protocol [10], which allows a single writer and multiple readers (SWMR). The chunk metadata management is distributed among the S-DSM servers by calculating a modulo on the chunk id.

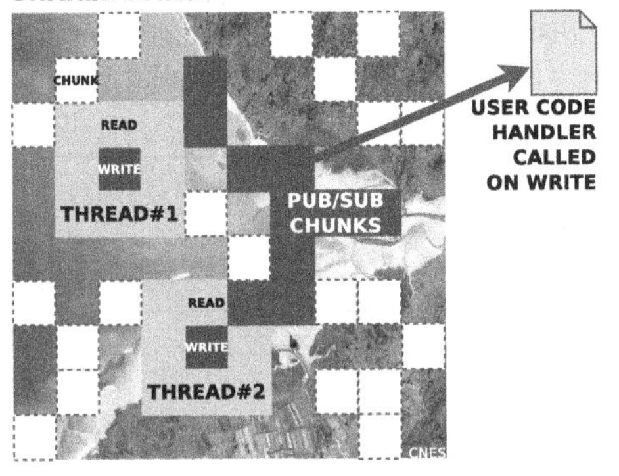

Fig. 1. Event coding in shared memory. Application to the parallel processing of tiles.

As a motivating example, we consider a parallel HPC application as illustrated in Fig. 1. The purpose is to calculate the sea level for each time step by applying a wave propagation model. After each iteration, some specific places on the map are monitored to detect if there is a threat to the population. The base map is represented as a set of chunks in the shared memory, each chunk covering a square surface (a tile). Several threads navigate the chunks to update values. Some other threads monitor the critical chunks (represented in red color). One realistic constraint is that it is not possible to modify the HPC code to manage the critical aspect of the calculation. Instead, we expect a smooth and non-intrusive integration of the critical code regarding the HPC code.

A first approach is to use one rendez-vous and one monitoring thread per critical chunk. Each time a HPC thread calculates a critical chunk, it invokes the corresponding rendez-vous and releases the critical threads. This is a static approach regarding the number of critical chunks and this requires to modify the HPC code to invoke rendez-vous. A second approach is based on polling the critical chunks: a set of monitoring threads continuously access the critical chunks for new values. It possibly generates useless requests and network activity in the S-DSM. It is also prone to skipping some updates between two accesses, unless implementing a dual rendez-vous producer-consumer pattern.

A more elegant approach is to rely on a event-based publish-subscribe (PS) mechanism. Monitoring threads subscribe to critical chunks and get notified each time the chunk has been modified. This approach is transparent for the HPC code and allows dynamic subscription of threads to critical chunks. In this paper, we propose to design and implement this publish-subscribe mechanism within the S-DSM runtime.

3 Event Programming with Memory Chunks

The publish-subscribe paradigm is defined by a set of mutable objects (publishers) and a set of subscribers. There is a many-to-many relationship between publishers and subscribers. Each time the mutable object is changed, it publishes the information to all its subscribers. The information can be a simple notification, an update or the complete data. We propose to merge the publish-subscribe model with the shared memory programming model, with a few modifications to the user API and the S-DSM runtime. The basic idea is to use chunks as mutable publishing objects and to extend the distributed metadata management for chunk coherence on the S-DSM servers with publish-subscribe metadata management. We consider the three following listings.

```
1   void main_publisher() {
2     mychunk = MALLOC(chunkid, size); /* allocate shared data in S-DSM */
3     WRITE(mychunk);                  /* ask for the write lock */
4      foo(mychunk);                   /* in this scope it is possible to write chunk */
5     RELEASE(mychunk);                /* release the write lock */
6   }
```

```
1   void main_subscriber() {
2     mychunk = LOOKUP(chunkid);          /* fetch information about previously allocated chunk */
3     SUBSCRIBE(mychunk, subscriber_handler, parameters);
4                                          /* subscribe to the chunk with given user handler */
5   }
```

```
1   void subscriber_handler(chunk, parameters) {
2     WRITE(chunk);                    /* ask for the write lock */
3      foo(chunk, parameters);         /* in this scope it is possible to read and write chunk */
4     RELEASE(chunk);                  /* release the write lock */
5     UNSUBSCRIBE(chunk);              /* unsubscribe to the chunk, this handler wont be call */
6                                      /* afterwards, all publish notifications are discarded, */
7                                      /* including the RELEASE in this function */
8   }
```

The first listing implements the publisher role. This code only makes use of regular S-DSM primitives. The publish-subscribe API is used by subscribers, as presented by the second listing. The subscribe primitive registers a user handler (a pointer to a local function) and some user parameters to a given chunk. Each time the chunk is modified -from anywhere in the S-DSM- this handler is called on the subscribing task. Finally, a handler function example is given in the third listing. Within the function it is possible to access shared data, subscribe to other chunks and unsubscribe to any chunk. The same handler function can be used to subscribe different chunks. Publish-subscribe events are *sequentialized* on each client and the corresponding handlers are called in the notification message delivering order. This choice has several ins and outs. First, the user code is easier to write because there is no local concurrency to manage. Second, this implies a tight design of the message handling in the S-DSM runtime: the main issue being that if a user code is currently running, and if it waits for a particular message from the S-DSM servers (e.g. a read or write acknowledgment message), then it has to postpone the treatment of this publish notification. The message is then pushed to an event pending list, to be later replayed. We propose the following task model, illustrated by the sequence diagram given in Fig. 2.

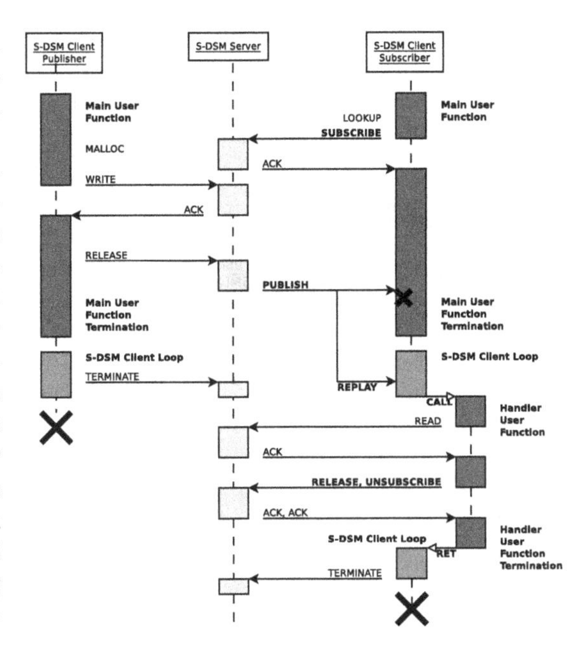

Fig. 2. Sequence diagram for shared memory access and publish-subscribe events. S-DSM server can be replicated.

A user task is defined by a mandatory *main* user function and several optional *handler* functions. The S-DSM runtime bootstraps on the main function. At the end of this function, it falls back to the builtin S-DSM client *loop* function that waits for incoming events such as publish notifications. If there are messages postponed in the event pending list, then they are locally replayed. If the task has no active chunk subscriptions, nor postponed messages in the pending list, then it effectively terminates.

The PS mechanism can work in two modes: (1) the notification mode only triggers a call to the user handler and (2) the push mode embeds a chunk update. This second mode can prefetch data if the user handler accesses the chunk. In the remaining of this paper we only consider the notification mode. The PS mechanism is not allowed to by-pass the consistency protocol and it is not possible to access the chunk outside the consistency scope. PS is a loosely coupled protocol and, for a given chunk, the only causal dependency between a PS notification and an access to the chunk within the handler is that the chunk version accessed is greater or equal to the chunk version that triggered the publish event. The notification and the shared access are not atomic, and several writes can occur on the chunk in-between. However, it is possible to implement a producer-consumer pattern with PS using two chunks as implemented in the application used for the experiments.

4 Experiments with an Heterogeneous Micro-server

Experiments have been conducted onto a RECS|Box heterogeneous micro-server. The form factor is a standard 1U rackable server that is composed by a backplane onto which it is possible to plug computing nodes. Figure 3 presents the micro-server configuration used for all experiments. Two Intel i7 nodes and two Arm-based nodes, the latter embedding 4 Cortex A15 processors each. We do not use the FPGA with Cortex A9 processor. The network is heterogeneous in terms of latencies and bandwidth. The ethernet interface of Cortex A15 processors is implemented over USB with an internal switch within the node to connect the 4 processors. This explains the poor network performances when accessing these processors. Power consumption is monitored by contacting the remote control unit using the REST protocol.

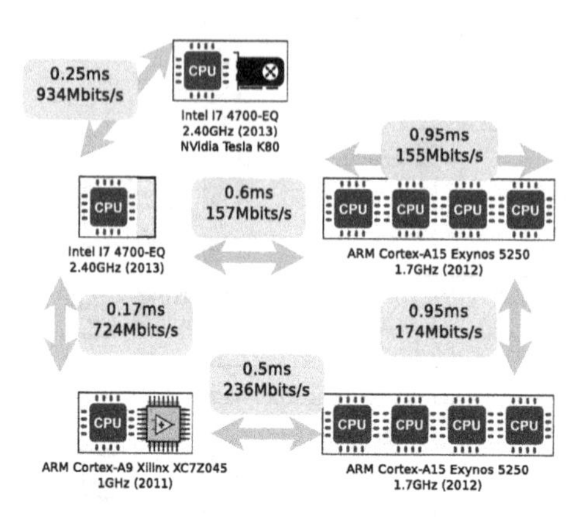

Fig. 3. Heterogeneous Christmann RECS| Box Antares Microserver. Latencies are given by *Ping* and throughputs by *Iperf*. If not specified, we assume roughly the same performances as similar links.

We consider a video processing application composed by one input task for video decoding and frame scheduling, N frame processing tasks, and one task for video encoding. The processing tasks perform edge detection using a $3 * 3$ stencil convolution, followed by line detection using a hough transform. While the convolution complexity is constant, the hough transform complexity is data-dependent: the complexity differs from one frame to another. Above a detection threshold, a pixel is represented as a sinusoid in the intermediate transformed representation. In this intermediate representation, above a second detection threshold, a pixel is represented as a line in the final output image. Both transform operations require the use of double-precision sinus and cosinus functions, which is quite demanding in terms of computational power. To illustrate the software heterogeneity, the processing task has been written in different technologies: sequential C, Pthread (4 threads), OpenMP, OpenCL and OpenCV (using the builtin OpenCV functions).

The application has been implemented using rendez-vous (RR for round-robin scheduling) and publish-subscribe (PS) synchronization functions over the S-DSM. Figure 4 represents the task interactions in both implementations. For each processing task, the input and output frames are stored into memory buffers that are allocated within the S-DSM chunks. The scheduling and buffer synchronization patterns differ in the RR and PS implementations: in the top half part of the figure, frames are written into the input buffers following a round-robin scheduling strategy implemented by the producer-consumer pattern based on rendez-vous synchronization. In the RR implementation, tasks will process the same number of frames (plus one extra frame depending on the video length). If there is a small parallelism degree -a small number of processing tasks- and if a task performs slowly, then this task becomes a bottleneck due to the round-robin strategy that will hang on this particular task until it has finished the job. In the second half part of the figure, the PS implementation, processing tasks are notified each time a new frame has been written into their associated input buffer. In turn, both encoding and decoding tasks are notified each time a processed

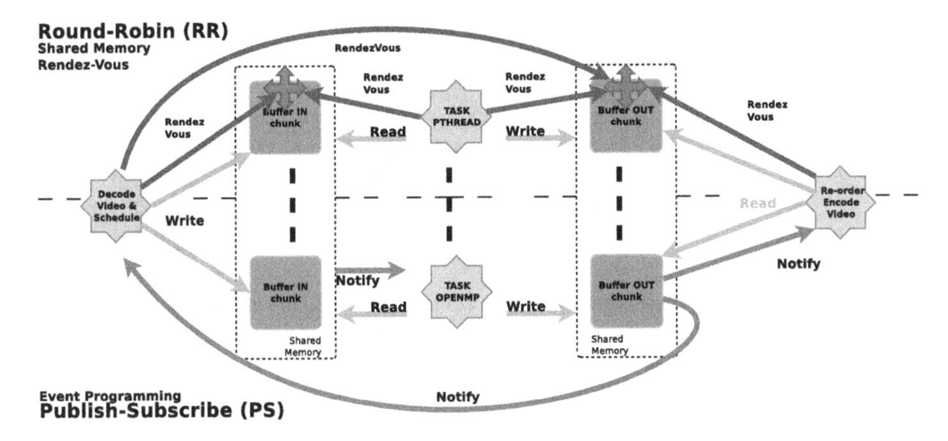

Fig. 4. Description of the video processing application. Top half part is the round-robin (RR) synchronization pattern while the second half part is the publish-subscribe (PS) pattern. The producer-consumer pattern is implemented using a mix of PS notification events and R/W shared memory access.

frame has been written to an output buffer. In that case, the encoding task reads this buffer and writes to the output, while the decoding task decodes the next frame and writes to the corresponding input buffer. This synchronization implements an eager scheduling strategy based on a mix of publish-subscribe notifications and S-DSM write events. The input is a 1-minute video file, with a total of 1730 frames and a resolution of 1280×720 pixels. Processing a frame using Pthread or OpenMP takes around 0.2s on a Core i7 (346s if we extrapolate to 1730 frames) and 0.9s on a Cortex A15 (1557s for 1730 frames). In OpenCV, it takes 0.05s on the Core i7 without external GPU (86.5s for 1730 frames). However, the OpenCV implementation provided by *libopencv* differs from other implementations and delivers quite different results.

Different configurations and mappings of the application are presented in Fig. 5 and labeled from A to F. The heterogeneity is given for processing tasks only. For technical reasons, decoding and encoding tasks are implemented in OpenCV and are always deployed on Core i7. For each configuration, Fig. 6 presents the number of frames processed by each task. The RR scheduling policy evenly distributes the workload among the tasks while the PS implementation reveals how tasks can process at different speeds depending on the hardware and the software choices.

PS Performs Better with Software Heterogeneity. In configuration A, a set of 4 processing tasks implemented with similar technologies -Pthread and OpenMP- are deployed on two i7 processors. Processing times are very close for both RR and PS implementations with a quite similar distribution of frames among the tasks. In configuration B, two tasks are implemented in OpenMP and two tasks in OpenCV, the latter being a faster code. All tasks are running on two i7 processors. The PS version performs better than RR by allowing the OpenCV tasks to process more frames than OpenMP.

	NODES		TASKS		HETEROGENEITY		TIME (s)		W
	i7	A15	Proc	Serv	Hardware	Software	RR	PS	
A	2	0	4	1	i7	Pthread OpenMP	220	218	58
B	2	0	4	1	i7	OpenMP OpenCV	177	153	58
C	1	8	8	1	A15	Sequential Pthread OpenMP	286	401	85
D	2	8	10	1	i7 A15	Pthread OpenMP	233	359	114
E	2	8	10	2	i7 A15	Pthread OpenMP	221	209	114
F	2	8	8	4	i7 A15	Pthread OpenMP	286	198	114

Fig. 5. Different configurations of the video processing application. For each configuration, the table gives the number of Intel Core i7 and Arm Cortex A15 processors used, the number of processing tasks (*Proc*), S-DSM data servers (*Serv*), the heterogeneity in terms of hardware and software, the total processing time for round-robin (RR) and publish-subscribe (PS) and the average instantaneous power consumption of the RECS|Box micro-server.

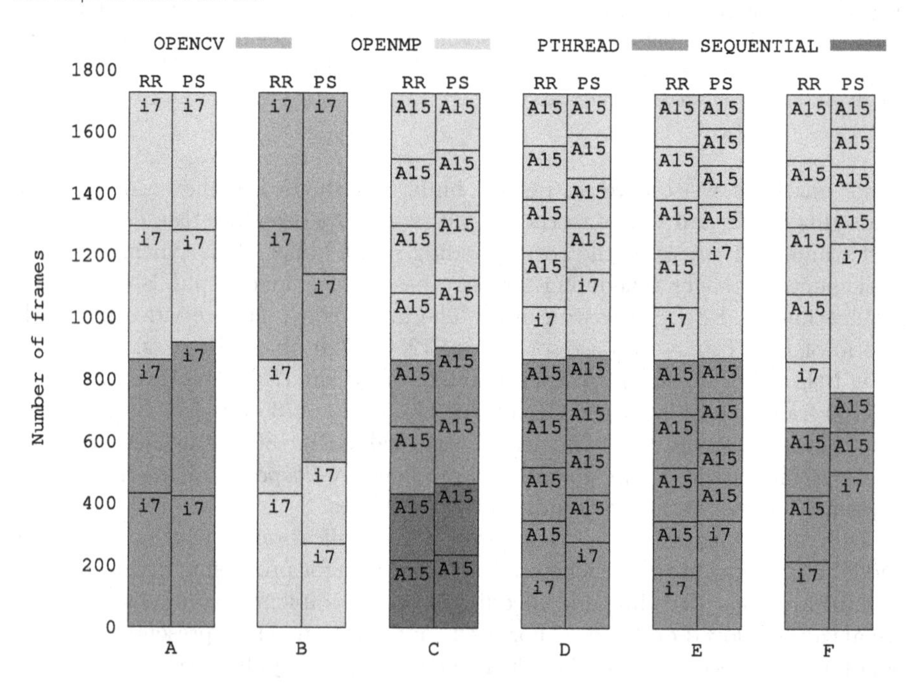

Fig. 6. Number of frames processed by each task for both RR and PS implementations. The software technology and the processor type into which the task is mapped are also displayed.

RR Performs Better with Low-Performance Network. In configuration C, 8 tasks are deployed over eight A15 processors. For technical reasons the decoding and encoding tasks require to be deployed on the i7 processor. Two processing tasks are implemented in a sequential C code, two in Pthread and four in OpenMP. While we were able to get the expected speedup between the sequential and the parallel implementations on Core i7 (almost 4 times faster), we observe that the sequential implementation performs slightly better than the parallel ones onto Cortex A15. However, the PS implementation is not adapted to this configuration, due to the poor network capabilities of our testbed, especially considering the latencies with the Arm baseboards. In that case, the RR implementation provides a better use of the network by avoiding bursts of small messages. In configuration D, 10 processing tasks are deployed over the two i7 and eight A15 processors. The PS implementation distributes more frames to the tasks running on the i7 processors than to the A15. However, as for configuration C, it does not perform well compared to the RR implementation. The S-DSM is deployed using one server and all memory access requests and publish-subscribe notifications are converging to the same i7 node.

PS Benefits from Distributed Metadata Management. Configurations E and F respectively use 2 and 4 S-DSM servers to manage data and metadata. In configuration E, S-DSM servers are deployed over the two i7 processors. The PS implementation largely benefits from this configuration, going from 359 s with one server to 209 s with two servers. In configuration F, two more S-DSM servers are deployed, with a total of one server per baseboard. While this approach involves more communications between servers and slows down the RR implementation, it is well adapted to the PS event-based implementation which performs slightly better than configuration E. This is quite a new result for the proposed S-DSM for which it is rarely worth to distribute the data and metadata management among different servers at this scale when using regular shared access primitives. Instead, we notice that the publish-subscribe mechanism requires a better load balance of events if the network is slow, even for small configurations.

PS Balances Idle Times Among Tasks. Figure 7 presents the execution time per task for both RR and PS implementations using configuration F. For each task the time is decomposed into three parts: (1) the *Sync MP* corresponds

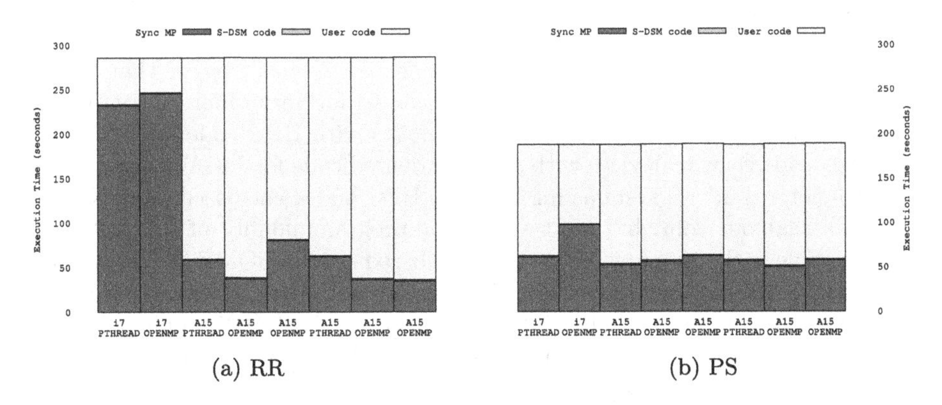

(a) RR

(b) PS

Fig. 7. S-DSM and application time per task for both RR and PS implementations using configuration F. Figures 7a and b use the same vertical scale.

to the time spent in the message passing receive primitive. This mainly happens while waiting for a ack message when accessing the shared memory, a rendez-vous release or a publish-subscribe notification. For HPC applications, this *Sync MP* time should be avoided because it reveals that the task is waiting rather than processing data. (2) The *S-DSM code* time corresponds to the local S-DSM data management. It is usually not significant, with less than 0.7% of the task total execution time in this example. (3) The *User code* corresponds to the time spent in the user code execution, excluding S-DSM calls. In the RR implementation, tasks running on i7 processors spend up to 86% of the time waiting on S-DSM rendez-vous, compared to 12% to 28% for tasks running on the A15 processors. In the PS implementation, while drastically decreasing the total computing time (more than 1.5 faster), all tasks spend between 27% and 51% of their time waiting for the next S-DSM events.

5 Related Works

Distributed shared memory and publish-subscribe systems have been widely studied in the literature for the past decades. Most of the DSM systems, starting with IVY [12] only provide mechanisms for implementing the shared memory paradigm. Cache coherence protocols based on write-invalidate or write-update policies such as MESI [10] are quite close to the publish-subscribe pattern: memories that host a copy of the data are in fact subscribing to its modifications. However, the event is defined by the sole protocol, whether it is a change of the data status in the metadata structure or the update of the data in the memory. There is no third-party application nor user code that can be called on such event. Event-based programming can be used to implement a DSM, as proposed in this system [13], which describes a DSM implemented using the Java event-based distributed system. Our contribution is to implement an event-based distributed system on top of the S-DSM, which is the opposite approach. Publish-subscribe systems have been successfully used for GUIs, internet services, multicasting in mobile networks [2,6] and managing immutable shared data in peer-to-peer (P2P) systems [11,15]. The PS programming paradigm is quite different from shared memory and as far as we know, there is no such system that merge both paradigms. These two paradigms are shaped for very different computing contexts: homogeneous reliable computing nodes with HPC code for DSM and heterogeneous volatile devices with service-oriented code for PS. With the emergence of heterogeneous systems mixing both HPC and event-based applications, we think that our contribution can ease the programmability of the platform. One example is the integration of the event-based system SOME/IP [19] within the AUTOSAR specification standard for future automotive systems, in which heterogeneous computing nodes will have to deal with both HPC applications for vehicle guidance and service-oriented applications for entertainment. The design of the video processing application used in this paper is very close to a dataflow application, in which a set of tasks communicate using explicit channels. Some dataflow runtimes include StarPU [5] designed for heterogeneous architectures with a complementary S-DSM used for internal data management. However, the programming model exposed to the user is pure dataflow, and not a mix of both shared memory and PS paradigms as proposed in this paper.

6 Conclusion

Heterogeneous distributed architectures are expected to be deployed in future technological systems for data centers, industry and automotive. Each application field relies on historical programming models and we propose to merge both shared memory with publish-subscribe models, building a bridge between very different application contexts. We found the underlying mechanisms very similar, leading to a quite straightforward integration. This work contributes with (1) a programming model that merges shared memory and publish-subscribe, (2) a task model that bootstraps on the main user code and terminates with the event-based model and (3) experiments on a heterogeneous micro-server. The experiments show that the choice between shared memory and PS should be made according to the application configuration and the execution platform.

Acknowledgments. This work received support from the H2020-ICT-2015 European Project M2DC - Modular Microserver Datacentre - under Grant Agreement number 688201.

References

1. Amza, C., et al.: TreadMarks: shared memory computing on networks of workstations. IEEE Comput. **29**(2), 18–28 (1996)
2. Anceaume, E., Datta, A.K., Gradinariu, M., Simon, G.: Publish/subscribe scheme for mobile networks. In: Proceedings of the Second ACM International Workshop on Principles of Mobile Computing, POMC 2002, pp. 74–81. ACM, New York (2002)
3. Antoniu, G., Bougé, L.: DSM-PM2: a portable implementation platform for multithreaded DSM consistency protocols. In: Mueller, F. (ed.) HIPS 2001. LNCS, vol. 2026, pp. 55–70. Springer, Heidelberg (2001). https://doi.org/10.1007/3-540-45401-2_5
4. Antoniu, G., Bougé, L., Jan, M.: JuxMem: an adaptive supportive platform for data-sharing on the grid. Scalable Comput. Pract. Exp. (SCPE) **6**(3), 45–55 (2005)
5. Augonnet, C., Thibault, S., Namyst, R., Wacrenier, P.-A.: StarPU: a unified platform for task scheduling on heterogeneous multicore architectures. In: Sips, H., Epema, D., Lin, H.-X. (eds.) Euro-Par 2009. LNCS, vol. 5704, pp. 863–874. Springer, Heidelberg (2009). https://doi.org/10.1007/978-3-642-03869-3_80
6. Banavar, G., Chandra, T., Mukherjee, B., Nagarajarao, J., Strom, R.E., Sturman, D.C.: An efficient multicast protocol for content-based publish-subscribe systems. In: Proceedings. 19th IEEE International Conference on Distributed Computing Systems (Cat. No.99CB37003), pp. 262–272 (1999)
7. Bershad, B.N., Zekauskas, M.J., Sawdon, W.A.: The Midway distributed shared memory system. In: Proceedings of the 38th IEEE International Computer Conference (COMPCON Spring 1993), pp. 528–537, Los Alamitos, CA, February 1993 (1993)

8. Bisiani, R., Forin, A.: Multilanguage parallel programming of heterogeneous machines. IEEE Trans. Comput. **37**(8), 930–945 (1988)
9. Cudennec, L.: Software-distributed shared memory over heterogeneous micro-server architecture. In: Heras, D.B., Bougé, L. (eds.) Euro-Par 2017. LNCS, vol. 10659, pp. 366–377. Springer, Cham (2018). https://doi.org/10.1007/978-3-319-75178-8_30
10. Culler, D., Singh, J., Gupta, A.: Parallel Computer Architecture: A Hardware/-Software Approach. The Morgan Kaufmann Series in Computer Architecture and Design, 1st edn. Morgan Kaufmann, San Francisco (1998)
11. Ginzler, T.: A robust and scalable peer-to-peer publish/subscribe mechanism. In: 2012 Military Communications and Information Systems Conference (MCC), pp. 1–6, October 2012
12. Li, K.: IVY: a shared virtual memory system for parallel computing. In: Proceedings of 1988 International Conference on Parallel Processing, pp. 94–101. University Park, August 1988
13. Mazzucco, M., Morgan, G., Panzieri, F., Sharp, C.: Engineering distributed shared memory middleware for Java. In: Meersman, R., Dillon, T., Herrero, P. (eds.) OTM 2009. LNCS, vol. 5870, pp. 531–548. Springer, Heidelberg (2009). https://doi.org/10.1007/978-3-642-05148-7_40
14. Morin, C., Kermarrec, A.M., Banatre, M., Gefflaut, A.: An efficient and scalable approach for implementing fault-tolerant dsm architectures. IEEE Trans. Comput. **49**(5), 414–430 (2000)
15. Nakayama, H., Duolikun, D., Enokido, T., Takizawa, M.: A P2P model of publish/subscribe systems. In: 2014 Ninth International Conference on Broadband and Wireless Computing, Communication and Applications, pp. 383–388, November 2014
16. Nelson, J., et al.: Latency-tolerant software distributed shared memory. In: 2015 USENIX Annual Technical Conference (USENIX ATC 2015), pp. 291–305. USENIX Association, Santa Clara, CA (2015)
17. Pinheiro, E., Chen, D., Dwarkadas, H., Parthasarathy, S., Scott, M.: S-DSM for heterogeneous machine architectures (2000)
18. Santo, M.D., Ranaldo, N., Sementa, C., Zimeo, E.: Software distributed shared memory with transactional coherence - a software engine to run transactional shared-memory parallel applications on clusters. In: 2010 18th Euromicro Conference on Parallel, Distributed and Network-based Processing, pp. 175–179, February 2010
19. Völker, L.: SOME/IP–die middleware für ethernet-basierte kommunikation. Hanser automotive networks, November 2013

Towards Application-Centric Parallel Memories

Giulio Stramondo(✉), Cătălin Bogdan Ciobanu, Ana Lucia Varbanescu, and Cees de Laat

University of Amsterdam, Amsterdam, The Netherlands
{g.stramondo,c.b.ciobanu,a.l.varbanescu,delaat}@uva.nl

Abstract. Many applications running on parallel processors and accelerators are bandwidth bound. In this work, we explore the benefits of parallel (scratch-pad) memories to further accelerate such applications. To this end, we propose a comprehensive approach to designing and implementing application-centric parallel memories based on the polymorphic memory-model called PolyMem. Our approach enables the acceleration of a memory-bound region of an application by (1) analyzing the memory access to extract parallel accesses, (2) configuring PolyMem to deliver maximum speed-up for the detected accesses, and (3) building an actual FPGA-based parallel-memory accelerator for this region, with predictable performance. We validate our approach on 10 instances of Sparse-STREAM (a STREAM benchmark adaptation with sparse memory accesses), for which we design and benchmark the corresponding parallel-memory accelerators in hardware. Our results demonstrate that building parallel-memory accelerators is feasible and leads to performance gain, but their efficient integration in heterogeneous platforms remains a challenge.

Keywords: Polymorphic parallel memory
Memory bandwidth improvement · Parallel-memory accelerator

1 Introduction

Many heterogeneous systems are currently based on massively parallel accelerators (e.g., GPUs), built for compute-heavy applications. Although these accelerators offer significantly larger memory bandwidth than regular CPUs, many kernels using them are bandwidth-bound. New technologies hold promise for further bandwidth gain, but their adoption depends on the processor vendors, and can therefore be slow. Instead, our work addresses the need for increased bandwidth by enabling more parallelism in the memory system. In other words, for bandwidth-bound applications, this work demonstrates how to build heterogeneous platforms using parallel-memory accelerators.

Designing and/or implementing application-specific parallel memories is non-trivial [3]. Writing the data efficiently, reading the data with a minimum number

G. Mencagli et al. (Eds.): Euro-Par 2018 Workshops, LNCS 11339, pp. 481–493, 2019.
https://doi.org/10.1007/978-3-030-10549-5_38

of accesses and maximum parallelism, and using such memories in real applications are significant challenges. In this paper, we describe our comprehensive approach to designing, building, and using parallel-memory application-specific accelerators. Our parallel memory is designed based on PolyMem [5], a polymorphic parallel memory model with a given set of predefined parallel access patterns. Our approach follows four stages: (1) analyze the memory access trace of the given application to extract parallel memory accesses (Sect. 2), (2) configure PolyMem to maximize the performance of the memory system for the given application (Sects. 3.1, 3.2 and 3.3), (3) compute the (close-to-)optimal mapping and scheduling of application concurrent memory accesses to PolyMem accesses (Fig. 1, Sect. 3.4), and (4) implement the actual accelerator (using MAX-PolyMem), also embedding its management into the host code (Sect. 4.1).

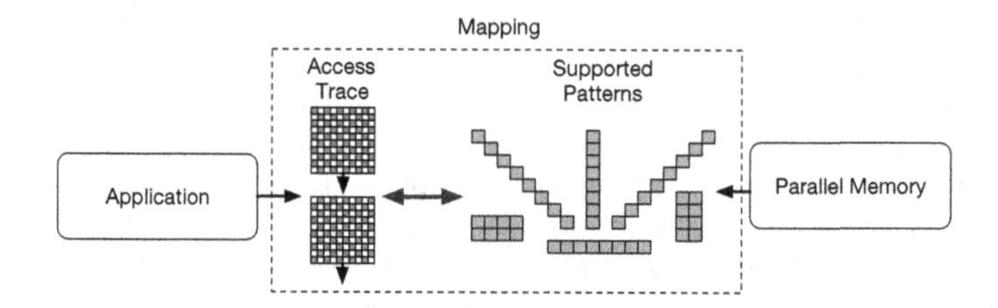

Fig. 1. Customizing parallel memories. Our research focuses on the mapping of the access trace from the application to the parallel access patterns of the parallel memory.

The performance of our accelerators is assessed using two metrics: speed-up against an equivalent accelerator with a sequential memory, and efficiency. Blased on a simple, yet accurate model that estimates the bandwidth of the resulting memory system. Using this estimate and benchmarking data, we could further estimate the overall performance gain of the application using the newly built heterogeneous system.

We validate our approach using 10 Sparse STREAM instances: the original (dense) and 9 variants with various sparsity levels (Sect. 4). We demonstrate how our method enables a seamless analysis and implementation of 10 accelerators in hardware (using a Maxeler FPGA board). Finally, using real benchmarking data from the PolyMem-based heterogeneous systems, we validate our performance model.

In summary, our contribution in this paper is four-fold:

- We present a methodology to analyze and transform application access traces into a sequence of parallel memory accesses.
- We provide a systematic approach to optimally configure a polymorphic parallel memory (e.g., PolyMem) and schedule the set of memory accesses to maximize the performance of the resulting memory system.
- We define and validate a model that predicts the performance of our parallel-memory system.

- We present empirical evidence that the designs generated using our approach can be implemented in hardware as parallel-memory accelerators, delivering the predicted performance.

2 Preliminaries and Terminology

In this section we present the terminology and basic definitions necessary to understand the remainder of this work.

2.1 Parallel Memories

Definition 1 (Parallel Memory). *A Parallel Memory (PM) is a memory that enables the access to multiple data elements in parallel.*

A parallel memory can be realized combining a set of independent memories - referred to as *sequential memories.* The *width of the parallel memory*, identified by the number of sequential memories used in the implementation, represents the maximum number of elements that can be read in parallel. The *capacity* of the parallel memory refers to the amount of data that it can store.

A specific element contained in a PM is identified by its *location*, a combination of a *memory module identifier* (to specify which sequential memory hosts the data) and an *in-memory address* (to specify where within that memory the element is stored). We call this pair *the parallel memory location* of the data element. Formally, thus, $loc(A[I]) = (m_k, addr), k = [0..M)$, where $A[I]$ represents an element of the application - see Sect. 2.2, m_k is the memory module identifier, M is the width of the PM, and $addr$ is the in-memory address.

Our approach focuses on *non-redundant* parallel memories. These memories use a one-to-one mapping between the coordinate of an element in the application space and a memory location. Non-redundant parallel memories can use the full capacity of all the memory resources available, and data consistency is guaranteed by avoiding data replication. However, these parallel memories restrict the possible parallel accesses: only elements stored in different memories can be accessed in parallel (see Sect. 2.2).

2.2 The Application

We use the term *application* to refer to the entity using the PM to read/write data - e.g., a hardware element directly connected to the PM, or a software application interfaced with the PM.

Without loss of generality, we will consider the data of an application to be stored in an array A of N dimensions. Each data element can then be identified by a tuple containing N coordinates $I = (i_0, i_1, ..., i_{N-1})$, which are said to be the coordinates of element $A[I] = A[i_0][i_1]...[i_{N-1}]$ in the *application space.*

An application *memory access* is a read/write operation which accesses $A[I]$. A *concurrent access* is a set of memory accesses, $A[I_j], j = 1..P$, which the application can perform concurrently. An *application memory access trace* is a temporal series of *concurrent accesses*. Finally, a *parallel memory access* is an access to multiple data elements which actually happens in parallel.

Ideally, to maximize the performance of an application, any concurrent access should be a parallel access, happening in one memory cycle. However, when the size of a concurrent access (P) is larger than the width of the PM (M), a scheduling step is required, to schedule all P accesses on the M memories. Our goal is to systematically minimize the number of parallel accesses for each concurrent access in the application trace. We do so by tweaking both the memory configuration and the scheduling itself.

Tweaking the Memory Configuration. To specify a M-wide parallel access to array A – stored in the PM –, one can explicitly enumerate M addresses $(A[I_0]...A[I_{M-1}])$, or use an *access pattern*. The access pattern is expressed as a M-wide set of N-dimensional offsets - i.e.,$\{(o_{0,0}, o_{0,1}, ..., o_{0,N-1}) - (o_{M-1,0}, o_{M-1,1}, ..., o_{M-1,N-1})\}$. Using a reference address - i.e. $A[I]$ - and the access pattern makes it possible to derive all M addresses to be accessed. For example, for a 4-wide access (M = 4) in a 2D array (N = 2), where the accesses are at the N,E,S,W elements, the access pattern is $\{(-1,0), (0,-1), (1,0), (0,1)\}$. When combining the pattern with a reference address - e.g., (4, 4) - we obtain a set of M element coordinates - e.g, $\{(3,4), (4,3), (5,4), (4,5)\}$. We call the operation of instantiating a memory access pattern into a set of addresses based on a reference address *resolving the pattern*. In Sect. 3.2 we will use the function *resolve_pattern(p,a)* - where p is an access pattern and a is a reference address - to indicate this operation.

Definition 2 (Conflict-Free Parallel Access). *A set of* Q *memory accesses* $A[I_0]..A[I_{Q-1}]$ *form a parallel memory access iff it constitutes a conflict-free parallel access, namely:*

$$\forall (A[I_i], A[I_j])$$
$$where\ i \neq j, 0 \leq i, j \leq Q-1, Q = M$$
$$loc(A[I_i]) = (m_i, addr_i), loc(A[I_j]) = (m_j, addr_j)$$
$$m_i \neq m_j.$$

To map the access to an element in application space to a parallel access in PM space, we need to define a mapping function that guarantees M-wide conflict free accesses. Determining the function to use is a key challenge in defining a custom parallel memory.

Definition 3 (Memory Mapping Function). *The Memory Mapping Function (MMF) maps an application memory access to its parallel memory location.*

$$MMF : (A[I], M, D[I]) \rightarrow (m_k, addr_k), k = [0..M)$$

where $I = (i_0, i_1, ..., i_{N-1})$ *are the coordinates of the access in the application space,* M *is the width of the parallel memory, and* $D[I]$ *are the sizes of each dimension of the application space array.*

We note that due to the restriction that only conflict-free accesses can be parallel accesses, there is a limited set of access patterns that a parallel memory can support. These patterns are an immediate consequence of the MMF.

A PM configuration is the pair (MMF, C), where MMF is a mapping function and C is the capacity of the PM. Customizing a parallel memory entails finding, for a given application, the configuration that minimizes the number of parallel accesses to the PM.

In the remainder of this paper we focus on a methodology to configure a custom parallel memory with the right M, C, and MMF for a given application (see Sect. 3 and further).

Scheduling Concurrent Accesses. Once the parallel memory configuration is known, the transformation between the application concurrent accesses and the memory parallel accesses is necessary. We call this transformation *scheduling*, and note it can be static - i.e., computed pre-runtime, per concurrent access - or dynamic - i.e., computed at runtime. In this work, we assume static scheduling is possible, and the actual schedule is an outcome of our methodology (see Sect. 3 and further).

3 Scheduling an Application Access Trace to a PM

In this section we describe two approaches for scheduling an application access trace using a set of PM parallel access patterns. The first one finds an optimal solution to this problem - the minimum number of PM accesses that cover the application access trace - using ILP. The second one proposes an alternative to ILP, in the form of a heuristic method which trades-off optimality for speed. Finally, we end this section with an overview of our full approach towards application-centric parallel memories and a simple predictive model to calculate the performance of the resulting memory system.

3.1 The Set Covering Problem

We express the problem of scheduling an application access trace onto a set of PM accesses as a particular instance of the *set covering* NP-complete problem [12].

Definition 4 (Set Covering [12]). *Given a universe* $\mathbb{U}$ *of* n *elements, a collection of sets* $\mathbb{S} = \{S_1, ..., S_k\}$, *with* $S_i \subseteq \mathbb{U}$, *and a cost function* $c : \mathbb{S} \to Q+$, *find a minimum-cost subset of* $\mathbb{S}$ *that covers all elements of* $\mathbb{U}$.

The set cover can be formulated as an integer program:

$$\text{minimize} \quad \sum_{S_i \in \mathbb{S}} c(S_i) \cdot x_{S_i}$$

$$\text{subject to} \quad \sum_{S_i : e \in S_i} x_{S_i} \geq 1, \quad e \in \mathbb{U}.$$

In this formulation, $x_{S_i} = \{0, 1\}$ is a variable indicating if set S_i is part of the solution, $c(S_i)$ is the cost of set S_i, and the solution is constrained to have for each element $e \in \mathbb{U}$ at least one set $S_i : e \in S_i$.

3.2 From Concurrent Accesses to Set Covering

An optimal schedule of an application access trace on a set of PM parallel accesses can be found by reducing this problem to a set covering one, and leveraging the ILP formulation discussed in the previous section. Although an application access trace contains a list of application concurrent accesses, we schedule each of those separately. For every application concurrent access, the universe $\mathbb{U}$ is formed by all accesses. From the PM predefined parallel access patterns, we define $\mathbb{S}$ as the collection of all possible parallel accesses in PM (see Algorithm 1). Finally, the solution obtained using an ILP solver, $\mathbb{S}_{min}, \mathbb{S}_{min} \subseteq \mathbb{S}$, is a list of sets which optimally cover the concurrent accesses, and will be converted back into a sequence of parallel memory accesses.

Algorithm 1. Generation of the Collection of Sets

```
1: 𝕊 ← ∅
2: 𝔸 ← {all application elements}
3: 𝕌 ← {all accessed elements}
4: ℙ ← {PM parallel access patterns}
5: for p ∈ ℙ do
6:     for a ∈ 𝔸 do
7:         pa ← resolve_pattern(p, a).
8:         S_pa ← pa ∩ 𝕌.
9:         𝕊 ← 𝕊 ∪ S_pa
10:    end for
11: end for
12: return 𝕊.
```

Algorithm 1 shows how to generate $\mathbb{S}$, from which the minimal coverage will be extracted. Set $\mathbb{P}$ contains the list of PM conflict-free accesses patterns, and it is obtained from the PM configuration. Set $\mathbb{A}$ contains the coordinates of the application data. Each pair of an application element and an access pattern (i.e., elements from $\mathbb{A}$ and $\mathbb{P}$, respectively) is resolved into a set of coordinates of application elements, pa, by *resolve_pattern* (see Sect. 2.1); To map our problem to the ILP formulation above we need to guarantee that the union of the collection of subsets in $\mathbb{S}$ is equal to the universe $\mathbb{U}$. This is done by removing the elements that are not being accessed in the concurrent access -i.e. the elements in $\mathbb{A}$ but not in $\mathbb{U}$- from the parallel access pa. The elements of $\mathbb{S}$ will be all these S_{pa} sets, for which it holds that $\bigcup_{S_{pa} \in \mathbb{S}} S_{pa} = \mathbb{U}$.

To solve our original problem, we are interested in finding the minimum collection of sets $\mathbb{S}_{min}$ such that $\bigcup_{S \in \mathbb{S}_{min}} S = \mathbb{U}$ and $\mathbb{S}_{min} \subseteq \mathbb{S}$, so the cost function will be defined as $c(S_{pa}) = 1, \forall S_{pa} \in \mathbb{S}$. Once $\mathbb{S}, \mathbb{U}, c$ are defined, an ILP solver can be used to compute $\mathbb{S}_{min}$ - the minimum collection of sets that covers the universe $\mathbb{U}$.

3.3 An Heuristic Approach

As our preliminary results show that ILP is a major bottleneck in our system, speed-wise, we also investigate the possibility to offer an alternative to the ILP formulation for solving the scheduling problem. Therefore, we have designed and implemented a heuristic approach, based on a greedy algorithm (see Algorithm 2). Our heuristic is based on [12], and the solution is guaranteed to be within an harmonic factor from the optimal solution (extracted with the ILP approach).

Algorithm 2. Heuristic Application Trace Scheduling

1: $\mathbb{U} \leftarrow$ {all accessed elements}
2: $\mathbb{S} \leftarrow$ {possible parallel accesses}
3: $\mathbb{S}_h \leftarrow \varnothing$
4: $E \leftarrow \mathbb{U}$
5: **while** $E \neq \varnothing$ **do**
6: Find $S_{pa} \in \mathbb{S}$ s.t. $|E \backslash S_{pa}|$ is minimum.
7: $\mathbb{S}_h \leftarrow \mathbb{S}_h \cup S_{pa}$.
8: $E \leftarrow E \backslash S_{pa}$
9: **end while**
10: **return** $\mathbb{S}_h$.

Algorithm 2 shows our heuristic approach. E is a set used to keep track of the elements still to be covered with a parallel access, and it is initialized with $\mathbb{U}$, the set containing all the elements in the concurrent access. $\mathbb{S}$ contains all parallel accesses from $\mathbb{A}$ for a given PM configuration (Algorithm 1, Sect. 3.2). In each iteration, the parallel access $S_{pa} \in \mathbb{S}$, which contains the maximum number of elements that still needs to be covered, is added to the solution, and the elements covered by S_{pa} are removed from E. Once all the elements in the application concurrent access have been covered, the algorithm returns the set of parallel access $\mathbb{S}_h$ containing the solution.

3.4 The Complete Approach

Our complete approach is presented in Fig. 2. We start from the *Application Access Trace*, a description of the concurrent accesses in the application, discussed in detail in Sect. 2.2. We test different parallel memory configuration by providing different *Configuration Files* to our *Memory Simulator*. Each *Configuration File* contains details regarding mapping scheme, number of parallel lanes and capacity of the parallel memory. The *Memory Simulator* produces all the available parallel accesses, compatible with the given parallel memory *Configuration File*, that cover elements contained in the *Application Access Trace*. The set of parallel accesses is then given as input to our ILP or Heuristic solver - implemented as described in Sects. 3.2 and 3.3. The *Solver* selects the minimum number of parallel accesses that fully cover the elements in the *Application*

Access Trace, thus producing a *Schedule* of parallel memory accesses. The *Schedule* can then directly be used in the hardware implementation of the application parallel memory.

An important side-effect of our approach is that the information contained in the schedule can further be used to accurately estimate the performance of the generated memory system. Thus, to calculate the achievable average bandwidth of the memory system for the given access trace, we can "penalize" the theoretical bandwidth (i.e., assuming that all lanes are fully used) by our efficiency metric: $BW_{real} = BW_{peak} \times Efficiency = (Frequency * Bitwidth * Lanes) \times \frac{N_{seq}}{N_{elements}}$. $Frequency$ is the frequency the PM is operating at, $Bitwidth$ is the size of each element stored in the PM and $Lanes$ represents the amount of elements that can be accessed in parallel; N_{seq} is the number of required sequential accesses and $N_{elements}$ is the total number of elements accessed by the PM using a *Schedule.*

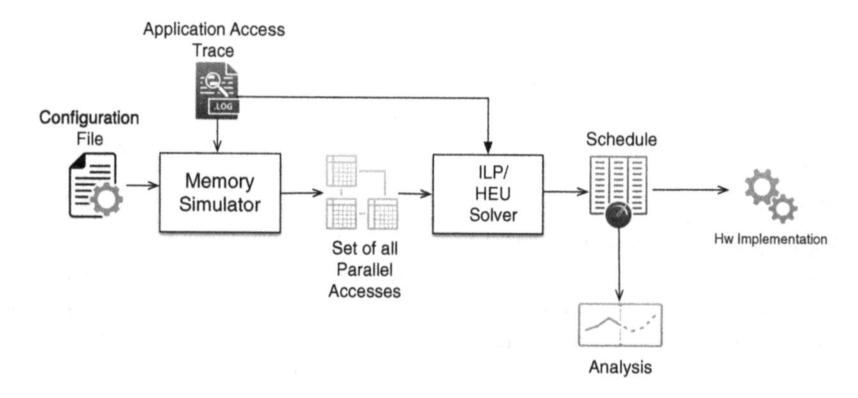

Fig. 2. An overview of our complete approach.

4 Experiments and Results

We evaluate the feasibility and performance of our approach by designing and implementing 10 parallel-memory accelerators on an FPGA-based system. We use a Maxeler Vectis board, equipped with a Xilinx Virtex-6 SX475T FPGA[1] featuring 475k logic cells and 4 MB of on-chip BRAMs.

4.1 MAX-PolyMem

Our parallel memory is based on PolyMem, a design inspired by the polymorphic register file [6]. The hardware implementations and performance analysis presented in this section are all based on the Maxeler version of PolyMem, MAX-PolyMem [5].

[1] Xilinx Virtex-6 Family Overview: http://xilinx.com/support/documentation/data_sheets/ds150.pdf.

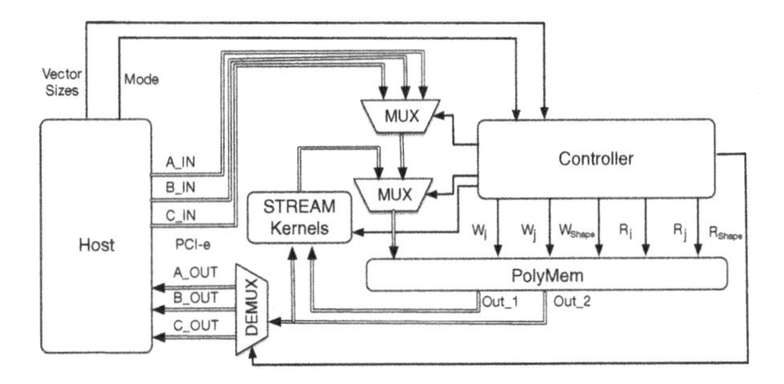

Fig. 3. The implementation of the STREAM benchmark for MAX-PolyMem (figure updated from [5]). All transfers between host (the CPU) and PolyMem (on the FPGA) are done via the PCIe link.

PolyMem is a non-redundant parallel memory, using multiple lanes to enable parallel data access to bi-dimensional data structures, and a specialized hardware module that enables parallelism for multiple access patterns. For example, an 8-lane PolyMem allows reading/writing 8 elements at a time from/to a 2D memory. The access shapes supported by PolyMem, defined as bi-dimensional shapes, are Row, Column, Rectangle, Transposed Rectangle, Main Diagonal, and Secondary Diagonal. Due to its multi-view design [6], PolyMem supports several *access schemes*, i.e, it can perform memory operations with different access patterns without reconfiguration:

- ReO: Rectangle.
- ReRo: Rectangle, Row, Diagonal, Sec. Diagonal.
- ReCo: Rectangle, Column, Diagonal, Sec. Diagonal.
- RoCo: Row, Column, Rectangle.
- ReTr: Rectangle, Transposed Rectangle.

4.2 Sparse STREAM

To prove the feasibility of our approach, from application access traces to hardware, we adapt the STREAM benchmark [2,10], a well-known tool for memory bandwidth estimation in modern computing systems, to support sparse accesses.

The original STREAM benchmark uses three *dense* vectors - A, B and C - and proposes four kernels: Copy ($C = A$), Scale ($A = q \cdot B$), Sum ($A = B + C$), and Triad ($A = B + q \cdot C$).

We have designed a version of STREAM for MAX-PolyMem [5]. A high-level view of our design[2], is presented in Fig. 3.

However, the original STREAM does not challenge our approach because it uses dense, regular accesses. We therefore propose Sparse STREAM, an adaptation of STREAM which allows 2D arrays and configurable sparse accesses. Table 1 presents 10 possible variants of Sparse STREAM, labeled based on their

[2] STREAM for MAX-PolyMem is open-source and available online [1].

Table 1. The 10 variants of the STREAM benchmark and the predicted performance of the calculated schedules for two schemes (ReRo and RoCo). The other schemes are omitted because they are not competitive for these patterns. In the patterns, only the `R` elements need to be read.

Pattern description			ReRo Scheme				RoCo Scheme				Selected
Density	Pattern	N_{seq}	N_{par}	$N_{elements}$	Speed-up	Efficiency	N_{par}	$N_{elements}$	Speed-up	Efficiency	Scheme
20	`RR________RR____`	17408	4369	34952	3.98	49.81	4369	34952	3.98	49.81	ReRo
25	`R___R___R___R___`	21760	10880	87040	2.00	25.00	2816	22528	7.73	96.59	RoCo
33	`R__R__R__R__R__R`	29013	3724	29792	7.79	97.39	9671	77368	3.00	37.50	ReRo
40	`RRRR____RRRR____`	34816	8687	69496	4.01	50.10	8687	69496	4.01	50.10	ReRo
50	`R_R_R_R_R_R_R_R_`	43519	10880	87040	4.00	50.00	5504	44032	7.91	98.83	RoCo
60	`RRRRRR____RRRRRR`	52224	8821	70568	5.92	74.01	8821	70568	5.92	74.01	ReRo
66	`RR_RR_RR_RR_RR_R`	58026	7350	58800	7.89	98.68	9710	77680	5.98	74.70	ReRo
75	`RRR_RRR_RRR_RRR_`	65279	10880	87040	6.00	75.00	8192	65536	7.97	99.61	RoCo
80	`RRRRRRRR__RRRRRR`	69632	8806	70448	7.91	98.84	8806	70448	7.91	98.84	ReRo
100	`RRRRRRRRRRRRRRRR`	87040	10880	87040	8.00	100.00	10880	87040	8.00	100.00	ReRo

read access density. The main difference between these variants is its number of sequential accesses, N_{seq}.

We apply our methodology for each variant. Thus, for each variant, we obtain the (close-to-) optimal schedule per access scheme. The schedule is characterized by the number of parallel accesses N_{par}, and the total number of accessed elements $N_{elements}$ (Sect. 3), from which we calculate speed-up and efficiency per access scheme. We present these results for two schemes (namely, ReRo and RoCo) in Table 1. We select the best performing to test in hardware.

The final step in our approach is the translation from a schedule to a hardware implementation of our parallel-memory accelerator. The key challenge is to enable the controller (see Fig. 3) to orchestrate the parallel memory operations based on the given schedule. Our current prototype stores the schedule, which contains information regarding the required sequence of parallel accesses (coordinates, shape, and mask), in an on-chip `Schedule memory`.

4.3 Results

We have implemented all 10 STREAM variants in hardware by configuring MAX-PolyMem, for each test-case, with a memory of 261120 elements (i.e., the maximum capacity available fitting the arrays A, B, C and the `schedule memory`), and the best scheme (see Table 1). We have measured the performance of each STREAM component and compared it against our bandwidth estimation.

We measure the bandwidth of our 10 Sparse STREAM kernels (average over 10000 runs)*[3]. The results - predicted vs. measured - are presented in Fig. 4. We make the following observations:

- Our performance model (see Sect. 3) accurately predicts the performance of the memory system (below 1% error in most cases).

[3] The overhead of uploading/downloading the arrays to PolyMem is not included in these results.

- For 6 out of the 9 sparse STREAM variants, we can achieve close to optimal speed-up due to our parallel memory being multi-view and polymorphic.
- For S-25, S-50, and S-75, the performance gain versus choosing the alternative scheme used in this experiment is, according to Table 1, of 70%, 50%, and 24%, respectively.
- Our STREAM PolyMem design uses only 25.98% of the logic available in the Vectis Maxeler board. More information regarding the resource usage is available in [5].

Overall, our experiments are successful: we demonstrated that the schedule generated by our approach can be used in real-hardware, and we showed that the measured performance is practically the same with the predicted one.

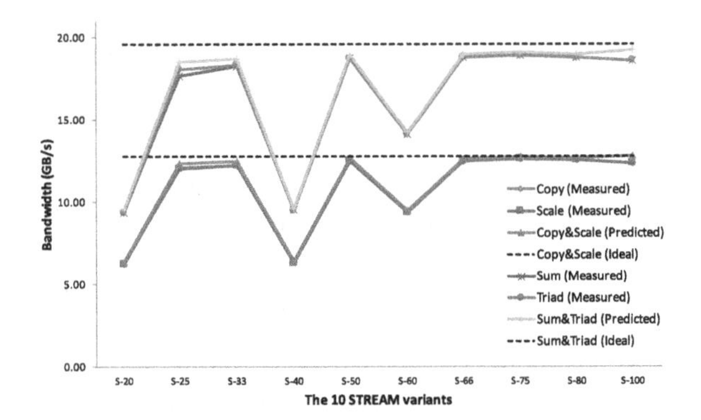

Fig. 4. The performance results (measured, predicted, and ideal) for the 10 different variants of the STREAM benchmark. The horizontal lines indicate the theoretical bandwidth of MAX-PolyMem, configured with 8-byte data, 8 lanes, and 2 (for Copy and Scale) or 3 (for Sum or Triad) parallel operations. Running at 100 MHz, MAX-PolyMem can reach up to 12.8 GB/s for 1-operand benchmarks and up to 19.6 GB/s for 2-operand benchmarks.

5 Related Work

Research on using parallel memories to improve system memory bandwidth has started in the 70s, and remains of interest today. Parallel memories that use a set of predefined mapping functions to enable specifically shaped parallel accesses have improved to better support more shapes [7–9], multiple views, and polymorphic access [6]. Approaches that derive an application-specific mapping function [13,15] have also emerged, constantly improving the efficiency and performance of the generated memory systems. The current version of this work uses a polymorphic parallel memory with fixed shapes, to which we add the novel analysis and configuration methodology.

As for building such memories in hardware, a lot of research has been invested in building application-specific caches for FPGAs. Although successful, such research [4,11,14] does not (yet) address parallel and/or polymorphic memories. Our work fills this gap, by showing how to efficiently design a polymorphic, multi-view parallel memory embedded into an FPGA-based accelerator.

6 Conclusion and Future Work

Modern accelerators, currently embedded in heterogeneous systems, offer massive parallelism for compute-intensive applications, but often suffer from memory bandwidth limitations. Our work investigates the benefits of building accelerators with application-specific parallel memories as a solution to alleviate this bottleneck. Our approach is especially effective for applications with large sets of concurrent accesses.

To this end, we proposed an end-to-end workflow which analyzes the application access trace, configures and builds a custom non-redundant parallel memory (e.g., PolyMem), optimized for the data-intensive kernel of interest, generates our parallel-memory accelerator in hardware, and embeds it in the original host code.

We have empirically validated our approach using Sparse STREAM with 10 different access densities. We demonstrated that we can instantiate and benchmark all 10 designs in real hardware (i.e., a Maxeler system and the MAX-PolyMem version). Our experimental results demonstrate clear bandwidth gains, and closely match our model's predictions. Our on-going work focuses on the analysis of more applications. In the near future, we aim to improve/automate the access traces extraction, a more efficient integration of the parallel-memory accelerator into the host application, and an extension of the model towards accurate full-application performance prediction.

References

1. STREAM PolyMem MaxJ Code. https://github.com/giuliostramondo/PolyMemStream
2. The STREAM benchmark website. https://cs.virginia.edu/stream/
3. Budnik, P., Kuck, D.J.: The organization and use of parallel memories. IEEE Trans. Comput. **100**(12), 1566–1569 (1971)
4. Chung, E.S., Hoe, J.C., Mai, K.: CoRAM: an in-fabric memory architecture for FPGA-based computing. In: FPGA 2011, pp. 97–106 (2011)
5. Ciobanu, C.B., Stramondo, G., de Laat, C., Varbanescu, A.L.: MAX-PolyMem: high-bandwidth polymorphic parallel memories for DFEs. In: IPDPSW 2018 (RAW 2018) (2018)
6. Ciobanu, C.: Customizable register files for multidimensional SIMD architectures. Ph.D. thesis, Delft University of Technology, Delft, Netherlands, March 2013
7. Gou, C., Kuzmanov, G., Gaydadjiev, G.N.: SAMS multi-layout memory: providing multiple views of data to boost SIMD performance. In: ICS, pp. 179–188. ACM (2010)
8. Harper, D.T.: Block, multistride vector, and FFT accesses in parallel memory systems. IEEE Trans. Parallel Distrib. Syst. **2**(1), 43–51 (1991)

9. Kuzmanov, G., Gaydadjiev, G., Vassiliadis, S.: Multimedia rectangularly addressable memory. IEEE Trans. Multimed. **8**, 315–322 (2006)
10. McCalpin, J.D.: A survey of memory bandwidth and machine balance in current high performance computers. IEEE TCCA Newslett. **19**, 25 (1995)
11. Putnam, A.R., Bennett, D., Dellinger, E., Mason, J., Sundararajan, P.: CHiMPS: a high-level compilation flow for hybrid CPU-FPGA architectures. In: FPGA 2008, p. 261 (2008)
12. Vazirani, V.V.: Approximation Algorithms. Springer, Heidelberg (2013). https://doi.org/10.1007/978-3-662-04565-7
13. Wang, Y., Li, P., Zhang, P., Zhang, C., Cong, J.: Memory partitioning for multidimensional arrays in high-level synthesis. In: DAC, p. 12. ACM (2013)
14. Yang, H.J., Fleming, K., Winterstein, F., Chen, A.I., Adler, M., Emer, J.: Automatic construction of program-optimized FPGA memory networks. In: FPGA 2017, pp. 125–134 (2017)
15. Yin, S., Xie, Z., Meng, C., Liu, L., Wei, S.: Multibank memory optimization for parallel data access in multiple data arrays. In: ICCAD 2016, pp. 1–8 (2016)

Fast Heuristic-Based GPU Compiler Sequence Specialization

Ricardo Nobre(✉), Luís Reis, and João M. P. Cardoso

Faculty of Engineering, University of Porto, INESC TEC, Porto, Portugal
{ricardo.nobre,luis.cubal}@fe.up.pt, jmpc@acm.org

Abstract. Iterative compilation focused on specialized phase orders (i.e., custom selections of compiler passes and orderings for each program or function) can significantly improve the performance of compiled code. However, phase ordering specialization typically needs to deal with large solution space. A previous approach, evaluated by targeting an x86 CPU, mitigates this issue by first using a training phase on reference codes to produce a small set of high-quality reusable phase orders. This approach then uses these phase orders to compile new codes, without any code analysis. In this paper, we evaluate the viability of using this approach to optimize the GPU execution performance of OpenCL kernels. In addition, we propose and evaluate the use of a heuristic to further reduce the number of evaluated phase orders, by comparing the speedups of the resulting binaries with those of the training phase for each phase order. This information is used to predict which untested phase order is most likely to produce good results (e.g., highest speedup). We performed our measurements using the PolyBench/GPU OpenCL benchmark suite on an NVIDIA Pascal GPU. Without heuristics, we can achieve a geomean execution speedup of 1.64×, using cross-validation, with 5 non-standard phase orders. With the heuristic, we can achieve the same speedup with only 3 non-standard phase orders. This is close to the geomean speedup achieved in our iterative compilation experiments exploring thousands of phase orders. Given the significant reduction in exploration time and other advantages of this approach, we believe that it is suitable for a wide range of compiler users concerned with performance.

Keywords: GPU · Phase ordering · Optimization

1 Introduction

Compilers optimize a function/program by applying a set of analysis and transformation operations over a representation of its source code (see, e.g., [2]). Those operations are implemented in compiler passes, each typically implementing a well delimited operation with a specific purpose, such as unrolling loops.

The set of compiler passes considered, and the order in which they are executed, can have a measurable impact in the quality of the final solution, for one

G. Mencagli et al. (Eds.): Euro-Par 2018 Workshops, LNCS 11339, pp. 494–505, 2019.
https://doi.org/10.1007/978-3-030-10549-5_39

or more given metrics of interest in the context of software compilation targeting Central Processing Units (CPUs) [16] and hardware compilation targeting Field-Programmable Gate Arrays (FPGAs) [10]. On Graphics Processing Units (GPUs), using this technique can also yield considerable improvements (e.g., up to 5× when targeting a NVIDIA Pascal-based GPU [15]).

The problem of finding orders of compiler passes (also called *compiler sequences* or *phase orders*) that result in better optimization (e.g., vs –O3) of a given function/program, for a given target and objective metric, is known as the *phase ordering* problem. The number of compiler passes available in current compilers is high and increasing (e.g., LLVM 3.3 has 157 passes, LLVM 3.9 has 245 passes). In LLVM, compiler phase ordering is accessible through passing ordered lists of flags to the LLVM Optimizer command-line tool (*opt*). Although the user interface is simple, the amount of available compiler passes results in a too large number of combinations to try manually. Moreover, compiler passes can have complex interactions (positive or negative) with other passes depending on when in the compilation process they are executed and depending on static and/or dynamic features of the function/program being compiled. Due to these factors, phase ordering is generally considered a difficult problem.

GPUs are widely used in a number of heterogeneous systems, such as smartphones, personal computers and supercomputers. Therefore, the performance of these systems strongly depends on how effectively GPUs are used. Purini and Jain [16] previously developed an approach for fast phase ordering, and evaluated it on CPUs. They found that their approach produced binaries that were comparable to slower state-of-the-art alternatives. In this paper, we evaluate their kind of approach in the context of OpenCL kernel compilation for GPUs. Going one step further, we propose and experiment with the use of a simple heuristic to make the approach more effective in generating suitable compiled code.

The rest of the paper is organized as follows. Section 2 provides background, including the description of aspects we believe to be important for an approach to address in order for it to suit a large number of compiler users concerned with optimization. Section 3 presents a selection of work in the field of Design Space Exploration (DSE) of compiler phase ordering, including the DSE approach that we augment with an heuristic. The heuristic we propose and evaluate in this paper is described in Sect. 4. Section 5 describes our experimental setup, including the target GPU and the OpenCL kernels used in our experiments. The experimental results are presented in Sect. 6. Finally, concluding remarks about the work presented in this paper are presented in Sect. 7.

2 Background and Motivation

This section presents what we believe are the important qualities a phase ordering specialization approach must have in order for it to suit a large number of compiler users and use cases.

2.1 Concerns Related with Phase Ordering

Given how difficult it can be to manually derive effective compiler phase orders, multiple automatic approaches have been proposed (see, e.g., [10,15,16]). Most approaches presented in the state-of-the-art, given a new program/function, generate new (i.e., previously untested) sequences for evaluation. Using these sequences without strenuous validation can result in a number of unwanted scenarios. These include the premature halting of the compiler execution, broken compiled code, or even the generation of compiled code that is functionally different than it should, which is arguably the worst possible outcome as it can be difficult to detect. Moreover, a number of the approaches suffer from an unacceptably high DSE overhead and/or they sacrifice too much in terms of the quality of the solutions.

Assuring Functional Correctness. It is known that even production compilers have bugs. Eide and Regehr evaluated thirteen production-quality C compilers and, for each, were able to find cases where incorrect code to access volatile variables was generated [9]. Iterative approaches for automatic phase ordering, such as the ones based on genetic algorithms or simulated annealing, typically rely on the generation and evaluation of a large number of compiler sequences (e.g., hundreds, thousands) during DSE to achieve considerable improvements in the compiled code in relation to an already optimized baseline (e.g., produced using the most aggressive optimization level). The number of sequences that can be generated by these iterative approaches is very large, so naturally most of them were not previously validated by the compiler writers, and expecting them to be exhaustively tested is not realistic. Therefore, compiler bugs are often exposed by these iterative methods. When custom compiler pass sequences are used, there is an high risk of side effects caused by bugs in any given compiler pass not previously detected by the battery of tests performed by the compiler developers. Even the validation of individual compiler passes is often incomplete. Zhao et al. [20] were able to create a formally verified version of the `mem2reg` pass, though they needed to rewrite the pass to do so and write 50,000 lines of proof scripts and infrastructure. However, despite this significant effort, the formally verified pass was less optimized than the original non-verified pass.

Balancing Exploration Overhead and Solution Quality. DSE on top of standard compilation can add a considerable overhead. This is aggravated in cases where more than one execution per compiled version is required in order to cover multiple execution flows, which might be required for a more thorough validation of the generated compiled code. Exploration overhead might be significant for most compiler users, to be further aggravated if the execution time of the function/program is considerable (e.g., a function/program that even compiled with GCC/Clang –O3 takes 1 h to execute). In some cases, certain techniques can be used to reduce execution time of a function/program while still maintaining it representative of the original function/program (e.g., reduce number of iterations of an outer loop) in a way that the same set of compiler knobs found for the code version modified in preparation for DSE can be used on the original version with comparable improvements. However, these techniques might not be straightforward to implement automatically. Either way, independently of the execution time for a given function/program, performing fewer compilations and executing the compiled code fewer times is preferable.

2.2 What Can Make an Approach Suitable to Most Compiler Users?

A considerable number of DSE approaches from the state-of-art are not suitable to most compiler users because of they require non-trivial validation by the final compiler user side and/or they require a large number of iterations to considerably improve most codes.

Figure 1 presents the different roles that actors in an approach of such type can take. To significantly lessen the requirement of validating (at the final user side) the functional correctness of the code compiled with the use of custom phase orders, we can evaluate only compiler sequences that have been previously demonstrated to work well on a set of representative functions/programs. Considerable efficiency (regarding number of compilations/evaluations) can be achieved by selecting a small, yet highly representative, set of these sequences.

Group	Compiler Developers	Phase Order Developers	Final Developers
Description	No changes needed (in LLVM's case) May also be the "phase order developers"	Develop target-aware phase orders with automated tools	Compile their programs Using the given phase orders and compilers
Result	Compiler	Set of phase orders	Final optimized program

Fig. 1. Roles in a type of approach that uses predefined custom phase orders.

3 Related Work

To the best of our knowledge, Cooper et al. [8] were the first to propose iterative compilation as a means to find phase orders to improve the quality of the compiled code with respect to a given metric. They used iterative compilation in the form of a Genetic Algorithm (GA) as a way to minimize the footprint of compiled code. Cooper et al. [7] explore compiler optimization phase ordering testing different randomized search algorithms based on genetic algorithms, hill climbers and randomized sampling. Almagor et al. [3] rely on GAs, hill climbers, and greedy constructive algorithms to explore compiler phase ordering at program-level to a simulated SPARC processor. Nobre [13] presents results for the use of a approach that relies in simulated annealing to specialize compiler sequences in the context of software and hardware compilation. More recently, Nobre et al. [14] presented an approach based on sampling over a graph representing transitions between compiler passes, targeting the LEON3 microarchitecture.

Agakov et al. [1] present a methodology to reduce the number of evaluations of the program being compiled with iterative approaches. Models are generated taking into account program features and the shapes of compiler sequence spaces generated from iteratively evaluating a reference set of programs. These models are used to focus the iterative exploration for a new program, targeting the TI C6713 and AMD Au1500 embedded processors. Kulkarni and Cavazos [11] proposed an approach that formulates the phase ordering challenge as a Markov process where the current state of a function being optimized conforms to the Markov property (i.e., the current state must have all the information to decide what to do next). Instead of suggesting complete compiler sequences, these authors use a neural network to propose the next compiler pass based on current code features. Sher et al. [19] describe a compilation system that relies on evolutionary neural networks for phase ordering. Neural networks constructed with reinforcement learning output a set of probabilities of use for each compiler pass, which is then sampled to generate compiler sequences based on the input program/function features. Martins et al. [12] propose the use of a clustering method to reduce the exploration space in the context of compiler pass phase order exploration. Amir et al. [5] present an approach for compiler phase ordering that relies on predictive modeling, using dynamic features to suggest the next compiler phase to execute to maximize execution performance given the current status; and more recently, they presented MICOMP, an approach that performs phase ordering of the compiler passes in the sequences represented by LLVM optimization levels using sub-sequences and machine learning to predict the speedup of using combinations of subsequences [4].

Purini and Jain [16] presented and evaluated a type of approach that devises an universal set of compiler sequences that covers the program space of a reference set of programs. Given a new program, all and only sequences from that predefined set of sequences are evaluated. The authors demonstrated, using LLVM 3.3 to target a computer with an X86 CPU, that sets of compiler sequences that perform well on a set of reference functions can also be suitable to compile other functions to the same target. Purini and Jain demonstrated that these sets can be quite small (e.g., 10 in what they call the *Best-10* approach), while still being able to achieve considerable binary execution performance improvements. Comparing with other DSE approaches, this type of approach results in fast evaluation at the user/programmer-side as the set of representative sequences is small. This makes it feasible to perform an exhaustive offline validation, in a manner similar to that of the standard optimization levels (e.g., –O3). This is important because validation at the user-side would normally be expensive, involving the comparison the outputs of the compiled functions/programs with sets of expected outputs for representative inputs, and even that might be insufficient as it may not cover all binary program paths.

The type of approach presented by Purini and Jain has a *training* phase, performed offline by the phase order developers; and an online phase, performed when a new program is compiled. In the training phase, other DSE methods are used to produce a large number of phase orders and corresponding metric improvements, of which a small set (K sequences) is selected.

In the online phase, only the sequences from the K set are evaluated. The validation of these sequences can be performed offline.

Purini and Jain presented multiple approaches to obtain the representative set of sequences, of which we opted to use the following:

1. Select the sequence that improves more kernels;
2. Select the sequence that combined with all previously selected sequences, maximizes the number of improved kernels. Use geomean as a tiebreaker;
3. Repeat 2. until K sequences ($K = 10$, in their paper) were selected.

4 Our Approach

Purini and Jain's approach [16] consists of generating a set of K sequences for each platform/compiler, and then using those sequences to compile any new programs/functions. However, if a user prefers to test fewer than K sequences, it is still possible to do so, by using the following algorithm:

1. Evaluate Seq. 1 (i.e., the first sequence extracted offline);
2. Evaluate the next sequence (i.e., by extraction order);
3. Repeat 2. until all K sequences were evaluated, the number of evaluations or time the user is willing to wait for is achieved, or the compiled code is sufficiently improved over baseline.

In this approach, the order of evaluation of the compiler sequences is always the same because, when the K set is constructed, each new sequence added is the one that best complements the sequences already obtained, so testing them in-order tends to yield better results, on average. We extend upon this type of approach by proposing the use of an heuristic to make the order of evaluation of the compiler sequences of the K set tuned to the code being compiled based on the impact of the previously evaluated sequences. This still circumvents the need to perform feature engineering and to classify code based on static and/or dynamic features. The only feature is the metric that one wants phase ordering to improve (e.g., performance). To the best of our knowledge, we are the first to evaluate this type of phase ordering approach.

4.1 Proposed Heuristic

Given a new code to compile, the end-user of the type of approach presented in [16] might not want to evaluate all K sequences. If less than K sequences are to be evaluated at the end-user side, then selecting which of those sequences to evaluate is important. We will refer to the sequences from the K set that are to be evaluated for a given new code as the T set (where $1 \leq T \leq K$).

If no information about a given new code being compiled is taken into account, then giving preference to the evaluation of sequences added first to the K set during the training phase seems to be a good (though as we will see below, not optimal) approach. For instance, if the end-user only wants to evaluate 3 custom compiler phase orders, then Seqs. 1 to 3 would be evaluated in-order. In this scenario, the order in which the sequences from the T set are to be evaluated is not important, given all are evaluated. However, order of evaluation can be important in a scenario where it is not known from start at the user side how many custom compiler phase orders are to be evaluated. In the later case, first evaluating sequences from the T set with lower index likely yields better results.

Other than all K sequences having been evaluated (i.e., $T = K$), other possible stopping conditions for the process of evaluating sequences from the K set (from lower index to higher index) can be, for instance, reaching a given improvement over baseline or a maximum compilation/evaluation overhead.

It is important to note that, when evaluating less than K sequences, it is not always the best choice to evaluate the subsequent custom sequences form the K set that have lower index. The best subset of sequences from the K set to evaluate depends on the particular code being compiled.

We propose and evaluate an heuristic, that we formulated in order to allow achieving comparable improvements over baseline while requiring evaluating fewer custom phase orders from a given K set. Given information about the specific code being compiled, the end-result of using the heuristic is the evaluation of a particular sub-selection of the K sequences. Notice that an heuristic that is not suitable can result in losing efficiency over evaluating the sequences with lower index from the K set. The first compiler phase order is always evaluated, as it is by far the phase order that is most generic and other phase orders are selected to be part of K for their ability to improve upon the sequences with lower index.

The heuristic selects the next sequence from the K set to evaluate based on the impact of the custom sequence from the K set previously evaluated. The heuristic replaces point 2 of the process that selects the next sequence from the K set to evaluate (see Sect. 4). Instead of evaluating sequences by the order they were extracted from the initial set of pairs of sequences and fitness values, the algorithm chooses the sequence that is predicted to be the most likely to result in the highest speedup. It compares the result (e.g., speedup) of the last tested sequence with that of each training program to find which one had the closest result and verifies which of the untested K sequences produced the best results for that program.

4.2 Example

Consider the hypothetical example of Table 1, with $K = 4$ sequences. When compiling a code, the approach would first compile and measure the impact of using Seq. 1. Suppose that the speedup for this sequence is 5.5×. This means that the training code that is most similar to this case is CODE3, so the next sequence to test is Seq. 4 (as it has the highest speedup for CODE3 out of the 3 sequences that have not yet been tested).

Table 1. Hypothetical example of speedups for a set of sequences on a set of reference programs/functions.

Ref. code	Seq. 1	Seq. 2	Seq. 3	Seq. 4	Seq. 5
CODE1	2×	1×	2×	3×	0.2×
CODE2	4×	2×	0.1×	0.4×	0.1×
CODE3	6×	0.1×	0.1×	6×	1.2×

5 Experimental Setup

We used a workstation with an Intel Xeon E5-1650 v4 CPU, running at 3.6 GHz (4.0 GHz Turbo) and 64 GB of Quad-channel ECC DDR4 at 2133 MHz. For the experiments we relied on Ubuntu 16.04 64-bit with the NVIDIA CUDA 8.0 toolchain (released in Sept. 28, 2016) and the NVIDIA 378.13 Linux Display Driver (released in Feb. 14, 2017).

The GPU is an EVGA NVIDIA GeForce GTX 1070 graphics card (08G-P4-6276-KR) with a 1607/1797 MHz base/boost graphics clock (NVIDIA GP104 GPU) and 8 GB of 256 bit GDDR5 memory.

The kernel mode driver is set to keep the GPU initialized at all instances and the preferred performance mode is set to maximum performance to reduce the occurrence of extreme GPU and memory frequency variation during execution of the GPU kernels. All execution time metrics reported in this paper correspond to the average over 30 executions.

5.1 Kernels

In this paper we use the PolyBench/GPU benchmark suite [17] kernels. We selected this particular benchmark as it is freely available and thus contributes to making the results presented in this paper reproducible.

PolyBench/GPU is a collection of 15 kernels implemented for GPUs using CUDA, OpenCL, and HMPP; including convolution kernels (2DCONV, 3DCONV), linear algebra (2MM, 3MM, ATAX, BICG, GEMM, GESUMMV, GRAMSCH, MVT, SYR2K, SYRK), data-mining (CORR, COVAR), and stencil computations (FDTD-2D). We use the default datasets so that reproducibility of our results is more straightforward.

5.2 Compilation and Execution Flow with Specialized Phase Ordering

We use Clang compiler's OpenCL frontend with the `libclc` library to generate an LLVM IR representation of a given input OpenCL kernel. Then, we use the LLVM Optimizer tool (`opt`) to optimize the IR using a specific optimization strategy represented by a compiler phase order, and we link this optimized IR with the `libclc` OpenCL functions for our target using `llvm-link`. Finally, using Clang, we generate the PTX representation of the kernel from the bytecode resulting from the previous step, using the `nvptx64-nvidia-nvcl` target.

For specialized phase ordering, we use *offline compilation*, i.e., we compile the source code to PTX using Clang/LLVM and pass the resulting PTX code to the `clCreateProgramWithBinary` function.

5.3 Data Used for Devising a Small Set of Sequences

The OpenCL kernels from each of the benchmarks have been compiled/tested with a set of 10,000 randomly generated compiler phase orders (the same set was used with all OpenCL codes) in the context of the work presented by Nobre et al. [15]. The data resulting from this strenuous evaluation is the input to the phase order extraction method used in the training phase. Only sequences that produce code that passes validation may be selected for the K set.

Each phase order is composed of 256 LLVM pass instances (can include repeated calls to the same pass) and the LLVM passes to consider for these sequences were selected from a list with all LLVM 3.9 passes except the ones that resulted in compilation and/or execution problems when used individually to compile the PolyBench/GPU OpenCL kernels.

6 Experimental Results

This section presents the results for the experiments performed to evaluate the efficiency of the proposed heuristic.

The evaluation of the approach was performed using 2-fold cross-validation. Randomly distributing the 15 PolyBench [17] kernels between two non-intersecting groups resulted in a group with `2DCONV`, `2MM`, `3MM`, `COVAR`, `GEMM`, `MVT` and `SYRK`; and another with `3DCONV`, `ATAX`, `BICG`, `CORR`, `FDTD-2D`, `GESUMMV`, `GRAMSCHM`, and `SYR2K`. The geometric mean metrics reported in this section consider the speedups obtained on all 15 codes.

The baseline used to calculate the speedups obtained when compiling the OpenCL codes using custom phase orders is the execution time of OpenCL versions generated by offline compilation using Clang/LLVM with `-O3`.

Note that the speedups reported in this paper with the use of custom phase orders would not be considerably higher or smaller if using other optimization levels or online compilation as baseline, because all standard optimization levels appear to be very similar for these kernels (see Nobre et al. [15]).

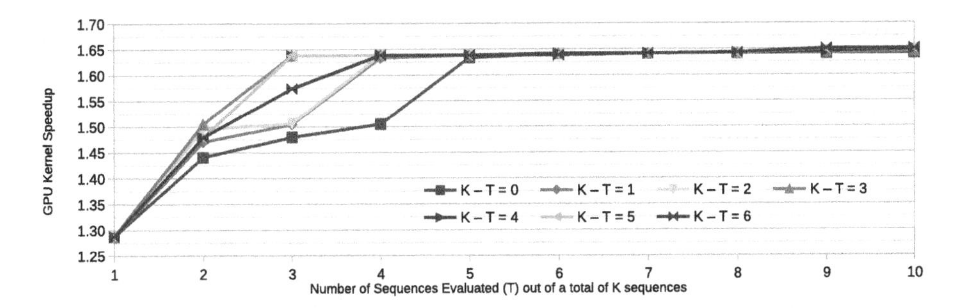

Fig. 2. Speedup achieved on tested kernels as a function of the number of evaluated sequences (T). Each line (K − T) represents a number of *excluded* sequences.

6.1 Impact of the Heuristic

Figure 2 depicts the speedups over baseline, considering different values (from 0 to 6) for the number of sequences excluded from evaluation, and different values for T (number of custom sequences from the K set that are evaluated).

As seen in Fig. 2, the ideal number of excluded sequences ($K - T$) is between 3 and 5. If too few sequences are excluded, then this method is not substantially different from Purini's approach (particularly when $K - T = 0$). If too many sequences are excluded, then for the same number of tested sequences (T), that means the compiler sequence selector must select from a higher number of available sequences of K. Since each additional generated sequence tends to be worse than all previous ones, that means that higher values of K imply worse average sequence quality.

For between 3 and 5 excluded sequences, a speedup of 1.638× is achieved with the evaluation of only 3 custom compiler sequences. Not relying on the heuristic ($K - T = 0$) required 5 evaluations to achieve compiled code with similar performance (1.633×). The ratio of improvement in efficiency with the use of the heuristic increases if considering even fewer evaluations. For the spectrum of values for the number of excluded sequences, evaluating only 2 custom compiler sequences results in compiled code that is similar in terms of performance with the compiled code obtained when relying on 4 evaluations without the heuristic.

Performing more that 3 evaluations (5 if not using the heuristic) does not result in significantly performance improvements of the compiled code. The geomean speedup obtained considering the use of the best individually found compiler sequence (per OpenCL code) from the 10,000 compiler sequences evaluated during the training phase is 1.653× (calculated using the same baseline, Clang/LLVM with –O3), making even the geomean speedup obtained with only 3 evaluations 0.99% of the former.

6.2 Generated GPU Code with Phase Ordering vs. Baseline

The performance increase with the use of phase ordering can be attributed to the use of different unroll factors, different memory loads (single combined instruction vs. multiple instructions) and moving memory stores out of a loop. A more detailed analysis can be found in Nobre et al. [15].

7 Conclusions

This paper presented and evaluated in the context of improving the performance of code targeting a NVIDIA Pascal GPU, a heuristic-based extension to a previous approach evaluated in the context of specialized phase orders for CPUs. This type of approach has characteristics that make it potentially more suitable to a larger number of users and use-cases: fast and efficient exploration at the final user side and possibility of pre-validating all the sequences used by the final users. The proposed heuristic helps making evaluation at the user-side faster.

When considering very low numbers of compilations/evaluations, relying on the heuristic to accelerate iterative compilation resulted in achieving compiled GPU code of comparable binary execution performance while requiring significantly fewer compilations/executions. For instance, 2 evaluations of custom phase orders using the heuristic achieves performance similar to 4 evaluations without the heuristic, and 3 evaluations with the heuristic is comparable to 5 evaluations without the heuristic. Moreover, performing only the evaluation of 3 custom compiler sequences results in achieving a geometric mean speedup of 1.64×, while using the best sequence individually found for each code results in a performance improvement of 1.65×.

We are currently evaluating the impact of a number of modifications to the heuristic presented in this paper, such as considering features other than the speedups obtained with the use of a single compiler sequence (the previously evaluated sequence) when computing the distance metric, and using other distance metrics. Ongoing work also includes evaluating the approach with other GPUs, including GPUs from other vendors (e.g., AMD). In addition, we plan to evaluate with OpenCL kernels from other benchmarks with versions targeting GPUs, such as Rodinia [6] and SNU NPB Suite [18].

We believe that the use of the proposed heuristic can make optimization through specialization of compiler sequences accessible to an even larger number of compiler users.

Acknowledgements. This work was partially supported by the TEC4Growth project, "NORTE-01-0145-FEDER-000020", financed by the North Portugal Regional Operational Programme (NORTE 2020) under the PORTUGAL 2020 Partnership Agreement, and through the European Regional Development Fund (ERDF). Reis acknowledges the support by FCT through PD/BD/105804/2014.

References

1. Agakov, F., et al.: Using machine learning to focus iterative optimization. In: CGO 2006, pp. 295–305. IEEE Computer Society, Washington, DC (2006)
2. Aho, A.V., Lam, M.S., Sethi, R., Ullman, J.D.: Compilers: Principles, Techniques, and Tools, 2nd edn. Addison-Wesley Longman Publishing Co., Inc., Boston (2006)

3. Almagor, L., et al.: Finding effective compilation sequences. In: LCTES 2004, pp. 231–239. ACM, New York (2004)
4. Ashouri, A.H., Bignoli, A., Palermo, G., Silvano, C., Kulkarni, S., Cavazos, J.: Micomp: mitigating the compiler phase-ordering problem using optimization subsequences and machine learning. ACM TACO **14**(3), 29 (2017)
5. Ashouri, A.H., Bignoli, A., Palermo, G., Silvano, C.: Predictive modeling methodology for compiler phase-ordering. In: PARMA-DITAM 2016, pp. 7–12. ACM, New York (2016)
6. Che, S., et al.: Rodinia: a benchmark suite for heterogeneous computing. In: IEEE IISWC, October 2009
7. Cooper, K.D., et al.: Exploring the structure of the space of compilation sequences using randomized search algorithms. J. Supercomput. **36**(2), 135–151 (2006)
8. Cooper, K.D., Schielke, P.J., Subramanian, D.: Optimizing for reduced code space using genetic algorithms. In: LCTES 1999, pp. 1–9. ACM, New York (1999)
9. Eide, E., Regehr, J.: Volatiles are miscompiled, and what to do about it. In: Proceedings of the 8th ACM International Conference on Embedded Software, EMSOFT 2008, pp. 255–264. ACM, New York (2008)
10. Huang, Q., et al.: The effect of compiler optimizations on high-level synthesis-generated hardware. ACM TRETS **8**(3), 14:1–14:26 (2015)
11. Kulkarni, S., Cavazos, J.: Mitigating the compiler optimization phase-ordering problem using machine learning. In: OOPSLA 2012, pp. 147–162. ACM, New York (2012)
12. Martins, L.G.A., Nobre, R., Cardoso, J.M.P., Delbem, A.C.B., Marques, E.: Clustering-based selection for the exploration of compiler optimization sequences. ACM TACO **13**(1), 8:1–8:28 (2016)
13. Nobre, R.: Identifying sequences of optimizations for HW/SW compilation. In: FPL 2013, pp. 1–2, September 2013
14. Nobre, R., Martins, L.G.A., Cardoso, J.a.M.P.: A graph-based iterative compiler pass selection and phase ordering approach. In: LCTES 2016, pp. 21–30. ACM, New York (2016)
15. Nobre, R., Reis, L., Cardoso, J.M.P.: Impact of compiler phase ordering when targeting GPUs. In: Heras, D.B., Bougé, L. (eds.) Euro-Par 2017. LNCS, vol. 10659, pp. 427–438. Springer, Cham (2018). https://doi.org/10.1007/978-3-319-75178-8_35
16. Purini, S., Jain, L.: Finding good optimization sequences covering program space. ACM TACO **9**(4), 56:1–56:23 (2013)
17. Scott Grauer-Gray, L.N.P.: Polybench/GPU: Implementation of Polybench codes for GPU processing (2012). http://web.cs.ucla.edu/~pouchet/software/polybench/GPU/index.html
18. Seo, S., Jo, G., Lee, J.: Performance characterization of the NAS parallel benchmarks in OpenCL. In: IISWC 2011, pp. 137–148. IEEE Computer Society, Washington, DC (2011)
19. Sher, G., Martin, K., Dechev, D.: Preliminary results for neuroevolutionary optimization phase order generation for static compilation. In: ODES 2014, pp. 33–40. ACM, New York (2014)
20. Zhao, J., Nagarakatte, S., Martin, M.M., Zdancewic, S.: Formal verification of SSA-based optimizations for LLVM. SIGPLAN Not. **48**(6), 175–186 (2013)

Accelerating Online Change-Point Detection Algorithm Using 10 GbE FPGA NIC

Takuma Iwata(✉), Kohei Nakamura, Yuta Tokusashi, and Hiroki Matsutani

Keio University, 3-14-1 Hiyoshi, Kohoku-ku, Yokohama 223-8522, Japan
{iwata,nakamura,tokusasi,matutani}@arc.ics.keio.ac.jp

Abstract. In statistical analysis and data mining, change-point detection that identifies the change-points which are times when the probability distribution of time series changes has been used for various purposes, such as anomaly detections on network traffic and transaction data. However, computation cost of a conventional AR (Auto-Regression) model based approach is too high and infeasible for online. In this paper, an AR model based online change-point detection algorithm, called ChangeFinder, is implemented on an FPGA (Field Programmable Gate Array) based NIC (Network Interface Card). The proposed system computes the change-point score from time series data received from 10 GbE (10 Gbit Ethernet). More specifically, it computes the change-point score at the 10 GbE NIC in advance of host applications. This paper aims to reduce the host workload and improve change-point detection performance by offloading ChangeFinder algorithm from host to the NIC. As evaluations, change-point detection in the FPGA NIC is compared with a baseline software implementation and those enhanced by two network optimization techniques using DPDK and Netfilter in terms of throughput. The result demonstrates 16.8x improvement in change-point detection throughput compared to the baseline software implementation. The throughput achieves 83.4% of the 10 GbE line rate.

1 Introduction

Due to advances in information and communication technology, data sets exchanged over networks are growing rapidly in size and the number. As the data sets grow, high-bandwidth becomes more important for data analysis and pattern recognition. Change-point detection is a method to identify the change-points which are times when the probability distribution of time series changes. Popular applications of the change-point detection are related to a security field [13], such as detecting a sudden increase in traffic volume by computer virus and worm. It is also used in other applications fields, such as transaction data, resource management, and trend analysis [3].

In a conventional change-point detection algorithm [5], the computational cost is too high to use it as an online algorithm. ChangeFinder algorithm [8]

G. Mencagli et al. (Eds.): Euro-Par 2018 Workshops, LNCS 11339, pp. 506–517, 2019.
https://doi.org/10.1007/978-3-030-10549-5_40

solves this issue and can be used as an online change-point detection. However, its computational cost is still high to detect change-points from data received via high bandwidth networks, such as 1 Gbps and 10 Gbps, due to heavy workload imposed to the host.

In this paper, change-point detection using ChangeFinder algorithm is implemented on an FPGA (Field Programmable Gate Array) based NIC (Network Interface Card). The proposed system computes the change-point score from time series data received from 10 GbE (10 Gbit Ethernet). More specifically, ChangeFinder algorithm implemented in the FPGA NIC computes the score in advance of host applications. This paper aims to reduce the host workload and improve change-point detection performance by offloading ChangeFinder algorithm from host to the NIC. As evaluations, change-point detection in the FPGA NIC is compared with a baseline software implementation and those enhanced by two network optimization techniques using DPDK and Netfilter in terms of throughput. The result demonstrates 16.8x improvement in change-point detection throughput compared to the baseline software implementation, while keeping the same change-point detection accuracy.

The rest of this paper is organized as follows. Section 2 introduces ChangeFinder algorithm and related FPGA-based accelerators. Section 3 designs the ChangeFinder module and Sect. 4 integrates it in the FPGA NIC. Section 5 evaluates area and throughput. Section 6 concludes this paper.

2 Background

In statistical analysis and data mining, change-point detection has been used for various purposes, such as step detection, edge detection, and anomaly detection. Since AR model is a primary approach to describe time-varying process, in this section, we will start with a conventional change-point detection based on AR model.

2.1 AR Model: A Conventional Way

Let $x_1^n = x_1, ..., x_n$ denote a time-series, and it is divided into x_1^t and x_{t+1}^n by a time point t, where $x_1^t = x_1, ..., x_t$ and $x_{t+1}^n = x_{t+1}, ..., x_n$. Assuming the k-th order AR model, the conditional probability density function of x_t is given as follows.

$$p(x_t|x_{t-k}^{t-1}) = \frac{1}{(2\pi)^{d/2}|\Sigma|^{1/2}} \exp\left[-\frac{(x_t-\omega_t)^T\Sigma^{-1}(x_t-\omega_t)}{2}\right], \quad (1)$$

where d and Σ denote the number of data dimensions and a covariance matrix, respectively.

ω_t is given as follows.

$$\omega_t = \sum_{i=1}^{k} \alpha_i(x_{t-i} - \mu) + \mu, \quad (2)$$

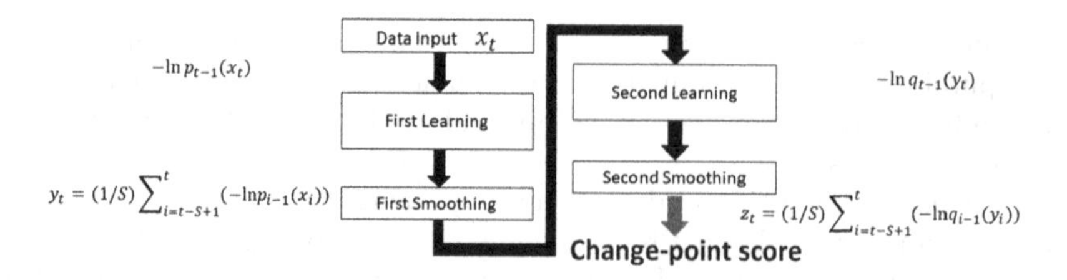

Fig. 1. Flowchart of ChangeFinder

where $\alpha_1, ..., \alpha_k$ and μ are model parameters.

Let $\hat{\omega_t}$ denote an estimated ω_t calculated by Eq. 2 using estimated model parameters. The model fitting error for x_1^n is thus given as follows.

$$I(x_1^n) = \sum_{t=1}^{n} ||x_t - \hat{\omega_t}||^2 \tag{3}$$

Here, time t is detected as a change-point when $I(x_1^t) + I(x_{t+1}^n)$ is sufficiently small compared to $I(x_1^n)$. Although this method is simple, computation cost is $O(n^2)$ and thus cannot be used for online change-point detection.

2.2 ChangeFinder Algorithm

The above mentioned problem is addressed by SDAR (Sequentially Discounting Auto-Regression model learning) algorithm [15]. ChangeFinder algorithm employs SDAR algorithm for the online change-point detection. It has been proven to be efficient. As one of promising applications, for example, [11] utilizes the SDAR-based change-point detection for detecting fraudulent calls. Apache Hivemall [1], which is a machine learning library on Apache Hive, releases a software module of ChangeFinder. But its hardware design has not been discussed.

Overview. Figure 1 shows the ChangeFinder algorithm that consists of two learning phases. Each step is described below.

Step 1 (Data Input) x_t is received at time point t.

Step 2 (First Learning) For each t, an AR model is built. More specifically, a sequence of probability density functions $p_t(x) : t = 1, 2, ...$ is obtained by the SDAR model, which will be explained later. Please note that p_{t-1} is learned based on x^{t-1}. The "outlier" score at x_t is calculated as follows.

$$Score(x_t) = -\log p_{t-1}(x_t) \tag{4}$$

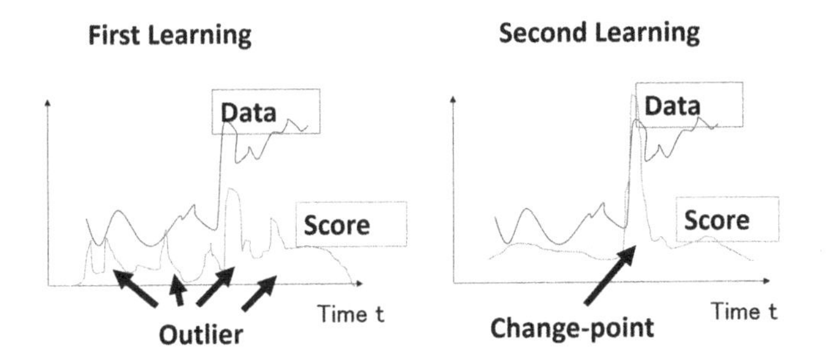

Fig. 2. Two-phase learning of ChangeFinder

Step 3 (First Smoothing) For each t, a moving average of the outlier scores (obtained in Step 2) in a time window is calculated, More specifically, a sequence of moving averages of the outlier scores $y_t : t = 0, 1, 2...$ is obtained as follows.

$$y_t = \frac{1}{T} \sum_{i=t-T+1}^{t} Score(x_i), \tag{5}$$

where T is the length of a time window.

Steps 4 & 5 (Second Learning & Smoothing) For each t, an AR model is built for the new time-series data $y_t : t = 0, 1, 2, ...$ (obtained in Step 3), and a sequence of new probability density functions $q_t(x) : t = 1, 2, ...$ is obtained by the SDAR model as well as Step 2. A smoothing step is also applied as well as Step 3. Thus, a sequence of the moving averages $z_t : t = 0, 1, 2, ...$ is obtained as follows.

$$z_t = \frac{1}{T} \sum_{i=t-T+1}^{t} (-\ln q_{t-1}(y_t)) \tag{6}$$

Here, z_t is denoted as the "change-point" score at time t. A higher change-point score z_t indicates a higher possibility of change-point at time t. As shown in Fig. 2, by using the two-phase learning, outliers are eliminated by the first smoothing step and thus only the change-points where the probability distribution of time series changes are extracted.

SDAR Model. SDAR model is used for online discounting learning that relies on AR model. ChangeFinder algorithm uses SDAR model to obtain the sequences of probability density functions $p_t(x)$ and $q_t(x)$. These probability density functions are derived from ω_t and Σ in Eq. 1. To obtain these parameters,

SDAR model is used as follows.

$$\hat{\mu} := (1 - r)\hat{\mu} + rx_t \tag{7}$$

$$C_j := (1 - r)C_j + r(x_t - \hat{\mu})(x_{t-j} - \hat{\mu})^T \tag{8}$$

$$\hat{x}_t := \sum_{i=1}^{k} \hat{\omega}_i(x_{t-i} - \hat{\mu}) + \hat{\mu} \tag{9}$$

$$\hat{\Sigma} := (1 - r)\hat{\Sigma} + r(x_t - \hat{x}_t)(x_t - \hat{x}_t)^T \tag{10}$$

Here, r is a discounting rate. A smaller r indicates a greater influence on past data. For each t, an weighted average $\hat{\mu}$ is updated using r and x_t in Eq. 7. Based on $C_j : j = 1, ..., k$ obtained in Eq. 8, estimated $\omega_1, ..., \omega_k$ (denoted as $\hat{\omega_1}, ..., \hat{\omega_k}$) are derived so that the following equation is satisfied.

$$\sum_{i=1}^{k} \omega_i C_{j-i} = C_j \tag{11}$$

Then $\hat{\omega_1}, ..., \hat{\omega_k}$ are used for Eq. 9.

By introducing the discounting effect, SDAR model can be used for online learning on non-stationary time-series data. In addition, the computation cost is reduced down to $O(n)$ and thus it is preferred for online change-point detection.

2.3 Related Work

In this paper, change-point detection using ChangeFinder algorithm is implemented on an FPGA NIC. NPCUSUM (Non-Parametric Cumulative SUM) is a classic and simple change-point detection algorithm. In [4], it is implemented on a high-speed FPGA NIC in order to detect attacks from network. The network attack detection using NPCUSUM is illustrated below.

$$S_0 = 0 \tag{12}$$

$$S_n = max\{0, S_{n-1} + X_n - \hat{\mu} - \epsilon\hat{\theta}\}, \tag{13}$$

where X_n denotes input data. $\hat{\mu}$ is an estimated value of X_n before an attack, $\hat{\theta}$ is that after the attack, and ϵ is a tuning parameter. An attack from the network is detected when S_n becomes unstable and changes drastically. Although it is quite simple to implement, $\hat{\mu}$ and $\hat{\theta}$ must be known in advance, which limits the applications of NPCUSUM.

There are some prior works that present FPGA-based outlier detection that detects anomaly values (not change-points). In [6], LOF (Local Outlier Factor) algorithm is accelerated by using an FPGA. Normal data are filtered at the NIC and only anomaly data are transferred to the host machine to reduce data size.

Although our target is change-point detection to detect trend changes, ChangeFinder algorithm can be used for both the change-point detection and outlier detection. Actually, the result of the first learning phase $Score(x_t)$ is used as outlier score, while the final output z_t is used as change-point score. Please note that this paper is the first work that accelerates ChangeFinder algorithm that supports both the change-point and outlier detections by using FPGA NIC.

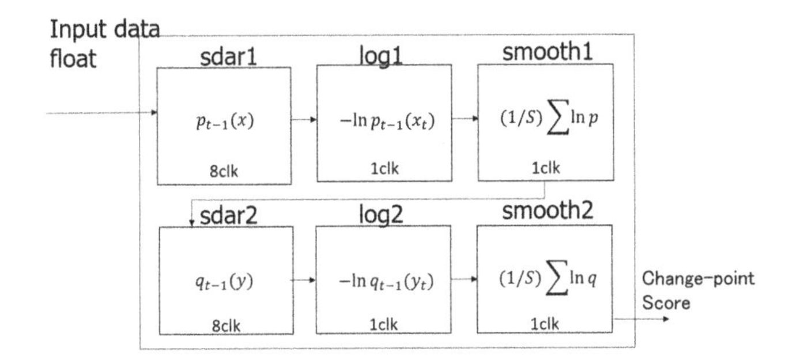

Fig. 3. Pipeline of ChangeFinder module

3 ChangeFinder on FPGA

In this section, ChangeFinder module on FPGA is illustrated. It is integrated into an FPGA NIC in Sect. 4. ChangeFinder module is written in C. As a high-level synthesis tool we use Xilinx Vivado HLS for the implementation.

3.1 Pipeline Structure

Figure 3 illustrates an overview of ChangeFinder module. It consists of pipelined six stages as mentioned in Section 2.2. As input data, a 32-bit float value is fed to the module. It is processed as follows.

- *sdar1*: A probability density function $p_t(x)$ for input data x_t in the first learning phase is computed.
- *log1*: A logarithmic loss of the probability density function is computed as an outlier score.
- *smooth1*: A moving average y_t of the outlier scores is computed as a result of the first learning phase.
- *sdar2, log2, and smooth2*: A change-point score z_t is computed by the same operations as the first phase.

These stages are operated at 125 MHz. In Fig. 3, the number in each pipeline stage indicates the minimum interval between two input data in the stage. For example, "1clk" indicates that new data can be accepted in every cycle. Thus, *log1*, *smooth1*, *log2*, and *smooth2* can accept new data every cycle, while *sdar1* and *sdar2* accept new data in every eight cycles. Please note that *sdar1* and *sdar2*, *log1* and *log2*, and *smooth1* and *smooth2* are identical, respectively. In the following, *sdar1*, *log1*, and *smooth1* modules are illustrated.

3.2 Detail of Each Module

Figure 4 shows *sdar* module. Its inputs are r and x_t. r is a discounting parameter. Based on it, $(1-r)$ is computed. x_t is an input float value. The outputs are $\hat{x}$ and $\hat{\Sigma}$. $\hat{x}$ is an estimated value of x_t and $\hat{\Sigma}$ is that of Σ_t.

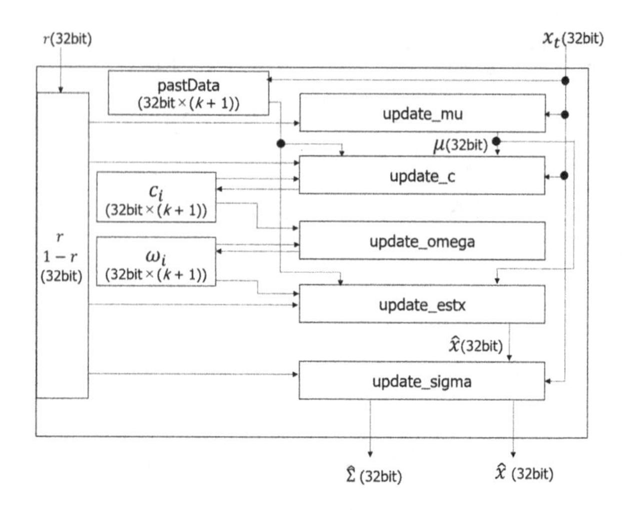

Fig. 4. *sdar* module

As shown, *sdar1* is further divided into five pipelined submodules: *update_mu*, *update_c*, *update_omega*, *update_estx*, and *update_sigma*. x_t is stored in $(k+1)$ 32-bit registers (pastData in the figure) to refer to past k data, where k is the order of AR model. C_i and ω_i are accumulated in $(k+1)$ 32-bit registers, respectively.

x_t, r, and $(1-r)$ are fed to *update_mu* submodule. *update_mu* submodule is corresponding to Eq. 7 and computes μ. *update_c* submodule is corresponding to Eq. 8 and updates C_i registers. *update_omega* submodule updates ω_i registers based on Eq. 11. *update_estx* submodule is corresponding to Eq. 9. It computes $\hat{x}_t$. Finally, *update_sigma* submodule is corresponding to Eq. 10. It computes $\hat{\Sigma}$.

These five submodules work in a pipelined manner. As a result, *sdar1* module accepts new data x_t in every eight cycles.

Log module performs a logarithmic computation as in Eq. 4. It is fully pipelined and can accept new data in every cycle.

Then *smooth* module computes a moving average of recent T data as in Eq. 5. The maximum T is set to 16 in our design. It is also fully pipelined and can accept new data in every cycle.

4 ChangeFinder on FPGA NIC

ChangeFinder module is implemented on a 10 GbE FPGA NIC. It is denoted as ChangeFinder NIC in this paper. It performs change-point detection for each numerical value coming from the 10 GbE network. The change-point score computed at the NIC is passed to a host application so that it can identify changes in given time series data.

In this paper, NetFPGA-SUME [17] is adopted as a 10 GbE FPGA NIC. It has four 10 GbE interfaces. Packets received by these interfaces are processed at an on-board FPGA and the results are transferred to a host machine via a PCI-Express Gen3 x8 interface. We use 10 GbE MAC IP core provided by Xilinx. We also use Reference NIC design provided by NetFPGA project [2] as a standard 10 GbE NIC function.

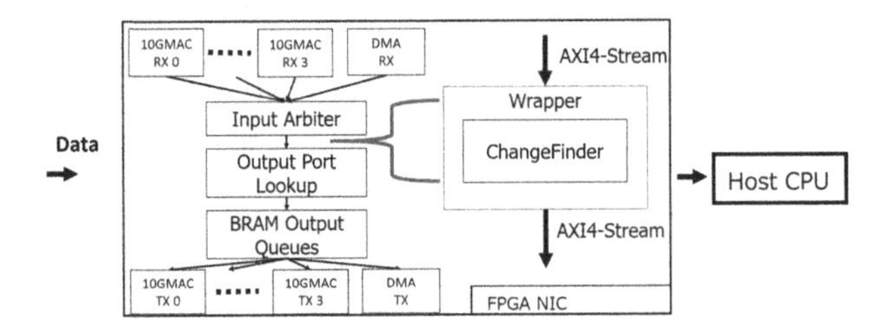

Fig. 5. ChageFinder on FPGA NIC

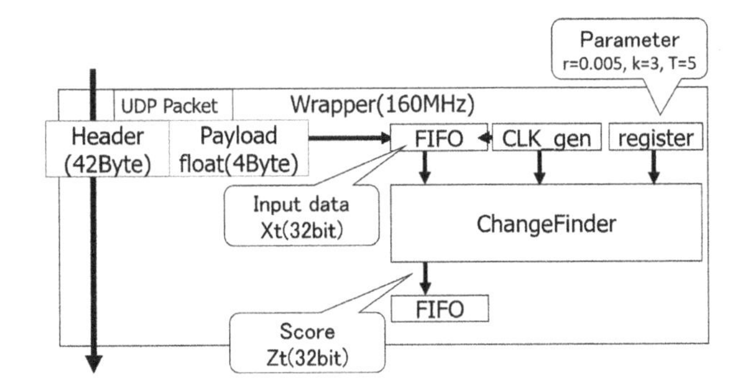

Fig. 6. Connection between wrapper and ChangeFinder modules

We implemented a wrapper module along the datapath of Reference NIC design so that all the received packets go through the wrapper module. Then ChangeFinder module designed with Xilinx Vivado HLS is implemented inside the wrapper module. Figure 5 shows a block diagram of ChangeFinder NIC consisting of ChangeFinder module and Reference NIC. In Reference NIC, packets received by the four 10 GbE interfaces (i.e., RX0 to RX3) and host DMAC are arbitrated at Input Arbiter module. Then, an output port is selected among the four 10 GbE interfaces (i.e., TX0 to TX3) and host DMAC for each packet. Packets are stored and transmitted via BRAM Output Queues corresponding to the selected output ports. Packets are transferred between these modules as AXI4 stream [14]. The wrapper module is implemented between Input Arbiter and Outport Lookup modules. We use UDP/IP as transport/network layer protocols. ChangeFinder module computes a change-point score for each incoming packet destined to a specific UDP port. All the other packets including ARP and ICMP just skip the wrapper module without any additional delay.

Figure 6 illustrates the wrapper module and input/output signals of ChangeFinder module. A clock generator of 125 MHz and parameter registers are implemented for ChangeFinder module. In addition, an input asynchronous FIFO buffer is inserted between them, because ChangeFinder module is operating at 125 MHz and Reference NIC is operating at 160 MHz.

The wrapper module identifies packets that contain sample data. Then it extracts the sample data and feeds them to ChangeFinder module. The packet conveys sample data x_t in a 32-bit float format in a UDP payload. UDP packets with a specific destination port number are extracted as sample packets and they are fed to the input FIFO buffer. As tuning parameters, AR model order k, discounting rate r, and smoothing window size T are stored in the parameter registers. They are fed to ChangeFinder module in addition to input data x_t when ChangeFinder module is ready. Then the change-point score z_t is computed and fed to an output asynchronous FIFO buffer. The score z_t can be embedded in the original packet and passed to host application.

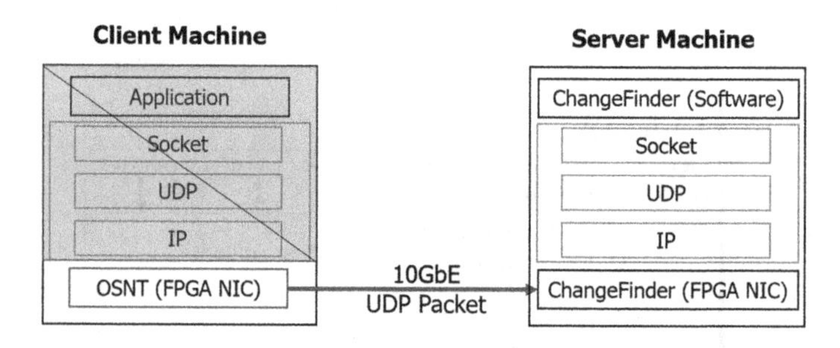

Fig. 7. Evaluation environment for throughput

5 Evaluations

5.1 Evaluation Environment

The target 10 GbE FPGA NIC is NetFPGA-SUME that has a Xilinx Virtex-7 XC7VX690T FPGA and four SFP+ 10 GbE interfaces. It is mounted to a host machine via PCI-Express Gen3 x8 interface. We use Xilinx Vivado HLS version 2016.4 for the implementation. Reference NIC part is operating at 160 MHz, while the proposed ChangeFinder module is running at 125 MHz.

Figure 7 shows the evaluation environment using two machines and Table 1 shows their specification.

The client and server machines are connected by a SFP+ direct attached cable for 10 GbE. The client machine has an FPGA NIC with OSNT (Open Source Network Teste) installed, which is a hardware packet generator, and sends packets to the server. In the server machine, the proposed ChangeFinder module is implemented on the FPGA NIC and processes incoming time series data. We measured the number of sample data processed at the ChangeFinder module per a second as throughput.

Table 1. Machines used in the environment

	Server (host) machine	Client machine
CPU	Intel Core i5-4460	Intel Core i5-4460
OS	Ubuntu 14.04	CentOS 6.6
NIC	NetFPGA-SUME (Proposal) Intel X520-DA2 (Software)	NetFPGA-10G for OSNT

5.2 Area Utilization

Table 2 shows area utilization of ChangeFinder NIC including ChangeFinder module and Reference NIC. As shown in Table 2, ChangeFinder module consumes 5.1 to 12.1% of the FPGA resources. Even with 10 GbE NIC functionality, the entire resource utilizations are less than or equal to 18.8%.

Table 2. Resources used in ChageFinder NIC

	ChangeFinder	ChangeFinder + Reference NIC
DSP	437 (12.1%)	437 (12.1%)
FF	44,519 (5.1%)	100,403 (11.6%)
LUT	45,836 (10.6%)	81,517 (18.8%)

5.3 Throughput

As mentioned above, OSNT at the client machine transmits time series data at 10 GbE line rate to the server machine, and the number of sample data processed in one second at the server machine is measured as throughput.

The proposed ChangeFinder NIC is compared with three software-based counterparts implemented in C: Baseline, DPDK, and Netfilter. In Baseline, a ChangeFinder program is running on the application layer. In DPDK, although the ChangeFinder program is running on the application layer, the program directly accesses the NIC without kernel UDP/IP stack. In Netfilter, the ChangeFinder program is implemented as a kernel module.

Figure 8 shows their throughput. The proposed ChangeFinder module is denoted as FPGA(sim) and the ChangeFinder NIC consisting of ChangeFinder and Reference NIC modules is denoted as FPGA(actual). FPGA(sim) throughput is derived by the number of cycles, pipeline structure (i.e., interval), and operating frequency of the ChangeFinder module. FPGA(actual) is the measured throughput. The proposed FPGA(actual) achieves 16.8x throughput improvement compared to Baseline. It is much higher than those with software-based optimizations by DPDK and Netfilter.

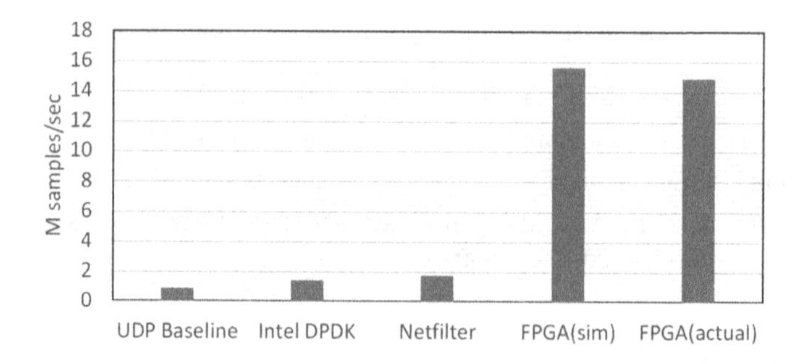

Fig. 8. Throughput of change-point detection [samples/sec]

In practical use cases, a specific field of received packets is extracted and fed to ChangeFinder module. In this experiment, we used 46-Byte UDP/IP packets containing a single 32-bit float value. This assumption is pessimistic in terms of throughput. Since internal data width of Reference NIC is 256 bits, these *sdar* modules are not bottleneck when packet length is greater than or equal to 256 Bytes. Considering the packet length of 46 Bytes[1], the proposed FPGA(actual) achieves 83.4% of 10 GbE line rate.

6 Summary

Toward anomaly detection, change-point detection is used to look for change in a probability distribution of time series, while outlier detection is used to look for entity being away from the mean of a probability distribution. ChangeFinder algorithm based on SDAR model supports both the outlier and change-point detections and can be used for online use. This paper is the first work that accelerates ChangeFinder algorithm using FPGA and integrates it into NetFPGA-SUME for high-speed change-point detection at 10 GbE NICs. The proposed ChangeFinder NIC is compared to a UDP baseline and two software-based optimizations, i.e., DPDK and Netfilter. The throughput is much higher than these counterparts and it is 16.8x higher than the UDP baseline. The throughput is corresponding to 83.4% of the 10 GbE line rate. To achieve full 10 GbE line rate or more, as future work, we are considering the possibility to use multiple ChangeFinder modules while keeping their consistency. A demonstration video of current design can be found in [16].

Acknowledgements. This work was supported by JST CREST Grant Number JPMJCR1785, Japan.

[1] In addition to the packet length, Ethernet preamble, FCS, and IFG are also considered.

References

1. Apache Hivemall. http://hivemall.incubator.apache.org/
2. The NetFPGA Project. http://netfpga.org/
3. Aminikhanghahi, S., Cook, D.J.: A survey of methods for time series change point detection. Knowl. Inf. Syst. **51**(2), 339–367 (2017)
4. Benacek, P., Blazek, R.B., Cejka, T., Kubatova, H.: Change-point detection method on 100 Gb/s ethernet interface. In: Proceedings of the ACM/IEEE Symposium on Architectures for Networking and Communications Systems (ANCS 2014), pp. 245–246, June 2014
5. Guralnik, V., Srivastava, J.: Event detection from time series data. In: Proceedings of the International Conference on Knowledge Discovery and Data Mining (KDD 1999), pp. 33–42, August 1999
6. Hayashi, A., Matsutani, H.: An FPGA-based In-NIC Cache approach for lazy learning outlier filtering. In: Proceedings of the International Conference on Parallel, Distributed, and Network-Based Processing (PDP 2017), pp. 15–22, March 2017
7. Hayashi, A., Tokusashi, Y., Matsutani, H.: A line rate outlier filtering FPGA NIC using 10 GbE interface. ACM SIGARCH Comput. Archit. News **43**(4), 22–27 (2015)
8. Takeuchi, J., Yamanishi, K.: A unifying framework for detecting outliers and change points from time series. IEEE Trans. Knowl. Data Eng. **18**(4), 482–492 (2006)
9. Kawahara, Y., Sugiyama, M.: Change-point detection in time-series data by direct density-ratio estimation. In: Proceedings of the SIAM International Conference on Data Mining (SDM 2009), pp. 389–400, April 2009
10. Pu, Y., Peng, J., Huang, L., Chen, J.: An efficient KNN algorithm implemented on FPGA based heterogeneous computing system using OpenCL. In: Proceedings of the International Symposium on Field-Programmable Custom Computing Machines (FCCM 2015), pp. 167–170, May 2015
11. Saaid, F., Nur, D., King, R.: Change points detection of vector autoregressive model using SDVAR algorithm. In: Proceedings of the 5th Annual ASEARC Conference, pp. 18–21, February 2012
12. Urabe, Y., Yamanishi, K., Tomioka, R., Iwai, H.: Real-time change-point detection using sequentially discounting normalized maximum likelihood coding. In: Huang, J.Z., Cao, L., Srivastava, J. (eds.) PAKDD 2011. LNCS, vol. 6635, pp. 185–197. Springer, Heidelberg (2011). https://doi.org/10.1007/978-3-642-20847-8_16
13. Wang, H., Zhang, D., Shin, K.G.: Change-point monitoring for the detection of DoS attacks. IEEE Trans. Dependable Secure Comput. **1**(4), 193–208 (2004)
14. Xilinx: AXI Reference Guide (2011)
15. Yamanishi, K., Takeuchi, J.: A unifying framework for detecting outliers and change points from non-stationary time series data. In: Proceedings of the International Conference on Knowledge Discovery and Data Mining (KDD 2002), pp. 676–681, July 2002
16. YouTube: Accelerating ChangeFinder using 10Gbps FPGA NIC. https://www.youtube.com/watch?v=wgTcBfkE5hY
17. Zilberman, N., Audzevich, Y., Covington, G.A., Moore, A.W.: NetFPGA SUME: toward 100 Gbps as research commodity. IEEE Micro **34**(5), 32–41 (2014)

OS-ELM-FPGA: An FPGA-Based Online Sequential Unsupervised Anomaly Detector

Mineto Tsukada[1(✉)], Masaaki Kondo[2], and Hiroki Matsutani[1]

[1] Keio University, 3-14-1 Hiyoshi, Kohoku-ku, Yokohama, Japan
{tsukada,matutani}@arc.ics.keio.ac.jp
[2] The University of Tokyo, 7-3-1 Hongo, Bunkyo-ku, Tokyo, Japan
kondo@hal.ipc.i.u-tokyo.ac.jp

Abstract. Autoencoder, a neural-network based dimensionality reduction algorithm has demonstrated its effectiveness in anomaly detection. It can detect whether an input sample is normal or abnormal by just training only with normal data. In general, Autoencoder is built on backpropagation-based neural networks (BP-NNs). When BP-NNs are implemented in edge devices, they are typically specialized only for prediction with weight matrices precomputed offline due to the high computational cost. However, such devices cannot be immediately adapted to time-series trend changes of input data. In this paper, we propose an FPGA-based unsupervised anomaly detector, called OS-ELM-FPGA, that combines Autoencoder and an online sequential learning algorithm OS-ELM. Based on our theoretical analysis of the algorithm, the proposed OS-ELM-FPGA completely eliminates matrix pseudoinversions while improving the learning throughput. Simulation results using open-source datasets show that OS-ELM-FPGA achieves favorable anomaly detection accuracy compared to CPU and GPU implementations of BP-NNs. Learning throughput of OS-ELM-FPGA is 3.47x to 27.99x and 5.22x to 78.06x higher than those of CPU and GPU implementations of OS-ELM. It is also 3.62x to 36.15x and 1.53x to 43.44x higher than those of CPU and GPU implementations of BP-NNs.

1 Introduction

Autoencoder, a neural-network-based dimensionality reduction algorithm has demonstrated its effectiveness in anomaly detection [3,4,15,17]. Autoencoder constrains the number of hidden nodes to be less than those of input and output nodes, and is trained so that it reconstructs input data in its output. When the reconstruction error between the input and output data is converged well, the dimensionality reduction is completed in the hidden nodes. Since the model uses input data as target data, we can train it in a unsupervised manner.

In a context of anomaly detection, the model is trained using only normal data. When input data that have different patterns from the normal data are

G. Mencagli et al. (Eds.): Euro-Par 2018 Workshops, LNCS 11339, pp. 518–529, 2019.
https://doi.org/10.1007/978-3-030-10549-5_41

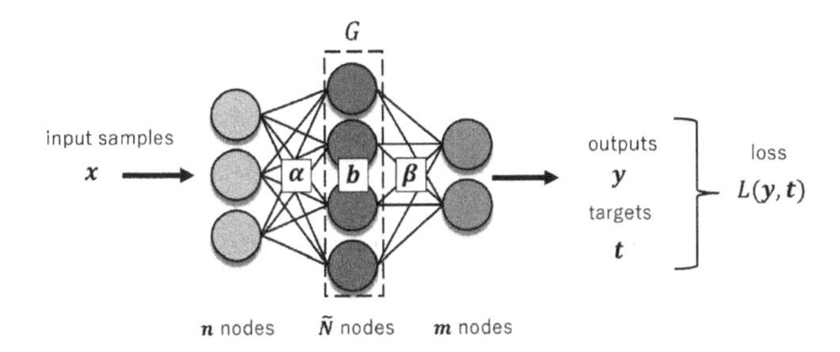

Fig. 1. Single Hidden Layer Feedforward Network (SLFN)

fed to the model, the reconstruction error will increase. If the error exceeds a threshold, the input data can be considered as abnormal data.

In general, Autoencoder is usually built on backpropagation-based neural networks (BP-NNs), and their training is accelerated with GPU-based massively parallel batch processing. For this reason, when BP-NNs are implemented in edge devices, they are typically specialized only for prediction with weight matrices precomputed offline. However, such prediction-only systems cannot immediately follow trend changes of input data. Thus, an anomaly detector that can train online is a primary solution for practical problems where input data trend or noise pattern shift dynamically as time goes by.

In this paper, by making use of Autoencoder and an online sequential learning algorithm OS-ELM, we propose an FPGA-based unsupervised anomaly detector, called OS-ELM-FPGA. OS-ELM [13] is one of neural-network-based convex optimization models. It can train faster than BP-NNs and always find the global optimal solution for its weight matrices at each training. Our theoretical analysis of the algorithm demonstrates the proposed OS-ELM-FPGA completely eliminates costly matrix inversions while improving the learning throughput by fixing the batch size to one.

The rest of this paper is organized as follows. Section 2 briefly introduces OS-ELM and anomaly detection using Autoencoder as background for OS-ELM-FPGA. Section 3 introduces related work. Section 4 proposes our OS-ELM-FPGA and Sect. 5 illustrates the implementation. Section 6 evaluates it in terms of learning throughput, prediction throughput, anomaly detection accuracy, and resource utilization. Section 7 summarizes this paper.

2 Preliminaries

2.1 ELM and OS-ELM

Before introducing OS-ELM, we briefly introduce ELM (Extreme Learning Machine) [9] as background.

ELM is one of single hidden layer feedforward neural networks (SLFNs) illustrated in Fig. 1. In an SLFN, m-dimensional k outputs $\boldsymbol{y} \in \boldsymbol{R}^{k \times m}$ corresponding to n-dimensional k input samples $\boldsymbol{x} \in \boldsymbol{R}^{k \times n}$ are computed by $\boldsymbol{y} = G(\boldsymbol{x} \cdot \boldsymbol{\alpha} + \boldsymbol{b})\boldsymbol{\beta}$, where $\boldsymbol{\alpha} \in \boldsymbol{R}^{n \times \tilde{N}}$ and $\boldsymbol{b} \in \boldsymbol{R}^{\tilde{N}}$ are parameters of the hidden layer. The former is the weight matrix connecting the input layer and the hidden layer, while the latter is the bias vector of the hidden nodes. $\boldsymbol{\beta} \in \boldsymbol{R}^{\tilde{N} \times m}$ is a weight matrix connecting the hidden layer and the output layer, and G is an activation function applied to the hidden nodes.

If the SLFN with $\tilde{N}$ hidden nodes can approximate m-dimensional k targets $\boldsymbol{t} \in \boldsymbol{R}^{k \times m}$ with zero error, it implies that there exists $\boldsymbol{\beta}$ that satisfies the following equation.

$$G(\boldsymbol{x} \cdot \boldsymbol{\alpha} + \boldsymbol{b})\boldsymbol{\beta} = \boldsymbol{t} \tag{1}$$

Then, if we define $\boldsymbol{H} \equiv G(\boldsymbol{x} \cdot \boldsymbol{\alpha} + \boldsymbol{b}) \in \boldsymbol{R}^{k \times \tilde{N}}$, the optimized weight matrix $\hat{\boldsymbol{\beta}}$ is calculated as follows.

$$\hat{\boldsymbol{\beta}} = \boldsymbol{H}^{\dagger}\boldsymbol{t}, \tag{2}$$

where $\boldsymbol{H}^{\dagger}$ is a pseudoinverse of $\boldsymbol{H}$. It can be computed with SVD (Singular Value Decomposition). By just updating the initial $\boldsymbol{\beta}$ with $\hat{\boldsymbol{\beta}}$, the training phase completes. The weight matrix $\boldsymbol{\alpha}$ does not have to be updated once initialized with random values. Furthermore, $\hat{\boldsymbol{\beta}}$ is always the global optimal solution, while BP-NNs is required to address the local minima problem [8]. Please note that ELM assumes all the training samples are available at the training phase in advance.

OS-ELM (Online Sequential Extreme Learning Machine) [13] is an ELM-based algorithm extended to learn input samples one-by-one or chunk-by-chunk.

Given the ith chunk of k_i training samples $\{\boldsymbol{x}_i \in \boldsymbol{R}^{k_i \times n}, \boldsymbol{t}_i \in \boldsymbol{R}^{k_i \times m}\}$, we have to find the optimized $\boldsymbol{\beta}_i$ that minimizes the following prediction error.

$$\left\| \begin{bmatrix} \boldsymbol{H}_0 \\ \vdots \\ \boldsymbol{H}_i \end{bmatrix} \boldsymbol{\beta}_i - \begin{bmatrix} \boldsymbol{t}_0 \\ \vdots \\ \boldsymbol{t}_i \end{bmatrix} \right\|, \tag{3}$$

where $\boldsymbol{H}_i \equiv G(\boldsymbol{x}_i \cdot \boldsymbol{\alpha} + \boldsymbol{b})$. According to the original paper [13], $\boldsymbol{\beta}_i$ can be sequentially computed with the following equation.

$$\begin{aligned} \boldsymbol{P}_i &= \boldsymbol{P}_{i-1} - \boldsymbol{P}_{i-1}\boldsymbol{H}_i^T(\boldsymbol{I} + \boldsymbol{H}_i\boldsymbol{P}_{i-1}\boldsymbol{H}_i^T)^{-1}\boldsymbol{H}_i\boldsymbol{P}_{i-1} \\ \boldsymbol{\beta}_i &= \boldsymbol{\beta}_{i-1} + \boldsymbol{P}_i\boldsymbol{H}_i^T(\boldsymbol{t}_i - \boldsymbol{H}_i\boldsymbol{\beta}_{i-1}) \end{aligned} \tag{4}$$

Specially, $\boldsymbol{P}_0$ and $\boldsymbol{\beta}_0$ can be computed as $\boldsymbol{P}_0 = (\boldsymbol{H}_0\boldsymbol{H}_0^T)^{-1}$, $\boldsymbol{\beta}_0 = \boldsymbol{P}_0\boldsymbol{H}_0^T\boldsymbol{t}_0$. As shown in Eq. 4, $\boldsymbol{\beta}_i$ can be computed without any memories and retraining for the past training samples.

2.2 Anomaly Detection Using Autoencoder

Autoencoder [7] is one of unsupervised learning models that reduces dimensions of input data in its hidden nodes. The model uses input data as target data, and is trained to reconstruct the input data in its output. Since the number of hidden nodes is constrained to be less than those of input and output nodes, when the reconstruction error (e.g., mean squared error and mean absolute error) between the input and the output data is converged well, the dimensionality reduction of the input data is completed in the hidden nodes.

In a context of anomaly detection using Autoencoder, the model is trained only with normal data. When input data that have different patterns from normal data (i.e., abnormal data) are fed, the reconstruction error will increase. If the error exceeds a threshold, the corresponding input data can be considered as abnormal data. Please note that this method does not require any abnormal data or labeling during training. Although PCA (Principal Component Analysis) is often mentioned as a similar model, Sakurada *et al.* showed that Autoencoder can detect subtle anomalies that PCA fails to detect [17] and is easy to apply nonlinear transformation without complex computations that kernel PCA [14] typically requires.

3 Related Work

3.1 Anomaly Detection Using OS-ELM

Since online sequential learning algorithms can follow time-series variability of input data, such algorithms are suitable for anomaly detection where we often have to deal with the nonstationarity. In the past few years, several studies on anomaly detection using OS-ELM have been reported. Singh *et al.* proposed an OS-ELM-based network traffic IDS (Intrusion Detection System) to train fast and accurately on huge amount of network traffic data with a limited memory. Bosman *et al.* presented a decentralized anomaly detection system that can detect abnormality in wireless sensor networks using OS-ELM in an unsupervised manner [11]. Although the above studies apply OS-ELM to anomaly detection, we use OS-ELM in conjunction with Autoencoder. As far as we know, this paper is the first work that uses OS-ELM-based Autoencoder for anomaly detection.

3.2 Hardware Implementation of OS-ELM

Although several hardware implementations of ELM have been reported [16,18,19], there are very few reports on that of OS-ELM. Bosman *et al.* proposed a fixed-point implementation of OS-ELM and its stability correction mechanism for resource-limited embedded devices [10], but they focused on software implementation. In this paper, we implement OS-ELM on an FPGA for the first time and propose an efficient design based on our theoretical analysis discussed in Sect. 4.

4 Analysis on OS-ELM Algorithm

OS-ELM update formula (i.e., Eq. 4) mainly consists of two types of matrix operations: (1) matrix product and (2) matrix inversion. When we assume the number of computational iterations for a matrix product $\boldsymbol{A} \in \boldsymbol{R}^{p \times q} \cdot \boldsymbol{B} \in \boldsymbol{R}^{q \times r}$

is pqr, and that for a matrix inversion $\boldsymbol{C}^{-1} \in \boldsymbol{R}^{r \times r}$ is r^3, the total numbers of iterations for these matrix operations in the update formula are calculated as follows.

$$\begin{aligned} I_{prod} &= 4k\tilde{N}^2 + k(2k + 2m + n)\tilde{N} \\ I_{inv} &= k^3, \end{aligned} \tag{5}$$

where I_{prod} and I_{inv} denote the total numbers of iterations for the matrix products and the matrix inversions, respectively. n, $\tilde{N}$, and m are the numbers of input, hidden, and output nodes of OS-ELM. k is the batch size. For example, we calculated the number of iterations for $\boldsymbol{H}_i\boldsymbol{P}_{i-1}\boldsymbol{H}_i^T$ by dividing it into the following two steps: (1) $\boldsymbol{H}_i \in \boldsymbol{R}^{k\times\tilde{N}} \cdot \boldsymbol{P}_{i-1} \in \boldsymbol{R}^{\tilde{N}\times\tilde{N}}$ and (2) $\boldsymbol{H}_i\boldsymbol{P}_{i-1} \in \boldsymbol{R}^{k\times\tilde{N}} \cdot \boldsymbol{H}_i^T \in \boldsymbol{R}^{\tilde{N}\times k}$, then computing the total number of these iterations $I = k\tilde{N}^2 + k^2\tilde{N}$.

Assuming that I_k denotes the total number of the iterations of matrix products and matrix inversions in OS-ELM update formula when the batch size is k, we can derive the following equation.

$$\begin{aligned} I_k &= I_{prod} + I_{inv} \\ &= 4k\tilde{N}^2 + k(2k + 2m + n)\tilde{N} + k^3 \\ &= k(4\tilde{N}^2 + (2k + 2m + n)\tilde{N} + k^2) \\ &\geq k(4\tilde{N}^2 + (2 + 2m + n)\tilde{N} + 1) = kI_1 \end{aligned} \tag{6}$$

This equation implies that OS-ELM can train at the same or higher learning throughput (i.e., $I_k \geq kI_1$) by fixing the batch size to one. In software frameworks, as actually shown in Sect. 6.3, they suffer from a low throughput at small batch sizes because of software specific overheads, such as dynamic memory allocation and library calls. On the other hand, the proposed FPGA-based implementation of OS-ELM can fully enjoy the insight from Eq. 6, since it is free from any software specific overheads.

Moreover, we can completely eliminate the costly matrix inversions in OS-ELM update formula. Because the size of the target matrix $(\boldsymbol{I} + \boldsymbol{H}_i\boldsymbol{P}_{i-1}\boldsymbol{H}_i^T)$ is $k \times k$, its inverse matrix can be easily calculated by computing its reciprocal when $k = 1$. In this case, OS-ELM update formula can be transformed as follows.

$$\begin{aligned} \boldsymbol{P}_i &= \boldsymbol{P}_{i-1} - \frac{\boldsymbol{P}_{i-1}\boldsymbol{h}_i^T\boldsymbol{h}_i\boldsymbol{P}_{i-1}}{1 + \boldsymbol{h}_i\boldsymbol{P}_{i-1}\boldsymbol{h}_i^T} \\ \boldsymbol{\beta}_i &= \boldsymbol{\beta}_{i-1} + \boldsymbol{P}_i\boldsymbol{h}_i^T(\boldsymbol{t}_i - \boldsymbol{h}_i\boldsymbol{\beta}_{i-1}), \end{aligned} \tag{7}$$

where $\boldsymbol{h} \in \boldsymbol{R}^{\tilde{N}}$ is a special case of $\boldsymbol{H} \in \boldsymbol{R}^{k\times\tilde{N}}$ when $k = 1$.

Thanks to the above trick, the proposed OS-ELM-FPGA can train without any costly matrix inversions. It reduces the hardware resources and significantly accelerates the learning throughput. It is possible to further improve the training/prediction throughput by computing matrix products in parallel.

5 Design and Implementation

We implemented the proposed OS-ELM-FPGA using Xilinx Vivado HLS 2016.4 as a toolchain for synthesizing hardware modules written in high-level languages such as C/C++. We chose Xilinx Virtex-7 XC7VX690T as the target FPGA and 100 MHz as the target frequency.

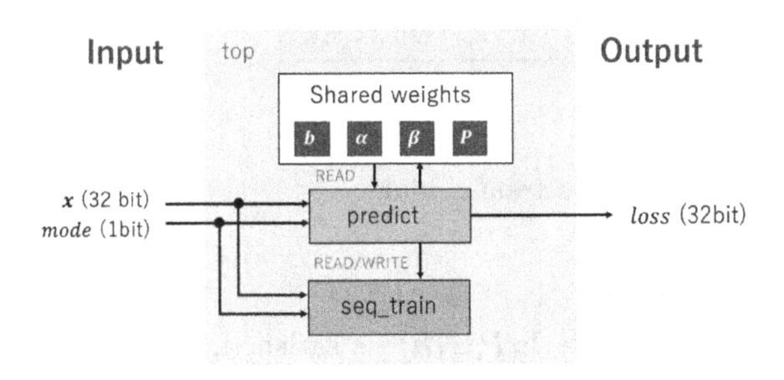

Fig. 2. Block diagram of OS-ELM-FPGA

5.1 Top Module

Figure 2 shows an overview of OS-ELM-FPGA. Since OS-ELM-FPGA uses Autoencoder, the number of input nodes of the network is same as that of output nodes.

top module consists of the following two modules: (1) *seq_train* and (2) *predict* modules. *seq_train* module is to train sequentially on a given input sample $\boldsymbol{x}$, and update shared weight matrices $\boldsymbol{\beta}$ and $\boldsymbol{P}$. *predict* module is to predict a loss (i.e., a reconstruction error) by computing $loss = L(\boldsymbol{x}, \boldsymbol{y})$ where L is a loss function and $\boldsymbol{y}$ denotes an output of the network. Here, we used MAE (Mean Absolute Error) $L(\boldsymbol{x}, \boldsymbol{y}) = \frac{1}{n}\sum_{i=1}^{n}|x_i - y_i|$ as a loss function. Since OS-ELM produces exactly the same learning result regardless of which loss function is used unlike BP-NNs, we recommend to use a loss function that consumes less hardware resources such as MAE.

A 1-bit input signal, named *mode*, determines whether to predict or train on given input samples. When the value is 0 or 1, prediction or training is performed, respectively. In our implementation, all the decimal numbers are represented by 32-bit fixed-point numbers (i.e., 10-bit integer and 22-bit decimal parts).

5.2 Seq_train Module and Predict Module

seq_train module executes OS-ELM-FPGA update formula (i.e., Eq. 7). Figure 3 shows the processing flow of the module. If $1 + \boldsymbol{h}_i\boldsymbol{P}_{i-1}\boldsymbol{h}_i^T$ is close to 0, $\frac{\boldsymbol{P}_{i-1}\boldsymbol{h}_i^T\boldsymbol{h}_i\boldsymbol{P}_{i-1}}{1+\boldsymbol{h}_i\boldsymbol{P}_{i-1}\boldsymbol{h}_i^T}$ will diverge, which makes the training significantly unstable. In our implementation, we set a threshold EPSILON to 1e-4 to detect singular

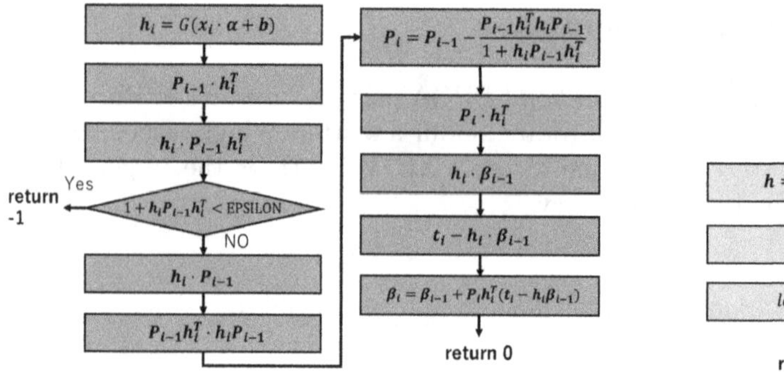

Fig. 3. Flowchart of Seq_train module

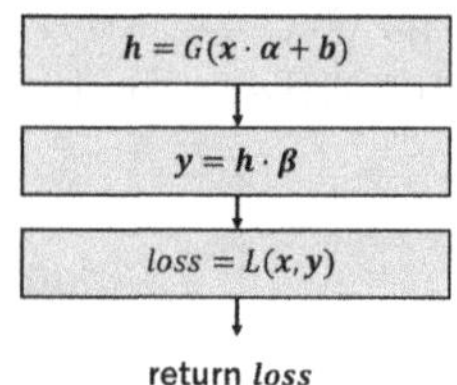

Fig. 4. Flowchart of predict module

matrices. If EPSILON $> 1 + \boldsymbol{h}_i \boldsymbol{P}_{i-1} \boldsymbol{h}_i^T$ is satisfied, OS-ELM-FPGA stops the training and discards the input data for learning stability.

predict module computes output data on given input data by computing matrix/vector products and then the corresponding loss value (i.e., reconstruction error) is computed. Figure 4 shows the processing flow. All the matrix/vector products in *seq_train* module and *predict* module can be accelerated by parallel execution of N product-sums in the innermost loop. This parameter should be tuned by considering the area and performance trade-offs.

6 Evaluations

In this section, OS-ELM-FPGA is evaluated in terms of anomaly detection accuracy, learning throughput, and FPGA resource utilization.

OS-ELM-FPGA is compared with the following four software counterparts: ① OS-ELM(CPU), ② OS-ELM(GPU), ③ BP-NN(CPU), ④ and BP-NN(GPU). ①/② is CPU/GPU implementation of OS-ELM, while ③/④ is CPU/GPU implementation of BP-NN. These counterparts are evaluated on a common server machine (Intel Core i7-6700 (3.4 GHz), NVIDIA GTX 1070 (VRAM 8 GB), DDR4 RAM (32 GB)).

To implement all the four software counterparts, we use Tensorflow [12] (ver 1.6.0). The model size (the numbers of input, hidden, and output nodes) of each implementation is set to 784, 32, and 784 respectively. For OS-ELM-FPGA and OS-ELM(CPU/GPU), we use the linear function $f(\boldsymbol{x}) = \boldsymbol{x}$ as an activation function in their hidden nodes, because it produced better anomaly detection accuracy than other nonlinear functions. In this paper, all the matrix/vector products in OS-ELM-FPGA are fully parallelized in the way mentioned in Sect. 5.2.

For BP-NN(CPU) and BP-NN(GPU), we use relu [20] function in their hidden nodes, and sigmoid [6] function in their output nodes. We use Adam [5] (learning rate $= 0.001$, $\beta_1 = 0.9$, $\beta_2 = 0.999$) as the optimization algorithm for them. For all the implementations, we use MAE $L(\boldsymbol{x}, \boldsymbol{y}) = \frac{1}{n} \sum_{i=1}^{n} |x_i - y_i|$

as the loss function as mentioned in Sect. 5.1. AVX (Advanced Vector eXtensions) instructions are used for all the CPU implementations to optimize their performance.

6.1 Anomaly Detection Accuracy

Evaluation Procedure. First, we train each model with a normal training dataset and then perform prediction to compute loss values for a normal validation dataset. Second, we calculate the mean μ and the standard deviation σ of these loss values. Finally, we perform prediction again to calculate another loss values (i.e., $loss$) on a mixed dataset that consists of the normal validation dataset and an abnormal dataset. If $\frac{loss-\mu}{\sigma} > \theta$ is satisfied, the corresponding input sample is detected as abnormal.

Datasets. For the normal dataset, we use MNIST dataset (Fig. 5, 10-class 28×28 gray-scale images) [2]. This dataset consists of 60,000 training samples and 10,000 validation samples. For the abnormal dataset, we use Fashion-MNIST dataset (Fig. 6, 10-class 28×28 gray-scale images) [1]. The dataset also consists of 60,000 training samples and 10,000 validation samples. We use the 10,000 validation samples as abnormal samples. All the samples are fed to OS-ELM-FPGA as $28 \times 28 = 784$-dimensional vector data.

Settings. All the images' pixel values are normalized into [0,1]. The weight matrix $\boldsymbol{\alpha}$ of OS-ELM(CPU/GPU) is initialized with uniform distribution along [0, 1] and then $\boldsymbol{P_0}$ and $\boldsymbol{\beta_0}$ are computed. $\boldsymbol{\alpha}$, $\boldsymbol{P_0}$, and $\boldsymbol{\beta_0}$ of OS-ELM-FPGA are initialized with the same values. Regarding the training procedure, OS-ELM(CPU/GPU) and OS-ELM-FPGA are trained with all the training samples only once (i.e., one epoch), because it makes no sense to train iteratively on the same dataset in OS-ELM algorithm. On the other hand, BP-NN(CPU) and BP-NN(GPU) are trained for ten epochs, because they could not obtain comparable anomaly detection accuracy with one epoch. For all the implementations except for OS-ELM-FPGA, the batch size is set to 64.

Results. Table 1 shows the evaluation results of OS-ELM-FPGA and the four counterparts in terms of precision, recall, and f-measure. In this paper, precision (denoted by P) means a percentage of actual abnormal samples to all the samples detected as abnormal, while recall (denoted by R) is a percentage of samples detected as abnormal to all the actual abnormal samples. F-measure (denoted

Fig. 5. MNIST

Fig. 6. Fashion-MNIST

Table 1. Anomaly detection accuracy

Implementation	θ	P	R	F
OS-ELM-FPGA	1.0	0.852	0.922	0.886
OS-ELM(CPU)	1.0	**0.858**	**0.926**	**0.891**
OS-ELM(GPU)	1.0	0.856	0.924	0.889
BP-NN(CPU)	1.0	0.852	0.908	0.879
BP-NN(GPU)	1.0	0.851	0.901	0.875
OS-ELM-FPGA	3.0	0.996	**0.770**	**0.868**
OS-ELM(CPU)	3.0	0.996	0.765	0.865
OS-ELM(GPU)	3.0	**0.996**	0.747	0.854
BP-NN(CPU)	3.0	0.991	0.662	0.794
BP-NN(GPU)	3.0	0.992	0.669	0.799

Table 2. FPGA resource utilization of OS-ELM-FPGA

	BRAM	DSP	FF	LUT
Used	816	3,347	182,825	330,881
Available	2,940	3,600	866,400	433,200
Utilization	27%	92%	21%	76%

by F) means a harmonic mean of precision and recall. Here, we call f-measure as "anomaly detection accuracy".

Anomaly detection accuracy of OS-ELM-FPGA is higher than those of BP-NN(CPU) and BP-NN(GPU) by up to 9.74%. Considering that they are trained for ten epochs while OS-ELM-FPGA is once, we can say OS-ELM-FPGA achieved better anomaly detection accuracy in a short training time. The result of OS-ELM-FPGA is slightly different from the other OS-ELM counterparts, because we use 32-bit fixed-point to handle the numerical values instead of 32-bit floating-point.

Please note that fixing batch size to one does not affect the accuracy, because OS-ELM always produce the same training result regardless of the batch size.

6.2 FPGA Resource Utilization

OS-ELM-FPGA is evaluated in terms of FPGA resource utilization. Table 2 shows the result. As described in Sect. 5, the target FPGA is Xilinx Virtex-7 XC7VX690T. As shown in the table, all the resource utilizations are less than their limit, though we fully parallelized all the matrix/vector products in OS-ELM-FPGA. The target FPGA device is not the state-of-the-art FPGA already and we can expect faster training/prediction throughput by using the latest FPGAs.

6.3 Sequential Learning Throughput

OS-ELM-FPGA is compared with the counterparts in terms of learning throughput by varying the batch size. Figure 7 shows the result. Since the batch size of OS-ELM-FPGA is one, its learning throughput is constant regardless of x-axis (batch size) in the graph. As shown in Fig. 7, although OS-ELM(CPU) can train faster than BP-NN(CPU) at small batch sizes, the tendency is inverted at big batch sizes since the computational cost for a matrix inversion in OS-ELM

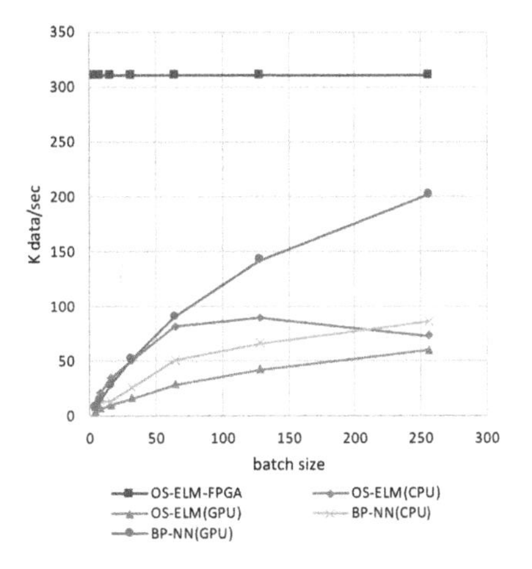

Fig. 7. Comparison of learning throughput

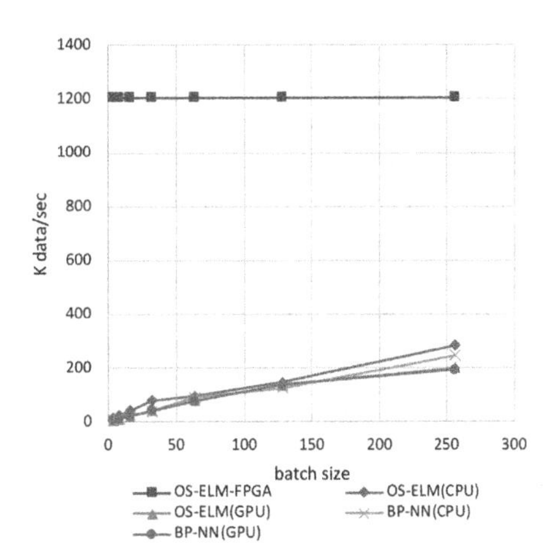

Fig. 8. Comparison of prediction throughput

update formula is proportional to the cube of the batch size. In the context of realtime anomaly detection, it is required to detect abnormal samples immediately after the samples are fed to the detector, thus small batch sizes are preferred in this case. This is a benefit of OS-ELM compared to BP-NNs. In addition, since OS-ELM-FPGA eliminates the computational bottleneck of OS-ELM by fixing the batch size to one, and computes matrix products in parallel, its learning throughput is 3.47x to 27.99x higher than OS-ELM(CPU), and 5.22x to 78.06x higher than OS-ELM(GPU), respectively. It is 3.62x to 36.15x and 1.53x to 43.44x higher than BP-NN(CPU) and BP-NN(GPU), respectively.

Regarding the GPU implementations, while BP-NN(GPU) significantly accelerates its learning throughput, OS-ELM(GPU) suffers from a lower throughput than OS-ELM(CPU). Since a matrix inversion in OS-ELM algorithm is difficult to execute in parallel because of a number of conditional operations, OS-ELM(GPU) could not accelerate the learning throughput efficiently. This result indicates that OS-ELM is less suitable for GPU acceleration than BP-NNs.

On the other hand, since the proposed OS-ELM-FPGA completely eliminates the matrix inversion, it achieves the best learning throughput among all the counterparts for all the batch sizes.

6.4 Prediction Throughput

OS-ELM-FPGA is compared with the counterparts in terms of prediction throughput by varying the batch size. Figure 8 shows the result. Regarding the CPU implementations, OS-ELM(CPU) achieved a slightly higher prediction throughput than that of BP-NN(CPU), because BP-NN(CPU) uses nonlinear activation functions while OS-ELM(CPU) does not use them.

Regarding the GPU implementations, although they execute prediction computations (e.g., matrix products, and matrix sums) in parallel, their throughput decreases on the contrary. When a model size is small like SLFNs, data transfer overheads between a host and GPU devices become major bottlenecks. For this reason, OS-ELM(GPU) and BP-NN(GPU) failed to accelerate the prediction speed. On the other hand, OS-ELM-FPGA is completely free from the data transfer overheads and achieves 4.23x to 83.98x and 6.04x to 183.79x higher throughput than OS-ELM(CPU) and OS-ELM(GPU), respectively. It is also 4.90x to 198.85x and 6.25x to 213.06x higher than NN-GPU(CPU) and NN-BP(GPU), respectively.

7 Summary

In this paper, we proposed an FPGA-based unsupervised anomaly detector, called OS-ELM-FPGA, that combines Autoencoder and an online sequential learning algorithm OS-ELM. Our theoretical analysis demonstrated that the design of OS-ELM-FPGA completely eliminates matrix pseudoinversions while improving the learning throughput. As a result, OS-ELM-FPGA can train and predict using only basic matrix operations, such as matrix product, addition, and subtraction. Simulation results using a hand-written digits dataset and a fashion items dataset showed that OS-ELM-FPGA achieved favorable anomaly detection accuracy compared to CPU and GPU implementations of BP-NN in a short training time. Learning throughput of OS-ELM-FPGA is 3.47x to 27.99x and 5.22x to 78.06x higher than CPU and GPU implementations of OS-ELM, while 3.62x to 36.15x and 1.53x to 43.44x higher than CPU and GPU implementations of BP-NN.

Please note that this paper is the first work that combines OS-ELM and Autoencoder and eliminates the matrix inversions for the efficient FPGA-based online sequential learning unsupervised anomaly detector. In anomaly detection for industries, because environmental noise differs by place and time, our online sequential unsupervised approach is preferable since it can adapt to a given environment online. As future work, we will extend this work to use multiple OS-ELM-FPGA instances in an ensemble manner to improve the expression capability. We will also conduct comprehensive comparisons between OS-ELM-FPGA and some other methods (e.g., PCA and kernel PCA) on more practical scenario using real industrial data.

Acknowlegements. This work was supported by JST CREST Grant Number JPMJCR1785, Japan.

References

1. Fashion-MNIST: A Novel Image Dataset for Benchmarking Machine Learning Algorithms. https://github.com/zalandoresearch/fashion-mnist
2. MNIST: Handwritten digit database. http://yann.lecun.com/exdb/mnist/
3. Zhou, C., Paffenroth, C.: Anomaly detection with robust deep autoencoders. In: Proceedings of the ACM SIGKDD International Conference on Knowledge Discovery and Data Mining, pp. 665–674, August 2017

4. Chicco, D., Sadowski, P., Baldi, P.: Deep autoencoder neural networks for gene ontology annotation predictions. In: Proceedings of the ACM Conference on Bioinformatics, Computational Biology, and Health Informatics, pp. 533–540, September 2014
5. Kingma, D.P., Ba, J.: Adam: A Method for Stochastic Optimization. CoRR abs/1412.6980, January 2014
6. Cybenko, G.: Approximation by superpositions of a sigmoidal function. Math. Control Signals Syst. **2**(4), 303–314 (1989)
7. Hinton, G., Salakhutdinov, R.: Reducing the dimensionality of data with neural networks. Science **313**(5786), 504–507 (2006)
8. Marco, G., Alberto, T.: On the problem of local minima in backpropagation. IEEE Trans. Pattern Anal. Mach. Intell. **14**(1), 76–86 (1992)
9. Huang, G.B., Zhu, Q.Y., Siew, C.K.: Extreme learning machine: a new learning scheme of feedforward neural networks. In: Proceedings of the International Joint Conference on Neural Networks, pp. 985–990, July 2004
10. Bosman, H.H.W.J., Liotta, A., Iacca, G., Wörtche, H.J.: Online extreme learning on fixed-point sensor networks. In: Proceedings of the IEEE International Conference on Data Mining Workshops, pp. 319–326, December 2013
11. Bosman, H.H.W.J., Iacca, G., Tejada, A., Wörtche, H.J., Liotta, A.: Spatial anomaly detection in sensor networks using neighborhood information. Inf. Fusion **33**, 41–56 (2017)
12. Abadi, M., et al.: TensorFlow: Large-Scale Machine Learning on Heterogeneous Systems, March 2016. https://www.tensorflow.org/
13. Liang, N.Y., Huang, G.B., Saratchandran, P., Sundararajan, N.: A fast and accurate online sequential learning algorithm for feedforward networks. IEEE Trans. Neural Netw. **17**(6), 1411–1423 (2006)
14. Wang, Q., et al.: Kernel Principal Component Analysis. In: Artificial Neural Networks. pp. 583–588, July 1997
15. Fakoor, R., Ladhak, F., Nazi, A., Huber, M.: Using deep learning to enhance cancer diagnosis and classification. In: Proceedings of the International Conference on Machine Learning, vol. 28, August 2013
16. Decherchi, S., Gastaldo, P., Leoncini, A., Zunino, R.: Efficient digital implementation of extreme learning machines for classification. IEEE Trans. Circ. Syst. II: Express Briefs **59**(8), 496–500 (2012)
17. Mayu, S., Takehisa, Y.: Anomaly detection using autoencoders with nonlinear dimensionality reduction. In: Proceedings of the Workshop on Machine Learning for Sensory Data Analysis, pp. 4–11, July 2014
18. Yeam, T.C., Ismail, N., Mashiko, K., Matsuzaki, T.: FPGA implementation of extreme learning machine system for classification. In: Proceedings of the IEEE Region 10 Conference, pp. 1868–1873, November 2017
19. Frances, V., et al.: Hardware implementation of real-time extreme learning machine in FPGA: analysis of precision, resource occupation and performance. Comput. Electr. Eng. **51**, 139–156 (2016)
20. Nair, V., Hinton, G.: Rectified linear units improve restricted boltzmann machines. In: Proceedings of the International Conference on Machine Learning, pp. 807–814, June 2010

LSDVE - Workshop on Large Scale Distributed Virtual Environments

Workshop on Large Scale Distributed Virtual Environments (LSDVE)

Workshop Description

The Sixth Workshop on Large Scale Distributed Virtual Environments (LSDVE 2018) was held in Turin, Italy. For the sixth time, this workshop was organized in conjunction with the Euro-Par annual series of international conferences. The main aim of the sixth edition of the workshop has been to provide a venue for researchers to present and discuss important aspects of large scale networked collaborative applications and of the platforms supporting them.

Several novel applications have emerged in the area of large scale networked applications: social networks, distributed cryptocurrencies, blockchains. In particular, blockchain technology which has been proposed for cryptocurrencies has been recently been applied to different areas, like IoT, e-health, financial services. Peer to peer, Internet of Things, Smart-cities, distributed sensing are examples of modern ICT paradigms that aim to describe globally cooperative infrastructures built upon objects' intelligence and self-configuring capabilities. The workshop has been a venue for researchers to present and discuss important aspects of large scale networked collaborative applications and of the platforms supporting them. The workshop's aim is to investigate open challenges for such applications, related to both the applications design and to the definition of proper supports. Some important challenges are, for instance, exploitation of the classical blockchain technology to support collaborative applications, discussion on alternative distributed consensus algorithms, privacy and security issues.

This year, the workshop has included two sessions. The papers presented in the first session regard blockchain technology, in particular the first one presents a framework for the secure sharing of health-data on a blockchain, while the second one discusses which are the drivers behind adoption of blockchain technology. The second session includes papers regarding mobility in a smart city environment, experiments on an Android-based Oportunistic Network and a novel approach for community detection in Distributed Online Social Networks.

We wish to thank all who helped to make this sixth edition of the workshop a success: authors submitting papers, colleagues who refereed the submitted papers, the numerous collegues who attended the sessions, and finally the Euro-Par 2018 organizers whose invaluable support greatly helped in the organisation of this sixth edition of the workshop.

Organization

Program Chairs

Laura Ricci	Department of Computer Science, Pisa, Italy
Barbara Guidi	Department of Computer Science, Pisa, Italy
Radu Prodan	University of Klagenfurt, Austria

Program Committee

Michele Amoretti	University of Parma, Italy
Massimo Bartoletti	University of Cagliari, Italy
Stefano Bistarelli	University of Perugia, Italy
Emanuele Carlini	IIT, CNR, Pisa, Italy
Jose Antonio Fernandes de Macedo	Federal University of Cearà, Brasil
Marco Furini	UNIMORE, Italy
Ombretta Gaggi	University of Padova, Italy
Kalman Graffi	University of Dusseldorf, Germany
Barbara Guidi	University of Pisa, Italy
Dragi Kimovski	University of Klagenfurt, Austria
Pedro Garcia Lopez	Universitat Rovira i Virgili, Spain
Alberto Montresor	University of Trento, Italy
Paolo Mori	IIT, CNR, Pisa, Italy
Symeon Papadopoulos	CERTH, Greece
Dana Petcu	West University of Timisoara, Romania
Radu Prodan	University of Klagenfurt, Austria
Laura Ricci	University of Pisa, Pisa, Italy

The Drivers Behind Blockchain Adoption: The Rationality of Irrational Choices

Tommy Koens(✉) and Erik Poll

Radboud University, Nijmegen, The Netherlands
{tkoens,erikpoll}@cs.ru.nl

Abstract. There has been a huge increase in interest in blockchain technology. However, little is known about the drivers behind the adoption of this technology. In this paper we identify and analyze these drivers, using three real-world and representative scenarios. We confirm in our analysis that blockchain is not an appropriate technology for some scenarios, from a purely technical point of view. The choice for blockchain technology in such scenarios may therefore seem as an irrational choice. However, our analysis reveals that there are non-technical drivers at play that drive the adoption of blockchain, such as philosophical beliefs, network effects, and economic incentives. These non-technical drivers may explain the rationality behind the choice for blockchain adoption.

Keywords: Blockchain · Distributed ledger · Technical drivers
Non-technical drivers

1 Introduction

Blockchain technology has received a huge interest ever since its inception in the cryptocurrency Bitcoin [22]. Indeed, on a global scale companies and governments [27] are looking for applications of this technology [13]. Cryptocurrencies, in particular Bitcoin, are the best-known and most successful scenario where blockchain technology has been adopted, but many other applications of blockchain have been proposed, such as supply chain management [28], identity management [15], and smart energy grids [29].

However, the justification for using a blockchain in many of these scenarios is unclear. Indeed, many papers have argued that using a blockchain is not the best – or not even a good – solution for particular scenarios [17]. This has led to the proposal of methodologies for deciding if blockchain is an appropriate solution for a given scenario, from a technical point of view [25,39]. However, non-technical drivers are not typically discussed in most of the computer science literature. In this paper we try to look beyond this technical view, and we also consider the non-technical drivers behind the choice for blockchain in real-world scenarios.

T. Koens—Supported by ING.

G. Mencagli et al. (Eds.): Euro-Par 2018 Workshops, LNCS 11339, pp. 535–546, 2019.
https://doi.org/10.1007/978-3-030-10549-5_42

To do this, we consider in Sect. 3 three real-world scenarios in which blockchain technology is used, namely, the cryptocurrency Bitcoin, the identity management solution uPort, and a supply chain scenario for agricultural products, namely table grapes. Here we also identify and analyze the drivers behind the adoption of blockchain for these scenarios. We distinguish four categories of drivers: technical properties, philosophical beliefs, network effects, and economic incentives. Furthermore, we discuss the appropriateness of blockchain technology for each scenario. We argue that using a blockchain is not an appropriate solution for some of the scenarios if we only take a technological perspective. This may seem that using blockchain in these scenarios is an irrational choice. Based on this analysis, Sect. 4 discusses the non-technical drivers that may explain blockchain adoption. Here we argue that there is a rationality behind blockchain adoption if we also take non-technical drivers into account. Section 5 discusses related work, Sect. 6 future work, and Sect. 7 summarizes our conclusions.

2 Background

This section provides a generic description of blockchain technology and introduces the decision model by Wüst and Gervais [39] for determining if blockchain technology is appropriate for a particular scenario.

The novel part of blockchain technology is having a consortium of unknown participants to reach consensus [26]. Typically, participants in blockchain technology consist of users and miners. At any time, a user may propose a new state of the ownership of a token by means of a transaction. A transaction, contains at least the sender's account, the receiver's account, the number of tokens transferred, a timestamp and a signature of the sender.

Miners propose new ledger states, but only after having solved a cryptographic puzzle. The idea here is to prevent multiple, different ledger states being proposed. The participant who first solves the puzzle is allowed to propose a new state of the ledger. Miners propose new ledger states by collecting user transactions and proposing these as a set, called a block. Since the unique identifier of the previous block is included in the new proposed block, a chain of blocks is created, hence the term blockchain.

Blockchain may be useful in a scenario which contains certain properties. Therefore, to determine if blockchain is an appropriate technology for a particular scenario, several blockchain decision models have been proposed.

2.1 Blockchain Decision Models

Wüst and Gervais [39] proposed a model to determine if blockchain technology is appropriate for a particular problem. Several such models have been proposed, as discussed by, for example, Meunier [20]. We chose the model of Wüst and Gervais because it provides a detailed description of the decisions that have to be made, leaving less room for misinterpretation. Their model consist of a decision tree based on the following scenario properties:

(a) *Storing state.* Refers to the need of storing data that may change both in volume and in content over time.
(b) *Number of writers.* Multiple writers (also known as miners) must be present, that have a common interest in agreeing on the validity of the stored state.
(c) *Is there a Trusted Third Party?* A Trusted Third Party (TTP) is a centralized entity that could manage changes and updates the state. A TTP, if present, may also control who can read the state stored.
(d) *Are all writers known?* This refers to knowing the identity of all writers.
(e) *Are all writers trusted?* When writers are trusted, they are expected not to behave maliciously. When writers are not trusted, they may behave maliciously.
(f) *Public verifiability of state.* This property determines who may read the state stored on the blockchain, and verify the integrity of the ledger.

Based on these six properties, the model determines one of four possible solutions as the best solution for the scenario:

1. *Permissionless blockchain.* Anyone may join the network and read from the state stored, and write to the blockchain.
2. *Public permissioned blockchain.* A limited set of participants may write to the blockchain. Anyone may join the network and read the state.
3. *Private permissioned blockchain.* A limited set of participants may join the network, and write a new state. Only this set can read the state.
4. *Don't use blockchain.* This end state is reached when one of the properties (a), (b), (c), or (e) above is not met.

3 Scenarios

The following paragraphs present three scenarios in which blockchain is used. We chose these for two reasons. First, these are real-life and representative scenarios where a blockchain is used. Second, these scenarios are generally well known to be related with blockchain technology. For each scenario we propose a set of blockchain adoption drivers (see Table 1) and we group these drivers into:

- *Scenario properties.* These drivers, (a)–(f) above, focus on the rationale for using blockchain from a technological perspective.
- *Philosophical beliefs.* These drivers focus on the rationale for using blockchain based on the participants' beliefs.
- *Network effects.* Here we propose drivers where existing participants influence new participants in using blockchain technology.
- *Economic incentives.* These drivers are based on financial gain, or preventing potential financial losses, by one of the parties involved in the scenario.

Table 1. Blockchain technology adoption drivers

Category	Drivers	Bitcoin	uPort	Supply chain
Scenario properties	Storing state	•	•	•
	Multiple writers	•	•	•
	Can not use TTP	•		
	Writers unknown	•	•	
	Writers untrusted	•		
	Public verifiability	•	•	•
Philosophical beliefs	Will not use TTP	•		
	Decentralization need	•	•	
	Enhanced privacy	•	•	
	Alternative system	•	•	•
	Political reasons	•		
Network effects	Driven by community	•		
	Curiosity	•	•	•
	Cool to use	•	•	•
Economic incentives	Marketing product		•	•
	Selling mining equipm.	•		
	Selling consultancy	•		•
	Charging for platform			•
	FOMO	•		•
	Alternative investment	•		

The scenario properties are inherent characteristics of a scenario, which we consider *technical properties*. The other three driver categories are more about preferences or motivations of the participants, which we consider *non-technical properties*. This categorization is important because it allows us to determine what drives blockchain adoption.

3.1 Scenario 1 - Bitcoin

Scenario Description. In Nakamoto's work [22] a decentralized payment system is envisioned. The essence is to have a consortium of unknown participants achieve consensus [26]. To achieve this, Bitcoin uses a public permissionless blockchain, allowing anyone to participate.

Each participant owns one or more Bitcoin accounts. An account is identified by a public cryptographic key, and managed by the corresponding private key. Each account may hold a number of tokens, which represent a value, and can be seen as 'coins'. Coin ownership can be transferred by transactions. A transaction, in principle, contains the account of the sender, the account of the receiver, the number of coins transferred, and the signature of the sender. Transactions created by participants are collected by other participants called miners. These miners independently solve a moderately-hard cryptographic puzzle. The miner that solves the puzzle first, obtains the privilege to propose a new state of accounts, based on the transactions collected. A miner proposes a new state by presenting a sequence of transactions called a block. Note that only miners may write to the blockchain. Each block holds the hash of its previous block, linking all blocks into a block-chain.

Scenario Properties. This scenario has all the properties for the use of blockchain to be the right solution according to the scheme of Wüst and Gervais: we have to store state, there are multiple writers, there is (by design) no Trusted Third Party (TTP), the writers are unknown and untrusted, and the state should be publicly verifiable. In other words, the properties of this scenario provide a clear technical rationale to use blockchain.

Philosophical Beliefs. Bitcoin's pseudonymous inventor Nakamoto states that 'What is needed is an electronic payment system based on cryptographic proof instead of trust' [22]. Clearly, Bitcoin is specifically designed not to have a TTP. Also, many of its participants are motivated by political reasons to use Bitcoin [30]. For example, when national governments prevented WikiLeaks from receiving donations by blocking credit card transactions [33], Bitcoin could be used as an alternative payment system to circumvent these restrictions. Furthermore, given the pseudonymous nature of all accounts in Bitcoin, payments are more privacy-friendly than centralized bank payments.

Network Effects. Bitcoin has received considerable media attention in the last few years [13,21,37]. This causes a network effect, where people consider Bitcoin 'cool to use' [3]. Also, at this point in time several issues remain which hinder global adoption, such as scalability [4], high transaction fees, price volatility and energy consumption [23]. These problems are hard to solve, which has led to a growing academic interest in blockchain technology to tackle them [32,40].

Economic Incentives. Several companies have a direct economic interest in the success of Bitcoin. As miners nowadays need special dedicated hardware, hardware vendors supplying this hardware have a clear economic interest in the success of Bitcoin. Furthermore, many companies, including established firms and young startups [35], offer blockchain consultancy services, some of which are related to Bitcoin. These companies also have a strong economic incentive, namely to sell consulting services.

Finally, given the broad global attention to blockchain technology, there is the fear of missing out (FOMO) [34]. This may lead to that some parties buy bitcoins, as well as other cryptocurrencies, to mitigate the risk of having missed the bandwagon when it turns out the technology becomes a success. For example, public media has extensively reported on the rise of the value of Bitcoin. This triggered other, new participants to also invest in Bitcoin, as these participants also hope for a profitable investment in Bitcoin. Indeed, uninformed participants consider Bitcoin as an alternative investment [13]. However, as Bitcoin is not backed by any government nor gold, these investments are fueled largely by speculation.

3.2 Scenario 2 - uPort

Scenario Description. This second scenario addresses an identity management solution. Such solutions aim to facilitate the management of identifiers, authentication, personal information, and the presentation of this information to other parties. Typically, in these solution schemes, a trusted identity provider such as a government, issues attributes to a participant. These participants store their attributes on their mobile device. This allows a verifying party such as a retailer, to verify the validity of the attributes issued.

Several companies (e.g. Consensys, Evernym, and IBM) advertise their blockchain-based identity solution. Here we focus on uPort [36] by Consensys. uPort is an identity management solution that uses the Ethereum blockchain [38] for so-called account recovery. In this account recovery process the user reclaims ownership of a unique number, called a persistent identifier (PI). This then allows participants to easily (re-)obtain attributes from issuing parties, by proving ownership of this PI.

The uPort app allows a device, such as a smart phone, to connect to a specific smart contract on Ethereum. This contract contains a unique number represented by the PI, which is linked to the participant's public key. When, for example, the device holding the attributes and private key is lost, a participant may prove to be the owner of the PI. Ownership of this PI is proven by requesting multiple trusted parties to state that, indeed, the participant is linked the unique number, after which the user can link a new public key to the PI. Currently, uPort seems to be the only identity management solution that offers recovery of a PI.

Scenario Properties. In this scenario, state in the form of a smart contract is stored on the publicly verifiable Ethereum blockchain. From a participant perspective, all writers to the contract holding the persistent identifier are known, since these are the parties (e.g. friends or government) trusted by the participant. In this scenario the owner of a smart contract, including its trustees, can write to the contract. Furthermore, a centralized party, for example the issuing party of the attributes, could store the unique number related to the attributes of a participant. Therefore, following the model of Wüset and Gervais, there is no technical rationale to use blockchain technology in this scenario as all writers are trusted.

Philosophical Beliefs. The mission of uPort states that "we believe that everyone has the right to control their own digital identity" [36]. Blockchain technology offers a platform that can be used by everyone and, therefore, using a blockchain is in the interest of uPort. From a company perspective, offering such a platform is based on principles that drive uPort, such as company purpose, economic principles, and social impact. However, from a technical perspective there is no need to use blockchain for the unique number recovery, as explained above.

Network Effects. Blockchain technology offers multiple functionalities, such as storing of data, reaching consensus, and an audit trail. As companies often wonder how blockchain functionalities can benefit their company, curiosity may have played a role in blockchain adoption in this scenario.

Economic Incentives. The uPort app points to a perceived single source of truth, the blockchain. When more participants would adopt the uPort app, uPort would gain more exposure, recognition, and funding. Still, the need for blockchain technology can be questioned. Ethereum, despite its novel design, currently contains several issues such as scalability [4], energy consumption [23], and lack of decentralization [12]. Instead, an independent group of trusted third parties could be used to manage the unique identifier of the smart contract. However, blockchain technology is also a marketing tool to arouse interest in a product [3] which in this scenario is the identity solution, or to arouse interest in an organization [1,2].

3.3 Scenario 3 - Agricultural Products Supply Chain

Scenario Description. In this third scenario a public permissioned blockchain called Hyperledger Fabric by IBM [5] is used. This blockchain tracks certificates in a supply chain of table grapes. In this scenario [11], a farmer in South Africa produces organic grapes, and presents such a claim to a certification authority. This authority issues a certificate to the farm, allowing the farm to certify its grapes. Grapes are stored in boxes, which are identified by a unique barcode.

To ensure a correct certification process, certification authorities are accredited by an accreditation authority. The certification authority stores the certificate it receives from an accreditation authority on the blockchain. Additionally, details of the certification authority are stored on the blockchain, so that anyone may see which party certified a farm. This entire process is audited. An auditor may revoke the certificate issued by the certification authority, for example, after the discovery of unauthorized pesticides [31] being used in the production of the fruits. An auditor also may revoke accreditations made by the accreditation authority. Here, both revocation types are recorded on the blockchain.

The grape boxes are shipped to resellers in Europe, after which the grapes are sold to supermarkets, and eventually to customers. Since it is unknown who may purchase the grapes, public verifiability is required. This allows all parties involved to query the blockchain for the validity of the organic certificate. Also, change of ownership is recorded in the blockchain, and provenance of the labeled boxes can be determined. From this description we observe that there are multiple, known writers. However, these writers are not trusted, as can be observed from the cascading audit trail from farmer to auditor.

Scenario Properties. In this scenario the origin and background of the grapes are stored on the blockchain. Furthermore, multiple writers are present, such as certificate authorities and auditors. Finally, the state stored must be publicly verifiable, as consumers verifying the grape origins must read from the blockchain. Furthermore, in this scenario it is clear that writers are not trusted, because there exists an extensive audit trail. However, blockchain technology does not replace the audit trail. In this scenario blockchain technology introduces a decentralized administrative system in which audit findings are stored. In fact, even with blockchain technology, audits still must be performed to ensure that each party involved follows the regulations. Although blockchain technology may offer insight in the entire audit trail, a shared centralized database could achieve the same. This database could be managed by the highest auditing authority in this grape scenario, as this is the final trusted party in the supply chain. Therefore, as there may exists a TTP, according to Wüst and Gervais [39], there is no technical rationale to use a blockchain in this scenario.

Philosophical Beliefs. In this scenario, blockchain technology is used as an alternative to a centralized solution. However, in any solution for this supply chain scenario, some form of trust is third parties is unavoidable, because trust has to be placed in auditors that audit the entire certification process. Furthermore, there is also trust in the shipping company for not changing the content of the grape boxes. For example, it would be feasible to exchange the contents of the boxes containing organic grapes with those boxes containing non-organic grapes during transport. Therefore, in essence, trust is placed in the integrity of the information stored on the blockchain. All participants rely that the information on the blockchain is correct only by trusting the auditors.

Network Effects. As blockchain is a complex technology, companies may experiment with it by creating proof of concepts. Indeed, the aim of the original scenario [11] was to provide a proof of concept based on blockchain technology. As other technologies, such as a centralized database, seem not to be considered, we assume that the use of blockchain technology is also driven by curiosity.

Economic Incentives. It benefits the technology supplier (here IBM) to use blockchain in this scenario, as it may provide related consulting services. Furthermore, the successful implementation of its technology serves as a platform for future scenarios. In such scenarios both the technology as well as consultancy may be provided. We therefore argue that in this scenario blockchain adoption is also driven by company principles.

Furthermore, in this scenario FOMO may also be a driver for blockchain adoption. Here, FOMO applies to all parties involved considering the potential of blockchain technology. However, as other technologies are not considered in [11], only blockchain seems to offer a solution to track certificates.

4 Discussion

All technical conditions must be met to ensure the appropriateness of using blockchain, if we follow the scheme of Wüst and Gervais [39]. However, in the uPort and supply chain scenarios only some technical drivers are addressed. Indeed, blockchain is used in both scenarios, despite that there appears to be no technical rationale to use blockchain, according to Wüst and Gervais [39]. Clearly, the scenario properties suggested in [39] alone are insufficient in explaining blockchain adoption.

As can be observed from Table 1, the majority of drivers for blockchain adoption in each of the three scenarios is non-technical. However, the technology supports at least one underlying technical property in a scenario, such as storing of state. Therefore, we conjecture that blockchain adoption is driven by a combination of both technical and non-technical drivers.

Furthermore, we observe that in each scenario a TTP *could* be used. Therefore, blockchain technology is not needed for any of these scenarios, according to [39]. However, in the Bitcoin scenario there used to be an underlying academic problem, namely, how can a consortium of unknown participants reach consensus. Nakamoto [22] aims to answer that question by introducing blockchain technology. Therefore, a rationale exists to use blockchain in the Bitcoin scenario.

5 Related Work

Although several models exists to determine technology acceptance, the Technology Acceptance Model [8] is most employed [7]. Blockchain technology and the Technology Acceptance Model (TAM) are discussed in, for example, [10], [3]. TAM is used to determine technology adoption based on two major considerations, *perceived usefulness* and *perceived ease of use* by the intended user. Depending on the research domain, TAM has been extended with other considerations such as 'perceived playfulness' for the web acceptance, and 'perceived user resources' in bulletin boards systems [14]. In our work we distinguish four considerations (i.e. the driver categories) for the adoption of blockchain.

Debabrata and Albert argue that blockchain may eliminate fraud in supply chain management [9]. However, eliminating fraud only by using a blockchain in the grape scenario is impossible. A TTP must remain present to verify the claims made by the farmers, certification authorities, and accreditation authorities. Here, blockchain cannot replace the trust in human observation of a complex process.

Seebacher and Schüritz propose that the qualitative aspects of transparency and autonomy play a role in blockchain adoption [24]. In addition to these two aspects, in our work we argue that blockchain adoption lies in both the technical and non-technical drivers, and we identified a total of 20 drivers.

6 Future Work

In our work we have shown that technical and non-technical drivers exist for blockchain technology adoption. Various models have been suggested to support this decision making process, as discussed in Sect. 2. These models, however, do not mention alternatives to blockchain. A further analysis, and a possible extension of these models is needed to determine if blockchain is appropriate.

Also, trust in a third party appears to be a much broader concept than the trust a blockchain can offer. In fact, this technology appears to provide trust in integrity of the data recorded on the blockchain. However, we assume that the trust needed by a participant goes beyond integrity of data alone. Therefore, it is unlikely that blockchain can fully replace a TTP. Additionally, the concept of trust has been defined in many ways [19]. For example, one way of defining trust is the willingness to depend, meaning that you make yourself vulnerable to another person in a situation by relying on them [18]. However, these many definitions also makes that the concept of trust is diffuse, and it is unclear what is defined as a *Trusted* Third Party. How blockchain shifts trust, and which types of trust are affected by blockchain also seem interesting subjects for further explorationBlock.

Furthermore, additional scenarios that involve blockchain technology could be analyzed in order to determine the value of blockchain technology over alternative technological solutions. Here, possibly more drivers for blockchain technology adoption may be found. Also, extending this work by adding weights to the drivers may be part of future work. Adding weight to drivers allow for determining which driver influences blockchain technology adoption most.

7 Conclusion

Many people have questioned the rationale behind blockchain adoption [6,16]. To support such claims, methodologies have been proposed to see if blockchain suits a particular scenario [20,39]. Such methodologies are mainly based on technical drivers, which are properties inherent to a scenario. In real-life scenarios we see that sometimes a blockchain-based solution is chosen even if these methodologies would argue against that.

Given the inherent lack of technical drivers in some scenarios, the choice for blockchain technology may seem irrational. Our novel insight is that blockchain adoption may be explained by non-technical drivers, namely philosophical beliefs, network effects and economic incentives. These drivers may explain, after all, the rationale behind blockchain adoption. Our work can be generalized to other scenarios that involve cryptocurrencies, identity management solutions and supply chains, as it is likely that similar scenarios contain the same drivers.

References

1. Liao, S.: Tea, juice, and vape companies add 'blockchain' to their names to profit on bitcoin mania. https://www.theverge.com/2017/12/21/16805598/companies-blockchain-tech-cryptocurrency-tea
2. McDermott, J.: Company stock prices have been going up every time they even mention using blockchain. https://melmagazine.com/a-companys-stocks-have-been-going-up-even-if-it-just-mentions-blockchain-2f8c02472422
3. Baur, A.W., Bühler, J., Bick, M., Bonorden, C.S.: Cryptocurrencies as a disruption? Empirical findings on user adoption and future potential of Bitcoin and co. In: Janssen, M., et al. (eds.) I3E 2015. LNCS, vol. 9373, pp. 63–80. Springer, Cham (2015). https://doi.org/10.1007/978-3-319-25013-7_6
4. Buterin, V.: Ethereum scalability research and development subsidy programs. https://blog.ethereum.org/2018/01/02/ethereum-scalability-research-development-subsidy-programs/

5. Cachin, C.: Architecture of the hyperledger blockchain fabric. In: Workshop on Distributed Cryptocurrencies and Consensus Ledgers, July 2016
6. Carter, L., Ubacht, J.: Blockchain applications in government. In: Proceedings of the 19th Annual International Conference on Digital Government Research: Governance in the Data Age, p. 126. ACM (2018)
7. Dauda, S.Y., Lee, J.: Technology adoption: a conjoint analysis of consumers preference on future online banking services. Inf. Syst. **53**, 1–15 (2015)
8. Davis, F.D.: A Technology Acceptance Model for Empirically Testing New End-User Information Systems: Theory and Results. Ph.D. thesis, Massachusetts Institute of Technology (1985)
9. Debabrata, G., Albert, T.: A Framework for implementing blockchain technologies to improve supply chain performance (2018). http://hdl.handle.net/1721.1/113244
10. Folkinshteyn, D., Lennon, M.: Braving Bitcoin: a technology acceptance model (TAM) analysis. J. Inf. Technol. Case Appl. Res. **18**(4), 220–249 (2016)
11. Ge, L., et al.: Blockchain for agriculture and food. No. 2017–112, Wageningen Economic Research (2017)
12. Gencer, A.E., Basu, S., Eyal, I., van Renesse, R., Sirer, E.G.: Decentralization in Bitcoin and ethereum networks. arXiv preprint arXiv:1801.03998 (2018)
13. Glaser, F., Zimmermann, K., Haferkorn, M., Weber, M., Siering, M.: Bitcoin - asset or currency? Revealing users' hidden intentions. In: Proceedings of the 22nd European Conference on Information Systems, Tel Aviv, June 2013
14. Hsu, C.L., Lu, H.P.: Why do people play on-line games? An extended TAM with social influences and flow experience. Inf. Manag. **41**(7), 853–868 (2004)
15. Liang, X., Shetty, S., Tosh, D., Kamhoua, C., Kwiat, K., Njilla, L.: Provchain: a blockchain-based data provenance architecture in cloud environment with enhanced privacy and availability. In: Proceedings of the 17th IEEE/ACM International Symposium on Cluster, Cloud and Grid Computing, pp. 468–477. IEEE Press (2017)
16. Mattila, J., Seppälä, T., Holmström, J.: Product-centric information management: a case study of a shared platform with blockchain technology (2016)
17. Maull, R., Godsiff, P., Mulligan, C., Brown, A., Kewell, B.: Distributed ledger technology: applications and implications. Strat. Chang. **26**(5), 481–489 (2017)
18. Mayer, R.C., Davis, J.H., Schoorman, F.D.: An integrative model of organizational trust. Acad. Manag. Rev. **20**(3), 709–734 (1995)
19. McKnight, D.H., Chervany, N.L.: What is trust? A conceptual analysis and an interdisciplinary model. In: AMCIS 2000 Proceedings, p. 382 (2000)
20. Meunier, S.: When do you need blockchain? Decision models. https://medium.com/@sbmeunier/when-do-you-need-blockchain-decision-models-a5c40e7c9ba1
21. Möser, M.: Anonymity of Bitcoin transactions: an analysis of mixing services. In: Proceedings of Münster Bitcoin Conference (2013)
22. Nakamoto, S.: Bitcoin: a peer-to-peer electronic cash system (2008). https://bitcoin.org/bitcoin.pdf
23. O'Dwyer, K.J., Malone, D.: Bitcoin mining and its energy footprint. In: Proceedings of the Irish Signals and Systems Conference, pp. 280–285 (2014)
24. Omran, Y., Henke, M., Heines, R., Hofmann, E.: Blockchain-driven supply chain finance: towards a conceptual framework from a buyer perspective (2017). https://www.alexandria.unisg.ch/251095/
25. Peck, M.E.: Blockchain world-do you need a blockchain? This chart will tell you if the technology can solve your problem. IEEE Spectr. **54**(10), 38–60 (2017)
26. Perlman, R.: Blockchain: hype or hope? Login **42**(2), 68–72 (2017)

27. Peters, G.W., Panayi, E.: Understanding modern banking ledgers through blockchain technologies: future of transaction processing and smart contracts on the internet of money. In: Tasca, P., Aste, T., Pelizzon, L., Perony, N. (eds.) Banking Beyond Banks and Money. NEW, pp. 239–278. Springer, Cham (2016). https://doi.org/10.1007/978-3-319-42448-4_13
28. Pilkington, M.: 11 blockchain technology: principles and applications. In: Research Handbook on Digital Transformations, p. 225 (2016)
29. Pop, C., Cioara, T., Antal, M., Anghel, I., Salomie, I., Bertoncini, M.: Blockchain based decentralized management of demand response programs in smart energy grids. Sensors **18**(1), 162 (2018)
30. Ron, D., Shamir, A.: Quantitative analysis of the full Bitcoin transaction graph. In: Sadeghi, A.-R. (ed.) FC 2013. LNCS, vol. 7859, pp. 6–24. Springer, Heidelberg (2013). https://doi.org/10.1007/978-3-642-39884-1_2
31. SABS Standards Division: South African National Standard, Organic Agriculture - Production and Processing. http://www.agro-organics.co.za/wp-content/uploads/2016/10/SABS-TC2110_N0009_SANS1369_ED1_SABSTC2110_DSS_secured.pdf
32. Seebacher, S., Schüritz, R.: Blockchain technology as an enabler of service systems: a structured literature review. In: Za, S., Drăgoicea, M., Cavallari, M. (eds.) IESS 2017. LNBIP, vol. 279, pp. 12–23. Springer, Cham (2017). https://doi.org/10.1007/978-3-319-56925-3_2
33. Swan, M.: Blockchain: Blueprint for a New Economy. O'Reilly Media Inc., Sebastopol (2015)
34. Swartz, L.: blockchain dreams: imagining techno-economic alternatives after Bitcoin. In: Another Economy Is Possible: Culture and Economy in a Time of Crisis, pp. 82–105. Polity Cambridge (2017)
35. Underwood, S.: Blockchain beyond Bitcoin. Commun. ACM **59**(11), 15–17 (2016)
36. uPort: Open identity system for the decentralized web. https://www.uport.me/
37. Urquhart, A.: Price clustering in bitcoin. Econ. Lett. **159**, 145–148 (2017)
38. Wood, G.: Ethereum: a secure decentralised generalised transaction ledger. Ethereum Proj. Yellow Pap. **151**, 1–32 (2014)
39. Wüst, K., Gervais, A.: Do you need a blockchain? IACR Cryptology ePrint Archive **2017**, 375 (2017)
40. Yli-Huumo, J., Ko, D., Choi, S., Park, S., Smolander, K.: Where is current research on blockchain technology? A systematic review. PloS one **11**(10), e0163477 (2016)

Field Experiment on the Performance of an Android-Based Opportunistic Network

Andre Ippisch(✉), Philipp Brühn, and Kalman Graffi

Heinrich-Heine-University Düsseldorf,
Universitätsstraße 1, 40225 Düsseldorf, Germany
{ippisch,philipp.bruehn,graffi}@hhu.de

Abstract. Android smartphones ubiquitously available, they are mobile and have sophisticated communication opportunities. With Opportunistic Networks, we can use the wireless connectivity of smartphones and other smart devices to relay messages in store-carry-forward fashion from one node to another to implement novel data-oriented applications. We can use these networks for high-bandwidth local data transfers, in cases with low or no connectivity, such as in third-world countries or remote areas, or in cases where communication should not leave any traces. In the last years, we developed an Android application for Opportunistic Networking, named *opptain*, that can be deployed on off-the-shelf unrooted smartphones and smart devices, enabling to harness this idea by simply installing an app. As the quality of such networks is essential, we implemented a test framework for Android-based opportunistic networks to run tests and aggregate results automatically. In this paper, we present the evaluation results of a field experiment we conducted with the *opptain* application, in which we used 26 devices to evaluate the outcome typical use cases. The tests show that the expected quality is reached and provides robust performance for various applications. In total, *opptain*, the testing environment, as well as the results themselves, are promising; for an office scenario in which interference is more common than in other possible scenarios, we achieved encouraging results.

Keywords: Opportunistic Networks · Android · Smartphones
Smart devices · Field tests · Measurement study

1 Introduction

Opportunistic Networks (OppNets) are disorganized Delay Tolerant Networks (DTNs) with typically not existing end-to-end paths between nodes at a given time. Nodes in OppNets can be represented by, among others, human-carried equipment like smartphones, tablets, and other smart devices. Since there is no end-to-end path between nodes, *Store, Carry and Forward* routing is used in these networks. By this, messages can be passed on from node to node in

G. Mencagli et al. (Eds.): Euro-Par 2018 Workshops, LNCS 11339, pp. 547–558, 2019.
https://doi.org/10.1007/978-3-030-10549-5_43

the proximity, whenever an opportunity of data exchange occurs, which happens through the mobility of the nodes. We can classify routing schemes into flooding-based and utility-based approaches. The simple Epidemic [10] routing approach is a flooding-based routing scheme which replicates messages to every encountered node that does not yet own a message copy. One of the utility-based routing schemes, on the other hand, is PRoPHET [5] which relays messages only if the connected node has higher delivery predictability.

Researchers working on OppNets are only able to simulate sufficiently large networks. For simulating OppNets, there are multiple tools available [1], such as *The ONE Simulator* [4] and *PeerfactSim.KOM* [2]. We can take results from the simulators to improve real-life OppNets, but it is also desirable that results of real-life OppNets improve the parameters of the simulator.

Real implementations of OppNets are limited to communicating devices handed out by one organizer. One example is the Sámi Network Connectivity project [6] which provides network connectivity to nomadic reindeer herders. The authors of [7] give another example which describes conference badges which are used by researchers to connect and exchange research interests. If there is a match, the user is made aware of the communication partner and a conversation is initialized. Additional information about their research can be exchanged automatically and used by the device owner after the conference. These current use cases only support a limited number of participants.

We use non-rooted off-the-shelf Android devices to establish OppNets on mobile devices and thus opening the opportunity for OppNets with millions or billions of users. Android devices "continue to capture roughly 85% of the worldwide smartphone volume"[1]. *opptain* [3] is an Android-based application to establish OppNets on smartphones and other smart devices. We are working on *opptain* with regard to connection possibilities, routing schemes, forwarding strategies, drop policies, security, and multiple signal way transmissions. We implemented several routing schemes, forward and drop policies and have multiple third-party applications available. Implemented routing schemes are PRoPHET, Epidemic, and (Binary) Spray & Wait/Focus [8,9]. The third-party applications can use the provided API to use the opptain network; under ongoing development are catastrophe, chat, file sharing, and gaming applications, as well as a distributed database. This shows the wide range of applications possible to run through this local, trace-less communication.

To test opptain and to create automatically running field tests, we developed a test framework application. This framework helps to distribute a settings file to all test devices opportunistically. All devices start the test at the same time, and after the test period, all individual results are aggregated on one device for evaluation.

The goal of this paper is to show that Android-based OppNets are capable of successfully transmitting and delivering data such as chat messages or files. By establishing such an OppNet, messages and files that are not time crucial can be

[1] See https://www.gartner.com/newsroom/id/3859963.

transmitted locally and without an Internet connection. This is interesting for a variety of situations.

During an *office scenario*, for example, there are both messages and files that are not time crucial among others that cannot be delayed and have to be transmitted in almost real-time like in prioritized emails. The former mentioned messages and files, however, can be transmitted via our OppNet.

Another example is a *catastrophe scenario* where there may be a loss of Internet connection to communicate with each other. Crucial in this scenario would be people in need of help which could be asked for with the help of an OppNet built up by smartphones from exactly those people involved. A message or rather request for help could be either answered or carried along by every participant in range and later on received by another person and delivered successfully respectively.

Also, our OppNet is applicable for situations with no infrastructure in general like areas with strict Internet surveillance going on, where communication must be hidden or is otherwise blocked. In such a *censorship-risky scenario*, people can communicate through an OppNet to stay connected and self-sufficient.

opptain may also be deployed in great rural areas without infrastructure. In a *village scenario*, there is a large area to cover for transmitting messages between villages or small towns. In this use case, delay is not crucial considering inter-village movement is rather slow.

The contributions of this paper are the following:

- We developed a methodology for evaluating Android-based OppNets.
- We developed a test framework for the evaluation, for which different routing protocols, forward and drop policies, TTLs or many different OppNet-related variations can be tested.
- We ran an initial field test with 26 devices. We created a testbed of devices and ran it with real people in our university building representing a use case.
- We present and discuss the findings of this field experiment.

The results show that we can use an Android-based OppNet to forward information in office scenarios. We discuss how we can use these results for the prediction of other scenarios, like catastrophe situations.

2 Methodology for Evaluating Opportunistic Networks

In this section, we present the methodology to evaluate OppNets in general, and specific for Android-based OppNets. We define the metrics that are used to evaluate OppNets and the message states to determine those. After that, we define our experimental setup to test the opptain application in a field experiment.

At the end of this section, we defined our test setup and metrics to present the evaluation in the next section.

2.1 Message States

In this section, we define the state of a message in the network. In OppNets a message can either be at the sending node, a relaying node, or the destination.

The essential *message states* are the following:

1. *'generated'* describes that a message is generated at some node.
2. *'received'* describes that the message is forwarded to a relay node but not the destination.
3. *'delivered'* describes that the message reached its destination.
4. *'reacted'* describes that a new message is generated in reaction to a delivered message. The delivered message's origin serves as the new recipient.

Both, simulators and our test framework track these message states as input for the metrics' formulas. We show these metrics in the following section.

2.2 Metrics

In this section we present the metrics for evaluation of our network. We identify *Delivery Ratio* and *Delay* as the primary metrics and *Overhead Ratio* and *Hop Count* as secondary metrics. While these four metrics can be used in OppNets generally, two additional metrics, *Client Time* and *Hotspot Time*, are important metrics for our specific Android-based OppNet.

The metrics used in this paper are the following:

1. *Delivery Ratio* is the ratio between delivered messages and generated ones. Therefore, it is calculated with

$$DR = M_{Delivered}/M_{Generated} \tag{1}$$

   where M is the sum of messages and DR is the calculated delivery ratio. As there are no end-to-end paths in OppNets, message delivery is not guaranteed. Therefore, *Delivery Ratio* is an essential measure for OppNets.
2. *Delay* is the time that successfully delivered messages need to reach their destination. Therefore, it is calculated with

$$D = TS_{Delivered} - TS_{Generated} \tag{2}$$

   where TS is the time in seconds and D is the calculated delay. As messages are relayed in store-carry-forward fashion *Delay* is used to measure the quality of the network.
3. *Overhead Ratio* is the ratio between transmissions and delivered messages. Therefore, it is calculated with

$$OR = M_{Transmitted}/M_{Delivered} \tag{3}$$

$$M_{Transmitted} = M_{Received} + M_{Delivered} \tag{4}$$

   where M is the sum of messages and OR is the calculated overhead ratio. We track *Overhead Ratio* as most routing protocols create message copies and all copies are transmitted more often than necessary.

4. *Hop Count* is the number of hops that are necessary to deliver a message.
5. *Client/Hotspot Time* is the duration a device is either hotspot or client. Android devices are not able to connect in ad-hoc fashion but use the Wi-Fi infrastructure mode [3]. Due to these limitations a device is either a tethering hotspot or acts as a client, and the devices have to be in different states to transfer data. The duration of *Client Time* and *Hotspot Time* show how long the devices are in each state, respectively.

2.3 Setup of Field Test

In this section, we describe the setup of our field tests. The goal of this evaluation and field test is to show how an Android-based OppNet performs in a typical office scenario with reasonable demand for data exchange. An office scenario provides us the possibility to test our network application in a realistic environment. We handed out 26 pre-configured, unrooted Android mobile devices, out of which 18 were mobile and eight static during office time.

With the help of our test framework, it is possible to set parameters in opptain. Possible settings are routing protocol, TTL, message size, the time interval in which messages are generated, the probability to *react* to a delivered message. These settings can be changed in a simulator as well so that a supportive comparison in a simulator is doable. A simulator could also emulate the network and opportunistic meetings, based on our field study. In the field test, the devices are spread to users. Our test framework can aggregate the data and log the message states on sending, relaying and receiving devices. Thus, the field tests could be reproduced in simulation.

In our test setup, we choose an overall test duration of five hours since these are the core hours of an average office day in our test environment. Crucial during this time are TTL and routing protocols as those are varied parameters. For routing, we choose either Epidemic [10] or PRoPHET [5] with a *routingMinP* of 0.4 and 150 and 300 min TTL respectively. The randomly generated messages are at a fixed size of 10 Kb. The response probability is set to 70 which implies that there is a 70% chance that there will be a direct reaction to a delivered message.

We choose to model the network into four communication islands (subnetworks) to simulate opportunistic behavior through individual offices. Islands 2 and 4 each consist of four devices whereas island 1 consists of ten and island 3 of eight devices. Communication between islands is only possible if the participants move around within the range of other participants' devices.

We chose to run two field tests simultaneously. Both networks are defined that only devices of the own network can connect to each other. Running two field test at the same time has two advantages: First, we can cope with possible outages of devices. Second, we can compare two test runs with the same parameters, pattern of movement, and social interaction of the participants. A disadvantage might be the WiFi interference of the networks to each other, but in a typical office scenario, there already is WiFi interference.

Table 1. Numerical results

Network	Min	Max	Avg
All	0.48	15844.26	1375.03
Reacted	0.48	15519.59	660.77
1	0.57	15519.59	842.99
2	0.90	2327.90	109.55
3	1.34	8351.99	621.41
4	2.60	5743.31	203.13

(a) Delay (s)

Network	Min	Max	Avg
All	38.31	71.44	60.85
Reacted	67.90	86.66	79.60
1	49.15	86.61	75.25
2	0.00	100.00	68.88
3	6.52	80.79	51.22
4	0.00	100.00	85.94

(b) Delivery Ratio (%)

Network	Min	Max	Avg
All	4.44	6.39	5.15
Reacted	2.58	3.78	3.11
1	4.05	9.34	6.32
2	2.48	10.20	4.83
3	2.56	30.00	8.63
4	2.95	10.91	4.99

(c) Overhead Ratio

Network	Min	Max	Avg
All	1.00	7.00	1.97
1	1.00	4.00	1.39
2	1.00	1.00	1.00
3	1.00	3.00	1.24
4	1.00	1.00	1.00

(d) Hop Count

Network	Min	Max	Avg
All	0.099	328.028	43.472
1	0.099	325.007	48.453
2	9.803	40.936	22.923
3	0.109	328.028	49.790
4	15.271	57.210	34.745

(e) Client Time (s)

Network	Min	Max	Avg
All	30.014	234.191	53.476
1	30.069	234.191	57.500
2	30.014	77.045	47.219
3	30.017	137.158	53.655
4	33.013	70.048	48.026

(f) Hotspot Time (s)

3 Performance of Real World Opportunistic Networks

In this section, we evaluate the performance of real-world OppNets based on the metrics described in the last section. In the end, results are related to one another and discussed.

The measurements indicate as the main result that the OppNet for our test purpose is at all events capable of reliably transmitting data with an average delay of 1375.03 s and a delivery ratio of 60.85%. In the following, we depict the results of our field tests. Note that we evaluate the overall average of all field tests merged with all sub-networks and additionally we evaluate the overall average of all field tests partitioned by every single sub-network.

Figure 3 shows results separated by test runs. The first two characters indicate the number of the test and its duplication; the three digits indicate the TTL of 150 and 300 min respectively. The last character indicates the routing protocol used for testing (either [e]pidemic or [p]RoPHET).

Thus, we can analyze every single sub-network completely encapsulated from each other without intersection (see Table 1). In this case, we consider only messages *generated*, *received*, *delivered* and *reacted* inside this sub-network. Therefore, these messages are just a subset of all messages and no inter-sub-network transmissions are considered. That is why it is not possible to compare the overall overhead ratio of all field tests to that of only a single sub-network.

Delay. On average a message's delay was 1375.03 s (~23 min) from its creation time until it was successfully delivered. The value of the upper bound is 15844.23 s (~4.4 h) and therefore about 11.5 times higher than the average value. With a value of roughly just half of a second, the lower bound shows a rather

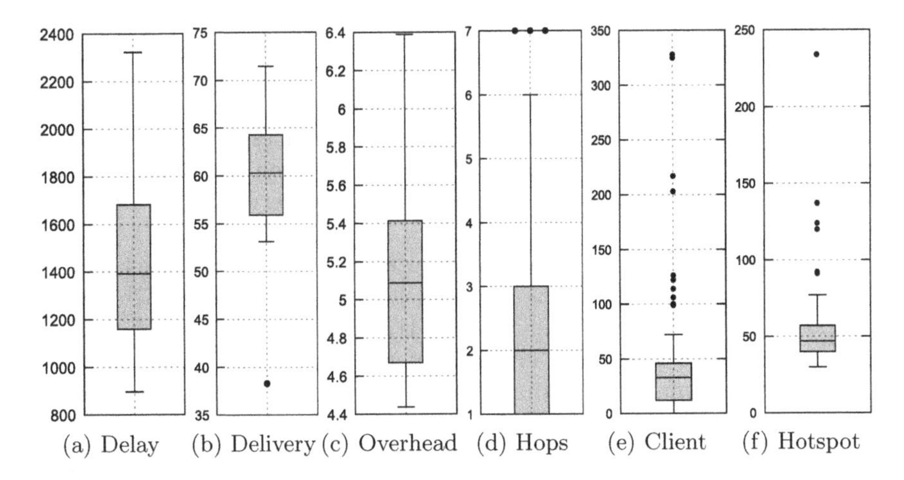

Fig. 1. Box plots of the metrics

fast transmission. Thus, the highest delay of all field tests is almost as long as the overall test duration.

50% of delay per message is in the range of around 1150 s (~19 min) to 1700 s (~28 min). The upper 25% of delay is between approximately 1700 and 2250 s (~37.5 min) (see Fig. 1a).

Sub-networks 1 and 3 show an average delay of 842.99 (~14 min) and 621.41 s (~10.3 min) respectively whereas sub-networks 2 and 4 present a faster transmission (see Table 1) of 109.41 (~1.8 min) and 203.13 s (~3.4 min). Also, the upper bounds correspond in this manner. As of sub-networks 1 and 3, there is a maximum delay of 15519.59 and 8341.99 s. Sub-networks 2 and 4 show us a delay of 2327.90 and 5741.31 s.

Delivery Ratio. Having a closer look at the delivery ratio we see that of all generated messages on average 60.85% arrived at their randomly selected destination. The upper and lower bounds are at 71.44 and 38.31%. 50% of the delivery ratios are between about 56 and 64%, and the upper 25% are in the range of around 64 and 72%. There is one outlier set at the absolute minimum of 38.31% (see Fig. 1b). As for the sub-networks values of the lower bound strongly differ from each other ranging from 0 to 49.15% delivery rate. The upper bound ranges from 71.44 to 100%.

Overhead Ratio. The overhead ratio of all field tests shows us that for every message delivered to its destination 5.15 messages were received by relay nodes on an average. Thus, it appears that for one message to be successfully delivered almost 40% of all nodes received this message. We see that the upper and lower limits are 6.39 and 4.44 respectively. There is no significantly high or low value relative to the average value, so it seems all networks were flooded with messages almost evenly. This appears to be plausible considering that the test framework randomly generates messages in a uniformly distributed span of time. So the more messages are generated, the more can and will be transmitted. Also, since we only use routing protocols on the basis of flooding messages are spread very broadly. This behavior was presumed during preparation. 50% of all overhead is set between 4.8 and 5.4 generated messages per delivery. 25% set from 5.4 to 6.39 messages (see Fig. 1c).

As for the sub-networks, there are more broad ranges from lower to upper bounds. At a maximum, there is an overhead of 30 messages (4.67 times the overall average value). At a minimum, there is an overhead of 2.48 messages (1.73 times the overall average value). The average values differ by 3.48 messages (sub-network 3) at maximum and by 0.16 (sub-network 4) at minimum. It is evident that sub-network 3's upper limit is quite elevated compared to the corresponding average's value (see Table 1) That is because numerous messages did not reach their destination. However, this is only the worst-case of all field tests and the average value distributed across all field tests is much more significant. Such a peak might happen inside an OppNet since the results of our study are entirely dependent on human movement and interaction with each other.

Hop Count. The average hop count is oscillating around two hops and is almost constant through all field test. The maximum value over all four sub-networks ranges from 1 to 7. Half of all hops of all networks and all tests are in the range of 1 to 3 (see Fig. 1d). While 22.5% of all hops are in the range of 3 to 6 hops, only 2.5% of all hops are placing at 7 hops. Sub-networks 2 and 4 have an average of 1 hop, which is the only possible option since each sub-network consists of two devices.

Client Time Versus Hotspot Time. The overall time a device resides in client state is about 43 s compared to about 53 s in hotspot state (see Fig. 1e and f). In sub-networks 1 and 3 there is a maximum of 325 and 328 s (~5 min) respectively in client state and for both sub-networks a minimum of one-tenth of a second. This seems to be a very small value and is due to the mode of operation of opptain which may not be able to establish this state and continue to its next one entirely. In hotspot state, there is a maximum of 234 and 137 s and a minimum of 30 s.

50% of all devices reside in a range of about 10 to 49 s in client task. The upper 22.5% range from 49 to about 75 s whereas the top 2.5% of all client times range from 100 to a maximum of 328 s.

50% of hotspot times reside in the range of roughly 48 to 53 s. Thus, this task is oscillating around 50 s at an average. The upper 22.5% range from about 53 to 80 s. However the last 2.5% of the upper bound ranges from about 95 to 234 s.

In sub-networks 2 and 4, the ranges of client task and hotspot task combined set from 22.923 s to 48.026 s. Thus, sub-networks 2 and 4 show a more narrow span of time in contrast to sub-networks 1 and 3.

Table 2. Numerical results of message states

Nw.	Min	Max	Avg
All	539	726	663.38
1	63	102	84.13
2	4	9	5.75
3	41	60	50.88
4	5	15	8.63

(a) Generated Messages

Nw.	Min	Max	Avg
All	2344	4778	3637.62
1	602	1314	1068.5
2	0	129	75
3	121	779	395.63
4	2	124	102.5

(b) Received Messages

Nw.	Min	Max	Avg
All	367	983	724,25
1	298	488	399,63
2	0	128	74,38
3	80	382	223,75
4	2	123	102

(c) Delivered Messages

Nw.	Min	Max	Avg
All	271	742	545
1	43	234	137,88
2	0	38	15,25
3	5	119	57,13
4	0	30	16,88

(d) Reacted Messages

Message States. Figure 2 and Table 2 show a distribution of the four predominant states a message can be in. As for generated messages, there is an average of 663.38 over 5 h test duration. Thus, about 2.1 messages per minute are generated. On an average 545 messages are resent as a reaction of delivered ones. Roughly 720 messages are delivered. Included in those are also messages reacted on. With an average of 3637.62 messages, received messages are about 5.5 times the size of generated ones.

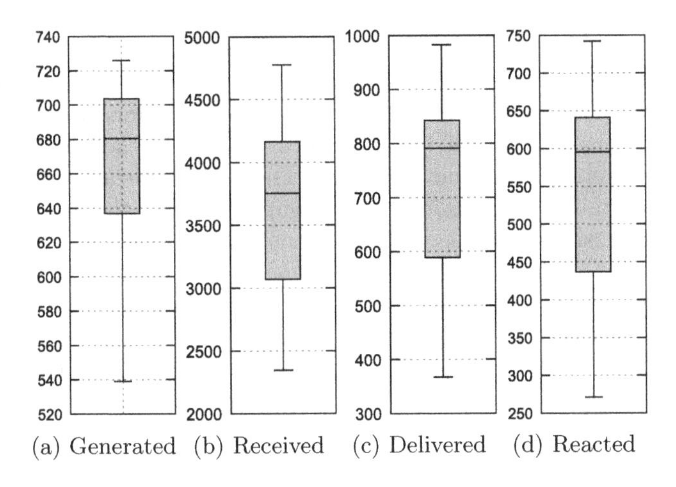

(a) Generated (b) Received (c) Delivered (d) Reacted

Fig. 2. Number of messages for each state

Reacted Messages. Delivered messages are reacted on at an average of 75.25%. That produced an overhead of 3.11 received messages per delivery. Thus, that is nearly two-thirds of the overall overhead ratio (see Table 1). Messages reacted on are delivered at an average of 79.6% with a delay of 660.77 s (~11 min).

These numbers allow identifying possible use cases of OppNet-based applications on Android-based smartphones in an office environment.

4 Discussion

In this section, we correlate the previously described outcome of our field tests. First, we compare the individual test runs among each other emphasizing commonalities and differences, followed by a general discussion of all results.

A test run with a TTL of 300 min was expected to be much worse concerning overhead ratio than a run with a TTL of 150 min as there would be much more transferable messages inside the network. Both are conducted with the Epidemic routing protocol. The equivalent test runs *1A-150e* & *1B-150e* and *3A-300e* & *3B-300e* show however that this assumption cannot be verified evidently.

Epidemic routing supposedly produces a higher overhead than its modified version PRoPHET which uses a threshold value and algorithms to determine a suitable node to forward a message to. Also, it was expected that PRoPHET presents a superior ratio between overhead and delivery meaning there would be the same delivery ratio with less overhead ratio. These assumptions are also not supported.

Test run *3A-300e* presents the highest values in overhead ratio, delay and hop count plus the lowest delivery ratio (see Fig. 3). In theory, a high overhead ratio can be linked to an elevated hop count and slow transmission. We would expect both high delivery ratio and high overhead ratio combined since the chance would be higher to deliver a message with an elevated overhead ratio.

The delay of *1A-150e* and *1B-150e* is very low in comparison to the other test runs. This can be explained with the possibility that the TTL may run out and messages eventually are not delivered. The high overhead ratio of *3A-300e* and *3B-300e* is an indication for this assumption. Also, there is a possibility that the client tasks and hotspot tasks did not run in favor of each other. It is an issue of smartphones that two devices may not be able to connect to each other because a client may only connect to a hotspot and not to another client. Nevertheless, this is the only option for unrooted devices to interact with each other without user interaction. It is the same with a hotspot that cannot connect to another hotspot.

It is striking that test run *3B-300e* presents the lowest overhead combined with the highest delivery ratio while supposedly being the same as *3A-300e* in configuration and pattern of movement. This vast difference in delay and overhead can be explained by the fact that one device failed during test run *3B-300e*. Thus, potentially relevant data is lost, and results are tampered. The failed device taken in account, the delivery ratio would be equal or even higher than it already is. It is also important to see how important the message ferry devices are in such networks.

In the test runs *1A-150e* and *1B-150e*, overhead ratio, delivery ratio and delay are all roughly similar to those of test runs *4A-300p* and *4B-300p* respectively. This is quite interesting since the first tests are performed with a TTL of 150 min and with Epidemic routing as the last two tests are set up with 300 min of TTL and the PRoPHET routing protocol. Thus, both groups of tests run on an entirely different configuration.

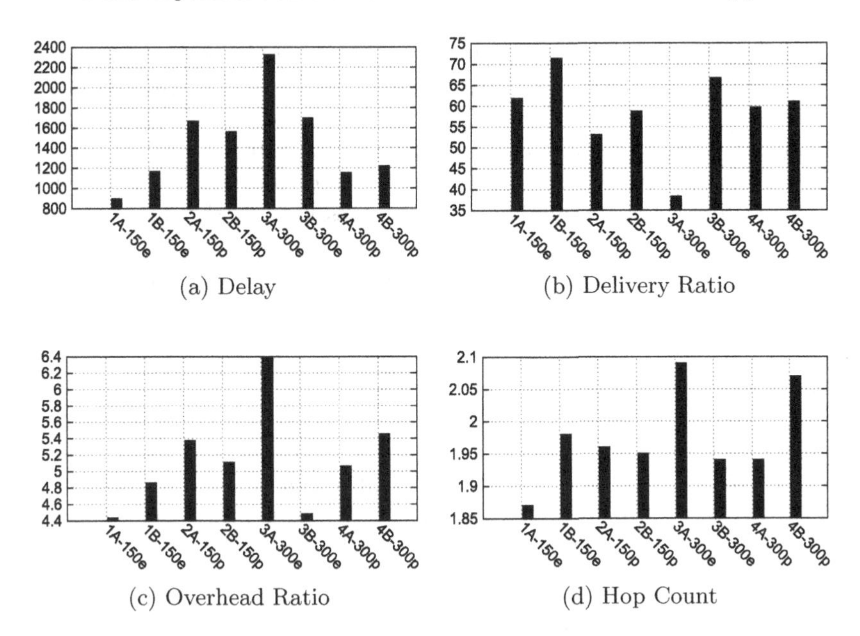

Fig. 3. Evaluation analysis according to the various setups

Almost the same results are presented looking at Table 1. Reacted messages are delivered at a maximum rate of almost 90% plus with nearly half of the overhead of all messages and with a comparatively low delay of 400 to 600 s.

These results are a strong indication that both setups fit quite well for a use case in a scenario in which messages are exchanged continuously and are supposed to be reacted on, such as in an office scenario.

5 Conclusion

This section concludes the previously presented results and correlates these with realistic scenarios and use cases of OppNets.

Our evaluation shows that our smartphone-based OppNets can successfully deliver data such as chat messages or files. We show that it is possible for participants to engage in a conversation and keep it maintained, though, with a certain delay. Thus, OppNets can practically be used to sustain a local communication structure with specific use cases. The results pose possibilities for a few real-life scenarios like an average office day, catastrophe or censorship situations or the village scenario. The used parameters may be applied to all of those situations.

Since it is essential that the vast majority of messages are delivered, we propose to neglect overhead ratio in favor of delivery ratio. As we can see from the results, all proposed scenarios rely on the social interaction of people in general. Therefore, our OppNet only works through people's movement and performs even better with an equal distribution of participants inside the network area.

Our OppNet may not be suitable for real-time transmission (for example VoIP) since it is not guaranteed that there is a stable and constant connection at all times. However, overall delay in a chat or mail conversation generally poses no significant problem as long as time is no crucial factor.

For the future, we plan further testing in larger scenarios with the applications sketched in the introduction. This includes varying the message size, the message creation frequency, and the mobility patterns to support more scenarios. There are many parameters in general which can be adjusted and have to be evaluated.

References

1. Cheraghi, A., Amft, T., Sati, S., Hagemeister, P., Graffi, K.: The state of simulation tools for P2P networks on mobile ad-hoc and opportunistic networks. In: IEEE ICCCN 2016: Proceedings of the International Conference on Computer Communication and Networks, pp. 1–7 (2016)
2. Graffi, K.: PeerfactSim.KOM: a P2P system simulator - experiences and lessons learned. In: IEEE P2P 2011: Proceedings of the International Conference on Peer-to-Peer Computing, pp. 154–155 (2011)
3. Ippisch, A., Graffi, K.: Infrastructure mode based opportunistic networks on android devices. In: 2017 IEEE 31st International Conference on Advanced Information Networking and Applications (AINA), pp. 454–461 (2017). https://doi.org/10.1109/AINA.2017.32
4. Keränen, A., Ott, J., Kärkkäinen, T.: The ONE simulator for DTN protocol evaluation. In: SIMUTools 2009: Proceedings of the 2nd International Conference on Simulation Tools and Techniques. ICST, New York, NY, USA (2009)
5. Lindgren, A., Doria, A., Davies, E., Grasic, S.: RFC 6693: probabilistic routing protocol for intermittently connected networks. IETF (2012)
6. Lindgren, A., Doria, A., Lindblom, J., Ek, M.: Networking in the land of northern lights: two years of experiences from DTN system deployments. In: Wireless Networks and Systems for Developing Regions (2008)
7. Mühlhäuser, M.: Handbook of Research on Ubiquitous Computing Technology for Real Time Enterprises. Handbook of Research On... Series. IGI Global (2008). https://books.google.de/books?id=PQjsqETjwhYC
8. Spyropoulos, T., Psounis, K.: Spray and wait: an efficient routing scheme for intermittently connected mobile networks. In: Proceedings of the ACM SIGCOMM Workshop on Delay-Tolerant Networking (2005)
9. Spyropoulos, T., Psounis, K., Raghavendra, C.S.: Spray and focus: efficient mobility-assisted routing for heterogeneous and correlated mobility. In: Proceedings of the IEEE International Conference on Pervasive Computing and Communications - Workshops (PerCom Workshops), pp. 79–85 (2007)
10. Vahdat, A., Becker, D.: Epidemic routing for partially-connected ad hoc networks. Technique report, Department of Computer Science, Duke University, USA, vol. 20, no. 6 (2000)

Distributed Computation of Mobility Patterns in a Smart City Environment

Eugenio Cesario, Franco Cicirelli, and Carlo Mastroianni(✉)

ICAR-CNR, Rende, CS, Italy
{cesario,cicirelli,mastroianni}@icar.cnr.it

Abstract. This paper copes with the issue of extracting mobility patterns in a urban computing scenario. The computation is parallelized by partitioning the territory into a number of regions. In each region a computing node collects data from a set of local sensors, analyzes the data and coordinates with neighbor regions to extract the mobility patterns. We propose and analyze a "local" synchronization approach, where computation regarding a specific region is performed using the information received from a subset of neighbor regions. When opposed to the usual approach, where the computation proceeds after collecting the results from all the regions, our approach offers notable benefits: reduction of computation time, real-time model extraction, better support to local decisions. The paper describes the model of local synchronization by means of a Petri net and analyzes the performance in terms of the ability of the system of keeping the pace with the data collected by sensors. The analysis is based on a real world dataset tracing the movements of taxis in the urban area of Beijing.

Keywords: Smart city · Mobility patterns · Local synchronization
Parallel computation

1 Introduction

This paper presents a novel approach that can be used for the execution of distributed smart city applications. We consider a scenario in which the parallelization of computation is performed by partitioning the territory into regions, and each region is assigned a portion of the computation, for which the input data has been collected locally. The sample application analyzed in this paper is the extraction of mobility patterns traced by people and vehicles over a city area, aiming at providing useful real-time information about mobility-related phenomena. To this purpose, we assume the existence of a network of sensors distributed in a city, which collect data about traffic, road, weather conditions, noise, etc. The analysis of such data, performed in coordination among the nodes, can provide useful real-time insights for transport users and traffic operators and can help to tackle a vast variety of mobility situations, e.g., congestion, safety, tolling.

G. Mencagli et al. (Eds.): Euro-Par 2018 Workshops, LNCS 11339, pp. 559–572, 2019.
https://doi.org/10.1007/978-3-030-10549-5_44

The presented approach exploits the fact that useful information can be obtained by analyzing the data related to a local area of the territory. Specifically, if the computing node assigned to a region is able to process local data together with data coming from a subset of neighbor regions, it is possible to rapidly extract mobility patterns regarding a significant portion of the city. With this approach, the computation does not require the *all–to–all* or *global* synchronization among the nodes (i.e., all the nodes need to synchronize and collect all the data before proceeding to computation), as typical with the master-slave paradigm. Instead, the opportunity emerges of synchronizing the computation only among a limited number of parallel nodes, without the need for a central coordinator node. With this "local" synchronization, a computation at one node can proceed after being notified about the mobility patterns discovered in neighbor nodes, and can then concatenate those patterns with the ones discovered locally. This allows mobility patterns to be available much more rapidly, while the patterns regarding the whole territory can still be made available by progressively extending the area covered by the local patterns.

In a previous work, we assessed the benefits of local synchronization in a context where the objective is to predict the Internet traffic generated by mobile users in a city avenue [4,5], in a monodimensional scenario. Here we focus on a different and more general application case where the scenario is bidimensional and real-time analysis is crucial, as the computation needs to keep the pace with the production of data. We consider the case in which the computation is step-based, i.e., at the end of a predetermined time interval (i.e., an hour) it is possible to process the data regarding that time interval. The main benefits of local synchronization are:

- *Faster computation.* Local synchronization allows the overall computation to proceed faster, see Sect. 5. Intuitively, with global synchronization a long execution at a node compels all the other nodes to wait, thus slowing down the overall computation, while with local synchronization only the neighbor nodes (i.e., the nodes assigned to neighbor regions) need to wait before proceeding to the next step;
- *Real-time model extraction.* The previous benefit applies both to offline and online computation. In the latter case, a further advantage is that a faster computation helps to keep the pace with the data collected by sensors;
- *Better support to local decisions.* With local synchronization mobility patterns are available earlier, enabling a faster reaction to local events, e.g., a traffic congestion. This is particularly useful if the territory partitioning follows the administrative organization. For example, based on the extracted patterns, decisions on the traffic management in a city district can be performed automatically or semi-automatically;
- *Better data traffic management.* With local synchronization, data is transmitted among neighbor nodes, which is an advantage – in terms of data traffic, congestion avoidance and battery consumption in the case of wireless transmission – with respect to the case when all the data is delivered to a single node.

In this paper we focus on the first two advantages. We have modeled the local and global synchronization paradigms through a Petri net and, starting from real data extracted from a dataset regarding the mobility of users in the city of Beijing, China, we have performed a set of experiments varying the partitioning of the territory and the computational power of the nodes. We came to the conclusion that local synchronization allows the system to keep the pace with data production in a wider set of scenarios than global synchronization.

The rest of the paper is organized as follows: Sect. 2 discusses some related work; Sect. 3 describes the problem of extracting mobility patterns in an urban scenario; Sect. 4 presents the Petri net that models the computation; Sect. 5 reports performance results regarding the ability of local synchronization to timely process the generated data; Sect. 6 concludes the paper and suggests some avenues for future work.

2 Related Work

The availability of urban and environmental data enables to extract mobility-related knowledge and achieve real-time traffic prediction that can support citizens in their everyday mobility. For example, it is possible to predict travel events and conditions (travel times over the street segments, traffic jams, slowed down traffic, congestion points, start-stop locations, availability of parking places) and road infrastructure conditions (bumpy road, slippery road surface, damaged road surface location).

Discovering mobility patterns from object movements is a very challenging task and several approaches to deal with it have been proposed in the literature [2,3,8,9]. In [3] a sequential approach to discovery hidden periodic patterns in spatiotemporal data is proposed. In particular, authors define the spatiotemporal periodic pattern mining problem and propose an algorithm for retrieving maximal periodic patterns. Moreover, they devise a specialized index structure, aimed at supporting more efficient execution of spatiotemporal queries over the discovered patterns. A parallel approach to estimate an object future location, based on pattern information and recent movements, is proposed in [2]; specifically, the discovered trajectory patterns are stored in the TPT (Trajectory Pattern Tree), a tree data structure exploited for an efficient and accurate prediction of future locations. In [8] the big data generated from mobile devices is analyzed in parallel at different locations and a final model is extracted by aggregating several local models following a master-worker paradigm. In particular, human mobility patterns are discovered by learning data-adaptive representations for cellular network data that are distributed across a set of interconnected nodes. In [9] a cooperative smart driving direction system is presented, where GPS-equipped taxis are employed as mobile sensors aimed at probing the traffic rhythm of a city. In particular, the main idea is to exploit the intelligence of experienced taxi drivers so as to provide a user with the practically fastest route to a given destination at a given departure time.

3 Distributed Mobility Analysis in a Smart City

The analysis of mobility data is conceived for a scenario in which a city is partitioned into N regions, and for each region a computing node (e.g., a Raspberry unit) collects and processes data coming from the sensors located in the region. As mentioned in the introductory section, mobility patterns discovered in a region can be concatenated with those discovered in neighbor regions, so as to obtain patterns covering a wider area. The partitioning of the city in regions can follow the administrative organization of the city, i.e., the shapes of the city districts. However, for the sake of simplicity, and to allow a readier analysis of the performance results, in this paper we consider equally-sized regions, uniformly distributed over a two-dimensional grid, as represented in Fig. 1.

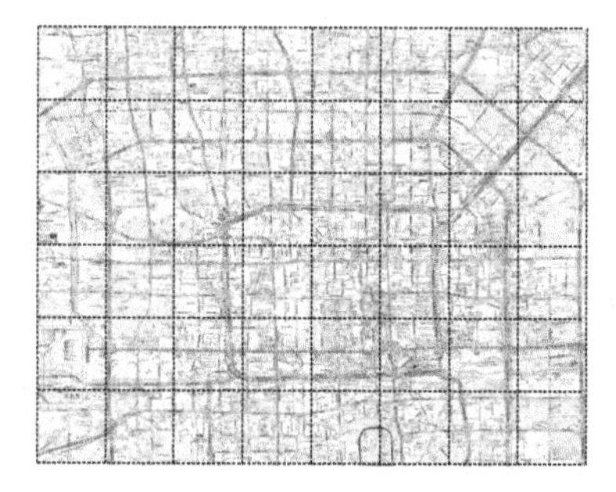

Fig. 1. A city partitioned through a bidimensional grid. This map represents the city of Beijing.

The discovery of mobility patterns is usually modeled in literature as a frequent itemset mining problem [3]. Let us suppose N sensors $s_1, ..., s_N$ that collect streams of urban mobility data in a region. Specifically, each sensor s_i collect a data stream of data $D_i = \{v_i^{t_1}, v_i^{t_2}, \cdots, v_i^{t_n}, \cdots\}$, where each $v_i^{t_j}$ represents the value of a given observed measure (intensity of traffic, average speed, occupation of the lane, etc.) at the sampling time t_j. A common approach to assist mobility services is the discovery of *frequent mobility patterns* from such data. A frequent mobility pattern is represented in the form $v_i^{t_1} v_j^{t_2} \cdots v_k^{t_s}$, where the elements of the pattern represent item values that co-occur together with a high frequency (higher than a given threshold value). The mechanisms of association allow to identify the conditions that tend to occur simultaneously, or the patterns that repeat in certain conditions. As an example, a frequent pattern can represent the flow of vehicles along the city avenues, i.e., the observation that a large number of vehicles have been observed at a given location during a time interval and have been later observed in a successive time interval in adjacent locations. Moreover, rules can be derived from mobility patterns, in the form $v_i^{t_1} v_j^{t_2} \cdots \rightarrow^c v_k^{t_s}$ with time constraints $t_1 < t_2 < \ldots < t_s$. The blocks on the left and on the right are the premises and the consequence of the rule, respectively, and c is its confidence

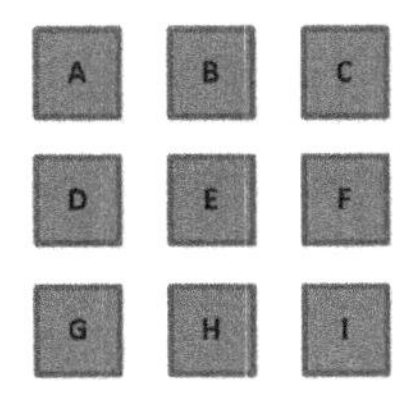

Fig. 2. Transitions modelling a grid partitioning of a city territory.

(meaning that when the premise event occurs then the consequence event will happen with probability c).

The discovery of mobility patterns has been performed by running an algorithm for frequent items and itemsets mining that we described and assessed in [1], and then by assembling the patterns discovered locally with those received by neighbor regions. The assembling operation consists in concatenating a pattern discovered in the local region with another pattern discovered in one of the adjacent regions, in the case that these two patterns overlap on the border between the two regions. In this way, two local patterns are joined and a longer inter-region pattern is discovered. This approach requires the definition of a synchronization barrier: the computation at one node, at a given step, can proceed only after receiving the results of the computation performed by neighbor nodes in the previous step. The formalization is provided in the next section.

4 The Petri Net Computational Model

The parallel computation process described in this paper is modeled by using a Petri net [6]. This formalism has been chosen because it allows to represent and analyze the main issues related to the parallel and distributed nature of the examined scenario, in particular concerning the synchronization aspects. The city territory is partitioned into multiple regions through a bidimensional grid, and the computation step – aiming at deriving the mobility patterns – is modeled by considering a timed Petri net transition for each region. In Fig. 2 we report the case in which a territory is partitioned into nine regions and, as a consequence, nine Petri net transitions are considered. The layout of the transitions mirrors the topological and neighborhood relationship among the corresponding city regions. For instance, the transition A is associated with a city region which has three neighbors, respectively modeled by the transitions B, D and E.

In the following we derive a Petri net modeling the case of local synchronization, while at the end of this section we focus on the case of global synchronization. Figure 3 shows the Petri net associated with a single region, in this case, region E, chosen here because it is the one having the largest number of neighbors in Fig. 2. Beyond the transition associated with the computation, a further transition, i.e., transition P in the figure, is defined to model the data acquisition process. The acquisition process is performed through sensors that are spread over the territory. We assume that at each region this data is produced and collected at regular intervals of time, e.g., every hour, at a single node. The time interval is denoted as T_{prod}. The transition P is used to inform the computation transitions of all the regions that the data has been collected for the last time interval and is ready to be analyzed.

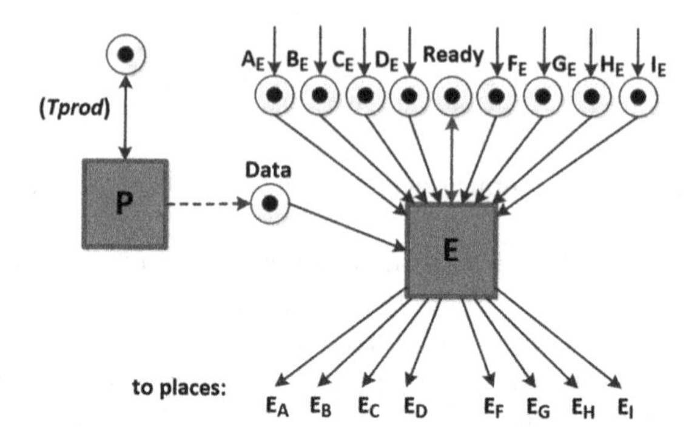

Fig. 3. Details of the Petri net model related to a single region in the city.

With reference to Fig. 3, the node at region E (also referred to as node E in the following) can execute the next computation step when: (i) the node has completed the previous computation step (ii) the node has received the results related to the previous computation at the neighbor regions and (iii) the data collected by the sensors during the last time interval has been collected and consigned to the node. In terms of the Petri net formalism, the transition E is connected by inbound arcs to ten input *places*, and in accordance with Petri net rules [7], the transition is *enabled*, and the computation can start, if all the input places hold at least one *token*. More in detail, the transition at node E is enabled when there is one token at the input place *Ready*, meaning that the previous step has been executed by node E, one token at the place *Data*, meaning that the sensor data is available, and one token at each of the eight remaining input places, meaning that all the eight neighbor nodes have completed the execution of the previous step. As an example, one token is produced at the input place A_E when the transition A has completed its execution and node A has transmitted the results to node E.

Once the node E has completed the computation step, it communicates the results to its neighbors. This is modeled by the Petri net as follows: after the firing of E, a token is consumed at each input place, and a new token is generated (i) in the place *Ready* and (ii) through the outbound arcs shown in the figure, in the input places of all the node E's neighbors, i.e., in the input place E_A of the neighbor A, in the input place E_B of the neighbor B, and so forth.

Figure 4 shows a portion of the whole Petri net model, which includes the Petri net of node E and the analogous Petri nets of the other nodes. For the sake of readability, the input places used by a node X to synchronize with its neighbors are collapsed into a single place, labeled as NG_X, and the arc that

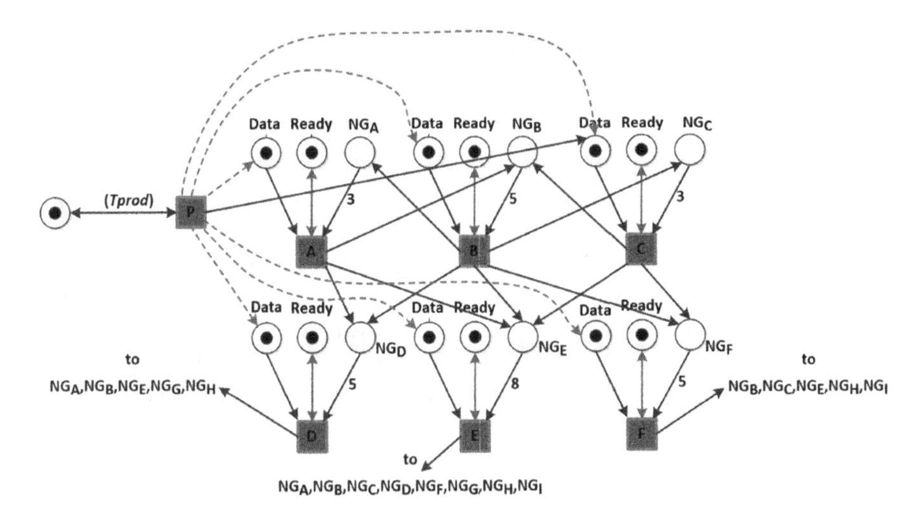

Fig. 4. A Petri net of the proposed computational model.

connects this place to the transition X has a weight equal to the number of X's neighbors. For example, the eight places labeled as A_E, B_E, C_E, D_E, F_E, G_E, H_E, I_E in Fig. 3 are now substituted with a single node NG_E connected to node E with an arc having a weight equal to eight. Analogously, the outgoing arcs directed to the input places of neighbor nodes are substituted with a single arc on which the input places are specified[1].

From the definition of the Petri net models, it emerges that the time experienced at a generic node i at the end of the step $k+1$, denoted ad $T_i(k+1)$, is determined by the recursive expression (1):

$$T_i(k+1) = max\left(T_i(k), max(T_{Ngh(i)}(k)),\ T_{prod_i}(k)\right) +\ T_{comp_i}(k+1) \qquad (1)$$

where $T_{Ngh(i)}(k)$ is the set containing the times experienced at all the nodes that are adjacent to node i at the end of the step k, $T_{prod_i}(k)$ is the time at which the data related to step k has been consigned by the local sensors to node i, and $T_{comp_i}(k+1)$ is the time needed by node i to compute the step $k+1$.

In the case of global synchronization, the approach for synchronization is centralized: at each step a central entity receives the results (i.e., the local mobility patterns) from every node that has completed the step, and after receiving the results from all the nodes, sends an ack to every node to trigger the execution of the next step. For brevity, here we do not show the Petri net that models the global synchronization case.

[1] Even with these simplifications, the Petri net maintains the desired semantics if we assume that: (i) the computation at each region has a progressive step number, (ii) each token holds the step number of the related computation, (iii) in a NG_X input place, only the tokens having the same step number can be used to enable the transition.

5 Experimental Evaluation

In this section we analyze the performance of the sample parallel application, i.e., the prediction of mobility patterns for an urban scenario (Sect. 3). In this paper we focus on the computational efficiency, while we do not discuss the semantics of the extracted patterns, nor the way they are obtained by concatenating those discovered in neighbor regions, which is left to a future work.

The main objective is to analyze the advantages deriving from the local synchronization strategy, with respect to the usual global synchronization strategy. We developed a Matlab simulator that reproduces the local synchronization model, in particular the recursive expression (1) of Sect. 4, and the global synchronization model. The execution times of the nodes are established by considering the real execution times obtained when executing the algorithm for mobility pattern analysis on a real dataset, namely *T-Drive Trajectory Data Sample* [10]. T-Drive is a collection of GPS traces describing the movement of taxis in the city of Beijing, China. In this fashion, we were able to assess the expected performance of local and global synchronization for a real scenario. Section 5.1 describes the T-Drive dataset and the scenario of interest, while Sect. 5.2 reports some interesting performance results.

5.1 Dataset Description and Scenario of Interest

The temporal span of the T-Drive dataset is one week. The number of vehicles tracked is 10,357. The total distance covered by the trajectories reaches almost 9 million kilometers, with 15 millions of locations (geographic points). The total data size amounts to about 772 MB. The original dataset was preprocessed to make it suitable for the analysis. In particular, we cleaned the data by removing all the points with unreliable position (i.e., coordinates with clear errors in latitude-longitude values) and those outside the city area of interest. The final dataset counts about 61,500 daily trajectories, each containing the set of points traced by a single taxi during a day.

The T-Drive dataset has been used to simulate a scenario where streams of data are collected by sensors distributed in the regions and analyzed to discover frequent mobility patterns in a city. As mentioned in Sect. 3, the analysis has been performed by running an algorithm for frequent itemsets mining that we presented in [1], and then by assembling the patterns discovered locally with those received by neighbor regions.

Since the conditions in urban environments change dynamically, the generation rate of data and the processing times vary during the day and among the regions. For this reason, we split the T-Drive data by considering time windows of one hour, and we executed the algorithm by analyzing the volume of data generated in those time windows. To analyze the statistical behavior of the algorithm execution time, we clustered the computation time by hour (for example, a cluster includes the execution times obtained from 5:00 pm to 6:00 pm of all the different days), computed the average of each cluster and then normalized each computation time with respect to the average of its cluster.

The distribution of the normalized execution times is reported in Fig. 5. The figure also reports the probability density function of a normal distribution with same mean and standard deviation. The two distributions appear very similar, which is confirmed by the fact that the Pearson coefficient is higher than 0.95. In conclusion, approximating the execution times with a normal curve is a reasonable assumption.

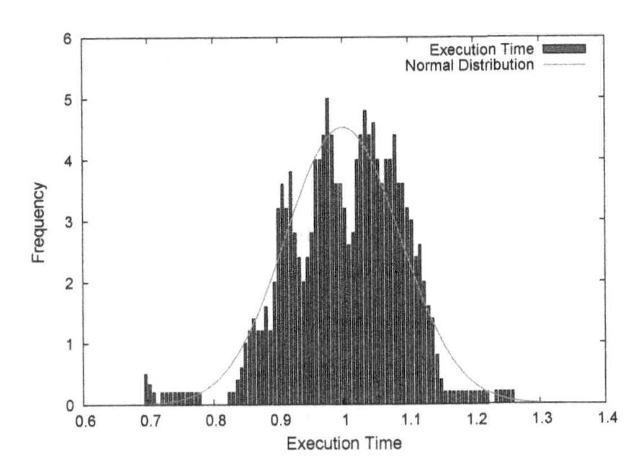

Fig. 5. Histogram of the normalized execution time of the algorithm for frequent itemsets mining. A normal distribution with same mean and standard deviation is also reported.

Though we base the analysis on the real data related to a specific city, in this case Beijing, we aim to assess the performance for a more general scenario, so as to draw conclusions that are related to the use of the local synchronization approach in general, and that are not tied to a given city only. To this aim, we define an experimental frame as indicated in the following:

1. we consider a city partitioned into N regions through a bidimensional grid, with square numbers of equally sized-regions, i.e., $N = 2 \times 2, 3 \times 3$, etc.
2. we assume that the extraction of mobility patterns is executed on each region by a computing node that receives and collects the mobility data produced at sensors every time interval T_{prod}, which is set to 1 h. Therefore each computing step is associated with the computation performed on the data of a specific hour;
3. we assume that the users are distributed uniformly in the area of interest. When considering the central area of Beijing, we found this assumption reasonable. The rationale of this assumption is that the analysis of a uniform scenario is preliminary to subsequently understand what happens in a non-uniform scenario, which will be the subject of further studies;
4. all the N computing nodes are assumed to have the same computation power;
5. this computation power of nodes is varied by adopting the following approach. We assume that the average time that would be needed by a single node to

perform the computation at a single step for the entire area is T_{serial}. Then, we define $R = T_{serial}/T_{prod}$ and vary the values of this ratio by varying the value of T_{serial}. Clearly the computation power of nodes in inversely proportional to the ratio R;

6. the *average computation time*, T_{node}, defined as the average time needed to perform the computation on a single node, is assumed to be proportional to the number of users located in the corresponding region, and then to the area of the region. Therefore, when the area is partitioned into N regions, $T_{node} = T_{serial}/N$. When considering the definition of R given in the previous item, it follows that $T_{node} = (R \cdot T_{prod})/N$;
7. the time needed to communicate (transmit and receive) data with the neighbor nodes is negligible with respect to the computation time. This assumption is reasonable because the nodes only need to transmit synthetic models, i.e., the results of the mobility pattern analysis, which can be done in a few seconds.

5.2 Experiments

The performance analysis was performed by using a Matlab simulator that reproduces the local and global synchronization models, as discussed at the beginning of Sect. 5, under the assumptions listed in the previous subsection. The local computation times used in the simulator are extracted from a normal distribution with average equal to $T_{node} = (R \cdot T_{prod})/N$ (see item 6 in Sect. 5.1)[2]. To analyze the benefits of local synchronization in the case that different degrees of variability are experienced, the standard deviation σ of the normal distribution was taken as a parameter, and it was set to three different values, i.e., $0.25 \cdot T_{node}$, $0.5 \cdot T_{node}$ and $1.0 \cdot T_{node}$. The number of simulated steps is equal to n_{step}. The evaluated performance indices were the following:

- the average step time T_{step}, defined as the average time to perform a computational step on all the nodes. It is computed as the time to execute n_{step} steps of the Petri net model divided by n_{step}. This index allows to assess the ability of the system to timely process the data coming from sensors. More in particular, the system does not keep the pace with data production (in the following, we say that it is "unstable" for brevity) when T_{step} is larger than the acquisition interval T_{prod}, while it keeps the pace (it is "stable") when $T_{step} = T_{prod}$. The value of T_{step} cannot be lower than T_{prod}, because the computation of a step must wait for the arrival of the related data;
- the fraction of missed deadlines, F_{miss}, defined as the fraction of times that a node receives new data coming from the sensors (the data produced during the interval T_{prod}) before completing the computation related to the previous bunch of data, i.e., the fraction of times that a single node does not keep the pace with data production.

[2] Negative values of the normal distribution are discarded and re-extracted.

The experiments were carried out when setting T_{prod} to one hour and the number of steps n_{step} to 720, corresponding to 30 days with the chosen value of T_{prod}. Furthermore, we considered different numbers and computation powers of nodes, more in particular, values of $N \in \{2, 4, 9, 16, 25\}$, and values of R ranging between 1 and 12.

Figure 6 shows the values of the two performance indices versus the value of R, when setting the number of nodes to 9, 16 and 25, and the value of the standard deviation σ to $0.25 \cdot T_{node}$. In the left figure we can see that the system is stable (i.e., $T_{step} = 1$ hour) when the computation is partitioned on 25 nodes. When using 16 nodes, the system is stable with local synchronization, but it is unstable with global synchronization when R is greater than 11. When using 9 nodes, we notice that there is an interval of values of R, between 6 and 7, for which the system is stable with local synchronization and unstable with global synchronization. The values of F_{miss} confirm this behavior: when the system is stable the fraction of missed deadlines is zero or negligible, while this index increases up to 1 when the system becomes unstable.

In Figs. 7 and 8 we report the performance values obtained when assuming a larger variability of local computation times, as detailed in the captions. When comparing these results to those in Fig. 6, we can notice two interesting phenomena:

- when the variability increases, the system tends to be unstable even with low values of R, i.e., with high values of the computation power of nodes. For example, with $R = 10$, the system is stable ($T_{step} = 1$ hour) with $\sigma = 0.25 \cdot T_{node}$ when using 16 and 25 nodes, with both local and global synchronization; it is stable with $\sigma = 0.5 \cdot T_{node}$ only when using 25 nodes, irrespective of the type of synchronization; it is stable with $\sigma = 1.0 \cdot T_{node}$ only when using 25 nodes and local synchronization;
- when the variability increases, the advantage of local synchronization increases as well. For example, if Fig. 8 is observed, we can notice that there is a significant range of R values (between 8 and 10 for the case $N = 25$) for which the system is stable with local synchronization but unstable with global synchronization.

The reported results confirm the benefits brought by local synchronization. Indeed, in some scenarios with local synchronization it is possible to keep the pace with data production, while it is impossible with global synchronization and it would be required to either increase the number of nodes (which means install more computing nodes and sustain larger costs) or increase their computational power. It will be important to assess this interesting outcome when removing the simplifying assumption of uniform user distribution. When the distribution is non-uniform, it can be useful to modify the territory partitioning, for example by defining smaller regions where the user density is higher. Indeed, this is one of the issues of our current research work in this field.

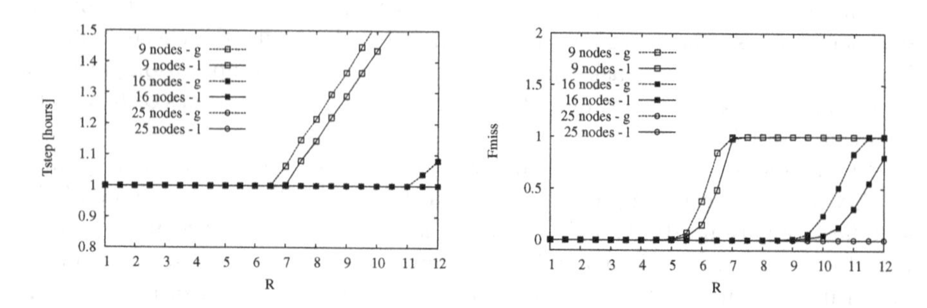

Fig. 6. Values of T_{step} and F_{miss} versus the ratio R, with $N = 9, 16$ and 25, and σ equal to $0.25 \cdot T_{node}$. Characters "g" and "l" in the legend refer to global and local synchronization, respectively.

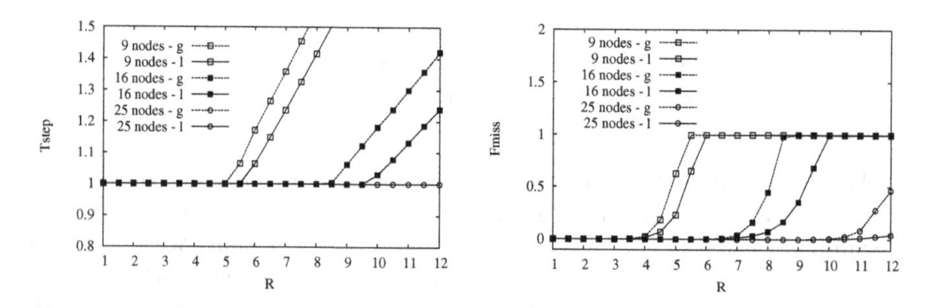

Fig. 7. Values of T_{step} and F_{miss} versus the ratio R, with $N = 9, 16$ and 25, and σ equal to $0.5 \cdot T_{node}$. Characters "g" and "l" in the legend refer to global and local synchronization, respectively.

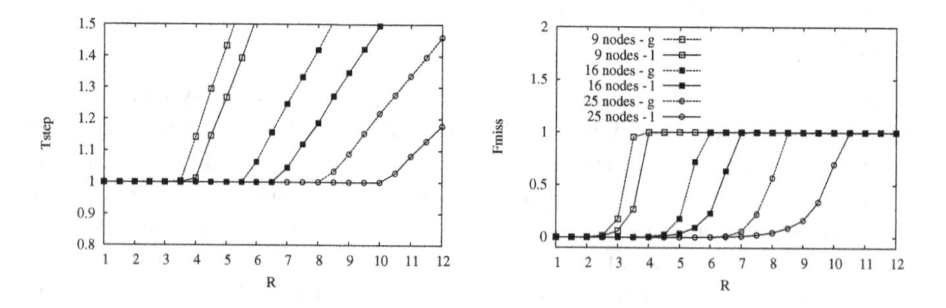

Fig. 8. Values of T_{step} and F_{miss} versus the ratio R, with $N = 9, 16$ and 25, and σ equal to $1.0 \cdot T_{node}$. Characters "g" and "l" in the legend refer to global and local synchronization, respectively. The legend is not shown in the left figure for the sake of readability.

6 Conclusion

In this paper, we presented an original approach based on local synchronization which is exploitable for the execution of distributed smart city applications. The main idea is to speed up the computation by limiting the overhead induced by the synchronization of the parallel nodes operating in different regions of the city. Specifically, with the presented *local* synchronization approach, each node needs to synchronize only with a set of neighbor nodes, instead of all the other nodes as required by the classical master-slave paradigm. As a specific application domain, the extraction of mobility patterns in an urban area was considered. Results, based on the analysis of a real dataset, showed that local synchronization helps to better keep the pace with the production of data in the environment, and that the advantage increases with the variability of execution times. This work has focused on the computation performance of the mobility patterns analysis. We have not discussed the semantics of the extracted patterns, nor the way they are obtained by concatenating those discovered in neighbor regions, but we intend to focus on this aspect in a future work. Other interesting research avenues are:

- extend the mobility patterns analysis to other city contexts;
- apply the approach to other smart city applications like those related to traffic management, transportation systems, and crowd monitoring and control;
- improve the approach so as to consider scenarios having a non-uniform and dynamic distribution of the workload among city regions;
- enrich the approach by furnishing a theoretical framework for the local synchronization approach.

References

1. Cesario, E., Mastroianni, C., Talia, D.: A multi-domain architecture for mining frequent items and itemsets from distributed data streams. J. Grid Comput. **12**(1), 153–168 (2014)
2. Jeung, H., Liu, Q., Shen, H., Tao Zhou, X.: A hybrid prediction model for moving objects. In: Proceedings of the 2008 IEEE 24th International Conference on Data Engineering, ICDE 2008, pp. 70–79. IEEE Computer Society (2008)
3. Mamoulis, N., Cao, H., Kollios, G., Hadjieleftheriou, M., Tao, Y., Cheung, D.W.: Mining, indexing, and querying historical spatiotemporal data. In: Proceedings of the Tenth ACM International Conference on Knowledge Discovery and Data Mining, KDD 2004, pp. 236–245. ACM (2004)
4. Mastroianni, C., Cesario, E., Giordano, A.: Balancing speedup and accuracy in smart city parallel applications. In: Desprez, F., et al. (eds.) Euro-Par 2016. LNCS, vol. 10104, pp. 224–235. Springer, Cham (2017). https://doi.org/10.1007/978-3-319-58943-5_18
5. Mastroianni, C., Cesario, E., Giordano, A.: Efficient and scalable execution of smart city parallel applications. In: Concurrency and Computation: Practice and Experience (2017). http://dx.doi.org/10.1002/cpe.4258. Early view
6. Murata, T.: Petri nets: properties, analysis and applications. Proc. IEEE **77**(4), 541–580 (1989)

7. Peterson, J.L.: Petri nets. ACM Comput. Surv. **9**(3), 223–252 (1977)
8. Wu, T., Rustamov, R.M., Goodall, C.: Distributed learning of human mobility patterns from cellular network data. In: 51st Annual Conference on Information Sciences and Systems (CISS) (2017)
9. Yuan, J., Zheng, Y., Xie, X., Sun, G.: T-Drive: enhancing driving directions with taxi drivers' intelligence. IEEE Trans. Knowl. Data Eng. **25**(1), 220–232 (2013)
10. Yuan, J., et al.: T-Drive: driving directions based on taxi trajectories. In: Proceedings of the 18th SIGSPATIAL International Conference on Advances in Geographic Information Systems, GIS 2010, pp. 99–108. ACM (2010)

Exploiting Community Detection to Recommend Privacy Policies in Decentralized Online Social Networks

Andrea De Salve[1](✉), Barbara Guidi[2], and Andrea Michienzi[2]

[1] Istituto di Informatica e Telematica, Consiglio Nazionale delle Ricerche, Via G. Moruzzi, 1, Pisa, Italy
andrea.desalve@iit.cnr.it

[2] Department of Computer Science, University of Pisa, Largo Bruno Pontecorvo, Pisa, Italy
{guidi,andrea.michienzi}@di.unipi.it

Abstract. The usage of Online Social Networks (OSNs) has become a daily activity for billions of people that share their contents and personal information with the other users. Regardless of the platform exploited to provide the OSNs' services, these contents' sharing could expose the OSNs' users to a number of privacy risks if proper privacy-preserving mechanisms are not provided. Indeed, users must be able to define its own privacy policies that are exploited by the OSN to regulate access to the shared contents. To reduce such users' privacy risks, we propose a Privacy Policies Recommended System (PPRS) that assists the users in defining their own privacy policies. Besides suggesting the most appropriate privacy policies to end users, the proposed system is able to exploits a certain set of properties (or attributes) of the users to define permissions on the shared contents. The evaluation results based on real OSN dataset show that our approach classifies users with a higher accuracy by recommending specific privacy policies for different communities of the users' friends.

Keywords: Decentralized online social networks
Recommendation system · Privacy · Privacy policies · Security

1 Introduction

The usage of Online Social Networks (OSNs) has become a daily activity for billions of people who share several private information on current OSNs, exposing them to privacy leaking. Indeed, current OSNs are free to use, and they make money by selling private data to advertisers. The last scandal involves Facebook and private data collected by Cambridge Analytica[1].

[1] https://www.theguardian.com/technology/2018/apr/04/facebook-cambridge-analytica-user-data-latest-more-than-thought.

G. Mencagli et al. (Eds.): Euro-Par 2018 Workshops, LNCS 11339, pp. 573–584, 2019.
https://doi.org/10.1007/978-3-030-10549-5_45

During the last decade, several solutions have been proposed to overcome the problem of current OSNs. One of the main promising is the decentralization of social services. Decentralized Online Social Networks (DOSNs) guarantee a higher level of privacy because data is distributed and users can have more control over their personal data. The access control is one of the most used technique to prevent privacy leaking in DOSNs. Indeed, the majority of existing DOSNs provide a set of privacy policies based on the knowledge derived from the relationships, content or profile information, etc...

In this paper we propose a new approach to define a Privacy Policy Recommendation System (PPRS) based on community detection in DOSNs. The motivation of this work is that users with common attributes are more likely to be friends and often form dense communities [15]. For this reason, our methodology exploits a set of attributes which describe properties of the users (such as location and school information). By considering the homophily between users [6], we compute communities based on the social graph and we exploit a decision tree learning algorithm to suggest privacy policies for such communities.

The evaluation conducted on real dataset shows that the proposed approach shall be capable of providing higher level of accuracy by correctly classifying the 80% of the users' friends in the proper community while exploiting different attributes of the users.

The paper is organized as follows. In Sect. 2 we propose an overview of the state of the art of privacy in OSNs. In Sect. 3 we introduce our approach. In Sect. 4 we describe the dataset used to evaluate our approach. Section 5 shows the evaluation of the approach, and finally, in Sect. 6 we propose our conclusion and future improvements.

2 Related Work

Nowadays, the most popular OSNs are based on centralized architectures where private data are stored in centralized storages which are under the control of the administrations. The centralized management of data exposes to several privacy risks. Indeed, malicious users, the service provider, and third-party applications can access users' private data. As explained in [11], the main attacks in OSNs are:

- Privacy breaches: attacks to strike the users' privacy. Three primary parties interact are involved: the service provider, the users, and third-party applications.
- Viral Marketing: spamming and phishing attacks which exploit information extracted from user profiles.
- Network Structural Attacks: the most famous one is the Sybil attack, in which an individual entity masquerades as multiple simultaneous identities.
- Malware Attacks: usage of OSNs to spread malicious software.

One of the main solution to the privacy issue in OSNs has been the introduction of Decentralized Online Social Networks (DOSNs) in order to overcome the centralization of data [17]. Several works have been proposed during the last ten years which exploits P2P solutions to implement the underlying architecture [1,4,12]. An important characteristic of DOSNs is that they provide the capability to define privacy preferences on the contents produced and exchanged to define which users are allowed to see such contents [8]. Typically, privacy policies are simple statements which specify the main attributes a user can have to access contents (such as friendship type, interests, work, school,...). In detail, a DOSN proposes a privacy model [8] defined as the capability of DOSNs to provide privacy policies to specify the set of members who can access contents, and a privacy policy management which guarantees that these policies are enforced on each content by using proper security mechanisms.

3 Our Approach

Our scenario consists of a DOSNs in which each user has information about its ego network, which includes the principal user (*ego*) together with the actors they are connected to (*alters*) and all the links among these alters [2]. Each user of the DOSNs can define privacy policies to manage the access to its content [9], and it is characterized by a set of attributes, such as information about personal profile (date of birthday, hometown, school, etc.) or information about its preferences (music, movies). Each ego node knows the friends' attributes and it can exploit them to express their privacy preferences on these friends.

3.1 Privacy Policy Recommendation

The first step of the PPRS is the application of a community detection algorithm to each ego network. The algorithm we used is DEMON [3] because it can be adapted to an ego centric approach and it is computationally not expensive, as explained in [13]. We extract the communities in the so called *ego minus ego*: a network made of the ego network of a user where we remove the ego itself and all edges connected to it. In this work, the community detection algorithm has been configured to return a set of non-overlapped communities where each alter can belong to only one community in the same ego network. The case of overlapped communities is left as future work because it demands more investigation and consideration than the case of disjointed communities. Each community has an identifier, and this identifier is used as a user's attribute, and it is inserted in the attributes list of each ego to identify how its alters are clustered. At the end of this phase, each ego node u has an array of attributes for each alter f which contains: the values of the f's attributes $p_1(f)$, $p_2(f)$, $p_3(f)$, and the communities $C = \{C_{id} | f \in C_{id}\}$ of u.

The second step consists in the definition of decision trees which let us to classify users. An example of decision trees is shown in Fig. 1. In Fig. 1(a) we propose an example of six users with both their school attribute and the community label associated. We exploit the *School* and *Hometown* attributes to build the decision tree shown in Fig. 1(b). Finally, a privacy policy of a community

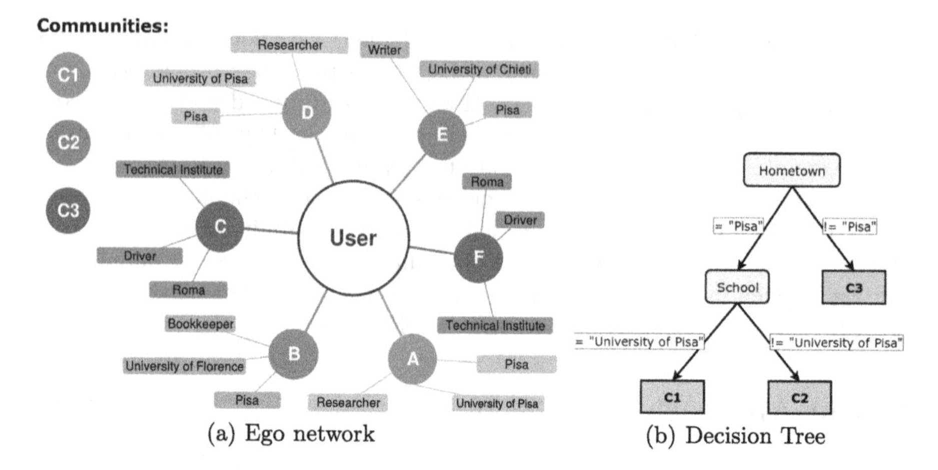

(a) Ego network (b) Decision Tree

Fig. 1. Example of the PPRS executed on the ego network (Fig. 1(a)) of a user with 6 friends having attributes and community label associated. The results of the PPRS is the decision tree shown in Fig. 1(b)

can be provided by considering the attributes on each path from the leaves of the community to the root of the decision tree. Thereafter, the conditions on the attributes resulting from the model can be translated by the PPRS into a privacy policy format. As for instance, the most part of privacy policy languages leverage XML for defining constraints that must be satisfied by attributes of the users [9]. Finally, the PPRS is able to suggest the most suitable privacy policies to the user.

4 The Dataset

Information about attributes of Facebook users have been gathered by a Facebook application (originally described in [5]), called SocialCircles![2], which exploits the Facebook API to retrieve a set of social information about the registered users which contain information about friends of registered users and the friendship relations existing between them, profile information, and information about interactions between registered users and their friends, such as posts, comments, likes, tags and photo. Due to technical reasons (time needed to fetch all data and storage capacity), we restrict the interaction information retrieved up to 6 months prior to user application registration. The dataset we use contains 205 complete Ego Networks, for a total of 95.716 users (ego and their friends). In the following of this section we will present in more detail the collected data to understand better its nature.

[2] https://www.facebook.com/SocialCircles-244719909045196/.

4.1 Features of the Dataset

We used the information collected from the OSNs to extract different features of users that can be exploited as attributes by the PPRS. Such features (or attributes) are properties of the users that can be either obtained from the users' profile (such as, age, sex, number of common friends, etc.) or derived from the OSNs information (such as tie strength and trustiness). An overview of the statistical properties that quantitatively describes the features obtained from our collection of information are listed below.

Friends and Common friends. We first analyze the degree distribution of our dataset. The graph of Fig. 2(a) shows the Cumulative Distribution Function (CDF) of the number of friends of the registered users as well as the degree distribution of the entire sample (all users). The graph clearly indicates that 50% of the registered users have at most 432 friends in their ego networks while the most part of them (about 90%) have at most 1000 friends. In addition, the CDF of the whole set of the users in our sample points out the presence of a higher number of users (about 85%) having only one friendship relation. According to [5], this is caused by Facebook privacy setting that could not allow our application to collect enough information related to the friends of the registered users.

We focus on the number of common friends between users by measuring the number of mutual friends that each alter shares with the ego. As shown by Fig. 2(b), the CDF of the number of common friends has exponential shape, resulting in about 10% of the friendship relations between the egos and their alters with any friends in common while about 50% of them have less than 8 mutual friends.

Age and Gender. We investigate the gender distribution by measuring the fraction of male and female users who have registered to our application. Figure 2(c) shows the gender distribution for both the set of registered users and of all users in the dataset, as well as the median number of male and female users' friends of the registered users. We can observe that registered users registered consist of about 127 (63%) men and 76 (37%) women while the whole set of users (all users) is more balanced and it consists of about 54% men and 45% women. The typical users established, on average, 202 (55%) friendships with men and 161 (45%) friend relationships with women.

We investigated the distribution of ages in our dataset by measuring the difference between the birthday date and the current date. Figure 2(d) shows the distribution of the ages for all the users in the dataset and for the set of registered users. We observed that about 20% of the registered users and 40% of all the users did not specify their birthday date or they provided an age of 0. The median age of the registered users (30 years old) is higher than those of all users (27 years old).

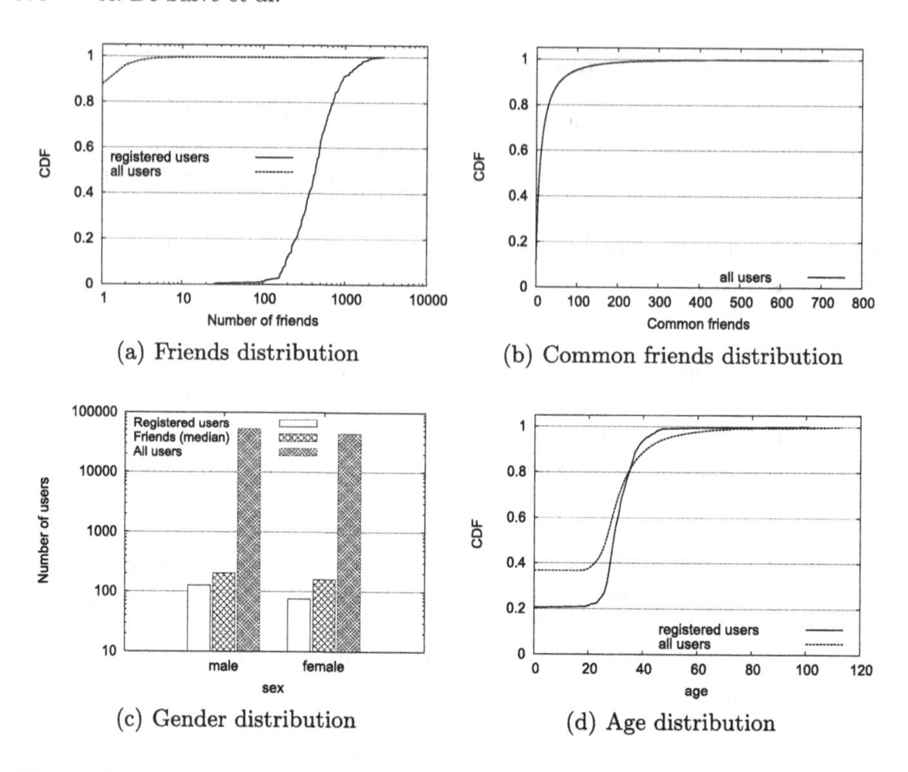

(a) Friends distribution
(b) Common friends distribution
(c) Gender distribution
(d) Age distribution

Fig. 2. General description of the statistical characteristics of the Facebook dataset.

Hometown and Current Location. Geographical locations of the users are also collected and they can be exploited to measure the distance or proximity between users. The map in Fig. 3 indicates the geographical location that users have specified in their Facebook profiles. In particular, we consider the hometown (Fig. 3(a)) and the current location (Fig. 3(b)) of users because they could affect their interaction patterns. The most part of the collected users have hometown location and current location placed in Europe, where the application was initially disseminated. However, the maps indicate that our application had spread also in America and a large portion of users came from North America.

Dunbar's Circles. An interesting analysis with respect of the OSNs is the characterization of the *ego network* of the user (introduced in Sect. 3). Indeed, many studies showed that the number of active relationships that a user can establish in his ego network is limited (about 150), the so called *Dunbar number* [10]. Figure 4(a) summarizes the average number of friends in each circle as well as their 95% confidence interval in square brackets while the frequency of contacts is used to estimate the tie strength between users. In particular, the closest circle, called *support clique* (circle 0), consist of 4 [±0.17] and the typical frequency of contact between individuals is estimated to be at least once weekly. The second circle is the *sympathy group* (circle 1), being the set of individuals contacted at

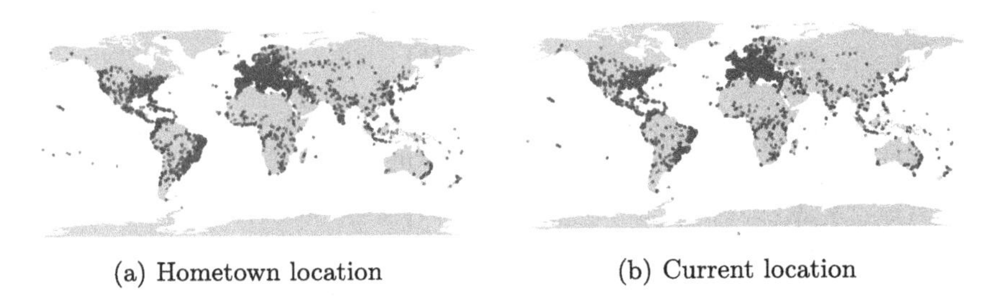

(a) Hometown location (b) Current location

Fig. 3. Geographic map representing the hometown and current location of the users.

least monthly and it consists of 13 [±0.48] users. The next circle is the *affinity group* (circle 2) which consists of 33 [±1.21] users, and finally the outermost circle is the *active network* (circle 3), which consists of 84 [±3.2] users. The total number of users that belong to the Dunbar's circles is equals to 134 [±5] while any other contact is considered to be a simple acquaintance. In particular, acquaintances are friends of an ego e that are occasionally contacted by e and the total number of acquaintances of an ego is equals to 391 [±15]. The procedure performed to obtain the Dunbar's circles are described in more detail in [5].

Community Structure. A significant property of OSNs is the community structure, i.e., densely connected groups of users which are sparely connected to other users. An important step for the PPRS is to identify, for each ego network, to which community a specific user belongs to. For this reason, we consider the ego networks of registered users and we utilize the community detection algorithm exploited in [6,13] to compute both the number and the structure of the communities. The total number of communities discovered in this step is equal to 2237 and in Fig. 4(b) we show the CDF of the community size. The average size of communities is about 60 contacts while about 80% of communities has less than 250 nodes. Figure 4(c) shows the average number of communities discovered in ego networks having different number of alters. The plot indicates that the number of communities defined by users is weakly correlated with the number of users' friends: as long as the number of users' friends increases the number of communities of such users remains bounded to 30 while the average and median number of communities for each ego network is about 14.

We focused on the size of the communities discovered in each ego network and we showed in Fig. 4(d) the average size of the communities defined by users having different number of friends. We observe that the size of the communities of users strongly depends on the number of friendships established by such users, resulting in left skewed distribution with average and median community size equal to 444 and 176, respectively.

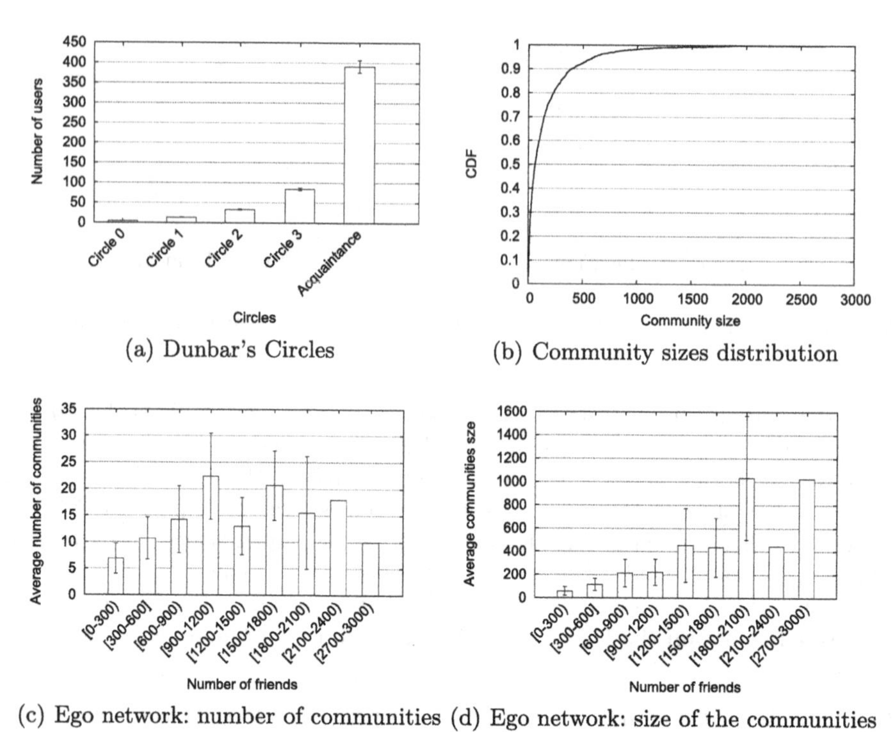

(a) Dunbar's Circles (b) Community sizes distribution

(c) Ego network: number of communities (d) Ego network: size of the communities

Fig. 4. Analysis of the Dunbar-based and static communities of the ego network

5 Experimental Methodology and Results

We focused on the evaluation of the classification task, i.e., on the capability of the PPRS to correctly identify the communities of users in each ego network by exploiting the users' attributes derived from the users' profiles.

5.1 Training and Classification Algorithm

Since our dataset is a collection of registered users, we considered the ego network of each registered user individually for the classification task. Given an ego network of the registered user u, we perform a transformation phase on the original dataset in order to construct an input dataset which contains a record R for each friend in the ego network. The record R consists of the set of attributes that a registered user u wants to exploit to define privacy policies on his ego network. In particular, the attributes are derived from the dataset's features (described in Sect. 4.1) and they include, for each friend f of u: *a)* the sex of f, *b)* the age of f, *c)* the number of common friends between u and f, *d)* the distance (in meters) between the hometown location of u and f, *e)* the distance (in meters) between the current location of u and f, and *f)* the Dunbar's circle to which f belongs, in the ego network of u. In addition to these attributes, a target attribute is created for each friend f of the registered user u to indicate the community to which the user f belongs, in the ego network of u, and it is used as (discrete, unordered) class label by the classification task. For this reason, we create a class $label(c)$ for each community c in the ego network of the registered user u and we set the target attribute of each friend f in the community c to the class $label(c)$. The goal of the classification task is to create a model for each registered user u that can be used to classify each friend f of u in the proper community c, based on a number of attributes related to f:

$$[gender, year, comm, distH, distC, dunbarCircle] \Rightarrow label(c) \tag{1}$$

The model of each registered user u is created by exploiting the C4.5 Decision Tree Learner [16], that is one of the most used methods for classification decision tree. The algorithm builds a hierarchical decision tree which is used for classifying the class label of a user. The attributes of f are used by the tree to routes f towards a leaf node which contains a class label of the community in the ego network of u. The conditions on internal nodes of the tree are generated by splitting the domain of attributes in two partitions (i.e., using a binary split) and the Gini index is used as a quality measure to calculate such splitting point.

5.2 Results Validation

In order to evaluate the models resulting from the supervised learning algorithm we collected several performance measures for each decision tree of a registered user u. The box plot of Fig. 5(a) shows the minimum, lower quartile, median, upper quartile, and maximum, of different tree properties. In particular, we consider the number of leaves in the tree (*#Leaves*), the size of the tree model (*Tree size*), and both the number of friends correctly and incorrectly classified in their community (*Correct* and *Incorrect*, respectively). The decision trees of the registered users have an average number of leaves equals to 76 [±0.31], which account for an average size of 151 [±0.63]. The size of the tree clearly depends on the number of leaves but, in general, the 80% of the trees have less than 120 leaves. The attributes selected from the users allow to correctly classify about 396 [±1.3] friends in the proper community while the average number of incorrectly classified friends is equals to 80 [±0.4]. Indeed, the amount of friends correctly classified by the model is high: 80% of the registered users have correctly classified at most 535 friends in their ego network while the number of friends incorrectly classified by the model is less than 130.

As shown by Fig. 5(b), the average fraction of friends correctly identified in each ego network amounts to 85.6% with average relative absolute error equals to 44 [±0.05] while only 14.3% of the friends cannot be classified by exploiting the selected attributes. In particular, the most part of the registered users (about 80%) have classified an average fraction of friends which ranges between 80% and 95%. Figure 5(c) shows the average error rate is quite low (about 0.14) while the median Kappa index, which measures the degree of accuracy and reliability of the classification task, is equal to 0.64. As explained also in [7],

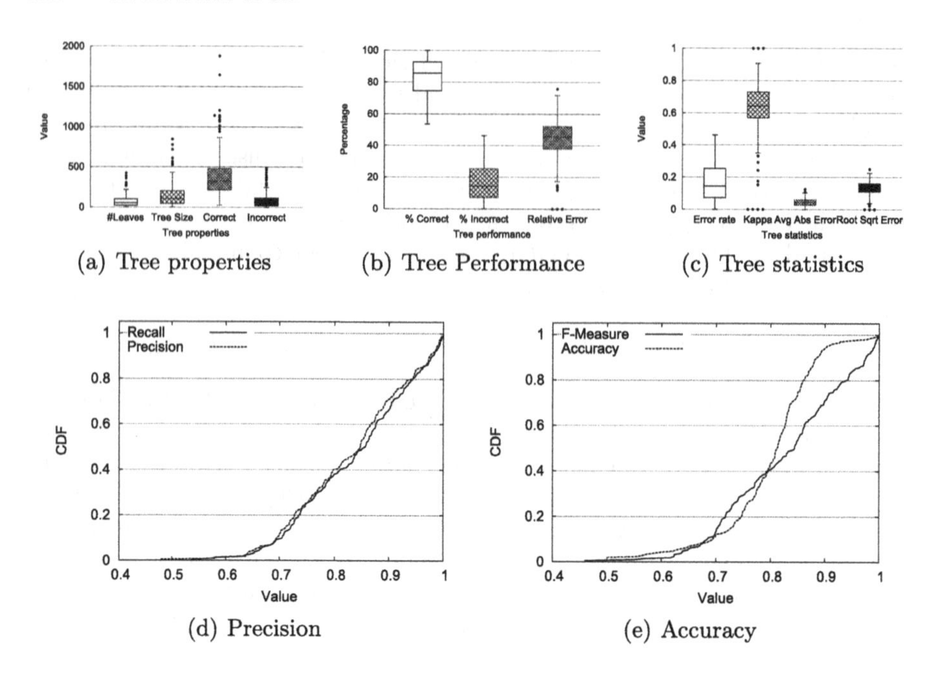

(a) Tree properties (b) Tree Performance (c) Tree statistics

(d) Precision (e) Accuracy

Fig. 5. Analysis of the performance of the classification task

depending on the value of kappa, the index can be interpreted as [14]: *(i)* no agreement if $k \in [0, 0.2]$, *(ii)* fair agreement if $k \in [0.21, 0.4]$, *(iii)* moderate agreement if $k \in [0.41, 0.6]$, *(iv)* substantial agreement if $k \in [0.61, 0.8]$, and (v) perfect agreement if $k \in [0.81, 1]$. Instead, the error of the predicted probability distribution (Avg Abs Error) and the root mean square error (Root Sqrt Error) are quite low and their media value does not exceed 0.13.

We investigated in more detail the ability of the predictors to correctly derive the community to which users belong to. Figure 5(d) shows the CDF of the recall and precision on the resulting models. As we expected, the recall of the classifier in predicting the community of the users is very high (about 0.84) and the precision of the most part of the users (80%) is higher that than 0.75. In addition, the predictors show to have similar precision, indicating that the most part of users are correctly classified by the models by exploiting the values of the users' attributes.

The last step in our analysis consists in evaluating the accuracy of the results, indicating the ability of the model to classify friends that belong to different communities while the *F-measure* summarizes the performance of each predictor. We showed in Fig. 5(e) the CDF of both the accuracy and the F-measure of the models. The average accuracy achieved by the model is 0.83 [$\pm$0.0004] and it is to the median accuracy (about 0.80), suggesting that about 50% of the models expose an accuracy higher than 0.80. Figure 6(a) shows the average performance achieved by models which are build on users having different number of friends, while Fig. 6(b) shows the attributes' importance which is measured as

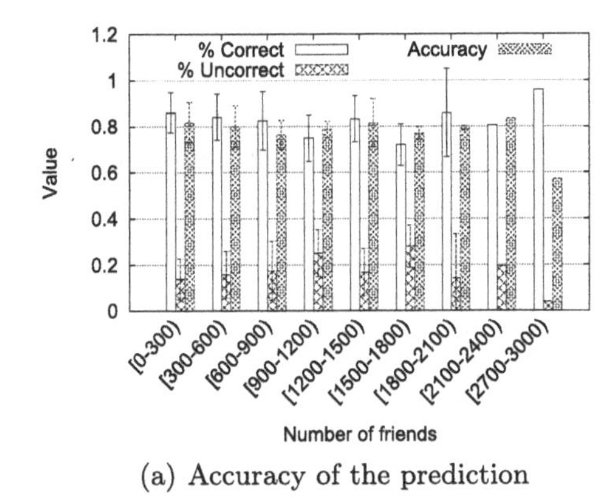

(a) Accuracy of the prediction

Attributes	Rank
Distance current location	0,205
Age	0,200
Sex	0,191
Common friends	0,165
Distance hometown location	0,146
Dunbar Circles	0,093

(b) Attribute importance

Fig. 6. Analysis of the accuracy of the model for ego network having different size.

the information gain provided by an attribute in order to identify the class label of a community. The graph clearly indicates that the most part of the models have either accuracy or fraction of correctly classified friends higher than 0.8 while some users (those in the ranges [900–1200] and [1500,1800]) expose a lower accuracy because the attributes specified by friends cannot be used to correctly classify them in the proper community.

6 Conclusion

In this paper, we focused on the privacy issues related to the contents sharing in Distributed Online Social Networks (DOSNs) by proposing a Privacy Policy Recommendation System (PPRS) that suggests to users the most appropriate privacy policy that expressing the groups of friends who can read the content they share. In particular, the privacy policy specify the authorized users in terms of a set of features encoded by attributes. Those attributes model different properties of users (such as gender, age, common relationship, preferences, location, etc.) and they are exploited by the PPRS to predict the privacy preference a user would give to their friends. We investigated the capability of the PPRS to select the attributes of the privacy policies by considering a real dataset obtained from Facebook, and the communities of friends arising from the friendships defined by each user. The experimental results performed on six attributes reveal that the PPRS is able to suggest privacy policies which correctly grant access to about 80% of the members of the communities, achieving higher level of accuracy.

We plan to enhance the proposed system by introducing proper mechanisms that adjust the conditions generated on each attribute by the PPRS in order to refine the set of authorized members. A further extension is also the investigation of the effect that different configuration parameters have on the performance of the classification algorithm.

References

1. Bielenberg, A., Helm, L., Gentilucci, A., Stefanescu, D., Zhang, H.: The growth of diaspora - a decentralized online social network in the wild. In: INFOCOM Workshops, pp. 13–18. IEEE (2012)
2. Conti, M., De Salve, A., Guidi, B., Pitto, F., Ricci, L.: Trusted dynamic storage for dunbar-based P2P online social networks. In: Meersman, R., et al. (eds.) OTM 2014. LNCS, vol. 8841, pp. 400–417. Springer, Heidelberg (2014). https://doi.org/10.1007/978-3-662-45563-0_23
3. Coscia, M., Rossetti, G., Giannotti, F., Pedreschi, D.: Demon: a local-first discovery method for overlapping communities. In: Proceedings of the 18th ACM KDD, pp. 615–623 (2012)
4. Cutillo, L.A., Molva, R., Strufe, T.: Safebook: a privacy-preserving online social network leveraging on real-life trust. IEEE Commun. Mag. **47**(12), 94–101 (2009)
5. De Salve, A., Dondio, M., Guidi, B., Ricci, L.: The impact of user's availability on on-line ego networks: a facebook analysis. Comput. Commun. **73**, 211–218 (2016)
6. De Salve, A., Guidi, B., Ricci, L.: Evaluation of structural and temporal properties of ego networks for data availability in DOSNs. Mob. Netw. Appl. **23**(1), 155–166 (2018)
7. De Salve, A., Mori, P., Ricci, L.: Evaluating the impact of friends in predicting user's availability in online social networks. In: Guidotti, R., Monreale, A., Pedreschi, D., Abiteboul, S. (eds.) PAP 2017. LNCS, vol. 10708, pp. 51–63. Springer, Cham (2017). https://doi.org/10.1007/978-3-319-71970-2_6
8. De Salve, A., Mori, P., Ricci, L.: A survey on privacy in decentralized online social networks. Comput. Sci. Rev. **27**, 154–176 (2018)
9. De Salve, A., Mori, P., Ricci, L., Al-Aaridhi, R., Graffi, K.: Privacy-preserving data allocation in decentralized online social networks. In: Jelasity, M., Kalyvianaki, E. (eds.) DAIS 2016. LNCS, vol. 9687, pp. 47–60. Springer, Cham (2016). https://doi.org/10.1007/978-3-319-39577-7_4
10. Dunbar, R.: The social brain hypothesis. Brain **9**(10), 178–190 (1998)
11. Gao, H., Hu, J., Huang, T., Wang, J., Chen, Y.: Security issues in online social networks. IEEE Internet Comput. **15**(4), 56–63 (2011)
12. Guidi, B., Amft, T., De Salve, A., Graffi, K., Ricci, L.: DiDuSoNet: A P2P architecture for distributed dunbar-based social networks. Peer-to-Peer Netw. Appl. **9**(6), 1177–1194 (2016)
13. Guidi, B., Michienzi, A., Rossetti, G.: Dynamic community analysis in decentralized online social networks. In: Heras, D.B., Bougé, L. (eds.) Euro-Par 2017. LNCS, vol. 10659, pp. 517–528. Springer, Cham (2018). https://doi.org/10.1007/978-3-319-75178-8_42
14. Landis, J.R., Koch, G.G.: The measurement of observer agreement for categorical data. Biometrics **33**, 159–174 (1977)
15. Mislove, A., Viswanath, B., Gummadi, K.P., Druschel, P.: You are who you know: inferring user profiles in online social networks. In: Proceedings of the third ACM International Conference on Web search and Data mining, pp. 251–260 (2010)
16. Quinlan, J.R.: C4. 5: Programs for Machine Learning. Elsevier, Amsterdam (2014)
17. Yeung, C.-m.A., Liccardi, I., Lu, K., Seneviratne, O., Berners-Lee, T.: Decentralization: the future of online social networking. In: W3C Workshop on the Future of Social Networking Position Papers, vol. 2, pp. 2–7 (2009)

ComeHere: Exploiting Ethereum for Secure Sharing of Health-Care Data

Matteo Franceschi[1(✉)], Davide Morelli[1,4], David Plans[1,4], Alan Brown[1], John Collomosse[2], Louise Coutts[2], and Laura Ricci[3]

[1] Center for Digital Economy, University of Surrey, Guildford, UK
mfranceschi94@gmail.com, {d.morelli,d.plans,alan.w.brown}@surrey.ac.uk
[2] Center for Vision, Speech and Signal Processing, University of Surrey, Guildford, UK
{j.collomosse,l.v.coutts}@surrey.ac.uk
[3] Department of Computer Science, University of Pisa, Pisa, Italy
laura.ricci@unipi.it
[4] BioBeats Group LTD, London, UK
{davide,david}@biobeats.com

Abstract. The problem of protecting sensitive data like medical records, and enabling the access only to authorized entities is currently a challenge. Current solutions often require trusting some centralized entity which is in charge of managing the data. The disruptive technology of blockchains may offer the possibility to change the current scenario and give to the users the control on their personal data.

In this paper we propose ComeHere, a system able to store medical records and to exploit the blockchain technology to control and track the access right transfer on the blockchain. The paper shows the current status of the project, presents a preliminary proof-of-concept implementation and discusses the future improvements of the system, and some critical issues which are still open.

Keywords: Ethereum · Healthcare · Blockchain

1 Introduction

The huge amount of personal data produced by different networked services, (social networks, health care services, selling services,...), are currently scattered among numerous data servers owned by different companies. The end users do not really have the control over their data and have to trust several entities which manage them, hoping they maintain the privacy of users' data. However, their trust is, in many cases, misplaced, because these entities handle users' data in a hardly controllable and verifiable way. Logging events generated by users to keep track of how data is used may be a solution, but in general, it is not implemented, and, in any case, no guarantee against log tampering is given.

A nagging problem is that of sensitive data such as medical records which may be scattered between numerous servers and encoded in different ways. When

G. Mencagli et al. (Eds.): Euro-Par 2018 Workshops, LNCS 11339, pp. 585–596, 2019.
https://doi.org/10.1007/978-3-030-10549-5_46

a user moves from a healthcare entity to another one, often he or she has to ask for their own data. Furthermore, research groups need to gather lots of medical data from a large number of individuals to support their researches and patients have to trust those groups to maintain their privacy and data secure. However, the tools to guarantee that only the proper entities access data and that gathered data remains anonymous are often inadequate.

Medical data pose several challenges, some of the most important are summarized in [2]. These data are sensitive and should be handled with the highest security standards. In particular, amongst other requirements, users should be able to delete their data; data should be exempt from tampering; only allowed entities should be able to access and process users data; all additions, deletions, and modifications of data should be logged, and all actors participating in the data handling system should be accountable for their actions. A system designed to fulfill security requirements would only allow access to a restricted set of agents, requiring explicit user consent to grant access to new agents. However, there are several cases in which requiring explicit consent could be impractical or would be detrimental to users best interests, e.g. to allow access to medical doctors in an emergency, or to allow researchers to develop drugs that the user might need in the future.

The blockchain technology [1] has recently been proposed as a solution to many of these problems. At a high level, the blockchain is a publicly accessible, append-only, tamper-free, distributed and replicated ledger of the same type of data. Using the blockchain technology and its characteristic to support tracking of medical data is a novel research field. Even without completely eliminating a centralized trusted entity, the blockchain technology could help to define a public and trusted log, storing how users data is accessed and shared, enforcing accountability for data access. Of course, control over data has to be guaranteed to their real owners. Data may be encrypted and shared on the blockchain so there is no way for people except who knows the right decryption key to access the data. Furthermore sharing data on the blockchain must be done carefully because, as already mentioned, it's an append-only data structure so it's impossible to remove data from it.

The ComeHere project exploits the blockchain technology to create a shared, trusted log of all the actions made over the data. This log is guaranteed to be tamper-proof and the creation of its record is delegated to trusted code running on the blockchain therefore not modifiable and publicly audible by every party that use the system. The difference between a traditional storage system and ComeHere is that the way data is shared, requested, saved etc. is publicly audible and impossible to tamper.

The structure of the paper is the following: Sect. 2 presents a brief introduction to blockchain technology, in particular Ethereum, and analyzes some existing proposals close to our system. Section 3 describes the general structure and architecture of ComeHere focusing, in particular, on the role of each smart contract. Section 5 shows how the system is implemented and the necessary steps to execute each action available to the users. Some preliminary results are presented in Sect. 6, and finally, Sect. 7 concludes the paper pointing out some open problems and future directions that ComeHere will take.

2 Background and Related Work

2.1 The Ethereum Blockchain

Blockchain technology allows creating an immutable, distributed and secure database of arbitrary data. A distributed consensus protocol gives the rules on how to manage and update the database (in particular decides what valid data is to add). The first usage of the blockchain technology was as a support for the Bitcoin cryptocurrency [6], in this scenario the database is used to record the transaction between entities. ComeHere exploits the Ethereum blockchain [7] which takes the idea of the Bitcoin blockchain and adds the possibility to execute distributed applications defined through a Turing complete programming language. The protocol has *ether* as currency. Entities in the blockchain, masked with a pseudonym (addresses), can exchange value between them by sending transactions to the network which are validated and update the global state. To validate a transaction, miners in the network have to execute the Ethereum consensus algorithm called *Ethash* which is based on PoW (i.e. Proof-of-Work). The main characteristic of the Ethereum protocol is the possibility to use the blockchain not only to store value but also code. Users can send transactions carrying executable Turing complete code, the *smart contracts*. Transactions can create smart contracts which deploy their code and link that to a public address. Any new transaction sent to this address triggers the execution of one of the functions inside the deployed smart contract. Transactions carry the function parameters needed for the execution. To validate such transactions the code has to be executed, and this can possibly update the global state which can be seen as the state the EVM, i.e. the Ethereum Virtual Machine, a virtual machine that runs all the code stored inside the blockchain. Miners actually execute the code inside the smart contract and they are rewarded for this: to each instruction of the EVM it's assigned a price proportional to the difficulty of that instruction. This price is called *gas*. So a transaction will have a total gas cost which is the sum of gas of every single instruction that has to be executed. Each transaction specifies two parameters *gas limit* and *gas price*, the former is the maximum amount of gas the transaction is allowed to consume, the latter is the amount that the user creating the transaction is willing to pay for each gas consumed.

2.2 Blockchain and Access Control

The use of blockchain for giving permission and access to data has been recently proposed, in particular for sensible records like health care data. The main reason why we are trying to use this technology instead of standard and consolidated ones is that the blockchain gives audibility and removes the need for trusting who maintains personal data. The code is publicly readable and checkable, hosted in the blockchain, we don't need anymore to trust closed systems that promise functionalities we don't have any control over. A general approach to the use of blockchain as an access control is presented in [3,4] where they implement the standard XACML directly in the blockchain. In [5] the authors implement a typology of smart contract that pairs each patient to a medical provider and stores pointers to data (as SQL queries) of the patient in the provider's database. [8] proposes a system where private blockchains are used to directly store the data encrypted and HDGs (i.e. Healthcare Data Gateway) which are off chain software are used as gatekeeper for the access to such data.

3 The ComeHere System: General Architecture

This paper proposes the ComeHere system, the Fig. 1 shows an high level representation of the system architecture. The system includes a trusted centralized server that maintains personal and sensitive healthcare data and exploits the Ethereum public blockchain to create a public audible log of the history of the data managed by the system. This log is made using 4 smart contracts communicating with each other, the server queries the smart contracts to give access to data and the rights to access any data can be verified by anyone checking the smart contract.

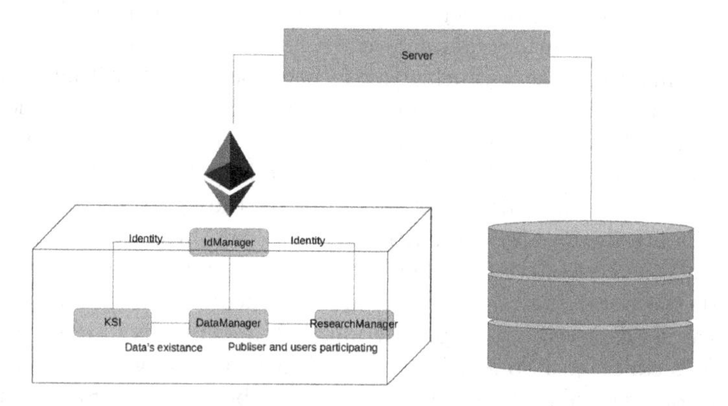

Fig. 1. Representation of the interaction and the structure of the ComeHere system

The aim of the system is to transform the provision of personal healthcare by commodifying and brokering personal healthcare data (e.g. from WBS, mobile devices or the IoT) to healthcare providers, enabling them to optimize preventative healthcare and helping to achieve a more efficient healthcare system. The system establishes the technical, logistic and socio-economic feasibility of the use of a public blockchain as an access-control manager to personal healthcare data. In particular, ComeHere aims to change the present paradigm where healthcare providers have to find people to base their study on. This system offers to healthcare providers an already established pool of people which will be informed about the researches the providers are carrying on. Who is willing to participate decides to opt-in giving the authorization to share personal and anonymous data to them.

There are two types of actors in the system: *institutions* which use the system to gather data to support their research and *participants* which take part in researches and create data for them.

The system is formed by a centralized server and a blockchain where four smart contracts have been deployed. The functions of the smart contracts are the following ones:

- *IdManager.* Maintains the digital identity of the registered users
- *ResearchManager.* Maintains public information about published researches and the list of participants of each research
- *KSI.* Keyless Signature Infrastructure, maintains information about submitted data and stores the hash of all the data submitted as an anti-tamper proof
- *DataManager.* Maintains authorization to store and retrieve data, and implements the real log of the access and storage of all the data managed by ComeHere.

Every user is publicly identified by their Ethereum address. The personal information which links an address to a person or institution is maintained securely in the centralized server. The registration is done sending personal data to the server that stores it in its database, and a message signed with their Ethereum private key which proves they own the address. The server may request additional information from the user and the registration is completed when the address is saved on the *IdManager.* After the registration, only the Ethereum address is required to interact with the system.

Institutions can publish researches by sending a transaction to the *ResearchManager* smart contract with all the needed information that are saved directly on the blockchain. The server maintains in its database a link to the published research. Participants can request the list of the researches to the server which gathers all the information from the *ResearchManager* and sends them to the participant. If a participant decides to opt in a research, he/she sends a transaction to the *ResearchManager* which logs that he/she is now participating in that research.

Participants are requested to publish data for researches. Data is stored in the server database, while the blockchain is used to guarantee their correct usage. First, the hash of the data is sent to the *KSI smart contract.* This proves that data won't be changed when submitted and after it is saved. Then data is submitted to the server which checks the identity of the submitter and that the hash of the data exists. The server logs on the blockchain the reception of the data. At this point, the participant submits an authorization to the blockchain that requests to save his data. The server sets in the blockchain a unique id that identifies the data in its server and adds this id to the list of the research data's id.

To retrieve the data submitted for their researches, institutions send a transaction to the *DataManager* to log and authorize the request to retrieve data. Then, they send the request to the server which asks the *DataManager* to check if the authorization has been submitted, if the authorization is found, the server retrieves the list of data's id from the blockchain and sends those data, saved in its database, to the institution.

4 ComeHere: The Smart Contracts

Each smart contract defines a set of public functions that can be called by every registered user and some private functions reserved to the server which is the only one that has the right to use them. Examples of private functions are those setting the unique ID of some data or registering new users in the system. Those functions can't be public but are a prerogative of the server.

4.1 Keyless Signature Infrastructure

This smart contract allows registered users to publish the hash of their data, those hash are also timestamped and the sender address is logged. The hash is used as an anti-tamper proof for the data. The centralized server can invoke two more functions of the smart contract which permit to log the event corresponding to the reception of the data and to set the data unique id when it is saved (Fig. 2).

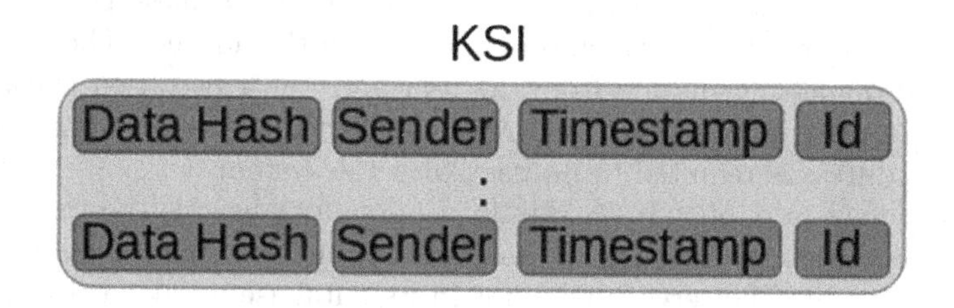

Fig. 2. Data stored in the KSI smart contract

4.2 IdManager

The smart contract saves the registered users of the system with their roles and the permissions set during the registration process. Only the server has the rights to register new users. In particular, institutions that retrieve data first need to be identified by the system. The smart contract permits also to check the role of every registered user. No personal information is stored in the blockchain: users are identified by their address and the server maintains a link between the address and the personal information (Fig. 3).

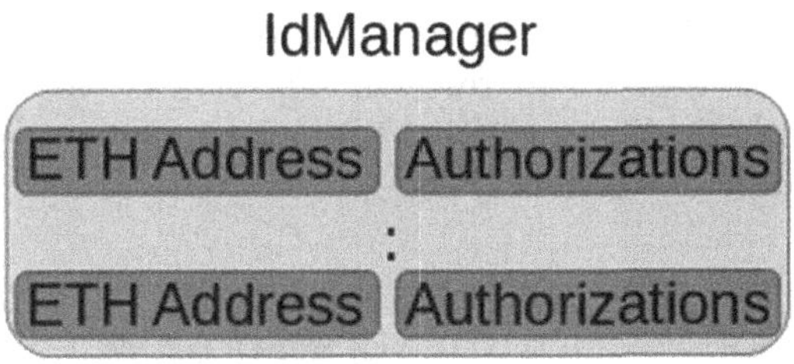

Fig. 3. Data stored in the IdManager smart contract

4.3 ResearchManager

The smart contract allows registered institutions to publish new researches. The data they provide is the research period and an URL where the user may find further information about the research. Participants can utilize the smart contract to participate in published researches (Fig. 4).

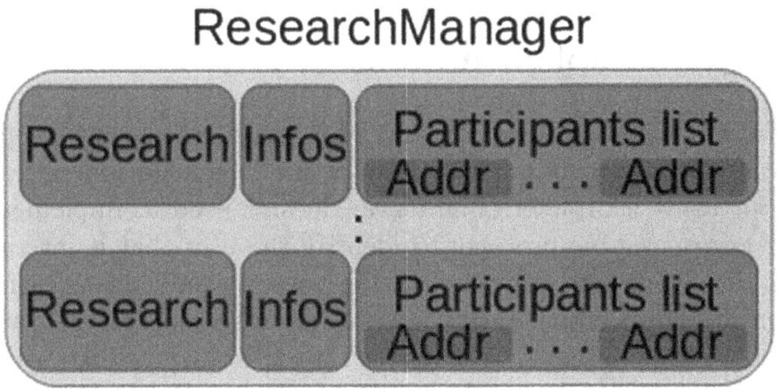

Fig. 4. ResearchManager smart contract is used to publish researches. It stores research's public info and the Ethereum address of each participant is added to the participants list

4.4 DataManager

The smart contract logs requests to store and retrieve data from the server database. Participants send a request to save data submitting the hash and the project id of the data. The smart contract checks if the user is authorized to perform this action and if the server has previously received the data. Institutions can submit authorization to retrieve data for their researches, the smart contract checks if the institution has the rights to send the authorization, in particular if the research has started and has not finished yet. The server uses this smart contract to set the unique ID of the data and also adds that ID to the list of research's data. This smart contract is also used when an institution asks the server to get the data for its research. The smart contract first checks the existence of an authorization submitted within a day and retrieves the list of ids of data to send to the institution (Fig. 5).

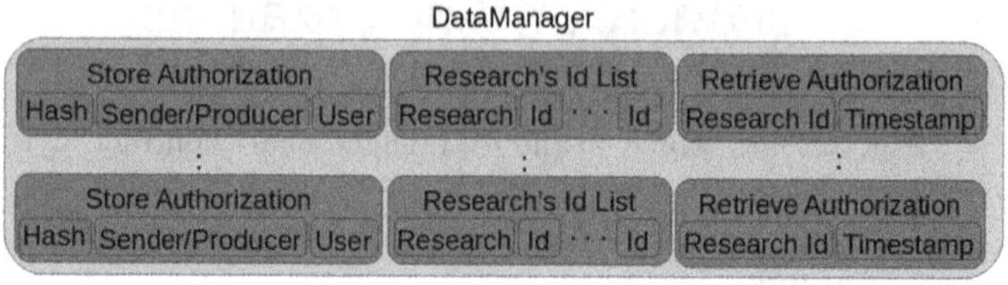

Fig. 5. DataManager has three different type of data structures: store authorization used to store submitted data, Research's Id List which maintains for each research the list of data Id relatives to that research and retrieve authorization used to log when a retrieve request is made.

5 ComeHere: Implementation

The server is implemented as a simple HTTP server which already gives all the functionalities described, but it can also be used by sending requests directly to it, without using a browser. The server doesn't need to implement any registration or cryptographic protocol to identify the user that is interacting with it, because the blockchain provides all the security and identification needed. The interaction between the server and the blockchain is realized by exploiting the standard *web3.js* library and *truffle-contract*[1] library to instantiate and use the smart contracts. The smart contracts are written using Solidity. Solidity is a contract-oriented language which is compiled into a bytecode executable by the Ethereum Virtual Machine.

The server monitors in real time when a new research is published and a new request to save data is received. The identification of a user requires the server to request from that user a signed message with its Ethereum address private key which proves its identity and the signature is directly controlled by the smart contracts code as an additional trust check.

The website pages provided by the server use *Metamask* plugin[2] which injects its own implementation of the standard *web3.js* library to interact with the smart contracts and Ethereum blockchain.

As already mentioned, even if the server does not expose a proper API at the moment, it's already possible to send requests directly from the application without standard authentication protocols. This is possible because each request made to the server will be authenticated using the blockchain smart contracts.

[1] https://github.com/trufflesuite/truffle-contract.
[2] https://metamask.io.

5.1 Registration

The registration is made by the server sending a transaction to the IdManager smart contract. The address of the user to register is sent in the transaction along with a message signed with that address's private key and parameters chosen by the server to set the permissions of the new user (e.g. possible permissions are the ability to create or retrieve data and to publish researches). The smart contract checks that the signed message is valid and registers the user in the system.

5.2 Publishing Research

A registered institution with the authorization of publishing researches can send a transaction to the ResearchManager smart contract to publish a new research. The smart contract checks the authorization of the user, then stores all the information in the public blockchain. The smart contract also fires an event that informs that a new research has been published and the server stores the id of the new research in its database. Other applications can also receive the event and act accordingly, for example, a notification server can wait for those events and push a notification on the mobile phone of a user.

5.3 Participating in a Research

A registered user can send a transaction to the ResearchManager smart contract to opt-in a research. The smart contract checks that the user is registered in the system and then adds its public address to the research's list of participants.

5.4 Submitting Data for Research

A user submits data to the system by sending to the *KSI smart contract* a transaction with the hash of the data. This contract first checks if the user is registered and has the authorization to submit data. If this condition is true, it stores the hash of the data with its timestamp and the address of the user. Afterwards, the user sends the data to the server with its hash signed with its private key.

The server again checks that the user is registered and authorized, then verifies the signature and if all these conditions are satisfied, it sends a transaction to the KSI smart contract to log that it received the data, then it sends a positive response to the user. The user, at this point, can send an authorization request to save its data to the *DataManager smart contract* calling the method *submitAuthorization*. This method includes the hash of the data to save and the id of the research for which data is saved. The smart contract checks that the user of the data is participating in the research he is submitting data for and that the sender of the data is also the owner of it. Then checks that the hash of the data exists and has been sent by the same user who sent this message and that has been received by the server. In this case, it stores the new authorization and fires an event that requests to save the sent data. The server waits for these events and it is the only authorized to submit a transaction to the *DataManager smart contract* which adds the Id of the data to the research's id list and sets the same Id on the *KSI smart contract.*

We plan to extend the ComeHere system to let users called *Data Producers* to submit data on behalf of other participants and this is the reason for the complexity of the procedure to submit data. If users submit data for themselves, it is enough to publish the hash of data to the *KSI smart contract* and then save it to the database. In the more general case, where Data Producers submit data on behalf of other users, they have to send the authorization request and the end user decides to authorize to save the data or not.

5.5 Retrieving Data for Research

When an institution wants to retrieve the data that has been previously submitted for its research, it needs first to submit an authorization request to the *DataManager smart contract*, the authorization is used as a timestamped retrieval requests to be stored on the log. The institutions send a transaction which includes the ID of the research to retrieve data for and the *DataManager* checks that the sender is also who published the research and that the research has not been yet concluded. Note that each authorization is timestamped and is valid for a day. Then the institution sends the request to the server which requires it to sign a message with its personal Ethereum address private key to prove its identity, then ask the DataManager to retrieve the research's list of data Id. The DataManager checks again that authorization not yet expired exists, and, in this case, it sends to the server the list of data's id to send to the institution. In this case, the authorizations to retrieve data are just a log of the number and time of the requests because when a user decides to participate in a research it gives the consent to give the institution its data.

As a future work, ComeHere will also permit institutions, medical staff or others entities called *Data Retriever* to request data from a user. In this case, the authorization request is stored on the blockchain and the owner of the data decides to give the authorization to access its data.

6 Experiments

We conducted a preliminary set of experiments on a 'proof of concept' system including the server and a private Ethereum network running on our machines, with just a node which validates all the incoming transactions. Even if in our test every transaction is instantly mined, we can evaluate the average time required to execute an operation like submitting new data to be at least 50 s in a real Ethereum network, where a new block is mined approximately every 10 s.

We created 50 users that submitted random data each day for 9 days for a single project. The simulation showed that with a fixed gas price of 5 gwei for transaction (the standard gas price swings between 2 and 5 gwei in this moment) a total of 0.376352 ether was spent by the users which is equivalent to 283,85$ (at an ethereum price of 755,35$[3]) each user spent 0.00752832 ether which is 5,68$. This may be an issue with the utilization of this system because people won't willingly spend their own money to give data for free for researches. Including a reward system for users or using another type of blockchain, for instance, a permissioned one could resolve this problem.

Over the time of the simulation, the amount of space occupied in the blockchain global state was 259.2 kbyte, not counting the space occupied by each block mined during the process. We need to take in consideration the space that this system occupies because blockchain space is expensive. The blockchain is replicated in every node of the network so 259.2 kbyte are replicated in thousands of others machines. We plan to solve this problem by defining a hierarchical solution including user's node which does not store an entire copy of the blockchain but connects to full nodes which maintain a full copy of the blockchain. Users' nodes can send transactions and interact with the smart contracts using full nodes.

7 Conclusions and Future Work

In this paper we presented ComeHere, a work in progress system to maintain medical data secure and give permissions over them through the use of the blockchain technology. The current implementation is a system where users publish their own medical data. In a real scenario, users never create medical and biometrical data for themselves but hospitals, medical staffs, care services create data for them. In the future, we plan to modify the system so that these third parties could create, submit and also retrieve data for users. The system offers a trusted environment where institutions may gather data for their research projects. The system gives the possibility to store and retrieve data to third parties so giving users a unique place where they can safely store and manage all their data. The user approves requests from third parties to submit or retrieve their data. The blockchain makes this possible, by registering the user's decision in a tamper-free distributed ledger. We plan to develop a full version of the server and to implement a real API. A mobile app will be created to interact with the system and also to enable interaction with other healthcare applications.

Some real-world problems have to be addressed before making ComeHere a publicly available system. For example, in every cryptocurrency, there is no way to recover a lost private key and who lose it automatically lose all his funds. Even if losing funds is already a big loss, it's not even comparable to losing access to all your medical history. A system must be designed to address this problem. The other problem that we need to address is the fact that we can keep track of data while it's inside ComeHere environment but when a user gives access to some data to third parties actually trusting those third parties and trusting how his data will be managed, we lose the traceability over that piece of data. After these and others minor problems have been addressed we think that ComeHere

[3] https://coinmarketcap.com/currencies/ethereum/.

will be a really successful and groundbreaking platform that uses one of the most discussed and researched technology of this time.

Acknowledgements. This research was partly sponsored by the UK's Engineering and Physical Sciences Research Council, grant number EP/P03196X/1, under the project: Co-operative Models for Evidence-based Healthcare Redistribution (CoME-HeRe), and also by BioBeats Group LTD, a UK company.

References

1. Bashir, I.: Mastering blockchain: distributed ledgers, decentralization and smart contracts explained (2017)
2. Bujari, A., Furini, M., Mandreoli, F., Martoglia, R., Montangero, M., Ronzani, D.: Standards, security and business models: key challenges for the IoT scenario. Mob. Netw. Appl. **23**(1), 147–154 (2018)
3. Di Francesco Maesa, D., Mori, P., Ricci, L.: Blockchain based access control. In: Chen, L.Y., Reiser, H.P. (eds.) DAIS 2017. LNCS, vol. 10320, pp. 206–220. Springer, Cham (2017). https://doi.org/10.1007/978-3-319-59665-5_15
4. Di Francesco Maesa, D., Mori, P., Ricci, L.: Blockchain based access control services. In: IEEE International Symposium on Recent Advances on Blockchain and Its Applications, Halifax, Canada (2018)
5. Ekblaw, A., Azaria, A., Halamka, J.D., Lippman, A.: A case study for blockchain in healthcare: "medrec" prototype for electronic health records and medical research data. In: Proceedings of IEEE Open & Big Data Conference, vol. 13, p. 13 (2016)
6. Nakamoto, S.: Bitcoin: a peer-to-peer electronic cash system (2008)
7. Wood, G.: Ethereum: a secure decentralised generalised transaction ledger. Ethereum Proj. Yellow Pap. **151**, 1–32 (2014)
8. Yue, X., Wang, H., Jin, D., Li, M., Jiang, W.: Healthcare data gateways: found healthcare intelligence on blockchain with novel privacy risk control. J. Med. Syst. **40**(10), 218 (2016)

Med-HPC - Workshop on Advances in High-Performance Bioinformatics, Systems Biology

Workshop on Advances in High-Performance Bioinformatics, Systems Biology (Med-HPC)

Workshop Description

The aim of Med-HPC workshop is to provide an opportunity to express and confront views on HPC trends, challenges, and state-of-the art in several application fields of Computational and Systems biology.

Its motivation is then due to the fact that a computational approach to biology is dealing with an enormous availability of data and an extreme complexity in the modeling and analysis of life systems. Therefore these issues make the scaling-up promise of High Performance Computing extremely appealing.

Currently, the possibility of parallelising algorithms and analysis techniques exploiting the various HPC emerging frameworks is receiving a lot of interest. Examples include the porting of legacy applications to clusters, e.g. those for genome analysis, and the use of distributed technologies, cloud computing, on-chip super-computing, GPUs, and massively parallel architectures for the treatment of high-throughput data-sets (e.g. Xeon Phi implementations).

In this first edition, we have received 7 articles for review, from 4 countries. At the end of the peer-reviewing process, 5 articles were selected for oral presentation The review process took into account the quality of the papers, their innovative ideas and their applicability to heterogeneous settings. Then, the acceptance of a paper were established through careful discussions among reviewers.

Finally, we would like to thank Med-HPC 2016 Program Committee, who made the workshop possible. I would also like to thank Euro-Par for hosting our community, and the Euro-Par workshop chairs Gabriele Mencagli and Dora Blanco Heras for their help and support.

Organization

Program Chairs

Marco Beccuti	University of Turin, Italy
Francesca Cordero	University of Turin, Italy
Pietro Lio'	University of Cambridge, UK
Ivan Merelli	Consiglio Nazionale delle Ricerche (CNR), Italy

Program Committee

Marzio Pennisi	University of Catania, Italy

Niccolo Totis	University of Turin, Italy
Laura Follia	University of Turin, Italy
Giulio Ferrero	University of Turin, Italy
Luciano Milanesi	Consiglio Nazionale delle Ricerche (CNR), Italy
Daniela Besozzi	University of Milano-Bicocca, Italy
Paolo Cazzaniga	University of Bergamo, Italy

BaaS - Bioinformatics as a Service

Ritesh Krishna(✉), Vadim Elisseev(✉), and Samuel Antao

IBM Research, SciTech Daresbury, Warrington WA4 4AD, UK
{ritesh.krishna,samuel.antao}@uk.ibm.com,vadim.v.elisseev@ibm.com

Abstract. Genomics and related technologies, collectively known as *Omics*, have transformed life sciences research. These technologies produce mountain of data that needs to be managed and analysed. Rapid developments in the Next Generation Sequencing technologies have helped genomics become mainstream, but the compute support systems, meant to enable genomics, have lagged behind. As genomics is making inroads into personalised health care and clinical settings, it is paramount that a robust compute infrastructure be designed to meet the growing needs of the field. Infrastructure design to deal with *omics* datasets is an active area of research and a critical one, for *omics* to be adopted in industrial healthcare and clinical settings. In this paper, we propose a blueprint for an *as-a service* compute infrastructure for fast and scalable processing of *omics* datasets. We explain our approach with help of a well-known bioinformatics workflow and a compute environment that can be tailored to achieve portability, reproducibility and scalability using modern High Performance Computing systems.

Keywords: Bioinformatics · HPC · Containers · Genomics Workflows

1 Introduction

Biology is a Big Data discipline, driven largely by the advancements in instrumentation that produce vast quantity of data. The key technologies are collectively known as *Omics*, consisting of genomics, transcriptomics, proteomics, metabolomics and several imaging techniques. Researchers often use a combination, or variations, of omics techniques (*multi-omics*) to understand biological systems in a comprehensive manner. Each of these omics techniques, can generate data in order of hundreds of gigabytes per experiment. The data magnitude scales up vastly in mulit-omics studies. While the omics revolution, provides us a magnifier to look at biology at a fine resolution, its success largely depends on the underlying data management techniques. Big Data and Omics, are fast evolving techniques in their respective domains, and it is becoming increasingly clear that the success of omics-revolution depends on highly scalable computing provisions that provide cost and energy efficient processing capabilities.

At the same time there are two important trends emerging in the Information Technologies industry: (*a*) Delivery of compute and storage resources *as-a-service*

G. Mencagli et al. (Eds.): Euro-Par 2018 Workshops, LNCS 11339, pp. 601–612, 2019.
https://doi.org/10.1007/978-3-030-10549-5_47

to provide various degrees of abstractions (platform as a service, software as a service, etc.) aimed to simplify interaction between end users and computational infrastructure, (*b*) Application of High Performance Computing (HPC) towards *Data Centric (DC) architecture* [14] that are designed to better handle workflows like the ones in *omics*.

In this paper, we will attempt to provide a road-map for Bioinformatics as a Service (BaaS) for distributed computing infrastructure, which can take advantage of modern HPC architectures to enable large scale *omics* data processing. We will focus on the Next Generation Sequencing (NGS) technologies, primarily applied for genomics and transcriptomics, and the main computational tasks involved in efficient processing of these datasets. We will explain our approach using a computational pipeline developed for processing whole transcriptomics datasets, also known as RNA-Seq datasets that are playing a central role in adaptation of NGS in clinical settings.

2 Motivation

Genomics data is growing at an unprecedented rate [15]. Much of the published raw data is available at the Sequence Read Archive (SRA) maintained by NIH/NCBI or its partnering institutions at EMBL-EBI (ENA - European Nucleotide Archive) and DNA Database of Japan (DDBJ). The magnitude of data produced from each experiment depends on many factors like the choice of sequencing platform, organism(s) being sequenced, expected read coverage, experimental goals etc. [5]. While a human whole genome sequencing data straight from the Illumina sequencer at 30x coverage is expected to be around 200 GB in size per sample [1], the whole transcriptome data can be much smaller around 2–10 GB in the similar settings [16]. An experiment will usually contain multiple samples and replicates. Specialised databases, like The Cancer Genome Atlas, ICGC etc., focus on cancer genomics and contain tens of thousands of samples obtained from a wider population. These samples need to be studied in tandem to create a comprehensive understanding of biological processes and phenotypes of interest. The very first steps towards creating a biological understanding from a set of *omics* data, is to process the dataset through appropriate bioinformatics pipelines. The pipelines churn through the raw datasets and create a reduced representation in form of community standard compressed file formats like SAM/BAM/VCF etc. These files create a basis for downstream data analysis through appropriate statistical and computational routines to generate biological insights.

2.1 Anatomy of a RNA-Seq Pipeline

RNA-Seq datasets are obtained to understand a range of biological phenomena, including understanding alternate gene splicing, gene fusion, changes in gene expression over time, or difference in gene expressions over different groups or treatments. Here, we will present a brief overview of a well accepted RNA-Seq data processing pipeline, called Tuxedo protocol [17], to lay the basis for our case-study. For simplicity, we assume that the experiment compares gene expression across only two conditions: wild-type vs mutant, and we want to compare the transcriptome profiles across conditions. The *de facto* standard for storing the output from a genome sequencer is the FASTQ format, a text based format that contains both the biological sequence as well as quality score. FASTQ files provide the starting point for the bioinformatics pipeline. For a typical paired-end read dataset, there would be a pair of FASTQ files for each technical replicate. Ideally, each experiment would contain several technical replicate for each biological replicate. The main computational steps involved in the protocol are read mapping, transcript assembly and detection of differentially expressed genes or transcripts. Figure 1 shows the information flow in the pipeline and the main tools used. The Tuxedo pipeline is based on TopHat [9] and Cufflinks [18] set of tools. TopHat is used to map reads from input FASTQ files to a user provided reference genome database and annotations. The read alignments are reported in form of compressed BAM files that are further processed through Cufflink to generate assembled transcripts for each condition. These assemblies are merged together by Cuffmerge to create a unified final transcript assembly file, which provides basis for comparing gene and transcript expression in each condition. The detection of differentially expressed gene or transcript is performed by Cuffdiff. Cuffdiff can also be used to perform an additional step of grouping transcripts into biologically relevant groups by performing a combined analysis of input FASTQ files with the final assembled transcripts. The results from Cuffdiff can be processed through a R [12] based package called CummeRbund for statistically relevant visualisation and final reporting. The entire pipeline consists of several stages, where some stages can be accelerated by employing efficient parallel and data movement strategies.

2.2 Scope for Parallel Constructs

While Fig. 1 shows an execution plan for a single sample with paired-end input files for two conditions, in reality, each experiment can consist of multiple samples and multiple conditions. Each pair of files, representing a particular sample under a particular condition, needs to be independently mapped and assembly-called using TopHat and Cufflinks respectively. These steps can be performed in an embarrassingly parallel way by assigning a dedicated resource - e.g. node, core, or accelerator - for each pair of files. When all the pair of FASTQ files have been processed to generate their respective BAM and GTF files, they need to be merged together through Cuffmerge to generate a final transcript assembly that needs to be analysed as a whole. Further, if there is a plan to perform grouping of reads through Cuffdiff, then this task is also specific to each pair of input files and can be performed independently in an asynchronous manner. In order to achieve significant speedup in case of large input FASTQ files on scales on tens of gigabytes, one can divide FASTQ files in chunks of manageable sizes and perform read mapping and assembly calling for each chunk and combine the BAMs and GTFs in the end. These strategies of divide and compute at certain stages in the pipeline provide means to manage memory, time and compute resources.

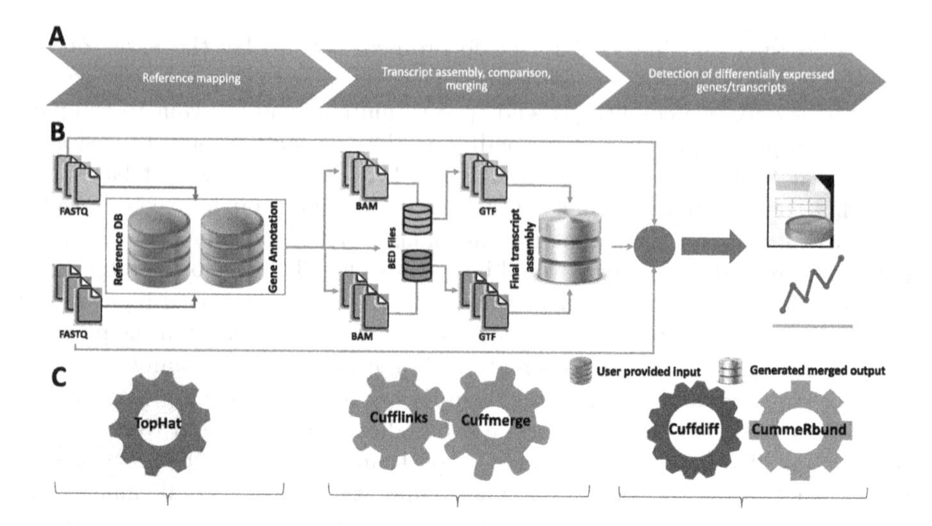

Fig. 1. The Tuxedo pipeline: (A) There are three main tasks in the pipeline - read mapping, transcript assembly, and detection of differential genes and transcripts. (B) The information flow in the pipeline and outputs produced at each stage. The input FASTQ files, shown in Orange and Light Blue, represent data from two experimental conditions. The same colour scheme is used to represent all the intermediate files generated for each condition. The steps in the pipeline are drawn to align with the sub-task listed in panel A. The input files are processed through different stages using tools as shown in the panel C of the figure. Each stage generates a set of output files that are used for downstream analysis. (C) List of tools grouped according to the sub-tasks listed in panel A. (Color figure online)

2.3 Portability and Reproducibility

While Tuxedo is a well understood and adopted pipeline, portability and reproducibility are two fundamental problems in bioinformatics. A typical workflow in bioinformatics requires a number of independently developed components that are stitched together through shell scripts, workflow standards or traditional programming constructs. These components are generally developed independently, using heterogeneous software engineering practices, by different research groups. Development of a pipeline that runs on a wide variety of platforms, and produces reproducible results is an important consideration in a clinical setting. The tools in a pipeline like Tuxedo offer a number of command-line arguments that need to be configured carefully and consistently to perform a reproducible study. The pipeline itself should be portable across compute architectures. The portability can be achieved through use of container technology like Docker [4], and reproducibility can be achieved using recently developed workflow languages like Common Workflow Language (CWL) [3]. To put reproducibility in context of our use case, lets focus on the first two steps in the pipeline, which are invocations of TopHat and Cufflinks respectively. The following boxes show how a call to these tools will look like when executed from a command-line interface.

```
tophat2 -p 8 -G user_annotation.gtf -o tophat_output
reference_genome Exp_R1_1.fq Exp_R1_2.fq

cufflinks -p 8 -o cufflinks_output tophat_output accepted_hits.bam
```

Both TopHat and Cufflinks come with a range of command line arguments to provide specific instructions to the tool depending on the input data. Here we use only the necessary arguments for demonstration purposes. In both TopHat and Cufflinks calls, switches like -p, -o represent the number of processors to use, and the name of output directories respectively. In TopHat, there is an additional switch -G to indicate the user provided annotation file. In order to achieve reproducibility, it is vital that the repeated execution of these tools involve the *same* arguments every time they are executed. Suppose, a new user comes with additional information about a particular dataset and decides to execute TopHat with an additional parameter *–library-type fr-secondstrand* which forces TopHat to perform read alignment in a different manner, the results will be different from what will otherwise be produced in the default mode, and the reproducibility will not be achieved. Specifications like CWL, provide a framework to facilitate on-demand construction of command-line calls and data movement in a consistent manner across environments. A user would directly manipulate a CWL representation as opposed to explicitly setting command line options.

Figure 2 shows a Rabix [19] enabled visualisation of the CWL code for TopHat and Cufflinks. Toolkits like Rabix, provide a graphical interface to enable a bench-biologist to create pipelines in CWL, without worrying about the language specifications. While at the same time, these tools provide an environment for experienced programmers to write complex CWL pipelines. The visualisation can be quite useful to understand and debug a pipeline with tens of intermediate steps and multiple input parameters. The combination of workflow languages with containers are increasingly being adopted by the bioinformatics community, and truly provide a plug-and-play environment for development of workflows and pipelines. These constructs provide a modular environment to introduce a new step, or, modify an existing one, without disturbing the rest of the pipeline. This is extremely handy as some bioinformatics pipelines can involve tens of steps and tools where maintaining a synchronisation between the components can be a tiresome and error-prone process.

3 Bioinformatics as a Service (*BaaS*)

The Tuxedo pipeline discussed in the previous sections is an example of a typical bioinformatics workflow, where a set of tools are stitched together to achieve a specific goal. While the tools in Tuxedo were developed by the same research group, it is often not the case in large bioinformatics workflows, where tools are developed by independent research groups, and a bioinformatician often mixes and matches among a set of available alternatives to prepare a workflow for

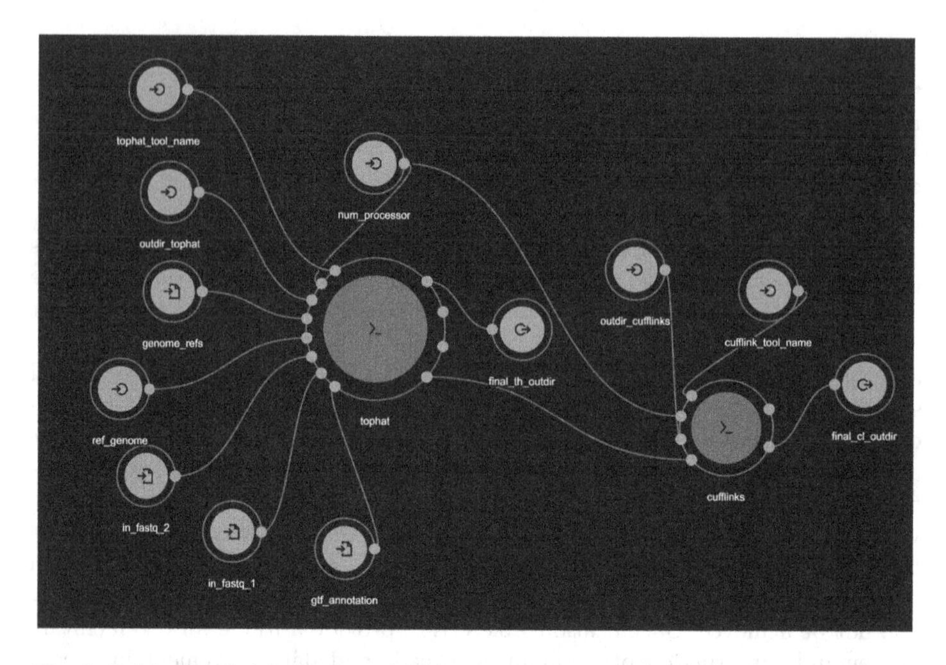

Fig. 2. Rabix based visualisation of CWL representation of TopHat and Cufflinks commands and their interconnectedness in the pipeline. The num_processor stands for -p in the above text. final_th_dir corresponds to -o tophat_output in the TopHat call and so on.

specific requirement. Different tools have different compute requirements and are diverse in their design and implementation. These are some fundamental problems in using different tools as components in a workflow: (*a*) Installation of the components –One can use a bioinformatics software, only if the software can be installed first. The software must be developed with good design and development practises. Many bioinformatics software can fail at this point itself. The dependent third party libraries can often be outdated, have obscure origin or not maintained anymore. The effort in trying to stitch dozens of such components together, where each component first needs to be built and tested before it can be a part of the pipeline can be daunting. (*b*) Security/Resilience –Due to the reasons mentioned above, one would not want an entire server to go down because a badly designed program misused the machine resources. At the very least, we expect the application to fail gracefully and the server to recover with minimum downtime. (*c*) Continuous changing landscape of the genomic technology –Genomics is among the fastest growing industries. The sequencing platforms, and the chemistry driving those platforms, both have been evolving rapidly, increasing the quality and quantity of the data produced. As a result, the software landscape is dynamic too, as it needs to keep pace with the latest platform updates. This dynamics require that there be a provision that a new software can be tested by easily plugging into the existing pipeline and discarded without affecting the entire workflow.

3.1 Essential Components

Our plan for implementing genomic pipelines *as-a-service* is shown in Fig. 3. We use a combination of HPC and virtualisation technologies, to build scalable, high performing and portable solutions, which can be used across private, public and hybrid Cloud environments. As a proof of concept we plan to use Docker, IBM®Spectrum LSF™ [7] and CWLEXEC [8]. All these components provide interoperable building blocks for creating *as-a-service* pipelines. Cluster design shown in Fig. 3 can be deployed in a private, public or hybrid Cloud. Portability can be achieved through custom-built Docker containers for each component in the workflow. Note that while our design is based on IBM POWER™ architectures, using the IBM-provided middle-ware components, the same design remains valid for building pipelines across different architectures.

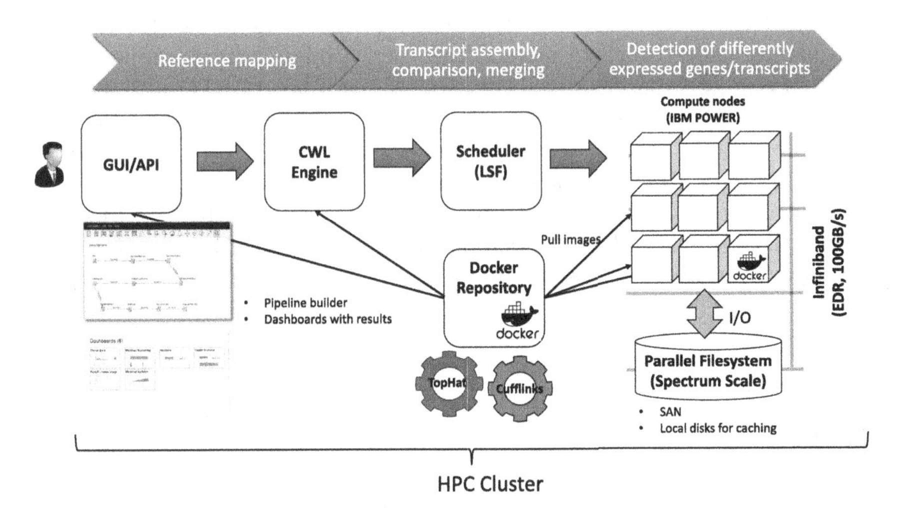

Fig. 3. *BaaS* workflow. Major components: GUI front-end for submission and displaying results, CWL engine, batch scheduler like IBM Spectrum LSF, HPC cluster with high bandwidth Infiniband interconnect, parallel high performance filesystem and Docker repository. Note that both shared and node local storage can be used for better I/O performance.

3.2 Pipeline Execution

In the proposed environment, the control flow of the pipeline is as follows:

1. User creates the desired workflow using a graphical interface, or directly through CWL language constructs
2. The workflow specification is parsed by the CWL engine and translated into submission scripts understandable by a scheduler.
3. Pipeline jobs are submitted to a scheduler in the order prescribed in the CWL flow. Scheduler ensures optimal job placement on compute nodes.

4. Jobs are started on compute nodes. Required components like TopHat and Cufflink are pulled from a Docker repository on demand.
5. All stages of a pipeline are completed, results are forwarded to the user.

Note that multiple instances of the above flow can be executed concurrently within the same HPC cluster following the scheme provided in Sect. 2.2. Data accesses from multiple pipelines are handled by the high performing parallel file system.

Figure 4 shows control flow of a single Pipeline instance as sequences of jobs with dependencies. Each stage of the pipeline consists of multiple concurrent jobs, with each job operating on a chunk of data. A special *wait* job waits for all jobs in a given stage to finish, and kicks off jobs for the next stage in the pipeline. In our context, it could be understood as Cufflinks will be executed only after TopHat has finished the mapping process and a BAM file for each FASTQ pair is available. Similarly, Cuffmerge will be executed only after all the GFT files are available before they are merged together. Similar wait constructs will be applied in case of Cuffdiff as well. In case, of the input FASTQ files divided in chunks and mapped individually, the system will wait for all the chunks to be mapped and results merged together to create a unified BAM. This sequence is repeated as many times as there are stages in the pipeline. It is important to note that all dependencies of each job - data availability, other jobs, etc. - are known to a scheduler and not hidden inside a job. This assures the best possible HPC resource utilisation and high throughput.

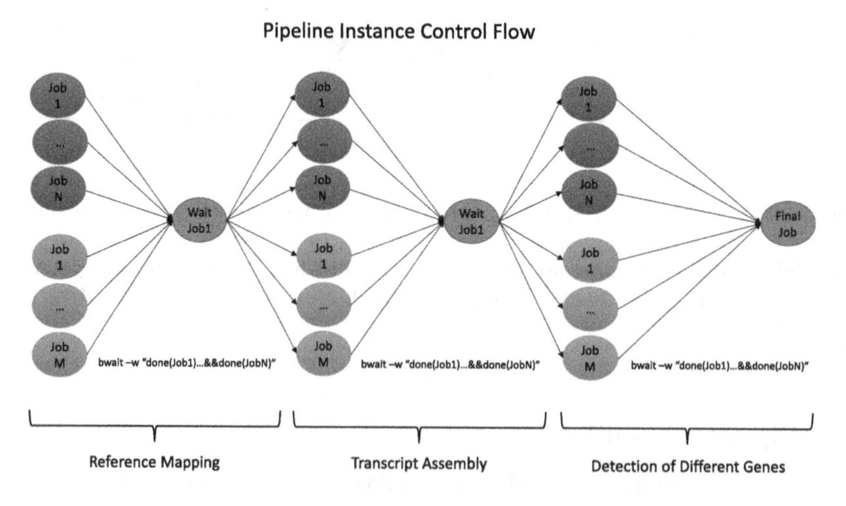

Fig. 4. Pipeline Instance Control Flow. Each stage consists of multiple concurrent jobs. Special "wait" jobs are used for synchronisation between stages. "Final" job is responsible for post-processing of the overall pipeline results.

4 *BaaS* in Data-Centric Systems

For a biologist, studying transcriptional activities, pipelines like Tuxedo provide a way to create meaningful insights from raw sequence data. The results are often in form of ASCII files and plots (like in Tuxedo) that provide the basis for further downstream analysis where specific biological questions can be asked, like understanding the interaction between differentially expressed genes of interest through a network perspective, or clustering of genes according to their functional profiles, or inference of phylogenetic relationships etc. Tuxedo like pipelines are independent but essential cog in a larger bioinformatics workflows, and a compute framework must make provisions to provide analytical capabilities to the results produced by such pipelines. The nature of questions that we ask from computational biology perspective varies as the field itself, and so can be the computational requirements. In order to realise *BaaS*, it is essential that we provide provisions to manage heterogeneous compute resources in the target data-centric systems to cater to different computational needs that arise in downstream analysis.

4.1 Heterogeneous Systems

Heterogeneous Systems have several types of processing elements and memory hierarchies, in contrast to the traditional systems with single type of processing element and a fixed memory hierarchy. Performance and compute density is obtained by specialised hardware tailored to compute patterns commonly found in scientific applications [10] making them suitable for compute intensive tasks in bioinformatics studies. Accelerators, in particular, Graphical Processing Units (GPUs) becoming integral elements of heterogeneous systems. We are seeing increasing examples of new software in bioinformatics exploiting GPUs [11], including tasks like read-mapping as achieved via TopHat in our case study, and examples of phylogenetic inferences [13], network biology etc. [2] as required for Post-Tuxedo downstream analysis.

One of the consequences of using accelerators is the necessity of using different memory spaces and move data efficiently between them. The intricacies around system heterogeneity pose an extra burden on users, as they now have to control where and when code should be executed and data be moved. Sophisticated interconnect between hardware and middleware, like NVLINK, and supporting development ecosystems like gpuR [6] etc. are increasingly being applied in bioinformatics studies [11].

As the benefits of using accelerators like GPUs become more apparent to users, we anticipate the presence of accelerated code and dependences to accelerator toolchains to become increasingly more frequent in the application used and developed in bioinformatics. For an end-user, in a heterogenous environment, to use a Tuxedo like pipeline, this will require two major considerations: (*i*) complex specification of resources in the pipeline, and (*ii*) increased scheduling complexity.

Specification of Heterogeneous Resources in the Pipeline. The resource requirements for a tool within a pipeline needs to be communicated to the scheduler, so the schedular can determine *where* and *how* a given application in the pipeline can be launched. *Where* because the schedule needs to forward the workload to machines that possess that resource (e.g. not all nodes may have a GPU). In some cases a given resource can be a hard dependence, i.e. the application only works if that resource is present, or it can be an option dependency, i.e. the application would perform better if that resource is present. Further, it is not uncommon that an application requires the environment or one of its arguments to specify the number of resources available to drive the partition of the problem at hand. This can be tackled by the creation of CWL nodes with attributes known to the scheduler that would be a dependence to the application. E.g. for the CWL representation in Fig. 2, the node `num_processor` would be provision of special attributes so that the scheduler knows the type of processors the application requires and its number. If the number of processors does not affect the results, an attribute would mark this node so that the scheduler could set the number at runtime depending on the number of resources it has available at a given time.

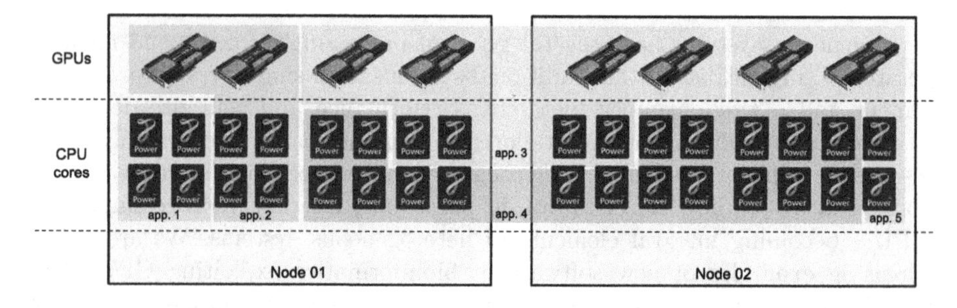

Fig. 5. Scheduling example for a set of application in a heterogeneous system with 4 NVIDIA GPUs and 16 Power 8 CPUs per core. In a given node, applications should use resources unused by applications already running there. The resource allocation can span across more than one node. Performance optimisation may involve migrating work once resources belonging to an application that finishes are released so that communication between all resources used by the other applications is more efficient.

Scheduling Complexity. Deploying an *as-a-service* platform for bioinformatics, necessarily implies that in a given system, multiple pipelines, each one with multiple independent jobs, will be running at a given time, and the scheduler must ensure that the system resources are utilised to the fullest. In a heterogenous environment, it is important that resources in a given machine are shared by different applications. If a given application only use CPUs, preventing the use of GPUs in that machine by some other application would hurt occupancy and, therefore, waste resources. Virtualisation of resources is therefore a must in order to obtain the right partition of resources from a given machine to be used by an application as shown in Fig. 5. That will also facilitate migration of resources between nodes to improve locality in the set of resources bound by an application. Modern scheduling tools have evolved to recognise accelerators like GPUs as a system resource in its own right and will be part of the *BaaS* design.

5 Conclusions

Even though Life Sciences is a vast field, DNAs are the fundamental unit of life, and central to all the biological questions. *Omics* technologies aim to understand DNA and its products, and are rapidly changing biology into a data-intensive discipline. Large amount of data requires efficient compute infrastructure for data processing. The infrastructure must be contextualised according to the discipline it aims to support. Bioinformatics has its own needs due to the nature of datasets and the computational tasks involved. *BaaS* is an attempt to address some of the typical computational requirements that arise from a Bioinformatics study. Though *BaaS* is presented in this paper as a blueprint, it utilises some well understood ideas and is easy to implement. We anticipate, as the NGS technologies progress in future, we will see many variations of field experiments and the rapid rise in produced data. We are already seeing a flood of data in Single cell sequencing experiments that are fast becoming mainstream. As the technology improves, so will the audacity of the experimental questions being asked, and so will be the amount of data produced. In our opinion, in order to under the central dogma of biology through the prism of *omics* data, we will need clever algorithms running on a range of compute devices as envisioned in *BaaS*. The specifications for *BaaS* as mentioned in this paper are by no means complete, as there are several important issues we didn't touch upon and would be useful for future improvements in the design. In this paper, we focussed only on the core functional aspect of *BaaS* as how jobs can be installed, scheduled and executed. To enhance the design of *BaaS* further, there must be considerations on the scope and role of its users and administrators, provisions for efficient data movement from a user's location to the compute cluster, cost effectiveness and benefits to the end-user, provisions for data sharing, and several other issues specific to Bioinformatics domain.

References

1. Robison, R.J.: How big is the human genome? https://medium.com/precision-medicine/how-big-is-the-human-genome-e90caa3409b0
2. Bhattacharya, A., Cui, Y.: A GPU-accelerated algorithm for biclustering analysis and detection of condition-dependent coexpression network modules. Sci. Rep. **7**(1) (2017). Article no. 4162
3. CWL working group: Common workflow language (2016). https://www.commonwl.org/
4. Docker: Docker (2018). https://www.docker.com/
5. Ekblom, R., Wolf, J.B.W.: A field guide to whole-genome sequencing, assembly and annotation **7**(9), 1026–1042. https://doi.org/10.1111/eva.12178

6. gpuR: gpuR repository page (2018). https://cran.r-project.org/web/packages/gpuR/index.html
7. IBM: IBM Spectrum LSF (2017). https://developer.ibm.com/storage/products/ibm-spectrum-lsf/
8. IBM: CWLEXEC (2018). https://github.com/IBMSpectrumComputing/cwlexec
9. Kim, D., Pertea, G., Trapnell, C., Pimentel, H., Kelley, R., Salzberg, S.L.: TopHat2: accurate alignment of transcriptomes in the presence of insertions, deletions and gene fusions **14**, R36. https://doi.org/10.1186/gb-2013-14-4-r36
10. Kim, N.S., Chen, D., Xiong, J., Hwu, W.W.: Heterogeneous computing meets near-memory acceleration and high-level synthesis in the post-moore era. IEEE Micro 37(4), 10–18 (2017). https://doi.org/10.1109/MM.2017.3211105
11. Nobile, M.S., Cazzaniga, P., Tangherloni, A., Besozzi, D.: Graphics processing units in bioinformatics, computational biology and systems biology. Brief. Bioinform. **18**(5), 870–885 (2017)
12. R Core Team: R: A Language and Environment for Statistical Computing. R Foundation for Statistical Computing, Vienna, Austria (2013). http://www.R-project.org/
13. Ronquist F., et al.: MrBayes 3.2: Efficient Bayesian phylogenetic inference and model choice across a large model space. Syst. Biol. **61**(3), 539–542 (2012)
14. Sadasivam, S.K., Thompto, B.W., Kalla, R., Starke, W.J.: IBM power9 processor architecture. IEEE Micro **37**(2), 40–51 (2017). https://doi.org/10.1109/MM.2017.40
15. Stephens, Z.D., et al.: Big data: astronomical or genomical? **13**(7), e1002195. https://doi.org/10.1371/journal.pbio.1002195
16. Tebani, A., Afonso, C., Marret, S., Bekri, S.: Omics-based strategies in precision medicine: toward a paradigm shift in inborn errors of metabolism investigations **17**(9), 1555. https://doi.org/10.3390/ijms17091555
17. Trapnell, C., et al.: Differential gene and transcript expression analysis of RNA-seq experiments with TopHat and Cufflinks **7**(3), 562–578. https://doi.org/10.1038/nprot.2012.016
18. Trapnell, C., et al.: Transcript assembly and abundance estimation from RNA-seq reveals thousands of new transcripts and switching among isoforms **28**(5), 511–515. https://doi.org/10.1038/nbt.1621
19. Various: Rabix website (2018). http://rabix.io/

Disaggregating Non-Volatile Memory for Throughput-Oriented Genomics Workloads

Aaron Call[1,2(✉)], Jordà Polo[1], David Carrera[1,2], Francesc Guim[3], and Sujoy Sen[3]

[1] Barcelona Supercomputing Center (BSC), Barcelona, Spain
{aaron.call,jorda.polo,david.carrera}@bsc.es
[2] Universitat Politècnica de Catalunya (UPC), Barcelona, Spain
[3] Intel Corporation, Santa Clara, USA
{francesc.guim,sujoy.sen}@intel.com

Abstract. Massive exploitation of next-generation sequencing technologies requires dealing with both: huge amounts of data and complex bioinformatics pipelines. Computing architectures have evolved to deal with these problems, enabling approaches that were unfeasible years ago: accelerators and Non-Volatile Memories (NVM) are becoming widely used to enhance the most demanding workloads. However, bioinformatics workloads are usually part of bigger pipelines with different and dynamic needs in terms of resources. The introduction of Software Defined Infrastructures (SDI) for data centers provides roots to dramatically increase the efficiency in the management of infrastructures. SDI enables new ways to structure hardware resources through disaggregation, and provides new hardware composability and sharing mechanisms to deploy workloads in more flexible ways. In this paper we study a state-of-the-art genomics application, SMUFIN, aiming to address the challenges of future HPC facilities.

Keywords: Genomics · Disaggregation · Composability · NVM
NVMeOF · Characterization · Orchestration

1 Introduction

The genetic basis of disease is increasingly becoming more accessible thanks to the emergence of Next Generation Sequencing platforms, which have extremely reduced the costs and increased the throughput of genomic sequencing. For the first time in history, personalized medicine is close to becoming a reality through the analysis of each patient's genome. Genomic variations, between patients or among cells of the same patient, have been identified to be the direct cause, or a predisposition to genetic diseases: from single nucleotide variants to structural

G. Mencagli et al. (Eds.): Euro-Par 2018 Workshops, LNCS 11339, pp. 613–625, 2019.
https://doi.org/10.1007/978-3-030-10549-5_48

variants, which can correspond to deletions, insertions, inversions, translocations and copy number variations, ranging from a few nucleotides to large genomic regions.

The exploitation of genomic sequencing should involve the accurate identification of all kinds of variants, in order to derive a correct diagnosis and to select the best therapy. For clinical purposes, it is important that this computational process be carried out within an effective timeframe. But a simple sequencing experiment typically yields thousands of millions of reads per genome, which have to be stored and processed. As a consequence, the analysis of genomes with diagnostic and therapeutic purposes is still a great challenge, both in the design of efficient algorithms and at the level of computing performance.

The field of computational genomics is quickly evolving in a continuous seek for more accurate results, but also looking for improvements in terms of performance and cost-efficiency. In parallel, computing architectures have also evolved, enabling approaches that were unfeasible only years ago. The use of Non-Volatile Memories (NVM) and accelerators has been widely adopted for all kinds of workloads with the introduction of NVMe cards, GPUs, and FPGAs for some of the most demanding computing challenges. Genomics workloads today have a larger variety of requirements related to the compute platforms they run in. Workloads are tuned to work optimally on specific configurations of compute, memory, and storage. On top of that, current genomics workloads and pipelines tend to be composed of multiple phases with different behaviors and resource requirements.

One such example in the context of variant calling is SMUFIN [15], a state-of-the-art method that performs a direct comparison of normal and tumor genomic samples from the same patient without the need of a reference genome, leading to more comprehensive results. In its original implementation, published in Nature [15] in 2014, this novel approach required significant amounts of resources in a supercomputing facility. Since then, it has been optimized and adapted to scale up and make the most of Non-Volatile Memory [1].

Beyond Non-Volatile Memories and accelerators, new technological advances currently under development, such as Software Defined Infrastructures, are dramatically changing the data center landscape. One of the key features of Software Defined Infrastructures is *disaggregation*, which allows dynamically attaching and detaching resources from physical nodes with just a software operation, removing the constraints of getting hardware components statically confined to servers. This paper takes a modern genomics workload, SMUFIN, evaluates disaggregation mechanisms when running it, and describes how characterization can be used to guide the orchestration of a genomics pipeline.

The rest of the paper is structured as follows. Section 2 provides an overview of the foundations of SMUFIN, the variant-calling method studied in this paper. Section 3 introduces resource disaggregation and the technology used to implement it. Next, Sect. 4 characterizes disaggregation mechanisms using SMUFIN. Section 5 shows how characterization can be used to guide orchestration. And finally, Sect. 6 discussed related work and Sect. 7 concludes.

2 SMUFIN: A Throughput-Oriented Genomics Workload

Most currently available methods for detecting genomic variations rely on an initial step that involves aligning sequence reads to a reference genome generally using Burrows-Wheeler transform [12], which has an impact not only on performance, but also on the accuracy of results. First, tumoral reads that carry variation may be harder or impossible to align against a reference genome. Second, the use of references also leads to interference with millions of inherited (germline) variants that affect the actual identification of somatic changes, consequently decreasing the final reliability and applicability of the results. The initial alignment also has an impact on subsequent analysis since most methods are tuned to identify only a particular kind or size of mutation [14]. Alternative methods that don't rely on the initial alignment of sequenced reads against a reference genome have been developed. In particular, the application used in this work is based on SMUFIN [15], a reference-free approach based on a direct comparison between normal and tumoral samples from the same patient. The basic idea behind SMUFIN can be summarized in the following steps: (i) input two sets of nucleic acid reads, normal and tumoral; (ii) build frequency counters of substrings in the input reads; and (iii) compare branches to find imbalances, which are then extracted as candidate positions for variation.

Internally, SMUFIN consists of a set of checkpointable stages that are combined to build fully fledged workloads (Fig. 1). These stages can be shaped on computing platforms depending on different criteria, such as availability or cost-effectiveness, allowing executions to be adapted to its environment. Data can be split into one or more *partitions*, and each one of these partitions can then be placed and distributed as needed: sequentially in a single machine, in parallel in multiple nodes, or even in different hardware depending on the characteristics of the stage. Data partitioning can be effectively used to adapt executions to a particular level of resources made available to SMUFIN, because it imposes a trade-off between computation and IO. This data partitioning can be achieved by going multiple times through the input data set that corresponds to each stage: *Prune*, *Count*, and *Filter*. In practice, systems with high-end capabilities will not require a high level of partitioning and hence IO, what ends up with scale-up solutions; on the opposite side of the spectrum, lower-end platforms are able to run the algorithm by partitioning data and duplicating IO, leading to scale-out solutions. The goal of each one of the stages is as follows:

- *Prune*: Discards sequences from the input by generating a bloom filter of k-mers that have been observed in the input more than once. Allows lowering memory requirements at the expense of additional computation and IO.
- *Count*: Builds a frequency table of normal and tumoral k-mers in the input sequences. More specifically, k-mer counters are used to detect imbalances when comparing two samples.
- *Filter*: Selects k-mers with imbalanced frequencies, which are candidates for variation, while also building indexes of sequences with such k-mers.

- *Merge*: Reads and combines multiple filter indexes from different partitions into single, unified indexes. Merging indexes only involves simple operations such as concatenation, OR on bitmaps, and appending.
- *Group*: Matches candidate sequences that belong to the same region. First, selecting reads that meet certain criteria, and then retrieving related reads by looking up those that contain the same imbalanced k-mers.

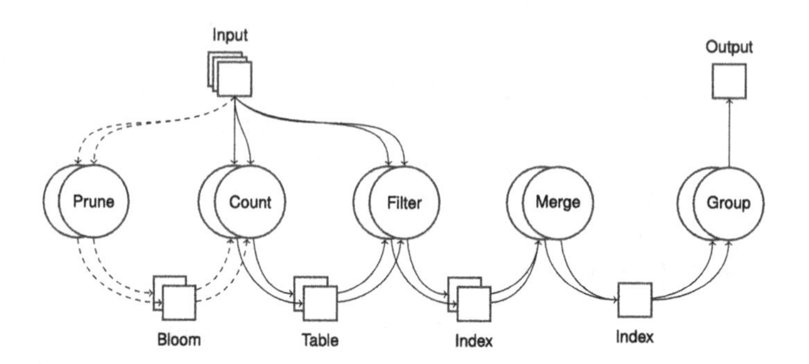

Fig. 1. SMUFIN's variant calling architecture: overview of stages and its data flow

One of the main characteristics of the current version of SMUFIN [1] is its ability to use NVM as memory extension. This can be exploited in two different ways. First, using an NVM optimized Key-Value Store such as RocksDB, and second, using a custom optimized swapping mechanism to flush memory directly to the device. When such memory extensions are available, a maximum size for the data structures is set; once such size is reached, data is flushed to the memory extension while a new empty structure becomes available. Generally speaking, bigger sizes are recommended: they help avoid duplicate data, and also lead to higher performance, as writing big chunks to a Non-Volatile Memory allows to exploit internal parallelism typical of flash drives [2].

SMUFIN's performance greatly benefits from NVM, as shown in Fig. 2, which compares an execution in 16 machines in a supercomputing facility (left) and a scale-up execution in a single node with NVM enabled (right). The latter leads to faster executions and lower power consumption. NVM can be leveraged in some way in most SMUFIN stages, and the experiments performed in this paper are focused on *Merge* using the RocksDB-based implementation, which is one of the most IO intensive of the pipeline. However, other stages have similar characteristics and the same techniques can be used elsewhere.

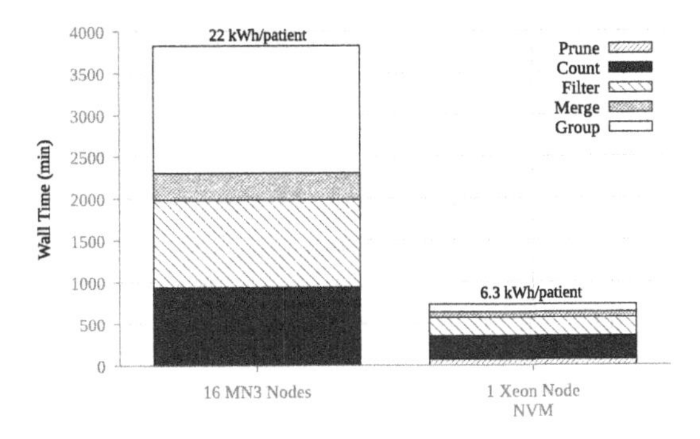

Fig. 2. Aggregate CPU time of a SMUFIN execution running in 16 MareNostrum nodes and in 1 Xeon-based node with NVM. Power consumption per execution (one patient) shown for reference.

3 Resource Disaggregation

Traditional data centers usually contain homogeneous and heterogeneous compute platforms (also referred to as computing nodes or servers). These platforms are statically composed by computing, memory, storage, fabric, and/or accelerator components, and they are usually stored in racks. However, in the last few years there has been a trend towards new technologies that allow disaggregating resources over the network, increasing flexibility and easying the management of such data centers.

This paper analyzes the use of one of those new technologies: *NVMe Over Fabrics* (NVMeOF). First off, NVMe [17] is an interface specification for accessing direct-attached NVM via a regular PCI Express bus. On the other hand NVMeOF [4] is an emerging network protocol used to communicate nodes with NVMe devices over a networking fabric. The architecture of NVMeOF allows scaling to large numbers of devices, and supports a range of different network fabrics, usually through Remote Direct Memory Access (RDMA) so as to eliminate middle software layers and provide very low latency.

Disaggregating NVMe over the network with NVMeOF allows new mechanisms to scale-up and improve efficiency of genomics workloads:

Resource Sharing. As workloads perceive remote NVMe as physically attached to their compute nodes, those can be partitioned, and each one of these partitions can then be exposed to the computational nodes as an exclusive resource. This translates into workload-unaware resource sharing, which in turn can lead to improved resource efficiency by maximizing usage.

Resource Composition. Certain resources can be aggregated and exposed as a single, physically attached resource. Instead of accessing individual units, accessing combined resources enables increased capacities that can lead to improved performance. For instance, two SSD disks with a bandwidth of 2 GB/s each can be composed and exposed as a single one with twice as much capacity and bandwidth, providing a total of 4 GB/s.

4 Characterizing Resource Disaggregation on SMUFIN

In a continuous need to deal with increasingly larger amounts of data, genomics workloads are quickly adapting, and NVM technologies have become widely used as a key component in the memory-storage hierarchy. This Section explores how disaggregating NVM might have an impact on genomics workloads, and in particular SMUFIN. As part of the evaluation, resource sharing and composition are analyzed using NVMeOF in an attempt to scale-up and shape the performance of the workload.

4.1 Experimental Environment

The experiments are conducted in an environment as depicted in Fig. 3.

The NVMe drives are used by SMUFIN as a memory extension over fabric to store temporary data structures required to accelerate the computation. As the drives are dual-controller, two NVMe devices – of half its physical size – are exposed by the system for each physical device. In order to expose a single NVMe consisting of its two controllers, or to unify several NVMe devices, Intel Rapid Storage Technology [9] (RST) is used. RST composes a RAID0 of the controllers which becomes exposed over fabric as a single NVMe card. Mellanox OFED 4.0-2.0.0.1 drivers were used for the InfiniBand HCA adapters. The drivers included modules for NVMe over fabrics as well, both the target and the client. Kernel 4.8.0-39 was used under Ubuntu server 16.10 operating system in all nodes.

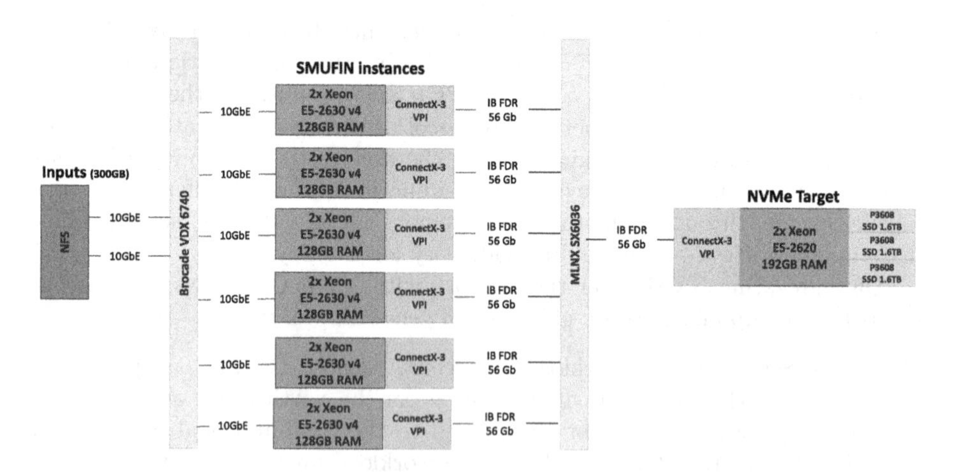

Fig. 3. Experiments environment

We use SMUFIN on its merge stage, as explained in Sect. 2. In the following evaluations each SMUFIN instance reads and processes a sample DNA input (+300 GB) from a NFS shared storage, while the shared NVMe devices are used as memory extension for temporary data and final output. SMUFIN has been implemented to maximize sequential writes to the devices, and this behavior has been verified by analyzing its access pattern. A block trace sample of requested blocks to the device was generated using Linux's *blktrace*, and the trace was then fed to the algorithm provided by [3] to calculate the percentage of sequential write accesses. This method identified 88% of sequential writes after adapting the algorithm to consider accesses in which the final address matched the initial address of many immediately following requests, thus accounting for file appends.

4.2 Direct-Attached Storage vs NVMe over Fabrics

The performance of NVMeOF has been studied in the literature [7], and found not to show any significant degradation when compared to *local* directly-attached storage (DAS). Additionally, in this section we perform our own experiments running up to 3 instances of SMUFIN in the same node: against a directly-attached NVMe device and against NVMeOF. Each instance processes the same dataset, generating ≈150 GB, with an average use of bandwidth of 477 MB/s per SMUFIN instance. The NVMe device is capable of handling 2 GB/s bandwidth under sequential write pattern, as is the SMUFIN scenario. Figure 4 shows average execution time and deviation after repeating the executions six times. As it can be observed, when running one and two instances on local storage (Fig. 4a) there is no performance degradation when disaggregating NVMe over fabrics (Fig. 4b). However, when running three concurrent instances there is a significant degradation of 6% when using NVMeOF.

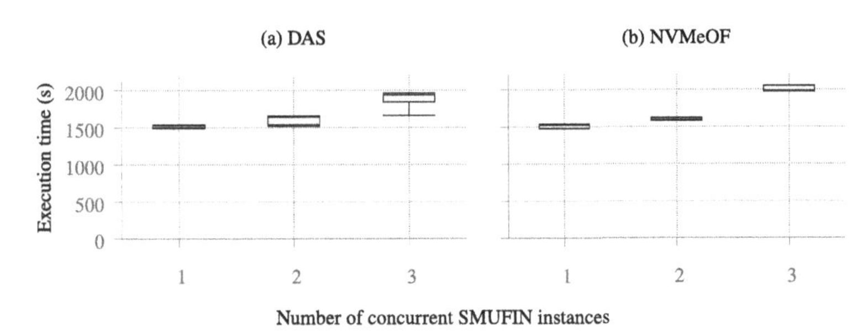

Fig. 4. Boxplot of execution time of Direct-Attached Storage (DAS) and NVMeOF when running 1x, 2x and 3x SMUFIN instances on the same node

On the other hand there is a certain performance degradation scaling up to three instances in both scenarios. Analyzing this behavior, up to two instances, the host's memory can handle all the intermediate data generated by SMUFIN and the NVMe becomes only used to output final data. However, with three instances the memory becomes a bottleneck and intermediate data not fitting in memory gets flushed to the NVMe device more frequently. Is in this scenario when degradation is observed and performance comparison against NVMeOF is worse. Figure 5 depicts memory usage on the three scenarios (1, 2 and 3 SMUFIN on the same node, directly-attached) over a period of 1500 s, evidencing the memory bottleneck.

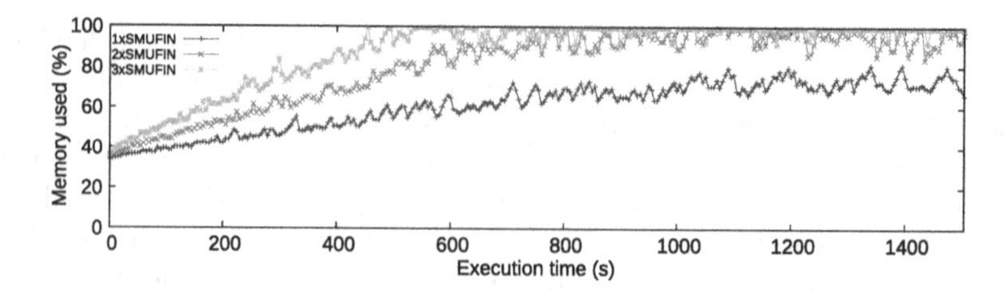

Fig. 5. Memory usage on 1x, 2x, 3x SMUFIN scenarios using Direct-Attached NVMe on a period of 1500 s

4.3 Resource Sharing and Composability

When multiple workloads share resources and hence compete for its usage, their execution time compared to a dedicated execution in isolation degrades when a threshold is reached, as shown in previous section. In this section we explore if degradation still occurs when running up to six concurrent instances, all of them using partitions from the same set of NVMe devices and running on separate nodes to avoid the aforementioned interferences.

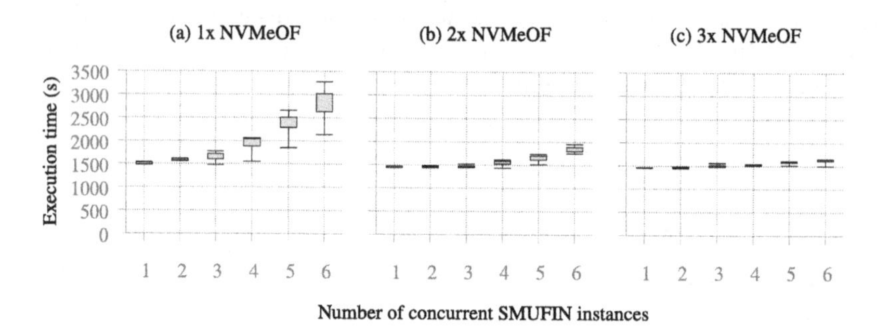

Fig. 6. Boxplots showing how execution time evolves when running multiple SMUFIN instances: sharing a single device (1xNVMe), or sharing on composed nodes (2xNVMe, 3xNVMe)

Figure 6a represents the box plot of individual execution times under different configurations, along with its quartiles, median, and standard deviation. In (a) only one NVMe SSD is used. It can be observed running three instances separately against a single device do not degrade as significantly as running under the same node. However, performance degradation is still experienced when certain resource sharing threshold is reached.

When disaggregating NVMe over fabrics we can benefit of composing several NVMe devices and expose them as a single one. Under composition, profiling data shows that the Intel driver balances the bandwidth evenly through all composed devices. It is also observed that provided bandwidth scales linearly with the number of devices, hence under 2 and 3-compositions 4 GB/s and 6 GB/s of sequential write speed can be reached respectively (each individual drive provides 2 GB/s). Through composition, performance degradation can be mitigated. Compositions of two and three NVMe SSD exposed as a single target to clients increases the bare-performance, as a composition multiplies the total available bandwidth. The evolution of execution time respect composition level is presented in Figs. 6b and c. In the 2-composition scenario, up to 3 sharing workloads obtain the same performance as if running alone in a single NVMe. The level of concurrency can be increased without introducing significant degradation using a composition of 3 NVMe, being able to have six sharing workloads with a similar performance as when running alone in a single device. Thus, workloads indeed benefit of resource composition. However, in all scenarios performance degradation still occurs on reaching a certain threshold, larger as more devices are used. Under 2-NVMe compositions it is at four workloads, whereas on the 3-composition the tendency is observed at six instances threshold.

4.4 Bandwidth

We observed performance degradation when a certain sharing ratio of resources is reached. Despite composition increases this threshold, degradation still occurs regardless of composition. As the memory bottleneck was removed and cannot be found on the network bandwidth, we analyze the target NVMe bandwidth.

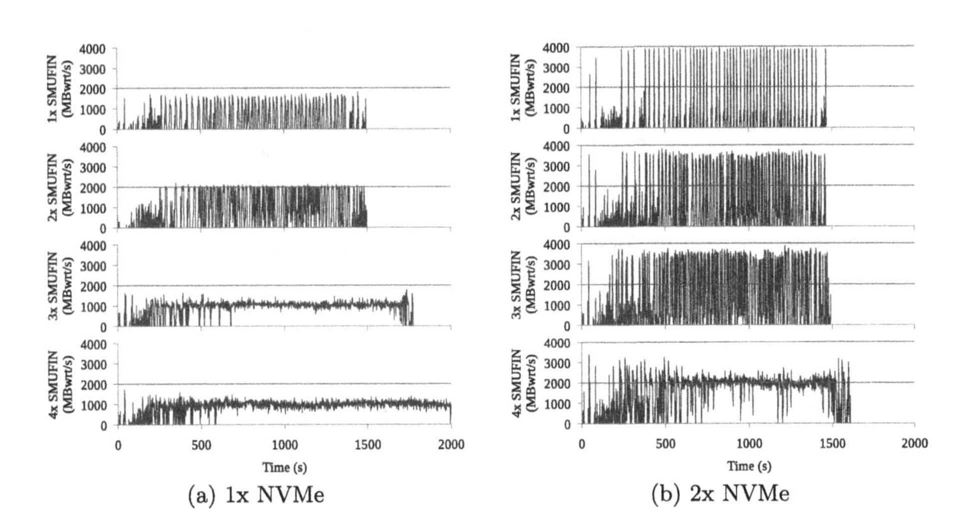

(a) 1x NVMe (b) 2x NVMe

Fig. 7. Bandwidth measured from the NVMe pool server for 1x, 2x, 3x and 4x instances of SMUFIN

Figures 7a and b show the NVMe bandwidth over time for experiments running up to four concurrent SMUFIN instances in the single-resource and the

2-composed resource configuration. The solid horizontal lines indicate the maximum bandwidth for sequential write that the resources can provide (2 GB/s in single-resource configuration, 4 GB/s for the composed scenario).

From the figures it can be appreciated, on one hand, that resource composition scales linearly, doubling the maximum available bandwidth of a single resource. In both scenarios, two important characteristics can be noticed as more concurrent instances are included in the experiment: (1) the bandwidth observed from the NVMe perspective is steadier; (2) the bandwidth that the NVMe device is capable of delivering is reduced as more concurrent instances are added. Running a single instance, the full bandwidth of the combined NVMe can be used with bursts at the maximum 4 GB/s. However as more concurrent executions are added these bursts make use of less bandwidth until reaching saturation levels, decreasing significantly.

5 Towards Efficient Orchestration of Shared and Composed Resources

Previous sections have shown how NVMe disaggregation provides new ways to use resources through resource sharing and composition. However, its behavior is not obvious a priori: heavy resource sharing may have a negative impact on performance, whereas composition may help increase sharing ratios without degradation. Therefore, deciding whether to compose a resource or to share it among many workloads is not trivial decision. With the help of workload characterization, platform orchestrator will be able to make more informed and smarter decisions.

In Fig. 8 we present different orchestration policies that could be managed with our data. The figure shows our cluster running five concurrent instances of SMUFIN, and three different resource allocation strategies for the instances: (a) sharing a single device, (b) sharing two NVMe devices, and (c) one instance-dedicated device and the remaining four instances on a shared NVM device. This example was run under the same setup as in Sect. 4. When the SMUFIN instances use two composed devices (b) it leads to faster executions times than using a single device (a). However, when using a dedicated device to run a single instance and a shared device to run the remaining four (c), the dedicated-device does not grant that instance an improved performance compared to a fully shared scenario using both devices (b). Intuitively it might be believed that just sharing all the resources under composition is the obvious winning strategy. However this approach does not consider arriving workloads might have a time requirement for completion, and upon arrival of those workloads, if the resources are fully occupied serving others the orchestrator will be unable to meet the requirement. Other concerns might be power consumption or total cost of ownership (as more resources, more expensive it becomes to run). Therefore, the strategy to follow must consider the trade-off between execution time and requirements of current and incoming workloads to maximize the granted quality of service, which in the case of genomics might be critical. The work on those policies is out of the scope of this paper and left as future work.

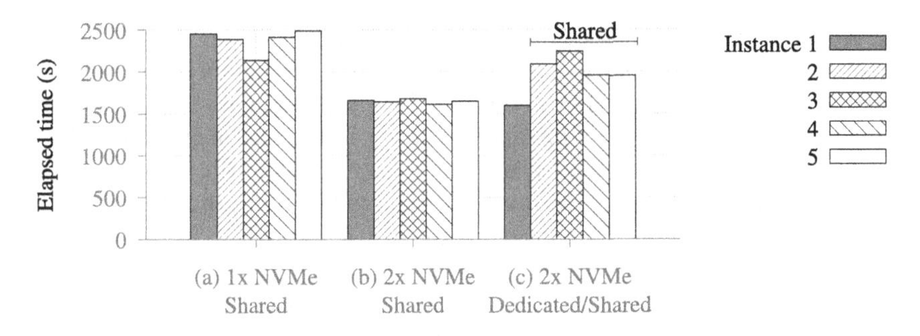

Fig. 8. Execution time of 5 SMUFIN instances under different scenarios

6 Related Work

Genomics workloads and pipelines in general are a good fit for disaggregation, but prior to this paper applications haven't explored its large-scale explotation. A number of different approaches to parallelize whole genome analysis in HPC systems have been proposed in the literature [10,13,16], but these tend simply adapt existing algorithms without considering or taking complete advantage of next generation computing platforms.

Resource disaggregation is being increasingly studied in the literature. In [6], the authors examine the network requirements for disaggregating resources at rack- and data-center levels. Minimum requirements are measured in terms of network bandwidth and latency. Those requirements must be such so that a given set of applications doesn't experiment any performance degradation when disaggregation memory or other resources over the fabric. [11] implements NVMe disaggregation, but unlike the work presented in this paper, the authors focus on a custom software layer to expose devices instead of using the NVMeOF standard. On the other hand, [18] evaluates the impact of FPGA disaggregation. In terms of Software-Defined Infrastructures, Intel Rack Scale [8] is a prototype system that allows dynamic composition of nodes. It fully disaggregates resources in pools, such as CPU, storage, memory, FPGA, GPU, etc. Facebook has engaged with Intel developing its own prototype, the Facebook Disaggregated Rack [5].

7 Conclusions

This paper evaluates resource sharing and composition benefits for NVM-centric workloads in the context of disaggregated datacenters. This work takes SMUFIN, a real production workload in the field of Computational Genomics, leveraging remote NVMe devices as memory extension. This paper presents a comprehensive characterization of SMUFIN's resource consumption patterns. It is shown NVMe is utilized in a sequential write pattern. A performance comparison between directly-attached NVMe and NVMeOF is then presented and shown that as long the system's memory is capable of handling SMUFIN instances there is no degradation. To increase concurrency disaggregating over fabrics allows to share the same resource across multiple nodes running instances, as well as the possibility of composition. Thus, through disaggregation we are able to handle more concurrent SMUFIN instances without individual degradation. On the other hand, reaching the resources' sharing ratio limit significantly degrades performance as the utilization of the available bandwidth diminishes, never reaching its maximum. Thus the NVMe becomes the bottleneck.

Finally the paper briefly explains how the results of this characterization could be used to implement data-center scheduling policies in order to maximize the efficiency in terms of Quality of Service. Quality of Service could be understood in terms of execution time, so all workloads should be completing its executions within a certain requested time-frame. The work on those policies is left as future work.

Acknowledgment. This work is partially supported by the European Research Council (ERC) under the EU Horizon 2020 programme (GA 639595), the Spanish Ministry of Economy, Industry and Competitivity (TIN2015-65316-P) and the Generalitat de Catalunya (2014-SGR-1051).

References

1. Cadenelli, N., Polo, J., Carrera, D.: Accelerating k-mer frequency counting with GPU and non-volatile memory. In: Proceedings of the 19th IEEE International Conference on High Performance Computing and Communications (HPCC). IEEE Computer Society, December 2017
2. Chen, F., Lee, R., Zhang, X.: Essential roles of exploiting internal parallelism of flash memory based solid state drives in high-speed data processing. In: 2011 IEEE 17th International Symposium on High Performance Computer Architecture, pp. 266–277, February 2011
3. Ciciani, B., et al.: Automated workload characterization in cloud-based transactional data grids. In: 2012 IEEE 26th International Parallel and Distributed Processing Symposium Workshops Ph.D. Forum, pp. 1525–1533, May 2012
4. NVMexpress: NVMe over fabrics overview. Tech. rep., NVM express (2017). http://www.nvmexpress.org/wp-content/uploads/nvme_over_fabrics.pdf
5. Facebook: Facebook disaggregated rack (2016). http://goo.gl/6h2Ut
6. Gao, P.X., et al.: Network requirements for resource disaggregation. In: Proceedings of the 12th USENIX Conference on Operating Systems Design and Implementation. USENIX Association, Berkely, CA, USA, November 2016
7. Guz, Z., Li, H.H., Shayesteh, A., Balakrishnan, V.: NVMe-over-fabrics performance characterization and the path to low-overhead flash disaggregation. In: Proceedings of the 10th ACM International Systems and Storage Conference SYSTOR 2017, pp. 16:1–16:9. ACM, New York (2017)
8. Intel: Intel rack scale design. Tech. Rep. 332937–004, Intel Corporation, August 2016. http://www.intel.com/content/dam/www/public/us/en/documents/guides/platform-hardware-design-guide.pdf
9. Intel: Rapid storage (2017). http://www.intel.com/content/www/us/en/support/technologies/intel-rapid-storage-technology-intel-rst.html

10. Kawalia, A., et al.: Leveraging the power of high performance computing for next generation sequencing data analysis: tricks and twists from a high throughput exome workflow. PloS one **10**(5), e0126321 (2015)
11. Klimovic, A., Litz, H., Kozyrakis, C.: Reflex: remote flash & local flash. In: Proceedings of the Twenty-Second International Conference on Architectural Support for Programming Languages and Operating Systems ASPLOS (2017)
12. Li, H., Durbin, R.: Fast and accurate short read alignment with burrows-wheeler transform. Bioinformatics **25**(14), 1754–1760 (2009)
13. Li, R., et al.: SNP detection for massively parallel whole-genome resequencing. Genome Res. **19**(6), 1124–1132 (2009)
14. Medvedev, P., Stanciu, M., Brudno, M.: Computational methods for discovering structural variation with next-generation sequencing. Nat. Methods **6**, S13–S20 (2009)
15. Moncunill, V., et al.: Comprehensive characterization of complex structural variations in cancer by directly comparing genome sequence reads. Nat. Biotechnol. **32**(11), 1106–1112 (2014)
16. Puckelwartz, M.J., et al.: Supercomputing for the parallelization of whole genome analysis. Bioinformatics **30**(11), 1508 (2014)
17. Sivashankar, S., Ramasamy, S.: Design and implementation of non-volatile memory express. In: 2014 International Conference on Recent Trends in Information Technology, Chennai, India, April 2014
18. Weerasinghe, J., Abel, F., Hagleitner, C., Herkersdorf, A.: Disaggregated FPGAs: network performance comparison against bare-metal servers, virtual machines and linux containers. In: Proceedings of the 8th IEEE International Conference on Cloud Computing Technology and Science, December 2016

GPU Accelerated Analysis of Treg-Teff Cross Regulation in Relapsing-Remitting Multiple Sclerosis

Marco Beccuti[1(✉)], Paolo Cazzaniga[2,3], Marzio Pennisi[4], Daniela Besozzi[5], Marco S. Nobile[3,5], Simone Pernice[1], Giulia Russo[6], Andrea Tangherloni[5], and Francesco Pappalardo[7]

[1] Department of Computer Science, University of Torino, Torino, Italy
beccuti@di.unito.it
[2] Department of Human and Social Sciences, University of Bergamo, Bergamo, Italy
paolo.cazzaniga@unibg.it
[3] SYSBIO.IT Centre of Systems Biology, Milano, Italy
[4] Department of Mathematics and Computer Science, University of Catania, Catania, Italy
mpennisi@dmi.unict.it
[5] Department of Informatics, Systems and Communication, University of Milano-Bicocca, Milano, Italy
[6] Department of Biomedical and Biotechnological Sciences, University of Catania, Catania, Italy
[7] Department of Drug Sciences, University of Catania, Catania, Italy

Abstract. The computational analysis of complex biological systems can be hindered by two main factors. First, modeling the system so that it can be easily understood and analyzed by non-expert users is not always possible, especially when dealing with systems of Ordinary Differential Equations. Second, when the system is composed of hundreds or thousands of reactions and chemical species, the classic CPU-based simulators could not be appropriate to efficiently derive the behavior of the system. To overcome these limitations, in this paper we propose a novel approach that combines the descriptive power of Stochastic Symmetric Nets–a Petri Net formalism that allows modeler to describe the system in a parametric and compact manner–with LASSIE, a GPU-powered deterministic simulator that offloads onto the GPU the calculations required to execute many simulations by following both fine-grained and coarse-grained parallelization strategies. This pipeline has been applied to carry out a parameter sweep analysis of a relapsing-remitting multiple sclerosis model, aimed at understanding the role of possible malfunctions in the cross-balancing mechanisms that regulate peripheral tolerance of self-reactive T lymphocytes. From our experiments, LASSIE achieves around 97× speed-up with respect to the sequential execution of the same number of simulations.

M. Beccuti, P. Cazzaniga and M. Pennisi—Equally contributed.

G. Mencagli et al. (Eds.): Euro-Par 2018 Workshops, LNCS 11339, pp. 626–637, 2019.
https://doi.org/10.1007/978-3-030-10549-5_49

Keywords: Multiple sclerosis · GPGPU computing · Petri nets
Parameter sweep analysis

1 Introduction

The Immune System (IS) is the ensemble of cells and molecules that protects living organisms from foreign pathogens. This complex machinery consists in a set of mechanisms whose complexity depends on the evolutionary level of the host. In mammals, besides the innate immunity, the adaptive immunity represents the most effective weapon against viruses and bacteria, thanks to its ability to specifically recognize and act against pathogens (specificity), to discriminate between self and non-self, and to remember previously encountered pathogens in order to act more rapidly (memory). While being extremely effective, adaptive immunity is not faultless. A breakdown of the mechanisms that allow the IS to discriminate between self and non-self antigens may lead to harmful effects, such as the arise of autoimmune diseases. Multiple sclerosis (MS), a disease of the Central Nervous System (CNS), falls within those.

MS is a chronic inflammatory disease that causes the removal of myelin sheath created by oligodendrocytes from axons, leading to a reduced functionality of the CNS. It is well known that a genetic predisposition correlates with MS [8]. Moreover, environmental and dietary factors may play an important role. Epstein-Barr virus (EBV) may trigger the disease onset [17,18], while it is supposed that vitamin D could help in preventing MS [11]. Symptoms include weakness and fatigue, blurry vision, speech problems, numbness and tingling, dizziness, lack of coordination and uncontrolled bodily functions. The most common form of MS (80–90% of the total insurgence) is Relapsing-Remitting MS (RRMS) [20], where relapses (periods of disease progression) are followed by periods of remission (total or partial recovery from symptoms). RRMS usually occurs in the age of 20–40, with a women-to-men ratio of 2:1. When left untreated, 65% of RRMS cases turn after 15–25 years to more severe MS forms [7].

Even if the etiology of MS is not fully understood, the common shared hypothesis suggests that self-reactive T lymphocytes may be activated in the periphery by an external trigger (i.e., EBV). Activated T cells can overcome the blood brain barrier and go through the CNS [24]. Once in the brain, self-reactive cells cause inflammatory events that negatively affect both myelin and oligodendrocytes, also involving other IS entities such as B lymphocytes, macrophages, and microglia. It is worth noting that relapses usually represent the clinical correlates of inflammatory bouts. Self-reactive T lymphocytes represent one of the main actors in the development and progression of the disease, as such cells tend to decrease in the peripheral blood while increasing in the spinal fluid when relapses occur. Furthermore, homeostasis of regulatory T cells (Treg) and effectors T cells (Teff) is fundamental in preventing autoimmunity [9,13]. More precisely, a breakdown of the peripheral tolerance mechanisms, such as the lack of functionality or deficiency of Treg functions, may bring to uncontrolled activation and proliferation of effectors T cells [19].

This hypothesis has been confirmed by Vélez de Mendizábal *et al.* [23], with the use of an Ordinary Differential Equations (ODEs) model capable of reproducing the behavior of RRMS. However, this model represented a very simplistic scenario, by avoiding to explicitly include the trigger of the disease represented by an external factor such as the EBV, as well as the occurrence of neural damage represented by the loss of myelin and/or the death of oligodendrocytes. Furthermore, the model totally missed to give any description of the spatial evolution of the disease. These issues were fulfilled by an agent based model (ABM) capable of better describing, from a temporal and spatial points of view, the typical shape of RRMS [16]. It must be said that, due to the significant computational efforts needed to run thousands of ABM simulations, a deeper analysis of the model parameters that may influence the disease progression was not carried out.

To cope with these aspects, in this paper we propose a new framework for the analysis of this type of biological systems, in which a graphical formalism is exploited to facilitate the model creation and the simulation of its behavior. In detail, Stochastic Symmetric Net (SSN) [6], a high-level Petri Nets formalism, is used to describe the system in a *parametric* and *compact* manner. Then, from the SSN model an ODE system is automatically derived and solved through a numerical integrator that exploits a High Performance Computing solution. In particular, a GPU-based simulation algorithm of ODE systems is suitable in this context [15], since models translated from SSNs into set of equations typically involve thousands of reactions and/or chemical species. It is therefore necessary to accelerate the numerical integration to achieve thorough analyses of the system. Here we exploit an improved version of LASSIE [22], a GPU-powered deterministic simulator capable of realizing both a fine-grained and a coarse-grained parallelization, meaning that the calculations required by a single simulation are distributed over the GPU cores, as well as multiple simulations that run in a parallel fashion on the GPU.

We show that this novel framework that combines SSNs with LASSIE may provide a good compromise between its effectiveness in terms of model description and solution, and the mathematical and computational skills needed to generate, simulate and analyse models.

The paper is structured as follows. In Sect. 2 we briefly recall the basic notions of SSN and the functioning of LASSIE, while in Sect. 3 we describe the SSN model of MS. In Sect. 4 we present our developed framework and the results of the parameter sweep analysis executed on the RRMS model. We conclude in Sect. 5 with some final remarks and future directions of this work.

2 Background

In this section we introduce all the definitions, notations and methods used in the rest of the paper. We first introduce the SSN formalism and then we describe how to translate a SSN model into the corresponding (symbolic) ODE system. Finally, we briefly describe LASSIE, the GPU-powered deterministic simulator exploited to realize the analysis of the RRMS model.

2.1 The SSN Formalism

Stochastic Symmetric Net (SSN) is a high-level graphical formalism that extends Stochastic Petri Net (SPN) formalism with *colored tokens* [6], so that an information can be associated with tokens flowing in the net. This feature allows for a more compact system representation that can be exploited during both the construction and the solution of the model [1,3,6]. SSN is a bipartite directed graph with two types of nodes, called *places* and *transitions*.

The places, graphically represented as circles, correspond to the variables describing the state of the system. Places can contain colored tokens, whose colors are defined by the *color domain cd*() associated with any place. The place color domains are thus defined as Cartesian products of *color classes* C_i, or by the neutral element ϵ consisting of a neutral color as in ordinary Petri Nets. A color class C_i can be partitioned into *static sub-classes* $C_{i,1} \cup \ldots \cup C_{i,l}$. Then, the colors of a class represent entities of the same nature (e.g., regulatory T cells), but only the colors within a static sub-class are guaranteed to behave similarly (e.g., regulatory T cells in active state). Moreover, a color class is ordered if and only if it is possible to define on it a successor function, denoted by ++, which determines a circular order on its elements. For instance, in the SSN model in Fig. 1, three color classes are defined: *State* denoting the cell state, *PosX* and *PosY* encoding the cell position on a grid representing a tissue portion. The color class *State* is divided into two static sub-classes N and A, which refer to the cell states *Naive* and *Active*, respectively. Differently, the ordered color classes *PosX* and *PosY* are not divided into static sub-classes. According to this color definition, the color domain of places *Treg* and *Teff* is *State*$\times$ *PosX*$\times$ *PosY*. Differently, the color domain of places *ODC* and *EBV* is *PosX* $\times$ *PosY*.

The transitions, graphically represented as boxes, correspond to the system events. The possible colored instances of a transition are defined by the *color domain cd*() associated with any transition. The transition color domains are thus expressed through a list of typed variables, whose types are selected among the color classes C_i. The variables associated with a transition appear in the functions labeling its arcs, so that a transition instance binds each variable to a specific color of proper type. Then, a *guard* can be used to introduce restrictions on the allowed instances of a transition. Such restrictions are defined as Boolean expression over the color domain of the transition, and their terms, called *basic predicates*, allow one (*i*) to compare colors assigned to variables of the same or different type ($x = y, x \neq y$); (*ii*) to test whether a color element belongs to a given static sub-class ($x \in C_{i,j}$); (*iii*) to compare the static sub-classes of the colors assigned to two variables ($x, y \in C_{i,j}$). For instance, the color domain of transition *TeffActivation* in Fig. 1 is *State* $\times$ *State* $\times$ *PosX* $\times$ *PosY*. The guard $[m \in N \ \wedge \ n \in A]$ is associated with this transition to mimics the activation of a Naive Teff cell.

The functions labeling arcs are formally expressed as sums of tuples where each tuple element is chosen from a set of predefined *basic functions*, whose domains and co-domains are respectively color classes and multisets on color classes. The basic functions in SSN formalism can be grouped as follows: *projection functions*, denoted by a variable in the transition color domain (e.g., m, x and y appearing in the arc expression $< m, x, y >$ labeling several arcs in net); *successor functions*, denoted by $x++$, where x is a variable in the transition color domain whose type is an ordered class; a constant function returning all elements in a class (or sub-class), indicated as *classname.All*. Input, output arcs are denoted by $I, O[p,t] : cd(t) \rightarrow Bag[cd(p)]$, where $Bag[A]$ is the set of all possible multisets that may be built on set A.

The state of an SSN, called *marking*, is defined by the number of colored tokens in each place. For instance, a marking for the model in Fig.1, assuming $N = \{n\}$, $A = \{a\}$, $PosX = \{x_1, \ldots, x_n\}$ and $PosY = \{y_1, \ldots, y_n\}$, is

$$m = Treg(10\langle n, x_1, y_2\rangle) + Teff(12\langle a, x_2, y_2\rangle),$$

representing the state in which there are 10 Treg cells in position x_1, y_2 and 12 Teff cells in position x_2, y_2.

The evolution of the system is given by the firing of an enabled transition, where the enabling condition and the state change associated with each transition instance are specified by means of *arc functions* labeling the arcs connecting a place to this transition and vice versa. Given the color identifying an instance of the transition t, the arc function labeling the arc connecting t to a place p provides the (multi)set of colored tokens that will be either added to or removed from p. In the SSNs, the firing of an enabled transition instance $\langle t, c\rangle$ occurs after a random delay sampled from a negative exponential distribution whose rate is given by:

$$\omega(t,c) = \begin{cases} r_i & cond_i(c)\ \forall i = 1, \ldots, n, \\ r_{n+1} & otherwise, \end{cases}$$

where $cond_i$ is a Boolean expression comprising standard predicates on the transition color instance. In this manner, the firing rate r_i of a transition instance can depend only on the static sub-classes of the objects assigned to the transition parameters and on the comparison of variables of the same type. We assume that the conditions $cond_i$ are mutually exclusive. So doing, the stochastic process mimicking the dynamic of SSN models is a Continuous Time Markov Chain (CTMC), where the states are identified with SSN markings and the state changes correspond to the marking changes in the SSN.

If we assume that all the transitions of the SSN use an infinite server policy, the transition rate from state m to state m' in the CTMC can be written as:

$$q_{m,m'} = \sum_{\forall t,c: m \xrightarrow{\langle t,c\rangle} m'} \omega(t,c) e(m,t,c),$$

where $e(m, t, c)$ is the enabling degree of the transition instance $\langle t, c \rangle$ in marking m, defined as:

$$e(m, t, c) = \min_{(p_j, c'): I[p_j, t](c)(c') \neq 0} \left\lfloor \frac{m(p_j)(c')}{I[p_j, t](c)(c')} \right\rfloor.$$

According to these assumptions, the temporal behavior of an SSN model can be derived by means of analytic or numerical approaches [21]. However, in the case of very complex models, the underlying CTMC can not be derived or/and solved due to the well-known state space explosion problem. To deal with these cases, whenever the stochasticity of the modeled system can be neglected (e.g., due to huge number of cells), the so-called deterministic approach [12] can be exploited, assuming that the behavior of entities contained in a place of the net is described with an ODE and that the whole model is specified with a system of ODEs, one for each place of the net.

2.2 From SSN Models to ODEs

Starting from Kurtz's results [12], in [3] we described how to efficiently derive an ODE system that provides a good deterministic approximation for the stochastic behavior of the corresponding SSN model. Practically, a SSN model is firstly translated into its equivalent SPN through the unfolding procedure [3], which consists of replicating places and transitions as many times as the cardinalities of the corresponding color domains. Hence, colors disappear in the unfolded model and the complex behavior due to color combinations, color arc functions and color transition guards, is encoded with a net structure in which tokens are indistinguishable entities and new transitions, places and arcs are introduced to account for the different actions performed by instances of the same transition on colored tokens. Note that the name of new places (transitions) in the unfolded net is defined by associating with the original name of the place (transition) in the SSN one possible element of its color domain. For instance, the unfolding of the SSN p place, with $cd(p) = C \times C$ and $C = \{c1, c2\}$, will provide four places: $p_{c1,c1}$, $p_{c1,c2}$, $p_{c2,c1}$ and $p_{c2,c2}$.

When the unfolded SPN model is derived, the average number of tokens in each place of the unfolded net is approximated through the following ODE:

$$\frac{dx_i(\nu)}{d\nu} = \sum_{j=1}^{|T|} s(t_j, x(\nu))(O[p_i, t_j] - I[p_i, t_j]), \tag{1}$$

where $x(\nu)$ is a vector of real numbers representing the average number of tokens in the model places at time ν, T is the set of the net transitions, and $s(t_j, x(\nu))$ is a function defining the speed of transition t_j in the state $x(\nu)$ as follows:

$$s(t_j, x(\nu)) = \omega(t_j) \min_{l: I(p_l, t_j) \neq 0} \frac{x_l(\nu)}{I[p_l, t_j]}. \tag{2}$$

2.3 LASSIE: GPU-Powered Simulation of Large-Scale Models

LASSIE is a GPU-powered deterministic simulator that can be easily used without any specific GPU programming or ODE modeling skills [22]. LASSIE was designed to perform deterministic simulations of large-scale biochemical models, distributing all required calculations on the cores of the GPU. LASSIE requires as input a biological system formalized as a reaction-based model [4,10] under the assumption of mass-action kinetics [14], as in the case of SSN models translated into ODE systems (see Sect. 2.2). LASSIE was developed using the most widespread GPU computing library, namely, Nvidia Compute Unified Device Architecture (CUDA), which allows programmers to exploit the GPUs for general-purpose computational tasks (GPGPU computing).

In this work, we make use of an improved version of LASSIE that realizes both a fine-grained and a coarse-grained parallelization of the simulations. This means that two different levels of parallelism are implemented: (*i*) the numerical integration of ODEs required by a single simulation is parallelized on the GPU cores, and (*ii*) many simulations of the same model characterized by different initial conditions and kinetic parameters are executed in a parallel fashion on the same GPU. The second level of parallelization was introduced to the aim of fully occupying the GPU cores, and to further accelerate the analysis of large-scale models of biological systems.

3 Treg-Teff Cross Regulation in RRMS

Our case study, as already anticipated in Sect. 1, refers to the cross regulation mechanism between Treg and Teff cells in RRMS. T cells are a type of white blood cells that play a central role in the human immune system. Indeed, they implement the adaptive immunity that tailors the immune response of the body to specific pathogens. T cells are commonly divided into various populations, including Cytotoxic CD8 T lymphocytes, also known as effectors T cells (Teff), the main effectors of cellular-mediated immunity that can directly attack infected or cancer cells, and CD4 T helper lymphocytes, essential to boost the immune functions by activating other immune cells. More recently, regulatory T cells (Treg) have been discovered as one of the main actors in modulating the immune system in order to maintain tolerance to self-antigens and to prevent autoimmune diseases. In particular, Treg cells are usually responsible of controlling the Teff functionalities suppressing their potentially deleterious activities. Teff cells can be inhibited by Treg cells through cell-to-cell contact and immunosuppressive cytokines. Furthermore, Treg proliferation can be stimulated as a consequence of the suppression of Teff cells. In our study we consider the activation of self-reactive Teff and Treg cells due to an EBV infection that, through a process called antigenic mimicry, misleads such cells. In this situation, in healthy people, Treg cells are able to control the spread of Teff cells activated by EBV. Instead, in diseased people a breakdown of the regulation mechanism, represented by a malfunction of Treg activities, leads to widespread inflammatory events driven by Teff cells that erroneously attack the Myelin Based Protein (MBP), a major structural component of myelin that is expressed by oligodendrocytes (ODC) in the central nervous system. This attack can irredeemably damage myelin sheath of neurons leading to the occurrence of demyelinating diseases as MS.

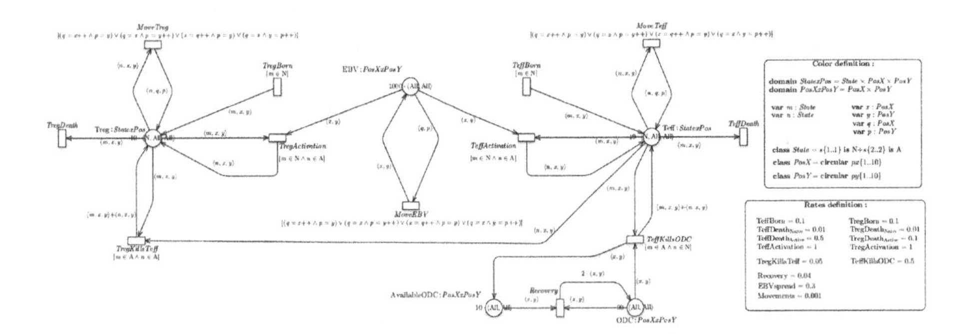

Fig. 1. SSN model describing Treg-Teff cross regulation in multiple sclerosis.

Figure 1 shows the SSN model describing our case study. The color class *State* divided into two sub-classes (i.e. *Naive* and *Active*) represents the cell status, while the ordered color classes *PosX* and *PosY* encode the cell position considering the tissue portion as spherical grid. The marking of places *Teff* (resp. *Treg*) provides the number of active and inactive Teff (resp. Treg) cells in each grid position. Similarly, the marking of places *EBV* and *ODC* represents the concentration of EBVs and ODCs in each grid position.

The Teff, Treg, and EBV diffusion process is modeled by the transitions *MoveTeff*, *MoveTreg* and *MoveEBV*. The proliferation of inactive Teff and Treg cells is modeled by the firing of the transitions *TeffBorn* and *TregBorn*, while their natural death by the firing of the transitions *TregDeath* and *TeffDeath*. The activation of a Teff cell due to the contact with EBV is modeled by the transition *TeffActivation*. Similarly, the transition *TregActivation* represents the activation of a Treg cell due to the contact with EBV. The transition *TeffKill-sODC* describes the attack of Teff against ODCs causing the axonal damage. Moreover, as a feedback, the Teff cell will be duplicated. The partial recovery (recoverable damage) of ODC functions up to their initial value is instead represented by the transition *recovery*. Finally, the transition *TregKillsTeff* is used to model the already described down regulation functions of Treg cells against Teff cells.

4 Results

4.1 Framework Architecture

In this section we describe the architecture of the prototype framework that we developed for the study of Treg-Teff cross regulation in RRMS. This framework is integrated in GreatSPN [2], a well-known suite for the analysis of Discrete Event Dynamic Systems described through Petri Net formalisms. In details, our framework exploits the GreatSPN GUI to draw an SSN model and to derive the corresponding ODE system from an SSN model, while LASSIE [22] is used for solving the generated ODE system. The architecture of this prototype framework is depicted in Fig. 2: GreatSPN is used as graphical interface for constructing the model and as solution manager for activating the solution process. The solution manager executes in the correct order the framework components, and manages the models/data exchanges between them.

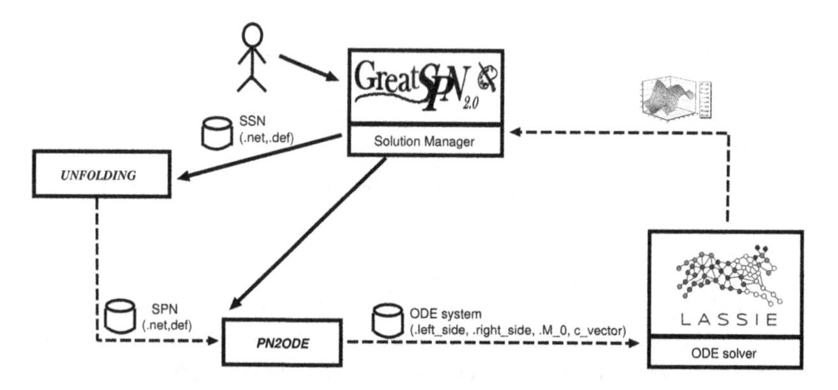

Fig. 2. Schematization of the prototype framework combining GreatSPN suite with LASSIE (the components are shown by rectangles, component invocations by solid arrows, models/data exchanges by dashed arrows).

Thus, the solution process comprises three steps:

1. *Unfolding* to derive the unfolded SPN model from an SNN model, as described in Sect. 2;
2. *PN2ODE* to generate the ODE system from an SPN model, as formalized in Sect. 2. Then, the derived ODE system is exported according to the LASSIE input format;
3. *LASSIE* to solve the generated ODE system by offloading onto the GPU all the calculations required by the numerical integration of all parallel simulations.

4.2 Computational Results

To test the effectiveness of the pipeline presented in Sect. 4.1, we performed a parameter sweep analysis (PSA) [5] on the RRMS model, in which one kinetic parameter was varied within a given sweep interval (chosen with respect to a fixed reference value for each parameter). For this test we exploited a Nvidia GeForce GTX Titan Z (2880 cores, clock 876 MHz, RAM 6 GB).

The RRMS model depicted in Fig. 1 was converted into an ODE system characterized by 3200 reactions and 700 chemical species. The PSA was performed by generating a set of different initial conditions—corresponding to different parameterizations of the model—and then automatically executing the parallel deterministic simulations with LASSIE. The initial marking, the transition rates and the grid size used in the experiments are reported in Fig. 1. The kinetic constant associated with the firing of the *TregKillsTeff* transition was varied by taking 640 different values equally distributed in the interval $[10^{-3}, 1]$ days^{-1}. We recall here that the firing rate of such transition is fundamental to describe the possible malfunction of Treg cells activities, which may lead to a breakdown of the peripheral tolerance and thus to the insurgence of the disease.

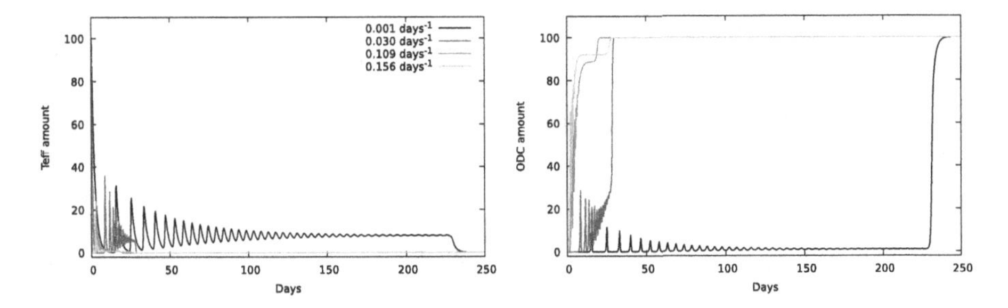

Fig. 3. Dynamics of Teff (left) and ODC (right) with different values of the kinetic constant associated with the *TregKillsTeff* transition. (Color figure online)

The results of this analysis are reported in Fig. 3, where we can observe that for values of the kinetic constant higher than 0.109 days^{-1}, Treg cells are able to control the spread of Teff cells (left panel, yellow and purple lines) and consequently to avoid the appearing of the disease. This is also visible on the ODC plot (right panel, yellow and purple lines) that shows how the amount of ODC, even if initially lowered due to the Teff actions, goes rapidly back to its maximum value, suggesting that any damage has been avoided or recovered at most (recoverable damage). This outcome well describes the scenario of healthy people, in which the peripheral tolerance is able to compensate for a genetic predisposition in developing the disease. For values of the kinetic constant lower than 0.109 days^{-1}, an oscillatory behavior of Teff starts to appear (left panel, red line), becoming more and more pronounced as the value of the kinetic constant decreases (i.e., left panel, black line). In this scenario, it is possible to observe that the amount of ODC decreases to around zero in correspondence to each peak in the number of Teff (left panel, red and black lines), suggesting an ongoing inflammation that causes neural damage, and thus the possibility of relapses in correspondence of each peak in the Teff amount. Interestingly, a fixed initial quantity of EBV seems to be sufficient to start such oscillatory behavior that can be correlated to multiple relapses. This is somewhat different from the models presented in [16,23], where each relapse was triggered by a single spread of virus.

For what concerns the computational time required to execute the PSA on the GPU, by considering the time necessary to run a single simulation with a C++ implementation of Dormand and Prince method, exploiting a single core of a CPU Intel Core i7-6700HQ, 2.6 GHz, we estimated a speed-up around 97× on the Nvidia GeForce GTX Titan Z, thanks to the parallelization provided by LASSIE.

5 Conclusions

In this paper we presented a novel framework for the analysis of complex biological systems. This framework combines the descriptive power of Stochastic Symmetric Nets, which allows one to provide a graphical representation of complex biological systems in a compact and parametric way, with a tool that automatically derives a system of ODEs corresponding to the net. The resulting ODEs system is typically composed of hundreds or thousands of reactions and/or chemical species; it is therefore essential to accelerate the simulations by means of a High Performance Computing solution. In our framework we exploit LASSIE, a GPU-powered deterministic simulator capable of realizing both a fine-grained and a coarse-grained parallelization strategy.

The framework presented here was applied to a complex biological system of relapsing-remitting multiple sclerosis, consisting in 3200 reactions and 700 chemical species. In particular, we realized a parameter sweep analysis to investigate the effects of possible malfunctions in the Teff-Treg cross regulation mechanisms that involve a break of peripheral tolerance and bring to the occurrence of relapses. Thanks to the acceleration provided by LASSIE, we obtained around 97× speed-up with respect to a CPU-based execution of the same analysis.

As a future extension of this work, on the one hand, we plan to execute extensive analyses of the parameter space of the model to better understand the underlying mechanisms of multiple sclerosis; on the other hand, we will assess the performance of our framework on different GPUs and on multi-GPU systems.

References

1. Baarir, S., Beccuti, M., Dutheillet, C., Franceschinis, G., Haddad, S.: Lumping partially symmetrical stochastic models. Perform. Eval. **68**(1), 21–44 (2010)
2. Babar, J., Beccuti, M., Donatelli, S., Miner, A.: GreatSPN enhanced with decision diagram data structures. In: Lilius, J., Penczek, W. (eds.) PETRI NETS 2010. LNCS, vol. 6128, pp. 308–317. Springer, Heidelberg (2010). https://doi.org/10.1007/978-3-642-13675-7_19
3. Beccuti, M., et al.: From symmetric nets to differential equations exploiting model symmetries. Comput. J. **58**(1), 23–39 (2015)
4. Besozzi, D.: Reaction-based models of biochemical networks. In: Beckmann, A., Bienvenu, L., Jonoska, N. (eds.) CiE 2016. LNCS, vol. 9709, pp. 24–34. Springer, Cham (2016). https://doi.org/10.1007/978-3-319-40189-8_3

5. Besozzi, D., Cazzaniga, P., Pescini, D., Mauri, G., Colombo, S., Martegani, E.: The role of feedback control mechanisms on the establishment of oscillatory regimes in the Ras/cAMP/PKA pathway in S. cerevisiae. EURASIP J. Bioinf. Syst. Biol. **2012**(1), 10 (2012)
6. Chiola, G., Dutheillet, C., Franceschinis, G., Haddad, S.: Stochastic well-formed coloured nets for symmetric modelling applications. IEEE Trans. Comput. **42**(11), 1343–1360 (1993)
7. Compston, A., Coles, A.: Multiple sclerosis. The Lancet **372**(9648), 1502–1517 (2008)
8. Compston, G., et al.: McAlpine's Multiple Sclerosis, 4th edn. Elsevier, Amsterdam (2013)
9. Fontenot, J.D., Rudensky, A.Y.: A well adapted regulatory contrivance: regulatory T cell development and the forkhead family transcription factor Foxp3. Nat. Immunol. **6**(4), 331–337 (2005)
10. Gillespie, D.T.: A general method for numerically simulating the stochastic time evolution of coupled chemical reactions. J. Comput. Phys. **22**, 403–434 (1976)
11. Goodin, D.S.: The causal cascade to multiple sclerosis: a model for MS pathogenesis. PLoS One **4**(2), e4565 (2009)
12. Kurtz, T.G.: Solutions of ordinary differential equations as limits of pure jump Markov processes. J. Appl. Probab. **1**(7), 49–58 (1970)
13. Lund, J.M., Hsing, L., Pham, T.T., Rudensky, A.Y.: Coordination of early protective immunity to viral infection by regulatory T cells. Science **320**(5880), 1220–1224 (2008)
14. Nelson, D.L., Cox, M.M.: Lehninger Principles of Biochemistry. W. H. FreemanCo., New York (2004)
15. Nobile, M.S., Besozzi, D., Cazzaniga, P., Mauri, G.: GPU-accelerated simulations of mass-action kinetics models with cupSODA. J. Supercomput. **69**(1), 17–24 (2014)
16. Pennisi, M., Rajput, A.M., Toldo, L., Pappalardo, F.: Agent based modeling of Treg-Teff cross regulation in relapsing-remitting multiple sclerosis. BMC Bioinform. **14**(Suppl 16), S9 (2013)
17. Pohl, D.: An altered immune response to Epstein-Barr virus in multiple sclerosis. J. Neurol. Sci. **286**(1–2), 62–4 (2009)
18. Ponsonby, A.L., et al.: Exposure to infant siblings during early life and risk of multiple sclerosis. JAMA **293**(4), 463–469 (2005)
19. Sakaguchi, S., Sakaguchi, N., Asano, M., Itoh, M., Toda, M.: Immunologic self-tolerance maintained by activated T cells expressing IL-2 receptor alpha-chains (CD25). Breakdown of a single mechanism of self-tolerance causes various autoimmune diseases. J. Immunol. **155**(3), 1152–1164 (1995)
20. Sospedra, M., Martin, R.: Immunology of multiple sclerosis. Annu. Rev. Immunol. **23**, 683–747 (2005)
21. Stewart, W.J.: Introduction to the Numerical Solution of Markov Chains. Princeton University Press, Princeton (1995)
22. Tangherloni, A., Nobile, M.S., Besozzi, D., Mauri, G., Cazzaniga, P.: LASSIE: simulating large-scale models of biochemical systems on GPUs. BMC Bioinform. **18**(1), 246 (2017)
23. Vélez De Mendizábal, N., et al.: Modeling the effector-regulatory T cell cross-regulation reveals the intrinsic character of relapses in Multiple Sclerosis. BMC Syst. Biol. **5**, 114 (2011)
24. Yadav, S.K., Mindur, J.E., Ito, K., Dhib-Jalbut, S.: Advances in the immunopathogenesis of multiple sclerosis. Curr. Opin. Neurol. **28**(3), 206–219 (2015)

Cross-Environment Comparison of a Bioinformatics Pipeline: Perspectives for Hybrid Computations

Nico Curti[1(✉)], Enrico Giampieri[1], Andrea Ferraro[2], Cristina Vistoli[2], Elisabetta Ronchieri[2], Daniele Cesini[2], Barbara Martelli[2], Cristina Duma Doina[2], and Gastone Castellani[1]

[1] Department of Physics and Astronomy, University of Bologna, Bologna, Italy
nico.curti2@unibo.it
[2] INFN-CNAF, Bologna, Italy

Abstract. In this work a previously published bioinformatics pipeline was reimplemented across various computational platforms, and the performances of its steps evaluated. The tested environments were: (I) dedicated bioinformatics-specific server (II) low-power single node (III) HPC single node (IV) virtual machine. The pipeline was tested on a use case of the analysis of a single patient to assess single-use performances, using the same configuration of the pipeline to be able to perform meaningful comparison and search the optimal environment/hybrid system configuration for biomedical analysis. Performances were evaluated in terms of execution wall time, memory usage and energy consumption per patient. Our results show that, albeit slower, low power single nodes are comparable with other environments for most of the steps, but with an energy consumption two to four times lower. These results indicate that these environments are viable candidates for bioinformatics clusters where long term efficiency is a factor.

Keywords: Whole genome sequencing · Bioinformatic pipeline Low-power · GATK-LODn pipeline

1 Introduction

Biomedical data are growing both in size and breath of possible uses. Of special importance are the so called biomedical big data, blanket term describing data generated from several machines and used to describe the health state of a person:

1. **Next generation sequencing NGS.** NGS technology. RNA-seq: experimental procedure, challenges and opportunities in statistical data analysis. ChIP-Seq: experimental procedure and statistical data analysis.

N. Curti and E. Giampieri contributed equally to this work.

G. Mencagli et al. (Eds.): Euro-Par 2018 Workshops, LNCS 11339, pp. 638–649, 2019.
https://doi.org/10.1007/978-3-030-10549-5_50

2. **Proteomics and Metabolomics.** LC/MS technology, challenges in data processing. Biological pathways.
3. **Biomedical imaging.** Imaging techniques, acquisition methods and data structures/characteristics for different imaging modalities.
4. **Statistical Analysis of Imaging Data.** Data processing techniques, study designs, analysis strategies, research questions and goals. Radiomics.
5. **Brain Networks and Imaging Genetics.** The importance of brain networks in differentiating between healthy and mentally ill subjects, methods on how to estimate the brain network which may or may not rely on additional clinical, demographic and genetic information.
6. **Molecular genetics and population genetics.** Biological backgrounds for statistical genetics, concepts from population genetics that are most relevant to association analysis.
7. **Genetic association studies.** Tests for association, challenges especially in the context of genome-wide association studies (GWAS), including how to correct for population stratification and multiple testing.

These datasets are known to contain vast amount of information, especially when connected together to enhance the power of the biological modeling [2,7].

Genetic information is important in studying cancer, as frequently the process is kickstarted from a small subset of mutations in the genetic code of the cell [5]. These mutations can, via genomic instability, generate a wide variety of mutations in the cancerous cells, often different not only from case to case, but even inside a single case. To address this problem and to find interesting treatment target, identifying the original mutations is necessary, and this requires an in depth analysis of the genome of both healthy and tumoral tissues, possibly across several subjects.

With the increasing demand of resources from ever-growing datasets, it is not favorable to focus on single server execution, and is better to distribute the computation over cluster of less powerful nodes. The computational pipeline also has to manage a high number of subjects, and several steps of the analyses are not trivial to be done in a highly parallel way. Thus, the importance of system statistics management as the efficiency usage of available resources are crucial to reach a compromise between computational execution time and energy cost. For these reasons our main focus is on the performance evaluation of a single subject without using all the available resources, as these could be more efficiently allocated to concurrently execute several subjects at the same time. Due to the nature of the employed algorithms, not all steps can exploit the available cores in a highly efficient way: some scales sublinearly with the number of cores, some have resource access bottleneck. Other tools are simply not implemented with parallelism in mind, often because they are the result of the effort of small teams that prefer to focus their attention on the scientific development side rather than the computational one.

Moreover in order to obtain an optimal execution of bioinformatics pipelines, each analysis step might need very different resources. This means that any suboptimal component of a server could act as a bottleneck, requiring bleeding edge technology if all the steps are to be performed on a single machine. Hybrid systems could be a possible solution to these issues, but designing them requires detailed information about how to partition the different steps of the pipeline. This work explores the different behavior of a recent pipeline on different computing environments as a starting point for this partition.

1.1 GATK-LODn Pipeline

This pipeline has been developed in 2016 by Valle et al. [9], and codifies a new approach aimed to Single Nucleotype Polimorphism (SNP) identification in tumors from Whole Exome Sequencing data (WES). WES is a type of "next generation sequencing" data [1,8,11], focused on the part of the genome that actually codifies proteins (the exome). Albeit known that non-transcriptional parts of the genome can affect the dynamic of gene expression, the majority of cancers inducing mutations are known to be on the exome, thus WES data allow to focus the computational effort on the most interesting part of the genome. Being the exome in human approximately 1% of the total genome, this approach helps significantly in reducing the number of false positives detected by the pipeline. The different sizes of next generation sequencing dataset are shown in Table 1.

The GATK-LODn pipeline is designed to combine results of two different SNP-calling softwares, GATK [6] and MuTect [4]. These two softwares employ different statistical approaches for the SNP calling: GATK examines the healthy tissue and the cancerous tissue independently, and identifies the suspect SNPs by comparing them; Mutect compares healthy and cancerous tissues at the same time and has a more strict threshold of selection. In identifying more SNPs, GATK has a higher true positive calling than Mutect, but also an higher number of false positives. On the other end Mutect has few false positives, but often does not recognize known SNPs. The two programs also call different set of SNPs, even when the set size is similar. The pipeline therefore uses a combination of the two sets of chosen SNPs to select a single one, averaging the strictness of Mutect with the recognition of known variants of GATK.

The pipeline workflow includes a series of common steps in bioinformatics analysis and in the common bioinformatics pipelines. It includes also a sufficient representative sample of tools for the performances statistical analysis. In this way the results extracted from the single steps analysis could be easily generalized to other standard bioinformatics pipelines.

1.2 System Resources Management

As mentioned earlier, a bioinformatics pipeline consists of various steps that could be independent or sequential from each other. Each step could need more or less resources (e.g. memory and threads). So the optimal pipeline execution is closely related to the amount of available resources. The number of samples (patients) to process can penalize performances. There are two main optimization strategies: the first is to improve the efficiency of a single run on a single

Table 1. Typical dataset size for a single patient of different types of next generation sequencing. BAM file size refers to the size of the binary file containing the reads from the machine.

	Coverage	No. of reads	Read length	BAM file size	NGS size
Whole genome	37.7x	975,000,000	115	82 GB	104 GB
Whole genome	38.4x	3,200,000,000	36	138 GB	193 GB
Exome	40x	110,000,000	75	5.7 GB	7.1 GB

patient and the second is to employ massive parallelization on various samples. In both cases we have to know the necessary resources of the pipeline (and in a fine grain the resources of each step) and the optimal concurrency strategy to be applied to our workflow (see Fig. 1). In the analyses we want to highlight limits and efficiencies of the most common computational environments used in big data analytics, without any optimization strategy of the codes or systems.

We also focused on a single patient analysis, the base case study to design a possible parallelization strategy. This is especially relevant for the multi-sample parallelization, that is the most promising of the two optimization strategies, as it does not rely on specific implementations of the softwares employed in the pipeline.

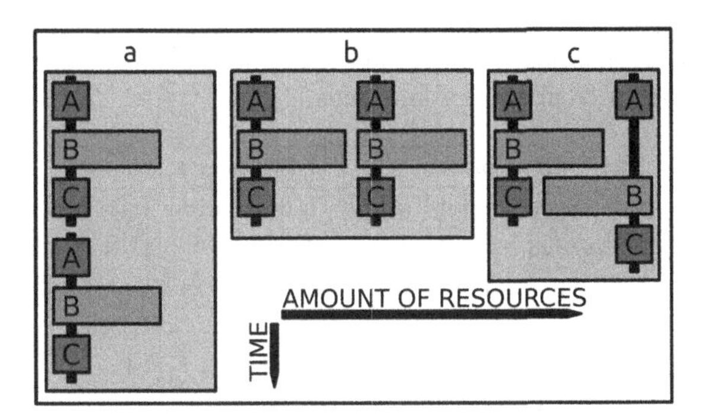

Fig. 1. Examples of concurrency workflow of two processes. The first case (a) represents a simple (naive) sequential workflow; the second (b) highlights a brute force parallelization; the third (c) is the case of a perfect match between the available resources and the requested resources. Often brute force parallelization of pipelines done as in the image b ends up overlapping the most computationally intensive steps. Measuring the minimum viable requirements for the execution allow to better allocate resources as seen in the image c.

2 Materials and Methods

The pipeline was implemented on 5 computational environments: 1 server grade machine (Xeon E52640), 1 HPC node (Xeon E52683), 2 low power machines

(Xeon D and Pentium J) and one virtual machine built on an AMD Opteron hypervisor. The characteristics of each node are presented in Table 2.

The server-grade node is a typical node used for bioinformatics computation, and as such features hundreds of GB of memory with multiple cores per motherboard: for these reasons we chose it as reference machine and the following results are expressed in relation to it.

The two low-power machines are designed to have a good cost-to-performance ratio, especially for the running cost[1]. These machines have been proven to be a viable solution for high performance computations [3]. Their low starting and running cost mean that a cluster of these machines would be more accessible for research groups looking forward to increase their computational power.

The last node is a virtual machine, designed to be operated in a cloud environment.

The monitoring tool used is Telegraf, which is an agent written in Go for collecting, processing, aggregating, and writing metrics. Each section of the pipeline sends messages to the Telegraf daemon independently.

Regardless of the number of cores of each machine we restrict the number of cores used to only two to compare the statistics: this restriction certainly penalize the environment with multiple cores but with a view of maximizing

Table 2. Characteristics of the tested computational environments. Electrical costs are estimated as 0.25 €/kWh; CPU frequencies are reported in GHz; TDP: Thermal Design Power, an estimation indicator of maximum amount of heat generated by a computer chip when a "real application" runs.

Class	Server grade machines		Low power machines		Virtual machine
CPU	Intel Xeon	Intel Xeon	Intel Pentium	Intel Xeon	AMD Opteron
Version	E5-2683v3	E5-2640v2	J4205	D-1540	6386 SE
Microarchitecture	Haswell	Ivy Bridge EP	Apollo Lake	Broadwell	Piledriver
Launch date	Q3'14	Q3'13	Q4'16	Q1'15	Q3'12
Lithography	22 nm	22 nm	14 nm	14 nm	32 nm
Cores/threads	14/28	8/16	4/4	8/16	16
Base/Max Freq	2.00/3.00	2.00/2.50	1.50/2.60	2.00/2.60	2.80/3.50
L2 Cache	35 MB	20 MB	2 MB	12 MB	16 MB
TDP	120 W	95 W	10 W	45 W	115 W
Total CPUs	2	2	1	1	1
Total cores/threads	28/56	16/32	4/4	8/16	16
Total Memory	256 GB	252 GB	8 GB	32 GB	60 GB
System power	240 + 60 W	190 + 60 W	10 + 2 W	45 + 10 W	115 + 10 W
Electrical costs	650 €/year	550 €/year	26 €/year	120 €/year	273€ /year
System price	4000–6000 €	3000–5000 €	100–130 €	900–1200 €	2000-3000€

[1] Running cost is evaluated as the energy consumption that the node requires per subject, assuming that the consumption scales linearly with the number of cores used in the individual step.

the parallelizations and minimize the energy cost it is the playground to compare all the available environments. Another restriction is applied to the chosen architectures: since available low-power machines provides only x86-architectures also the other environments are forced to work in x86 to allow the statistics comparison.

2.1 Dedicated Bioinformatics Server

The reference node for the tests is one of the servers employed for bioinformatics analyses by the authors. This is a single node with 252 GB memory, 125 TB storage and 2 CPU E5-2640v2, with 16 cores each.

This machine was designed to be able to sustain most commonly performed bioinformatics pipelines, using high volume memory and storage.

2.2 HPC Cluster Hardware Configuration

The HPC cluster is composed by 27 Infiniband interconnected worker nodes, which provide 640 core (Hyperthreaded, E5-2640 cpu), 48 HT cores X5650, 48 HT cores E5-2620, 168 HT cores E5-2683v3, 15 GPUs (8 Tesla K40, 7 Tesla K20, 2 x (4GRID K1)), 2 MICs (2 x Xeon Phi 5100).

A dedicated storage has been setup for the cluster. Storage is accessible by all the nodes through the GPFS file system. In particular the setup includes 2 disks servers, 60 TB of shared disk space, 4 TB for shared home directories. Disks servers are equipped with dual 10 Gb/s Ethernet.

Worker nodes are connected each other via Infiniband (QDR) and are equipped with 1 Gb Ethernet interfaces for storage and network traffic. Home, data and softwares directories are located on a dedicated GPFS file system and shared between all the cluster nodes. The LSF batch system (version 9.1.3) is used to manage job submission to the cluster nodes. The execution environment is shared with a number of other users, therefore in order to measure resource usage, it has been necessary to monitor our jobs from within.

2.3 The Low-power Cluster

The nodes of the cluster are located in a I.N.F.N. facility located in Bologna (Italy) and are based on the current state-of-the-art low-power processors technology. Low power processors are gaining interest in many scientific applicative fields. Designed for the embedded, mobile or consumer market, they are progressively reducing the performance gap with server grade environments, with the added values of keeping a competitive edge on the bill of material and electrical energy costs.

In particular, low power Systems-on-Chip (SoCs) are designed to meet the best computing performance with the lowest power consumption. The SoCs superior performance/consumption ratio is driven by the growing demands for energy-saving boards in mobile and embedded industries. Indeed, the primary design goal for SoCs has been low power consumption because of their use in battery-powered devices or rugged industrial embedded devices. On the contrary, the current server grade CPUs were designed to meet high performance demand required by data center power-hungry clients. Moving away from their embedded and consumer worlds, SoCs are becoming a valid alternative environment for scientific applications without sacrificing too much the performances of server grade CPUs.

The low-power cluster is equipped with nodes based on ARMv7, ARMv8 and x86 low-power environments and is currently used for scientific benchmarks and real-time application tests. Nevertheless, in this work we have only considered x86-based low-power environments because they do not require porting compiling issues and because on the basis of our experience other low-power architectures (i.e. ARM based) are equivalent to x86 low-power platform in term of CPU performance. GPU-enhanced applications can result in a different scenario between ARM and x86 platforms, however, the software pipeline in this work were developed for CPU only.

We chose the following two x86 low-power architectures because they are deployed in different fields of applications: the extremely low-power Intel Pentium J Series (Apollo Lake code name) and the high-performance low-power Intel Xeon D Family (Broadwell code name). We would stress the fact that the Intel Xeon D Family is on the edge of the low-power boundary definition, as shown in the last two rows at the bottom of the Table 2 with the thermal design power (TDP) and median Bill Of Material (BOM) of each platform, but we chose it because it is a natural glue between the low-power platforms and the server-grade platforms.

2.4 Virtual Machine

The virtual machine used in our tests is made available by the project Cloud@CNAF with 16 VCPUs, 60 GB RAM and an attached persistent storage volume of 1 TB. A small list of the benefits from an end-user point of view is: lower computer costs; flexibility and scalability; virtually unlimited storage capacity; increased data reliability; easier group collaboration; device independent.

The Cloud@CNAF IaaS (Infrastructure as a Service) is based on OpenStack, a free and open-source cloud-computing software platform and it has all the services deployed using a High-Availability (HA) setup or in a clustered manner (for ex. using a Percona XtraDB MySQL clustering solution for the deployment of the DBs). It is able to satisfy diversified users needs of compute and storage resources, having available, up to now, 66 hypervisors, with a total of approximately 1400 CPUs, 4 TB of memory and more than 70 TB of storage. The hypervisors range from SuperMicro nodes with 2 × 8 Core AMD Opteron Processor 6320, 64 GB of memory to 2 × 12 AMD Opteron Processor 6238, 80 GB of memory, connected to a PowerVault MD3660i through a GPFS cluster, acting as backend for the cloud VMs ephemeral storage and the persistent, block-storage one.

2.5 Pipeline Steps

The pipeline steps that have been examined are a subset of all the possible steps: we only focus on those whose computational requirements are higher and thus require the most computational power. These steps are:

1. **mapping:** takes all the reads of the subjects and maps them on the reference genome;
2. **sort:** sorts the sequences based on the alignment, to improve the reconstruction steps;
3. **markduplicates:** checks for read duplicates (that could be imperfections in the experimental procedures and would skew the results);
4. **buildbamindex:** indexes the dataset for faster sorting;
5. **indexrealigner:** realigns the created data index to the reference genome;
6. **BQSR:** base quality score recalibration of the reads, to improve SNPs detection;
7. **haplotypecaller:** determines the SNPs of the subject;
8. **hardfilter:** removes the least significant SNPs.

The following statistics were evaluated:

1. **memory per function:** estimate percentage of the total memory available to the node used for each individual step of the pipeline;
2. **energy consumption:** estimated as the time taken by the step, multiplied by the number of cores used in the step and the power consumption per core (TDP divided by the available cores). As mentioned before this normalization unavoidably penalize the multi-core machines but give us a term of comparison between the different environment;
3. **elapsed time:** wall time of each step.

The pipeline was tested on the patient data from the 1000 genome project with access code NA12878, sample SRR1611178. It is referred as a Gold Standard reference dataset [10]. It is generated with an Illumina HiSeq2000 platform, SeqCap EZ Human Exome Lib v3.0 library and have a 80x coverage. As Gold Standard reference it is commonly used as benchmark of new algorithm and for our purpose can be used as valid prototype of genome.

3 Results

Memory occupation is one of the major drawbacks of the bioinformatics pipelines, and one of the greater limits to the possibility of parallel computation of multiple subjects at the same time. As it can be seen in Fig. 2, the memory occupation is comprised between 10% and 30% on all the nodes. This is due to the default behavior of the GATK libraries to reserve a fixed percentage of the total memory of the node. The authors could not find any solution to prevent this behavior from happening. As it can be noticed, in the node with the greatest amount of total memory (both Xeon E5 and the virtual machine) the

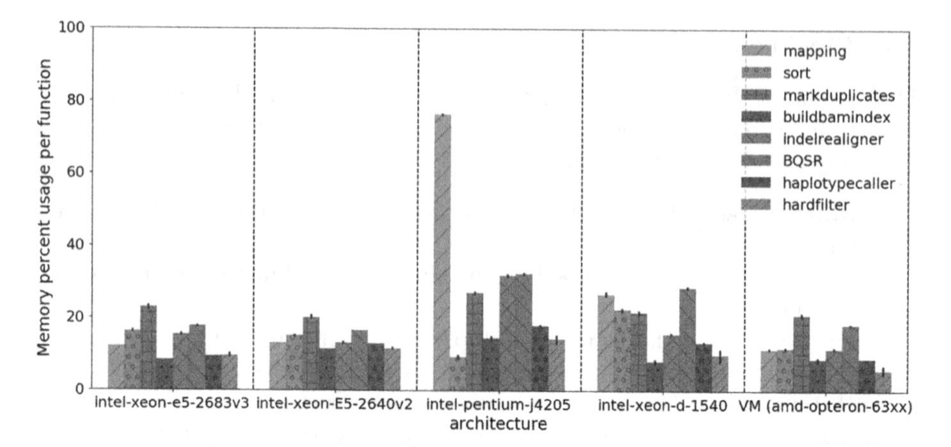

Fig. 2. Memory used for each step of the pipeline. Due to the GATK memory allocation strategy, all steps use a baseline amount of memory proportional to the available memory. Smaller nodes, like the low power ones, require more memory as the baseline allocated memory is not sufficient to perform the calculation.

requested memory is approximately stable, as is always sufficient for the required task. The memory allocation is less stable in the nodes with a limited memory (Xeon D and Pentium J), as GATK might requires more memory than what initially allocated to perform the calculation. The exception to this behavior is the "mapping" step, that uses a fixed amount of memory independently from the available one (between 5 and 7 GB). This is due to the necessity of loading the whole human reference genome (version hg19GRCh37) to align each individual read to it. All the other steps do not require the human reference genome but can work on the individual reads, allowing greater flexibility in memory allocation.

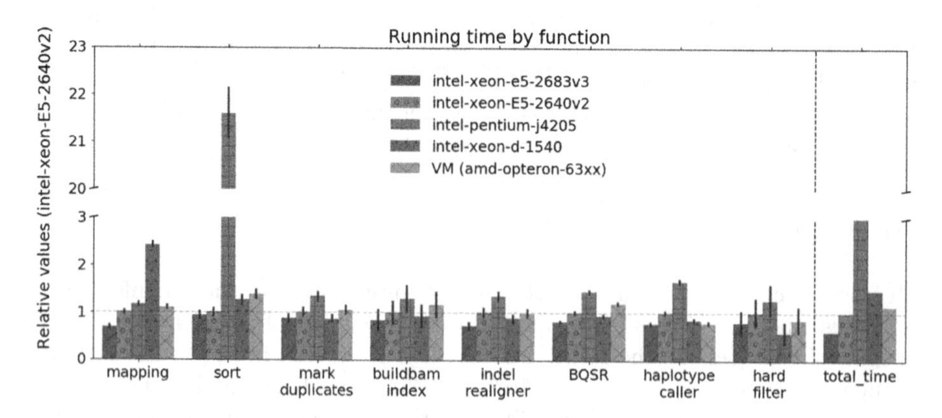

Fig. 3. Time elapsed per step of the pipeline, and total elapsed time. In the sorting step, Pentium J is 20 times slower than the reference, probably due to the limited cache size.

As can be seen in Figs. 3 and 4, this increase of memory consumption does not correspond to a proportional improvement of the time elapsed in the computation.

The elapsed time for each step and for the whole pipeline can be seen in Fig. 3. It can be seen that there is a non consistent trend in the behavior of the different environments. Aside from the most extreme low power machine, the pentium J, the elapsed times are on average higher for the low power and slightly higher for the cloud node, but the time for the individual rule can vary. In the sorting step, Pentium J is 20 times slower than the reference. This is probably due to the limited cache and memory size of the pentium J, that are both important factors determining the execution time of a sorting algorithm and are both at least four to six times smaller than the other machines. The HPC machine, the Xeon E52683, is consistently faster than the reference node.

The energy consumption per step can be seen in Fig. 4. The low power machines are consistently less than half the baseline consumption. Even considering the peak of consumption due to the long time required to perform the sorting, the most efficient low power machine, the pentium J, consumes 40% of the reference, and the Xeon D consumes 60% of the reference. The HPC machine, the Xeon E52683, have consumption close to the low power nodes, balancing out the higher energy consumption with a faster execution speed. The virtual machine has the highest consumption despite the fact that the execution time of the whole pipeline is comparable to the reference due to the high TDP compared to its execution time.

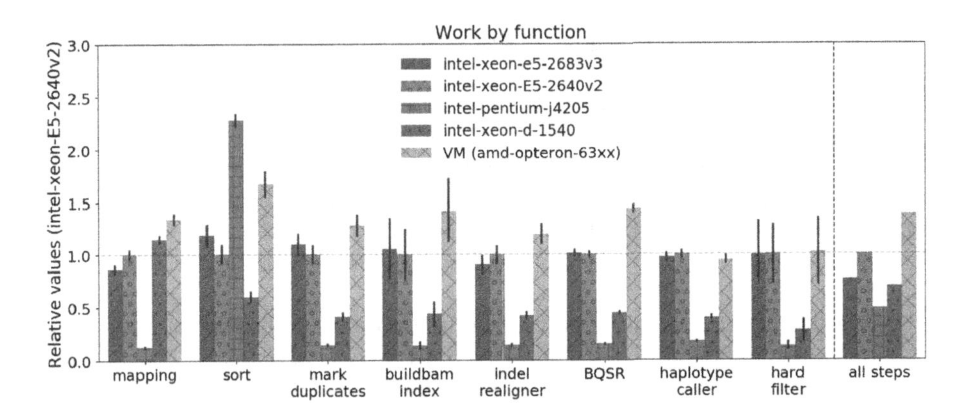

Fig. 4. Energy consumption per pipeline step and on the whole pipeline. Energy consumption is estimated as the time taken by the step, multiplied by the number of cores used in the step and the power consumption per core (TDP divided by the available cores).

4 Discussion and Conclusions

Bioinformatic pipelines are one of the most important uses of biomedical big data and, at the same time, one of the hardest to optimize, both for their extreme requisites and the constant change of the specification, both in input-output data format and program API.

This makes the task of pipeline optimization a daunting one, especially for the final target of the results; physicians and biologists could lack the technical expertise (and time) required to optimize each new version of the various softwares of the pipelines. Moreover, in a verified pipeline updating the software included without a long and detailed crossvalidation with the previous one is often considered a bad practice: this means that often these pipelines are running with underperforming versions of each software.

Clinical use of these pipelines is growing, in particular with the rise of the concept of "personalized medicine", where the therapy plan is designed on the specific genotype and phenotype of the individual patient rather than on the characteristic of the overall population. This would increase the precision of the therapy and thus increase its efficacy, while cutting considerably the trial and error process required to identify promising target of therapy. This requires the pipelines to be evaluated in real time, for multiple subjects at the same time (and potentially with multiple samples per subject). To perform this task no single node is powerful enough, and thus it is necessary to use clusters. This brings the need to evaluate which is the most cost and time efficient node that can be employed.

In the cost assessment there are several factors that need to be considered aside of the initial setup cost, namely cost for running the server and opportunity cost for obsolescence. Scaled on medium sized facilities, such the one that could be required for a hospital, this cost could quickly overcome the setup cost. This cost does also include not only the direct power consumption of the nodes, but also the required power for air conditioning to maintain them in the working temperature range. Opportunity costs are more complex, but do represent the loss of possibility of using the most advanced technologies due to the cost of the individual node of the cluster. Higher end nodes require a significant investment, and thus can not be replaced often.

With this perspective in mind, we surmise that energy efficient nodes present an interesting opportunity for the implementation of these pipelines. As shown in this work, these nodes have a low cost per subject, paired with a low setup cost. This makes them an interesting alternative to traditional nodes as a workhorse node for a cluster, as a greater number of cores can be bought and maintained for the same cost.

Given the high variability of the performances in the various steps, in particular with the sorting and mapping steps, it might be more efficient to employ a hybrid environment, where few high power nodes are used for specific tasks, while the bulk of the computation is done by the energy efficient nodes. This is true even for those steps that can be massively parallelized, such as the mapping, as they benefit mainly from a high number of processors rather than few powerful ones. In this work we focused only on CPUs computation, but another possibility could be an hybrid-parallelization approach in which the use of a single GPU accelerator can improve the parallelization of the slower steps. Each pipeline workflow requires its own analyses and tuning to reach the best performances and the right parallelization strategy based on the use which it is intended but a low energy node approach is emerging as a good alternative to the more expensive and common solutions.

References

1. Behjati, S., Tarpey, P.S.: What is next generation sequencing? Arch. Dis. Child. Educ. Pract. Edition **98**(6), 236–238 (2013). http://ep.bmj.com/lookup/doi/10.1136/archdischild-2013-304340
2. Castellani, G., et al.: Systems medicine of inflammaging. Brief. Bioinform. **17**(3), 527–540 (2016). https://doi.org/10.1093/bib/bbv062
3. Cesini, D., et al.: Power-efficient computing: experiences from the COSA project. Sci. Program. **2017** (2017). http://www.sciencedirect.com/science/article/pii/S0092867400816839
4. Cibulskis, K., et al.: Sensitive detection of somatic point mutations in impure and heterogeneous cancer samples. Nat. Biotechnol. **31**(3), 213–219 (2013). http://www.nature.com/doifinder/10.1038/nbt.2514
5. Hanahan, D., Weinberg, R.A.: The hallmarks of cancer. Cell **100**(1), 57–70 (2000). http://www.sciencedirect.com/science/article/pii/S0092867400816839
6. McKenna, A., et al.: The genome analysis toolkit: a MapReduce framework for analyzing next-generation DNA sequencing data. Genome Res. **20**(9), 1297–1303 (2010). https://doi.org/10.1101/gr.107524.110
7. Pooley, R.: Bridging the culture gap. No. 767 (2005)
8. Shendure, J., Ji, H.: Next-generation DNA sequencing. Nat. Biotechnol. **26**(10), 1135–1145 (2008). http://www.nature.com/doifinder/10.1038/nbt1486
9. do Valle, Í.F., et al.: Optimized pipeline of MuTect and GATK tools to improve the detection of somatic single nucleotide polymorphisms in whole-exome sequencing data. BMC Bioinform. **17**(S12), 341 (2016). http://bmcbioinformatics.biomedcentral.com/articles/10.1186/s12859-016-1190-7
10. Zook, J.M., et al.: Integrating human sequence data sets provides a resource of benchmark SNP and indel genotype calls. Nat. Biotechnol. **32**, 246 (2014)
11. Zwolak, M., Di Ventra, M.: Colloquium: physical approaches to DNA sequencing and detection. Rev. Mod. Phys. **80**(1), 141–165 (2008)

High Performance Computing for Haplotyping: Models and Platforms

Andrea Tangherloni[1(✉)], Leonardo Rundo[1,5], Simone Spolaor[1], Marco S. Nobile[1,6], Ivan Merelli[2], Daniela Besozzi[1], Giancarlo Mauri[1,6], Paolo Cazzaniga[3,6], and Pietro Liò[4]

[1] Department of Informatics, Systems and Communication, University of Milano-Bicocca, Milan, Italy
andrea.tangherloni@disco.unimib.it
[2] Institute of Biomedical Technologies, Italian National Research Council, Segrate, Italy
[3] Department of Human and Social Sciences, University of Bergamo, Bergamo, Italy
[4] Computer Laboratory, University of Cambridge, Cambridge, UK
[5] Institute of Molecular Bioimaging and Physiology, Italian National Research Council, Cefalù, PA, Italy
[6] SYSBIO.IT Centre of Systems Biology, Milano, Italy

Abstract. The reconstruction of the haplotype pair for each chromosome is a hot topic in Bioinformatics and Genome Analysis. In Haplotype Assembly (HA), all heterozygous Single Nucleotide Polymorphisms (SNPs) have to be assigned to exactly one of the two chromosomes. In this work, we outline the state-of-the-art on HA approaches and present an in-depth analysis of the computational performance of GenHap, a recent method based on Genetic Algorithms. GenHap was designed to tackle the computational complexity of the HA problem by means of a *divide-et-impera* strategy that effectively leverages multi-core architectures. In order to evaluate GenHap's performance, we generated different instances of synthetic (yet realistic) data exploiting empirical error models of four different sequencing platforms (namely, Illumina NovaSeq, Roche/454, PacBio RS II and Oxford Nanopore Technologies MinION). Our results show that the processing time generally decreases along with the read length, involving a lower number of sub-problems to be distributed on multiple cores.

Keywords: Future-generation sequencing
Genome Analysis Haplotype Assembly
High Performance Computing · Master-Slave paradigm

1 Introduction

The advent of second-generation sequencing technologies revolutionized the field of genomics, enabling a more complete view and understanding of the genome of different species. However, despite their great contribution to the field, the

G. Mencagli et al. (Eds.): Euro-Par 2018 Workshops, LNCS 11339, pp. 650–661, 2019.
https://doi.org/10.1007/978-3-030-10549-5_51

data produced by these technologies are still unsuitable for several applications, including Haplotype Assembly (HA). This problem consists in assigning all heterozygous Single Nucleotide Polymorphisms (SNPs) to exactly one of the two homologous chromosomes, leveraging data from sequencing experiments. The short length of the reads produced by second-generation sequencing technologies might be not long enough to span over a relevant number of SNP positions, leading to the reconstruction of short haplotype blocks [8,43] and ultimately hindering the possibility of reconstructing the full haplotypes.

In recent years, however, a third-generation of sequencing technologies was developed and paved the way to the production of sequencing data characterized by reads covering hundreds of kilobases, thus able to span different SNP loci at once [16,32,33]. Unfortunately, the increase in length comes at the cost of a decrease in the accuracy of the reads, compared to the short and precise ones produced by second-generation sequencing technologies, such as NovaSeq (Illumina Inc., San Diego, CA, USA) [31]. In order to compensate for this inadequacy, there is a need for increasing the read coverage. Formally, the coverage of a sequencing experiment is the average number of times that each nucleotide is expected to be covered by a read. This value is given by the following relationship:

$$\text{cov} = (L \cdot N)/G, \tag{1}$$

where cov stands for the coverage, L for the read length, N for the number of reads and G for the length of the haploid region of the genome on which the reads are mapped [20]. Equation (1) shows that longer reads or a higher amount of reads are needed to increase the coverage. In practice, an average coverage higher than 30$\times$ is the *de facto* standard for accurate SNP detection [38]. Along with the HA issues, novel challenges—e.g., poliploidity, metagenomics, analysis of cancer cell heterogeneity and chromosomal capture experiments—require sequencing data with a high coverage.

In this paper, we briefly describe the state-of-the-art on haplotype computational tools, providing a taxonomy based on the employed computational techniques. Then, we focus on GenHap [40], an evolutionary method that exploits High Performance Computing (HPC) architectures. We show how GenHap performs on data produced by four different sequencing platforms, namely:

- Illumina NovaSeq (Illumina Inc., San Diego, CA, USA) [31]: the most used and widespread platform belonging to the class of second-generation sequencing technologies, able to produce a huge number of short and precise reads (up to 150 bp);
- Roche/454 (Roche AG, Basel, Switzerland) [23]: a second-generation sequencing technology able to produce accurate and slightly longer reads than Illumina sequencers (up to 700 bp);
- PacBio RS II (Pacific Biosciences of California Inc., Menlo Park, CA, USA) [32,33]: a third-generation sequencing technology able to produce long reads (up to 30000 bp);

- Oxford Nanopore Technologies (ONT) MinION (ONT Ltd., Oxford, United Kingdom) [16,17,36]: the latest developed third-generation sequencing technology, able to produce reads that are tens of kilobases long.

The manuscript is structured as follows. Section 2 describes and classifies the most used HA approaches, focusing on HPC potential provided by GenHap. The achieved results, in terms of scalability and efficiency on multi-core architectures, are shown and analyzed in Sect. 3. Finally, future directions and possible fruitful connections with other research fields, such as machine learning and security in distributed computing, are mentioned in Sect. 4.

2 HPC in Haplotype Assembly

Current human Whole Genome Sequencing (WGS) approaches do not generally provide phasing information, limiting the identification of clinically-relevant samples, estimation of compound heterozygosity as well as population-level phenomena, including haplotype diversity and Linkage Disequilibrium patterns that could help to resolve migratory patterns and mutation origins [7].

Several computational HA approaches for human genome phasing have been proposed in literature [7]. Most of these methods solve the NP-hard Minimum Error Correction (MEC) problem, which aims at inferring the haplotype pair that yields two disjoint sets of the sequencing reads characterized by the minimum number of SNP values to be corrected [41]. An additional variant of MEC exists, called weighted MEC (wMEC) [14], which takes into account also the information concerning the quality of the reads.

In what follows, we concisely describe the most diffused HA methods and graphically represent them by means of a "phylogenetic tree"-like diagram (Fig. 1). Then, we focus on the functioning of the distributed GenHap implementation on multi-core architectures [40].

2.1 Related Work

Beagle [5] is one of the earliest heuristic approaches based on Hidden Markov Models (HMMs). Considering the genotype information of an individual, Beagle finds the most likely haplotype pair among different possible haplotype solutions. It has a quadratic computational complexity with respect to the input data.

SHAPEIT [10] starts from genotyping data related to a population and, given the genotype data of an individual, exploits an HMM-based approach to estimate the haplotype pair. The population data are used to apply constraints on the graph, which denotes all possible haplotypes compatible with the input data, in order to determine the haplotype of that individual. At each iteration, SHAPEIT has a linear complexity with respect to the number of haplotypes.

Eagle2 [22] is a phasing algorithm that exploits the Burrows-Wheeler transform to encode the information from large external reference panels. It relies on an HMM to explore only the most relevant phase paths among all possible paths. The authors showed that Eagle is 20 times faster than SHAPEIT [10].

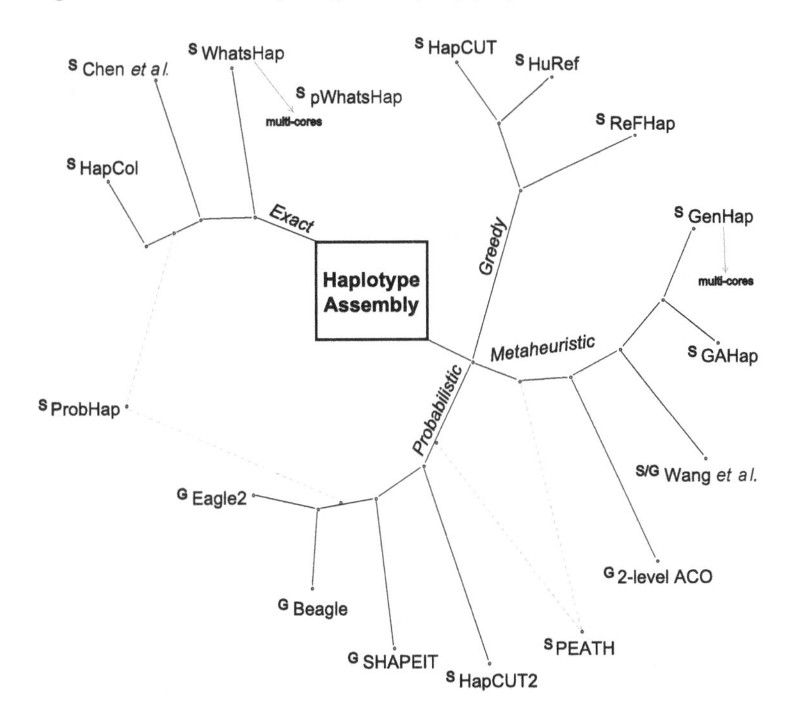

Fig. 1. The "phylogeny" of haplotyping methods. Over the past few years, the repertoire of tools for haplotyping has rapidly expanded. A "phylogenetic tree"-like diagram is used here to depict the division of the algorithms in 4 different classes, namely: exact, greedy, probabilistic, metaheuristic. Hybrid methods are connected with dashed lines to the implemented multiple computational techniques. The orange superscript denotes the analyzed data: sequencing (S) and genotyping (G). Methods that solve either the MEC or the wMEC problem are denoted with blue or magenta, respectively. Finally, the HA methods that exploit HPC are highlighted with a green arrow directed to the used computational resources. See text in Sect. 2.1 for descriptions of the most common software representatives of branches, and for the definitions of abbreviations. (Color figure online)

HapCUT [1] leverages sequencing data (i.e., the entire set of reads is considered) instead of population genotypes. It infers the haplotype pair of an individual by partitioning the set of reads solving the MEC problem. The MEC problem is reduced to the max-cut problem, which is greedily solved over the graph representation of the input instance.

HapCUT2 [12] is a recent heuristic approach that exploits a haplotype likelihood model for the sequencing reads. A partial likelihood function is used to evaluate the likelihood of a subset of the fragments. Differently from its previous version (HapCUT [1]), which is based on a greedy max-cut algorithm, HapCUT2 optimizes the likelihood to find a max-cut in graph representation of the input instance.

ProbHap [18] relies on an exact likelihood optimization technique to solve a generalized version of the MEC problem. It exploits a dynamic programming algorithm capable of exactly optimizing a likelihood function, which is specified by a probabilistic graphical model that generalizes the MEC problem.

ReFHap [11] is based on a heuristic algorithm to find the max-cut. ReFHap solves the Maximum Fragments Cut (MFC) problem instead of the classic MEC problem. The max-cut problem is reduced to the MFC problem, which is addressed using a greedy approach.

HuRef [21] is a heuristic approach that aims at inferring the heterozygous variants of an individual. It is based on a greedy algorithm that iteratively refines the initial partial haplotype solutions. The authors leveraged this HA approach to study non-SNP genetic alterations considering the diploid nature of the human genome.

Chen et al. [6] proposed an exact approach for the MEC problem using an integer linear programming solver. First, the fragment matrix is decomposed into small independent sub-matrices. Each of these sub-matrices is used to define an integer linear programming problem that is then exactly solved.

WhatsHap [29] is an exact method relying on a dynamic programming algorithm used to solve wMEC. It implements a fixed parameter tractable algorithm, where the fixed parameter is the maximum coverage of the input instance, to deal with the NP-hardness of the wMEC problem. This method does not assume the all-heterozygosity of the phased positions.

pWhatsHap [4] is an efficient version of WhatsHap [29], which was designed to leverage multi-core architectures in order to obtain a relevant reduction of the execution time required by WhatsHap. The proposed implementation exploits the physical shared memory of the underlying architecture to avoid data communication among threads.

HapCol [30] implements a dynamic programming algorithm to solve an alternative version of the wMEC problem, called k-MEC, which is used to take into account the distribution of sequencing errors of future-generation technologies. In this strategy, the number of corrections per column is bounded by the parameter k. No all-heterozygous assumption is required.

Two-Level ACO [2] is based on the Ant Colony Optimization (ACO) technique, which is a metaheuristic designed to deal with combinatorial problems on graphs generated starting from the genotyping data given as input. This approach is based on the pure parsimony criterion to find the smallest set of distinct haplotypes that solves the HA problem.

Probabilistic Evolutionary Algorithm with Toggling for Haplotyping (PEATH) [26] is based on the Estimation of Distribution Algorithm (EDA), which is a metaheuristic suitable for continuous problems. During each iteration of EDA, the promising individuals are used to build probabilistic models that are sampled to explore the search space. This metaheuristic is exploited to deal with noisy sequencing reads, aiming at inferring one haplotype, under the all-heterozygous assumption.

Wang et al. [41] relies on Genetic Algorithms (GAs), which are a family of metaheuristics designed to tackle combinatorial and discrete problems. This method was proposed to address an extended version of the MEC problem in which genotyping data are considered during the SNP correction process.

GAHap [42] uses GAs to infer the haplotype pair of an individual working on nucleotide strings. During the optimization, GAHap solves the MEC problem by means of a majority rule that takes into account allele frequencies. No all-heterozygous assumption is required.

GenHap [40] is a novel computational method based on GAs to solve the wMEC problem. This method exploits a *divide-et-impera* approach to partition the entire problem into smaller and manageable overlapped sub-problems. In order to solve in parallel the sub-problems, GenHap was developed using a Master-Slave approach to leverage multi-core architectures.

2.2 GenHap: A Distributed Computing Implementation for HA

Hereafter, we briefly recall the peculiarities of GenHap [40], by focusing on the HPC implementation. GenHap tackles the HA problem by solving the wMEC problem, exploiting an approach based on GAs. Since the execution time and the problem difficulty increase with the number of reads and SNPs of the input data, GenHap follows a *divide-et-impera* approach [24] in which the wMEC problem is efficiently solved by splitting the fragment matrix $\mathbf{M}$ into $\Pi = \lfloor m/\gamma \rfloor$ sub-matrices consisting of γ reads (where γ depends on the coverage value and on the nature of the sequencing technology). By so doing, the problem difficulty is reduced by solving the sub-problems by means of independent GA executions that eventually converge to solutions having two sub-haplotypes with the least number of corrections to the SNP values. Finally, these sub-haplotypes are combined to achieve the complete haplotype pair. It is worth noting that GenHap considers all phased positions [19] as heterozygous during the optimization phase with GAs. As soon as the sub-haplotypes are obtained, all possible uncorrected heterozygous sites are removed and the correct value is assigned by checking the columns of the sub-partitions.

GenHap makes use of a Master-Slave distributed programming paradigm [39] to speed up the overall execution (Fig. 2) [35]. It was developed using the C++ programming language and the Message Passing Interface (MPI) specifications to leverage multi-core Central Processing Units (CPUs). The Master-Slave strategy of GenHap consists of the following phases: **(1)** the Master process (MPI rank 0) proceeds by (*i*) allocating the necessary resources, (*ii*) partitioning the matrix into Π sub-matrices, and (*iii*) offloading the data onto the available Σ Slave processes. Each Slave σ (with MPI rank $1 \leq \sigma \leq \Sigma$) proceeds by randomly generating the initial population of the GA; **(2)** each Slave executes the assigned wMEC sub-task by means of an independent GA instance. If multiple cores are available, the Slave processes are executed in a parallel fashion; **(3)** as soon as the wMEC sub-tasks are terminated, the Master process recombines the sub-solutions received from the Slaves, and yields the complete wMEC solution.

According to the GA settings analysis provided in [40], we used here 100 individuals, tournament selection with size equal to 10 individuals, crossover and mutation rates equal to 0.9 and 0.05, respectively. Finally, the elitism strategy is exploited to copy the best individual from the current population into the next one without undergoing the genetic operators.

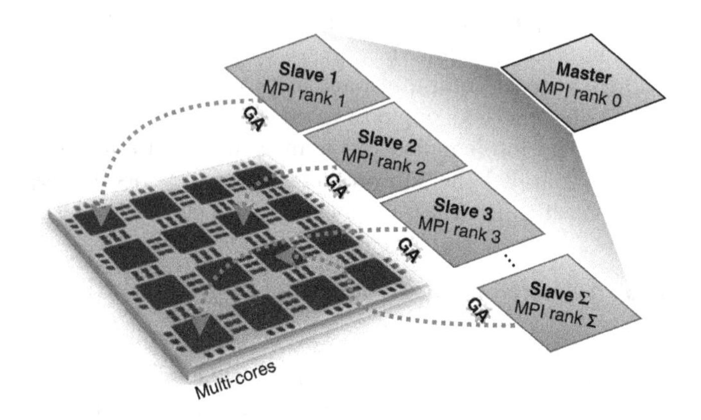

Fig. 2. Graphical representation of the Master-Slave approach implemented by GenHap: the Master process handles all the Σ Slaves by sending one or more sub-partitions to each Slave, which then solves the assigned wMEC sub-task leveraging a core.

3 Test Battery and Results

In what follows, we present some computational results obtained by considering different sequencing technologies, namely: Illumina NovaSeq, Roche/454, PacBio RS II, and ONT MinION. In [40], GenHap was shown to be faster than HapCol achieving up to 20× speed-up on PacBio RS II instances, reconstructing haplotypes characterized by a very low haplotype error rate. Moreover, GenHap was capable of solving in about 10 min a real PacBio RS II instance characterized by #SNPs $\simeq$ 28000 and #reads $\simeq$ 140000, with average and maximum coverages equal to 29 and 565, respectively. Notice that a direct comparison with the only other parallel method, pWhatsHap [4], was not possible since the source code of that tool is no longer publicly available.

In order to assess the computational performance of GenHap, we used the General Error-Model based SIMulator (GemSIM) toolbox [25] to generate different instances of synthetic (yet realistic) data, compliant with these sequencing technologies. GemSIM generates the instances relying on empirical error models and distributions learned from real NGS data. A detailed description of the whole pipeline is described in [40]. For each sequencing technology, we generated a single instance varying the following parameters: (*i*) #SNPs $\in$

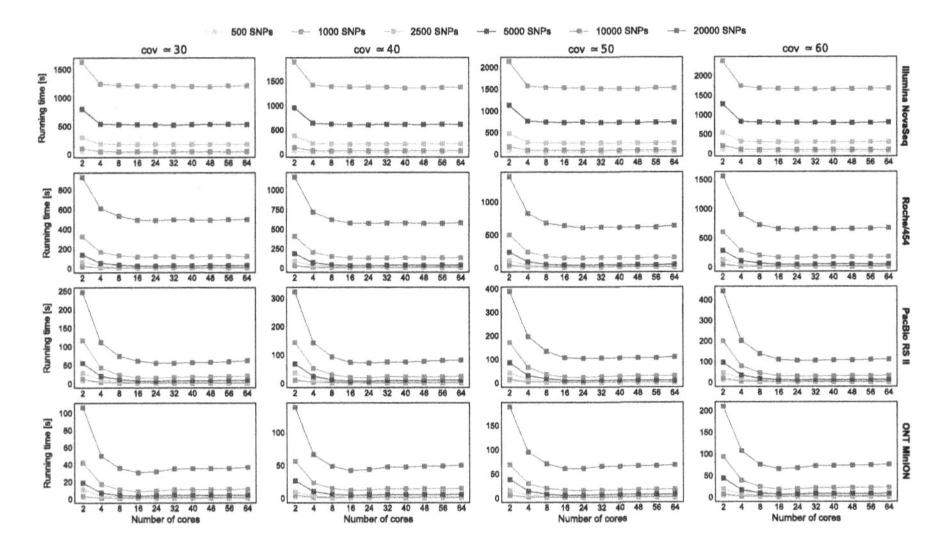

Fig. 3. Comparison of the running time required by GenHap on sequencing data generated by four sequencing technologies (Illumina NovaSeq, Roche/454, PacBio RS II, ONT MinION) by varying the coverage values. Note that the instances generated using the Illumina NovaSeq technology and characterized by #SNPs = 20000 required more RAM than the amount of memory available on the computing nodes used for the tests. The tests were executed by increasing the number of cores exploited to run GenHap, to evaluate the scalability of the implementation based on distributed computing.

$\{500, 1000, 5000, 10000, 20000\}$; (*ii*) cov $\in \{\sim 30\times, \sim 40\times, \sim 50\times, \sim 60\times\}$; (*iii*) average $f_{\text{SNPs}} = 200$ (i.e., one SNP every 200 bp exists [13,27]).

These instances were used to evaluate the scalability of GenHap by varying the number of cores, that is, #cores $\in \{2, 4, 8, 16, 24, 32, 40, 48, 56, 64\}$. All tests were performed on the MARCONI supercomputer, which is based on the Lenovo NeXtScale System® platform (Morrisville, NC, USA), provided by the Italian inter-university consortium CINECA (Bologna, Italy). Three different partitions running on CentOS 7.2 are available on this supercomputer:

*A*1 Broadwell (BDW) partition consists of 720 compute nodes, each one equipped with 2 Intel® Xeon® E5-2697 v4 (18 cores at 2.30 GHz) and 128 GB RAM;
*A*2 Knights Landing (KNL) partition consists of 3600 compute nodes, each one equipped with an Intel® Knights Landing (68 cores at 1.40 GHz and 16 GB MCDRAM), which is the next-generation of the Intel® Xeon Phi™ product family for many-core architectures, and 93 GB RAM;
*A*3 Skylake (SKL) partition consists of 92 compute nodes, each one equipped with 2 Intel® Xeon® 8160 CPU (18 cores at 2.10 GHz) and 192 GB RAM.

Our analysis was carried out by using the computing nodes of partition *A*2, which was chosen due to the availability of a higher number of computing cores.

Figure 3 depicts the running times required by GenHap to infer the pairs of haplotypes. As expected, the processing time generally decreases along with the read length: indeed, according to Eq. (1), the same coverage can be obtained by means of long reads coupled with a lower number of reads. This circumstance leads to a lower number of sub-problems to be solved, reducing the necessary computational effort. Moreover, the lowest running time is achieved on the instances generated relying on the ONT MinION, which is capable of producing long reads (up to 6000 bp) with accuracy greater than 92%. As a matter of fact, the amount of SNPs to be corrected decreases when reads characterized by high accuracy are taken into account, allowing the GA instances to have a fast convergence to the optimal solutions. The results obtained for each sequencing platform are summarized as follows. (*i*) Illumina NovaSeq: independently from the coverage, the lowest running time is achieved by exploiting 24 cores to parallelize the GA instances when #SNPs = 10000. When #SNPs $<$ 10000, 16 or 24 cores require the minimum running time to infer the haplotype pairs; (*ii*) Roche/454: when #SNPs $\geq$ 5000, the best GenHap's performance is achieved by exploiting 16 or 24 cores, otherwise the best choice is 24 cores; (*iii*) PacBio RS II: in every test, the fastest executions are generally obtained by exploiting 24 cores to parallelize the GA instances, except when #SNPs = 500 is taken into account. In this case, the running time decreases when 16 cores are exploited to effectively distribute the GA instances on multiple cores. Since the reads generated by relying on this technology have a low accuracy (approximately 87%), which makes the problem more difficult to be solved (i.e., the amount of SNPs to be corrected increases), the scalability of GenHap is emphasized; (*iv*) ONT MinION: in all tests, the best choice is 16 cores that allow for efficiently distributing the computational load. In every test, a number of cores greater than 24 does not reduce the running time since the overhead introduced by MPI is not entirely mitigated by the required computational load. Furthermore, when the number of sub-problems is lower than the number of available cores, our Master-Slave approach exploits a number of cores equal to the number of sub-problems. On the one hand, when technologies producing short reads are considered, the number of haplotype blocks increases along with #SNPs. Since these blocks are solved sequentially and are generally characterized by a number of sub-problems lower than the available cores, 16 or 24 cores allow for balancing the computational load. On the other hand, technologies producing long reads generate a small number of reads that lead to a low number of sub-problems to be solved. Notice that exploiting the accuracy of the reads produced using Illumina NovaSeq, Roche/454 and ONT MinION, the GA instances have a fast convergence to the optimal solutions requiring only a dozen of generations.

4 Conclusion and Future Trends

In this paper, we presented a complete overview on the currently available HA computational tools, focusing on the potential of HPC in this research area. In particular, we investigated the computational performance of GenHap [40], a recent evolutionary method leveraging multi-core architectures.

As a future development, we plan to extend GenHap to deal with HA in organisms characterized by different ploidity. Differently from diploid organisms having two copies of each chromosome set, polyploid organisms have multiple copies of their chromosome sets. Polyploidy has gained scientific interest in the study of the ongoing species diversification phenomena [28]. This characteristic is mainly present in plant genomes, but also in animals (such as salmonid fishes and African clawed frogs) [34]. In these comparative genomic studies, haplotype-aware assemblies play a crucial role in elucidating genetic and epigenetic regulatory evolutionary aspects. Unfortunately, the computational burden of the HA problem is emphasized in the case of polyploid haplotypes with respect to diploids [9]. Therefore, HPC represents a key element for efficient, accurate, and scalable methods for HA of both diploid and polyploid organisms.

An interesting future trend in Genome Analysis is related to its connection with machine learning. As a matter of fact, deep learning has been successfully applied in population genetic inference and learning informative features of data [37]. Combining population genetics inference and HA can provide insights on patterns regarding the genetic diversity in DNA polymorphism data, especially for rapid adaptation and selection [15].

An additional issue worth of notice is that, although the integration of various types of information (e.g., electronic health records and genome sequences) conveys a wealth of information, it is giving rise to unique challenges in bioinformatics analysis even in terms of secure genomic information sharing [3]. With reference to secure Genome-Wide Association Study (GWAS) in distributed computing environments, multi-party computation schemes based on conventional cryptographic techniques achieve limited performance in practice [7]. Therefore, HPC could become an enabling factor also in this context.

Acknowledgment. We acknowledge the CINECA for the availability of High Performance Computing resources and support.

References

1. Bansal, V., Bafna, V.: HapCUT: an efficient and accurate algorithm for the haplotype assembly problem. Bioinformatics **24**(16), i153–i159 (2008)
2. Benedettini, S., Roli, A., Di Gaspero, L.: Two-level ACO for haplotype inference under pure parsimony. In: Dorigo, M., Birattari, M., Blum, C., Clerc, M., Stützle, T., Winfield, A.F.T. (eds.) ANTS 2008. LNCS, vol. 5217, pp. 179–190. Springer, Heidelberg (2008). https://doi.org/10.1007/978-3-540-87527-7_16
3. Bianchi, L., Liò, P.: Opportunities for community awareness platforms in personal genomics and bioinformatics education. Brief. Bioinform. **18**(6), 1082–1090 (2016)
4. Bracciali, A., et al.: pWhatsHap: efficient haplotyping for future generation sequencing. BMC Bioinform. **17**(Suppl. 11), 342 (2016)
5. Browning, S.R., Browning, B.L.: Rapid and accurate haplotype phasing and missing-data inference for whole-genome association studies by use of localized haplotype clustering. Am. J. Hum. Genet. **81**(5), 1084–1097 (2007)
6. Chen, Z.Z., Deng, F., Wang, L.: Exact algorithms for haplotype assembly from whole-genome sequence data. Bioinformatics **29**(16), 1938–1945 (2013)
7. Choi, Y., Chan, A.P., Kirkness, E., Telenti, A., Schork, N.J.: Comparison of phasing strategies for whole human genomes. PLoS Genet. **14**(4), e1007308 (2018)

8. Daly, M.J., Rioux, J.D., Schaffner, S.F., Hudson, T.J., Lander, E.S.: High-resolution haplotype structure in the human genome. Nat. Genet. **29**(2), 229 (2001)
9. Das, S., Vikalo, H.: SDhaP: haplotype assembly for diploids and polyploids via semi-definite programming. BMC Genomics **16**(1), 260 (2015)
10. Delaneau, O., Marchini, J., Zagury, J.F.: A linear complexity phasing method for thousands of genomes. Nat. Methods **9**(2), 179 (2012)
11. Duitama, J., Huebsch, T., McEwen, G., Suk, E., Hoehe, M.: ReFHap: a reliable and fast algorithm for single individual haplotyping. In: Proceedings of the First ACM International Conference on Bioinformatics and Computational Biology, pp. 160–169. ACM (2010)
12. Edge, P., Bafna, V., Bansal, V.: HapCUT2: robust and accurate haplotype assembly for diverse sequencing technologies. Genome Res. **27**(5), 801–812 (2017)
13. Gabriel, S.B., et al.: The structure of haplotype blocks in the human genome. Science **296**(5576), 2225–2229 (2002)
14. Greenberg, H.J., Hart, W.E., Lancia, G.: Opportunities for combinatorial optimization in computational biology. INFORMS J. Comput. **16**(3), 211–231 (2004)
15. Hermisson, J., Pennings, P.S.: Soft sweeps and beyond: understanding the patterns and probabilities of selection footprints under rapid adaptation. Methods Ecol. Evol. **8**(6), 700–716 (2017)
16. Jain, M., Fiddes, I.T., Miga, K.H., Olsen, H.E., Paten, B., Akeson, M.: Improved data analysis for the MinION Nanopore sequencer. Nat. Methods **12**(4), 351 (2015)
17. Jain, M., et al.: Nanopore sequencing and assembly of a human genome with ultra-long reads. Nat. Biotechnol. **36**(4), 338 (2018)
18. Kuleshov, V.: Probabilistic single-individual haplotyping. Bioinformatics **30**(17), i379–i385 (2014)
19. Kuleshov, V., et al.: Whole-genome haplotyping using long reads and statistical methods. Nat. Biotechnol. **32**(3), 261–266 (2014)
20. Lander, E.S., Waterman, M.S.: Genomic mapping by fingerprinting random clones: a mathematical analysis. Genomics **2**(3), 231–239 (1988)
21. Levy, S., et al.: The diploid genome sequence of an individual human. PLoS Biol. **5**(10), e254 (2007)
22. Loh, P.R., et al.: Reference-based phasing using the haplotype reference consortium panel. Nat. Genet. **48**(11), 1443 (2016)
23. Luo, C., Tsementzi, D., Kyrpides, N., Read, T., Konstantinidis, K.T.: Direct comparisons of Illumina vs. Roche 454 sequencing technologies on the same microbial community DNA sample. PloS One **7**(2), e30087 (2012)
24. Maisto, D., Donnarumma, F., Pezzulo, G.: Divide et impera: subgoaling reduces the complexity of probabilistic inference and problem solving. J. R. Soc. Interface **12**(104), 20141335 (2015)
25. McElroy, K.E., Luciani, F., Thomas, T.: GemSIM: general, error-model based simulator of next-generation sequencing data. BMC Genomics **13**(1), 74 (2012)
26. Na, J.C., Lee, J.C., Rhee, J.K., Shin, S.Y.: PEATH: single individual haplotyping by a probabilistic evolutionary algorithm with toggling. Bioinformatics **34**(11), 1801–1807 (2018)
27. Nachman, M.W.: Single nucleotide polymorphisms and recombination rate in humans. Trends Genet. **17**(9), 481–485 (2001)
28. Otto, S.P., Whitton, J.: Polyploid incidence and evolution. Annu. Rev. Genet. **34**(1), 401–437 (2000)
29. Patterson, M., et al.: WhatsHap: weighted haplotype assembly for future-generation sequencing reads. J. Comput. Biol. **22**(6), 498–509 (2015)

30. Pirola, Y., Zaccaria, S., Dondi, R., Klau, G., Pisanti, N., Bonizzoni, P.: HapCol: accurate and memory-efficient haplotype assembly from long reads. Bioinformatics **32**(11), 1610–1617 (2015)
31. Quail, M.A., et al.: A large genome center's improvements to the Illumina sequencing system. Nat. Methods **5**(12), 1005 (2008)
32. Rhoads, A., Au, K.F.: PacBio sequencing and its applications. Genomics Proteomics Bioinform. **13**(5), 278–289 (2015)
33. Roberts, R.J., Carneiro, M.O., Schatz, M.C.: The advantages of SMRT sequencing. Genome Biol. **14**(6), 405 (2013)
34. Rodriguez, F., Arkhipova, I.R.: Transposable elements and polyploid evolution in animals. Curr. Opin. Genet. Dev. **49**, 115–123 (2018)
35. Rundo, L., et al.: MedGA: a novel evolutionary method for image enhancement in medical imaging systems. Expert Syst. Appl. **119**, 387–399 (2019)
36. Senol Cali, D., Kim, J.S., Ghose, S., Alkan, C., Mutlu, O.: Nanopore sequencing technology and tools for genome assembly: computational analysis of the current state, bottlenecks and future directions. Brief. Bioinform., bby017 (2018)
37. Sheehan, S., Song, Y.S.: Deep learning for population genetic inference. PLoS Comput. Biol. **12**(3), e1004845 (2016)
38. Sims, D., Sudbery, I., Ilott, N.E., Heger, A., Ponting, C.P.: Sequencing depth and coverage: key considerations in genomic analyses. Nat. Rev. Genet. **15**(2), 121 (2014)
39. Tangherloni, A., Rundo, L., Spolaor, S., Cazzaniga, P., Nobile, M.S.: GPU-powered multi-swarm parameter estimation of biological systems: a master-slave approach. In: Proceedings of the 26th Euromicro International Conference on Parallel, Distributed and Network-based Processing (PDP), pp. 698–705. IEEE (2018)
40. Tangherloni, A., et al.: GenHap: a novel computational method based on genetic algorithms for haplotype assembly. BMC Bioinform. (2018, in press)
41. Wang, R., Wu, L., Li, Z., Zhang, X.: Haplotype reconstruction from SNP fragments by minimum error correction. Bioinformatics **21**(10), 2456–2462 (2005)
42. Wang, T.C., Taheri, J., Zomaya, A.Y.: Using genetic algorithm in reconstructing single individual haplotype with minimum error correction. J. Biomed. Inform. **45**(5), 922–930 (2012)
43. Zhang, K., Calabrese, P., Nordborg, M., Sun, F.: Haplotype block structure and its applications to association studies: power and study designs. Am. J. Hum. Genet. **71**(6), 1386–1394 (2002)

PCDLifeS - Workshop on Parallel and Distributed Computing for Life Sciences: Algorithms, Methodologies and Tools

Workshop on Parallel and Distributed Computing for Life Sciences: Algorithms, Methodologies, and Tools (PDCLifeS)

Workshop Description

Advancements in Life Sciences are largely driven by the development of powerful technologies and computational tools. Applications range from drug discovery and personalized medical therapies to improved agricultural and green energy production. However, the solution of world-real problems requires a multidisciplinary approach and poses new challenges to the field of High Performance Computing (HPC) at different levels:

- the modeling and simulation of complex phenomena (human organ functions, evolution of diseases, sustainable energy systems, etc.);
- the processing and analysis of massive amounts of data produced by modern technologies (omics and genome sequencing, functional and anatomical imaging, High-Content Screening, etc.);
- the extracting, merging and understanding of information from different sources (merging different types of images, bridging imaging and omics features, etc.);
- the storage, security, and availability of datasets (in order to gather information, compare results, reproduce the experiments, etc.).

The main goal of the PDCLifeS workshop was to foster discussion and collaboration among researchers from different backgrounds (bioinformatics, mathematics, physics, engineering, etc.), as well as to promote interest in algorithms, methodologies, and tools of HPC to face the challenges related to different branches of Life Sciences (Biology, Biomedicine, Bioengineering, Ecology, etc.).

The first edition of PDCLifeS was held in Turin, Italy, in conjunction with EuroPar 2018, and it has received 8 papers for review, from 4 countries. The reviewing process selected only 5 high-quality papers for the workshop schedule. The workshop had also a presentation by an invited speaker.

Organization

Program Chairs

Laura Antonelli	National Research Council of Italy
Salvatore Cuomo	University of Naples Federico II

Program Committee

Andrew Adamatzky	University of the West of England, UK
Stefano Berrone	Politecnico di Torino, Italy
Mario Cannataro	Università Magna Grecia, Catanzaro, Italy
Claudia Di Napoli	National Research Council, Italy
Daniela di Serafino	Università della Campania "Luigi Vanvitelli", Italy
Jing Gong	KTH Royal Institute of Technology, Sweden
Mario Rosario Guarracino	National Research Council, Italy
Gwanggil Jeon	Incheon National University, South Korea
Jason J. Jung	Chung-Ang University, Korea
Mario Nicodemi	Università degli Studi di Napoli Federico II, Italy
Domenico Talia	Università della Calabria, Italy
Jose Carlos Valeverde	University of Castilla la Mancha, Spain
Pierangelo Veltri	Università Magna Grecia, Italy

Effect of Spatial Decomposition on the Efficiency of k Nearest Neighbors Search in Spatial Interpolation

Naijie Fan[1], Gang Mei[1(✉)], Zengyu Ding[1], Salvatore Cuomo[2], and Nengxiong Xu[1]

[1] School of Engineering and Technology, China University of Geosciences (Beijing), Beijing 100083, China
gang.mei@cugb.edu.cn

[2] Department of Mathematics and Applications "R. Caccioppoli", University of Naples Federico II, Naples, Italy

Abstract. Spatial interpolations are commonly used in geometric modeling for life science applications. In large-scale spatial interpolations, it is always needed to find a local set of data points for each interpolated point using the k Nearest Neighbor (kNN) search procedure. To improve the computational efficiency of kNN search, spatial decomposition structures such as grids and trees are employed to fastly locate the nearest neighbors. Among those spatial decomposition structures, the uniform grid is the simplest one, and the size of the grid cell could strongly affect the efficiency of kNN search. In this paper, we evaluate the effect of the size of uniform grid cell on the efficiency of kNN search. Our objective is to find the relatively optimal size of grid cell by considering the distribution of scattered points (i.e., the data points and the interpolated points). We employ the Standard Deviation of points' coordinates to measure the spatial distribution of scattered points. For the irregularly distributed scattered points, we perform several series of kNN search procedures in two dimensions. Benchmark results indicate that: in two dimensions, with the increase of the Standard Deviation of points' coordinates, the relatively optimal size of the grid cell decreases and eventually converges. The relationships between the Standard Deviation of scattered points' coordinates and the relatively optimal size of grid cell are also fitted. The fitted relationships could be applied to determine the relatively optimal grid cell in kNN search, and further, improve the computational efficiency of spatial interpolations.

Keywords: Spatial interpolation · k nearest neighbors (kNN) search
Uniform grid · Spatial distribution · Standard error

1 Introduction

A spatial interpolation algorithm is the method in which the attributes at some known locations (data points) are used to predict the attributes at some unknown

G. Mencagli et al. (Eds.): Euro-Par 2018 Workshops, LNCS 11339, pp. 667–679, 2019.
https://doi.org/10.1007/978-3-030-10549-5_52

locations (interpolated points). Spatial interpolation algorithms, such as the Inverse Distance Weighting (IDW) [15], Kriging [24], Moving Least Squares method (MLS) [19], Radial Basis Functions (RBFs) Interpolation [5–7]. Different interpolation methods are widely used in various scientific fields, such as Geographic Information System (GIS) [9,10], geometric modeling [2,11], image processing [8,18], numerical analysis [25,27].

Interpolation algorithms are widely used in the field of life science applications. Liu et al. [13] proposed a hybrid approach to shape-based interpolation of stereotactic atlases of the human brain. Volkau et al. [26] combined a minimal distance map and cubic splines to reconstruct the subcortical structures of the Talairach-Tournoux atlas. Parrot et al. [23] focused on interpolation of scalar values in the 3-D gird of input data. Pan et al. [22] compared filter interpolation, ordinary interpolation and general partial volume interpolation in medical image interpolation.

In large-scale spatial interpolations, to improve the computational efficiency of interpolating, it always uses a local set of data points rather than the global set of data points to predict the interpolation value of each interpolated points. Thus, it commonly needs to find a local set of data points for each interpolated point using several approaches such as the k Nearest Neighbor (kNN) search procedure.

For example, Li et al. [12] proposed the Random kNN (a novel generalization of traditional nearest-neighbor modeling) for pattern analysis and modeled with high-dimensional data. Al Aghbari [1] studied the multiple kNN queries processing techniques in constrained spatial networks. Nutanong [20] studied an efficient algorithm for moving k Nearest Neighbor queries. Roberto Cavoretto [4] proposed an efficient scheme for the computation of triangular Shepard method. Mei [17] presented an efficient AIDW interpolation algorithm on the GPU by utilizing a fast kNN search method.

The space decomposition data structures such as RP-tree [21], VP-tree [14], k-d tree [3], and uniform grid [17] are employed to accelerate the kNN search procedure. Among those space decomposition structures, the uniform grid is the simplest. And a critical issue in creating the uniform grid is the size of grid cell since it could strongly affect the search efficiency and cannot be too small or too large. To the best of our knowledge, there is currently no research work specifically focusing on determining the optimal size of grid cell in the kNN search.

Based on our previous work [7,16,17], in this paper we first evaluate the effect of the size of uniform grid cell on the efficiency of kNN search, and then attempt to find the relatively optimal size of grid cell by considering the distribution of scattered points.

This paper is organized as follows. Section 2 briefly describes the kNN search that is commonly used in spatial interpolation. Section 3 introduces our benchmark tests. Section 4 presents and discusses the test results. Finally, Sect. 5 draws several conclusions.

2 Background: kNN Search in Spatial Interpolation

The kNN search algorithm is directly derived from our previous work [7,16,17]. And more details on the process of the kNN search are described as follows.
Step 1: Creating an even grid

The creating of an even planar grid is straightforward. We first determine the planar rectangular region for partitioning by finding the minimum and maximum x and y coordinates of all points. Then, the numbers of rows and columns of the grid can be easily determined by dividing the rectangle with the width of the square cell; see a simple illustration in Fig. 1.

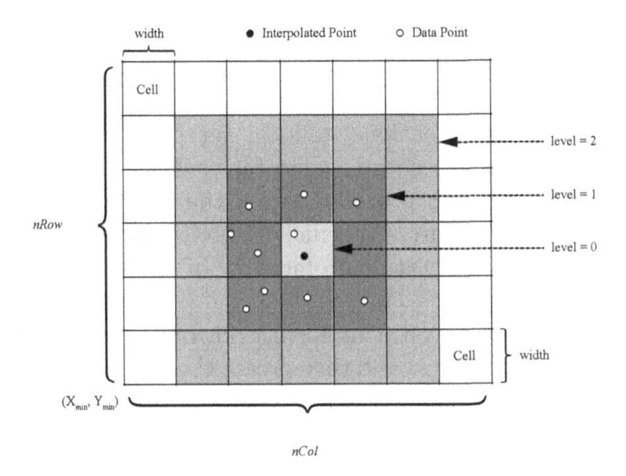

Fig. 1. Creation of an even grid according to the minimum and maximum coordinates of all the data points and interpolated points in two dimensions. (This figure is directly derived from our previous work [17].)

Step 2: Distributing data points into cells

The objective of distributing all data points into the grid cells is to find out in which grid cell each data point is located. The distributing of each data point is in fact to determine the row and column indices of the cell in which it locates. Since the grid cells are indexed sequentially first by rows and then by columns, the procedure of distributing can be easily carried out. First, the differences between the coordinates of a data point and the minimum coordinates of all cells are calculated; then the indices of column and row can be determined by dividing the above differences with the cell width.
Step 3: Determining data points in each cell

The objective of this step is to determine the number and the indices of those data points located in the same cell. The number of data points located in the same cell can be determined with the use of a *segmented* parallel reduction. After sorting all data points according to cell indices, the data points are sequentially stored in a group of segments; each segment is flagged with the cell index and contains the indices of data points locating in the same cell. The number of those data points located in the same cell can be obtained by performing a reduction for each segment. Moreover, the head index of the first point of each segment can be determined using segmented parallel scan.

Step 4: Searching nearest neighbors

The process of kNN search for each interpolated point can be summarized as the following substeps: (1) locating the interpolate point into the even grid, (2) determining the level of cell expanding (see Fig. 1), and (3) finding the k nearest neighbors within the local region. More details on searching the nearest neighboring data points for each interpolated points were presented in our previous work [17].

3 Methods

In large-scale spatial interpolations, a local set of data points is always to be used to predict the interpolation value for each interpolated point. Therefore, there are commonly two procedures: (1) the kNN search procedure, and (2) the interpolating procedure. An efficient kNN search procedure would be helpful to improve the computational efficiency of the entire process of spatial interpolation.

In the kNN search based on a uniform grid, one of the critical steps is to determine the size of the grid cell and then create the even grid. When attempting to search for k nearest data points, the levels of grid cells are constantly expanded to find required number of data points. When the data points are intensive, the grid cell could be too large and contain too many points. In this case, the number of data points locating in the current level of grid cells is far more than the required k; and the redundant data points need to be removed by sorting. This removal may cost significant extra computational consumption. In contrast, if the grid cell is very small, it needs to expand several times to cover enough number of data points. The expanding could also cost significant extra computational consumption.

In summary, the size of the uniform grid cell could strongly affect the computational efficiency of the kNN search procedure, and it could not be too large or too small. Our objective in this paper is to find the relatively optimal size of grid cell by considering the distribution of scattered points.

In this paper, several factors may affect the determination of grid cell size which include the value of k, the data points' density, and two metrics of data distribution (i.e., the mean and Standard Deviation).

The basic idea in this paper is as follows. By changing the size of grid cells, the efficiency of kNN search is first analyzed, and then the influences of the several factors on the size of grid cells are discussed. Finally, we fit the relationships between the several factors and the relatively optimal size of the grid cell.

The sizes of grid cells are constant for the same distribution of data points in the original formula, we multiply the original formula by a coefficient w in this paper, the original formula for calculating the $cellWidth$ is described in

Eq. (1) in two dimensions. The used formula for changing the $cellWidth$ in two dimensions is described in Eq. (2).

$$cellWidth_0^{2D} = \sqrt{A_{Box}/dnum_{2D}} \tag{1}$$

$$cellWidth_{used}^{2D} = w_{2D} \times cellWidth_0^{2D} \tag{2}$$

where, $cellWidth_0^{2D}$ is the size of the original grid cell in two dimensions, $cellWidth_{used}^{2D}$ is the size of the used grid cell in two dimensions, w_{2D} is the coefficient in two dimensions, $dnum_{2D}$ is the number of known data points in two dimensions, A_{Box} is the area of the Boundary Box, and V_{Box} is the volume of the Boundary Box. The relationship between each factor and the coefficient $\boldsymbol{w}$ of grid cell size will be directly discussed subsequently.

4 Results and Discussion

4.1 Benchmark Environment and Testing Data

We carry out five groups of benchmark tests in two-dimensions on a powerful workstation computer. The specifications of the employed workstations are listed in Table 1.

Table 1. Specifications of the employed workstation computer for performing benchmark tests

Specifications	Details
CPU	Intel Xeon E5-2650 v3
CPU Frequency	2.30 GHz
CPU RAM	144 GB
CPU Core	40
GPU	Quadro M5000
GPU Memory	8 GB
GPU Core	2048
OS	Windows 7 Professional
Compiler	Visual Studio 2010
CUDA Version	v8.0

For each group of the two-dimensional testing data, each set of data points is created by randomly distributing on a parametric surface; the equation of the parametric surface is demonstrated in Eq. (3). More specifically, both x and y coordinates are randomly generated in the range of 0–1000, while the associated value is simply calculated according to Eq. (3) after the x and y coordinates have been determined. The generation of five sets of interpolated points is the same as that of the data points. Both x and y coordinates of each interpolated points are randomly generated in the range of 0–1000.

$$\begin{aligned} f(x,y) = {} & 750\exp\left[\frac{(9x/1000-2)^2+(9y/1000-2)^2}{4}\right] \\ & +750\exp\left[\frac{(9x/1000+1)^2}{49}+\frac{(9y/1000+1)}{10}\right] \\ & -200\exp\left[(9x/1000-4)^2+(9y/1000-7)^2\right] \\ & +500\exp\left[\frac{(9x/1000-7)^2+(9y/1000-3)^2}{4}\right] \end{aligned} \quad (3)$$

4.2 Benchmark Results in Two-Dimensions

The test data in two-dimensions are listed in Table 2, including the number of irregularly distributed data points, and the number of interpolated points, respectively. For the irregularly distributed data points, the number of interpolated points is the same.

Table 2. Test data in two-dimensional benchmark tests

Data set	Num. of irregularly distributed data points	Num. of interpolated points
Size 1	67766	72301
Size 2	140157	144601
Size 3	263199	287977
Size 4	455637	580194
Size 5	723576	1149231

Influence of the Value of k on the Relatively Optimal Coefficient w of Grid Cell Size for Irregularly Distributed Scattered Points. This subsection discusses the effect of different k values and different point densities on the relatively optimal coefficient w of grid cell size for irregularly distribution scattered points. When the points' spatial distribution is irregular, the mean value is 500 and the Standard Deviation value is 166. In the benchmark tests, the k values specified as 10, 20, 50, 100, and 200 for irregularly distribution scattered points is discussed in this section.

The benchmark results illustrated in Fig. 2 indicate that: when the point density is set as the Size 1 and the w is approximately 3.0, the highest efficiency can be achieved for different values of k. Moreover, the trends of the fitted curves are similar when configuring different values of k. For other four-point densities (i.e., the sizes of data points), almost the same conclusions can be drawn. It can be concluded that: the k value is of weak effect on the relatively optimal coefficient w of grid cell size for irregularly distributed scattered points, see Fig. 3.

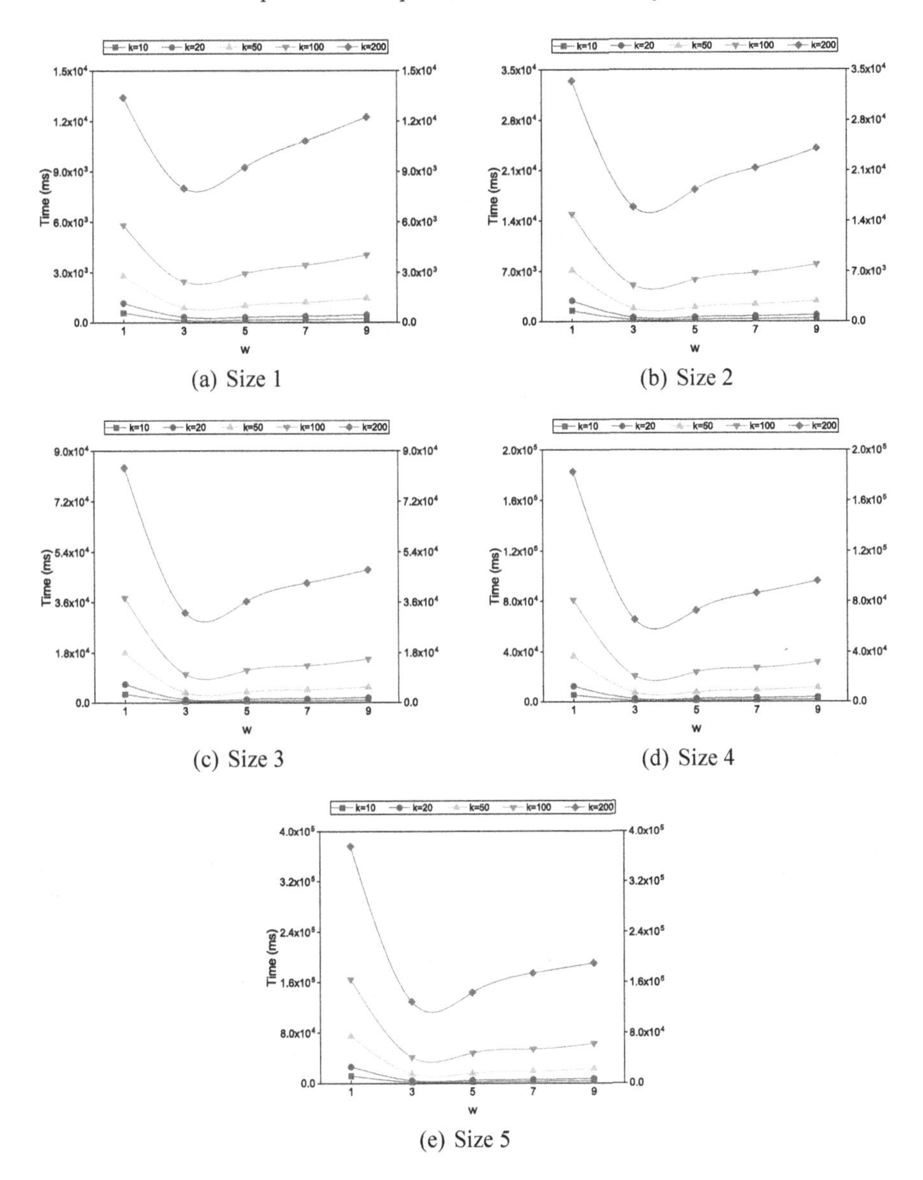

(a) Size 1

(b) Size 2

(c) Size 3

(d) Size 4

(e) Size 5

Fig. 2. Influence of the value of k on the coefficient w of grid cell size for irregularly distributed scattered points.

Influence of Point Density on the Relatively Optimal Coefficient w of Grid Cell Size for Irregularly Distributed Scattered Points. This subsection specifically discusses the relationship between different point densities and the coefficient w of grid cell size by fixing the k values. In the benchmark tests, the point densities were specified as Size 1, Size 2, Size 3, Size 4, and Size 5 for irregularly distribution scattered points.

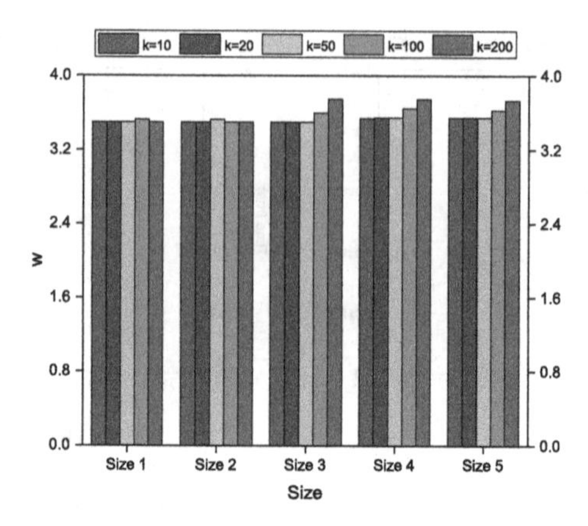

Fig. 3. The relatively optimal coefficient w of grid cell size when setting different values of k for irregularly distributed scattered points.

The benchmark results illustrated in Fig. 4 indicate that: when the value of k is set as the 10 and the w is approximately 3.0, the highest efficiency can be achieved for different point densities. Moreover, the trends of the fitted curves are similar when configuring different point densities. For other values of k, almost the same conclusions can be drawn for irregularly distributed scattered points. It can be concluded that: the points densities are of weak effect on the relatively optimal coefficient w of grid cell size for irregularly distributed scattered points, see Fig. 5.

Influence of Mean of Points' Coordinates on the Relatively Optimal Coefficient w of Grid Cell Size for Irregularly Distributed Scattered Points. This subsection specifically discusses the relationship between different mean of points' coordinates and the coefficient w of grid cell size by fixing other factors. In the benchmark tests, the mean of points' coordinates was specified as (400,400), (600,400), (600,600), and (400,600). The number of data points is 67766, the number of interpolated points is 72301, the Standard Deviation value is 200, and the value of k is 50.

The benchmark results illustrated in Fig. 6 indicate that: the trends of the fitted curves are similar when configuring different mean of points' coordinates, the highest efficiency corresponding to the relatively optimal coefficient w of grid cell size is close to 2.5 for different mean of points' coordinates. It can be concluded that: the mean of points' coordinates is of weak effect on the relatively optimal coefficient w of grid cell size for irregularly distributed scattered points.

Influence of Standard Deviation of Points' Coordinates on the Relatively Optimal Coefficient w of Grid Cell Size for Irregularly Distributed Scattered Points. This subsection specifically discusses the relationship between different Standard Deviation and the coefficient w of grid cell size by fixing other factors. In the benchmark tests, the number of data points is 67766, the number of interpolated points is 72301, the mean of x and y is 500,

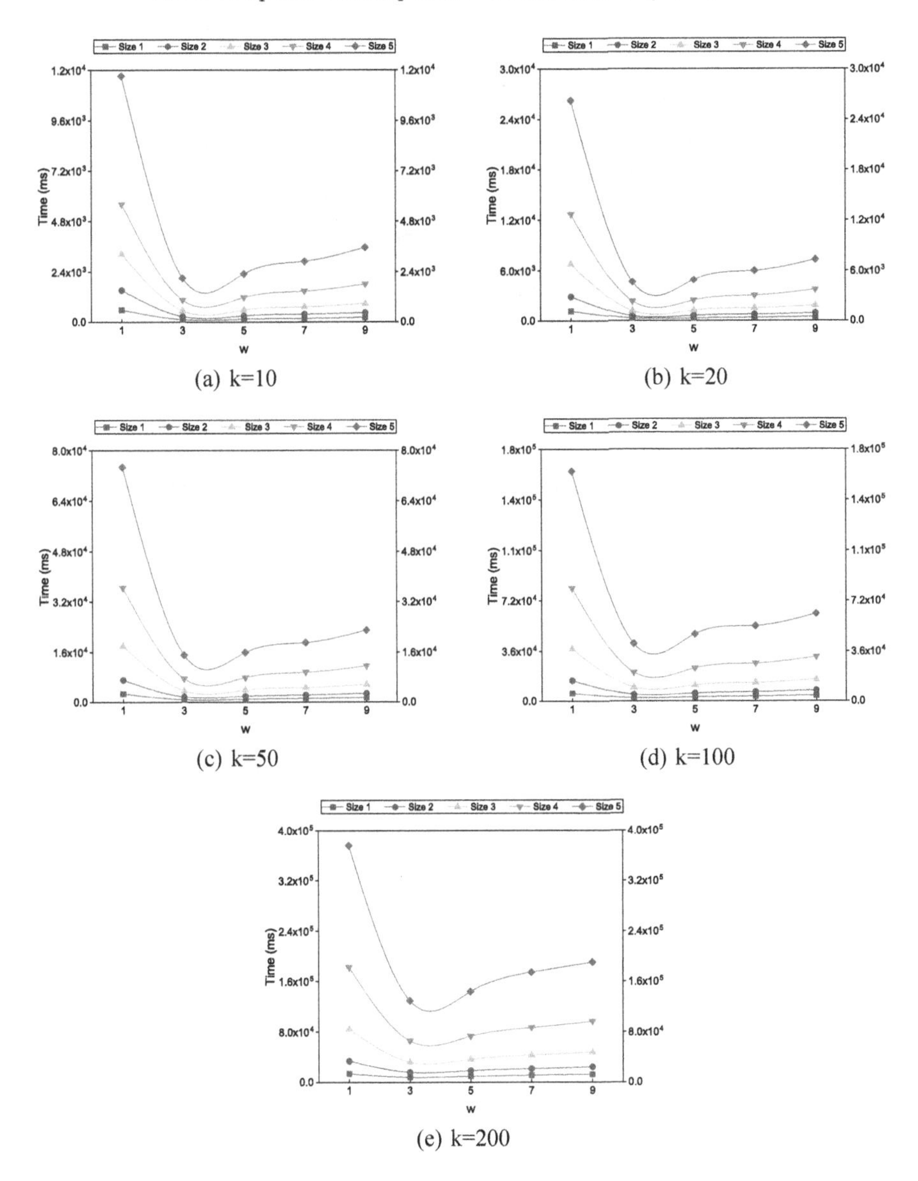

(a) k=10

(b) k=20

(c) k=50

(d) k=100

(e) k=200

Fig. 4. Influence of point densities on the coefficient w of grid cell size for irregularly distributed scattered points.

and the value of k is 50. The Standard Deviation was specified as 100, 130, 160, 190, 200, 250, 300, 350, and 400. The benchmark results indicate that with the increase of the Standard Deviation of points' coordinates, the relatively optimal size of the grid cell decreases and eventually converges, see Table 3. We have also fitted the relationships between the Standard Deviation of scattered points'

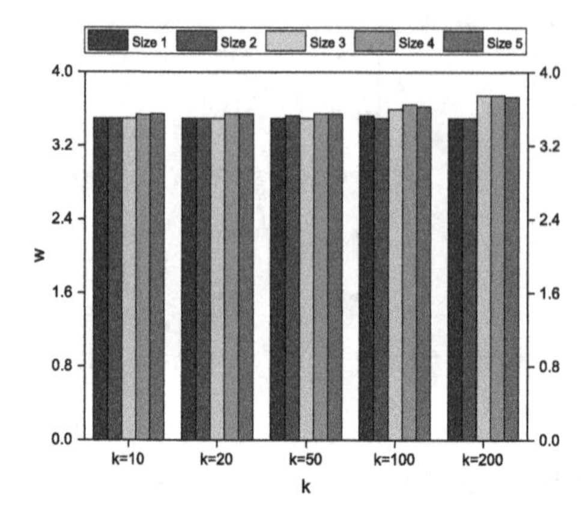

Fig. 5. The relatively optimal coefficient w of grid cell size when setting different point densities for irregularly distributed scattered points.

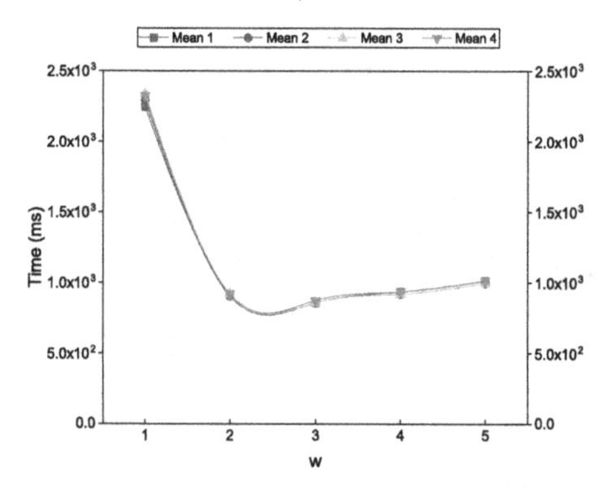

Fig. 6. Influence of mean on the relatively optimal coefficient w of grid cell size for irregularly distributed scattered points.

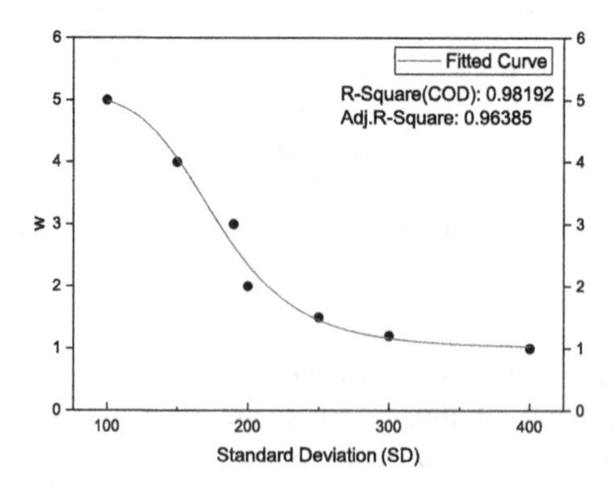

Fig. 7. The fitted curve indicating the relationships between the Standard Deviation and the relatively optimal coefficient w of grid cell size in two-dimensions.

coordinates and the relatively optimal size of the grid cell in two-dimensions, see Fig. 7, the fitted relationship is described in Eq. (4).

$$w = \frac{4.09003}{1 + (\sigma + 178.4079)^{6.20917}} + 1.00546 \tag{4}$$

To evaluate the Goodness of Fit, we use the COD (Coefficient of Determination) to measure the fitted equation. The COD of fitted equation is 0.98192, which indicates the fitting is good.

Table 3. The optimal coefficient w of grid cell size corresponding to different Standard Deviations in two-dimensions

Standard Deviation	100	150	190	200	250	300	400
w	5	4	3	2	1.5	1.2	1

5 Conclusion

In this paper, we have investigated the effect of the decomposition of uniform grid on the computational efficiency of the kNN search procedure used in spatial interpolations. More precisely, we have evaluated the influence of the size of grid cell on the efficiency of the kNN search procedure. Our objective is to find a relatively optimal size of the grid cell. We have performed several series of benchmark based on irregularly distributed scattered points, and found that the distribution of scattered points, which is measured by the Standard Deviation of points' coordinates, is of strong influence on the determination of the relatively optimal size of the grid cell. More specifically, the benchmark results indicate that: in two dimensions, with the increase of the Standard Deviation of points' coordinates, the relatively optimal size of the grid cell decreases and eventually converges. We have also fitted the relationships between the Standard Deviation of scattered points' coordinates and the relatively optimal size of the grid cell, the COD of fitted equation is 0.98192, which indicates the fitting is good. The fitted relationships could be employed to determine the relatively optimal grid cell in kNN search, and further, improve the computational efficiency of spatial interpolations that could be commonly used in the geometric modeling for life science applications.

In this paper, we have only evaluated the effect of the size of grid cell on the efficiency of kNN search executed on the CPU. In the kNN search procedure, there are several logic routines. It has been widely learned that the same logic routines executed on the CPU and GPU may lead to dramatically different efficiencies. Thus, the relationships between the distributions of scattered points between the relatively optimal size of the grid cell obtained on the CPU may differ from those achieved on the GPU. In the future, we will address this problem.

Acknowledgements. This work was supported by the Natural Science Foundation of China (Grant Numbers 11602235 and 41772326), the China Postdoctoral Science Foundation (2015M571081), the Fundamental Research Funds for the Central Universities (2652017086).

References

1. Al Aghbari, Z., Al-Hamadi, A.: Efficient KNN search by linear projection of image clusters. Int. J. Intell. Syst. **26**(9), 844–865 (2011)
2. Allen, G., Gandevia, S., Mckenzie, D.: Reliability of measurements of muscle strength and voluntary activation using twitch interpolation. Muscle Nerve **18**(6), 593–600 (1995)
3. Beliakov, G., Li, G.: Improving the speed and stability of the k-nearest neighbors method. Pattern Recognit. Lett. **33**(10), 1296–1301 (2012)
4. Cavoretto, R., Rossi, A.D., Dell'Accio, F., Tommaso, F.D.: Fast computation of triangular shepard interpolants. J. Comput. Appl. Math. (2018). https://doi.org/10.1016/j.cam.2018.03.012
5. Cuomo, S., Galletti, A., Giunta, G., Marcellino, L.: Reconstruction of implicit curves and surfaces via RBF interpolation. Appl. Numer. Math. **116**(1), 157–171 (2017)
6. Cuomo, S., Galletti, A., Giunta, G., Starace, A.: Surface reconstruction from scattered point via RBF interpolation on GPU. In: Ganzha, M., Maciaszek, L., Paprzycki, M (eds.) 2013 Federated Conference on Computer Science and Information Systems (Fedcsis), pp. 433–440 (2013)
7. Ding, Z., Mei, G., Cuomo, S., Xu, N., Tian, H.: Performance evaluation of GPU-accelerated spatial interpolation using radial basis functions for building explicit surfaces. Int. J. Parallel Program. **46**(5), 963–991 (2018)
8. Dong, W., Zhang, L., Lukac, R., Shi, G.: Sparse representation based image interpolation with nonlocal autoregressive modeling. IEEE Trans. Image Process. **22**(4), 1382–1394 (2013)
9. Huang, F., Bu, S., Tao, J., Tan, X.: OpenCL implementation of a parallel universal Kriging algorithm for massive spatial data interpolation on heterogeneous systems. ISPRS Int. J. Geo Inf. **5**(6), 96 (2016)
10. Huang, F., Liu, D., Tan, X., Wang, J., Chen, Y., He, B.: Explorations of the implementation of a parallel IDW interpolation algorithm in a Linux cluster-based parallel GIS. Comput. Geosci. **37**(4), 426–434 (2011)
11. Lehmann, T., Gonner, C., Spitzer, K.: Survey: interpolation methods in medical image processing. IEEE Trans. Med. Image **18**(11), 1049–1075 (1999)
12. Li, S., Harner, E.J., Adjeroh, D.A.: Random KNN. In: Zhou, Z.H., et al. (eds.) 2014 IEEE International Conference on Data Mining Workshop (ICDMW), pp. 629–636 (2014)
13. Liu, J., Nowinski, W.L.: A hybrid approach to shape-based interpolation of stereotactic atlases of the human brain. Neuroinformatics **4**(2), 177–198 (2006)
14. Liu, S.g., Wei, Y.w.: Fast nearest neighbor searching based on improved VP-tree. Pattern Recognit. Lett. **60–61**, 8–15 (2015)
15. Mei, G.: Evaluating the power of GPU acceleration for IDW interpolation algorithm. Sci. World J. **2014**, 8 (2014)
16. Mei, G., Xu, L., Xu, N.: Accelerating adaptive inverse distance weighting interpolation algorithm on a graphics processing unit. R. Soc. Open Sci. **4**(9), 170436 (2017)

17. Mei, G., Xu, N., Xu, L.: Improving GPU-accelerated adaptive IDW interpolation algorithm using fast kNN search. SpringerPlus **5**, 1389 (2016)
18. Meijering, E.: A chronology of interpolation: from ancient astronomy to modern signal and image processing. Proc. IEEE **90**(3), 319–342 (2002)
19. Mirzaei, D.: Analysis of moving least squares approximation revisited. J. Comput. Appl. Math. **282**, 237–250 (2015)
20. Nutanong, S., Zhang, R., Tanin, E., Kulik, L.: V*-kNN: an efficient algorithm for moving k nearest neighbor queries. In: ICDE: 2009 IEEE International Conference on Data Engineering, pp. 1519–1522 (2009)
21. Pan, J., Manocha, D.: Bi-level locality sensitive hashing for k-nearest neighbor computation. In: 2012 IEEE 28th IEEE International Conference on Data Engineering, pp. 378–389 (2012)
22. Pan, M.s., Yang, X.l., Tang, J.t.: Research on interpolation methods in medical image processing. J. Med. Syst. **36**(2), 777–807 (2012)
23. Parrott, R., Stytz, M., Amburn, P., Robinson, D.: Towards statistically optimal interpolation for 3-D medical imaging. IEEE Eng. Med. Biol. Mag. **12**(3), 49–59 (1993)
24. Pesquer, L., Cortes, A., Pons, X.: Parallel ordinary Kriging interpolation incorporating automatic variogram fitting. Comput. Geosci. **37**(4), 464–473 (2011)
25. Shankar, V., Wright, G.B., Kirby, R.M., Fogelson, A.L.: A radial basis function (RBF)-finite difference (FD) method for diffusion and reaction-diffusion equations on surfaces. J. Sci. Comput. **63**(3), 745–768 (2015)
26. Volkau, I., Aziz, A., Nowinski, W.: Indirect interpolation of subcortical structures in the Talairach-Tournoux atlas, vol. 5367, pp. 533–537 (2004)
27. Wang, J., Liu, G.: A point interpolation meshless method based on radial basis functions. Int. J. Numer. Methods Eng. **54**(11), 1623–1648 (2002)

Understanding Chromatin Structure: Efficient Computational Implementation of Polymer Physics Models

Simona Bianco[1], Carlo Annunziatella[1], Andrea Esposito[1,2], Luca Fiorillo[1], Mattia Conte[1], Raffaele Campanile[1], and Andrea M. Chiariello[1(✉)]

[1] Dipartimento di Fisica, Università di Napoli Federico II, and INFN Napoli, Complesso Universitario di Monte Sant'Angelo, 80126 Naples, Italy
chiariello@na.infn.it

[2] Berlin Institute for Medical Systems Biology, Max-Delbrück Centre (MDC) for Molecular Medicine, Robert-Rössle Straße, 13125 Berlin-Buch, Germany

Abstract. In recent years the development of novel technologies, as Hi-C or GAM, allowed to investigate the spatial structure of chromatin in the cell nucleus with a constantly increasing level of accuracy. Polymer physics models have been developed and improved to better interpret the wealth of complex information coming from the experimental data, providing highly accurate understandings on chromatin architecture and on the mechanisms regulating genome folding. To investigate the capability of the models to explain the experiments and to test their agreement with the data, massive parallel simulations are needed and efficient algorithms are fundamental. In this work, we consider general computational Molecular Dynamics (MD) techniques commonly used to implement such models, with a special focus on the Strings & Binders Switch polymer model. By combining this model with machine learning computational approaches, it is possible to give an accurate description of real genomic loci. In addition, it is also possible to make predictions about the impact of structural variants of the genomic sequence, which are known to be linked to severe congenital diseases.

Keywords: Molecular dynamics · Chromatin · Polymer physics

1 Introduction

The 3D conformation of chromosomes in the nucleus is important since it is deeply linked to genome regulation [1–5]. The development of new experimental technologies such as Hi-C [6] and GAM [7] allowed to have powerful tools to investigate genome structure. Indeed, they can measure the frequency of physical contacts between any pairs of DNA regions, with high accuracy and genome-wide. This kind of data are typically collected in contact maps, which reveal non-random patterns of interaction that highlight the complex organization of chromatin in the nucleus.

G. Mencagli et al. (Eds.): Euro-Par 2018 Workshops, LNCS 11339, pp. 680–691, 2019.
https://doi.org/10.1007/978-3-030-10549-5_53

From the analysis of Hi-C data it was discovered, for instance, that chromosomes can be partitioned into *compartment A/B* domains [6], approximately 10 Mb wide regions, associated with active and repressed chromatin respectively.

At lower genomic scales, it has emerged that chromosomes are also divided into a sequence of megabase-sized domains, called Topological Associating Domains (TADs, [8, 9]), where chromatin tend to interact preferentially. Such domains interact non-randomly with each other giving rise to higher order structures, called meta-TADs [10, 11], extending up to entire chromosome scales. Additionally, TADs have non-trivial internal structures [12, 13]. More recently, some of the molecular factors necessary to chromatin folding are also being identified (for instance, CTCF and active or poised transcription factories [14, 15]).

Importantly, it has been also shown that modifications of the chromatin architecture can be associated to human diseases [16, 17], highlighting even more the importance of the genome folding problem.

To better understand the information coming from such an amount of experimental data and to quantitatively explain the spatial organization of chromatin in the nucleus, theoretical models from Polymer Physics have been developed [18–21]. Such models represent powerful tools to investigate chromosome structure, since they can successfully explain many general features of genome folding [22–32]. On the other hand, in order to accurately evaluate their prediction efficacy, it is crucial to set up an efficient computational implementation. In this work, we will focus our attention on the Strings & Binders Switch (SBS) polymer model [22, 23], that has been shown to recapitulate some important features of genome folding, as observed from the experimental Hi-C and GAM data [7, 15, 23, 28].

In Sect. 2, we will describe some general computational methods to implement the SBS model using Molecular Dynamics (MD) techniques [28, 33], and we will try to highlight the importance of High Performance Computing (HPC) resources to fully explore the advantages and the limitations of the model. Importantly, we also stress that the described theoretical and computational methods are of absolutely general validity (see e.g. [36–38]) and are broadly used in the field [25, 28–31]. Next, in Sect. 3, we will show how the combination of such MD methods with a machine learning-like approach, based on the so-called *PRISMR* algorithm [17], allow to go beyond the description of average structural properties of chromatin and explain the folding of real genomic loci. We will describe how the algorithm works and evaluate its performance by applying it on an exemplificative case of study. Notably, the method also allows to make predictions about the impact on chromatin structure produced by genomic mutations, as deletions or duplications [17, 28].

2 Molecular Dynamics Simulations

2.1 The Polymer Chain

In these kind of systems, a coarse-grained model of the chromatin filament is typically used. Here, a standard bead-on-a-chain polymer describes a chromosome, or a fixed genomic locus, and each bead represents a certain amount of genomic content, expressed in number of bases. The self-avoiding-walk (SAW) polymer chain is made of N consecutives beads, with a diameter equal to σ. To model the hard-core nature of the particles, between any two beads i and j there is a truncated Lennard-Jones (LJ) potential V_{LJ} [36], that is:

$$V_{LJ} = \begin{cases} 4\varepsilon\left[\left(\frac{\sigma}{r_{ij}}\right)^{12} - \left(\frac{\sigma}{r_{ij}}\right)^{6}\right] + \varepsilon & r < 2\sigma^{1/6} \\ 0 & otherwise \end{cases} \quad (1)$$

where σ is the diameter of a bead, $r_{ij} = |\boldsymbol{r}_i - \boldsymbol{r}_j|$ is the center-to-center distance and $\varepsilon = k_B T$ defines the intensity of the interaction (expressed in $k_B T$ units, T temperature of the system and k_B the Boltzmann constant). As shown in Fig. 1, panel a (blue curve), such potential is a continuous decreasing positive function of r_{ij}, being 0 for $r_{ij} < 2^{1/6}\sigma$. In this way, we take into account excluded volume effects between the beads.

The bonds between two consecutive beads in the chain are modelled with a *finitely extensible nonlinear elastic* (FENE) potential V_{FENE}:

$$V_{FENE} = -\frac{k_{FENE} R_0^2}{2} ln\left[1 - \left(\frac{|\boldsymbol{r}_{i+1} - \boldsymbol{r}_i|}{R_0}\right)^2\right] \quad (2)$$

originally introduced in [36] and now broadly used in literature [28–31]. In the expression, $\boldsymbol{r}_i$ and $\boldsymbol{r}_{i+1}$ are the position of neighboring beads on polymer, k_{FENE} is the strength of the FENE spring and R_0 is its maximal extension. As shown in Fig. 1, panel a, yellow curve, the FENE potential is close to a harmonic potential for values of the distance $r = |\boldsymbol{r}_{i+1} - \boldsymbol{r}_i|$ near to zero ($r \to 0$) and diverges for $r \to R_0$, representing the maximal length of the bond.

The resulting total potential, $V(r) = V_{LJ} + V_{FENE}$ represent the interaction experienced by two consecutive beads on the chain. As can be seen from Fig. 1, panel a

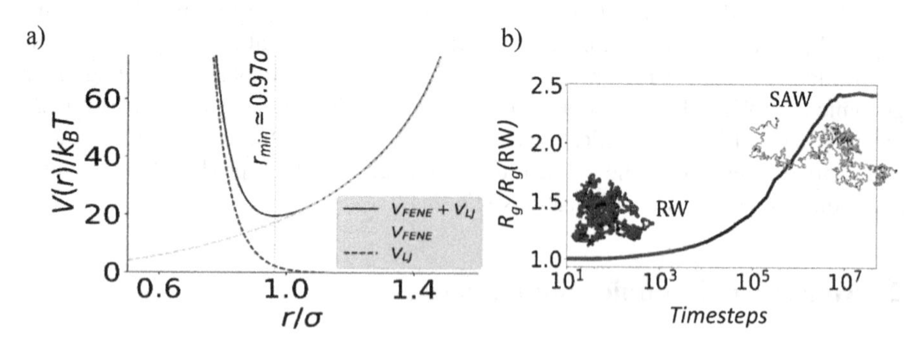

Fig. 1. (a) In this plot, the Fene potential (yellow curve) and the purely repulsive hard-core LJ potential (blue curve) are shown. The potential between two consecutive beads on the chain is the sum of these two contributions (green curve). The vertical dashed line is the minimum of the potential, and gives the average distance between two consecutive beads. (b) The gyration radius in the transition from the RW state to the SAW states. Adapted from [33]. (Color figure online)

(green curve), its minimum corresponds to the mean distance between consecutives beads on the chain and depends on the potential parameters. Here, the parameters used are $k_{FENE} = 30\,k_BT/\sigma^2$ and $R_0 = 1.6\sigma$, which have been typically employed in chromatin models [28–31].

2.2 Preparations of the SAW

A SAW polymer state can be obtained in the following way [28, 31, 36]: first, it is generated a Random-Walk (RW) chain configuration. Its average bond length is taken to be equal to the minimum of the bonding potential (e.g., 0.97 σ with the previous FENE parameters). Then, excess overlap between the beads of the chain are softly removed by replacing the hard-core LJ repulsive potential with:

$$V_{soft} = A\left(1 + \cos\frac{\pi r}{2^{1/6}\sigma}\right) \tag{3}$$

where A is a normalization factor linearly increasing during the simulation [28, 31, 36].

This potential does not diverge at small distances, so the Langevin equations (see below) can be easily integrated for enough time-steps to completely remove the overlap and to reach the equilibrium SAW state.

A fundamental quantity used to check whether the polymer SAW state (and in general any equilibrium state) has been approached is the gyration radius [23, 28, 35] R_g:

$$R_g = \sqrt{\frac{1}{N}\sum\nolimits_{i=1}^{N}(\boldsymbol{r}_i - \boldsymbol{r}_{CM})^2} \tag{4}$$

where N is the number of beads, $\boldsymbol{r}_{CM}$ is the position of the center of mass of the chain and $\boldsymbol{r}_i$ is the position of its i-th bead. This quantity can be used as an estimation of the polymer size. In Fig. 1, Panel b, it is shown the gyration radius R_g from an ensemble of real MD simulations, as a function of time t during the dynamics: when it reaches a plateau, the equilibrium SAW state is reached.

2.3 The Strings and Binders Switch Model

In the *Strings & Binders* Switch (SBS) model, a chromatin filament (the *string*) is represented as the just described SAW polymer chain. Additionally, the beads interact with diffusing molecules (the *binders*) distributed in the environment at a concentration c. They can bridge pairs of different beads and allow the formation of loops in the polymer. The interaction intensity is energy E_{int}. The folding of the polymer is driven by the interaction between beads and binders. As widely discussed in literature, for this system different equilibrium thermodynamics phases exist, depending on the value of control parameters, E_{int} and c [23, 28, 29]. A schematic cartoon of the SBS model is shown in Fig. 2, panel a, showing the case with only one type of binders and binding sites (all in red). For values of E_{int} and c above a threshold, the polymer is able to collapse from a SAW state to a globule conformation, in the so-called coil-globule, switch-like, transition. Extensive details can be found in [23, 28, 29]. More complex situations, as real genomic loci, require different types of beads (and correspondingly cognate binders), which can be schematically represented by different "colors" [17, 28]. This is discussed in detail below.

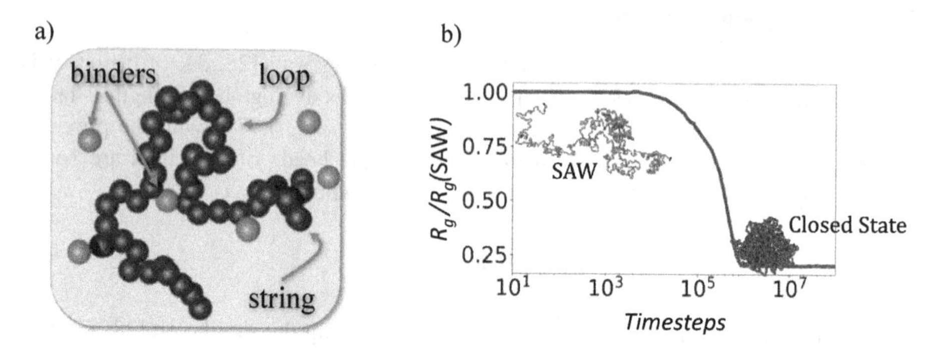

Fig. 2. (a) Schematic representation of the SBS model. (b) The folding dynamics is followed by monitoring the gyration radius. Adapted from [33]. (Color figure online)

In the MD implementation, the binders are modelled as hard-core particles, so they interact with any other bead or binder through the above LJ potential of Eq. (1). The interaction between a binder and its cognate beads on the polymer is modelled by the truncated LJ potential described above, with a higher cut-off distance in order to include the attractive part in the potential. The expression for this potential V_{int} is then:

$$V_{int} = \begin{cases} 4\varepsilon_{int}\left[\left(\frac{\sigma_{bb}}{r}\right)^{12} - \left(\frac{\sigma_{bb}}{r}\right)^{6} - \left(\frac{\sigma_{bb}}{r_{int}}\right)^{12} + \left(\frac{\sigma_{bb}}{r_{int}}\right)^{6}\right] & r < r_{int} \\ 0 & otherwise \end{cases} \quad (5)$$

In the above formula, σ_{bb} is the sum of bead and binder radii (typically, $\sigma_{bb} = 1\ \sigma$, that is beads and binders have the same radius), ε_{int} modulates the attractive interaction intensity (see following expression), r is the center-to-center distance between the binder and the polymer bead and r_{int} is the cut-off distance. As V_{int} goes to zero when $r = r_{int}$, beads and binders interact if their distance is shorter than the range r_{int}. The interaction energy E_{int} is the minimum (in absolute value) of the potential V_{int}:

$$E_{int} = |\min(V_{int})| = \left|4\varepsilon_{int}\left[\left(\frac{\sigma_{bb}}{r_{int}}\right)^{6} - \left(\frac{\sigma_{bb}}{r_{int}}\right)^{12} - \frac{1}{4}\right]\right|$$

Typical parameters are $r_{int} = 1.5\sigma$, $\varepsilon_{int} = 12k_BT$ and $\sigma_{bb} = 1\sigma$ [17, 28].

2.4 Folding Dynamics

Once the potential parameters have been set (LJ or soft), the system evolves according to the Langevin equation [34, 36]

$$m\frac{d^2\boldsymbol{x}(t)}{dt^2} = -\zeta\frac{d\boldsymbol{x}(t)}{dt} - \nabla V + \boldsymbol{\xi}(t) \tag{6}$$

where m and $\boldsymbol{x}(t)$ are respectively the mass and the position (in vector notation) of the particle, ζ is the friction coefficient, V the total potential on the particle, and $\boldsymbol{\xi}(\mathrm{t})$ is the random noise term representing the collisions with the molecules in the fluid. Basically, the system is simulated under Brownian motion conditions. The components of the noise term have a Gaussian probability distribution with zero mean and a time correlation given by:

$$\langle \xi_i(\mathrm{t})\xi_j(\mathrm{t}') \rangle = 2k_B T\zeta\ \delta_{ij}\delta(t-t') \tag{7}$$

where T is the temperature of the system and $\xi_i(\mathrm{t})$ is the *i-th* component of the noise vector.

The simulations are typically performed in dimensionless units. A typical value for the dimensionless friction coefficient is $\zeta = 0.5$ [36], and it is widely used in chromatin modelling [25, 28–31]. The other standard [36] dimensionless MD parameters are $\varepsilon = k_B T = 1$ (energy scale), $\sigma = 1$ (length scale) and $m = 1$ (mass).

Usually, the system is confined in a cubic simulation box, having edge size D and periodic boundary conditions. Roughly, the size D of the box edge is at least as large as the gyration radius of the polymer in its open SAW conformation, in order to minimize finite size effects [33].

2.5 Efficiency of the MD Implementation

As the simulation starts, the beads and the binders interact, and the polymer, if the values of E_{int} and c are high enough (see above), folds according to the coil-globule transition. This process is monitored by the gyration radius R_g (defined in Eq. 4), which has a sharp drop since the polymer reduces consistently its size in this transition. In Fig. 2, panel b, R_g is shown as a function of the time steps, for a polymer made of $N = 1000$ beads.

Note that the MD time required in order to complete the transition of this (very simple) system, is quite small ($\sim 10^6$ single time steps). Of course, this number strongly depends on the system complexity, as the total number of particles (beads and binders), the number of binding sites and the interaction energy E_{int}. All these details are crucial when the simulated polymer aims to model a real genomic region, where the complexity is determined from a machine learning approach informed with the experimental data (see next section). More details can also be found in refs. [28, 29].

Analogously, the real computational time required to reach the equilibrium depends not only on the just mentioned parameters, but also on other details as the sampling frequency of the physical quantities (as the particle positions).

In order to have reliable results and robust distributions for the interesting quantities, each system needs to be simulated several times, i.e. an ensemble average is required. Again, the require number of independent runs to produce reliable ensemble averages depends on the system complexity. As order of magnitude, one hundred of replicates, for each system parameter choice, is a convenient amount.

Several established MD software exist to perform this kind of simulations. A very important example is LAMMPS, a publicly available and efficient MD code [37], optimized for parallel computing and broadly used in the field [17, 25, 28–31].

3 *PRISMR*: A New Machine Learning Approach to Investigate Chromatin Spatial Structure

3.1 The Idea Behind the *PRISMR* Algorithm

As stated in the Introduction, novel experimental technologies have been developed to quantitatively investigate the three-dimensional structure of chromosomes. Specifically, the Hi-C method [6] allow to measure the spatial contact frequency of any pair of genomic loci. That is, in a population of cells, it gives the number of times two genomic loci are in spatial proximity. Such contact frequencies are collected in a matrix (one for each chromosome), where each bin x_{ij} gives the frequency between the locus i and the locus j. Typically, this kind of data are represented as heat-maps, where the contact frequencies are associated to a fixed color scheme. Examples of Hi-C data are shown below.

This experimental data can be combined with the above discussed polymer model to reconstruct the 3D structure of real genomic regions.

In its simplest version, that is one type of binding site and one type of binders, the SBS model is able to explain the long-range average contact probability profile [23, 28]. By introducing another color, other general features can be explained, as the TADs, metaTADs and A/B compartments [28, 29]. By generalizing this approach, it is possible to explain the architectural features of a specific DNA region. The idea is to find, starting from an experimental Hi-C contact map, a SBS polymer able to recapitulate the features contained in that Hi-C contact map. In general, this polymer will have several different types of binding sites, conveniently located along the polymer chain (Fig. 3, left panel). To find the number of types and their positions, we developed a machine learning computational procedure, named *PRISMR* (Polymer-based Recursive Statistical Inference Method), where the best polymer is found by minimizing a cost function H, with a standard Simulated Annealing Monte Carlo procedure. Specifically, H is made of two terms: the distance between the experimental Hi-C map and the model contact map, and a Bayesian term that penalizes the addition of binding sites, in order to avoid overfitting. Full details can be found in ref. [17]. Importantly, the described procedure can be applied to every locus of the genome and for every cell line, provided that the required experimental data are available.

Once the binding sites arrangement along the polymer chain is obtained, MD simulations are performed. The potentials and the associated parameters employed in the simulations have been extensively discussed in the previous section. This is

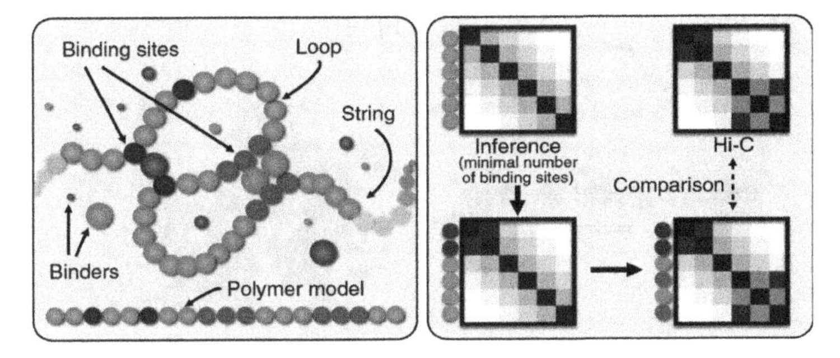

Fig. 3. The *PRISMR* algorithm aims to find the best binding sites configurations describing the contact map. On the left, a schematic polymer with different binding sites. On the right, a graphical scheme of *PRISMR* computational procedure. Adapted from [17].

definitely the most computational demanding step, since it requires the use of massive parallel simulations, whereas the number of single processors strongly depends on the system complexity. The simulation is performed until the equilibrium state is achieved (see previous section). Additionally, the same system needs to be simulated several times, in order to have a reliable set of replicates and compute robust statistics.

3.2 Example of *PRISMR* Performance: The *Sox9* Locus

The performance of the procedure has been successfully tested on several loci (see [17, 28, 29] and reviews in [33, 38, 39]). Here we report the test case of the *Sox9* locus, an important genomic region in mammals, involved in male sexual development, whose mutations are linked to genetic diseases, such as skeletal malformation and sex-reversal syndromes [40]. The procedure has been applied on a $L = 6$ Mb region around the *Sox9* gene, genomic coordinates chr11:109-115 Mb. The experimental contact map (Hi-C data from [8]) is shown Fig. 4, panel a, upper matrix, in mouse embryonic cells (mESC-J1). In general, given a Hi-C matrix with a resolution of n base pairs (that is, each bin represents a genomic window of n base pairs) describing a genomic region L bases long, the corresponding matrix has a size $N \times N$, with $N = L/n$. In the Hi-C data used in the *Sox9* case, $n = 40$ kb and $L = 6$ Mb, so $N = 150$ and the experimental matrix has a size of 150×150.

To explain the complexity of the patterns in the data, *PRISMR* extracts the number of types and the sequence of the binding sites. Here, 15 different types of binding sites had to be introduced, with their cognate binders [28]. Once the algorithm returns the polymer, we can perform MD simulations with the above described methods, and study the three-dimensional conformations. From them, we can re-compute the contact map, based on the physical distances between the beads of the polymer, and compare it with the experimental maps. In Fig. 4, panel a, bottom matrix, is shown the resulting simulated map, which captures very accurately most of features contained in the experimental Hi-C map. This demonstrates that the simulated 3D structures could represent the real 3D architecture of the locus. In Fig. 4, panel b, a snapshot from a real MD simulation is shown.

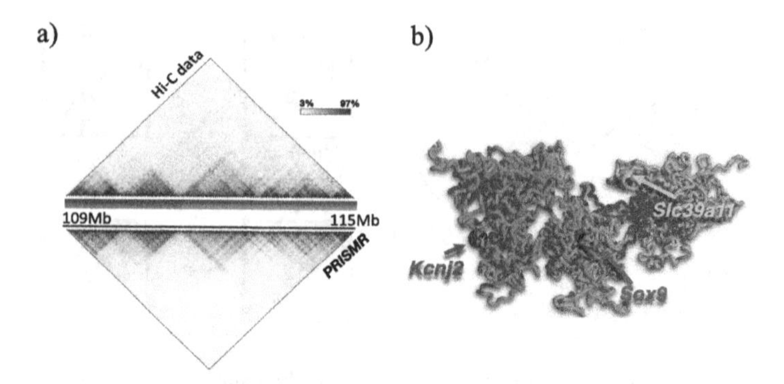

Fig. 4. (a) Comparison between experimental Hi-C contact map (upper matrix, chr11:109-115 Mb, data from [8]) with the result of *PRISMR* (bottom matrix). The limits in the colorbar refers to the distributions percentiles of the represented data. (b) 3D structure of the *Sox9* locus obtained from a real MD simulation, with some important genes highlighted. Adapted from [28]. (Color figure online)

If the genomic region to model is increased of a factor b, the size of the corresponding matrix is increased of factor b^2. This means that the data size rapidly increases with the size of the genomic region to investigate. To give a sense of the scales involved, the whole mouse chromosome 11, which contain the discussed *Sox9* region and has an intermediate genomic length (122 Mb) among the other chromosomes, at 40 kb resolution has a linear size $N > 3000$, and a Hi-C of approximately 3000×3000. Furthermore, more accurate databases are becoming available, with very high resolutions (up to 1 kb [14]), making huge the amount of the data and very difficult their management. In this sense, HPC computational resources become, once again, essential in order to model larger loci using more accurate datasets.

3.3 *PRISMR* Can Be Used to Predict Structural Variant Effects

An important application of the *PRISMR* algorithm is the possibility to make predictions of the effects of genomic structural variants at a given locus on its 3D structure. The polymer model of the considered locus, inferred by the algorithm trained on its wild type (WT) experimental contact matrix (Fig. 3), can in fact be used to implement in-silico any genomic mutation, like deletions, inversions or duplications (schematically shown in Fig. 5). For example, to model a deletion, it is enough to remove the piece of polymer located at the deleted genomic region and, without any fitting parameter, simply re-run the ensemble of MD simulations on the mutated polymer. This way an ensemble of 3D configurations is obtained for the mutated system and its average contact matrix can be computed (Fig. 5). The model predictions of the effects of a set of structural variants at the *Epha4* locus, known to be implicated in human limb malformations, have been indeed experimentally tested and confirmed by independent Capture Hi-C experiment [17].

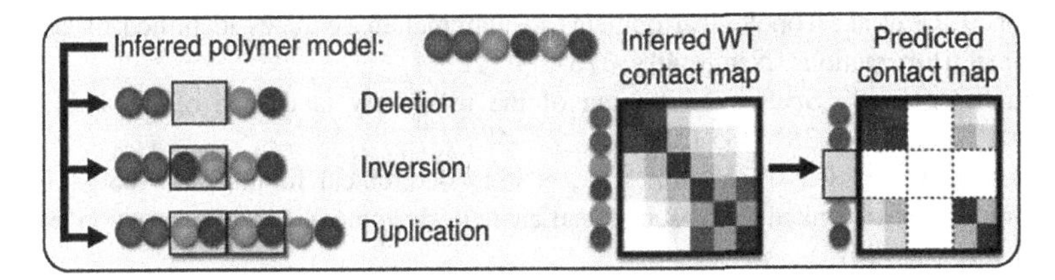

Fig. 5. The effects of structural variants, like deletions, inversions and duplications, on chromatin 3D folding can be predicted in-silico. Adapted from [17].

3.4 Conclusions

The development of polymer models, based on theoretical and computational classical methods, has allowed to quantitatively interpret genome contact data, revealing a powerful tool to investigate chromatin spatial organization. Here, we focused our attention on the SBS model, and recalled in detail the computational ingredients necessary to build a fast and efficient MD implementation. To fully exploit the power of this model (and of any other model in general), High Performance Computing is necessary, and becomes crucial to simulate increasingly more complex polymer systems, as large genomic regions described by high resolution data. In this way, it would be possible to give a more accurate description of the genome structure and the mechanisms orchestrating its folding. In the next years, the challenge is to produce models of better quality, taking into account finer details, and, on the other hand, improving the efficiency of the computational tools [41]. That must be combined with the integration and an efficient management of constantly increasing experimental databases [41], in order to get a deeper understanding of chromatin organization and its links to gene regulation.

References

1. Misteli, T.: Beyond the sequence: cellular organization of genome function. Cell **128**, 787–800 (2007)
2. Lanctôt, C., Cheutin, T., Cremer, M., Cavalli, G., Cremer, T.: Dynamic genome architecture in the nuclear space: regulation of gene expression in three dimensions. Nat. Rev. Genet. **8**, 104–115 (2007)
3. Bickmore, W.A., van Steensel, B.: Genome architecture: domain organization of interphase chromosomes. Cell **152**(6), 1270–1284 (2013)
4. Tanay, A., Cavalli, G.: Chromosomal domains: epigenetic contexts and functional implications of genomic compartmentalization. Curr. Opin. Genet. Dev. **23**, 197–203 (2013)
5. Dekker, J., Mirny, L.: 3D genome as moderator of chromosomal communication. Cell **164** (6), 1110–1121 (2016)
6. Lieberman-Aiden, E., et al.: Comprehensive mapping of long-range interactions reveals folding principles of the human genome. Science **326**, 289–293 (2009)
7. Beagrie, R., et al.: Complex multi-enhancer contacts captured by genome architecture mapping. Nature **543**(7646), 519–524 (2017)

8. Dixon, J.R., et al.: Topological domains in mammalian genomes identified by analysis of chromatin interactions. Nature **485**, 376–380 (2012)
9. Nora, E.P., et al.: Spatial partitioning of the regulatory landscape of the X-inactivation centre. Nature **485**, 381–385 (2012)
10. Fraser, J., Ferrai, C., Chiariello, A.M., et al.: Hierarchical folding and reorganisation of chromosomes are linked to transcriptional changes during cellular differentiation. Mol. Syst. Biol. **11**, 852 (2015)
11. Chiariello, A.M., et al.: The scaling features of the 3D organization are highlighted by a transformation à la Kadanoff on HiC data. EPL **120**, 40004 (2017)
12. Sexton, T., et al.: Three-dimensional folding and functional organization principles of the Drosophila genome. Cell **148**, 458–472 (2012)
13. Phillips-Cremins, J.E., et al.: Architectural protein subclasses shape 3D organization of genomes during lineage commitment. Cell **153**, 1281–1295 (2013)
14. Rao, S.S.P., et al.: A 3D map of the human genome at kilobase resolution reveals principles of chromatin looping. Cell **159**, 1665–1680 (2014)
15. Barbieri, M., et al.: Active and poised promoter states drive folding of the extended HoxB locus in mouse embryonic stem cells. Nat. Struct. Mol. Biol. **24**, 515–524 (2017)
16. Lupiáñez, D.G., Kraft, K., Heinrich, V., et al.: Disruptions of topological chromatin domains cause pathogenic rewiring of gene-enhancer interactions. Cell **161**(5), 1012–1025 (2015)
17. Bianco, S., et al.: Polymer physics predicts the effects of structural variants on chromatin architecture. Nat. Gen. **50**, 662–667 (2018)
18. Emanuel, M., Radja, N.H., Henriksson, A., Schiessel, H.: The physics behind the larger scale organization of DNA in eukaryotes. Phys. Biol. **6**, 025008 (2009)
19. Tark-Dame, M., van Driel, R., Heermann, D.W.: Chromatin folding–from biology to polymer models and back. J. Cell Sci. **124**, 839–845 (2011)
20. Barbieri, M., Scialdone, A., Gamba, A., Pombo, A., Nicodemi, M.: Polymer physics, scaling and heterogeneity in the spatial organisation of chromosomes in the cell nucleus. Soft Matter **9**, 8631–8635 (2013)
21. Nicodemi, M., Pombo, A.: Models of chromosome structure. Curr. Opin. Cell Biol. **28**, 90–95 (2014)
22. Nicodemi, M., Prisco, A.: Thermodynamic pathways to genome spatial organization in the cell nucleus. Biophys. J. **96**, 2168–2177 (2009)
23. Barbieri, M., et al.: Complexity of chromatin folding is captured by the strings and binders switch model. Proc. Natl. Acad. Sci. U.S.A. **109**, 16173–16178 (2012)
24. Bohn, M., Heermann, D.W.: Diffusion-driven looping provides a consistent framework for chromatin organization. PLoS ONE **5**(8), e12218 (2010)
25. Sanborn, A.L., Rao, S.S.P., Huang, S.-C., et al.: Chromatin extrusion explains key features of loop and domain formation in wild-type and engineered genomes. Proc. Natl. Acad. Sci. U.S.A. **112**, E6456–E6465 (2015)
26. Fudenberg, G., Imakaev, M., Lu, C., et al.: Formation of chromosomal domains by loop extrusion. Cell Rep. **15**, 1–12 (2016)
27. Brackley, C.A., et al.: Nonequilibrium chromosome looping via molecular slip links. Phys. Rev. Lett. **108**, 158103 (2017)
28. Chiariello, A.M., Annunziatella, C., Bianco, S., Esposito, A., Nicodemi, M.: Polymer physics of chromosome large-scale 3d organization. Sci. Rep. **6**, 29775 (2016)
29. Annunziatella, C., Chiariello, A.M., Bianco, S., Nicodemi, M.: Polymer models of the hierarchical folding of the Hox-B chromosomal locus. Phys. Rev. E **94**, 042402 (2016)
30. Rosa, A., Everaers, R.: Structure and dynamics of interphase chromosomes. PLoS Comput. Biol. **4**, e1000153 (2008)

31. Brackley, C.A., Taylor, S., Papantonis, A., Cook, P.R., Marenduzzo, D.: Nonspecific bridging-induced attraction drives clustering of DNA-binding proteins and genome organization. Proc. Natl. Acad. Sci. U.S.A. **110**, E3605–E3611 (2013)
32. Jost, D., Carrivain, P., Cavalli, G., Vaillant, C.: Modeling epigenome folding: formation and dynamics of topologically associated chromatin domains. Nucleic Acids Res. **42**, 9553–9561 (2014)
33. Annunziatella, C., Chiariello, A.M., Esposito, A., Bianco, S., Fiorillo, L., Nicodemi, M.: Molecular dynamics simulations of the strings and binders switch model of chromatin. Methods **142**, 81–88 (2018)
34. Allen, M.P., Tildesley, D.J.: Computer Simulation of Liquids. Oxford University Press, Oxford (1987)
35. de Gennes, P.G.: Scaling Concepts in Polymer Physics. Cornel University Press, Ithaca (1979)
36. Kremer, K., Grest, G.S.: Dynamics of entangled linear polymer melts: a molecular-dynamics simulation. J. Chem. Phys. **92**(8), 5057–5086 (1990)
37. Plimpton, S.: Fast parallel algorithms for short-range molecular dynamics. J. Comput. Phys. **117**, 1–19 (1995)
38. Bianco, S., Chiariello, A.M., Annunziatella, C., Esposito, A., Nicodemi, M.: Predicting chromatin architecture from models of polymer physics. Chromosome Res. **25**, 25–34 (2017)
39. Chiariello, A.M., et al.: A polymer physics investigation of the architecture of the murine orthologue of the 7q11.23 human locus. Front. Neurosci. **11**, 559 (2017)
40. Franke, M., et al.: Formation of new chromatin domains determines pathogenicity of genomic duplications. Nature **538**(7624), 265–269 (2016)
41. Dekker, J., et al.: The 4D nucleome project. Nature **549**, 219–226 (2017)

Towards Heterogeneous Network Alignment: Design and Implementation of a Large-Scale Data Processing Framework

Marianna Milano[1,2], Pierangelo Veltri[1,2], Mario Cannataro[1,2], and Pietro H. Guzzi[1,2](✉)

[1] Department of Medical and Surgical Science, University Magna Græcia, Catanzaro, Italy
[2] Data Analytics Research Centre, University of Catanzaro, Catanzaro, Italy
{m.milano,veltri,cannataro,hguzzi}@unicz.it

Abstract. The importance of the use of networks to model and analyse biological data and the interplay of bio-molecules is widely recognised. Consequently, many algorithms for the analysis and the comparison of networks (such as alignment algorithms) have been developed in the past. Recently, many different approaches tried to integrate into a single model the interplay of different molecules, such as genes, transcription factors and microRNAs. A possible formalism to model such scenario comes from node coloured networks (or heterogeneous networks) implemented as node/ edge-coloured graphs. Consequently, the need for the introduction of alignment algorithms able to analyse heterogeneous networks arises. To the best of our knowledge, all the existing algorithms are not able to mine heterogeneous networks. We propose a two-step alignment strategy that receives as input two heterogeneous networks (node-coloured graphs) and a similarity function among nodes of two networks extending the previous formulations. We first build a single alignment graph. Then we mine this graph extracting relevant subgraphs. Despite this simple approach, the analysis of such networks relies on graph and subgraph isomorphism and the size of the data is still growing. Therefore the use of high-performance data analytics framework is needed. We here present HetNetAligner a framework built on top of Apache Spark. We also implemented our algorithm, and we tested it on some selected heterogeneous biological networks. Preliminary results confirm that our method may extract relevant knowledge from biological data reducing the computational time.

Keywords: Heterogeneous network · Network alignment
Apache Spark

1 Introduction

The importance of the use of networks to model and analyse biological data is widely recognised [11]. For instance, networks have been used to model interactions among biological macromolecules inside cells, such as protein-protein

G. Mencagli et al. (Eds.): Euro-Par 2018 Workshops, LNCS 11339, pp. 692–703, 2019.
https://doi.org/10.1007/978-3-030-10549-5_54

interactions (PPI), or gene-gene interactions [2]. Usually, these models contain a single node type (e.g. proteins or genes) and simple (i.e. uncoloured and eventually weighted) edges. For example, in protein-protein interaction (PPI) networks, nodes are proteins while edges are their interactions and associated weights model the reliability of the discovered interactions.

The use of networks has enabled the discovery of many biological insights related to cells and related to disease development and progression [5,18]. Consequently, many approaches have led to the introduction of data models, databases and algorithms of analysis. Nevertheless, the interplay of molecules inside cells is always made by molecules of different types (e.g. genes, proteins and ribonucleic acids [8]. Consequently, the possible integration in a single comprehensive model of heterogeneous data is still a challenge. In the scenario we envision, a single network containing both different kinds of nodes and different kinds of edges may model the reality inside cells [16]. One of the best formalism to model such scenario comes from heterogeneous networks implemented as node/ edge-coloured graphs. [7]. For example, data have been collected on how proteins are related to diseases, and how drugs interact with proteins. Consequently, a single network may represent proteins, drugs and diseases as nodes of different kind or colour.

The possible scenarios of analysis of such networks involve many tasks [16], and we here focus on the local alignment of networks. Local network alignment has been defined in the past for homogeneous network (LNA_{hom}), and it has been formalised in many papers, from those we recall the approaches of Berg and Lassig [1] and the subsequent formalisation by Mina and Guzzi [15]. Many LNAs_{hom} are based on a two-step strategy: (i) initially they merge two input networks in a single one (referred to as alignment graph), (ii) the alignment graph is then analysed to extract relevant subnetworks (or communities).

Here we extend this approach to consider heterogeneous network by proposing a two-way strategy to align heterogeneous networks: (i) initially merge two input networks in a single one (referred to as heterogeneous alignment graph), (ii) then we analyse the alignment graph to extract relevant subnetworks (or communities).

Even though the single formulation dimension of real networks is still growing due to the introduction of novel technological platforms and on the integration of different data sources. Consequently, the development of novel approaches able to leverage computational resource offered by high computational platforms such as clusters and novel programming models tailored to big data is a crucial challenge. For these aims, after the formulation of the problem of the alignment for heterogeneous networks, we here propose a high-performance framework for the alignment based on Apache Spark. We present some preliminary results that demonstrate the advantage of the use of such approach.

2 Related Work

Local Network Alignment (LNA) algorithms were developed initially for homogeneous networks to find multiple and unrelated regions of isomorphism, i.e.

same graph structure, between the input networks, where each region implies a mapping independently of other regions. The strategy consists of the mapping or set of mappings between subsets of nodes such that their similarity is maximal over all possible subsets. These subnetworks correspond to conserved patterns of interactions that can represent a conserved motif or pattern of activities. To the best of our knowledge, currently, there is not an algorithm for local alignment of heterogeneous networks. Therefore we here present main approaches for homogeneous networks.

The first work by Berg and Lassig [1] proposed the first formalisation for network alignment in biology. Then, the work [13] proposed an LNA algorithm tailored for biological networks based on the theory of evolution of genes (the so-called duplication-divergence model).

AlignNemo [3] algorithm, given the networks of two organisms, enables the discovery of subnetworks of proteins related to biological function and topology of interactions. The algorithm can handle sparse interaction data with an expansion process that at each step explores the local topology of the networks beyond the proteins directly interacting with the current solution. AlignMCL [15] is a local alignment algorithm that represents an evolution of previous algorithm AlignNemo. AlignMCL builds the local alignment, by merging all the input data in a single graph, *alignment graph*, that is afterwards examined, and by using the Markov cluster algorithm MCL [6], to extract the conserved subnetworks. The main contribution of AlignMCL consists of the ability to extract functional modules, represented as local dense subgraphs, without the imposition of any particular topology.

LocalAli [10] is a local network alignment algorithm based on a maximum-parsimony evolutionary model for the build of local alignment among multiple networks as functionally conserved modules. LocalAli uses the maximum-parsimony evolutionary model to infer the evolutionary tree of networks nodes. Then, LocalAli extracts local alignments as conserved modules that have been evolved from a common ancestral module.

3 Local Alignment of Heterogeneous Networks

We develop a framework for the local alignment of heterogeneous biological networks. We formally define the computational problem matches, mismatches, and gaps.

3.1 Heterogeneous Network Alignment Problem

An heterogeneous biological network is modeled by a node colored graph $G_{het} = (V_{het}, E_{het}, C)$, where V_{het} is a set of coloured nodes, $E_{het} \subseteq V_{het} \times V_{het}$ and C is a set of colors that define a coverage of V_{het}. We extend the formulation provided in [13], therefore given two heterogeneous networks $G_{het1} = (V_{het1}, E_{het1}, C)$ and $G_{het2} = (V_{het2}, E_{het2}, C)$, a subset of node pair $L \subseteq V_{het1} \times V_{het2}$, induces a local alignment L_{ali} of G_{het1} and G_{het2} under a scoring function F that measure the similarity among nodes of two input networks $F : V_{het1} \times V_{het2} \rightarrow [0, 1]$, and under a match, mismatch and gap schema. Formally, the local alignment may relate node of different colors. Considering the topology, and the distance between nodes participating in the input networks we may find clear three possible cases.

Given two pair of nodes of the input networks $(v_{11}, v_{12}) \in G_{het1}$ and $(v_{21}, v_{22}) \in G_{het2}$, there is a match if both v_{11}, v_{12} and v_{21}, v_{22} are connected in input networks. There is a mismatch if only a pair of nodes is connected to a network. There is a gap if a pair of nodes is connected ant the other two nodes are at a distance k lower than δ.

Figure 1 depicts this scenario.

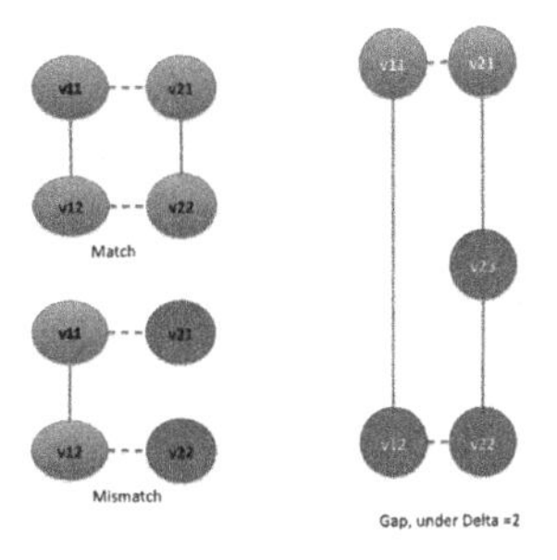

Fig. 1. Framework.

Clearly, for each match, mismatch and gap we may associate a scoring using a function Q that takes into account both the similarity of nodes and the topology. Consequently, the problem of finding a local alignment may be formulated as the finding of a subset of node pairs that maximise the overall score Q_{max}.

Since the general formulation is computationally hard [1], we propose a heuristic algorithm to solve the problem based on two main steps:

1. **Building of the Alignment Graph**: starting from two node-coloured graphs, and a similarity function among nodes of these graphs, we build a weighted alignment graph.
2. **Analysis of the Alignment Graph**: the alignment graph is then analysed to extract communities using Markov clustering algorithm [6].

Thus the more general formulation of the network alignment problem is to find a $L \subseteq V_{het1} \times V_{het2}$ that maximise a function Q.

3.2 Heterogeneous Alignment Graph

The alignment graph $G = (V_{al}, E_{al})$ is a node-colored graph that is built starting from two input graphs $G_1 = (V_1, E_1)$, and $G_2 = (V_2, E_2)$. Each node $v_{al} \in V_{al}$ represent a pair of nodes of the input graphs, therefore $V_{al} \subset V_1 \times V_2$. For the sake of the simplicity we consider only the integration of two nodes of the same color, but the extension may be easily obtained. Edges of the alignment graph are inserted by the presence of the edges relating corresponding nodes on two input graphs. Edges are weighted by using a scoring function that extends the match-mismatch-gap score of the classical alignment graph. Given two nodes of the alignment graph, the corresponding nodes of the input graph may be connected or not, and may be of the same colour or not. Intuitively, the best case is when nodes are connected and of the same colour. The scoring function should take into account this consideration by considering six possible cases of match, mismatch and gap and two possible sub-cases for each one, homogeneous and heterogeneous. We first introduce these cases.

Match. Given two nodes of the alignment graph $v_{al,1} = (v_{11}, v_{21})$ and $v_{al,2} = (v_{21}, v_{22})$, an **homogeneous match** is established when the input nodes are adjacent and all the nodes have the same color. Given two nodes of the alignment graph $v_{al,1} = (v_{11}, v_{21})$ and $v_{al,2} = (v_{21}, v_{22})$, an **heterogeneous match** is established when the input nodes are adjacent and the input nodes have the a different color. Figure 2 depicts this scenario.

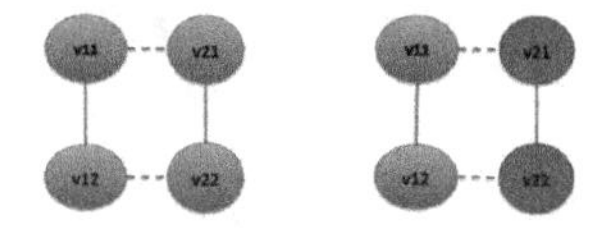

Fig. 2. Match

Mismatch. Given two nodes of the alignment graph $v_{al,1} = (v_{11}, v_{21})$ and $v_{al,2} = (v_{21}, v_{22})$, an **homogeneous mismatch** is established when the input nodes are adjacent only in a single network and all the nodes have the same color. Given two nodes of the alignment graph $v_{al,1} = (v_{11}, v_{21})$ *and* $v_{al,2} = (v_{21}, v_{22})$, an **heterogeneous mismatch** is established when the input nodes are adjacent only in a single network and the input nodes have the a different color. Figure 3 depicts this scenario.

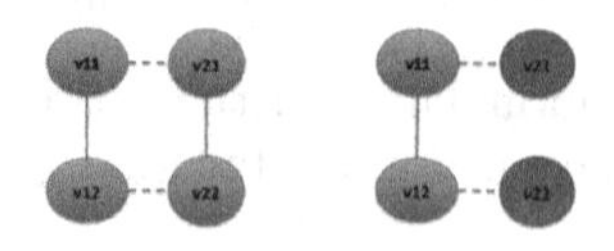

Fig. 3. Mismatch

Gap. Given two nodes of the alignment graph $v_{al,1} = (v_{11}, v_{21})$ and $v_{al,2} == (v_{21}, v_{22})$, an **homogeneous gap** is established when the input nodes are adjacent only in a single network and they are at distance lower than Δ (gap threshold) in the other network and all the nodes have the same color. Given two nodes of the alignment graph $v_{al,1} = (v_{11}, v_{21})$ *and* $v_{al,2} == (v_{21}, v_{22})$, an **heterogeneous gap** is established when the input nodes are are adjacent only in a single network and they are at distance lower than Δ in the other network and the input nodes have the a different color. Figure 4 depicts this scenario.

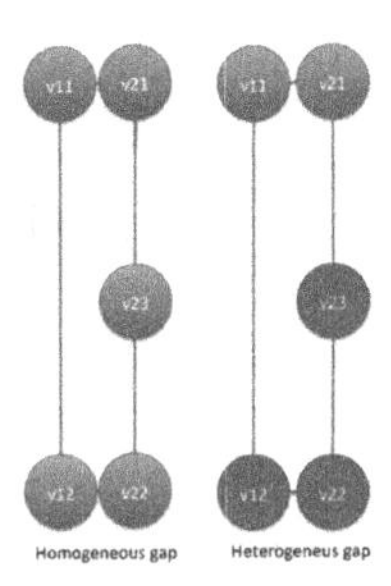

Fig. 4. Gap

3.3 Weighting the Edges

Clearly, after the building of the edges of the alignment graph, there is the need to weight each edge using an ad-hoc scoring function F and the gap threshold Δ. This function should emphasise matches and should penalise mismatch and gaps. The nature of the scoring function has a high impact on the resulting alignment graph and on the alignment itself.

4 Sequential Implementation in R

At first, we implemented our algorithm using the R programming language [12].

The algorithm takes as input two heterogeneous networks $G_{het1} = (V_{het1}, E_{het1}, C)$ and $G_{het2} = (V_{het2}, E_{het2}, C)$, a subset of node pair matched according to a similarity functions and builds the local alignment of G_{het1} and G_{het2} under a scoring function F and under a match, mismatch and gap schema.

The Network analysis were performed using the igraph [4] R Package. The Fig. 5 show the workflow algorithm.

Step 1-Import heterogeneous networks and similarity nodes: the algorithm receives as input two input node-coloured graphs and the list of matched pair nodes. For simplicity, we consider two different colours to model the nodes of the heterogeneous networks.

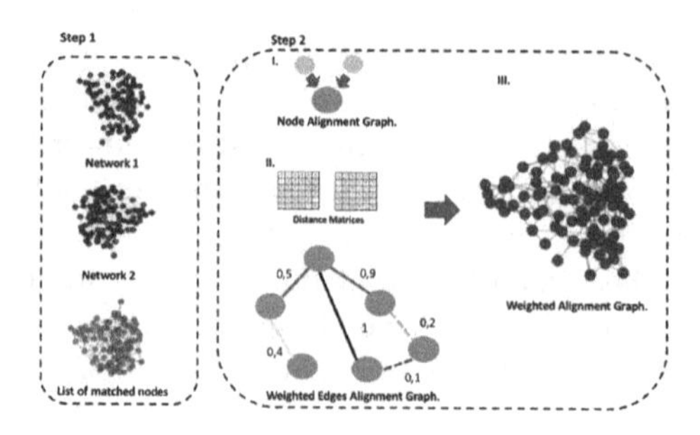

Fig. 5. Workflow of algorithm on R.

Step 2-Building of the Alignment Graph: The algorithm builds an alignment graph represented as a weighted graph.

Step 2.1-Node Alignment Graph Definition: The algorithm defines the nodes of the alignment graph represented by the pair of nodes matched by the similarity considerations. Thus, the nodes of the alignment graph are composite nodes representing pairs of similar nodes of two input networks

Step 2.2-Edges Building and Edges Weighting Step: The algorithm proceeds to insert the edges of the alignment graph considering the presence of corresponding edges in both networks, or the presence of at least an edge in one of the input networks. While the edges are inserted, the algorithm apply an edge scoring strategy to weights each edge. The algorithm computes a distance matrix for each input networks and set a distance threshold Δ that relies on the distance of nodes in the input networks. According to these, the algorithm weights the edges of the alignment graph. The edges are weighted by considering six cases of match homogeneous/heterogeneous, mismatch homogeneous/heterogeneous and gap homogeneous/heterogeneous. In case of match homogeneous, the algorithm assigns a score equals to 1 to the edge, whereas the weight of edge is equal to 0.9 in match heterogeneous case. Instead, when the algorithm finds a mismatch homogeneous weights the edge with 0.5, while in mismatch heterogeneous case the weight edge is equal to 0.4. Finally, in gap homogeneous case and gap heterogeneous the weights edge are equals to 0.2 and 0.1 The process ends when none edge is added.

Finally, the Markov clustering algorithm is used.

5 High Performance Computing on Apache Spark

Apache Spark [19] is a framework for big data analytics and processing built on top of the Hadoop MapReduce experience.

Hadoop MapReduce has found many applications in Bioinformatics and computational biology [17]. Recently, the analysis of (big) data in bioinformatics has caused the need for the introduction of high computational platforms for processing (big) data generated from technological platforms. The common paradigm for big data analytics involves the distribution of computations in a set of machines (or a cluster) that share data in a shared file system. Among the other programming models, the Hadoop's MapReduce API has gained an important role. Usually, the Hadoop MapReduce API operate in a remote data centre that is accessed through web interface. Hadoop [20] is a software framework available for Linux platforms that enable in a natural way the access and the use of the computational power of a cluster. Main characteristics of Hadoop are (i) robust, fault-tolerant Hadoop Distributed File System (HDFS), (ii) Map-Reduce programming model. The HDFS allows parallel processing across the nodes of the cluster using the MapReduce paradigm.

Hadoop uses a Fault-tolerant, shared-nothing architecture based on the constraint that tasks are mutually independent. Therefore the failure of a node requires the restart of a single node.

Hadoop employs a Map/Reduce execution engine [19] to realize a fault-tolerant distributed computing system over the large data sets stored in the cluster's distributed file system. The critical idea of the Map/Reduce engine is the processing workflow that is subdivided in two main stages Map and Reduce. Each computation has many separate Map and Reduce steps, each step is done in parallel. Each node operates on a subset of the initial dataset. Therefore, each node run a Map function on such dataset. The output of such step is a set of records stored as key-value pairs. In the second stage, (Reduce Stage), records must be grouped considering keys. Therefore, for any key there is a Reducer, running on a node, that group all the records of the key until all the data from the Map stage has been transferred to the appropriate machine. The Reduce stage produces another set of key-value pairs, as final output. Despite the simplicity and the constraint of the use of key-value pairs, this programming model may be used on a broad set of problems and tasks.

The Apache Spark framework is based on MapReduce programming model improving its weaknesses. Apache Spark is an open-source cluster computing framework for significant data processing offering to the user an easy way to access map reduce programming on a cluster. Spark extend the Map-Reduce capabilities: it runs more faster [19] and it simplifies the use by providing a rich set of API in Python, Java, Scala and R. The core concept of SPARK is the distributed data frame that has been used in many applications including large queries, machine learning, and graph processing.

6 A Framework for Graph Alignment in Apache Spark

We designed HetNetAligner, a framework for heterogeneous graph aligner over Spark. Main modules of HetNetAligner, as depicted in Fig. 6, are:

- **A User Interface:** that is responsible for interacting with users. User Interface has two main instances: a command line that accept instruction using the command line and a graphical user interface (currently under development) that simplify the user commands.
- **NetworkX Libraries** [9]**:** HetNetHaligner uses the NetworkX libraries for managing input and output of graphs.

- **Graph Clustering Libraries:** we used the mLib [14] to analyse the graph efficiently.

Currently, we designed the overall architecture of the HetNetAligner framework, and we implemented main modules to test the effectiveness of our approach.

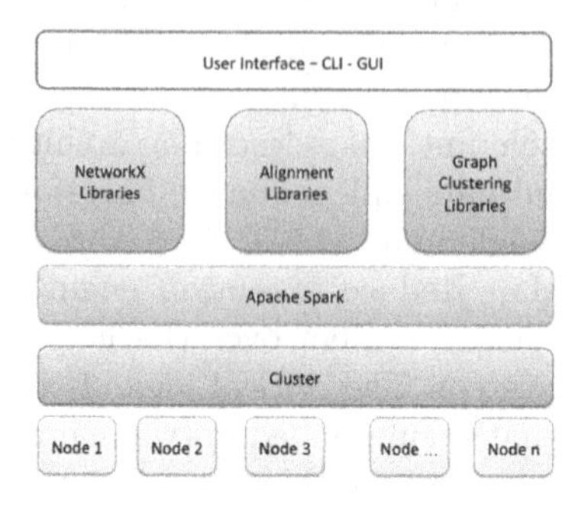

Fig. 6. The architecture of HetNetALigner.

6.1 Implementation of the Heterogeneous Graph Alignment Algorithm

The implementation of the alignment algorithm in Spark is based on five main steps as described in the following algorithm.

```
Algorithm 1: Alignment Graph Building
Input: Graph 1, Graph 2
Output: Alignment Graph.
1: Building of Node List
2: Building Empty Adjacency Matrix
3: Parallelization of the Adjacency Matrix
4: Parallel Calculation of Edges and Weights
5: End
```

Step 1 and two are performed sequentially. After building of the empty adjacent matrix, this matrix is spread among nodes using distributed matrix abstraction of Spark (Fig. 7).

7 Results

7.1 Dataset

The dataset consisted of 12 synthetic networks. We built the synthetic networks using a random graph generator according to the Erdos-Renyi model.

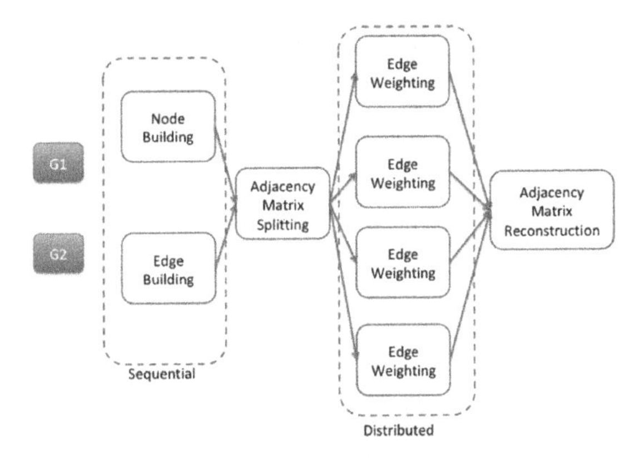

Fig. 7. Implementation of the algorithm on Spark.

We set all model network instances to the same size of 9500 nodes, and we vary the number of edges. Then, we randomly assign each node a colour out of 2 possible colours because the existing random graph generators are not designed to produce heterogeneous networks. The Table 1 shows the network parameters.

Table 1. Details of synthetic networks used for experiments

Network	Nodes	Edge
N1	9500	341000
N2	9500	342000
N3	9500	334000
N4	9500	320000
N5	9500	353000
N6	9500	333000
N7	9500	333000
N8	9500	338000
N9	9500	449000
N10	9500	406000
N11	9500	438000
N12	9500	416000

All the experiments were performed on an Intel Xeon(R) Processor (3.4 Ghz, 4 core, and 8 threads) with 16 Gbytes of memory running an Ubuntu OS ver 18.04.

We configured the Apache Spark environment and the HetNetAligner framework. We measured both the quality of the alignment and the increase of the performances when varying the number of clusters. We compared each network with itself, and we increased the number of cores using 1, 2, 4 and 16 cores. Figure 8 shows the scalability of our algorithm considering the time to build the alignment. We should note the time to build the alignment is reduced for each network.

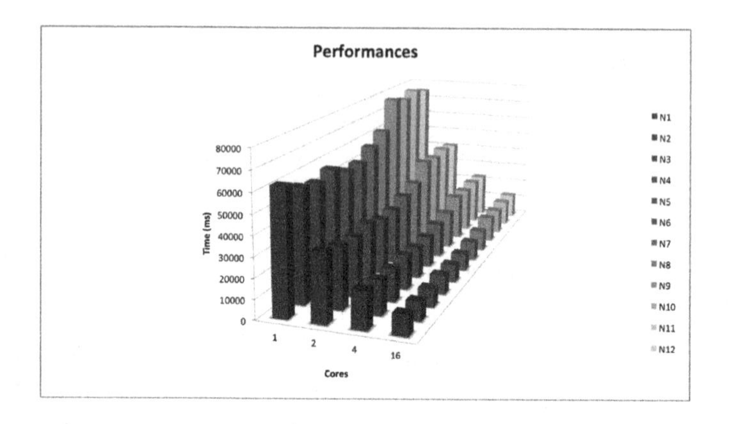

Fig. 8. Scalability of HetNetAligner.

8 Conclusion

We here presented HetNetAligner a framework built on top of Apache Spark. We also implemented our algorithm, and we tested it on some selected heterogeneous biological networks. Preliminary results confirm that our method may extract relevant knowledge from biological data reducing the computational time. Future work will regard the implementation of the whole framework.

Acknowledgements. This work has been partially supported by Fondo di Finanziamento per le Attivitá Base di Ricerca (FFABR 2017) of Prof. Pietro Hiram Guzzi.

References

1. Berg, J., Lässig, M.: Local graph alignment and motif search in biological networks. Proc. Natl. Acad. Sci. U. S. A. **101**(41), 14689–14694 (2004)
2. Cannataro, M., Guzzi, P.H., Veltri, P.: Protein-to-protein interactions: technologies, databases, and algorithms. ACM Comput. Surv. (CSUR) **43**(1), 1 (2010)
3. Ciriello, G., Mina, M., Guzzi, P.H., Cannataro, M., Guerra, C.: Alignnemo: a local network alignment method to integrate homology and topology. PLoS ONE **7**(6), e38107 (2012)
4. Csardi, G., Nepusz, T.: The igraph software package for complex network research. InterJournal Complex Syst. **1695**(5), 1–9 (2006)

5. Di Martino, M.T., et al.: Integrated analysis of micrornas, transcription factors and target genes expression discloses a specific molecular architecture of hyperdiploid multiple myeloma. Oncotarget **6**(22), 19132 (2015)
6. Enright, A.J., Van Dongen, S., Ouzounis, C.A.: An efficient algorithm for large-scale detection of protein families. Nucleic Acids Res. **30**(7), 1575–1584 (2002)
7. Gligorijevic, V., Malod-Dognin, N., Przulj, N.: Integrative methods for analyzing big data in precision medicine. Proteomics **16**(5), 741–758 (2016)
8. Guzzi, P.H., Di Martino, M.T., Tagliaferri, P., Tassone, P., Cannataro, M.: Analysis of miRNA, mRNA, and TF interactions through network-based methods. EURASIP J. Bioinform. Syst. Biol. **2015**(1), 1–11 (2015)
9. Hagberg, A., Swart, P., Chult, D.S.: Exploring network structure, dynamics, and function using networkx. Technical report, Los Alamos National Lab. (LANL), Los Alamos, NM, United States (2008)
10. Hu, J., Reinert, K.: Localali: an evolutionary-based local alignment approach to identify functionally conserved modules in multiple networks. Bioinformatics **31**(3), 363–372 (2014)
11. Ideker, T., Nussinov, R.: Network approaches and applications in biology. PLoS Comput. Biol. **13**(10), e1005771 (2017)
12. Ihaka, R., Gentleman, R.: R: a language for data analysis and graphics. J. Comput. Graph. Stat. **5**(3), 299–314 (1996)
13. Koyuturk, M., Kim, Y., Topkara, U., Subramaniam, S., Szpankowski, W., Grama, A.: Pairwise alignment of protein interaction networks. J. Comput. Biol. **13**(2), 182–199 (2006)
14. Meng, X., et al.: MLlib: machine learning in apache spark. J. Mach. Learn. Res. **17**(1), 1235–1241 (2016)
15. Mina, M., Guzzi, P.H.: Improving the robustness of local network alignment: design and extensive assessmentof a Markov clustering-based approach. IEEE/ACM Trans. Comput. Biol. Bioinform. **11**(3), 561–572 (2014)
16. Navarro, C., Martínez, V., Blanco, A., Cano, C.: ProphTools: general prioritization tools for heterogeneous biological networks. GigaScience **6**(12), 1–8 (2017)
17. Taylor, R.C.: An overview of the Hadoop/MapReduce/HBase framework and its current applications in bioinformatics. In: BMC Bioinformatics, vol. 11, p. S1. BioMed Central (2010)
18. Yap, P.-T., Wu, G., Shen, D.: Human brain connectomics: networks, techniques, and applications [life sciences]. IEEE Signal Process. Mag. **27**(4), 131–134 (2010)
19. Zaharia, M., et al.: Apache spark: a unified engine for big data processing. Commun. ACM **59**(11), 56–65 (2016)
20. Zikopoulos, P., Eaton, C., et al.: Understanding Big Data: Analytics for Enterprise Class Hadoop and Streaming Data. McGraw-Hill Osborne Media, New York (2011)

A Parallel Cellular Automaton Model For Adenocarcinomas in Situ with Java: Study of One Case

Antonio J. Tomeu-Hardasmal[1](✉), Alberto G. Salguero-Hidalgo[1], and Manuel I. Capel[2]

[1] Department of Computer Science, University of Cádiz, 11519 Puerto Real, Spain
{antonio.tomeu,alberto.salguero}@uca.es

[2] Department of Software Engineering, University of Granada, 18071 Granada, Spain
mcapel@ugr.es

Abstract. Adenocarcinomas are tumors that originate in the lining epithelium of the ducts that form the endocrine glands of the human body. Infiltrating breast and one of the most frequent neoplasms among female population, and the early detection of the disease is then fundamental and, for this reason, a profound knowledge of the biology of tumor at this phase is essential. Among the distinct tools that contribute to this knowledge, computational simulation is more frequently used every day. The availability of fast and efficient computations that allow the simulation of tumor dynamics in situ, under a wide range of different parameters, is an important research topic. Based on cellular automata, this paper proposes a generic simulation model for the Adenocarcinomas In Situ (CIS). We applied it to the breast ductal adenocarcinoma in situ (DCIS), modeling our cells with the genomic load that we currently know that the tumor starts, and proposing a numerical coding method for the genome that allows efficient computational management. We propose a parallelization scheme using data parallelism, and we show the acceleration achieved in multiple nodes of our cluster of processors.

Keywords: Adenocarcionomas in situ · Cellular automaton
Data partition · Parallel processing · *Speedup*

1 Introduction

It is estimated that one in eight women [8] will suffer breast cancer, being approximately 80% of them ductal carcinomas. Likewise, one in every nine men will suffer a prostate cancer. Thus, the incidence of these neoplasms in the adult population and the magnitude of the health problem they imply will be very important. Early detection is aimed at identifying the disease when it has not yet acquired infiltrating character, and it is limited to glandular ducts (in situ),

G. Mencagli et al. (Eds.): Euro-Par 2018 Workshops, LNCS 11339, pp. 704–715, 2019.
https://doi.org/10.1007/978-3-030-10549-5_55

i.e. the glandular parenchyma not was infiltrated yet. At this point, the disease can only be root out with surgery that removes the affected segment of the duct, and a safety margin free of disease, while preserving the rest of the patient's breast, with a success rate of more than 90%. In the case of prostate carcinomas, prostate-specific antigen, which has traditionally been used as a tumor marker, it has been found out that is unaccurate in screening the disease for men. In both cases, the characterization of the disease when is still in situ becomes of great interest, and for this, computer simulation can be an excellent tool to investigate it. Carcinogenesis is a phenomenon in which one or multiple mutations on certain genes allow the cells to reproduce and survive abnormally, under a selection process that results in uncontrolled tumor growth characterized by infiltrating nature. There are many mathematical models in the literature that contain the knowledge we currently have about genes involvement in neoplasms [1–3,6,7,9,11], which study the mutations that neoplasms can develop to originate a CIS. In this paper, we propose a three-dimensional cellular automaton based CIS model to simulate a generic glandular duct and to analyze how the mutations in the cells of the simulated duct become CIS. We also apply the model to known breast intraductal adenocarcinoma data, parallelize it and we study its natural development with respect to the parallel model and the acceleration achieved.

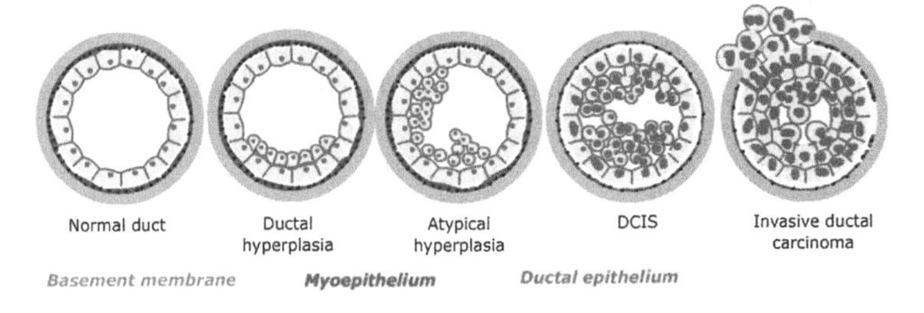

Fig. 1. Natural development of Adenocarcinomas in Situ (CIS), from a normal duct to an infiltrated one.

2 Biology of Breast Adenocarcinomas in Situ

If not detected and treated, the natural development of these tumours is the progression to an infiltrating adenocarcinoma, as shown in Fig. 1. In the case of the human breast, it is now known that within a normal duct the two types of cells that form the ducts originate from a single class of progenitor cell that, by cellular differentiation, leads to two germ lines that conclude in the two cited types of cells. Ductal adenocarcinomas initially have a local character and then grow to infiltrate and reach the duct.

It is known that those women with genetic predisposition to breast cancer accumulate inherited specific mutations [16,17], and thus, an estimate points out that up to 12% the number of cases is due to this circumstance, not mentioning other genes that may be involved. In addition it is now known that mutations in the BRCA1, BRCA2, PTEN and TP53 genes increase the likelihood of suffering from ductal carcinoma. In the model proposed here, this genetic predisposition will be taken into account by means of a logical variable HMG. In our simulation, all the *stem* cells of the duct will be defined with the genetic predisposition incorporated into their genome.

The meaning of the four genes that we will consider in the simulation is illustrated in Table 1. In it, the first and second columns collect the modeled genes and their function in physiological conditions. When one or several of the genes suffer damage, the behavior of the cell that contains it becomes malignant. When a chain of specific mutations occurs it inexorably leads to the proliferation of ductal carcinoma, first local, and then infiltrating, breaking the duct and expanding to the glandular parenchyma.

Table 1. Pathological functioning of genes.

Gen	Operation with damages
BRCA1	The cell dies
BRCA2	Neoplastic reproduction
PTEN	Neoplastic reproduction
PTEN	Does not inhibit neoplastic reproduction
TP53	Cell survival with damage to proto-oncogenes
TP53	Cell survival with damage to the double-layer architecture

3 Cellular Automata

A cellular automaton (CA) [5,15,18] is as a 4-tuple $(\zeta, \varepsilon, N^I, \rho)$ where:

- ζ is a discrete regular network of cells (or nodes) together with some border conditions set for the finite dimension net case, which are of use to define neighboring conditions of cells at the net frontier.In our case, we have the mathematical representation of a 3D-cubic: $\zeta = \{r : r = (r_1, r_2, r_3) \in Z^3\}$.
- ε is a finite set (usually, with an algebraic Abelian ring structure) of states that the network of cells can take on.
- N^I is a finite set of cells that define the neighbor cells with which a given cell of the network can interaction.
- The transition function ρ that defines how any cell's state can change depending on time and on its neighbor cells own state N^I.

Given the previous definitions, any area of cells can be defined as the network ζ included in the real 3D space R^d that uniformly covers a portion of the d-dimensional Euclidean space. Each cell is labeled by its position $r \in \zeta$. The layout of cells is spatially specified by the connections that any cell holds with its closest neighbors, which are obtained by connecting pairs of cells following a regular pattern. For any spatial coordinate r, the neighborhood grid $N_b(r)$ consists of a list of neighbor cells that is defined by

$$N_b(r) = \{r + c_i : c_i \in N_b, i = 1, \cdots, b\} \tag{1}$$

Where b is the *coordination number* or, in other words, the number of the grid neighbors that directly interact with the cell at coordinate r. N_b denotes the elements in that pattern as $c_i \in R^d$, $i = 1, \cdots, b$.

$$\zeta = \{r : r \in \mathbb{Z}^3\} \tag{2}$$

The total number of cells available is usually denoted by $|\zeta|$. The entire set of neighboring cells whose states affect any cell r is defined by the *interaction vicinity* $N_b^I(r)$ function, $N_b^I(r) = \{r + c_i : c_i \in N_b^I\}$.

Any cell's neighborhood can be chosen in different ways, though we choose for our simulation the vicinity schema of Moore [5], where any cell has as neighbors only its surrounding cells. Furthermore, each cell $r \in \zeta$ has a state $s(r) \in \varepsilon$. A global configuration of the automaton $s \in \varepsilon^{|\zeta|}$ is determined by the state of all the cells on the grid. Finally, model's temporal evolution dynamics is determined by the function of transition ρ that specifies the changes in any cell state according to its previous state, and the interaction with closest-cells neighborhood given by $\rho : \varepsilon^{\mu} \rightarrow \varepsilon$ where $\mu = |N_b^I|$. The rule is proved to be spatially homogeneous and does not therefore explicitly depends on the position of a given cell [14]. Extensions of the previous definition to include temporary or spatial homogeneity are feasible. If the CA is deterministic, the function of transition yields only one feasible change of state, whereas if it is stochastic, the new cell's state is given by a specific distribution of probability.

4 Modelling Breast Adeconocarcinoma Ductal in Situ with Cellular Automata

To model the duct, a cellular automaton [12,13] assuming a three-dimensional ζ grid with $20 \times 20 \times 200$ nodes is used, which is built from the two-dimensional model proposed in [14], by just adding an additional dimension. Each node may contains a cell. Although a human ductal cell has a genome composed of multiple genes with millions of DNA bases, we will limit ourselves to consider only the four genes in the model involved in the pathogenesis of the DICS, which are encoded by 32 bits integers. The genetic load of a cell is then modeled by an ordered tuple of the form $GC = (brca1, brca2, pten, tp53)$. The tuple GC is encoded in its turn by a single integer using the pairing function given by the Eq. 3. The three dimensional version of *Moore*'s neighborhood and a null boundary condition is used to give the ends of the duct a biological coherence.

$$\langle x, y \rangle = 2^x(2y + 1) - 1 \tag{3}$$

This function, which is a bijection, may be nested by means of the expression.

$$\langle\langle brca1, brca2, \rangle, \langle pten, tp53 \rangle\rangle \tag{4}$$

It allows the encoding of the entire genome of a cell in a single positive integer by using a compact and reasonably efficient way. In this way, each node of the ζ grid of the cellular automaton contains a pair of positive numbers that respectively code the cell type and its genetic load, which in turn are re-encoded by applying the pairing function to both data, so that the node contains a unique number in $\mathbb{Z}^+$. Decoding the integer to update that genetic load when a cell mutates or for any other reason is trivial, given the encoding technique exposed, by simply using the decoding functions $r(z)$ and (z), described in the Eqs. 5 and 6. The set of possible cell types[1] of the grid is $S = \{free, basal, luminal, myoephitelial\}$ and, as we have said, they are numerically coded.

$$l(z) = min_{x \leq z}[(\exists y)_{\leq z}](z = \langle x, y \rangle) \quad (5)$$

$$r(z) = min_{y \leq z}[(\exists x)_{\leq z}](z = \langle x, y \rangle) \quad (6)$$

The three given functions are primitive recursive [4] and, therefore, computable. The nodes of the grid are synchronously updated node by node of the duct. The cells are updated according to the probability of mutation and its neighborhood environment. Both variables define the transition function ρ. The selection and updating of the 8×10^4 nodes of the grid defines a generation. The number of generations varies depending on the length of the natural history of the tumor being simulated, increasing or decreasing the number of generations of the simulation. The grid is initialized by a completely deterministic algorithm that creates a base membrane and places a small number of progenitor cells in its interior, which reproduce to form a double layer duct, though we will apply it to the breast ducts here. Each section of the duct contains approximately 45–50 luminal cells. Originally, all the cells are located on the duct have a healthy genome, which is represented by 32 bits equal to zero. Mutations are modeled by nullifying the value of one or several bits of a gene. The `HMG` *flag* allows us to execute the model considering an inherited genetic predisposition to contract the disease, using a Monte-Carlo method. The algorithm to obtain a simulation of the duct compatible with the histological structure of a human breast is shown below[2].

```
1 Algorithm SetUp
2 Input: empty grid
3 Output: grid with initial states for nodes
4 Method:
5
6 1. With radial symmetry put basal_cells to define basal
     membrane;
```

[1] Basal cells: they form the outer layer of tissue that surrounds the duct; luminal and myoephitelial cells: form the internal structure of a normal duct (see Fig. 1); free represents the internal space of the duct that is empty.

[2] For the sake of clarity, we have abstracted the necessary coding and decoding steps that allow us to modify the state of a node of the reticle or the genome of a cell located in that node. However, the reader should always bear in mind that any reading or writing to node in the grid requires that state modification.

```
7      stem_cells=[];
8      //seeding stem cells...
9   2. for(i=0; i<200; i++){
10      cx=random(0, 19);
11      cy=random(0, 19);
12      cz=random(0,199);
13      grid[x][y][z]=stem;
14      stem_cells.add((x, y, z));
15     }
16     //putting mutations in stem cells...
17  3. if(HMG==true)
18       for iterator in stem_cells{
19         x=iterator(x);
20         y=iterator(y);
21         z=iterator(z);
22         mutate(grid[x][y][z], all_gens, 15%);
23       }
24     //making the rest of duct...
25  4. While(free_places){
26     5. for all cells in grid
27          reproduce(grid[x][y][z], adjacent, hierarchy);
28     6. for all !(stem_cell) in grid
29          migrate(grid[x][y][z], vacant_neighboring,
               radial_symemtry);
30     }
```

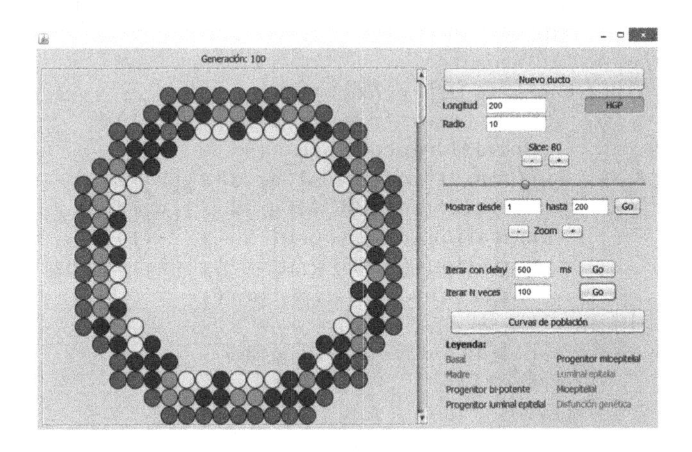

Fig. 2. Initial state for a layer of the duct.

When the previous simulation is executed in the Java language, a grid is obtained that coherently models the normal histological structure of a human duct (Fig. 2), and all the cells generated in the grid remain inside, adopting the double layer structure illustrated in Fig. 1 for the normal state of the duct.

During the reproduction phase, modeled on line number 5, all the cells of the grid get divided and take up the adjacent places, wherever there is enough room for them. The inherited genetic load can be mutated, according to the mutation rate set as a parameter of the `mutate` method, to which we have given a value of 15%, which reasonably encompasses the various real causes that can lead to this type of mutations, and that include the environment, the genetics and even the type of the cell [7]. Since all genes are mutated through the method, including those that control both mitosis and programmed cell death, the cells of the duct resulting from the routine `SetUp` will eventually lead to neoplastic pathology. Once the grid is in its initial state, it is necessary to make it evolve over time, which is the responsibility of the `Evolve` algorithm.

```
1  Algorithm Evolve
2  Input: grid in t-time
3  Output: grid in (t+1)-time
4  Method:
5
6  //now, the transition function...
7  1. for all cells in grid{
8        //normal apoptosis...
9       2. if((mutations(BRCA1(grid[x][y][z]))
10             +mutations(TP53(grid[x][y][z])))>32)
11           grid[x][y][z]=free; //cell dies
12      //normal apoptosis...
13      3. if(mutations(TP53(grid[x][y][z]))<16 && (
14             !adjacent_basal(grid[x][y][z]) ||
15             !adjacent_myopithelial(grid[x][y][z])))
16             grid[x][y][z]=free; //cell dies
17       //anormal apoptosis...
18      4. if(stem(grid[x][y][z])){
19           5. if(adjacent_free(grid[x][y][z]))
20                normal_reproduction();
21           6. if((mutations(BRCA1(grid[x][y][z]))+
22                   mutations(BRCA1(grid[x][y][z])+
23                mutations(PTEN(grid[x][y][z])+
24                mutations(TP53(grid[x][y][z])))>64)
25                cancerous_reproduction()
26         }
27       7. for all !(stem_cell) in grid
28             migrate();
29    }
```

In the previous algorithm, the methods `BRCA1`, `BRCA2`, `PTEN` and `TP53` takes the integer that encodes the genome of a cell in the grid and extracts the 32-bit integer that encodes the gene according to the name of the method; the `mutations` method takes a numerically coded gene as its argument and returns the number of mutations it presents, as an integer between 0 and 32. The methods `adjacent_basal` and `adjacent_myopithelial` allow us to know the type of the cells that form the *Moore*'s neighborhood cube of a given cell while the method **adjacent_free** gets the free nodes on the neighborhood of the node given as argument. On the other hand, there is also available a set of four methods that allow us to know the type of the cell that is in a node of the grid. The subroutine **normal_reproduction** allows parents to be reproduced correctly around their local cubic neighborhood, preserving the double layer structure of the duct. The subroutine **cancerous_reproduction**, allows parents to be reproduced at points in their local cubic neighborhood, but does not respect the double-layer structure of the duct, and ended up forming an intraductal carcinoma in situ. Note that for a parent to reproduce in this way, it is necessary that the total sum of mutations present in their four genes is greater than half the positions that the four genes encode. Finally, a simulation is carried out using a given number of discrete time steps, in which each of them the described algorithm **Evolve** is executed. When a critical number of mutations is reached, cells begin to proliferate uncontrollably, filling the duct lumen and forming the carcinoma in situ. Figure 3 illustrates this for a segment of the duct consisting of fifty layers, where the neoplastic transformation has taken place and the malignant cells have begun to fill the duct lumen, without infiltrating the base membrane.

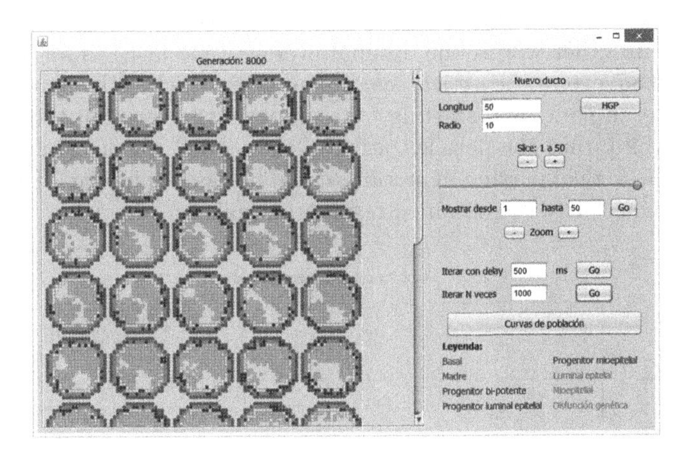

Fig. 3. Simulation for a full duct by layers. Neoplastic cells (yellow) are filling the inside of the duct. (Color figure online)

5 Implementation

The previous model was implemented using the Java programming language, and parallelizing the initial, sequential version. The parallelization employed the principles of symmetric multiprocessing with data parallelism, dividing the grid in its longitudinal dimension z into cubic sections that were processed by different threads on a dedicated *core* to each one of them [18].

A security condition is implemented to ensure the consistency of the simulation, which consists of forcing a thread trying to write in the bilayer section of the neighboring sub-table to consult the state of the node in which it intends to write after the acquisition of the lock, since the thread responsible for that sub-grid reticle could have occupied that node in its own writing time [15]. The execution tests were developed on four different nodes of the cluster of our university. Each node has two Intel®Xeon™ E5 processors at 2.6 GHz, which yield 20.8 Gflops together, with 128 GB memory and without hyperthreading activated. The entry node operates the HP Cluster Management Utility on Red Hat Enterprise Linux for HPC and the processing nodes the version *Compute Node* of the same operating system. The version of the Java development kit used was Oracle 1.8.0.151-1.b12.el7_4.

6 Measurements and Results Discussion

Figures 4 and 5 show the average times and *speedups* obtained, for 5×10^3 generations. Once computed, the simulation stopped. Average times ans *speedups* were obtained by computing the same simulation in different nodes of our cluster It can be seen that both time and speedup curves reach their bests values for eight parallel threads and that these values get worse if the number of parallel tasks is increased. In other words, the optimal average time is 4.18 s for a maximum speedup of 5.85, over a theoretical maximum of 16, which is the number of cores available in each node, and starting from an optimal sequential time of 24.45 s. One might think that the parallelization of the model, which barely gets up to half of the theoretical maximum *speedup*, could be easily improved. However, the following items clarify the obtained results rationale:

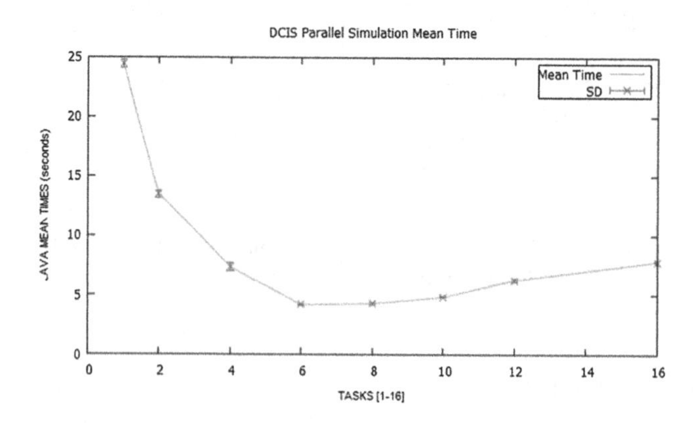

Fig. 4. Execution times (Mean ± Standard Deviation).

- It must be remembered that the contact zones between sub-reticles, controlled by different threads, are protected by a mutually exclusive lock, which introduces undesirable latencies that are however necessary to guarantee the coherence of the state of the nodes in the grid. This directly induces an

overload of the execution time that is proportional to the number of parallel threads (and contact zones). This shortcoming was identified in previous work [15] and by other authors in [10].
- Although the introduction of different reading and writing grids allow the threads to process the nodes that are not in the contact areas of the grid in a fully parallel manner, this is not the case of the nodes in those areas. Here, the thread that wants to write to a node located in the contact area, once it has got the permission to do it, cannot just use the neighborhood data in the reading grid, but has also to check the writing grid to verify that there is enough free space for the modification, because another thread may have occupied that space as the result of a mitosis. This also induces execution overloads.
- It is also worth mentioning that each node of the grid encodes a lot of information by using a single positive integer (type of cell that occupies the node, and BRCA1, BRCA, PTEN and TP53 genes). This introduces a heavy load process for decoding (and encoding, when appropriate) the information in the neighborhood of a cell.

One could think that the representation of the state and the genome of a cell by means of a class `gridCell.java` could improve the results, although the measures obtained by using an alternative implementation, discarded that. The space occupied in the *heap* of the Java Virtual Machine by the nodes modeled as classes, and the need of navigate through their respective references to reach them, increases the global process times and decreases the *speedups*. In short, the three previous items justify why those *seepdups* have been obtained, being the second one of particular relevance, and also being coherent with models that develop similar simulation dynamics in two dimensions, such as the results published in [10] and in [15]. The parallelization is worthwhile by itself, besides the proposed method is very general, and applicable to other types of tumors where, depending on the transition function with which they are modeled, the speedup could be slightly improved.

Regarding the biological fidelity of the model, we have compared the simulation with a real specimen, using the number of neoplastic cells in the duct as a as variable that changes over time (number of generations). In the real case, the genetic predisposition was verified by means of immunohistochemical method, while in our case the corresponding *flag* of the simulation was activated. The classic gompertzian behavior [7] that describes the tumor dynamics for both *in vivo* and *in vitro* were observed, which tends to occupy all available tissue domain with a quasi-exponential acceleration from a specific time instant. We see that the simulation *in silico* is compatible with biological and histological observations, with an acceptable degree of fidelity in terms of the global dynamics of neoplastic growth *in situ* refers.

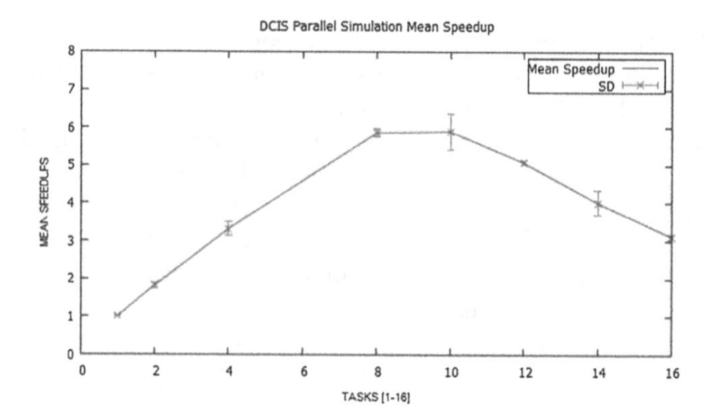

Fig. 5. Speedups (Mean ± Standard Deviation).

7 Conclusions and Future Works

In this work we have proposed a general procedure for the parallel simulation of adenocarcinomas *in situ* by using cellular automata-based model. A change of the transition function of the cellular automaton and the genetic load model allows us to adapt it to different types of glandular neoplasms, before they adopt infiltrating character. From the proposed algorithms, a parallel implementation has been developed using the Java language with symmetric multiprocessing by means of data parallelism for the study of a case: breast ductal adenocarcinoma *in situ*. The parallel simulation in the cluster of our University achieved a significant reduction of the processing times (Fig. 4), getting a maximum *speedup* factor of 5.85 (Fig. 5); it has also allowed us to identify an important limitation to the scalability of the proposed method, derived from the need to have under mutual exclusion control the nodes of the simulation grid located in contact zones that separate the data spaces reserved for different threads, which we already had identified in a previous work [15] for a two dimensional simulation. This limitation is typical of the nature of the problem and, therefore, cannot be ignored. The fidelity of the proposed model to the biological reality has also been checked, showing that the simulation achieves a more than acceptable fidelity with respect to the usual behavior in this type of neoplasms. Our future work is focused in:

- the application of the developed model to other glandular neoplasms *in situ*.
- the development of a data partitioning scheme that allows parallel simulations on GPU architectures.

References

1. Altrock, P.M., Liu, L.L., Michor, F.: The mathematics of cancer: integrating quantitative models. Nat. Rev. Cancer **15**, 730–745 (2015)
2. Byrne, H.M., Alarcon, T., Owen, M.R., Webb, S.D., Maini, P.K.: Modelling aspects of cancer dynamics: a review. Philos. Trans. Roy. Soc. **364**(1843), 1563–1578 (2006)
3. Byrne, H.M.: Dissecting cancer through mathematics: from the cell to the animal model. Nat. Rev. Cancer **10**, 221–230 (2010)
4. Davis, M., Sigal, R., Weyuker, E.: Computability, Complexity and Languages. Academic Press, Cambridge (1994)
5. Deutsch, A., Dormann, S.: Cellular Automaton Modeling of Biological Pattern Formation. Birkhäuser, Boston (2005)
6. Edelman, L.B., Eddy, J.A., Price, N.D.: *In silico* models of cancer. Syst. Biol. Med. Adv. Rev. **2**, 438–439 (2010)
7. Enderling, H., Chaplain, M., Anderson, A., Vaidya, J.: A mathematical model of breast cancer development, local treatment and recurrence. J. Theor. Biol. **246**(2), 245–259 (2007)
8. Erbas, B., Provenzano, E., Armes, J., Gertig, D.: The natural history of ductal carcinoma in situ of the breast: a review. Breast Cancer Res. Treat. **97**(2), 135–144 (2006)
9. Gatenby, R.A., Gawlinski, E.T.: A reaction-diffusion model of cancer invasion. Cancer Res. **56**(24), 5745–5753 (1996)
10. Giordano, A., et al.: Parallel execution of cellular automata through space partitioning: the landslide simulation Sciddicas3-Hex case study. In: Proceeding of 25th Euromicro International Conference on Parallel, Distributed and Network-based Processing (PDP), pp. 505–510 (2017)
11. Gevertz, J.L., Gillies, G.T., Torquato, S.: Simulating tumor growth in confined heterogeneous environments. Phys. Biol. **5**(3), 036010 (2008)
12. Kam, Y., Rejniak, K.A., Anderson, A.R.A.: Cellular modeling of cancer invasion: integration of *in silico* and *in vitro* approaches. J. Cell. Physiol. **227**(2), 431–438 (2012)
13. Monteagudo, A., Santos, J.: Studying the capability of different cancer hallmarks to initiate tumor growth using a cellular automaton simulation. Application in a cancer stem cell context. Biosystems **115**, 46–58 (2014)
14. Norton, K.-A., Wininger, M., Bhanot, G., Ganesan, S., Barnardh, N., Shinbrotb, T.: A 2D mechanistic model of breast ductal carcinoma in situ (DCIS) morphology and progression. J. Theor. Biol. **263**(4), 393–406 (2009)
15. Salguero-Hidalgo, A.G., Capel-Tunon, M.I., Tomeu-Hardasmal, A.J.: Parallel cellular automaton tumor growth model. In: Proceedings of 12th International Conference on Practical Applications of Computational Biology and Bioinformatics (to appear)
16. Silva, A.S., Gatenby, R.A., Gillies, R.J., Yunesa, J.A.: A quantitative theoretical model for the development of malignancy in ductal carcinoma in situ. J. Theor. Biol. **262**(4), 601–613 (2009)
17. Sottoriva, A., et al.: Cancer stem cell tumor model reveals invasive morphology and increased phenotypical heterogeneity. Cancer Res. **70**(1), 46–56 (2010)
18. Tomeu-Hardasmal, A.J., Salguero-Hidalgo, A.G., Capel-Tunon, M.I.: Speeding up tumor growth simulations using parallel programming and cellular automata. IEEE Lat. Am. Trans. **14**(11), 4603–4619 (2016)

Performance Evaluation for a PETSc Parallel-in-Time Solver Based on the MGRIT Algorithm

Valeria Mele[1(✉)], Diego Romano[2], Emil M. Constantinescu[3], Luisa Carracciuolo[2], and Luisa D'Amore[1]

[1] University of Naples Federico II, Naples, Italy
valeria.mele@unina.it
[2] Italian National Research Council - CNR, Rome, Italy
[3] Mathematics and Computer Science Division, Argonne National Laboratory, Chicago, IL, USA

Abstract. We herein describe the performance evaluation of a modular implementation of the MGRIT (MultiGrid-In-Time) algorithm within the context of the PETSc (the Portable, Extensible Toolkit for Scientific computing) library. Our aim is to give the PETSc users the opportunity of testing the MGRIT parallel-in-time approach as an alternative to the Time Stepping integrator (TS), when solving their problems arising from the discretization of linear evolutionary models. To this end, we analyzed the performance parameters of the algorithm in order to underline the relationship between the configuration factors and problem characteristics, intentionally overlooking any accuracy issue and spacial parallelism.

Keywords: Parallelism-in-time · Performance evaluation Multigrid reduction · MGRIT · Linear systems · PETSc

1 Introduction

Scientific applications in life science and in many other fields can benefit from the Parallel In Time (PINT) methods which have the potential to extract additional parallelism in many applications governed by evolutionary models, allowing for concurrency also along the temporal dimension. Consider as an example the analysis, the reconstruction and the denoising of ultrasound images arising from 2D/3D echocardiography [2,18,24]. In the European Exascale Software Initiative (EESI) 2014 roadmap, PINT approaches are recommended to the end of developing efficient applications for Exascale computing, thus taking a significant step beyond "traditional" HPC. On the other side, the deployment of application codes by means of scientific libraries, such as PETSc (the Portable, Extensible Toolkit for Scientific computing) [1], can be considered as a good investment [2] to maximize the availability of PinT algorithms for scientific applications.

G. Mencagli et al. (Eds.): Euro-Par 2018 Workshops, LNCS 11339, pp. 716–728, 2019.
https://doi.org/10.1007/978-3-030-10549-5_56

Recent advances in PETSc regarded the improvement of multilevel, multidomain and multiphysics algorithms. The most relevant capabilities allow users to test different solvers (linear, nonlinear, and time stepping) for their complex simulations, without making premature choices about algorithms and data structures [1]. Neverthless, PETSc does not provide any parallel-in-time support.

The MultiGrid-In-Time (MGRIT) algorithm is a PINT approach based on Multigrid Reduction (MGR) techniques [3]. Although we know that it is implemented in the software package XBraid [4], we are developing a modular multilevel parallel implementation [5] based on PETSc. The main goal of our approach is to provide a model predicting the performance gain achievable using the MGRIT approach instead of a timemarching integrator, independently of wheather parallelism in the space dimension is introduced or not. The performance model in [7], instead, aims to selecting the best parallel configuration (i.e. how much parallelism is to be devoteted to space vs. time). Therefore, we analyze the performance parameters of the algorithm in the mathematical framework presented in other works by the same authors [8]. We intentionally overlook spacial parallelism. In this way we describe the performance improvement regardless of the execution time needed to implement the characteristic function of the problem. We believe that both performance models could be employed for the successful implementation of the MGRIT algorithm [9].

In the second section we describe the basic idea of the algorithm to be implemented, summarizing the main results described in other works [3,7,10,11]. In the third section we briefly define the tools of the performance evaluation framework we need. In the fourth one we give some details about the PETSc implementation of MGRIT and write a performance model to describe the expected performance gain, depending mainly on the number of processors, the number of time-discretization points and of grids levels. Finally, in the last section we introduce what we are currently working on and what are the next planned steps.

2 MGRIT Algorithm. Basic Idea

The basic idea of MGRIT comes from the two-grid formulation of the Parareal method [11] for solving an Ordinary Differential Equation (ODE) and its discretization

$$u_t = f(u,t), \text{ with } u(0) = u_0 \text{ and } t \in [0,T]. \tag{1}$$

$$u(t+\delta t) = \Phi(u(t), u(t+\delta t)) + g(t+\delta t). \tag{2}$$

where Φ is a linear (or nonlinear) operator that encapsulates the chosen time stepping solver, and g incorporates all solution independent terms. The application of Φ is either a matrix vector multiplication, e.g. forward Euler, or a spatial solver, e.g. backward Euler [13].

The MGRIT algorithm is detailed in several works [3,7,10,13]. Briefly, let $t_i = i\delta_t$, $i = 0,1,...,N$ be a discretization of $[0,T]$ with spacing $\delta_t = \frac{T}{N}$ (this mesh will be called F-grid), and $t_j = j\Delta T$, where $j = 0,1,...,N_\Delta$ with $N_\Delta = \frac{N}{m}$

and $m > 1$ (called C-grid). We rewrite the problem 2 on the F-grid, denoted as *Fine problem*:

$$A(u) = \begin{bmatrix} I & 0 & \cdots & 0 & 0 \\ -\Phi_0 & I & \cdots & 0 & 0 \\ 0 & -\Phi_1 & \cdots & 0 & 0 \\ \vdots & & & & \\ 0 & 0 & \cdots & -\Phi_{N-1} & I \end{bmatrix} \cdot \begin{bmatrix} u_0 \\ u_1 \\ \vdots \\ u_N \end{bmatrix} = \begin{bmatrix} g_0 \\ g_1 \\ \vdots \\ g_N \end{bmatrix} = g \tag{3}$$

that corresponds to a C-grid problem obtained by introducing the appropriate interpolation and restriction operators P and R (see definitions in [10] and description in [9]). Then the multigrid reduction approximates A_Δ by B_Δ which is based on a new coarse propagator $\Phi_{\Delta,i}$ arising from the re-discretization of problem 2 on the C-grid, and which is less expensive to evaluate. In this way we have to solve the so-called *Coarse problem*:

$$B_\Delta = \begin{bmatrix} I & 0 & \cdots & 0 & 0 \\ -\Phi_{\Delta,0} & I & \cdots & 0 & 0 \\ 0 & -\Phi_{\Delta,1} & \cdots & 0 & 0 \\ \vdots & & & & \\ 0 & 0 & \cdots & -\Phi_{\Delta,N-1} & I \end{bmatrix} \cdot \begin{bmatrix} u_{\Delta,0} \\ u_{\Delta,1} \\ \vdots \\ u_{\Delta,N} \end{bmatrix} = \begin{bmatrix} g_{\Delta,0} \\ g_{\Delta,0} \\ \vdots \\ g_{\Delta,0} \end{bmatrix} = g_\Delta \tag{4}$$

Let us assume that the model equations in (1) are linear so that the Φ_i are linear, and we let $\Phi_i \equiv \Phi$, $i = 1, 2, \ldots, N$. Then, Parareal can be derived as an approximate Schur-complement approach with F-relaxation (relaxation[1] applied on the so-called fine points, or F-points, that are the points on the F-grid and not also on the C-grid), i.e. a two-level multigrid method. Mainly MGRIT algorithm extends the Parareal approach on more grids. This means that it uses discretization, relaxation, restriction, and projection operators for each grid-level, according to different kinds of cycles. The key difference from Parareal relies on a new relaxation operator called the **FCF-relaxation**. In practice it is the application of the F-relaxation and the C-relaxation repeated one after another once or more times [7].

The MGRIT algorithm for solving the linear case, as detailed in [3], is listed in Algorithm 1.

where:

- l is the current level, $0 \leq l \leq L$ and $L$is the coarsest level,
- m_l is the coarsening step at each level l, with $m_0 = 1$, and δ_l is the discretization time step at each level l, where $\delta_l = \delta_{l-1} \cdot m_l$
- N_l is the number of time steps for each l, with $N_0 > N_1 > ... > N_L$ and A_l is the matrix at level l
- $u^{(l)}$ and $g^{(l)}$ are the solution and right hand side vectors at level l,

[1] *Relaxation* meaning the solution of (3) by using an iterative method (see [12] for details).

Algorithm 1. $\mathbf{MGRIT}(l)$ - Linear MGRIT algorithm at level l

if l is the coarsest level L **then**
  Solve the Coarse problem $A_L\mathbf{u}^{(L)} = \mathbf{g}^{(L)}$
else
  Apply FCF-relaxation to $A_l\mathbf{u}^{(l)} = \mathbf{g}^{(l)}$
  Compute and restrict residual using injection $\mathbf{g}^{(l+1)} = R_{Inj}(\mathbf{g}^{(l)} - A_l\mathbf{u}^{(l)})$
  Recursively call $\mathbf{MGRIT}(l+1)$ to solve on next level
  Correct using *ideal interpolation* $\mathbf{u}^{(l)} \leftarrow \mathbf{u}^{(l)} + P\mathbf{u}^{(l+1)}$
end if

- R_{Inj} is the restriction/injection operator from a level to the coarser one and P is the *ideal interpolation* (see [3]) corresponding to an injection from the coarser level to a finer one, followed by an F-relaxation with a zero right-hand side (see [13]).

3 Preliminary Concepts and Definitions

The increasing need for parallel and scalable software, ready to exploit the new exascale architectures, leads to the development of many performance models, mainly based on architecture features [19–23,26] or especially made for choosen algorithm classes [25,27–29]. The model we present here is mainly focused on the dependencies among the computational tasks of the algorithm and is meant to be as general as possible.

We start by giving the definition of *dependency relation* on a set.

Definition 1 (Dependency relation). *Let $\mathcal{E}$ be a set and let $\pi_{\mathcal{E}}$ be a strict partial order relation on $\mathcal{E}$ describing a* dependency relation *between the elements. We say that any element of $\mathcal{E}$, say A, depends on another element of $\mathcal{E}$, say B, if $A\pi_{\mathcal{E}}B$, and we write $A \leftarrow B$. If A and B do not depend on each other we write $A \not\leftarrow B$.*

Then, consider the set of all the computational problems Γ and any element $B_N \in \Gamma$ where N is the input data size, called the *problem size.* Any B_N can always be decomposed in at least one finite set of other computational problems, that we call *decomposition of* B_N. Given a decomposition in k subproblems B_{N_i}, called D_k, and, taking into account the dependencies among the subproblems, we build a *dependency matrix* $\mathcal{M}_{D_k}$ where in each row we essentially put subproblems independent of one another and dependent on those in the previous rows. Let us introduce the dependency relation π_{D_k} such that $B_{N_i}\pi_{D_k}B_{N_j}$ with $i \neq j$ if and only if the solution of B_{N_j} must be found before the one of B_{N_i}.

Definition 2 (Dependency Matrix). *Given the partially ordered set (D_k, π_{D_k}), the matrix M_{D_k}, of size $r_{D_k} \times c_{D_k}$, whose elements $d_{i,j}$, are s.t. $\forall i \in [0, r_{D_k} - 1]$ and $\forall s, j \in [0, c_{D_k} - 1]$ it is $d_{i,j} \not\leftrightarrow d_{i,s}$ and s.t. $\forall i \in [1, r_{D_k} - 1]$ $\exists q \in [0, c_{D_k} - 1]$ s.t. $d_{i,j} \leftarrow d_{i-1,q}$ $\forall j \in [0, c_{D_k} - 1]$, while the other elements are set equal to zero, is called the dependency matrix.*

Given D_k, c_{D_k} is the *concurrency degree* of B_N, and r_{D_k} is the *dependency degree* of B_N, according to the actual decomposition, so that the dependency degree measures the amount of dependencies intrinsic to the chosen decomposition. The number and size of sub-problems a problem is decomposed into determine the granularity of the decomposition. Granularity has a major consequence in the level of detail required for an algorithm to be analysed with this approach.

The decomposition matrix allows us to identify some properties of the algorithm design, such as the concurrency available in a problem when we choose a decomposition rather than another. So the first question must be about how to decompose the problem. That is pretty obvious, but it can lead to algorithm characteristics that we want to emphasize and possibly exploit.

At this point we define the Scale up, using the cardinality of two decompositions.

Definition 3 (Scale Up). *Let us consider the following two decomposition D_{k_i} and D_{k_j} of B_N, with cardinalities $k_j \neq k_i$, the ratio $SC(D_{k_i}, D_{k_j}) := \frac{k_i}{k_j}$ is called scale-up factor of D_{k_j} measured with respect to D_{k_i}.*

The next step is to assign the identified subproblems to the computing machine. First we introduce the machine $\mathcal{M}_P$ equipped with $P \geq 1$ processing elements with specific logical-operational capabilities[2] called computing operators of $\mathcal{M}_P$, and denoted by the function[3] $I[\cdot] : B_N \in \Gamma \longrightarrow S(B_N) \in S$ where S is the set of the solutions of all the problems in Γ and $S(B_N)$ is the solution of B_N. Given $\mathcal{M}_P$, the set without repetitions $Cop_{\mathcal{M}_P} = \{I^j\}_{j \in [0,q-1]}$, where $q \in \mathbb{N}$, characterizes logical-operational capabilities of the machine $\mathcal{M}_P$.

Definition 4 (Algorithm). *Given the problem decomposition D_k, an algorithm solving B_N on $\mathcal{M}_P$, is the partially ordered set $(A_{k,P}, \pi_{A_{k,P}})$, with not necessarily distinct elements, where $A_{k,P} = \{I^{i_0}, I^{i_1}, ... I^{i_k}\}$ such that $I^{i_j} \in Cop_{\mathcal{M}_P}$ and*

$$\forall B_{N_\nu} \in D_k(B_N) \quad \exists! I^{i_j} \in A_{k,P} : I^{i_j}[B_{N_\nu}] = S(B_{N_\nu}). \tag{5}$$

There is a bijective correspondence $\gamma : B_{N_\nu} \in D_k \longleftrightarrow I^{i_j} \in A_{k,P}$. Every ordered subset of $A_{k,P}$ is called sub-algorithm *of $A_{k,P}$.*

By virtue of the property 5, operators of $A_{k,P}$ inherit the dependencies existing between subproblems in D_k, but not the independencies, because, for example, two operators may depend on the availability of computing units of $\mathcal{M}_P$ during their executions [6].

Let AL_{B_N} (or simply AL) be the set of algorithms that solve B_N, obtained by varying $\mathcal{M}_P$, P and D_k. Let us associate each algorithm of AL to a decomposition suited for $\mathcal{M}_P$, which means that we introduce the surjective correspondence

[2] Such as basic operations (arithmetic,...), special functions evaluations (sin, cos, ...), solvers (integrals, equations system, non linear equations...).

[3] An operator can be an algorithm itself, from a finer granularity point of view.

$\psi : A_{k,P} \in AL \longrightarrow D_k$, which induces an equivalence relationship ϱ of AL to itself, such that

$$\varrho(A_{k,P}) = \{\widetilde{A_{k,P}} \in AL : \psi(\widetilde{A_{k,P}}) = \psi(A_{k,P})\}. \tag{6}$$

Therefore, $\varrho(A_{k,P})$ is the set of algorithms of AL associated with the same decomposition D_k[4]. Hence, ϱ induces the quotient set $\frac{AL}{\varrho}$, the elements of which are disjoint subsets of AL determined by ϱ, that is they are *equivalence classes* under ϱ. In the following we consider $A_{k,P}$ as a representative of its equivalence class in AL.

Definition 5 (Complexity). *The cardinality of $A_{k,P}$ is called complexity of $A_{k,P}$. It is denoted as $C(A_{k,P})$. That is $C(A_{k,P}) := card(A_{k,P}) = k$.*

Notice that, by virtue of the property 5, it holds that

$$card(A_{k,P}) = card(D_k(\mathcal{B}_{N_r})) = k, \quad \forall\, A_{k,P} \in \varrho(A_{k,P}). \tag{7}$$

and so $C(A_{k,P}) = k$ equals the number of non empty elements of M_{D_k} (see Definition 2). This means that each algorithm belonging to the same equivalence class according to ϱ has the same complexity. Thus an integer (the complexity) is associated with each element $\varrho(A_{k,P})$ of quotient set $\frac{AL}{\varrho}$ and induces an ordering relation between the equivalence classes in $\frac{AL}{\varrho}$. Therefore there is a minimum complexity for algorithms that solve the problem $\mathcal{B}_{N_r}$.

Let us better define the order relation on the algorithm set, as a second dependency relation $\pi_{A_{k,P}}$ such that $I^{i_j}\pi_{A_{k,P}}I^{i_r}$ with $j \neq r$ if and only if I^{i_j} solves a subproblem dependent on the one solved by I^{i_r}, and/or the execution of I^{i_j} needs to wait for the execution of I^{i_r} to use the same computing resource.

Definition 6 (Execution matrix). *Given the partially ordered set $(A_{k,P}, \pi_{A_{k,P}})$, the matrix $\mathcal{E}_{k,P}$, of size $r_{\mathcal{E}_{k,P}} \times c_{\mathcal{E}_{k,P}}$, with*[5] *$c_{\mathcal{E}_{k,P}} = P$, whose elements $e_{i,j}$, are s.t. $\forall i \in [0, r_{\mathcal{E}_{k,P}} - 1]$ and $\forall s,\, j \in [0, P-1]$ it is $e_{i,j} \not\leftrightarrow e_{i,s}$ and s.t. $\forall i \in [1, r_{\mathcal{E}_{k,P}} - 1] \quad \exists q \in [0, P-1]$ s.t. $e_{i,j} \leftarrow e_{i-1,q} \quad \forall j \in [0, P-1]$, while the other elements are set equal to zero, is called the execution matrix.*

Inside an equivalency class, the algorithm solving a problem according to a decomposition that is executed on a machine with just one processor is a *sequential algorithm* and its execution matrix has just one column, since $P = 1$. In general, the execution matrix size describes the *cost* of the algorithm. In case of empty spaces in the matrix, they represent the algorithm *overhead.*

The number of rows $r_{\mathcal{E}_{k,P}}$ is directly related to the execution time of the algorithm executed with that number P of processing units. Note that in order to compare two algorithms we must ensure that they are described by the same

---

[4] In this set the algorithms can have different value of P.

[5] In general $c_E \leq P$, but we can exclude cases where dependencies between subproblems do not allow us to use all the computing units available, i.e. in which $c_E < P$, because they can easily be taken back to the case where $c_E = P$.

kind of operators, or with the same granularity. In particular, if all the operators have the same execution time t, the *algorithm execution time* is proportional to $r_{\mathcal{E}_{k,P}}$ and the *Speed Up* can be defined for an algorithm, in its equivalency class, as the ratio between its complexity and the number of rows. More specifically, if $A_{k,P}$ is an algorithm built according to the decomposition D_k and executed on a machine with P processing units, we give the following definitions

Definition 7 (Execution time). *The quantity* $T(A_{k,P}) := r_{\mathcal{E}_{k,P}} \cdot t$ *is called execution time of* $A_{k,P}$.

Definition 8 (Speed Up). *Given the algorithms* $A_{k,P}$ *executed with* P *computing units the ratio* $S(A_{k,P}) := \frac{C(A_{k,P})}{r_{\mathcal{E}_{k,P}}}$ *is called Speed Up of* $A_{k,P}$ *in its equivalency class.*

This rewrites the classical speed up formula, so we can say that the ideal value is P, and we can also show that, varying P, it is limited by the concurrency degree of the problem in the same decomposition.

Briefly, given two different decompositions D_{k_i} and D_{k_j}, with $k_j \neq k_i$, given two different machines with two different number of processors $P_1 = 1$ and $P > 1$, for the two corresponding algorithms we define the *General Speed Up* of the parallel one respect to the sequential one, as the product of the *Scale Up* between the two decompositions and the classical speed up of the parallel one.

Definition 9 (General Speed Up). *The ratio*

$$GS(A_{k_j,P}, A_{k_i,1}) := SC(D_{k_i}, D_{k_j}) \cdot S(A_{k_j,P}) = \frac{k_i}{k_j} \cdot \frac{k_j}{r_{\mathcal{E}_{A_{k_j},P}}} = \frac{r_{\mathcal{E}_{A_{k_i},1}}}{r_{\mathcal{E}_{A_{k_j},P}}}$$

is called General Speed Up of $A_{k_j,P}$ *respect to* $A_{k_i,1}$.

Note that the ideal value of the General Speed Up is not limited by the number of processing units P.

4 The PETSc Based Implementation of MGRIT for the Linear Case

At the top of the PETSc hierarchy there are the object to solve ODEs and nonlinear systems, built on other objects needed to solve linear systems. In particular, the TS (TimeStepping) library provides a framework to solve ODEs and DAEs arising from the discretization of time-dependent PDEs. Users shall essentially provide the F function, the G function (if nonzero), the initial condition and the Jacobian.

We are now developing a kind of "parallel TS", based on MGRIT, to be compared with the already provided sequential ones. The idea is to "simply" solve the linear system using a linear solver with a multigrid preconditioner.

The first step of the implementation is to provide the data structure to handle the time dimension together with the space ones, in the context of the PETSc

DM or Distributed objects. This means (1) to provide the basic operations for the new type, (2) to handle the coarsening factor, and (3) to provide the user interface to the function which describes the way of operating for Φ, that is the spacial solver, and the time discretization calls.

Everything about the coarsening of the grids along the levels, the distribution of the points among the processes and the communications is handled by the PETSc DA (DistributedArray) object linked to the solvers in a fully transparent fashion. Users can tune the behavior of the solver and thus the actual structure of the scheme through the option setting (including tolerance and initial guess for all the operators involved) at runtime.

The second step is the implementation of F- and C-relaxations that must be set as down and up smoothers of the multigrid scheme, tunable (even at runtime) by the user to fit his/her own problem, according to the PETSc design. Users will still control all the parameters and solver choices even at runtime.

4.1 The Performance Model

First, we notice that the application of Φ is the dominant task. In case of explicit time stepping each application of Φ corresponds to a matrix-vector product, whose execution time will be constant. In case of implicit time stepping, each application of Φ equates itself to a system solver. Using an optimal space solver and fixing the stopping tolerance or the number of iterations and the initial guess choice for the spacial solver, the work required for one time step evaluation can be considered constant across all time levels (and associated time step sizes)[6] [10].

Let $\Phi_{i,j}$ be the subproblem of evaluating the function Φ at any instant $u_{\delta_i,j}$, with $i = 0, ...L$ and $j = 1, ...N_l$, and $\phi_{i,j}$ the operator to solve it. Notice that there is no evaluation at the first instant of each grid.

Let $N_{F_l} := N_l - N_{l+1}$ be the number of F-points and N_{l+1} be the number of C-points at each level l of MGRIT algorithm. The relation between the number of F-points and C-points depends on the coarsening factor m that can be the same for all levels or possibly different for each one. In Algorithm 1, we note that if L is the coarsest level, and the solver of the system on the coarsest-grid is sequential, this will involve at least one ϕ-execution for each time step on the L-th grid. It means that if L is the coarsest level there are N_L executions of ϕ. Otherwise, for each level $l < L$,

- the FCF-relaxation involves N_{F_l} F-relaxation steps (or ϕ-executions), which can be performed in parallel, N_{l+1} C-relaxation steps (or ϕ-executions), which can be performed in parallel, F-relaxation steps (or ϕ-executions), which can be performed in parallel,
- computing the residual requires one ϕ-execution for each time step on the $(l+1)$-th grid, that is N_{l+1}, which can be performed in parallel,

[6] For the sake of brevity we discuss here the execution of only one V-Cycle, as described in Algorithm 1. The number of iterations of the multigrid cycles can be considered later.

- the ideal interpolation requires N_{F_l} F-relaxation steps (or ϕ-executions), which can be performed in parallel.

Let us now define the *dependency matrix* $\mathcal{M}_D$ (see Definition 2 in Sect. 3) of the time-space problem to be solved, according to its decomposition in the space subproblems $\Phi_{i,j}$, for $i = 0, \dots, L$ and $j = 1, \dots, Np$ where $Np \in \{N_{F_l}, N_{l+1}, N_L\}$ and where in each row we essentially put subproblems independent of one another and dependent on those in the previous rows (the $\mathcal{M}_D$ matrix is well described in [9]).

The *concurrency degree* of the problem decomposed in this way is c_D, i.e. the maximum number of simultaneous Φ evaluations. Since $N_{F_l} > N_{l+1}$ and $N_{F_l} > N_{F_{l+1}}$, which means that the number of F-points at any level is greater than the number of C-points at the same level and greater than the F-points at the next level, $c_D = N_{F_0}$.

The *dependency degree* is $r_D = 5 \cdot L + N_L$, since, with L+1 levels, we have (1) 3 rows for each FCF-relaxation, that means $3 \cdot L$ rows, (2) 1 row for each residual computation, that means L rows, which are the longest rows in the matrix, or with the largest numbers of columns, (3) N_L rows for the coarsest-grid solver, (4) 1 row for each ideal interpolation (F-relaxation), that means L rows.

Consider now a computing architecture with P processing elements, where $P = \frac{c_D}{np}$ (this condition states that the points on the finest grid are equally distributed among the processors, that is c_D is a multiple of P) and $np \in \mathbf{N}$ and $P <= N_L$ (this condition states that on the coarsest grid each processor holds at least one point).

We can define the *execution matrix* $\mathcal{E}_P$ of MGRIT (see Definition 6, in Sect. 3), consisting of the operators $\phi_{i,k \cdot P+j}$, with $i = 0, \dots, L$ and $j = 1, ...P$ and $k = 1, \dots, \frac{N_{F_L}}{P}$ for F-relaxation or $k = 1, \dots, \frac{N_{l+1}}{P}$ for C-relaxation and residual computation, considering that, for each level, the number of points of the grid is a multiple of P[7] (the $\mathcal{E}_P$ matrix is well described in [9]).

Consider now the algorithm $A_{N_0,1}$, which solves (2) with the same discretization in time on the finest grid (same initial guess and same tolerance) but without introducing MGR or any parallelism, that means using a sequential time-stepping approach with the same discretization techniques and parameters as used by MGRIT on the finest grid. $A_{N_0,1}$ is made of N_0 executions of ϕ, leading to the execution matrix $\mathcal{E}_1$ with one column and N_0 rows (the $\mathcal{E}_1$ matrix is well described in [9]).

[7] This is without loss of generality, as, otherwise, the number of rows is still the same but with just some empty elements.

We can prove the following (proof in [9]):

Theorem 1. *Let us assume that MGRIT algorithm runs on a computing architecture with* $P <= N_L$ *processing elements, where* $P = \frac{N_0}{np}$ *and* $np \in \mathbf{N}$. *Let* t_ϕ *be the execution time of* ϕ, $\forall l \in [0, L]$.
Let us say that it reaches the same accuracy as $A_{N_0,1}$ *in* ν *iterations. Then the general speed-up* $GS(MGRIT_{N_{MGRIT},P}, A_{N_0,1})$ *of MGRIT with respect to* $A_{N_0,1}$ *is*

$$GS(MGRIT_{N_{MGRIT},P}, A_{N_0,1}) = \frac{N_0}{\nu \cdot \left(\sum_{l=0}^{L-1}\left(3 \cdot \frac{N_{F_l}}{P} + 2 \cdot \frac{N_{l+1}}{P}\right) + N_L\right)} \quad (8)$$

5 Conclusions and Future Work

Summarizing, we introduced a mathematical framework to propose a speed-up model for our implementation of MGRIT algorithm. It describes the impact of several factors (i.e. the number of time steps and the number of processors) on the dependencies among operators and thus on the algorithm performance, regardless of the execution of ϕ. Any choice related to its implementation affects the unit time t_ϕ and/or the numerical accuracy of the results. The required accuracy will limit one or more parameters in a way that is beyond the scope of this paper. If Φ is nonlinear, each application becomes an iterative nonlinear solver, whose conditioning usually depends on the time step size [13].

The main topics we are now focusing on are the following:

- definition of a *memory access matrix* to take into account the communications that can significantly affect the *software speed up* limiting the number of processing elements and grid levels to be used,
- parallel implementation of Φ, to handle different levels of parallelism, exploiting the capabilities of heterogeneous architectures, such as multicore clusters and GPUs, to efficiently treat the parallelism in the spacial dimension [14–17],
- validation of all the results arising from this designing approach through the execution of the resulting software prototype on a suited set of problems. The validation activities should provide the PETSc users with the needed guidelines to efficiently use the new TS object to solve their problems.

Acknowledgments. The research was carried out during a collaboration between the University of Naples Federico II (Naples, Italy) and the Argonne National Laboratory (Chicago, Illinois, USA).

It has received funding from European Commission under H2020-MSCA-RISE NASDAC project (grant agreement n. 691184).

This work was also supported by GNCS INdAM.

References

1. Balay, S., et al.: Petsc User Manual. Revision 3.7 Report number ANL-95/11 Rev. 3.7 127241, United States: N. p., 2016. Web (2016). https://doi.org/10.2172/1255238
2. Murli, A., Boccia, V., Carracciuolo, L., D'Amore, L., Laccetti, G., Lapegna, M.: Monitoring and migration of a PETSc-based parallel application for medical imaging in a grid computing PSE. In: Gaffney, P.W., Pool, J.C.T. (eds.) Grid-Based Problem Solving Environments. ITIFIP, vol. 239, pp. 421–432. Springer, Boston, MA (2007). https://doi.org/10.1007/978-0-387-73659-4_25
3. Falgout, R.D., Friedhoff, S., Kolev, T.V., MacLachlan, S.P., Schroder, J.B.: Parallel time integration with multigrid. SIAM J. Sci. Comput. **36**(6), C635–C661 (2014). https://doi.org/10.1137/130944230
4. XBraid: Parallel multigrid in time. http://llnl.gov/casc/xbraid
5. Carracciuolo, L., D'Amore, L., Mele, V.: Toward a fully parallel multigrid in time algorithm in PETSc environment: a case study in ocean models. In: IEEE proceedings of International Conference on High Performance Computing & Simulation (HPCS) 2015, Amsterdam, pp. 595–598 (2015). https://doi.org/10.1109/HPCSim.2015.7237098
6. Tjaden, G.S., Flynn, M.J.: Detection and parallel execution of independent instruction. IEEE Trans. Comput. **19**(10), 889–895 (1970). https://doi.org/10.1109/T-C.1970.222795
7. Gahvari, H., et al.: A performance model for allocating the parallelism in a multigrid-in-time solver. In: Proceedings of 7th International Workshop on Performance Modeling, Benchmarking and Simulation of High Performance Computing Systems (PMBS), Salt Lake City, UT, 2016, art. no. 7836411, pp. 22–31. IEEE Press (2017). https://doi.org/10.1109/PMBS.2016.008
8. D'Amore, L., Mele, V., Laccetti, G., Murli, A.: Mathematical approach to the performance evaluation of matrix multiply algorithm. In: Wyrzykowski, R., Deelman, E., Dongarra, J., Karczewski, K., Kitowski, J., Wiatr, K. (eds.) PPAM 2015. LNCS, vol. 9574, pp. 25–34. Springer, Cham (2016). https://doi.org/10.1007/978-3-319-32152-3_3
9. Mele, V., Costantinescu, E.M., Carracciuolo, L., D'Amore, L.: A PETSc parallel-in-time solver based on MGRIT algorithm. Concurrency Comput.: Practice Exp. e4928 (2018). https://doi.org/10.1002/cpe.4928
10. Schroder, J.B., Falgout, R.D., Manteuffel, T.A., O'Neill, B.: Multigrid reduction in time for nonlinear parabolic problems: a case study. SIAM J. Sci. Comput. **39**(5), S298–S322 (2017)
11. Lions, J.L., Maday, Y., Turinici, G.: A parareal in time discretization of PDEs. Comptes Rendus de l'Academie des Sci. - Ser. I - Math. **332**, 661–668 (2001). https://doi.org/10.1016/S0764-4442(00)01793-6
12. Gander, M.J., Vandewalle, S.: Analysis of the parareal time-parallel time-integration method. SIAM J. Sci. Comput. **29**, 556–578 (2007). https://doi.org/10.1137/05064607X
13. Falgout, R.D., Friedhoff, S., Kolev, T.V., MacLachlan, S.P., Schroder, J.B., Vandewalle, S.: Multigrid methods with space-time concurrency. SIAM J. Sci. Comput. (2015). https://doi.org/10.1007/s00791-017-0283-9
14. Cuomo, S., De Michele, P., Piccialli, F.: 3D data denoising via nonlocal means filter by using parallel GPU strategies. Comput. Math. Methods Med. **2014**, 14 (2014). https://doi.org/10.1155/2014/523862. Article ID 523862

15. Cuomo, S., De Michele, P., Piccialli, F.: A (multi) GPU iterative reconstruction algorithm based on Hessian penalty term for sparse MRI. Int. J. Grid Utility Comput. **9**(2), 139–156 (2018). https://doi.org/10.1504/IJGUC.2018.091720
16. Piccialli, F., Cuomo, S., De Michele, P.: A regularized MRI image reconstruction based on Hessian penalty term on CPU/GPU systems. Procedia Comput. Sci. **18**, 2643–2646 (2013). https://doi.org/10.1016/j.procs.2013.06.001. ISSN 1877–0509
17. D'Amore, L., Marcellino, L., Mele, V., Romano, D.: Deconvolution of 3D fluorescence microscopy images using graphics processing units. In: Wyrzykowski, R., Dongarra, J., Karczewski, K., Waśniewski, J. (eds.) PPAM 2011. LNCS, vol. 7203, pp. 690–699. Springer, Heidelberg (2012). https://doi.org/10.1007/978-3-642-31464-3_70
18. Maddalena, L., Petrosino, A., Laccetti, G.: A fusion-based approach to digital movie restoration. Pattern Recogn. **42**(7), 1485–1495 (2009)
19. Gregoretti, F., Laccetti, G., Murli, A., Oliva, G., Scafuri, U.: MGF: a grid-enabled MPI library. Future Gen. Comput. Syst. **24**(2), 158–165 (2008)
20. Laccetti, G., Lapegna, M., Mele, V., Romano, D., Murli, A.: A double adaptive algorithm for multidimensional integration on multicore based HPC systems. Int. J. Parallel Program. **40**(4), 397–409 (2012). https://doi.org/10.1007/s10766-011-0191-4
21. Laccetti, G., Lapegna, M., Mele, V., Romano, D.: A study on adaptive algorithms for numerical quadrature on heterogeneous GPU and multicore based systems. In: Wyrzykowski, R., Dongarra, J., Karczewski, K., Waśniewski, J. (eds.) PPAM 2013. LNCS, vol. 8384, pp. 704–713. Springer, Heidelberg (2014). https://doi.org/10.1007/978-3-642-55224-3_66
22. Laccetti, G., Lapegna, M., Mele, V., Montella, R.: An adaptive algorithm for high-dimensional integrals on heterogeneous CPU-GPU systems. Concurrency Comput.: Practice Exp. **2018**, e4945 (2018). https://doi.org/10.1002/cpe.4945
23. Laccetti, G., Lapegna, M., Mele, V.: A loosely coordinated model for heap-based priority queues in multicore environments. Int. J. Parallel Program. **44**(4), 901–921 (2016). https://doi.org/10.1007/s10766-015-0398-x
24. D'Amore, L., Casaburi, D., Galletti, A., Marcellino, L., Murli, A.: Integration of emerging computer technologies for an efficient image sequences analysis. Integr. Comput.-Aided Eng. **18**(4), 365–378 (2011). https://doi.org/10.3233/ICA-2011-0382
25. Arcucci, R., D'Amore, L., Celestino, S., Laccetti, G., Murli, A.: A scalable numerical algorithm for solving Tikhonov regularization problems. In: Wyrzykowski, R., Deelman, E., Dongarra, J., Karczewski, K., Kitowski, J., Wiatr, K. (eds.) PPAM 2015. LNCS, vol. 9574, pp. 45–54. Springer, Cham (2016). https://doi.org/10.1007/978-3-319-32152-3_5
26. Boccia, V., Carracciuolo, L., Laccetti, G., Lapegna, M., Mele, V.: HADAB: enabling fault tolerance in parallel applications running in distributed environments. In: Wyrzykowski, R., Dongarra, J., Karczewski, K., Waśniewski, J. (eds.) PPAM 2011. LNCS, vol. 7203, pp. 700–709. Springer, Heidelberg (2012). https://doi.org/10.1007/978-3-642-31464-3_71
27. Murli, A., Cuomo, S., D'Amore, L., Galletti, A.: Numerical regularization of a real inversion formula based on the Laplace transform's eigen function expansion of the inverse function. Inverse Probl. **23**(2), 713 (2007)

28. D'Amore, L., Campagna, R., Mele, V., Murli, A., Rizzardi, M.: ReLaTIve. An Ansi C90 software package for the real Laplace transform inversion. Numer. Algorithms **63**(1), 187–211 (2013). https://doi.org/10.1007/s11075-012-9636-0
29. Murli, A., D'Amore, L., Laccetti, G., Gregoretti, F., Oliva, G.: A multi-grained distributed implementation of the parallel Block Conjugate Gradient algorithm. Concurrency Comput. Practice Exp. **22**(15), 2053–2072 (2010). https://doi.org/10.1002/cpe.1548

RePara - Workshop on Reengineering for Parallelism in Heterogeneous Parallel Platforms

Workshop on Reengineering for Parallelism in Heterogeneous Parallel Platforms (RePara)

Workshop Description

The RePara workshop aims to join experts from related disciplines to share recent advances in different areas contributing to better transformation of new and legacy applications to different programming models for diverse computing devices in the context of parallel heterogeneous architectures.

One of the approaches to keep satisfying the increasing demand for computing power, is the use of heterogeneous highly parallel architectures combining different kinds of processors (CPUs, GPUs, DSPs, FPGAs, and other accelerators). While this approach has allowed significant performance and energy efficiency benefits, heterogeneous systems are often highly difficult to program with existing tools. To reduce the cost of system development, refactoring and reengineering techniques emerge as a solution which may help to balance ease-of-development with better performance, better reliability, and lower maintenance costs.

The RePara workshop was born in 2015 as a forum to foster exchange of ideas in the area of Reengineering software for parallel platforms with a special focus on parallelism. This has been the fourth edition of the workshop. Previous editions were held in Helsinki, Finland (co-located with IEEE ISPA 2015), Toulouse, France (co-located with IEEE ScalCom 2016), and Bologna, Italy (co-located with ParCo 2017).

This year the workshop consisted of one invited talk accompanied by technical presentations. The workshop was very well attended (around 30 participants) and each presentation was followed by participation of the audience interacting with presenters.

We received a total of 7 articles for review from 7 different countries. After a comprenhensive review process we selected 4 papers for oral presentation at the workshop. The review process focused on scientific advancement and technical quality of papers. Every paper was reviewed by at least 4 different members of the program committee. Final decisions were taken by consensus after additional discussions by the program committee.

We would like to thank all authors for submitting their work to the workshop. We would also like to express our gratitude to all PC members for their efforts during the review process and the high quality of their reviews. Finally, but not least, we are very grateful to EuroPara workshops chairs, Dora B. Heras and Gabriele Mencagli, for their very hard work and excellent support helping us to make RePara 2018 a reality.

Organization

Program Chairs

J. Daniel Garcia	University Carlos III of Madrid, Spain
Marco Danelutto	University of Pisa, Italy

Program Committee

Marco Aldinucci	University of Torino, Italy
Rafael Asenjo	University of Málaga, Spain
Jesús Carretero	University Carlos III of Madrid, Spain
Rudolf Ferenc	University of Szeged, Hungary
Fracisco Javier García-Blas	University Carlos III of Madrid, Spain
María Angeles González	University of Málaga, Spain
Sergei Gorlatch	University of Münster, Germany
Cristoph Kessler	University of Linköping, Sweden
Andreas Koch	University of Darmstadt, Germany
Jürgen Mottok	OTH Regensburg, Germany
Marc Reichenbach	Friedrich-Alexander Universität Erlangen-Nürnberg, Germany
Lutz Schubert	University of Ulm, Germany
Massimo Torquati	University of Pisa, Italy
John Wickerson	Imperial College, UK

Programmable HSA Accelerators for Zynq UltraScale+ MPSoC Systems

Wolfgang Bauer[1(✉)], Philipp Holzinger[1], Marc Reichenbach[1], Steffen Vaas[1], Paul Hartke[2], and Dietmar Fey[1]

[1] Department of Computer Science, Chair of Computer Architecture, Friedrich-Alexander-University Erlangen-Nürnberg (FAU), Martensstraße 3, 91058 Erlangen, Germany
{WolfgangM.Bauer,Philipp.Holzinger,Marc.Reichenbach, Steffen.Vaas,Dietmar.Fey}@fau.de

[2] Xilinx, Inc., 2100 Logic Drive, San Jose, CA 95124-3400, USA
phartke@xilinx.com

Abstract. Modern algorithms for virtual reality, machine learning or big data find its way into more and more application fields and result in stricter power per watt requirements. This challenges traditional homogeneous computing concepts and drives the development of new, heterogeneous architectures. One idea to attain a balance of high data throughput and flexibility are GPU-like soft-core processors combined with general purpose CPUs as hosts. However, the approaches proposed in recent years are still not sufficient regarding their integration in a shared hardware environment and unified software stack. The approach of the *HSA Foundation* provides a complete communication definition for heterogeneous systems but lacks FPGA accelerator support. Our work presents a methodology making soft-core processors HSA compliant within MPSoC systems. This enables high level software programming and therefore eases the accessibility of soft-core FPGA accelerators. Furthermore, the integration effort is kept low by fully utilizing the *HSA Foundation* standards and toolchains.

Keywords: Heterogeneous system architecture · FPGA
Programmable accelerator · HSA foundation · Zynq ultrascale+
Nyuzi processor

1 Introduction

Modern computing applications keep growing requirements in terms of execution time and power consumption. This development can be observed for high-performance computing, desktop environments, as well as in embedded systems. However, the upcoming end of Moore's law limits the prospects of traditional CPU centered computing. In the future these requirements can only be satisfied by increasingly heterogeneous systems. Such environments exploit the benefits of

G. Mencagli et al. (Eds.): Euro-Par 2018 Workshops, LNCS 11339, pp. 733–744, 2019.
https://doi.org/10.1007/978-3-030-10549-5_57

CPUs, GPUs, DSPs and FPGAs by executing each task on the best suited. This way heterogeneous systems can be designed combining different architectures in order to attain the highest energy efficiency. For embedded systems this concept can be further extended by integrating all cores on a single die.

Contrary to all benefits of heterogeneous architectures, software development is getting more and more complex with the rising amount of different parts. Therefore, various programming models and language extensions, like CUDA, OpenCL or OpenMP, have been introduced to reduce the programming complexity by abstracting architecture specific properties. Some of them also hide data communication between different hardware units. However, most of the existing standards are either proprietary or lack exact definitions regarding communication from a hardware point of view. To close this gap the Heterogeneous System Architecture Foundation (HSA Foundation[1]) specified a low-level programming model and system software infrastructure to support heterogeneous computing architectures [10]. This facilitates the extension of new HSA compliant acceleration devices to existing systems without any changes to the application source code.

HSA Foundation standards are already established in the desktop computers from AMD and their graphics cards [3,12]. Recent embedded devices, such as smartphones, also incorporate HSA compliant chips [14]. Unfortunately, FPGAs which are a good choice for heterogeneous systems due to their high peak performance and low power consumption, are currently not fully supported. Due to their highly flexible nature, finding a mapping is significantly more complex and needs to be further investigated. This means up to now, new, emerging SoC architectures e.g. from Xilinx or Altera, which contain processor cores and an FPGA part, could not benefit from HSA Foundation standards. This limits the flexibility of these powerful embedded devices. Therefore, in this paper we show a new methodology to make SoCs, containing a CPU and FPGA part, HSA compliant. Due to the interface's open definition between software runtime and hardware the HSA environment is ideally suitable handling the FPGA's communication to other components in heterogeneous systems.

To demonstrate our concept, we chose a Xilinx SoC containing an ARM application processor deployed as controlling host unit and a FPGA part as hardware accelerator. Traditionally, such FPGA based hardware accelerators are described with custom HDL code, which makes the accessibility of FPGA accelerators rather low. Therefore, to preserve the flexibility and to avoid language restrictions, we use in this paper highly configurable and customizable soft-core accelerators, to unite flexibility and pragmatism of FPGAs. Those cores enable the execution of multiple application tasks without the need of resynthesis and reloading, but can also be adapted for the application, e.g. by adding custom instruction units.

This paper is structured as follows: First, competing concepts and similar approaches are evaluated in Sect. 2. Afterwards in Sect. 3 the used hardware platform, the necessary fundamentals of the HSA Foundation standards and

[1] http://www.hsafoundation.com.

the architecture of the selected GPU like soft-core are explained. Then Sect. 4 describes the derived hardware setup and software toolchain. The detailed results are presented in Sect. 5. Lastly Sect. 6 summarizes the paper and briefly covers possibilities for future work.

2 Related Work

The most promising alternative to programmable soft-core GPUs for using an FPGA from a common language is high-level synthesis (HLS). However, instead of compiling to an accelerator's instruction set architecture (ISA), the functionality of the kernel itself is mapped to an application-specific hardware circuit. While in its simplest form only the kernel itself is translated to HDL [17], there exist more sophisticated solutions generating the hardware connection as well as software interfacing automatically. The most prominent ones are the commercial Xilinx SDAccel [16] and the Intel FPGA SDK for OpenCL [2]. Both are based on the vendor neutral and well known OpenCL standard to ease the usage for developers. An academic approach to HLS was for example done by LegUp [8]. It provides FPGA accessibility via *pthreads* or OpenMP [9], but also tries to get a step further by automatically determining and offloading frequently used code sections. While this process usually leads to better results than code execution on a soft-core processor, it has major drawbacks. Since each kernel can only execute a specific program, the time-consuming synthesis and FPGA reconfiguration has to be done anew for each kernel in the application. Therefore, a more flexible approach based on soft-core accelerators is advantageous.

Further approaches rely on application-specific instruction set processors (ASIP). The ISA of those cores is optimized for a certain application-field. For example in [15] an ASIP for power quality monitoring was developed. In comparison to hard-wired solutions ASIPs require a slight resource overhead and provide slightly less performance, but offer programming flexibility without resynthesis as big benefit. This strategy works well for processing intense tasks, but in times of Internet-of-Things even more flexibility is necessary to realize communication protocols like for example OPC UA or TCP/IP. Thus, a combined system-on-a-chip architecture consisting of multiple general-purpose embedded CPU- and accelerator cores (MPSoC) is required, to obtain a low-power solution at sufficient performance and flexibility. Nevertheless, the performance enhancement of ASIPs can only be exploited when using their rather complex instructions, like FFT- or mean value calculations. Current compilers are incapable to map standard source code to those specific instructions, so developers have to use architecture-specific functions to benefit from such architectures. That practice cumbers the flexible source-code portability from and to other architectures.

While many open source processors like LEON3[2], OpenRISC[3], Amber ARM-compatible core[4] and various RISC-V[5] implementations are available for scalar

[2] http://www.gaisler.com.

[3] https://openrisc.io.

[4] https://opencores.org/project/amber.

[5] https://riscv.org.

data processing, the variety for soft-core GPU architectures is more reduced. Al-Dujaili et al. extended the mentioned LEON3 processor by adding parallelization and synchronization features to support the CUDA execution model with their Guppy GPU-like soft-core processor [1]. An other approach is pursued by the FlexGrip project [4] and the MIAOW project [5]. The developed architectures are based on proprietary Nvidia or AMD GPUs and modeled according to available information. Due to ISA compatibility the existing vendor toolchains can be used for code generation.

Al Kadi et al. proposed the FGPU [11] with a MIPS-based ISA, which is extended by further vector-processing instructions to execute OpenCL kernels. It provides hardware support for scheduling work items to multiple computing units conveniently to the SIMT programming model and includes an LLVM-backend. In contrast to this the Nyami [6], or later Nyuzi [7], presented by Jeff Bush et al. uses a more general purpose architecture utilizing wide vector registers with predicated execution vicarious to the Intel Xeon Phi architecture. It also uses its own ISA similar to MIPS-ISA and, besides integer arithmetic, floating point operations are supported as well. Due to the LLVM-backend many languages providing LLVM-frontends can be translated to the processor's ISA.

The selection of available source languages is currently quite limited for all these approaches and there is little freedom of choice. A common low-level standard like the HSA specifications can reduce the time to develop language frontends and diversify the existing solutions.

3 Fundamentals

3.1 MPSoC Platform

The Xilinx Zynq UltraScale+ MPSoC integrates a quad-core ARM Cortex-A53 MPCore based processing system (PS) and Xilinx programmable logic (PL) in a single device [18]. The 16 nm FinFET+ PL communicates with the PS through 6,000 interconnects that are organized into twelve 128-bit high-performance ARM AMBA AXI4 ports each providing different capabilities. The high-performance AXI4 ports provide access from the PL to DDR and high-speed interconnect in the PS. The PL can be tightly or loosely coupled to the A53 APUs via two-way coherent, I/O (one-way) coherent, or non-coherent transactions. Address translation is provided by the system memory management unit (SMMU) on select AXI4 interfaces.

3.2 HSA Specifications

In this paper we leverage the HSA Foundation standards [10] and its existing ecosystem to improve the integrability of heterogeneous SoCs. This provides a new level of flexibility for developers of embedded systems. The specifications consist of three main parts:

- The *Programmer's Reference Manual* defines the HSA intermediate language (HSAIL) which abstracts the target ISA.

- The *Runtime Programmer's Reference Manual* defines the vendor neutral hardware communication API a language runtime is expected to target.
- The *Platform System Architecture Specification* defines the underlying hardware model which the software toolchain is targeting.

To utilize all features the HSA ecosystem provides an application developer does not need to use any HSA specific constructs. Instead the programming language can freely be chosen among the available HSA compiler frontends. When the application software is compiled the compiler is expected to separate kernel from host code and generate all HSA runtime API calls needed. To provide an enhanced flexibility with regards to the actual accelerator hardware a special virtual language is used as an intermediate representation of accelerator kernel code.

This language is called HSAIL and has a textual form which resembles Nvidia's PTX. Its binary representation is BRIG. For all purposes of this paper HSAIL and BRIG are equivalent and can be converted into each other. Similar to CUDA and OpenCL, a separation of kernels into work-groups and work-items is also used in this execution model. A common workflow is splitted into the two steps. First, the source code of a supported language is compiled to HSAIL. Afterwards, either at compile time or runtime, this intermediate code is *finalized* to the accelerator ISA. Finalization is very lightweight, because most time consuming steps like register allocation already happened in the previous compile process that produces low-level BRIG. This is possible due to the minimum hardware requirements defined in the Platform System Architecture Specification. With this concept the dispatch latency can be reduced compared to direct compilation from LLVM-IR/SPIR.

A reference to these kernels in target ISA is embedded in an AQL kernel dispatch packet. These packets have a special format and compliant hardware is expected to be able to interpret it. Besides the actual binary all associated meta information like the grid size are also included. To submit a job to an accelerator core such a packet just needs to be written to a user-mode queue provided by the device. All further processing is then in the responsibility of the hardware.

3.3 LibHSA Library

In order to logically and physically connect a programmable accelerator in the PL to the ARM cores in the PS a connector is needed. In particular these components must adhere to the protocol specified by the HSA Foundation. With LibHSA the first implementation of such a system was presented by Reichenbach et al. [13]. Its core component is a self-developed, lightweight, 64 bit CPU based on the MIPS III ISA. It acts as an AQL *packet processor* and manages all incoming tasks dispatched via the HSA runtime. After interpreting the AQL packet, the packet processor issues the execution command described in Fig. 1 to a suitable accelerator core. As bus protocol the widespread AXI4 standard has been incorporated to decrease the needed integration effort for new cores.

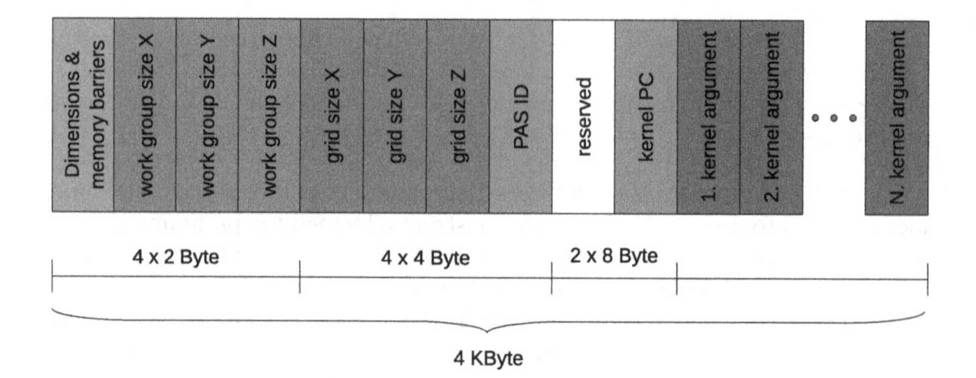

Fig. 1. Execution command format of the packet processor to the accelerator cores.

Additionally a fixed interface of an accelerator has been defined such that cores can be freely interchanged.

In the following LibHSA is used to connect the accelerator core to the ARM host in an HSA compatible way. However, in the original paper they only demonstrated a MIPS CPU in the PL as a host. An implementation for a faster and highly energy-efficient ARM CPU has not been presented yet. Therefore, some adaptions had to be made in this paper.

3.4 Nyuzi Vector Processor

The accelerator core used in this paper is the open source, 32 bit Nyuzi vector processor[6]. It was designed by Jeff Bush for highly parallel applications [7]. The simultanious multi threading (SMT) capable, multi-core architecture incorporates floating point and integer SIMD execution units. Its memory subsystem consists of coherent, set associative L1 and L2 caches. All vector instructions support predication allowing individual lanes of the vector to be masked to avoid branches for diverging program flow paths. The data communication is established via two separate bus systems. On the one hand the IO-bus is used for uncached peripheral small data transfers without any protocol overhead besides access arbitration. On the other hand memory transactions with the remaining system are carried out by an AXI4-full interface with 32 bit addresses and adjustable data width.

The Nyuzi processor is parameterized and can be easily modified to contain the desired number of cores. Moreover, the cache size, number of vector lanes, and threads per hardware core can be also configured. To program the parallel processor architecture of Nyuzi the project includes a complete LLVM compiler toolchain which utilizes all of the hardware features.

[6] http://nyuzi.org/.

4 Environment

4.1 Hardware Structure

The general hardware setup can be seen in Fig. 2. Compared to the setup Reichenbach et al. proposed in [13] the accelerator cores are no longer limited to fixed function accelerators. Now programmable soft-core architectures are also possible. Moreover, with our extention their custom MIPS host processor can be replaced by a high-performance ARM ASIC. Our design is the same for all Zynq-based designs from low-cost *UltraZed* and *Ultra96* boards to the high-end *Sidewinder-100*. On the host side the *ARM Cortex A-53* is used for the reasons explained in Sect. 3.1. It dispatches all tasks which need to be accelerated to the *Nyuzi vector processor*. The connection between these main components is realized with the LibHSA library described in Sect. 3.3. It acts as middleware between host and accelerator to provide a uniform HSA-based interface and communication protocol. The central component is the *packet processor* which manages all submitted kernels. Since the task dispatch always follows the HSA specifications there is no difference between the instruction sets of different host processors. This means on the software side any programming language with an HSA backend is supported including upcoming, future backends. However, the physical connection on the hardware level differs making adaptions necessary.

First, the way to send and receive interrupts differs between the Zynq ARM core and MIPS host processor. While Reichenbach et al.'s custom MIPS has dedicated pins for all needed in- and outgoing interrupts, this had to be changed to GPIO for the ARM processor.

Secondly, in the Zynq system there is only one main DRAM memory region where data is shared and this is accessible with the same addresses from PS an PL. This means in contrast to a x86/PCIe setup the shared virtual memory requirement is trivially satisfied in the Zynq MPSoC system.

Lastly, in an MPSoC system the DRAM is accessed via the Zynq IP core. Here, cache coherency can be established with the integrated CCI-400. This means no additional hardware units or software changes to the packet processor are needed to fulfill this requirement. However, not all accelerators (like Nyuzi) support cache snooping via ACE, such that this property can be relaxed if the specific application doesn't need it. For that reason, to have both, high-throughput DMA and (one-way) cache coherency, the AXI HPC ports were used to access the DRAM from PL.

On the accelerator side LibHSA uses its own protocol since no requirements are stated in the HSA specification. As explained in [13] accelerator cores can be usually easily adapted with connector components provided by LibHSA. However, the Nyuzi vector processor additionally lacks abilities like system wide memory barriers to make it suitable for shared, heterogeneous processing with other hardware components. Therefore, more adaptions need to made which are explained in the following Sect. 4.2.

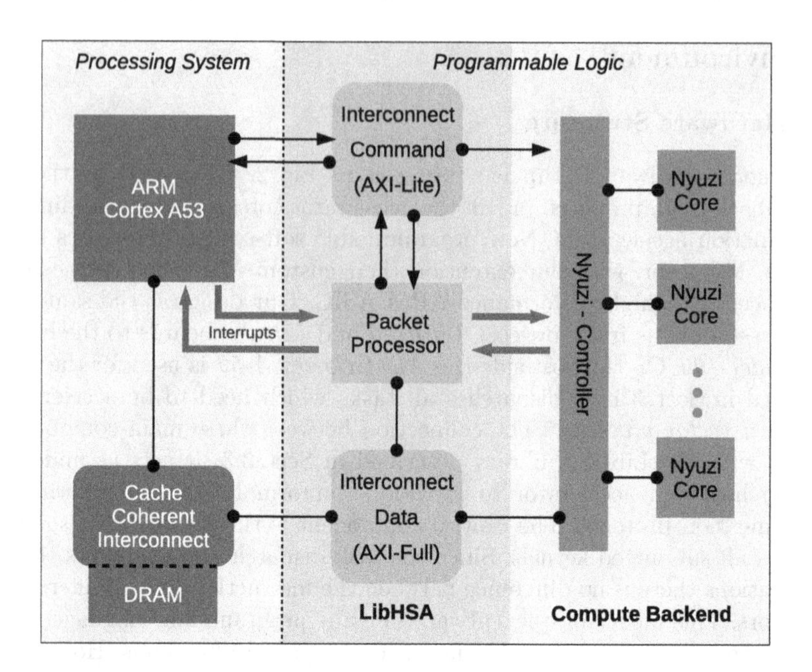

Fig. 2. Overview of the system components. The design is splitted into three main parts. On the right hand side there is the host subsystem with ARM, DRAM and cache-coherent interconnect. These parts are exclusively located in the PS. The accelerator cores can be seen on the left hand side. They are part of the programmable logic and are interchangeable at runtime. Both parts are connected via the LibHSA library in the middle section. It ensures the HSA conformance of the accelerator cores.

4.2 Nyuzi Adapter

The Nyuzi architecture is designed to run as host processor in a computing system, not as co-processor, offering two data bus systems and an interrupt interface to communicate with its environment. In order to minimize the management overhead inside the compute units a dedicated hardware component, the Nyuzi-controller, is added. This can accept AQL packets via a separate AXI-LITE interface and can schedule work items directly on specific Nyuzi hardware threads assigned to one core. After a thread is completed, it disables itself monitored by the Nyuzi controller to schedule the next work item on the now available thread.

Work item related information, e.g. item id or group dimensions, is also retained for each thread in the Nyuzi controller. To avoid cache invalidations and unwanted replacements the work item meta information is transfered over the separate IO-bus allowing simple 32 bit read and write transactions. In the original Nyuzi design each write or read will cause a pipeline rollback because the IO-bus was intended to perform for slow peripheral memory accesses. To speedup IO-bus requests the execution was pipelined into four stages according to a best case access scenario. Therefore, only bus conflicts will lead to pipeline rollbacks.

The cache system is coherent over all cores but is not capable of communicating to external components. Therefore, the L2 cache was extended with global flushing and invalidation functionality enabling HSA memory fences. The added flush controller waits till all L1 caches have finished their write requests and flushes all dirty cache lines afterwards. For cache invalidation all valid bits in L2 and L1 caches are cleared after flushing the L2 cache.

4.3 HSAIL/BRIG Finalization

The executed kernel functions are compiled from any supported high level language into the HSA intermediate representation, BRIG. Due to developers providing an LLVM-backend for Nyuzi code generation the BRIG program is first transformed into the LLVM intermediate representation (LLVM-IR). Because of the lacking tooling support on the side of the HSA Foundation this step is accomplished using a self written tool supporting all instructions required for the example kernels. For better utilization of the vector register and arithmetic the used kernels are automatically vectorized, based on kernels' LLVM-IR for better reusability. The basic concept is to compute 16 work item in concurrent X dimension with one kernel call. Therefore, within the kernel the API-call returning the X-id is searched and replaced with a vector of ascending, adjacent ids. Instructions using this now vectorized id have to expand each other operand by ether expanding the scalar value or vectorization. Using vectorized operands transforms the instruction result into a vectorized value, which is recursively for all instructions. Control flow divergence evoked by vectorized branch conditions lead to the reorganization of the control flow graph with the addition of executions masks for predicated instruction execution.

5 Results

The presented results are based on the hardware boards described in Sect. 4.1. The Nyuzi accelerator is synthesized with four different configurations regarding the amount of cores and cache sizes, two for the UltraZed board and two for the Sidewinder-100 board. Due to the selection of benchmark programs no floating point unit is configured in all variants. Table 1 shows the chosen configurations combined with the required hardware resource using Vivado version 2017.2 as synthesis toolchain. The complete FPGA resources are split into the static part, the LibHSA environment, and the configurable part, the accelerator cores.

On the software side the host program is running bare metal on one ARM core and starts various benchmark kernels using a reduced HSA-runtime. The selected pure integer programs are:

- *Vec Add*: The simple addition of two vector with 2^{15} values.
- *Mat Mul*: Multiplication of a 2048×100 and a 100×100 matrix.

Table 1. FPGA resource utilization for LibHSA environment and Nyuzi-core configurations on the UltraZed and Sidewinder MPSoC platforms

Platform	Component	LUTs [k]	FFs [k]	BRAM	DSPs
UltraZed	LibHSA Environment	8.3 (11.8 %)	7.1 (5 %)	8 (4 %)	0 (0 %)
	1-Core, Cache-Sizes: 32 KB-L1 256 KB-L2	40.9 (58 %)	24.5 (17 %)	96.5 (45%)	160 (44%)
	2-Cores, Cache-Sizes: 4 KB-L1 16 KB-L2	57.4 (81 %)	33.6 (24 %)	78.5 (36%)	128 (36%)
Sidewinder-100	LibHSA Environment	8.3 (1.6 %)	7.0 (0.7 %)	8 (0.8 %)	0 (0 %)
	4-Cores, Cache-Sizes: 16 KB-L1 128 KB-L2	117 (22 %)	65 (6.2 %)	171 (17 %)	256 (13 %)
	8-Cores, Cores-Sizes: 32 KB-L1 256 KB-L2	229 (44 %)	124 (12 %)	345 (35 %)	512 (26 %)

Table 2. Runtime comparison of different benchmark program kernels running on different Nyuzi configurations and the ARM Cortex A53

	Vec Add	Mat Mul	Gauss 3 × 3	Gauss 5 × 5	Diff of Gauss
1 Nyuzi-Cores @150 MHz	10.6 ms	15.3 s	164.4 ms	336.2 ms	588.4 ms
2 Nyuzi-Cores @100 MHz	4.83 ms	129.2 s	86.0 ms	186.7 ms	377.9 ms
4 Nyuzi-Cores @150 MHz	1.87 ms	312.5 ms	15.0 ms	28.3 ms	57.8 ms
8 Nyuzi-Cores @100 MHz	1.90 ms	90.0 ms	10.4 ms	14.2 ms	38.8 ms

- *Gauss 3 × 3*: Application of a 3 × 3 convolution filter to a 512 × 512 image.
- *Gauss 5 × 5*: Application of a 5 × 5 convolution filter to a 512 × 512 image.
- *Diff of Gauss*: This programs calculates the absolute value of the difference of *Gauss 5 × 5* and *Gauss 3 × 3*.

The resulting execution times for one kernel call can be seen in Table 2. Furthermore, it demonstrates the achieved PL-frequencies. The time measurements are accomplished using the ARM's real time clock, and are averaged over 100 runs. Attention should be paid to the difference in memory access times of both hardware platforms with the Sidewinder-100 board performing around four times faster than the UltraZed board. The kernel execution includes the transfer from the ARM's cache into the Nyuzi's cache, the actual kernel execution, and the flushing backing into the cache system of the ARM. Therefore, primarily memory bound kernels, like *Vec Add*, hardly scale with the rising amount of computing cores. This scaling can be distinguished clearly for the three convolution filter kernels. The unpropotional trend of execution time for the *Mat Mul* kernel can be explained with the variation of the cache size matching the problem size superiorly.

6 Conclusion

In this paper we presented a methodology to utilize highly configurable and programmable soft-core accelerators by making MPSoC systems HSA compliant. The high flexibility regarding the front end programing language and standardized communication interface substantially could improve the accessibility these accelerators.

We could demonstrate a HSA based heterogeneous system connecting an ARM host CPU to the existing GPU like Nyuzi processor using software and hardware components of LibHSA [13]. The necessary extensions to the Nyuzi core on hardware level and the LibHSA environment were described. On the software side a finalizer provides the conversion from intermediate BRIG code to Nyuzi ISA.

All in all we could show that the HSA Foundation standards can reduce the overall complexity of heterogeneous platforms, like the Zynq UltraScale+. Moreover, the Zynq capabilities itself are well suited to implement an HSA-based system on top of it. Furthermore, the overhead in the system introduced by the HSA standard is only negligible. The HSA runtime API allows easy dispatching of tasks to the accelerator cores with no knowledge of hardware specifics required.

The host code is currently running bare metal on an ARM core. In the future an adaptation for a full Linux operating system can make it even simpler to deploy an easily usable, heterogeneous, multi-user system on Zynq basis. In addition, other accelerator cores could replace the currently used Nyuzi processor. Furthermore, it is conceivable to integrate LibHSA's packet processor as a separate ASIC in the MPSoC system and use its capabilities to bring the HSA functionality to embedded devices without needing additional logic resources.

Acknowledgments. We want to thank Xilinx and Fidus Systems for providing the used Zynq hardware platforms necessary to conduct our research.

References

1. Al-Dujaili, A., Deragisch, F., Hagiescu, A., Wong, W.: Guppy: a GPU-like soft-core processor. In: 2012 International Conference on Field-Programmable Technology, FPT 2012, Seoul, Korea (South), 10–12 December 2012, pp. 57–60. IEEE (2012)
2. Altera: Implementing FPGA Design with the OpenCL Standard, November 2013. https://www.altera.com/en_US/pdfs/literature/wp/wp-01173-opencl.pdf
3. AMD: ROCm: Open Platform For Development, Discovery and Education around GPU Computing, April 2016. https://gpuopen.com/compute-product/rocm/
4. Andryc, K., Merchant, M., Tessier, R.: Flexgrip: A soft GPGPU for FPGAS. In: 2013 International Conference on Field-Programmable Technology (FPT), pp. 230–237, December 2013
5. Balasubramanian, R., et al.: MIAOW - an open source RTL implementation of a GPGPU. In: 2015 IEEE Symposium in Low-Power and High-Speed Chips, COOL CHIPS XVIII, Yokohama, Japan, 13–15 April 2015, pp. 1–3. IEEE (2015)
6. Bush, J., Dexter, P., Miller, T.N., Carpenter, A.: Nyami: a synthesizable GPU architectural model for general-purpose and graphics-specific workloads. In: 2015 IEEE International Symposium on Performance Analysis of Systems and Software, ISPASS 2015, Philadelphia, PA, USA, 29–31 March 2015, pp. 173–182. IEEE Computer Society (2015)
7. Bush, J., Khasawneh, M.A., Mahmoud, K.Z., Miller, T.N.: NyuziRaster: Optimizing rasterizer performance and energy in the Nyuzi open source GPU. In: 2016 IEEE International Symposium on Performance Analysis of Systems and Software (ISPASS), pp. 204–213. IEEE (2016)

8. Canis, A., et al.: LegUp: high-level synthesis for FPGA-based processor/accelerator systems. In: Proceedings of the 19th ACM/SIGDA International Symposium on Field Programmable Gate Arrays, FPGA 2011, ACM, New York, NY, USA, pp. 33–36 (2011)
9. Choi, J., Brown, S., Anderson, J.: From software threads to parallel hardware in high-level synthesis for FPGAs. In: 2013 International Conference on Field-Programmable Technology (FPT), pp. 270–277. IEEE (2013)
10. HSA Foundation: HSA Foundation Specification Version 1.1, May 2016. http://www.hsafoundation.com/standards/
11. Kadi, M.A., Huebner, M.: Integer computations with soft GPGPU on FPGAs. In: 2016 International Conference on Field-Programmable Technology (FPT), pp. 28–35, December 2016
12. Mukherjee, S., Sun, Y., Blinzer, P., Ziabari, A.K., Kaeli, D.: A comprehensive performance analysis of HSA and OpenCL 2.0. In: 2016 IEEE International Symposium on Performance Analysis of Systems and Software (ISPASS), pp. 183–193. IEEE (2016)
13. Reichenbach, M., Holzinger, P., Häublein, K., Lieske, T., Blinzer, P., Fey, D.: LibHSA: one step towards mastering the era of heterogeneous hardware accelerators using FPGAs. In: 2017 Conference on Design and Architectures for Signal and Image Processing (DASIP), pp. 1–6. IEEE (2017)
14. Samsung: A Mobile Processor That Goes Beyond Mobile Innovation, April 2016. http://www.samsung.com/semiconductor/minisite/exynos/products/mobileprocessor/exynos-9-series-8895/
15. Vaas, S., Reichenbach, M., Fey, D.: An application-specific instruction set processor for power quality monitoring. In: 2016 IEEE International Parallel and Distributed Processing Symposium Workshops (IPDPSW), pp. 181–188, May 2016
16. Xilinx: The Xilinx SDAccel Development Environment (2014). https://www.xilinx.com/publications/prod_mktg/sdx/sdaccel-backgrounder.pdf
17. Xilinx: Vivado Design Suite User Guide: High-Level Synthesis, October 2014. https://www.xilinx.com/support/documentation/sw_manuals/xilinx2017_2/ug902-vivado-high-level-synthesis.pdf
18. Xilinx: Xilinx Zynq UltraScale+ Device Technical Reference Manual, December 2017. https://www.xilinx.com/support/documentation/user_guides/ug1085-zynq-ultrascale-trm.pdf

Service Level Objectives via C++11 Attributes

Dalvan Griebler[1,3(✉)], Daniele De Sensi[2], Adriano Vogel[1], Marco Danelutto[2], and Luiz Gustavo Fernandes[1]

[1] School of Technology, Pontifical Catholic University of Rio Grande do Sul, Porto Alegre, Brazil
dalvan.griebler@acad.pucrs.br
[2] Department of Computer Science, University of Pisa, Pisa, Italy
[3] Laboratory of Advanced Research on Cloud Computing, Três de Maio Faculty, Três de Maio, Brazil

Abstract. In recent years, increasing attention has been given to the possibility of guaranteeing Service Level Objectives (SLOs) to users about their applications, either regarding performance or power consumption. SLO can be implemented for parallel applications since they can provide many control knobs (*e.g.*, the number of threads to use, the clock frequency of the cores, etc.) to tune the performance and power consumption of the application. Different from most of the existing approaches, we target sequential stream processing applications by proposing a solution based on C++ annotations. The user specifies which parts of the code to parallelize and what type of requirements should be enforced on that part of the code. Our solution first automatically parallelizes the annotated code and then applies self-adaptation approaches at run-time to enforce the user-expressed objectives. We ran experiments on different real-world applications, showing its simplicity and effectiveness.

Keywords: Parallel programming
Adaptive and autonomic computing · Power-aware computing
Domain-specific language

1 Introduction

The rich stream processing application domain motivated the creation of different parallel programming environments/tools to speed up the computation of data stream. In multi-core systems, this is typically exploited by using linear or non-linear pipeline structures [15]. To this purpose, state-of-the-art framework such as Streamit, TBB, and FastFlow provide different programming approaches and interfaces with a reasonable performance scalability for this domain [1,16,19]. Although these frameworks are equipped with high-level patterns implementation to express the parallelism, they are still closer to expert system programmers rather than to the application domain programmers. Seeking to provide domain-specific and suitable abstractions for stream parallelism,

G. Mencagli et al. (Eds.): Euro-Par 2018 Workshops, LNCS 11339, pp. 745–756, 2019.
https://doi.org/10.1007/978-3-030-10549-5_58

SPar was created. Different from these frameworks, application programmers are invited to express parallelism with SPar through C++11 annotation without the need for rewriting/restructuring the sequential source code semantics [10].

Moreover, stream processing applications usually have unpredictable load fluctuations and uncertain end of execution (may never end) characteristics [3]. Therefore, besides the need for improving performance through the efficient exploitation of the multi-core parallelism, there are other major concerns such adaptive and autonomic computing, power-aware computing, and efficient resource usage [9,13]. In this direction, NORNIR was created to be a simple interface and runtime support to dynamically and automatically control the resources allocated to the application according to the user needs [7]. However NORNIR, like most existing self-adaptive solutions, only works on parallel applications.

In this paper, we propose the use of the Service Level Objective (SLO) concept [18] for sequential stream processing applications. The idea is that the programmer annotates the code by using the SPar language, synergistically specifying both the parallelism exploitation and the SLO. Based on the code annotations, SPar generates a parallel code with the NORNIR runtime system, which will dynamically adapt the parallel execution to meet the SLO. We simplify the SLO definition by introducing new attributes in SPar. The simplicity is delivered by integrating SPar annotation syntax with new attributes to specify SLO about throughput, power consumption, system utilization or a combination of these. Our approach could also be applied to REPARA project[1], which provides a set of C++11 attributes to introduce parallelism [6].

This paper is organized as follows. In Sect. 2 we analyze the related work in this area. Then, in Sect. 3 we introduce the SPar domain-specific language and in Sect. 4 we describe how we extended it to consider SLO. In Sect. 5 we perform our evaluation and, eventually, in Sect. 6 we draw the conclusions, and we outline some possible future directions for this work.

2 Related Work

In the literature, there are different studies targeting power consumption, throughput, and system utilization objectives. Among them, the approach of Maggio el al. [13] monitors generic applications and supports the specification of a target performance (throughput) in the parallel code. It efficiently manages the CPU cores, adapting the amount of resource usage needed. However, it supposes that the parallel application has already been implemented, and does not provide any mechanism to introduce SLO in sequential programs.

Concerning stream parallel processing for real-time data analytic, Floratou et al. [9] introduced the notion of self-regulation in Twitter's Heron framework, called Dhalion. The user defines a target throughput as an SLO parameter for Dhalion. The self-regulator engine handles the number of process and number of instances in a cloud infrastructure to provide the specified throughput. In the experiments, the results revealed that the system can dynamically adapt

[1] http://repara-project.eu/.

resources and automatically reconfigure to meet SLOs. We differently proposed three target SLOs (throughput, energy, utilization) to be expressed in sequential source codes for multi-core systems. Our adaptive runtime uses system knobs and applies machine learning algorithms to dynamically adapt CPU frequency and the number of active threads to meet SLO requirements.

There are studies focusing on high-level abstractions for energy saving on data parallelism [2,17]. They provide compiler directives for expressing energy consumption and performance objectives in OpenMP. While Shafik et al. [17] can minimize energy consumption on both sequential and parallel applications, they do not provide any means to explicitly control the performance of the application. On the other hand, in Alessi et al. [2], OpenMPE is proposed adding a new construct and two clauses (objectives) for OpenMP. Their solution was implemented using a source-to-source compiler, which recognizes the new directives and control the number of threads used by OpenMP and applies DVFS to satisfy the SLOs expressed by the user. This is probably the closest work to the approach we are proposing in this work. The main difference is that, while Alessi et al. [2] targets batch applications (i.e. applications for which all the input data is already available in memory) implemented through OpenMP, we provide support for stream processing applications, exposing ad-hoc SLOs for these applications such as system utilization.

3 SPar: High-Level Stream Parallelism

SPar[2] is an internal Domain-Specific Language (DSL) designed to support high-level stream parallelism for application programmers [10]. With SPar, instead of rewriting the source code, the programmer introduces C++ annotations (standard `C++-11` [14]) using five attributes, representing the main properties of stream processing applications. The `ToStream` attribute identifies the beginning of a stream region, which can be viewed as an assembly line. The `Stage` attribute marks a stage in the assembly line and as many as necessary can be declared. Auxiliary attributes can be used inside the attribute list of an annotation sentence. The `Input` and `Output` respectively attributes are used to specify the input

```
1  [[spar::ToStream]] while(1){
2    frame f = read_frame();
3    if(f.empty()) break;
4    [[spar::Stage,spar::Input(f),spar::
       Output(f),spar::Replicate(n)]]
5    for (int i=0; i<f.length(); i++) {
6      f[i] = convert(f[i]);
7    }
8    [[spar::Stage,spar::Input(f)]]{
9      write_frame(f);
10   }
11 }
```

Listing 1.1. SPar code example.

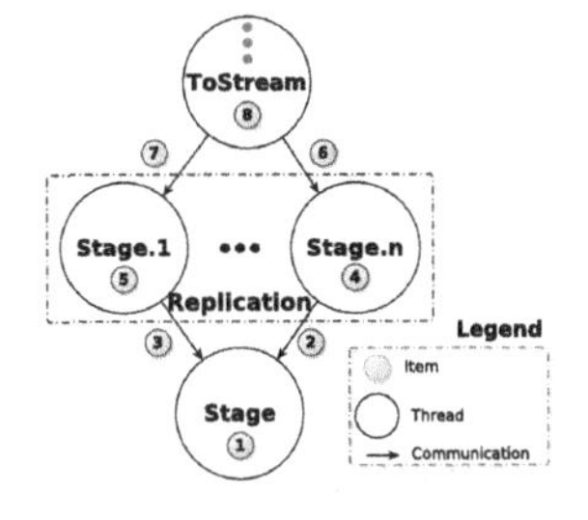

Fig. 1. Parallel activity graph.

[2] SPar website: https://gmap.pucrs.br/spar.

and output stream items, while the `Replicate` attribute is used for replicating stateless stages to increase the degree of parallelism.

Listing 1.1 provides a short code example annotated with SPar attributes. This example represents a typical use case of stream parallelism, where there is a sequence of operations to be performed on each stream element. The parallel activity graph produced by the SPar compiler for Listing 1.1 is shown in Fig. 1. SPar generates the parallel code with the FastFlow library [1], which implements different parallel patterns [15] for stream processing computations. SPar compiler parses the code of Listing 1.1 and represents the code with an Abstract Syntax Tree (AST) [10]. Traversing the AST, it performs a semantic analysis of the attributes to further make the source-to-source transformation. In this step, SPar compiler finds the best parallel pattern that meets the parsed annotation schema. In the case of Listing 1.1, it will generate parallel code with three stages where one of them have replicated instances. There will be situations where there will be different compositions of stages and replicated instances. By default, elements are scheduled from the `ToStream` stage to the `Stage.x` stages in a round-robin way. However, it is possible to use an on-demand policy by specifying the `-spar_ondemand` flag to the SPar compiler. If the data needs to be received from the last stage in the same order it was produced by the `ToStream` stage, the programmer can specify the `-spar_ordered` flag to the SPar compiler.

4 Service Level Objective for Stream Parallelism

Service Level Objectives (SLOs) are traditionally included in Service Level Agreements (SLAs), which are contracts to manage the quality of service delivered by or received by a provider [18]. An SLA contract defines the acceptable levels of service by user and attainable levels of service by a provider. The SLO is a target value or a range of values for a certain level of service to be delivered and the level of service is measured by a Service Level Indicator (SLI). A typical structure of SLO can be written $SLI \leq target$ or $lower\_bound \leq SLI \leq upper\_bound$ [4]. When an SLO is violated, the system will autonomously react to guarantee the quality of service and SLA. Our design goal is to simplify the usability of SLO for stream parallel applications, on top of an existing parallel programming tool. Since SPar already provides high-level parallel programming abstractions and allows us to extend its annotations, we made our proof of concept on top of it. We will concentrate for the moment on three different SLOs (throughput, power, and utilization), which can be expressed by using standard `C++11` attributes that will be described in the following section.

4.1 Attributes

The proposed attributes have to be used along with a `ToStream` annotation, which identifies the beginning of a stream parallelism region, so that the SLO is applied to this particular region. Listing 1.2 presents how the code looks like when expressing a power consumption SLO of 60 w. It is worth noting that, beside the `slo::Power` attribute, no other modification is required with respect to the original SPar code (Listing 1.1). The following list enumerates the attributes we added to SPar in this work, to support SLOs.

```
[[spar::ToStream, slo::Power(60)]] while
    (1){
  frame f = read_frame();
  if(f.empty()) break;
  [[spar::Stage,spar::Input(f),spar::
    Output(f),spar::Replicate(n)]]
  for (int i=0; i<f.length(); i++) {
    f[i] = convert(f[i]);
  }
  [[spar::Stage,spar::Input(f)]]{
   write_frame(f);
  }
}
```

Listing 1.2. SPar code example with power consumption SLO.

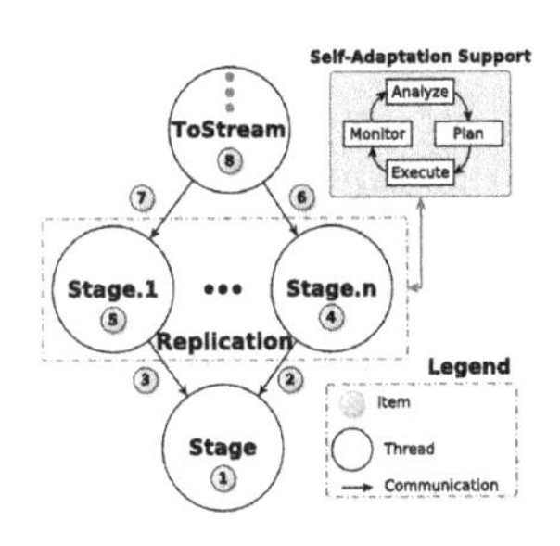

Fig. 2. Parallel activity graph with self-adaptation support.

slo::Power(<max-watts>) is the attribute used to specify the power consumption SLO. The user can specify the maximum power consumption in Watts. If no other attributes are specified, NORNIR will implicitly find the configuration with the highest throughput among those with a power consumption lower than `<max-watts>`.

slo::Throughput(<min-items/second>) is the attribute used to specify the application throughput SLO. The user can specify the minimum throughput required in items per second. If a power consumption SLO is not explicitly set, NORNIR will implicitly find the configuration with the lowest power consumption among those with a throughput greater than `<min-items/second>`.

slo::Utilization(min-percentage) is the attribute used to specify the application utilization SLO. The user can specify the minimum utilization required in percentage. Utilization represents the percentage of time that the system is active (i.e. actively processing input elements) over a time interval. Having a low utilization is often associated to a low power efficiency, since resources may be active but performing useless activities (i.e. actively waiting for new elements to be processed). If a power consumption SLO is not explicitly set, NORNIR will implicitly find the configuration with the lowest power consumption among those with a greater utilization number than `<min-percentage>`.

4.2 Implementation and Self-adaptation Support with Nornir

In the SPar compiler, we registered the new SLO attributes and performed the semantic analysis traversing the source code AST. Since the SLO attributes belong only to the `ToStream` attribute list, we stored it along with the SPar

AST [10]. In the source-to-source code transformation, we generate the same parallel patterns originally designed. However, we check if there is an SLO attribute to generate code with NORNIR in the situations where SPar annotation generates a stage with replicated instances.

To provide the specified SLO, we couple a self-adaptive runtime to the activity graph (Fig. 2). In this work, we rely on the NORNIR self-adaptive runtime support [7]. NORNIR monitors the application throughout its entire execution, dynamically changing the number of resources used by the application to satisfy the requirements expressed by the user. For example, NORNIR may decide to reduce the number of replicated stages of the application to decrease its power consumption, or to increase the clock frequency of the cores to increase its throughput[3]. NORNIR can rely on different algorithms to decide how many resources to add/remove, either based on machine learning techniques [8] or on heuristics. In both cases, when the application starts, NORNIR spends some time in collecting data about the application in different configurations. These data are used to build prediction models which will be used to find the optimal configuration according to the objectives specified by the user. If no feasible solutions are found, NORNIR will select the configuration with performance and power consumption closest to the user requirements. More information about this algorithm can be found in [8].

Besides providing the possibility to control existing parallel applications (by inserting instrumentation calls in the existing code), NORNIR can also be used as a programming framework (by relying on the FASTFLOW framework) for implementing stream-parallel applications with an embedded self-adaptation support. In this work, we exploited this second possibility, so that SPar can translate sequentially annotated code into self-adaptive NORNIR parallel code.

While the integration with SPar allows to use NORNIR in a simple and transparent way, it is worth noting that NORNIR could also be used on other frameworks different from SPar.

5 Experiments

In this section, we evaluate our approach over some real-world applications. We will first introduce the considered applications. Then, we will compare the code generated by SPar with some handwritten parallel implementations, both regarding maximum performance achieved and in terms of productivity. Eventually, we will analyze the self-adaptation capabilities of our solution under different scenarios.

All the experiments have been executed on a dual-socket NUMA machine with two Intel Xeon E5-2695 Ivy Bridge CPUs running at 2.40 GHz featuring 24 cores (12 per socket). The machine exposes 13 frequency levels, ranging from 1.2 GHz to 2.4 GHz, at steps of 0.1 GHz. Each core has 2-way hyperthreading,

[3] Since the number of replicas is dynamically changed during the execution, the number of replicas specified with the `spar::Replicate` attribute now represents the maximum number of replicas that can be active at any time.

32 KB private L1, 256 KB private L2 and 30 MB of L3 shared with the cores on the same socket. The machine has 64 GB of DDR3 RAM. We used Linux 3.14.49 $\times$ 86_64 shipped with CentOS 7.1 and `gcc` version `4.8.5`. For all our experiments we disabled the hyper-threading feature.

5.1 Applications

In this section, we briefly describe the real-world application set, input loads, and parallel implementations. For a detailed description of how *Lane Detection* and *Person Recognition* have been parallelized by using SPar please refer to [12], while for *Pbzip2* more details can be found in [11].

Lane Detection is a video processing application to detect road lanes, implemented by using the OpenCV library. To introduce parallelism in the sequential code, we annotated it with SPar by identifying three stages: (i) a first stage which reads the frames; (ii) another stage, replicated a number of times, which processes the frames in parallel; (iii) a last stage which displays the frames in the proper order, with the lanes properly marked. As input workload, we used a 22 MB MPEG-4 video (640 $\times$ 360 pixels).

Person Recognition is an application used to recognize people in a video. The parallel structure of this application is similar to *Lane Detection*, with the middle stage detecting the faces from the crowd and searching in an image database to classify each face detected. As input workload, we used a 4.8 MB MPEG-4 video (640 $\times$ 360 pixels) along with a training set of 10 face images of 150 $\times$ 150 pixels.

Pbzip application is a parallel implementation of the `bzip2` block-sorting files compressor[4]. This is a very coarse grained application characterized by a stream parallel programming model. We annotated the SPar version with three stages, where the middle stage is replicated. The input compressed file used for our experiments has 6.3 GB containing a dump of all abstracts present in the English Wikipedia extracted on 01/12/2015.

5.2 Comparison with Handwritten Implementations

Before evaluating the ability to satisfy SLO specified by the user we want to prove that, from a performance standpoint, the code generated by SPar is comparable with a handwritten implementation. On the other hand, we would like to show that our solution reduces the code intrusion required to transform a sequential application into a parallel one. As reference implementations for *Pbzip* we consider the original Pthreads version, while for *Lane Detection* and *Person Recognition* applications we consider the handwritten FastFlow versions described in [12].

[4] http://compression.ca/pbzip2/.

Performance. To measure the maximum performance, we executed both the reference and our solution generated versions by running them with 24 threads (to have at most one thread per core). For our generated version, we did not specify any SLO, but we still monitor the application by using NORNIR. By doing so, we monitor both the overhead introduced by the interaction with the self-adaptive support and possible inefficiencies in the generated code. As shown by the results in Table 1, for *Lane Detection* and *Person Recognition*, the overhead is negligible (below 1.5%). For *Pbzip2*, there is a slight improvement caused by the use of FASTFLOW as runtime support, while the reference implementation was based on Pthreads.

Table 1. Performance improvement with respect to a handwritten implementation. Negative values mean that SPar version is slower than the handwritten one. For LOC Reduction, negative values mean that SPar version is more concise than the handwritten one.

	PBZIP2	Lane detection	Person recognition
Performance improvement (%)	+0.48%	−1.45%	−0.92%
LOC reduction (%)	−15.86%	−21.51%	−24.49%

Code Intrusion. To measure the code intrusion, we rely on Lines of Code (LOC) metric. Despite that LOC is not universally accepted, it is commonly used to compare different implementations of the same application [20]. For our measurements, we only considered the source files containing the code relevant for the parallelization. In all the cases, parallelizing an application by using SPar requires a lower code intrusion with respect to Pthreads or FastFlow [10,11], since it usually only requires introducing some annotations in the already existing sequential code. Also, the SLOs attributes requires minimal effort.

5.3 Self-adaptation Analysis

To analyze the self-adaptation capabilities of the parallel code automatically generated by our solution, we first require the application to have a greater throughput number than the sequential version while minimizing the power consumption.

Table 2. Power consumption reduction obtained by a parallel application with the same throughput of the sequential one.

	PBZIP2	Lane detection	Person recognition
Power consumption reduction (%)	−9.43%	−10.37%	−7.39%

The target of this first experiment is to prove that parallelization is not only useful for improving the performance of an application, but it can also be used to reduce its power consumption. In a nutshell, we want to prove that a parallel application with the same performance of the sequential one has lower power consumption. We show the results of this test in Table 2.

The interpretation we would like to give to these results is that, even if the performance of a sequential application is satisfactory, parallelizing it may still be useful for reducing its power consumption. This effect occurs since by increasing the number of replicas (and thus the number of cores used by the application), we can reduce the clock frequency while keeping the same performance. Since the power consumption increases linearly with the number of cores but more than quadratically with the clock frequency [5], running an application on more cores at a lower frequency is usually more energy efficient than running it on fewer cores at a higher frequency. Having tools and methodologies for doing that automatically and with low code intrusion, like those we are describing in this work is of paramount importance for enabling such techniques in real-world scenarios.

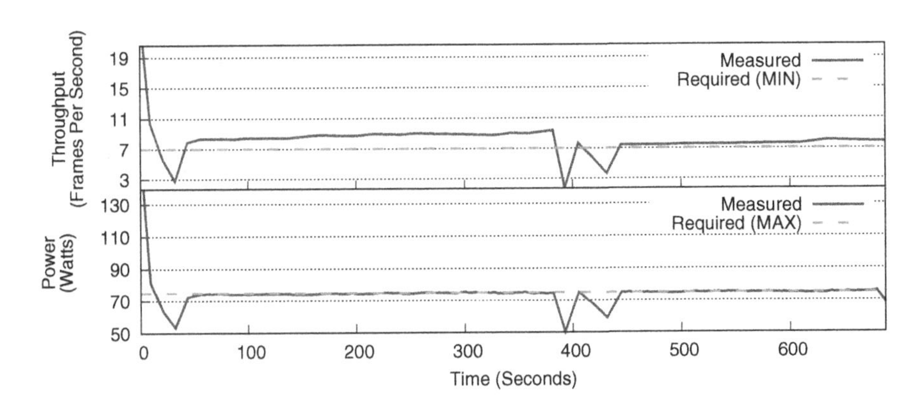

Fig. 3. *Person recognition* application with `slo::Throughput(7)` and `slo::Power(75)`.

We now analyze the time behavior of different applications for different types of SLO. In Fig. 3, we show how throughput and power change in time when the user requires a greater throughput number than 7 frames per seconds and a power consumption lower than 75 w for the *Person Recognition* application. In the first 40 s of the execution, our runtime changes the configuration a few times to collect some data which will then be used to predict the best configuration according to the user requirements. This behaviour depends from the specific algorithm we used in NORNIR and other algorithms, which avoid such fluctuations could be used as well. Around 390 s from the beginning, the application enters a different phase of its execution, and our runtime needs to update the prediction models by collecting new data. This different phase impacts in the throughput and power consumption fluctuations, occurring around 400 s from the beginning.

In Fig. 4 we analyze a different scenario, where the user requires a greater throughput number than 20 blocks per second and power consumption lower than 65 W for the *Pbzip* application. In this test, we add some external noise to show that our runtime succeeds in providing the required SLO even in the presence of unexpected behaviors. In particular, besides the usual calibration done in the first seconds of execution, after 50 s from the start of *Pbzip*, we start another application on the same machine. Since the two applications share some resources (*i.e.*, cores, memory, among others), the throughput of *Pbzip2* starts to decrease. In response to this issue, our runtime recomputes the prediction models, now considering the presence of external interference. As a consequence, as we can see from the bottom part of Fig. 4, our runtime increases the number of replicas of the middle stage from 12 to 14. When the other interfering application terminates (around 120 s from the start of *Pbzip2*), our runtime recomputes the models and decreases the number of replicas from 14 to 13. As we can see from the two upper parts of the figure, our runtime satisfies the user requirements throughout the entire execution (excepts for the phases where the models are computed), independently from the presence of other applications running on the system.

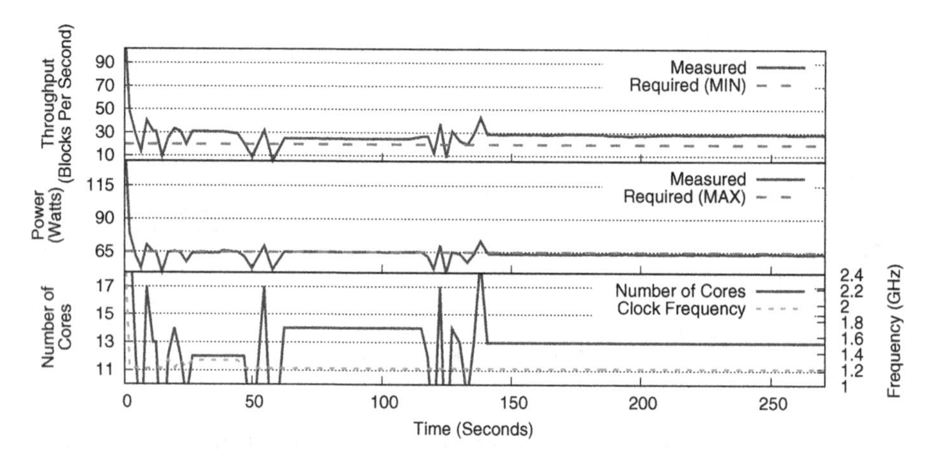

Fig. 4. *Pbzip2* application with `slo::Throughput(20)` and `slo::Power(65)`.

In the last experiment, which we report in Fig. 5, we analyze the *Lane Detection* application, in a scenario where it produces no more than 50 frames per seconds. In such case, using all the available resources could be inefficient, since they could be idle for most of the time. To avoid such scenario, we set a utilization SLO of 80%. In the upper part of Fig. 5, we report the utilization when an SLO is specified and when it is not specified. In the bottom part, we report the power consumption. As shown by the result when an SLO is not specified, the utilization would be around 20%. This utilization means that the threads of the application would spend 80% of the time waiting for new frames to arrive. By requiring a minimum utilization of 80%, our runtime decreases the number of resources allocated to the application, decreasing the power consumption from 90 W to 55 W. This event occurs without decreasing the overall performance of the application. Indeed, the threads still spend some time waiting for new data, but it is reduced from 80% to 5% (the utilization is around 95%).

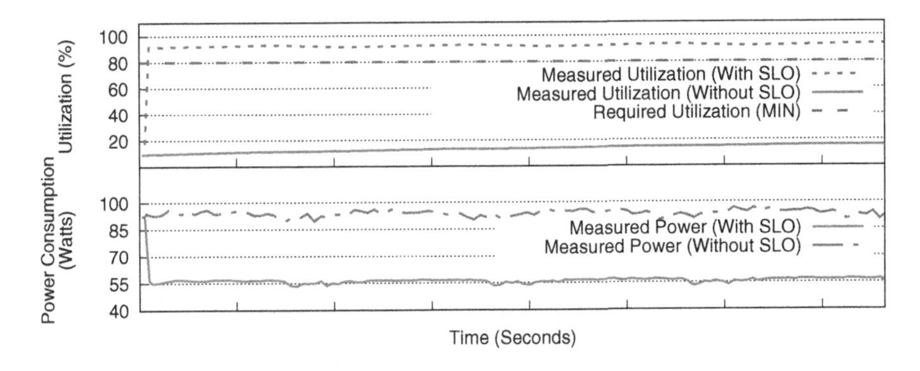

Fig. 5. *Lane detection* application with `slo::Utilization(80)`.

6 Conclusions and Future Work

In this paper we provided the possibility to express SLO on the sequential code, using automatic parallelization and self-adaptation of resources such as the number of replicas (and, consequently, the number of cores) and clock frequency. We described how we extended the SPar source-to-source compiler to support different types of SLO and we performed an experimental evaluation showing the effectiveness of our approach. The results demonstrated that by using self-adaptation, under certain conditions, we reduced the power consumption up to 42%. Also, we reduced the power consumption by 9.06% while not decreasing the performance with respect to the sequential version. Lines of code are reduced 20% in average with respect to a handwritten implementation, which shows the simplicity of our solution. As a future work, we intend to consider other types of SLO such as execution time and energy consumption (*i.e.*, integral of power consumption over time). Moreover, we would like to extend our work by considering more applications and different or more heterogeneous workloads.

Acknowledgements. This study was financed in part by the Coordenação de Aperfeiçoamento de Pessoal de Nivel Superior - Brasil (CAPES) - Finance Code 001, by the EU H2020-ICT-2014-1 project RePhrase (No. 644235), and by the FAPERGS 01/2017-ARD project ParaElastic (No. 17/2551-0000871-5).

References

1. Aldinucci, M., Danelutto, M., Kilpatrick, P., Torquati, M.: FastFlow: high-level and efficient streaming on multi-core. In: Programming Multi-core and Many-core Computing Systems, PDC, vol. 1, p. 14. Wiley (2014)
2. Alessi, F., Thoman, P., Georgakoudis, G., Fahringer, T., Nikolopoulos, D.S.: Application-level energy awareness for OpenMP. In: Terboven, C., de Supinski, B.R., Reble, P., Chapman, B.M., Müller, M.S. (eds.) IWOMP 2015. LNCS, vol. 9342, pp. 219–232. Springer, Cham (2015). https://doi.org/10.1007/978-3-319-24595-9_16

3. Andrade, H.C.M., Gedik, B., Turaga, D.S.: Fundamentals of Stream Processing. Cambridge University Press, New York (2014)
4. Beyer, B., Jones, C., Petoff, J., Murphy, N.R.: Site Reliability Engineering. O'Reilly, Boston (2016)
5. Chandrakasan, A.P., Brodersen, R.W.: Minimizing power consumption in digital CMOS circuits. Proc. IEEE **83**(4), 498–523 (1995)
6. Danelutto, M., Garcia, J.D., Sanchez, L.M., Sotomayor, R., Torquati, M.: Introducing parallelism by using REPARA C++11 attributes. In: Euromicro International Conference on Parallel, Distributed, and Network-Based Processing, pp. 354–358. IEEE (2016)
7. De Sensi, D., De Matteis, T., Danelutto, M.: Simplifying self-adaptive and power-aware computing with Nornir. Future Gener. Comput. Syst. **87**, 136–151 (2018)
8. De Sensi, D., Torquati, M., Danelutto, M.: A reconfiguration algorithm for power-aware parallel applications. ACM Trans. Architect. Code Optim. **13**(4), 43:1–43:25 (2016)
9. Floratou, A., Agrawal, A., Graham, B., Rao, S., Ramasamy, K.: Dhalion: self-regulating stream processing in heron. Proc. VLDB Endowment **10**, 1825–1836 (2017)
10. Griebler, D., Danelutto, M., Torquati, M., Fernandes, L.G.: SPar: a DSL for high-level and productive stream parallelism. Parallel Process. Lett. **27**(01), 20 (2017)
11. Griebler, D., Hoffmann, R.B., Danelutto, M., Fernandes, L.G.: High-level and productive stream parallelism for Dedup, Ferret, and Bzip2. Int. J. Parallel Program., 1–19 (2018)
12. Griebler, D., Hoffmann, R.B., Danelutto, M., Fernandes, L.G.: Higher-level parallelism abstractions for video applications with SPar. In: Parallel Computing is Everywhere, Proceedings of the International Conference on Parallel Computing, ParCo 2017, pp. 698–707. IOS Press, Bologna (2017)
13. Maggio, M., Hoffmann, H., Santambrogio, M.D., Agarwal, A., Leva, A.: Controlling software applications via resource allocation within the heartbeats framework. In: IEEE Conference on Decision and Control, pp. 3736–3741. IEEE (2010)
14. Maurer, J., Wong, M.: Towards support for attributes in C++ (revision 6). Technical report, The C++ Standards Committee (2008)
15. McCool, M., Robison, A.D., Reinders, J.: Structured Parallel Programming: Patterns for Efficient Computation. Morgan Kaufmann, Burlington (2012)
16. Reinders, J.: Intel Threading Building Blocks. O'Reilly, Newton (2007)
17. Shafik, R.A., Das, A., Yang, S., Merrett, G., Al-Hashimi, B.M.: Adaptive energy minimization of OpenMP parallel applications on many-core systems. In: Parallel Programming and Run-Time Management Techniques, pp. 19–24 (2015)
18. Sturm, R., Morris, W., Jander, M.: Foundations of Service Level Management. SAMS, Boston (2000)
19. Thies, W., Karczmarek, M., Amarasinghe, S.: StreamIt: a language for streaming applications. In: Horspool, R.N. (ed.) CC 2002. LNCS, vol. 2304, pp. 179–196. Springer, Heidelberg (2002). https://doi.org/10.1007/3-540-45937-5_14
20. Weyuker, E.J.: Evaluating software complexity measures. IEEE Trans. Softw. Eng. **14**(9), 1357–1365 (1988)

InKS, a Programming Model to Decouple Performance from Algorithm in HPC Codes

Ksander Ejjaaouani[1,2(✉)], Olivier Aumage[3,4], Julien Bigot[1], Michel Mehrenberger[5], Hitoshi Murai[6], Masahiro Nakao[6], and Mitsuhisa Sato[6]

[1] Maison de la Simulation, CEA, CNRS, Univ. Paris-Sud, UVSQ Université Paris-Saclay, Gif-sur-Yvette, France
julien.bigot@cea.fr
[2] Inria, Nancy, France
ksander.ejjaaouani@inria.fr
[3] Inria, Bordeaux, France
olivier.aumage@inria.fr
[4] LaBRI, Bordeaux, France
[5] IRMA, Université de Strasbourg, Strasbourg, France
mehrenbe@math.unistra.fr
[6] Riken AICS, Kobe, Japan
{h-murai,masahiro.nakao,msato}@riken.jp

Abstract. Existing programming models tend to tightly interleave algorithm and optimization in HPC simulation codes. This requires scientists to become experts in both the simulated domain and the optimization process and makes the code difficult to maintain and port to new architectures. This paper proposes the InKS programming model that decouples these two concerns with distinct languages for each. The simulation algorithm is expressed in the InKS_{pia} language with no concern for machine-specific optimizations. Optimizations are expressed using both a family of dedicated optimizations DSLs (InKS_{O}) and plain C++. InKS_{O} relies on the InKS_{pia} source to assist developers with common optimizations while C++ is used for less common ones. Our evaluation demonstrates the soundness of the approach by using it on synthetic benchmarks and the Vlasov-Poisson equation. It shows that InKS offers separation of concerns at no performance cost.

Keywords: Programming model · Separation of concerns HPC · DSL

1 Introduction

It is more and more common to identify simulation as the *third pillar of science* together with theory and experimentation. Parallel computers provide the computing power required by the more demanding of these simulations. The

G. Mencagli et al. (Eds.): Euro-Par 2018 Workshops, LNCS 11339, pp. 757–768, 2019.
https://doi.org/10.1007/978-3-030-10549-5_59

complexity and heterogeneity of these architectures do however force scientists to write complex code (using vectorization, parallelization, accelerator specific languages, etc.) These optimizations heavily depend on the target machine and the whole code has to be adapted whenever it is ported to a new architecture.

As a result, scientists have to become experts in the art of computer optimizations in addition to their own domain of expertise. It is very difficult in practice to maintain a code targeting multiple distinct architectures. One fundamental cause for this situation is the tight interleaving of two distinct concerns imposed by most programming models. On the one hand, the algorithm comes from the expertise of the domain scientist and does not depend on the target architecture. On the other hand, optimization is the expertise of optimization specialists and has to be adapted for every new architecture.

Many approaches have been proposed to improve this situation in the form of libraries or languages. Approaches based on automated optimization processes typically isolate the algorithmic aspects very well but restrict their domain of applicability and/or the range of supported optimizations. Approaches based on optimization tools and libraries enable optimization specialists to express common optimizations very efficiently but leave others mixed with the algorithm.

In this paper, we propose the Independent Kernel Scheduling (InKS) programming model to separate algorithm from optimization choices in HPC simulation codes. We define the InKS_{pia} language used to express the algorithm of an application independently of its optimization. Such a program can be optimized with the InKS_{O} family of domain-specific languages (DSLs) for common optimizations or C++ for less common optimizations.

This paper makes the following contributions: **(1)** it defines the InKS programming model and its *platform-independent algorithmic* language InKS_{pia}; **(2)** it proposes an implementation of InKS with two optimization DSLs, $\text{InKS}_{\text{O/Loop}}$ and $\text{InKS}_{\text{O/XMP}}$; and **(3)** it evaluates the approach on the synthetic NAS parallel benchmarks [3] and on the 6D Vlasov-Poisson solving with a semi-Lagrangian method.

The remaining of the paper is organized as follows. Section 2 presents and analyzes related work. Section 3 describes the InKS programming model and its implementation. Section 4 presents the 6D Vlasov-Poisson problem and its implementation using InKS while Sect. 5 evaluates the approach. Finally, Sect. 6 concludes the paper and identifies some perspectives.

2 Related Works

Many approaches are used to implement optimized scientific simulations. A first widely used approach is based on imperative languages such as Fortran, C or C++. Libraries like MPI extend this to distributed memory with message passing. Abstractions very close to the actual execution machine make fine-tuning possible to achieve good performance on any specific architecture. It does however require encoding complex optimizations directly in the code. As there is no language support to separate the algorithm and architecture-specific optimizations, tedious efforts have to be applied [10] to support performance portability. Algorithm and optimizations are instead often tightly bound together in codes.

A second approach is thus offered by tools (libraries, frameworks or language extensions) that encode classical optimizations. *OpenMP* [5] or *Kokkos* [4] support common shared-memory parallelization patterns. *E.g*, Kokkos offers multi-dimensional arrays and iterators for which efficient memory mappings and iteration orders are selected independently. *E.g*, *UPC* [8] or XMP [14] support the partitioned global address space paradigm. In XMP, directives describe array distribution and communications between nodes. These tools offer gains of productivity when the optimization patterns they offer fit the requirements. The separation of optimizations from the main code base also eases porting between architectures. Even if expressed more compactly optimizations do however remain mixed with the algorithm and only cover part of the requirements.

A third approach pushes this further with tools that automate the optimization process. For example, *PaRSEC* [11] or *StarPU* [1] support the many-tasks paradigm. In StarPU, the user expresses its code as a DAG of tasks with data dependencies that is automatically scheduled at runtime depending on the available resources. Another examples are *SkeTo* [18] or *Lift* [16] that offer algorithmic skeletons. Lift offers a limited set of parallel patterns whose combinations are automatically transformed by an optimizing compiler. Automating optimization improves productivity and clearly separate these optimizations which improves portability. The tools do however not cover the whole range of potential optimizations such as the choice of work granularity inside tasks. The algorithm remains largely interleaved with optimization choices even with this approach.

A last approach is based on DSLs that restrict optimizations, such as *Pochoir* [17] or *PATUS* [6], DSLs for stencil problems. In Pochoir, the user only specifies a stencil (computation kernel and access pattern), boundary conditions and a space-time domain while all optimizations are handled by a compiler. DSLs restrict the developer to the expression of the algorithm only, while optimizations are handled independently. This ensures a very good separation of these aspects. The narrower the target domain is, the more efficient domain and architecture-specific optimizations are possible. However, it makes it less likely for the tool to cover the needs of a whole application. Real-world applications can fall at the frontier between the domains of distinct DSLs or not be covered by a single one. Performance then depends on the choice of DSLs to use and the best choice depends on the target architecture leading to new portability issues.

To summarize, one can consider a continuum of approaches from very general approaches where the optimization process is manual to more and more domain specific where the optimization process can be automated. The more general approaches support a large range of optimizations and application domains but yield high implementation costs and low separation of concerns and portability. The more automated approaches reduce implementation costs and offer good separation of concerns and portability but restrain the range of supported domains and optimizations. Ideally, one would like to combine all these advantages: **(1)** the domain generality of imperative languages, **(2)** the ease of optimization offered by dedicated tools and **(3)** the separation of concerns and performance portability offered by DSLs. The following section describes the InKS programming model that aims to combine these approaches to offer such a solution.

3 The InKS Programming Model

This section describes the core of our contribution, the InKS programming model. This approach is based on the use of distinct languages to express algorithm and optimization choices; thus enforcing their separation. The *algorithm* of the simulation consists in the set of values computed, the formula used to produce each of them as well as the simulation inputs and outputs. We include in *optimization choices* all that is not the algorithm, such as the choice of a computing unit for each computation, their ordering, the choice of a location in memory for each value, etc. Multiple optimization choices can differ in performance but simulation results depend on the algorithm only.

The InKS approach is summarized in Fig. 1. The InKS$_{\text{pia}}$ language is used to express the algorithm with no concern for optimization choices. A compiler generates non-optimized, generic choices automatically from this specification for test purposes. The InKS$_{\text{O}}$ family of DSLs is used to define common optimizations efficiently while C++ is used to describe arbitrarily complex optimizations. Many versions of the optimization choices can be devised to optimize for multiple targets.

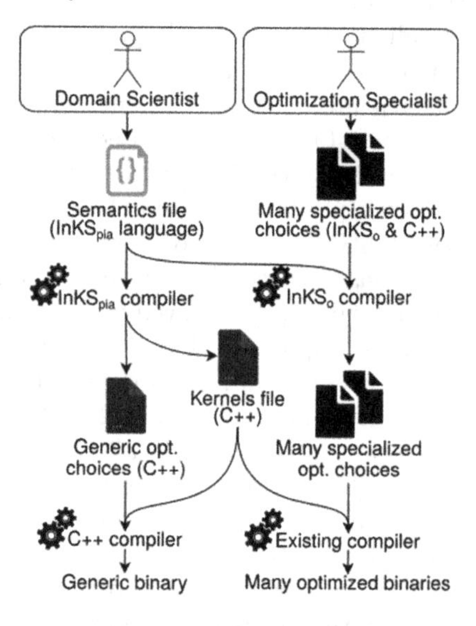

Fig. 1. The InKS model

The remaining of the section describes InKS$_{\text{pia}}$ and proposes two preliminary InKS$_{\text{O}}$ DSLs. InKS$_{\text{O/XMP}}$ handles domain decomposition and inter-node communications while InKS$_{\text{O/Loop}}$ focuses on efficient loops.

The InKS$_{\text{pia}}$ *language.* In InKS$_{\text{pia}}$ [2] (illustrated in Listing 1), values are stored in infinite multidimensional arrays based on dynamic single assignment (DSA, each coordinate can only be written once). Memory placement of each coordinate is left unspecified. Computations are specified by *kernel* procedures that **(1)** take as parameters data arrays and integer coordinates; **(2)** specify the coordinate they might read and will write in each array; and **(3)** define either a C++ or InKS implementation. An InKS implementation defines kernels *validity domains*: coordinates where C++ kernels can generate values in arrays. Kernel execution order is left unspecified. The simulation entry point is a kernel marked *public*. This specifies a parameterized task graph (PTG) [7]. This representation covers a large range of problems but imposes a few limitations. Mostly, all the problem parameters must be known at launch time, it does for example not support adaptive mesh or time-steps. It is still possible to express these concerns outside InKS_{pia} and call the InKS implementation multiple times with different parameters.

The InKS_{pia} compiler [2] extracts C++ functions from InKS_{pia} kernels and generates a function with correct but non-optimized loops and memory allocations to execute them. Arbitrarily complex versions of these can also be written manually in plain C++ and rely on existing optimization tools. These functions can be called from any existing code whose language supports the C calling convention. However, that approach requires information present in InKS_{pia} to be repeated. The InKS_{O} DSLs thus interface optimization tools with InKS_{pia}.

```
1 kernel stencil3(x, t): ( double A(2) {in: (x-1:x+1, t) | out: (x, t+1)} )
2     #CODE(C) A(x, t+1) = 0.5*A(x, t-1) + 0.25*(A(x-1, t-1)+A(x+1, t-1)); #END
3 public kernel inks_stencil(DIM_X, N_ITER):
4         ( double A_decl(2) {in: (0:DIM_X, 0) | out: (1:DIM_X-1, N_ITER-1)} )
5     #CODE(INKS) stencil3(1:DIM_X-1, 1:N_ITER-1):(A_decl) #END
```

Listing 1: 1D stencil computation on a 2D domain in InKS_{pia}

```
1 #pragma xmp nodes p6d[pV3][pV2][pV1][pZ][pY][pX]
2 #pragma inks decompose dynamic % f6d // dynamic allocation of f6d algorithmic array
3     (8:, 7:, 6, 5, 4, 3, 2, 1) // dimension reordering, dim 7 & 8 are folded
4     with t6d onto p6d // block decomposition mapped on the XMP topology
5 // Dynamic halo exchange on the 4th dimension, halo sizes are computed automatically
6 #pragma inks exchange periodic f6d(4, advection4) to R and L
7 /*R and L are now allocated buffers and contain the halo values: */ foo(R, L);
```

Listing 2: 6D decomposition and dynamic halo exchange in $\text{InKS}_{\text{O/XMP}}$

```
1 double (f6d*)[][][][][]; // need to declare f6d global, valid in xmp
2 #pragma xmp nodes p6d[pV3][pV2][pV1][pZ][pY][pX] // xmp 6d cartesian node topology
3 #pragma xmp template t6d[:][:][:][:][:][:] // xmp 6d logical array
4 #pragma xmp distribute t6d [block][block][block][block][block][block] onto p6d
5 // map element of f6d to element of t6d
6 #pragma xmp align f6d[n][m][l][k][j][i] with t6d[n][m][l][k][j][i]
7 #pragma xmp template_fix t6d[N][M][L][K][J][I]
8 f6d = (double(*)[M][L][K][J][I]) xmp_malloc(xmp_desc_of(f6d), N, M, L, K, J, I);
```

Listing 3: XMP code generated for the `f6D` decomposition of Listing 2

The $\text{InKS}_{\text{O/XMP}}$ *Optimization Language.* $\text{InKS}_{\text{O/XMP}}$ (illustrated in Listing 2) handles distributed memory domain decomposition by combining C and directives based on XMP and adapted for InKS. The compiler replaces these directives by C and XMP code (Listing 3). The `inks decompose` directive supports static or dynamic allocation of arrays from the algorithm. The domain size is extracted from InKS_{pia} source and the user only has to specify its mapping onto memory. As in XMP, $\text{InKS}_{\text{O/XMP}}$ supports domain decomposition mapped onto an XMP topology. In addition, it supports dimension reordering and folding which consists in reusing the same memory address for subsequent indices in a given dimension. This feature is important to reuse memory due to the DSA nature of InKS_{pia} arrays. The `exchange` directive supports halo exchanges. The required halo size is automatically extracted from the algorithm and the user only has to specify when to execute the communications and in what dimension. While XMP requires halo values to be stored contiguously with the domain,

INKS$_{\mathsf{O/XMP}}$ support a dynamic halo extension where halo values are stored in dedicated, dynamically allocated buffers to reduce memory footprint.

```
1 /*** advec.iks InKSpia algorithmic file ***/
2 kernel advection3 (i, j, k, l, m, n, t, K, step) : (
3     double f6d { in: (i, j, 0:K, l, m, n, t, step-1) | out: (i, j, k, l, m, n, t, step) },
4     int disp {in: (n)}, double coef {in: (n, 0:4)} )
5 #CODE (C) /* ... */ #END
6
7 public kernel main_code(t, I, J, K, L, M, N, Niter): ( double coef(2), int disp(1)
8     double f6d(6) { in: (i, j, 0:K, l, m, n, t, step-1) | out: (i, j, k, l, m, n, t,
          step) } )
9 #CODE(INKS)
10   /* ... */
11   advection3 (0:I, 0:J, 0:K, 0:L, 0:M, 0:N, 1:Niter, K, 2) : (f6d, disp, coef)
12   /* ... */
13 #END
14
15 /*** advec.iloop InKSo/Loop optimization choices file ***/
16 loop advection3_loops(t, I, J, K, L, M, N, Niter) : advection3 { // set "t" value
17   // "Set" not specified -> loop bounds are computed, with a fixed "t"
18   Order: n, m, l, j, i, k; // order of the loop
19   Block: 16; // blocking on the inner dimension k
20   Buffer: f6d(3); } // copy the third dimension of f6d to a 1d buffer
```

Listing 4: A loop nest in INKS$_{\mathsf{pia}}$ optimized in INKS$_{\mathsf{O/Loop}}$

```
1 /* for all N, M, L, J, do */ for (int i=0; i<I; i+=blockSize){
2   for(int ci=-halo_size; ci<0; ++ci) /*Copy to buffer*/
3     for(int ii=0; ii<blockSize; ++ii) buff.buff_in[...] = left[...];
4   for(int ci=0; ci<K; ++ci)
5     for(int ii=0; ii<blockSize; ++ii) buff.buff_in[...] = f6d[...];
6   for(int ci=sizeK; ci<sizeK+halo_size; ++ci)
7     for(int ii=0; ii<blockSize; ++ii) buff.buff_in[...] = right[...];
8   for(int idb=0; idb<size_block; ++idb) /*Computation*/
9     for(int k=0; k<K; ++k) advection3(buff, idb+i, j, k, l, m, n);
10  for(int ci=0; ci<K; ++ci) /*Copy to f6d*/
11    for(int ii=0; ii<block_size; ++ii) f6d[...] = buff.buff_out[...];}
```

Listing 5: C++ code generated for the loop nest of Listing 4

The INKS$_{\mathsf{O/Loop}}$ *Optimization Language.* INKS$_{\mathsf{O/Loop}}$ (illustrated in Listing 4) offers to specify manually loop nests for which the compiler generates plain C++ loops (Listing 5). Plain C++ is usable with INKS$_{\mathsf{O/Loop}}$. The `loop` keyword introduces a nest optimization with a name, the list of parameters from the algorithm on which the loop bounds depend and a reference to the optimized kernel. Loop bounds can be automatically extracted from INKS$_{\mathsf{pia}}$, but the `Set` keyword makes it possible to restrict these bounds. The `Order` keyword specifies the iteration order on the dimensions and the `Block` keyword enables the user to implement blocking. It takes as parameters the size of block for the loops starting from the innermost one. If there are less block sizes than loops, the remaining loops are not blocked. The `Buffer` keyword supports copying data in a local buffer before computation and back after to ensure data continuity and improve vectorization. The compiler uses data dependencies from the algorithm to check the validity of the loops order and generate vectorization directives where possible.

4 The 6D Vlasov/Poisson Problem

The 6D Vlasov-Poisson equation, presented in (1), describes the movement of particles in a plasma and the resulting electric field. We study its resolution for a single species on a 6D Cartesian mesh with periodic boundary conditions. We solve the Poisson part using a fast Fourier transform (FFT) and rely on a Strang splitting (order 2 in time) for the Vlasov part. This leads to 6 1D advections: 3 in the space dimensions (x_1, x_2, x_3) and 3 in the velocity dimensions (v_1, v_2, v_3). Each 1D advection relies on a Lagrange interpolation of degree 4. In the space dimensions, we use a semi-Lagrangian approach where the stencil is not applied around the destination point but at the foot of characteristics, a coordinate known at runtime only. This is described in more details in [15].

$$\begin{cases} \frac{\partial f(t,x,v)}{\partial t} + v.\nabla_x f(t,x,v) - E(t,x).\nabla_v f(t,x,v) = 0 \\ -\Delta\phi(t,x) = 1 - \rho(t,x) \\ E(t,x) = -\nabla\phi(t,x) \\ \rho(t,x) = \int f(t,x,v)dv \end{cases} \tag{1}$$

The main unknown is f (`f6D` in the code), the distribution function of particles in 6D phase space. Due to the Strang splitting, a first half time-step of advections is required after `f6D` initialization but before the main time-loop. These advections need the electric field E as input. E is obtained through the FFT-based Poisson solver that in turn needs the charge density ρ as input. ρ is computed by a reduction of `f6D`. The main time-loop is composed of 3 steps: advections in space dimensions, computation of the charge density (reduction) and electric field (Poisson solver) and advections in velocity dimensions.

The 6D nature of `f6D` requires a lot of memory, but the regularity of the problem means it can be distributed in blocks with good load-balancing. Halos are required to hold values of neighbors for the advections. Connected halo zones would increase the number of points in all dimensions and consume too much memory. Split advections mean that halos are required in a single dimension at a time though. We therefore use dynamic halos composed of two buffers, one for each boundary of the advected dimension (denoted *"right"* and *"left"*) as shown on Fig. 2. Listing 2 corresponds to the InKS$_{\text{O/XMP}}$ implementation of this strategy.

Advections are the main computational cost of the problem, accounting for 90% of the sequential execution time. Six loops surround the stencil computation of each advection and in a naive version, the use of a modulo to handle periodicity and application along non-contiguous dimensions slow down the computation. To enable vectorization and improve cache use, we copy `f6D` elements into contiguous buffers along with the *left* and *right* halos. Advections are applied on these buffers before copying them back into `f6D`. Blocking further improves performance by copying 16 elements at a time. Listing 5 corresponds to the InKS$_{\text{O/Loop}}$ implementation of these optimizations.

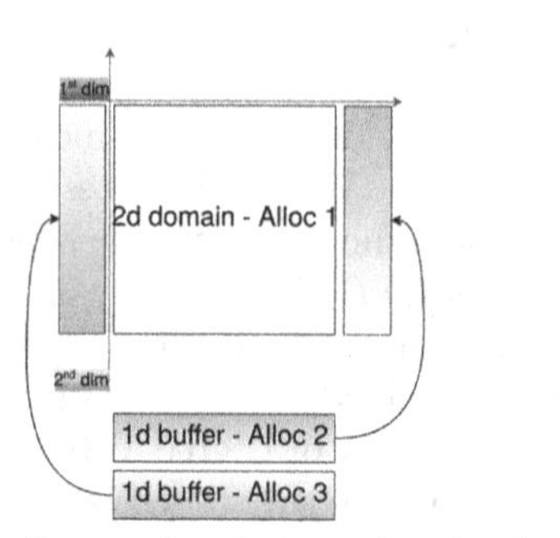

(a) Buffers used as halo regions in the first dimension

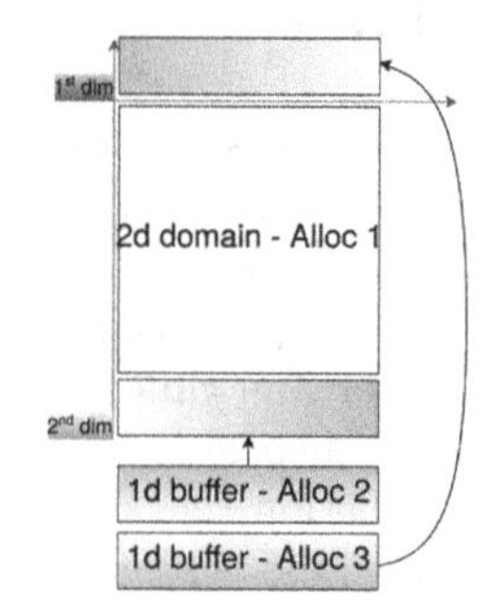

(b) Buffers used as halo regions in the second dimension

Fig. 2. Dynamic halo exchange representation on a 2D domain

5 Evaluation

This section evaluates the INKS model on the NAS parallel benchmark, a simple stencil code and the 6D Vlasov-Poisson problem. Plain C++ is used for the synthetic benchmarks optimization while $\text{INKS}_{\text{O/XMP}}$, $\text{INKS}_{\text{O/Loop}}$, plain C++ and C with XMP are used for Vlasov-Poisson. All codes are compiled with Intel 18 compiler (`-O3 -xHost`), Intel MPI 5.0.1 and executed on the *Poincare* cluster (Idris, France) with 32 GB RAM and two Sandy Bridge E5-2670 CPUs per node and a QLogic QDR InfiniBand interconnect.

5.1 Synthetic Benchmarks

We have implemented 4 out of the 5 sequential NAS benchmark kernels (`IS`, `FT`, `EP` and `MG`) in INKS_{pia} and optimized them with plain C++. The C++ version [9], is used as reference. We have also implemented a 3D heat equation resolution by finite differences (7-point stencil) with two distinct C++ optimization strategies from a single INKS_{pia} source. Both strategies comes from the reference [12]. One uses double buffering (Heat/Buf) and the other implements a cache oblivious strategy (Heat/Obl).

The NAS `CG` kernel relies on indirections not expressible in the PTG model of INKS_{pia}. Its implementation would thus have to rely on a large C++ kernel whose optimization would be mixed with the algorithm. INKS_{pia} can however be used to express all other NAS kernels as well as the 3D heat equation solver. Even if not as expressive as C or Fortran, INKS_{pia} covers the needs of a wide range of simulation domains and offers abstractions close to the execution machine rather than from a specific simulation domain. Among others, it can express computations such as FFTs or stencils with input coordinates unknown at compile-time.

INKS separates the specification of algorithm and optimization in distinct files. Multiple optimization strategies can be implemented for a single algorithm,

Table 1. Execution time of the C++ and InKS implementations of the sequential NAS benchmark, class B - time/iteration of the 3D heat equation (7point stencil), size (1024^3) - median and standard deviation of 10 executions - GNU complexity score of the implementation.

	Execution time (second)			Complexity	
Benchmark	Reference	InKS	Rel. dev.	Ref.	InKS
NAS/FT	62.43 (±0.57)	62.86 (±0.71)	0.68%	6	5
NAS/IS	3.39 (±0.00)	3.44 (±0.00)	1.47%	55	52
NAS/MG	5.10 (±0.02)	4.73 (±0.06)	−7.25%	20	12
NAS/EP	76.43 (±0.21)	76.47 (±0.22)	0.05%	19	19
Heat/Buf	3.05 (±0.01)	2.97 (±0.06)	−2.58%	5	3
Heat/Obl	2.43 (±0.01)	2.05 (±0.02)	−15.59%	22	13

as shown for the 3D heat equation where each relies on a specific memory layout and scheduling. It thus offers a clear separation of algorithm and optimization.

Finding the right metric to evaluate the easiness of writing a code is a difficult question. As illustrated in Listing 4 however, algorithm expression in InKS_{pia} is close to the most naive C implementation where loops are replaced by InKS validity domains with no worry for optimization. The specification of optimization choices is close to their expression in C++. Table 1 compares the GNU complexity score of InKS optimizations to the reference code. InKS scores are slightly better because kernels extracted from the algorithm hide computations and thus, part of the complexity. In addition, the use of C++ to write optimizations let optimization specialists reuse their preexisting knowledge of this language. These considerations should not hide the fact that some information has to be specified both in the InKS_{pia} and C++ files with this approach leading to more code overall.

Regarding performance, the InKS approach makes it possible to express optimizations that do not change the algorithm. Optimizations of the four NAS parallel benchmarks and 3D heat equation solver in InKS were trivial to implement and their performance match or improve upon the reference as presented in Table 1. Investigation have shown that Intel ICC 18 does not vectorize properly the reference versions of Heat/Obl and NAS/MG. The use of the Intel `ivdep` directive as done on the InKS versions leads to slightly better performance.

5.2 Vlasov-Poisson

We evaluate $\text{InKS}_{\text{O/XMP}}$ and $\text{InKS}_{\text{O/Loop}}$ on Vlasov-Poisson separately as they target different optimizations and are not usable together currently. A first experiment focuses on the sequential aspects with the intra-node optimization of the v_1 advection using either $\text{InKS}_{\text{O/Loop}}$ or plain C++. A second experiment focuses on the parallel aspects with the charge density computation, the Poisson solver and a halo exchange optimized either with C/XMP or with $\text{InKS}_{\text{O/XMP}}$. The reference is the Fortran/MPI implementation from the Selalib library [13].

Distinct files for both concerns in InKS makes possible to write a unique InKS$_{\mathsf{pia}}$ algorithm and multiple versions of optimization choices. Four optimization choices are implemented based on one InKS$_{\mathsf{pia}}$ source : (1) InKS$_{\mathsf{O/XMP}}$, (2) C with XMP, (3) InKS$_{\mathsf{O/Loop}}$ and (4) plain C++. This proves, to some extent, that the separation of concerns is respected. As of now, InKS$_{\mathsf{O/XMP}}$ and InKS$_{\mathsf{O/Loop}}$ are not usable together since InKS$_{\mathsf{O/Loop}}$ relies on C++ that XMP does not support. We plan to address this limitation in the future.

For the v_1 advection, both the C++ and InKS$_{\mathsf{O/Loop}}$ optimizations of the InKS code achieve performance similar to the reference as shown in Table 2. For the parallel aspects, the InKS$_{\mathsf{O/XMP}}$ optimization offers performance similar to XMP as shown on Fig. 3. The performance is comparable to MPI on the reduction operation but MPI is faster on the Poisson solver and the halo exchanges. At the moment, it seems that XMP does not optimize local copies which slows down the Poisson solver. Besides, XMP directives used for the halo exchanges are based on MPI RMA which make the comparison with MPI Send/Receive complex. Still, MPI is much harder to program: more than 350 lines of MPI and Fortran are required to handle domain decomposition, remapping for FFT and halo exchange in Selalib vs. 50 lines in XMP and 15 in InKS$_{\mathsf{O/XMP}}$.

Table 2. Comparison between Fortran, C++ and InKS$_{\mathsf{O/Loop}}$ version of the v_1 advection on a 32^6 grid (double precision) on a single E5-2670 core with vectorization. Median of 12 executions

Version	Time/advection	GFLOP/s	% Peak core perf.
Selalib (Fortran)	4.81 s	1.12	5.36%
InKS (C++)	3.76 s	1.43	6.87%
InKS (InKS$_{\mathsf{O/Loop}}$)	3.61 s	1.49	7.16%

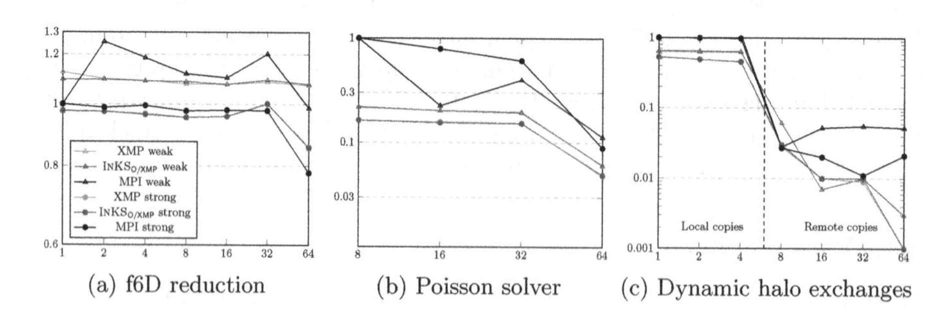

(a) f6D reduction (b) Poisson solver (c) Dynamic halo exchanges

Fig. 3. Weak and strong scaling for 3 parts of the Vlasov-poisson solver up to 64 nodes (1 process/node) on a 32^6 grid divided among processes (strong scaling) or 16^6 grid per process (weak scaling). Median of 10 executions.

The InKS$_O$ family of DSLs enables the developer to specify optimization choices only while algorithmic information is extracted from InKS$_{pia}$ code. This is illustrated by Listings 2, presenting the InKS$_{O/XMP}$ 6D domain decomposition, and 3, presenting the XMP version. Both are equivalent, but the InKS$_{O/XMP}$ expects only optimization choices parameters. Hence, one can test another memory layout, such as a different dimension ordering, by changing only a few parameters, while multiple directives must be modified in XMP. Similarly, with InKS$_{O/Loop}$ (Listing 4), developers can easily test different optimization choices that would be tedious in plain C++. Since InKS$_{O/XMP}$ and InKS$_{O/Loop}$ are respectively usable with C and C++, InKS does not restrict the expressible optimization choices: one can still implement optimizations not handled by InKS$_O$ in C/C++. Moreover, operations such as halo size computation or vectorization capabilities detection are automatized using the algorithm. In summary, the approach enables optimization specialists to focus on their specialty which make the development easier.

6 Conclusion and Future Works

In this paper, we have presented the InKS programming model to separate algorithm (InKS$_{pia}$) and optimization choices (InKS$_O$ & C++) and its implementation supporting two DSLs : InKS$_{O/Loop}$ for loop optimizations and InKS$_{O/XMP}$ for domain decomposition. We have evaluated InKS on synthetic benchmarks and on the Vlasov-Poisson solving. We have demonstrated its generality and its advantages in terms of separation of concerns to improve maintainability and portability while offering performance on par with existing approaches.

While this paper demonstrates the interest of the InKS approach, it still requires some work to further develop it. We plan to apply the InKS model on a range of different problems. We will improve the optimization DSLs; base InKS$_{O/Loop}$ on existing loop optimization tools and ensure good interactions with InKS$_{O/XMP}$. We also want to target different architectures to demonstrate the portability gains of the InKS approach.

References

1. Augonnet, C., Thibault, S., Namyst, R., Wacrenier, P.A.: StarPU: a unified platform for task scheduling on heterogeneous multicore architectures. Concurr. Comput.: Pract. Exper. **23**(2), 187–198 (2011). https://doi.org/10.1002/cpe.1631
2. Aumage, O., Bigot, J., Ejjaaouani, K., Mehrenberger, M.: INKS, a programming model to decouple performance from semantics in simulation codes. Technical report (2017). https://hal-cea.archives-ouvertes.fr/cea-01493075
3. Bailey, D.H., et al.: The NAS parallel benchmarks. Int. J. Supercomput. Appl. **5**(3), 63–73 (1991)
4. Carter Edwards, H., Trott, C.R., Sunderland, D.: Kokkos: Enabling manycore performance portability through polymorphic memory access patterns. J. Parallel Distrib. Comput. **74**(12), 3202–3216 (2014). https://doi.org/10.1016/j.jpdc.2014.07.003, http://www.sciencedirect.com/science/article/pii/S0743731514001257

5. Chandra, R., Dagum, L., Kohr, D., Maydan, D., McDonald, J., Menon, R.: Parallel Programming in OpenMP. Morgan Kaufmann Publishers Inc., San Francisco (2001)
6. Christen, M., Schenk, O., Burkhart, H.: PATUS: a code generation and autotuning framework for parallel iterative stencil computations on modern microarchitectures. In: 2011 IEEE International Parallel and Distributed Processing Symposium (IPDPS), pp. 676–687. IEEE, May 2011. https://doi.org/10.1109/ipdps.2011.70
7. Cosnard, M., Jeannot, E.: Compact DAG representation and its dynamic-scheduling. J. Parallel Distrib. Comput. **58**(3), 487–514 (1999). https://doi.org/10.1006/jpdc.1999.1566, http://www.sciencedirect.com/science/article/pii/S0743731599915666
8. El-Ghazawi, T., Carlson, W., Sterling, T., Yelick, K.: UPC: distributed Shared Memory Programming (Wiley Series on Parallel and Distributed Computing). Wiley, Hoboken (2005)
9. Griebler, D., Löff, J., Fernandes, L., Mencagli, G., Danelutto, M.: Efficient NAS benchmark kernels with C++ parallel programming, January 2018
10. Höhnerbach, M., Ismail, A.E., Bientinesi, P.: The vectorization of the tersoff multi-body potential: an exercise in performance portability. In: Proceedings of the International Conference for High Performance Computing, Networking, Storage and Analysis SC 2016, pp. 7:1–7:13. IEEE Press, Piscataway (2016). http://dl.acm.org/citation.cfm?id=3014904.3014914
11. Hoque, R., Herault, T., Bosilca, G., Dongarra, J.: Dynamic task discovery in parsec: a data-flow task-based runtime. In: Proceedings of the 8th Workshop on Latest Advances in Scalable Algorithms for Large-Scale Systems ScalA 2017, pp. 6:1–6:8. ACM, New York (2017). https://doi.org/10.1145/3148226.3148233
12. Kamil, S.: Stencilprobe: a microbenchmark for stencil applications (2012). http://people.csail.mit.edu/skamil/projects/stencilprobe/. Accessed 25 Aug 2017
13. Kormann, K., Reuter, K., Rampp, M., Sonnendrücker, E.: Massively parallel semi-lagrangian solution of the 6D Vlasov-Poisson problem, October 2016
14. Lee, J., Sato, M.: Implementation and performance evaluation of xcalablemp: a parallel programming language for distributed memory systems. In: 2010 39th International Conference on Parallel Processing Workshops, pp. 413–420, September 2010. https://doi.org/10.1109/ICPPW.2010.62
15. Mehrenberger, M., Steiner, C., Marradi, L., Crouseilles, N., Sonnendrücker, E., Afeyan, B.: Vlasov on GPU (vog project)******. In: Proceedings ESAIM, vol. 43, pp. 37–58 (2013). https://doi.org/10.1051/proc/201343003
16. Steuwer, M., Remmelg, T., Dubach, C.: Lift: a functional data-parallel IR for high-performance GPU code generation. In: 2017 IEEE/ACM International Symposium on Code Generation and Optimization (CGO), pp. 74–85, February 2017. https://doi.org/10.1109/CGO.2017.7863730
17. Tang, Y., Chowdhury, R.A., Kuszmaul, B.C., Luk, C.K., Leiserson, C.E.: The Pochoir stencil compiler. In: Proceedings of the Twenty-third Annual ACM Symposium on Parallelism in Algorithms and Architectures SPAA 2011, pp. 117–128. ACM (2011). https://doi.org/10.1145/1989493.1989508
18. Tanno, H., Iwasaki, H.: Parallel skeletons for variable-length lists in sketo skeleton library. In: Proceedings of the 15th International Euro-Par Conference on Parallel Processing Euro-Par 2009, pp. 666–677. Springer, Heidelberg (2009). https://doi.org/10.1007/978-3-642-03869-3_63

Refactoring Loops with Nested IFs for SIMD Extensions Without Masked Instructions

Huihui Sun[1,2](✉), Sergei Gorlatch[1], and Rongcai Zhao[2]

[1] University of Münster, Münster, Germany
{huihuisun,gorlatch}@uni-muenster.de
[2] National Digital Switching System Engineering and Technological Research Center, Zhengzhou, China

Abstract. Most CPUs in heterogeneous systems are now equipped with SIMD (Single Instruction Multiple Data) extensions that operate on short vectors in parallel to enable high performance. Refactoring programs for such systems relies on vectorization, i.e., transforming into a form with SIMD-instructions. We improve the state of the art in refactoring loops with nested IF-statements that are notoriously difficult to vectorize. For IF-statements whose conditions are independent of the loop variable, we improve the classical *loop unswitching* method, such that it can tackle nested IFs. For IF-statements whose conditions change with loop iterations, we develop a novel *IF-select transformation* method: (1) it can work with arbitrarily nested IFs, and (2) while previous methods rely on either masked instructions or hardware support for predicated execution, our method works for SIMD extensions without such operations (as found, e.g., in IBM Power8 and ARM Cortex-A8). Our experimental evaluation for the SPEC CPU2006 benchmark suite is conducted on an SW26010 processor used in the Sunway TaihuLight supercomputer (#2 in the TOP500 list); it demonstrates the performance advantages of our implemented approach over the vectorizer of the Open64 compiler.

Keywords: SIMD extensions · Nested IF-statements
Loop vectorization · Loop unswitching · IF-select transformation

1 Motivation and Related Work

Most modern processors are equipped with SIMD (Single Instruction Multiple Data) extensions that operate on short vectors in parallel to enable high performance. To use this performance potential, programs must be refactored to a form with SIMD instructions; this is traditionally called *vectorization*. Manual vectorization via hand-written instrinsics is tedious, error-prone and unportable. Therefore, automatic vectorization is an indispensable part of most modern compilers, such as the commercial compiler ICC [11], as well as open-source compilers Open64 [3], GCC [6], and LLVM [14].

G. Mencagli et al. (Eds.): Euro-Par 2018 Workshops, LNCS 11339, pp. 769–781, 2019.
https://doi.org/10.1007/978-3-030-10549-5_60

There are three classic vectorization approaches: (1) loop vectorization [18] combines multiple occurrences of a scalar operation across consecutive loop iterations into one SIMD instruction, (2) basic block or SLP (Superword Level Parallelism) vectorization [13] transforms a group of isomorphic operations into one SIMD instruction, and (3) WFV (Whole Function Vectorization) [12] converts multiple instances of a kernel into SIMD instructions. These approaches are restricted: in particular, IF-statements lead to the control flow divergence that makes vectorization difficult.

Several methods were suggested to overcome this restriction, but they work only in special cases. The *loop unswitching* method [19] requires that the IF-condition remains the same across loop iterations. The *IF conversion* method [2] targets vector computers with explicit hardware support for predicated execution, where instructions from both paths of the branch are executed speculatively, and each instruction is then associated with a dedicated predicated register that determines whether this instruction should modify processor state. In this paper, we develop vectorization methods for processors with SIMD extensions that do not have explicit hardware support for predicated execution. Shin et al. [16] extend the classic SLP method to work in the presence of IF-statements. Our approach is similar to [16], except that we extend loop vectorization to work in the presence of arbitrarily nested IF-statements; we discuss further differences below. In comparison with the WFV method [12], we vectorize loops rather than functions in data-parallel languages (like CUDA or OpenCL). The state-of-the-art compilers such as LLVM depend on masked instructions to vectorize IF-statements, and need to fall back on IF-cascades on architectures without masked instructions, which makes automatic vectorization futile on such architectures. In our recent work [8], we extend the WFV vectorizer for SIMD extensions without masked instructions. Also Smith et al. [17] describe using masked vector instructions for vectorization, while we target architectures without masked instructions.

Summarizing, we aim at improving the state-of-the-art methods of refactoring by vectorization, that currently cannot generate efficient SIMD code for loops with arbitrarily nested IF-statements without hardware support for predicated execution or masked instructions. We cover two cases depending on whether the IF-condition changes across the loop iterations: (1) for loop-independent IF-statements, we extend the *loop unswitching* method to arbitrarily nested IF-statements; (2) for loop-dependent IF-statements, we develop a novel *IF-select transformation* method which works for loops with arbitrarily nested IF-statements on SIMD extensions without hardware support for predicated execution and masked instructions. We integrate our approach into the Open64 compiler [3] and evaluate it on an SW26010 processor [7] with a 256-bit SIMD extension as used in the Sunway TaihuLight supercomputer (#2 in the TOP500 list [20]). Experiments on a set of benchmarks from SPEC CPU2006 [9] with loops containing IF-statements confirm the efficiency of our approach.

In the remainder of the paper, Sect. 2 introduces the background on refactoring via vectorization and our target architecture model. Section 3 presents our vectorization approach for loops with nested IF-statements. Experimental results are presented in Sect. 4, and Sect. 5 concludes the paper.

2 Background: SIMD Extensions and Vectorization

We target modern heterogeneous systems that comprise CPUs with SIMD extensions, but without masked instructions, such as IBM Power8 [10], ARM Cortex-A8 [4], and SW26010 [7]. While the existing frameworks like FastFlow [1] and REPARA [5] can distribute workload among different cores using manual refactoring based on parallel patterns, we aim at automated refactoring within one core using vectorization. We use the SW26010 processor as our example: each core of it employs a 256-bit SIMD extension that works on 256 bits in parallel: it can be one long int (256-bit) operation, or 8 integer operations, or 4 floating point operations. Without loss of generality, we work in this paper with 64-bit floating point values, i.e., 4 operations can be executed simultaneously on such values.

Figure 1 illustrates a simple example of refactoring via vectorization: Fig. 1(a) shows a loop with regular computations, so it is straightforwardly vectorizable. Figure 1(b) shows the vectorization result using SIMD intrinsics, i.e., C-style functions providing access to SIMD instructions. For simplicity, we call these intrinsics *instructions*. A SIMD extension executes a loop iteration in Fig. 1(b) in parallel as follows: load the operands from memory to vectors, add the two vectors, and store the result vector into memory.

```
1 for(i=0;i<1024;i++)
2 {
3   c[i]=a[i]+b[i];
4 }
```

(a)

```
1 for(i=0;i<1024;i=i+4)
2 {
3   simd_load(v_a,&a[i]);
4   simd_load(v_b,&b[i]);
5   v_c=simd_vaddd(v_a,v_b);
6   simd_store(v_c, &c[i]);
7 }
```

(b)

Fig. 1. (a) An easily vectorizable loop; (b) The loop after vectorization

Table 1 shows the SIMD instructions used in this paper, with the names as used in the SW26010 processor. We only list the instructions for double precision floating point parameters; the vector type `doublev4` means 4 packed 64-bit double elements.

An important feature of our target architecture model is that we do not assume the existence of dedicated predicate registers, while many previous approaches to vectorization (e.g., [2]) rely on these registers and the corresponding predicated execution modus. Such registers can be found, e.g., in conventional vector processors, but not in modern CPUs with SIMD extensions. We also do not require from our target SIMD extensions to provide masked instructions

Table 1. Specific SIMD instructions used in this paper

Instruction	Operation	Input	Output	Functional description
simd_load	Load	doublev4 va, double *addr	void	Load 4 double elements into vector va from contiguous memory starting from *addr
simd_store	Store	doublev4 va, double *addr	void	Store 4 elements of vector va into contiguous memory starting from *addr
simd_vaddd	Addition	doublev4 va, vb	doublev4	Add 4 elements of va with 4 elements of vb element-wise, return the result
simd_vsubd	Subtraction	doublev4 va, vb	doublev4	Subtract 4 elements of va from 4 elements of vb element-wise, return the result
simd_vseleq	Select	doublev4 va, vb, vc	doublev4	Test the value of va element-wise: if it equals 0, then return the element of vb, otherwise return the element of vc
simd_vfcmplt	Comparison	doublev4 va, vb	doublev4	Compare the value of va and vb element-wise; if va $<$ vb, then the element of vc is assigned 1.0, otherwise 0

that are present, e.g., in the Intel AVX extension and used in some vectorization methods [17]. Summarizing, we aim at covering a broader class of target architectures than most of previous approaches.

3 Vectorization of Loops with IF-statements

Figure 2 shows the overall structure of our vectorization approach. For clarity, we assume that there is only a single, probably nested, IF-statement in the loop. For multiple IF-statements, we process them ordinally.

The first step in Fig. 2, *SIMD preanalysis*, checks whether vectorization can be applied to the loop legally. We mainly rely on the traditional four criteria of legal vectorization: (1) there are no dependence cycles between the statements in the loop body; (2) the loop is countable [15], i.e., the number of iterations of the loop is known before entering the loop body; (3) there is only one exit from the loop; (4) the loop is the innermost loop.
Note that the IF-statement may be nested, such that either the THEN or ELSE block or both have at least one IF-statement. Each IF-statement in a candidate loop is put into one of two categories:

- *a loop-independent IF-statement*, if its condition remains the same across loop iterations;
- *a loop-dependent IF-statement*, if its condition changes with loop iterations.

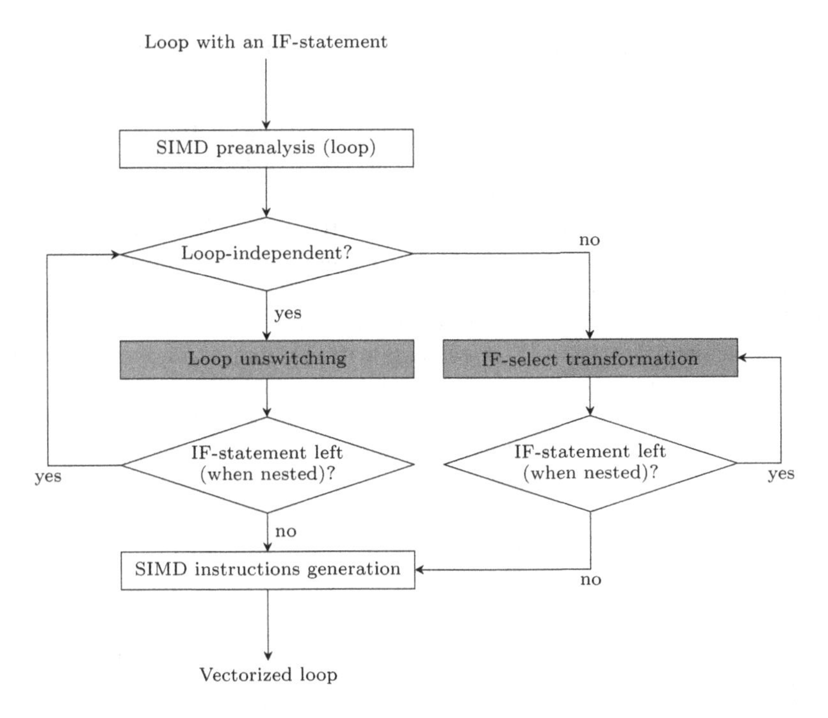

Fig. 2. Overview of our vectorization approach for a loop with a single, possibly nested IF-statement

According to these two cases, we apply two vectorization methods in Fig. 2:

- If the IF-statement is loop-independent, we apply our improved *loop unswitching* method (described in Sect. 3.1) to move the condition testing of the IF-statement outside of the loop. If the IF-statement is nested, we first tackle the outermost IF-statement, then tackle the inner IF-statement in the THEN or ELSE block and so on, until there is no IF-statement left, or until we encounter a loop-dependent IF-statement.
- If the IF-statement is loop-dependent, we apply our novel *IF-select transformation* (described in Sect. 3.2) that converts control dependences (IF) into data dependences (select). If the IF-statement is nested, we first tackle the innermost IF-statement in the corresponding THEN or ELSE block, then tackle the outer IF-statement and so on, until there is no IF-statement left.

The output of our method is the loop without IF-statements, for which equivalent SIMD instructions can be generated straightforwardly like in Fig. 1. The following two subsections describe the two core methods (the highlighted parts in Fig. 2) in detail.

3.1 Vectorizing Loop-Independent IFs: Loop Unswitching

The *loop unswitching* method, originally proposed in [19], is applied to a loop with a loop-independent IF-statement: the idea is to move the condition testing of the IF-statement outside of the loop; the original loop is duplicated, and a copy of it is placed inside of both THEN and ELSE blocks of the resulting IF-statement. Note that, besides enabling vectorization, loop unswitching also optimizes the program, because the testing of the IF-condition is performed only once outside of the loop, rather than repetitively in each loop iteration.

Our modification of the original loop unswitching method [19] allows it to be applied to arbitrarily nested IF-statements within a loop if all of them are loop-independent: we first apply loop unswitching to the outermost IF-statement, and then we apply loop unswitching iteratively to the both copies of the loop with respect to their outermost IF-statements, and so on, see Fig. 2. However, repetitive loop unswitching may lead to an exponential increase of code size, thus hindering the compiler to do other optimizations. We empirically impose a limit of 4 passes of this transformation for nested IF-statements, which is found to be a good solution via experimental evaluation.

3.2 Vectorizing Loop-Dependent IFs: IF-select Transformation

As described above, the classical loop unswitching method is only applicable to loop-independent IF-statements. For a loop-dependent IF-statement, we follow the idea of [16] to transform the IF-statement into *select* statements. However, our approach proceeds very differently from [16], where the original IF conversion [2] is applied to transform a program with IF-statements into an equivalent program with predicated statements, which are then transformed into select statements. This transformation relies on the PHG (Predicate Hierarchy Graph) representing the nesting relations among predicates. Our approach generates select statements directly, without generating predicated statements: we also avoid building and analyzing the PHG.

The idea of our approach is that we generate select statements by matching the statements in the THEN block with the statements in the ELSE block and combining each pair of matched statements into a select statement. We say that statements are matched if they define the same variable. For example, in the statement `if(cond){dst=val1;} else{dst=val2;}`, the statements in the THEN and ELSE blocks both define `dst`, so they are matched, and we can combine them into one select statement `dst=select(cond,val1,val2)`. In contrast, if there are no matched statements for the current statement in the THEN or the ELSE block, then we assume that there is a fictitious statement `dst=dst` to match with the current statement, and we combine the original statement with the fictitious statement into one select statement. For example, in the statement `if(cond){dst=val1;}`, there is no ELSE part and thus no matched statement, therefore, for this single statement we generate the select statement `dst=select(cond,val1,dst)`. We denote the former case that generates a select statement for two matched statements as *Rule 1*, and the latter case that generates a select statement for a single unmatched statement as *Rule 2*.

Algorithm 1 shows the pseudocode of our *IF-select transformation* method applied to an IF-statement in a loop. We first create a new block `sel_wn` to store the newly generated select statements (line 2). Then we sequentially traverse the statements in the THEN and ELSE blocks (line 6): we initialize the flag `matched` as FALSE (line 7) at the beginning of each traversal pass, and then we try to match the statements in the THEN and ELSE blocks and generate corresponding select statements according to Rule 1 and Rule 2 (line 8–44). Eventually, if `sel_wn` is not empty (line 45), we replace the original IF-statement with `sel_wn` (line 46), otherwise, we leave the IF-statement unchanged.

We describe in the following how we match statements and generate select statements, especially when there are flow dependences in the block. We begin with traversing the ELSE block from the current statement and looking for a matching statement (line 10–14) for the current statement in the THEN block. If there is no matching statement (Case 1), then we generate a select statement according to Rule 2 (line 16) and we turn to the next statement in the THEN block (line 17). If we find a matching statement that is the current statement in the ELSE block (Case 2), then we combine these two statements and generate a select statement according to Rule 1 (line 20), and we turn to the next statements in the THEN and ELSE blocks (line 21–22).

Otherwise, if the matching statement is not the current statement in the ELSE block (Case 3), then we reset flag `matched` to FALSE (line 24), and then we turn to looking for a matching statement in the THEN block (line 26–30) for the current statement in the ELSE block. If there is no matching statement in the THEN block (line 31), then we generate a select statement according to Rule 2 (line 32), and we turn to the next statement in the ELSE block (line 33). If a matching statement for the current statement is found, then it means that the order of these two statements is different in the THEN and ELSE blocks: e.g., `dst1` is defined before `dst2` in the THEN block and after `dst2` in the ELSE block. In this case, we check whether there is a flow dependence between the memory accesses in these two statements (line 35). If no flow dependence is found from `then_stmt` to `then_iter`, then we change the order of these two statements in the THEN block by moving `then_stmt` after `then_iter`. Likewise, if no flow dependence is found from `else_stmt` to `else_iter`, then we change the order of these two statements in the ELSE block by moving `else_stmt` after `else_iter`. Otherwise, we retain the IF-statement unchanged, ignore all select statements generated before, and return (line 41). After detecting flow dependences and reordering statements, we generate select statements according to Rule 1 (line 36) and turn to the next statements in the THEN and ELSE blocks (line 37–38). Note that case 3 enables us to generate select statements even when there is a flow dependence between the statements in the THEN or ELSE block. If we would simply add all matched statements to `sel_wn` and perform an analysis for detecting a cyclic dependence afterward, we may end up with inconsistent semantics by ignoring flow dependences.

Algorithm 1. IF-select Transformation

```
1  Function IF-selectTransformation(IF)
2      build a new block sel_wn ;                      // store the generated select statements
3      get the Array_Dependence_Graph as ADG;
4      then_stmt=get_first(IF.then);   // initiate the current statement in the THEN block
5      else_stmt=get_first(IF.else);   // initiate the current statement in the ELSE block
6      while then_stmt!=NULL | else_stmt!=NULL do
7          BOOL matched = FALSE;
8          if then_stmt != NULL then
9              else_iter=else_stmt;
10             while else_iter!=NULL & matched ==FALSE do
11                 if else_iter is matched with then_stmt then
12                     matched = TRUE ;                     // find the matched else_iter
13                 else
14                     else_iter=get_next(else_iter);
15             if matched==FALSE then                                    // Case 1
16                 generate select statement (Rule 2) and insert it into sel_wn;
17                 then_stmt=get_next(then_stmt);
18             else
19                 if else_iter == else_stmt then                        // Case 2
20                     generate select statements (Rule 1) and insert it into sel_wn;
21                     then_stmt=get_next(then_stmt);
22                     else_stmt=get_next(else_stmt);
23                 else                                                  // Case 3
24                     matched = FALSE;
25                     then_iter=then_stmt;
26                     while then_iter!=NULL & matched ==FALSE do
27                         if then_iter is matched with else_stmt then
28                             matched = TRUE ;            // find the matched then_iter
29                         else
30                             then_iter=get_next(then_iter);
31                     if matched==FALSE then
32                         generate select statement (Rule 2) and insert it into sel_wn;
33                         else_stmt=get_next(else_stmt);
34                     else
35                         if Forward_Motion(then_stmt, then_iter, ADG) |
                            Forward_Motion(else_stmt, else_iter, ADG) then
36                             generate select statements (Rule 1) and insert it into sel_wn;
37                             then_stmt=get_next(then_stmt);
38                             else_stmt=get_next(else_stmt);
39                         else
40                             sel_wn = NULL;
41                             return;
42         else if else_stmt != NULL then                                // Case 4
43             generate select statement (Rule 2) and insert it into sel_wn;
44             else_stmt=get_next(else_stmt);
45     if sel_wn != NULL then
46         replace IF with sel_wn;
```

If we are done with all statements in the THEN block and there are still statements in the ELSE block (Case 4), then for the current statement in the ELSE block we generate a select statement according to Rule 2 (line 43), and we turn to the next statement in the ELSE block (line 44), until we are also done with all statements in the ELSE block.

We further extend our IF-select transformation method (Algorithm 1) to handle nested loop-dependent IF-statements: we tackle the IF-statements starting from the innermost one and moving to the outermost, see Fig. 2.

```
1 for(i=0;i<1024;i++)
2 {
3  if(a[i]<b[i])
4  {
5   if(a[i]<10)
6     c[i]=a[i]+b[i];
7   else
8     c[i]=a[i]-b[i];
9   }
10 }
```

(a)

```
1 for(i=0;i<1024;i++)
2 {
3  if(a[i]<b[i])
4  {
5    c[i]=select(a[i]<10,a[i]+
         ↪ b[i],a[i]-b[i]);
6   }
7 }
```

(b)

```
1 for(i=0;i<1024;i++)
2 {
3  c[i]=select(a[i]<b[i],select(a[i]<10,
         ↪ a[i]+b[i],a[i]-b[i]),c[i]);
4 }
```

(c)

```
1 for(i=0;i<1024;i=i+4)
2 {
3  simd_load(v_a,&a[i]);
4  simd_load(v_b,&b[i]);
5  v_add=simd_vaddd(v_a,v_b);
6  v_sub=simd_vsubd(v_a,v_b);
7  v_cond1=simd_vfcmplt(v_a,v_10);
8  v1=simd_vseleq(v_cond1,v_sub,v_add);
9  simd_load(v_c,&c[i]);
10 v_cond2=simd_vfcmplt(v_a,v_b);
11 v2=simd_vseleq(v_cond2,v_c,v1);
12 simd_store(v2,&c[i]);
13 }
```

(d)

Fig. 3. (a) A loop with a nested loop-dependent IF-statement; (b) Apply IF-select transformation to the innermost IF-statement; (c) Apply IF-select transformation to the outermost IF-statement; (d) Vectorized code with SIMD instructions

Figure 3(a) illustrates how we vectorize a nested loop-dependent IF-statement. According to Algorithm 1, we first transform the innermost IF-statement to a select statement (Rule 1), with the result in Fig. 3(b). Then we transform the outermost IF-statement to a select statement (Rule 2), with the result in Fig. 3(c). Finally, we generate SIMD instructions as shown in Fig. 3(d).

4 Experimental Evaluation and Results

We integrated our presented vectorization approach for loops with nested IF-statements into the Open64 compiler [3] by adding to it our improved methods of loop unswitching (Sect. 3.1) and IF-select transformation (Sect. 3.2). The SIMD preanalysis and the generation of SIMD instructions shown in Fig. 2 have been slightly adapted in order to exploit our proposed vectorization methods.

Table 2. Benchmark kernels with IF-statements from SPEC CPU2006

Program	Kernel	Kernel runtime (%)	Application category	IF-stmt type
429.mcf	primal_bea_mpp	49.95	Combinatorial optimization	Nested
456.hmmer	P7Viterbi	99.53	Search gene sequence database	Nested
464.h264ref	SetupFastFullPelSearch	40.93	Video compression	Nested
454.calculix	e_c3d	69.12	Structural mechanics	Nested
482.sphinx3	vector_gautbl_eval_logs3	38.67	Speech recognition	Single
458.sjeng	std_eval	15.11	Pattern recognition	Nested
462.libquantum	quantum_toffoli	63.41	Physics and quantum computing	Nested

We conduct our experiments on the programs with IF-statements from the SPEC CPU2006 benchmark suite [9], listed in Table 2. Out of 29 programs in SPEC CPU2006, the 7 programs in the table contain IF-statements in their most time-consuming loops; 6 of these programs have nested IF-statements within loops. Our experimental platform is an SW26010 processor with a 256-bit dedicated SIMD extension, running under Linux Redhat Enterprise 5.

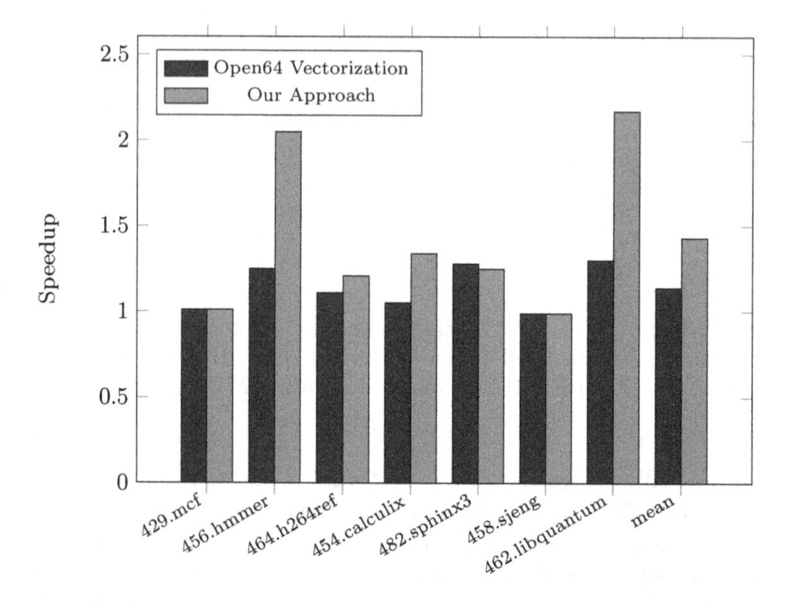

Fig. 4. Kernel speedups: our approach compared with the Open64 vectorization

For the seven benchmarks listed in Table 2, both kernel and whole-program speedups are presented. We compare two vectorization approaches: the Open64 compiler vectorization (performing loop unswitching and IF conversion) and our approach. All programs are compiled with the same flags: -O3, -LNO:simd=1. The execution time of a kernel or program is measured as the average of 20 runs. The results are within a few percent over each run. The speedups are calculated as compared with the execution on the same SW26010 processor, but without vectorization, i.e., when the SIMD extension is not used.

Figure 4 shows the kernel speedups. The mean kernel speedup achieved by our approach is 1.43x compared to the non-vectorization baseline and 1.25x compared to the Open64 vectorization. Our approach outperforms Open64 vectorization for 4 out of 7 programs and matches it for 3 remaining programs. We attribute the performance gains as follows. For 454.calculix, our loop unswitching method is applied twice to the two-level nested loop-independent IF-statement. For 456.hmmer, there is a two-level nested IF-statement: firstly, our loop unswitching method is applied to the outermost loop-independent IF-statement, and then our IF-select transformation is applied to the innermost loop-dependent

IF-statement, the same is done for 464.h264ref. For 462.libquantum, our IF-select transformation is applied to the two-level nested loop-dependent IF-statement. Our approach achieves a speedup similar to the Open64 vectorizer for 482.sphinx3, because its IF-statement is not nested. The remaining 2 programs which show no improvement are 429.mcf and 458.sjeng: they are not vectorized. For 429.mcf, its IF-statement contains pointers where dependence cycles are conservatively assumed and, therefore, the surrounding loop is excluded from vectorization. For 458.sjeng, there is a three-level nested loop-dependent IF-statement, however, the dependence cycles between the indirected arrays exclude the loop from vectorization in the SIMD preanalysis phase.

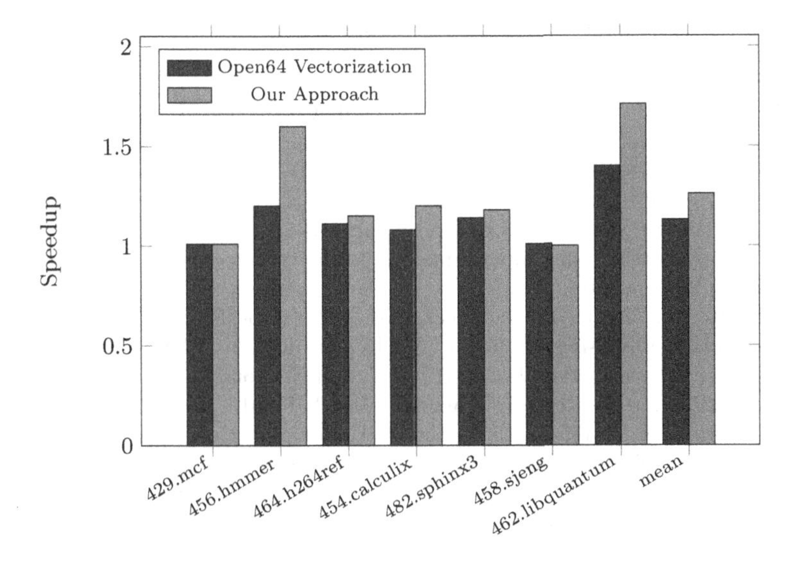

Fig. 5. Whole-program speedups: our approach compared with the Open64 vectorization

Figure 5 shows the whole-program speedups. The mean whole-program speedup achieved by our approach is 1.26x compared to the non-vectorization baseline and 1.11x compared to the Open64 vectorization. In most cases, the achieved whole-program speedups are consistent with the cumulative speedups of the most-time consuming kernels.

5 Conclusions

In this paper, we present an approach to refactoring loops with nested IF-statements by vectorizing them. Our new contributions to the state of the art in program vectorization are as follows:

- for loop-independent IF-statements, our modified loop unswitching method extends previous work to the case of arbitrarily nested IF-statements;

- for loop-dependent IF-statements, we develop a novel *IF-select transformation* method for targeting arbitrarily nested IF-statements and for SIMD extensions without predicated execution and masked instructions.

We integrate our approach into the Open64 compiler and we experimentally confirm its advantages using SPEC CPU2006 benchmarks on the SW26010 processor used in the Sunway TaihuLight supercomputer (#2 in the TOP500 list).

References

1. Aldinucci, M., Danelutto, M., Kilpatrick, P., Meneghin, M., Torquati, M.: Accelerating code on multi-cores with FastFlow. In: Proceedings of the 17th International Conference on Parallel Processing (Euro-Par), pp. 170–181 (2011). https://doi.org/10.1007/978-3-642-23397-5_17
2. Allen, J.R., Kennedy, K., Porterfield, C., et al.: Conversion of control dependence to data dependence. In: Proceedings of the Symposium on Principles of Programming Languages (POPL), Austin, Texas, USA, pp. 177–189 (1983). https://doi.org/10.1145/567067.567085
3. AMD: Using the x86 Open64 Compiler Suite (2012). For x86 Open64 version 4.5.2
4. ARM. https://developer.arm.com/products/processors/cortex-a/cortex-a8. Accessed 24 Sept 2018
5. Danelutto, M., Garcia, J.D., Sanchez, L.M., Sotomayor, R., Torquati, M.: Introducing parallelism by using REPARA C++11 attributes. In: 24th Euromicro International Conference on Parallel, Distributed, and Network-Based Processing (PDP), pp. 354–358 (2016). https://doi.org/10.1109/PDP.2016.115
6. Free Software Foundation: Using the GNU Compiler Collection (GCC). https://gcc.gnu.org/onlinedocs/gcc/. Accessed 24 Sept 2018
7. Fu, H., Liao, J., Yang, J., et al.: The Sunway TaihuLight supercomputer: system and applications. Sci. China Inf. Sci. **59**, 1–16 (2016)
8. Haidl, M., Moll, S., Klein, L., Sun, H., Hack, S., Gorlatch, S.: PACXXv2 + RV: an LLVM-based portable high-performance programming model. In: Proceedings of the Fourth Workshop on the LLVM Compiler Infrastructure in HPC, pp. 7:1–7:12 (2017). https://doi.org/10.1145/3148173.3148185
9. Henning, J.L.: SPEC CPU2006 benchmark descriptions. ACM SIGARCH Comput. Arch. News **34**, 1–17 (2006)
10. IBM. https://www.ibm.com/systems/power/hardware/power8/. Accessed 24 Sept 2018
11. Intel: Intel C++ Compiler Developer Guide and Reference (2017). Version 18.0
12. Karrenberg, R., Hack, S.: Whole-function vectorization. In: Proceedings of the International Symposium on Code Generation and Optimization (CGO), Chamonix, France, pp. 141–150 (2011). https://doi.org/10.1109/CGO.2011.5764682
13. Larsen, S., Amarasinghe, S.P.: Exploiting superword level parallelism with multimedia instruction sets. In: Proceedings of the Conference on Programming Language Design and Implementation (PLDI), Vancouver, Britith Columbia, Canada, pp. 145–156 (2000). https://doi.org/10.1145/358438.349320
14. Lattner, C., Adve, V.S.: LLVM: a compilation framework for lifelong program analysis and transformation. In: Proceedings of the International Symposium on Code Generation and Optimization (CGO), San Jose, CA, USA, pp. 75–88 (2004)

15. Naishlos, D.: Autovectorization in GCC. In: Proceedings of the GCC Developers Summit, Ottawa, Ontario, Canada, pp. 105–118 (2004)
16. Shin, J., Hall, M.W., Chame, J.: Superword-level parallelism in the presence of control flow. In: Proceedings of the International Symposium on Code Generation and Optimization (CGO), San Jose, CA, USA, pp. 165–175 (2005)
17. Smith, J.E., Faanes, G., Sugumar, R.A.: Vector instruction set support for conditional operations. In: Proceedings of the International Symposium on Computer Architecture (ISCA), Vancouver, BC, Canada, pp. 260–269 (2000)
18. Sreraman, N., Govindarajan, R.: A vectorizing compiler for multimedia extensions. Int. J. Parallel Program. **28**, 363–400 (2000)
19. Thomas, J., Allen, F., Cocke, J.: A Catalogue of Optimizing Transformations. Prentice-Hall, Englewood Cliffs (1971)
20. TOP500. https://www.top500.org/lists/2018/06/. Accessed 24 Sept 2018

Resilience - Workshop on Resiliency in High Performance Computing with Clouds, Grids, and Clusters

Workshop on Resiliency in High Performance Computing in Clouds, Grids, and Clusters (Resilience)

Workshop Description

Clouds, Grids, and Clusters are three different computational paradigms with the potential to support High Performance Computing (HPC) and enterprise IT infrastructure. Currently, they consist of hardware, management, and usage models particular to different computational regimes (e.g., high performance cluster systems designed to support tightly coupled scientific simulation codes typically utilize high-speed interconnects and commercial cloud systems designed to support software as a service (SAS) typically do not). However, in order to support HPC, all must at least utilize large numbers of resources and hence effective HPC in any of these paradigms must address the same issue of resiliency at a very large-scale.

Recent trends in HPC systems have clearly indicated that future increases in performance, in excess of those resulting from improvements in single-processor performance, will be achieved through corresponding increases in system scale, i.e., using a significantly larger component count. As the raw computational performance of the world's fastest HPC systems increases from today's current multi-petascale to next-generation exascale capability and beyond, their number of computational, networking, and storage components will grow from the ten-to-one-hundred thousand compute nodes of today's systems to several hundreds of thousands of compute nodes in the foreseeable future. This substantial growth in system scale, and the resulting component count, poses a challenge for HPC system and application software with respect to reliability, availability and serviceability (RAS).

Resilience is a critical challenge as HPC systems continue to increase component counts, individual component reliability decreases, and software complexity increases. Application correctness and execution efficiency, in spite of frequent faults, errors, and failures, is essential to ensure the success of the extreme-scale HPC systems, cluster computing environments, Grid computing infrastructures, and Cloud computing services.

Resilience for HPC systems encompasses a wide spectrum of fundamental and applied research and development, including theoretical foundations, fault detection and prediction, monitoring and control, end-to-end data integrity, enabling infrastructure, and resilient solvers and algorithm-based fault tolerance. This workshop brings together experts in the community to further research and development in HPC resilience and to facilitate exchanges across the computational paradigms of extreme-scale HPC, cluster computing, Grid computing, and Cloud computing.

The goal of this workshop is to bring together experts in the area of fault tolerance and resilience for HPC to present the latest achievements and to discuss the challenges ahead. The Resilience 2018 workshop program included presentations of 4 high-quality peer-reviewed papers as well as an opportunity for discussions among the participants from research, academia, and industry.

Organization

Workshop Chairs

Stephen L. Scott	Tennessee Tech University, USA
Chokchai (Box) Leangsuksun	Louisiana Tech University, USA

Workshop Program Chairs

Patrick G. Bridges	University of New Mexico, USA
Christian Engelmann	Oak Ridge National Laboratory, USA

Program Committee (PC)

Ferrol Aderholdt	Middle Tennessee State University, USA
Rizwan Ashraf	Oak Ridge National Laboratory, USA
Wesley Bland	Intel Corporation, USA
Hans-Joachim Bungartz	Technical University of Munich, Germany
Marc Casas	Barcelona Supercomputer Center, Spain
Zizhong Chen	University of California at Riverside, USA
Robert Clay	Sandia National Laboratories, USA
Miguel Correia	Universidade de Lisboa, Portugal
Nathan DeBardeleben	Los Alamos National Laboratory, USA
James Elliott	Sandia National Laboratories, USA
Kurt Ferreira	Sandia National Laboratories, USA
Saurabh Hukerikar	NVIDIA, USA
Dieter Kranzlmueller	Ludwig-Maximilians University of Munich, Germany
Ignacio Laguna	Lawrence Livermore National Laboratory, USA
Scott Levy	University of New Mexico, USA
Dirk Pflueger	University of Stuttgart, Germany
Alexander Reinefeld	Zuse Institute Berlin, Germany
Rolf Riesen	Intel Corporation, USA
Yves Robert	ENS Lyon, France
Thomas Ropars	Universite Grenoble Alpes, France
Martin Schulz	Lawrence Livermore National Laboratory, USA
Keita Teranishi	Sandia National Laboratories, USA

Do Moldable Applications Perform Better on Failure-Prone HPC Platforms?

Valentin Le Fèvre[1(✉)], George Bosilca[2], Aurelien Bouteiller[2], Thomas Herault[2], Atsushi Hori[3], Yves Robert[1,2], and Jack Dongarra[2,4]

[1] Laboratoire LIP, École Normale Supérieure de Lyon & Inria, Lyon, France
{valentin.le-fevre,yves.robert}@inria.fr
[2] University of Tennessee, Knoxville, TN, USA
{bosilca,bouteill,herault,dongarra}@icl.utk.edu
[3] RIKEN Center for Computational Science, Kobe, Japan
ahori@riken.jp
[4] University of Manchester, Manchester, UK

Abstract. This paper compares the performance of different approaches to tolerate failures using checkpoint/restart when executed on large-scale failure-prone platforms. We study (i) Rigid applications, which use a constant number of processors throughout execution; (ii) Moldable applications, which can use a different number of processors after each restart following a fail-stop error; and (iii) GridShaped applications, which are moldable applications restricted to use rectangular processor grids (such as many dense linear algebra kernels). For each application type, we compute the optimal number of failures to tolerate before relinquishing the current allocation and waiting until a new resource can be allocated, and we determine the optimal yield that can be achieved. We instantiate our performance model with a realistic applicative scenario and make it publicly available for further usage.

Keywords: Resilience · Spare nodes · Moldable applications
Checkpoint · Restart · Allocation length · Wait time

1 Introduction

Consider a long-running job that requests N processors from the batch scheduler. Resilience to fail-stop errors[1] is provided by a Checkpoint/Restart (CR) mechanism, which is the de-facto standard approach for High-Performance Computing (HPC) applications. After each failure, the application restarts from the last checkpoint but the number of available processors decreases, assuming the application can continue execution after a failure (e.g., using ULFM [3]). Until which point should the execution proceed before requesting a new allocation with N fresh resources from the batch scheduler?

[1] We use the terms *fail-stop error* and *failure* indifferently.

G. Mencagli et al. (Eds.): Euro-Par 2018 Workshops, LNCS 11339, pp. 787–799, 2019.
https://doi.org/10.1007/978-3-030-10549-5_61

The answer depends upon the nature of the application. For a RIGID application, the number of processors must remain constant throughout the execution. The question is then to decide the number F of processors (out of the N available initially) that will be used as spares. With F spares, the application can tolerate F failures. The application always executes with $N-F$ processors: after each failure, then it restarts from the last checkpoint and continues executing with $N-F$ processors, the faulty processor having been replaced by a spare. After F failures, the application stops when the $(F+1)$st failure strikes, and relinquishes the current allocation. It then asks for a new allocation with N processors, which takes a *wait time*, D, to start (as other applications are most likely using the platform concurrently). The optimal value of F obviously depends on the value of D, in addition to the application and resilience parameters. The wait time typically ranges from several hours to several days if the platform is over-subscribed (up to 10 days for large applications on the K-computer [24]). The metric to optimize here is the (expected) application yield, which is the fraction of useful work per second, averaged over the N resources, and computed in steady-state mode (expected value for multiple batch allocations of N resources).

For a MOLDABLE application, the problem is different: here we assume that the application can use a different number of processors after each restart. The application starts executing with N processors; after the first failure, the application recovers from the last checkpoint and is able to continue with only $N-1$ processors, albeit with a slowdown factor $\frac{N-1}{N}$. After how many failures F should the application decide to stop[2] and accept to produce no progress during D, in order to request a new allocation? Again, the metric to optimize is the application yield.

Finally, consider an application which must have a given shape (or a set of given shapes) in terms of processor layout. Typically, these shapes are dictated by the algorithm. In this paper, we use the example of a GRIDSHAPED application, which is required to execute on a rectangular processor grid whose size can dynamically be chosen. Most dense linear algebra kernels (matrix multiplication, LU, Cholesky and QR factorizations) are GRIDSHAPED applications, and perform more efficiently on square processor grids than on elongated rectangle ones. The application starts with a square $p \times p$ grid of $N = p^2$ processors. After the first failure, execution continues on a $p \times (p-1)$ rectangular grid, keeping $p-1$ processors as spares for the next $p-1$ failures. After p failures, the grid is shrunk again to a $(p-1) \times (p-1)$ square grid, and so on. We address the same question: after how many failures F should the application stop working on a smaller processor grid and request a new allocation, in order to optimize the application yield?

[2] Another limit is induced by the total application memory Mem_{tot}. There must remain at least ℓ live processors such that $Mem_{tot} \leq \ell \times Mem_{ind}$, where Mem_{ind} is the memory of each processor. We ignore this contraint in the paper but it would be straightforward to take it into account.

The major contribution of this paper is to present a detailed performance model and to provide analytical formulas for the expected yield of each application type. Due to lack of space, we instantiate the model for a single applicative scenarios, for which we draw comparisons across application types. Our model is publicly available [21] so that more scenarios can be explored. Notably, the paper qualifies the optimal number of spares for the optimal yield, and the optimal length of a period between two full restarts; it also qualifies how much the yield and total work done within a period are improved by deploying MOLDABLE applications w.r.t. RIGID applications.

The rest of the paper is organized as follows. Section 2 provides an overview of related work. Section 3 is devoted to formally defining the performance model. Section 4 provides formulas for the yield of RIGID, MOLDABLE and GRIDSHAPED applications. These formulas are instantiated through the applicative scenario in Sect. 5, to compare the different results. Finally, Sect. 6 provides final remarks and hints for future work.

2 Related Work

We first survey related work on checkpoint-restart. Then we discuss previous contributions on MOLDABLE applications.

Checkpoint-Restart. Checkpoint/restart (CR) is the most common strategy employed to protect applications from underlying faults and failures on HPC platforms. Generally, CR periodically outputs snapshots (*i.e.*, checkpoints) of the application global, distributed state to some stable storage device. When a failure occurs, the last stored checkpoint is retrieved and used to restart the application.

A widely-used approach for HPC applications is to use a fixed checkpoint period (typically one or a few hours), but it is sub-optimal. Instead, application-specific metrics can (and should) be used to determine the optimal checkpoint period. The well-known Young/Daly formula [8,25] yields an application optimal checkpoint period, $\sqrt{2\mu C}$ seconds, where C is the time to commit a checkpoint and μ the application Mean Time Between Failures (MTBF) on the platform. We have $\mu = \frac{\mu_{ind}}{N}$, where N is the number of processors enrolled by the application and μ_{ind} is the MTBF of an individual processor [17].

The Young/Daly formula minimizes platform waste, defined as the fraction of job execution time that does not contribute to its progress. The two sources of waste are the time spent taking checkpoints (which motivates longer checkpoint periods) and the time needed to recover and re-execute after each failure (which motivates shorter checkpoint periods). The Young/Daly period achieves the optimal trade-off between these sources to minimize the total waste.

For RIGID applications, both [18,26] report some experimental study to determine the optimal number of processors and of spares that should be used. Furthermore, the optimal number of resources for a perfectly parallel job is computed via an iterative relaxation procedure in [18] and through analytical formulas in [5].

Moldable and GridShaped Applications. RIGID and MOLDABLE applications have been studied for long in the context of scientific applications. A detailed survey on various application types (RIGID, MOLDABLE, malleable) was conducted in [10]. Resizing application to improve performance has been investigated by many authors, including [6,19,22,23] among others. A related recent study is the design of a MPI prototype for enabling tolerance in MOLDABLE MapReduce applications [13].

The TORQUE/Maui scheduler has been extended to support evolving, malleable, and MOLDABLE parallel jobs [20]. In addition, the scheduler may have system-wide spare nodes to replace failed nodes. In contrast, our scheme does not assume a change of behavior from the batch schedulers and resource allocators, but utilizes job-wide spare nodes: a node set including potential spare nodes is allocated and dedicated to a job at the time of scheduling, that can be used by the application to restart within the same job after a failure.

An experimental validation of the feasibility of shrinking application on the fly is provided in [2]. In this paper, the authors used an iterative solver application to compare two recovery strategies, shrinking and spare node substitution. They use ULFM, the fault-tolerant extension of MPI that offers the possibiliity of dynamically resizing the execution after a failure. In [11,15], the authors studied MOLDABLE and GRIDSHAPED applications that continue executing after some failures. They focus on the performance degradation incurred after shrinking or spare node substitution, due to less efficient communications (in particular collective communications). A major difference with our work is that these studies focus on recovery overhead and do not address overall performance nor yield.

3 Performance Model

This section reviews the key parameters of the performance model. Some assumptions are made to simplify the computation of the yield. We discuss possible extensions in Sect. 6.

Application/Platform Framework. We consider perfectly parallel applications that execute on homogeneous parallel platforms. Without loss of generality, we assume that each processor has unit speed: we only need to know that the total amount of work done by p processors within T seconds requires $\frac{p}{q}T$ seconds with q processors.

Mean Time Between Failures (MTBF). Each processor is subject to failures which are IID (independent and identically distributed) random variables following an Exponential probability distribution of mean μ_{ind}, the individual processor MTBF. Then the MTBF of a section of the platform comprised of i processors is given by $\mu_i = \frac{\mu_{ind}}{i}$ [17].

Checkpoints. Processors checkpoint periodically, using the optimal Young/ Daly period [8,25]: for an application using i processors, this period is $\sqrt{2C_i\mu_i}$, where C_i is the time to checkpoint with i processors[3]. We consider two cases to define C_i. In both cases, the overall application memory footprint is considered constant at Mem_{tot}, so the size of individual checkpoints is inversely linear with the number of participating/surviving processors. In the first case, the I/O bandwidth is the bottleneck (which is often the case in HPC platforms – it takes only a few processors to saturate the I/O bandwidth); then the checkpoint cost is constant and given by $C_i = \frac{Mem_{tot}}{\tau_{io}}$, where τ_{io} is the aggregated I/O bandwidth. In the second case, the processor network card is the bottleneck (which is the case for in-memory checkpointing, or checkpointing to NVRAM), and the checkpoint cost is inversely proportional to number of active processors: $C_i = \frac{Mem_{tot}}{\tau_{xnet} \times i}$, where τ_{xnet} is the available network bandwidth, and $\frac{Mem_{tot}}{i}$ the checkpoint size.

We denote the recovery time with i processors as R_i. For all simulations we use $R_i = C_i$, assuming that the read and write bandwidths are identical.

Objective. We consider a long-lasting application that requests a resource allocation with N processors. We aim at deriving the optimal number of failures F that should be tolerated before paying the wait time and requesting a new allocation. We aim at maximizing the *yield* $\mathcal{Y}$ of the application, defined as the fraction of time during the allocation length and wait time where the N resources perform useful work. Of course a spare does not perform useful work when idle, and no processor is active during wait time, which explains that the yield will always be smaller than 1. We will derive the value of F that maximizes $\mathcal{Y}$ for the three application types.

4 Expected Yield

This section is the core of the paper. We compute the expected yield for each application type, RIGID, MOLDABLE and GRIDSHAPED.

4.1 Rigid Application

We first consider a RIGID application that can be parallelized at compile-time to use any number of processors but cannot change this number until it reaches termination. There are N processors allocated to the application. We use $N - F$ for execution and keep F as spares. The execution is protected from failures by checkpoints of duration C_{N-F}. Each failure striking the application will incur an in-place restart of duration R_{N-F}, using a spare processor to replace the faulty one. However, when the $(F + 1)^{st}$ failure strikes, the job will have to stop and

[3] In [8], the optimal checkpoitning period is $\sqrt{2C_i\mu_i} + C_i$, but we use $\sqrt{2C_i\mu_i}$ as derived in [17]. Note that both formulas are only first-order approximations and collapse when C_i is small in front of the MTBF μ_i. The exact formula for the optimal checkpointing period is given in [17].

perform a full restart, waiting for a new allocation of N processors to be granted by the job scheduler.

We define $\mathcal{T}_R$ as the expected duration of an execution period until the application is ready to continue after the $(F+1)^{st}$ failure strikes. We compute $\mathcal{T}_R$ using several first-order approximations. In particular, we ignore scenarios where failures strike during checkpoint, recovery or re-execution, thereby neglecting the probability of two failures within a short time window. Also, we approximate the time lost after a failure as half the checkpointing period. Finally, we assume an integer number of checkpointing periods in between failures. The first failure is expected to strike after μ_N seconds, the second failure μ_{N-1} seconds after the first one, and so on. Without any overhead, the length of a period would be $\sum_{i=N}^{N-F} \mu_i$. Except for the last failure, each failure incurs some overhead only if it strikes the application. This happens with probability $\frac{N-F}{i}$, where i is the current number of live processors. In that case, the failure requires a restart and some re-execution, namely half the checkpoint period in average. The application always uses $N-F$ processors, hence the checkpoint period remains equal to $\sqrt{2C_{N-F}\mu_{N-F}}$. On the contrary, if the failure strikes a spare, there is no overhead. The last failure always requires a wait time, and then a restart and re-execution. Therefore, we derive:

$$\mathcal{T}_R = \sum_{i=N}^{N-F} \mu_i + \sum_{i=N}^{N-F+1} \frac{N-F}{i} \left(R_{N-F} + \frac{\sqrt{2C_{N-F}\mu_{N-F}}}{2} \right) + D + R_{N-F} + \frac{\sqrt{2C_{N-F}\mu_{N-F}}}{2}$$

What is the total amount of work $\mathcal{W}_R$ computed during a period? During the sub-period of length μ_i, there are $\frac{\mu_i}{\sqrt{2C_{N-F}\mu_{N-F}}}$ checkpoints, each of length C_{N-F}, and each processor works during $\frac{\mu_i}{1+\frac{C_{N-F}}{\sqrt{2C_{N-F}\mu_{N-F}}}}$ seconds. There are $N-F$ processors at work, hence

$$\mathcal{W}_R = (N-F) \cdot \sum_{i=N}^{N-F} \frac{\mu_i}{1 + \frac{C_{N-F}}{\sqrt{2C_{N-F}\mu_{N-F}}}}$$

During the duration $\mathcal{T}_R$ of the period, in the absence of failures and protection, the application could have used all N processors to compute. Thus the effective yield with protection for the application during $\mathcal{T}_R$ is reduced to $\mathcal{Y}_R$:

$$\mathcal{Y}_R = \frac{\mathcal{W}_R}{N \cdot \mathcal{T}_R}$$

4.2 Moldable Application

We now consider a Moldable application that can use a different number of processors after each restart. The application starts executing with N processors; after the first failure, the application recovers from the last checkpoint and is able to continue with only $N-1$ processors after paying the restart cost R_{N-1}, albeit with a slowdown factor $\frac{N-1}{N}$ of the parallel work per time unit.

We define $\mathcal{T}_M$ as the expected duration of an execution period until the $(F+1)^{st}$ failure strikes. Without any overhead, the length of a period would be $\sum_{i=N}^{N-F} \mu_i$, the same as for RIGID applications. But there are few differences. First, each failure strikes the application, since it always uses all live processors. Second, the checkpoint period increases after each failure, since the number of live processors decreases. Third, the re-execution after a failure (except the last one) incurs a slowdown factor because we move from i processors to $i-1$ processors. Fourth and finally, the re-execution after the last failure is performed faster, because there are more live processors. Altogether, we derive that

$$\mathcal{T}_M = \sum_{i=N}^{N-F} \mu_i + \sum_{i=N}^{N-F+1} \left(R_{i-1} + \frac{i}{i-1} \cdot \frac{\sqrt{2C_i\mu_i}}{2} \right) + D + R_N + \frac{N-F}{N} \frac{\sqrt{2C_{N-F}\mu_{N-F}}}{2}$$

To compute the total amount of work $\mathcal{W}_M$ during a period, we proceed as before and consider each sub-period. During the sub-period of length μ_i, there are $\frac{\mu_i}{\sqrt{2C_i\mu_i}}$ checkpoints, each of length C_i, and each processor works during $\frac{\mu_i}{1+\frac{C_i}{\sqrt{2C_i\mu_i}}}$ seconds. And there are i processors at work during that sub-period. Altogether:

$$\mathcal{W}_M = \sum_{i=N}^{N-F} i \times \frac{\mu_i}{1 + \frac{C_i}{\sqrt{2C_i\mu_i}}}, \qquad \text{and } \mathcal{Y}_M = \frac{\mathcal{W}_M}{N \cdot \mathcal{T}_M}$$

where $\mathcal{Y}_M$ is the yield of the MOLDABLE application.

4.3 GridShaped Application

Finally, we consider a GRIDSHAPED application, defined as a moldable execution which requires a rectangular processor grid. The application starts with a square $p \times p$ grid of $N = p^2$ processors. After the first failure, execution continues on a $p \times (p-1)$ rectangular grid, keeping $p-1$ processors as spares for the next $p-1$ failures. After p failures, the grid is shrunk again to a $(p-1) \times (p-1)$ square grid, and the execution continues on this reduced-size square grid. After how many failures F should the application stop, in order to maximize the application yield? The derivation of the expected length of a period and of the total work are more complicated for GRIDSHAPED than for RIGID and MOLDABLE. Due to lack of space, we refer to the extended version [12], as well as to the publicly available software [21], for detailed formulas and an algorithm to compute the optimal value of F.

5 Applicative Scenario

As an applicative scenario, we consider a platform with 22,250 nodes (150^2), with a node MTBF of 20 years, and an application that would take 2 min to checkpoint (at 22,250 nodes). In other words, we let $N = 22,500$, $\mu_{ind} = 20y$ and $C_i = C = 120s$. These values are inspired from existing platforms: the Titan supercomputer at OLCF [14], for example, holds 18,688 nodes, and experiences a few node failures per day, implying a node MTBF between 18 and 25 years. The filesystem has a bandwidth of 1.4 TB/s, and nodes altogether aggregate 100 TB of memory, thus a checkpoint that would save 30% of that system should take in the order of 2 min to complete. Further experiments varying N, μ_{ind} and with several scenarios for checkpoint costs are available in the extended version [12].

Figure 1 shows the yield that can be expected if doing a full restart after an optimal number of failures, as a function of the wait time, for the three kind of applications considered (Rigid, Moldable and GridShaped). We also plot the expected yield when the application experiences a full restart after each failure (NoSpare). First, one sees that the three approaches that avoid paying the cost of a wait time after every failure experience a comparable yield, while the performance of the NoSpare approach quickly degrades to a small efficiency (30% when the wait time is around 14 h).

The zoom box to differentiate the Rigid, Moldable and GridShaped yield shows that the Moldable approach has a slightly higher yield than the other ones, but only for a minimal fraction of the yield. This is expected, as the Moldable approach takes advantage of all living processors, while the GridShaped and Rigid approaches sacrifice the computing power of the spare nodes waiting for the next failure. However, the size of the gain is small to the point of being negligible. The GridShaped approach experiences a yield that changes in steps. Both these phenomenons are explained by the next figure.

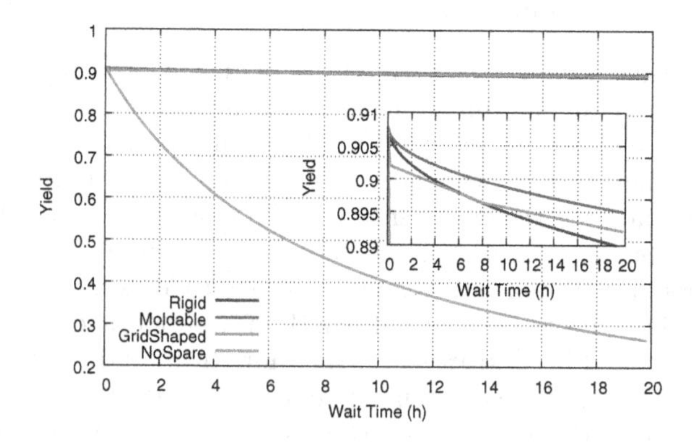

Fig. 1. Optimal yield as function of the wait time, for the different types of applications.

Figure 2 shows the number of failures after which the application should do a full restart, to obtain an optimal yield, as a function of the wait time, for the

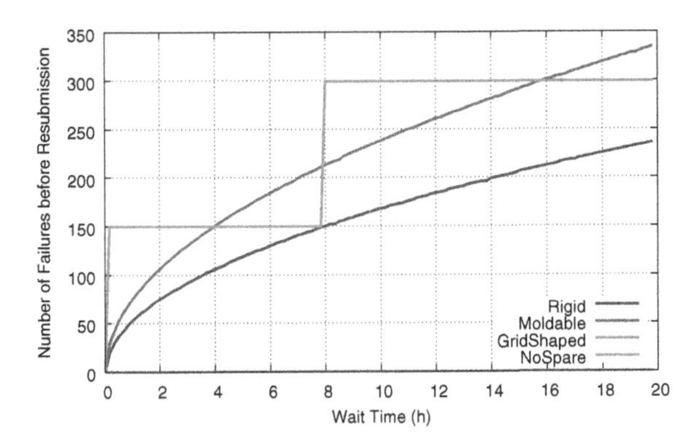

Fig. 2. Optimal number of failures tolerated between two full restarts, as function of the wait time, for the different types of applications.

three kind of applications considered. We observe that this optimal is quickly reached: even with long wait times (e.g. 10 h), 200 to 250 failures (depending on the method) should be tolerated within the allocation before relinquishing it. This is small compared to the number of nodes: less than 1% of the resource should be dedicated as spares for the RIGID approach, and after losing 1% of the resource, the MOLDABLE approach should request a new allocation.

This is remarkable, taking into account the poor yield obtained by the approach that does not tolerate failures within the allocation. Even with a small wait time (assuming the platform would be capable of re-scheduling applications that experience failures in less than 2 h), Fig. 1 shows that the yield of the NOSPARE approach would decrease to 70%. This represents a waste of 30%, which is much higher than the recommended waste of 10% for resilience in the current HPC platforms recommendations [4, 7]. Comparatively, provisioning only 1% of additional resources as spares within the allocations, would allow to achieve a yield over 88%, for every approach considered, when the wait time does not exceed 20 h.

The GRIDSHAPED approach experiences steps that correspond to using all the spares created when redeploying the application over a smaller grid before relinquishing the allocation. As illustrated in Fig. 1, the yield evolves in steps, changing the slope of a linear approximation radically when redeploying over a smaller grid. This has for consequence that the maximal yield is always at a slope change point, thus at the frontier of a new grid size. It is still remarkable that even with very small wait times, it is more beneficial to use spares (and thus to lose a full row of processors) than to redeploy immediately.

Figure 3 shows the length of an allocation providing the optimal yield (best value of F). After such a duration, the job will have to fully restart in order to maintain the optimal yield. This figure illustrates the real difference between the RIGID and MOLDABLE approaches: although both approaches are capable of extracting the same yield, the MOLDABLE approach can do so with significantly longer periods between full restarts. This is important when considering real life applications, because this means that the applications using a MOLDABLE approach have a higher chance to complete before the first full restart, and overall will always complete in a lower number of allocations than the RIGID approach.

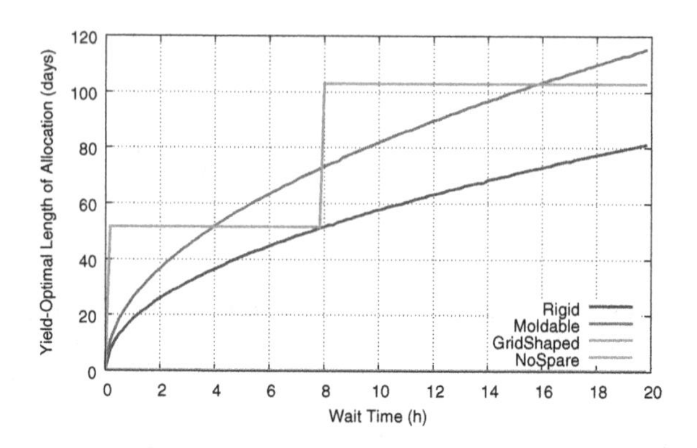

Fig. 3. Optimal length of allocations, for the different types of applications.

Finally, Fig. 4 shows an upper limit of the duration of the wait time in order to guarantee a given yield for the three applications. In particular, we see that to reach a yield of 90%, an application which would restart its job at each fault would need that restart to be done in less than 6 min whereas the RIGID and GRIDSHAPED approaches need a full restart in less than 3 h approximately. This bound goes up to 7 h for the MOLDABLE approach. In comparison, with a wait time of 1 h, the yield obtained using NOSPARE is only 80%. This shows that, using these parameters, it seems impossible to guarantee the recommended waste of 10% without tolerating (a small) number of failures before rescheduling the job.

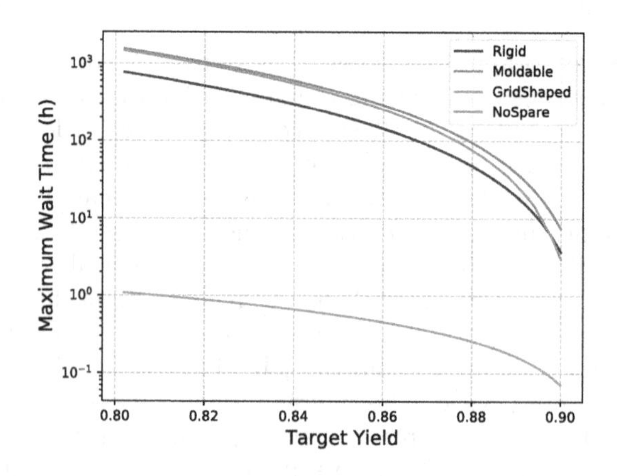

Fig. 4. Maximum wait time allowed to reach a target yield.

6 Conclusion

In this paper, we have compared the performance of RIGID, MOLDABLE and GRIDSHAPED applications when executed on large-scale failure-prone platforms. For each application type, we have computed the optimal number of faults that should be tolerated before requesting a new allocation, as a function of the wait time. Through a realistic applicative scenario inspired by state-of-the-art platforms, we have shown that the three application types experience an optimal yield when requesting a new allocation after experiencing a number of failures that represents a small percentage of the initial number of resources (hence a small percentage of spares for RIGID applications), and this even for large values of the wait time. On the contrary, the NOSPARE strategy, where a new allocation is requested after each failure, sees its yield dramatically decrease when the wait time increases. We also observed that MOLDABLE applications enjoy much longer execution periods in between two re-allocations, thereby decreasing the total execution time as compared to RIGID applications (and GRIDSHAPED applications lying in between).

Future work will be devoted to exploring more applicative scenarios. We also intend to extend the model in several directions. On the application side, we aim at dealing with non-perfectly parallel applications but instead with applications whose speedup profile obeys Amdahl's law [1]. We will also introduce a more refined speedup profile for GRIDSHAPED applications, with an execution speed that depends on the grid shape (a square being usually faster than an elongated rectangle). On the resilience side, we will address forward-recovery schemes, such as ABFT [9,16], in replacement of, or in combination with, checkpoint-restart techniques.

References

1. Amdahl, G.: The validity of the single processor approach to achieving large scale computing capabilities. In: AFIPS Conference Proceedings, vol. 30, pp. 483–485. AFIPS Press (1967)
2. Ashraf, R.A., Hukerikar, S., Engelmann, C.: Shrink or substitute: handling process failures in HPC systems using in-situ recovery. CoRR abs/1801.04523 (2018). http://arxiv.org/abs/1801.04523
3. Bland, W., Bouteiller, A., Herault, T., Bosilca, G., Dongarra, J.: Post-failure recovery of MPI communication capability: design and rationale. Int. J. High Perform. Comput. Appl. **27**(3), 244–254 (2013). https://doi.org/10.1177/1094342013488238, http://hpc.sagepub.com/content/27/3/244.abstract
4. Cappello, F., Geist, A., Gropp, W., Kale, S., Kramer, B., Snir, M.: Toward exascale resilience: 2014 update. Supercomput. Front. Innov. **1**(1), 5–28 (2014)
5. Cavelan, A., Li, J., Robert, Y., Sun, H.: When Amdahl meets Young/Daly. In: Cluster 2016. IEEE Computer Society Press (2016)
6. Cirne, W., Berman, F.: Using moldability to improve the performance of supercomputer jobs. J. Parallel Distrib. Comput. **62**(10), 1571–1601 (2002)
7. CORAL: Collaboration of Oak Ridge, Argonne and Livermore National Laboratorie: Draft CORAL-2 build statement of work. Technical report LLNL-TM-7390608, Lawrence Livermore National Laboratory, 30 March 2018

8. Daly, J.T.: A higher order estimate of the optimum checkpoint interval for restart dumps. Future Gener. Comp. Syst. **22**(3), 303–312 (2006)
9. Du, P., Bouteiller, A., et al.: Algorithm-based fault tolerance for dense matrix factorizations. In: PPoPP, pp. 225–234. ACM (2012)
10. Dutot, P., Mounié, G., Trystram, D.: Scheduling parallel tasks approximation algorithms. In: Leung, J.Y. (ed.) Handbook of Scheduling - Algorithms, Models, and Performance Analysis. CRC Press (2004)
11. Fang, A., Fujita, H., Chien, A.A.: Towards understanding post-recovery efficiency for shrinking and non-shrinking recovery. In: Hunold, S., et al. (eds.) Euro-Par 2015. LNCS, vol. 9523, pp. 656–668. Springer, Cham (2015). https://doi.org/10.1007/978-3-319-27308-2_53
12. Fèvre, V.L., et al.: Do moldable applications perform better on failure-prone HPC platforms? Research report RR-9174, INRIA (2018)
13. Guo, Y., Bland, W., Balaji, P., Zhou, X.: Fault tolerant MapReduce-MPI for HPC clusters. In: Proceedings of the International Conference for High Performance Computing, Networking, Storage and Analysis, SC 2015, Austin, TX, USA, 15–20 November 2015, pp. 34:1–34:12 (2015)
14. Gupta, S., Patel, T., Engelmann, C., Tiwari, D.: Failures in large scale systems: long-term measurement, analysis, and implications. In: Proceedings of the International Conference for High Performance Computing, Networking, Storage and Analysis, SC 2017, New York, NY, USA, pp. 44:1–44:12 (2017)
15. Hori, A., Yoshinaga, K., Herault, T., Bouteiller, A., Bosilca, G., Ishikawa, Y.: Sliding substitution of failed nodes. In: Proceedings of the 22nd European MPI Users' Group Meeting, EuroMPI 2015, pp. 14:1–14:10. ACM, New York (2015). https://doi.org/10.1145/2802658.2802670
16. Huang, K.H., Abraham, J.A.: Algorithm-based fault tolerance for matrix operations. IEEE Trans. Comput. **33**(6), 518–528 (1984)
17. Hérault, T., Robert, Y. (eds.): Fault-Tolerance Techniques for High-Performance Computing. Springer, Heidelberg (2015). https://doi.org/10.1007/978-3-319-20943-2
18. Jin, H., Chen, Y., Zhu, H., Sun, X.H.: Optimizing HPC fault-tolerant environment: an analytical approach. In: Proceedings of the ICPP 2010 (2010)
19. Moreira, J.E., Naik, V.K.: Dynamic resource management on distributed systems using reconfigurable applications. IBM J. Res. Dev. **41**(3), 303–330 (1997)
20. Prabhakaranw, S.: Dynamic resource management and job scheduling for high performance computing. Ph.D. thesis, Technische Universität Darmstadt (2016)
21. Simulation software: computing the yield (2018). https://github.com/vlefevre/continuability
22. Sudarsan, R., Ribbens, C.J.: Design and performance of a scheduling framework for resizable parallel applications. Parallel Comput. **36**(1), 48–64 (2010)
23. Sudarsan, R., Ribbens, C.J., Farkas, D.: Dynamic resizing of parallel scientific simulations: a case study using LAMMPS. In: Allen, G., Nabrzyski, J., Seidel, E., van Albada, G.D., Dongarra, J., Sloot, P.M.A. (eds.) ICCS 2009. LNCS, vol. 5544, pp. 175–184. Springer, Heidelberg (2009). https://doi.org/10.1007/978-3-642-01970-8_18

24. Yamamoto, K., et al.: The K computer operations: experiences and statistics. Procedia Comput. Sci. (ICCS) **29**, 576–585 (2014)
25. Young, J.W.: A first order approximation to the optimum checkpoint interval. Commun. ACM **17**(9), 530–531 (1974)
26. Zheng, Z., Yu, L., Lan, Z.: Reliability-aware speedup models for parallel applications with coordinated checkpointing/restart. IEEE Trans. Comput. **64**(5), 1402–1415 (2015)

FINJ: A Fault Injection Tool for HPC Systems

Alessio Netti[1(✉)], Zeynep Kiziltan[1], Ozalp Babaoglu[1], Alina Sîrbu[2], Andrea Bartolini[3], and Andrea Borghesi[3]

[1] Department of Computer Science and Engineering, University of Bologna, Bologna, Italy
{alessio.netti,zeynep.kiziltan,ozalp.babaoglu}@unibo.it
[2] Department of Computer Science, University of Pisa, Pisa, Italy
alina.sirbu@unipi.it
[3] Department of Electrical, Electronic and Information Engineering, University of Bologna, Bologna, Italy
{a.bartolini,andrea.borghesi3}@unibo.it

Abstract. We present FINJ, a high-level fault injection tool for High-Performance Computing (HPC) systems, with a focus on the management of complex experiments. FINJ provides support for custom workloads and allows generation of anomalous conditions through the use of fault-triggering executable programs. FINJ can also be integrated seamlessly with most other lower-level fault injection tools, allowing users to create and monitor a variety of highly-complex and diverse fault conditions in HPC systems that would be difficult to recreate in practice. FINJ is suitable for experiments involving many, potentially interacting nodes, making it a very versatile design and evaluation tool.

Keywords: Exascale systems · Resiliency
Fault detection · Monitoring · Benchmarking · Open-source

1 Introduction

Motivation. High-Performance Computing (HPC) systems have become indispensable for economic growth and scientific progress in our modern society. As the performance of HPC systems increases, the value of the results they produce increases through higher-fidelity simulations, better predictive models and analysis of greater quantities of data. The resulting techniques, policy decisions and vastly-improved manufacturing processes in areas such as agriculture, engineering, transportation, materials, energy, health care, security and the environment are bound to impact most aspects of our lives. Today, HPC systems are also being used as fundamental "instruments" to achieve groundbreaking results in basic sciences ranging from particle physics to cosmology. Yet, many important problems in various fields remain unsolvable with current computational resources. *Exascale* HPC systems, capable of 10^{18} operations per second, are believed to

G. Mencagli et al. (Eds.): Euro-Par 2018 Workshops, LNCS 11339, pp. 800–812, 2019.
https://doi.org/10.1007/978-3-030-10549-5_62

be essential for solving such problems [2]. Reaching exascale performance is the *moonshot* for modern HPC systems with many nations and companies engaged in an *arms race* towards achieving it.

Exascale systems, when they arrive, will come at a significant cost: scaling current technologies to exascale performance through massive parallelism will result in systems that have prohibitively-high levels of power consumption [17] and excessively-high failure rates [4]. Thus, to be usable in production environments with acceptable *Quality of Service* levels, exascale systems need to improve their power efficiency and resiliency by several orders of magnitude.

In our terminology, a *fault* is defined as an anomalous behavior at the software or hardware level that can lead to illegal system states (*errors*) and, in the worst case, to service interruptions (*failures*) [7]. In this paper, we limit our attention to improving the resiliency of HPC systems through the use of mechanisms for predicting, detecting and preventing errors and failures. An important technique in this endeavor is *fault injection*: the deliberate triggering of faults in a system so as to observe their behavior in a controlled environment, enable development of new prediction and response techniques and testing of existing ones [11]. For fault injection to be effective, dedicated tools are necessary, allowing users to trigger complex and realistic fault scenarios in a reproducible manner.

Related Work. Fault injection for prediction and detection purposes has been a topic of great interest in recent years. In [6,8,9,16], the authors employed software-based fault injection techniques to observe the behavior and performance variations of HPC systems in anomalous conditions, and to detect such faults using system performance metrics. However, while characterizing the fault-simulating programs that were used, these works do not focus on the tools used to inject and coordinate the faults themselves in the system.

Several studies have proposed fault injection tools with varying levels of abstraction. Calhoun et al. [3] devised a compiler-level fault injection tool focused on memory bit-flip errors, targeting HPC applications. De Bardeleben et al. [5] proposed a logic error-oriented fault injection tool. This tool is designed to inject faults in virtual machines, by exploiting emulated machine instructions through the open-source virtual machine and processor emulator (QEMU). Both works focus on low-level fault-specific tools and do not provide functionality for the injection of complex workloads, and for the collection of produced data, if any.

Stott et al. [15] proposed NFTAPE, a high-level and generic tool for fault injection. This tool is designed to be integrated with other fault injection tools and triggers at various levels, allowing for the automation of long and complex experiments. The tool however has aged considerably, and is not publicly available. A similar fault injection tool was proposed by Naughton et al. [14], however, to the best of our knowledge, it has never progressed past the prototype stage and is also not publicly available. Moreover, both tools require users to write a fair amount of wrapper and configuration code, resulting in a complex setup process. The Gremlins Python package[1] also supplies a high-level fault injector.

[1] https://github.com/toddlipcon/gremlins.

However, it does not support workload or data collection functionalities, and experiments on multiple nodes cannot be performed.

Joshi et al. [12] introduced the PREFAIL tool, which allows for the injection of failures at any code entry point in the underlying operating system. This tool, like NFTAPE, employs a coordinator process for the execution of complex experiments. It is targeted at a specific type of fault (code-level errors) and does not permit performing experiments focused on performance degradation and interference, among other fault types. Similarly, the tool proposed by Gunawi et al. [10], named FATE, allows the execution of long experiments; furthermore, it is focused on reproducing specific fault sequences, simulating real scenarios. Like PREFAIL, it is limited to a specific fault type, namely I/O errors, thus greatly limiting its scope.

Contributions. The main contribution of this paper is the design and implementation of FINJ, an easy-to-use open-source Python tool for fault injection targeted at HPC systems, with workload management capabilities. A relevant feature of FINJ is the possibility of seamless integration with other injection tools targeted at specific fault types, thus enabling users to coordinate faults from different sources and different system levels. By using FINJ's *workload* feature, users can also specify lists of applications to be executed and faults to be triggered on multiple nodes at specific times with specific durations. FINJ thus represents a high-level, flexible tool, enabling users to perform complex and reproducible experiments, aimed at revealing the complex relations that may exist between faults, application behavior and the system itself. FINJ is also extremely easy to use: it can be set up and executed in a matter of minutes, and does not require the writing of additional code in most of its usage scenarios. To the best of our knowledge, FINJ is the first portable, open-source tool that allows users to perform and control complex injection experiments, that can be integrated with heterogeneous fault types and that includes workload support, while retaining ease of use and a quick setup time.

Organization. The rest of the paper is structured as follows. In Sect. 2, we describe the FINJ architecture (Sect. 2.1), its components (Sect. 2.2) and their implementation (Sect. 2.3). In Sect. 3, we present a simple use case to show how FINJ can be deployed, while Sect. 4 concludes the paper.

2 FINJ Architecture

In this Section we discuss how fault injection is achieved in FINJ. We then present its architecture, together with some implementation details. Due to its portable and modular nature, customizing FINJ for different purposes is easy.

2.1 Architecture Overview

Fault injection in FINJ is achieved through *tasks* that are executed on target nodes: each task corresponds to a particular application, which can either be

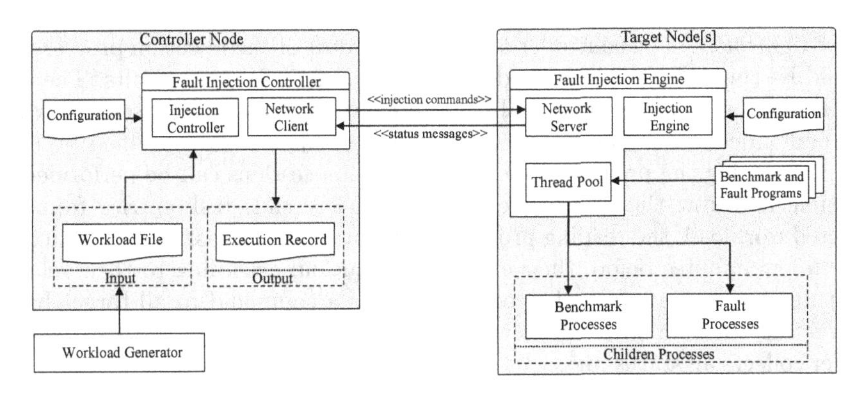

Fig. 1. Architecture of the FINJ tool showing the division between a controller node (left) and a target node (right).

a benchmark program or a fault-triggering program. As demonstrated in [15], this approach allows for the integration in FINJ of any low-level fault injection framework that can be triggered by using an executable program or a shell script. A task is defined by the following attributes:

- *args*: the full shell command required to run the selected task. The command must refer to an executable file that can be accessed from the target hosts;
- *timestamp*: the time in seconds at which the task must be started, relative to the starting time of the injection session;
- *duration*: the task's *maximum allowed* duration, expressed in seconds, after which it will be abruptly terminated. This duration can serve as an *exact* duration as well, with FINJ restarting the task if it finishes earlier, and terminating it if it lasts more. This behavior depends on the FINJ configuration (see Sect. 2.2). A duration of 0 implies that the task is always allowed to run until its termination;
- *isFault*: defines whether the task corresponds to a fault-triggering program, or to a benchmark application;
- *seqNum*: a sequence number used to uniquely identify the task;
- *cores*: the list of CPU cores that the task is allowed to use on target nodes, enforced through a *NUMA Control* policy [13]; this attribute is optional.

A set of tasks defines a *workload*, which is a succession of scheduled fault and benchmark executions at specific times, reproducing a realistic working environment for the fault injection process. A particular execution of a given workload then constitutes an *injection session*. Many fault programs are supplied with FINJ, allowing users to experiment with a variety of anomalies out-of-the-box.

FINJ consists of two basic components: a fault injection *controller*, and a fault injection *engine*. The two components correspond to processes that must be run on the nodes subject to injection experiments. Communication between them is achieved through TCP *sockets* using a simple message-based protocol. The high-level structure of the FINJ architecture is illustrated in Fig. 1.

FINJ Controller. The controller is the orchestrator of the injection process, and should be run on an external node that is not affected by the faults. The controller maintains connections to all nodes involved in the injection session, which run fault injection *engine* instances and whose addresses are specified by users when launching the program. Therefore, injection sessions can be performed on multiple nodes at the same time. The controller reads task entries from the selected workload: the reading process is incremental, and tasks are read in real-time a few minutes before their expected execution, according to their relative time-stamp. For each task the controller sends a command to all target hosts, instructing them to start the new task at the specified time. Finally, the controller collects all status messages produced by the target hosts, and stores them in a separate file for each host. These status messages are related to the start and termination of each single task, besides status changes in the host (for example, when connection is lost and re-established).

FINJ Engine. The engine is structured as a daemon, perpetually running on nodes that are expected to be subject to injection sessions. The engine waits for task commands to be received from remote controller instances. Engines can be connected to multiple controllers at the same time, and status messages will be sent to all of them. However, task commands are accepted from one controller at a time, which is defined as the *master* of the injection session. The engine manages received task commands by assigning them to a dedicated thread from a *pool*. The thread manages all aspects related to the execution of the task, such as spawning the necessary subprocesses and sending status messages to controllers when relevant events (such as the start or termination of the task) occur. Whenever a fault causes a target node to crash and reboot, controllers are able to re-establish and recover the previously running injection session, given that the engine is set up to be executed at boot time on the target node.

2.2 Components

FINJ is based on a highly modular architecture, and therefore it is very easy to customize single components in order to add or tune features.

Network. Engine and controller instances communicate through a network layer in the FINJ tool. Communication is achieved through a simple message-based protocol employing TCP sockets. This design choice is motivated by the fact that the volume of data sent during injection sessions is extremely low, while high reliability is a desirable quality. Users can still integrate their preferred transport method with little effort, thanks to FINJ's highly modular nature.

Specifically, a message *client* and *server* were implemented: clients are used by FINJ controllers in order to connect to servers hosted on FINJ engine instances. Messages can then be either *commands*, related to single tasks and imposed by controllers, or *status* messages, which are sent by engines and are related to status changes in their system. All messages are in the form of *dictionaries*. This component also handles resiliency features such as automatic re-connection from clients to servers, since temporary connection losses are to be expected in a fault injection context.

Thread Pool. Task commands in FINJ engines are assigned to a thread in a pool as they are received: each thread manages all aspects of a task assigned to it. Specifically, the thread sleeps until the scheduled starting time of the task (according to its time-stamp); then, it spawns a subprocess running the specified task, and sends a message to all connected controllers to inform them of the event. At this point, the thread waits for the task's termination, depending on its duration and on the current configuration. Finally, the thread sends a new status message to all connected hosts informing them of the task's termination, and returns to sleep. The amount of threads in the pool, which is a configurable parameter, determines the maximum number of tasks that can be executed concurrently. Since threads in the pool are started only once during the engine's initialization, and wake up for minimal amounts of time when a task needs to be started or terminated, we expect their impact on performance to be negligible.

Input and Output. In FINJ, input and output of all data related to injection sessions are performed by controller instances, and are handled by *reader* and *writer* entities. By default, these employ the CSV format, which was chosen due to its extreme simplicity and generality, but they can be easily customized by users for other formats. *Input* in FINJ is constituted by *workload* files: as mentioned in Sect. 2.1, these files include one entry for each task that must be executed in the injection session. Using the CSV format makes workload files extremely readable, and manually writing workloads corresponding to highly specific test cases can be easily achieved as well. FINJ *output*, instead, is made up of two parts. The first is the *execution log*, which contains entries corresponding to status changes in the target node, namely the start and termination of tasks, errors that are encountered if any, and connection loss or recovery events. The second part of FINJ output is related to tasks: all output text written to the *stdout* or *stderr* channels during their execution, if any, is reported to controllers, and is stored in separate plain-text files in a directory alongside the main output file, each named according to the task's name and sequence number.

Configuration. The FINJ tool's runtime behavior is customizable by means of a configuration file. This file is in JSON format and includes several options that alter the behavior of either controller or engine instances. Among the basic options, it is possible to specify the listening TCP port for engine instances, and the list of addresses of target hosts, to which controller instances should connect at launch time. The latter is useful when injection sessions must be performed on large sets of nodes, whose addresses can be conveniently stored in a file. More complex options are also available: for instance, it is possible to define a series of commands corresponding to tasks that must be launched together with FINJ, and must be terminated with it. This option proves especially useful when users wish to set up monitoring frameworks, such as the *Lightweight Distributed*

Metric Service (LDMS) [1], to be launched together with FINJ in order to collect system performance metrics during injection sessions.

Workload Generation. While writing workload files manually is possible, this is time-consuming and not desirable for long injection sessions. Therefore, we implemented in FINJ a *workload generation* tool, which can be used to automatically generate workload files with certain statistical features, while trying to combine flexibility and ease of use. The workload generation process is controlled by three parameters: a maximum *time span* for the total duration of the workload expressed in seconds, a statistical distribution for the *duration* of tasks, and another one for their *inter-arrival* times. These distributions are separated in two sets, for fault and benchmark tasks, thus amounting to a total of four. They can be either specified analytically by the user or can be fitted from real data, thus reproducing realistic behavior.

A workload is composed as a series of fault and benchmark tasks that are selected from a list of possible shell commands. To control the composition of workloads, users can optionally associate to each command a probability for its selection during the generation process, and a list of CPU cores for its execution, as explained in Sect. 2.1. By default, commands are picked uniformly. Having defined its parameters, the workload generation process is then fairly simple: tasks are randomly generated in order to achieve statistical features close to those specified as input, and are written to an output CSV file, until the maximum imposed time span is reached. Alongside the full workload, a *probe* file is also produced: this workload file contains one entry for each task type, all with a short fixed duration, and represents a lightweight workload version. This file can be used during the setup phase to test the correct configuration of the system, making sure that all tasks are correctly found and executed on the target hosts, without having to run the entire heavy workload.

2.3 Implementation

FINJ is implemented in Python, an object-oriented, high-level interpreted programming language[2], and can be used on all major operating systems. All FINJ dependencies are included in the Python distribution, and the only optional external dependency is the *scipy* package, which is needed for the workload generation functionality. The source code is publicly available on GitHub[3] under the MIT license, together with its documentation, usage examples and several fault-triggering programs. FINJ works on Python versions 3.4 and above.

In Fig. 2 we illustrate the class diagram for the FINJ tool. The *engine* and *controller* entities are respectively represented by the *InjectorEngine* and *InjectorController* classes. Users can instantiate these classes and start injection sessions directly, by using the *listen* method to put the engine in listening mode, and the *inject* method of the controller, which allows to start the injection session

[2] https://www.python.org/events/python-events/.
[3] https://github.com/AlessioNetti/fault_injector.

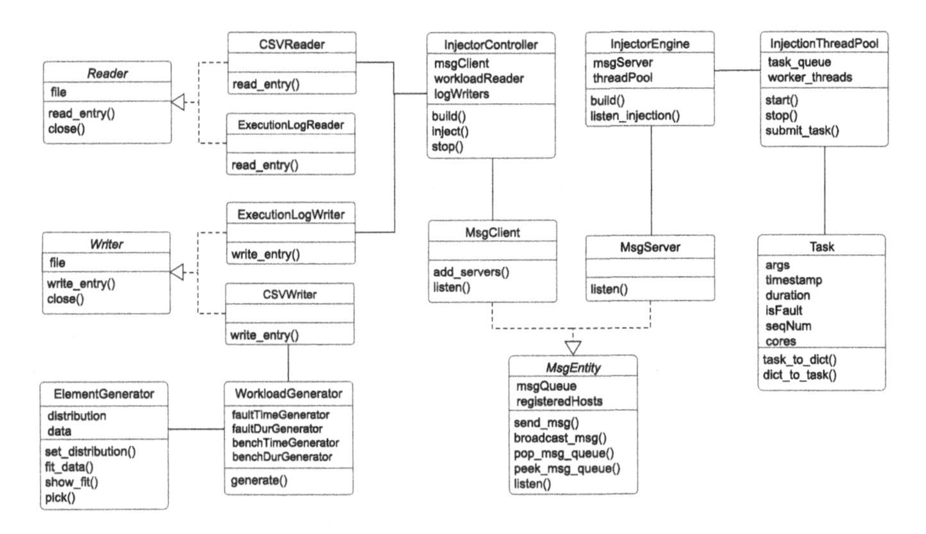

Fig. 2. Class diagram of the FINJ tool.

itself. However, scripts are supplied with FINJ to create controller and engine instances from a command-line interface, simplifying the process. This method will be discussed in Sect. 3. The *InjectionThreadPool* class, instead, supplies the thread pool implementation used to execute and manage tasks.

The network layer of the tool is represented by the *MsgClient* and *MsgServer* classes, which implement the message and queue-based client and server used for communication. Both classes are implementations of the *MsgEntity* abstract class, which provides the interface for sending and receiving messages, and implements the basic mechanisms that regulate the access to the underlying queue.

Input and output are instead handled by the *Reader* and *Writer* abstract classes and their implementations: *CSVReader* and *CSVWriter* handle the reading and writing of workload files, while *ExecutionLogReader* and *ExecutionLogWriter* handle execution logs generated by injection sessions. Since these classes are all implementations of abstract interfaces, it is easy for users to customize them for different formats. Tasks are modeled by the *Task* class that contains all attributes specified in Sect. 2.1.

Lastly, access to the workload generator is provided through the *WorkloadGenerator* class, which is the interface used to set up and start the generation process. This class is backed by the *ElementGenerator* class, which offers basic functionality for fitting data and generating random values. This class acts as a wrapper on scipy's *rv_continuous* class, which generates random variables.

3 Using FINJ

In this Section we demonstrate the flow of execution of FINJ through a concrete example carried out on a real HPC node and provide insight on its overhead.

```
timestamp;duration;seqNum;isFault;cores;args
0;1723;1;False;0-7;./hpl lininput
355;244;2;True;6;sudo ./cpufreq 258
914;291;3;True;4;./leak 316
```

Fig. 3. A sample CSV workload that can be used with FINJ.

3.1 Sample Execution

In this Section we will consider a sample fault injection session carried out using FINJ. The employed workload file, named *sample.csv*, is illustrated in Fig. 3. The test was carried out on one node of an HPC system equipped with two Intel Xeon E5-2630 v3 CPUs, each with 8 cores, 128 GB of RAM, and running CentOS 7.3. The *finj_engine* and *finj_controller* Python scripts are supplied with FINJ to start *engine* and *controller* instances respectively. Their usage is explained on the GitHub repository for the tool, together with all configuration options.

In this workload, the first task is the Intel Distribution[4] for the well-known *High-Performance Linpack* (HPL) benchmark, optimized for Intel Xeon CPUs. This task starts at time 0 in the workload, and has a maximum allowed duration of 30 min. The following two tasks are fault-triggering programs: *cpufreq* uses the Intel P-State driver in the Linux kernel[5] to dynamically reduce the maximum allowed CPU frequency, emulating performance degradation, while *leak* [16] creates a memory leak in the system, eventually using all available RAM. The cpufreq program requires appropriate permissions, so that users can access the files controlling Linux CPU governors. The HPL benchmark was run with 8 threads, pinned on the first 8 cores of the machine, while the cpufreq and leak tasks were forced to run on cores 6 and 4 respectively. Also note that the tasks must be available at the specified path on the systems running the FINJ engine, which in this case is relative to the location of the launching script.

Having defined the workload, the injection engine and controller must be started. Using the default configuration, and supposing that the test must be performed locally, this can be accomplished with the two following commands:

```
python finj_engine -p 30000 &
python finj_controller -w sample.csv -a localhost:30000
```

In the code above, the *-p* argument indicates the listening TCP port for the engine instance. The *-a* argument is instead the list of engine addresses to which the controller should connect, and *-w* is the path of the CSV workload file to be injected. The controller instance will then connect to the engine and start executing the workload, storing all output in a unique CSV file for each target host. When this process is finished, the controller terminates. The output CSV files for our example have the format shown in Fig. 4: each entry represents a status change event, which in this case is the start or termination of tasks, and

[4] https://software.intel.com/en-us/mkl-windows-developer-guide-overview-of-the-intel-distribution-for-linpack-benchmark.

[5] https://www.kernel.org/doc/Documentation/cpu-freq/intel-pstate.txt.

```
timestamp;type;args;seqNum;duration;isFault;cores;error
1529172604;command_session_s;None;None;None;None;None;None
1529172624;status_start;./hpl lininput;1;1723;False;0-7;None
1529172979;status_start;sudo ./cpufreq 258;2;258;True;6;None
1529173237;status_end;sudo ./cpufreq 258;2;258;True;6;None
1529173538;status_start;./leak 316;3;316;True;4;None
1529173855;status_end;./leak 316;3;316;True;4;None
1529174347;status_end;./hpl lininput;1;1723;False;0-7;None
1529174348;command_session_e;None;None;None;None;None;None
```

Fig. 4. A sample output file produced by FINJ after an injection session for the workload specified in Fig. 3.

is flagged with its absolute time-stamp on the target host. In addition, we also find an *error* field, detailing possible errors that were encountered. Note that the file is opened and closed by session *start* and *end* entries: the presence of these ensures that the injection process did not encounter errors and that the entire workload was processed successfully. It can be clearly seen from this experiment how easily a FINJ experiment can be configured and started on multiple cores.

At this point, the data generated by FINJ can be easily compared with other data, for example performance metrics collected through a monitoring framework, in order to better understand the system's behavior under faults. For this test, we used the LDMS framework [1] to collect performance metrics on the target host at each second, for the duration of the injection session. In Fig. 5 we show the total RAM usage and the CPU frequency of core 0. The benchmark's profile is simple, showing a constant CPU frequency while RAM usage slowly increases as the application performs tests on increasing matrix sizes. The effect of our fault programs, marked in gray, can be clearly observed in the system: the *cpufreq* fault causes a sudden drop in CPU frequency, resulting in reduced performance and longer computation times, while the *leak* fault causes a steady, linear increase in RAM usage. Even though saturation of the available RAM is not reached, this peculiar behavior can be used for prediction purposes.

3.2 Overhead of FINJ

We also performed tests in order to evaluate the overhead that FINJ may introduce. To do so, we employed the same system used in Sect. 3.1 together with the HPL benchmark, this time configured to use all 16 cores of the machine. We run the HPL benchmark 20 times directly, and then repeated the same process by using a FINJ workload. FINJ was once again instantiated locally. In both conditions the HPL benchmark scored an average running time of roughly 320 seconds, therefore leading us to conclude that the impact of FINJ on running applications is negligible, as expected from the implementation.

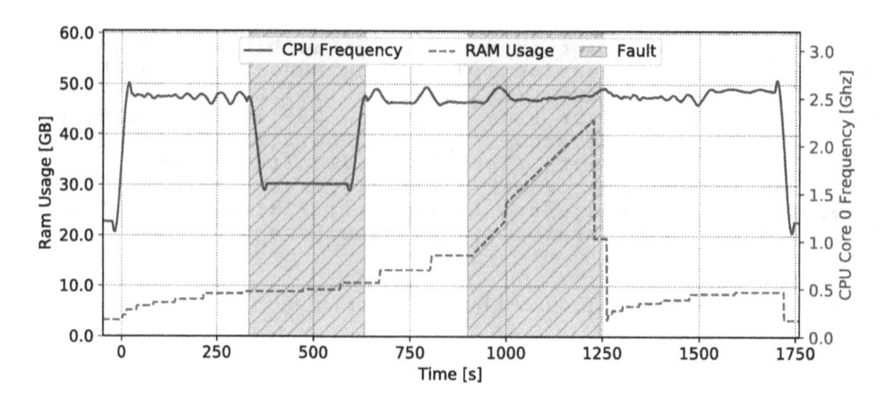

Fig. 5. CPU Frequency and RAM Usage, as monitored on the target system during the sample injection session.

4 Conclusions

We have presented FINJ, a high-level, easy-to-use tool for fault injection and monitoring in HPC systems. FINJ allows for the automation of complex experiments, and for reproducing anomalous behaviors in a deterministic, simple way. FINJ is open-source and implemented in Python, an object-oriented interpreted programming language available on all major operating systems, and has no dependencies for its core operation. This, together with the simplicity of its command-line interface, makes the deployment of FINJ on large-scale systems trivial. Since FINJ is based on the use of tasks, which are external executable programs, users can integrate the tool with any existing lower-level fault injection framework that can be triggered in such way, and ranging from the application level to the kernel, or even hardware level. The use of workloads in FINJ also allows to reproduce complex, specific fault conditions in HPC systems, and to reliably perform experiments involving multiple nodes at the same time.

As future work, we plan to perform scalability studies on the FINJ tool, by deploying it on a large-scale HPC environment. We have already performed extensive testing on the system presented in Sect. 3 with excellent preliminary results. Also, we plan to implement the ability to build workloads in which the order of tasks is defined by *causal* relationships rather than time-stamps, which might simplify the triggering of extremely specific anomalous states in a given system. We will also integrate multiple network transport methods to choose from besides TCP, so as to extend the range of systems FINJ can be applied to.

Acknowledgements. A. Netti has been supported by a research fellowship from the *Oprecomp-Open Transprecision Computing* project. A. Sîrbu has been partially funded by the EU project *SoBigData Research Infrastructure—Big Data and Social Mining Ecosystem* (grant agreement 654024).

References

1. Agelastos, A., et al.: The lightweight distributed metric service: a scalable infrastructure for continuous monitoring of large scale computing systems and applications. In: Proceedings of SC 2014, pp. 154–165. IEEE (2014)
2. Ashby, S., Beckman, P., Chen, J., Colella, P., Collins, B., Crawford, D., et al.: The opportunities and challenges of exascale computing. In: Summary Report of the Advanced Scientific Computing Advisory Committee (ASCAC) Subcommittee, pp. 1–77 (2010)
3. Calhoun, J., Olson, L., Snir, M.: FlipIt: an LLVM based fault injector for HPC. In: Lopes, L., et al. (eds.) Euro-Par 2014. LNCS, vol. 8805, pp. 547–558. Springer, Cham (2014). https://doi.org/10.1007/978-3-319-14325-5_47
4. Cappello, F., Geist, A., Gropp, W., Kale, S., Kramer, B., Snir, M.: Toward exascale resilience: 2014 update. Supercomput. Front. Innovations **1**(1), 5–28 (2014)
5. DeBardeleben, N., Blanchard, S., Guan, Q., Zhang, Z., Fu, S.: Experimental framework for injecting logic errors in a virtual machine to profile applications for soft error resilience. In: Alexander, M., et al. (eds.) Euro-Par 2011. LNCS, vol. 7156, pp. 282–291. Springer, Heidelberg (2012). https://doi.org/10.1007/978-3-642-29740-3_32
6. Ferreira, K.B., Bridges, P., Brightwell, R.: Characterizing application sensitivity to OS interference using kernel-level noise injection. In: Proceedings of SC 2008, p. 19. IEEE Press (2008)
7. Gainaru, A., Cappello, F.: Errors and faults. In: Herault, T., Robert, Y. (eds.) Fault-Tolerance Techniques for High-Performance Computing. CCN, pp. 89–144. Springer, Cham (2015). https://doi.org/10.1007/978-3-319-20943-2_2
8. Guan, Q., Chiu, C.C., Fu, S.: CDA: a cloud dependability analysis framework for characterizing system dependability in cloud computing infrastructures. In: Proceedings of PRDC 2012, pp. 11–20. IEEE (2012)
9. Guan, Q., Fu, S.: Adaptive anomaly identification by exploring metric subspace in cloud computing infrastructures. In: Proceedings of SRDS 2013, pp. 205–214. IEEE (2013)
10. Gunawi, H.S., et al.: FATE and DESTINI: a framework for cloud recovery testing. In: Proceedings of NSDI 2011, p. 239 (2011)
11. Hsueh, M.C., Tsai, T.K., Iyer, R.K.: Fault injection techniques and tools. Computer **30**(4), 75–82 (1997)
12. Joshi, P., Gunawi, H.S., Sen, K.: PREFAIL: a programmable tool for multiple-failure injection. In: ACM SIGPLAN Notices, vol. 46, pp. 171–188. ACM (2011)
13. Lameter, C.: Numa (non-uniform memory access): an overview. Queue **11**(7), 40 (2013)
14. Naughton, T., Bland, W., Vallee, G., Engelmann, C., Scott, S.L.: Fault injection framework for system resilience evaluation: fake faults for finding future failures. In: Proceedings of Resilience 2009, pp. 23–28. ACM (2009)
15. Stott, D.T., Floering, B., Burke, D., Kalbarczpk, Z., Iyer, R.K.: NFTAPE: a framework for assessing dependability in distributed systems with lightweight fault injectors. In: Proceedings of IPDS 2000, pp. 91–100. IEEE (2000)

16. Tuncer, O., et al.: Diagnosing performance variations in HPC applications using machine learning. In: Kunkel, J.M., Yokota, R., Balaji, P., Keyes, D. (eds.) ISC 2017. LNCS, vol. 10266, pp. 355–373. Springer, Cham (2017). https://doi.org/10.1007/978-3-319-58667-0_19
17. Villa, O., Johnson, D.R., O'connor, M., Bolotin, E., Nellans, D., Luitjens, J., et al.: Scaling the power wall: a path to exascale. In: Proceedings of SC 2014, pp. 830–841. IEEE (2014)

Performance Efficient Multiresilience Using Checkpoint Recovery in Iterative Algorithms

Rizwan A. Ashraf(✉) and Christian Engelmann

Computer Science and Mathematics Division, Oak Ridge National Laboratory, Oak Ridge, TN 37831, USA
{ashrafra,engelmannc}@ornl.gov

Abstract. In this paper, we address the design challenge of building multiresilient iterative high-performance computing (HPC) applications. Multiresilience in HPC applications is the ability to tolerate and maintain forward progress in the presence of both soft errors and process failures. We address the challenge by proposing performance models which are useful to design performance efficient and resilient iterative applications. The models consider the interaction between soft error and process failure resilience solutions. We experimented with a linear solver application with two distinct kinds of soft error detectors: one detector has high overhead and high accuracy, whereas the second has low overhead and low accuracy. We show how both can be leveraged for verifying the integrity of checkpointed state used to recover from both soft errors and process failures. Our results show the performance efficiency and resiliency benefit of employing the low overhead detector with high frequency within the checkpoint interval, so that timely soft error recovery can take place, resulting in less re-computed work.

Keywords: High-performance computing · Resilience · Soft errors Process failures · Fault injection · Checkpoint restart Design patterns · Iterative algorithms · Linear solver · Performance Analytical models

This work was sponsored by the U.S. Department of Energy's Office of Advanced Scientific Computing Research. This manuscript has been authored by UT-Battelle, LLC under Contract No. DE-AC05-00OR22725 with the U.S. Department of Energy.

G. Mencagli et al. (Eds.): Euro-Par 2018 Workshops, LNCS 11339, pp. 813–825, 2019.
https://doi.org/10.1007/978-3-030-10549-5_63

1 Introduction

Reliable operation of extreme-scale computing systems is a significant challenge due to evolving system architectures, hardware components and software, and sheer scale of these systems. Since it is difficult and costly to build reliable high-performance computing (HPC) systems, its users or application developers need to devise solutions which can ensure predictable outcome in the presence of an array of faults, errors, and failures. Broadly, HPC applications are affected by soft errors and hard errors. Soft errors are transient in nature, caused mostly due to cosmic radiation particles interacting with various electronic components in the computing system. On the other hand, permanent failures in the system affect components such as memory, processor, system software, and eventually the applications executing on the HPC system.

Complete resilience of HPC applications requires tackling both soft errors and process failures, or hereafter referred to as *multiresilience*. The manner in which both errors impact applications is unique. Some kind of soft errors can eventually cause a process failure, such as via corruption of a pointer variable, or loop index variable. Most soft errors will corrupt the data of the application. Hard errors which eventually cause a process or compute node failure are relatively easy to detect. Whereas, it may not always be possible to detect soft errors, i.e., they may silently corrupt the state of the application with no obvious symptoms, which is usually referred to as *silent data corruption (SDC)*. SDCs can have significantly varying consequences on the outcome of the application, ranging from negligible effect on correctness to unusable results. Therefore, it is important to be able to design applications which can tolerate and make useful forward progress in the presence of both soft errors and process failures.

We leverage a design pattern oriented approach to implement multiresilient HPC applications [1]. Design patterns provide concrete and repeatable solutions to commonly occurring problems. Based on this idea, previous work [9] identifies and formalizes design patterns for solution of resilience problems occurring in HPC systems. In this work, we focus on performance models for design patterns used for soft error and process failure resilience. These models serve as a guide to build optimal, efficient and reliable HPC applications. Specifically, we focus on iterative HPC applications, which can tolerate soft errors by taking additional time to converge to a solution [4,10]. We are interested in the combination of soft error detection and checkpoint-based recovery which has minimal impact on application execution time and provides acceptable level of tolerance to soft errors. Previous work has identified combination of soft error detection with checkpoints by identifying the optimal number of verifications to perform within a checkpoint interval [2]. However, the prior work assumes ideal soft error detectors. On the contrary, we focus on practical detectors which might leave some soft errors undetected and corrupt checkpointed state, yet provide a satisfactory solution at the cost of additional iterations beyond the error free case.

Checkpointing is commonly used in HPC applications to recover from process failures [9]. It involves checkpointing the application state to a stable storage at regular intervals and its utilization in the event of a process failure.

The application rollbacks to the last known good checkpoint and continues execution. A checkpointing based approach becomes complicated with the presence of soft errors since the state which is being checkpointed may be corrupted, and the iterative application can become stuck and make no progress. Therefore, it is important to verify the integrity of the checkpoint before it is stored to a stable storage. This check provides a loose guarantee that the application will keep on making forward progress.

In this paper, we develop performance models for multiresilience to both soft and hard errors using checkpoint-based recovery, which is a well-utilized method in the field. In our experiments, we compare the performance of two distinct soft error detectors. One detector is high overhead and high accuracy, whereas the other detector is low overhead and low accuracy. We investigate through experiments and derive analytical models to assess whether it is better to use a high overhead detector less often or a low overhead detector more often. A tradeoff exists since the low overhead detector can cause the application to consume more iterations to converge as compared to the case when high overhead detector is used. This tradeoff is investigated in our work. We perform our experiments with a Generalized Minimal Residual (GMRES) solver implemented using Trilinos and Open MPI User Level Failure Mitigation (ULFM) [3] in C++ programming language. The experiments are performed on an in-house Linux cluster with 960 processing cores as described in Sect. 5.

2 Soft Error Resilience

In this section, the two distinct soft error resilience design patterns utilized in our work are discussed. Without loss of generality and encompassing the scope of our work to iterative applications, we introduce the patterns based on a linear solver. The solver solves for the solution vector x in the system of equations of the form: $Ax = b$, where matrix A and right hand vector b are known. Soft errors can corrupt the state of the solver, which is composed of both static and dynamic states. The static state in this case forms the matrix A and the vector b, whereas the dynamic state is represented by the solution vector x. The remaining state of the solver which is required for achieving computational results is the environment state. The environmental state includes the variables associated with the runtime system of the message passing library (e.g., Open MPI), pointers, index variables, etc. Corruption of any of the above mentioned state categorizations can cause slowdowns, unbounded errors or fatal crashes.

The SDC detection patterns assist in catching these abnormalities exploiting common algorithmic characteristics of the solver. The two patterns namely: "Monotonicity Violation" and "Bounded Computations" are listed in Tables 1 and 2 respectively. In the first case, the use of the pattern relies on the property of the solver that it is always making forward progress with increasing iteration count, i.e., a characteristic of iterative algorithms. This pattern can be utilized in all iterative applications which use a quality metric to determine convergence of the algorithm. To reduce the possibility of a false positive detection using

Table 1. Resilience pattern: monotonicity violation

Pattern name	Monotonicity violation
Problem	SDC Detection in iterative algorithms
Context	Check the progress of algorithm at each iteration by inspecting the quality metric
Forces	Applicable for iterative algorithms where quality metric is monotonically non-increasing
Solution	Calculate quality metric at each iteration and check violation by comparing the quality metric from previous iteration
Capability	The need to calculate quality metric frequently increases computation and communication between parallel processes
Protection domain	SDCs in static and dynamic state can be detected
Resulting context	Enables timely recovery of iterative algorithm state
Rationale	Inexpensive method as compared to redundant computation

this pattern, the difference from prior iteration can be bounded within certain limit. For detection in the GMRES solver, we utilize the residual which is a measurement of the error in the current solution. The residual at iteration or time step k is defined as: $r_k = b - Ax_k$. The residual has the property of being monotonically decreasing in the GMRES solver [8]. Over the course of iterative computations, if for any reason, this property is violated, we infer the presence of soft errors, and initiate recovery. The calculation of residual is a costly operation because it involves matrix vector multiplication, Ax_k. The matrix multiplication is a global operation across all the parallel processes and involves both parallel computation and communication. However, this high overhead detector is able to catch soft errors with high accuracy.

The GMRES solver does not need to calculate the residual at every iteration to determine convergence since it can use the 2-norm of the result obtained from solving the least squares problem as an indicator for convergence [8]. The residual only needs to be calculated after convergence has been indicated and it is used to certify that convergence criteria has been met, i.e., the residual falls below a certain user-specified threshold value. Even though the value of 2-norm can be used as an indicator of errors, we rely on the more accurate residual as a quality metric for use within the monotonicity violation resilience pattern. As far as our low overhead detector is concerned, we rely on inexpensive invariant checks, as highlighted by the bounded computations design pattern in Table 2. It involves checking of an invariant condition which is done locally. In case of GMRES solver, projection lengths produced during the orthogonalization phase are bounded by Frobenius norm of matrix A. This condition on the projections can be checked relatively inexpensively, since each parallel process iterates over its projection lengths locally. These are a good indicator of the corruption of state due to soft errors [8]. However, it is not a high accuracy detector.

Table 2. Resilience pattern: bounded computations

Pattern name	Bounded computations
Problem	SDC Detection in critical computations
Context	Check the progress and integrity of algorithm by inspecting the outputs produced during critical computations
Forces	Applicable for algorithms with identifiable critical computations and deterministic lower and upper bounds
Solution	Compare key outputs produced during critical computations against lower and/or upper bounds
Capability	Utilize implicit calculations and local invariant checking
Protection domain	SDCs in static and dynamic state can be detected
Resulting context	Enables timely recovery of the iterative algorithm state
Rationale	Inexpensive method as compared to redundant computation

Once soft errors are detected, checkpoints are utilized for soft rollback. To be able to minimize the amount of re-computations, it is best to perform soft error detections frequently such that the rollback takes place quickly, i.e., we fail fast. Otherwise, if only a single detection or verification is performed prior to the checkpoint, then the whole interval which is usually composed of multiple iterations needs to be re-computed. This is because soft errors cause data corruption unlike process failures which cause disruption in the parallel environment and are relatively easy to detect. The resilience to process failures and aspects for multiresilience are discussed in the next section.

3 Process Failure Resilience and Multiresilience

In distributed applications based on the message passing programming model, the failure of even one process in the parallel environment causes a fatal crash of the application in most implementations. Recent proposal to integrate ULFM in Message-Passing Interface (MPI) addresses some of the challenges associated with handling process failures [3]. For example, ULFM implementation based on Open MPI provides the ability to reliably detect process failures using a consensus algorithm. It also provides the ability to continue execution despite the presence of process failures, by reconstructing communication objects. However, it does not provide the ability to recover application state and this is left on to the users to enable exploitation of unique traits of each application. Multiple methods exist to recover application state including forward and backward recovery of application state [9]. Methods which use application-oblivious checkpointing tend to have high storage and performance overheads as compared to an approach which only stores the minimal state required to resume computation. In this work, we utilize application-assisted checkpointing. For example, we only checkpoint the dynamic state of the solver at regular intervals, whereas the static state of the solver only needs to be checkpointed at the start and redistributed after each process failure to sustain future failures.

The checkpoint restart design pattern to recover from process failures is widely utilized [9]. Recovery from process failure can be accomplished via spares or using only the surviving processes. In this work, we utilize spare processes to recover from failures since it avoids the need to re-balance the workload among surviving processes. We also use in-memory checkpointing [12], whereby the highly optimized point-to-point connectivity between nodes in the HPC system is utilized to store the checkpoints in the memories of assigned nodes in the system. We maintain two copies of the checkpoint, one is maintained locally, and the other one is maintained at a neighboring process. This arrangement helps to recover checkpointed state in case of failure of one process. The approach can be extended to handle multiple process failures by maintaining extra level of redundancy at more than two processes. This is beyond the scope of this work. In a multiresilient implementation, the local checkpoints can be used to recover from soft errors relatively inexpensively compared to the communication overhead required in case of process failure. Thus, performing multiple soft error detections within the interval is feasible since errors can be caught early and timely recovery can be performed.

In a multiresilient solution, it is also important to verify the integrity of the state being checkpointed, since use of corrupt state in recovery can hinder the ability of the iterative application to make forward progress. It may be possible to store multiple checkpoints, and jump back to older ones, in case no forward progress is determined, however it results in high overheads as well as the challenge of determining when the soft error might have started the corruption of checkpoints. Therefore, it is important to perform soft error detection to look for obvious abnormalities in the state being checkpointed. After the memory store, we assume that the checkpointed state will not be corrupted. However, with double in-memory checkpoints it is possible to drop this assumption.

4 Performance Model for Multiresilience

In this section, we develop analytical models to investigate performance characteristics of multiresilient iterative applications. We focus on the combination of soft error detection and mitigation patterns, and process failure mitigation patterns that reduce the time-to-solution. Specifically, we are interested in finding which kind of detector to use and how often to use it within a single checkpoint interval given their overheads. We assume two types of soft error detectors D_1, a high overhead and high accuracy detector, and D_2, a low overhead and low accuracy detector, with overheads quantified in software implementation as T_{D_1} and T_{D_2}, respectively. In case of GMRES, T_{D_1} is mostly composed of the overhead of calculating the residual and T_{D_2} is composed of the overhead of iterating through multiple projection lengths and performing the comparisons. It is noteworthy to mention that if we assume both D_1 and D_2 to be ideal detectors, i.e., they can detect each and every soft error, then choosing the low-overhead detector D_2 is the obvious choice. As opposed to prior work [2], we define our detectors to be non-ideal and are therefore interested in the overall impact on time-to-solution. With a generic software detector having a overhead T_D, the time-to-solution for an iterative application in the error- and failure-free case (T_{FF}) is quantified as:

$$T_{FF} = T_{work} N_{FF} + \lfloor N_{FF} \gamma_{check} \rfloor (T_D N_D + T_{check}) \quad (1)$$

Here, T_{work} represents the time spent doing useful work inside a single iteration of the application, N_{FF} represents the number of iterations required to converge to a solution when no error or failure occurs, γ_{check} represents the factor or frequency with which checkpoints are taken (assumes checkpoints are only taken at the completion of an iteration, e.g., a value of 1/20 means checkpoint is taken after every 20 iterations), T_{check} represents time spent performing the checkpoint, and N_D represents the number of soft error detections done within a single checkpoint interval. The rate with which to take the checkpoints is dependent on the cost of performing the checkpoint and failure rate of the HPC system [7]. A tradeoff exists between frequency of checkpoints which causes overhead in case of failure-free execution and the amount of re-computation in case of failure which may be high if checkpoints are not taken frequently. We assume γ_{check} to be constant for our analysis. Other parameters are dependent on the application and vary depending on the workload used.

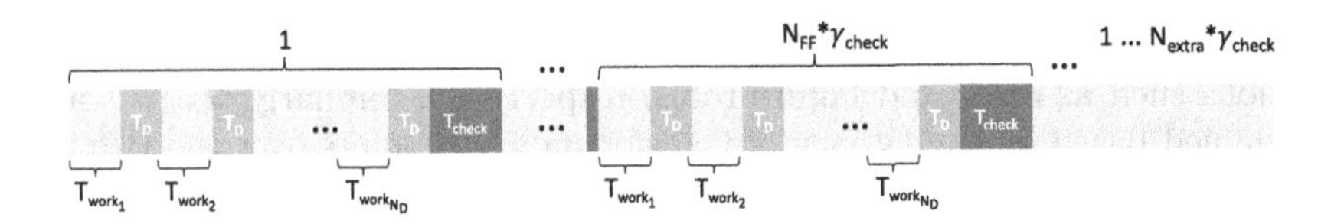

Fig. 1. The multiresilient checkpointing and fail-fast recovery approach.

Now, we model the time-to-solution in the presence of both detected soft errors and process failures, T_{fail}. This is composed of the following components: (1) error- and failure-free total time, (2) overhead incurred due to re-computation after recovery from detected soft-errors and process failures, (3) recovery overheads of detected errors and failures, and (4) extra work done beyond error free case due to presence of bounded errors or undetected soft errors in the state of the application. With these overheads, T_{fail} can be quantified as:

$$\begin{aligned} T_{fail} = T_{FF} + N_{SE}(T_{recompSE} + T_{SEr}) + N_{PF}(T_{recompPF} + T_{PFr}) \\ + T_{work} N_{extra} + \lfloor \gamma_{check} N_{extra} \rfloor (T_D N_D + T_{check}), \quad \text{where,} \end{aligned} \quad (2)$$

$$\begin{aligned} T_{recompSE} &= ((1 + 2 + 3 + \ldots + N_D)/N_D).((T_{work} \gamma_{check}^{-1})/N_D + T_D) \\ &= 0.5\ (N_D + 1).((T_{work} \gamma_{check}^{-1})/N_D + T_D), \quad \text{and,} \end{aligned} \quad (3)$$

$$T_{recompPF} = (T_{work} \gamma_{check}^{-1} + T_D N_D)/2 \quad (4)$$

Here, N_{SE} is the expected number of soft errors which are detected and is therefore dependent on the type and frequency with which the detector is utilized (note, this represents each instance when the detector positively flags corruption of state which may include multiple soft errors in practice); $T_{recompSE}$ and T_{SEr} represent the re-computation and recovery overheads after recovery from a single successful soft error detection, respectively; N_{PF} represents the expected number of process failures which are detected; $T_{recompPF}$ and T_{PFr} represent re-computation and recovery overheads associated with detected process failures, respectively; N_{extra} represents the expected number of extra iterations taken by the iterative application beyond the error-free case. In Fig. 1, the periodic placement of soft error detectors is shown. We assume that the detectors are placed such that the interval is divided into equal sized chunks which may compose multiple iterations of useful work depending on N_D. Irrespective of the original location of the soft fault, the error only has a chance to be detected upon the execution of a detector. If the first detector after the checkpoint catches an error, then only one chunk of work and one detection need to be recomputed. Similarly, if the second detector catches an error, then two chunks of work and two detections starting from the last restart location need to be recomputed, and so on. Following this observation and assuming the fault is equally likely to strike in each chunk, the average value for re-computation due to detected soft errors can be estimated as in Eq. 3. On the other hand, a process failure is detected almost immediately due to its disruptive nature, therefore, based on a uniform distribution, the average amount of work recomputed is estimated as in Eq. 4.

Other parameters such as N_{SE} and N_{PF} also depend on the system specifications such as error and failure rates, respectively. Similarly, T_{check} can be determined based on the latency of transferring checkpoints over the HPC network and the size of the checkpoint [5]. The values for other parameters are best estimated through statistical fault injection experiments. In the next experiment and results section, we find the value of N_D for each type of soft error detector which minimizes T_{fail}. We also estimate N_{extra} and N_{SE} in terms of type and frequency of detector used, although they are strongly application dependent.

5 Experiments and Results

In our experiments, we utilize the FT-GMRES solver which has been implemented using the Trilinos framework [8]. Trilinos provides the ability to solve large scale problems using an array of parallel programming models on a variety of computing platforms. Our implementation is done using ULFM 1.1 built on top of Open MPI 1.7.1. ULFM provides the ability to detect failed processes and remove them from communication objects. In our previous work, we modified FT-GMRES to support multiresilience including the ability to utilize spare processes to recover from process failures [1]. This work provides an in-depth analysis of how to choose the right soft error detector in a multiresilient setup.

We perform our experiments on a Linux cluster with 40 nodes with 2 AMD Opteron processors each (48 cores per node) interconnected with 1 Gbps ethernet. We solve a linear problem with a sparse matrix A which has about 7 million rows and 186 million non-zero elements using 512 cores. The GMRES solver is able to converge to a solution in 320 iterations in the fault free (N_{FF}) case. We perform fault injection in our experiments to determine the multiresilience of the solver and various parameters of interest. In all cases, the number of process failures and the time window in which these are injected are the same, and are based on an exponential distribution. The checkpoints are also performed at the same rate, e.g., we set $\gamma_{check} = 1/20$ for all our experiments. With this setup, the variables associated with process failures have bounded values. Soft errors are injected randomly into computed data (e.g., the resultant vector produced after a sparse matrix vector multiplication operation) after almost every 10 iterations of useful work. The error and failure rates are fixed across all our experiments. Enough fault injection experiments (at least 100 for each case) are performed in each case to keep the coefficient of variation low.

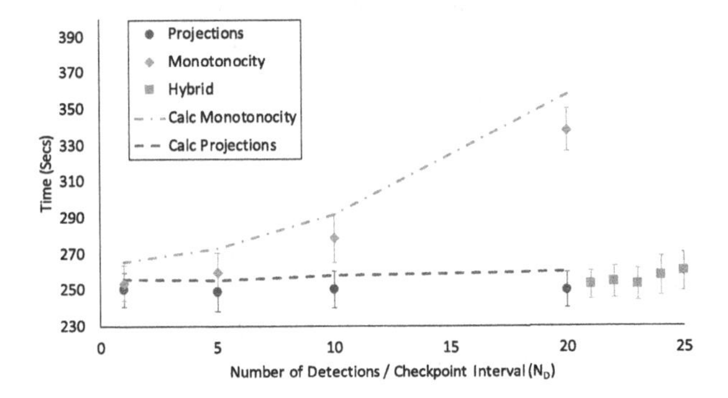

Fig. 2. The effect on total time-to-solution (average and std. dev.) with different number of soft error detections inside a single checkpoint interval. Performance estimates from proposed analytical models in Eqs. 1 and 2 are also plotted.

The overall time-to-solution for FT-GMRES with the two soft error detectors, i.e., monotonicity violation and bounded computations (projections), is shown in Fig. 2. The effect of performing increasing number of soft error detections inside a single checkpoint interval (note: a max of 20 detections can be performed) on time-to-solution shows the runaway effect when using the high-overhead detector, especially when $N_D > 5$. In our experiments, on average we measured about 90 fold higher overhead for monotonicity detector compared to bounded computations detector. Thus, using the high accuracy detector too often starts to dominate the time-to-solution nullifying any other positive effects. However, the disparity among overheads of accurate and inaccurate detectors is high for FT-GMRES solver. Consequently, the conclusions may differ for other applications depending on the tradeoff between penalty of extra work with low accuracy detector and overhead of using the high accuracy detector. The estimations obtained from the performance models proposed in Eqs. 1 and 2 are also plotted in Fig. 2, demonstrating a decent bound on time-to-solution with both detectors in FT-GMRES solver. Some observations on the parameters in our models are: T_{check} is dominated by the time to store the checkpoint in remote memory, $T_{SEr} << T_{PFr}$ recovering checkpoint from local memory is orders of magnitude faster than process failure recovery, and N_{extra} and N_{SE} depend on the type of the detector and the frequency (N_D) with which it is used.

Based on the performance of the two detectors, we also evaluate an additional type of detector, which is a hybrid of the monotonicity violation and bounded computations detectors. In this case, we perform the low overhead detection at every iteration of the solver, whereas the high overhead detector is performed up to 5 times inside a single checkpoint interval. The time-to-solution with the hybrid soft error detector is shown in Fig. 2. The hybrid detector gives mid-tier overall performance, with interesting implications on total iteration count and soft error detection success rate as discussed hereafter.

Results in Fig. 3 show the total number of iterations taken by the solver to converge to a solution with each type of detector while using different number of detections inside a single checkpoint interval. The total iteration count here includes all the re-computations after each soft error and process failure recovery, and the extra iterations taken by the solver to converge to a solution beyond the fault free case. Overall, increasing the use of low overhead detector does not effect the iteration count drastically when compared to the high overhead detector. For example, the total iterations decrease at a rate of 0.08 and 0.71 per detection when using bounded computations and monotonicity patterns, respectively. The hybrid approach seems to provide the fastest decrease in total iteration count among all cases. These results correspond directly to the number of additional iterations taken by the solver beyond the fault free case, N_{extra}. Our estimations for N_{extra} range between 18 and 46 for the high accuracy detector, and between 51 and 60 for the low accuracy detector. These results show that there is more overhead due to additional iterations for the low accuracy detector including extra checkpoints as compared to high accuracy detector.

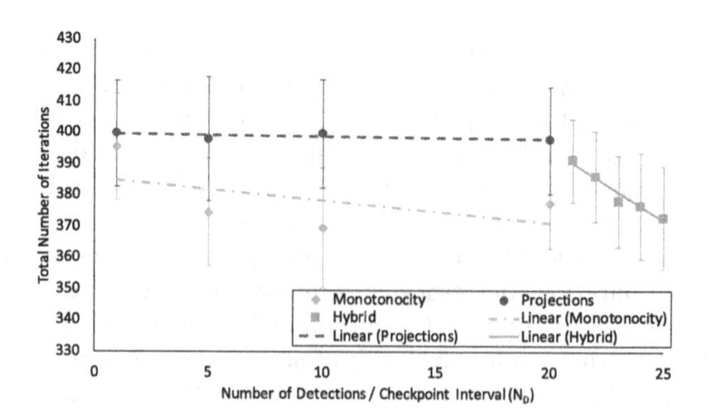

Fig. 3. The effect on total iterations (average and std. dev.) to converge to a solution with different number of soft error detections inside a single checkpoint interval. Includes re-computations with errors and extra iterations beyond error-free case.

The detection accuracy of each soft error detector is shown in Fig. 4. Here, the undetected soft errors may cause any of the following cases: negligible effect on the outcome or convergence of the solver, extra work to converge to a solution, and increased chances of inducing a process failure. Another possibility is that the solver does not converge to a solution in allocated time, which is not listed earlier since sufficient time is given to the solver in our experiments. The results in Fig. 4 also provide a good estimate for expected number of soft errors detected N_{SE} in each case. We estimate N_{SE} by averaging the number of soft errors detected across all runs. On average, the high accuracy detector catches between 1 and 2 soft errors, whereas the low accuracy detector catches between 0 and 1 soft errors in each run depending on the number of detections performed in each interval. A significantly higher number of soft errors are injected compared to those which are detected in line with the premise of our work. As expected, the bounded computations soft error detection pattern achieves lower accuracy than the monotonicity violation pattern. The low accuracy detector seems to surpass the lowest accuracy achieved by high accuracy detector with $N_D > 15$. The use of high accuracy detector at low frequency combined with low accuracy detector at highest frequency is seen to provide matching or better accuracy than the high accuracy detector in most cases. Overall, the hybrid detector is able to detect soft errors more often reducing the overheads due to extra iterations and therefore is able to provide significantly better resilience than the low overhead detector with up to 4% more performance overhead.

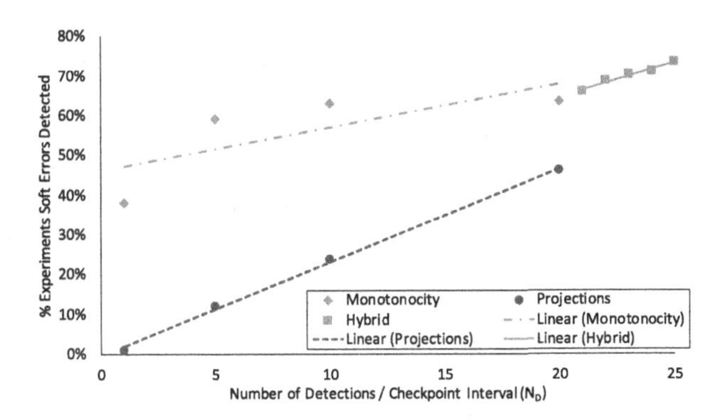

Fig. 4. Variation of soft error detection rate (total number of experiments in which soft errors were successfully detected out of all experiments) when different number of soft error detections are performed inside a single checkpoint interval.

6 Related Work

Previous works in the design of resilient iterative methods have focused on tolerance to either soft errors [4,10] or process failures [6], but not both together. Most recently, design patterns have been utilized for implementation of multiresilient solutions in HPC applications [1]. The catalog of design patterns [9] comprehensively describes various resilience solutions, a layered hierarchy of the patterns and a patterns language. The use of algorithmic approaches to detect soft errors for sparse linear algebra and a linear solver are demonstrated in [11] and [8], respectively. In this work, we develop a performance model which aids in the selection and tuning of soft error detectors in conjunction with a checkpoint-based recovery approach, which is widely applicable [5,12]. Related work [2] developed a performance model for checkpoint-based recovery in presence of both soft errors and process failures, however, it assumes ideal soft error detection and therefore does not consider the special case of iterative algorithms. Furthermore, we also test the efficacy of our performance models via experiments with a linear solver.

7 Conclusion

We demonstrate the design of performance efficient multiresilient linear solver application. Checkpoint restart is shown to be an effective recovery approach in our multiresilient solution. Our approach shows the appropriate combination of soft error and process failure resilience solutions. We evaluate two different type of soft error detectors in our work and investigate the tradeoffs of using them under non-ideal detection conditions. Results evaluate the affect of using the detectors with different frequency on time-to-solution, the number of extra iterations taken by the solver beyond the fault free case, and the rate of successful soft error detections in simulated fault injection experiments. A hybrid approach which uses the high overhead and high accuracy detector sparingly combined with a low overhead detector and low accuracy detector at every iteration is observed to have similar or better detection success rate as using a high overhead detector at every iteration with significantly less impact on time-to-solution.

Acknowledgements. This material is based upon work supported by the U.S. Department of Energy, Office of Science, Office of Advanced Scientific Computing Research, program manager Lucy Nowell, under contract number DE-AC05-00OR22725.

References

1. Ashraf, R.A., Hukerikar, S., Engelmann, C.: Pattern-based modeling of multiresilience solutions for high-performance computing. In: Proceedings of the 2018 ACM/SPEC International Conference on Performance Engineering (2018)
2. Benoit, A., Cavelan, A., Robert, Y., Sun, H.: Optimal resilience patterns to cope with fail-stop and silent errors. Report RR-8786, LIP - ENS Lyon (October 2015)

3. Bland, W., Bouteiller, A., Herault, T., Bosilca, G., Dongarra, J.: Post-failure recovery of MPI communication capability. Int. J. High Perform. Comput. Appl. **27**(3), 244–254 (2013)
4. Bronevetsky, G., de Supinski, B.: Soft error vulnerability of iterative linear algebra methods. In: 22nd Annual International Conference on Supercomputing (2008)
5. Cao, J., Arya, K., Garg, R., Matott, S., Panda, D.K., Subramoni, H., Vienne, J., Cooperman, G.: System-level scalable checkpoint-restart for petascale computing. In: IEEE 22nd International Conference on Parallel and Distributed Systems (2016)
6. Chen, Z.: Algorithm-based recovery for iterative methods without checkpointing. In: 20th International Symposium on High Performance Distributed Computing (2011)
7. Daly, J.: A higher order estimate of the optimum checkpoint interval for restart dumps. Futur. Gener. Comput. Syst. **22**(3), 303–312 (2006)
8. Elliott, J., Hoemmen, M., Mueller, F.: Evaluating the impact of SDC on the GMRES iterative solver. In: 2014 IEEE 28th International Parallel and Distributed Processing Symposium, pp. 1193–1202 (May 2014)
9. Hukerikar, S., Engelmann, C.: Resilience design patterns: a structured approach to resilience at extreme scale (version 1.2). Technical report ORNL/TM-2017/745, Oak Ridge National Laboratory, Oak Ridge, TN, USA (August 2017)
10. Jaulmes, L., Casas, M., Moretó, M., Ayguadé, E., Labarta, J., Valero, M.: Exploiting asynchrony from exact forward recovery for DUE in iterative solvers. In: International Conference for High Performance Computing, Networking, Storage and Analysis (2015)
11. Sloan, J., Kumar, R., Bronevetsky, G.: An algorithmic approach to error localization and partial recomputation for low-overhead fault tolerance. In: 43rd Annual IEEE/IFIP International Conference on Dependable Systems and Networks (2013)
12. Zheng, G., Shi, L., Kale, L.V.: FTC-Charm++: an in-memory checkpoint-based fault tolerant runtime for Charm++ and MPI. In: 2004 IEEE International Conference on Cluster Computing, pp. 93–103 (September 2004)

A Lightweight Approach to GPU Resilience

Max Baird(✉), Christian Fensch, Sven-Bodo Scholz, and Artjoms Šinkarovs

Heriot-Watt University, Edinburgh, Scotland
{mmb1,c.fensch,s.scholz,a.sinkarovs}@hw.ac.uk

Abstract. Resilience for HPC applications typically is implemented as a CPU-based rollback-recovery technique. In this context, long running accelerator computations on GPUs pose a major challenge as these devices usually do not offer any means of interrupt. This paper proposes a solution to the aforementioned problem: it suggests a novel approach that rewrites GPU kernels so that a soft interrupt of their execution becomes possible. Our approach is based on the Compute Unified Device Architecture (CUDA) by Nvidia and works by taking advantage of CUDA's execution model of partitioning threads into blocks. In essence, we rewrite the kernel so that each block determines whether it should continue execution or return control to the CPU. By doing so we are able to perform a premature interrupt of kernels.

Keywords: HPC · GPU · Resilience

1 Introduction

A large number of high-performance systems these days are equipped with GPGPUs [2,6,7,13,15], as they provide higher energy efficiency and offer a significantly larger degree of parallelism than traditional multi-core CPUs. As a result, the number of compute cores on such systems becomes very large, which in turn, increases the probability of hardware failures. This brings the problem of resilience to hardware failures, which is known to be a challenging topic already [3,5], to the next level. First, the mean time between failures (MTBF) for a single node becomes shorter. Second, resilience for failing GPU nodes requires special treatment.

The de-facto resilience technique today is *application checkpointing*. A checkpointing system pauses the running application and takes a snapshot of its state. The state is either captured automatically by recording register values and the state of the memory of a paused process (*e.g.* by using software such as BLCR [1]) or by explicit stores of relevant data (*e.g.* by using libraries such as FTI [4]). On restore, the captured state is restored and the application restarts its execution from the latest checkpoint. For applications that use GPUs, the described checkpointing mechanism will not work without further measures. GPU kernels do not run as a part of any operating system processes. Even if a process is suspended,

G. Mencagli et al. (Eds.): Euro-Par 2018 Workshops, LNCS 11339, pp. 826–838, 2019.
https://doi.org/10.1007/978-3-030-10549-5_64

the GPU kernels keep on running. Actually, at the time of writing, we are not aware of any hardware mechanisms to interrupt a running GPU kernel.

This behavior poses a serious problem to automated checkpoint mechanisms such as BLCR: as the GPU cannot be interrupted, it is not possible to save a stable snapshot of the GPU state. Checkpoints are only possible between kernel invocations. The problem is intensified, as the size of memory on the GPUs increases, resulting in longer runs of the individual kernels [18,19]. In the case of long kernel execution times, explicit stores of relevant data do not help either as snapshots can only be orchestrated between kernel executions. Furthermore, snapshots require all relevant data to be present on the host.

This paper focuses on finding a solution to the GPU kernel snapshotting and restoring problem in a checkpointing-system agnostic way. We propose an approach that is based on the observation that most GPU kernels schedule orders of magnitude more threads than a GPU can physically execute concurrently. While it is not possible to interrupt an individual thread, a thread can voluntarily stop its execution. Thus, in principle, we are able to interrupt a kernel execution, after the currently running threads have terminated.

We describe a technique on how to rewrite CUDA kernels so that they become "interruptible", and we provide a library[1] with a concise API to simplify this task. We demonstrate how the proposed approach can be used by modifying the code of a real world application. We measure the overheads that our approach brings, using real-world and synthetic benchmarks, concluding that typically the overheads are below 0.2%. This shows that the proposed approach can be used in combination with any checkpointing system for applications that use GPUs.

2 Mechanism Description

The key idea of our approach lies in the observation that due to resource constraints, it is not possible to schedule all kernel threads simultaneously, instead, threads are scheduled in blocks. After all threads in a block are terminated, they are replaced by remaining threads of the compute kernel. This staggered starting makes it possible to instrument every thread at the beginning of its execution with a check of a shared interrupt variable and terminate the execution if the variable is set to a specific value. As a result, a kernel can be forced to terminate in a very short time.

Issuing an interrupt. In order to implement the interrupt mechanism, we use a memory-mapped integer variable that is shared between the host and the device. On the host we define a variable and ask the CUDA driver to share it with the GPU:

```
1 int *timeout = 0;
2 cudaHostAlloc(timeout, sizeof (int), cudaHostAllocMapped);
```

[1] Freely available at https://bitbucket.org/maxbaird/cuda_backup.

For a host to issue an interrupt, it writes a value 1 into a shared variable `*timeout`. The host waits for the kernel to terminate then transfers data from the GPU. After that the value of `*timeout` can be set back to 0 so that further kernel invocations could perform some useful work.

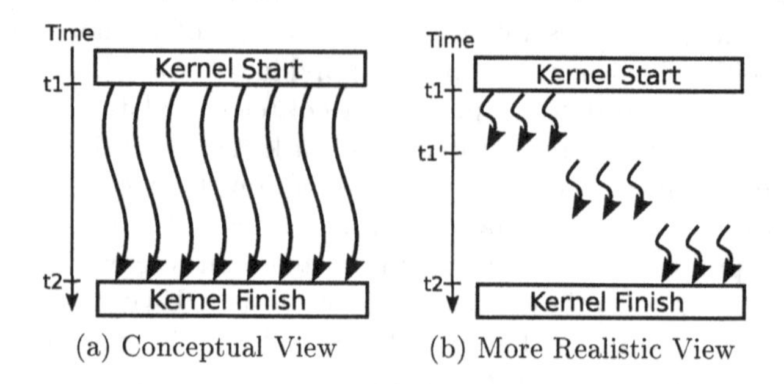

(a) Conceptual View (b) More Realistic View

Fig. 1. GPU multithread execution model. (a) shows the conceptual view with all threads running in parallel, while in reality (b) the number of concurrent executing threads is limited by hardware resources.

Interrupting a kernel. The CUDA execution model [11] suggests that all the threads are launched simultaneously and the kernel runs till all the threads are completed (see Fig. 1a). However, in reality, threads are scheduled in blocks as it is shown in Fig. 1b.

While indeed a thread cannot be interrupted once it has been started, a thread can decide to interrupt itself. Such a decision can be based on checking the state of a global variable at the start of execution. According to the model from Fig. 1a, this approach would not work: all threads check the variable at the same time and then either all continue or interrupt. However, using the more realistic model, the threads that have not been scheduled will observe a change in the variable and will interrupt. As a result, the kernel terminates faster than the case where we wait for all threads to complete, as we only have to:

- wait for all the currently scheduled threads to complete; and
- execute all the remaining threads where the first statement within every such a thread will terminate its execution.

Consider a host issuing an interrupt at time $t1$ in Fig. 1b. The kernel can complete at $t1' + \max((c \times n), t_r)$, where c is the time it takes to execute one conditional per block (GPU executes in a lock-step), n is the number of remaining unscheduled blocks, and t_r is the time to finish already scheduled threads.

Snapshotting. After a kernel has been interrupted, the host copies all data that will be necessary to restart the kernel. In the simplest case, these data include inputs of the kernel and partial outputs of the kernel. In addition, we need to perform a bit of bookkeeping via a boolean array which tracks which threads have been executed to completion. At the start of each thread, we check whether this thread has yet to run. At the end of each thread, we update this boolean array to indicate that it has completed. At every snapshot, we also copy this array back to the host.

Restarting. Restarting a kernel is straight-forward: we copy all the kernel-relevant data back to the GPU and launch the kernel again. We use above mentioned mask to prevent already completed threads from executing again.

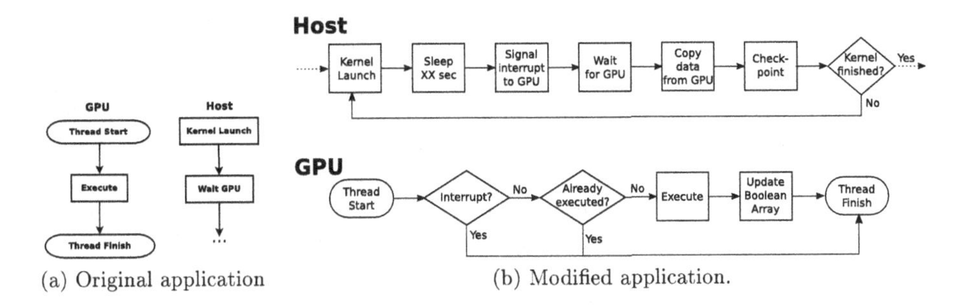

(a) Original application

(b) Modified application.

Fig. 2. How to apply the proposed technique to the original application.

2.1 Integration with Checkpointing System

Once the GPU kernel has been interrupted and all the relevant data has been copied to host, it is safe to snapshot the global state of the application. However, as most checkpointing systems are not aware of GPUs, it is difficult to predict when the checkpointing will happen, and, as a consequence, when to capture the state of running kernels. Our solution to this is to make kernel snapshots every n time units. After each snapshot, the host checks the boolean array for any unfinished threads. If such threads exists, then the kernel is relaunched. This process continues iteratively until all threads are executed.

To apply the proposed technique, we modify the kernel and the code that invokes the kernel as shown in Fig. 2. The wait time on the host should ideally fall within the MTBF.

2.2 Synchronisation Within Kernels

The approach presented so far works for kernels that do not use explicit synchronisation because explicit synchronisation breaks the proposed approach. The reason for this is that threads within blocks are not necessarily scheduled all at the same time. Threads within blocks are split in warps and if a warp is stalled for any reason the scheduler is free to replace it with another warp. Consider the case of a kernel with explicit synchronization, and after the first warp reaches the synchronization point, an interrupt occurs. In this case all the other warps will skip their executions, but threads from the first warp will never leave synchronisation point, resulting in a hung kernel.

Our solution to this problem is to terminate the entire block when we receive an interrupt from the host. To do this, the value of `timeout` is only read once by thread zero of warp zero and stored in a variable local to the block. A block-level synchronisation point is set immediately after the read of `timeout` so that no warps can proceed until `timeout` has been read. After all warps have synchronised, the block-local variable is checked to determine whether or not the block should be executed.

A final note about synchronization, CUDA 9.0 introduced grid and multi-device synchronization along with co-operative groups to the programming model. Co-operative groups extends the CUDA model to organise groups of co-operating threads so that programmers can express the granularity of communicating threads. The approach presented in this paper is unaffected by kernels using co-operative groups because co-operative groups are within blocks and still obey block level synchronization. Our approach cannot work if a kernel performs grid or multi-device synchronization because our mechanism would cause the kernel to hang if some blocks terminate early before reaching the grid synchronization point and other blocks are already in wait of synchronization. In summary, the advantages of this approach are as follows:

1. Only makes sense for long running kernels
2. The kernels must be resource intensive enough to exhaust the parallelism in the GPU
3. Does not work for kernels that perform grid or multi-device synchronization
4. May not be suitable for kernels that consume most of the GPU memory

2.3 Implementation

For the adoption of the proposed approach we introduce an API[2] that facilitates adjustment of applications. The core of the API consists of three macros: `BACKUP_KERNEL_DEF`, `BACKUP_CONTINUE`, `BACKUP_KERNEL_LAUNCH` and a wrapper around `cudaMalloc`. Assuming that an application has one kernel, we replace `cudaMalloc` with its `BACKUP_` version. We adjust kernel definitions as follows:

```
1 __global__ void
2 kernel_name (/* args */){
3     /* kernel body */
4 }
```

```
1 __global__ void
2 BACKUP_KERNEL_DEF (kernel_name ,
3                        /* args */){
4     BACKUP_CONTINUE ();
5     /* kernel body */
6 }
```

[2] The API with its documentation and examples can be found at https://bitbucket.org/maxbaird/cuda_backup.

We replace kernel invocation as follows:

```
1 kernel_name<<<blocks,
2                 threads>>>
3         (/* args */);
```

```
1 BACKUP_KERNEL_LAUNCH
2     (kernel_name, blocks,
3      threads, /* args */);
```

When we rewrite a kernel definition, the macros extend the arguments with a boolean mask array to log which threads ran previously, and they insert the code that checks for the interrupts and the code that terminates the entire block of threads if the interrupt has been received. The `BACKUP_cudaMalloc` memory wrapper collects the allocated data structures that the kernels need so that we can transfer them back from the GPU to the host for the purpose of snapshotting. The macro that wraps the launch of the kernel defines a loop that launches the kernel, waits for a certain time, sets the interrupt and transfers the data (captured by `BACKUP_cudaMalloc` wrapper) from the GPU.

For a complete example, please refer to *demo* directory https://goo.gl/BKvcxX where we demonstrate how the proposed API applies to an application with a kernel that adds two vectors. We provide an original code *vecadd-original.cu* and its modified version *vecadd-modified.cu* that uses our API.

Currently, the API is restricted to applications with a single kernel and only provides a wrapper for `cudaMalloc`. Allocations done via `cudaMallocManaged` automatically work because they are managed by the unified memory system which means that data is readily available at snapshot time. Wrappers for the remaining CUDA allocation functions like `cudaMalloc3D` and `cudaMemcpy2D` are missing. These limitations are only of a technical nature and will be fixed in the foreseeable future.

3 Experimental Setup

In order to evaluate the proposed mechanism we use a real-world application, PBOOST [19] and an artificial example. Ideally, it would have been more suitable to use an established benchmarking suite such as the Rodinia benchmarks instead of an artificial example. However, these benchmarks do not run long enough on our hardware to escape measurement noise and provide conclusive results. A simple kernel is best to isolate and measure the sources of overhead. PBOOST is a tool for parallel permutation tests in genome-wide association studies which concern single nucleotide polymorphism pairs and their association with diseases via the combination of their main effects and interactions. On our system PBOOST runs for about 38 min. The modified version of PBOOST can be found at https://goo.gl/84pNQs. All the modifications to the code are implemented using our API.

We also use the artificial kernel in Listing 1.1 to perform an in-depth analysis of the overheads introduced by our mechanism.

```
1 __global__ void
2 kernel(unsigned long long n, unsigned long long *res){
3   unsigned long long x = 0;
4   for(unsigned long long i = 0; i < n; i++){
5     x++;
6   }
7   *res = x;
8 }
```

Listing 1.1. Artificial kernel for evaluating overheads

We deliberately choose such a trivial kernel, so that we get 100% occupancy on the GPU. All experiments are performed on a AMD Opteron 6376 system with four sockets running Scientific Linux Release 7.4 (Nitrogen), kernel version 3.10.0. The system is fitted with 512 GB of RAM, running at 800 MHz and an NVIDIA TITAN-XP GPU, which is connected via PCIe x16. The TITAN-XP can execute 61,440 threads simultaneously using its 30 streaming multiprocessors (SM). For our experiments we use CUDA 9.0 with a driver version 384.81. Each application is executed 10 times to eliminate measurement noise. We report the average execution time and 90% confidence intervals. In addition, we note kernel configurations in the tripple-chevron CUDA notation: `<<<blocks, threads>>>`; where `blocks` represents the number of blocks of threads and `threads` represents the number of threads per block.

4 Evaluation

Figure 3 shows the execution times of PBOOST with an increasing number of snapshots. The application runs for approximately 38 minutes and the variation of execution time is within 5 s (0.2%) when performing 0 to 6 interrupts. We see that in this particular example, the execution time of the application with our mechanism enabled is the same as that of the vanilla version within the measurement error.

Despite such a low overhead looking very promising, this result is not conclusive. In order to understand the nature of the overheads that our mechanism really brings, we study them in isolation. We investigate how expensive is it to do:

1. Conditional checks in each thread
2. Soft interrupts of a kernel
3. Memory transfers

For these experiments we will use the kernel from Listing. 1.1.

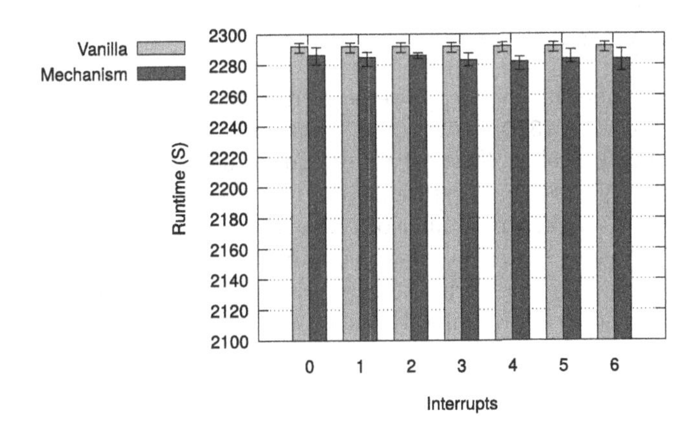

Fig. 3. Absolute runtimes of modified application

4.1 Conditional Checks Overheads

Every thread needs to perform two conditional checks (interrupt and did it already execute) to determine whether to continue or not, so the goal of this experiment is to determine the cost of having these extra checks. To avoid also measuring any overhead that may come from the GPU scheduler, we use a kernel configuration that matches the number of simultaneous threads that can be executed by the GPU. As the TITAN-XP can execute 61,440 threads simultaneously, we use a configuration of `<<<60, 1024>>>`. The results in Fig. 4a show that the conditional checks is significant if number of operations, and by extension runtime, is very small. However this becomes irrelevant for the cases, we are interested in. Figure 4b shows that the overhead remains minimal for much larger values of n.

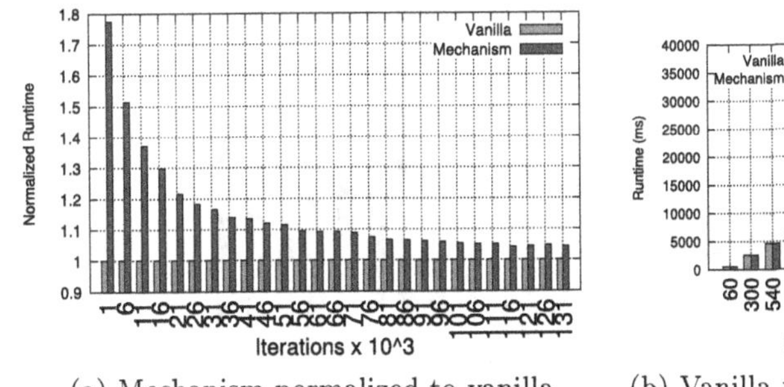

(a) Mechanism normalized to vanilla

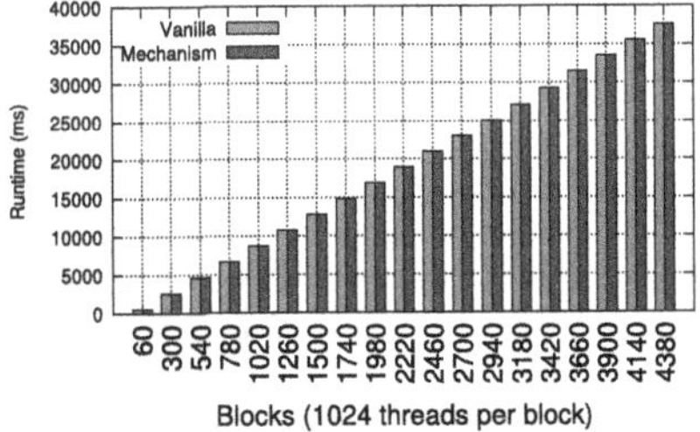

(b) Vanilla vs Mechanism. $n = 67 \times 10^6$

Fig. 4. Overhead of conditional check

4.2 Interrupt Overheads

In order to examine this overhead, we performed set $n = 1.6 \times 10^9$ with a kernel configuration of <<<`1320, 1024`>>>. This configuration is needed to be able to interrupt the kernel at least 20 times. To be able to interrupt a kernel N times, at least $(N + 1) \times s \times t$ threads are required, where s is the number of SMs and t is the maximum number of threads an SM can execute. No memory transfers were made. Figure 5a shows the absolute runtime for each interrupt and Fig. 5b shows the time each interrupt adds to the vanilla execution. We see that for a runtime of approximately 3 min, each interrupt adds between 34 ms to 85 ms; the variability of which can be attributed to measurement noise.

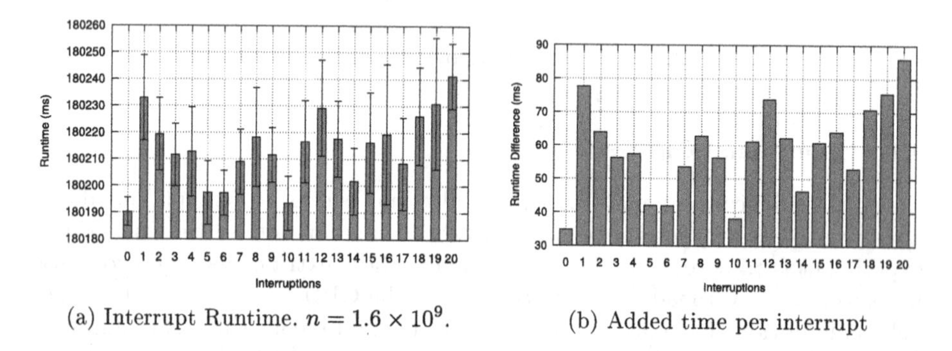

(a) Interrupt Runtime. $n = 1.6 \times 10^9$. (b) Added time per interrupt

Fig. 5. Overheads of soft interrupts. Kernel configuration <<<`1320, 1024`>>>

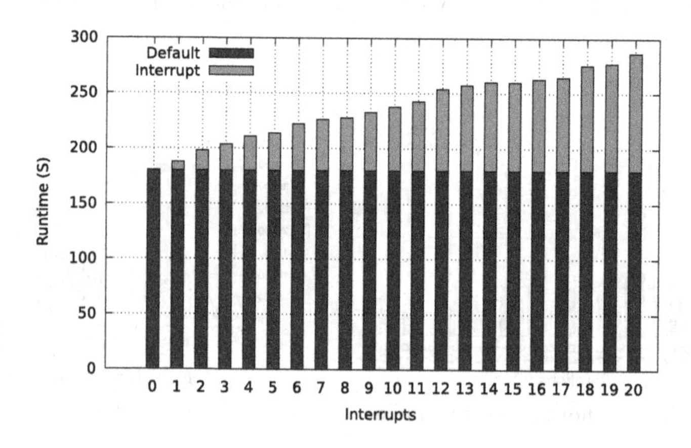

Fig. 6. $n = 1.6 \times 10^9$. Kernel configuration <<<`1320, 1024`>>>. Single memory copy of 11.9 GB made at each interrupt

4.3 Data Transfer Overheads

To measure this overhead, we set $n = 1.6 \times 10^9$ with 98.3% (11.9 GB) of GPU memory allocated. At each interrupt, all GPU allocated memory is transferred back to the device. The results in Fig. 6 show that having to perform large memory transfers at each interrupt noticeably increases the overhead.

The first two experiments show that practical overheads of checking a conditional or doing a software interrupt are close to zero. Memory overheads on the other head, can be quite expensive, but we did not observe them in PBOOST. The reason for this is that despite the kernel runs for such a long time, it only uses 213 MB of the GPU memory, which can be copied very quickly.

5 Related Work

CheCUDA [16] and NVCR [10] are presented as checkpoint/restart tools both of which take a similar approach to GPU fault tolerance. The former works by hooking into basic CUDA driver API calls to record status changes on the device, writing those changes into a file at checkpoint time and using this file to re-initialise the device at restart. NVCR works in a similar way but deletes all CUDA resources before checkpointing and restores them right after checkpointing. Both approaches need the kernel to run to completion and depend on the CUDA runtime to automatically detach itself from the running process and destroy its context. Unfortunately the CUDA runtime stopped doing this from version 3.2 and onward when support for 64-bit device side memory space was added. This is a problem because an existing context at checkpoint time will have its information captured. Restarting an application with this information will fail because the context is no longer attached to the device.

A possible way to circumvent the limitation of CUDA's runtime remaining attached would be to mimic the approach taken by CheCL [17]. CheCL is implemented in the context of OpenCL and transparently provides checkpointing capabilities by substituting the OpenCL shared library with its own version. This allows CheCL to decouple the process from the OpenCL runtime by forwarding all API calls to a proxy process that executes the real API function.

Virtual machines (VMs) are a viable option to achieve both fault tolerance and process migration. Along these lines vCuda [9] and GVIM [8] are proposed as a GPGPU computing solution for applications running on VMs. The advantage of a VM is that it inherently decouples the application from the GPU hardware interface thus simplifying the checkpoint step. This means that API calls need to be intercepted and redirected to the guest OS resulting in large communication overheads and performance degradation.

CudaCR [14] and VOCL [12] are presented as schemes for soft error recovery for GPUs and coprocessors respectively. CudaCR captures the GPU state within the kernel to be able to roll back to a previous state if a soft error occurs. VOCL provides a transparent virtualization layer between applications and the OpenCL runtime. This allows the capture of API calls so that they can be replayed if a soft error occurs. It is worthy to note that CudaCR does address soft errors for long running kernels, however in contrast to our work, neither of these approaches specifically target hardware failures. Approaches mentioned in this section need to wait for GPU kernels to complete before taking a checkpoint; to the best of our knowledge none consider the case of a long-running kernel.

6 Conclusions and Future Work

This paper proposes a solution to the problem of checkpointing applications that use GPU kernels. We present a mechanism that periodically captures a state of the running GPU kernels. With such a mechanism in place, we can use any existing checkpointing system to make snapshots of an application, while a GPU kernel is still running. It is guaranteed by the construction of our mechanism that any such a snapshot captures enough of a state to safely restore the application.

The key insight of this approach lies in the observation that not all the threads of the kernel start at the same time. Such a delay makes it possible to instrument the thread to check for the interrupt and terminate voluntarily if the interrupt has been received. As we have demonstrated on a real-world and synthetic examples, the runtime overhead of the proposed mechanism is very small. We have implemented a library with a compact API which makes our approach straight-forwardly applicable to existing applications. The implementation is freely available at BitBucket.

The effectiveness of the proposed approach enables several future directions of research. First of all, the straightforward nature of our API suggests an automated instrumentation of GPU kernels should be easily possible. Secondly, we would like to integrate our approach with an existing checkpointing system. All we need to do is to make sure that the system makes a snapshot at the time when we captured the state of a kernel ("Checkpoint" stage in Fig. 2b). The checkpointing system could also set or change the time we wait after the kernel launch, so that the snapshotting frequency could be altered.

As our experiments show, the amount of data that is transferred to enable checkpointing dominates the overall overhead. The amount of data that we currently copy at every interrupt/kernel restart is a conservative over approximation. The blocks of results that have been computed do not need to be copied to the GPU. However, figuring out whether it is safe to copy data partially is far from trivial. Despite being inspired by the needs of resilience, our interrupt mechanism has further uses. Fail early scenarios can use our approach so that GPUs return as soon as possible if the system has already started failing and a rollback has to occur. It can also be used for fault injection testing on GPUs which is difficult if kernels run to completion.

Acknowledgements. This work was supported in part by grants EP/N028201/1 and EP/L00058X/1 from the Engineering and Physical Sciences Research Council (EPSRC) as well as the James Watt Scholarship of Heriot-Watt University.

References

1. Hargrove, P.H., Duell, J.C.: Berkeley lab checkpoint/restart (BLCR) for Linux clusters. J. Phys. Conf. Ser. **46**, 494–499 (2006). https://doi.org/10.1088/1742-6596/46/1/067
2. Gõddeke, D., Strzodka, R., Mohd-Yusof, J., McCormick, P.: Exploring weak scalability for FEM calculations on a GPU-enhanced cluster. Parallel Comput. **33**(10–11), 685–699 (2007). https://doi.org/10.1016/j.parco.2007.09.002
3. Egwutuoha, I.P., Levy, D., Selic, B., Chen, S.: A survey of fault tolerance mechanisms and checkpoint/restart implementations for high performance computing systems. J. Supercomput. **65**(3), 1302–1326 (2013). https://doi.org/10.1007/s11227-013-0884-0
4. Bautista-Gomez, L., Tsuboi, S., et al.: FTI: high performance fault tolerance interface for hybrid systems. In: 2011 International Conference for High Performance Computing. IEEE (2011). https://doi.org/10.1145/2063384.2063427
5. Cappello, F., Geist, A., et al.: Toward exascale resilience. Int. J. High Perform. Comput. Appl. **23**(4), 374–388 (2009). https://doi.org/10.1177/1094342009347767
6. DeBardeleben, N., et al.: GPU behavior on a large HPC cluster. In: an Mey, D., et al. (eds.) Euro-Par 2013. LNCS, vol. 8374, pp. 680–689. Springer, Heidelberg (2014). https://doi.org/10.1007/978-3-642-54420-0_66
7. Fan, Z., Qiu, F., et al.: GPU cluster for high performance computing. In: Proceedings of the 2004 ACM/IEEE Conference on Supercomputing, SC 2004, p. 47 (2004). https://doi.org/10.1109/SC.2004.26
8. Gupta, V., et al.: GViM: GPU-accelerated virtual machines. In: Proceedings of the 3rd ACM Workshop on System-Level Virtualization for High Performance Computing, HPCVirt 2009, pp. 17–24. ACM (2009). https://doi.org/10.1145/1519138.1519141
9. Shi, L., Chen, H., et al.: vCUDA: GPU-accelerated high-performance computing in virtual machines. IEEE Trans. Comput. **61**(6), 804–816 (2009). https://doi.org/10.1109/IPDPS.2009.5161020
10. Nukada, A., et al.: NVCR: a transparent checkpoint-restart library for NVIDIA CUDA. In: 2011 IEEE IPDPS Workshops and Phd Forum, pp. 104–113. IEEE (2011). https://doi.org/10.1109/IPDPS.2011.131
11. NVIDIA: CUDA C programming guide (2017)
12. Peña, A.J., Bland, W., Balaji, P.: VOCL-FT: introducing techniques for efficient soft error coprocessor recovery. In: Proceedings of the International Conference for High Performance Computing, Networking, Storage and Analysis, SC 2015, pp. 1–12. IEEE (2015). https://doi.org/10.1145/2807591.2807640
13. Phillips, J.C., et al.: Adapting a message-driven parallel application to GPU-accelerated clusters. In: Proceedings of the 2008 ACM/IEEE Conference on Supercomputing, SC 2008. IEEE (2008). https://doi.org/10.1109/SC.2008.5214716
14. Pourghassemi, B., et al.: CudaCR: an in-kernel application-level checkpoint/restart scheme for CUDA-enabled GPUs. In: 2017 IEEE International Conference on Cluster Computing (CLUSTER), pp. 725–732. IEEE (2017). https://doi.org/10.1109/CLUSTER.2017.100
15. Showerman, M., et al.: QP: a heterogeneous multi-accelerator cluster. In: 10th LCI International Conference on High-Performance Clustered Computing (2009)
16. Takizawa, H., et al.: CheCUDA: a checkpoint/restart tool for CUDA applications. In: 2009 International Conference on PDCAT, pp. 408–413. IEEE (2009). https://doi.org/10.1109/PDCAT.2009.78

17. Takizawa, H., et al.: CheCL: transparent checkpointing and process migration of OpenCL applications. In: 2011 IEEE International IPDPS. IEEE (2011). https://doi.org/10.1109/IPDPS.2011.85
18. Mohamed, H., Osipyan, H., Marchand-Maillet, S.: Multi-core (CPU and GPU) for permutation-based indexing. In: Traina, A.J.M., Traina, C., Cordeiro, R.L.F. (eds.) SISAP 2014. LNCS, vol. 8821, pp. 277–288. Springer, Cham (2014). https://doi.org/10.1007/978-3-319-11988-5_26
19. Yang, G., et al.: PBOOST: a GPU-based tool for parallel permutation tests in genome-wide association studies. Bioinformatics **31**(9), 1460–1462 (2015). https://doi.org/10.1093/bioinformatics/btu840

Author Index

Printed in the United States
By Bookmasters